75 YEARS *of the* OSCAR

THE OFFICIAL HISTORY OF THE ACADEMY AWARDS

ROBERT OSBORNE

ABBEVILLE PRESS · PUBLISHERS · NEW YORK · LONDON

Editor: Bruce Davis, Mikel Gordon
Designer: Advantage Graphics
Photography Archivist: Val Almandarez
Historian: Patrick Stockstill, Libby Wertin
75th Anniversary Logo: Deaf Eye Design

Library of Congress Cataloging-in-Publication Data
Osborne, Robert A.
75 Years of the Oscar: the official history of the Academy
Awards / by Robert Osborne
    p. cm.
    Bibliography: p.
    Includes Index
    1. Academy of Motion Picture Arts and Sciences
2. Academy Awards (Motion pictures). 3. Motion pictures—
United States—History.
I. Title. II. Title: 75 Years of the Oscar.
PN1993.5.U6014 1989 791.43'079-dc19 88 30487
ISBN 0-7892-0787-0

Table of Contents

The Beginning...

In 1928, no one knew better than Mary Pickford how much the motion picture industry needed one all-encompassing organization as a focal point for unbiased judgments, coordination and cool thinking in the often-scrambled movie community known as Hollywood. Miss Pickford had been a part of the movie business almost from its beginning, watching the nickelodeon novelty grow with lightning speed into what had become, by the end of the 1920s, the fourth largest industry in America. The movies — silent but golden — had captured the imagination and the pocketbooks of the world, but until the Academy of Motion Picture Arts and Sciences was formed, no one had organized the moviemakers themselves into a single, cohesive force. And the time had come.

The 1920s had been, in fact, a time of great changes everywhere, a dynamic period of transition. After World War I ended in 1918, the United States had been undergoing an invigorating decade of technological and cultural breakthroughs, one after another, stockpiling inventions and creations faster than at any other period in the country's history. Growth was particularly swift in the area of mass communications and, by the end of the 1920s, all the current major communications media had attained some degree of maturity, except of course for television.

Statistics on the motion picture industry itself were staggering. By 1928, the American film colony alone was producing over five hundred feature-length films (and hundreds of short subjects) each year for a weekly audience of one hundred million ticket-buyers in twenty-three thousand theaters across the nation. Hollywood, California — that little suburb that had mushroomed just outside of Los Angeles — had firmly established itself, without any premeditation, as the film capital of the world. That's when problems began, problems that brought about an organization encompassing all filmmakers.

World leadership in any field has distinct disadvantages, and Hollywood was getting all the slaps synonymous with success. The attacks came from everywhere. Church groups charged that the medium foisted harmful influences on unsuspecting patrons, and Parent-Teacher Associations criticized Hollywood's preoccupation with adult themes. Everyone had something to say about the personal conduct of the town's citizenry, often blown out of proportion for publicity purposes, then eagerly reported by the world's press, egged on by aggressive studio publicity departments. The government, too, often cast a critical eye on Hollywood, eager to show the moviemakers how to use, or how not to use, their undeniable influence over the masses.

The handwriting was on the wall: outside censorship of the film industry was inevitable unless the industry took hasty steps to police itself. In order to head off the possibility of outside control, a group of film producers gathered

What The Academy Means
To Me

The Academy is the League of Nations of the Motion Picture Industry. It is our open forum where all branches can meet and discuss constructive solutions to problems with which each is confronted. In the past we have never been able to get together on a common ground and in making this possible the Academy has conferred a great service. The producer, star, featured player, cinematographer — in fact, every individual can come into the Academy with any problem or proposal and feel that all barriers are leveled, that in this open court his voice carries the same weight as that of any other person, regardless of position and standing. There is no greater force for coordination, no greater avenue for constructive and intelligent cooperation for advancement than that offered by the Academy of Motion Picture Arts and Sciences.

Mary Pickford
Academy Bulletin, April 2, 1928

Janet Gaynor

William Cameron Menzies

together in 1922 and hired Will H. Hays, a former Postmaster General under President Warren Harding, to head up a new self-policing body for the industry. Hays was to set guidelines for films, censor the offenders of good taste and give a stamp of approval to acceptable products, all of which the film community was to accept en masse. Everyone hoped the distinguished Hays name would help alleviate those outside criticisms, with the knowledge that the moviemakers themselves were doing something constructive to police the screen. Hays' leadership was the stimulus for the first movie production code, but it still didn't prevent all attempts at outside interference with films and filmmakers. Despite the good intentions and tough policies of Mr. Hays, a few states and several cities still decided to establish their own local censorship boards to pass on motion picture content, and these boards often rejected films previously cleared by Hays and his Hollywood code office.

There was another source of confusion in the industry: a new trend toward unionism. Los Angeles had long been known as a haven for non-union employment, and union organizers felt that the motion picture industry could be used as a tool to bring unions into the unorganized labor town. It started slowly at first. In November of 1926, a Studio Basic Agreement was signed between nine film studios and unions representing carpenters, painters, electricians, stagehands and musicians. At the same time, an attempt to form a screen-

writer's guild was defeated, and a major effort to organize talent groups by Actors Equity Association, the stage union covering performers, had failed. Still, more change was inevitable, one way or another.

Public interest in silent films was also on the wane, and the motion picture industry was in a serious state of mechanical overhaul. Technological advances were being made by various studios, but each was keeping its knowledge a heavily guarded secret, leading to chaos in the manufacture and distribution of prints, even the silent ones, to theaters. There were as many standards as there were studios, and in the face of a falling market, producers needed all the cooperation they could muster, particularly with the impending changeover to sound-on-film. They needed, first and foremost, a central clearinghouse and exchange for ideas, a common ground where the development of new equipment could be discussed, and procedures could be shared that would benefit the entire industry.

In January of 1927, just five weeks after the Studio Basic Agreement was a fact of Hollywood life, the first seed-idea for the Academy of Motion Picture Arts and Sciences was planted. It happened during a Sunday dinner at the Santa Monica beach home of M-G-M's powerful studio chief Louis B. Mayer, during a conversation between Mayer and three of his guests, actor Conrad Nagel, director Fred Niblo and producer Fred Beetson. The men agreed there should be one organized group that could

Introduction

On May 4, 1927, the articles of incorporation for the Academy of Motion Picture Arts and Sciences were filed with the California Secretary of State and the Academy came into formal existence. Though planning meetings had been taking place for several months before that, the first official meeting of the Academy was held on May 6, and by May 11 the first roster of 230 members was printed.

benefit the entire industry, help solve technological problems, aid in arbitrating labor disputes, and assist Will Hays in policing screen content. Stimulated by the idea, the four men planned a dinner for the following week, which would be attended by representatives from all the creative branches of the motion picture industry who, it was hoped, would be equally willing to support such an organization.

The men meant business. On January 11, 1927, thirty-six people gathered at the Ambassador Hotel in Los Angeles, listened to the proposal, and applauded the whole idea. These film industry leaders became the official founders of the International Academy of Motion Picture Arts and Sciences (the "International" was later dropped during incorporation proceedings). The thirty-six, besides Mayer, Nagel, Niblo and Beetson, were J.A. Ball, Richard Barthelmess, Charles H. Christie, George Cohen, Cecil B. DeMille, Douglas Fairbanks, Joseph W. Farnham, Cedric Gibbons, Benjamin Glazer, Sid Grauman, Milton Hoffman, Jack Holt, Henry King, Jesse Lasky, M.C. Levee, Frank Lloyd, Harold Lloyd, Edwin Loeb, Jeanie MacPherson, Bess Meredyth, Mary Pickford, Roy Pomeroy, Harry Rapf, Joseph Schenck, Milton Sills, John Stahl, Irving Thalberg, Raoul Walsh, Harry Warner, Jack L. Warner, Carey Wilson and Frank Woods.

After that, things moved swiftly. Articles of incorporation were presented by mid-March, and the first officers were elected: Douglas Fairbanks (president), Fred Niblo (vice president), M.C. Levee (treasurer) and Frank Woods (secretary). On May 4, 1927, the state of California granted the Academy a charter as a non-profit corporation, and a week later, on May 11, 1927, a festive and official organizational banquet took place in the Crystal Ballroom of the Biltmore Hotel in Los Angeles with three hundred guests in attendance. That night, two hundred and thirty of them joined the new Academy as pioneer members, by signing a check for one hundred dollars. "Our purpose is positive, not negative," Fairbanks told them. "We are formed to do, not un-do."

On June 20, 1927, the Academy founders further committed the goals of the new organization in a statement, which declared:

The Academy will take aggressive action in meeting outside attacks that are unjust.

It will promote harmony and solidarity among the membership and among different branches.

It will reconcile internal differences that may exist or arise.

It will adopt such ways and means as are proper to further the welfare and protect the honor and good repute of the profession.

It will encourage the improvement and advancement of the arts and sciences of the profession by the interchange of constructive ideas and by awards of merit for distinctive achievement.

It will take steps to develop the greater power and influence of the screen.

In a word, the Academy proposes to do for the motion picture profession in all its branches what other great national and international bodies have done for other arts and sciences and industries.

The organization of the Academy of Motion Picture Arts and Sciences consisted of different groups, each with equal representation on the Board of Directors (later changed to the Board of Governors), and each group with a semi-autonomous branch organization of its own. Initially, there were five main branches — Producers, Actors, Directors, Writers and Technicians — but the number of branches has gradually been increased over the years to reflect the greater diversity of activity and specialization in the production of motion pictures. More of that later.

The Academy was intended as an exclusive, invitational organization, and its opinions and actions were to be those of the organization, not necessarily of the entire industry. Still, in 1927, the Academy was (and still is some seventy-five years later) used to solve industry-wide problems. From the beginning, no attempt at "membership drives" has ever been made. Membership in the Academy is still by invitation only. Qualification for membership is based on distinctive achievements in one of the branches of motion picture production covered by the Academy.

In May, 1927, the Academy rented a suite of offices at 6912 Hollywood Boulevard to serve as temporary headquarters for the organization. A new history had begun.

As forefathers run, this was a pretty impressive group. It included Wallace Beery, Francis X. Bushman, Lon Chaney, Ronald Colman, Michael Curtiz, C.B. and William DeMille, Douglas Fairbanks, Cedric Gibbons, John Gilbert, D.W. Griffith, Jean Hersholt, Carl Laemmle, Jesse Lasky, Harold Lloyd, Louis B. Mayer, Colleen Moore, Ramon Novarro, Mary Pickford, Norma Shearer, Gloria Swanson, Norma Talmadge, Irving Thalberg, Erich Von Stroheim, Raoul Walsh, Darryl Zanuck and a good many other legendary names.

Their motives — or the motives of some among them at any rate — have been questioned. If you read the minutes of the early meetings though, or look over the transcriptions of speeches from the Academy's earliest public occasions, it's hard not to be impressed with the high ideals of our founders.

As the book you're about to begin makes clear, they wanted an organization that would keep its members abreast of new technical developments affecting their art. They wanted a voice that could speak for the industry when the industry was maligned or misunderstood. And they wanted an organization that would help educate the wide public about motion pictures, partly by endorsing the most distinguished achievements in the field each year.

The Academy they formed is more than sixty years old now. For those of us who have inherited the organization and the aims it set down for itself, a little reflection seems in order. I'd like to think that if those 230 original members could look over our shoulders as we go about our various activities these days, they'd be agreeably surprised at how closely the Academy that exists today resembles the one they set out to create.

It's not all that common after all for an organization to live up to its idealistic early hopes for itself. That we in the Academy have pretty much accomplished that strikes me as cause, not for smugness or complacency certainly, but perhaps for a pause and a small warm wave of good feeling...before we hitch up our belts, take a hard look ahead and continue into the seventh decade of Academy history.

Robert E. Wise, President
Academy of Motion Picture Arts and Sciences
1985-1988

1927-1937
The Academy's First Decade

May, 1927: the same month the Academy of Motion Picture Arts and Sciences was officially born, air mail pilot Charles A. Lindbergh stunned the world by making the first non-stop New York-to-Paris flight, alone aboard his *Spirit of St. Louis* monoplane. In Washington, D.C., Calvin Coolidge was President of the United States, in New York Mae West was holding forth on Broadway in a play called *Sex,* and across the country moviegoers were paying an average of 25¢ for a ticket each time they went to the movies. Moviegoers were also still mourning the death of Rudolph Valentino nine months before. Out in Hollywood, Grauman's Chinese Theatre opened its doors for the first time on May 18 (showing Cecil B. DeMille's *King of Kings* plus a spectacular stage presentation) and movie makers had their minds on a myriad of matters, one of them the worrisome possibility of talking pictures, launched by Warner Bros. with some Vitaphone short subjects the previous year.

At the Academy, the first order of business was a labor dispute that was threatening to erupt within the motion picture industry. The West Coast managers of the major motion picture studios—including Metro-Goldwyn-Mayer, Paramount, Fox, Universal, Warner Bros. and United Artists—were being severely pressured by their New York superiors and Manhattan bankers to impose a ten percent salary cut on all Hollywood studio personnel as a means of reducing production costs. A full-scale strike by studio employees was imminent; they were arguing that costs could—and should—be slashed elsewhere, not at the employee-salary level. The Producers Branch of the new Academy stepped in, effected a meeting with the other Academy branches to discuss the proposed cut and its ramifications, arbitrated the differences and ultimately managed to have the proposed salary cut withdrawn altogether.

Another early order of business was a search for larger headquarters. The Academy's office at 6912 Hollywood Boulevard was barely large enough for small committee meetings, much less for an organization with several hundred members. In June of 1927, one month after the Academy's official incorporation, the Building and Finance Committee submitted a proposal for construction of a new building, but the idea was rejected by the Board for lack of funds. In November of the same year, the Academy found suitable office space on the mezzanine floor of the Roosevelt Hotel, located at 7010 Hollywood Boulevard. There the Academy began accumulating a complete file of professional periodicals from all over the world, and plans were made for an eventual library.

The following year, in May, 1928, the Board approved the installation of screening facilities in the Club Lounge of the hotel. The most complete and up-to-date equipment available was ordered, and the plan was for imme-

---

EDITOR'S NOTE

We wish to express our appreciation to the Academy Award winners who have responded to our request for their Oscar memories. More than one hundred and twenty have sent us their personal remembrances. A selection of their comments is presented for the enjoyment of our readers.

NORMA SHEARER

"I wish to take this glorious opportunity to express my deep affection and admiration for all those wonderful people in the motion picture business it has been my privilege to know and admire and to call my friends throughout the years."

Norma Shearer
Best Actress, 1929-30

HELEN HAYES

"Advice to young actors winning Oscars: Enjoy! Don't wait years to find out what that award can give you in comfort and confidence. As an actor grows older, no matter how long his memory, it is hard to hold on to that delicious feeling of his youth — of being best. That Oscar sitting on the mantel is a good reminder. I treasure mine for just that."

Helen Hayes
Best Actress, 1931-32
Best Supporting Actress, 1970

LEWIS MILESTONE

"From my first Oscar, handed me by Douglas Fairbanks in 1929, a small and (by today's standards) informal family celebration, to the present worldwide interest in the Oscar presentations, the growth of the Academy Awards proves indeed the cultural and educational benefits of the Academy...the Supreme Court of the Screen."

Lewis Milestone
Best Director, 1927-28; 1929-30

BETTE DAVIS

"I have always felt proud of my Oscars and my numerous nominations. This pride is due to the fact it was the result of voters from the members of my own profession.

This, of course, is a great compliment for one's work. I hope each winner of an Oscar is as thrilled as I was when I received mine."

Bette Davis
Best Actress, 1935; 1938

Some Founders of the Academy: (Standing) Cedric Gibbons, J.A. Ball, Carey Wilson, George Cohen, Edwin Loeb, Fred Beetson, Frank Lloyd, Roy Pomeroy, John Stahl, Harry Rapf; (Seated) Louis B. Mayer, Conrad Nagel, Mary Pickford, Douglas Fairbanks, Frank Woods, M.C. Levee, Joseph M. Schenck, Fred Niblo.

diate installation. But seven months later, the "immediate installation" still had not taken place, due to the tremendous demand by theater owners all over the country for sound equipment to cash in on the sudden impact of talking pictures. An appeal was made to the equipment manufacturers and—finally—the desired facilities for the Academy were completed six months later, in April, 1929. And it was worth the wait, as the Academy's screening room was equipped with Vitaphone, Movietone and every other sound system then used by the industry.

During the Academy's first decade, there were other moves, necessitated by the organization's rapid expansion. In June, 1930, a suite of offices in the Professional Building at 7046 Hollywood Boulevard was rented, where the Academy could have space for its increased staff of four executives, three assistants and six clerks. By December, the library

Richard Arlen, (unidentified), Douglas Fairbanks, Benjamin Glazer, Janet Gaynor, Karl Struss, Frank Borzage

KATHARINE HEPBURN

"Prizes are given. Prizes are won. They are the result of competition. Any way you want to look at it, from birth to death we are competing.

My first competition. A track meet. The three-legged race. I won it. My next was a diving contest. I was doing several very complicated dives badly. My friend and competitor was doing several very simple dives well. She won it. I resented it deeply. But there it was. There is a terrible agony in competition. You have to pretend that you don't care if you lose. We have home movies of all those early competitions. Cry at the beginning. Cry during the race. Cry when you win. Cry when you lose.

No way. Too much of a strain. I'll avoid that. But I didn't. I encountered The Super Cry.

I grew up. I went to work. And I found that I had entered a business which had a thing called — THE ACADEMY AWARD. People from all over the world see the different competitors do their stuff. The winning of the prize in any department is a boost to business. The winning of Best Picture. Best Director. Best Actor. Best Actress. This is a Super Boost.

The effort to win votes by advertising, selling, begging, organizing in full swing in all media. Then the terrible Night. Telecast worldwide. All dressed up. Here I am a competitor. And I care. I care desperately. Will I be the one to...

Oh dear me. Let's avoid that, I said to myself. So I never went. But I had to be honest enough with myself to wonder — What is it, Kathy? Are you afraid that you won't win?

One year when I was not in the running myself I was asked to present the Thalberg Award to Lawrence Weingarten. I just could not in all conscience refuse. So I rushed on. And then I rushed off. But do you know what — they all stood up. They stood up for me. All those people. Those people whose votes through the years had given me the prize. They had voted me in. Not once, but twice — and a half. They stood. They clapped. They gave me their respect and their affection. It was a revelation — the generous heart of the industry. The pat on the back from one's peers.

However maddening, infuriating, embarrassing and seemingly artificial these occasions are. However

drummed up. The truth of the matter is still pure. The Academy Awards are in all good faith. An attempt to honor a person or a product of our industry. And they have maintained in essence a purity, a simple — well, truth.

This year by our vote you are the best.

Well, there must be something to it. It's gone on for sixty years. It must be healthy.

One can quibble. How does anyone know which performance? Which picture? It's an Art —

Well, hell — let's face it. How does anyone know anything? It's our track meet. It's painful but it's thrilling."

Katharine Hepburn
Best Actress, 1932-33; 1967; 1968; 1981

was acknowledged as having one of the most complete collections of information on the motion picture industry anywhere in existence.

Moving again in 1935, the accounting and executive offices shifted to the Taft Building on the corner of Hollywood and Vine, right in the center of Hollywood, while the library relocated to 1455 North Gordon Street. The library was growing so rapidly that in 1936 the Academy's first full-time librarian, Margaret Herrick, was hired to oversee its burgeoning collection of periodicals and other film materials.

During the initial decade, the Academy also began initiating a few publications of its own, as a service to its members and the industry in general. In 1928 the Academy published its first book, *Report on Incandescent Illumination*, based on the contents of a series of Academy-sponsored seminars that had been given earlier in the year with the help of the American Society of Cinematographers and Producers Association. This had been attended by one hundred and fifty interested cinematographers. (Another series of lectures on sound technique, sponsored by the Academy to help familiarize novices with the vast technical requirements of sound-on-film, was the basis for a second book, *Recording Sound for Motion Pictures*, which was published in 1931.) In 1929, *Introduction to the Photoplay* was published, based on lectures given during a new film course at the University of Southern California in cooperation with the Academy's College Affairs Committee.

The Academy tried its hand at publishing a magazine, too, but without much success. During the period, *Motion Picture Arts and Sciences* was premiered, featuring Academy news and distributed only to Academy members. It was published in November, 1927, and lasted for the one issue. In

Henry B. Walthall, D.W. Griffith

1928, the organization made plans to purchase an existing publication titled *Hollywood*, intending to circulate it nationally, but dropped the idea when the plans for widespread distribution were not feasible.

Other Academy efforts in the publications field have been more durable. In 1933, the *Screen Achievement Records Bulletin* was born, listing film production titles and complete credits for directors and writers; today it is still published, now called the *Annual Index to Motion Picture Credits*, and expanded to include complete credits

of productions, cross-indexed by title, individual, production company and specific craft. The *Academy Players Directory* began in 1937, showing then—as now—photographs of actors, with the name of their agents or industry contacts, as a service to casting directors. The *Players Directory* is still being published two times a year, now with over 17,000 performers in recent issues, all given the same amount of space, regardless of their credits or fame, and all available for assignment.

One of the primary reasons for the formation of the Academy was to counter

CLAUDETTE COLBERT

"What can one say about receiving the Academy Award except, 'I was so happy, excited, etc., etc., etc.'

In my particular case, added to all these emotions was utter astonishment! I was convinced that we could not win because a comedy had never won—so convinced, that I was actually boarding the Santa Fe Super Chief for New York when I was whisked back to the Biltmore Hotel to accept the Oscar while they held the train. It was quite a scenario!!!"

Claudette Colbert
Best Actress, 1934

GALE SONDERGAARD

"I came to Hollywood in 1935, not to seek a career in motion pictures but rather to accompany my husband, Herbert Biberman, New York Theater Guild director, who was about to embark on his new career as director of films.

Although I was already a stage actress and had played leading roles on Broadway, I sincerely believed that I did not belong in motion pictures.

Much to my amazement, it then happened that Mervyn LeRoy cast me as Faith Paleologue in Anthony Adverse—*and then, to my even greater amazement, in 1936 I won the first Academy Award ever given to an actress in a supporting role.*

My new career was on its way. I love the Academy of Motion Picture Arts and Sciences."

Gale Sondergaard
Best Supporting Actress, 1936

HERMES PAN

"The Academy of Motion Picture Arts and Sciences is, and always has been, a great stimulus and encouragement to all involved in the film industry.

Needless to say, the highlight of my career was a night many years ago at the old Biltmore Hotel ballroom, when I heard a voice saying 'And the winner is—Hermes Pan.'"

Hermes Pan
Dance Direction, 1937

the unfavorable publicity focusing on the film industry at the time. Through succeeding years it has continued to do its share of public relations work for the entire movie community. Some of its early attempts to improve the industry's image and create good will with the public included such efforts as Academy contributions to the Mississippi River Relief Fund. Prior to the official organization charter date, the Academy raised funds for the relief of suffering flood victims in the Mississippi Basin, and on May 12, 1927, just one day after the organization dinner of May 11, the Academy presented a check to the Fund for over thirty-five thousand dollars, which was over one-quarter of the total donation from the entire city of Los Angeles.

As a further good will gesture, the Academy opened its facilities to outside organizations and groups for meetings. Advance screenings of as-yet-unreleased motion pictures were held for the benefit of opinion-makers from major churches in the community, plus certain educational and fraternal institutions. The value of having influential community leaders approve Hollywood product was, at the time, of inestimable help to the industry. And though the Academy was never intended to be the official spokesman for the entire film community, it has often served as a clearinghouse for inquiries from the press, private individuals, civic organizations and others.

Another public relations "first" came when the Academy began arranging visits with studio personnel from foreign nations, as in 1930 when leading representatives from the Russian film industry met with Hollywood executives and technicians to exchange ideas and knowledge. In November of the same year, the Academy initiated a successful practice of having some of its members tour to various cities in the

Norma Shearer

United States, talking to civic groups, schools and leaders of industry.

Through the early years, the Academy often became involved in studio problems and union matters, but such endeavors were never its strongest suit, despite being one of the original reasons for the formation of the organization. By the time the first decade of the Academy of Motion Picture Arts and Sciences was over, it was completely out of the arbitration business.

There was no denying a troublesome period loomed with the launching of sound films. Talking pictures had done a great deal to alleviate some weighty box-office problems that had been plaguing the industry, but the national Depression in 1931 was another crip-

pler. It pushed several studios to the brink of bankruptcy and sent Universal and RKO Radio into receivership. In March of 1933 came the final blow: from Washington, D.C., the new President, Franklin D. Roosevelt, declared a bank holiday. In order to survive, Hollywood studios had frenzied meetings, uncertain if they should continue, scratch production plans or shut their gates altogether. In the meantime, several companies suspended salaries.

The Academy jumped in to do what it could to help a difficult situation. It formed an Emergency Committee and recommended a temporary pay cut of 50% for studio employees as opposed to total shutdown, which everyone feared would be a death blow to several of the troubled companies. An adjusted scale was also devised by the Emergency Committee to provide additional aid for low-salaried employees. The plan was to remain in effect for a limited, eight-week period (March 6–April 30, 1933). One provision was that the Academy be given permission to inspect companies' financial records to ensure that all was conducted fairly, as agreed. The accounting firm of Price Waterhouse & Co. was hired for auditing; it was the Academy's first utilization of the company which in 1936 was given charge of officially tabulating results of Academy Awards balloting.

Basically, the Academy's aid in the 1933 crisis was a success—both in helping to get a badly bruised industry moving again, and by demonstrating the value of the Academy in producing measures for the industry-at-large. At the end of the "freeze" period, the crisis had ebbed, the panic had given way to optimism and all studios returned their employees to full salary as promised, with the exception of the Warner Bros. company. Its failure to do so enraged Darryl F. Zanuck, one of the studio's

---

LUISE RAINER

"The Academy Award—what shall I say? I shall jot down, quickly, as it comes to my mind:

Still in my early twenties, only a few months in Hollywood, I made my first film. It made me a star. It was then I first heard of 'the Academy Award.' What was it? I should soon learn. I never had much thought of any award beyond the wondrous contact and the warmth that I was fortunate to receive from many while spending my teens on the stage in Vienna and Berlin; my driving force was love and enthusiasm for my work and great hope to develop as an actress.

In my first year in Hollywood I started and finished my second film, The Great Ziegfeld. *Mr. Louis B. Mayer did not want me to do the film: 'Anna Held is out of it before the film is halfway through,' he said. 'You are a star now and you can't do it!' I hoped to make something of the two-minute telephone scene. It brought me my first Academy Award.*

Immediately after, I started The Good Earth. *Irving Thalberg cast me. Mr. Mayer was against that, too: 'She has to be a dismal-looking slave and grow old; but*

Luise is a young girl; we just have made her glamorous—what are you doing?' It brought me my second Academy Award as the best actress of the year. It happened in two successive years.

How did I feel about it? As often in life, big events or the importance of them are felt less at the time than later. There was a great deal of photographing, much clamour, more so than the 'glamour' it is believed to be. Above all, a change of one's image felt by others but not by oneself. One was acclaimed, now; therefore one's doings, one's motives, one's every utterance seemed to have greater dimension and therefore suddenly became suspect. It seemed harder to continue one's work quietly. Shortly later I left Hollywood.

I have often heard the Academy Award to be a bad omen. I don't think it need be. Except, maybe, that the industry seemed to feel that having an Academy Award-winner on their hands was sufficient to overcome bad story material as was, often, handed out afterwards to stars under long-term contract. However, to build anything good it needs solid material, so it does not slip through your fingers like sand. This is what I felt then.

Now I feel that it is wonderful to have received two Academy Awards!"

Luise Rainer
Best Actress, 1936; 1937

production heads, and he quit the company in protest. Zanuck subsequently formed his own 20th Century Productions, which initially released through United Artists distribution channels, then merged in 1936 with the Fox Film Corporation.

The Warner Bros. action also had an effect on the Academy hierarchy. Academy President Conrad Nagel was accused by some of supporting the studio in its action, and he received a vote of no confidence from the Academy Board of Directors and consequently resigned, succeeded by J. Theodore Reed.

The incident proved to weaken the Academy's ability to hold its constituents' faith as an impartial arbiter and was one reason the Academy began easing away from involvement in labor relations. Reed took upon himself—as a first order of Academy business—the job of drafting a new constitution, one free of politics and any self-serving interests that might apply to any Academy officer in the future.

More trouble loomed directly ahead. Union militancy again presented itself in June, 1933, when President Roosevelt introduced his National Industrial Recovery Act, a further effort of Washington to loosen the binds imposed by the Depression. The main thrust of the National Recovery Act was to suspend various anti-trust laws, allowing an industry such as the motion picture business to regulate itself, following self-imposed codes. The lengthy code, drawn up by the Motion Pictures Code Committee, infuriated almost everyone, especially performers. They were without a union, or organization, and they eyed this code as another example of dictatorship by the major studio executives. Since the Academy numbered many of those executives among its membership and—at the same time—made rather weak protestations at code

Fredric March, wife Florence Eldridge

hearings, suspicions grew that the Academy was on the side of the "enemy" and was no longer inclined to act in the best interests of actors, as it had often done in the past.

In July, 1933, a number of actors dropped their Academy membership and broke away to form the Screen Actors Guild union. A mass defection began when the specific rules in the code were released and discovered to contain such irritating items as strict salary controls, licensing of agencies and other dominating provisions. Important actors such as Paul Muni, Gary Cooper, Fredric March, James Cagney and George Raft were among the defectors, additionally angered because Academy President Reed had been one of the authors of the code. By Novem-

ber, over 1,000 actors had joined the new Screen Actors Guild. The strong anti-Academy resentment lasted even after the National Recovery Administration was declared unconstitutional by the United States Supreme Court on May 27, 1935. It continued even through 1936, including the eighth Academy Awards presentation banquet on March 5, 1936, when several guilds and unions boycotted the annual dinner, causing many actors, writers and craftsmen to be absent. Because of the boycott, screenwriter Dudley Nichols became the first individual to refuse an Academy Award. After his name was announced as winner of the 1935 Screenplay Award (for *The Informer*), he announced that he could not accept because to do so would imply tacit approval of the

---

FRANK CAPRA

"Late in 1935 (during the preparation of Mr. Deeds*), the Board of Governors of the Academy of Motion Picture Arts and Sciences bestowed on me the dubious honor of electing me president.*

I say 'dubious' because the president would be presiding at a deathwatch. The Academy had become the favorite whipping boy of Hollywood. Its membership slashed from six hundred to four hundred, its officers to one, loyal, underpaid, executive secretary Margaret Herrick—the Academy's alter ego. With few dollars in its treasury—and fewer in sight—the odds were ten to one the Academy would fold and Oscar would acquire the patina of a collector's item.

Why? Because the polyarchic Academy—governed by management, technicians, and creative talent—was caught in the middle of Hollywood's first labor war between management and talent. The producing companies did everything short of asking for the National Guard to prevent actors, writers, and directors from organizing into guilds. The guilds were organized. But their siege of company ramparts was to last five long

years—years of strife and strikes—before management capitulated and accepted the guilds as the bargaining agents for talent.

However, in 1935 the labor war was in full cry. Actor Ronald Reagan, writer John Howard Lawson and director King Vidor led the fight for their respective guilds.

Part of talent's strategy was to wreck the Academy in order to deny management the box office promotional values of the Oscars. Oddly enough, short-sighted company heads couldn't care less. The Academy had failed them as an instrument of salary cuts during the bank-closing crisis. They withdrew their memberships and financial support, leaving the derelict organization in the care of a few staunch Academy-oriented visionaries dedicated to the cultural advancement of the arts and sciences of filmmaking, and to the continuance of the Awards—the most valuable, but least expensive, item of worldwide public relations ever invented by any industry.

It is an honor to name the few unsung idealists who crossed all economic battle lines to prevent the destruc-

tion of Hollywood's lone bastion of culture:

Writers: Howard Estabrook, Jane Murfin, Waldemar Young, Edwin Burke;

Producers: David O. Selznick, Darryl F. Zanuck, Sam Briskin, Fred Leahy, DeWitt Jennings, Graham Baker;

Technicians: Nathan Levinson, John Arnold, Van Nest Polglase;

Directors: Cecil B. DeMille, Frank Lloyd.

This group elected me to lead them in the Academy's fight for survival. What motivated my instant acceptance—pride or service? I am not sure. But I was sure that the upcoming Academy Awards banquet of March, 1936, loomed dark and discouraging; that things could get worse before they got 'worser.'

Boycott rumors were rife. Officers of the Screen Actors and Screen Writers Guilds sent telegrams to all members urging them not to attend the Academy dinner, and not to accept any Oscars.

To keep the Academy's head above water, we grabbed at the following straws: for the first time, we allowed films made in England to compete for the Oscars; we

Helen Hayes

Academy, and therefore weaken his own union or guild.

In 1937, while Frank Capra presided over the Academy, the bylaws were again rewritten, taking the Academy further from involvement in labor-management arbitrations and negotiations. It hadn't been a successful foray, but it couldn't be dismissed as a weakening disaster for the Academy, either. The Academy had managed to achieve success in settling some disputes that had plagued the industry from time to time; it helped introduce collective bargaining to the industry and, intended or not, had aided in the development of strong labor unions.

During its early years, the Academy experienced several erratic shifts in the size of its membership. Going from an initial enrollment of 230 members, the Academy roll expanded to 374 members in November, 1928, mushrooming to over 800 members in 1932, dropped drastically to just 400 members after the 1933 protest, then grew again by the end of the first decade.

If labor relations had temporarily caused the Academy's membership lists to shrink, the Awards of Merit always caused public interest to grow. And nothing would probably have surprised the Academy founders more. When the Academy was first organized in 1927, the Awards of Merit committee was only one of several general committees established, and the presentation of Awards definitely a secondary matter.

The original seven members of the Awards committee were Richard Barthelmess, D.W. Griffith, Henry King, Sid Grauman, Bess Meredyth, J. Stuart Blackton and Cedric Gibbons. Gibbons served as chairman. Griffith and Barthelmess were later replaced by Charles Rosher and George Fawcett. During its initial meetings, the committee gave thought to the development of some sort of Academy Awards presentation, but the idea was put aside due to more urgent matters. In May, 1928—a full year after the Academy was organized—the subject was again brought up and actively pursued. By July, it was suggested by the committee and approved by the Board to present awards in twelve categories.

Most outstanding production
Achievement by an actor
Achievement by an actress
Achievement in dramatic directing
Achievement in comedy directing
Achievement in cinematography
Achievement in art directing
Achievement in engineering effects
Achievement in original story writing
Achievement in writing adaptation
Achievement in title writing
Most artistic or unique production

The first awards, it was agreed, would be for motion pictures that had been released in the Los Angeles area between August 1, 1927, and July 31, 1928. In order to consider properly all qualifying films, studios were asked to supply the Academy with a list of pictures released within those dates, and the reminder list was sent on to the membership from which they were to make the initial nominations for Awards. The deadline was August 15, 1928, after which five Boards of Judges (one from each of the Academy's branches) were appointed to consider the ten achievements in each category accumulating the largest vote totals, narrowing those ten finalists down to three recommendations. Then came a Central Board of Judges—made up of *one* member from each branch—who made the final decision as to who would be the winner. The two remaining finalists would be singled out for "honorable mention."

The five men who made the decision on the first Academy Awards were Frank Lloyd (representing the Directors Branch), Sid Grauman (Producers Branch), Alec Francis (Actors Branch), Tom Geraghty (Writers Branch) and A. George Volck (Technicians Branch).

Unlike in later years, nominees were not publicly announced in advance of the final balloting. The decision on winners was made at an Academy conclave on Friday, February 15, 1929, a full six months after the closing date for submission of nominations, and the results were announced to the press the following Monday. The Awards themselves were officially presented three months later, on May 16, 1929.

The second Awards year, only seven categories were honored: Production, Performance by an Actor, Performance by an Actress, Direction, Writing, Cinematography and Art Direction. Sound pictures became eligible for the first time, having been excluded from consideration the first time around,

established the Supporting Actor and Supporting Actress categories; we also established the 'Irving G. Thalberg Memorial Award' for outstanding contribution in the production of films. But our top caper to hype the attendance was to persuade the giant of all filmmakers, D.W. Griffith, to come out of his retired oblivion and accept from the Academy a special statuette for his legendary pioneering in films.

Griffith's name was magic. The boycott fizzled. Bette Davis was present to receive her Best Actress trophy for Dangerous; *Victor McLaglen was there to clutch a Best Actor award for* The Informer.

But neither John Ford nor Dudley Nichols showed up for their Best Directing and Best Writing Oscars awarded The Informer. *Ford accepted the trophy later. Nichols did not. He was quoted in a trade paper as having said: 'To accept it would be to turn my back on nearly a thousand members of the Writers Guild...'*

By prayers and incantations, and the Board members putting up their own money for the statuettes, plus some fancy begging on my part (each year I had to plead with the officers of the talent guilds to allow me to mail Academy ballots to their Guild members) the Academy deathwatch kept the grim reaper away until 1939.

Then came a massive transfusion of new blood. The writers, actors, and directors, having signed their newly won basic agreements with management, returned to the Academy fold virtually en masse. The Academy was reorganized into a self-supporting institution dedicated solely to cultural goals. And it was off and running! Today, its Oscars are the world's number one news event of the year."

Frank Capra
Best Director, 1934; 1936; 1938

primarily because the Academy judges weren't sure how to evaluate the new phenomenon of talking pictures on a yardstick with silents. The period of eligibility remained seasonal—August 1 to July 31—and remained so until the sixth Awards. In 1933, it was decided to begin using the calendar year (January 1 to December 31) as the Academy's eligibility period for Awards consideration, but since the preceding cut-off date had been July 31, 1932, all the films released in Los Angeles between August 1–December 31, 1932, would be left unjudged unless the Academy incorporated them into the 1933 "calendar" year. They did. The sixth Awards eligibility period therefore, incorporated seventeen months, from August 1, 1932 through December 31, 1933. Since 1934, the Academy's official year is a calendar one, and eligibility limited to films exhibited theatrically in the Los Angeles area.

Through the years, there have been constant changes in other areas of voting, as well. The process by which winners are selected remained the same for the second Awards year, but was broadened the third year (and remained so through the eighth Awards year) so that both the nomination procedure and the final voting was done by the full Academy membership. In 1936, the nominations were made by a special Awards Nominating Committee, appointed by President Frank Capra, with the final vote then done by the full Academy membership.

New categories have been adopted, then dropped or honed at the discretion of the Academy, such as awards for Dance Direction, One-reel and Two-reel short subjects, and awards distinguishing between color films and black-and-white ones. Two significant—and long-lasting—Awards were introduced near the end of the Academy's first decade: awards for Performance by an Actor in a Supporting Role, and Performance by an Actress in a Supporting Role. Like other aspects of the voting structure, the designation of a "supporting role" as opposed to a "leading role" has changed through the years. Originally it was decided by the studios, who based it on a performer's billing status. At times, studios have made the decision, but arbitrarily; other years, it has been left to the discretion of the performer himself. As of the Academy's thirty-seventh year, it was left to the discretion of the Academy member doing the voting.

The original constitution and bylaws provided for the conferring of honorary Academy memberships on "any person distinguished for public service or eminence in the industry, or by reason of any contribution made thereto." The first honorary membership was given to Thomas Edison at the organizational banquet on May 11, 1927; the second went to George Eastman at the 1930 Awards ceremony.

With the Academy's growing involvement in research through the years, the category for Scientific or Technical Achievement was established for the 1930-31 Awards. This Award may be given in any of three classes:

Class I — for basic achievements which influence the advancement of the industry as a whole.

Class II — for high level of engineering or technical merit.

Class III — for accomplishments which are valuable contributions to the progress of the industry.

The Irving G. Thalberg Memorial Award, given for consistently high quality of production and presented in the form of a bronze likeness of Thalberg's head, was first bestowed at the 1937 Awards ceremony, held March 10, 1938. The former production chief of Metro-Goldwyn-Mayer studios had died in September, 1936.

The Awards themselves are presented in several forms and, like the various rules and categories themselves, have changed through the years, only becoming somewhat standarized in the middle 1940s. Actor and actress winners have always received full-sized statuettes, although in earlier years the statue itself was mounted on a lower base than it has been since the post-World War II period. Winners in the Supporting Actor and Supporting Actress divisions only began receiving full-sized statuettes at the March 2, 1944, ceremony; for the first seven years honoring that category, recipients received Academy plaques.

Initially, film editors chosen for recognition received certificates of merit (1934-1935), then Academy plaques (1936 thru 1943), then statuettes (beginning in 1944). Most of the other categories honored by the Academy have had equally varied histories in respect to the form of Award given each winner. Basically, they are given either as (a) full-size statuettes, representing a knight holding a crusader's sword and standing on a reel of film whose spokes signify the five original branches of the Academy—Actors, Writers, Directors, Producers and Technicians; or (b) Academy plaques, containing a small replica of the Academy symbol; or (c) certificates of merit, or scrolls. In the technical division, Class I Award winners receive a statuette, Class II winners receive an Academy plaque and Class III winners are given a certificate of merit. Honorary Awards may be given in the form of a statuette, a scroll, a life membership or any other design ordered by the Board of Governors. For several years, beginning with the 1934 Awards year, juvenile players received miniature replicas of the Academy statuette. Edgar Bergen, at the 1937 Awards year ceremony, was presented a miniature wooden statuette with a moveable mouth, in honor of his creation of Charlie McCarthy. All nomi-

BOB HOPE

"Being invited to add my comments to the others in this fascinating and unique book is the realization of a lifelong dream. At long last, I take my place among a galaxy of Oscar winners! And I consider this request from the Academy as an apology for not giving me an award for my acting.

My spectacular lack of success in winning an Oscar is too well known to be repeated here. Nonetheless, I consider myself eminently qualified to air my thoughts and feelings about movies because like just about everyone else, I'm a movie fan. I love pictures...and everything about them...making them, and even more, watching them.

Music, literature, painting, and all the other arts have made incalculable contributions to the world. But, in my view, movies are the most influential, the most marvelous, and the most universal art form known to man!

When you consider that movies are a product of this century, the growth and accomplishments of the film industry have been nothing less than miraculous.

Just by shelling out the price of a ticket, you can escape from the cares and problems of real life, and be transported to another wondrous world, a magical world where nothing is impossible. A world inhabited by the most diverse, the most gifted and the most beautiful people ever assembled in such profusion, whose only mission is to thrill, charm and entertain us.

The film industry has survived every change, every crisis, and despite the inevitable prophets of doom, movies are more alive, more innovative, and more marvelous than ever. No other medium can match its scope, its magnetism, or the masterful way in which it has made come alive for us every facet of human experience.

It is fitting that we pay this tribute to the movies...the fabulous art that has given us great drama, mystery, superb comedy that has inspired us, lifted our spirits, and brought us all those dedicated, brilliant and beautiful people. All that and popcorn too!

I'm proud and privileged to have been a part of the magical, mystical and marvelous illusion called...movies."

Bob Hope
Special Award, 1940; 1944
Honorary Award, 1952; 1965
Jean Hersholt Humanitarian Award, 1959

Victor McLaglen, Bette Davis and D.W. Griffith

ability to adapt in a changing world and industry. More problems were ahead, but the beginning years of the new organization had at least created a firm foundation on which to build. And by the time the second decade began, the presentation of the Academy Awards themselves were already an indelible part of the public's consciousness, far beyond the invisible walls of a place called Hollywood.

ACADEMY PRESIDENTS, THE FIRST DECADE

May 1927–October 1927	*Douglas Fairbanks*
October 1927–October 1928	*Douglas Fairbanks*
October 1928–October 1929	*Douglas Fairbanks*
October 1929–October 1930	*William C. deMille*
October 1930–October 1931	*William C. deMille*
October 1931–October 1932	*M.C. Levee*
October 1932–April 1933	*Conrad Nagel*
April 1933–August 1933	*J. Theodore Reed*
August 1933–October 1934	*J. Theodore Reed*
October 1934–October 1935	*Frank Lloyd*
October 1935–October 1936	*Frank Capra*
October 1936–October 1937	*Frank Capra*

nees receive certificates of nomination.

The Academy statuette was designed in 1928 by M-G-M's art director Cedric Gibbons and hasn't been altered since, except for that higher pedestal beginning in the 1940's. It stands thirteen and one-half inches tall, weighs eight and one-half pounds and is made of britannium and is gold plated. Since 1949, the statuettes have been numbered, starting with No. 501. Sculptor George Stanley received a fee of $500 to execute the original statue from Gibbons' design.

Sometime during the first decade, the nickname of "Oscar" was born and, at various times, three people have been credited with the abbreviation: Margaret Herrick, the Academy's librarian and later its executive director, actress Bette Davis and columnist Sidney Skolsky. The actual author has never been definitely established, but the nickname caught on like wildfire, warmly embraced by newsmen, fans and Hollywood citizenry who were finding it increasingly cumbersome to refer to the Academy's Award of Merit as "the Academy's gold statue," "the Academy Award statuette" or, worse, "the trophy." Earlier the trade paper Weekly Variety attempted to give the statue the nickname "the iron man," but it never caught fire. "Oscar" did, and remains ironclad.

Under any name, the Academy Awards and the Academy itself had become prestigious parts of the film community by the end of the first decade, and the organization had been internally strengthened by growing pains and the

1927-28
The First Year

Nineteen hundred and twenty-nine was a year of transition and activity all across the United States. Herbert Hoover succeeded Calvin Coolidge as president, construction began on the Empire State Building, Knute Rockne's Notre Dame football team became the year's national champion, Wall Street had its thundering crash and the motion picture industry began wiring for sound. In the midst of it all, on May 16, 1929 (postponed from May 9), the first Academy Awards were presented at a black-tie dinner, held in the Blossom Room of the Hollywood Roosevelt Hotel, a full three months after the winners had been announced to the press, industry and public. The dinner also marked the second anniversary of the Academy's organization, but little business was done that night beyond the presentation of the Academy's awards of merit and certificates of honorable mention. It was a relaxed, festive "family" evening, attended by two hundred and seventy, most of them Academy members, along with guests of members who were invited to attend (at a slight charge of five dollars to their hosts).

After a dinner of Filet of Sole *Saute au Buerre,* Half Broiled Chicken on Toast, New String Beans and Long Branch Potatoes, preceded by Consomme Celestine, Academy President Douglas Fairbanks explained to the gathering how the awards selections had been made: after Academy members made initial suggestions, twenty Academy-appointed judges designated official nominees and five other judges made the final decisions. Fairbanks then made the official presentations while William C. deMille called the winners to the head table. In explaining the difficulty the five final judges had in making their selections, he commented, "It is a bit like asking, 'Does this man play checkers better than that man plays chess?' "

Twelve awards were presented at this first dinner, and twenty additional certificates of honorable mention were given to runners-up in each of the awards categories. Most of the winners were present, except best actor winner Emil Jannings (for *The Last Command* and *The Way of All Flesh*) who had left Hollywood for his home in Europe. Said deMille, "Mr. Jannings arrives in Berlin today; he was presented with his statuette before he left, and carried it with him to Germany." (He thus became the first individual to actually receive an Academy statuette, later called an "Oscar.") All the honored films were silent ones, and *Wings* was chosen the outstanding picture of the year, Janet Gaynor was named best actress for her work in three films (*7th Heaven, Street Angel* and *Sunrise*) and the Academy, for the first and only time, gave awards for both dramatic direction (presented to Frank Borzage for *7th Heaven*) and comedy direction (Lewis Milestone for *Two Arabian Knights*). Special awards went to Warner Bros. for producing *The Jazz Singer* (accepted by Warner Bros.' executive Darryl F. Zanuck) and to

Best Actress: **Janet Gaynor** *in* 7th Heaven *(immediate right; directed by Frank Borzage),* Street Angel *(right, middle; directed by Borzage), and* Sunrise *(far right, with George O'Brien; directed by F.W. Murnau), all Fox films. New to the screen, Janet Gaynor was the Academy's first Award-winning actress, chosen on the basis of three films, all of them silent. Later, she smoothly adjusted to the coming of sound films and was again nominated in 1937, for her performance in* A Star is Born.

Best Picture: Wings *(Paramount; produced by Lucien Hubbard) was the story of World War I aviation and, specifically, two American aviators (Charles 'Buddy' Rogers and Richard Arlen) both in love with the same hometown beauty (Clara Bow). It was a silent film, directed by William A. Wellman, accompanied in many engagements by a musical score composed and synchronized by John S. Zamecnick. Wings was also visual, touching, great fun and the kind of red-blooded entertainment with which the motion picture industry first found its mass audience and support.*

Best Actor: Emil Jannings *in* The Last Command *(Paramount; directed by Josef Von Sternberg) and* The Way of All Flesh *(Paramount; directed by Victor Fleming). Jannings was born in Brooklyn but raised in Germany; at the peak of his career as a great figure in the German film industry, he went to Hollywood and stayed until the advent of talking pictures. He was not only the first actor to win an Academy Award, but the first person ever presented an Academy statuette. After being announced as a winner, he was photographed with his award before the actual ceremony, then left for Europe and never again returned to the United States. By definition, that also makes him the first no-show winner at an Academy Award presentation.*

Charles Chaplin for writing, producing, acting in and directing *The Circus.* Said deMille, "Mr. Chaplin is not here tonight, due to cold feet, but he has wired his high appreciation of the honor."

Once the awards were presented, there were addresses by Mary Pickford, Professor Walter R. Miles (of Stanford University), Dean Waugh (of the University of Southern California), Mrs. Edward Jacobs (of the Federated Women's Clubs), Sir Gilbert Parker, Cecil B. DeMille and three of the original thirty-six Academy founders: Fred Niblo, Conrad Nagel and Louis B. Mayer. After that, a reel of talking film, photographed at Paramount's Long Island, New York, studios and showing Adolph Zukor visiting with Douglas Fairbanks, was shown, then Al Jolson—in person —brought the evening to a close.

Years later, Miss Gaynor recalled the evening. "Naturally, I was thrilled," she said. "But being the first year, the Academy had no background or tradition and it naturally didn't mean what it has come to mean. Had I known then what it would come to mean in the next few years, I'm sure I would have been overwhelmed. But I still remember that night as very special, a warm evening, and a room filled with important people and nice friends." She also admitted that at the time the real high point for her had been not the award but "the chance to meet the dashing Douglas Fairbanks!"

Special Award: to Warner Bros. *for producing* The Jazz Singer *(above, with Al Jolson), "the pioneer outstanding talking picture which has revolutionized the industry." The film opened during the Academy's initial (and basically silent)* eligibility year, August 1, 1927 to August 1, 1928; by the time the Awards were actually presented in May of 1929, sound-on-film had become a country-wide sensation, and silent films were suddenly passe.

Best Dramatic Director: **Frank Borzage** *(with Charles Farrell sitting in the trench) for* 7th Heaven *(Fox). Borzage made a bona fide classic, in the best tradition of silent screen romance, with his adaptation of Austin Strong's stage play* about a young Montmartre waif whose faith and loyalty bring her lover back from the World War I battlefield. The film was additionally honored for Benjamin Glazer's writing adaptation.

NOTE: For the first Academy Awards, all awards could be for a single achievement, for several achievements, or for the whole body of work during the qualifying year. That is why multiple titles are listed by some names, and no titles at all by others. All achievements not receiving the First Award (*) in each category received "Honorable Mention" certificates.

OUTSTANDING PICTURE

THE RACKET, The Caddo Company, Paramount Famous Lasky. Produced by Howard Hughes.
7TH HEAVEN, Fox. Produced by William Fox.
*****WINGS**, Paramount Famous Lasky. Produced by Lucien Hubbard.

UNIQUE AND ARTISTIC PICTURE

CHANG, Paramount Famous Lasky.
THE CROWD, M-G-M.
*****SUNRISE**, Fox.

ACTOR

RICHARD BARTHELMESS in *The Noose*, First National, and *The Patent Leather Kid*, First National.
*****EMIL JANNINGS** in *The Last Command*, Paramount Famous Lasky, and *The Way of All Flesh*, Paramount Famous Lasky.

ACTRESS

LOUISE DRESSER in *A Ship Comes In*, DeMille Pictures, Pathé Exchange.
*****JANET GAYNOR** in *7th Heaven*, Fox, *Street Angel*, Fox, and *Sunrise*, Fox.
GLORIA SWANSON in *Sadie Thompson*, Gloria Swanson Productions, UA.

DIRECTING

(Comedy Picture)
(NOTE: Award not given after this year.)
*****LEWIS MILESTONE** for *Two Arabian Knights*, The Caddo Company, UA.
TED WILDE for *Speedy*, Harold Lloyd Corp., Paramount Famous Lasky.
CHARLES CHAPLIN, ". . . The Academy Board of Judges on merit awards for individual achievements in motion picture arts during the year ending August 1, 1928, unanimously decided that your name should be removed from the competitive classes, and that a special first award be conferred upon you for writing, acting, directing and producing *The Circus*. The collective accomplishments thus displayed place you in a class by yourself." Letter from the Academy to Mr. Chaplin, dated February 19, 1929.

(Dramatic Picture)
*****FRANK BORZAGE** for *7th Heaven*, Fox.
HERBERT BRENON for *Sorrell and Son*, Feature Productions, UA.
KING VIDOR for *The Crowd*, M-G-M.

WRITING

(Adaptation)
ALFRED COHN, *The Jazz Singer*, Warner Bros.
ANTHONY COLDEWAY, *Glorious Betsy*, Warner Bros.
*****BENJAMIN GLAZER**, *7th Heaven*, Fox.

(Original Story)
LAJOS BIRO, *The Last Command*, Paramount Famous Lasky.
*****BEN HECHT**, *Underworld*, Paramount Famous Lasky.

(Title Writing)
(NOTE: Award not given after this year.)
GERALD DUFFY, *The Private Life of Helen of Troy*, First National.
*****JOSEPH FARNHAM**.
GEORGE MARION, JR.

CINEMATOGRAPHY

GEORGE BARNES, *The Devil Dancer*, Samuel Goldwyn, UA, *The Magic Flame*, Samuel Goldwyn, UA, and *Sadie Thompson*, Gloria Swanson Productions, UA.
*****CHARLES ROSHER**, *Sunrise*, Fox.
*****KARL STRUSS**, *Sunrise*, Fox.

ART DIRECTION

ROCHUS GLIESE, *Sunrise*, Fox.
*****WILLIAM CAMERON MENZIES**, *The Dove*, Joseph M. Schenck Productions, UA, and *Tempest*, Art Cinema, UA.
HARRY OLIVER, *7th Heaven*, Fox.

ENGINEERING EFFECTS

(NOTE: Award not given after this year.)
RALPH HAMMERAS.
*****ROY POMEROY**, *Wings*, Paramount Famous Lasky.
NUGENT SLAUGHTER.
(NOTE: Though no specific titles were indicated during the presentation on May 16, 1929 or in the official results from the Central Board of Judges for the honorable mentions above, Academy records indicate that Mr. Slaughter was most often mentioned in connection with *The Jazz Singer*.)

SPECIAL AWARDS

TO WARNER BROS. for producing *The Jazz Singer*, the pioneer outstanding talking picture, which has revolutionized the industry. (statuette)
TO CHARLES CHAPLIN for acting, writing, directing and producing *The Circus*. (statuette)

*INDICATES WINNER

Special Award: Charles Chaplin *(above) in* The Circus. *Chaplin was very much in evidence during the Academy's first Awards year, initially nominated for and then withdrawn from both acting and comedy direction awards when he was voted a Special Award by the Academy Board of Governors for "versatility and genius in writing, acting, directing and producing* The Circus." *Forty-three years later, in a far different world and industry, he again received a special award from the Academy.*

Best Comedy Direction: Lewis Milestone *for* Two Arabian Knights *(United Artists) with William Boyd and Mary Astor (right). For the first and only year, the Academy distinguished between comedy direction and dramatic direction, in two separate voting categories; hereafter, they were judged as one body. Milestone won a second Academy Award two years later for his very dramatic* All Quiet on the Western Front.

1928-29
The Second Year

Talking pictures were firmly established as a Hollywood fact of life by the time the second Academy Awards were presented April 3, 1930, six months after the stock market crash, covering motion pictures exhibited in the Los Angeles area during the eligibility period of August 1, 1928, to July 31, 1929. Still, enough silent films were being made, or in release, to cause some confusion at the Academy office as to whether there should be separate awards categories for silent films *and* sound films. "The development of talking pictures has made individual achievement of artists more difficult to judge," said Academy Secretary Frank Woods, adding, "Sound has brought in a new element of screen art and a host of new people." After considerable discussion, it was decided no special distinction would be made in voting between the new talking pictures and silent ones.

Once again, as in the first voting year, only five individuals made the final selection of award winners. M-G-M's first all-talking picture, *The Broadway Melody,* was chosen best picture, Warner Baxter was chosen best actor for *In Old Arizona,* the screen's first outdoor talkie, Mary Pickford, one of the Academy founders, was named best actress for *Coquette,* which had been her initiation to sound films, and Frank Lloyd was named best director. In total, only seven awards were given, seven less than in the previous year. All the presentations were made by the new Academy President William C. deMille, and the banquet was held, not at the Biltmore Hotel or the Hollywood Roosevelt as before, but at the splendid Cocoanut Grove of the Ambassador Hotel in Los Angeles.

For the next formative years, it was inevitable the awards structure would undergo changes while the Academy leaders experimented with the best ways to utilize the awards of merit as a constructive arm of the Academy organization, and a worthwhile complement to the entire motion picture industry.

It was just as inevitable that the early years would also be inundated with "firsts." It was at the Academy banquet honoring the 1928-29 achievements that the first radio broadcast of an Academy Awards ceremony took place. A local Los Angeles radio station, KNX, did on-the-spot coverage of the festivities for one hour, beginning at 10:30 p.m. Pacific Standard Time. The annual presentation has been broadcast ever since, either on radio, or television, or both.

Best Picture: **The Broadway Melody** *(M-G-M; produced by Harry Rapf) starred Bessie Love and Charles King along with Anita Page, and was the first sound film to win the Academy's best picture award. The story was conventional by later yardsticks (two sisters, working in vaudeville, both fall in love with a successful Broadway song-and-dance man) but was particularly impressive in its day, surrounded by the novelty of sound on film. It contained a big "Wedding of the Painted Doll" musical sequence in color hues, and prompted M-G-M to produce three more musicals with the Broadway Melody label during the next ten years, all of them starring dancer Eleanor Powell. The original was also remade 11 years later as* Two Girls on Broadway *with Joan Blondell and Lana Turner as the show biz sisters.*

Nominations 1928-29

NOTES: For the second Academy Awards, all awards could be for a single achievement, for several achievements, or for the whole body of work during the qualifying year.

There were no announcements of nominations, no certificates of nomination or honorable mention, and only the winners (*) were revealed during the awards banquet. Though not official nominations, the additional names in each category, according to in-house records, were under consideration by the various boards of judges.

Frank Lloyd (Direction) and Hans Kraly (Writing) were each considered for their work on more than one picture, but in each case the document signed by the Academy's central board of judges singled out a particular film as the basis for their awards.

OUTSTANDING PICTURE

ALIBI, Feature Productions, UA. Produced by Roland West.
*THE BROADWAY MELODY, M-G-M. Produced by Harry Rapf.
THE HOLLYWOOD REVUE, M-G-M. Produced by Harry Rapf.
IN OLD ARIZONA, Fox. Winfield Sheehan, studio head.
THE PATRIOT, Paramount Famous Lasky. Produced by Ernst Lubitsch.

ACTOR

GEORGE BANCROFT in *Thunderbolt*, Paramount Famous Lasky.
*WARNER BAXTER in *In Old Arizona*, Fox.
CHESTER MORRIS in *Alibi*, Feature Productions, UA.
PAUL MUNI in *The Valiant*, Fox.
LEWIS STONE in *The Patriot*, Paramount Famous Lasky.

ACTRESS

RUTH CHATTERTON in *Madame X*, M-G-M.
BETTY COMPSON in *The Barker*, First National.
JEANNE EAGELS in *The Letter*, Paramount Famous Lasky.
CORRINE GRIFFITH in *The Divine Lady*, First National.
BESSIE LOVE in *The Broadway Melody*, M-G-M.
*MARY PICKFORD in *Coquette*, Pickford, UA.

DIRECTING

LIONEL BARRYMORE for *Madame X*, M-G-M.
HARRY BEAUMONT for *The Broadway Melody*, M-G-M.
IRVING CUMMINGS for *In Old Arizona*, Fox.
*FRANK LLOYD for *The Divine Lady*, First National.
FRANK LLOYD for *Weary River*, First National, and *Drag*, First National.
ERNST LUBITSCH for *The Patriot*, Paramount Famous Lasky.

WRITING

TOM BARRY, *The Valiant*, Fox, and *In Old Arizona*, Fox.
ELLIOTT CLAWSON, *The Leatherneck*, Ralph Block, Pathé Exchange, *Sal of Singapore*, Pathé Exchange, *Skyscraper*, DeMille Pictures, Pathé Exchange, and *The Cop*, DeMille Pictures, Pathé Exchange.
*HANS KRALY, *The Patriot*, Paramount Famous Lasky.
HANS KRALY, *The Last of Mrs. Cheyney*, M-G-M.
JOSEPHINE LOVETT, *Our Dancing Daughters*, Cosmopolitan, M-G-M.
BESS MEREDYTH, *Wonder of Women*, M-G-M, and *A Woman of Affairs*, M-G-M.

CINEMATOGRAPHY

GEORGE BARNES, *Our Dancing Daughters*, Cosmopolitan, M-G-M.
*CLYDE DE VINNA, *White Shadows in the South Seas*, Cosmopolitan, M-G-M.
ARTHUR EDESON, *In Old Arizona*, Fox.
ERNEST PALMER, *Four Devils*, Fox, and *Street Angel*, Fox.
JOHN SEITZ, *The Divine Lady*, First National.

ART DIRECTION

HANS DREIER, *The Patriot*, Paramount Famous Lasky.
*CEDRIC GIBBONS, *The Bridge of San Luis Rey* and other pictures, M-G-M.
MITCHELL LEISEN, *Dynamite*, Pathé Exchange, M-G-M.
WILLIAM CAMERON MENZIES, *Alibi*, Art Cinema, UA, and *The Awakening*, Samuel Goldwyn, UA.
HARRY OLIVER, *Street Angel*, Fox.

SPECIAL AWARDS

None given this year.

*INDICATES WINNER

Best Director: **Frank Lloyd** *(above, sitting in lower chair with Corrine Griffith) for* The Divine Lady *with Miss Griffith and Marie Dressler. Lloyd was again an Academy Award winner in 1932-33 for* Cavalcade, *and served one term as Academy President, in 1934-35.*

Best Actress: **Mary Pickford** *as Norma Beasant (above, surrounded by beaus) in* Coquette *(United Artists; directed by Sam Taylor). It was quite an event for moviegoers when Mary Pickford's voice was heard on the screen for the first time. A long-time staple of silent films, her introduction to sound also gave her an intense, adult role to play, as a small-* town *Southern flirt who wreaks havoc on all the men in her life. Four years later, Miss Pickford played her last screen role (in 1933's* Secrets*) but stayed active as a producer and business woman. In the Academy's 1975 award year she was again presented a statuette, an honorary one, for her overall contributions to the film medium.*

Best Actor: **Warner Baxter** *as The Cisco Kid in* In Old Arizona *(Fox; directed by Irving Cummings). Baxter (left) was a last-minute replacement to play O. Henry's troubadouring bandido who robs the rich and aids the poor; Raoul Walsh had been first choice but was injured in a Utah location accident during early filming. Baxter again played the Kid in two sequels,* The Cisco Kid *(1931) and* The Return of the Cisco Kid *(1939) before Cesar Romero and then Duncan Renaldo took over the character in a series of minor-budget but profitable "Cisco" sagebrushers.*

1929-30
The Third Year

Voting rules were changed drastically for the Academy's third presentation of awards, honoring motion pictures shown in the Los Angeles area between August 1, 1929 and July 31, 1930. No longer did a handful of judges make the big decisions. Now, both the original nominations and the final awards were voted by the entire Academy membership, which had grown to total over four hundred people, and the policy remained the same for the next five years (until 1936). The ceremony was held at the Fiesta Room of the Ambassador Hotel in Los Angeles on November 5, 1930, only seven months after the last presentation, in order to pick up a time lag and present awards closer to their eligibility deadlines.

Academy members, for the first time, were charged a fee to attend the banquet (ten dollars per person) and it was a complete sellout. Guests listened to a pre-dinner address by Will H. Hays, president of the Motion Picture Producers and Distributors Organization, and a post-dinner talk by Thomas A. Edison. Edison and George Eastman were both given honorary Academy memberships for their pioneering in the film medium. Academy Vice President Conrad Nagel presided over the evening, and awards were presented by Louis B. Mayer, Lawrence Grant and John Cromwell. Eight awards were given, and it was the last year so few would be dispersed.

All Quiet on the Western Front and *The Big House* were the most honored films, with two awards each. *All Quiet* was named as best picture, and for its director Lewis Milestone; *The Big House* was honored for Frances Marion's writing achievement and in a new category, sound recording, won by Norma Shearer's brother, Douglas Shearer. Norma Shearer was named best actress, offically for *The Divorcee*, and George Arliss was chosen best actor for *Disraeli*. The Arliss win marked another Academy "first": it was the first time a performer was honored by Academy voters for re-creating a role on screen which he or she had performed previously on the legitimate stage. (Arliss had not only done "Disraeli" on stage but had also starred in an earlier silent film version of the play.) Other awards went to *With Byrd at the South Pole* for its cinematography and *King of Jazz* for its art direction.

Sound on film now fully dominated the industry; the transitional period from the silent era was over. Interestingly, talking pictures had severely curbed the careers of several silent screen stars, but others were enhanced by the spoken word, and flourished, a fact underscored by the 1929–30 awards. Three of the year's nominees—Ronald Colman, Greta Garbo and Gloria Swanson—were stars who had bridged the gap successfully and were honored for performances in their initial sound films.

Best Picture: **All Quiet on the Western Front** *(Universal; produced by Carl Laemmle, Jr.) and* **Best Director:** **Lewis Milestone** *for* All Quiet on the Western Front. *Erich Maria Remarque's savage anti-war novel traced the steps of seven German schoolboys of 1914 as they come to face fear, filth, death and other horrors of battle during four years of World War I combat, a daring subject for the screen and dubious commercial material for audiences concerned with a national Depression. But it was an enormous success, skillfully made, won Academy Awards for producer Laemmle and director Milestone, and gave stimulus to the careers of its cast, including (right) Lew Ayres and Louis Wolheim.*

Nominations 1929-30

NOTE: For the third Academy Awards no certificates of nomination were given out, and, in the categories of Art Direction, Cinematography, Sound Recording and Writing, only the titles of the nominated films and their companies were announced; no individual names were listed. When the winners were revealed, only the names of the individuals involved with the *winning* achievements were announced. The names of those credited with the other nominated achievements in those four categories are indicated here in parentheses.

OUTSTANDING PRODUCTION

*ALL QUIET ON THE WESTERN FRONT, Universal. Produced by Carl Laemmle, Jr.
THE BIG HOUSE, Cosmopolitan, M-G-M. Produced by Irving G. Thalberg.
DISRAELI, Warner Bros. Produced by Jack L. Warner, with Darryl F. Zanuck.
THE DIVORCEE, M-G-M. Produced by Robert Z. Leonard.
THE LOVE PARADE, Paramount Famous Lasky. Produced by Ernst Lubitsch.

ACTOR

*GEORGE ARLISS in *Disraeli*, Warner Bros., and *The Green Goddess*, Warner Bros.
(NOTE: Though the awards ballot listed both films in Arliss's nomination, the award was announced for only the *Disraeli* performance. Why this was has not been established; it might possibly have been because the original report from the Acting Branch Board of Judges only listed this one performance in the results of the nominations voting, or it could have resulted from voters indicating a preference for the *Disraeli* performance over that in *Goddess* on their final ballots.)
WALLACE BEERY in *The Big House*, Cosmopolitan, M-G-M.
MAURICE CHEVALIER in *The Big Pond*, Paramount Publix, and *The Love Parade*, Paramount Famous Lasky.
RONALD COLMAN in *Bulldog Drummond*, Samuel Goldwyn, UA, and *Condemned*, Samuel Goldwyn, UA.
LAWRENCE TIBBETT in *The Rogue Song*, M-G-M.

ACTRESS

NANCY CARROLL in *The Devil's Holiday*, Paramount Publix.
RUTH CHATTERTON in *Sarah and Son*, Paramount Famous Lasky.
GRETA GARBO in *Anna Christie*, M-G-M, and *Romance*, M-G-M.
*NORMA SHEARER in *The Divorcee*, M-G-M, and *Their Own Desire*, M-G-M.
(NOTE: Though the awards ballot listed both films in Shearer's nomination, the award was announced for only the performance in *The Divorcee*. Why this was has not been established; it might possibly have been because the original report from the Acting Branch Board of Judges only listed this one performance in the results of the nominations voting, or it could have resulted from voters indicating a preference for the *Divorcee* performance over that in *Desire* on their final ballots.)
GLORIA SWANSON in *The Trespasser*, Joseph P. Kennedy Productions, UA.

DIRECTING

CLARENCE BROWN for *Anna Christie*, M-G-M, and *Romance*, M-G-M.
ROBERT LEONARD for *The Divorcee*, M-G-M.
ERNST LUBITSCH for *The Love Parade*, Paramount Famous Lasky.
*LEWIS MILESTONE for *All Quiet on the Western Front*, Universal.
KING VIDOR for *Hallelujah*, M-G-M.

WRITING

ALL QUIET ON THE WESTERN FRONT, Universal. (George Abbott, Maxwell Anderson and Del Andrews)
*THE BIG HOUSE, Cosmopolitan, M-G-M. Frances Marion.
DISRAELI, Warner Bros. (Julian Josephson)
THE DIVORCEE, M-G-M. (John Meehan)
STREET OF CHANCE, Paramount Famous Lasky. (Howard Estabrook)

CINEMATOGRAPHY

ALL QUIET ON THE WESTERN FRONT, Universal. (Arthur Edeson)
ANNA CHRISTIE, M-G-M. (William Daniels)
HELL'S ANGELS, The Caddo Company, UA. (Gaetano Gaudio and Harry Perry)
THE LOVE PARADE, Paramount Famous Lasky. (Victor Milner)
*WITH BYRD AT THE SOUTH POLE, Paramount Publix. Joseph T. Rucker and Willard Van Der Veer.

ART DIRECTION

BULLDOG DRUMMOND, Samuel Goldwyn, UA. (William Cameron Menzies)
*KING OF JAZZ, Universal. Herman Rosse.
THE LOVE PARADE, Paramount Famous Lasky. (Hans Dreier)
SALLY, First National. (Jack Okey)
THE VAGABOND KING, Paramount Publix. (Hans Dreier)

SOUND RECORDING

(New category)
*THE BIG HOUSE, Cosmopolitan, M-G-M. Douglas Shearer for the M-G-M Studio Sound Dept.
THE CASE OF SERGEANT GRISCHA, RKO Radio. (John Tribby for the RKO Radio Studio Sound Dept.)
THE LOVE PARADE, Paramount Famous Lasky. (Franklin Hansen for the Paramount Famous Lasky Studio Sound Dept.)
RAFFLES, Samuel Goldwyn, UA. (Oscar Lagerstrom for the United Artists Studio Sound Dept.)
SONG OF THE FLAME, First National. (George Groves for the First National Studio Sound Dept.)

SPECIAL AWARDS

None given this year.

*INDICATES WINNER

Best Actress: **Norma Shearer** *as Jerry (above, with Conrad Nagel) in* The Divorcee *(M-G-M; directed by Robert Leonard). The official Academy voting ballot for 1929-30 lists Miss Shearer with a single nomination encompassing two achievements (*The Divorcee *and* Their Own Desire*) but her award was officially presented solely for the first-named film, in which she played a free-spirited woman involved with a broken marriage and her ex-husband's best friend. How, or why, the single designation was made is now a mystery to everyone, including Academy researchers (and, in the years before her death in 1983, to Miss Shearer herself). But the following year, a rule change stated that in the future "no performer shall be entitled to more than one nomination, with the achievement polling the highest vote to be listed in case the individual may have received enough votes for different achievements to be entitled to more than one nomination."*

Best Actor: **George Arliss** *as Benjamin Disraeli (left, with Joan Bennett) in* Disraeli *(Warner Bros.; directed by Alfred E. Green). Arliss was a successful stage actor who popularly became known as the First Gentleman of the Talking Screen, and he was also the screen's dean of biography. He played* Disraeli *in the legitimate theater for five years before it became an early sound feature; predominantly set at No. 10 Downing Street in London, the movie covered the political manipulations of Prime Minister Disraeli to outwit Russia and acquire the Suez Canal for England and Queen Victoria. It concentrated on characterization and ideas rather than action.*

The Academy had gained a solid, national reputation by its fifth anniversary, which was also the fourth year of presenting Academy Awards for screen achievement. From Washington, D.C., President Herbert Hoover sent Vice President Charles Curtis to attend the 1930-31 awards banquet, held November 10, 1931, at the Biltmore Hotel in Los Angeles. Curtis, attending with his socially prominent sister Mrs. Dolly Gann, told the Academy members and guests, "I have come to you tonight from the capital of our country to pay my respects to the creative minds of the world's greatest and most influential enterprise, the motion picture." Movies had been a great morale booster during the year, which had been one of massive unemployment and a nationwide Depression. The Academy had also solidified its public image by establishing an extensive library dealing solely with motion pictures, helping inaugurate college film courses, organizing lectures on mechanical innovations and other activities.

Lawrence Grant was the master of ceremonies, and speakers joining Vice President Curtis included new Academy President M.C. Levee, past President William C. deMille, Louis B. Mayer, Conrad Nagel and California Governor James Rolph, Jr.; non-member guests included eastern film executives and visiting journalists from all over the United States, the first time the nation's news media paid rapt attention to an Academy Awards function. It was car-ried on a local radio station (KHJ) plus the entire Don Lee-Columbia radio network on the Pacific Coast.

Cimarron received three awards: for best picture, writing adaptation and art direction. Norman Taurog was named best director for *Skippy.* Lionel Barrymore was saluted as best actor for *A Free Soul,* and Marie Dressler won the best actress statuette for *Min and Bill.* Norma Shearer, the previous year's best actress winner, was asked to present the latter award and did so. Later, the program planners realized she inadvertently could have been placed in the embarrassing position of announcing herself as the winner, since she was again a nominee. Since that night, there has been an unwritten rule that previous *actress* honorees would present awards to winning *actors,* and vice versa. Also, the outcome of the balloting had always been disclosed a week or more in advance of the actual presentation; this year, Academy officials took extra precautions to keep the results of voting a secret, not giving names of winners to the press until late in the day of the awards.

One of the nominees drew attention when he fell asleep during the festivities. As the speeches wore on, ten-year-old Jackie Cooper, nominated as best actor for *Skippy,* snoozed with his head resting on the ample shoulder of Marie Dressler. When she was called to receive her award, young Cooper, still sleeping, had to be eased onto his mother's lap.

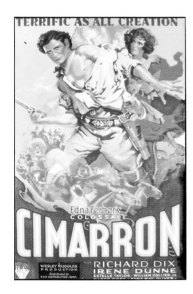

Best Picture: **Cimarron** *(RKO Radio; produced by William LeBaron) covered the rise of Oklahoma from early pioneer days to statehood, based on Edna Ferber's sweeping novel. Richard Dix (right, with Irene Dunne) was a homesteader in the great Oklahoma landrush of 1888 who lost his claim, became a newspaper editor and during the next four decades helped turn the overnight camp of Osage into a respectable town.* Cimarron *also won Academy Awards for writing adaptation (by Howard Estabrook) and art direction (by Max Rée) and is the only motion picture with a distinctly western flavor to have won a best picture award until the Academy's 63rd year when* Dances With Wolves *took home a statuette. This was followed two years later by Best Picture-winner* Unforgiven.

Nominations 1930-31

Best Director: **Norman Taurog** *for* Skippy *(Paramount), adapted from Percy Crosby's widely read comic strip of the day. Jackie Cooper was Skippy and Robert Coogan played Sooky (above), a couple of kids endeavoring to acquire enough money to buy Sooky's mongrel dog back from the local dogcatcher, to no avail. Taurog, Cooper and Coogan reteamed later in 1931 for a sequel,* Sooky, *and Taurog was again nominated in 1938 for his direction of* Boys Town.

OUTSTANDING PRODUCTION

*CIMARRON, RKO Radio. Produced by William LeBaron.
EAST LYNNE, Fox. Winfield Sheehan, studio head.
THE FRONT PAGE, Caddo, UA. Produced by Howard Hughes.
SKIPPY, Paramount Publix. Adolph Zukor, studio head.
TRADER HORN, M-G-M. Produced by Irving G. Thalberg.

ACTOR

*LIONEL BARRYMORE in *A Free Soul*, M-G-M.
JACKIE COOPER in *Skippy*, Paramount Publix.
RICHARD DIX in *Cimarron*, RKO Radio.
FREDRIC MARCH in *The Royal Family of Broadway*, Paramount Publix.
ADOLPHE MENJOU in *The Front Page*, Caddo, UA.

ACTRESS

MARLENE DIETRICH in *Morocco*, Paramount Publix.
*MARIE DRESSLER in *Min and Bill*, M-G-M.
IRENE DUNNE in *Cimarron*, RKO Radio.
ANN HARDING in *Holiday*, Pathé.
NORMA SHEARER in *A Free Soul*, M-G-M.

DIRECTING

CIMARRON, RKO Radio. Wesley Ruggles.
A FREE SOUL, M-G-M. Clarence Brown.
THE FRONT PAGE, Caddo, UA. Lewis Milestone.
MOROCCO, Paramount Publix. Joseph Von Sternberg.
*SKIPPY, Paramount Publix. Norman Taurog.

WRITING

(Adaptation)

*CIMARRON, RKO Radio. Howard Estabrook.
THE CRIMINAL CODE, Columbia. Seton I. Miller and Fred Niblo, Jr.
HOLIDAY, Pathé. Horace Jackson.
LITTLE CAESAR, Warner Bros.-First National. Francis Faragoh and Robert N. Lee.
SKIPPY, Paramount Publix. Joseph Mankiewicz and Sam Mintz.

(Original Story)

*THE DAWN PATROL, Warner Bros.-First National. John Monk Saunders.
THE DOORWAY TO HELL, Warner Bros. Rowland Brown.
LAUGHTER, Paramount Publix. Harry d'Abbadie d'Arrast, Douglas Doty and Donald Ogden Stewart.
THE PUBLIC ENEMY, Warner Bros. John Bright and Kubec Glasmon.
SMART MONEY, Warner Bros. Lucien Hubbard and Joseph Jackson.

CINEMATOGRAPHY

CIMARRON, RKO Radio. Edward Cronjager.
MOROCCO, Paramount Publix. Lee Garmes.
THE RIGHT TO LOVE, Paramount Publix. Charles Lang.
SVENGALI, Warner Bros. Barney "Chick" McGill.
*TABU, Paramount Publix. Floyd Crosby.

ART DIRECTION

*CIMARRON, RKO Radio. Max Rée.
JUST IMAGINE, Fox. Stephen Goosson and Ralph Hammeras.
MOROCCO, Paramount Publix. Hans Dreier.
SVENGALI, Warner Bros. Anton Grot.
WHOOPEE, Goldwyn, UA. Richard Day.

SOUND RECORDING

SAMUEL GOLDWYN-UA STUDIO SOUND DEPT.
M-G-M STUDIO SOUND DEPT.
*PARAMOUNT PUBLIX STUDIO SOUND DEPT.
RKO RADIO STUDIO SOUND DEPT.

SPECIAL AWARDS

None given this year.

SCIENTIFIC OR TECHNICAL

(New category)

CLASS I (statuette)

ELECTRICAL RESEARCH PRODUCTS, INC., RCA-PHOTOPHONE, INC., and RKO RADIO PICTURES, INC., for noise reduction recording equipment.
DuPONT FILM MANUFACTURING CORP. and EASTMAN KODAK CO. for super-sensitive panchromatic film.

CLASS II (certificate)

FOX FILM CORP. for effective use of synchro-projection composite photography.

CLASS III (honorable mention)

ELECTRICAL RESEARCH PRODUCTS, INC., for moving coil microphone transmitters.
RKO RADIO PICTURES, INC., for reflex type microphone concentrators.
RCA-PHOTOPHONE, INC., for ribbon microphone transmitters.

*INDICATES WINNER

Best Actress: **Marie Dressler** *as Min (above, with Wallace Beery) in* Min and Bill *(directed by George Hill). She had a bulky figure, unforgettable face and enormous talent, and in* Min and Bill *Marie Dressler walked the treacherous line between comedy and pathos with enormous distinction. As Min, she was a good-hearted old boozer who runs a broken-down waterfront hotel, works hard, constantly battles with a hulking beau (Beery), raises a foundling and ultimately gets led off to jail for killing the foundling's wayward mother. Dressler, one of Hollywood's boxoffice favorites of the 1930s, died at the height of her career, on July 28, 1934, just three years after her Academy Award triumph.*

Best Actor: **Lionel Barrymore** *as Stephen Ashe (above, with Norma Shearer) in* A Free Soul *(M-G-M; directed by Clarence Brown). They didn't make actors any better, or better liked, than Lionel Barrymore, and he always claimed* A Free Soul *was his favorite screen role. In it, he played a heavy-drinking, free-thinking criminal lawyer whose unconventional behavior is adopted by his spoiled daughter; at the finale, he delivered a 14 minute courtroom soliloquy that was considered a high mark in screen acting for the period. Earlier, Barrymore was under consideration for a 1928-29 Academy Award as director of* Madame X, *starring Ruth Chatterton.*

1931-32
The Fifth Year

A tie occurred for the first time at the 1931–32 awards ceremony, honoring films released between August 1, 1931 and July 31, 1932 in the Los Angeles area. Academy rules stated that duplicate awards were to be given when any contender came within three votes of a winner on the final ballot, and Wallace Beery, for his performance in *The Champ*, received only one less vote than Fredric March who starred in *Dr. Jekyll and Mr. Hyde*, so both officially shared recognition as the year's best actor. Later, rules were changed so that a tie is declared only when nominees receive the *exact* same number of final votes.

The banquet was held November 18, 1932, in the Ambassador Hotel's Fiesta Room, just eight days after Franklin D. Roosevelt's election as the thirty-second President of the United States in a landslide victory. Conrad Nagel, was master of ceremonies, and the most-honored films were *The Champ* and *Bad Girl* with two awards each. *Grand Hotel* was named best picture, Helen Hayes was best actress for *The Sin of Madelon Claudet*, and Frank Borzage won his second award as director, for *Bad Girl*. The awards categories themselves had increased to a total of ten, with the addition of a new division honoring short subjects and won by Walt Disney for his cartoon *Flowers and Trees*. Disney also was given an honorary award for his creation of Mickey Mouse and, during his lifetime, was destined to win more Academy Awards than any other individual.

The year caused two particularly interesting happenings. The Academy, attempting to stimulate excellence in motion picture achievements from all countries and all sources, had previously welcomed non-Hollywood product in its awards lists. However, some voters had been disturbed that the preceding year *Tabu*, filmed in the South Seas by the late German director F.W. Murnau, had received the Academy's cinematography award over a home-town achievement. The Academy was asked to qualify the requirements for its 1931–32 cinematography award to read, "for the best achievement in cinematography of a black-and-white picture photographed in America under normal production conditions." (The 1931–32 nomination for the French-made *A Nous la Liberté* in the art direction category caused a similar qualification in 1932–33.) In later years, however, as industry sentiments matured, the Academy again showed its respect for foreign-made films by according them equal status with domestic product.

The Fredric March–Wallace Beery tie also triggered the first of many "quotable quotes" given by Academy winners throughout the years. By coincidence, both actors had adopted children shortly before winning their awards. "Under the circumstances," said Mr. March during his acceptance speech, "it seems a little odd that Wally and I were both given awards for the best male performance of the year."

28

Best Picture: **Grand Hotel** *(M-G-M; produced by Irving Thalberg) created a new screen formula in which all-star casts and unrelated characters were brought together in a common and dramatic environment. In the case of* Grand Hotel, *it was a plush Berlin hotel during a 48-hour period, based on a Vicki Baum novel and subsequent play which had been financed by M-G-M. Edmund Goulding directed the film and the cast included Greta Garbo and John Barrymore (right), as well as Joan Crawford, Wallace Beery and Lionel Barrymore, each of whom was usually the solo star of his or her own Metro film. Also known as the film in which Garbo first said "I vant to be alone" (not once but, in fact, three times), it was later updated by M-G-M in 1945 as* Weekend at the Waldorf *and was also remade as a 1960 German film starring Michele Morgan.*

Best Actor: Fredric March *as Henry Jekyll and as Mr. Hyde (above) in* Dr. Jekyll and Mr. Hyde *(Paramount; directed by Rouben Mamoulian). Many distinguished actors have had a field day playing the two-faced doctor created by Robert Louis Stevenson in his fascinating tale of a man who dreams of releasing the evil desires in every man's sub-* conscious. *James Cruze, Sheldon Lewis, John Barrymore, Spencer Tracy, Paul Massie and Anthony Perkins are among those who have had a go at it on screen; none, however, has been more successful than Fredric March in the first sound version of the horror story. Virtually unrecognizable as the alter-ego Hyde, wearing false teeth, putty nose, gorilla hands* and makeup which took three hours to apply, March won the *Academy Award for his performance. He won again in 1946 for* The Best Years of Our Lives *and received five award nominations during his lifetime.*

Best Actor: Wallace Beery *as Champ (left, with Jackie Cooper) in* The Champ *(M-G-M; directed by King Vidor). Beery once said, "I have no art in my soul, I don't try to be different. I'm just plain me in every picture and the public continues to accept me." However, Beery was seen in two widely divergent roles during the 1931-32 awards year, as the crooked industrialist in* Grand Hotel *and as a drunken, ex-champion prizefighter in* The Champ, *and showed his enormous power as an actor in both. When Academy Award votes were counted, Beery's performance in the latter film had come within one vote of Fredric March in* Dr. Jekyll and Mr. Hyde, *so under Academy rules of the day, both officially shared honors and received statuettes as the year's best actor.*

Shanghai Express *(Paramount), starred Marlene Dietrich and Clive Brook (left) as two passengers on a train journey to Shanghai, amid rebel unrest in China, sharing secrets and staterooms with the likes of Anna May Wong, Warner Oland, Eugene Pallette and others. It won an Academy Award for Lee Garmes' atmospheric cinematography; Garmes had also photographed Miss Dietrich's two previous American-made films,* Morocco *and* Dishonored.

Best Director: Frank Borzage *for* Bad Girl *(Fox) starring Sally Eilers and James Dunn (left). Strangely mistitled,* Bad Girl *covered a year in the life of a likable fellow and girl, from their first meeting, through marriage, to the birth of a son, set against a background of New York tenement life. Borzage, a specialist in directing effective, sentimental stories, had earlier won the Academy Award for his direction of* 7th Heaven *during the first awards year.*

Nominations 1931-32

Best Actress: Helen Hayes *as Madelon (above, with Neil Hamilton) in* The Sin of Madelon Claudet *(M-G-M; directed by Edgar Selwyn). Helen Hayes had made a few film appearances as a juvenile during the movies' silent era, but* The Sin of Madelon Claudet *was her much-heralded introduction to screen audiences after she'd made a notable success as a Broadway star. It was also a tear-jerker of the dampest sort, based on Edward Knoblock's play* The Lullaby, *about a young Parisian girl who falls in love with an American artist, bears an illegitimate child, then goes from mistress to party girl to barfly to street-walker to scrubwoman, in an effort to raise money so her unsuspecting son can have a good life. Audiences in 1931 reveled in it, and in Miss Hayes' rich performance. She was again an Academy Award winner 38 years later, as 1970's best supporting actress in* Airport.

A new category, honoring short subjects, was inaugurated with the 1931-32 awards, with the award for best comedy short going to Hal Roach's The Music Box *starring Oliver Hardy and Stan Laurel (right), a hilarious featurette in which the indefatigable comedy team battled the challenge of delivering a piano up a seemingly endless flight of Los Angeles hillside stairs. Ironically, for all the timeless comedy delivered on screen by Laurel and Hardy, this was their only movie which went on to receive an Academy Award.*

OUTSTANDING PRODUCTION

ARROWSMITH, Goldwyn, UA. Produced by Samuel Goldwyn.
BAD GIRL, Fox. Winfield Sheehan, studio head.
THE CHAMP, M-G-M. Produced by King Vidor.
FIVE STAR FINAL, First National. Produced by Hal B. Wallis.
*****GRAND HOTEL**, M-G-M. Produced by Irving Thalberg.
ONE HOUR WITH YOU, Paramount Publix. Produced by Ernst Lubitsch.
SHANGHAI EXPRESS, Paramount Publix. Adolph Zukor, studio head.
THE SMILING LIEUTENANT, Paramount Publix. Produced by Ernst Lubitsch.

ACTOR

*****WALLACE BEERY** in *The Champ*, M-G-M.
ALFRED LUNT in *The Guardsman*, M-G-M.
*****FREDRIC MARCH** in *Dr. Jekyll and Mr. Hyde*, Paramount Publix.

ACTRESS

MARIE DRESSLER in *Emma*, M-G-M.
LYNN FONTANNE in *The Guardsman*, M-G-M.
*****HELEN HAYES** in *The Sin of Madelon Claudet*, M-G-M.

DIRECTING

*****BAD GIRL**, Fox. Frank Borzage.
THE CHAMP, M-G-M. King Vidor.
SHANGHAI EXPRESS, Paramount Publix. Josef Von Sternberg.

WRITING

(Adaptation)
ARROWSMITH, Goldwyn, UA. Sidney Howard.
*****BAD GIRL**, Fox. Edwin Burke.
DR. JEKYLL AND MR. HYDE, Paramount Publix. Percy Heath and Samuel Hoffenstein.

(Original Story)
*****THE CHAMP**, M-G-M. Frances Marion.
LADY AND GENT, Paramount Publix. Grover Jones and William Slavens McNutt.
THE STAR WITNESS, Warner Bros. Lucien Hubbard.
WHAT PRICE HOLLYWOOD, RKO Radio. Adela Rogers St. Johns and Jane Murfin.

CINEMATOGRAPHY

ARROWSMITH, Goldwyn, UA. Ray June.
DR. JEKYLL AND MR. HYDE, Paramount Publix. Karl Struss.
*****SHANGHAI EXPRESS**, Paramount Publix. Lee Garmes.

ART DIRECTION

A NOUS LA LIBERTE (French). Lazare Meerson.
ARROWSMITH, Goldwyn, UA. Richard Day.
*****TRANSATLANTIC**, Fox. Gordon Wiles.

SOUND RECORDING

M-G-M STUDIO SOUND DEPT.
*****PARAMOUNT PUBLIX STUDIO SOUND DEPT.**
RKO RADIO STUDIO SOUND DEPT.
WARNER BROS.-FIRST NATIONAL STUDIO SOUND DEPT.

SHORT SUBJECTS

(New category)

(Cartoons)
*****FLOWERS AND TREES**, Disney, UA.
IT'S GOT ME AGAIN, Schlesinger, Warner Bros.
MICKEY'S ORPHANS, Disney, Columbia.

(Comedy)
THE LOUD MOUTH, Mack Sennett, Paramount Publix.
*****THE MUSIC BOX**, Hal Roach, M-G-M. (Laurel & Hardy)
SCRATCH-AS-CATCH-CAN, RKO Radio.

(Novelty)
SCREEN SOUVENIRS, Paramount Publix.
SWING HIGH, M-G-M.
*****WRESTLING SWORDFISH**, Mack Sennett, Educational.

SPECIAL AWARD

TO WALT DISNEY for the creation of Mickey Mouse. (statuette)

SCIENTIFIC OR TECHNICAL

CLASS I (statuette)
None

CLASS II (certificate)
TECHNICOLOR MOTION PICTURE CORP. for its color cartoon process.

CLASS III (honorable mention)
EASTMAN KODAK CO. for its Type II-B sensitometer.

*****INDICATES WINNER**

31

Some befuddled confusion accompanied the 1932-33 Academy party, the type of unrehearsed fun that has added to the folklore of Hollywood's annual awards night. Will Rogers, already a legendary humorist and sometime actor, was host and, in presenting the award for director of the year, drawled on at length about "my good friend Frank," and "Frank's rise to prominence," finally finishing his introduction by commanding, "Come and get it, Frank." Nominee Frank Capra was out of his seat and halfway to the podium when he realized another nominee, Frank Lloyd for *Cavalcade,* was the actual winner. Capra later returned to his seat from what he later described goodnaturedly as "the longest crawl in history." During the festivities, host Rogers also invited actress nominees May Robson and Diana Wynyard to the speakers' table, leading many people to anticipate there had been a tie; Rogers kissed them both, told them they had delivered "sparkling performances," and announced the absent Katharine Hepburn as the winner for *Morning Glory.*

During the evening, March 16, 1934, in the Fiesta Room of the Ambassador Hotel, fourteen awards categories were honored, including a new one for assistant directors. *Cavalcade,* with its trio of awards, including best picture, won the most honors from Academy voting. Charles Laughton was named best actor for *The Private Life of Henry VIII,* the first time a performer in a British-made film had been an Academy Award winner. Also, second and third place runners-up in all categories were announced, a practice later discontinued shortly after the certified public accounting firm of Price Waterhouse & Co. began tabulating ballots for the Academy. *Cavalcade* was followed by *A Farewell to Arms,* then *Little Women,* in number of votes as the best picture; Paul Muni and May Robson were first runners-up for acting awards, and Leslie Howard and Diana Wynyard were second runners-up. Frank Capra was the second choice for director, and George Cukor was third choice.

For the first and only time, more than a twelve-month span was used as the awards eligibility period; instead, the 1932-33 awards covered seventeen months, from August 1, 1932, to December 31, 1933, in order to allow future Academy Awards to be based on a calendar year, rather than a seasonal one. The awards have remained on a calendar basis ever since.

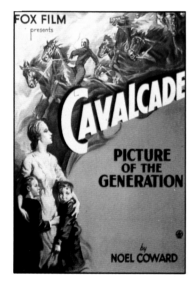

FOX FILM
presents

CAVALCADE

PICTURE
OF THE
GENERATION

by
NOEL COWARD

***Best Picture:* Cavalcade** *(Fox Film Corporation) and* ***Best Director:* Frank Lloyd** *for* Cavalcade. *Based on the play by Noel Coward, with a screenplay by Reginald Berkeley,* Cavalcade *was a sweeping, episodic composition with a British flavor and British cast, but filmed in Hollywood. It told of the effect of world events on the home life and family of a married couple (Diana Wynyard and Clive Brook) during the decades between New Year's Eve 1899 and the same evening 33 years later, a patriotic pageant with a universal theme and appeal for families of any country. William S. Darling was also honored for his art direction.*

Best Actor: **Charles Laughton** *as King Henry in* The Private Life of Henry VIII *(United Artists; directed in England by Alexander Korda). Laughton's performance was the first in a non-Hollywood film to win the Academy Award, and a vastly good-natured portrait of England's bulky monarch (1491-1547) whose six marriages complicated the future reigns of his country and brought about the independence of the Church of England. Laughton played it with flamboyant spice and among his most memorable moments was a scene when he dined a la Henry, ripping a chicken apart with his hands, devouring the food, belching and generally having a grand gastronomical time. Laughton again played Henry 21 years later in 1953's* Young Bess *with Jean Simmons as his daughter Elizabeth.*

Best Actress: **Katharine Hepburn** *as Eva Lovelace (left, with C. Aubrey Smith) in* Morning Glory *(RKO Radio; directed by Lowell Sherman). A year after her striking screen debut in* A Bill of Divorcement, *and concurrent with another 1933 success,* Little Women, *Miss Hepburn played a stagestruck young actress, self-confident, talkative and ambitiously determined to become "the finest actress in the world," with Adolphe Menjou and Douglas Fairbanks, Jr., as two important men in her private-public life. It was Hepburn's first contact with the Academy Awards but far from her last. She was destined to become (along with Meryl Streep [13 times]) the most nominated and most Oscared (4 Awards) performer during the Academy's first 75 years of giving prizes.*

Little Women *(RKO Radio; produced by Merian C. Cooper, with Kenneth MacGowan) was Louisa May Alcott wrapped up in the persona of (above) Joan Bennett as Amy,* *Spring Byington as Marmee, Frances Dee as Meg, Jean Parker (at piano) as Beth and Katharine Hepburn as Jo. It won for the writing adaptation of Miss Alcott's popular novel* *by screenwriters Victor Heerman and Sarah Y. Mason. George Cukor directed.*

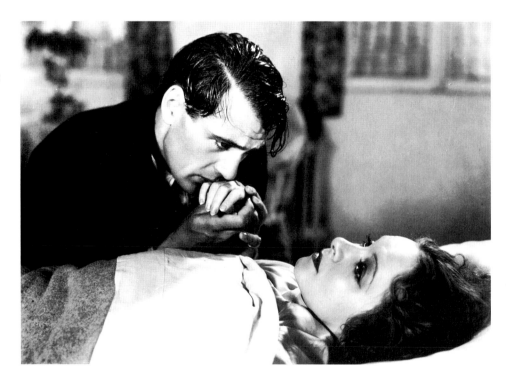

A Farewell to Arms *(Paramount) received two awards: for cinematography (by Charles Bryant Lang, Jr.) and sound recording (by Harold C. Lewis). It was based on the 1930 Ernest Hemingway book and directed by Frank Borzage, with (left) Gary Cooper as the American lieutenant serving with the Italian ambulance corps who falls in love with Helen Hayes as an English nurse, during wartime. The film opted for a happy ending, as opposed to Hemingway's more tragic one, something audiences often demanded in the 1930s. It was a distinguished, well-admired film and inspired two later versions: a revamped adaptation called Force of Arms (1950) with William Holden and Nancy Olson, and a remake in 1957 with Rock Hudson and Jennifer Jones, produced by David O. Selznick. Helen Hayes later called the 1932 version "my own favorite movie in which I appeared."*

OUTSTANDING PRODUCTION

*CAVALCADE, Fox. Winfield Sheehan, studio head.
A FAREWELL TO ARMS, Paramount. Adolph Zukor, studio head.
42ND STREET, Warner Bros. Produced by Darryl F. Zanuck.
I AM A FUGITIVE FROM A CHAIN GANG, Warner Bros. Produced by Hal B. Wallis.
LADY FOR A DAY, Columbia. Produced by Frank Capra.
LITTLE WOMEN, RKO Radio. Produced by Merian C. Cooper, with Kenneth MacGowan.
THE PRIVATE LIFE OF HENRY VIII, London Films, UA (British). Produced by Alexander Korda.
SHE DONE HIM WRONG, Paramount. Produced by William LeBaron.
SMILIN' THROUGH, M-G-M. Produced by Irving Thalberg.
STATE FAIR, Fox. Winfield Sheehan, studio head.

ACTOR

LESLIE HOWARD in *Berkeley Square*, Fox.
*CHARLES LAUGHTON in *The Private Life of Henry VIII*, London Films, UA (British).
PAUL MUNI in *I Am a Fugitive from a Chain Gang*, Warner Bros.

ACTRESS

*KATHARINE HEPBURN in *Morning Glory*, RKO Radio.
MAY ROBSON in *Lady for a Day*, Columbia.
DIANA WYNYARD in *Cavalcade*, Fox.

DIRECTING

*CAVALCADE, Fox. Frank Lloyd.
LADY FOR A DAY, Columbia. Frank Capra.
LITTLE WOMEN, RKO Radio. George Cukor.

WRITING

(Adaptation)
LADY FOR A DAY, Columbia. Robert Riskin.
*LITTLE WOMEN, RKO Radio. Victor Heerman and Sarah Y. Mason.
STATE FAIR, Fox. Paul Green and Sonya Levien.

(Original Story)
*ONE WAY PASSAGE, Warner Bros. Robert Lord.
THE PRIZEFIGHTER AND THE LADY, M-G-M. Frances Marion.
RASPUTIN AND THE EMPRESS, M-G-M. Charles MacArthur.

CINEMATOGRAPHY

*A FAREWELL TO ARMS, Paramount. Charles Bryant Lang, Jr.
REUNION IN VIENNA, M-G-M. George J. Folsey.
THE SIGN OF THE CROSS, Paramount Publix. Karl Struss.

ART DIRECTION

*CAVALCADE, Fox. William S. Darling.
A FAREWELL TO ARMS, Paramount. Hans Dreier and Roland Anderson.
WHEN LADIES MEET, M-G-M. Cedric Gibbons.

SOUND RECORDING

*A FAREWELL TO ARMS, Paramount. Paramount Studio Sound Dept., Franklin B. Hansen, Sound Director.
42ND STREET, Warner Bros. Warner Bros. Studio Sound Dept., Nathan Levinson, Sound Director.
GOLD DIGGERS OF 1933, Warner Bros. Warner Bros. Studio Sound Dept., Nathan Levinson, Sound Director.
I AM A FUGITIVE FROM A CHAIN GANG, Warner Bros. Warner Bros. Studio Sound Dept., Nathan Levinson, Sound Director.

ASSISTANT DIRECTOR

(New category)
PERCY IKERD, Fox.
*WILLIAM TUMMEL, Fox.
*CHARLES DORIAN, M-G-M.
BUNNY DULL, M-G-M.
JOHN S. WATERS, M-G-M.
*CHARLES BARTON, Paramount.
SIDNEY S. BROD, Paramount.
ARTHUR JACOBSON, Paramount.
EDDIE KILLEY, RKO Radio.
DEWEY STARKEY, RKO Radio
*FRED FOX, UA.
BENJAMIN SILVEY, UA.
*SCOTT BEAL, Universal.
JOE McDONOUGH, Universal.
W.J. REITER, Universal.
AL ALBORN, Warner Bros.
*GORDON HOLLINGSHEAD, Warner Bros.
FRANK X. SHAW, Warner Bros.
(NOTE: Multiple awards given this year only.)

SHORT SUBJECTS

(Cartoons)
BUILDING A BUILDING, Disney, UA.
THE MERRY OLD SOUL, Lantz, Universal.
*THREE LITTLE PIGS, Disney, UA.

(Comedy)
MISTER MUGG, Universal. (Comedies)
A PREFERRED LIST, Louis Brock, RKO Radio. (Headliner Series #5)
*SO THIS IS HARRIS, Louis Brock, RKO Radio. (Special)

(Novelty)
*KRAKATOA, Joe Rock, Educational. (Three-reel Special)
MENU, Pete Smith, M-G-M. (Oddities)
THE SEA, Educational. (Battle for Life)

SPECIAL AWARDS

None given this year.

SCIENTIFIC OR TECHNICAL

CLASS I (statuette)
None.

CLASS II (certificate)
ELECTRICAL RESEARCH PRODUCTS, INC., for their wide range recording and reproducing system.
RCA-VICTOR CO., INC., for their high-fidelity recording and reproducing system.

CLASS III (honorable mention)
FOX FILM CORP., FRED JACKMAN and WARNER BROS. PICTURES, INC., and SIDNEY SANDERS of RKO Studios, Inc. for their development and effective use of the translucent cellulose screen in composite photography.

*INDICATES WINNER

Three Little Pigs *(right) won the year's award for best cartoon short subject, only the second year that category had been included in the award structure and the second Disney win in a row (following 1931–32's* Flowers and Trees). *Over the next decades, The Walt Disney Company would accomplish an incredible record of wins in the short subject categories: 23 Academy Awards, 13 of them for animation, seven for live-action shorts, three for documentaries. And as the Disney organization began branching into feature-length movies with* Snow White and the Seven Dwarfs, *even more Academy attention was to come.*

1934
The Seventh Year

When the nominees for the 1934 awards were announced, the Academy was bombarded with protests, the first time there had been such massive critical argument with the selections. The crux of the irritation was the fact that in the best actress category the names of Bette Davis (for *Of Human Bondage*) and Myrna Loy (in *The Thin Man*), two of the year's most respected performances, were missing. Newspaper editorials, telegrams and telephone calls assailed the Academy, reaching a high enough pitch that voting rules were temporarily abandoned and the Academy announced, on January 16, 1935, that voters would be allowed to disregard the printed ballot and write in any name they preferred.

On the night of the awards, February 27, 1935, nearly a thousand guests jammed into the Biltmore Bowl of the Los Angeles Biltmore Hotel to hear the outcome, realizing there was a good chance none of the original nominees would ultimately be declared winners, despite the fact that many members had marked their ballots before the "write-in" free-for-all was allowed. When the final results were announced, everyone had reason to be surprised. The "overlooked" performers, it was announced, including Bette Davis and Myrna Loy, did not win, place or show. A single picture, *It Happened One Night,* walked off with five of the evening's awards, including best picture, actor (Clark Gable), actress (Claudette Colbert), director (Frank Capra) and writing adaptation (Robert Riskin), the first time one picture had been so prominent in a single awards year.

Claudette Colbert, not expecting to win, was in the process of boarding a train to New York when Academy officials found her and informed her of the results. Santa Fe officials held up the locomotive as she was rushed off to collect her prize, dressed in a tailored suit for travel. She arrived at the banquet, received her award from host-presenter Irvin S. Cobb, posed for photographs, then was whisked back to the train.

Later, when the voting order was officially made known, it was stated that Miss Colbert's runners-up were Norma Shearer, then Grace Moore, all of them official nominees. Clark Gable was followed by Frank Morgan and William Powell, also official nominees. However, Academy records are now in evidence which show that the public announcement was not entirely accurate. Indeed, Miss Colbert came in first, followed by Norma Shearer, but write-in choice Bette Davis was third. Why the incorrect information was announced is unknown today. The men's ranking order was as announced.

Music was honored for the first year, in two categories (song and music score), and a film editing division was also inaugurated. Shirley Temple received a special award in the form of a miniature statuette, in recognition of her contributions during the year as a screen juvenile. And for the first time, the eligibility period for awards consideration was based on a calendar year (January 1 to December 31, 1934) rather than a seasonal period.

Best Picture: **It Happened One Night** *(Columbia; produced by Harry Cohn),* **Best Director:** Frank Capra *(right),* **Best Actor:** Clark Gable *as Peter Warne, and* **Best Actress:** Claudette Colbert *as Ellie Andrews (opposite page) in* It Happened One Night. *It was one of those happy celluloid accidents, difficult to analyze and impossible to reproduce intentionally.* Night Bus, *the original script, had been kicking around studios for several months. No one expected it to be such a runaway hit, but it was exactly the kind of entertainment that appealed to a Depression-weary country, and its appeal is just as potent today. It marked Gable's first go at playing comedy, and was one of three strong 1934 roles for Miss Colbert, along with* Cleopatra *and* Imitation of Life. *It was also the first of Capra's three awards as best director. For the next 41 years (until 1975's* One Flew Over the Cuckoo's Nest*), it would also remain the only film to win the Academy's prizes for picture, actor, actress and director. It also won a fifth award, for Robert Riskin's invaluable writing adaptation.*

37

Cleopatra *(Paramount; produced by Cecil B. DeMille) was DeMillian spectacle at its showiest, a superb example of the kind of eye-feast which the motion picture medium could serve better than any other. Claudette Colbert (left) played the Egyptian queen, involved with court intrigue, Mark Antony, asps and a thousand or so extras, and the film won the Academy Award for Victor Milner's cinematography. It was not Oscar's last encounter with Cleo-of-the-Nile. Joseph L. Mankiewicz's mammoth 1963 version also won an Academy Award for its cinematography, along with three other statues for excellence.*

In the constant attempt to rightfully honor deserving movie contributors, the Academy introduced another new category with the 1934 awards, the one for music. The first best song winner was "The Continental," introduced by Ginger Rogers and Fred Astaire (left), along with Erik Rhodes and a platoon of dancers in a lengthy sequence in RKO's The Gay Divorcee. *The song was written by Con Conrad and Herb Magidson and among its competitors for the award was another song written for the Astaire-Rogers team, "Carioca" from* Flying Down to Rio. *Ginger herself would go on to win an Academy Award, sans music, as best actress for 1940's* Kitty Foyle; *Fred was voted an honorary Oscar in 1949 for his contributions to the movie musical genre.*

Nominations 1934

Special Award: **Shirley Temple** *(above, with Irvin S. Cobb). "When Santa Claus brought you down Creation's chimney, he brought the loveliest Christmas present that has ever been given to the world," said Cobb as he presented a miniature statuette to Shirley Temple for her contributions during the year to screen entertainment. There were nine Temple features in 1934, including* Little Miss Marker *which had made her a major screen attraction, America's favorite tot, and, at the age of six, one of the most famous females in the world.*

OUTSTANDING PRODUCTION

THE BARRETTS OF WIMPOLE STREET, M-G-M. Produced by Irving Thalberg.
CLEOPATRA, Paramount. Produced by Cecil B. DeMille.
FLIRTATION WALK, First National. Produced by Jack L. Warner and Hal Wallis, with Robert Lord.
THE GAY DIVORCEE, RKO Radio. Produced by Pandro S. Berman.
HERE COMES THE NAVY, Warner Bros. Produced by Lou Edelman.
THE HOUSE OF ROTHSCHILD, 20th Century, UA. Produced by Darryl F. Zanuck, with William Goetz and Raymond Griffith.
IMITATION OF LIFE, Universal. Produced by John M. Stahl.
*****IT HAPPENED ONE NIGHT**, Columbia. Produced by Harry Cohn.
ONE NIGHT OF LOVE, Columbia. Produced by Harry Cohn, with Everett Riskin.
THE THIN MAN, M-G-M. Produced by Hunt Stromberg.
VIVA VILLA, M-G-M. Produced by David O. Selznick.
THE WHITE PARADE, Fox. Produced by Jesse L. Lasky.

ACTOR

*****CLARK GABLE** in *It Happened One Night*, Columbia.
FRANK MORGAN in *The Affairs of Cellini*, 20th Century, UA.
WILLIAM POWELL in *The Thin Man*, M-G-M.

ACTRESS

*****CLAUDETTE COLBERT** in *It Happened One Night*, Columbia.
GRACE MOORE in *One Night of Love*, Columbia.
NORMA SHEARER in *The Barretts of Wimpole Street*, M-G-M.

DIRECTING

*****IT HAPPENED ONE NIGHT**, Columbia. Frank Capra.
ONE NIGHT OF LOVE, Columbia. Victor Schertzinger.
THE THIN MAN, M-G-M. W.S. Van Dyke.

WRITING

(Adaptation)
*****IT HAPPENED ONE NIGHT**, Columbia. Robert Riskin.
THE THIN MAN, M-G-M. Frances Goodrich and Albert Hackett.
VIVA VILLA, M-G-M. Ben Hecht.

(Original Story)
HIDE-OUT, M-G-M. Mauri Grashin.
*****MANHATTAN MELODRAMA**, Cosmopolitan, M-G-M. Arthur Caesar.
THE RICHEST GIRL IN THE WORLD, RKO Radio. Norman Krasna.

CINEMATOGRAPHY

THE AFFAIRS OF CELLINI, 20th Century, UA. Charles Rosher.
*****CLEOPATRA**, Paramount. Victor Milner.
OPERATOR 13, Cosmopolitan, M-G-M. George Folsey.

ART DIRECTION

THE AFFAIRS OF CELLINI, 20th Century, UA. Richard Day.
THE GAY DIVORCEE, RKO Radio. Van Nest Polglase and Carroll Clark.
*****THE MERRY WIDOW**, M-G-M. Cedric Gibbons and Frederic Hope.

SOUND RECORDING

THE AFFAIRS OF CELLINI, 20th Century, UA. United Artists Studio Sound Dept., Thomas T. Moulton, Sound Director.
CLEOPATRA, Paramount. Paramount Studio Sound Dept., Franklin Hansen, Sound Director.
FLIRTATION WALK, First National. Warner Bros.-First National Studio Sound Dept., Nathan Levinson, Sound Director.
THE GAY DIVORCEE, RKO Radio. RKO Radio Studio Sound Dept., Carl Dreher, Sound Director.
IMITATION OF LIFE, Universal. Universal Studio Sound Dept., Theodore Soderberg, Sound Director.
*****ONE NIGHT OF LOVE**, Columbia. Columbia Studio Sound Dept., John Livadary, Sound Director.
VIVA VILLA, M-G-M. M-G-M Studio Sound Dept., Douglas Shearer, Sound Director.
THE WHITE PARADE, Jesse L. Lasky, Fox. Fox Studio Sound Dept., E.H. Hansen, Sound Director.

FILM EDITING

(New category)
CLEOPATRA, Paramount. Anne Bauchens.
*****ESKIMO**, M-G-M. Conrad Nervig.
ONE NIGHT OF LOVE, Columbia. Gene Milford.

MUSIC

(New category)

(Song)
CARIOCA (*Flying Down to Rio*, RKO Radio); Music by Vincent Youmans. Lyrics by Edward Eliscu and Gus Kahn.
*****THE CONTINENTAL** (*The Gay Divorcee*, RKO Radio); Music by Con Conrad. Lyrics by Herb Magidson.
LOVE IN BLOOM (*She Loves Me Not*, Paramount); Music by Ralph Rainger. Lyrics by Leo Robin.

(Score)
THE GAY DIVORCEE, RKO Radio. RKO Radio Studio Music Dept.; Max Steiner, head. Score by Kenneth Webb and Samuel Hoffenstein.
THE LOST PATROL, RKO Radio. RKO Radio Studio Music Dept.; Max Steiner, head. Score by Max Steiner.
*****ONE NIGHT OF LOVE**, Columbia. Columbia Studio Music Dept.; Louis Silvers, head. Thematic music by Victor Schertzinger and Gus Kahn.
(NOTE: From 1934–37, best score was considered a music department achievement and award was presented to department head instead of to the composer.)

ASSISTANT DIRECTOR

CLEOPATRA, Paramount. Cullen Tate.
IMITATION OF LIFE, Universal. Scott Beal.
*****VIVA VILLA**, M-G-M. John Waters.

SHORT SUBJECTS

(Cartoons)
HOLIDAY LAND, Mintz, Columbia.
JOLLY LITTLE ELVES, Universal.
*****THE TORTOISE AND THE HARE**, Disney, UA.

(Comedy)
*****LA CUCARACHA**, RKO Radio. (Special)
MEN IN BLACK, Columbia. (Broadway Comedies)
WHAT, NO MEN!, Warner Bros. (Broadway Brevities)

(Novelty)
BOSOM FRIENDS, Educational. (Treasure Chest)
*****CITY OF WAX**, Educational. (Battle for Life)
STRIKES AND SPARES, M-G-M. (Oddities)

SPECIAL AWARDS

TO SHIRLEY TEMPLE, in grateful recognition of her outstanding contribution to screen entertainment during the year 1934. (miniature statuette)

SCIENTIFIC OR TECHNICAL

CLASS I (statuette)
None.

CLASS II (plaque)
ELECTRICAL RESEARCH PRODUCTS, INC., for their development of the vertical cut disc method of recording sound for motion pictures (hill and dale recording).

CLASS III (citation)
COLUMBIA PICTURES CORP.;
BELL AND HOWELL CO.

*****INDICATES WINNER**

1935
The Eighth Year

Sometime in 1935, or thereabouts, the Academy Award statuette acquired an indelible nickname. For years, industry members and newspaper reporters had been forced to refer clumsily to "the Academy statuette" or "the golden trophy" or "the statue of merit," but suddenly it became widely known as, simply, "Oscar." The name of the person responsible for initiating the new name is not conclusively documented, but through the years, three people have been credited. Margaret Herrick, then the Academy's librarian and later its executive director, is said to have named the statue after an uncle, a Mr. Oscar Pierce. Hollywood columnist Sidney Skolsky claimed to have first called it Oscar after an old vaudeville joke ("Will you have a cigar, Oscar?") because he was weary of finding synonyms when writing about the Academy Award statuette. Bette Davis is also said to have been the originator, naming the award after her husband, Harmon Oscar Nelson, Jr., whom, she claimed, aspects of the statuette resembled. Only one thing is certain: sometime in the mid-1930s, the name "Oscar" arrived. And stayed.

The 1935 awards were held March 5, 1936, at the Biltmore Hotel and, as in the preceding year, write-in votes were allowed. During the year, the Academy had also retained the public accounting firm of Price Waterhouse & Co. to tabulate ballots, a job earlier left to the staff and judges at the Academy headquarters. Cinematographer Hal Mohr

became the first, and only, write-in Oscar winner. Mr. Mohr later said, "I think there had been some industry antagonism towards me because I had been very active in a 1933 strike, and I wasn't nominated for *A Midsummer Night's Dream.* But write-ins were allowed then, and I was unshaven, sitting at home in my work clothes and the phone rang. It was Eddie Blackburn, a friend, at the Biltmore Bowl and he told me I'd won and to get the hell down there. I shaved, threw on a tux, and with my wife jumped in a cab and was there in an hour. I'm very proud of that award."

Pioneer director D.W. Griffith received a special award from the Academy and, in turn, he presented the acting awards. As in previous years, runners-up were again disclosed. Bette Davis was named best actress for *Dangerous,* with Katharine Hepburn and Elisabeth Bergner as her runners-up. Victor McLaglen was named best actor for *The Informer,* competing with three actors from *Mutiny on the Bounty:* Clark Gable, Charles Laughton and Franchot Tone. Paul Muni, not a nominee, came in second on the ballots (for *Black Fury*) and Laughton came in third. *Mutiny on the Bounty* was named best picture, followed by *The Informer,* followed by *Captain Blood.* John Ford was named best director for *The Informer,* followed by *Captain Blood's* Michael Curtiz, who had not been an official nominee, then Henry Hathaway for *The Lives of a Bengal Lancer.* It was the last year

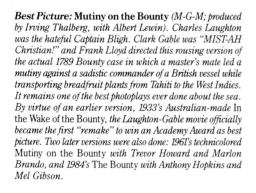

***Best Picture:* Mutiny on the Bounty** *(M-G-M; produced by Irving Thalberg, with Albert Lewin). Charles Laughton was the hateful Captain Bligh. Clark Gable was "MIST-AH Christian!" and Frank Lloyd directed this rousing version of the actual 1789 Bounty case in which a master's mate led a mutiny against a sadistic commander of a British vessel while transporting breadfruit plants from Tahiti to the West Indies. It remains one of the best photoplays ever done about the sea. By virtue of an earlier version, 1933's Australian-made* In the Wake of the Bounty, *the Laughton-Gable movie officially became the first "remake" to win an Academy Award as best picture. Two later versions were also done: 1961's technicolored* Mutiny on the Bounty *with Trevor Howard and Marlon Brando, and 1984's* The Bounty *with Anthony Hopkins and Mel Gibson.*

write-in votes were allowed by the Academy.

Writer Dudley Nichols, voted the Oscar for his screenplay of *The Informer,* also became the first to decline an Academy Award. He took the stand, he said, not to demean the honor, but because of antagonism between several industry guilds and the Academy over union matters, which resulted in many members boycotting the 1935 awards party. It was not the last time an Academy Awards night would be used to underline either a political or a personal stand.

41

Best Actor: **Victor McLaglen** *as Gypo Nolan and* ***Best Director:*** **John Ford** *for* The Informer *(RKO Radio). RKO bosses had been reluctant to film writer Liam O'Flaherty's story about a drunken, boastful Irishman in Dublin during the Irish Revolutionary troubles of 1922 who sells out his best pal to the police for a 20-pound note, then spends the money on a drunken spree, and is eventually "executed" by his fellow Revolutionists. They relented only after endless badgering by director Ford, who then made what many regard as one of the* genuine screen masterpieces, dominated by the towering performance of McLaglen as the tragic Gypo. *The Informer* is the first film to noticeably benefit financially from winning Academy Awards; although made for a modest $200,000, it was not a box office success during its original release, but after winning four awards (including one for Dudley Nichols' screenplay and another for Max Steiner's score) was rebooked into theaters and attracted a sizable audience.

Broadway Melody of 1936 *M-G-M; produced by John W. Considine, Jr.) contained a musical sequence with (above, right) June Knight and Robert Taylor and hardtapping* *accomplices singing and dancing to "I've Got A Feeling You're Fooling," for which choreographer Dave Gould received an award in a new category, honoring dance direction.* *Choreography in motion pictures was similarly honored for the next two years, then discontinued as a yearly award.*

***Best Actress:* Bette Davis** *(with Allison Skipworth, left) as Joyce Heath in* Dangerous *(Warner Bros.; directed by Alfred E. Green). Legend has it that Bette Davis received her 1935 Oscar because voters had overlooked her performance in* Of Human Bondage *the preceding awards year; Miss Davis herself said she suspects it was so. Nevertheless, her* Dangerous *performance as a self-centered, neurotic and destructive ex-Broadway star is eminently Oscar-worthy, and elevates a short (78 minutes) and relatively undistinguished film into a substantial, crackling drama.*

Nominations 1935

OUTSTANDING PRODUCTION

ALICE ADAMS, RKO Radio. Produced by Pandro S. Berman.
BROADWAY MELODY OF 1936, M-G-M. Produced by John W. Considine, Jr.
CAPTAIN BLOOD, Warner Bros.-Cosmopolitan. Produced by Hal Wallis, with Harry Joe Brown and Gordon Hollingshead.
DAVID COPPERFIELD, M-G-M. Produced by David O. Selznick.
THE INFORMER, RKO Radio. Produced by Cliff Reid.
LES MISERABLES, 20th Century, UA. Produced by Darryl F. Zanuck.
THE LIVES OF A BENGAL LANCER, Paramount. Produced by Louis D. Lighton.
A MIDSUMMER NIGHT'S DREAM, Warner Bros.-First National. Produced by Henry Blanke.
*__MUTINY ON THE BOUNTY__, M-G-M. Produced by Irving Thalberg, with Albert Lewin.
NAUGHTY MARIETTA, M-G-M. Produced by Hunt Stromberg.
RUGGLES OF RED GAP, Paramount. Produced by Arthur Hornblow, Jr.
TOP HAT, RKO Radio. Produced by Pandro S. Berman.

ACTOR

CLARK GABLE in *Mutiny on the Bounty*, M-G-M.
CHARLES LAUGHTON in *Mutiny on the Bounty*, M-G-M.
*__VICTOR McLAGLEN__ in *The Informer*, RKO Radio.
FRANCHOT TONE in *Mutiny on the Bounty*, M-G-M.

ACTRESS

ELISABETH BERGNER in *Escape Me Never*, Wilcox, UA (British).
CLAUDETTE COLBERT in *Private Worlds*, Paramount.
*__BETTE DAVIS__ in *Dangerous*, Warner Bros.
KATHARINE HEPBURN in *Alice Adams*, RKO Radio.
MIRIAM HOPKINS in *Becky Sharp*, Pioneer, RKO Radio.
MERLE OBERON in *The Dark Angel*, Goldwyn, UA.

DIRECTING

*__THE INFORMER__, RKO Radio. John Ford.
THE LIVES OF A BENGAL LANCER, Paramount. Henry Hathaway.
MUTINY ON THE BOUNTY, M-G-M. Frank Lloyd.

WRITING

(Original Story)
BROADWAY MELODY OF 1936, M-G-M. Moss Hart.
THE GAY DECEPTION, Lasky, Fox. Don Hartman and Stephen Avery.
*__THE SCOUNDREL__, Paramount. Ben Hecht and Charles MacArthur.

(Screenplay)
*__THE INFORMER__, RKO Radio. Dudley Nichols.
THE LIVES OF A BENGAL LANCER, Paramount. Achmed Abdullah, John L. Balderston, Grover Jones, William Slavens McNutt and Waldemar Young.
MUTINY ON THE BOUNTY, M-G-M. Jules Furthman, Talbot Jennings and Carey Wilson.

CINEMATOGRAPHY

BARBARY COAST, Goldwyn, UA. Ray June.
THE CRUSADES, Paramount. Victor Milner.
LES MISERABLES, 20th Century, UA. Gregg Toland.
*__A MIDSUMMER NIGHT'S DREAM__, Warner Bros. Hal Mohr.
(NOTE: *A Midsummer Night's Dream* was not a nominee but won the award as a write-in choice. Write-in votes were allowed in 1934 and 1935 but since then have not been counted in Academy tallies.)

ART DIRECTION

*__THE DARK ANGEL__, Goldwyn, UA. Richard Day.
THE LIVES OF A BENGAL LANCER, Paramount. Hans Dreier and Roland Anderson.
TOP HAT, RKO Radio. Carroll Clark and Van Nest Polglase.

SOUND RECORDING

THE BRIDE OF FRANKENSTEIN, Universal. Universal Studio Sound Dept., Gilbert Kurland, Sound Director.
CAPTAIN BLOOD, Warner Bros. Warner Bros.-First National Studio Sound Dept., Nathan Levinson, Sound Director.
THE DARK ANGEL, Goldwyn, UA. United Artists Studio Sound Dept., Thomas T. Moulton, Sound Director.
I DREAM TOO MUCH, RKO Radio. RKO Radio Studio Sound Dept., Carl Dreher, Sound Director.
THE LIVES OF A BENGAL LANCER, Paramount. Paramount Studio Sound Dept., Franklin Hansen, Sound Director.
LOVE ME FOREVER, Columbia. Columbia Studio Sound Dept., John Livadary, Sound Director.
*__NAUGHTY MARIETTA__, M-G-M. M-G-M Studio Sound Dept., Douglas Shearer, Sound Director.
$1,000 A MINUTE, Republic. Republic Studio Sound Dept.
THANKS A MILLION, 20th Century-Fox. 20th Century-Fox Studio Sound Dept., E.H. Hansen, Sound Director.

FILM EDITING

DAVID COPPERFIELD, M-G-M. Robert J. Kern.
THE INFORMER, RKO Radio. George Hively.
LES MISERABLES, 20th Century, UA. Barbara McLean.
THE LIVES OF A BENGAL LANCER, Paramount. Ellsworth Hoagland.
*__A MIDSUMMER NIGHT'S DREAM__, Warner Bros. Ralph Dawson.
MUTINY ON THE BOUNTY, M-G-M. Margaret Booth.

MUSIC

(Song)
CHEEK TO CHEEK (*Top Hat*, RKO Radio); Music and Lyrics by Irving Berlin.
LOVELY TO LOOK AT (*Roberta*, RKO Radio); Music by Jerome Kern. Lyrics by Dorothy Fields and Jimmy McHugh.
*__LULLABY OF BROADWAY__ (*Gold Diggers of 1935*, Warner Bros.-First National); Music by Harry Warren. Lyrics by Al Dubin.

(Score)
*__THE INFORMER__, RKO Radio. RKO Radio Studio Music Dept.; Max Steiner, head. Score by Max Steiner.
MUTINY ON THE BOUNTY, M-G-M. M-G-M Studio Music Dept.; Nat W. Finston, head. Score by Herbert Stothart.
PETER IBBETSON, Paramount. Paramount Studio Music Dept.; Irvin Talbot, head. Score by Ernst Toch.
(NOTE: Until 1938, Best Score was considered a music department achievement and award was presented to department head instead of to composer.)

ASSISTANT DIRECTOR

DAVID COPPERFIELD, M-G-M. Joseph Newman.
LES MISERABLES, 20th Century, UA. Eric Stacey.
*__THE LIVES OF A BENGAL LANCER__, Paramount. Clem Beauchamp and Paul Wing.

DANCE DIRECTION

(New category)
BUSBY BERKELEY for "Lullaby of Broadway" number and "The Words Are in My Heart" number from *Gold Diggers of 1935* (Warner Bros.-First National).
BOBBY CONNOLLY for "Latin from Manhattan" number from *Go Into Your Dance* (Warner Bros.-First National) and "Playboy from Paree" number from *Broadway Hostess* (Warner Bros.-First National).
*__DAVE GOULD__ for "I've Got a Feeling You're Fooling" number from *Broadway Melody of 1936* (M-G-M) and "Straw Hat" number from *Folies Bergère* (20th Century, UA).
SAMMY LEE for "Lovely Lady" number and "Too Good to Be True" number from *King of Burlesque* (20th Century-Fox).
HERMES PAN for "Piccolino" number and "Top Hat, White Tie, and Tails" number from *Top Hat* (RKO Radio).
LEROY PRINZ for "Elephant Number—It's the Animal in Me" number from *Big Broadcast of 1936* (Paramount) and "Viennese Waltz" number from *All the King's Horses* (Paramount).
BENJAMIN ZEMACH for "Hall of Kings" number from *She* (RKO Radio).

SHORT SUBJECTS

(Cartoons)
THE CALICO DRAGON, Harman-Ising, M-G-M.
*__THREE ORPHAN KITTENS__, Disney, UA.
WHO KILLED COCK ROBIN?, Disney, UA.

(Comedy)
*__HOW TO SLEEP__, M-G-M. (Miniature)
OH, MY NERVES, Columbia. (Broadway Comedies)
TIT FOR TAT, Roach, M-G-M. (Laurel & Hardy)

(Novelty)
AUDIOSCOPIKS, M-G-M.
CAMERA THRILLS, Universal.
*__WINGS OVER MT. EVEREST__, Educational.

SPECIAL AWARD

TO DAVID WARK GRIFFITH, for his distinguished creative achievements as director and producer and his invaluable initiative and lasting contributions to the progress of the motion picture arts. (statuette)

SCIENTIFIC OR TECHNICAL

CLASS I (statuette)
None.

CLASS II (certificate)
AGFA ANSCO CORP. for their development of the Agfa infra-red film.
EASTMAN KODAK CO. for their development of the Eastman Pola-Screen.

CLASS III (honorable mention)
METRO-GOLDWYN-MAYER STUDIO;
WILLIAM A. MUELLER of Warner Bros.-First National Studio Sound Dept.;
MOLE-RICHARDSON CO.;
DOUGLAS SHEARER and **M-G-M STUDIO SOUND DEPT.;**
ELECTRICAL RESEARCH PRODUCTS, INC.;
PARAMOUNT PRODUCTIONS, INC.;
NATHAN LEVINSON, director of Sound Recording for Warner Bros.-First National Studio.

*__INDICATES WINNER__

Prior to 1936, acting done by supporting performers, or "featured players," was either judged by Academy voters alongside the work of leading actors, or ignored totally. During Oscar's initial eight years, the only supporting performances that managed to earn Academy nominations were those of Lewis Stone in *The Patriot* (1928-29), Frank Morgan in *The Affairs of Cellini* (1934) and Franchot Tone in *Mutiny on the Bounty* (1935), and each of them lost to work done by starring players with considerably more on-screen time. In the Academy's ninth year, the unintentional slighting was corrected and the organization began honoring an actor and an actress for their work in that area each year thereafter. Walter Brennan in *Come and Get It* and Gale Sondergaard in *Anthony Adverse* were the first supporting winners, and they were presented Academy Award plaques. Full-sized Oscar statuettes were not given to supporting performers until the 1943 awards year.

Voting rules again changed, after six years. Nominations for awards were made by a special committee of fifty individuals appointed by Academy President Frank Capra, with equal representation from each of the Academy's branches, and the final decisions were made by a vote of all Academy members. The big winner of the year was *Anthony Adverse* with four awards, including the one for Miss Sondergaard, plus cinematography, music score and film editing. Paul Muni was chosen best actor for *The Story of Louis Pasteur,* Luise Rainer won as best actress for *The Great Ziegfeld,* and the latter was also named the year's best picture. Frank Capra won his second Oscar as director, for *Mr. Deeds Goes to Town. The March of Time,* a unique short subject series, received a special award statuette for its "significance and for having revolutionized one of the most important branches of the industry, the newsreel." Outside the regular cinematography category, W. Howard Greene and Harold Rosson were given special award plaques for their color cinematography of *The Garden of Allah,* starring Marlene Dietrich, the first time the Academy had acknowledged the use of color in a motion picture.

The awards ceremony itself was held March 4, 1937, at the Biltmore Hotel, attended by over fifteen hundred Academy members and guests, with George Jessel as master of ceremonies. Except for Victor McLaglen's presentation of the actor award to Paul Muni (wearing a beard for his current filming of *The Life of Emile Zola*), all the awards were presented by Jessel. Norma Shearer, nominated for *Romeo and Juliet,* attended the festivities with Louis B. Mayer; it was her first public appearance following the death of her husband, Irving G. Thalberg, on September 14, 1936. Among the winners was Walt Disney, who picked up his fifth straight Oscar for producing the best cartoon of the year. In the writing category, Pierre Collings and Sheridan Gibney of *The Story of Louis Pasteur* won the awards in both the original story and the screenplay divisions, the only time such a double win has ever occurred.

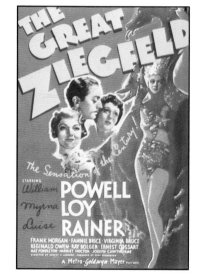

Best Picture: **The Great Ziegfeld** *(M-G-M; produced by Hunt Stromberg) and* **Best Actress:** **Luise Rainer** *as Anna Held (right, with Robert Grieg and William Powell) in* The Great Ziegfeld. *Universal studios spent a year planning a film based on the life of Broadway's spectacular showman Florenz Ziegfeld, then sold the project to M-G-M which used the full resources of that studio to produce a gargantuan, lavish entertainment. It was directed by Robert Z. Leonard with Powell as Ziegfeld, rising from an 1893 sideshow promoter to his eventual success as a New York impressario, and Miss Rainer as Anna Held, the famous stage beauty with whom he had a stormy marriage and divorce, but continued to love. The cast included Myrna Loy as Billie Burke (Ziegfeld's later wife, and widow), Fannie Brice, Frank Morgan, Gilda Gray, Ray Bolger, Leon Errol, and encompassed some 23 songs and seven spectacular production numbers. Still, it is best remembered for one simple scene of a woman and a telephone, as Miss Rainer playing Anna calls her ex-husband to congratulate him on his forthcoming marriage and emotionally begins, "Hello, Flo?...yes, this is Anna..."*

Best Actor: **Paul Muni** *as Louis Pasteur in* The Story of Louis Pasteur *(Warner Bros.; directed by William Dieterle). Pasteur deviated from the Hollywood formula for biographies, skipping the early life of the famous French medical genius and concentrating on his battles with the French Academy of Medicine over sterilization of medical instruments, and the search for a rabies cure. It was unlikely screen material, but in the hands of director Dieterle and actor Muni, was an unqualified success, critically and commercially. Muni, despite a limited catalog of screen roles, received five Oscar nominations but in accepting his one and only Oscar thanked a single individual, his make-up man. Said Muni, "Perc Westmore helped me feel like Pasteur. He deserves as much credit as I for this award."*

Best Supporting Actor: **Walter Brennan** *as Swan Bostrom (here with Edward Arnold) in* Come and Get It *(United Artists; directed by Howard Hawks and William Wyler). Brennan became the first male winner of the Academy's new award designation for supporting performances, as the Swedish lumberjack pal of Arnold in the adaptation of Edna Ferber's novel about a Wisconsin lumber dynasty; later, Brennan marries a saloon singer (Frances Farmer) whom Arnold has jilted. During the next four years, Brennan won two more supporting actor awards, a remarkable Academy record.*

Best Supporting Actress: Gale Sondergaard *as Faith Paleologue (left with Fredric March) in* Anthony Adverse *(Warner Bros.; directed by Mervyn LeRoy). Miss Sondergaard was the first winner of an Oscar for a supporting performance by an actress, playing a woman scheming for wealth and position in the time of Napoleon, and a thorn to the title character, played by Fredric March. The film was based on Hervey Allen's massive adventure novel and won more Academy Awards than any other film of the year, including Oscars for cinematography (Gaetano Gaudio), music score (Leo Forbstein) and film editing (Ralph Dawson). Sondergaard herself, a versatile actress often type-cast by Hollywood as a villainess, virtually disappeared from films after the early 1950s when she was implicated in the House Un-American Activities committee investigations that briefly swept the entire film community.*

Best Director: Frank Capra *(far left, with Gary Cooper) for* Mr. Deeds Goes to Town *(Columbia). Capra had previously won an Oscar two years before for 1934's* It Happened One Night, *and had another one in his future for 1938's* You Can't Take It With You. *With* Mr. Deeds, *he again tackled a favorite Capra topic: what happened when an average American guy gets thrown in with devious sophisticates, in this case a small town fellow named Longfellow Deeds (Cooper) who has just inherited $20 million and gets taken, at least, temporarily, by New Yorkers such as Jean Arthur, George Bancroft and Douglas Dumbrille.*

Nominations 1936

OUTSTANDING PRODUCTION

ANTHONY ADVERSE, Warner Bros. Produced by Henry Blanke.
DODSWORTH, Goldwyn, UA. Produced by Samuel Goldwyn, with Merritt Hulbert.
*__THE GREAT ZIEGFELD__, M-G-M. Produced by Hunt Stromberg.
LIBELED LADY, M-G-M. Produced by Lawrence Weingarten.
MR. DEEDS GOES TO TOWN, Columbia. Produced by Frank Capra.
ROMEO AND JULIET, M-G-M. Produced by Irving Thalberg.
SAN FRANCISCO, M-G-M. Produced by John Emerson and Bernard H. Hyman.
THE STORY OF LOUIS PASTEUR, Warner Bros. Produced by Henry Blanke.
A TALE OF TWO CITIES, M-G-M. Produced by David O. Selznick.
THREE SMART GIRLS, Universal. Produced by Joseph Pasternak, with Charles R. Rogers.

ACTOR

GARY COOPER in *Mr. Deeds Goes to Town*, Columbia.
WALTER HUSTON in *Dodsworth*, Goldwyn, UA.
*__PAUL MUNI__ in *The Story of Louis Pasteur*, Warner Bros.
WILLIAM POWELL in *My Man Godfrey*, Universal.
SPENCER TRACY in *San Francisco*, M-G-M.

ACTRESS

IRENE DUNNE in *Theodora Goes Wild*, Columbia.
GLADYS GEORGE in *Valiant Is the Word for Carrie*, Paramount.
CAROLE LOMBARD in *My Man Godfrey*, Universal.
*__LUISE RAINER__ in *The Great Ziegfeld*, M-G-M.
NORMA SHEARER in *Romeo and Juliet*, M-G-M.

SUPPORTING ACTOR

(New category)
MISCHA AUER in *My Man Godfrey*, Universal.
*__WALTER BRENNAN__ in *Come and Get It*, Goldwyn, UA.
STUART ERWIN in *Pigskin Parade*, 20th Century-Fox.
BASIL RATHBONE in *Romeo and Juliet*, M-G-M.
AKIM TAMIROFF in *The General Died at Dawn*, Paramount.

SUPPORTING ACTRESS

(New category)
BEULAH BONDI in *The Gorgeous Hussy*, M-G-M.
ALICE BRADY in *My Man Godfrey*, Universal.
BONITA GRANVILLE in *These Three*, Goldwyn, UA.
MARIA OUSPENSKAYA in *Dodsworth*, Goldwyn, UA.
*__GALE SONDERGAARD__ in *Anthony Adverse*, Warner Bros.

DIRECTING

DODSWORTH, UA. William Wyler.
THE GREAT ZIEGFELD, M-G-M. Robert Z. Leonard.
*__MR. DEEDS GOES TO TOWN__, Columbia. Frank Capra.
MY MAN GODFREY, Universal. Gregory La Cava.
SAN FRANCISCO, M-G-M. W.S. Van Dyke.

WRITING

(Original Story)
FURY, M-G-M. Norman Krasna.
THE GREAT ZIEGFELD, M-G-M. William Anthony McGuire.
SAN FRANCISCO, M-G-M. Robert Hopkins.
*__THE STORY OF LOUIS PASTEUR__, Warner Bros. Pierre Collings and Sheridan Gibney.
THREE SMART GIRLS, Universal. Adele Comandini.

(Screenplay)
AFTER THE THIN MAN, M-G-M. Frances Goodrich and Albert Hackett.
DODSWORTH, Goldwyn, UA. Sidney Howard.
MR. DEEDS GOES TO TOWN, Columbia. Robert Riskin.
MY MAN GODFREY, Universal. Eric Hatch and Morris Ryskind.
*__THE STORY OF LOUIS PASTEUR__, Warner Bros. Pierre Collings and Sheridan Gibney.

CINEMATOGRAPHY

*__ANTHONY ADVERSE__, Warner Bros. Gaetano Gaudio.
THE GENERAL DIED AT DAWN, Paramount. Victor Milner.
THE GORGEOUS HUSSY, M-G-M. George Folsey.

ART DIRECTION

ANTHONY ADVERSE, Warner Bros. Anton Grot.
*__DODSWORTH__, Goldwyn, UA. Richard Day.
THE GREAT ZIEGFELD, M-G-M. Cedric Gibbons, Eddie Imazu and Edwin B. Willis.
LLOYD'S OF LONDON, 20th Century-Fox. William S. Darling.
THE MAGNIFICENT BRUTE, Universal. Albert S. D'Agostino and Jack Otterson.
ROMEO AND JULIET, M-G-M. Cedric Gibbons, Frederic Hope and Edwin B. Willis.
WINTERSET, RKO Radio. Perry Ferguson.

SOUND RECORDING

BANJO ON MY KNEE, 20th Century-Fox. 20th Century-Fox Studio Sound Dept., E.H. Hansen, Sound Director.
THE CHARGE OF THE LIGHT BRIGADE, Warner Bros. Warner Bros. Studio Sound Dept., Nathan Levinson, Sound Director.
DODSWORTH, Goldwyn, UA. United Artists Studio Sound Dept., Thomas T. Moulton, Sound Director.
GENERAL SPANKY, Roach, M-G-M. Hal Roach Studio Sound Dept., Elmer A. Raguse, Sound Director.
MR. DEEDS GOES TO TOWN, Columbia. Columbia Studio Sound Dept., John Livadary, Sound Director.
*__SAN FRANCISCO__, M-G-M. M-G-M Studio Sound Dept., Douglas Shearer, Sound Director.
THE TEXAS RANGERS, Paramount. Paramount Studio Sound Dept., Franklin Hansen, Sound Director.
THAT GIRL FROM PARIS, RKO Radio. RKO Radio Studio Sound Dept., J.O. Aalberg, Sound Director.
THREE SMART GIRLS, Universal. Universal Studio Sound Dept., Homer G. Tasker, Sound Director.

FILM EDITING

*__ANTHONY ADVERSE__, Warner Bros. Ralph Dawson.
COME AND GET IT, Goldwyn, UA. Edward Curtiss.
THE GREAT ZIEGFELD, M-G-M. William S. Gray.
LLOYD'S OF LONDON, 20th Century-Fox. Barbara McLean.
A TALE OF TWO CITIES, M-G-M. Conrad A. Nervig.
THEODORA GOES WILD, Columbia. Otto Meyer.

MUSIC

(Song)
DID I REMEMBER (*Suzy*, M-G-M); Music by Walter Donaldson. Lyrics by Harold Adamson.
I'VE GOT YOU UNDER MY SKIN (*Born To Dance*, M-G-M); Music and Lyrics by Cole Porter.
A MELODY FROM THE SKY (*The Trail of the Lonesome Pine*, Paramount); Music by Louis Alter. Lyrics by Sidney Mitchell.
PENNIES FROM HEAVEN (*Pennies from Heaven*, Columbia); Music by Arthur Johnston. Lyrics by Johnny Burke.
*__THE WAY YOU LOOK TONIGHT__ (*Swing Time*, RKO Radio); Music by Jerome Kern. Lyrics by Dorothy Fields.
WHEN DID YOU LEAVE HEAVEN (*Sing, Baby, Sing*, 20th Century-Fox); Music by Richard A. Whiting. Lyrics by Walter Bullock.

(Score)
*__ANTHONY ADVERSE__, Warner Bros. Warner Bros. Studio Music Dept.; Leo Forbstein, head. Score by Erich Wolfgang Korngold.
THE CHARGE OF THE LIGHT BRIGADE, Warner Bros. Warner Bros. Studio Music Dept.; Leo Forbstein, head. Score by Max Steiner.
THE GARDEN OF ALLAH, Selznick, UA. Selznick International Pictures Music Dept.; Max Steiner, head. Score by Max Steiner.
THE GENERAL DIED AT DAWN, Paramount. Paramount Studio Music Dept.; Boris Morros, head. Score by Werner Janssen.
WINTERSET, RKO Radio. RKO Radio Studio Music Dept.; Nathaniel Shilkret, head. Score by Nathaniel Shilkret.
(NOTE: Through 1937, Best Score was considered a music department achievement and award was presented to department head instead of composer.)

ASSISTANT DIRECTOR

ANTHONY ADVERSE, Warner Bros. William Cannon.
*__THE CHARGE OF THE LIGHT BRIGADE__, Warner Bros. Jack Sullivan.
THE GARDEN OF ALLAH, Selznick, UA. Eric G. Stacey.
THE LAST OF THE MOHICANS, Reliance, UA. Clem Beauchamp.
SAN FRANCISCO, M-G-M. Joseph Newman.

DANCE DIRECTION

BUSBY BERKELEY for "Love and War" number from *Gold Diggers of 1936* (Warner Bros.).
BOBBY CONNOLLY for "1000 Love Songs" number from *Cain and Mabel* (Warner Bros.).
*__SEYMOUR FELIX__ for "A Pretty Girl Is Like a Melody" number from *The Great Ziegfeld* (M-G-M).
DAVE GOULD for "Swingin' the Jinx" number from *Born To Dance* (M-G-M).
JACK HASKELL for "Skating Ensemble" number from *One in a Million* (20th Century-Fox).
RUSSELL LEWIS for "The Finale" number from *Dancing Pirate* (RKO Radio).
HERMES PAN for "Bojangles of Harlem" number from *Swing Time* (RKO Radio).

SHORT SUBJECTS

(Cartoons)
*__COUNTRY COUSIN__, Disney, UA.
OLD MILL POND, Harman-Ising, M-G-M.
SINBAD THE SAILOR, Paramount.

(One-reel)
*__BORED OF EDUCATION__, Roach, M-G-M. (Our Gang)
MOSCOW MOODS, Paramount. (Headliners)
WANTED, A MASTER, M-G-M. (Peter Smith Specialties)

(Two-reel)
DOUBLE OR NOTHING, Warner Bros. (Broadway Brevities)
DUMMY ACHE, RKO Radio. (Edgar Kennedy Comedies)
*__THE PUBLIC PAYS__, M-G-M. (Crime Doesn't Pay)

(Color)
*__GIVE ME LIBERTY__, Warner Bros. (Broadway Brevities)
LA FIESTA DE SANTA BARBARA, M-G-M. (Musical Revues)
POPULAR SCIENCE J-6-2, Paramount.

SPECIAL AWARDS

TO MARCH OF TIME for its significance to motion pictures and for having revolutionized one of the most important branches of the industry—the newsreel. (statuette)
TO W. HOWARD GREENE and **HAROLD ROSSON** for the color cinematography of the Selznick International Production, *The Garden of Allah*. (plaques)

SCIENTIFIC OR TECHNICAL

CLASS I (statuette)
DOUGLAS SHEARER and the **M-G-M STUDIO SOUND DEPARTMENT** for the development of a practical two-way horn system and a biased Class A push-pull recording system.

CLASS II (plaque)
E.C. WENTE and the **BELL TELEPHONE LABORATORIES** for their multi-cellular high-frequency horn and receiver.

CLASS III (citations)
RCA MANUFACTURING CO., INC. (3 citations); **ELECTRICAL RESEARCH PRODUCTS, INC.; UNITED ARTISTS STUDIO CORP.**

*INDICATES WINNER

47

1937
The Tenth Year

Luise Rainer became the first performer to win a second Academy Award; at the same time, she also was the first actor or actress to win two awards in succession. At the 1937 Oscar ceremony, she was named best actress for *The Good Earth,* and other Oscars went to best actor Spencer Tracy in *Captains Courageous,* director Leo McCarey for *The Awful Truth,* supporting actor Joseph Schildkraut for *The Life of Emile Zola* and supporting actress Alice Brady for *In Old Chicago. Zola* won three awards, the highest total of the evening, including best picture and screenplay.

The actual presentation banquet was delayed one week (to March 10, 1938), due to a major rain and flood which had incapacitated the Los Angeles area. When the party finally took place at the Biltmore Hotel, more than thirteen hundred guests attended, the largest turnout to date at an Academy Awards function. Comedian Bob Burns was the master of ceremonies and, during the evening, W.C. Fields presented a special award to Mack Sennett for his contributions to screen comedy. Darryl F. Zanuck of the recently merged 20th Century-Fox studios received the first Irving G. Thalberg Memorial Award, established in the name of the late M-G-M producer, which is given to a creative producer whose work reflects a consistently high quality of motion picture production. Ventriloquist Edgar Bergen was also called to the podium to receive a special miniature wooden

Oscar statuette, with a hinged and movable mouth, on behalf of his wooden comedy creation Charlie McCarthy. The award for dance direction was given for the last time, to Hermes Pan; since 1937, choreography in motion pictures has been honored only on an occasional basis, in the form of a special award.

In its continuing attempt to find the most democratic means of selecting winners, the Academy again changed its voting rules and, for the first time, invited members of *all* industry-related guilds and unions, including the Screen Extras Guild, to join with Academy members in selecting both the award nominees and final winners, with the result that twelve thousand people now participated in the voting. This policy continued for eight years, until 1944, when the Screen Extras were disqualified from participation.

There was another first in 1937: John Lee Mahin became the first individual to refuse an Academy nomination, for his co-authorship of the *Captains Courageous* screenplay, in protest over the way the Writers Branch of the awards committee had been selected.

As before, newspapers in the area had been furnished with the names of award winners at 8:30 p.m. on the evening of the presentations, but were pledged to keep the news secret until late editions. Luise Rainer was at home in house slippers when the Academy committee noted her absence and phoned to tell her she had won for the second year in a row. She hastily chang-

Best Picture: **The Life of Emile Zola** *(Warner Bros.; produced by Henry Blanke) with Paul Muni, right. Directed by William Dieterle, Zola followed 1936's The Story of Louis Pasteur as another meticulous Muni-Dieterle-Warners screen biography, and covered the early career of the brilliant French novelist, but concentrated the majority of its footage on Zola's fight for the underdog in the famous Dreyfus case. The cast included Gale Sondergaard, Donald Crisp, Gloria Holden, Louis Calhern, Erin O'Brien-Moore (as the real-life Nana) and Joseph Schildkraut, who also won an Oscar as Dreyfus.*

ed into an evening gown and hurried to the Biltmore with husband Clifford Odets. Winner Alice Brady was confined at home with a broken ankle, and Mrs. Spencer Tracy accepted the award for her husband, who was recovering from a major operation at Good Samaritan Hospital. When his Oscar was later sent to be inscribed, it came back incorrectly engraved to "Dick Tracy." Luckily, the error was caught before the statuette was sent on to Spencer Tracy and it was corrected.

Best Actor: **Spencer Tracy** *as Manuel in* Captains Courageous *(M-G-M; directed by Victor Fleming). Tracy portrayed Rudyard Kipling's happy-go-lucky, simple Portuguese fisherman who befriends a spoiled English lad (played by Freddie Bartholomew, above with Tracy) and teaches him the values of honesty and obedience to orders. The role required the actor to sing several old-time sea chants and speak with a Portuguese accent, both of which he claimed made him extremely nervous. His talented shipmates included Lionel Barrymore, Charles Grapewin, Mickey Rooney, John Carradine, Jack LaRue and (on shore) Melvyn Douglas, and the film brought Tracy his first Academy Award. The following year he won a second one for* Boys Town.

Best Actress: **Luise Rainer** *as O-Lan in* The Good Earth *(M-G-M; directed by Sidney Franklin). Miss Rainer won her second Academy Award in succession as the passive but earthstrong farm wife to Wang (played by Paul Muni), characters originally created by Pearl S. Buck in her epic 1931 novel.* Earth *also won an Oscar for Karl Freund's cinematography, and was dedicated to production genius Irving Thalberg who died shortly after filming had been completed.*

Best Supporting Actress: **Alice Brady** *as Molly O'Leary in* In Old Chicago *(20th Century-Fox; directed by Henry King). Miss Brady, a famous stage actress best known for playing flittery society ladies, won her Academy trophy for playing the decidedly unflittery Mrs. O'Leary, a lady with three sons (Tyrone Power, Don Ameche and Tom Brown) and the cow who accidentally started the great Chicago fire of 1871. Miss Brady had a busy year in 1937, also appearing in five other films; she died in 1939, only one and a half years after winning her Academy Award.*

OUTSTANDING PRODUCTION

THE AWFUL TRUTH, Columbia. Produced by Leo McCarey, with Everett Riskin.
CAPTAINS COURAGEOUS, M-G-M. Produced by Louis D. Lighton.
DEAD END, Goldwyn, UA. Produced by Samuel Goldwyn, with Merritt Hulbert.
THE GOOD EARTH, M-G-M. Produced by Irving Thalberg, with Albert Lewin.
IN OLD CHICAGO, 20th Century-Fox. Produced by Darryl F. Zanuck, with Kenneth MacGowan.
*****THE LIFE OF EMILE ZOLA**, Warner Bros. Produced by Henry Blanke.
LOST HORIZON, Columbia. Produced by Frank Capra.
ONE HUNDRED MEN AND A GIRL, Universal. Produced by Charles R. Rogers, with Joe Pasternak.
STAGE DOOR, RKO Radio. Produced by Pandro S. Berman.
A STAR IS BORN, Selznick International, UA. Produced by David O. Selznick.

ACTOR

CHARLES BOYER in *Conquest*, M-G-M.
FREDRIC MARCH in *A Star Is Born*, Selznick, UA.
ROBERT MONTGOMERY in *Night Must Fall*, M-G-M.
PAUL MUNI in *The Life of Emile Zola*, Warner Bros.
*****SPENCER TRACY** in *Captains Courageous*, M-G-M.

ACTRESS

IRENE DUNNE in *The Awful Truth*, Columbia.
GRETA GARBO in *Camille*, M-G-M.
JANET GAYNOR in *A Star Is Born*, Selznick, UA.
*****LUISE RAINER** in *The Good Earth*, M-G-M.
BARBARA STANWYCK in *Stella Dallas*, Goldwyn, UA.

SUPPORTING ACTOR

RALPH BELLAMY in *The Awful Truth*, Columbia.
THOMAS MITCHELL in *The Hurricane*, Goldwyn, UA.
*****JOSEPH SCHILDKRAUT** in *The Life of Emile Zola*, Warner Bros.
H.B. WARNER in *Lost Horizon*, Columbia.
ROLAND YOUNG in *Topper*, Roach, M-G-M.

SUPPORTING ACTRESS

*****ALICE BRADY** in *In Old Chicago*, 20th Century-Fox.
ANDREA LEEDS in *Stage Door*, RKO Radio.
ANNE SHIRLEY in *Stella Dallas*, Goldwyn, UA.
CLAIRE TREVOR in *Dead End*, Goldwyn, UA.
DAME MAY WHITTY in *Night Must Fall*, M-G-M.

DIRECTING

*****THE AWFUL TRUTH**, Columbia. Leo McCarey.
THE GOOD EARTH, M-G-M. Sidney Franklin.
THE LIFE OF EMILE ZOLA, Warner Bros. William Dieterle.
STAGE DOOR, RKO Radio. Gregory La Cava.
A STAR IS BORN, Selznick, UA. William Wellman.

WRITING

(Original Story)

BLACK LEGION, Warner Bros. Robert Lord.
IN OLD CHICAGO, 20th Century-Fox. Niven Busch.
THE LIFE OF EMILE ZOLA, Warner Bros. Heinz Herald and Geza Herczeg.
ONE HUNDRED MEN AND A GIRL, Universal. Hans Kraly.
*****A STAR IS BORN**, Selznick, UA. William A. Wellman and Robert Carson.

(Screenplay)

THE AWFUL TRUTH, Columbia. Vina Delmar.
CAPTAINS COURAGEOUS, M-G-M. Marc Connelly, John Lee Mahin and Dale Van Every.
*****THE LIFE OF EMILE ZOLA**, Warner Bros. Heinz Herald, Geza Herczeg and Norman Reilly Raine.
STAGE DOOR, RKO Radio. Morris Ryskind and Anthony Veiller.
A STAR IS BORN, Selznick, UA. Alan Campbell, Robert Carson and Dorothy Parker.

CINEMATOGRAPHY

DEAD END, Goldwyn, UA. Gregg Toland.
*****THE GOOD EARTH**, M-G-M. Karl Freund.
WINGS OVER HONOLULU, Universal. Joseph Valentine.

ART DIRECTION

CONQUEST, M-G-M. Cedric Gibbons and William Horning.
A DAMSEL IN DISTRESS, RKO Radio. Carroll Clark.
DEAD END, Goldwyn, UA. Richard Day.
EVERY DAY'S A HOLIDAY, Major Prods., Paramount. Wiard Ihnen.
THE LIFE OF EMILE ZOLA, Warner Bros. Anton Grot.
*****LOST HORIZON**, Columbia. Stephen Goosson.
MANHATTAN MERRY-GO-ROUND, Republic. John Victor Mackay.
THE PRISONER OF ZENDA, Selznick, UA. Lyle Wheeler.
SOULS AT SEA, Paramount. Hans Dreier and Roland Anderson.
WEE WILLIE WINKIE, 20th Century-Fox. William S. Darling and David Hall.
WALTER WANGER'S VOGUES OF 1938, Wanger, UA. Alexander Toluboff.
YOU'RE A SWEETHEART, Universal. Jack Otterson.

MUSIC

(Song)

REMEMBER ME (*Mr. Dodd Takes the Air*, Warner Bros.); Music by Harry Warren. Lyrics by Al Dubin.
*****SWEET LEILANI** (*Waikiki Wedding*, Paramount); Music and Lyrics by Harry Owens.
THAT OLD FEELING (*Walter Wanger's Vogues of 1938*, Wanger, UA); Music by Sammy Fain. Lyrics by Lew Brown.
THEY CAN'T TAKE THAT AWAY FROM ME (*Shall We Dance*, RKO Radio); Music by George Gershwin. Lyrics by Ira Gershwin.

Best Supporting Actor: **Joseph Schildkraut** *(right) as Capt. Alfred Dreyfus in* The Life of Emile Zola. *A major asset to the year's best picture, Schildkraut portrayed the real-life French Army officer who was disgraced and unjustly accused of treason in 1894 and sentenced to life imprisonment on Devil's Island, a penalty comparable to death. William Dieterle was his director. Despite his Academy Award win for 1937, Schildkraut's subsequent screen career followed a teeter-totter pattern, from second leads in major studio epics and supporting roles in Republic westerns to occasional starring roles in important works, such as 1959's* The Diary of Anne Frank. *On stage, his true forte, he was never less than above-the-title.*

WHISPERS IN THE DARK (*Artists and Models*, Paramount); Music by Frederick Hollander. Lyrics by Leo Robin.

(Score)

THE HURRICANE, Goldwyn, UA. Samuel Goldwyn Studio Music Dept.; Alfred Newman, head. Score by Alfred Newman.

IN OLD CHICAGO, 20th Century-Fox. 20th Century-Fox Studio Music Dept.; Louis Silvers, head. (No composer credit.)

THE LIFE OF EMILE ZOLA, Warner Bros. Warner Bros. Studio Music Dept.; Leo Forbstein, head. Score by Max Steiner.

LOST HORIZON, Columbia. Columbia Studio Music Dept.; Morris Stoloff, head. Score by Dimitri Tiomkin.

MAKE A WISH, Lesser. RKO Radio Studio Music Dept.; Dr. Hugo Riesenfeld, musical director. Score by Dr. Hugo Riesenfeld.

MAYTIME, M-G-M. M-G-M Studio Music Dept.; Nat W. Finston, head. Score by Herbert Stothart.

*ONE HUNDRED MEN AND A GIRL, Universal. Universal Studio Music Dept.; Charles Previn, head. (No composer credit.)

PORTIA ON TRIAL, Republic. Republic Studio Music Dept.; Alberto Colombo, head. Score by Alberto Colombo.

THE PRISONER OF ZENDA, Selznick, UA. Selznick International Pictures Music Dept.; Alfred Newman, musical director. Score by Alfred Newman.

QUALITY STREET, RKO Radio. RKO Radio Studio Music Dept.; Roy Webb, musical director. Score by Roy Webb.

SNOW WHITE AND THE SEVEN DWARFS, Disney, RKO Radio. Walt Disney Studio Music Dept.; Leigh Harline, head. Score by Frank Churchill, Leigh Harline and Paul J. Smith.

SOMETHING TO SING ABOUT, Grand National. Grand National Studio Music Dept.; C. Bakaleinikoff, musical director. Score by Victor Schertzinger.

SOULS AT SEA, Paramount. Paramount Studio Music Dept.; Boris Morros, head. Score by W. Franke Harling and Milan Roder.

WAY OUT WEST, Roach, M-G-M. Hal Roach Studio Music Dept.; Marvin Hatley, head. Score by Marvin Hatley.

(NOTE: Through 1937, Best Score was considered a music department achievement and award was presented to department head instead of to composer.)

SOUND RECORDING

THE GIRL SAID NO, Grand National. Grand National Studio Sound Dept., A.E. Kaye, Sound Director.

HITTING A NEW HIGH, RKO Radio. RKO Radio Studio Sound Dept., John Aalberg, Sound Director.

*THE HURRICANE, Goldwyn, UA. United Artists Studio Sound Dept., Thomas T. Moulton, Sound Director.

IN OLD CHICAGO, 20th Century-Fox. 20th Century-Fox Studio Sound Dept.; E.H. Hansen, Sound Director.

THE LIFE OF EMILE ZOLA, Warner Bros. Warner Bros. Studio Sound Dept., Nathan Levinson, Sound Director.

LOST HORIZON, Columbia. Columbia Studio Sound Dept., John Livadary, Sound Director.

MAYTIME, M-G-M. M-G-M Studio Sound Dept., Douglas Shearer, Sound Director.

ONE HUNDRED MEN AND A GIRL, Universal. Universal Studio Sound Dept., Homer Tasker, Sound Director.

TOPPER, Hal Roach, M-G-M. Hal Roach Studio Sound Dept., Elmer Raguse, Sound Director.

WELLS FARGO, Paramount. Paramount Studio Sound Dept., L.L. Ryder, Sound Director.

FILM EDITING

THE AWFUL TRUTH, Columbia. Al Clark.

CAPTAINS COURAGEOUS, M-G-M. Elmo Vernon.

THE GOOD EARTH, M-G-M. Basil Wrangell.

*LOST HORIZON, Columbia. Gene Havlick and Gene Milford.

ONE HUNDRED MEN AND A GIRL, Universal. Bernard W. Burton.

ASSISTANT DIRECTOR

(Not given after this year.)

*IN OLD CHICAGO, 20th Century-Fox. Robert Webb.

THE LIFE OF EMILE ZOLA, Warner Bros. Russ Saunders.

LOST HORIZON, Columbia. C.C. Coleman, Jr.

SOULS AT SEA, Paramount. Hal Walker.

A STAR IS BORN, Selznick, UA. Eric Stacey.

DANCE DIRECTION

(Not given after this year.)

BUSBY BERKELEY for "The Finale" number from *Varsity Show* (Warner Bros.).

BOBBY CONNOLLY for "Too Marvelous for Words" number from *Ready, Willing and Able* (Warner Bros.).

DAVE GOULD for "All God's Children Got Rhythm" number from *A Day at the Races* (M-G-M).

SAMMY LEE for "Swing Is Here to Stay" number from *Ali Baba Goes to Town* (20th Century-Fox).

HARRY LOSEE for "Prince Igor Suite" number from *Thin Ice* (20th Century-Fox).

*HERMES PAN for "Fun House" number from *Damsel in Distress* (RKO Radio).

LEROY PRINZ for "Luau" number from *Waikiki Wedding* (Paramount).

SHORT SUBJECTS

(Cartoons)

EDUCATED FISH, Paramount.

THE LITTLE MATCH GIRL, Mintz, Columbia.

*THE OLD MILL, Disney, RKO Radio.

(One-reel)

A NIGHT AT THE MOVIES, M-G-M. (Robert Benchley)

*PRIVATE LIFE OF THE GANNETS, Educational.

ROMANCE OF RADIUM, M-G-M. (Pete Smith Specialties)

(Two-reel)

DEEP SOUTH, RKO Radio. (Radio Musical Comedies)

SHOULD WIVES WORK, RKO Radio. (Leon Errol Comedies)

*TORTURE MONEY, M-G-M. (Crime Doesn't Pay)

(Color)

THE MAN WITHOUT A COUNTRY, Warner Bros. (Broadway Brevities)

*PENNY WISDOM, M-G-M. (Pete Smith Specialties)

POPULAR SCIENCE J-7-1, Paramount.

SPECIAL AWARDS

TO MACK SENNETT "for his lasting contribution to the comedy technique of the screen, the basic principles of which are as important today as when they were first put into practice, the Academy presents a Special Award to that master of fun, discoverer of stars, sympathetic, kindly, understanding comedy genius, Mack Sennett." (statuette)

TO EDGAR BERGEN for his outstanding comedy creation, Charlie McCarthy (wooden statuette).

TO THE MUSEUM OF MODERN ART FILM LIBRARY for its significant work in collecting films dating from 1895 to the present and for the first time making available to the public the means of studying the historical and aesthetic development of the motion picture as one of the major arts (scroll certificate).

TO W. HOWARD GREENE for the color photography of *A Star Is Born*. (This Award was recommended by a committee of leading cinematographers after viewing all the color pictures made during the year.) (plaque)

1937 IRVING G. THALBERG MEMORIAL AWARD

(First year presented)

TO DARRYL F. ZANUCK.

SCIENTIFIC OR TECHNICAL

CLASS I (statuette)

AGFA ANSCO CORP. for Agfa Supreme and Agfa Ultra Speed pan motion picture negatives.

CLASS II (plaque)

WALT DISNEY PRODS., LTD., for the design and application to production of the Multi-Plane Camera.

EASTMAN KODAK CO. for two fine-grain duplicating film stocks.

FARCIOT EDOUART and PARAMOUNT PICTURES, INC., for the development of the Paramount dual screen transparency camera setup.

DOUGLAS SHEARER and the M-G-M STUDIO SOUND DEPT. for a method of varying the scanning width of variable density sound tracks (squeeze tracks) for the purpose of obtaining an increased amount of noise reduction.

CLASS III (citation)

JOHN ARNOLD and the M-G-M STUDIO CAMERA DEPT.;

JOHN LIVADARY, director of Sound Recording for Columbia Pictures Corp.;

THOMAS T. MOULTON and the UNITED ARTISTS STUDIO SOUND DEPT.;

RCA MANUFACTURING CO., INC.;

JOSEPH E. ROBBINS and PARAMOUNT PICTURES, INC.;

DOUGLAS SHEARER and the M-G-M STUDIO SOUND DEPT.

*INDICATES WINNER

The outbreak of World War II, outside Hollywood's boundaries but certainly within its consciousness, had a distinct effect on all elements connected with the motion picture industry and the Academy of Motion Picture Arts and Sciences as well.

It was not the first introduction the Academy had to the world of the military. Back in 1930, at the government's request, the Academy had been called upon to help pave the way for a training program in which Signal Corps officers could learn about motion picture production in order to produce military training films. Sponsored and planned by the Academy, one Signal Corps officer per year for eight years was trained in the intricacies of photography, editing, mixing, sound and other elements, by visiting actual film departments at work. With the outbreak of World War II, the studios opened their doors even wider to aid the war effort.

Darryl F. Zanuck, head of 20th Century-Fox studios and chairman of the Academy's Research Council, recognized the need for well-made training films for newly inducted military personnel, and he immediately volunteered the Council's complete cooperation. With the encouragement of the Academy's Board of Governors, the Council set to work arranging for major motion picture studios, including 20th Century-Fox, Metro-Goldwyn-Mayer, Paramount and Warner Bros., to produce training films of all kinds on a non-profit basis. The studios used existing equipment and facilities to do the work, and charged the government only for film stock and film processing and a few labor salaries not waived by unions. From the start of the war until mid-1943, over four hundred training shorts and related featurettes were delivered to the armed services, covering a wide range of subjects, including *Combat Counter-Intelligence* and *The Articles of War,* as well as *Sex Hygiene* and *Safeguarding Military Information.*

The war also had an effect on the Academy's actual Awards-night galas, at that time held in posh dining rooms of Los Angeles and Hollywood hotels, such as the Hollywood Roosevelt, the Ambassador or the Biltmore. Not only was growing interest in the Academy causing space problems and overcrowded conditions, but Academy officials also reasoned it was not in the best interests of the organization to dispense industry Oscars at elegant banquets at a time when much of the world was suffering a lack of food and the indignities of a calamitous war. So on March 2, 1944, honoring film achievements during the calendar year of 1943, the festivities were held for the first time in an actual theater, Grauman's Chinese in Hollywood, without an accompanying gala dinner-dance.

There was also another major change in Oscar during the second decade of existence: beginning with the 1940 Awards, presented February 27, 1941, winners were no longer divulged in advance, and the names of recipients

MICKEY ROONEY

I am grateful and proud to be a part of the wonderful work of the Academy of Motion Picture Arts and Sciences."

Mickey Rooney
Special Award, 1938
Honorary Award, 1982

MIKLOS ROZSA

"At the time I received my Oscars, they meant a great deal to me careerwise, and I am very grateful for them."

Miklos Rozsa
Music (Scoring Dramatic or
Comedy Picture), 1945; 1947; 1959

ANNE REVERE

"The nomination for my 'Mrs. Brown' in National Velvet *brought me great joy, but as an orphan with no studio to champion my cause, I had little hope of winning the Oscar.*

On the eve of the great day, the odds-on favorite was Warner Bros.' talented young starlet Ann Blyth, for her notable performance in Mildred Pierce.

Next morning the papers reported the surprising winner: ANNE REVERE, the talented young Warner Bros.' starlet!

The surprise, I think, doubled my pleasure."

Anne Revere
Best Supporting Actress, 1945

were kept completely secret in sealed and guarded envelopes until the statuettes were formally handed to the winners.

Then as now, change has always been an integral part of the Academy story, part of a determination on the part of the Academy to stay in step with changing industry styles and technological innovations. Rules change yearly—as have voting requirements and category designations—all in an attempt to do right by the industry and the Academy itself. Among the important changes made between 1938 and 1947 were several Academy constitutional bylaws. In December of 1939, for example, the bylaws were revised to group the five existing Academy branches—Producers, Directors, Actors, Writers and Technicians—into two main categories, the Arts Branches and the Sciences Branches. In 1946, memberships were defined into three specific types: active, honorary and life; earlier, they had also included fellowship memberships and foundation memberships. The number of Academy branches was also increased from five to eight, with the addition of branches for Music, Short Subjects and Public Relations. Later it was increased to a total of twelve. The Technicians branch was retired in favor of more specifically defined branches for Cinematographers, Film Editors, Art Directors (which includes Costume Designers), Sound and Miscellaneous, the latter to cover those not included elsewhere.

Guy Lombardo, Judy Garland, Mickey Rooney at 1939 (12th) Awards

MARY ASTOR

"It was war time when I received my award. And since metal was precious, all the winners in other than Best Actor, Best Actress and Best Picture were given small metal plaques. Of course I was delighted with the honor, and I thanked everyone with a pretty little speech. (I'm grateful now that we had no TV coverage then!)

Over the years and after my retirement, I felt something was lacking. I had won an Oscar—and yet I hadn't.

In my book, A Life On Film, I describe my feelings, and in parentheses I wrote: (Hey Academy! I would dearly love to have a real Oscar!)

So now I have my real Golden Boy standing on my bookshelf beside the faded little plaque of 1942."

Mary Astor
Best Supporting Actress, 1941

CLAUDE JARMAN JR.

"Even at the age of twelve, it was an overwhelming experience to receive an Oscar. Years later I still feel the same way."

Claude Jarman, Jr.
Special Award, 1946

DORE SCHARY

"Herewith—some memories:

I remember Frank Capra's face when it was announced: 'And the winner is Frank Capra!'

I remember Eric Johnston, who in 1942 presented: 'As an honored guest, the distinguished Ambassador from Japan—I mean China.'

I remember Clare Booth Luce saying as she presented the writers award: 'And the winner is John Husston!'

A moment later John, in accepting, said 'Thank you, Miss Looka!'

I remember the year the program simply ran out of TV time.

I remember the night that Frank Lloyd and Frank Capra were both nominated—and as the announcer said, 'And the winner is Frank...' both Franks got up. But the winner was Lloyd.

And finally I remember when I got my Oscar. It was a golden moment—just as golden as shining Oscar. Warmest and best wishes."

Dore Schary
Writing (Original Story), 1938

LAURENCE OLIVIER

"My thoughts for a special award for Henry V in 1947 and for Hamlet in '48 for performance and best picture were for each and both of the most delighted kind and my gratitude of the heartfelt fullest."

Laurence Olivier
Special Award, 1946
Best Actor, 1948
Honorary Award, 1978

There was another significant rule change in 1941: unlike times past, an Academy Award winner was no longer able to sell "or otherwise dispose of (an Oscar statuette), nor permit it to be sold or disposed of by operation of law without first offering to sell it back to the Academy for ten dollars." This protection was sealed when the Academy Award design was officially copyrighted on September 2, 1941.

As the importance, prestige and fame of the Academy Awards presentation ceremonies continued to grow, other Academy functions also continued to expand, and with far-reaching effects. By 1941, the archival and reference library of the Academy had grown to such an extent it was ranked as one of the most complete collections on motion pictures anywhere in the world. The library now included almost every book published in English about motion pictures, production information on nearly 20,000 motion pictures produced since 1896, plus still photographs and scripts from many significant productions. The library continued to develop its extensive biography files of clippings and still photographs on actors, actresses, directors and other film people.

There was a special clipping file established dealing solely with the effects of the war on the motion picture industry, and in the archives prints, in both 35mm and 16mm, encompassing features and short subjects. In order to provide a tangible record of Oscar's screen achievements, the Academy also began a project to acquire a print from studios of every film that has received an Academy Award nomination. That practice lapsed for several years before being resumed in the 1980's.

With such an extensive collection of tangible material, the Academy was also able to aid and support film research under the guidance of the Academy Foundation, created during this period

to take charge of the educational and cultural activities of the Academy.

The Foundation was officially incorporated on January 31, 1944, as a separate unit from the Academy, in order to be eligible to receive gifts of private funding and certain tax-exemption privileges. The Foundation accepts bequests and donations from estates, governmental agencies, other foundations, the motion picture industry and the general public, and uses the funds to administer educational, cultural and film archival activities.

The ties between the Academy and educational groups actually started long before the Academy Foundation came into being. On May 24, 1927, only days after the initial organizational banquet, Cecil B. DeMille and Milton Sills, representing the Academy, met with the then-president of the University of Southern California regarding the establishment of cinema classes at the school, with the Academy's assistance. Further aid was later given to such schools as Yale, Purdue, Columbia, the University of Oregon and others. In 1943, the Academy helped the University of California at Los Angeles (UCLA) organize extensive courses on the motion picture field, and later remained closely affiliated with the school in an advisory capacity.

The cooperation with schools and educational institutions continued. The Academy supplied a constant flow of information on the movie spectrum to students around the world, in the form of clippings, still photographs, scripts, journal references and other kinds of requested information. Later, in 1972, the Academy, in conjunction with the Academy Foundation, established the National Film Information Service to offer access by mail to the extensive holdings of the library, so historians, students, scholars, teachers and film programmers living outside the Los

James Stewart (13th Awards)

Joan Crawford (18th Awards)

54

ALEXANDER GOLITZEN

"To be nominated (and as many times as I have) comes always as a surprise and with great appreciation as one realizes that it was approved by one's own kind.

Then comes the 'day'—and winning an 'Oscar' (whether the first, second, etc., etc. is always a thrill').

In the 'old' days there was no celebration, ball, etc., so one merely collected one's statuette and celebrated with close friends. In my case (when I won the first one) we met at Jimmy Wong Howe's Restaurant (he was a great cameraman), and this is where I made my acceptance speech."

Alexander Golitzen
Art Direction (Color), 1943; 1960
Art Direction (Black-and-white), 1962

CELESTE HOLM

"When I was making my first film in 1946, I met a dear man named Gabe York who was in the publicity department. I never knew his title—but he came down on the set to talk to me, and before I knew it we were talking about the films that had meant a great deal to us per-

sonally, and why. There weren't a whole lot of them—some of them were foreign, which seemed heretical, seated as we were on the back lot at 20th Century-Fox. But all of them had shown people as not only fascinating but valuable—that to be human was a wonderful thing to be.

'I want to make movies that say something,' I said, 'for people to keep.'

Gabe York wore glasses that made his eyes look enormous. 'From Hollywood?' he asked, and his eyes looked even bigger.

'Well,' I said, 'I can try.'

Two years later I was sitting in my assigned seat at the Academy Awards presentations in the old Shrine Auditorium (which always smelled softly of elephants). Quite early in the proceedings I heard, '...and the winner,' spoken by Donald Crisp, 'for her role in Gentleman's Agreement, Celeste Holm.'

I literally could not move, the lights were so sudden and so intense. My husband muttered, 'Get up, get up.'

I didn't, so he and the man on my right hoisted me to my feet. I had not expected to win; Ethel Barrymore

was also in the same category.

In a dream I walked toward the stage and as I started up the steps, I hoped I would not stumble up the inside of my ruffled petticoat. I didn't, and I found myself facing that huge, warm ocean of appreciation. And then I was supposed to say something. I hadn't prepared anything because I was sure I would not win. And I suddenly thought of Gabe York.

'I thought,' I said slowly, looking for the words from a full heart, 'that I'd already received the greatest reward an actress can have—of being in a picture that brings understanding, in a world that seems to need it so much.' As I left the dazzle of the stage, into the dark wings there was Gabe. 'You did it!' he said.

And I leaked happy tears all over his tuxedo."

Celeste Holm
Best Supporting Actress, 1947

Harold Russell, Shirley Temple, Claude Jarman, Jr. (19th Awards)

Teresa Wright (15th Awards)

Angeles area could also take advantage of the library's fund of knowledge.

The Academy Foundation was also deeply involved in restoring an invaluable collection of Paper Prints at the Library of Congress. From 1894 to 1912, all motion pictures had been copyrighted via photographic reproductions on paper of their individual frames. These "paper prints" were then stored in the Copyright Office in Washington, D.C., and forgotten. In the 1940s, Howard Walls, a Library of Congress employee, discovered over two and one-half million feet of dusty copies stored there, including newsreels with priceless footage of early presidential inaugurations, coverage of the Boer and Spanish-American wars, and other films of historical interest no longer available from other sources. There were also many theatrical features in the collection, long since assumed to have been lost. Walls was immediately appointed curator of the collection for the Library

of Congress and began the task of transferring the positive paper prints to motion picture film, but was soon stopped when Congress abruptly voted to end the Motion Picture Division, due to wartime cutbacks. The Academy Foundation then took over, and hired Walls to continue as curator. Walls was eventually succeeded by Kemp Niver, a film restoration specialist, and the job was completed ten years later.

In 1946, the Academy again found itself in need of more room. A twenty-five-year-old building, known as the Marquis Theater and functioning as a neighborhood cinema, located at 9038 Melrose Avenue, was purchased from the West Coast theater chain and became the new Academy of Motion Picture Arts and Sciences' headquarters. The main floor of the building housed a 950-seat theater, and allowed greater seating capacity for members than the Academy had earlier enjoyed; its projection booth and sound facilities were

soon redesigned by the Research Council to make it one of the most acoustically perfect theaters anywhere. The upper floor, designed for executive offices and the library, allowed sorely needed room for those ever-expanding files and other material. By the end of the decade, the library was averaging three hundred visiting researchers per week, including studio personnel, Academy members, college students and others needing assistance. Several thousand phone calls were also coming in each month, asking for specific pieces of information on some facet or another of the movie world or the Academy operation.

By 1947, Academy membership had reached a new high of 1600, the war was over, Oscar was in a new home and there were new challenges and projects ahead. One of them was an attempt to set into motion a series of twelve documentary featurettes that would help inform the public about specific facets

HAROLD RUSSELL

"Winning two 'Oscars' for my first commercial motion-picture is and was a thrill almost beyond description. The Best Years of Our Lives *was Hollywood's tribute to the servicemen and women of World War II and the awards it won reflected that feeling. Personally, my Oscars brought me in contact with the field of rehabilitation and the opportunity to work with disabled people in the areas of education and employment. For all of this, I am very grateful to the wonderful people of the motion picture industry."*

Harold Russell
Best Supporting Actor, 1946
Special Award, 1946

GREER GARSON

"On the night I was given my Oscar I tried impulsively to express not only thanks but some honest thoughts about the Awards system. Hardly tactful timing, perhaps. I was said to have given the longest acceptance speech ever. It wasn't, really. It just seemed that way to a roomful of weary listeners at midnight. However,

maybe I can claim modestly to have triggered a needed overhaul of the Awards program, that gradually transformed it from the original rather loosely organized informal dinner-dance evening for Industry members, to a split-second, elaborately staged, spectacular gala for an audience of millions.

Of course I treasure my statuette. And I treasure several nominations just as much, because I have always thought the nominations themselves should be considered the Awards. For actors, acting is not a competition but a sharing and blending of experiences and imaginings.

I am forever proud of being part of this industry and this Academy."

Greer Garson
Best Actress, 1942

JACK CARDIFF

"When Madame Curie received the Nobel Prize and Churchill was knighted by the Queen, they must have felt the same orbital elation I experienced when I won my Oscar.

I am unashamedly conceited about it. It would be most difficult for any visitor to my house to avoid seeing it, shimmering its golden glow, beckoning homage like a god.

The visitor says, 'Is that really an Oscar?' and I take it off the shelf with a Peter Sellers smirk and condescendingly let it be handled. They weigh it and stroke it reverently, murmuring the usual things — 'Never thought I'd hold a real Oscar…is it real gold, etc.' and then it goes back in the middle of my other trophies.

But proud as I am of my Golden Globes, the New York Film Critics' Award and others, my Oscar stands out in Olympian detachment like a dazzling beacon to artistic endeavour, and whenever I gaze at it I always seem to grow a few inches taller."

Jack Cardiff
Cinematography (Color), 1947

of film production and industry life, plus concurrently improve the public image of the industry, something Hollywood always seemed to need. Spearheaded by the Academy and underwritten by the Producers Association, the films were made at various cooperating studios, and budgeted so that the financial returns from the distribution of the first five made would pay the costs of the entire dozen planned. The series, including *The Actor, The Writer, The Director, The Sound Man, The Cinematographer, The Costume Designer, Moments in Music, History Brought to Life, Movies Are Adventure, Let's Go to the Movies* and *This Theater and You*, was not finished until into the Academy's third decade, but in later years, through distribution in 16mm to schools, libraries and universities, it proved to be one of the Academy's most worthwhile legacies to the understanding of Hollywood and its work.

Academy Headquarters, 1946-1975

ACADEMY PRESIDENTS, THE SECOND DECADE

October 1937–October 1938 . . . . *Frank Capra*
October 1938–December 1939 . . . . *Frank Capra*
December 1939–December 1940 . . . . . *Walter Wanger*
January 1941–October 1941 . . . . *Walter Wanger*
October 1941–December 1941 . . . .*Bette Davis**
December 1941–October 1942 . . . . *Walter Wanger*
October 1942–October 1943 . . . . *Walter Wanger*
October 1943–October 1944 . . . . *Walter Wanger*
October 1944–October 1945 . . . . *Walter Wanger*
October 1945–May 1947 . . . .*Jean Hersholt*

**Resigned during first term*

Ginger Rogers, Bob Hope (13th Awards)

David O. Selznick, Vivien Leigh (12th Awards)

56

ANNE BAXTER

"Oscar, Oscar, wherefore art thou, Oscar? It's easy to lose things when you move. I lost my Oscar. He vanished between van and new threshold or fell prey to the sticky fingers of a souvenir-happy moving man, but in either case—gone. Getting his duplicate was a polite hassle, complete with affidavits, details, descriptions and seventy-five dollars.

I moved yet again, under particularly horrendous circumstances, and undid the royal blue, golden-corded felt bag cradling Oscar's stand-in, only to watch him crash out in two gleaming hunks—not lost or stolen this time. Broken. Will I try, try again? Yes. Because nothing else will so sharply bring into focus an emotional peak.

Through the years, awards have mushroomed as after a cloudburst, but there is only one Oscar. Belittle, scoff at or denigrate him as you will, when your name comes bounding out of that microphone I defy adrenal glands of marble not to quiver. In memoriam, I still cringe at my acceptance mumbles and leaky eyes and at looking fatly stuffed into a pompous navy blue lace dress, but it's a moment impossible to plan.

The best response I can remember was Jimmy Cagney's. He won for Yankee Doodle Dandy at the last monkey-draped Cocoanut Grove Awards Dinner. I can see him now, stepping energetically up to the mike and carving the hush neatly with: 'It's nice to know some people think a job has been well done. Thank you.' Wish I'd said that."

Anne Baxter
Best Supporting Actress, 1946

TERESA WRIGHT

"The Academy Award ceremonies of 1942, our first war year, was an evening of mixed emotions for all of us who had worked on Mrs. Miniver. Willie Wyler, in service overseas, could not be with us to share the thrill of Miniver winning six awards. It was also an unbelievably exciting night for me, as I had been nominated for two awards, for my second and third films: best performance by an actress in a starring role in Pride of the Yankees, as well as the supporting role in Mrs. Miniver.

A memory that I recall with affection was an evening when I had been asked to present an award. I was sitting in a dark corner backstage at Grauman's Chinese Theatre as nervous as if I had to perform. Suddenly I realized I shared the darkness with a beautiful man: white curly hair, sad-comic face, huge harp; my favorite Marx brother. I was so delighted to see him that I couldn't keep my eyes off him; a fact which he noticed because he broke his famous silence to say, 'Young lady, are you flirting with me?'"

Teresa Wright
Best Supporting Actress, 1942

GINGER ROGERS

"In 1940 there were no television cameras to record my gratitude when I received an 'Oscar' for my performance in Kitty Foyle. Now—at long last—I have the opportunity to say to my peers of the Academy—thank you for that marvelous tribute."

Ginger Rogers
Best Actress, 1940

Joan Fontaine, Olivia de Havilland (14th Awards)

Greer Garson, James Cagney (15th Awards)

Fredric March, Loretta Young, Price Waterhouse Representative (20th Awards)

LORETTA YOUNG

"There is something about a dark horse winning that brings the house down. In 1947, I was the dark horse, the house was the Shrine Auditorium! All those hands clapping made lots of noise. Beautiful noise! And I allowed myself the luxury of believing it was indeed all for me. For over twenty years, I'd been more than satisfied with the work itself, without a nod from the Academy—now the 'jackpot'!

I guess primarily it was a good night for me because it meant the industry looked at me as more than just 'pretty as usual, Period.' Acceptance! A great word, great for the heart and soul. Great for the ego, the actor's source. My self-confidence soared and in a strange way it has never wavered since, at least not in any serious way.

Soon, wise friends were reminding me 'the Oscar is only the icing on the cake.' I agreed with them, I still do. But, my, oh, my, what a lovely taste that icing had, and still has!

Every time I open the guest coat closet, in my front hall, and see Oscar residing on a shelf, all by himself,

with the automatic door light shining down on him, I enjoy a small wave of gratitude and I'm delighted all over again to have been chosen a winner.

In my professional life, more than once, it's occurred to me there are only two material things in my life that I've never gotten used to. One, the Oscar statuette residing in my home, with my name on it. The other, for no sensible reason I know of, is my Rolls-Royce car. Unless it's because they both make me feel like a movie star, and I like that. I like it a lot!"

Loretta Young
Best Actress, 1947

MARGARET O'BRIEN

"The Academy Awards have the same mystique for actors as for audiences and I must admit it was a delightful assignment to look back and recollect when my mother told me we would be attending the Academy Awards and that there was a possibility that I might receive an Oscar for my performance in Meet Me In St. Louis. I was typically excited and apprehensive. I think my reaction pleased my mother, but what she

didn't realize was that my excitement was the possibility of receiving the award from my very secret heartthrob, Bob Hope, and my apprehension was the possibility that one of the false teeth that the studio made me wear to cover my missing baby teeth might fall out as they often did while we were making the film. Nevertheless, all went well. My false teeth held fast, I received the Oscar, and the handsome Bob Hope presented it to me. As a matter of fact, he even hugged me; he hugged most of the other actresses too, but I was the only one he both hugged and lifted."

Margaret O'Brien
Special Award, 1944

RICHARD RODGERS

"Oscar Hammerstein II and I won an Oscar for 'It Might As Well Be Spring' in 1945. The only thing that could have made me happier than this award was the song itself."

Richard Rodgers
Music (Song), 1945

Across the world, grim war clouds continued to cover Europe as the Academy of Motion Picture Arts and Sciences entered its second decade, and Hollywood itself was having some troubled times as well. Box office attendance had taken an alarming dip which—coupled with possible revenue losses from the dwindling European film market—caused jitters within the industry. Oscar night, however, was an unparalleled success, the biggest to date, held on February 23, 1939, in the Biltmore Bowl of the Los Angeles Biltmore Hotel.

For the second year, both the nominations and the final vote for award winners were made by 12,000 Hollywood citizens (Academy members, plus members of various industry guilds and unions). Three of the four acting winners (Spencer Tracy, Bette Davis, Walter Brennan) had won before, so they were familiar faces in the winners' circle, as was director Frank Capra, who collected his third Oscar in that luminous category. There was no official master of ceremonies at the award banquet, and most of the acting statuettes were presented by character actor Cedric Hardwicke and new matinee idol Tyrone Power. Shirley Temple, ten years old and Hollywood's boxoffice queen, presented Walt Disney with one large honorary Oscar and seven miniature ones on behalf of his animated feature *Snow White and the Seven Dwarfs*. Miniature-sized Academy Awards also went to Universal's Deanna Durbin (age seven-

teen) and M-G-M's Mickey Rooney (age eighteen) for their juvenile performances during the preceding year. Biggest single winner of all 1938 films was Warner Bros.' colorful *The Adventures of Robin Hood,* which won three Academy Awards, but the best picture prize itself went to Mr. Capra's infectious *You Can't Take It With You,* just the kind of warm and comical entertainment to take everyone's mind off uneasy ledger sheets in the bookkeeping departments, and that impending crisis overseas.

Best Picture: **You Can't Take It with You** *(Columbia; produced by Frank Capra) and* **Best Director:** **Frank Capra** *for* **You Can't Take It with You.** *The zany story of an eccentric clan by the name of Vanderhof (with some Sycamores thrown in), it was based on the Pulitzer Prize-winning play by George S. Kaufman and Moss Hart, and starred (right) James Stewart and Jean Arthur along with scene-stealers such as Lionel Barrymore, Edward Arnold, Spring Byington, Mischa Auer, Donald Meek, H.B. Warner, Eddie (Rochester) Anderson and Ann Miller. As with most Capra capers, it had a generous supply of cracker-barrel philosophy mixed in with its daffy doings and feisty comedy. It also marked a third Oscar win for Capra as a director, after previous wins in 1934 and 1936.*

Best Actress: **Bette Davis** *as Julie Marsden in* Jezebel *(Warner Bros.; produced by Henry Blanke). Under the meticulous direction of William Wyler, Bette Davis won her second Oscar as a willful, headstrong Southern belle in pre-Civil War New Orleans who ultimately sacrifices herself for the man she loves (Henry Fonda). The film was made with all the finest resources at the command of a major motion picture company like Warner Bros.; it was also the real turning point in the Davis career, the first in a series of film performances which during the next eight years were unmatched by any other American actress.*

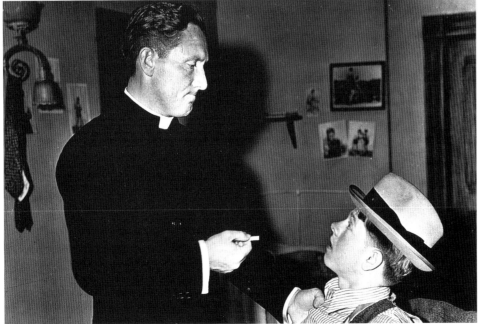

Best Actor: **Spencer Tracy** *as Father Flanagan in* Boys Town *(M-G-M; directed by Norman Taurog). An Academy Award winner for the second consecutive year, Tracy played the real-life Flanagan, a man who founded a community 12 miles outside Omaha in 1920 to help turn juvenile delinquents into responsible citizens. Mickey Rooney (left, with Tracy) costarred, and the film's success inspired a sequel in 1941,* Men of Boys Town, *again with Rooney and Tracy as Father Flanagan. Tracy sent his* Boys Town *Oscar to Flanagan, and it still remains at Boys Town, Nebraska, today.*

Snow White and the Seven Dwarfs *(released by RKO; produced by Walt Disney) received a Special Honorary Award salute in 1938: one full-size statuette and seven miniature ones to the man who pioneered the animated feature.* Snow White *had been nominated for an Oscar (in the music category) the preceding year, eligible then since it had first opened in Los Angeles during that calendar year, on Dec. 20, 1937. But most audiences saw* Snow *during 1938, and it was too much of a success and too revolutionary (and too loved) for Oscar to ignore, thus the 1938 honorary nod.*

Best Supporting Actor: Walter Brennan *as Peter Goodwin in* Kentucky *(20th Century-Fox; produced by Darryl F. Zanuck). Supporting Loretta Young (left, watching a race with Brennan), Richard Greene and some Technicolored and thoroughbred horses, Brennan helped beautiful Loretta save her family plantation with a long-shot victory at the Kentucky Derby. Directed by David Butler, it brought Brennan his second Academy Award in three years, and a third one was still to come.*

Best Supporting Actress: Fay Bainter *as Aunt Belle in* Jezebel. *Miss Bainter, a noted stage actress who also regularly contributed to films, won her supporting Oscar playing the stern but sympathetic friend of the hard-to-love vixen played by Bette Davis (left, being comforted by Bainter). Curiously, Fay Bainter also competed with Davis for the year's best actress prize, nominated in that category for her performance in* White Banners, *making her the first performer to be nominated the same year in both the "best" an "best supporting" categories.*

Nominations 1938

OUTSTANDING PRODUCTION

THE ADVENTURES OF ROBIN HOOD, Warner Bros. Produced by Hal B. Wallis, with Henry Blanke.
ALEXANDER'S RAGTIME BAND, 20th Century-Fox. Produced by Darryl F. Zanuck, with Harry Joe Brown.
BOYS TOWN, M-G-M. Produced by John W. Considine, Jr.
THE CITADEL, M-G-M (British). Produced by Victor Saville.
FOUR DAUGHTERS, Warner Bros.-First National. Produced by Hal B. Wallis, with Henry Blanke.
GRAND ILLUSION, R.A.O., World Pictures (French). Produced by Frank Rollmer and Albert Pinkovitch.
JEZEBEL, Warner Bros. Produced by Hal B. Wallis, with Henry Blanke.
PYGMALION, M-G-M (British). Produced by Gabriel Pascal.
TEST PILOT, M-G-M. Produced by Louis D. Lighton.
*****YOU CAN'T TAKE IT WITH YOU,** Columbia. Produced by Frank Capra.

ACTOR

CHARLES BOYER in *Algiers,* Wanger, UA.
JAMES CAGNEY in *Angels with Dirty Faces.* Warner Bros.
ROBERT DONAT in *The Citadel,* M-G-M (British).
LESLIE HOWARD in *Pygmalion,* M-G-M (British).
*****SPENCER TRACY** in *Boys Town,* M-G-M.

ACTRESS

FAY BAINTER in *White Banners,* Warner Bros.
*****BETTE DAVIS** in *Jezebel,* Warner Bros.
WENDY HILLER in *Pygmalion,* M-G-M (British).
NORMA SHEARER in *Marie Antoinette,* M-G-M.
MARGARET SULLAVAN in *Three Comrades,* M-G-M.

SUPPORTING ACTOR

*****WALTER BRENNAN** in *Kentucky,* 20th Century-Fox.
JOHN GARFIELD in *Four Daughters,* Warner Bros.
GENE LOCKHART in *Algiers,* Wanger, UA.
ROBERT MORLEY in *Marie Antoinette,* M-G-M.
BASIL RATHBONE in *If I Were King,* Paramount.

SUPPORTING ACTRESS

*****FAY BAINTER** in *Jezebel,* Warner Bros.
BEULAH BONDI in *Of Human Hearts,* M-G-M.
BILLIE BURKE in *Merrily We Live,* Roach, M-G-M.
SPRING BYINGTON in *You Can't Take It With You,* Columbia.
MILIZA KORJUS in *The Great Waltz,* M-G-M.

DIRECTING

ANGELS WITH DIRTY FACES, Warner Bros. Michael Curtiz.
BOYS TOWN, M-G-M. Norman Taurog.
THE CITADEL, M-G-M (British). King Vidor.
FOUR DAUGHTERS, Warner Bros. Michael Curtiz.
*****YOU CAN'T TAKE IT WITH YOU,** Columbia. Frank Capra.

WRITING

(Original Story)

ALEXANDER'S RAGTIME BAND, 20th Century-Fox. Irving Berlin.
ANGELS WITH DIRTY FACES, Warner Bros. Rowland Brown.
BLOCKADE, Wanger, UA. John Howard Lawson.
*****BOYS TOWN,** M-G-M. Eleanore Griffin and Dore Schary.
MAD ABOUT MUSIC, Universal. Marcella Burke and Frederick Kohner.
TEST PILOT, M-G-M. Frank Wead.

(Screenplay)

BOYS TOWN, M-G-M. John Meehan and Dore Schary.
THE CITADEL, M-G-M (British). Ian Dalrymple, Elizabeth Hill and Frank Wead.
FOUR DAUGHTERS, Warner Bros. Lenore Coffee and Julius J. Epstein.
*****PYGMALION,** M-G-M (British). George Bernard Shaw; adaptation by Ian Dalrymple, Cecil Lewis and W.P. Lipscomb.
YOU CAN'T TAKE IT WITH YOU, Columbia. Robert Riskin.

CINEMATOGRAPHY

ALGIERS, Wanger, UA. James Wong Howe.
ARMY GIRL, Republic. Ernest Miller and Harry Wild.
THE BUCCANEER, Paramount. Victor Milner.
*****THE GREAT WALTZ,** M-G-M. Joseph Ruttenberg.
JEZEBEL, Warner Bros. Ernest Haller.
MAD ABOUT MUSIC, Universal. Joseph Valentine.
MERRILY WE LIVE, Roach, M-G-M. Norbert Brodine.

SUEZ, 20th Century-Fox. Peverell Marley.
VIVACIOUS LADY, RKO Radio. Robert de Grasse.
YOU CAN'T TAKE IT WITH YOU, Columbia. Joseph Walker.
THE YOUNG IN HEART, Selznick, UA. Leon Shamroy.

ART DIRECTION

*****THE ADVENTURES OF ROBIN HOOD,** Warner Bros. Carl J. Weyl.
THE ADVENTURES OF TOM SAWYER, Selznick, UA. Lyle Wheeler.
ALEXANDER'S RAGTIME BAND, 20th Century-Fox. Bernard Herzbrun and Boris Leven.
ALGIERS, Wanger, UA. Alexander Toluboff.
CAREFREE, RKO Radio. Van Nest Polglase.
GOLDWYN FOLLIES, Goldwyn, UA. Richard Day.
HOLIDAY, Columbia. Stephen Goosson and Lionel Banks.
IF I WERE KING, Paramount. Hans Dreier and John Goodman.
MAD ABOUT MUSIC, Universal. Jack Otterson.
MARIE ANTOINETTE, M-G-M. Cedric Gibbons.
MERRILY WE LIVE, Roach, M-G-M. Charles D. Hall.

SOUND RECORDING

ARMY GIRL, Republic. Republic Studio Sound Dept., Charles Lootens, Sound Director.
*****THE COWBOY AND THE LADY,** Goldwyn, UA. United Artists Studio Sound Dept., Thomas Moulton, Sound Director.
FOUR DAUGHTERS, Warner Bros. Warner Bros. Studio Sound Dept., Nathan Levinson, Sound Director.
IF I WERE KING, Paramount. Paramount Studio Sound Dept., L.L. Ryder, Sound Director.
MERRILY WE LIVE, Roach, M-G-M. Hal Roach Studio Sound Dept., Elmer Raguse, Sound Director.
SWEETHEARTS, M-G-M. M-G-M Studio Sound Dept., Douglas Shearer, Sound Director.
SUEZ, 20th Century-Fox. 20th Century-Fox Studio Sound Dept., Edmund Hansen, Sound Director.
THAT CERTAIN AGE, Universal. Universal Studio Sound Dept., Bernard B. Brown, Sound Director.
VIVACIOUS LADY, RKO Radio. RKO Radio Studio Sound Dept., James Wilkinson, Sound Director.
YOU CAN'T TAKE IT WITH YOU, Columbia. Columbia Studio Sound Dept., John Livadary, Sound Director.

FILM EDITING

*****THE ADVENTURES OF ROBIN HOOD,** Warner Bros. Ralph Dawson.
ALEXANDER'S RAGTIME BAND, 20th Century-Fox. Barbara McLean.
THE GREAT WALTZ, M-G-M. Tom Held.
TEST PILOT, M-G-M. Tom Held.
YOU CAN'T TAKE IT WITH YOU, Columbia. Gene Havlick.

MUSIC

(New classifications)

(Song)

ALWAYS AND ALWAYS (*Mannequin,* M-G-M); Music by Edward Ward. Lyrics by Chet Forrest and Bob Wright.
CHANGE PARTNERS AND DANCE WITH ME (*Carefree,* RKO Radio); Music and Lyrics by Irving Berlin.
THE COWBOY AND THE LADY (*The Cowboy and the Lady,* Goldwyn, UA); Music by Lionel Newman. Lyrics by Arthur Quenzer.
DUST (*Under Western Stars,* Republic); Music and Lyrics by Johnny Marvin.
JEEPERS CREEPERS (*Going Places,* Warner Bros.); Music by Harry Warren. Lyrics by Johnny Mercer.
MERRILY WE LIVE (*Merrily We Live,* Roach, M-G-M); Music by Phil Craig. Lyrics by Arthur Quenzer.
A MIST OVER THE MOON (*The Lady Objects,* Columbia); Music by Ben Oakland. Lyrics by Oscar Hammerstein II.
MY OWN (*That Certain Age,* Universal); Music by Jimmy McHugh. Lyrics by Harold Adamson.
NOW IT CAN BE TOLD (*Alexander's Ragtime Band,* 20th Century-Fox); Music and Lyrics by Irving Berlin.
*****THANKS FOR THE MEMORY** (*Big Broadcast of 1938,* Paramount); Music by Ralph Rainger. Lyrics by Leo Robin.

(Scoring)

*****ALEXANDER'S RAGTIME BAND,** 20th Century-Fox. Alfred Newman.
CAREFREE, RKO Radio. Victor Baravalle.
GIRLS SCHOOL, Columbia. Morris Stoloff and Gregory Stone.
GOLDWYN FOLLIES, Goldwyn, UA. Alfred Newman.
JEZEBEL, Warner Bros. Max Steiner.
MAD ABOUT MUSIC, Universal. Charles Previn and Frank Skinner.
STORM OVER BENGAL, Republic. Cy Feuer.
SWEETHEARTS, M-G-M. Herbert Stothart.
THERE GOES MY HEART, Hal Roach, UA. Marvin Hatley.

TROPIC HOLIDAY, Paramount. Boris Morros.
THE YOUNG IN HEART, Selznick, UA. Franz Waxman.

(Original Score)

*****THE ADVENTURES OF ROBIN HOOD,** Warner Bros. Erich Wolfgang Korngold.
ARMY GIRL, Republic. Victor Young.
BLOCKADE, Wanger, UA. Werner Janssen.
BLOCKHEADS, Roach, UA. Marvin Hatley.
BREAKING THE ICE, RKO Radio. Victor Young.
THE COWBOY AND THE LADY, Goldwyn, UA. Alfred Newman.
IF I WERE KING, Paramount. Richard Hageman.
MARIE ANTOINETTE, M-G-M. Herbert Stothart.
PACIFIC LINER, RKO Radio. Russell Bennett.
SUEZ, 20th Century-Fox. Louis Silvers.
THE YOUNG IN HEART, Selznick, UA. Franz Waxman.

SPECIAL AWARDS

TO DEANNA DURBIN and **MICKEY ROONEY** for their significant contribution in bringing to the screen the spirit and personification of youth, and as juvenile players setting a high standard of ability and achievement. (miniature statuette trophies)
TO HARRY M. WARNER in recognition of patriotic service in the production of historical short subjects presenting significant episodes in the early struggle of the American people for liberty. (scroll)
TO WALT DISNEY for *Snow White and the Seven Dwarfs,* recognized as a significant screen innovation which has charmed millions and pioneered a great new entertainment field for the motion picture cartoon. (one statuette — seven miniature statuettes)
TO OLIVER MARSH and **ALLEN DAVEY** for the color cinematography of the M-G-M production *Sweethearts.* (plaques)
For outstanding achievements in creating special photographic and sound effects in the Paramount production *Spawn of the North:* special effects by **GORDON JENNINGS,** assisted by **JAN DOMELA, DEV JENNINGS, IRMIN ROBERTS** and **ART SMITH;** transparencies by **FARCIOT EDOUART,** assisted by **LOYAL GRIGGS;** sound effects by **LOREN RYDER,** assisted by **HARRY MILLS, LOUIS H. MESENKOP** and **WALTER OBERST.** (plaques)
TO J. ARTHUR BALL for his outstanding contributions to the advancement of color in motion picture photography. (scroll)

SHORT SUBJECTS

(Cartoons)

BRAVE LITTLE TAILOR, Disney, RKO Radio.
MOTHER GOOSE GOES HOLLYWOOD, Disney, RKO Radio.
*****FERDINAND THE BULL,** Disney, RKO Radio.
GOOD SCOUTS, Disney, RKO Radio.
HUNKY AND SPUNKY, Paramount.

(One-reel)

THE GREAT HEART, M-G-M. (Miniature)
*****THAT MOTHERS MIGHT LIVE,** M-G-M. (Miniature)
TIMBER TOPPERS, 20th Century-Fox. (Ed Thorgensen-Sports)

(Two-reel)

*****DECLARATION OF INDEPENDENCE,** Warner Bros. (Historical Featurette)
SWINGTIME IN THE MOVIES, Warner Bros. (Broadway Brevities)
THEY'RE ALWAYS CAUGHT, M-G-M. (Crime Doesn't Pay)

1938 IRVING G. THALBERG MEMORIAL AWARD

TO HAL B. WALLIS

SCIENTIFIC OR TECHNICAL

CLASS I (statuette)
None.

CLASS II (plaque)
None.

CLASS III (citation)
JOHN AALBERG and the **RKO RADIO STUDIO SOUND DEPT.;**
BYRON HASKIN and the **SPECIAL EFFECTS DEPT.** of **WARNER BROS. STUDIO.**

*****INDICATES WINNER**

1939
The Twelfth Year

From start (with the January release of *Gunga Din*) to finish with the December unveiling of *The Light That Failed*), the calendar year of 1939 produced probably more bona fide great entertainments and classics than any similar period in moviemaking annals. At Academy Award time, the competition was unintentionally outlandish, but eight of the features survived to win Oscars: *Gone With the Wind, The Wizard of Oz, Stagecoach, Wuthering Heights, The Rains Came, Mr. Smith Goes to Washington, When Tomorrow Comes* and *Goodbye, Mr. Chips.*

Gone With the Wind, in fact, set a new Oscar numbers record, with eight awards, plus the Irving G. Thalberg award for its producer David O. Selznick. Winning writer Sidney Howard, credited with sole authorship of the final *G.W.T.W.* script, became the Academy's first posthumous winner. He had died in a Massachusetts farm accident in August, 1939, while the film was still in production. Douglas Fairbanks, Sr., the first president of the Academy, was also posthumously honored at the 1939 award ceremony, held February 29, 1940, at the Cocoanut Grove of the Los Angeles Ambassador Hotel; Fairbanks had died two months before, and his special award was accepted by his son, Douglas, Jr.

For the first time, Bob Hope was an Oscar night master of ceremonies ("What a wonderful thing, this benefit for David Selznick," he kidded.) It was the last year the names of winners were told to the press prior to the actual presentation of awards. As in previous times, the Academy tipped off journalists in advance of the festivities, but under strict instructions the results were not to be printed prior to the ceremonial handing out of Oscars. The *Los Angeles Times,* however, jumped the gun and heralded the winners' names in their 8:45 p.m. edition, which could be easily read by nominees and guests on their way to the award banquet. It brought on an Academy decision that holds to this day: ever after, the names of the winners would be kept a stony secret from *everyone*—except two representatives of a tight-lipped tabulating firm—until the actual moment of presentation. Thus, "The envelope please..." was born.

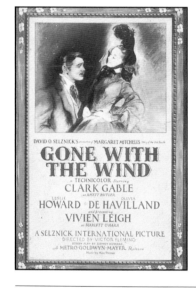

Best Actress: Vivien Leigh *as Scarlett O'Hara and* Best Supporting Actress: *Hattie McDaniel as Mammy (right) in* Gone with the Wind. *Entering films in 1931, Hattie McDaniel had become a welcome staple by the time she played Scarlett O'Hara's no-nonsense Mammy. Via her performance she became the first Black ever nominated for an Academy Award, and the first to win. The performance of 26-year-old Vivien Leigh as the determined Scarlett still stands as one of the best-liked and most durable pieces of acting ever committed to film.*

Best Picture: Gone with the Wind *(Released by M-G-M; produced by David O. Selznick). Long-winded by 1939 standards at 222 minutes, with intermission, Margaret Mitchell's famous novel about a Southern belle and Civil War survival became the epic of the year and—unknown at the time—probably the most famous motion picture of all time. One of the great reasons for its popularity can be summed up simply: it moves.*

Best Director: Victor Fleming *for* Gone with the Wind. *Fleming (right, in jacket and tie, directing William Bakewell as a dispatch rider and Vivien Leigh) took over direction on the Selznick epic after the film began with George Cukor in charge; later, both Sam Wood and William Cameron Menzies helmed certain scenes, but Fleming was the only director officially credited when the film was released.*

Best Supporting Actor: Thomas Mitchell *as Doc Boone in* Stagecoach *(United Artists; produced by Walter Wanger). Mitchell, also a veteran of the* Gone with the Wind *cast, won his Oscar for another 1939 triumph: as a heavy-drinking doctor who rises to his finest hour delivering a baby during a stagecoach trek. John Ford directed, and made a bona fide western classic at the same time. Bing Crosby played Doc when* Stagecoach *was remade in 1966.*

64

OUTSTANDING PRODUCTION

DARK VICTORY, Warner Bros. Produced by David Lewis.

*****GONE WITH THE WIND,** Selznick, M-G-M. Produced by David O. Selznick.

GOODBYE, MR. CHIPS, M-G-M (British). Produced by Victor Saville.

LOVE AFFAIR, RKO Radio. Produced by Leo McCarey.

MR. SMITH GOES TO WASHINGTON, Columbia. Produced by Frank Capra.

NINOTCHKA, M-G-M. Produced by Sidney Franklin.

OF MICE AND MEN, Hal Roach, UA. Produced by Lewis Milestone.

STAGECOACH, Wanger, UA. Produced by Walter Wanger.

THE WIZARD OF OZ, M-G-M. Produced by Mervyn LeRoy.

WUTHERING HEIGHTS, Goldwyn, UA. Produced by Samuel Goldwyn.

ACTOR

*****ROBERT DONAT** in *Goodbye, Mr. Chips,* M-G-M (British).

CLARK GABLE in *Gone With the Wind,* Selznick, M-G-M.

LAURENCE OLIVIER in *Wuthering Heights,* Goldwyn, UA.

MICKEY ROONEY in *Babes in Arms,* M-G-M.

JAMES STEWART in *Mr. Smith Goes to Washington,* Columbia.

ACTRESS

BETTE DAVIS in *Dark Victory,* Warner Bros.

IRENE DUNNE in *Love Affair,* RKO Radio.

GRETA GARBO in *Ninotchka,* M-G-M.

GREER GARSON in *Goodbye, Mr. Chips,* M-G-M (British).

*****VIVIEN LEIGH** in *Gone With the Wind,* Selznick, M-G-M.

SUPPORTING ACTOR

BRIAN AHERNE in *Juarez,* Warner Bros.

HARRY CAREY in *Mr. Smith Goes to Washington,* Columbia.

BRIAN DONLEVY in *Beau Geste,* Paramount.

*****THOMAS MITCHELL** in *Stagecoach,* Wanger, UA.

CLAUDE RAINS in *Mr. Smith Goes to Washington,* Columbia.

SUPPORTING ACTRESS

OLIVIA DE HAVILLAND in *Gone With the Wind,* Selznick, M-G-M.

GERALDINE FITZGERALD in *Wuthering Heights,* Goldwyn, UA.

*****HATTIE McDANIEL** in *Gone With the Wind,* Selznick, M-G-M.

EDNA MAY OLIVER in *Drums Along the Mohawk,* 20th Century-Fox.

MARIA OUSPENSKAYA in *Love Affair,* RKO Radio.

DIRECTING

*****GONE WITH THE WIND,** Selznick M-G-M. Victor Fleming.

GOODBYE, MR. CHIPS, M-G-M (British). Sam Wood.

MR. SMITH GOES TO WASHINGTON, Columbia. Frank Capra.

STAGECOACH, Wanger, UA. John Ford.

WUTHERING HEIGHTS, Goldwyn, UA. William Wyler.

SHORT SUBJECTS

(Cartoons)

DETOURING AMERICA, Warner Bros.

PEACE ON EARTH, M-G-M.

THE POINTER, Disney, RKO Radio.

*****THE UGLY DUCKLING,** Disney, RKO Radio.

(One-reel)

*****BUSY LITTLE BEARS,** Paramount. (Paragraphics)

INFORMATION PLEASE, RKO Radio.

PROPHET WITHOUT HONOR, M-G-M. (Miniature)

SWORD FISHING, Warner Bros. (Vitaphone Varieties)

(Two-reel)

DRUNK DRIVING, M-G-M. (Crime Doesn't Pay)

FIVE TIMES FIVE, RKO Radio. (Special)

*****SONS OF LIBERTY,** Warner Bros. (Historical Featurette)

FILM EDITING

*****GONE WITH THE WIND,** Selznick, M-G-M. Hal C. Kern and James E. Newcom.

GOODBYE, MR. CHIPS, M-G-M (British). Charles Frend.

MR. SMITH GOES TO WASHINGTON, Columbia. Gene Havlick and Al Clark.

THE RAINS CAME, 20th Century-Fox. Barbara McLean.

STAGECOACH, Wanger, UA. Otho Lovering and Dorothy Spencer.

ART DIRECTION

BEAU GESTE, Paramount. Hans Dreier and Robert Odell.

CAPTAIN FURY, Roach, UA. Charles D. Hall.

FIRST LOVE, Universal. Jack Otterson and Martin Obzina.

*****GONE WITH THE WIND,** Selznick, M-G-M. Lyle Wheeler.

LOVE AFFAIR, RKO Radio. Van Nest Polglase and Al Herman.

MAN OF CONQUEST, Republic. John Victor Mackay.

MR. SMITH GOES TO WASHINGTON, Columbia. Lionel Banks.

THE PRIVATE LIVES OF ELIZABETH AND ESSEX, Warner Bros. Anton Grot.

THE RAINS CAME, 20th Century-Fox. William Darling and George Dudley.

STAGECOACH, Wanger, UA. Alexander Toluboff.

THE WIZARD OF OZ, M-G-M. Cedric Gibbons and William A. Horning.

WUTHERING HEIGHTS, Goldwyn, UA. James Basevi.

MUSIC

(Song)

FAITHFUL FOREVER *(Gulliver's Travels,* Paramount); Music by Ralph Rainger. Lyrics by Leo Robin.

I POURED MY HEART INTO A SONG *(Second Fiddle,* 20th Century-Fox); Music and Lyrics by Irving Berlin.

*****OVER THE RAINBOW** *(The Wizard of Oz,* M-G-M); Music by Harold Arlen. Lyrics by E.Y. Harburg.

WISHING *(Love Affair,* RKO Radio); Music and Lyrics by Buddy de Sylva.

(Scoring)

BABES IN ARMS, M-G-M. Roger Edens and George E. Stoll.

FIRST LOVE, Universal. Charles Previn.

THE GREAT VICTOR HERBERT, Paramount. Phil Boutelje and Arthur Lange.

THE HUNCHBACK OF NOTRE DAME, RKO Radio. Alfred Newman.

INTERMEZZO, Selznick, UA. Lou Forbes.

MR. SMITH GOES TO WASHINGTON, Columbia. Dimitri Tiomkin.

OF MICE AND MEN, Roach, UA. Aaron Copland.

THE PRIVATE LIVES OF ELIZABETH AND ESSEX, Warner Bros. Erich Wolfgang Korngold.

SHE MARRIED A COP, Republic. Cy Feuer.

*****STAGECOACH,** Wanger, UA. Richard Hageman, Frank Harling, John Leipold and Leo Shuken.

SWANEE RIVER, 20th Century-Fox. Louis Silvers.

THEY SHALL HAVE MUSIC, Goldwyn, UA. Alfred Newman.

WAY DOWN SOUTH, Lesser, RKO Radio. Victor Young.

(Original Score)

DARK VICTORY, Warner Bros. Max Steiner.

ETERNALLY YOURS, Wanger, UA. Werner Janssen.

GOLDEN BOY, Columbia. Victor Young.

GONE WITH THE WIND, Selznick, M-G-M. Max Steiner.

GULLIVER'S TRAVELS, Paramount. Victor Young.

THE MAN IN THE IRON MASK, Small, UA. Lud Gluskin and Lucien Moraweck.

Best Actor: Robert Donat *as Mr. Chipping (above, with unbilled former student) in* Goodbye, Mr. Chips *(M-G-M; produced by Victor Saville). A touching tribute to teachers everywhere, Donat played a shy and scholarly schoolmaster in England who builds careers and character during several generations of Brookfield schoolboys. Conceived in Hollywood,* the film was made in England at the M-G-M studios there, and co-starred Greer Garson as the ill-fated Mrs. Chips. Sam Wood, who also helped out on Gone with the Wind, directed. Thirty years later, Peter O'Toole played a musicalized Mr. Chips in a 1969 remake.

The Wizard of Oz *(M-G-M; produced by Mervyn LeRoy) won Oscars for Original Music Score, Song ("Over the Rainbow") plus a special miniature statuette for Judy Garland* *(above, being photographed on the yellow brick road with Jack Haley as the Tin Man and Ray Bolger as the Straw Man). It was also nominated for art direction (but lost to* Gone with *the Wind) and in a new category honoring special effects (where* The Rains Came *was the final winner).*

MAN OF CONQUEST, Republic. Victor Young.
NURSE EDITH CAVELL, RKO Radio. Anthony Collins.
OF MICE AND MEN, Roach, UA. Aaron Copland.
THE RAINS CAME, 20th Century-Fox. Alfred Newman.
*THE WIZARD OF OZ, M-G-M. Herbert Stothart.
WUTHERING HEIGHTS, Goldwyn, UA. Alfred Newman.

SOUND RECORDING

BALALAIKA, M-G-M. M-G-M Studio Sound Dept., Douglas Shearer, Sound Director.
GONE WITH THE WIND, Selznick, M-G-M. Samuel Goldwyn Studio Sound Dept., Thomas T. Moulton, Sound Director.
GOODBYE, MR. CHIPS, M-G-M (British). Denham Studio Sound Dept., A.W. Watkins, Sound Director.
THE GREAT VICTOR HERBERT, Paramount. Paramount Studio Sound Dept., Loren Ryder, Sound Director.
THE HUNCHBACK OF NOTRE DAME, RKO Radio. RKO Radio Studio Sound Dept., John Aalberg, Sound Director.
MAN OF CONQUEST, Republic. Republic Studio Sound Dept., C.L. Lootens, Sound Director.
MR. SMITH GOES TO WASHINGTON, Columbia. Columbia Studio Sound Dept., John Livadary, Sound Director.
OF MICE AND MEN, Roach, M-G-M. Hal Roach Studio Sound Dept., Elmer Raguse, Sound Director.
THE PRIVATE LIVES OF ELIZABETH AND ESSEX, Warner Bros. Warner Bros. Studio Sound Dept., Nathan Levinson, Sound Director.
THE RAINS CAME, 20th Century-Fox. 20th Century-Fox Studio Sound Dept., E.H. Hansen, Sound Director.
*WHEN TOMORROW COMES, Universal. Universal Studio Sound Dept., Bernard B. Brown, Sound Director.

WRITING

(Original Story)

BACHELOR MOTHER, RKO Radio. Felix Jackson.
LOVE AFFAIR, RKO Radio. Mildred Cram and Leo McCarey.
*MR. SMITH GOES TO WASHINGTON, Columbia. Lewis R. Foster.
NINOTCHKA, M-G-M. Melchior Lengyel.
YOUNG MR. LINCOLN, 20th Century-Fox. Lamar Trotti.

(Screenplay)

*GONE WITH THE WIND, Selznick, M-G-M. Sidney Howard.

GOODBYE, MR. CHIPS, M-G-M (British). Eric Maschwitz, R.C. Sherriff and Claudine West.
MR. SMITH GOES TO WASHINGTON, Columbia. Sidney Buchman.
NINOTCHKA, M-G-M. Charles Brackett, Walter Reisch and Billy Wilder.
WUTHERING HEIGHTS, Goldwyn, UA. Ben Hecht and Charles MacArthur.

CINEMATOGRAPHY

(New classifications)

(Black-and-White)

STAGECOACH, Wanger, UA. Bert Glennon.
*WUTHERING HEIGHTS, Goldwyn, UA. Gregg Toland.

(Color)

*GONE WITH THE WIND, Selznick, M-G-M. Ernest Haller and Ray Rennahan.
THE PRIVATE LIVES OF ELIZABETH AND ESSEX, Warner Bros. Sol Polito and W. Howard Greene.

SPECIAL EFFECTS

(New category)

GONE WITH THE WIND, Selznick, M-G-M. John R. Cosgrove, Fred Albin and Arthur Johns.
ONLY ANGELS HAVE WINGS, Columbia. Roy Davidson and Edwin C. Hahn.
THE PRIVATE LIVES OF ELIZABETH AND ESSEX, Warner Bros. Byron Haskin and Nathan Levinson.
*THE RAINS CAME, 20th Century-Fox. E.H. Hansen and Fred Sersen.
TOPPER TAKES A TRIP, Roach, UA. Roy Seawright.
UNION PACIFIC, Paramount. Farciot Edouart, Gordon Jennings and Loren Ryder.
THE WIZARD OF OZ, M-G-M. A. Arnold Gillespie and Douglas Shearer.

SPECIAL AWARDS

TO DOUGLAS FAIRBANKS (Commemorative Award)—recognizing the unique and outstanding contribution of Douglas Fairbanks, first president of the Academy, to the international development of the motion picture. (statuette)
TO THE MOTION PICTURE RELIEF FUND—acknowledging the outstanding services to the industry during the past year of the Motion Picture Relief Fund and its progressive leadership. Presented to **JEAN HERSHOLT**, President; **RALPH MORGAN**, Chairman of the Executive Committee; **RALPH**

BLOCK, First Vice-President; **CONRAD NAGEL**. (plaques)
TO JUDY GARLAND for her outstanding performance as a screen juvenile during the past year. (miniature statuette)
TO WILLIAM CAMERON MENZIES for outstanding achievement in the use of color for the enhancement of dramatic mood in the production of *Gone With the Wind*. (plaque)
TO TECHNICOLOR COMPANY for its contributions in successfully bringing three-color feature production to the screen. (statuette)

1939 IRVING G. THALBERG MEMORIAL AWARD

TO DAVID O. SELZNICK

SCIENTIFIC OR TECHNICAL

CLASS I (statuette)

None.

CLASS II (plaque)

None.

CLASS III (citation)

GEORGE ANDERSON of Warner Bros. Studio;
JOHN ARNOLD of Metro-Goldwyn-Mayer Studio;
THOMAS T. MOULTON, FRED ALBIN and the SOUND DEPARTMENT of the SAMUEL GOLDWYN STUDIO;
FARCIOT EDOUART, JOSEPH E. ROBBINS, WILLIAM RUDOLPH and PARAMOUNT PICTURES, INC.;
EMERY HUSE and RALPH B. ATKINSON of Eastman Kodak Co.;
HAROLD NYE of Warner Bros. Studio;
A.J. TONDREAU of Warner Bros. Studio;
F.R. ABBOTT, HALLER BELT, ALAN COOK and BAUSCH & LOMB OPTICAL CO.;
MITCHELL CAMERA CO.;
MOLE-RICHARDSON CO.;
CHARLES HANDLEY, DAVID JOY and NATIONAL CARBON CO.;
WINTON HOCH and TECHNICOLOR MOTION PICTURE CORP.;
DON MUSGRAVE and SELZNICK INTERNATIONAL PICTURES, INC.

*INDICATES WINNER

65

1940
The Thirteenth Year

Since the early nickelodeon days, movies had been an important entertainment toy for audiences, but as a new World War erupted in Europe, the toy began to gain recognition as a powerful tool for aiding the national defense and solidarity. President Franklin D. Roosevelt underscored that fact at the thirteenth Academy Awards banquet, held February 27, 1941, by giving a six-minute direct-line radio address from the White House in Washington, D.C., to the 1500 guests gathered at the Biltmore Bowl of the Los Angeles Biltmore Hotel, paying tribute to the work being done by Hollywood's citizenry. It was the first time an American president had participated in an Oscar evening, even indirectly, and the town was justifiably pleased and impressed.

Most of the guests were justifiably nervous, too. For the first time, the names of all the evening's winners were kept secret until the actual moment statuettes were placed in the hands of the winners. The Academy had hired Price Waterhouse & Co., a certified public accounting firm, to count the ballots, insure secrecy and thus avoid any future embarrassment of press leaks as had occurred in the past. So, to the fellowship and glamour synonymous with Oscars, the "surprise element" was now added.

For the second year in a row, independent producer David O. Selznick produced the picture honored as best of the year, *Rebecca*. The biggest single winner—with three awards—was also independently produced, Alexander Korda's *The Thief of Bagdad*. Walter Brennan became the first performer to win three Academy Awards for acting, this time for Samuel Goldwyn's *The Westerner*. James Stewart was honored as best actor for *The Philadelphia Story,* Ginger Rogers was named best actress for *Kitty Foyle,* and Jane Darwell was chosen best supporting actress for *The Grapes of Wrath*. Also for *Grapes,* John Ford won his second Oscar as best director. Bob Hope, the evening's master of ceremonies, received his first official Academy recognition: a silver plaque, in recognition of "his unselfish services to the motion picture industry." The acting awards were presented that night by the theater's most luminous acting couple, Alfred Lunt and Lynn Fontanne.

Best Picture: **Rebecca** *(United Artists; produced by David O. Selznick). From the atmospheric suspense novel by Daphne du Maurier,* Rebecca *was producer Selznick's first film following* Gone with the Wind, *and marked the Hollywood directorial debut of England's Alfred Hitchcock. The film opened with the famous line from the du Maurier novel ("Last night I dreamt I went to Manderley again...") and at Selznick's insistence included all the famous passages from the well-read story including (at right) the moment Joan Fontaine as the second wife of Laurence Olivier realizes she may never escape the ghostly presence of his first wife, the beautiful Rebecca, who died mysteriously.*

Best Actress: Ginger Rogers *as Kitty in* Kitty Foyle *(RKO Radio; directed by Sam Wood). Taking leave of her dancing shoes, Ginger Rogers (above) won the Oscar as the heroine of a popular Christopher Morley novel about a white-collar worker who has to choose between a rich married socialite (Dennis Morgan) and an industrious young doctor (James Craig). She also had a second major 1940 success via her performance in* Primrose Path, *directed by Gregory La Cava, which added to her new status as an exceptionally fine actress and helped put the Kitty Oscar on her mantel.*

Best Actor: James Stewart *as Mike Conner in* The Philadelphia Story *(M-G-M; produced by Joseph L. Mankiewicz). Stewart, directed by George Cukor, was a Spy magazine reporter assigned to cover the upcoming society marriage of a Philadelphia main liner (Katharine Hepburn, above) only to fall in love with the lady himself. Stewart's win, some have suggested, may have had less to do with his performance in* Philadelphia—*excellent as it was—and more to do with the fact he'd been overlooked by Oscar the previous year for 1939's* Mr. Smith Goes to Washington *and* Destry Rides Again.

Best Director: John Ford *(at left, with Henry Fonda) for* The Grapes of Wrath *(20th Century-Fox; produced by Darryl F. Zanuck, with Nunnally Johnson). It was the second Academy Award for Ford (after 1935's* The Informer*), and his picture remains one of the enduring pieces of cinema storytelling; John Steinbeck's saga of the Joad family's migration from the dust bowl of Oklahoma to a new beginning in California. There were more Oscars ahead for Ford, in 1941 for* How Green Was My Valley *and in 1952 for* The Quiet Man.

Best Supporting Actress: Jane Darwell *as Ma Joad in* The Grapes of Wrath. *Long a staple in Hollywood's ranks of familiar character faces, Miss Darwell had her finest screen hour as Steinbeck's indomitable Ma Joad, the undeviating strength at the core of the Joad clan. Among her most memorable scenes: saying goodbye, perhaps forever, to her son Tom (Henry Fonda, above), near the conclusion of the drama directed by John Ford.*

Best Supporting Actor: Walter Brennan *as Judge Roy Bean in* The Westerner *(United Artists; directed by William Wyler). Brennan, a previous award recipient in 1936 and 1938, became the Academy's first three-time winner among performers. In* The Westerner *he played the feisty real-life judge who held his court from behind the bar of a saloon in Vinegaroon, Texas, in the 1880s before dying in a gunbattle with a cowhand played by Gary Cooper (above, carrying Brennan). Brennan was again nominated for an Academy Award in 1941, for* Sergeant York, *again with Cooper.*

OUTSTANDING PRODUCTION

ALL THIS, AND HEAVEN TOO, Warner Bros. Produced by Jack L. Warner and Hal B. Wallis, with David Lewis.
FOREIGN CORRESPONDENT, Wanger, UA. Produced by Walter Wanger.
THE GRAPES OF WRATH, 20th Century-Fox. Produced by Darryl F. Zanuck, with Nunnally Johnson.
THE GREAT DICTATOR, Chaplin, UA. Produced by Charles Chaplin.
KITTY FOYLE, RKO Radio. Produced by David Hempstead.
THE LETTER, Warner Bros. Produced by Hal B. Wallis.
THE LONG VOYAGE HOME, Wanger, UA. Produced by John Ford.
OUR TOWN, Lesser, UA. Produced by Sol Lesser.
THE PHILADELPHIA STORY, M-G-M. Produced by Joseph L. Mankiewicz.
*****REBECCA,** Selznick, UA. Produced by David O. Selznick.

ACTOR

CHARLES CHAPLIN in *The Great Dictator,* Chaplin, UA.
HENRY FONDA in *The Grapes of Wrath,* 20th Century-Fox.
RAYMOND MASSEY in *Abe Lincoln in Illinois,* RKO Radio.
LAURENCE OLIVIER in *Rebecca,* Selznick, UA.
*****JAMES STEWART** in *The Philadelphia Story,* M-G-M.

ACTRESS

BETTE DAVIS in *The Letter,* Warner Bros.
JOAN FONTAINE in *Rebecca,* Selznick, UA.
KATHARINE HEPBURN in *The Philadelphia Story,* M-G-M.
*****GINGER ROGERS** in *Kitty Foyle,* RKO Radio.
MARTHA SCOTT in *Our Town,* Lesser, UA.

SUPPORTING ACTOR

ALBERT BASSERMANN in *Foreign Correspondent,* Wanger, UA.
*****WALTER BRENNAN** in *The Westerner,* Goldwyn, UA.
WILLIAM GARGAN in *They Knew What They Wanted,* RKO Radio.
JACK OAKIE in *The Great Dictator,* Chaplin, UA.
JAMES STEPHENSON in *The Letter,* Warner Bros.

SUPPORTING ACTRESS

JUDITH ANDERSON in *Rebecca,* Selznick, UA.
*****JANE DARWELL** in *The Grapes of Wrath,* 20th Century-Fox.
RUTH HUSSEY in *The Philadelphia Story,* M-G-M.
BARBARA O'NEIL in *All This, and Heaven Too,* Warner Bros.
MARJORIE RAMBEAU in *Primrose Path,* RKO Radio.

DIRECTING

*****THE GRAPES OF WRATH,** 20th Century-Fox. John Ford.
KITTY FOYLE, RKO Radio. Sam Wood.
THE LETTER, Warner Bros. William Wyler.
THE PHILADELPHIA STORY, M-G-M. George Cukor.
REBECCA, Selznick, UA. Alfred Hitchcock.

SPECIAL EFFECTS

THE BLUE BIRD, 20th Century-Fox. Fred Sersen and E.H. Hansen.
BOOM TOWN, M-G-M. A. Arnold Gillespie and Douglas Shearer.
THE BOYS FROM SYRACUSE, Universal. John P. Fulton, Bernard B. Brown and Joseph Lapis.
DR. CYCLOPS, Paramount. Farciot Edouart and Gordon Jennings.
FOREIGN CORRESPONDENT, Wanger, UA. Paul Eagler and Thomas T. Moulton.
THE INVISIBLE MAN RETURNS, Universal. John P. Fulton, Bernard B. Brown and William Hedgecock.
THE LONG VOYAGE HOME, Argosy-Wanger, UA. R.T. Layton, R.O. Binger and Thomas T. Moulton.
ONE MILLION B.C., Roach, UA. Roy Seawright and Elmer Raguse.
REBECCA, Selznick, UA. Jack Cosgrove and Arthur Johns.
THE SEA HAWK, Warner Bros. Byron Haskin and Nathan Levinson.
SWISS FAMILY ROBINSON, RKO Radio. Vernon L. Walker and John O. Aalberg.
*****THE THIEF OF BAGDAD,** Korda, UA. Lawrence Butler and Jack Whitney.
TYPHOON, Paramount. Farciot Edouart, Gordon Jennings and Loren Ryder.
WOMEN IN WAR, Republic. Howard J. Lydecker, William Bradford, Ellis J. Thackery and Herbert Norsch.

WRITING

(Slight alteration of classifications)

(Original Story)

*****ARISE, MY LOVE,** Paramount. Benjamin Glazer and John S. Toldy.
COMRADE X, M-G-M. Walter Reisch.
EDISON THE MAN, M-G-M. Hugo Butler and Dore Schary.
MY FAVORITE WIFE, RKO Radio. Leo McCarey, Bella Spewack and Samuel Spewack.
THE WESTERNER, Goldwyn, UA. Stuart N. Lake.

(Original Screenplay)

ANGELS OVER BROADWAY, Columbia. Ben Hecht.
DR. EHRLICH'S MAGIC BULLET, Warner Bros. Norman Burnside, Heinz Herald and John Huston.
FOREIGN CORRESPONDENT, Wanger, UA. Charles Bennett and Joan Harrison.
THE GREAT DICTATOR, Chaplin, UA. Charles Chaplin.
*****THE GREAT McGINTY,** Paramount. Preston Sturges.

(Screenplay)

THE GRAPES OF WRATH, 20th Century-Fox. Nunnally Johnson.
KITTY FOYLE, RKO Radio. Dalton Trumbo.
THE LONG VOYAGE HOME, Argosy-Wanger, UA. Dudley Nichols.
*****THE PHILADELPHIA STORY,** M-G-M. Donald Ogden Stewart.
REBECCA, Selznick, UA. Robert E. Sherwood and Joan Harrison.

FILM EDITING

THE GRAPES OF WRATH, 20th Century-Fox. Robert E. Simpson.
THE LETTER, Warner Bros. Warren Low.
THE LONG VOYAGE HOME, Argosy-Wanger, UA. Sherman Todd.
*****NORTH WEST MOUNTED POLICE,** DeMille, Paramount. Anne Bauchens.
REBECCA, Selznick, UA. Hal C. Kern.

CINEMATOGRAPHY

(Black-and-White)

ABE LINCOLN IN ILLINOIS, RKO Radio. James Wong Howe.
ALL THIS, AND HEAVEN TOO, Warner Bros. Ernest Haller.
ARISE, MY LOVE, Paramount. Charles B. Lang, Jr.
BOOM TOWN, M-G-M. Harold Rosson.
FOREIGN CORRESPONDENT, Wagner, UA. Rudolph Maté.
THE LETTER, Warner Bros. Gaetano Gaudio.
THE LONG VOYAGE HOME, Argosy-Wanger, UA. Gregg Toland.
*****REBECCA,** Selznick, UA. George Barnes.
SPRING PARADE, Universal. Joseph Valentine.
WATERLOO BRIDGE, M-G-M. Joseph Ruttenberg.

(Color)

BITTER SWEET, M-G-M. Oliver T. Marsh and Allen Davey.
THE BLUE BIRD, 20th Century-Fox. Arthur Miller and Ray Rennahan.
DOWN ARGENTINE WAY, 20th Century-Fox. Leon Shamroy and Ray Rennahan.
NORTH WEST MOUNTED POLICE, DeMille, Paramount. Victor Milner and W. Howard Greene.
NORTHWEST PASSAGE, M-G-M. Sidney Wagner and William V. Skall.
*****THE THIEF OF BAGDAD,** Korda, UA (British). George Perinal.

SOUND RECORDING

BEHIND THE NEWS, Republic. Republic Studio Sound Dept., Charles Lootens, Sound Director.
CAPTAIN CAUTION, Roach, UA. Hal Roach Studio Sound Dept., Elmer Raguse, Sound Director.
THE GRAPES OF WRATH, 20th Century-Fox. 20th Century-Fox Studio Sound Dept., E.H. Hansen, Sound Director.
THE HOWARDS OF VIRGINIA, Columbia. General Service Studio Sound Dept., Jack Whitney, Sound Director.
KITTY FOYLE, RKO Radio. RKO Radio Studio Sound Dept., John Aalberg, Sound Director.
NORTH WEST MOUNTED POLICE, Paramount. Paramount Studio Sound Dept., Loren Ryder, Sound Director.
OUR TOWN, Lesser, UA. Samuel Goldwyn Studio Sound Dept., Thomas Moulton, Sound Director.
THE SEA HAWK, Warner Bros. Warner Bros. Studio Sound Dept., Nathan Levinson, Sound Director.
SPRING PARADE, Universal. Universal Studio Sound Dept., Bernard B. Brown, Sound Director.
*****STRIKE UP THE BAND,** M-G-M. M-G-M Studio Sound Dept., Douglas Shearer, Sound Director.
TOO MANY HUSBANDS, Columbia. Columbia Studio Sound Dept., John Livadary, Sound Director.

ART DIRECTION

(New classification)

(Black-and-White)

ARISE, MY LOVE, Paramount. Hans Dreier and Robert Usher.
ARIZONA, Columbia. Lionel Banks and Robert Peterson.
THE BOYS FROM SYRACUSE, Universal. John Otterson.
THE DARK COMMAND, Republic. John Victor Mackay.
FOREIGN CORRESPONDENT, Wanger, UA. Alexander Golitzen.
LILLIAN RUSSELL, 20th Century-Fox. Richard Day and Joseph C. Wright.
MY FAVORITE WIFE, RKO Radio. Van Nest Polglase and Mark-Lee Kirk.
MY SON, MY SON, Small, UA. John DuCasse Schulze.
OUR TOWN, Lesser, UA. Lewis J. Rachmil.
*PRIDE AND PREJUDICE, M-G-M. Cedric Gibbons and Paul Groesse.
REBECCA, Selznick, UA. Lyle Wheeler.
THE SEA HAWK, Warner Bros. Anton Grot.
THE WESTERNER, Goldwyn, UA. James Basevi.

(Color)

BITTER SWEET, M-G-M. Cedric Gibbons and John S. Detlie.
DOWN ARGENTINE WAY, 20th Century-Fox. Richard Day and Joseph C. Wright.
NORTH WEST MOUNTED POLICE, DeMille, Paramount. Hans Dreier and Roland Anderson.
*THE THIEF OF BAGDAD, Korda, UA. Vincent Korda.

MUSIC

(Song)

DOWN ARGENTINE WAY (*Down Argentine Way*, 20th Century-Fox); Music by Harry Warren. Lyrics by Mack Gordon.
I'D KNOW YOU ANYWHERE (*You'll Find Out*, RKO Radio); Music by Jimmy McHugh. Lyrics by Johnny Mercer.
IT'S A BLUE WORLD (*Music in My Heart*, Columbia); Music and Lyrics by Chet Forrest and Bob Wright.
LOVE OF MY LIFE (*Second Chorus*, Paramount); Music by Artie Shaw. Lyrics by Johnny Mercer.
ONLY FOREVER (*Rhythm on the River*, Paramount); Music by James Monaco. Lyrics by John Burke.
OUR LOVE AFFAIR (*Strike Up the Band*, M-G-M); Music and Lyrics by Roger Edens and Arthur Freed.
WALTZING IN THE CLOUDS (*Spring Parade*, Universal); Music by Robert Stolz. Lyrics by Gus Kahn.

WHO AM I? (*Hit Parade of 1941*, Republic); Music by Jule Styne. Lyrics by Walter Bullock.
*WHEN YOU WISH UPON A STAR (*Pinocchio*, Disney, RKO Radio); Music by Leigh Harline. Lyrics by Ned Washington.

(Score)

ARISE, MY LOVE, Paramount. Victor Young.
HIT PARADE OF 1941, Republic. Cy Feuer.
IRENE, Imperadio, RKO Radio. Anthony Collins.
OUR TOWN, Lesser, UA. Aaron Copland.
THE SEA HAWK, Warner Bros. Erich Wolfgang Korngold.
SECOND CHORUS, Paramount. Artie Shaw.
SPRING PARADE, Universal. Charles Previn.
STRIKE UP THE BAND, M-G-M. Georgie Stoll and Roger Edens.
*TIN PAN ALLEY, 20th Century-Fox. Alfred Newman.

(Original Score)

ARIZONA, Columbia. Victor Young.
THE DARK COMMAND, Republic. Victor Young.
THE FIGHT FOR LIFE, U.S. Government-Columbia. Louis Gruenberg.
THE GREAT DICTATOR, Chaplin, UA. Meredith Willson.
THE HOUSE OF SEVEN GABLES, Universal. Frank Skinner.
THE HOWARDS OF VIRGINIA, Columbia. Richard Hageman.
THE LETTER, Warner Bros. Max Steiner.
THE LONG VOYAGE HOME, Argosy-Wanger, UA. Richard Hageman.
THE MARK OF ZORRO, 20th Century-Fox. Alfred Newman.
MY FAVORITE WIFE, RKO Radio. Roy Webb.
NORTH WEST MOUNTED POLICE, DeMille, Paramount. Victor Young.
ONE MILLION B.C., Roach, UA. Werner Heymann.
OUR TOWN, Lesser, UA. Aaron Copland.
*PINOCCHIO, Disney, RKO Radio. Leigh Harline, Paul J. Smith and Ned Washington.
REBECCA, Selznick, UA. Franz Waxman.
THE THIEF OF BAGDAD, Korda, UA. Miklos Rozsa.
WATERLOO BRIDGE, M-G-M. Herbert Stothart.

SHORT SUBJECTS

(Cartoons)

*MILKY WAY, M-G-M. (Rudolph Ising Series)
PUSS GETS THE BOOT, M-G-M. (Cat and Mouse Series)

A WILD HARE, Schlesinger, Warner Bros.

(One-reel)

LONDON CAN TAKE IT, Warner Bros. (Vitaphone Varieties)
MORE ABOUT NOSTRADAMUS, M-G-M.
*QUICKER 'N A WINK, Pete Smith, M-G-M.
SIEGE, RKO Radio. (Reelism)

(Two-reel)

EYES OF THE NAVY, M-G-M. (Crime Doesn't Pay)
SERVICE WITH THE COLORS, Warner Bros. (National Defense Series)
*TEDDY, THE ROUGH RIDER, Warner Bros. (Historical Featurette)

SPECIAL AWARDS

TO BOB HOPE, in recognition of his unselfish services to the motion picture industry. (special silver plaque)
TO COLONEL NATHAN LEVINSON for his outstanding service to the industry and the Army during the past nine years, which has made possible the present efficient mobilization of the motion picture industry facilities for the production of Army training films. (statuette)

1940 IRVING G. THALBERG MEMORIAL AWARD

None given.

SCIENTIFIC OR TECHNICAL

CLASS I (statuette)

20TH CENTURY-FOX FILM CORP. for the design and construction of the 20th Century Silenced Camera, developed by DANIEL CLARK, GROVER LAUBE, CHARLES MILLER and ROBERT W. STEVENS.

CLASS II (plaque)

None.

CLASS III (citation)

WARNER BROS. STUDIO ART DEPARTMENT and ANTON GROT.

*INDICATES WINNER

69

The Thief of Bagdad (*United Artists; produced by Alexander Korda) received the most Academy Awards of 1940: three, including statuettes for special effects (Lawrence Butler,* Jack Whitney), color cinematography (George Perinal) and color art direction (Vincent Korda). Made in England, the cast included Sabu, Conrad Veidt, John Justin, June Duprez and, pictured, Rex Ingram as an ill-tempered genie.

1941
The Fourteenth Year

War was now a grim reality. Just two months before the Academy was scheduled to hold the Oscar award banquet honoring achievements for the calendar year 1941, World War II for the United States erupted with the Japanese attack at Pearl Harbor. Then, on January 16, 1942, Carole Lombard—one of the town's top stars and most popular citizens—was killed in an airplane accident returning from a bond-selling tour. Initially, Academy officials decided it best to cancel the Oscar festivities altogether. Bette Davis, newly elected Academy president, suggested they be held, but in a large auditorium instead of a banquet hall, with the public invited to buy tickets, and those proceeds turned over to the Red Cross. After some discussion, the Academy governors vetoed the Davis plan, but decided to go ahead with the awarding of Oscars, under modified conditions. Formal attire was banned, the ceremony was labeled a "dinner" rather than a banquet and there were no searchlights fanning through the skies outside the Biltmore Hotel that night, February 26, 1942.

Bob Hope was the master of ceremonies, and the principal speaker was Wendell L. Willkie, the top man in the Republican party, allowing the GOP equal time among the film folk after the participation of President Roosevelt, a Democrat, the previous year. Biggest single winner of the evening was 20th Century-Fox's *How Green Was My Valley* with five awards, including best picture, best supporting actor Donald Crisp, and best director John Ford. It was Ford's third win, and his second one in two years. For the first time, two real-life sisters were among the nominees for best actress of the year, Olivia de Havilland for *Hold Back the Dawn* and—the winner—Joan Fontaine for *Suspicion*. Mary Astor received her plaque as best supporting actress for *The Great Lie*; she'd also been prominent in another major 1941 success, *The Maltese Falcon*. Orson Welles was personally nominated for four Oscars (as actor, director, producer and co-writer of *Citizen Kane*) and won in the original screenplay division, along with Herman J. Mankiewicz. Harry Segall won the best original story award for *Here Comes Mr. Jordan*, based on his play *Heaven Can Wait*; it was eligible as an "original" because the play had not yet been produced anywhere.

For the first time, the Academy recognized documentary film production; it would be an increasingly important genre in the war years ahead. It was also the last year for a while that the themes of Hollywood's productions would be an equal balance of romantic dramas, infectious musicals, warm comedies, dashing adventure stories and pure escapist fare. For the next several seasons, war would dominate the movies just as it did real life.

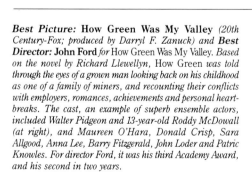

Best Picture: **How Green Was My Valley** *(20th Century-Fox; produced by Darryl F. Zanuck) and* **Best Director:** **John Ford** *for* How Green Was My Valley. *Based on the novel by Richard Llewellyn,* How Green *was told through the eyes of a grown man looking back on his childhood as one of a family of miners, and recounting their conflicts with employers, romances, achievements and personal heartbreaks. The cast, an example of superb ensemble actors, included Walter Pidgeon and 13-year-old Roddy McDowall (at right), and Maureen O'Hara, Donald Crisp, Sara Allgood, Anna Lee, Barry Fitzgerald, John Loder and Patric Knowles. For director Ford, it was his third Academy Award, and his second in two years.*

Best Actor: Gary Cooper *as Alvin York in* Sergeant York *(Warner Bros.; directed by Howard Hawks). York was a real-life Tennessee farmer who became a conscientious objector during World War I, then won fame as a soldier who single-handedly captured 132 German soldiers in the Argonne Forest on October 6, 1918, armed only with a Springfield rifle. As a movie, it was a perfect matching of actor and role. Left, Cooper is the backwoods York at a local bar with cohorts Ike (Ward Bond) and Buck (Noah Beery Jr.), facing Dickie Moore, with shotgun. Cooper won a second Oscar in 1952, and an honorary award in 1960.*

Best Actress: Joan Fontaine *as Lina Laidlaw in* Suspicion *(RKO Radio). Will he or won't he? As a shy British girl who entered into a hasty marriage with a mysterious charmer (Cary Grant, above at left), Miss Fontaine had growing reasons to believe her husband was possibly a murderer, with herself his intended victim. The thriller, based on Frances Iles'* Before the Fact, *reunited the actress with her* Rebecca *director, Alfred Hitchcock, and brought her an Academy Award despite competition from a strong field that included her sister, Olivia de Havilland. Miss Fontaine was also nominated two years later for 1943's* The Constant Nymph.

Best Supporting Actress: Mary Astor *as Sandra Kovack in* The Great Lie *(Warner Bros.) Miss Astor was also a screen contributor whose work stretched back to silent days, when she was usually cast as a sweet ingenue to John Barrymore, Douglas Fairbanks and others. In* The Great Lie, *directed by Edmund Goulding, she was no longer playing a softie but instead a brittle, spoiled concert pianist who creates mayhem in the lives of Bette Davis (above, with Astor) and George Brent.*

Best Supporting Actor: Donald Crisp *as Mr. Morgan in* How Green Was My Valley. *Crisp was one of the founding fathers of the entire motion picture industry, and one of its finest actors. He played General Grant in D.W. Griffith's* Birth of a Nation *(1915), became a silent screen director (among his successes: Buster Keaton's* The Navigator*), then devoted his time exclusively to character acting. In his Oscar-winning role, he played the patriarchal head of a closely-knit coal-mining clan.*

Citizen Kane *(RKO Radio; produced by Orson Welles) won one Academy Award, for the Original Screenplay by Welles and Herman J. Mankiewicz, and has become one of the most famous of all films in the 1941 catalog, some say the greatest motion picture yet made. Loosely based on the career of newspaper tycoon William Randolph Hearst, it marked the motion picture debut of Welles and many of his Mercury Players cast (including Joseph Cotton, Ruth Warrick, Everett Sloane, Paul Stewart and Agnes Moorehead).*

OUTSTANDING MOTION PICTURE

BLOSSOMS IN THE DUST, M-G-M. Produced by Irving Asher.
CITIZEN KANE, Mercury, RKO Radio. Produced by Orson Welles.
HERE COMES MR. JORDAN, Columbia. Produced by Everett Riskin.
HOLD BACK THE DAWN, Paramount. Produced by Arthur Hornblow, Jr.
*****HOW GREEN WAS MY VALLEY,** 20th Century-Fox. Produced by Darryl F. Zanuck.
THE LITTLE FOXES, Goldwyn, RKO Radio. Produced by Samuel Goldwyn.
THE MALTESE FALCON, Warner Bros. Produced by Hal B. Wallis.
ONE FOOT IN HEAVEN, Warner Bros. Produced by Hal B. Wallis.
SERGEANT YORK, Warner Bros. Produced by Jesse L. Lasky and Hal B. Wallis.
SUSPICION, RKO Radio. Produced by RKO Radio.

ACTOR

*****GARY COOPER** in *Sergeant York,* Warner Bros.
CARY GRANT in *Penny Serenade,* Columbia.
WALTER HUSTON in *All That Money Can Buy* (aka *The Devil and Daniel Webster*), RKO Radio.
ROBERT MONTGOMERY in *Here Comes Mr. Jordan,* Columbia.
ORSON WELLES in *Citizen Kane,* Mercury, RKO Radio.

ACTRESS

BETTE DAVIS in *The Little Foxes,* Goldwyn, RKO Radio.
OLIVIA DE HAVILLAND in *Hold Back the Dawn,* Paramount.
*****JOAN FONTAINE** in *Suspicion,* RKO Radio.
GREER GARSON in *Blossoms in the Dust,* M-G-M.
BARBARA STANWYCK in *Ball of Fire,* Goldwyn, RKO Radio.

SUPPORTING ACTOR

WALTER BRENNAN in *Sergeant York,* Warner Bros.
CHARLES COBURN in *The Devil and Miss Jones,* RKO Radio.
*****DONALD CRISP** in *How Green Was My Valley,* 20th Century-Fox.
JAMES GLEASON in *Here Comes Mr. Jordan,* Columbia.
SYDNEY GREENSTREET, in *The Maltese Falcon,* Warner Bros.

SUPPORTING ACTRESS

SARA ALLGOOD in *How Green Was My Valley,* 20th Century-Fox.
*****MARY ASTOR** in *The Great Lie,* Warner Bros.
PATRICIA COLLINGE in *The Little Foxes,* Goldwyn, RKO Radio.
TERESA WRIGHT in *The Little Foxes,* Goldwyn, RKO Radio.
MARGARET WYCHERLY in *Sergeant York,* Warner Bros.

DIRECTING

CITIZEN KANE, Mercury, RKO Radio. Orson Welles.
HERE COMES MR. JORDAN, Columbia. Alexander Hall.
*****HOW GREEN WAS MY VALLEY,** 20th Century-Fox. John Ford.
THE LITTLE FOXES, Goldwyn, RKO Radio. William Wyler.

SERGEANT YORK, Warner Bros. Howard Hawks.

MUSIC

(New classifications)

(Song)

BABY MINE (*Dumbo,* Disney, RKO Radio); Music by Frank Churchill. Lyrics by Ned Washington.
BE HONEST WITH ME (*Ridin' on a Rainbow,* Republic); Music and Lyrics by Gene Autry and Fred Rose.
BLUES IN THE NIGHT (*Blues in the Night,* Warner Bros.); Music by Harold Arlen. Lyrics by Johnny Mercer.
BOOGIE WOOGIE BUGLE BOY OF COMPANY B (*Buck Privates,* Universal); Music by Hugh Prince. Lyrics by Don Raye.
CHATTANOOGA CHOO CHOO (*Sun Valley Serenade,* 20th Century-Fox); Music by Harry Warren. Lyrics by Mack Gordon.
DOLORES (*Las Vegas Nights,* Paramount); Music by Lou Alter. Lyrics by Frank Loesser.
*****THE LAST TIME I SAW PARIS** (*Lady Be Good,* M-G-M); Music by Jerome Kern. Lyrics by Oscar Hammerstein II.
OUT OF THE SILENCE (*All American Co-Ed,* Roach, UA); Music and Lyrics by Lloyd B. Norlind.
SINCE I KISSED MY BABY GOODBYE (*You'll Never Get Rich,* Columbia); Music and Lyrics by Cole Porter.

(Scoring of a Dramatic Picture)

*****ALL THAT MONEY CAN BUY,** RKO Radio. Bernard Herrmann.
BACK STREET, Universal. Frank Skinner.
BALL OF FIRE, Goldwyn, RKO Radio. Alfred Newman.
CHEERS FOR MISS BISHOP, Rowland, UA. Edward Ward.
CITIZEN KANE, Mercury, RKO Radio. Bernard Herrmann.
DR. JEKYLL AND MR. HYDE, M-G-M. Franz Waxman.
HOLD BACK THE DAWN, Paramount. Victor Young.
HOW GREEN WAS MY VALLEY, 20th Century Fox. Alfred Newman.
KING OF THE ZOMBIES, Monogram. Edward Kay.
LADIES IN RETIREMENT, Columbia. Morris Stoloff and Ernst Toch.
THE LITTLE FOXES, Goldwyn, RKO Radio. Meredith Willson.
LYDIA, Korda, UA. Miklos Rozsa.
MERCY ISLAND, Republic. Cy Feuer and Walter Scharf.
SERGEANT YORK, Warner Bros. Max Steiner.
SO ENDS OUR NIGHT, Loew-Lewin, UA. Louis Gruenberg.
SUNDOWN, Wanger, UA. Miklos Rozsa.
SUSPICION, RKO Radio. Franz Waxman.
TANKS A MILLION, Roach, UA. Edward Ward.
THAT UNCERTAIN FEELING, Lubitsch, UA. Werner Heymann.
THIS WOMAN IS MINE, Universal. Richard Hageman.

(Scoring of a Music Picture)

ALL AMERICAN CO-ED, Roach, UA. Edward Ward.
BIRTH OF THE BLUES, Paramount. Robert Emmett Dolan.
BUCK PRIVATES, Universal. Charles Previn.
THE CHOCOLATE SOLDIER, M-G-M. Herbert Stothart and Bronislau Kaper.
*****DUMBO,** Disney, RKO Radio. Frank Churchill and Oliver Wallace.
ICE CAPADES, Republic. Cy Feuer.
THE STRAWBERRY BLONDE, Warner Bros. Heinz Roemheld.
SUN VALLEY SERENADE, 20th Century-Fox. Emil Newman.
SUNNY, RKO Radio. Anthony Collins.
YOU'LL NEVER GET RICH, Columbia. Morris Stoloff.

WRITING

(Original Story)

BALL OF FIRE, Goldwyn, RKO Radio. Thomas Monroe and Billy Wilder.
*****HERE COMES MR. JORDAN,** Columbia. Harry Segall.
THE LADY EVE, Paramount. Monckton Hoffe.
MEET JOHN DOE, Warner Bros. Richard Connell and Robert Presnell.
NIGHT TRAIN, 20th Century-Fox (British). Gordon Wellesley.

(Original Screenplay)

*****CITIZEN KANE,** Mercury, RKO Radio. Herman J. Mankiewicz and Orson Welles.
THE DEVIL AND MISS JONES, RKO Radio. Norman Krasna.
SERGEANT YORK, Warner Bros. Harry Chandlee, Abem Finkel, John Huston and Howard Koch.
TALL, DARK AND HANDSOME, 20th Century-Fox. Karl Tunberg and Darrell Ware.
TOM, DICK AND HARRY, RKO Radio. Paul Jarrico.

(Screenplay)
*HERE COMES MR. JORDAN, Columbia. Sidney Buchman and Seton I. Miller.
HOLD BACK THE DAWN, Paramount. Charles Brackett and Billy Wilder.
HOW GREEN WAS MY VALLEY, 20th Century-Fox. Philip Dunne.
THE LITTLE FOXES, Goldwyn, RKO Radio. Lillian Hellman.
THE MALTESE FALCON, Warner Bros. John Huston.

SPECIAL EFFECTS
ALOMA OF THE SOUTH SEAS, Paramount. Farciot Edouart, Gordon Jennings and Louis Mesenkop.
FLIGHT COMMAND, M-G-M. A. Arnold Gillespie and Douglas Shearer.
*I WANTED WINGS, Paramount. Farciot Edouart, Gordon Jennings and Louis Mesenkop.
THE INVISIBLE WOMAN, Universal. John Fulton and John Hall.
THE SEA WOLF, Warner Bros. Byron Haskin and Nathan Levinson.
THAT HAMILTON WOMAN, Korda, UA. Lawrence Butler and William H. Wilmarth.
TOPPER RETURNS, Roach, UA. Roy Seawright and Elmer Raguse.
A YANK IN THE R.A.F., 20th Century-Fox. Fred Sersen and E.H. Hansen.

CINEMATOGRAPHY
(Black-and-White)
THE CHOCOLATE SOLDIER, M-G-M. Karl Freund.
CITIZEN KANE, Mercury, RKO Radio. Gregg Toland.
DR. JEKYLL AND MR. HYDE, M-G-M. Joseph Ruttenberg.
HERE COMES MR. JORDAN, Columbia. Joseph Walker.
HOLD BACK THE DAWN, Paramount, Leo Tover.
*HOW GREEN WAS MY VALLEY, 20th Century-Fox. Arthur Miller.
SERGEANT YORK, Warner Bros. Sol Polito.
SUN VALLEY SERENADE, 20th Century-Fox. Edward Cronjager.
SUNDOWN, Wanger, UA. Charles Lang.
THAT HAMILTON WOMAN, Korda, UA. Rudolph Maté.

(Color)
ALOMA OF THE SOUTH SEAS, Paramount. Wilfred M. Cline, Karl Struss and William Snyder.
BILLY THE KID, M-G-M. William V. Skall and Leonard Smith.
*BLOOD AND SAND, 20th Century-Fox. Ernest Palmer and Ray Rennahan.
BLOSSOMS IN THE DUST, M-G-M. Karl Freund and W. Howard Greene.
DIVE BOMBER, Warner Bros. Bert Glennon.
LOUISIANA PURCHASE, Paramount. Harry Hallenberger and Ray Rennahan.

SHORT SUBJECTS
(Cartoons)
BOOGIE WOOGIE BUGLE BOY OF COMPANY B, Lantz, Universal.
HIAWATHA'S RABBIT HUNT, Schlesinger, Warner Bros.
HOW WAR CAME, Columbia. (Raymond Gram Swing Series)
*LEND A PAW, Disney, RKO Radio.
THE NIGHT BEFORE CHRISTMAS, M-G-M. (Tom and Jerry Series)
RHAPSODY IN RIVETS, Schlesinger, Warner Bros.
THE ROOKIE BEAR, M-G-M. (Bear Series)
RHYTHM IN THE RANKS, Paramount. (George Pal Puppetoon Series)
SUPERMAN NO. 1, Paramount.
TRUANT OFFICER DONALD, Disney, RKO Radio. (Donald Duck)

(One-reel)
ARMY CHAMPIONS, Pete Smith, M-G-M. (Pete Smith Specialties)
BEAUTY AND THE BEACH, Paramount. (Headliner Series)
DOWN ON THE FARM, Paramount. (Speaking of Animals)
FORTY BOYS AND A SONG, Warner Bros. (Melody Master Series)
KINGS OF THE TURF, Warner Bros. (Color Parade Series)
*OF PUPS AND PUZZLES, M-G-M. (Passing Parade Series)
SAGEBRUSH AND SILVER, 20th Century-Fox. (Magic Carpet Series)

(Two-reel)
ALIVE IN THE DEEP, Woodard Productions, Inc.
FORBIDDEN PASSAGE, M-G-M. (Crime Doesn't Pay)
THE GAY PARISIAN, Warner Bros. (Miniature Featurette Series)

Best Song: "The Last Time I Saw Paris," *sung by Ann Sothern (above, with Robert Young at the keyboard) in M-G-M's* Lady Be Good. *It was a beautiful song, and an emotional one for 1941, considering the Nazi occupation of France's City of Light. But many Academy members were noisily unmoved by the song's winning of the Oscar. For a reason. The song had been independently written in 1940 by Jerome Kern and Oscar Hammerstein II, and publicly performed before it was purchased by M-G-M and inserted into the Cole Porter movie musical, an itinerary at odds with the Academy's basic desire to reward songs specifically written for a movie score.*

*MAIN STREET ON THE MARCH, M-G-M. (Special)
THE TANKS ARE COMING, Warner Bros. (National Defense Series)

ART DIRECTION— INTERIOR DECORATION
(For the first year, certificates of merit were given to the Interior Decorators of the film receiving award for Art Direction)

(Black-and-White)
CITIZEN KANE, Mercury, RKO Radio. Perry Ferguson and Van Nest Polglase; Al Fields and Darrell Silvera.
THE FLAME OF NEW ORLEANS, Universal. Martin Obzina and Jack Otterson; Russell A. Gausman.
HOLD BACK THE DAWN, Paramount. Hans Dreier and Robert Usher; Sam Comer.
*HOW GREEN WAS MY VALLEY, 20th Century-Fox. Richard Day and Nathan Juran; Thomas Little.
LADIES IN RETIREMENT, Columbia. Lionel Banks; George Montgomery.
THE LITTLE FOXES, Goldwyn, RKO Radio. Stephen Goosson; Howard Bristol.
SERGEANT YORK, Warner Bros. John Hughes; Fred MacLean.
THE SON OF MONTE CRISTO, Small, UA. John DuCasse Schulze; Edward G. Boyle.
SUNDOWN, Wanger, UA. Alexander Golitzen; Richard Irvine.
THAT HAMILTON WOMAN, Korda, UA. Vincent Korda; Julia Heron.
WHEN LADIES MEET, M-G-M. Cedric Gibbons and Randall Duell; Edwin B. Willis.

(Color)
BLOOD AND SAND, 20th Century-Fox. Richard Day and Joseph C. Wright; Thomas Little.
*BLOSSOMS IN THE DUST, M-G-M. Cedric Gibbons and Urie McCleary; Edwin B. Willis.
LOUISIANA PURCHASE, Paramount. Raoul Pene du Bois; Stephen A. Seymour.

SOUND RECORDING
APPOINTMENT FOR LOVE, Universal. Universal Studio Sound Dept., Bernard B. Brown, Sound Director.
BALL OF FIRE, Goldwyn, RKO Radio. Samuel Goldwyn Studio Sound Dept., Thomas Moulton, Sound Director.
THE CHOCOLATE SOLDIER, M-G-M. M-G-M Studio Sound Dept., Douglas Shearer, Sound Director.
CITIZEN KANE, Mercury, RKO Radio. RKO Radio Studio Sound Dept., John Aalberg, Sound Director.
THE DEVIL PAYS OFF, Republic. Republic Studio Sound Dept., Charles Lootens, Sound Director.
HOW GREEN WAS MY VALLEY, 20th Century-Fox. 20th Century-Fox Studio Sound Dept., E.H. Hansen, Sound Director.
THE MEN IN HER LIFE, Columbia. Columbia Studio Sound Dept., John Livadary, Sound Director.
SERGEANT YORK, Warner Bros. Warner Bros. Studio Sound Dept., Nathan Levinson, Sound Director.
SKYLARK, Paramount. Paramount Studio Sound Dept., Loren Ryder, Sound Director.
*THAT HAMILTON WOMAN, Korda, UA. General Service Studio Sound Dept., Jack Whitney, Sound Director.
TOPPER RETURNS, Roach, UA. Hal Roach Studio Sound Dept., Elmer Raguse, Sound Director.

FILM EDITING
CITIZEN KANE, Mercury, RKO Radio. Robert Wise.
DR. JEKYLL AND MR. HYDE, M-G-M. Harold F. Kress.
HOW GREEN WAS MY VALLEY, 20th Century-Fox. James B. Clark.

THE LITTLE FOXES, Goldwyn, RKO Radio. Daniel Mandell.
*SERGEANT YORK, Warner Bros. William Holmes.

DOCUMENTARY
(New category)
ADVENTURES IN THE BRONX, Film Assocs.
BOMBER, U.S. Office for Emergency Management Film Unit.
CHRISTMAS UNDER FIRE, British Ministry of Information, Warner Bros.
*CHURCHILL'S ISLAND, Canadian Film Board, UA.
A LETTER FROM HOME, British Ministry of Information.
LIFE OF A THOROUGHBRED, 20th Century-Fox.
NORWAY IN REVOLT, March of Time, RKO Radio.
SOLDIERS OF THE SKY, 20th Century-Fox.
WAR CLOUDS IN THE PACIFIC, Canadian Film Board.

SPECIAL AWARDS
TO REY SCOTT for his extraordinary achievement in producing *Kukan*, the film record of China's struggle, including its photography with a 16mm camera under the most difficult and dangerous conditions. (certificate)
TO THE BRITISH MINISTRY OF INFORMATION for its vivid and dramatic presentation of the heroism of the RAF in the documentary film *Target For Tonight*. (certificate)
TO LEOPOLD STOKOWSKI and his associates for their unique achievement in the creation of a new form of visualized music in Walt Disney's production *Fantasia*, thereby widening the scope of the motion picture as entertainment and as an art form. (certificate)
TO WALT DISNEY, WILLIAM GARITY, JOHN N.A. HAWKINS and the RCA MANUFACTURING COMPANY, for their outstanding contribution to the advancement of the use of sound in motion pictures through the production of *Fantasia*. (certificates)

1941 IRVING G. THALBERG MEMORIAL AWARD
TO WALT DISNEY

SCIENTIFIC OR TECHNICAL
CLASS I (statuette)
None.

CLASS II (plaque)
ELECTRICAL RESEARCH PRODUCTS DIVISION OF WESTERN ELECTRIC CO., INC., for the development of the precision integrating sphere densitometer.
RCA MANUFACTURING CO. for the design and development of the MI-3043 Uni-directional microphone.

CLASS III (citation)
RAY WILKINSON and the PARAMOUNT STUDIO LABORATORY;
CHARLES LOOTENS and the REPUBLIC STUDIO SOUND DEPT.;
WILBUR SILVERTOOTH and the PARAMOUNT STUDIO ENGINEERING DEPT.;
PARAMOUNT PICTURES, INC., and 20TH CENTURY-FOX FILM CORP.;
DOUGLAS SHEARER and the METRO-GOLDWYN-MAYER STUDIO SOUND DEPT. and to LOREN RYDER and the PARAMOUNT STUDIO SOUND DEPARTMENT.

*INDICATES WINNER

73

1942
The Fifteenth Year

At the 1942 Academy Awards banquet, held March 4, 1943, at the Cocoanut Grove in the Los Angeles Ambassador Hotel, Greer Garson received the Oscar as best actress of the year for *Mrs. Miniver* and gave a speech which is still a subject for discussion. Legend has it that her "thank you" oratory lasted nearly an hour, causing Academy officials thereafter to put a time limit on all Academy acceptance speeches. As sometimes happens in Hollywood, the facts may have been devoured by exaggeration. Years later, Miss Garson said good-naturedly, "Reports on the length of my speech that night seem to be a bit like that one report of Mark Twain's death: slightly exaggerated. Actually, it was clocked at about five-and-a-half minutes, but I think the reason people remembered it is because I somewhat fractured a long-standing rule which was that a winner should simply say 'thank you' and then dissolve into a flood of tears and sit down. I felt very sincerely about what I had to say, that there were no losers in the room that night, that we were all winners, but I know I didn't do a long, one-woman fillibuster as the reports now have it. I admit I do have a gift of gab, and it seems to have gotten me in hot water that time, but I did use it to advantage later while selling war bonds all over the country." And the Academy did *not* put a limit to the length of acceptance speeches.

Mrs. Miniver also won five other Academy Awards, including those for best picture, best director William Wyler and best supporting actress Teresa Wright. It was a big year for Miss Wright; she was also nominated in the best actress category, for *The Pride of the Yankees*. James Cagney was named best actor for *Yankee Doodle Dandy* and Van Heflin was chosen best supporting actor for *Johnny Eager.* Four winners were chosen in the best documentary division, and thereafter that category was more clearly defined between "short subjects" and "features." Best song of the year was Irving Berlin's "White Christmas," introduced in *Holiday Inn* by Bing Crosby and Marjorie Reynolds. Berlin himself announced the winner in that category; when he opened the sealed envelope bearing his name, he told the on-lookers, "I'm glad to present the award. I've known the fellow for a long time."

Bob Hope was again master of ceremonies for the evening, Jeanette MacDonald sang the National Anthem, and the Oscar ceremony itself carried a distinctly military flavor, with honored guests from all branches of the military services. Before the actual winners were announced, Marine private Tyrone Power and Air Force private Alan Ladd unfurled an industry flag disclosing that 27,677 members of the motion picture industry were in uniform. For the first time, the usual bronze-filled, gold-plated Oscar statues were made out of plaster, due to wartime shortages; they were all replaced by the real thing when the war was over. It was also the last time Academy Awards were handed out at small, industry banquets. With a world at war and many facing starvation, it seemed insensitive to continue presenting awards at elegant dinner parties, so Oscar moved into a theater.

Best Picture: **Mrs. Miniver** *(M-G-M; produced by Sidney Franklin) and* **Best Director:** **William Wyler** *(right) for* Mrs. Miniver. *Wyler was in military action overseas when he was announced as 1942's Oscar winner as director; his award was accepted by his wife.* Mrs. Miniver *was a war picture without a battle scene but showed an English family's everyday adjustments to wartime problems with courage and warmth, and could not have come to the screen at a more apt time. It starred Greer Garson and Walter Pidgeon, supported by Teresa Wright, Dame May Whitty, Richard Ney, Henry Travers and Henry Wilcoxon.*

Best Actor: James Cagney *as George M. Cohan in* Yankee Doodle Dandy *(Warner Bros.; directed by Michael Curtiz). Cagney became the first actor to win an Academy Award for a musical performance, playing the theater's prolific actor-writer-musician Cohan, born on the fourth of July and a perennial flagwaver. It was a major change of pace for Cagney, best known for tough-guy roles such as in 1938's* Angels with Dirty Faces, *which brought him his first Academy Award nomination. After Dandy and his Oscar win, Cagney took leave from his long-time Warner Bros. employers to become an independent film actor and his appearances became rarer. But the quality of his work always remained first rate, and in 1955 he was again a nominee, for* Love Me or Leave Me. *He also played Cohan again in an unbilled cameo appearance in 1955's* The Seven Little Foys *with Bob Hope.*

Best Actress: Greer Garson *(near left) as Mrs. Miniver* and **Best Supporting Actress: Teresa Wright** *(far left) as Carol Beldon Miniver with* **Walter Pidgeon** *(center) in* Mrs. Miniver. *Norma Shearer had been the first choice to play Mrs. Miniver but turned down the role; Greer Garson was equally apprehensive, at age 33, of playing the mother of a mature and married son. But Miss Garson eventually relented, and her performance became one of the most popular of the World War II years, enthroning her as the First Lady of M-G-M and the new leading female draw at the nation's box offices. For five consecutive years (1941–45) she was an Academy Award nominee, book-ended by additional best actress nominations in 1939 and 1960. Teresa Wright played her daughter-in-law, tragically killed by German aircraft fire and bringing the war even closer to the close-knit Miniver family. Miss Wright was also a 1942 best actress nominee for* The Pride of the Yankees.

Best Supporting Actor: Van Heflin as *Jeff Hartnett* (above, holding Robert Taylor) in Johnny Eager (M-G-M; directed by Mervyn LeRoy). At age 32, Heflin became the youngest actor to that date to win an Academy Award. He played a booze-soaked friend and conscience to an underworld tough guy (Taylor) who came to a no-good end despite Heflin/Hartnett's loyalty-to-the-last. Heflin's career was curtailed during the war period but in subsequent years the roles got larger and he was always regarded as a welcome asset to any film in which he worked.

Woman of the Year (M-G-M; produced by Joseph L. Mankiewicz) marked the first screen teaming of Katharine Hepburn and Spencer Tracy (above), and won the original screenplay award for Michael Kanin and Ring Lardner, Jr. It was directed by George Stevens and matched a tough New York sportswriter (Tracy) with a society columnist (Hepburn); the Hepburn-Tracy chemistry was contagious, and inspired seven more pairings from Keeper of the Flame (1942) through Guess Who's Coming to Dinner (1967), twenty-five years later.

OUTSTANDING MOTION PICTURE

THE INVADERS, Ortus, Columbia (British). Produced by Michael Powell.
KINGS ROW, Warner Bros. Produced by Hal B. Wallis.
THE MAGNIFICENT AMBERSONS, Mercury, RKO Radio. Produced by Orson Welles.
*MRS. MINIVER, M-G-M. Produced by Sidney Franklin.
THE PIED PIPER, 20th Century-Fox. Produced by Nunnally Johnson.
THE PRIDE OF THE YANKEES, Goldwyn, RKO Radio. Produced by Samuel Goldwyn.
RANDOM HARVEST, M-G-M. Produced by Sidney Franklin.
THE TALK OF THE TOWN. Columbia. Produced by George Stevens.
WAKE ISLAND, Paramount. Produced by Joseph Sistrom.
YANKEE DOODLE DANDY, Warner Bros. Produced by Jack Warner and Hal. B. Wallis, with William Cagney.

ACTOR

*JAMES CAGNEY in *Yankee Doodle Dandy*, Warner Bros.
RONALD COLMAN in *Random Harvest*, M-G-M.
GARY COOPER in *The Pride of the Yankees*, Goldwyn, RKO Radio.
WALTER PIDGEON in *Mrs. Miniver*, M-G-M.
MONTY WOOLLEY in *The Pied Piper*, 20th Century-Fox.

ACTRESS

BETTE DAVIS in *Now, Voyager*, Warner Bros.
*GREER GARSON in *Mrs. Miniver*, M-G-M.
KATHARINE HEPBURN in *Woman of the Year*, M-G-M.
ROSALIND RUSSELL in *My Sister Eileen*, Columbia.
TERESA WRIGHT in *The Pride of the Yankees*, Goldwyn, RKO Radio.

SUPPORTING ACTOR

WILLIAM BENDIX in *Wake Island*, Paramount.
*VAN HEFLIN in *Johnny Eager*, M-G-M.
WALTER HUSTON in *Yankee Doodle Dandy*, Warner Bros.
FRANK MORGAN in *Tortilla Flat*, M-G-M.
HENRY TRAVERS in *Mrs. Miniver*, M-G-M.

SUPPORTING ACTRESS

GLADYS COOPER in *Now, Voyager*, Warner Bros.
AGNES MOOREHEAD in *The Magnificent Ambersons*, Mercury, RKO Radio.
SUSAN PETERS in *Random Harvest*, M-G-M.
DAME MAY WHITTY in *Mrs. Miniver*, M-G-M.
*TERESA WRIGHT in *Mrs. Miniver*, M-G-M.

DIRECTING

KINGS ROW, Warner Bros. Sam Wood.
*MRS. MINIVER, M-G-M. William Wyler.
RANDOM HARVEST, M-G-M. Mervyn LeRoy.
WAKE ISLAND, Paramount. John Farrow.
YANKEE DOODLE DANDY, Warner Bros. Michael Curtiz.

WRITING

(Original Story)
HOLIDAY INN, Paramount. Irving Berlin.
*THE INVADERS, Ortus, Columbia (British). Emeric Pressburger.
THE PRIDE OF THE YANKEES, Goldwyn, RKO Radio. Paul Gallico.
THE TALK OF THE TOWN, Columbia. Sidney Harmon.
YANKEE DOODLE DANDY, Warner Bros. Robert Buckner.

(Original Screenplay)
ONE OF OUR AIRCRAFT IS MISSING, Powell, UA (British). Michael Powell and Emeric Pressburger.
THE ROAD TO MOROCCO, Paramount. Frank Butler and Don Hartman.
WAKE ISLAND, Paramount. W.R. Burnett and Frank Butler.
THE WAR AGAINST MRS. HADLEY, M-G-M. George Oppenheimer.
*WOMAN OF THE YEAR, M-G-M. Michael Kanin and Ring Lardner, Jr.

(Screenplay)
THE INVADERS, Ortus, Columbia (British). Rodney Ackland and Emeric Pressburger.
*MRS. MINIVER, M-G-M. George Froeschel, James Hilton, Claudine West and Arthur Wimperis.
THE PRIDE OF THE YANKEES, Goldwyn, RKO Radio. Herman J. Mankiewicz and Jo Swerling.
RANDOM HARVEST, M-G-M. George Froeschel, Claudine West and Arthur Wimperis.

THE TALK OF THE TOWN, Columbia. Sidney Buchman and Irwin Shaw.

CINEMATOGRAPHY

(Black-and-White)
KINGS ROW, Warner Bros. James Wong Howe.
THE MAGNIFICENT AMBERSONS, Mercury, RKO Radio. Stanley Cortez.
*MRS. MINIVER, M-G-M. Joseph Ruttenberg.
MOONTIDE, 20th Century-Fox. Charles Clarke.
THE PIED PIPER, 20th Century-Fox. Edward Cronjager.
THE PRIDE OF THE YANKEES, Goldwyn, RKO Radio. Rudolph Maté.
TAKE A LETTER, DARLING, Paramount. John Mescall.
THE TALK OF THE TOWN, Columbia. Ted Tetzlaff.
TEN GENTLEMEN FROM WEST POINT, 20th Century-Fox. Leon Shamroy.
THIS ABOVE ALL, 20th Century-Fox. Arthur Miller.

(Color)
ARABIAN NIGHTS, Wanger, Universal. Milton Krasner, William V. Skall and W. Howard Greene.
*THE BLACK SWAN, 20th Century-Fox. Leon Shamroy.
CAPTAINS OF THE CLOUDS, Warner Bros. Sol Polito.
JUNGLE BOOK, Korda, UA. W. Howard Greene.
REAP THE WILD WIND, DeMille, Paramount. Victor Milner and William V. Skall.
TO THE SHORES OF TRIPOLI, 20th Century-Fox. Edward Cronjager and William V. Skall.

ART DIRECTION-
INTERIOR DECORATION

(Black-and-White)
GEORGE WASHINGTON SLEPT HERE, Warner Bros. Max Parker and Mark-Lee Kirk; Casey Roberts.
THE MAGNIFICENT AMBERSONS, Mercury, RKO Radio. Albert S. D'Agostino; Al Fields and Darrell Silvera.
THE PRIDE OF THE YANKEES, Goldwyn, RKO Radio. Perry Ferguson; Howard Bristol.
RANDOM HARVEST, M-G-M. Cedric Gibbons and Randall Duell; Edwin B. Willis and Jack Moore.
THE SHANGHAI GESTURE, Pressburger, UA. Boris Leven.
SILVER QUEEN, Sherman, UA. Ralph Berger; Emile Kuri.
THE SPOILERS, Universal. John B. Goodman and Jack Otterson; Russell A. Gausman and Edward R. Robinson.
TAKE A LETTER, DARLING, Paramount. Hans Dreier and Roland Anderson; Sam Comer.
THE TALK OF THE TOWN, Columbia. Lionel Banks and Rudolph Sternad; Fay Babcock.
*THIS ABOVE ALL, 20th Century-Fox. Richard Day and Joseph Wright; Thomas Little.

(Color)
ARABIAN NIGHTS, Wanger, Universal. Alexander Golitzen and Jack Otterson; Russell A. Gausman and Ira S. Webb.
CAPTAINS OF THE CLOUDS, Warner Bros. Ted Smith; Casey Roberts.
JUNGLE BOOK, Korda, UA. Vincent Korda; Julia Heron.
*MY GAL SAL, 20th Century-Fox. Richard Day and Joseph Wright; Thomas Little.
REAP THE WILD WIND, DeMille, Paramount. Hans Dreier and Roland Anderson; George Sawley.

SOUND RECORDING

ARABIAN NIGHTS, Universal. Universal Studio Sound Dept., Bernard B. Brown, Sound Director.
BAMBI, Disney, RKO Radio. Walt Disney Studio Sound Dept., Sam Slyfield, Sound Director.
FLYING TIGERS, Republic. Republic Studio Sound Dept., Daniel Bloomberg, Sound Director.
FRIENDLY ENEMIES, Small, UA. Sound Service, Inc., Jack Whitney, Sound Director.
THE GOLD RUSH, Chaplin, UA. RCA Sound, James Fields, Sound Director.
MRS. MINIVER, M-G-M. M-G-M Studio Sound Dept., Douglas Shearer, Sound Director.
ONCE UPON A HONEYMOON, RKO Radio. RKO Radio Studio Sound Dept., Steve Dunn, Sound Director.
THE PRIDE OF THE YANKEES, Goldwyn, RKO Radio. Samuel Goldwyn Studio Sound Dept., Thomas Moulton, Sound Director.
THE ROAD TO MOROCCO, Paramount. Paramount Studio Sound Dept., Loren Ryder, Sound Director.
THIS ABOVE ALL, 20th Century-Fox. 20th Century-Fox Studio Sound Dept., E.H. Hansen, Sound Director.
*YANKEE DOODLE DANDY, Warner Bros. Warner Bros. Studio Sound Dept., Nathan Levinson, Sound Director.
YOU WERE NEVER LOVELIER, Columbia. Columbia Studio Sound Dept., John Livadary, Sound Director.

FILM EDITING

MRS. MINIVER, M-G-M. Harold F. Kress.
*THE PRIDE OF THE YANKEES, Goldwyn, RKO Radio. Daniel Mandell.
THE TALK OF THE TOWN, Columbia. Otto Meyer.
THIS ABOVE ALL, 20th Century-Fox. Walter Thompson.
YANKEE DOODLE DANDY, Warner Bros. George Amy.

SPECIAL EFFECTS

THE BLACK SWAN, 20th Century-Fox. Fred Sersen, Roger Herman and George Leverett.
DESPERATE JOURNEY, Warner Bros. Byron Haskin and Nathan Levinson.
FLYING TIGERS, Republic. Howard Lydecker and Daniel J. Bloomberg.
INVISIBLE AGENT, Universal. John Fulton and Bernard B. Brown.
JUNGLE BOOK, Korda, UA. Lawrence Butler and William H. Wilmarth.
MRS. MINIVER, M-G-M. A. Arnold Gillespie, Warren Newcombe and Douglas Shearer.
THE NAVY COMES THROUGH, RKO Radio. Vernon L. Walker and James G. Stewart.
ONE OF OUR AIRCRAFT IS MISSING, Powell, UA (British). Ronald Neame and C.C. Stevens.
THE PRIDE OF THE YANKEES, Goldwyn, RKO Radio. Jack Cosgrove. Ray Binger and Thomas T. Moulton.
*REAP THE WILD WIND, DeMille, Paramount. Farciot Edouart, Gordon Jennings, William L. Pereira and Louis Mesenkop.

SHORT SUBJECTS

(Cartoons)

ALL OUT FOR V, 20th Century-Fox.
THE BLITZ WOLF, M-G-M.
*DER FUEHRER'S FACE, Disney, RKO Radio.
JUKE BOX JAMBOREE, Lantz, Universal.
PIGS IN A POLKA, Schlesinger, Warner Bros.
TULIPS SHALL GROW, Paramount. (George Pal Puppetoon)

(One-Reel)

DESERT WONDERLAND, 20th Century-Fox. (Magic Carpet Series)
MARINES IN THE MAKING, M-G-M. (Pete Smith Specialties)
*SPEAKING OF ANIMALS AND THEIR FAMILIES, Paramount. (Speaking of Animals)
UNITED STATES MARINE BAND, Warner Bros. (Melody Master Bands)

(Two-reel)

*BEYOND THE LINE OF DUTY, Warner Bros. (Broadway Brevities)
DON'T TALK, M-G-M. (Two-reel Special)
PRIVATE SMITH OF THE U.S.A., RKO Radio. (This Is America Series)

MUSIC

(Song)

ALWAYS IN MY HEART (Always in My Heart, Warner Bros.); Music by Ernesto Lecuona. Lyrics by Kim Gannon.
DEARLY BELOVED (You Were Never Lovelier, Columbia); Music by Jerome Kern. Lyrics by Johnny Mercer.
HOW ABOUT YOU? (Babes on Broadway, M-G-M); Music by Burton Lane. Lyrics by Ralph Freed.
IT SEEMS I HEARD THAT SONG BEFORE (Youth on Parade, Republic); Music by Jule Styne. Lyrics by Sammy Cahn.
I'VE GOT A GAL IN KALAMAZOO (Orchestra Wives, 20th Century-Fox); Music by Harry Warren. Lyrics by Mack Gordon.
LOVE IS A SONG (Bambi, Disney, RKO Radio); Music by Frank Churchill. Lyrics by Larry Morey.
PENNIES FOR PEPPINO (Flying With Music, Roach, UA); Music by Edward Ward. Lyrics by Chet Forrest and Bob Wright.
PIG FOOT PETE (Keep 'Em Flying, Universal); Music by Gene de Paul. Lyrics by Don Raye.
THERE'S A BREEZE ON LAKE LOUISE (The Mayor of 44th Street, RKO Radio); Music by Harry Revel. Lyrics by Mort Greene.
*WHITE CHRISTMAS (Holiday Inn, Paramount); Music and Lyrics by Irving Berlin.

(Scoring of a Dramatic or Comedy Picture)
(Slight alteration of classification)

ARABIAN NIGHTS, Universal. Frank Skinner.
BAMBI, Disney, RKO Radio. Frank Churchill and Edward Plumb.
THE BLACK SWAN, 20th Century-Fox. Alfred Newman.
THE CORSICAN BROTHERS, Small, UA. Dimitri Tiomkin.
FLYING TIGERS, Republic. Victor Young.
THE GOLD RUSH, Chaplin, UA. Max Terr.
I MARRIED A WITCH, Cinema Guild, UA. Roy Webb.
JOAN OF PARIS, RKO Radio. Roy Webb.
JUNGLE BOOK, Korda, UA. Miklos Rozsa.
KLONDIKE FURY, Monogram. Edward Kay.
*NOW, VOYAGER, Warner Bros. Max Steiner.
THE PRIDE OF THE YANKEES, Goldwyn, RKO Radio. Leigh Harline.
RANDOM HARVEST, M-G-M. Herbert Stothart.
THE SHANGHAI GESTURE, Pressburger, UA. Richard Hageman.
SILVER QUEEN, Sherman, UA. Victor Young.
TAKE A LETTER, DARLING, Paramount. Victor Young.
THE TALK OF THE TOWN, Columbia. Frederick Hollander and Morris Stoloff.
TO BE OR NOT TO BE, Lubitsch, UA. Werner Heymann.

(Scoring of a Musical Picture)

FLYING WITH MUSIC, Roach, UA. Edward Ward.
FOR ME AND MY GAL, M-G-M. Roger Edens and Georgie Stoll.
HOLIDAY INN, Paramount. Robert Emmett Dolan.
IT STARTED WITH EVE, Universal. Charles Previn and Hans Salter.
JOHNNY DOUGHBOY, Republic. Walter Scharf.
MY GAL SAL, 20th Century-Fox. Alfred Newman.
*YANKEE DOODLE DANDY, Warner Bros. Ray Heindorf and Heinz Roemheld.
YOU WERE NEVER LOVELIER, Columbia. Leigh Harline.

DOCUMENTARY

AFRICA, PRELUDE TO VICTORY, March of Time, 20th Century-Fox.
*BATTLE OF MIDWAY, U.S. Navy, 20th Century-Fox.
COMBAT REPORT, U.S. Army Signal Corps.
CONQUER BY THE CLOCK, Office of War Information, RKO Pathe. Frederic Ullman, Jr.
THE GRAIN THAT BUILT A HEMISPHERE, Coordinator's Office, Motion Picture Society for the Americas. Walt Disney.
HENRY BROWNE, FARMER, U.S. Department of Agriculture, Republic.
HIGH OVER THE BORDERS, Canadian National Film Board.
HIGH STAKES IN THE EAST, Netherlands Information Bureau.
INSIDE FIGHTING CHINA, Canadian National Film Board.
IT'S EVERYBODY'S WAR, Office of War Information, 20th Century-Fox.
*KOKODA FRONT LINE, Australian News Information Bureau.
LISTEN TO BRITAIN, British Ministry of Information.
LITTLE BELGIUM, Belgian Ministry of Information.
LITTLE ISLES OF FREEDOM, Warner Bros. Victor Stoloff and Edgar Loew.

The Black Swan (20th Century-Fox; produced by Robert Bassler) starred Tyrone Power and Maureen O'Hara (above) in the dazzling kind of Technicolor swashbuckling adventure which was a common (and always welcome) screen commodity in the 1940s. Swan was a cut above most; directed by Henry King and based on a Rafael Sabatini novel (with a Ben Hecht screenplay), it received an Oscar for its color cinematography by Leon Shamroy.

MR. BLABBERMOUTH, Office of War Information, M-G-M.
MR. GARDENIA JONES, Office of War Information, M-G-M.
*MOSCOW STRIKES BACK, Artkino (Russian).
NEW SPIRIT, U.S. Treasury Department. Walt Disney.
*PRELUDE TO WAR, U.S. Army Special Services.
THE PRICE OF VICTORY, Office of War Information, Paramount. Pine-Thomas.
A SHIP IS BORN, U.S. Merchant Marine, Warner Bros.
TWENTY-ONE MILES, British Ministry of Information.
WE REFUSE TO DIE, Office of War Information, Paramount. William C. Thomas.
WHITE EAGLE, Cocanen Films.
WINNING YOUR WINGS, U.S. Army Air Force, Warner Bros.
(NOTE: four winners this year only.)

SPECIAL AWARDS

TO CHARLES BOYER for his progressive cultural achievement in establishing the French Research Foundation in Los Angeles as a source of reference for the Hollywood motion picture industry. (certificate)
TO NOEL COWARD for his outstanding production achievement in In Which We Serve. (certificate)
TO METRO-GOLDWYN-MAYER STUDIO for its achievement in representing the American way of life in the production of the Andy Hardy series of films. (certificate)

1942 IRVING G. THALBERG MEMORIAL AWARD
TO SIDNEY FRANKLIN

SCIENTIFIC OR TECHNICAL

CLASS I (statuette)
None.

CLASS II (plaque)

CARROLL CLARK, F. THOMAS THOMPSON and the RKO RADIO STUDIO ART and MINIATURE DEPARTMENTS for the design and construction of a moving cloud and horizon machine.
DANIEL B. CLARK and the 20TH CENTURY-FOX CORP. for the development of a lens calibration system and the application of this system to exposure control in cinematography.

CLASS III (citation)

ROBERT HENDERSON and the PARAMOUNT STUDIO ENGINEERING and TRANSPARENCY DEPARTMENTS;
DANIEL J. BLOOMBERG and the REPUBLIC STUDIO SOUND DEPARTMENT.

*INDICATES WINNER

The Oscar ceremony moved from a banquet setting into a theater for the first time on March 2, 1944, when awards were given for movie world achievement during 1943. The site of the new-style gala was the large and legendary Grauman's Chinese Theatre on Hollywood Boulevard with a seating capacity of 2,258; increased attendance at the Academy's big night had made further banquets impractical so, after 15 years, the intimate little industry dinners became a thing of the past. The extra space afforded by Grauman's not only gave Oscar a new look but also gave the industry a chance to invite a large number of servicemen and women from all military branches to come share in the excitement.

Something else new was added, too. For the first time since the supporting actor and supporting actress categories were inaugurated in 1936, winners in those divisions were given full-size statues instead of plaques (and, so no one would feel slighted, the Academy in later years replaced earlier plaques with statuettes for all acting award winners). The two most honored motion pictures of the year were *The Song of Bernadette* with four awards, including best actress (Jennifer Jones), and *Casablanca* with three, including best picture and best director (Michael Curtiz). Photographers had a field day when Miss Jones arrived at the theater with Ingrid Bergman, both of them under contract to David O. Selznick, close friends and leading nominees for that best actress

trophy. Later, Miss Bergman told reporters, "I cried all the way through *Bernadette* because Jennifer was so moving and because I realized then I had lost the award."

Despite the fact the number of award categories had swelled to twenty-seven, as compared to seven in Oscar's first year, the only other movie to receive more than one award was *The Phantom of the Opera*, with nods for color cinematography and color art direction. Paul Lukas was chosen best actor for *Watch on the Rhine,* a role he created on the Broadway stage with great success, and the supporting award statuettes went to Charles Coburn in *The More the Merrier* and Katina Paxinou in *For Whom the Bell Tolls.* Warner Bros.' Hal Wallis received the Irving G. Thalberg award and, soon after, moved from Burbank over to Paramount to become an independent producer, one of the industry's most prolific and prestigious.

Awards for the evening were presented by Academy President Walter Wanger, producer Sidney Franklin, writer James Hilton, radio star Dinah Shore and actresses Greer Garson, Teresa Wright, Rosalind Russell and Carole Landis. Jack Benny was the master of ceremonies for a radio broadcast of the ceremony sent to Armed Forces fighting overseas. And that fighting was nearing an important campaign. Just three months after Oscar's sixteenth celebration, on D-Day, the sixth of June, 1944, the Allied invasion of Nazi-occupied West Europe would begin in Normandy, and World War II would be entering its final chapters.

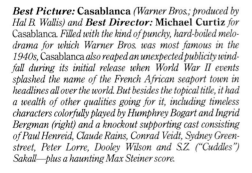

*Best Picture: **Casablanca** (Warner Bros.; produced by Hal B. Wallis) and **Best Director: Michael Curtiz** for* Casablanca. *Filled with the kind of punchy, hard-boiled melodrama for which Warner Bros. was most famous in the 1940s,* Casablanca *also reaped an unexpected publicity windfall during its initial release when World War II events splashed the name of the French African seaport town in headlines all over the world. But besides the topical title, it had a wealth of other qualities going for it, including timeless characters colorfully played by Humphrey Bogart and Ingrid Bergman (right) and a knockout supporting cast consisting of Paul Henreid, Claude Rains, Conrad Veidt, Sydney Greenstreet, Peter Lorre, Dooley Wilson and S.Z. ("Cuddles") Sakall—plus a haunting Max Steiner score.*

Best Actress: **Jennifer Jones** *as Bernadette in* The Song of Bernadette *(20th Century-Fox; directed by Henry King). A 24-year-old screen newcomer, Jennifer Jones (left) was luminous as the simple peasant girl of Lourdes who became the center of a spiritual tornado in the mid-1800s when she claimed to have seen a vision of the Virgin Mary while gathering firewood. Based on the novel by Franz Werfel, Bernadette was one of the year's most distinguished successes, and the year's biggest Oscar winner, with additional awards for cinematography, art direction and music score.*

Best Actor: **Paul Lukas** *as Kurt Muller in* Watch on the Rhine *(Warner Bros.; directed by Herman Shumlin). Lukas (left, with Janis Wilson and Eric Roberts) re-created his Broadway role of a gentle German engineer, married to an American (Bette Davis) and a member of the German Underground fighting Fascism. Lillian Hellman wrote the original play—a topical warning about the threat of Fascism infiltrating American homes.*

The Phantom of the Opera (Universal; produced by George Waggner) featured Claude Rains (above) as the mad musician who secretly lives in the catacombs under the Paris Opera House and saws down a crystal chandelier during a sold-out performance, and it won two Academy Awards: for color cinematography and color art direction. Universal was a specialist in the horror genre, but this remake of Lon Chaney's Phantom marked only the third time the studio had worked in the three-strip Technicolor genre (following 1942's Arabian Nights and 1943's White Savage).

OUTSTANDING MOTION PICTURE

*CASABLANCA, Warner Bros. Produced by Hal B. Wallis.
FOR WHOM THE BELL TOLLS, Paramount. Produced by Sam Wood.
HEAVEN CAN WAIT, 20th Century-Fox. Produced by Ernst Lubitsch.
THE HUMAN COMEDY, M-G-M. Produced by Clarence Brown.
IN WHICH WE SERVE, Two Cities, UA (British). Produced by Noel Coward.
MADAME CURIE, M-G-M. Produced by Sidney Franklin.
THE MORE THE MERRIER, Columbia. Produced by George Stevens.
THE OX-BOW INCIDENT, 20th Century-Fox. Produced by Lamar Trotti.
THE SONG OF BERNADETTE, 20th Century-Fox. Produced by William Perlberg.
WATCH ON THE RHINE, Warner Bros. Produced by Hal B. Wallis.

ACTOR

HUMPHREY BOGART in Casablanca, Warner Bros.
GARY COOPER in For Whom the Bell Tolls, Paramount.
*PAUL LUKAS in Watch on the Rhine, Warner Bros.
WALTER PIDGEON in Madame Curie, M-G-M.
MICKEY ROONEY in The Human Comedy, M-G-M.

ACTRESS

JEAN ARTHUR in The More the Merrier, Columbia.
INGRID BERGMAN in For Whom the Bell Tolls, Paramount.
JOAN FONTAINE in The Constant Nymph, Warner Bros.
GREER GARSON in Madame Curie, M-G-M.
*JENNIFER JONES in The Song of Bernadette, 20th Century-Fox.

SUPPORTING ACTOR

CHARLES BICKFORD in The Song of Bernadette, 20th Century-Fox.
*CHARLES COBURN in The More the Merrier, Columbia.
J. CARROL NAISH in Sahara, Columbia.
CLAUDE RAINS in Casablanca, Warner Bros.
AKIM TAMIROFF in For Whom the Bell Tolls, Paramount.

SUPPORTING ACTRESS

GLADYS COOPER in The Song of Bernadette, 20th Century-Fox.
PAULETTE GODDARD in So Proudly We Hail, Paramount.
*KATINA PAXINOU in For Whom the Bell Tolls, Paramount.
ANNE REVERE in The Song of Bernadette, 20th Century-Fox.
LUCILE WATSON in Watch on the Rhine, Warner Bros.

DIRECTING

*CASABLANCA, Warner Bros. Michael Curtiz.
HEAVEN CAN WAIT, 20th Century-Fox. Ernst Lubitsch.
THE HUMAN COMEDY, M-G-M. Clarence Brown.
THE MORE THE MERRIER, Columbia. George Stevens.
THE SONG OF BERNADETTE, 20th Century-Fox. Henry King.

WRITING

(Original Story)

ACTION IN THE NORTH ATLANTIC, Warner Bros. Guy Gilpatric.
DESTINATION TOKYO, Warner Bros. Steve Fisher.
*THE HUMAN COMEDY, M-G-M. William Saroyan.

THE MORE THE MERRIER, Columbia, Frank Ross and Robert Russell.
SHADOW OF A DOUBT, Universal, Gordon McDonnell.

(Original Screenplay)

AIR FORCE, Warner Bros. Dudley Nichols.
IN WHICH WE SERVE, Two-Cities-UA (British). Noel Coward.
THE NORTH STAR, Goldwyn, RKO Radio. Lillian Hellman.
*PRINCESS O'ROURKE, Warner Bros. Norman Krasna.
SO PROUDLY WE HAIL, Paramount. Allan Scott.

(Screenplay)

*CASABLANCA, Warner Bros. Julius J. Epstein, Philip G. Epstein and Howard Koch.
HOLY MATRIMONY, 20th Century-Fox. Nunnally Johnson.
THE MORE THE MERRIER, Columbia. Richard Flournoy, Lewis R. Foster, Frank Ross and Robert Russell.
THE SONG OF BERNADETTE, 20th Century-Fox. George Seaton.
WATCH ON THE RHINE, Warner Bros. Dashiell Hammett.

CINEMATOGRAPHY

(Black-and-White)

AIR FORCE, Warner Bros. James Wong Howe, Elmer Dyer and Charles Marshall.
CASABLANCA, Warner Bros. Arthur Edeson.
CORVETTE K-225, Universal. Tony Gaudio.
FIVE GRAVES TO CAIRO, Paramount. John Seitz.
THE HUMAN COMEDY, M-G-M. Harry Stradling.
MADAME CURIE, M-G-M. Joseph Ruttenberg.
THE NORTH STAR, Goldwyn, RKO Radio. James Wong Howe.
SAHARA, Columbia. Rudolph Maté.
SO PROUDLY WE HAIL, Paramount. Charles Lang.
*THE SONG OF BERNADETTE, 20th Century-Fox. Arthur Miller.

(Color)

FOR WHOM THE BELL TOLLS, Paramount, Ray Rennahan.
HEAVEN CAN WAIT, 20th Century-Fox. Edward Cronjager.
HELLO, FRISCO, HELLO, 20th Century-Fox. Charles G. Clarke and Allen Davey.
LASSIE COME HOME, M-G-M. Leonard Smith.
*THE PHANTOM OF THE OPERA. Universal. Hal Mohr and W. Howard Greene.
THOUSANDS CHEER, M-G-M. George Folsey.

ART DIRECTION-INTERIOR DECORATION

(Black-and-White)

FIVE GRAVES TO CAIRO, Paramount. Hans Dreier and Ernst Fegte; Bertram Granger.
FLIGHT FOR FREEDOM, RKO Radio. Albert S. D'Agostino and Carroll Clark; Darrell Silvera and Harley Miller.
MADAME CURIE, M-G-M. Cedric Gibbons and Paul Groesse; Edwin B. Willis and Hugh Hunt.
MISSION TO MOSCOW, Warner Bros. Carl Weyl; George J. Hopkins.
THE NORTH STAR, Goldwyn, RKO Radio. Perry Ferguson; Howard Bristol.
*THE SONG OF BERNADETTE, 20th Century-Fox. James Basevi and William Darling; Thomas Little.

(Color)

FOR WHOM THE BELL TOLLS, Paramount. Hans Dreir and Haldane Douglas; Bertram Granger.
THE GANG'S ALL HERE, 20th Century-Fox. James Basevi and Joseph C. Wright; Thomas Little.
*THE PHANTOM OF THE OPERA, Universal. Alexander Golitzen and John B. Goodman; Russell A. Gausman and Ira S. Webb.
THIS IS THE ARMY, Warner Bros. John Hughes and Lt. John Koenig; George J. Hopkins.
THOUSANDS CHEER, M-G-M. Cedric Gibbons and Daniel Cathcart; Edwin B. Willis and Jacques Mersereau.

Best Supporting Actress: Katina Paxinou as Pilar in For Whom the Bell Tolls (Paramount; directed by Sam Wood). Long recognized as the first lady of Greek theater and a vital force in that nation's Royal Theatre of Athens, Katina Paxinou made her first Hollywood film appearance—and won the Academy Award—as a powerful, strong-willed hill woman and guerrilla fighter in the Spanish Civil War. For Whom, based on the Ernest Hemingway novel, was one of the most touted films of the year, initially shown as a roadshow, reserved-seat attraction and well known for its romantic scenes (especially one in a sleeping bag, though innocent by later standards) featuring Ingrid Bergman and Gary Cooper (at left, with Paxinou).

SOUND RECORDING

HANGMEN ALSO DIE, Pressburger, UA. Sound Service, Inc., Jack Whitney, Sound Director.

IN OLD OKLAHOMA, Republic. Republic Studio Sound Dept., Daniel J. Bloomberg, Sound Director.

MADAME CURIE. M-G-M. M-G-M Studio Sound Dept., Douglas Shearer, Sound Director.

THE NORTH STAR, Goldwyn, RKO Radio. Samuel Goldwyn Studio Sound Dept., Thomas Moulton, Sound Director.

THE PHANTOM OF THE OPERA, Universal. Universal Studio Sound Dept., Bernard B. Brown, Sound Director.

RIDING HIGH, Paramount. Paramount Studio Sound Dept., Loren L. Ryder, Sound Director.

SAHARA, Columbia. Columbia Studio Sound Dept., John Livadary, Sound Director.

SALUDOS AMIGOS, Disney, RKO Radio. Walt Disney Studio Sound Dept., C.O. Slyfield, Sound Director.

SO THIS IS WASHINGTON, Votion, RKO Radio. RCA Sound, J.L. Fields, Sound Director.

THE SONG OF BERNADETTE, 20th Century-Fox. 20th Century-Fox Studio Sound Dept., E.H. Hansen, Sound Director.

THIS IS THE ARMY, Warner Bros. Warner Bros. Studio Sound Dept., Nathan Levinson, Sound Director.

*THIS LAND IS MINE, RKO Radio. RKO Radio Studio Sound Dept., Stephen Dunn, Sound Director.

FILM EDITING

*AIR FORCE, Warner Bros. George Amy.

CASABLANCA, Warner Bros. Owen Marks.

FIVE GRAVES TO CAIRO, Paramount. Doane Harrison.

FOR WHOM THE BELL TOLLS, Paramount. Sherman Todd and John Link.

THE SONG OF BERNADETTE, 20th Century-Fox. Barbara McLean.

SPECIAL EFFECTS

AIR FORCE, Warner Bros. Hans Koenekamp, Rex Wimpy and Nathan Levinson.

BOMBARDIER, RKO Radio. Vernon L. Walker, James G. Stewart and Roy Granville.

*CRASH DIVE, 20th Century-Fox. Fred Sersen and Roger Heman.

THE NORTH STAR, Goldwyn, RKO Radio. Clarence Slifer, R.O. Binger`and Thomas T. Moulton.

SO PROUDLY WE HAIL, Paramount. Farciot Edouart, Gordon Jennings and George Dutton.

STAND BY FOR ACTION, M-G-M. A. Arnold Gillespie, Donald Jahraus and Michael Steinore.

MUSIC

(Song)

CHANGE OF HEART (Hit Parade of 1943, Republic); Music by Jule Styne. Lyrics by Harold Adamson.

HAPPINESS IS A THING CALLED JOE (Cabin in the Sky, M-G-M); Music by Harold Arlen. Lyrics by E.Y. Harburg.

MY SHINING HOUR (The Sky's the Limit, RKO Radio); Music by Harold Arlen. Lyrics by Johnny Mercer.

SALUDOS AMIGOS (Saludos Amigos, Disney, RKO Radio); Music by Charles Wolcott. Lyrics by Ned Washington.

SAY A PRAYER FOR THE BOYS OVER THERE (Hers To Hold, Universal); Music by Jimmy McHugh. Lyrics by Herb Magidson.

THAT OLD BLACK MAGIC (Star Spangled Rhythm, Paramount); Music by Harold Arlen. Lyrics by Johnny Mercer.

THEY'RE EITHER TOO YOUNG OR TOO OLD (Thank Your Lucky Stars, Warner Bros); Music by Arthur Schwartz. Lyrics by Frank Loesser.

WE MUSTN'T SAY GOOD BYE (Stage Door Canteen, Lesser, UA); Music by James Monaco. Lyrics by Al Dubin.

YOU'D BE SO NICE TO COME HOME TO (Something To Shout About, Columbia); Music and Lyrics by Cole Porter.

*YOU'LL NEVER KNOW (Hello, Frisco, Hello, 20th Century-Fox); Music by Harry Warren. Lyrics by Mack Gordon.

(Scoring of a Dramatic or Comedy Picture)

THE AMAZING MRS. HOLLIDAY, Universal. Hans J. Salter and Frank Skinner.

CASABLANCA, Warner Bros. Max Steiner.

THE COMMANDOS STRIKE AT DAWN, Columbia. Louis Gruenberg and Morris Stoloff.

THE FALLEN SPARROW, RKO Radio. C. Bakaleinikoff and Roy Webb.

FOR WHOM THE BELL TOLLS, Paramount. Victor Young.

HANGMEN ALSO DIE, Pressburger, UA. Hanns Eisler.

HI DIDDLE DIDDLE, Stone UA. Phil Boutelje.

IN OLD OKLAHOMA, Republic. Walter Scharf.

JOHNNY COME LATELY, Cagney, UA. Leigh Harline.

THE KANSAN, Sherman, UA. Gerard Carbonara.

LADY OF BURLESQUE, Stromberg, UA. Arthur Lange.

MADAME CURIE, M-G-M. Herbert Stothart.

Best Supporting Actor: **Charles Coburn** *as Benjamin Dingle (flanked by Joel McCrea and Jean Arthur) in* The More the Merrier *(Columbia; directed by George Stevens). The setting was overcrowded, wartime Washington, D.C., and*

Coburn played a delightful old sharpie looking for a room to rent, which Jean Arthur happened to have. In 1966, the famous Coburn role reappeared in Walk, Don't Run *and was played by Cary Grant.*

THE MOON AND SIXPENCE, Loew-Lewin, UA. Dimitri Tiomkin.

THE NORTH STAR, Goldwyn, RKO Radio. Aaron Copland.

*THE SONG OF BERNADETTE, 20th Century-Fox. Alfred Newman.

VICTORY THROUGH AIR POWER. Disney, UA. Edward H. Plumb, Paul J. Smith and Oliver G. Wallace.

(Scoring of a Musical Picture)

CONEY ISLAND, 20th Century-Fox. Alfred Newman.

HIT PARADE OF 1943, Republic. Walter Scharf.

THE PHANTOM OF THE OPERA, Universal. Edward Ward.

SALUDOS AMIGOS, Disney, RKO Radio. Edward H. Plumb, Paul J. Smith and Charles Wolcott.

THE SKY'S THE LIMIT, RKO Radio. Leigh Harline.

SOMETHING TO SHOUT ABOUT, Columbia. Morris Stoloff.

STAGE DOOR CANTEEN, Lesser, UA. Frederic E. Rich.

STAR SPANGLED RHYTHM, Paramount. Robert Emmett Dolan.

*THIS IS THE ARMY, Warner Bros. Ray Heindorf.

THOUSANDS CHEER, M-G-M. Herbert Stothart.

SHORT SUBJECTS

(Cartoons)

THE DIZZY ACROBAT, Lantz, Universal. Walter Lantz, producer.

THE FIVE HUNDRED HATS OF BARTHOLOMEW CUBBINS, Paramount (Puppetoon). George Pal, producer.

GREETINGS, BAIT, Warner Bros. Leon Schlesinger, producer.

IMAGINATION, Columbia. Dave Fleischer, producer.

REASON AND EMOTION, Disney, RKO Radio. Walt Disney, producer.

*YANKEE DOODLE MOUSE, M-G-M. Frederick Quimby, producer.

(One-reel)

*AMPHIBIOUS FIGHTERS, Paramount. Grantland Rice, producer.

CAVALCADE OF THE DANCE WITH VELOZ AND YOLANDA, Warner Bros. (Melody Master Bands). Gordon Hollingshead, producer.

CHAMPIONS CARRY ON, 20th Century-Fox. (Sports Reviews). Edmund Reek, producer.

HOLLYWOOD IN UNIFORM, Columbia. (Screen Snapshots). Ralph Staub, producer.

SEEING HANDS, M-G-M. (Pete Smith Specialty). Pete Smith, producer.

(Two-reel)

*HEAVENLY MUSIC, M-G-M. Jerry Bresler and Sam Coslow, producers.

LETTER TO A HERO, RKO Radio. (This Is America). Fred Ullman, producer.

MARDI GRAS, Paramount. (Musical Parade). Walter MacEwen, producer.

WOMEN AT WAR, Warner Bros. (Technicolor Special). Gordon Hollingshead, producer.

DOCUMENTARY

(Short Subjects)

CHILDREN OF MARS, This Is America Series, RKO Radio.

*DECEMBER 7TH, U.S. Navy, Field Photographic Branch, Office of Strategic Services.

PLAN FOR DESTRUCTION, M-G-M.

SWEDES IN AMERICA, Office of War Information, Overseas Motion Picture Bureau.

TO THE PEOPLE OF THE UNITED STATES, U.S. Public Health Service, Walter Wanger Prods.

TOMORROW WE FLY, U.S. Navy, Bureau of Aeronautics.

YOUTH IN CRISIS, March of Time, 20th Century-Fox.

(Features)

BAPTISM OF FIRE, U.S. Army, Fighting Men Series.

BATTLE OF RUSSIA, Special Service Division of the War Department.

*DESERT VICTORY, British Ministry of Information.

REPORT FROM THE ALEUTIANS, U.S. Army Pictorial Service, Combat Film Series.

WAR DEPARTMENT REPORT, Field Photographic Branch, Office of Strategic Services.

SPECIAL AWARDS

TO GEORGE PAL for the development of novel methods and techniques in the production of short subjects known as Puppetoons (plaque)

1943 IRVING G. THALBERG MEMORIAL AWARD

TO HAL B. WALLIS

SCIENTIFIC OR TECHNICAL

CLASS I (statuette)

None.

CLASS II (plaque)

FARCIOT EDOUART, EARLE MORGAN, BARTON THOMPSON and the PARAMOUNT STUDIO ENGINEERING and TRANSPARENCY DEPARTMENTS for the development and practical application to motion picture production of a method of duplicating and enlarging natural color photographs, transferring the image emulsions to glass plates and projecting these slides by especially designed stereopticon equipment.

PHOTO PRODUCTS DEPARTMENT, E.I. duPONT de NEMOURS AND CO., INC. for the development of fine-grain motion picture films.

CLASS III (citation)

DANIEL J. BLOOMBERG and the REPUBLIC STUDIO SOUND DEPARTMENT;

CHARLES GALLOWAY CLARKE and the 20TH CENTURY-FOX STUDIO CAMERA DEPARTMENT;

FARCIOT EDOUART and the PARAMOUNT STUDIO TRANSPARENCY DEPARTMENT;

WILLARD H. TURNER and the RKO RADIO STUDIO SOUND DEPARTMENT.

*INDICATES WINNER

1944
The Seventeenth Year

Hollywood was in the midst of a labor strike on March 15, 1945, when the Academy honors for 1944 were handed out at Grauman's Chinese Theatre, Hollywood. The setting again was broadcast over network radio, via the American Broadcasting Company system. It was also the last time plaster statuettes were given to the winners. Wartime austerity still had its effect on Oscar but—happily—the news from Europe was optimistic. Within two months, Germany would surrender and the European siege would be over; by August, 1945, the Japanese would follow suit.

Once again, Bob Hope was master of ceremonies for the Academy party, sharing the job with director John Cromwell, whose *Since You Went Away* had been nominated in nine award categories. The two most honored films of the year were Darryl F. Zanuck's mammoth *Wilson* and Leo McCarey's gentle *Going My Way*, each nominated for ten awards. Ultimately, *Wilson* won five Oscars and *Going My Way* received seven, including those for best picture, best actor (Bing Crosby), best supporting actor (Barry Fitzgerald), best director (Leo Mc-Carey) and best song ("Swinging on a Star" by James Van Heusen and Johnny Burke). It was a particular triumph for Crosby, best known not as an actor, but as the country's best-selling crooner.

Ingrid Bergman was named best actress for *Gaslight*, and Ethel Barrymore was chosen best supporting actress for *None But the Lonely Heart*, her first film since *Rasputin and the Empress* in 1932. She was absent, but Miss Barrymore's award was accepted by RKO's Charles Koerner. Norma Shearer, retired from the screen for three years, presented the Irving G. Thalberg Memorial Award to Darryl F. Zanuck; it was the first time Thalberg's widow had presented the award herself.

Margaret O'Brien, age eight and a new star via four 1944 releases (*Jane Eyre*, *Lost Angel*, *The Canterville Ghost* and *Meet Me in St. Louis*), received a miniature statuette as the year's outstanding child actress and, years later, recalled the evening warmly. "I was very excited and apprehensive," she said. "Excited because I received the award from Bob Hope, who was my secret heartthrob, and apprehensive because I was afraid one of the false teeth the studio made me wear to cover my missing baby teeth might fall out, as they often did when I was working. Nevertheless, all went well. I was *thrilled* when Bob Hope later hugged me. As a matter of fact, he hugged most of the other actresses, too, but I felt special because I was the only one he both hugged *and* lifted."

82

Best Supporting Actress: **Ethel Barrymore** *as Ma Mott (here with Cary Grant) in* None But the Lonely Heart *(RKO Radio; directed by Clifford Odets). Long regarded as one of the genuine great ladies of the American stage, Miss Barrymore hadn't made a motion picture since 1932's* Rasputin and the Empress *when she played the sympathetic and terminally ill mother of cynical Ernie Mott (Grant), living in London's pre-World War II slums and destined to finally die of cancer in a prison hospital. Miss Barrymore also received Oscar nominations in 1946 (for* The Spiral Staircase*), 1947 (for* The Paradine Case*) and 1949 (for* Pinky*).*

Best Actress: **Ingrid Bergman** *(here with Charles Boyer) as Paula Alquist Anton in* Gaslight *(M-G-M; directed by George Cukor). It was a choice role, flawlessly played: a helpless, frightened young bride returns to the home where her aunt has been murdered, only to discover her new husband is attempting to drive her insane. Based on a play by Patrick Hamilton called* Angel Street, *the story had also been filmed as a 1940 British thriller starring Diana Wynyard, but was withheld from showing in the United States until 1952 due to Ingrid Bergman's Oscar-winning version. Bergman was to win Academy Awards again, in 1956 as best actress for* Anastasia *and in 1974 as best supporting actress for* Murder on the Orient Express.

83

Best Picture: **Going My Way** *(Paramount; produced and directed by Leo McCarey),* **Best Director: Leo McCarey** *and* **Best Actor: Bing Crosby** *as Father O'Malley and* **Best Supporting Actor: Barry Fitzgerald** *as Father Fitzgibbon in* Going My Way. *A warm and inspiring story of a frisky young priest on his first assignment in an insolvent New York parish, it provided Crosby with a challenging change of pace and gave Fitzgerald a unique niche in Oscar history: he became the first (and only) performer to be nominated both* as best actor and as best supporting actor for the same performance, something no longer possible under present voting rules. One of the year's most popular films, Going provided an ideal combination of entertainment and inspiration for a country in the midst of war and also inspired an immediate sequel, 1945's The Bells of St. Mary's with Crosby but without Fitzgerald. But they were later teamed twice again, in Welcome Stranger (1947) and Top o' the Morning (1949).

Laura *(20th Century-Fox; directed by Otto Preminger) won less Oscar attention in 1944 than* Wilson, *a much more heavily-hyped film from the same studio, but through the years* Laura, *not* Wilson, *has gone on to become a much-loved, genuine classic. Starring Dana Andrews (pictured staring at a portrait of costar Gene Tierney),* Laura *won an Oscar for Joseph LaShelle's black-and-white cinematography and was nominated in four other categories but, curiously, not for its most famous asset, a haunting musical score by David Raksin. Although there were 20 nominations in 1944 in the "scoring of a dramatic or comedy picture" category, Raksin's score was not one of them.*

BEST MOTION PICTURE

DOUBLE INDEMNITY, Paramount. Produced by Joseph Sistrom.
GASLIGHT, M-G-M. Produced by Arthur Hornblow, Jr.
*GOING MY WAY, Paramount. Produced by Leo McCarey.
SINCE YOU WENT AWAY, Selznick, UA. Produced by David O. Selznick.
WILSON, 20th Century-Fox. Produced by Darryl F. Zanuck.

ACTOR

CHARLES BOYER in *Gaslight,* M-G-M.
*BING CROSBY in *Going My Way,* Paramount.
BARRY FITZGERALD in *Going My Way,* Paramount.
CARY GRANT in *None But the Lonely Heart,* RKO Radio.
ALEXANDER KNOX in *Wilson,* 20th Century-Fox.

ACTRESS

*INGRID BERGMAN in *Gaslight,* M-G-M.
CLAUDETTE COLBERT in *Since You Went Away,* Selznick, UA.
BETTE DAVIS in *Mr. Skeffington,* Warner Bros.
GREER GARSON in *Mrs. Parkington,* M-G-M.
BARBARA STANWYCK in *Double Indemnity,* Paramount.

SUPPORTING ACTOR

HUME CRONYN in *The Seventh Cross,* M-G-M.
*BARRY FITZGERALD in *Going My Way,* Paramount.
CLAUDE RAINS in *Mr. Skeffington,* Warner Bros.
CLIFTON WEBB in *Laura,* 20th Century-Fox.
MONTY WOOLLEY in *Since You Went Away,* Selznick, UA.

SUPPORTING ACTRESS

*ETHEL BARRYMORE in *None But the Lonely Heart,* RKO Radio.
JENNIFER JONES in *Since You Went Away,* Selznick, UA.
ANGELA LANSBURY in *Gaslight,* M-G-M.
ALINE MacMAHON in *Dragon Seed,* M-G-M.
AGNES MOOREHEAD in *Mrs. Parkington,* M-G-M.

DIRECTING

DOUBLE INDEMNITY, Paramount. Billy Wilder.
*GOING MY WAY, Paramount. Leo McCarey.
LAURA, 20th Century-Fox. Otto Preminger.
LIFEBOAT, 20th Century-Fox. Alfred Hitchcock.
WILSON, 20th Century-Fox. Henry King.

WRITING

(Original Story)
*GOING MY WAY, Paramount. Leo McCarey.
A GUY NAMED JOE, M-G-M. David Boehm and Chandler Sprague.
LIFEBOAT, 20th Century-Fox. John Steinbeck.
NONE SHALL ESCAPE, Columbia. Alfred Neumann and Joseph Than.
THE SULLIVANS, 20th Century-Fox. Edward Doherty and Jules Schermer.

(Original Screenplay)
HAIL THE CONQUERING HERO, Paramount. Preston Sturges.
THE MIRACLE OF MORGAN'S CREEK, Paramount, Preston Sturges.
TWO GIRLS AND A SAILOR, M-G-M. Richard Connell and Gladys Lehman.
*WILSON, 20th Century-Fox. Lamar Trotti.
WING AND A PRAYER, 20th Century-Fox. Jerome Cady.

(Screenplay)
DOUBLE INDEMNITY, Paramount. Raymond Chandler and Billy Wilder.
GASLIGHT, M-G-M. John L. Balderston, Walter Reisch and John Van Druten.
*GOING MY WAY, Paramount. Frank Butler and Frank Cavett.
LAURA, 20th Century-Fox. Jay Dratler, Samuel Hoffenstein and Betty Reinhardt.
MEET ME IN ST. LOUIS, M-G-M. Irving Brecher and Fred F. Finkelhoffe.

CINEMATOGRAPHY

(Black-and-White)
DOUBLE INDEMNITY, Paramount. John Seitz.
DRAGON SEED, M-G-M. Sidney Wagner.
GASLIGHT, M-G-M. Joseph Ruttenberg.
GOING MY WAY, Paramount, Lionel Lindon.
*LAURA, 20th Century-Fox. Joseph LaShelle.
LIFEBOAT, 20th Century-Fox. Glen MacWilliams.
SINCE YOU WENT AWAY, Selznick, UA. Stanley Cortez and Lee Garmes.
THIRTY SECONDS OVER TOKYO. M-G-M. Robert Surtees and Harold Rosson.
THE UNINVITED, Paramount. Charles Lang.
THE WHITE CLIFFS OF DOVER, M-G-M. George Folsey.

(Color)
COVER GIRL, Columbia. Rudy Maté and Allen M. Davey.
HOME IN INDIANA, 20th Century-Fox. Edward Cronjager.
KISMET, M-G-M. Charles Rosher.
LADY IN THE DARK, Paramount. Ray Rennahan.
MEET ME IN ST. LOUIS, M-G-M. George Folsey.
*WILSON, 20th Century-Fox. Leon Shamroy.

ART DIRECTION-INTERIOR DECORATION

(Black-and-White)
ADDRESS UNKNOWN, Columbia. Lionel Banks and Walter Holscher; Joseph Kish.
THE ADVENTURES OF MARK TWAIN, Warner Bros. John J. Hughes; Fred MacLean.
CASANOVA BROWN, International, RKO Radio. Perry Ferguson; Julia Heron.
*GASLIGHT, M-G-M. Cedric Gibbons and William Ferrari; Edwin B. Willis and Paul Huldschinsky.
LAURA, 20th Century-Fox. Lyle Wheeler and Leland Fuller; Thomas Little.
NO TIME FOR LOVE, Paramount. Hans Dreier and Robert Usher; Sam Comer.
SINCE YOU WENT AWAY, Selznick, UA. Mark-Lee Kirk; Victor A. Gangelin.
STEP LIVELY, RKO Radio, Albert S. D'Agostino and Carroll Clark; Darrell Silvera and Claude Carpenter.

(Color)
THE CLIMAX, Universal, John B. Goodman and Alexander Golitzen; Russell A. Gausman and Ira S. Webb.
COVER GIRL, Columbia. Lionel Banks and Cary Odell; Fay Babcock.
THE DESERT SONG, Warner Bros. Charles Novi; Jack McConaghy.
KISMET, M-G-M. Cedric Gibbons and Daniel B. Cathcart; Edwin B. Willis and Richard Pefferle.
LADY IN THE DARK, Paramount. Hans Dreier and Raoul Pene du Bois; Ray Moyer.
THE PRINCESS AND THE PIRATE, Goldwyn, RKO Radio, Ernst Fegte; Howard Bristol.

*WILSON, 20th Century-Fox. Wiard Ihnen; Thomas Little.

FILM EDITING
GOING MY WAY, Paramount. Leroy Stone.
JANIE, Warner Bros. Owen Marks.
NONE BUT THE LONELY HEART, RKO Radio. Roland Gross.
SINCE YOU WENT AWAY, Selznick, UA. Hal C. Kern and James E. Newcom.
*WILSON, 20th Century-Fox. Barbara McLean.

SPECIAL EFFECTS
THE ADVENTURES OF MARK TWAIN, Warner Bros. Paul Detlefsen, John Crouse and Nathan Levinson.
DAYS OF GLORY, Robinson, RKO Radio. Vernon L. Walker, James G. Stewart and Roy Granville.
SECRET COMMAND, Columbia. David Allen, Ray Cory, Robert Wright, Russell Malmgren and Harry Kusnick.
SINCE YOU WENT AWAY, Selznick, UA. John R. Cosgrove and Arthur Johns.
THE STORY OF DR. WASSELL, DeMille, Paramount. Farciot Edouart, Gordon Jennings and George Dutton.
*THIRTY SECONDS OVER TOKYO, M-G-M. A. Arnold Gillespie, Donald Jahraus, Warren Newcombe and Douglas Shearer.
WILSON, 20th Century-Fox. Fred Sersen and Roger Heman.

SOUND RECORDING
BRAZIL, Republic. Republic Studio Sound Dept., Daniel J. Bloomberg, Sound Director.
CASANOVA BROWN, International, RKO Radio. Samuel Goldwyn Studio Sound Dept., Thomas T. Moulton, Sound Director.
COVER GIRL, Columbia. Columbia Studio Sound Dept., John Livadaray, Sound Director.
DOUBLE INDEMNITY, Paramount. Paramount Studio Sound Dept., Loren Ryder, Sound Director.
HIS BUTLER'S SISTER, Universal. Universal Studio Sound Dept., Bernard B. Brown, Sound Director.
HOLLYWOOD CANTEEN, Warner Bros. Warner Bros. Studio Sound Dept., Nathan Levinson, Sound Director.
IT HAPPENED TOMORROW, Arnold, UA. Sound Services, Inc., Jack Whitney, Sound Director.
KISMET, M-G-M. M-G-M Studio Sound Dept., Douglas Shearer, Sound Director.
MUSIC IN MANHATTAN, RKO Radio. RKO Radio Studio Sound Dept., Stephen Dunn, Sound Director.
VOICE IN THE WIND, Ripley-Monter, UA. RCA Sound, W. M. Dalgleish, Sound Director.
*WILSON, 20th Century-Fox. 20th Century-Fox Studio Sound Dept., E. H. Hansen, Sound Director.

MUSIC
(Song)
I COULDN'T SLEEP A WINK LAST NIGHT (*Higher and Higher*, RKO Radio); Music by Jimmy McHugh. Lyrics by Harold Adamson.
I'LL WALK ALONE (*Follow the Boys*, Feldman, Universal); Music by Jule Styne. Lyrics by Sammy Cahn.
I'M MAKING BELIEVE (*Sweet and Lowdown*, 20th Century-Fox); Music by James V. Monaco. Lyrics by Mack Gordon.
LONG AGO AND FAR AWAY (*Cover Girl*, Columbia); Music by Jerome Kern. Lyrics by Ira Gershwin.
NOW I KNOW (*Up in Arms*, Avalon, RKO Radio); Music by Harold Arlen. Lyrics by Ted Koehler.
REMEMBER ME TO CAROLINA (*Minstrel Man*, PRC); Music by Harry Revel. Lyrics by Paul Webster.
RIO DE JANEIRO (*Brazil*, Republic); Music by Ary Barroso. Lyrics by Ned Washington.
SILVER SHADOWS AND GOLDEN DREAMS (*Lady Let's Dance*, Monogram); Music by Lew Pollack. Lyrics by Charles Newman.
SWEET DREAMS SWEETHEART (*Hollywood Canteen*, Warner Bros.); Music by M.K. Jerome. Lyrics by Ted Koehler.
*SWINGING ON A STAR (*Going My Way*, Paramount); Music by James Van Heusen. Lyrics by Johnny Burke.
TOO MUCH IN LOVE (*Song of the Open Road*, Rogers, UA); Music by Walter Kent. Lyrics by Kim Gannon.
THE TROLLEY SONG (*Meet Me in St. Louis*, M-G-M); Music and Lyrics by Ralph Blane and Hugh Martin.

(Scoring of a Dramatic or Comedy Picture)
ADDRESS UNKNOWN, Columbia. Morris Stoloff and Ernst Toch.
THE ADVENTURES OF MARK TWAIN, Warner Bros. Max Steiner.
THE BRIDGE OF SAN LUIS REY, Bogeaus, UA. Dimitri Tiomkin.
CASANOVA BROWN, International, RKO Radio. Arthur Lange.
CHRISTMAS HOLIDAY, Universal. H.J. Salter.

DOUBLE INDEMNITY, Paramount. Miklos Rozsa.
THE FIGHTING SEABEES, Republic. Walter Scharf and Ray Webb.
THE HAIRY APE, Levey, UA. Michel Michelet and Edward Paul.
IT HAPPENED TOMORROW, Arnold, UA. Robert Stolz.
JACK LONDON, Bronston, UA. Frederic E. Rich.
KISMET, M-G-M. Herbert Stothart.
NONE BUT THE LONELY HEART, RKO Radio. C. Bakaleinikoff and Hanns Eisler.
THE PRINCESS AND THE PIRATE, Goldwyn, RKO Radio. David Rose.
*SINCE YOU WENT AWAY, Selznick, UA. Max Steiner.
SUMMER STORM, Angelus, UA. Karl Hajos.
THREE RUSSIAN GIRLS, R & F Prods., UA. Franke Harling.
UP IN MABEL'S ROOM, Small, UA. Edward Paul.
VOICE IN THE WIND, Ripley-Monter, UA. Michel Michelet.
WILSON, 20th Century-Fox. Alfred Newman.
WOMAN OF THE TOWN, Sherman, UA. Miklos Rozsa.

(Scoring of a Musical Picture)
BRAZIL, Republic. Walter Scharf.
*COVER GIRL, Columbia. Carmen Dragon and Morris Stoloff.
HIGHER AND HIGHER, RKO Radio. C. Bakaleinikoff.
HOLLYWOOD CANTEEN, Warner Bros. Ray Heindorf.
IRISH EYES ARE SMILING, 20th Century-Fox. Alfred Newman.
KNICKERBOCKER HOLIDAY, RCA, UA. Werner R. Heymann and Kurt Weill.
LADY IN THE DARK, Paramount. Robert Emmett Dolan.
LADY LET'S DANCE, Monogram. Edward Kay.
MEET ME IN ST. LOUIS, M-G-M. Georgie Stoll.
THE MERRY MONAHANS, Universal. H.J. Salter.
MINSTREL MAN, PRC. Leo Erdody and Ferdie Grofe.
SENSATIONS OF 1945, Stone, UA. Mahlon Merrick.
SONG OF THE OPEN ROAD, Rogers, UA. Charles Previn.
UP IN ARMS, Avalon, RKO Radio. Louis Forbes and Ray Heindorf.

SHORT SUBJECTS
(Cartoons)
AND TO THINK I SAW IT ON MULBERRY STREET, Paramount. (Puppetoon). George Pal, producer.
THE DOG, CAT AND CANARY, Columbia. (Screen Gems).
FISH FRY. Universal. Walter Lantz, producer.
HOW TO PLAY FOOTBALL, Disney, RKO Radio. Walt Disney, producer.
*MOUSE TROUBLE, M-G-M. Frederick C. Quimby, producer.
MY BOY, JOHNNY, 20th Century-Fox. Paul Terry, producer.
SWOONER CROONER, Warner Bros.

(One-reel)
BLUE GRASS GENTLEMEN, 20th Century-Fox. (Sports Review). Edmund Reek, producer.
JAMMIN' THE BLUES, Warner Bros. (Melody Master Bands). Gordon Hollingshead, producer.
MOVIE PESTS, M-G-M. (Pete Smith Specialty). Pete Smith, producer.
50TH ANNIVERSARY OF MOTION PICTURES, Columbia. (Screen Snapshots). Ralph Staub, producer.
*WHO'S WHO IN ANIMAL LAND. Paramount. (Speaking of Animals). Jerry Fairbanks, producer.

Special Award: Margaret O'Brien (left with Judy Garland in Meet Me in St. Louis) *as "the outstanding child actress of 1944." The Academy first presented miniature Oscar statuettes to pint-sized performers in 1934 when Shirley Temple was honored; since then, other juveniles similarly singled out have been Deanna Durbin and Mickey Rooney (1938), Judy Garland (1939), Peggy Ann Garner (1945), Claude Jarman, Jr. (1946), Ivan Jandl (1948), Bobby Driscoll (1949), Jon Whitely and Vincent Winter (1954) and Hayley Mills (1960). Since 1960, juvenile performers such as Patty Duke, Tatum O'Neal and others have had to win their Oscars in regular competitive categories, alongside their elders.*

(Two-reel)
BOMBALERA, Paramount. (Musical Parade). Louis Harris, producer.
*I WON'T PLAY, Warner Bros. (Featurette). Gordon Hollingshead, producer.
MAIN STREET TODAY, M-G-M. (Two-reel Special). Jerry Bresler, producer.

DOCUMENTARY
(Short Subjects)
ARTURO TOSCANINI, Motion Picture Bureau, Overseas Branch, Office of War Information.
NEW AMERICANS, This Is America Series, RKO Radio.
*WITH THE MARINES AT TARAWA, U.S. Marine Corps.

(Features)
*THE FIGHTING LADY, 20th Century-Fox and U.S. Navy.
RESISTING ENEMY INTERROGATION, U.S. Army Air Force.

SPECIAL AWARDS
TO MARGARET O'BRIEN, outstanding child actress of 1944. (miniature statuette).
TO BOB HOPE, for his many services to the Academy, a Life Membership in the Academy of Motion Picture Arts and Sciences.

1944 IRVING G. THALBERG MEMORIAL AWARD
TO DARRYL F. ZANUCK

SCIENTIFIC OR TECHNICAL
CLASS I (statuette)
None.

CLASS II (plaque)
STEPHEN DUNN and the RKO RADIO STUDIO SOUND DEPARTMENT and RADIO CORPORATION OF AMERICA for the design and development of the electronic compressor-limiter.

CLASS III (citation)
LINWOOD DUNN, CECIL LOVE and ACME TOOL MANUFACTURING CO.;
GROVER LAUBE and the 20TH CENTURY-FOX STUDIO CAMERA DEPARTMENT;
WESTERN ELECTRIC CO.;
RUSSELL BROWN, RAY HINSDALE and JOSEPH E. ROBBINS;
GORDON JENNINGS;
RADIO CORPORATION OF AMERICA and the RKO RADIO STUDIO SOUND DEPARTMENT;
DANIEL J. BLOOMBERG and the REPUBLIC STUDIO SOUND DEPARTMENT;
BERNARD B. BROWN and JOHN P. LIVADARY;
PAUL ZELL, S.J. TWINING and GEORGE SEID;
PAUL LERPAE.

*INDICATES WINNER.

85

1945
The Eighteenth Year

The year 1945 had been good for movies (critically, as well as at the box office) and a historic one for the world: President Roosevelt had died in office, World War II had ended, the first atom bomb was exploded on Hiroshima, the United Nations was founded in San Francisco and everyone began readjusting to peace. When it came time to salute 1945 with Oscars on March 7, 1946, at Grauman's Chinese Theatre, Hollywood again dressed up in tuxedos and finery as it had in those pre-war days, and the Hollywood staple—searchlights—again beamed over the city.

Most-nominated pictures of the year were *The Bells of St. Mary's,* a sequel to the previous year's Oscar-winning *Going My Way,* competing in eight categories, and *The Lost Weekend* with seven nominations. *Weekend* ultimately won four: best picture, best actor (Ray Milland), best director (Billy Wilder) and best screenplay (Charles Brackett and Wilder). Anne Revere was named best supporting actress for *National Velvet,* and James Dunn was chosen best supporting actor for *A Tree Grows in Brooklyn.* Biggest newsmaker of the evening, however, was Joan Crawford, named best actress for *Mildred Pierce.* A durable Hollywood headliner for twenty years, she was a first-time nominee for Oscar honors and in the midst of a major career comeback after several years of indifferent screen roles. Confined to bed at her Brentwood home (reportedly because of the flu and a fever), she was

unable to attend the ceremony so her award was accepted in her behalf by her director Michael Curtiz. But, she said later, "It was the greatest moment of my life."

Bob Hope and James Stewart were co-hosts of the awards program and additional Oscars were rather evenly distributed among a variety of fine films, including *The True Glory, Anchors Aweigh, Spellbound, State Fair, The Picture of Dorian Gray, Leave Her to Heaven, Marie-Louise, The House on 92nd Street* and *Frenchman's Creek.* For the last time, there were a myriad of nominees in the categories of sound recording (twelve), song (fourteen), scoring of a drama or comedy (twenty-one), and scoring of a musical (twelve); hereafter, there would be no more than five nominees in those divisions.

Outgoing Academy President Walter Wanger received a special plaque for his six-year term as head of the Academy, and Peggy Ann Garner of 1945's *A Tree Grows in Brooklyn, Junior Miss* and *Nob Hill* received a miniature statuette as the year's outstanding child actress. Perhaps the most significant award of the night was the special Oscar awarded to *The House I Live In,* a ten-minute short subject distributed by RKO and involving the talents of bobbysox idol Frank Sinatra, Frank Ross, Mervyn LeRoy and Albert Maltz. The film made a plea for racial tolerance, a growing concern now that the problems of a world war had been solved—at least temporarily.

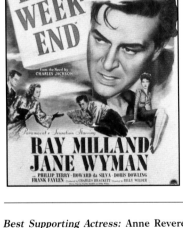

Best Supporting Actress: Anne Revere *(here with Elizabeth Taylor) as Mrs. Brown in* National Velvet *(M-G-M; directed by Clarence Brown). A long-time veteran of playing gentle, understanding mums with strong values, Anne Revere this time played the mother of a horse-loving girl who wants to race her horse in England's Grand National Steeplechase. Previously nominated as Jennifer Jones' mother in* The Song of Bernadette *in 1943, she was again an Oscar contender in 1947 as Gregory Peck's mother in* Gentleman's Agreement, *but her career in the 1950s and after was severely curtailed by accusations made during the 1950s House Un-American Activities investigations.*

Best Picture: **The Lost Weekend** (Paramount; produced by Charles Brackett), **Best Director:** **Billy Wilder** and **Best Actor:** **Ray Milland** as Don Birnam in The Lost Weekend. Decidedly off the beaten track among

1945 screen fare, it followed Milland as would-be writer on a booze-filled weekend in New York City, trying to hock his typewriter for set-ups, attempting to beg drinks and suffering the D.T.s, as audiences were let loose inside an alcoholic's psyche.

Producer Brackett and director Wilder also won Oscars for the Lost screenplay. Milland got his Oscar-winning role when the first choice to play Birnam, Broadway actor José Ferrer, was unavailable.

Best Actress: **Joan Crawford** as Mildred Pierce Baragon in Mildred Pierce (Warner Bros.; directed by Michael Curtiz). Bette Davis, Barbara Stanwyck and Ann Sheridan all turned down the role of James M. Cain's middle-class housewife who works as a waitress, becomes a wealthy business woman and ultimately tries to take the blame for a murder committed by her over-indulged daughter (Ann Blyth, left with Crawford). But Joan Crawford grabbed the part because her career was at a low ebb, and she'd been off the screen two years attempting to find a solid role to reestablish her reputation in Hollywood circles. Mildred Pierce did the trick, brought Joan Crawford back to the front ranks of stardom and made her an Academy Award winner.

Best Supporting Actor: James Dunn *as Johnny Nolan (with Peggy Ann Garner) in* A Tree Grows in Brooklyn *(20th Century-Fox; directed by Elia Kazan). Like Ray Milland, James Dunn won his Oscar for playing a man fond of the spirits; like Joan Crawford, he was in the midst of a comeback to screen prominence after several years of secondary roles. Young Miss Garner also received a miniature Oscar statuette as the oustanding child actress of the year for her performance as Dunn's daughter Francie, the pivotal character of* A Tree, *through whose eyes the popular story by Betty Smith unfolds.*

BEST MOTION PICTURE

ANCHORS AWEIGH, M-G-M. Produced by Joe Pasternak.
THE BELLS OF ST. MARY'S, Rainbow, RKO Radio. Produced by Leo McCarey.
*THE LOST WEEKEND, Paramount. Produced by Charles Brackett.
MILDRED PIERCE, Warner Bros. Produced by Jerry Wald.
SPELLBOUND, Selznick, UA. Produced by David O. Selznick.

ACTOR

BING CROSBY in *The Bells of St. Mary's,* Rainbow, RKO Radio.
GENE KELLY in *Anchors Aweigh,* M-G-M.
*RAY MILLAND in *The Lost Weekend,* Paramount.
GREGORY PECK in *The Keys of the Kingdom,* 20th Century-Fox.
CORNEL WILDE in *A Song To Remember,* Columbia.

ACTRESS

INGRID BERGMAN in *The Bells of St. Mary's,* Rainbow, RKO Radio.
*JOAN CRAWFORD in *Mildred Pierce,* Warner Bros.
GREER GARSON in *The Valley of Decision,* M-G-M.
JENNIFER JONES in *Love Letters,* Wallis, Paramount.
GENE TIERNEY in *Leave Her to Heaven,* 20th Century-Fox.

SUPPORTING ACTOR

MICHAEL CHEKHOV in *Spellbound,* Selznick, UA.
JOHN DALL in *The Corn Is Green,* Warner Bros.
*JAMES DUNN in *A Tree Grows in Brooklyn,* 20th Century-Fox.
ROBERT MITCHUM in *The Story of G.I. Joe,* Cowan, UA.
J. CARROL NAISH in *A Medal for Benny,* Paramount.

SUPPORTING ACTRESS

EVE ARDEN in *Mildred Pierce,* Warner Bros.
ANN BLYTH in *Mildred Pierce,* Warner Bros.
ANGELA LANSBURY in *The Picture of Dorian Gray,* M-G-M.
JOAN LORRING in *The Corn Is Green,* Warner Bros.
*ANNE REVERE in *National Velvet.* M-G-M.

DIRECTING

THE BELLS OF ST. MARY'S, RKO Radio. Leo McCarey.
*THE LOST WEEKEND, Paramount. Billy Wilder.
NATIONAL VELVET, M-G-M. Clarence Brown.
THE SOUTHERNER, Loew-Hakim, UA. Jean Renoir.
SPELLBOUND, Selznick, UA. Alfred Hitchcock.

WRITING

(Original Story)

THE AFFAIRS OF SUSAN, Wallis, Paramount. Laszlo Gorog and Thomas Monroe.
*THE HOUSE ON 92ND STREET, 20th Century-Fox. Charles G. Booth.
A MEDAL FOR BENNY, Paramount. John Steinbeck and Jack Wagner.
OBJECTIVE, BURMA!, Warner Bros. Alvah Bessie.
A SONG TO REMEMBER, Columbia. Ernst Marischka.

(Original Screenplay)

DILLINGER, Monogram. Philip Yordan.
*MARIE-LOUISE, Praesens Films (Swiss). Richard Schweizer.
MUSIC FOR MILLIONS, M-G-M. Myles Connolly.
SALTY O'ROURKE, Paramount. Milton Holmes.
WHAT NEXT, CORPORAL HARGROVE? M-G-M. Harry Kurnitz.

(Screenplay)

THE STORY OF G.I. JOE, Cowan, UA. Leopold Atlas, Guy Endore and Philip Stevenson.
*THE LOST WEEKEND, Paramount. Charles Brackett and Billy Wilder.
MILDRED PIERCE, Warner Bros. Ranald MacDougall.
PRIDE OF THE MARINES, Warner Bros. Albert Maltz.
A TREE GROWS IN BROOKLYN, 20th Century-Fox. Frank Davis and Tess Slesinger.

CINEMATOGRAPHY

(Black-and-White)

THE KEYS OF THE KINGDOM, 20th Century-Fox. Arthur Miller.
THE LOST WEEKEND, Paramount. John F. Seitz.
MILDRED PIERCE, Warner Bros. Ernest Haller.
*THE PICTURE OF DORIAN GRAY, M-G-M. Harry Stradling.
SPELLBOUND, Selznick, UA. George Barnes.

(Color)

ANCHORS AWEIGH, M-G-M. Robert Planck and Charles Boyle.
*LEAVE HER TO HEAVEN, 20th Century-Fox. Leon Shamory.
NATIONAL VELVET, M-G-M. Leonard Smith.
A SONG TO REMEMBER, Columbia. Tony Gaudio and Allen M. Davey.
THE SPANISH MAIN, RKO Radio. George Barnes.

ART DIRECTION-INTERIOR DECORATION

(Black-and-White)

*BLOOD ON THE SUN, Cagney, UA. Wiard Ihnen; A. Roland Fields.
EXPERIMENT PERILOUS, RKO Radio. Albert S. D'Agostino and Jack Okey; Darrell Silvera and Claude Carpenter.
THE KEYS OF THE KINGDOM, 20th Century-Fox. James Basevi and William Darling; Thomas Little and Frank E. Hughes.
LOVE LETTERS, Wallis, Paramount. Hans Dreier and Roland Anderson; Sam Comer and Ray Moyer.
THE PICTURE OF DORIAN GRAY, M-G-M. Cedric Gibbons and Hans Peters; Edwin B. Willis, John Bonar and Hugh Hunt.

(Color)

*FRENCHMAN'S CREEK, Paramount. Hans Dreier and Ernst Fegte; Sam Comer.
LEAVE HER TO HEAVEN, 20th Century-Fox. Lyle Wheeler and Maurice Ransford; Thomas Little.
NATIONAL VELVET, M-G-M. Cedric Gibbons and Urie McCleary; Edwin B. Willis and Mildred Griffiths.
SAN ANTONIO, Warner Bros. Ted Smith; Jack McConaghy.
A THOUSAND AND ONE NIGHTS, Columbia. Stephen Goosson and Rudolph Sternad; Frank Tuttle.

SOUND RECORDING

*THE BELLS OF ST. MARY'S, Rainbow, RKO Radio. RKO Radio Studio Sound Dept., Stephen Dunn, Sound Director.
FLAME OF BARBARY COAST, Republic. Republic Studio Sound Dept., Daniel J. Bloomberg, Sound Director.
LADY ON A TRAIN, Universal. Universal Studio Sound Dept., Bernard B. Brown, Sound Director.
LEAVE HER TO HEAVEN, 20th Century-Fox. 20th Century-Fox Studio Sound Dept., Thomas T. Moulton, Sound Director.
RHAPSODY IN BLUE, Warner Bros. Warner Bros. Studio Sound Dept., Nathan Levinson, Sound Director.
A SONG TO REMEMBER, Columbia. Columbia Studio Sound Dept., John Livadary, Sound Director.
THE SOUTHERNER, Loew-Hakim, UA. Sound Services, Inc., Jack Whitney, Sound Director.
THEY WERE EXPENDABLE, M-G-M. M-G-M Studio Sound Dept., Douglas Shearer, Sound Director.
THE THREE CABALLEROS, Disney, RKO Radio. Walt Disney Studio Sound Dept., C. O. Slyfield, Sound Director.
THREE IS A FAMILY, Master Productions, UA. RCA Sound, W. V. Wolfe, Sound Director.
THE UNSEEN, Paramount. Paramount Studio Sound Dept., Loren L. Ryder, Sound Director.
WONDER MAN, Goldwyn, RKO Radio. Samuel Goldwyn Studio Sound Dept., Gordon Sawyer, Sound Director.

FILM EDITING

THE BELLS OF ST. MARY'S, Rainbow, RKO Radio. Harry Marker.
THE LOST WEEKEND, Paramount. Doane Harrison.
*NATIONAL VELVET, M-G-M. Robert J. Kern.
OBJECTIVE, BURMA!, Warner Bros. George Amy.
A SONG TO REMEMBER, Columbia. Charles Nelson.

SPECIAL EFFECTS

CAPTAIN EDDIE, 20th Century-Fox. Fred Sersen, Sol Halprin, Roger Heman and Harry Leonard.
SPELLBOUND, Selznick, UA. Jack Cosgrove.
THEY WERE EXPENDABLE, M-G-M. A. Arnold Gillespie, Donald Jahraus, R.A. MacDonald and Michael Steinore.
A THOUSAND AND ONE NIGHTS, Columbia. L.W. Butler and Ray Bomba.
*WONDER MAN, Goldwyn, RKO Radio. John Fulton and A.W. Johns.

MUSIC

(Song)

ACCENTUATE THE POSITIVE (*Here Come the Waves,* Paramount); Music by Harold Arlen. Lyrics by Johnny Mercer.
ANYWHERE (*Tonight and Every Night,* Columbia);

The Picture of Dorian Gray (M-G-M; produced by Pandro S. Berman) featured Hurd Hatfield as Oscar Wilde's famous young sinner who stayed young while his portrait grew old, and won Harry Stradling an Academy Award for his moody and effective cinematography. Until the 1970s, only a few cinematographers were known outside industry circles, but the Academy has been honoring them since the first 1927-28 Awards ceremony.

Music by Jule Styne. Lyrics by Sammy Cahn.
AREN'T YOU GLAD YOU'RE YOU (*The Bells of St. Mary's,* Rainbow, RKO Radio); Music by James Van Heusen. Lyrics by Johnny Burke.
THE CAT AND THE CANARY (*Why Girls Leave Home,* PRC); Music by Jay Livingston. Lyrics by Ray Evans.
ENDLESSLY (*Earl Carroll Vanities,* Republic); Music by Walter Kent. Lyrics by Kim Gannon.
I FALL IN LOVE TOO EASILY (*Anchors Aweigh,* M-G-M); Music by Jule Styne. Lyrics by Sammy Cahn.
I'LL BUY THAT DREAM (*Sing Your Way Home,* RKO Radio); Music by Allie Wrubel. Lyrics by Herb Magidson.
*****IT MIGHT AS WELL BE SPRING** (*State Fair,* 20th Century-Fox); Music by Richard Rodgers. Lyrics by Oscar Hammerstein II.
LINDA (*The Story of G.I. Joe,* Cowan, UA); Music and Lyrics by Ann Ronell.
LOVE LETTERS (*Love Letters,* Wallis, Paramount); Music by Victor Young. Lyrics by Edward Heyman.
MORE AND MORE (*Can't Help Singing,* Universal); Music by Jerome Kern. Lyrics by E.Y. Harburg.
SLEIGHRIDE IN JULY (*Belle of the Yukon,* International, RKO Radio); Music by James Van Heusen. Lyrics by Johnny Burke.
SO IN LOVE (*Wonder Man,* Beverly Prods., RKO Radio); Music by David Rose. Lyrics by Leo Robin.
SOME SUNDAY MORNING (*San Antonio,* Warner Bros.); Music by Ray Heindorf and M.K. Jerome. Lyrics by Ted Koehler.

(Scoring of a Dramatic or Comedy Picture)
THE BELLS OF ST. MARY'S, Rainbow, RKO Radio. Robert Emmett Dolan.
BREWSTER'S MILLIONS, Small, UA. Lou Forbes.
CAPTAIN KIDD, Bogeaus, UA. Werner Janssen.
ENCHANTED COTTAGE, RKO Radio. Roy Webb.
FLAME OF BARBARY COAST, Republic. Dale Butts and Morton Scott.
G.I. HONEYMOON, Monogram. Edward J. Kay.
GUEST IN THE HOUSE, Guest in the House, Inc., UA. Werner Janssen.
GUEST WIFE, Green Tree, Prods., UA. Daniele Amfitheatrof.
THE KEYS OF THE KINGDOM, 20th Century-Fox. Alfred Newman.
THE LOST WEEKEND, Paramount. Miklos Rozsa.
LOVE LETTERS, Wallis, Paramount. Victor Young.
THE MAN WHO WALKED ALONE, PRC. Karl Hajos.
OBJECTIVE, BURMA!, Warner Bros. Franz Waxman.
PARIS—UNDERGROUND, Bennett, UA. Alexander Tansman.
A SONG TO REMEMBER, Columbia. Miklos Rozsa and Morris Stoloff.
THE SOUTHERNER, Loew-Hakim, UA. Werner Janssen.
*****SPELLBOUND,** Selznick, UA. Miklos Rozsa.
THE STORY OF G.I. JOE, Cowan, UA. Louis Applebaum and Ann Ronell.
THIS LOVE OF OURS, Universal, H.J. Salter.

THE VALLEY OF DECISION, M-G-M. Herbert Stothart.
THE WOMAN IN THE WINDOW, International, RKO Radio. Hugo Friedhofer and Arthur Lange.

(Scoring of a Musical Picture)
*****ANCHORS AWEIGH,** M-G-M. Georgie Stoll.
BELLE OF THE YUKON, International, RKO Radio. Arthur Lange.
CAN'T HELP SINGING, Universal. Jerome Kern and H.J. Salter.
HITCHHIKE TO HAPPINESS, Republic. Morton Scott.
INCENDIARY BLONDE, Paramount. Robert Emmett Dolan.
RHAPSODY IN BLUE, Warner Bros. Ray Heindorf and Max Steiner.
STATE FAIR, 20th Century-Fox. Charles Henderson and Alfred Newman.
SUNBONNET SUE, Monogram. Edward J. Kay.
THE THREE CABALLEROS, Disney, RKO Radio. Edward Plumb, Paul J. Smith and Charles Wolcott.
TONIGHT AND EVERY NIGHT, Columbia. Marlin Skiles and Morris Stoloff.
WHY GIRLS LEAVE HOME, PRC. Walter Greene.
WONDER MAN, Goldwyn, RKO Radio. Lou Forbes and Ray Heindorf.

SHORT SUBJECTS

(Cartoons)
DONALD'S CRIME, Disney, RKO Radio. (Donald Duck). Walt Disney, producer.
JASPER AND THE BEANSTALK, Paramount. (Jasper Puppetoon). George Pal, producer.
LIFE WITH FEATHERS, Warner Bros. (Merrie Melodies). Eddie Selzer, producer.
MIGHTY MOUSE IN GYPSY LIFE, 20th Century-Fox. (Terrytoon). Paul Terry, producer.
POET AND PEASANT, Universal. (Lantz Cartune). Walter Lantz, producer.
*****QUIET PLEASE!,** M-G-M. (Tom & Jerry Series). Frederick Quimby, producer.
RIPPLING ROMANCE, Columbia. (Color Rhapsodies).

(One-reel)
ALONG THE RAINBOW TRAIL, 20th Century-Fox. (Movietone Adventure). Edmund Reek, producer.
SCREEN SNAPSHOTS 25TH ANNIVERSARY, Columbia. (Screen Snapshots). Ralph Staub, producer.
*****STAIRWAY TO LIGHT,** M-G-M. (John Nesbitt Passing Parade). Herbert Moulton, producer.
STORY OF A DOG. Warner Bros. (Vitaphone Varieties). Gordon Hollingshead, producer.
WHITE RHAPSODY, Paramount. (Sportlights). Grantland Rice, producer.
YOUR NATIONAL GALLERY, Universal. (Variety Views). Joseph O'Brien and Thomas Mead, producers.

(Two-reel)
A GUN IN HIS HAND, M-G-M. (Crime Doesn't Pay).

Chester Franklin, producer.
THE JURY GOES ROUND 'N' ROUND, Columbia. (All Star Comedies). Jules White, producer.
THE LITTLE WITCH, Paramount. (Musical Parade). George Templeton, producer.
*****STAR IN THE NIGHT,** Warner Bros. (Broadway Brevities). Gordon Hollingshead, producer.

DOCUMENTARY

(Short Subjects)
*****HITLER LIVES?,** Warner Bros.
LIBRARY OF CONGRESS, Overseas Motion Picture Bureau, Office of War Information.
TO THE SHORES OF IWO JIMA, U.S. Marine Corps.

(Features)
THE LAST BOMB, U.S. Army Air Force.
*****THE TRUE GLORY,** Governments of Great Britain and USA.

SPECIAL AWARDS

TO WALTER WANGER for his six years service as President of the Academy of Motion Picture Arts and Sciences. (special plaque)
TO PEGGY ANN GARNER, outstanding child actress of 1945. (miniature statuette)
TO *THE HOUSE I LIVE IN,* tolerance short subject; produced by Frank Ross and Mervyn LeRoy; directed by Mervyn LeRoy; screenplay by Albert Maltz; song *The House I Live In,* music by Earl Robinson, lyrics by Lewis Allen; starring Frank Sinatra; released by RKO Radio. (statuette)
TO REPUBLIC STUDIO, DANIEL J. BLOOMBERG and the **REPUBLIC SOUND DEPARTMENT** for the building of an outstanding musical scoring auditorium which provides optimum recording and conditions and combines all elements of acoustic and engineering design. (certificates)

1945 IRVING G. THALBERG MEMORIAL AWARD

None given this year.

SCIENTIFIC OR TECHNICAL

Class I (statuette)
None.

CLASS II (plaque)
None.

CLASS III (citation)
LOREN L. RYDER, CHARLES R. DAILY and the **PARAMOUNT STUDIO SOUND DEPARTMENT.**
MICHAEL S. LESHING, BENJAMIN C. ROBINSON, ARTHUR B. CHATELAIN and **ROBERT C. STEVENS** of 20th Century-Fox Studio and **JOHN G. CAPSTAFF** of Eastman Kodak Co.

*****INDICATES WINNER**

1946
The Nineteenth Year

The Academy made a major change in its voting rules for the 1946 awards year. Instead of having nearly 10,000 members of the film community select the nominees and final Academy Award winners as they had during the past nine years, the rules were altered so the final decision would be made solely by bona fide Academy members. Not surprisingly, the announcement caused Academy membership rolls to swell from its 700 to a new high of 1,675. The new voting policy created a more reliable set of judges for the Academy, since votes would now be more specifically in the hands of craftspeople actually involved in picture making. Some say the new ruling also helped stimulate something the Academy has always abhorred: active campaigning for voter attention in trade publications.

There were other significant changes, as well. After three years of presenting the Oscars at Grauman's Chinese Theatre, the Academy moved its setting to the mammoth Shrine Auditorium with a seating capacity of 6,700 seats, five hundred more than the Radio City Music Hall in New York. Because of the extra capacity, the general public for the first time was allowed to buy tickets and attend, side by side with industry members. The program on March 13, 1947, was produced for the Academy by Mervyn LeRoy and hosted by Jack Benny.

Samuel Goldwyn's distinctly American *The Best Years of Our Lives* received seven of the 1946 awards, including those for best picture, best actor (Fredric March), best director (William Wyler) and best supporting actor (Harold Russell). It was the second time both March and Wyler were honored by the Academy. Olivia de Havilland was named the year's best actress for *To Each His Own,* and Anne Baxter was named best supporting actress for *The Razor's Edge.*

Two other films dealing with aspects of Americana—*The Yearling* and *The Jolson Story*—each won two awards, but in some ways Americana took a back seat to European films. It had not happened before in an Oscar competition, but films from overseas were almost as prominent as American products, with six English-made movies (*Henry V, Brief Encounter, Caesar and Cleopatra, Vacation from Marriage, The Seventh Veil* and *Blithe Spirit*) winning eleven of the year's nominations, and three of the final awards. Both France (with *Children of Paradise*) and Italy (via *Open City*) were also represented. It was a sign of things to come and, beginning the next awards year, the Academy began to specifically acknowledge the vibrant postwar contributions of the European cinema.

Best Picture: **The Best Years of Our Lives** *(RKO Radio; produced by Samuel Goldwyn),* **Best Director:** **William Wyler,** *Best Actor:* **Fredric March** *as Al Stephenson and* **Best Supporting Actor:** Harold Russell *as Homer Parrish. Some speculated that 1946 audiences wouldn't want to be reminded of the recent World War II and the complexities of returning to civilian life, but William Wyler and his company examined the problem so artfully in* The Best Years of Our Lives, *it became the picture of the year, and a genuine classic. Based on a blank-verse essay by Mackinlay Kantor titled* Glory for Me, *it examined the problems faced by three veterans (Harold Russell, Dana Andrews and Fredric March, right) when returning home after the war and readjusting to the lives they left behind. It brought March his second Oscar (the first, for 1931-32's* Dr. Jekyll and Mr. Hyde*); he played a devoted family man who suddenly finds his old bank job oddly unsatisfying. Russell, a nonprofessional and real-life arm amputee, won two Academy Awards as a sailor returning with his hands replaced by hooks. One was the supporting actor award, the second was a special award for "bringing hope and courage to his fellow veterans." The expert* Best Years *cast also included Myrna Loy, Teresa Wright, Virginia Mayo, Hoagy Carmichael, Gladys George, Cathy O'Donnell and Steve Cochran.*

Special Award: Laurence Olivier *(above) for "his outstanding achievements as actor, producer and director in bringing* Henry V *to the screen." Olivier made Henry in England during the war and despite limitations of money and production materials, and other adversities, it became the first successful Olivier adaptation of Shakespeare on the screen, although he'd appeared in celluloid Shakespeare before (1936's* As You Like It), *then solely as a performer.*

Best Actress: Olivia de Havilland *as Jody Norris (right, with Griff Barnett) in* To Each His Own *(Paramount; directed by Mitchell Leisen). The year 1946 marked an important screen comeback for Olivia de Havilland, important because she'd been unable to work for two years, waging a court battle against her home studio, Warner Bros., over an unenforced California law which limited to seven years the period any employer could enforce a contract against an employee, something Warner Bros. disputed. She won the case (officially on the books as The de Havilland Decision) and new freedom for all actors thereafter. When she returned to work, she had immediate success in two important dramas,* The Dark Mirror *and* To Each His Own, *and won the Academy Award for the latter. In it, she played an unwed mother who loses custody of her son, and becomes his "Aunt Jody" when he is adopted by another family. Spanning two wars and covering a 27-year period, the film required her to age from a fresh-faced young girl to a brusque, no-nonsense business woman and, after previous Academy nominations in 1939 and 1941, she became an Oscar winner. Three years later she won again, for* The Heiress.

The Yearling (*M-G-M; produced by Sidney Franklin*) *starred Jane Wyman, Claude Jarman, Jr. and Gregory Peck (above) as the embodiment of the Baxter family, from Mar-* *jorie Kinnan Rawlings' magnificent novel about life—and growing up—in the backwoods of Florida. One of the year's best-liked films, it won Academy Awards for color cinematog-* *raphy and color art direction, plus a special award to Jarman as the outstanding child actor of 1946.*

Best Supporting Actress: Anne Baxter *as Sophie MacDonald (in center at right, with John Payne) in* The Razor's Edge (*20th Century-Fox; directed by Edmund Goulding*). *Created in a novel by Somerset Maugham, and acted by Anne Baxter, Sophie MacDonald was one of the screen's memorable characters of the 1940s: a gentle young mother who loses her husband and child in an automobile accident, then becomes a tragic and alcoholic wanton in Paris whom an old friend (played by Tyrone Power) unsuccessfully attempts to rehabilitate. By a paradox, Anne Baxter was not the first choice for her Oscar-winning role; producer Darryl F. Zanuck originally had assigned it to Betty Grable, who refused to do it on the grounds that the role was beyond her range as an actress. The final Razor's cast also included Gene Tierney, Clifton Webb, Herbert Marshall, Frank Latimore (as Sophie's husband) and Lucile Watson.*

Nominations 1946

BEST MOTION PICTURE

*THE BEST YEARS OF OUR LIVES, Goldwyn, RKO Radio. Produced by Samuel Goldwyn.
HENRY V, Rank-Two Cities, UA (British). Produced by Laurence Olivier.
IT'S A WONDERFUL LIFE, Liberty, RKO Radio. Produced by Frank Capra.
THE RAZOR'S EDGE, 20th Century-Fox. Produced by Darryl F. Zanuck.
THE YEARLING, M-G-M. Produced by Sidney Franklin.

ACTOR

*FREDRIC MARCH in *The Best Years of Our Lives*, Goldwyn, RKO Radio.
LAURENCE OLIVIER in *Henry V*, Rank-Two Cities, UA (British).
LARRY PARKS in *The Jolson Story*, Columbia.
GREGORY PECK in *The Yearling*, M-G-M.
JAMES STEWART in *It's A Wonderful Life*, Liberty Films, RKO Radio.

ACTRESS

*OLIVIA DE HAVILLAND in *To Each His Own*, Paramount.
CELIA JOHNSON in *Brief Encounter*, Rank, U-I (British).
JENNIFER JONES in *Duel in the Sun*, Selznick International.
ROSALIND RUSSELL in *Sister Kenny*, RKO Radio.
JANE WYMAN in *The Yearling*, M-G-M.

SUPPORTING ACTOR

CHARLES COBURN in *The Green Years*, M-G-M.
WILLIAM DEMAREST in *The Jolson Story*, Columbia.
CLAUDE RAINS in *Notorious*, RKO Radio.
*HAROLD RUSSELL in *The Best Years of Our Lives*, Goldwyn, RKO Radio.
CLIFTON WEBB in *The Razor's Edge*, 20th Century-Fox.

SUPPORTING ACTRESS

ETHEL BARRYMORE in *The Spiral Staircase*, RKO Radio.
*ANNE BAXTER in *The Razor's Edge*, 20th Century-Fox.
LILLIAN GISH in *Duel in the Sun*, Selznick International.
FLORA ROBSON in *Saratoga Trunk*, Warner Bros..
GALE SONDERGAARD in *Anna and the King of Siam*, 20th Century-Fox.

DIRECTING

*THE BEST YEARS OF OUR LIVES, Goldwyn, RKO Radio. William Wyler.
BRIEF ENCOUNTER, Rank, U-I (British). David Lean.
IT'S A WONDERFUL LIFE, Liberty, RKO Radio. Frank Capra.
THE KILLERS, Hellinger, Universal. Robert Siodmak.
THE YEARLING, M-G-M. Clarence Brown.

WRITING

(Original Story)

THE DARK MIRROR, U-I. Vladimir Pozner.
THE STRANGE LOVE OF MARTHA IVERS, Wallis, Paramount. Jack Patrick.
THE STRANGER, International, RKO Radio. Victor Trivas.
TO EACH HIS OWN, Paramount. Charles Brackett.
*VACATION FROM MARRIAGE, London Films, M-G-M (British). Clemence Dane.

(Original Screenplay)

THE BLUE DAHLIA, Paramount. Raymond Chandler.
CHILDREN OF PARADISE, (French). Jacques Prevert.
NOTORIOUS, RKO Radio. Ben Hecht.
THE ROAD TO UTOPIA, Paramount. Norman Panama and Melvin Frank.
*THE SEVENTH VEIL, Rank, Universal (British). Muriel Box and Sydney Box.

(Screenplay)

ANNA AND THE KING OF SIAM, 20th Century-Fox. Sally Benson and Talbot Jennings.
*THE BEST YEARS OF OUR LIVES, Goldwyn, RKO Radio. Robert E. Sherwood.
BRIEF ENCOUNTER, Rank, U-I (British). Anthony Havelock-Allan, David Lean and Ronald Neame.
THE KILLERS, Hellinger, Universal. Anthony Veiller.
OPEN CITY, (Italian). Sergio Amidei and F. Fellini.

CINEMATOGRAPHY

(Black-and-White)

*ANNA AND THE KING OF SIAM, 20th Century-Fox. Arthur Miller.
THE GREEN YEARS, M-G-M. George Folsey.

(Color)

THE JOLSON STORY, Columbia. Joseph Walker.
*THE YEARLING, M-G-M. Charles Rosher, Leonard Smith and Arthur Arling.

ART DIRECTION-INTERIOR DECORATION

(Black-and-White)

*ANNA AND THE KING OF SIAM, 20th Century-Fox. Lyle Wheeler and William Darling; Thomas Little and Frank E. Hughes.
KITTY, Paramount. Hans Dreier and Walter Tyler; Sam Comer and Ray Moyer.
THE RAZOR'S EDGE, 20th Century-Fox. Richard Day and Nathan Juran; Thomas Little and Paul S. Fox.

(Color)

CAESAR AND CLEOPATRA, Pascal, UA (British). John Bryan.
HENRY V, Rank-Two Cities UA (British). Paul Sheriff and Carmen Dillon.
*THE YEARLING, M-G-M. Cedric Gibbons and Paul Groesse; Edwin B. Willis.

SOUND RECORDING

THE BEST YEARS OF OUR LIVES, Goldwyn, RKO Radio. Samuel Goldwyn Studio Sound Dept., Gordon Sawyer, Sound Director.
IT'S A WONDERFUL LIFE, Liberty, RKO Radio. RKO Radio Studio Sound Dept., John Aalberg, Sound Director.
*THE JOLSON STORY, Columbia. Columbia Studio Sound Dept., John Livadary, Sound Director.

FILM EDITING

*THE BEST YEARS OF OUR LIVES, Goldwyn, RKO Radio. Daniel Mandell.
IT'S A WONDERFUL LIFE, Liberty, RKO Radio. William Hornbeck.
THE JOLSON STORY, Columbia. William Lyon.
THE KILLERS, Hellinger, Universal. Arthur Hilton.
THE YEARLING, M-G-M. Harold Kress.

SPECIAL EFFECTS

*BLITHE SPIRIT, Rank-Two Cities, UA (British). Thomas Howard.
A STOLEN LIFE, Warner Bros. William McGann and Nathan Levinson.

MUSIC

(Song)

ALL THROUGH THE DAY (*Centennial Summer*, 20th Century-Fox); Music by Jerome Kern. Lyrics by Oscar Hammerstein II.
I CAN'T BEGIN TO TELL YOU (*The Dolly Sisters*, 20th Century-Fox); Music by James Monaco. Lyrics by Mack Gordon.
OLE BUTTERMILK SKY (*Canyon Passage*, Wanger, Universal); Music by Hoagy Carmichael. Lyrics by Jack Brooks.
*ON THE ATCHISON, TOPEKA AND THE SANTA FE (*The Harvey Girls*, M-G-M); Music by Harry Warren. Lyrics by Johnny Mercer.
YOU KEEP COMING BACK LIKE A SONG (*Blue Skies*, Paramount); Music and Lyrics by Irving Berlin.

(Scoring of a Dramatic or Comedy Picture)

ANNA AND THE KING OF SIAM, 20th Century-Fox. Bernard Herrmann.
*THE BEST YEARS OF OUR LIVES, Goldwyn, RKO Radio. Hugo Friedhofer.
HENRY V, Rank-Two Cities, UA (British). William Walton.
HUMORESQUE, Warner Bros. Franz Waxman.
THE KILLERS, Hellinger, Universal. Miklos Rozsa.

(Scoring of a Musical Picture)

BLUE SKIES, Paramount. Robert Emmett Dolan.
CENTENNIAL SUMMER, 20th Century-Fox. Alfred Newman.
THE HARVEY GIRLS, M-G-M. Lennie Hayton.
*THE JOLSON STORY, Columbia. Morris Stoloff.
NIGHT AND DAY, Warner Bros.. Ray Heindorf and Max Steiner.

SHORT SUBJECTS

(Cartoons)

*THE CAT CONCERTO, M-G-M. (Tom & Jerry). Frederick Quimby, producer.
CHOPIN'S MUSICAL MOMENTS, Universal. (Musical Miniatures). Walter Lantz, producer.
JOHN HENRY AND THE INKY POO, Paramount. (Puppetoon). George Pal, producer.
SQUATTER'S RIGHTS, Disney, RKO Radio. (Mickey Mouse). Walt Disney, producer.
WALKY TALKY HAWKY, Warner Bros. (Merrie Melodies). Edward Selzer, producer.

(One-reel)

DIVE-HI CHAMPS, Paramount. (Sportlights). Jack Eaton, producer.
*FACING YOUR DANGER, Warner Bros. (Sports Parade). Gordon Hollingshead, producer.
GOLDEN HORSES, 20th Century-Fox. (Movietone Sports Review). Edmund Reek, producer.
SMART AS A FOX, Warner Bros. (Varieties). Gordon Hollingshead, producer.
SURE CURES, M-G-M. (Pete Smith Specialty). Pete Smith, producer.

(Two-reel)

*A BOY AND HIS DOG, Warner Bros. (Featurettes). Gordon Hollingshead, producer.
COLLEGE QUEEN, Paramount. (Musical Parade). George Templeton, producer.
HISS AND YELL, Columbia. (All Star Comedies). Jules White, producer.
THE LUCKIEST GUY IN THE WORLD, Warner Bros.. (Two-reel Special). Jerry Bresler, producer.

DOCUMENTARY

(Short Subjects)

ATOMIC POWER, 20th Century-Fox.
LIFE AT THE ZOO, Artkino.
PARAMOUNT NEWS ISSUE #37, Paramount.
*SEEDS OF DESTINY, U.S. War Department.
TRAFFIC WITH THE DEVIL, M-G-M.

(Features)

None nominated this year.

SPECIAL AWARDS

TO LAURENCE OLIVIER for his outstanding achievement as actor, producer and director in bringing *Henry V* to the screen. (statuette)
TO HAROLD RUSSELL for bringing hope and courage to his fellow veterans through his appearance in *The Best Years of Our Lives*. (statuette)
TO ERNST LUBITSCH for his distinguished contributions to the art of the motion picture. (scroll)
TO CLAUDE JARMAN, JR., outstanding child actor of 1946. (miniature statuette)

1946 IRVING G. THALBERG MEMORIAL AWARD

TO SAMUEL GOLDWYN

SCIENTIFIC OR TECHNICAL

CLASS I (statuette)
None.

CLASS II (plaque)
None.

CLASS III (citation)
HARLAN L. BAUMBACH and the PARAMOUNT WEST COAST LABORATORY;
HERBERT E. BRITT;
BURTON F. MILLER and the WARNER BROS. STUDIO SOUND and ELECTRICAL DEPARTMENTS;
CARL FAULKNER of the 20th Century-Fox Studio Sound Department;
MOLE-RICHARDSON CO.;
ARTHUR F. BLINN, ROBERT O. COOK, C.O. SLYFIELD and the WALT DISNEY STUDIO SOUND DEPARTMENT;
BURTON F. MILLER and the WARNER BROS. STUDIO SOUND DEPARTMENT;
MARTY MARTIN and HAL ADKINS of the RKO Radio Studio Miniature Department;
HAROLD NYE and the WARNER BROS. STUDIO ELECTRICAL DEPARTMENT.

*INDICATES WINNER

93

It was the year of *Gentleman's Agreement* and *Life With Father* and *Forever Amber* and *The Egg and I,* but many people best remember the Academy's twentieth birthday party as the year of a wildly incorrect straw poll taken by a Hollywood trade publication. As was the custom, *Daily Variety* took a pre-show sampling of numerous Academy members asking how each voted in various awards categories, then published the results—and predictions—on Oscar day. On March 20, 1948, the paper bannered that night's winners for 1947 would probably be *Gentleman's Agreement* as best picture, Ronald Colman in *A Double Life* as best actor (in a narrow margin over Gregory Peck of *Gentleman's*) and Edmund Gwenn (in *Miracle on 34th Street*) and Celeste Holm (in *Gentleman's*) winning in the supporting divisions.

Among the nominees for best actress, the prediction was a "sure thing" for Rosalind Russell in *Mourning Becomes Electra* with her runners-up listed, in order, as Dorothy McGuire, Joan Crawford, Susan Hayward, and in the final spot, Loretta Young. By the end of the evening most of the guesses were correct, but in the case of best actress they could not have been more wrong. Not only did the anticipated "sure thing" fail to happen, but the winner was the trailing "dark horse," Loretta Young in *The Farmer's Daughter.* It was the last time such a poll was regularly published; thereafter, the Academy requested its members keep mum on how ballots were marked.

Basically, the 1947 awards were quite evenly distributed, with *Gentleman's Agreement* winning three (including Elia Kazan's as best director), *Miracle on 34th Street* receiving three, *A Double Life, Great Expectations* and *Black Narcissus* each winning two, and six other achievements winning one: *Body and Soul, Green Dolphin Street, Mother Wore Tights, The Bachelor and the Bobbysoxer, Song of the South,* and *The Bishop's Wife.* For the first time, the Academy specifically honored a foreign-language film, Italy's *Shoe-Shine,* as part of its special awards category; not until the 1956 awards year were foreign language films saluted in a category of their own, with nominations. Also honored with a special Oscar statuette was James Baskett, the endearing Uncle Remus of Walt Disney's *Song of the South.* A special award plaque went to another delight for the younger audiences, Ken Murray's *Bill and Coo,* the story of a humanized life style as enacted by birds. The Academy saluted it because "artistry and patience blended in a novel and entertaining use of the medium of motion pictures."

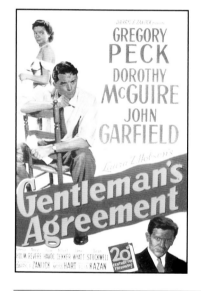

GREGORY **PECK** DOROTHY **McGUIRE** JOHN **GARFIELD**

Gentleman's Agreement

Best Actress: **Loretta Young** *as Katie Holstrom (right, with Keith Andes, James Arness and Lex Barker) in* The Farmer's Daughter *(RKO Radio; directed by H.C. Potter). Loretta Young, like Ronald Colman, was a long-time screen veteran when she won her Oscar. After early days as a child extra, she played her first role at age 14 in 1927's* Naughty But Nice *with Colleen Moore, then became the personification of an elegant leading lady—charming, well-groomed, classy—in frothy comedies, major spectacles and romantic dramas.* The Farmer's Daughter *had originally been planned for Ingrid Bergman, but it fit the Young talents perfectly: with a Swedish accent and blonde hair, she was a Minnesota farm girl who begins as the household maid of a Congressman (Joseph Cotton) and ultimately is elected to Congress herself.*

Best Picture: Gentleman's Agreement *(20th Century-Fox; produced by Darryl F. Zanuck),* **Best Director:** Elia Kazan *and* **Best Supporting Actress:** Celeste Holm *as Anne Dettrey (above, with Gregory Peck, John Garfield, Robert Karnes and Gene Nelson) in* Gentleman's Agreement. *In 1947, Hollywood used the screen to take microscopic looks at minority groups and prejudice running rampant in the United States; one of the most successful was* Gentleman's Agreement, *based on Laura Z. Hobson's powerful novel about a writer who poses as a Jew for six months in order to research a series of articles he intends to write on anti-Semitism. The cast included Dorothy McGuire, Anne Revere, Albert Dekker, June Havoc, Jane Wyatt, Dean Stockwell and Sam Jaffe. Celeste Holm, in her third screen role, won the Academy Award as a compassionate friend of the writer; she was later nominated for Academy Awards in 1949 (for* Come to the Stable*) and again in 1950 (for* All About Eve*). Kazan himself later said he felt* Gentleman's *"skated over the surface of an issue that needed a more penetrating treatment," but 1947 audiences and critics found it potent drama, a deft mix of preachment with entertainment.*

95

Best Actor: Ronald Colman *as Anthony John in* A Double Life *(Universal-International; directed by George Cukor). Ronald Colman won his first recognition in the movies' silent era opposite Lillian Gish in* The White Sister *(1923) and received ever-wider popularity when the screen learned to speak, due to his unique, resonant voice. On the celebration of his 25th year as a star, he had one of his most demanding roles, as an actor so immersed in playing Othello that his stage character begins to take possession of his off-screen personality.* A Double Life *was written by Ruth Gordon and Garson Kanin, co-starred Signe Hasso and Edmond O'Brien and gave Shelley Winters her first important screen role as a waitress murdered by the actor. Shakespearean veteran Walter Hampden coached Colman for the slices of* Othello *incorporated into the film. At left, Colman as the actor in performance.*

Special Award: Shoe-Shine from Italy (Lopert Films; produced in Italy by Paolo W. Tamburella) received an Academy Award from the Board of Governors because "the high quality of this Italian-made motion picture, brought to eloquent life in a country scarred by war, is proof to the world that the creative spirit can triumph over adversity." It was the first time the Academy had specifically honored a foreign-language film. Directed by Vittorio DeSica, Shoe-Shine was peopled with a cast of nonprofessional children and mirrored the struggle of two hungry, homeless boys to survive on the streets after the fall of Fascism in Italy. The gritty, realistic look of the film, coming as it did on the heels of Rossellini's Open City and other post-war European pictures, was to have a major effect on altering the glossy, glamourized look of Hollywood movies in the next decade.

MOTION PICTURE

THE BISHOP'S WIFE, Goldwyn, RKO Radio. Produced by Samuel Goldwyn.
CROSSFIRE, RKO Radio. Produced by Adrian Scott.
*GENTLEMAN'S AGREEMENT, 20th Century-Fox. Produced by Darryl F. Zanuck.
GREAT EXPECTATIONS, Rank-Cineguild, U-I (British). Produced by Ronald Neame.
MIRACLE ON 34TH STREET, 20th Century-Fox. Produced by William Perlberg.

ACTOR

*RONALD COLMAN in A Double Life, Kanin, U-I.
JOHN GARFIELD in Body and Soul, Enterprise, UA.
GREGORY PECK in Gentleman's Agreement, 20th Century-Fox.
WILLIAM POWELL in Life with Father, Warner Bros.
MICHAEL REDGRAVE in Mourning Becomes Electra, RKO Radio.

ACTRESS

JOAN CRAWFORD in Possessed, Warner Bros.
SUSAN HAYWARD in Smash Up—The Story of a Woman, Wanger, U-I.
DOROTHY McGUIRE in Gentleman's Agreement, 20th Century-Fox.
ROSALIND RUSSELL in Mourning Becomes Electra, RKO Radio.
*LORETTA YOUNG in The Farmer's Daughter, RKO Radio.

SUPPORTING ACTOR

CHARLES BICKFORD in The Farmer's Daughter, RKO Radio.
THOMAS GOMEZ in Ride the Pink Horse, U-I.
*EDMUND GWENN in Miracle on 34th Street, 20th Century-Fox.
ROBERT RYAN in Crossfire, RKO Radio.
RICHARD WIDMARK in Kiss of Death, 20th Century-Fox.

SUPPORTING ACTRESS

ETHEL BARRYMORE in The Paradine Case, Selznick Releasing Organization.
GLORIA GRAHAME in Crossfire, RKO Radio.
*CELESTE HOLM in Gentleman's Agreement, 20th Century-Fox.
MARJORIE MAIN in The Egg and I, U-I.
ANNE REVERE in Gentleman's Agreement, 20th Century-Fox.

DIRECTING

THE BISHOP'S WIFE, Goldwyn, RKO Radio. Henry Koster.
CROSSFIRE, RKO Radio. Edward Dmytryk.
A DOUBLE LIFE, Kanin, U-I. George Cukor.
*GENTLEMAN'S AGREEMENT, 20th Century-Fox. Elia Kazan.
GREAT EXPECTATIONS, Rank-Cineguild, U-I (British). David Lean.

WRITING

(Original Story)

A CAGE OF NIGHTINGALES, Lopert Films (French). Georges Chaperot and Rene Wheeler.
IT HAPPENED ON FIFTH AVENUE, Del Ruth, Allied Artists. Herbert Clyde Lewis and Frederick Stephani.
KISS OF DEATH, 20th Century-Fox. Eleazar Lipsky.
*MIRACLE ON 34TH STREET, 20th Century-Fox. Valentine Davies.
SMASH-UP—THE STORY OF A WOMAN, Wanger, U-I. Dorothy Parker and Frank Cavett.

(Original Screenplay)

*THE BACHELOR AND THE BOBBYSOXER, RKO Radio. Sidney Sheldon.
BODY AND SOUL, Enterprise, UA. Abraham Polonsky.
A DOUBLE LIFE, Kanin, U-I. Ruth Gordon and Garson Kanin.
MONSIEUR VERDOUX, Chaplin, UA. Charles Chaplin.
SHOE-SHINE, Lopert Films (Italian). Sergio Amidei, Adolfo Franci, C.G. Viola and Cesare Zavattini.

(Screenplay)

BOOMERANG!, 20th Century-Fox. Richard Murphy.
CROSSFIRE, RKO Radio. John Paxton.
GENTLEMAN'S AGREEMENT, 20th Century-Fox. Moss Hart.
GREAT EXPECTATIONS, Rank-Cineguild, U-I (British). David Lean, Ronald Neame and Anthony Havelock-Allan.
*MIRACLE ON 34TH STREET, 20th Century-Fox. George Seaton.

CINEMATOGRAPHY

(Black-and-White)

THE GHOST AND MRS. MUIR, 20th Century-Fox. Charles Lang, Jr.
*GREAT EXPECTATIONS, Rank-Cineguild, U-I (British). Guy Green.
GREEN DOLPHIN STREET, M-G-M. George Folsey.

(Color)

*BLACK NARCISSUS, Rank-Archer, U-I (British). Jack Cardiff.
LIFE WITH FATHER, Warner Bros. Peverell Marley and William V. Skall.
MOTHER WORE TIGHTS, 20th Century-Fox. Harry Jackson.

ART DIRECTION-SET DECORATION

(New classification)
(Winning art directors given statuettes; set decorator of the winning film given Academy plaque until 1955)

(Black-and-White)

THE FOXES OF HARROW, 20th Century-Fox. Lyle Wheeler and Maurice Ransford; Thomas Little and Paul S. Fox.
*GREAT EXPECTATIONS, Rank-Cineguild, U-I (British). John Bryan; Wilfred Shingleton.

(Color)

*BLACK NARCISSUS, Rank-Archers, U-I (British). Alfred Junge.
LIFE WITH FATHER, Warner Bros. Robert M. Haas; George James Hopkins.

SOUND RECORDING

*THE BISHOP'S WIFE, Goldwyn, RKO Radio. Samuel Goldwyn Studio Sound Dept., Gordon Sawyer, Sound Director.
GREEN DOLPHIN STREET, M-G-M. M-G-M Studio Sound Dept., Douglas Shearer, Sound Director.
T-MEN, Reliance Pictures, Eagle-Lion. Sound Services, Inc., Jack Whitney, Sound Director.

FILM EDITING

THE BISHOP'S WIFE, Goldwyn, RKO Radio. Monica Collingwood.
*BODY AND SOUL, Enterprise, UA. Francis Lyon and Robert Parrish.
GENTLEMAN'S AGREEMENT, 20th Century-Fox. Harmon Jones.
GREEN DOLPHIN STREET, M-G-M. George White.
ODD MAN OUT. Rank-Two Cities, U-I (British). Fergus McDonnell.

SPECIAL EFFECTS

*GREEN DOLPHIN STREET, M-G-M. A. Arnold Gillespie, Warren Newcombe, Douglas Shearer and Michael Steinore.
UNCONQUERED, DeMille, Paramount. Farciot Edouart, Devereux Jennings, Gordon Jennings, Wallace Kelley, Paul Lerpae and George Dutton.

MUSIC

(Song)

A GAL IN CALICO (The Time, Place and the Girl, Warner Bros.); Music by Arthur Schwartz. Lyrics by Leo Robin.
I WISH I DIDN'T LOVE YOU SO (The Perils of Pauline, Paramount); Music and Lyrics by Frank Loesser.
PASS THAT PEACE PIPE (Good News, M-G-M); Music and Lyrics by Ralph Blane, Hugh Martin and Roger Edens.
YOU DO (Mother Wore Tights, 20th Century-Fox); Music by Josef Myrow. Lyrics by Mack Gordon.
*ZIP-A-DEE-DOO-DAH (Song of the South, Disney, RKO Radio); Music by Allie Wrubel. Lyrics by Ray Gilbert.

(Scoring of a Dramatic or Comedy Picture)

THE BISHOP'S WIFE, Goldwyn, RKO Radio. Hugo Friedhofer.
CAPTAIN FROM CASTILE, 20th Century-Fox. Alfred Newman.
*A DOUBLE LIFE, Kanin, U-I. Miklos Rozsa.
FOREVER AMBER, 20th Century-Fox. David Raksin.
LIFE WITH FATHER, Warner Bros. Max Steiner.

(Scoring of a Musical Picture)

FIESTA, M-G-M. Johnny Green.
*MOTHER WORE TIGHTS, 20th Century-Fox. Alfred Newman.
MY WILD IRISH ROSE, Warner Bros.. Ray Heindorf and Max Steiner.
ROAD TO RIO, Paramount. Robert Emmett Dolan.
SONG OF THE SOUTH, Disney, RKO Radio. Daniele Amfitheatrof, Paul J. Smith and Charles Wolcott.

SHORT SUBJECTS

(Cartoons)

CHIP AN' DALE, Disney, RKO Radio. (Donald Duck).
Walt Disney, producer.

DR. JEKYLL AND MR. MOUSE, M-G-M. (Tom &
Jerry). Frederick Quimby, producer.

PLUTO'S BLUE NOTE, Disney, RKO Radio. (Pluto).
Walt Disney, producer.

TUBBY THE TUBA, Paramount. (Puppetoon). George
Pal, producer.

*TWEETIE PIE, Warner Bros. (Merrie Melodies).
Edward Selzer, producer.

(One-reel)

BROOKLYN, U.S.A., Universal-International. (Variety
Series). Thomas Mead, producer.

*GOODBYE MISS TURLOCK, M-G-M. (John Nesbitt
Passing Parade). Herbert Moulton, producer.

MOON ROCKETS, Paramount. (Popular Science).
Jerry Fairbanks, producer.

NOW YOU SEE IT, M-G-M. (Pete Smith Specialty).
Pete Smith, producer.

SO YOU WANT TO BE IN PICTURES, Warner Bros.
(Joe McDoakes). Gordon Hollingshead, producer.

(Two-reel)

CHAMPAGNE FOR TWO, Paramount. (Musical Parade
Featurette). Harry Grey, producer.

*CLIMBING THE MATTERHORN, Monogram.
(Special). Irving Allen, producer.

FIGHT OF THE WILD STALLIONS, U-I. (Special).
Thomas Mead, producer.

GIVE US THE EARTH, M-G-M. (Special). Herbert
Morgan, producer.

A VOICE IS BORN, Columbia. (Musical Featurette).
Ben Blake, producer.

DOCUMENTARY

(Short Subjects)

*FIRST STEPS, United Nations Division of Films and
Visual Education.

PASSPORT TO NOWHERE, RKO Radio. (This Is
America Series). Frederic Ullman, Jr., producer.

SCHOOL IN THE MAILBOX, Australian News and
Information Bureau.

(Features)

*DESIGN FOR DEATH, RKO Radio. Sid Rogell,
executive producer; Theron Warth and Richard O.
Fleischer, producers.

JOURNEY INTO MEDICINE, U.S. Department of
State, Office of Information and Educational Exchange.

THE WORLD IS RICH, British Information Services.
Paul Rotha, producer.

SPECIAL AWARDS

TO JAMES BASKETT for his able and heart-warming
characterization of Uncle Remus, friend and story
teller to the children of the world, in Walt Disney's
Song of the South. (statuette)

TO BILL AND COO, in which artistry and patience
blended in a novel and entertaining use of the
medium of motion pictures. (plaque)

TO SHOE-SHINE—the high quality of this Italian-
made motion picture, brought to eloquent life in a
country scarred by war, is proof to the world that the
creative spirit can triumph over adversity. (statuette)

TO COLONEL WILLIAM N. SELIG, ALBERT E.
SMITH, THOMAS ARMAT and GEORGE K.
SPOOR (one of) the small group of pioneers whose
belief in a new medium, and whose contributions to
its development, blazed the trail along which the
motion picture has progressed, in their lifetime, from
obscurity to world-wide acclaim. (statuettes)

1947 IRVING G. THALBERG MEMORIAL AWARD

None given this year.

SCIENTIFIC OR TECHNICAL

CLASS I (statuette)

None.

CLASS II (plaque)

C.C. DAVIS and ELECTRICAL RESEARCH
PRODUCTS, DIVISION OF WESTERN ELECTRIC
CO., for the development and application of an
improved film drive filter mechanism.

C.R. DAILY and the PARAMOUNT STUDIO FILM
LABORATORY, STILL and ENGINEERING
DEPARTMENTS for the development and first
practical application to motion picture and still
photography of a method of increasing film speed as
first suggested to the industry by E.I. duPont de
Nemours & Co.

Class III (citation)

NATHAN LEVINSON and the WARNER BROS.
STUDIO SOUND DEPARTMENT;

FARCIOT EDOUART, C.R. DAILY, HAL CORL, H.G.
CARTWRIGHT and the PARAMOUNT STUDIO
TRANSPARENCY and ENGINEERING
DEPARTMENTS;

FRED PONEDEL of Warner Bros. Studio;

KURT SINGER and the RCA-VICTOR DIVISION of
the RADIO CORPORATION OF AMERICA;

JAMES GIBBONS of Warner Bros. Studio.

*INDICATES WINNER

Great Expectations *(Universal-International; produced by Ronald Neame) won Academy Awards for Guy Green's black-and-white cinematography and John Bryan's black-and-white art direction (with set decoration by Wilfred Shingleton) and helped give a noticeable impetus to the popularity of British-made films in America's general movie market. At the time, most films from England only found acceptance in specialized art-houses. It was based on the adventurous Charles Dickens novel and featured John Mills, Valerie Hobson, Alec Guinness, Jean Simmons and (above) Martita Hunt and Anthony Wager.*

Best Supporting Actor: *Edmund Gwenn as Kris Kringle (left, with Natalie Wood) in* Miracle on 34th Street *(20th Century-Fox; directed by George Seaton). Is he or isn't he? In Valentine Davies' fresh and original screenplay, the man hired to be Macy's Santa Claus claims to be the real thing, and even gets sent as far as the Supreme Court on the question of his sanity. Edmund Gwenn won the Academy Award for his portrayal of Mr. Claus, alias Mr. Kringle, aided and abetted by Maureen O'Hara, John Payne and Thelma Ritter, among others. Mr. Davies also won an Oscar for his words.*

James Baskett's easy-going embodiment of Uncle Remus made such an impression on 1947 audiences that he was honored with a special Oscar at that year's ceremonies. Seen above with young admirers Bobby Driscoll and Luana Patten, Baskett, best known before Song of the South *as the fast-talking lawyer Gabby Gibson on radio's "Amos 'n' Andy" show, died only four months after receiving his award.*

1948-1957
The Academy's Third Decade

The war years (1942-1945) had been a period of prosperity for the motion picture industry. Movie attendance soared to 85 million paid admissions per week, which had been the best financial news for filmmakers since the introduction of sound in the late 1920s. But, when the war ended, a multiplicity of problems hit Hollywood that forced a complete revolution in the production and distribution of films. The effect on the industry, naturally, had a corresponding effect on the Academy.

For many years, major studios had either owned, been owned by or been connected to vast theater chains, insuring outlets for their constant supply of product. It was an unquestioned way of life for the companies, as was block-booking, in which films were rented to theaters in multiple numbers, sold by blocks, offering a guarantee of playdates for weaker films when packaged in a block with several strong ones. However, after the war, independent theater owners filed an antitrust suit against the studios, which resulted in companies like Metro-Goldwyn-Mayer (connected to Loew's theater chain), RKO Radio, Warner Bros. and 20th Century-Fox having to divest themselves of their theater-chain affiliations, and block-booking was similarly declared illegal, both of which cut off guaranteed incomes for the studios at a time when production costs were rising dramatically. Increasing taxes on personal income also encouraged actors, writers and directors to forego studio contracts for certain advantages offered by personal incorporation. Others were dropped by studios that no longer felt financially able to pay weekly salaries except to those artists who were currently at work on a production. There was confusion and upheaval everywhere because now, for the first time, in order to obtain top talent, film companies had to offer substantial salaries and percentages of pictures on a regular basis—rather than as an occasional enticement—which upped the cost of production budgets even higher.

The sudden popularity of television also exploded during the Academy's third decade, although it had been a dark cloud hovering over the industry as early as 1939. Wartime restrictions had limited the development of television and thus forestalled development of the formidable competition for a time. However, once the postwar manufacturing of sets resumed and programming improved—added to the fact that television was *free* to viewers once the initial investment in a receiver was made—attendance in movie theaters dropped sharply. It would have been enormously advantageous for the studios to have controlled the new medium, but they were thwarted by FCC regulations in their attempts to gain a foothold; they were also thwarted by the lack of vision of many in high decision-making places.

Competition between the two giant mass media appeared for a while to be

98

CLAIRE TREVOR

"There are many jokes—like what to say if you win. Bogart's advice to me was 'Tell 'em you don't owe anybody anything—you did it all by yourself.' This was a few days before the awards when I won it for Key Largo. *He was playing it cool in his usual 'screw you' Bogart character.*

So you try to play it cool and not care too much. You go to the theater and you see almost everyone you ever worked with—everyone you've always admired—and you're thrilled and nervous.

Then it narrows down to your category. There are years between the announcement of each nominee, and then—the winner's name.

There's sort of an explosion which makes you half dead and blind. Somehow you find yourself on the stage and you begin to hear the applause—and it doesn't stop! The proof is there, with every clap of the hand, that these are my people, whom I've worked with and loved all my life and they seem to love me back!

It's hard to say anything—it's hard not to cry. All the dues paid are overwhelmingly worthwhile. It's

pure glory.

That's what it meant to 'tough guy' Bogart too when he won for African Queen. *I know because I had presented an award and was one of the first to see him when he came backstage clutching his Oscar, beaming—full of glory!"*

Claire Trevor
Best Supporting Actress, 1948

KARL MALDEN

"To achieve within yourself the definition and understanding of a specific role is a challenge that, when successfully met, brings a glowing personal satisfaction.

To have that achievement recognized by the craftsmen and actors of the motion picture industry is an unrivalled thrill.

I received an Academy Award for a supporting role in A Streetcar Named Desire *when Oscar was only twenty-four years old. I have not forgotten it. I never will!"*

Karl Malden
Best Supporting Actor, 1951

Judy Holliday, José Ferrer, Gloria Swanson, George Cukor, Celeste Holm (23rd Awards)

James Stewart, Olivia de Havilland, Broderick Crawford, Jane Wyman (22nd Awards)

HOAGY CARMICHAEL

"Naturally, I was overjoyed at receiving my Oscar for the song 'In The Cool, Cool, Cool of the Evening.' I'm not sure that my lyricist, Johny Mercer, was as overjoyed as I because he already had a vulgar display of three Oscars at his home from former years.

Possibly we didn't deserve it because we both forgot to thank Jane Wyman and Danny Kaye for singing it the night of the Oscar show, and I'm not too sure we thanked Jane and Bing for making it a hit in the picture. On this occasion Johnny and I were pulling together, but once we were worlds apart when his song 'On the Atchison, Topeka and Santa Fe' beat out my 'Ole Buttermilk Sky.' "

Hoagy Carmichael
Music (Song), 1951

JOHN GREEN

"Since November 16, 1944, the date on which the Academy of Motion Picture Arts and Sciences invited me to regular membership in its music branch, the Academy and I have been 'going steady,' having an affair, a liaison, a constant assignation — call it what you will. Like any intense romance, it has had its ups, its downs, its highs, its lows, its tears and laughter (much more of the latter than the former), its awful problems with happy resolutions to most of them, its violent lovers' quarrels with equally violent kiss-and-make-up fests.

Don't ever sell Oscar short. Carpers, critics, detractors and out-and-out slanderers come and go, but Oscar sails on as the number one, most respected, most prestigious award of its kind worldwide. For me, no doorstop, no closet item he! My fourteen nominations and my five Oscars are on unashamedly proud, conspicuous and constant display in my home and office.

Ten times I have been music director and conductor of the Awards show. Having been present at several of the shows prior to my first time on the podium, and having been appalled at the number of missed or delayed music cues, endless repetition of the same meaningless fanfare, no real connection between the music in the pit and the achievements being honored, I am the one who dreamed up the actually simple device by which the right music for the specific achievement hits instantaneously with the last syllable of the announcement of the winner — and this despite the fact that the conductor and his players have absolutely no advance inkling of any kind as to who the winner will be. The double whammy of this has been that, while being regarded as some sort of a miracle of precision, the device has been used as alleged evidence that the secrecy of the Awards is a myth and that 'of course, the conductor and the orchestra know in advance.' Year after year I have been interviewed by every branch of the media (local, national and international) about this item. I have the impression that the proper and showmanly catching of music cues is finally being recognized for its true colors and is no longer being regarded as a piece of crafty chicanery."

John Green
Music (Scoring of a Musical Picture)
1948; 1951; 1961
Producer (One-reel Short Subject), 1953
Music (Scoring of a Musical Picture:
Original or Adaptation), 1968

a standoff. In order to block television from gaining any more ground, studios refused to permit their stars to appear on any TV programs, barred the use of film clips on the air waves and stood guard over their most precious asset: the valuable backlog of feature films accumulating in the vaults since the movies began. The deadlock was finally ended when the studios, desperate for production funds and feeling the pinch at the box office, finally relented and allowed stars still under contract to appear on certain television projects. They also began to use the new medium as a publicity tool for promoting new motion pictures made for theatrical showing. Further, they began releasing older blocks of their feature films to television, and the once-distinct lines drawn between the two media began disappearing dramatically. Probably no single thing made this fact more apparent than the twenty-fifth Academy Awards presentation on March 19, 1953, when Hollywood's Oscar ceremony was broadcast for the first time on television. Movie attendance across the country that night hit a new low, but the show collected the largest single audience in television's five-year commercial history, and the Academy helped to underscore dramatically the fact the two media could possibly work together for everyone's mutual benefit.

Thanks to that first televised Awards gala, a large chunk of the public had its first opportunity to watch an Oscar ceremony in progress, and saw more major stars and Hollywood creators on their television screens than had ever been seen before. A majority of the celebrities were making their live television debuts that evening and the collection of names either participating or attending was noteworthy, including the first two ladies to win Academy Awards, Janet Gaynor and Mary Pickford, in addition to movie names such as Loretta

Walter and John Huston (21st Awards)

Young, Greer Garson, Olivia de Havilland, Joan Fontaine, Cecil B. DeMille, Gloria Swanson, Harold Lloyd, Victor McLaglen, Luise Rainer, Paul Muni, James Stewart, Ginger Rogers, Jane Darwell, Donald Crisp, Teresa Wright, Charles Coburn, Joan Crawford, Ray Milland, Fredric March, Anne Baxter, Ronald Colman, Celeste Holm, Edmund Gwenn, Jane Wyman, Claire Trevor, Broderick Crawford, Dean Jagger, Kim Hunter, Darryl F. Zanuck, Walt Disney,

Frank Capra, Jean Hersholt, Dimitri Tiomkin, Piper Laurie, Tex Ritter, John Wayne, Shirley Booth, Gloria Grahame, Bob Hope and others. It set a precedent that became an Academy tradition; the Oscar telecast became the one television show, above all others, on which even stars who usually shied from the TV medium would willingly take part, without payment, in order to support their industry.

The Academy also had another brush

RED BUTTONS

"I am proud to own an Oscar. Some of the greatest people in the history of the world never got an Oscar.

Adam — who said in the Garden of Eden, 'I've got more ribs, have you got more girls?' — never got an Oscar.

Moses — who said at the Red Sea, 'Surf's up!' — never got an Oscar.

King Solomon — who said to his thousand wives, 'For better service, take a number' — never got an Oscar.

Amelia Earhart — who said, 'Stop looking for me; see if you can find my luggage' — never got an Oscar.

I repeat: I am proud to own an Oscar."

Red Buttons
Best Supporting Actor, 1957

DELBERT MANN

"I am sure I was in a state of shock. I guess I couldn't believe it was all real. I know that I lurched into the wings without a word of thanks or appreciation to anyone.

So I appreciate the opportunity to say thanks to Paddy, to Harold Hecht, who believed in Marty *so completely, to Ernie Borgnine, Betsy Blair, Joe Mantell and the rest of that beautiful company of actors, to a truly supportive staff—Paul Helmick, Joe LaShelle, Ted Haworth and all the others — and most of all to my mentor and teacher Fred Coe, who launched me and guided me and made my whole career possible.*

I wish I had pulled myself together enough to say it then. I'm glad to say it now!"

Delbert Mann
Best Director, 1955

KIM HUNTER

"As thrilled as I was to win my Oscar, I question the possibility of choosing 'Bests' in any artistic field. But this occasion shouldn't go by without also cheering for the countless individuals who've contributed as much or more to the excellence of motion pictures without receiving the Academy's glamorous, 'official' accolade."

Kim Hunter
Best Supporting Actress, 1951

GENE KELLY

"My relations with Oscar were always distant but remain quite warm in my memory. Let me explain: When I was nominated in 1945 for Anchors Aweigh, *I was away with the U.S. Naval Air Force. When I was actually presented with a Special Oscar in 1952, 'in appreciation of his versatility as an actor, singer, director and dancer, and specifically for his brilliant achievements in the art of choreography on film,' I was making a picture in Europe for M-G-M, and was told the good news over the long-distance telephone. That explains the distance factor, but the warmth, of course, remains with me forever."*

Gene Kelly
Honorary Award, 1951

DEAN JAGGER

"They said I would have to spend money advertising. I didn't spend two cents…and when I won…it was beautiful!"

Dean Jagger
Best Supporting Actor, 1949

Humphrey Bogart, Claire Trevor (24th Awards)

Marlene Dietrich, Italian Consul Mario Ungaro (23rd Awards)

March 19, 1953: Shirley Booth and the first Oscar telecast

DANIEL TARADASH

"I am grateful indeed to the Academy for two of the most thrilling moments in my life. Each was connected with an 'Oscar,' one that I won, one that I presented. The winner was for the Best Screenplay (adaptation from another medium) for From Here to Eternity. I can't say I was surprised because the film already had won extraordinary critical acclaim and commercial success, in part because it was based on a bold book which, in 1953, just 'couldn't be made.' Still, among the other screenplays nominated in my category were those for Roman Holiday and Shane, and these were certainly magnificent works of writing. So I was on tenterhooks until Kirk Douglas announced my name. And that moment, as I'm sure every 'Oscar' winner will testify, is one you never forget.

The second 'Oscar' delight came in 1972 when, as President of the Academy, I presented a Special Honorary Academy Award (an 'Oscar' statuette) to Charlie Chaplin. To be part of the climactic moment which included the return of Chaplin to Hollywood and the Academy taking him to its heart was a thrill which is still alive in my mind and will always continue to be."

Daniel Taradash
Writing (Screenplay), 1953

FRED ZINNEMANN

"Everything went blank when I heard my name being called as the Oscar winner for directing From Here to Eternity. There seemed to be lots of applause coming from far away throughout the Pantages Theatre, and a blinding light shone on my head. I only came to when I felt someone thump my back and shout 'Congratulations.' It was a friend and fellow nominee, George Stevens, who was seated directly behind me. From then on, everything became a golden blur."

Fred Zinnemann
Best Director, 1953; 1966

DIMITRI TIOMKIN

"I remember so vividly the fun, the excitement, the hopes and the natural disappointments leading to the final days of the Academy Award presentations.

By nature I have always been a 'sucker' for awards and recognition. I like them both. They help me to forget the necessary daily routine (or process of trying to make money!). The motion picture Academy developed in its members a sense of trial and responsibility, and a desire to better themselves. Now, in my old age, I would like to express my thanks that providence gave me the chance to participate, for so many years, in the excitements, triumphs, and sorrows connected with the results of that great night of Academy Awards decisions.

God bless you all. Be happy, healthy, stubborn and reasonable."

Dimitri Tiomkin
Music (Scoring of a Dramatic or Comedy Picture), 1952; 1954; 1958
Music (Song), 1952

ALEC GUINNESS

"With the proliferation of awards in the cinema there is only one that everyone knows about and that is the Oscar, and it is the most highly prized of all."

Alec Guinness
Best Actor, 1957
Honorary Award, 1979

with political involvement as its third decade came to an end, brought about by investigations that began in 1947 of Communist infiltration into the motion picture industry, conducted by the Committee on Un-American Activities of the House of Representatives in Washington, D.C. At these hearings, nineteen members of the motion picture industry were called as witnesses, and ten of them questioned the committee's right to interrogate, after which they became known as the "Unfriendly Ten." Those "ten" were blacklisted from employment within the motion picture industry and, in June of 1950, received jail sentences of up to one year. Though the Academy stayed clear of the blacklisting controversy, either directly or implied, it became involved later when certain scripts by writers involved in the so-called Un-American investigations became eligible for Oscar consideration although their authors were denied screen credit. This was based on a 1952 agreement between individual studios and the Screen Writers Guild. To avoid further confusion, at a meeting on February 6, 1957, the Academy revised a bylaw to read:

> "Any person who, before any duly constituted Federal legislative committee or body, shall have admittted that he is a member of the Communist party (and has not since publicly renounced the party), or who shall have refused to answer whether or not he is, or was, a member of the Communist party, or shall have refused to respond to a subpoena to appear before such a committee or body, shall not be eligible for an Academy Award so long as he persists in such a refusal."

It was a gesture made in the spirit of the political times, but it proved to be an embarrassment almost at once. The following year, several Academy members, including Academy President George Seaton, urged the repeal of the rule and, on January 12, 1959, it was revoked by the Academy's Board of Governors. The Board issued an official

Marlon Brando, Bette Davis (27th Awards)

GRACE KELLY

"Being nominated for an Academy Award by your fellow actors is quite an honor; winning one is a special honor and a fantastic, though numbing, experience.

After the nominations are announced, speculation begins and the fever mounts. This period of waiting seems to bring out the best and worst in everyone connected with the business. No one nominated escapes the jaundiced eye of criticism as to this one's worth and that one's talent. Even the Academy takes it on the nose. Why all this fuss? Is it really worthwhile? How important is an Oscar anyway? So-and-so never won an award and it didn't hurt her career, etc. Besides, who needs it?

Well, I suppose no one really needs it; but, believe me, it is awfully nice to have. When my turn came, I was longing to win, and wanted to so badly that I was afraid that I would stand up no matter which name was read out. I said to Don Hartman of Paramount, who was next to me, 'Hold me down, if it isn't my name.' And when it was, I kept asking him, 'Are you sure, are you sure?' Then, all I could think was, 'Just try to get up there, Grace, without tripping.' Well, I managed to make it without tripping on my dress or the steps, but didn't do so well on the speech."

Grace Kelly
Best Actress, 1954

ALAN JAY LERNER

"I have won three Oscars. The first was for the original screenplay for An American in Paris *in 1951, and I was not present because of an illness in the family. When I was nominated for the screenplay and song for* Gigi *in 1959, I was in the arena. I was more astonished and more incredulous when I was not there than when I was there, due, I suppose, to the fact that I am ill at ease in the hot lights. I remember feeling that no one knew how I felt—but, alas, today I do not remember how I felt. But it must have been lovely."*

Alan Jay Lerner
Writing (Story and Screenplay), 1951
Writing (Screenplay, Adapted), 1958
Music (Best Song/Lyrics), 1958

ERNEST BORGNINE

"It was one bet I hoped I'd lose. I had wagered a grand total of $1.98 with Jerry Lewis, who was the host of that year's show, that I wouldn't win. If you have an opportunity to look at an old film clip of that evening, you will notice that right after Grace Kelly opened the envelope and said, 'And the winner is Ernest Borgnine,' I rushed on stage and handed Jerry something. What I handed him was 198 pennies wrapped in a red sock belonging to my daughter. Two weeks later, when my life was starting to return to normal, a telegram arrived from Jerry saying, 'I saved the money, but spent the sock!'"

Ernest Borgnine
Best Actor, 1955

EVA MARIE SAINT

"I received the Oscar and one day later gave birth to Darrel. Both fellows have been a joy in my life."

Eva Marie Saint
Best Supporting Actress, 1954

statement calling the rule "unworkable and impractical to administer and enforce." The statement brought an official end to Hollywood's mystery-shrouded "blacklist" era.

As the third decade drew to a close, something new was also tried, briefly. At the 1957 Academy Awards ceremony, for the first time, the motion picture industry itself — instead of commercial sponsors — began financing the annual Oscar telecasts, and continued to do so for the telecasts honoring 1958 and 1959 achievements.

ACADEMY PRESIDENTS, THE THIRD DECADE

May 1947–May 1948	*Jean Hersholt*
May 1948–May 1949	*Jean Hersholt*
May 1949–May 1950	*Charles Brackett*
May 1950–May 1951	*Charles Brackett*
May 1951–May 1952	*Charles Brackett*
May 1952–May 1953	*Charles Brackett*
May 1953–May 1954	*Charles Brackett*
May 1954–May 1955	*Charles Brackett*
June 1955–May 1956	*George Seaton*
June 1956–May 1957	*George Seaton*

Judy Garland, Greer Garson, Jane Wyman at 1955's experimental telecast of the Oscar nominations

SAMMY CAHN

"I really believe that I have lost more Oscars than I have won (four, count them, four) and mainly because the membership thinks I have won so many. I actually lost thirteen straight times and was starting to feel like the eternal loser when I won for the first time with Jule Styne for 'Three Coins in the Fountain.' But the 'losers' are my favorite songs and stories. I would like to ask the Board of Governors not to seat the contestants in the same category together; it really makes for over-politeness and lousy acting. One year there we were seated behind our nemesis (or is it nemesi?) the talented team of Livingston & Evans. They were nominated for 'Buttons and Bows' and Nicholas Brodszky and I for 'Be My Love.' Now the contents of the Academy Awards envelopes are the best-kept secrets of all award shows, and I always felt that if I really was the winner someone would whisper in my ear, 'Relax, it is you!' No one ever does. So you devise little tricks of trying to catch a hint of the result. That year I watched the lips of the presenter after he had opened the envelope, and sure enough his lips formed the letter 'B' so Brodszky and

I started to rise when he said, 'Buttons and Bows.' Of course we slunk back in our seats, Brodszky snarling in my ear, 'It's a fix!' I smiled my customary loser's smile and said, 'If it were a fix, we would be up there!' The last time we thought we had a winner was the night when the genius James Van Heusen and I were nominated for 'Thoroughly Modern Millie,' and the songs against us were the formidable David and Bacharach smash 'The Look of Love' and an ingenious song called 'Talk to the Animals.' Well — there we were, all the contestants seated together. Bacharach turned to me and said, 'Looks like it's you again.' I, half-lying because I did think it could be me again, said, 'No way, you and Hal have never won and this has to be your year!' And so it went, 'No it's you!' and 'No it's you!' until they announced the winner for the best scoring of a musical, Elmer Bernstein! That could only mean that Van Heusen and I had to win for "Millie" because there just wasn't that much scoring to the film. By now I am half meaning it when I say to Hal and Burt, 'You two are a cinch!' I am sure you know that the winner was 'Talk to the Animals'! Finally let me say there is no

thrill quite like the thrill of hearing the man say 'and the winner is' and walking to the stage and being handed the Oscar. My 'cahn-tempt' is total for those who refuse it and for those who use it as a doorstop! Some doorstop! Mine are proudly displayed in my home, and I carry the miniature 'Oscars' in my pocket; they are the most marvelous 'worry-beads,' and I am never without them!"

Sammy Cahn
Music (Song), 1954; 1957; 1959; 1963

JANE WYMAN

"On your twenty-first birthday, it was my great privilege to bring you to my home, having been honored by you for my performance in Johnny Belinda.

Your artistic excellence and love have lived on through the years only because of the integrity, challenge and respect you command among our peers.

I hope you continue to bring as much joy to others as you did to me."

Jane Wyman
Best Actress, 1948

Grace Kelly, William Holden and the press (27th Awards)

Cinematographer Robert Burks, Claudette Colbert (28th Awards)

FRANK SINATRA

"I've been up and down in my life more often than a roller coaster on the Fourth of July. At thirty-eight years old, I was a has-been. Sitting by a phone that wouldn't ring. Wondering what happened to all the friends who grew invisible when the music stopped. Finding out fast how tough it is to borrow money when you're all washed up.

Yes, when 1953 slid down the pole in Times Square, my only collateral was a dream. A dream to end my nightmare. And what a dream it was.

It began when I dozed off after finishing an absolutely fascinating book written by a giant, James Jones. More than a book, it was a portrait of people I knew, understood and could feel, and in it I saw myself as clearly as I see myself every morning when I shave. I was Maggio. No matter who said what, I was Maggio, and Maggio was I. And I would prove it, up there on the big screen. I would prove it no matter how many tests I was asked to make, nor what the money. I was going to become Maggio if it was the last thing I ever did in life.

It was that gifted actress Mercedes McCambridge who woke me out of the dream. She stood there on the stage of the old RKO Pantages with half the world watching. I was never in better company than on that night of March 25, 1954. Eddie Albert had been brilliant in Roman Holiday. *In* Shane, *Brandon DeWilde and Jack Palance had more than proven they were winners. And Bob Strauss had pulled off a tour de force in* Stalag 17.

But God chose to smile on me that night. Mercedes, my dear, I don't know what was written on that slip of paper, but I'll thank you eternally for saying: 'And the winner is Frank Sinatra for From Here to Eternity.'

It's quite a dream. I still have it three nights a week. I'd have it seven nights a week, but I don't go to bed four nights a week.

Talk about being 'born again.' It's the one time in my life when I had such happiness I couldn't even share it with another human being. I ducked the party, lost the crowds and took a walk. Just me and Oscar. I think I relived my entire lifetime that night as I walked up and down the streets of Beverly Hills.

Even when the cop stopped me, he couldn't bring me down to earth. He was very nice about it, although I did have to wait till his partner got out of the cruiser to assure him I was who I said I was and that I hadn't stolen the statue I was carrying.

Since that night, the roller coaster evened out and every day is the Fourth of July.

Yes, I started out the third decade of the Academy of Motion Picture Arts and Sciences as the 'man least likely' and closed it out as a grateful human being, given a second shot at life.

As far as my thoughts are now in retrospect, I recall presenting a Special Oscar to Cary Grant on behalf of the Academy in 1969. In his gracious acceptance, Cary began by saying, 'Ours is a collaborative business.' True. Very true. We all help each other.

Just as armies of grips and boom men, lighting men and extras helped me on the set of Eternity *in 1953, so too, now on motion picture sets all over the world, people in our industry are helping other people in our industry. Just as Burt Lancaster, Monty Cliff, Deborah Kerr, Donna Reed, Ernie Borgnine and so many other*

Anna Magnani

warm people pushed me up on that stage of the Pantages by pushing me harder on the set in Hawaii, other artists continue in the Fraternity of Helpers which has long been the motion picture industry.

God bless you all."

Frank Sinatra, Best Supporting Actor, 1953
Jean Hersholt Humanitarian Award, 1970

EDMOND O'BRIEN

"If an actor does not have the right words, he'll never win anything.

I was lucky enough in The Barefoot Contessa *to have my words written, produced and directed by one of the great talents of our time, Mr. Joseph Mankiewicz. He also wrote* All About Eve, *etc., etc.*

One year before The Barefoot Contessa, *Joe Mankiewicz had directed me in his production of Shakespeare's* Julius Caesar.

Joe Mankiewicz actually wrote the part in Contessa *with me in mind. He sent me the script from Connecticut. I read it, called him and said, 'Yes!'*

It takes great writing and directing to win an Aca-

demy Award. I had them both, thanks to Joe Mankiewicz.

For me, an award from the Academy of Motion Picture Arts and Sciences is the most meaningful award in the film world. I have won other awards but the Academy Award is the one I treasure most."

Edmond O'Brien
Best Supporting Actor, 1954

GLORIA GRAHAME

"My deepest feeling about the Oscar is that the people with whom I worked liked what I did."

Gloria Grahame
Best Supporting Actress, 1952

MERCEDES McCAMBRIDGE

*"Some women have a sable,
Some women have a yacht,
But my lovely golden Oscar
Not many women have got —
And I am ever grateful."*

Mercedes McCambridge
Best Supporting Actress, 1949

FRED ASTAIRE

"I am of course delighted to have received my Honorary Academy Award given to me in 1949. Also to have been nominated for Best Supporting Actor in 1975.

In my opinion the whole Oscar thing is an exciting and inspiring experience for both the public and the performers."

Fred Astaire
Special Award, 1949

YUL BRYNNER

"My advice:

1. Be content to be just nominated.

2. When your name is called out, make sure you don't stumble on the way to the stage, which would entitle you only to a cheap laugh.

3. Never prepare an acceptance speech until you have your hands firmly on the Oscar, otherwise it will be haunting you in the years to come as an unfulfilled dream."

Yul Brynner
Best Actor, 1956

Academy Secretary Johnny Green belatedly presents Vivien Leigh her 1951 award in London

Miyoshi Umeki, Red Buttons (30th Awards)

JO VAN FLEET

"I have very vivid and warm feelings about that eventful night that I won the Oscar for East of Eden. I believe the voting was something different at that time. I know I was competing against myself for the nominations for I'll Cry Tomorrow and East of Eden.

I was working at Paramount at the time on Gunfight at the O.K. Corral. Edith Head kindly helped me get an evening gown, stole, gloves, etc. I was given a hair dryer in my dressing room, where I made myself up, did my own hair and dressed. I was picked up by Helen Rose's limousine and was escorted to the Awards ceremony by Sydney Guilleroff. The nominees for Best Supporting Actress were seated near the rear of the theater. When my name was called as having won, I simply did not hear it! Mr. Guilleroff said, poking me in the ribs, 'Go on. You won!' And I ran all the way down the aisle and up the steps. I was presented the Oscar by Edmond O'Brien, who was crying, and that almost made me cry too. (I did later.)

As I said, it was totally unexpected—my winning that night—and I took great pride in the fact that I did not put an advertisement in the trade papers, though I recall being asked to by some reporters who warned me that if I didn't advertise I had no chance of winning!!

Later, Jerry Lewis kindly gave me a film clip of my part of the ceremony, which I still have in my possession.

It was a great night, a beautiful experience and one I shall never forget."

Jo Van Fleet
Best Supporting Actress, 1955

DOROTHY MALONE

"CARRY ON!

At times when things seem perfect all about us.
And Lady Luck grants us a lucky star,
We must try to keep these memories forever,
For things cannot remain just as they are.

There are times when all our universe seems hopeless,
And all our hopes and dreams are smashed to bits.
It is then we have to keep our wits about us,
And strive against all odds to keep those wits!

For if all our happy moments were unending,
We wouldn't know the heartbreak when they're gone,
And learn to grit our teeth at disappointment—
To hold our head up high and carry on!"

Dorothy Malone
Best Supporting Actress, 1956

JACK LEMMON

"With whatever problems one faces in trying to decide which of five different performances is the best, there is still no question that the fortunate winner is receiving a very high honor indeed.

But there are many who may justifiably feel that the nomination itself is an equal honor.

Though the craft of acting is basically geared to a general audience acceptance, there is still the understandable and special pride that the actor feels when his peers deem his efforts to be worthy of an Oscar.

Long may that joy persist."

Jack Lemmon
Best Supporting Actor, 1955
Best Actor, 1973

Elizabeth Taylor, Walt Disney (26th Awards)

SIDNEY SHELDON

"In show business, where even the biggest names go through up and down periods of being 'hot' and 'cold,' there is one name that for the past sixty years has always been 'hot' — Oscar. Everybody wants him. Comes each January, studios spend millions of dollars in trade advertising, trying to coax Oscar onto their trophy shelves. It is rumored that certain stars would kill to get him. Myths and rumors surround Oscar: If you win him you'll never want again; if you win him, you'll never work again. It's all politics. Oscar can be bought. Oscar night is a glamorous, rigged spectacle. The nominees know in advance who's going to win. The myths are exactly that. Myths.

It is true Oscar winners do go through dry spells sometimes, but then, so do the losers. You can't advertise your way to an Oscar, nor is he for sale. He is awarded solely by the vote of one's peers.

As for knowing in advance who the winners are, I can refute that from my own experience. When a screenplay I wrote was nominated I was so sure I would not win that I did not even bother to think about

an acceptance speech. When my name was called, I was in a state of shock. I mumbled some ridiculous acceptance speech, grabbed Oscar and fled. No, the winners don't know in advance. The suspense of the evening is legitimate.

Over the years, since the evening I received my Oscar, I have been working on the acceptance speech I would like to have given. It is witty and warm, touching and modest, yet filled with sincerity. It begins, 'Ladies and gentlemen…' "

Sidney Sheldon
Writing (Original Screenplay), 1947

ELIA KAZAN

"I resigned from the Academy because I don't believe in lists, ten bests, awards and so on. The contrary fact remains that I sure as hell enjoyed getting my two Oscars. I wish the organization would become not less, but more active, actually do more about the Motion Picture Arts and Sciences. Or does it and I don't know about it?

Academy means Academy. The only thing I know

about the organization is the show it puts on once a year, which I watch with the rest of the movie fans and gossip hounds. It's sometimes fun, sometimes silly and every once in a while grand. I don't think the Academy is serious enough. At least whatever it has tried to do of more worth has never filtered down to me. Why hasn't it?"

Elia Kazan
Best Director, 1947; 1954
Honorary Award, 1998

IRENE SHARAFF

"I, of course, appreciate very much indeed the nominations and Oscars awarded me by the Academy and am glad for this opportunity to thank warmly the members of the Academy for noticing my work. It is recognition also of the many people in the costume departments and workrooms who worked with me to produce the results on film. Many, many happy returns to all of them, too!"

Irene Sharaff
Costume Design (Color),
1951; 1956; 1961; 1963
Costume Design (Black-and-white), 1966

1948
The Twenty-First Year

After two Oscar presentations at the Shrine Auditorium, the 1948 awards party on March 24, 1949, was given at the Academy's own theater, a 985-seat house. The primary reason for the change of locales (and the loss of some 5,750 extra seats at the Shrine) was because the major Hollywood studios—M-G-M, 20th Century-Fox, Warner Bros., Paramount and RKO Radio—had withdrawn their financial support of the awards in order to remove rumors that they had been trying to exert their influence on voters. The new, shrunken seating capacity made it impossible to accommodate more than a fraction of those who hoped to attend, and that last-minute withdrawal of studio support had left no time for Academy officials to raise the needed funds to rent a larger location.

But the show went on, produced for the Academy by William Dozier, with Johnny Green as musical director and Robert Montgomery as master of ceremonies; presenters included the previous year's winners (Ronald Colman, Loretta Young, Edmund Gwenn, Celeste Holm) plus new screen beauties like Ava Gardner, Elizabeth Taylor and Arlene Dahl. Warner Bros. dominated the year's nominations, with three of its films—*Johnny Belinda, The Treasure of the Sierra Madre* and *Key Largo*—pulling in a total of fifteen nominations.

But England clearly dominated Oscar itself. Two British-made imports, *Hamlet* and *The Red Shoes,* won six of the night's awards, including Oscars to *Hamlet* as best picture and to Laurence Olivier as best actor. Douglas Fairbanks, Jr. accepted the award for Olivier, who was in England.

Warner Bros. ultimately won five awards: Jane Wyman in *Johnny Belinda* as best actress; Claire Trevor in *Key Largo* as best supporting actress; and three awards for *Treasure,* including two for John Huston (as best director and for his screenplay) and one for his father, Walter Huston, as best supporting actor. Said the elder Huston in his acceptance speech: "Many, many years ago, I raised a son and I said to him, 'If you ever become a writer or director, please find a good part for your old man.'" Said Miss Trevor: "May my three sons grow up to give their old lady a part...."

In their constant attempt to clarify awards categories, and extend honors where justified, Academy officials decided in 1948 to—at last—honor the field of motion picture costume design, an area long neglected by Oscar. Nominees were separately classified between color films and those in black-and-white, and the first winners were Roger K. Furse for *Hamlet* (black-and-white costume design) and Dorothy Jeakins and Karinska for *Joan of Arc* (color costume design).

(right) **The Treasure of the Sierra Madre** *(Warner Bros.; produced by Henry Blanke) won Oscars for* **Best Director:** **John Huston** *and (pictured with Humphrey Bogart and Tim Holt)* **Best Supporting Actor:** **Walter Huston** *as Howard, a grizzled old-time prospector of an ill-fated expedition for gold into the treacherous Sierra Madre terrain in Mexico. Never before had a father-son team been similarly honored by the Academy; son John also received an Oscar for* Treasure's *best screenplay. Thirty-seven years later, John also directed his daughter Anjelica into an Oscar, with 1985's* Prizzi's Honor.

Best Picture: Hamlet *(Rank-Two Cities/Universal-International release; produced and directed by Laurence Olivier) and* **Best Actor: Laurence Olivier** *as the Prince of Denmark (above, dueling with Terence Morgan on the left)* in Hamlet. *Not until the dynamic Olivier came along did the movie medium seem a very advantageous place for Shakespeare's plays, although over 66 motion pictures had been based on his works since* Macbeth *in the silent days of 1905.* *Olivier seemed to have the key: he used the Bard as the basis for a movie that moved, and turned his* Hamlet *not only into a first-rate suspense thriller but also into the first film from a foreign land to win the Academy's best picture award.*

Best Actress: Jane Wyman *as Belinda McDonald (right, menaced by Stephen McNally) in* Johnny Belinda *(Warner Bros.; directed by Jean Negulesco). As a stage play,* Johnny Belinda *had not been a success, but a movie adaptation produced by Henry Blanke was one of 1948's most popular tickets, primarily due to Jane Wyman's pivotal performance as a deaf-mute farm girl in rural Nova Scotia who is befriended by a country doctor (Lew Ayres),and helped through the birth of an illegitimate son whom she names* Johnny. *Throughout the film's 103-minute running time, she didn't speak a word, and later in receiving her Oscar, she said, "I accept this very gratefully for keeping my mouth shut. I think I'll do it again...."*

Nominations 1948

***Best Supporting Actress:* Claire Trevor** *as Gaye Dawn in* Key Largo *(Warner Bros.; directed by John Huston). Long a Hollywood workhorse, and always a favorite with moviegoers, Claire Trevor won her Award playing the whiskey-soaked mistress of a cruel gangster (Edward G. Robinson, above with Trevor) on a rampage in Florida. She was also nominated for* Dead End *in 1937, and in 1954 for* The High and the Mighty.

MOTION PICTURE

*HAMLET, Rank-Two Cities, U-I (British). Produced by Laurence Olivier.
JOHNNY BELINDA, Warner Bros. Produced by Jerry Wald.
THE RED SHOES, Rank-Archers, Eagle-Lion (British). Produced by Michael Powell and Emeric Pressburger.
THE SNAKE PIT, 20th Century-Fox. Produced by Anatole Litvak and Robert Bassler.
THE TREASURE OF THE SIERRA MADRE, Warner Bros. Produced by Henry Blanke.

ACTOR

LEW AYRES in *Johnny Belinda*, Warner Bros.
MONTGOMERY CLIFT in *The Search*, Praesens Films, M-G-M (Swiss).
DAN DAILEY in *When My Baby Smiles at Me*, 20th Century-Fox.
*LAURENCE OLIVIER in *Hamlet*, Rank-Two Cities, U-I (British).
CLIFTON WEBB in *Sitting Pretty*, 20th Century-Fox.

ACTRESS

INGRID BERGMAN in *Joan of Arc*, Wanger-Sierra, RKO Radio.
OLIVIA DE HAVILLAND in *The Snake Pit*, 20th Century-Fox.
IRENE DUNNE in *I Remember Mama*, RKO Radio.
BARBARA STANWYCK in *Sorry, Wrong Number*, Wallis, Paramount.
*JANE WYMAN in *Johnny Belinda*, Warner Bros.

SUPPORTING ACTOR

CHARLES BICKFORD in *Johnny Belinda*, Warner Bros.
JOSÉ FERRER in *Joan of Arc*, Sierra, RKO Radio.
OSCAR HOMOLKA in *I Remember Mama*, RKO Radio.
*WALTER HUSTON in *The Treasure of the Sierra Madre*, Warner Bros.
CECIL KELLAWAY in *The Luck of the Irish*, 20th Century-Fox.

SUPPORTING ACTRESS

BARBARA BEL GEDDES in *I Remember Mama*, RKO Radio.
ELLEN CORBY in *I Remember Mama*, RKO Radio.
AGNES MOOREHEAD in *Johnny Belinda*, Warner Bros.
JEAN SIMMONS in *Hamlet*, Rank-Two Cities, U-I (British).
*CLAIRE TREVOR in *Key Largo*, Warner Bros.

DIRECTING

HAMLET, Rank-Two Cities, U-I (British). Laurence Olivier.
JOHNNY BELINDA, Warner Bros. Jean Negulesco.
THE SEARCH, M-G-M (Swiss). Fred Zinnemann.
THE SNAKE PIT, 20th Century-Fox. Anatole Litvak.
*THE TREASURE OF THE SIERRA MADRE, Warner Bros. John Huston.

CINEMATOGRAPHY

(Black-and-White)

A FOREIGN AFFAIR, Paramount. Charles B. Lang, Jr.
I REMEMBER MAMA, RKO Radio. Nicholas Musuraca.
JOHNNY BELINDA, Warner Bros. Ted McCord.
*THE NAKED CITY, Hellinger, U-I. William Daniels.
PORTRAIT OF JENNIE, Selznick Releasing Organization. Joseph August.

(Color)

GREEN GRASS OF WYOMING, 20th Century-Fox. Charles G. Clarke.
*JOAN OF ARC, Wanger-Sierra, RKO Radio. Joseph Valentine, William V. Skall and Winton Hoch.
THE LOVES OF CARMEN, Beckworth, Columbia. William Snyder.
THE THREE MUSKETEERS, M-G-M. Robert Planck.

WRITING

(New classifications)

(Motion Picture Story)

THE LOUISIANA STORY, Robert Flaherty, Lopert. Frances Flaherty and Robert Flaherty.
THE NAKED CITY, Hellinger, U-I. Malvin Wald.
RED RIVER, Hawks-Monterey, UA. Borden Chase.
THE RED SHOES, Rank-Archers, Eagle-Lion (British). Emeric Pressburger.
*THE SEARCH, M-G-M (Swiss). Richard Schweizer and David Wechsler.

(Screenplay)

A FOREIGN AFFAIR, Paramount. Charles Brackett, Billy Wilder and Richard L. Breen.

JOHNNY BELINDA, Warner Bros. Irmgard Von Cube and Allen Vincent.
THE SEARCH, M-G-M (Swiss). Richard Schweizer and David Wechsler.
THE SNAKE PIT, 20th Century-Fox. Frank Partos and Millen Brand.
*THE TREASURE OF THE SIERRA MADRE, Warner Bros. John Huston.

ART DIRECTION-SET DECORATION

(Black-and-White)

*HAMLET, Rank-Two Cities, U-I (British). Roger K. Furse; Carmen Dillon.
JOHNNY BELINDA, Warner Bros. Robert Haas; William Wallace.

(Color)

JOAN OF ARC, Wanger-Sierra, RKO Radio. Richard Day; Edwin Casey Roberts and Joseph Kish.
*THE RED SHOES, Rank-Archers, Eagle-Lion (British). Hein Heckroth, Arthur Lawson.

COSTUME DESIGN

(New category)

(Black-and-White)

B.F.'S DAUGHTER, M-G-M. Irene.
*HAMLET, Rank-Two Cities, U-I (British). Roger K. Furse.

(Color)

THE EMPEROR WALTZ, Paramount. Edith Head and Gile Steele.
*JOAN OF ARC, Wanger-Sierra, RKO Radio. Dorothy Jeakins and Karinska.

SOUND RECORDING

JOHNNY BELINDA, Warner Bros. Warner Bros. Sound Department; Col. Nathan O. Levinson, sound director.
MOONRISE, Republic. Republic Sound Department; Daniel J. Bloomberg, sound director.
*THE SNAKE PIT, 20th Century-Fox. 20th Century-Fox Sound Department; Thomas T. Moulton, sound director.

FILM EDITING

JOAN OF ARC, Wanger-Sierra, RKO Radio. Frank Sullivan.
JOHNNY BELINDA, Warner Bros. David Weisbart.
*THE NAKED CITY, Hellinger, U-I. Paul Weatherwax.
RED RIVER, Hawks-Monterey, UA. Christian Nyby.
THE RED SHOES, Rank-Archers, Eagle-Lion (British). Reginald Mills.

SPECIAL EFFECTS

DEEP WATERS, 20th Century-Fox. Ralph Hammeras, Fred Sersen, Edward Snyder and Roger Heman.
*PORTRAIT OF JENNIE, Selznick Releasing Organization. Paul Eagler, J. McMillan Johnson, Russell Shearman, Clarence Slifer, Charles Freeman and James G. Stewart.

SHORT SUBJECTS

(Cartoons)

*THE LITTLE ORPHAN, M-G-M (Tom & Jerry). Fred Quimby, producer.
MICKEY AND THE SEAL, Disney, RKO Radio. (Pluto). Walt Disney, producer.
MOUSE WRECKERS, Warner Bros. (Looney Tunes). Edward Selzer, producer.
ROBIN HOODLUM, UPA, Columbia. (Fox & Crow). United Productions of America, producer.
TEA FOR TWO HUNDRED, Disney, RKO Radio. (Donald Duck). Walt Disney, producer.

(One-reel)

ANNIE WAS A WONDER, M-G-M. (John Nesbitt Passing Parade). Herbert Moulton, producer.
CINDERELLA HORSE, Warner Bros. (Sports Parade). Gordon Hollingshead, producer.
SO YOU WANT TO BE ON THE RADIO, Warner Bros. (Joe McDoakes). Gordon Hollingshead, producer.
*SYMPHONY OF A CITY, 20th Century-Fox. (Movietone Specialty). Edmund H. Reek, producer.
YOU CAN'T WIN, M-G-M (Pete Smith Specialty). Pete Smith, producer.

(Two-reel)

CALGARY STAMPEDE, Warner Bros. (Technicolor Special). Gordon Hollingshead, producer.
GOING TO BLAZES, M-G-M. (Special). Herbert Morgan, producer.
SAMBA-MANIA, Paramount. (Musical Parade). Harry Grey, producer.
*SEAL ISLAND, Disney, RKO Radio. (True-Life Adventure). Walt Disney, producer.
SNOW CAPERS, U-I. (Special Series). Thomas Mead, producer.

The Red Shoes *(Rank-Archers, released by Eagle-Lion; produced and directed by Michael Powell and Emeric Pressburger)* starred Moira Shearer *(right, dancing* The Red Shoes Ballet *with Robert Helpmann and Leonide Massine) and won Oscars for color art direction and best score of a dramatic or comedy picture. Like* Hamlet, *it was a British-made stunner which elevated the movies' postwar image and found great favor with audiences and with Hollywood's Academy membership.*

Joan of Arc *(RKO Radio; produced by Walter Wanger) was the first film to win an Oscar for color costume design; prior to 1948, the field of costume design had not been honored by the Academy.* Joan of Arc *also received a special award for producer Wanger, and an Academy Award for color cinematography. It starred Ingrid Bergman (right) as the Maid of Orleans who effected the coronation of Charles VII in 1429 amid court intrigue and conspiracy.*

DOCUMENTARY

(Short Subjects)
HEART TO HEART, Fact Film Organization. Herbert Morgan, producer.
OPERATION VITTLES, U.S. Army Air Force.
*TOWARD INDEPENDENCE, U.S. Army.

(Features)
THE QUIET ONE, Mayer-Burstyn. Janice Loeb, producer.
*THE SECRET LAND, U.S. Navy, M-G-M. O.O. Dull, producer.

MUSIC

(Song)
*BUTTONS AND BOWS (*The Paleface,* Paramount), Music and Lyrics by Jay Livingston and Ray Evans.
FOR EVERY MAN THERE'S A WOMAN (*Casbah,* Marston, U-I); Music by Harold Arlen. Lyrics by Leo Robin.
IT'S MAGIC (*Romance on the High Seas,* Warner Bros.); Music by Jule Styne. Lyrics by Sammy Cahn.
THIS IS THE MOMENT (*That Lady In Ermine,* 20th Century-Fox); Music by Frederick Hollander. Lyrics by Leo Robin.
THE WOODY WOODPECKER SONG (*Wet Blanket Policy,* Lantz, UA Cartoon); Music and Lyrics by Ramey Idriss and George Tibbles.

(Scoring of a Dramatic or Comedy Picture)
HAMLET, Rank-Two Cities, U-I (British). William Walton.
JOAN OF ARC, Wanger-Sierra, RKO Radio. Hugo Friedhofer.
JOHNNY BELINDA, Warner Bros. Max Steiner.
*THE RED SHOES, Rank-Archers, Eagle-Lion (British). Brian Easdale.
THE SNAKE PIT, 20th Century-Fox. Alfred Newman.

(Scoring of a Musical Picture)
*EASTER PARADE, M-G-M. Johnny Green and Roger Edens.
THE EMPEROR WALTZ, Paramount. Victor Young.
THE PIRATE, M-G-M. Lennie Hayton.
ROMANCE ON THE HIGH SEAS, Warner Bros. Ray Heindorf.
WHEN MY BABY SMILES AT ME, 20th Century-Fox. Alfred Newman.

SPECIAL AWARDS
TO *MONSIEUR VINCENT* (French)—voted by the Academy Board of Governors as the most outstanding foreign language film released in the United States during 1948. (statuette)
TO IVAN JANDL, for the outstanding juvenile performance of 1948 in *The Search.* (miniature statuette)
TO SID GRAUMAN, master showman, who raised the standard of exhibition of motion pictures. (statuette)
TO ADOLPH ZUKOR, a man who has been called the father of the feature film in America, for his services to the industry over a period of forty years. (statuette)
TO WALTER WANGER for distinguished service to the industry in adding to its moral stature in the world community by his production of the picture *Joan of Arc.* (statuette)

1948 IRVING G. THALBERG MEMORIAL AWARD
TO JERRY WALD

SCIENTIFIC OR TECHNICAL

CLASS I (statuette)
None.

CLASS II (plaque)
VICTOR CACCIALANZA, MAURICE AYERS and the PARAMOUNT STUDIO SET CONSTRUCTION DEPARTMENT for the development and application of "Paralite," a new lightweight plaster process for set construction.
NICK KALTEN, LOUIS J. WITTI and the 20TH CENTURY-FOX STUDIO MECHANICAL EFFECTS DEPARTMENT for a process of preserving and flame-proofing foliage.

CLASS III (citation)
MARTY MARTIN, JACK LANNON, RUSSELL SHEARMAN and the RKO RADIO STUDIO SPECIAL EFFECTS DEPARTMENT;
A.J. MORAN and the WARNER BROS. STUDIO ELECTRICAL DEPARTMENT.

*INDICATES WINNER

111

In the late 1940s, Hollywood's entire approach to filmmaking began changing. Studios dropped long-term star contracts, the influence of television was growing, costs were being pared, new postwar personalities were attracting attention and stark semi-documentary films were gaining popularity with audiences.

One thing didn't change: the Academy's appreciation of quality films. On March 23, 1950, at the 1949 Academy Awards presentation, the most honored picture of the year was Paramount's *The Heiress* with four awards, including one to Olivia de Havilland as best actress, the second time she had been so honored in three years. Columbia's stark, powerful *All the King's Men* received three awards (best picture, Broderick Crawford as best actor, newcomer Mercedes McCambridge as best supporting actress) and *A Letter to Three Wives* won two, both of them for Joseph L. Mankiewicz (as best director, and author of best screenplay).

Best supporting actor was Dean Jagger in *12 O'Clock High,* a film also honored for its sound recording. The booming war story *Battleground* won two awards: one for Robert Pirosh's story and screenplay, and one for Paul Vogel's black-and-white cinematography.

The site for the awards was moved again, for the third time in four years, this time to the 2,812-seat RKO Pantages Theatre, the biggest motion picture house in Hollywood. The ceremony remained there for the next eleven years. Paul Douglas, a long-time stage veteran but new Hollywood name via Mankiewicz' *A Letter to Three Wives,* was the evening's M.C., and Johnny Green turned over his musical baton to Robert Emmett Dolan and was sole producer of the Academy show.

Two other special awards provided the evening with sizeable impact, primarily because they went to a pair of screen innovators who had never been honored before, both of whom were helpful in keeping the public on the big screen and away from that (supposedly) threatening television box. One went to Fred Astaire; it was presented by Ginger Rogers, with whom he had been reunited after a ten-year absence in 1949's *The Barkleys of Broadway.* The other special award went to Cecil B. DeMille for his 37 years of screen showmanship; *Samson and Delilah,* his first new film in two years, had not been released in Los Angeles in time for 1949 awards eligibility, but it was helpful in bringing public focus to a grand old filmmaker.

THE PULITZER PRIZE WINNING NOVEL BECOMES A VITAL, VERY GREAT MOTION PICTURE

COLUMBIA PICTURES presents
ROBERT ROSSEN'S PRODUCTION of
ALL THE KING'S MEN
BASED UPON THE PULITZER PRIZE NOVEL "ALL THE KING'S MEN" by ROBERT PENN WARREN

Best Picture: **All the King's Men** *(Columbia; produced and directed by Robert Rossen) and (at right)* **Best Actor:** **Broderick Crawford** *as Willie Stark and* **Best Supporting Actress:** **Mercedes McCambridge** *as Sadie Burke in* All the King's Men. *A bold and blunt drama based on Robert Penn Warren's Pulitzer Prize novel about a corrupt political boss who bore a close resemblance to Louisiana's powerful Huey Long, stopped by an assassin's bullet in 1935. It was a first film for Mercedes McCambridge, a veteran radio actress, and a bellringer for Crawford, who'd made three dozen films before but never had such a meaty role to play. The cast included Joanne Dru, John Ireland, John Derek and Shepperd Strudwick; Rossen also wrote the screenplay.*

Best Actress: **Olivia de Havilland** *as Catherine Sloper (above, with Ralph Richardson) in* The Heiress *(Paramount; directed by William Wyler). The Heiress was derived via a Broadway play from Henry James' novel* Washington Square, *about an awkward girl of the 1850s dominated by her wealthy father and bitterly disillusioned by a handsome fortune hunter, on whom she finally gets sweet revenge. Olivia de Havilland brilliantly played the multi-faceted woman and won the second Academy Award of her career; the picture itself also won more Oscars than any other 1949 film, including ones for art direction (black-and-white), costume design (black-and-white) and music score.*

The Barkleys of Broadway *saw Rogers and Astaire teamed together for the first time in a decade, in the tenth and last of their co-starring vehicles. Not the most distinguished picture in the series,* Barkleys *was nevertheless the only one of the ten shot in color, and though it received not a single music nomination it provided the occasion for a special "career" Oscar for the incomparable Fred Astaire—many of whose finest films were still ahead of him.*

She Wore a Yellow Ribbon (RKO Radio; directed by John Ford) was a big-boned and Technicolored western with John Wayne as a United States Cavalry captain leading troops through dangerous Indian territory. It won Winton Hoch the Oscar for color cinematography, and remains one of the best-liked films in the Ford-Wayne list of collaborations.

Best Supporting Actor: Dean Jagger as Major Stovall (above, with Gregory Peck) in 12 O'Clock High (20th Century-Fox; directed by Henry King). A personal production of Darryl F. Zanuck, 12 O'Clock High was a psychological drama of World War II, dealing with problems inside an American bomber base in England; Jagger was a middle-aged major assigned to the base which Peck—as a young general—turns into an inspired, forceful unit.

Best Director: Joseph L. Mankiewicz for A Letter to Three Wives (20th Century-Fox; produced by Sol Siegel) presented Ann Sothern, Linda Darnell and Jeanne Crain as three wives who receive a letter from a local friend informing them she has just run off with the husband of one. But which one? An intriguing premise, artfully handled, A Letter also won a second 1949 Academy Award for Mankiewicz: as author of the year's best screenplay. The following year, with 1950's All about Eve, he again won in the same two Oscar categories.

Nominations 1949

MOTION PICTURE

*ALL THE KING'S MEN, Rossen, Columbia. Produced by Robert Rossen.
BATTLEGROUND, M-G-M. Produced by Dore Schary.
THE HEIRESS, Paramount. Produced by William Wyler.
A LETTER TO THREE WIVES, 20th Century-Fox. Produced by Sol C. Siegel.
12 O'CLOCK HIGH, 20th Century-Fox. Produced by Darryl F. Zanuck.

ACTOR

*BRODERICK CRAWFORD in All the King's Men, Rossen, Columbia.
KIRK DOUGLAS in Champion, Kramer, UA.
GREGORY PECK in 12 O'Clock High, 20th Century-Fox.
RICHARD TODD in The Hasty Heart, Warner Bros.
JOHN WAYNE in Sands of Iwo Jima, Republic.

ACTRESS

JEANNE CRAIN in Pinky, 20th Century-Fox.
*OLIVIA DE HAVILLAND in The Heiress, Paramount.
SUSAN HAYWARD in My Foolish Heart, Goldwyn, RKO Radio.
DEBORAH KERR in Edward, My Son, M-G-M.
LORETTA YOUNG in Come to the Stable, 20th Century-Fox.

SUPPORTING ACTOR

JOHN IRELAND in All the King's Men, Columbia.
*DEAN JAGGER in 12 O'Clock High, 20th Century-Fox.
ARTHUR KENNEDY in Champion, Kramer, UA.
RALPH RICHARDSON in The Heiress, Paramount.
JAMES WHITMORE in Battleground, M-G-M.

SUPPORTING ACTRESS

ETHEL BARRYMORE in Pinky, 20th Century-Fox.
CELESTE HOLM in Come to the Stable, 20th Century-Fox.
ELSA LANCHESTER in Come to the Stable, 20th Century-Fox.
*MERCEDES McCAMBRIDGE in All the King's Men, Rossen, Columbia.
ETHEL WATERS in Pinky, 20th Century-Fox.

DIRECTING

ALL THE KING'S MEN, Rossen, Columbia. Robert Rossen.
BATTLEGROUND, M-G-M. William A. Wellman.
THE FALLEN IDOL, London Films, SRO (British). Carol Reed.
THE HEIRESS, Paramount. William Wyler.
*A LETTER TO THREE WIVES, 20th Century-Fox. Joseph L. Mankiewicz.

ART DIRECTION-SET DECORATION

(Black-and-White)

COME TO THE STABLE, 20th Century-Fox. Lyle Wheeler and Joseph C. Wright; Thomas Little and Paul S. Fox.
*THE HEIRESS, Paramount. John Meehan and Harry Horner; Emile Kuri.
MADAME BOVARY, M-G-M. Cedric Gibbons and Jack Martin Smith; Edwin B. Willis and Richard A. Pefferle.

(Color)

ADVENTURES OF DON JUAN, Warner Bros. Edward Carrere; Lyle Reifsnider.
*LITTLE WOMEN, M-G-M. Cedric Gibbons and Paul Groesse; Edwin B. Willis and Jack D. Moore.
SARABAND, Rank-Ealing, Eagle-Lion (British). Jim Morahan, William Kellner and Michael Relph.

WRITING

(New classifications)

(Motion Picture Story)

COME TO THE STABLE, 20th Century-Fox. Clare Booth Luce.
IT HAPPENS EVERY SPRING, 20th Century-Fox. Shirley W. Smith and Valentine Davies.
SANDS OF IWO JIMA, Republic. Harry Brown.
*THE STRATTON STORY, M-G-M. Douglas Morrow.
WHITE HEAT, Warner Bros. Virginia Kellogg.

(Screenplay)

ALL THE KING'S MEN, Rossen, Columbia. Robert Rossen.
THE BICYCLE THIEF, De Sica, Mayer-Burstyn (Italian). Cesare Zavattini.
CHAMPION, Kramer, UA. Carl Foreman.

THE FALLEN IDOL, London Films, SRO (British). Graham Greene.
*A LETTER TO THREE WIVES, 20th Century-Fox. Joseph L. Mankiewicz.

(Story and Screenplay)

*BATTLEGROUND, M-G-M. Robert Pirosh.
JOLSON SINGS AGAIN, Columbia. Sidney Buchman.
PAISAN, Rossellini, Mayer-Burstyn (Italian). Alfred Hayes, Federico Fellini, Sergio Amidei, Marcello Pagliero and Roberto Rossellini.
PASSPORT TO PIMLICO, Rank-Ealing, Eagle-Lion (British). T.E.B. Clarke.
THE QUIET ONE, Film Documents, Mayer-Burstyn. Helen Levitt, Janice Loeb and Sidney Meyers.

CINEMATOGRAPHY

(Black-and-White)

*BATTLEGROUND, M-G-M. Paul C. Vogel.
CHAMPION, Kramer, UA. Frank Planer.
COME TO THE STABLE, 20th Century-Fox. Joseph LaShelle.
THE HEIRESS, Paramount. Leo Tover.
PRINCE OF FOXES, 20th Century-Fox. Leon Shamroy.

(Color)

THE BARKLEYS OF BROADWAY, M-G-M. Harry Stradling.
JOLSON SINGS AGAIN, Columbia. William Snyder.
LITTLE WOMEN, M-G-M. Robert Planck and Charles Schoenbaum.
SAND, 20th Century-Fox. Charles G. Clarke.
*SHE WORE A YELLOW RIBBON, Argosy, RKO Radio. Winton Hoch.

SOUND RECORDING

ONCE MORE, MY DARLING, U-I. Universal-International Sound Department; Leslie I. Carey, sound director.
SANDS OF IWO JIMA, Republic. Republic Sound Department; Daniel J. Bloomberg, sound director.
*12 O'CLOCK HIGH, 20th Century-Fox. 20th Century-Fox Sound Department; Thomas T. Moulton, sound director.

FILM EDITING

ALL THE KING'S MEN, Rossen, Columbia. Robert Parrish and Al Clark.
BATTLEGROUND, M-G-M. John Dunning.
*CHAMPION, Kramer, UA. Harry Gerstad.
SANDS OF IWO JIMA, Republic. Richard L. Van Enger.
THE WINDOW, RKO Radio. Frederic Knudtson.

SPECIAL EFFECTS

*MIGHTY JOE YOUNG, Cooper, RKO Radio.
TULSA, Wanger, Eagle-Lion.

MUSIC

(Song)

*BABY, IT'S COLD OUTSIDE (Neptune's Daughter, M-G-M); Music and Lyrics by Frank Loesser.
IT'S A GREAT FEELING (It's a Great Feeling, Warner Bros.); Music by Jule Styne. Lyrics by Sammy Cahn.
LAVENDER BLUE (So Dear to My Heart, Disney, RKO Radio); Music by Eliot Daniel. Lyrics by Larry Morey.
MY FOOLISH HEART (My Foolish Heart, Goldwyn, RKO Radio); Music by Victor Young. Lyrics by Ned Washington.
THROUGH A LONG AND SLEEPLESS NIGHT (Come to the Stable, 20th Century-Fox); Music by Alfred Newman. Lyrics by Mack Gordon.

(Scoring of a Dramatic or Comedy Picture)

BEYOND THE FOREST, Warner Bros. Max Steiner.
CHAMPION, Kramer, UA. Dimitri Tiomkin.
*THE HEIRESS, Paramount. Aaron Copland.

(Scoring of a Musical Picture)

JOLSON SINGS AGAIN, Columbia. Morris Stoloff and George Duning.
LOOK FOR THE SILVER LINING, Warner Bros. Ray Heindorf.
*ON THE TOWN, M-G-M. Roger Edens and Lennie Hayton.

SHORT SUBJECTS

(Cartoons)

*FOR SCENT-IMENTAL REASONS, Warner Bros. (Looney Tunes). Edward Selzer, producer.
HATCH UP YOUR TROUBLES, M-G-M. (Tom & Jerry). Fred Quimby, producer.
MAGIC FLUKE, UPA, Columbia. (Fox & Crow). Stephen Bosustow, producer.
TOY TINKERS, Disney, RKO Radio. (Donald Duck). Walt Disney, producer.

(One-reel)

*AQUATIC HOUSE-PARTY, Paramount. (Grantland Rice Sportlights). Jack Eaton, producer.
ROLLER DERBY GIRL, Paramount. (Pacemaker). Justin Herman, producer.
SO YOU THINK YOU'RE NOT GUILTY, Warner Bros. (Joe McDoakes). Gordon Hollingshead, producer.
SPILLS AND CHILLS, Warner Bros. (Sports Review). Walton C. Ament, producer.
WATER TRIX, M-G-M. (Pete Smith Specialty). Pete Smith, producer.

(Two-reel)

BOY AND THE EAGLE, RKO Radio. William Lasky, producer.
CHASE OF DEATH, Irving Allen Productions. Irving Allen, producer.
THE GRASS IS ALWAYS GREENER, Warner Bros. Gordon Hollingshead, producer.
SNOW CARNIVAL, Warner Bros. Gordon Hollingshead, producer.
*VAN GOGH, Canton-Weiner. Gaston Diehl and Robert Haessens, producers.

COSTUME DESIGN

(Black-and-White)

*THE HEIRESS, Paramount. Edith Head and Gile Steele.
PRINCE OF FOXES, 20th Century-Fox. Vittorio Nino Novarese.

(Color)

*ADVENTURES OF DON JUAN, Warner Bros. Leah Rhodes, Travilla and Marjorie Best.
MOTHER IS A FRESHMAN, 20th Century-Fox. Kay Nelson.

DOCUMENTARY

(Short Subjects)

*A CHANCE TO LIVE, March of Time, 20th Century-Fox. Richard de Rochemont, producer.
1848, A.F. Films, Inc. French Cinema General Cooperative, producer.
THE RISING TIDE, National Film Board of Canada. St. Francis-Xavier University (Nova Scotia), producer.
*SO MUCH FOR SO LITTLE, Warner Bros. Edward Selzer, producer.

(Features)

*DAYBREAK IN UDI, British Information Services. Crown Film Unit, producer.
KENJI COMES HOME, A Protestant Film Commission Prod. Paul F. Heard, producer.

SPECIAL AWARDS

TO THE BICYCLE THIEF (Italian)—voted by the Academy Board of Governors as the most outstanding foreign language film released in the United States during 1949. (statuette)
TO BOBBY DRISCOLL, as the outstanding juvenile actor of 1949. (miniature statuette)
TO FRED ASTAIRE for his unique artistry and his contributions to the technique of musical pictures. (statuette)
TO CECIL B. DeMILLE, distinguished motion picture pioneer, for 37 years of brilliant showmanship. (statuette)
TO JEAN HERSHOLT, for distinguished service to the motion picture industry. (statuette)

1949 IRVING G. THALBERG MEMORIAL AWARD

None given this year.

SCIENTIFIC OR TECHNICAL

CLASS I (statuette)

EASTMAN KODAK CO. for the development and introduction of an improved safety base motion picture film.

CLASS II (plaque)

None.

CLASS III (citation)

LOREN L. RYDER, BRUCE H. DENNEY, ROBERT CARR and the PARAMOUNT STUDIO SOUND DEPARTMENT;
M.B. PAUL;
HERBERT BRITT;
ANDRE COUTANT and JACQUES MATHOT;
CHARLES R. DAILY, STEVE CSILLAG and the PARAMOUNT STUDIO ENGINEERING, EDITORIAL and MUSIC DEPARTMENTS;
INTERNATIONAL PROJECTOR CORP.;
ALEXANDER VELCOFF.

*INDICATES WINNER

Hollywood took some sharp jabs at the world of the legitimate theater in 1950's *All about Eve*, then told some equally painful truths about itself in *Sunset Boulevard*, easily two of the best films of the year. Between them, they were nominated for twenty-five Academy Awards. *Eve*, in fact, became Oscar's most-nominated film to that date, with fourteen acknowledgments, competing with itself in the categories best actress (Bette Davis and Anne Baxter) and best supporting actress (Celeste Holm and Thelma Ritter). There was an abundance of other good work, too: *Born Yesterday* (four nominations), *Samson and Delilah* (five), *The Third Man* (three), *Father of the Bride* (three), *The Asphalt Jungle* (four), *Annie Get Your Gun* (four), *King Solomon's Mines* (three), *Adam's Rib* (one), among others.

When awards were handed out, March 29, 1951, at the RKO Pantages Theatre in Hollywood, *Eve* and *Sunset* still held center stage with the biggest Oscar totals for the year. *All about Eve* was honored with six awards, including best picture, best director (Joseph L. Mankiewicz) and best supporting actor (George Sanders). Mankiewicz also won for best screenplay, making the second year in a row he had won in both the director and screenplay categories. *Sunset Boulevard* received three awards: best story and screenplay, best art direction and best dramatic score.

The world of the theater was also evident in the evening's other acting awards. Judy Holliday was named best actress for *Born Yesterday*, a role she had played extensively on the Broadway stage. José Ferrer was chosen best actor for *Cyrano de Bergerac*, which he had also played before on the boards. The same is true of Josephine Hull, named best supporting actress for *Harvey*. Louis B. Mayer, outgoing head of the M-G-M Studio empire, was voted an honorary Oscar for his distinguished service to the motion picture industry, and the Franco-Italian *The Walls of Malapaga* received an honorary award as the year's outstanding foreign language film.

The ceremony itself was produced by Richard L. Breen and hosted by Fred Astaire, but most of the winners (and several nominees) who were currently in New York plays held their own party at the La Zambra cafe there, listening to the results on an ABC radio broadcast. Back in Hollywood, Marlene Dietrich wore a dress that exposed the famous Dietrich legs to the knee and stole the show as she climbed the stairs to the stage to present an award. Thanks to Dietrich, the evening was blessed with showmanship, just as 1950 had been brightened by some superior films.

Sunset Boulevard *(Paramount; produced by Charles Brackett) gave Hollywood the same kind of naked examination* All About Eve *gave to Broadway with Gloria Swanson as a past-tense movie queen unable to make a transition into private life as a human being. It was directed by Billy Wilder, co-starred William Holden, Erich Von Stroheim and Nancy Olson, and won three Oscars, including writing statuettes for Wilder, Brackett and D.M. Marshman, Jr. Sunset Boulevard also helped make moviegoing decidedly worthwhile in the days when television was beginning to grab a foothold on the affection—and the pocketbooks—of audiences.*

Best Picture: All about Eve *(20th Century-Fox; produced by Darryl F. Zanuck)*, **Best Director:** Joseph L. Mankiewicz *(above, with Anne Baxter, Bette Davis and Marilyn Monroe)* and **Best Supporting Actor:** George Sanders *as Addison DeWitt in* All about Eve. *Mankiewicz used a Mary Orr short story, "The Wisdom of Eve," as a foun-*dation for his stingingly comic examination of the New York theatrical jungle and came up with a creative and original zinger ultimately nominated for a record fourteen Academy Awards, winning six of them. *All about Eve followed the inter-mingled lives of an aging Broadway actress, a young director, a dedicated playwright and his nonprofessional wife as they* are affected by a dangerously ambitious young actress. Sanders won his Oscar as a cynical critic who takes the girl under his wing. Everyone involved was meticulously cast, including Celeste Holm, Hugh Marlowe, Gary Merrill, Thelma Ritter and Gregory Ratoff.

Best Actor: José Ferrer *as Cyrano (above) in* Cyrano de Bergerac *(United Artists; directed by Michael Gordon)*. Cyrano, *produced by Stanley Kramer, was an adaptation of Edmond Rostand's famous love story about a poetic, swaggering swordsman in 17th-century Paris who possessed an oversized nose and a secret passion for a damsel named Roxanne; in the title role Ferrer gave a robustly appealing performance, wearing a lengthy 2¾-inch beak which was created by Josef and Gustaf Norin. Earlier, Pierre Magnier had played Cyrano in a silent 1925 movie version, and Ferrer again played him in a 1964 French film,* Cyrano and D'Artagnan. *Steve Martin played a modernized Cyrano in a 1987 comedy version called* Roxanne, *and Gerard Depardieu took on the role in 1990.*

Best Actress: Judy Holliday *as Billie Dawn in* Born Yesterday *(Columbia; directed by George Cukor)*. Judy Holliday played Billie Dawn on the Broadway stage for three years and 1,200 performances to enormous success but almost didn't get the movie role; Columbia studio boss Harry Cohn bought the property for Rita Hayworth, then spent two years also testing and considering every other young actress in Hollywood. When she did play it on film, Holliday was an instant success as the dumb blonde mistress of a corrupt tycoon (Broderick Crawford) who is tutored by a magazine writer (William Holden, above with Holliday) while visiting Washington, D.C., and learns to think for herself.

117

King Solomon's Mines *(M-G-M; produced by Sam Zimbalist). M-G-M actually took cast and crew to Africa to shoot the major portions of this remake of H. Rider Haggard's adventure classic about a safari into unchartered areas of the* continent, *searching for a lost explorer who had gone hunting for the legendary diamond mine. It starred Stewart Granger, Deborah Kerr and Richard Carlson (facing a rhino above), featured dozens of Watutsi natives and won Oscars for color* cinematography by Robert Surtees and the film editing of Ralph E. Winters and Conrad A. Nervig.

The Third Man *(Selznick Releasing Organization; directed by Carol Reed) won an Oscar for Robert Krasker's cinematography (black-and-white), most of it done on Vienna's cobbled and starkly colorful streets. Orson Welles (left) starred as a mystery man named Harry Lime, involved in postwar black marketeering, while eerie zither music hummed* The Third Man Theme *in the background. Graham Greene wrote the screenplay from his own novel.*

Best Supporting Actress: Josephine Hull *as Veda Louise Simmons in* Harvey *(Universal-International; directed by Henry Koster). Josephine Hull had an extremely abbreviated screen career—only three movies in the sound era—but two of those appearances preserved on film a pair of her most famous stage roles: the sweet little poison-serving aunt in* Arsenic and Old Lace, *and (at left surrounded by Billy Lynn and Victoria Horne) in* Harvey *as the daffy, long-suffering sister of a man who chums around with an invisible rabbit, for which she won an Academy Award. Her third and final film, in 1951, was called* The Lady from Texas.

Nominations 1950

MOTION PICTURE

*ALL ABOUT EVE, 20th Century-Fox. Produced by Darryl F. Zanuck.
BORN YESTERDAY, Columbia. Produced by S. Sylvan Simon.
FATHER OF THE BRIDE, M-G-M. Produced by Pandro S. Berman.
KING SOLOMON'S MINES, M-G-M. Produced by Sam Zimbalist.
SUNSET BOULEVARD, Paramount. Produced by Charles Brackett.

ACTOR

LOUIS CALHERN in *The Magnificent Yankee*, M-G-M.
*JOSÉ FERRER in *Cyrano de Bergerac*, Kramer, UA.
WILLIAM HOLDEN in *Sunset Boulevard*, Paramount.
JAMES STEWART in *Harvey*, U-I.
SPENCER TRACY in *Father of the Bride*, M-G-M.

ACTRESS

ANNE BAXTER in *All about Eve*, 20th Century-Fox.
BETTE DAVIS in *All about Eve*, 20th Century-Fox.
*JUDY HOLLIDAY in *Born Yesterday*, Columbia.
ELEANOR PARKER in *Caged*, Warner Bros.
GLORIA SWANSON in *Sunset Boulevard*, Paramount.

SUPPORTING ACTOR

JEFF CHANDLER in *Broken Arrow*, 20th Century-Fox.
EDMUND GWENN in *Mister 880*, 20th Century-Fox.
SAM JAFFE in *The Asphalt Jungle*, M-G-M.
*GEORGE SANDERS in *All about Eve*, 20th Century-Fox.
ERICH VON STROHEIM in *Sunset Boulevard*, Paramount.

SUPPORTING ACTRESS

HOPE EMERSON in *Caged*, Warner Bros.
CELESTE HOLM in *All about Eve*, 20th Century-Fox.
*JOSEPHINE HULL in *Harvey*, U-I.
NANCY OLSON in *Sunset Boulevard*, Paramount.
THELMA RITTER in *All about Eve*, 20th Century-Fox.

DIRECTING

*ALL ABOUT EVE, 20th Century-Fox. Joseph L. Mankiewicz.
THE ASPHALT JUNGLE, M-G-M. John Huston.
BORN YESTERDAY, Columbia. George Cukor.
SUNSET BOULEVARD, Paramount. Billy Wilder.
THE THIRD MAN, Selznick-London Films, SRO (British). Carol Reed.

WRITING

(Motion Picture Story)

BITTER RICE, Lux Films (Italian). Giuseppe De Santis and Carlo Lizzani.
THE GUNFIGHTER, 20th Century-Fox. William Bowers and Andre de Toth.
MYSTERY STREET, M-G-M. Leonard Spigelgass.
*PANIC IN THE STREETS, 20th Century-Fox. Edna Anhalt and Edward Anhalt.
WHEN WILLIE COMES MARCHING HOME, 20th Century-Fox. Sy Gomberg.

(Screenplay)

*ALL ABOUT EVE, 20th Century-Fox. Joseph L. Mankiewicz.
THE ASPHALT JUNGLE, M-G-M. Ben Maddow and John Huston.
BORN YESTERDAY, Columbia. Albert Mannheimer.
BROKEN ARROW, 20th Century-Fox. Albert Maltz.
FATHER OF THE BRIDE, M-G-M. Frances Goodrich and Albert Hackett.

(Story and Screenplay)

ADAM'S RIB, M-G-M. Ruth Gordon and Garson Kanin.
CAGED, Warner Bros. Virginia Kellogg and Bernard C. Schoenfeld.
THE MEN, Kramer, UA. Carl Foreman.
NO WAY OUT, 20th Century-Fox. Joseph L. Mankiewicz and Lesser Samuels.
*SUNSET BOULEVARD, Paramount. Charles Brackett, Billy Wilder and D.M. Marshman, Jr.

CINEMATOGRAPHY

(Black-and-White)

ALL ABOUT EVE, 20th Century-Fox. Milton Krasner.
THE ASPHALT JUNGLE, M-G-M. Harold Rosson.
THE FURIES, Wallis, Paramount. Victor Milner.
SUNSET BOULEVARD, Paramount. John F. Seitz.
*THE THIRD MAN, Selznick-London Films, SRO (British). Robert Krasker.

(Color)

ANNIE GET YOUR GUN, M-G-M. Charles Rosher.
BROKEN ARROW, 20th Century-Fox. Ernest Palmer.
THE FLAME AND THE ARROW, Norma-F.R., Warner Bros. Ernest Haller.
*KING SOLOMON'S MINES, M-G-M. Robert Surtees.
SAMSON AND DELILAH, DeMille, Paramount. George Barnes.

ART DIRECTION-SET DECORATION

(Black-and-White)

ALL ABOUT EVE, 20th Century-Fox. Lyle Wheeler and George Davis; Thomas Little and Walter M. Scott.
THE RED DANUBE, M-G-M. Cedric Gibbons and Hans Peters; Edwin B. Willis and Hugh Hunt.
*SUNSET BOULEVARD, Paramount. Hans Dreier and John Meehan; Sam Comer and Ray Moyer.

(Color)

ANNIE GET YOUR GUN, M-G-M. Cedric Gibbons and Paul Groesse; Edwin B. Willis and Richard A. Pefferle.
DESTINATION MOON, Pal, Eagle-Lion. Ernst Fegte; George Sawley.
*SAMSON AND DELILAH, DeMille, Paramount. Hans Dreier and Walter Tyler; Sam Comer and Ray Moyer.

COSTUME DESIGN

(Black-and-White)

*ALL ABOUT EVE, 20th Century-Fox. Edith Head and Charles LeMaire.
BORN YESTERDAY, Columbia. Jean Louis.
THE MAGNIFICENT YANKEE, M-G-M. Walter Plunkett.

(Color)

THE BLACK ROSE, 20th Century-Fox. Michael Whittaker.
*SAMSON AND DELILAH, DeMille, Paramount. Edith Head, Dorothy Jeakins, Elois Jenssen, Gile Steele and Gwen Wakeling.
THAT FORSYTE WOMAN, M-G-M. Walter Plunkett and Valles.

SOUND RECORDING

*ALL ABOUT EVE, 20th Century-Fox. 20th Century-Fox Sound Department; Thomas T. Moulton, Sound Director.
CINDERELLA, Disney, RKO Radio. Disney Sound Department; C.O. Slyfield, Sound Director.
LOUISA, U-I. Universal-International Sound Department; Leslie I. Carey, Sound Director.
OUR VERY OWN, Goldwyn, RKO Radio. Goldwyn Sound Department; Gordon Sawyer, Sound Director.
TRIO, Rank-Sydney Box, Paramount (British). Pinewood Studio Sound Department; Cyril Crowhurst, Sound Director.

FILM EDITING

ALL ABOUT EVE, 20th Century-Fox. Barbara McLean.
ANNIE GET YOUR GUN, M-G-M. James E. Newcom.
*KING SOLOMON'S MINES, M-G-M. Ralph E. Winters and Conrad A. Nervig.
SUNSET BOULEVARD, Paramount. Arthur Schmidt and Doane Harrison.
THE THIRD MAN, Selznick-London Films, SRO (British). Oswald Hafenrichter.

SPECIAL EFFECTS

*DESTINATION MOON, Pal, Eagle-Lion.
SAMSON AND DELILAH, DeMille, Paramount.

MUSIC

(Song)

BE MY LOVE (*The Toast of New Orleans*, M-G-M); Music by Nicholas Brodszky. Lyrics by Sammy Cahn.
BIBBIDY-BOBBIDI-BOO (*Cinderella*, Disney, RKO Radio); Music and Lyrics by Mack David, Al Hoffman and Jerry Livingston.
*MONA LISA (*Captain Carey*, USA, Paramount); Music and Lyrics by Ray Evans and Jay Livingston.
MULE TRAIN (*Singing Guns*, Republic); Music and Lyrics by Fred Glickman, Hy Heath and Johnny Lange.
WILHELMINA (*Wabash Avenue*, 20th Century-Fox); Music by Josef Myrow. Lyrics by Mack Gordon.

(Scoring of a Dramatic or Comedy Picture)

ALL ABOUT EVE, 20th Century-Fox. Alfred Newman.
THE FLAME AND THE ARROW, Norma, Warner Bros. Max Steiner.
NO SAD SONGS FOR ME, Columbia. George Duning.
SAMSON AND DELILAH, Paramount. Victor Young.
*SUNSET BOULEVARD, Paramount. Franz Waxman.

(Scoring of a Musical Picture)

*ANNIE GET YOUR GUN, M-G-M. Adolph Deutsch and Roger Edens.
CINDERELLA, Disney, RKO Radio. Oliver Wallace and Paul J. Smith.
I'LL GET BY, 20th Century-Fox. Lionel Newman.
THREE LITTLE WORDS, M-G-M. Andre Previn.
THE WEST POINT STORY, Warner Bros. Ray Heindorf.

SHORT SUBJECTS

(Cartoons)

*GERALD McBOING-BOING, UPA, Columbia. (Jolly Frolics Series). Stephen Bosustow, executive producer.
JERRY'S COUSIN, M-G-M. (Tom & Jerry Series). Fred Quimby, producer.
TROUBLE INDEMNITY, UPA, Columbia. (Mr. Magoo Series). Stephen Bosustow, executive producer.

(One-reel)

BLAZE BUSTERS, Warner Bros. (Vitaphone Novelties). Robert Youngson, producer.
*GRANDAD OF RACES, Warner Bros. (Sports Parade). Gordon Hollingshead, producer.
WRONG WAY BUTCH, M-G-M. (Pete Smith Specialty). Pete Smith, producer.

(Two-reel)

GRANDMA MOSES, Falcon Films, Inc., A.F. Films. Falcon Films, Inc., producer.
*IN BEAVER VALLEY, Disney, RKO Radio. (True-Life Adventure). Walt Disney, producer.
MY COUNTRY 'TIS OF THEE, Warner Bros. (Featurette Series). Gordon Hollingshead, producer.

DOCUMENTARY

(Short Subjects)

THE FIGHT: SCIENCE AGAINST CANCER, National Film Board of Canada in cooperation with the Medical Film Institute of the Association of American Medical Colleges. Guy Glover, producer.
THE STAIRS, Film Documents, Inc.
*WHY KOREA?, 20th Century-Fox Movietone. Edmund Reek, producer.

(Features)

*THE TITAN: STORY OF MICHELANGELO, Michelangelo Co., Classics Pictures, Inc. Robert Snyder, producer.
WITH THESE HANDS, Promotional Films Co., Inc. Jack Arnold and Lee Goodman, producers.

HONORARY AND OTHER AWARDS

(New classification)

TO GEORGE MURPHY for his services in interpreting the film industry to the country at large. (statuette)
TO LOUIS B. MAYER for distinguished service to the motion picture industry. (statuette)
TO *THE WALLS OF MALAPAGA* (Franco-Italian)— voted by the Board of Governors as the most outstanding foreign language film released in the United States in 1950. (statuette)

1950 IRVING G. THALBERG MEMORIAL AWARD

TO DARRYL F. ZANUCK

SCIENTIFIC OR TECHNICAL

CLASS I (statuette)
None.

CLASS II (plaque)

JAMES B. GORDON and the 20TH CENTURY-FOX STUDIO CAMERA DEPARTMENT for the design and development of a multiple image film viewer.
JOHN PAUL LIVADARY, FLOYD CAMPBELL, L.W. RUSSELL and the COLUMBIA STUDIO SOUND DEPARTMENT for the development of a multi-track magnetic re-recording system.
LOREN L. RYDER and the PARAMOUNT STUDIO SOUND DEPARTMENT for the first studio-wide application of magnetic sound recording to motion picture production.

CLASS III (citation)
None.

*INDICATES WINNER

Humphrey Bogart won his one and only Academy Award at the 1951 awards ceremony, held March 20, 1952, at the RKO Pantages Theatre in Hollywood. It obviously rattled the famous tough guy, who had gone to the ceremony, he told friends, expecting Marlon Brando to win. But the unexpected has always been a fascinating ingredient of the Academy Awards story. No matter what fortunetellers, Ouija boards and the crystal ball may predict, every year seems to produce a lively upset or two to make Oscar-watching especially interesting. Said Bogart when he received the best actor award for *The African Queen,* "It's a long way from the Belgian Congo to the Pantages Theatre, but I'd rather be here than there."

Another major surprise occurred in 1951 when Ronald Colman opened the sealed envelope and announced the musical *An American in Paris* as the year's best picture; only twice before had a musical been voted the Academy's highest accolade (*The Broadway Melody* in 1928-29, *The Great Ziegfeld* in 1936). Most awards-watchers predicted one of two heavy dramas—either *A Streetcar Named Desire* or *A Place in the Sun*—would be honored. Even M-G-M, producers of the winning film, were caught off guard, and ran a whimsical trade advertisement afterwards which had a caricature of the studio's Leo the Lion trademark, looking modestly at an Oscar statue, saying with some embarrassment, "Honestly I was just standing *in the Sun* waiting for *A Streetcar.*"

Danny Kaye was M.C. for the program; it was produced by Arthur Freed, with Johnny Green as musical director (and a set designed by Mitchell Leisen). *A Streetcar Named Desire* became the first motion picture to win three awards for acting: Vivien Leigh was named the year's best actress, Karl Malden was chosen best supporting actor and Kim Hunter was announced as best supporting actress. Miss Leigh was in New York, co-starring with husband Laurence Olivier in a stage production of *Antony and Cleopatra* and heard the news via radio.

Special Oscars were voted to Japan's *Rashomon* as the outstanding foreign language film, and to Gene Kelly for his screen versatility and choreographic contributions to *An American in Paris.* *Paris* and *A Place in the Sun* tied for the most wins of the night, with six each. No one knew it at the time, but something else unexpected was about to happen: after this year, television cameras would be a permanent part of the Academy Awards story.

Best Picture: **An American in Paris** *(M-G-M; produced by Arthur Freed). Exuberant moviemaking at its do-re-mi best,* An American in Paris *proved—if proof was needed—that nobody could make a musical quite like Hollywood, especially those artists in the prolific Arthur Freed unit at M-G-M. Vincente Minnelli directed, the score was wall-to-wall Gershwin, and Gene Kelly starred with 19-year-old Leslie Caron from the* Ballet des Champs Élysées *in Paris (right, in a portion of a 17½-minute ballet sequence which climaxed the film). The cast included Oscar Levant, Nina Foch and Georges Guetary; the finale featured 120 dancers working in settings and styles patterned after paintings of Paris by Utrillo, Toulouse-Lautrec, Dufy, Renoir, Rousseau and Van Gogh.*

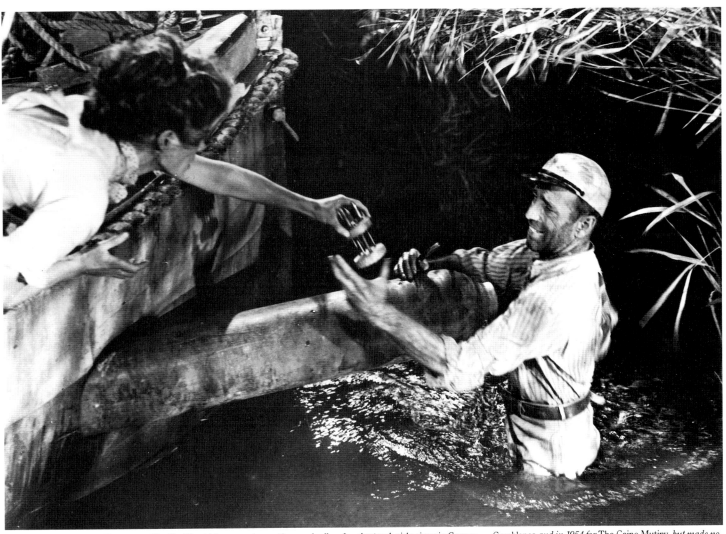

Best Actor: Humphrey Bogart *as Charlie Allnut (above, with Katharine Hepburn) in* The African Queen *(United Artists; directed by John Huston). Bogart played a scruffy, gin-loving vagabond aboard a 30-foot river steamboat heading* down a thousand miles of unchartered, risky rivers in German East Africa during World War I, battling the elements on one hand and, on the other, a chatty spinster who is accompanying him. Bogart was also nominated for Oscars in 1943 for Casablanca *and in 1954 for* The Caine Mutiny, *but made no secret of the fact he was not generally in favor of awards for actors. "The only true test would be to have every actor play* Hamlet *and decide who is best," he said.*

A Streetcar Named Desire *(Warner Bros.; directed by Elia Kazan) was based on the powerful play by Tennessee Williams and became the first motion picture to win three Academy Awards for acting, for (at left)* **Best Actress: Vivien Leigh** *as Blanche du Bois,* **Best Supporting Actress: Kim Hunter** *(next to Leigh) as Stella Kowalski, and* **Best Supporting Actor: Karl Malden** *(at right of Leigh, Hunter and Peg Hillias). It marked* the second Oscar for Vivien Leigh, this time as a desperate, faded beauty who hides her sexual maladjustments beneath a coquettish and ladylike surface then clashes with the animal honesty of her brother-in-law, played by Marlon Brando. Kim Hunter played her sister; Malden, a would-be suitor.

Special Award: **Rashomon** *(Japanese; produced by Jingo Minoura) received an Oscar statuette from the Board of Governors as the oustanding foreign language film released during 1951. It starred Toshiro Mifune and Machiko Kyo and told the story of a bandit attack and rape from three individual viewpoints. In 1964, director Martin Ritt used* Rashomon *as the basis for* The Outrage *with Paul Newman and Claire Bloom.*

MOTION PICTURE

*AN AMERICAN IN PARIS, M-G-M. Produced by Arthur Freed.
DECISION BEFORE DAWN, 20th Century-Fox. Produced by Anatole Litvak and Frank McCarthy.
A PLACE IN THE SUN, Paramount. Produced by George Stevens.
QUO VADIS, M-G-M. Produced by Sam Zimbalist.
A STREETCAR NAMED DESIRE, Feldman, Warner Bros. Produced by Charles K. Feldman.

ACTOR

*HUMPHREY BOGART in *The African Queen*, Horizon, UA.
MARLON BRANDO in *A Streetcar Named Desire*, Charles K. Feldman, Warner Bros.
MONTGOMERY CLIFT in *A Place in the Sun*, Paramount.
ARTHUR KENNEDY in *Bright Victory*, U-I.
FREDRIC MARCH in *Death of a Salesman*, Stanley Kramer, Columbia.

ACTRESS

KATHARINE HEPBURN in *The African Queen*, Horizon, UA.
*VIVIEN LEIGH in *A Streetcar Named Desire*, Charles K. Feldman, Warner Bros.
ELEANOR PARKER in *Detective Story*, Paramount.
SHELLEY WINTERS in *A Place in the Sun*, Paramount.
JANE WYMAN in *The Blue Veil*, Wald-Krasna, RKO Radio.

SUPPORTING ACTOR

LEO GENN in *Quo Vadis*, M-G-M.
*KARL MALDEN in *A Streetcar Named Desire*, Charles K. Feldman, Warner Bros.
KEVIN McCARTHY in *Death of a Salesman*, Kramer, Columbia.
PETER USTINOV in *Quo Vadis*, M-G-M.
GIG YOUNG in *Come Fill the Cup*, Warner Bros.

SUPPORTING ACTRESS

JOAN BLONDELL in *The Blue Veil*, Wald-Krasna, RKO Radio.
MILDRED DUNNOCK in *Death of a Salesman*, Kramer, Columbia.
LEE GRANT in *Detective Story*, Paramount.
*KIM HUNTER in *A Streetcar Named Desire*, Charles K. Feldman, Warner Bros.
THELMA RITTER in *The Mating Season*, Paramount.

DIRECTING

THE AFRICAN QUEEN, Horizon-Romulus, UA. John Huston.
AN AMERICAN IN PARIS, M-G-M. Vincente Minnelli.
DETECTIVE STORY, Paramount. William Wyler.
*A PLACE IN THE SUN, Paramount. George Stevens.
A STREETCAR NAMED DESIRE, Feldman, Warner Bros. Elia Kazan.

WRITING

(Motion Picture Story)

THE BULLFIGHTER AND THE LADY, Republic. Budd Boetticher and Ray Nazarro.
THE FROGMEN, 20th Century-Fox. Oscar Millard.
HERE COMES THE GROOM, Paramount. Robert Riskin and Liam O'Brien.
*SEVEN DAYS TO NOON, Boulting Bros., Mayer-Kingsley (British). Paul Dehn and James Bernard.
TERESA, M-G-M. Alfred Hayes and Stewart Stern.

(Screenplay)

THE AFRICAN QUEEN, Horizon-Romulus, UA. James Agee and John Huston.
DETECTIVE STORY, Paramount. Philip Yordan and Robert Wyler.
LA RONDE, Commercial Pictures (French). Jacques Natanson and Max Ophuls.
*A PLACE IN THE SUN, Paramount. Michael Wilson and Harry Brown.
A STREETCAR NAMED DESIRE, Feldman, Warner Bros. Tennessee Williams.

(Story and Screenplay)

*AN AMERICAN IN PARIS, M-G-M. Alan Jay Lerner.
THE BIG CARNIVAL, Paramount. Billy Wilder, Lesser Samuels and Walter Newman.
DAVID AND BATHSHEBA, 20th Century-Fox. Philip Dunne.
GO FOR BROKE!, M-G-M. Robert Pirosh.
THE WELL, Popkin, UA. Clarence Greene and Russell Rouse.

CINEMATOGRAPHY

(Black-and-White)

DEATH OF A SALESMAN, Kramer, Columbia. Frank Planer.
THE FROGMEN, 20th Century-Fox. Norbert Brodine.
*A PLACE IN THE SUN, Paramount. William C. Mellor.
STRANGERS ON A TRAIN, Warner Bros. Robert Burks.
A STREETCAR NAMED DESIRE, Feldman, Warner Bros. Harry Stradling.

(Color)

*AN AMERICAN IN PARIS, M-G-M. Alfred Gilks and John Alton.
DAVID AND BATHSHEBA, 20th Century-Fox. Leon Shamroy.
QUO VADIS, M-G-M. Robert Surtees and William V. Skall.
SHOW BOAT, M-G-M. Charles Rosher.
WHEN WORLDS COLLIDE, Pal, Paramount. John F. Seitz and W. Howard Greene.

ART DIRECTION-
SET DECORATION

(Black-and-White)

FOURTEEN HOURS, 20th Century-Fox. Lyle Wheeler and Leland Fuller; Thomas Little and Fred J. Rode.
HOUSE ON TELEGRAPH HILL, 20th Century-Fox. Lyle Wheeler and John DeCuir; Thomas Little and Paul S. Fox.
LA RONDE, Commercial Pictures (French). D'Eaubonne.
*A STREETCAR NAMED DESIRE, Feldman, Warner Bros. Richard Day; George James Hopkins.
TOO YOUNG TO KISS, M-G-M. Cedric Gibbons and Paul Groesse; Edwin B. Willis and Jack D. Moore.

When Worlds Collide *(Paramount; produced by George Pal) showed the havoc that happened—at least in the imagination of original authors Edwin Balmer and Philip Wylie—when another planet collided with Earth. It was voted an Oscar for special effects under a new 1951 Academy ruling which specified such an award would be presented only at such times there was an outstanding achievement deserving to be honored.*

(Color)

*AN AMERICAN IN PARIS, M-G-M. Cedric Gibbons
  and Preston Ames; Edwin B. Willis and Keogh
  Gleason.
DAVID AND BATHSHEBA, 20th Century-Fox. Lyle
  Wheeler and George Davis; Thomas Little and Paul
  S. Fox.
ON THE RIVIERA, 20th Century-Fox. Lyle Wheeler
  and Leland Fuller; Joseph C. Wright, Thomas Little
  and Walter M. Scott.
QUO VADIS, M-G-M. William A. Horning, Cedric
  Gibbons and Edward Carfagno; Hugh Hunt.
TALES OF HOFFMANN, Powell-Pressburger. Lopert
  (British). Hein Heckroth.

SHORT SUBJECTS

(Cartoons)

LAMBERT, THE SHEEPISH LION, Disney, RKO
  Radio. (Special). Walt Disney, producer.
ROOTY TOOT TOOT, UPA, Columbia (Jolly Frolics).
  Stephen Bosustow, executive producer.
*TWO MOUSEKETEERS, M-G-M. (Tom & Jerry). Fred
  Quimby, producer.

(One-reel)

RIDIN' THE RAILS, Paramount. (Sportlights). Jack
  Eaton, producer.
THE STORY OF TIME, A Signal Films Production by
  Robert G. Leffingwell, Cornell Film Company
  (British).
*WORLD OF KIDS, Warner Bros. (Vitaphone
  Novelties). Robert Youngson, producer.

(Two-reel)

BALZAC, Les Films Du Compass, A.F. Films, Inc.
  (French). Les Films Du Compass, producer.
DANGER UNDER THE SEA, U-I. Tom Mead,
  producer.
*NATURE'S HALF ACRE, Disney, RKO Radio. (True-
  Life Adventure). Walt Disney, producer.

DOCUMENTARY

(Short Subjects)

*BENJY, Made by Fred Zinnemann with the
  cooperation of Paramount Pictures Corp. for the Los
  Angeles Orthopaedic Hospital.
ONE WHO CAME BACK, Owen Crump, producer.
  (Film sponsored by the Disabled American Veterans,
  in cooperation with the United States Department of
  Defense and the Association of Motion Picture
  Producers.)
THE SEEING EYE, Warner Bros. Gordon
  Hollingshead, producer.

(Features)

I WAS A COMMUNIST FOR THE F.B.I., Warner Bros.
  Bryan Foy, producer.
*KON-TIKI, Artfilm Prod., RKO Radio (Norwegian). Olle
  Nordemar, producer.

SPECIAL EFFECTS

(NOTE: 1951 through 1953, Special Effects classified as an
  ''other'' award [not necessarily given each year]; hence,
  no nominations.)

*WHEN WORLDS COLLIDE, Pal, Paramount.

MUSIC

(Song)

*IN THE COOL, COOL, COOL OF THE EVENING
  (Here Comes the Groom, Paramount); Music by
  Hoagy Carmichael. Lyrics by Johnny Mercer.
A KISS TO BUILD A DREAM ON (The Strip, M-G-M);
  Music and Lyrics by Bert Kalmar, Harry Ruby and
  Oscar Hammerstein, II.
NEVER (Golden Girl, 20th Century-Fox); Music by
  Lionel Newman. Lyrics by Eliot Daniel.
TOO LATE NOW (Royal Wedding, M-G-M); Music by
  Burton Lane. Lyrics by Alan Jay Lerner.
WONDER WHY (Rich, Young and Pretty, M-G-M);
  Music by Nicholas Brodsky. Lyrics by Sammy Cahn.

(Scoring of a Dramatic or Comedy Picture)

DAVID AND BATHSHEBA, 20th Century-Fox. Alfred
  Newman.
DEATH OF A SALESMAN, Kramer, Columbia. Alex
  North.
*A PLACE IN THE SUN, Paramount. Franz Waxman.
QUO VADIS, M-G-M. Miklos Rozsa.
A STREETCAR NAMED DESIRE, Feldman, Warner
  Bros. Alex North.

(Scoring of a Musical Picture)

ALICE IN WONDERLAND, Disney, RKO Radio. Oliver
  Wallace.
*AN AMERICAN IN PARIS, M-G-M. Johnny Green and
  Saul Chaplin.
THE GREAT CARUSO, M-G-M. Peter Herman Adler
  and Johnny Green.

Best Director: George Stevens (at left, directing
Montgomery Clift and Elizabeth Taylor) for A Place in the
Sun, an adaptation of Theodore Dreiser's classic An American
Tragedy, which had earlier been filmed in 1931 by Paramount.
The dramatic A Place in the Sun gave enormous career boosts
to the popularity of Taylor and Clift, but started Shelley Winters
on a new career of essaying young character roles. It also won
Oscars for screenplay (by Michael Wilson and Harry Brown),
cinematography (by William C. Mellor), dramatic music score
(by Franz Waxman), film editing (by William Hornbeck) and
costume design (by Edith Head).

ON THE RIVIERA, 20th Century-Fox. Alfred
  Newman.
SHOW BOAT, M-G-M. Adolph Deutsch and Conrad
  Salinger.

COSTUME DESIGN

(Black-and-White)

KIND LADY, M-G-M. Walter Plunkett and Gile Steele.
THE MODEL AND THE MARRIAGE BROKER, 20th
  Century-Fox. Charles LeMaire and Renie.
THE MUDLARK, 20th Century-Fox. Edward
  Stevenson and Margaret Furse.
*A PLACE IN THE SUN, Paramount. Edith Head.
A STREETCAR NAMED DESIRE. Feldman, Warner
  Bros. Lucinda Ballard.

(Color)

*AN AMERICAN IN PARIS, M-G-M. Orry-Kelly, Walter
  Plunkett and Irene Sharaff.
DAVID AND BATHSHEBA, 20th Century-Fox. Charles
  LeMaire and Edward Stevenson.
THE GREAT CARUSO, M-G-M. Helen Rose and Gile
  Steele.
QUO VADIS, M-G-M. Herschel McCoy.
TALES OF HOFFMANN, Powell-Pressburger, Lopert
  (British). Hein Heckroth.

SOUND RECORDING

BRIGHT VICTORY, U-I. Leslie I. Carey, sound director.
*THE GREAT CARUSO, M-G-M. Douglas Shearer,
  sound director.
I WANT YOU, Goldwyn, RKO Radio. Gordon Sawyer,
  sound director.
A STREETCAR NAMED DESIRE, Feldman, Warner
  Bros. Col. Nathan Levinson, sound director.
TWO TICKETS TO BROADWAY, RKO Radio. John O.
  Aalberg, sound director.

FILM EDITING

AN AMERICAN IN PARIS, M-G-M. Adrienne Fazan.
DECISION BEFORE DAWN, 20th Century-Fox.
  Dorothy Spencer.
*A PLACE IN THE SUN, Paramount. William
  Hornbeck.
QUO VADIS, M-G-M. Ralph E. Winters.
THE WELL, Popkin, UA. Chester Schaeffer.

HONORARY AND OTHER AWARDS

TO GENE KELLY in appreciation of his versatility as
  an actor, singer, director and dancer, and specifically
  for his brilliant achievements in the art of
  choreography on film. (statuette)
TO RASHOMON (Japanese)—voted by the Board of
  Governors as the most outstanding foreign language
  film released in the United States during 1951.
  (statuette)

1951 IRVING G. THALBERG MEMORIAL AWARD

TO ARTHUR FREED

SCIENTIFIC OR TECHNICAL

CLASS I (statuette)

None.

CLASS II (plaque)

GORDON JENNINGS, S.L. STANCLIFFE and the
  PARAMOUNT STUDIO SPECIAL PHOTOGRAPHIC
  and ENGINEERING DEPARTMENTS for the design,
  construction and application of a servo-operated
  recording and repeating device.
OLIN L. DUPY of M-G-M Studio for the design,
  construction and application of a motion picture
  reproducing system.
RADIO CORPORATION OF AMERICA, VICTOR
  DIVISION, for pioneering direct positive recording
  with anticipatory noise reduction.

CLASS III (citation)

RICHARD M. HAFF, FRANK P. HERRNFELD,
  GARLAND C. MISENER and the ANSCO FILM
  DIVISION OF GENERAL ANILINE AND FILM CORP.;
FRED PONEDEL, RALPH AYRES and GEORGE
  BROWN of Warner Bros. Studio;
GLEN ROBINSON and the METRO-GOLDWYN-
  MAYER STUDIO CONSTRUCTION DEPARTMENT;
JACK GAYLORD and the METRO-GOLDWYN-
  MAYER STUDIO CONSTRUCTION DEPARTMENT;
CARLOS RIVAS of Metro-Goldwyn-Mayer Studio.

*INDICATES WINNER

Television loomed as a frightening ogre to most motion picture makers in the early 1950s. Hollywood studio bosses were justifiably concerned with the new medium's seemingly insatiable appetite, and rightfully worried about the public's growing interest in it as an entertainment source. Most studios went so far as to forbid their contractees to work for the competition, but sooner or later it was inevitable the walls would come tumbling down. It finally happened on March 19, 1953; television cameras covered the twenty-fifth Academy Awards presentation, and they have been an integral part of the Oscar story every year since.

It happened partly by default. The Academy had consistently turned down requests from the networks to buy the rights for TV coverage of the annual show, mainly to help protect the interests of the industry it represented. However, close to the time for the 1952 Oscar show to take form, several major film companies (Warner Bros., Columbia, Universal-International and Republic) refused to come up with their usual share of expenses to help underwrite the ceremony. The timing seemed right. Had NBC-RCA not made a $100,000 bid for radio and TV rights at that moment, there would have been no Oscar ceremony that year.

The show itself worked remarkably well for a first-timer. The presentation originated in Hollywood at the RKO Pantages Theatre with Bob Hope as M.C. A companion show took place in New York at the International Theatre, hosted by Conrad Nagel. Cameras switched back and forth from the two coasts, depending on which city held the presenter, or the winner. Johnny Green produced for the Academy, with Adolph Deutsch as musical director. Robert L. Welch produced for NBC-TV, and William A. Bennington directed for the network. The show was a refreshing novelty for home viewers, unaccustomed to seeing such a large collection of famous names, and it received the largest single audience to that date in television's five-year commercial history.

The Bad and the Beautiful won the most Oscars of the night, a total of five, including the best supporting actress award to Gloria Grahame. Gary Cooper (in *High Noon*) won the best actor award for the second time in his career, and Anthony Quinn was chosen best supporting actor (for *Viva Zapata!*); both men were working together on location in Mexico and absent from the festivities in Hollywood. Shirley Booth, in New York appearing on stage in *Time of the Cuckoo,* was named best actress for *Come Back, Little Sheba* and came close to taking a public pratfall when she rushed on stage to accept her award, and momentarily stumbled. John Ford was named best director for the fourth time in his career (this one for *The Quiet Man*) and, also for the fourth time, was not present to accept his statuette. Once again, there was also a major surprise when the best picture winner was

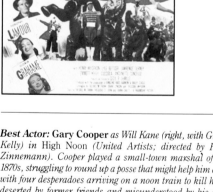
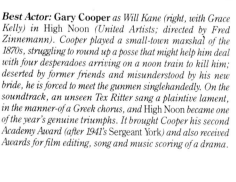

Best Actor: **Gary Cooper** *as Will Kane (right, with Grace Kelly) in* High Noon *(United Artists; directed by Fred Zinnemann). Cooper played a small-town marshal of the 1870s, struggling to round up a posse that might help him deal with four desperadoes arriving on a noon train to kill him; deserted by former friends and misunderstood by his new bride, he is forced to meet the gunmen singlehandedly. On the soundtrack, an unseen Tex Ritter sang a plaintive lament, in the manner-of a Greek chorus, and* High Noon *became one of the year's genuine triumphs. It brought Cooper his second Academy Award (after 1941's* Sergeant York) *and also received Awards for film editing, song and music scoring of a drama.*

announced. Decidedly a dark horse, Cecil B. DeMille's *The Greatest Show on Earth* was chosen, the first DeMille movie so honored by Oscar. The award was appropriately presented by another motion picture pioneer, Mary Pickford.

Best Actress: **Shirley Booth** *as Lola Delaney (right, with Burt Lancaster on the floor) in* Come Back, Little Sheba *(Paramount; directed by Daniel Mann). In the 1950s, juicy stage roles didn't often go to their original Broadway creators, even when they'd had as much critical success as Shirley Booth did playing Lola Delaney, a slovenly but good-hearted housewife who endlessly waddles around her home, munching chocolates, listening to radio soap operas, mourning her lost pup Sheba and inadvertently driving her husband to drink. When Hal Wallis transferred* Sheba *to film, however, he cast it with an eye more to interpretation than to box office and got both—a brilliant performance by Miss Booth in her last film role, and a successful moneymaker as well.*

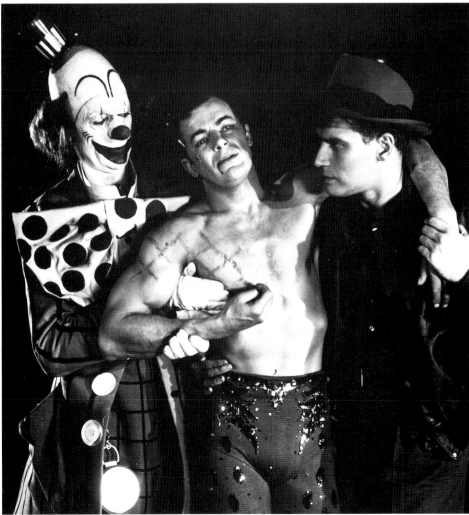

Best Picture: **The Greatest Show on Earth** *(Paramount; produced and directed by Cecil B. DeMille) was a 2-hour, 31-minute spectacle-drama using the Ringling Bros.-Barnum & Bailey Circus as a backdrop—and as a focal point. Among the cast were (at right) James Stewart as a clown hiding from the police, Cornel Wilde as an aerial star who falls during a performance and dooms his career, and Charlton Heston as the circus manager, struggling to keep the Big Top show going through thick and thin. Other co-stars included Betty Hutton, Dorothy Lamour, Gloria Grahame, Henry Wilcoxon and a tent full of others contributing to the splashy, rousing entertainment. The film also won an Academy Award for its story, while DeMille himself— Hollywood's old master showman—received the 1952 Irving G. Thalberg Memorial Award for consistent high quality of production.*

Best Director: John Ford *for* The Quiet Man *(Argosy, Republic; produced by Ford and Merian C. Cooper). John Wayne starred as an ex-prizefighter from Pittsburgh who returns to his Irish birthplace seeking peace and quiet and, instead, finds rough-and-tumble problems with a marriageable spitfire (Maureen O'Hara, above with Wayne), and her ill-tempered brother (Victor McLaglen). It was peopled with familiar Ford players (including Barry Fitzgerald, Ward Bond, Mildred Natwick, Arthur Shields and Frances Ford), filmed in Ireland in Technicolor, and acclaimed as one of the year's most robust delights. It also won Ford his fourth Oscar for direction, the largest total won by an individual in that category during Oscar's first 75 years.*

MOTION PICTURE

*THE GREATEST SHOW ON EARTH, DeMille, Paramount. Produced by Cecil B. DeMille.
HIGH NOON, Kramer, UA. Produced by Stanley Kramer.
IVANHOE, M-G-M. Produced by Pandro S. Berman.
MOULIN ROUGE, Romulus, UA. Produced by John Huston.
THE QUIET MAN, Argosy, Republic. Produced by John Ford and Merian C. Cooper.

ACTOR

MARLON BRANDO in *Viva Zapata!,* 20th Century-Fox.
*GARY COOPER in *High Noon,* Kramer, UA.
KIRK DOUGLAS in *The Bad and the Beautiful,* M-G-M.
JOSE FERRER in *Moulin Rouge,* Romulus, UA.
ALEC GUINNESS in *The Lavender Hill Mob,* Rank-Ealing, U-I. (British).

ACTRESS

*SHIRLEY BOOTH in *Come Back, Little Sheba,* Wallis, Paramount.
JOAN CRAWFORD in *Sudden Fear,* Kaufman, RKO Radio.
BETTE DAVIS in *The Star,* Friedlob, 20th Century-Fox.
JULIE HARRIS in *The Member of the Wedding,* Kramer, Columbia.
SUSAN HAYWARD in *With a Song in My Heart,* 20th Century-Fox.

SUPPORTING ACTOR

RICHARD BURTON in *My Cousin Rachel,* 20th Century-Fox.
ARTHUR HUNNICUTT in *The Big Sky,* Winchester, RKO Radio.
VICTOR McLAGLEN in *The Quiet Man,* Argosy, Republic.
JACK PALANCE in *Sudden Fear,* Kaufman, RKO Radio.
*ANTHONY QUINN in *Viva Zapata!,* 20th Century-Fox.

SUPPORTING ACTRESS

*GLORIA GRAHAME in *The Bad and the Beautiful,* M-G-M.
JEAN HAGEN in *Singin' in the Rain,* M-G-M.
COLETTE MARCHAND in *Moulin Rouge,* Romulus, UA.
TERRY MOORE in *Come Back, Little Sheba,* Wallis, Paramount.
THELMA RITTER in *With a Song in My Heart,* 20th Century-Fox.

DIRECTING

FIVE FINGERS, 20th Century-Fox. Joseph L. Mankiewicz.
THE GREATEST SHOW ON EARTH, DeMille, Paramount. Cecil B. DeMille.
HIGH NOON, Stanley Kramer, UA. Fred Zinnemann.
MOULIN ROUGE, Romulus, UA. John Huston.
*THE QUIET MAN, Argosy, Republic. John Ford.

WRITING

(Motion Picture Story)

*THE GREATEST SHOW ON EARTH, DeMille, Paramount. Frederick M. Frank, Theodore St. John and Frank Cavett.
MY SON JOHN, Rainbow, Paramount. Leo McCarey.
THE NARROW MARGIN, RKO Radio. Martin Goldsmith and Jack Leonard.
THE PRIDE OF ST. LOUIS, 20th Century-Fox. Guy Trosper.
THE SNIPER, Kramer, Columbia. Edna Anhalt and Edward Anhalt.

(Screenplay)

*THE BAD AND THE BEAUTIFUL, M-G-M. Charles Schnee.
FIVE FINGERS, 20th Century-Fox. Michael Wilson.
HIGH NOON, Kramer, UA. Carl Foreman.
THE MAN IN THE WHITE SUIT, Rank-Ealing, U-I (British). Roger MacDougall, John Dighton and Alexander Mackendrick.
THE QUIET MAN, Argosy, Republic. Frank S. Nugent.

(Story and Screenplay)

THE ATOMIC CITY, Paramount. Sydney Boehm.
BREAKING THE SOUND BARRIER, London Films, UA (British). Terence Rattigan.
*THE LAVENDER HILL MOB, Rank-Ealing, U-I (British). T.E.B. Clarke.
PAT AND MIKE, M-G-M. Ruth Gordon and Garson Kanin.
VIVA ZAPATA!, 20th Century-Fox. John Steinbeck.

CINEMATOGRAPHY

(Black-and-White)

*THE BAD AND THE BEAUTIFUL, M-G-M. Robert Surtees.
THE BIG SKY, Winchester, RKO Radio. Russell Harlan.
MY COUSIN RACHEL, 20th Century-Fox. Joseph LaShelle.
NAVAJO, Bartlett-Foster, Lippert. Virgil E. Miller.
SUDDEN FEAR, Kaufman, RKO Radio. Charles B. Lang, Jr.

(Color)

HANS CHRISTIAN ANDERSEN, Goldwyn, RKO Radio. Harry Stradling.
IVANHOE, M-G-M. F.A. Young.
MILLION DOLLAR MERMAID, M-G-M. George J. Folsey.
*THE QUIET MAN, Argosy, Republic. Winton C. Hoch and Archie Stout.
THE SNOWS OF KILIMANJARO, 20th Century-Fox. Leon Shamroy.

ART DIRECTION-SET DECORATION

(Black-and-White)

*THE BAD AND THE BEAUTIFUL, M-G-M. Cedric Gibbons and Edward Carfagno; Edwin B. Willis and Keogh Gleason.
CARRIE, Paramount. Hal Pereira and Roland Anderson; Emile Kuri.
MY COUSIN RACHEL, 20th Century-Fox. Lyle Wheeler and John DeCuir; Walter M. Scott.
RASHOMON, RKO Radio (Japanese). Matsuyama; H. Motsumoto.
VIVA ZAPATA!, 20th Century-Fox. Lyle Wheeler and Leland Fuller; Thomas Little and Claude Carpenter.

(Color)

HANS CHRISTIAN ANDERSEN, Goldwyn, RKO Radio. Richard Day and Clave; Howard Bristol.
THE MERRY WIDOW, M-G-M. Cedric Gibbons and Paul Groesse; Edwin B. Willis and Arthur Krams.

Best Supporting Actress: Gloria Grahame *as Rosemary Bartlow (left, with Dick Powell) in* The Bad and the Beautiful *(M-G-M; directed by Vincente Minnelli). It was a productive year for the actress with strong roles in four well-seen, well-liked releases:* The Greatest Show on Earth, Sudden Fear, Macao *and* The Bad and the Beautiful. *For the latter, playing the coquettish Southern-belle wife of a novelist-turned-screenwriter, she officially won her Academy Award.* The Bad *was also the year's most-honored film by the Academy, winning four additional Awards.*

*MOULIN ROUGE, Romulus, UA. Paul Sheriff; Marcel Vertes.
THE QUIET MAN, Argosy, Republic. Frank Hotaling; John McCarthy, Jr. and Charles Thompson.
THE SNOWS OF KILIMANJARO, 20th Century-Fox. Lyle Wheeler and John DeCuir; Thomas Little and Paul S. Fox.

COSTUME DESIGN

(Black-and-White)

AFFAIR IN TRINIDAD, Beckworth, Columbia. Jean Louis.
*THE BAD AND THE BEAUTIFUL, M-G-M. Helen Rose.
CARRIE, Paramount. Edith Head.
MY COUSIN RACHEL, 20th Century-Fox. Charles LeMaire and Dorothy Jeakins.
SUDDEN FEAR, Kaufman, RKO Radio. Sheila O'Brien.

(Color)

THE GREATEST SHOW ON EARTH, DeMille, Paramount. Edith Head, Dorothy Jeakins and Miles White.
HANS CHRISTIAN ANDERSEN, Goldwyn, RKO Radio. Clave, Mary Wills and Madame Karinska.
THE MERRY WIDOW, M-G-M. Helen Rose and Gile Steele.
*MOULIN ROUGE, Romulus, UA. Marcel Vertes.
WITH A SONG IN MY HEART, 20th Century-Fox. Charles LeMaire.

SOUND RECORDING

*BREAKING THE SOUND BARRIER, London Films, UA (British). London Film Sound Department.
HANS CHRISTIAN ANDERSEN, Goldwyn, RKO Radio. Goldwyn Sound Department; Gordon Sawyer, sound director.
THE PROMOTER, Rank-Neame, U-I (British). Pinewood Studios Sound Department.
THE QUIET MAN, Argosy, Republic. Republic Sound Department; Daniel J. Bloomberg, sound director.
WITH A SONG IN MY HEART, 20th Century-Fox. 20th Century-Fox Sound Department; Thomas T. Moulton, sound director.

FILM EDITING

COME BACK, LITTLE SHEBA, Wallis, Paramount. Warren Low.
FLAT TOP, Monogram. William Austin.
THE GREATEST SHOW ON EARTH, DeMille, Paramount. Anne Bauchens.
*HIGH NOON, Kramer, UA. Elmo Williams and Harry Gerstad.
MOULIN ROUGE, Romulus, UA. Ralph Kemplen.

SPECIAL EFFECTS

(NOTE: 1951 through 1953, Special Effects classified as an "other" award [not necessarily given each year]; hence, no nominations.)
*PLYMOUTH ADVENTURE, M-G-M.

MUSIC

(Song)

AM I IN LOVE (*Son of Paleface,* Paramount); Music and Lyrics by Jack Brooks.
BECAUSE YOU'RE MINE, (*Because You're Mine,* M-G-M); Music by Nicholas Brodszky. Lyrics by Sammy Cahn.
*HIGH NOON (DO NOT FORSAKE ME, OH MY DARLIN'), (*High Noon,* Kramer, UA); Music by Dimitri Tiomkin. Lyrics by Ned Washington.
THUMBELINA (*Hans Christian Andersen,* Goldwyn, RKO Radio); Music and Lyrics by Frank Loesser.
ZING A LITTLE ZONG, (*Just for You,* Paramount); Music by Harry Warren. Lyrics by Leo Robin.

(Scoring of a Dramatic or Comedy Picture)

*HIGH NOON, Kramer, UA. Dimitri Tiomkin.
IVANHOE, M-G-M. Miklos Rozsa.
THE MIRACLE OF FATIMA, Foy, Warner Bros. Max Steiner.
THE THIEF, Popkin, UA. Herschel Burke Gilbert.
VIVA ZAPATA!, 20th Century-Fox. Alex North.

(Scoring of a Musical Picture)

HANS CHRISTIAN ANDERSEN, Goldwyn, RKO Radio. Walter Scharf.
THE JAZZ SINGER, Warner Bros. Ray Heindorf and Max Steiner.
THE MEDIUM, Transfilm-Lopert (Italian). Gian-Carlo Menotti.
SINGIN' IN THE RAIN, M-G-M. Lennie Hayton.
*WITH A SONG IN MY HEART, 20th Century-Fox. Alfred Newman.

SHORT SUBJECTS

(Cartoons)

*JOHANN MOUSE, M-G-M. (Tom & Jerry). Fred Quimby, producer.
LITTLE JOHNNY JET, M-G-M. (M-G-M Series). Fred Quimby, producer.
MADELINE, UPA, Columbia. (Jolly Frolics). Stephen Bosustow, executive producer.
PINK AND BLUE BLUES, UPA, Columbia. (Mister Magoo). Stephen Bosustow, executive producer.
ROMANCE OF TRANSPORTATION, National Film Board of Canada. (Canadian). Tom Daly, producer.

(One-reel)

ATHLETES OF THE SADDLE, Paramount. (Sportlights Series). Jack Eaton, producer.
DESERT KILLER, Warner Bros. (Sports Parade). Gordon Hollingshead, producer.
*LIGHT IN THE WINDOW, Art Films Prods., 20th Century-Fox. (Art Series). Boris Vermont, producer.
NEIGHBOURS, National Film Board of Canada (Canadian). Norman McLaren, producer.
ROYAL SCOTLAND, Crown Film Unit, British Information Services (British).

(Two-reel)

BRIDGE OF TIME, London Film Prod., British Information Services (British).
DEVIL TAKE US, Theatre of Life Prod. (Theatre of Life Series). Herbert Morgan, producer.
THAR SHE BLOWS!, Warner Bros. (Technicolor Special). Gordon Hollingshead, producer.
*WATER BIRDS, Disney, RKO Radio. (True-Life Adventure). Walt Disney, producer.

DOCUMENTARY

(Short Subjects)

DEVIL TAKE US, Theatre of Life Prod. Herbert Morgan, producer.
THE GARDEN SPIDER (EPEIRA DIADEMA), Cristallo Films, I.F.E. Releasing Corp. (Italian). Alberto Ancilotto, producer.
MAN ALIVE!, UPA for the American Cancer Society. Stephen Bosustow, executive producer.
*NEIGHBOURS, National Film Board of Canada, Mayer-Kingsley, Inc. (Canadian). Norman McLaren, producer.

(Features)

THE HOAXTERS, M-G-M. Dore Schary, producer.
NAVAJO, Bartlett-Foster Prod., Lippert Pictures, Inc. Hall Bartlett, producer.
*THE SEA AROUND US, RKO Radio. Irwin Allen, producer.

HONORARY AND OTHER AWARDS

TO GEORGE ALFRED MITCHELL for the design and development of the camera which bears his name and for his continued and dominant presence in the field of cinematography. (statuette)
TO JOSEPH M. SCHENCK for long and distinguished service to the motion picture industry. (statuette)
TO MERIAN C. COOPER for his many innovations and contributions to the art of motion pictures. (statuette)
TO HAROLD LLOYD, master comedian and good citizen. (statuette)
TO BOB HOPE for his contribution to the laughter of the world, his service to the motion picture industry, and his devotion to the American premise. (statuette)
TO *FORBIDDEN GAMES* (French)—Best Foreign Language Film first released in the United States during 1952. (statuette)

1952 IRVING G. THALBERG MEMORIAL AWARD

TO CECIL B. DeMILLE

SCIENTIFIC OR TECHNICAL

CLASS I (statuette)

EASTMAN KODAK CO. for the introduction of Eastman color negative and Eastman color print film.
ANSCO DIVISION, GENERAL ANILINE AND FILM CORP., for the introduction of Ansco color negative and Ansco color print film.

CLASS II (plaque)

TECHNICOLOR MOTION PICTURE CORP. for an improved method of color motion picture photography under incandescent light.

CLASS III (citation)

PROJECTION, STILL PHOTOGRAPHIC and DEVELOPMENT ENGINEERING DEPARTMENTS of METRO-GOLDWYN-MAYER STUDIO;
JOHN G. FRAYNE and R.R. SCOVILLE and WESTREX CORP.;
PHOTO RESEARCH CORP.;
GUSTAV JIROUCH;
CARLOS RIVAS of Metro-Goldwyn-Mayer Studio.

*INDICATES WINNER

127

1953
The Twenty-Sixth Year

The year 1953 had been one of great Hollywood revitalization and enthusiasm, most of it connected to a wide-screen boom of Technicolored CinemaScope projection methods and 3-D gimmicks which were heavily promoted to lure audiences away from their television sets at home. Curiously, however, the big Oscar winners of the year—*From Here to Eternity, Roman Holiday* and *Stalag 17*—were all filmed in black-and-white, in standard-sized ratios, sans gimmicks of any kind. Once again, voters had obviously opted for quality, first and foremost.

On March 25, 1954, the night Hollywood recognized screen achievements for 1953 movies, Frank Sinatra was named best supporting actor for his work in *From Here to Eternity* and put the final stroke on a show business comeback of sizeable proportions. *Eternity* itself was named best picture, the first film to come along and tie the long-standing record of eight Academy Awards set by *Gone With the Wind* fourteen years before. Other winners for *Eternity* included Donna Reed (best supporting actress) and Fred Zinnemann (best director). Next most-honored film was *Roman Holiday,* with three awards, including one for Audrey Hepburn as best actress of the year. William Holden was named best actor for *Stalag 17.*

An estimated 43,000,000 television viewers watched the 1953 awards show which was again telecast over NBC-TV, with cut-ins from New York (when Audrey Hepburn won) and Philadelphia (where Shirley Booth presented the award to Holden by long distance). Donald O'Connor was master of ceremonies from the Pantages Theatre base in Hollywood; Fredric March was the M.C. in New York at the Century Theater. Audrey Hepburn was appearing on Broadway at the time in *Ondine* and, after her final curtain, was rushed by police motorcycle escort to the Century Theater just in time to hear her name announced. The show itself was given a two-hour running time by NBC and ran late, necessitating William Holden to cut his acceptance speech to a "thank you" before exiting into the wings. Mitchell Leisen produced for the Academy, Andre Previn was musical director and William A. Bennington (in Hollywood) and Gray Lockwood (in New York) shared directorial duties for NBC.

Most conspicuous man of the night, next to Oscar himself, was Walt Disney. During the course of the evening, he was called to the stage four times to accept awards for *The Alaskan Eskimo* (documentary short subject), *The Living Desert* (documentary feature), *Toot, Whistle, Plunk and Boom* (cartoon short) and *Bear Country* (two-reel short). No person—male or female—had personally collected so many Oscars in one session.

THE BOLDEST BOOK OF OUR TIME... HONESTLY, FEARLESSLY ON THE SCREEN!

BURT LANCASTER · MONTGOMERY CLIFT

FROM HERE TO ETERNITY

DEBORAH KERR

FRANK SINATRA · DONNA REED

Best Actor: **William Holden** *as Sefton in* Stalag 17 *(Paramount; directed by Billy Wilder). John Ericson created the role of Stalag's Sefton on Broadway; on film, Holden played the hero-heel, a cynical World War II prisoner in a German POW barracks who is suspected by his fellow inmates of being an informer. Previously, Holden had been nominated in 1950 for* Sunset Boulevard *(also directed by Billy Wilder) and was again nominated in 1976 for* Network. *Holden became slightly miffed the night of his Oscar victory when, because the telecast was running long, he was only allowed enough time to blurt out a hurried "Thank you" before having to exit the stage with his Stalag prize.*

Best Director: Fred Zinnemann *for* From Here to Eternity, *and* **Best Supporting Actress: Donna Reed** *as* Lorene *in* From Here to Eternity. *One reason for the* Eternity *impact was the casting of first-class players in off-* beat roles, among them Donna Reed (center, flanked by co-player Montgomery Clift and director Zinnemann), as a somewhat embittered play-for-pay hostess who falls in love with soldier Clift. The part was a far cry from the sweet and unspoiled ingenues she'd played at M-G-M, Paramount and Columbia for the preceding 12 years. She received the Oscar, and deservedly.

Best Supporting Actor: Frank Sinatra *as Angelo Maggio in* From Here to Eternity. *At first, no one but Frank Sinatra envisioned Frank Sinatra as* Eternity's *hard-luck Maggio, the feisty little Italian soldier who tragically locks horns with a sadistic stockade supervisor. Sinatra campaigned for the nonstarring role, won it although it had earlier been earmarked for Eli Wallach, and delivered a performance which sparked one of the genuinely impressive comebacks in Hollywood's scrapbook. He won the Academy Award, then two years later was nominated as 1955's best actor for* The Man with the Golden Arm, *and in 1971 received the Jean Hersholt Humanitarian Award. And since* Eternity, *his career has never been less than first-string.*

Best Picture: From Here to Eternity *(Columbia; produced by Buddy Adler) was based on James Jones' scorching novel about Army life at the Scofield Barracks in Hawaii just prior to the 1941 Japanese air attack, considered too salty to be ideal film material. But it became a powerful and tasteful blockbuster, acted by a meticulously-chosen cast including (above) Burt Lancaster and Deborah Kerr, and won eight Academy Awards, more than any film since* Gone with the Wind *of 1939.*

129

Best Actress: **Audrey Hepburn** *as Princess Anne (above)*
in Roman Holiday *(Paramount; directed by William Wyler).*
Audrey Hepburn made her initial impact in 1951 on
Broadway in Gigi, *then two years later had the same effect on*
moviegoers when she played the princess who sneaks away
from her royal duties while on a visit to Rome, and investigates

the Eternal City—incognito—with a reporter (Gregory Peck)
and a photographer (Eddie Albert). It was a genuinely
delightful performance, and won her the Oscar; after that,
she was also nominated for Sabrina *(1954),* The Nun's Story
(1959), Breakfast at Tiffany's *(1961) and* Wait until Dark
(1967) before she semi-retired from acting.

MOTION PICTURE

*FROM HERE TO ETERNITY, Columbia. Produced by
Buddy Adler.
JULIUS CAESAR, M-G-M. Produced by John
Houseman.
THE ROBE, 20th Century-Fox. Produced by Frank
Ross.
ROMAN HOLIDAY, Paramount. Produced by William
Wyler.
SHANE, Paramount. Produced by George Stevens.

ACTOR

MARLON BRANDO in *Julius Caesar,* 20th
Century-Fox.
RICHARD BURTON in *The Robe,* 20th Century-Fox.
MONTGOMERY CLIFT in *From Here to Eternity,*
Columbia.
*WILLIAM HOLDEN in *Stalag 17,* Paramount.
BURT LANCASTER in *From Here to Eternity,*
Columbia.

ACTRESS

LESLIE CARON in *Lili,* M-G-M.
AVA GARDNER in *Mogambo,* M-G-M.
*AUDREY HEPBURN in *Roman Holiday,* Paramount.
DEBORAH KERR in *From Here to Eternity,* Columbia.
MAGGIE McNAMARA, in *The Moon Is Blue,*
Preminger-Herbert, UA.

SUPPORTING ACTOR

EDDIE ALBERT in *Roman Holiday,* Paramount.
BRANDON DE WILDE in *Shane,* Paramount.
JACK PALANCE in *Shane,* Paramount.
*FRANK SINATRA in *From Here to Eternity,*
Columbia.
ROBERT STRAUSS in *Stalag 17,* Paramount.

SUPPORTING ACTRESS

GRACE KELLY in *Mogambo,* M-G-M.
GERALDINE PAGE in *Hondo,* Wayne-Fellows, Warner
Bros.
MARJORIE RAMBEAU in *Torch Song,* M-G-M.
*DONNA REED in *From Here to Eternity,* Columbia.
THELMA RITTER in *Pickup on South Street,* 20th
Century-Fox.

DIRECTING

*FROM HERE TO ETERNITY, Columbia. Fred
Zinnemann.
LILI, M-G-M. Charles Walters.
ROMAN HOLIDAY, Paramount. William Wyler.
SHANE, Paramount. George Stevens.
STALAG 17, Paramount. Billy Wilder.

Shane *(Paramount; produced by George Stevens) starred*
Alan Ladd (above, with Brandon De Wilde), Jean Arthur and
Van Heflin in a Technicolor outdoor drama filmed near the
Grand Tetons in Wyoming. A classic of its kind, it won an
Oscar for color cinematography, and its producer-director,
George Stevens, received 1953's Irving G. Thalberg Memorial
Award for "consistently high quality of production."

WRITING

(Motion Picture Story)

ABOVE AND BEYOND, M-G-M. Beirne Lay, Jr.
THE CAPTAIN'S PARADISE, London Films, Lopert-
UA (British). Alec Coppel.
LITTLE FUGITIVE, Burstyn Releasing. Ray `Ashley,
Morris Engel and Ruth Orkin.
*ROMAN HOLIDAY, Paramount. Dalton Trumbo.

(Screenplay)

THE CRUEL SEA, Rank-Ealing, U-I (British). Eric
Ambler.
*FROM HERE TO ETERNITY, Columbia. Daniel Taradash.
LILI, M-G-M. Helen Deutsch.
ROMAN HOLIDAY, Paramount. Ian McLellan Hunter
and John Dighton.
SHANE, Paramount. A.B. Guthrie, Jr.

(Story and Screenplay)

THE BAND WAGON, M-G-M. Betty Comden and
Adolph Green.
THE DESERT RATS, 20th Century-Fox. Richard Murphy.
THE NAKED SPUR, M-G-M. Sam Rolfe and Harold
Jack Bloom.
TAKE THE HIGH GROUND, M-G-M. Millard Kaufman.
*TITANIC, 20th Century-Fox. Charles Brackett, Walter
Reisch and Richard Breen.

CINEMATOGRAPHY

(Black-and-White)

THE FOUR POSTER, Kramer, Columbia. Hal Mohr.
*FROM HERE TO ETERNITY, Columbia. Burnett
Guffey.
JULIUS CAESAR, M-G-M. Joseph Ruttenberg.
MARTIN LUTHER, de Rochemont Assocs. Joseph C.
Brun.
ROMAN HOLIDAY, Paramount. Frank Planer and
Henry Alekan.

(Color)

ALL THE BROTHERS WERE VALIANT, M-G-M.
George Folsey.
BENEATH THE 12 MILE REEF, 20th Century-Fox.
Edward Cronjager.
LILI, M-G-M. Robert Planck.
THE ROBE, 20th Century-Fox. Leon Shamroy.
*SHANE, Paramount. Loyal Griggs.

ART DIRECTION-
SET DECORATION

(Black-and-White)

*JULIUS CAESAR, M-G-M. Cedric Gibbons and
Edward Carfagno; Edwin B. Willis and Hugh Hunt.
MARTIN LUTHER, de Rochemont Assocs. Fritz
Maurischat and Paul Markwitz.
THE PRESIDENT'S LADY, 20th Century-Fox. Lyle
Wheeler and Leland Fuller; Paul S. Fox.
ROMAN HOLIDAY, Paramount. Hal Pereira and Walter
Tyler.
TITANIC, 20th Century-Fox. Lyle Wheeler and
Maurice Ransford; Stuart Reiss.

(Color)

KNIGHTS OF THE ROUND TABLE, M-G-M. Alfred
Junge and Hans Peters; John Jarvis.
LILI, M-G-M. Cedric Gibbons and Paul Groesse; Edwin
B. Willis and Arthur Krams.
*THE ROBE, 20th Century-Fox. Lyle Wheeler and
George W. Davis; Walter M. Scott and Paul S. Fox.
THE STORY OF THREE LOVES, M-G-M. Cedric
Gibbons, Preston Ames, Edward Carfagno and
Gabriel Scognamillo; Edwin B. Willis, Keogh Gleason,
Arthur Krams and Jack D. Moore.
YOUNG BESS, M-G-M. Cedric Gibbons and Urie
McCleary; Edwin B. Willis and Jack D. Moore.

COSTUME DESIGN

(Black-and-White)

THE ACTRESS, M-G-M. Walter Plunkett.
DREAM WIFE, M-G-M. Helen Rose and Herschel McCoy.
FROM HERE TO ETERNITY, Columbia. Jean Louis.
THE PRESIDENT'S LADY, 20th Century-Fox. Charles
LeMaire and Renie.
*ROMAN HOLIDAY, Paramount. Edith Head.

(Color)

THE BAND WAGON, M-G-M. Mary Ann Nyberg.
CALL ME MADAM, 20th Century-Fox. Irene Sharaff.
HOW TO MARRY A MILLIONAIRE, 20th Century-
Fox. Charles LeMaire and Travilla.
*THE ROBE, 20th Century-Fox. Charles LeMaire and
Emile Santiago.
YOUNG BESS, M-G-M. Walter Plunkett.

The Robe (20th Century-Fox; produced by Frank Ross) was the first motion picture photographed and released in Cinema-Scope, a new wide-screen process requiring an anamorphic lens (and more horizontal screen) for projection. It was based on Lloyd C. Douglas' best-seller, starred Jean Simmons and Richard Burton (above, with Jay Robinson as Emperor Caligula) and won Academy Awards for color art direction and color costume design. 20th Century-Fox was also awarded a special statuette "in recognition of their imagination, showmanship and foresight in introducing the revolutionary process known as CinemaScope."

SOUND RECORDING

CALAMITY JANE, Warner Bros. Warner Bros. Sound Department; William A. Mueller, sound director.
*__FROM HERE TO ETERNITY,__ Columbia. Columbia Sound Department; John P. Livadary, sound director.
KNIGHTS OF THE ROUND TABLE, M-G-M. M-G-M Sound Department; A.W. Watkins, sound director.
THE MISSISSIPPI GAMBLER, U-I. Universal-International Sound Department; Leslie I. Carey, sound director.
THE WAR OF THE WORLDS, Pal, Paramount. Paramount Sound Department; Loren L. Ryder, sound director.

FILM EDITING

CRAZYLEGS, Bartlett, Republic. Irvine (Cotton) Warburton.
*__FROM HERE TO ETERNITY,__ Columbia. William Lyon.
THE MOON IS BLUE, Preminger-Herbert, UA. Otto Ludwig.
ROMAN HOLIDAY, Paramount. Robert Swink.
THE WAR OF THE WORLDS, Pal, Paramount. Everett Douglas.

SPECIAL EFFECTS

(NOTE: 1951 through 1953, Special Effects classified as an "other" award [not necessarily given each year]; hence, no nominations.)
*__THE WAR OF THE WORLDS,__ Pal, Paramount.

MUSIC

(Song)

THE MOON IS BLUE (The Moon Is Blue, Preminger-Herbert, UA); Music by Herschel Burke Gilbert. Lyrics by Sylvia Fine.
MY FLAMING HEART (Small Town Girl, M-G-M); Music by Nicholas Brodszky. Lyrics by Leo Robin.
SADIE THOMPSON'S SONG (BLUE PACIFIC BLUES) (Miss Sadie Thompson, Beckworth, Columbia); Music by Lester Lee. Lyrics by Ned Washington.
*__SECRET LOVE__ (Calamity Jane, Warner Bros.); Music by Sammy Fain. Lyrics by Paul Francis Webster.
THAT'S AMORE (The Caddy, Paramount); Music by Harry Warren. Lyrics by Jack Brooks.

(Scoring of a Dramatic or Comedy Picture)

ABOVE AND BEYOND, M-G-M. Hugo Friedhofer.
FROM HERE TO ETERNITY, Columbia. Morris Stoloff and George Duning.
JULIUS CAESAR, M-G-M. Miklos Rozsa.
*__LILI,__ M-G-M. Bronislau Kaper.
THIS IS CINERAMA, Cinerama Corp. Louis Forbes.

(Scoring of a Musical Picture)

THE BAND WAGON, M-G-M. Adolph Deutsch.
CALAMITY JANE, Warner Bros. Ray Heindorf.
*__CALL ME MADAM,__ 20th Century-Fox. Alfred Newman.
5,000 FINGERS OF DR. T., Kramer, Columbia. Frederick Hollander and Morris Stoloff.
KISS ME KATE, M-G-M. Andre Previn and Saul Chaplin.

SHORT SUBJECTS

(Cartoons)

CHRISTOPHER CRUMPET, UPA, Columbia. (Jolly Frolics). Stephen Bosustow, producer.
FROM A TO Z-Z-Z-Z, Warner Bros. (Looney Tunes). Edward Selzer, producer.
RUGGED BEAR, Disney, RKO Radio. (Donald Duck). Walt Disney, producer.
THE TELL TALE HEART, UPA, Columbia. (Cartoon Special). Stephen Bosustow, producer.
*__TOOT, WHISTLE, PLUNK AND BOOM.__ Disney, Buena Vista. (Special Music Series). Walt Disney, producer.

(One-reel)

CHRIST AMONG THE PRIMITIVES, IFE Releasing Corp. (Italian). Vincenzo Lucci-Chiarissi, producer.
HERRING HUNT, National Film Board of Canada, RKO Pathe, Inc. (Canadian). (Canada Carries On Series).
JOY OF LIVING, Art Film Prods., 20th Century-Fox. (Art Film Series). Boris Vermont, producer.
*__THE MERRY WIVES OF WINDSOR OVERTURE,__ M-G-M. (Overture Series). Johnny Green, producer.
WEE WATER WONDERS, Paramount. (Grantland Rice Sportlights Series). Jack Eaton, producer.

(Two-reel)

*__BEAR COUNTRY,__ Disney, RKO Radio. (True-Life Adventure). Walt Disney, producer.
BEN AND ME, Disney, Buena Vista (Cartoon Special Series). Walt Disney, producer.
RETURN TO GLENNASCAUL, Dublin Gate Theatre Prod., Mayer-Kingsley Inc.
VESUVIUS EXPRESS, 20th Century-Fox. (CinemaScope Shorts Series). Otto Lang, producer.
WINTER PARADISE, Warner Bros. (Technicolor Special). Cedric Francis, producer.

DOCUMENTARY

(Short Subjects)

*__THE ALASKAN ESKIMO,__ Disney, RKO Radio. Walt Disney, producer.
THE LIVING CITY, Encyclopaedia Britannica Films, Inc. John Barnes, producer.
OPERATION BLUE JAY, U.S. Army Signal Corps.

THEY PLANTED A STONE, World Wide Pictures, British Information Services (British). James Carr, producer.
THE WORD, 20th Century-Fox. John Healy and John Adams, producers.

(Features)

THE CONQUEST OF EVEREST, Countryman Films, Group 3 Ltd., UA (British). John Taylor, Leon Clore and Grahame Tharp, producers.
*__THE LIVING DESERT,__ Disney, Buena Vista. Walt Disney, producer.
A QUEEN IS CROWNED, J. Arthur Rank, U-I. (British). Castleton Knight, producer.

HONORARY AND OTHER AWARDS

TO PETE SMITH for his witty and pungent observations on the American scene in his series of "Pete Smith Specialties." (statuette)
TO 20TH CENTURY-FOX FILM CORPORATION in recognition of their imagination, showmanship and foresight in introducing the revolutionary process known as CinemaScope. (statuette)
TO JOSEPH I. BREEN for his conscientious, open-minded and dignified management of the Motion Picture Production Code. (statuette)
TO BELL AND HOWELL COMPANY for their pioneering and basic achievements in the advancement of the motion picture industry. (statuette)

131

1953 IRVING G. THALBERG MEMORIAL AWARD

TO GEORGE STEVENS

SCIENTIFIC OR TECHNICAL

CLASS I (statuette)

PROFESSOR HENRI CHRETIEN and **EARL SPONABLE, SOL HALPRIN, LORIN GRIGNON, HERBERT GRAGG** and **CARL FAULKNER** of 20th Century-Fox Studios for creating, developing and engineering the equipment, processes and techniques known as CinemaScope.
FRED WALLER for designing and developing the multiple photographic and projection systems which culminated in Cinerama.

CLASS II (plaque)

REEVES SOUNDCRAFT CORP. for their development of a process of applying stripes of magnetic oxide to motion picture film for sound recording and reproduction.

CLASS III (citation)

WESTREX CORP.

*__INDICATES WINNER__

Greta Garbo, retired from motion pictures for thirteen years and never an Academy Award winner during her active screen career, was voted an honorary Academy Award statuette at the 1954 awards, held March 30, 1955, and telecast both from Hollywood (with Bob Hope as M.C.) and from New York (with Thelma Ritter as hostess). Earlier in the year, Garbo had been the subject of a biographical series in *Life Magazine,* sparking a renewed interest in revivals of her films, capped by the Academy paying tribute to her timeless career. The elusive Garbo, of course, did not attend the ceremony; the award was accepted for her by Nancy Kelly.

Another major actress, this one a nominee, was also absent. Judy Garland, nominated for *A Star Is Born,* was a patient in Cedars of Lebanon Hospital, the mother of a day-old-son. NBC-TV, anticipating a possible Garland victory as best actress, had television equipment set up outside her hospital room window, balanced on a special scaffolding, ready for on-the-spot coverage, just in case. However, Grace Kelly, present at the Pantages Theatre in Hollywood, was ultimately announced as the year's best actress for *The Country Girl,* and quickly switched the focus away from Cedars. Biggest winner of the night was *On the Waterfront* with eight awards, including best picture, best actor (Marlon Brando), best supporting actress (Eva Marie Saint) and best director (Elia Kazan). With its total, it tied the all-time Oscar

record set by *Gone With the Wind* in 1939, and equalled by 1953's *From Here to Eternity.* Edmond O'Brien was chosen best supporting actor for *The Barefoot Contessa.*

Danny Kaye received an honorary Oscar for his unique talents and services to the Academy, the industry and the American people; and Japan's *Gate of Hell* was voted an honorary statuette as the year's finest foreign language film released in the United States. Dimitri Tiomkin, winner of the best music score award for *The High and the Mighty,* accepted his Oscar by thanking a few helpers by name: "Brahms, Bach, Beethoven, Richard Strauss and Johann Strauss…"

Two months earlier, on February 12, 1955, the announcement of nominees was made on a live telecast aired over NBC-TV and beamed from Romanoff's restaurant in Hollywood, Ciro's nightclub on the Sunset Strip, the Cocoanut Grove near downtown Los Angeles and the NBC-TV studios in Burbank. It was not considered a success and the experiment was never repeated in that specific form.

Best Supporting Actor: **Edmond O'Brien** *as Oscar Muldoon in* The Barefoot Contessa *(United Artists; directed by Joseph L. Mankiewicz). Humphrey Bogart, Ava Gardner and Rossano Brazzi were the stars of this brittle but glamorous assessment of the tragedy behind a beautiful actress-sex symbol's rise and death; Edmond O'Brien (here, with Marius Goring) won the Academy's highest honor as a sweating, harassed and overbearing press agent involved in their lives.*

Best Picture: **On the Waterfront** *(Columbia; produced by Sam Spiegel),* ***Best Director:*** **Elia Kazan** *and* ***Best Actor:*** **Marlon Brando** *as Terry Malloy and* ***Best Supporting Actress:*** **Eva Marie Saint** *as Edie Doyle in* On the Waterfront. *Produced on a small budget ($820,000) in an era when most picture makers were concentrating on new wide-screen processes and CinemaScopic projects, it stemmed from a series of crusading newspaper articles by Malcolm Johnson fashioned into a tight script by Budd Schulberg about brutality and corruption on the New York-New Jersey shipping docks. Brando played a longshoreman who awakens to the fact it's morally wrong to be enslaved by a crooked boss; Eva Marie Saint, in her first screen role, played his sensitive girlfriend who encourages the longshoreman's better instincts. Told in semi-documentary style, it was strong screen fare and 1954's most honored film with 12 nominations for awards and, ultimately, eight Oscars to its credit. Brando's role was originally to have been played by Frank Sinatra; he sued producer Spiegel and Columbia when they dropped him from the project and began filming with Brando in the leading role.*

133

Special Award: **Greta Garbo.** *Greta Garbo had been nominated for Academy Awards in 1929-30 (for* Anna Christie *and* Romance*), in 1937 (for* Camille*) and in 1939 (for* Ninotchka*) but had never been voted the final Oscar statuette. To make up for the oversight and, at last, to honor one of the industry's finest artists, the Board of Governors voted her a special 1954 Academy Award for "her unforgettable screen performances." Not unexpectedly, she didn't appear at the award ceremony to collect her prize.*

Best Actress: **Grace Kelly** *as Georgie Elgin (left, with William Holden) in* The Country Girl *(Paramount; directed by George Seaton). Uta Hagen created the role on Broadway; Jennifer Jones was originally set to star in the film version with William Holden and Bing Crosby but had to withdraw because of pregnancy. Grace Kelly, relatively new to the film scene, then got the part—against type—played the plain, embittered wife of an aging and alcoholic matinee idol who tries to cover up for her husband's weaknesses but is misunderstood in her motives. The preceding year, she had also been a part of the Oscar story, nominated for her supporting performance in* Mogambo *(1953). A year after winning her* Country Girl *prize, Grace Kelly permanently retired from acting to become Princess Grace of Monaco.*

(opposite page) **20,000 Leagues under the Sea** *(Buena Vista; produced by Walt Disney) was honored for color art direction and for special effects. Kirk Douglas, James Mason, Paul Lukas and Peter Lorre starred in the undersea adventure, based on the tales by Jules Verne, in which—among other perils—the men of the submarine* Nautilus *battle a giant squid.*

MOTION PICTURE

THE CAINE MUTINY, Kramer, Columbia. Produced by Stanley Kramer.
THE COUNTRY GIRL, Perlberg-Seaton, Paramount. Produced by William Perlberg.
*****ON THE WATERFRONT,** Horizon-American, Columbia. Produced by Sam Spiegel.
SEVEN BRIDES FOR SEVEN BROTHERS, M-G-M. Produced by Jack Cummings.
THREE COINS IN THE FOUNTAIN, 20th Century-Fox. Produced by Sol C. Siegel.

ACTOR

HUMPHREY BOGART in *The Caine Mutiny,* Kramer, Columbia.
*****MARLON BRANDO** in *On the Waterfront,* Horizon-American. Columbia.
BING CROSBY in *The Country Girl,* Perlberg-Seaton, Paramount.
JAMES MASON in *A Star Is Born,* Transcona, Warner Bros.
DAN O'HERLIHY in *Adventures of Robinson Crusoe,* Dancigers-Ehrlich, UA.

ACTRESS

DOROTHY DANDRIDGE in *Carmen Jones,* Preminger, 20th Century-Fox.
JUDY GARLAND in *A Star Is Born,* Transcona, Warner Bros.
AUDREY HEPBURN in *Sabrina,* Paramount.
*****GRACE KELLY** in *The Country Girl,* Perlberg-Seaton, Paramount.
JANE WYMAN in *The Magnificent Obsession,* Universal-International.

SUPPORTING ACTOR

LEE J. COBB in *On the Waterfront,* Horizon-American, Columbia.
KARL MALDEN in *On the Waterfront,* Horizon-American, Columbia.
*****EDMOND O'BRIEN** in *The Barefoot Contessa,* Figaro, UA.
ROD STEIGER in *On the Waterfront,* Horizon-American, Columbia.
TOM TULLY in *The Caine Mutiny,* Kramer, Columbia.

SUPPORTING ACTRESS

NINA FOCH in *Executive Suite,* M-G-M.
KATY JURADO in *Broken Lance,* 20th Century-Fox.
*****EVA MARIE SAINT** in *On the Waterfront,* Horizon-American, Columbia.
JAN STERLING in *The High and the Mighty,* Wayne-Fellows, Warner Bros..
CLAIRE TREVOR in *The High and the Mighty,* Wayne-Fellows, Warner Bros.

DIRECTING

THE COUNTRY GIRL, Perlberg-Seaton, Paramount. George Seaton.
THE HIGH AND THE MIGHTY, Wayne-Fellows, Warner Bros. William Wellman.
*****ON THE WATERFRONT,** Horizon, Columbia. Elia Kazan.
REAR WINDOW, Hitchcock, Paramount. Alfred Hitchcock.
SABRINA, Paramount. Billy Wilder.

WRITING

(Motion Picture Story)

BREAD, LOVE AND DREAMS, Titanus, I.F.E. Releasing (Italian). Ettore Margadonna.
*****BROKEN LANCE,** 20th Century-Fox. Philip Yordan.
FORBIDDEN GAMES, Times Film Corp. (French). Francois Boyer.
NIGHT PEOPLE, 20th Century-Fox. Jed Harris and Tom Reed.
THERE'S NO BUSINESS LIKE SHOW BUSINESS, 20th Century-Fox. Lamar Trotti.

(Screenplay)

THE CAINE MUTINY, Kramer, Columbia. Stanley Roberts.
*****THE COUNTRY GIRL,** Perlberg-Seaton, Paramount. George Seaton.
REAR WINDOW, Hitchcock, Paramount. John Michael Hayes.
SABRINA, Paramount. Billy Wilder. Samuel Taylor and Ernest Lehman.
SEVEN BRIDES FOR SEVEN BROTHERS, M-G-M. Albert Hackett, Frances Goodrich and Dorothy Kingsley.

(Story and Screenplay)

THE BAREFOOT CONTESSA, Figaro, UA. Joseph Mankiewicz.
GENEVIEVE, Rank-Sirius, U-I (British). William Rose.
THE GLENN MILLER STORY, U-I. Valentine Davies and Oscar Brodney.
KNOCK ON WOOD, Dena, Paramount. Norman Panama and Melvin Frank.
*****ON THE WATERFRONT,** Horizon, Columbia. Budd Schulberg.

CINEMATOGRAPHY

(Black-and-White)

THE COUNTRY GIRL, Perlberg-Seaton, Paramount. John F. Warren.
EXECUTIVE SUITE, M-G-M. George Folsey.
*****ON THE WATERFRONT,** Horizon, Columbia. Boris Kaufman.
ROGUE COP, M-G-M. John Seitz.
SABRINA, Paramount. Charles Lang, Jr.

(Color)

THE EGYPTIAN, 20th Century-Fox. Leon Shamroy.
REAR WINDOW, Hitchcock, Paramount. Robert Burks.
SEVEN BRIDES FOR SEVEN BROTHERS, M-G-M. George Folsey.
THE SILVER CHALICE, Saville, Warner Bros. William V. Skall.
*****THREE COINS IN THE FOUNTAIN,** 20th Century-Fox. Milton Krasner.

ART DIRECTION-
SET DECORATION

(Black-and-White)

THE COUNTRY GIRL, Perlberg-Seaton, Paramount. Hal Pereira and Roland Anderson; Sam Comer and Grace Gregory.
EXECUTIVE SUITE, M-G-M. Cedric Gibbons and Edward Carfagno; Edwin B. Willis and Emile Kuri.
LE PLAISIR, Meyer-Kingsley (French). Max Ophuls.
*****ON THE WATERFRONT,** Horizon, Columbia. Richard Day.
SABRINA, Paramount. Hal Pereira and Walter Tyler; Sam Comer and Ray Moyer.

(Color)

BRIGADOON, M-G-M. Cedric Gibbons and Preston Ames; Edwin B. Willis and Keogh Gleason.
DESIREE, 20th Century-Fox. Lyle Wheeler and Leland Fuller; Walter M. Scott and Paul S. Fox.
RED GARTERS, Paramount. Hal Pereira and Roland Anderson; Sam Comer and Ray Moyer.
A STAR IS BORN, Transcona, Warner Bros. Malcolm Bert, Gene Allen and Irene Sharaff; George James Hopkins.
*****20,000 LEAGUES UNDER THE SEA,** Disney, Buena Vista. John Meehan; Emile Kuri.

COSTUME DESIGN

(Black-and-White)

THE EARRINGS OF MADAME DE..., Arlan Pictures (French). Georges Annenkov and Rosine Delamare.
EXECUTIVE SUITE, M-G-M. Helen Rose.
INDISCRETION OF AN AMERICAN WIFE, DeSica, Columbia. Christian Dior.
IT SHOULD HAPPEN TO YOU, Columbia. Jean Louis.
*****SABRINA,** Paramount. Edith Head.

(Color)

BRIGADOON, M-G-M. Irene Sharaff.
DESIREE, 20th Century-Fox. Charles LeMaire and Rene Hubert.
*****GATE OF HELL,** Daiei, Edward Harrison (Japanese). Sanzo Wada.

A STAR IS BORN, Transcona, Warner Bros. Jean
Louis, Mary Ann Nyberg and Irene Sharaff.
THERE'S NO BUSINESS LIKE SHOW BUSINESS,
20th Century-Fox. Charles LeMaire, Travilla and
Miles White.

SOUND RECORDING

BRIGADOON, M-G-M. Wesley C. Miller, sound director.
THE CAINE MUTINY, Columbia. John P. Livadary,
sound director.
*THE GLENN MILLER STORY, U-I. Leslie I. Carey,
sound director.
REAR WINDOW, Hitchcock, Paramount. Loren L.
Ryder, sound director.
SUSAN SLEPT HERE, RKO Radio. John O. Aalberg,
sound director.

FILM EDITING

THE CAINE MUTINY, Kramer, Columbia. William A.
Lyon and Henry Batista.
THE HIGH AND THE MIGHTY, Wayne-Fellows,
Warner Bros. Ralph Dawson.
*ON THE WATERFRONT, Horizon, Columbia. Gene
Milford.
SEVEN BRIDES FOR SEVEN BROTHERS, M-G-M.
Ralph E. Winters.
20,000 LEAGUES UNDER THE SEA, Disney, Buena
Vista. Elmo Williams.

SPECIAL EFFECTS

(A regular Award category for the first time since 1950)
HELL AND HIGH WATER, 20th Century-Fox.
THEM! Warner Bros.
*20,000 LEAGUES UNDER THE SEA, Walt Disney
Studios.

MUSIC

(Song)
COUNT YOUR BLESSINGS INSTEAD OF SHEEP
(*White Christmas*, Paramount); Music and Lyrics by
Irving Berlin.
THE HIGH AND THE MIGHTY (*The High and the
Mighty*, Wayne-Fellows, Warner Bros.); Music by
Dimitri Tiomkin. Lyrics by Ned Washington.
HOLD MY HAND (*Susan Slept Here*, RKO Radio);
Music and Lyrics by Jack Lawrence and Richard
Myers.
THE MAN THAT GOT AWAY (*A Star Is Born*,
Transcona, Warner Bros.); Music by Harold Arlen.
Lyrics by Ira Gershwin.
*THREE COINS IN THE FOUNTAIN (*Three Coins in
the Fountain*, 20th Century-Fox); Music by Jule
Styne. Lyrics by Sammy Cahn.

(Scoring of a Dramatic or Comedy Picture)
THE CAINE MUTINY, Kramer, Columbia. Max Steiner.
GENEVIEVE, Rank-Sirius, U-I (British). Larry Adler.
(NOTE: Because of the political climate of the times,
GENEVIEVE's arranger and orchestra conductor Muir
Mathieson was credited as composer on American prints
of this British-made film, and was thus credited with the
nomination. Academy records have been updated to give

Mr. Adler his proper credit, which Mr. Mathieson had
never claimed.)
*THE HIGH AND THE MIGHTY, Wayne-Fellows,
Warner Bros. Dimitri Tiomkin.
ON THE WATERFRONT, Horizon, Columbia. Leonard
Bernstein.
THE SILVER CHALICE, Saville, Warner Bros. Franz
Waxman.

(Scoring of a Musical Picture)
CARMEN JONES, Preminger, 20th Century-Fox.
Herschel Burke Gilbert.
THE GLENN MILLER STORY, U-I. Joseph
Gershenson and Henry Mancini.
*SEVEN BRIDES FOR SEVEN BROTHERS, M-G-M.
Adolph Deutsch and Saul Chaplin.
A STAR IS BORN, Transcona, Warner Bros. Ray
Heindorf.
THERE'S NO BUSINESS LIKE SHOW BUSINESS,
20th Century-Fox. Alfred Newman and Lionel Newman.

SHORT SUBJECTS

(Cartoons)
CRAZY MIXED UP PUP, Lantz, U-I. Walter Lantz,
producer.
PIGS IS PIGS, Disney, RKO Radio. Walt Disney,
producer.
SANDY CLAWS, Warner Bros. Edward Selzer, producer.
TOUCHE, PUSSY CAT, M-G-M. Fred Quimby, producer.
*WHEN MAGOO FLEW, UPA, Columbia. Stephen
Bosustow, producer.

(One-reel)
THE FIRST PIANO QUARTETTE, 20th Century-Fox.
Otto Lang, producer.
THE STRAUSS FANTASY, M-G-M. Johnny Green,
producer.
*THIS MECHANICAL AGE, Warner Bros. Robert
Youngson, producer.

(Two-reel)
BEAUTY AND THE BULL, Warner Bros. Cedric
Francis, producer.
JET CARRIER, 20th Century-Fox. Otto Lang, producer.
SIAM, Disney, Buena Vista. Walt Disney, producer.
*A TIME OUT OF WAR, Carnival Prods., Denis and
Terry Sanders, producers.

DOCUMENTARY

(Short Subjects)
JET CARRIER, 20th Century-Fox. Otto Lang, producer.
REMBRANDT: A SELF-PORTRAIT, Distributors
Corp. of America. Morrie Roizman, producer.
*THURSDAY'S CHILDREN, British Information
Services (British). World Wide Pictures and Morse
Films, producers.

(Features)
THE STRATFORD ADVENTURE, National Film
Board of Canada, Continental (Canadian). Guy
Glover, producer.
*THE VANISHING PRAIRIE, Disney, Buena Vista.
Walt Disney, producer.

HONORARY AND OTHER AWARDS

TO BAUSCH & LOMB OPTICAL COMPANY for their
contributions to the advancement of the motion
picture industry. (statuette)
TO KEMP R. NIVER for the development of the
Renovare Process which has made possible the
restoration of the Library of Congress Paper Film
Collection. (statuette)
TO GRETA GARBO for her unforgettable screen
performances. (statuette)
TO DANNY KAYE for his unique talents, his service to
the Academy, the motion picture industry, and the
American people. (statuette)
TO JON WHITELEY for his outstanding juvenile
performance in *The Little Kidnappers*. (miniature
statuette)
TO VINCENT WINTER for his outstanding performance
in *The Little Kidnappers*. (miniature statuette)
TO *GATE OF HELL* (Japanese)—Best Foreign
Language Film first released in the United States
during 1954. (statuette)

1954 IRVING G. THALBERG MEMORIAL AWARD

None given this year.

SCIENTIFIC OR TECHNICAL

CLASS I (statuette)
PARAMOUNT PICTURES, INC., LOREN L. RYDER,
JOHN R. BISHOP and all the members of the
technical and engineering staff for developing a
method of producing and exhibiting motion pictures
known as VistaVision.

CLASS II (plaque)
None.

CLASS III (citation)
DAVID S. HORSLEY and the UNIVERSAL-
INTERNATIONAL STUDIO SPECIAL
PHOTOGRAPHIC DEPARTMENT; KARL FREUND
and FRANK CRANDELL of Photo Research Corp.;
WESLEY C. MILLER, J.W. STAFFORD, K.M.
FRIERSON and the METRO-GOLDWYN-MAYER
STUDIO SOUND DEPARTMENT;
JOHN P. LIVADARY, LLOYD RUSSELL and the
COLUMBIA STUDIO SOUND DEPARTMENT;
ROLAND MILLER and MAX GOEPPINGER of
Magnascope Corp.;
CARLOS RIVAS, G.M. SPRAGUE and the METRO-
GOLDWYN-MAYER STUDIO SOUND
DEPARTMENT;
FRED WILSON of the Samuel Goldwyn Studio Sound
Department;
P.C. YOUNG of the M-G-M Studio Projection Department
FRED KNOTH and ORIEN ERNEST of the Universal-
International Studio Technical Department.

*INDICATES WINNER

1955
The Twenty-Eighth Year

Before 1955, Oscars had been given to numerous revamped Broadway shows, novels and short stories, but at the twenty-eighth session, March 21, 1956, Academy members voted their top prize to a motion picture based on a *television* play. Never before had the film industry been so complimentary to its archenemy, the TV world. It was an omen of things to come.

Marty, in its transition from tube to big screen, received four of the 1955 awards including best picture, best actor (Ernest Borgnine) and best director (Delbert Mann), plus a screenplay award to the man who created it all, Paddy Chayefsky. Among the actors nominated alongside Borgnine was James Dean, who had been killed in an auto accident six months before, the first actor posthumously nominated for an Academy Award. The next year, he would again be nominated, for *Giant,* completed just prior to his death. Italy's vibrant Anna Magnani was named best actress for *The Rose Tattoo,* her first Hollywood-made movie; she was asleep at home in Rome when she received the news in a transatlantic telephone call.

Jack Lemmon was chosen best supporting actor for *Mister Roberts* and Jo Van Fleet was named best supporting actress for *East of Eden* (she had also been prominent in two other 1955-nominated films, *The Rose Tattoo* with Magnani, and *I'll Cry Tomorrow* with Susan Hayward). *Samurai* was voted an honorary award as the outstanding foreign language film, the second Japanese film in two years so recognized.

The Academy Award ceremony itself was again telecast on NBC-TV as a two-coast affair, with Jerry Lewis handling M.C. responsibilities in Hollywood, and Claudette Colbert sharing similar duties with Joseph L. Mankiewicz (for whom she almost made *All about Eve* six years before) in New York's Century Theater.

Robert Emmett Dolan and George Seaton co-produced for the Academy, and William A. Bennington again directed for the network. Most of the awards were presented by the year's acting nominees, or the previous year's winners. The main thrust of attention on this Academy Award night fell on Grace Kelly, on hand to present the year's best actor award. Three months before, she had announced both her engagement to Prince Rainier of Monaco and her screen retirement. The 1955 Academy Award show was her last public appearance before heading to New York days later, then on to Monaco for the wedding.

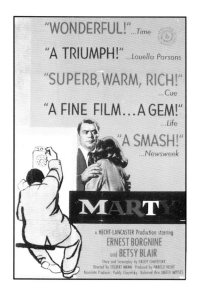

"WONDERFUL!"...Time

"A TRIUMPH!"...Louella Parsons

"SUPERB, WARM, RICH!"...Cue

"A FINE FILM...A GEM!"...Life

"A SMASH!"...Newsweek

MARTY

A HECHT-LANCASTER Production starring
ERNEST BORGNINE and BETSY BLAIR
Story and Screenplay by PADDY CHAYEFSKY
Directed by DELBERT MANN · Produced by HAROLD HECHT
Associate Producer: Paddy Chayefsky · Released thru UNITED ARTISTS

Best Supporting Actress: **Jo Van Fleet** *as Kate (right, with James Dean) in* East of Eden *(Warner Bros.; directed by Elia Kazan). Jo Van Fleet had three strong film roles in 1955: as Susan Hayward's ambitious mother in* I'll Cry Tomorrow, *as Anna Magnani's visitor in* The Rose Tattoo *and as the mysterious madam-mother of James Dean and Richard Davalos in* East of Eden. *For the latter, based on the book by John Steinbeck, she won the Academy Award; it was her first film appearance, and an auspicious debut for the New York-based actress.*

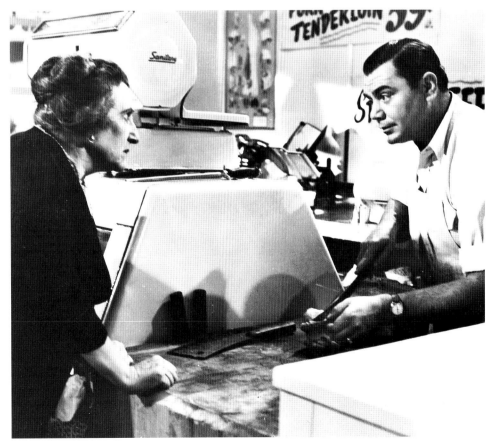

Best Actress: **Anna Magnani** *as Serafina Delle Rose (above, on the set with director Daniel Mann and Burt Lancaster) in* The Rose Tattoo *(Paramount; directed by Mann). Tennessee Williams originally wrote* The Rose Tattoo *for Italy's Anna to play on Broadway, but she rejected the offer because of her difficulty at the time with the English language; by the time Hal Wallis was ready to roll movie cameras on* Tattoo, *however, she was ready, and she delivered a blistering performance as the seamstress who neurotically worships the memory of a deceased (and unfaithful) husband.*

137

Best Picture: Marty *(United Artists; produced by Harold Hecht),* **Best Director:** *Delbert Mann and* **Best Actor:** **Ernest Borgnine** *as Marty (right, with Minerva Urecal) in* Marty. *Written by Paddy Chayefsky and originally done as a television play with Rod Steiger and Nancy Marchand,* Marty *became the first born-in-TV drama to win the Academy's best picture award. Made for a slim $343,000, it told the simple, poignant story of two lonely, plain-looking people (Ernest Borgnine and Betsy Blair) who find each other; Borgnine turned the role of the ordinary, fattish Brooklyn butcher into a star-making part and the picture additionally won the Academy's Screenplay Award for the man who started it all, author Chayefsky.*

Best Supporting Actor: **Jack Lemmon** as *Ensign Pulver in* Mister Roberts *(Warner Bros.; directed by John Ford and Mervyn LeRoy). The Thomas Heggen-Joshua Logan play of 1948 was perfect and robust screen material, one of the year's most popular pictures and allowed newcomer Lemmon, in his fourth film, to underscore his growing reputation as an ace new comedian. He played Roberts' wily and mischievous Pulver aboard the ship Reluctant during World War II, among a crew that included Henry Fonda, James Cagney and William Powell. He won a second Oscar in 1973 for* Save The Tiger, *this time in the leading actor division.*

MOTION PICTURE

LOVE IS A MANY-SPLENDORED THING, 20th Century-Fox. Produced by Buddy Adler.
*MARTY, Hecht-Lancaster, UA. Produced by Harold Hecht.
MISTER ROBERTS, Orange, Warner Bros. Produced by Leland Hayward.
PICNIC, Columbia. Produced by Fred Kohlmar.
THE ROSE TATTOO, Wallis, Paramount. Produced by Hal Wallis.

ACTOR

*ERNEST BORGNINE in *Marty,* Hecht-Lancaster, UA.
JAMES CAGNEY in *Love Me or Leave Me,* M-G-M.
JAMES DEAN in *East of Eden,* Warner Bros.
FRANK SINATRA in *The Man with the Golden Arm,* Preminger, UA.
SPENCER TRACY in *Bad Day at Black Rock,* M-G-M.

ACTRESS

SUSAN HAYWARD in *I'll Cry Tomorrow,* M-G-M.
KATHARINE HEPBURN in *Summertime,* Lopert-Lean, UA (Anglo-American).
JENNIFER JONES in *Love Is a Many-Splendored Thing,* 20th Century-Fox.
*ANNA MAGNANI in *The Rose Tattoo,* Wallis, Paramount.
ELEANOR PARKER in *Interrupted Melody,* M-G-M.

SUPPORTING ACTOR

ARTHUR KENNEDY in *Trial,* M-G-M.
*JACK LEMMON in *Mister Roberts,* Orange, Warner Bros.
JOE MANTELL in *Marty,* Hecht-Lancaster, UA.
SAL MINEO in *Rebel Without a Cause,* Warner Bros.
ARTHUR O'CONNELL in *Picnic,* Columbia.

SUPPORTING ACTRESS

BETSY BLAIR in *Marty,* Hecht-Lancaster, UA.
PEGGY LEE in *Pete Kelly's Blues,* Mark VII, Warner Bros.
MARISA PAVAN in *The Rose Tattoo,* Wallis, Paramount.
*JO VAN FLEET in *East of Eden,* Warner Bros.
NATALIE WOOD in *Rebel Without a Cause,* Warner Bros.

DIRECTING

BAD DAY AT BLACK ROCK, M-G-M. John Sturges.
EAST OF EDEN, Warner Bros. Elia Kazan.
*MARTY, Hecht-Lancaster, UA. Delbert Mann.
PICNIC, Columbia. Joshua Logan.
SUMMERTIME, Lopert, UA (Anglo-American). David Lean.

WRITING

(Motion Picture Story)

*LOVE ME OR LEAVE ME, M-G-M. Daniel Fuchs.
THE PRIVATE WAR OF MAJOR BENSON, U-I. Joe Connelly and Bob Mosher.
REBEL WITHOUT A CAUSE, Warner Bros. Nicholas Ray.
THE SHEEP HAS 5 LEGS, U.M.P.O. (French). Jean Marsan, Henry Troyat, Jacques Perret, Henri Verneuil and Raoul Ploquin.
STRATEGIC AIR COMMAND, Paramount. Beirne Lay, Jr.

(Screenplay)

BAD DAY AT BLACK ROCK, M-G-M. Millard Kaufman.
BLACKBOARD JUNGLE, M-G-M. Richard Brooks.
EAST OF EDEN, Warner Bros. Paul Osborn.
LOVE ME OR LEAVE ME, M-G-M. Daniel Fuchs and Isobel Lennart.
*MARTY, Hecht-Lancaster, UA. Paddy Chayefsky.

(Story and Screenplay)

THE COURT-MARTIAL OF BILLY MITCHELL, United States Pictures, Warner Bros. Milton Sperling and Emmet Lavery.
*INTERRUPTED MELODY, M-G-M. William Ludwig and Sonya Levien.
IT'S ALWAYS FAIR WEATHER, M-G-M. Betty Comden and Adolph Green.
MR. HULOT'S HOLIDAY, GBD International Releasing (French). Jacques Tati and Henri Marquet.
THE SEVEN LITTLE FOYS, Paramount. Melville Shavelson and Jack Rose.

CINEMATOGRAPHY

(Black-and-White)

BLACKBOARD JUNGLE, M-G-M. Russell Harlan.
I'LL CRY TOMORROW, M-G-M. Arthur E. Arling.
MARTY, Hecht-Lancaster, UA. Joseph LaShelle.
QUEEN BEE, Columbia. Charles Lang.
*THE ROSE TATTOO, Wallis, Paramount. James Wong Howe.

(Color)

GUYS AND DOLLS, Goldwyn, M-G-M. Harry Stradling.
LOVE IS A MANY-SPLENDORED THING, 20th Century-Fox. Leon Shamroy.
A MAN CALLED PETER, 20th Century-Fox. Harold Lipstein.
OKLAHOMA!, Hornblow, Magna Corp. Robert Surtees.
*TO CATCH A THIEF, Hitchcock, Paramount. Robert Burks.

ART DIRECTION- SET DECORATION

(For the first time, set decorators as well as art directors of winning films received a full-size Academy statuette, instead of certificate or plaque)

(Black-and-White)

BLACKBOARD JUNGLE, M-G-M. Cedric Gibbons and Randall Duell; Edwin B. Willis and Henry Grace.
I'LL CRY TOMORROW, M-G-M. Cedric Gibbons and Malcolm Brown; Edwin B. Willis and Hugh B. Hunt.
THE MAN WITH THE GOLDEN ARM, Preminger, UA. Joseph C. Wright; Darrell Silvera.
MARTY, Hecht-Lancaster, UA. Edward S. Haworth and Walter Simonds; Robert Priestley.
*THE ROSE TATTOO, Wallis, Paramount. Hal Pereira and Tambi Larsen; Sam Comer and Arthur Krams.

(Color)

DADDY LONG LEGS, 20th Century-Fox. Lyle Wheeler and John DeCuir; Walter M. Scott and Paul S. Fox.
GUYS AND DOLLS, Goldwyn, M-G-M. Oliver Smith and Joseph C. Wright; Howard Bristol.
LOVE IS A MANY-SPLENDORED THING, 20th Century-Fox. Lyle Wheeler and George W. Davis; Walter M. Scott and Jack Stubbs.
*PICNIC, Columbia. William Flannery and Jo Mielziner; Robert Priestley.
TO CATCH A THIEF, Hitchcock, Paramount. Hal Pereira and Joseph McMillan Johnson; Sam Comer and Arthur Krams.

Honorary Award: Samurai (Fine Arts Films; produced in Japan by Kazuo Takimura) starred Toshiro Mifune as a 16th-century villager who wants to become a samurai warrior, joins a losing war and ultimately ends his days as a missionary. The Academy honored Samurai *as the best foreign language film released in the United States during 1955, as chosen by the Board of Governors. Hereafter, beginning with the 1956 Awards, foreign films were honored in their own regular award category, with nominations, rather than as special or honorary awards.*

COSTUME DESIGN

(Black-and-White)

*I'LL CRY TOMORROW, M-G-M. Helen Rose.
THE PICKWICK PAPERS, Renown, Kingsley International (British). Beatrice Dawson.
QUEEN BEE, Columbia. Jean Louis.
THE ROSE TATTOO, Wallis, Paramount. Edith Head.
UGETSU, Daiei, Edward Harrison Releasing (Japanese). Tadaoto Kainoscho.

(Color)

GUYS AND DOLLS, Goldwyn, M-G-M. Irene Sharaff.
INTERRUPTED MELODY, M-G-M. Helen Rose.
*LOVE IS A MANY-SPLENDORED THING, 20th Century-Fox. Charles LeMaire.
TO CATCH A THIEF, Hitchcock, Paramount. Edith Head.
THE VIRGIN QUEEN, 20th Century-Fox. Charles LeMaire and Mary Wills.

SOUND RECORDING

LOVE IS A MANY-SPLENDORED THING, 20th Century-Fox. Carl W. Faulkner, sound director.
LOVE ME OR LEAVE ME, M-G-M. Wesley C. Miller, sound director.
MISTER ROBERTS, Warner Bros. William A. Mueller, sound director.
NOT AS A STRANGER, Kramer, UA. RCA Sound Department; Watson Jones, sound director.
*OKLAHOMA!, Hornblow, Magna. Todd-AO Sound Department; Fred Hynes, sound director.

FILM EDITING

BLACKBOARD JUNGLE, M-G-M. Ferris Webster.
THE BRIDGES AT TOKO-RI, Perlberg-Seaton, Paramount. Alma Macrorie.
OKLAHOMA!, Hornblow, Magna Corp. Gene Ruggiero and George Boemler.
*PICNIC, Columbia. Charles Nelson and William A. Lyon.
THE ROSE TATTOO, Wallis, Paramount. Warren Low.

SPECIAL EFFECTS

*THE BRIDGES AT TOKO-RI, Paramount.
THE DAM BUSTERS, Associated British, Warner Bros. (British).
THE RAINS OF RANCHIPUR, 20th Century-Fox.

MUSIC

(Song)

I'LL NEVER STOP LOVING YOU (Love Me or Leave Me, M-G-M); Music by Nicholas Brodszky. Lyrics by Sammy Cahn.
*LOVE IS A MANY-SPLENDORED THING (Love Is a Many-Splendored Thing, 20th Century-Fox); Music by Sammy Fain. Lyrics by Paul Francis Webster.

SOMETHING'S GOTTA GIVE (Daddy Long Legs, 20th Century-Fox); Music and Lyrics by Johnny Mercer.
(LOVE IS) THE TENDER TRAP (The Tender Trap, M-G-M); Music by James Van Heusen. Lyrics by Sammy Cahn.
UNCHAINED MELODY (Unchained, Bartlett, Warner Bros.); Music by Alex North. Lyrics by Hy Zaret.

(Scoring of a Dramatic or Comedy Picture)

BATTLE CRY, Warner Bros. Max Steiner.
*LOVE IS A MANY-SPLENDORED THING, 20th Century-Fox. Alfred Newman.
THE MAN WITH THE GOLDEN ARM, Preminger, UA. Elmer Bernstein.
PICNIC, Columbia. George Duning.
THE ROSE TATTOO, Wallis, Paramount. Alex North.

(Scoring of a Musical Picture)

DADDY LONG LEGS, 20th Century-Fox. Alfred Newman.
GUYS AND DOLLS, Goldwyn, M-G-M. Jay Blackton and Cyril J. Mockridge.
IT'S ALWAYS FAIR WEATHER, M-G-M. Andre Previn.
LOVE ME OR LEAVE ME, M-G-M. Percy Faith and George Stoll.
*OKLAHOMA!, Hornblow, Magna Corp. Robert Russell Bennett, Jay Blackton and Adolph Deutsch.

SHORT SUBJECTS

(Cartoons)

GOOD WILL TO MEN, M-G-M. Fred Quimby, William Hanna and Joseph Barbera, producers.
THE LEGEND OF A ROCK-A-BYE POINT, Lantz, U-I. Walter Lantz, producer.
NO HUNTING, Disney, RKO Radio. Walt Disney, producer.
*SPEEDY GONZALES, Warner Bros. Edward Selzer, producer.

(One-reel)

GADGETS GALORE, Warner Bros. Robert Youngson, producer.
*SURVIVAL CITY, 20th Century-Fox. Edmund Reek, producer.
3RD AVE. EL, Davidson Prods., Ardee Films. Carson Davidson, producer.
THREE KISSES, Paramount. Justin Herman, producer.

(Two-reel)

THE BATTLE OF GETTYSBURG, M-G-M. Dore Schary, producer.
*THE FACE OF LINCOLN, University of Southern California, Cavalcade Pictures. Wilbur T. Blume, producer.
ON THE TWELFTH DAY..., Go Pictures, George Brest & Assocs. George K. Arthur, producer.

SWITZERLAND, Disney, Buena Vista. Walt Disney, producer.
24 HOUR ALERT, Warner Bros. Cedric Francis, producer.

DOCUMENTARY

(Short Subjects)

THE BATTLE OF GETTYSBURG, M-G-M. Dore Schary, producer.
THE FACE OF LINCOLN, University of Southern California, Cavalcade Pictures. Wilbur T. Blume, producer.
*MEN AGAINST THE ARCTIC, Disney, Buena Vista. Walt Disney, producer.

(Features)

HEARTBREAK RIDGE, Rene Risacher Prod., Tudor Pictures (French). Rene Risacher, producer.
*HELEN KELLER IN HER STORY, Nancy Hamilton Presentation. Nancy Hamilton, producer.

HONORARY AND OTHER AWARDS

TO SAMURAI, The Legend of Musashi, (Japanese)— Best Foreign Language Film first released in the United States during 1955. (statuette)

1955 IRVING G. THALBERG MEMORIAL AWARD

None given this year.

SCIENTIFIC OR TECHNICAL

CLASS I (statuette)

NATIONAL CARBON CO. for the development and production of a high efficiency yellow flame carbon for motion picture color photography.

CLASS II (plaque)

EASTMAN KODAK CO. for Eastman Tri-X panchromatic negative film.
FARCIOT EDOUART, HAL CORL and the PARAMOUNT STUDIO TRANSPARENCY DEPT. for the engineering and development of a double-frame, triple-head background projector.

CLASS III (citation)

20TH CENTURY-FOX STUDIO and BAUSCH & LOMB CO.;
WALTER JOLLEY, MAURICE LARSON and R.H. SPIES of 20th Century-Fox Studio;
STEVE KRILANOVICH;
DAVE ANDERSON of 20th Century-Fox Studio;
LOREN L. RYDER, CHARLES WEST, HENRY FRACKER and PARAMOUNT STUDIO;
FARCIOT EDOUART, HAL CORL and the PARAMOUNT STUDIO TRANSPARENCY DEPARTMENT.

*INDICATES WINNER

ngrid Bergman received a rousing welcome back to the Hollywood (and international) movie scene on March 27, 1957, when she was announced as the Academy's best actress winner of 1956 for *Anastasia.* For the preceding six years, the star had worked exclusively in Italian-made films, most of them directed by her husband, Roberto Rossellini, none of them as commercially successful as her earlier work in Hollywood under the management of David O. Selznick. At the time of the Oscar announcement, she was in Paris, appearing on stage in *Tea and Sympathy,* and her award was accepted by former co-star Cary Grant.

Controversy erupted in the Academy's writing category. Early in 1956, the name of screenwriter Michael Wilson had been deleted from the credits of *Friendly Persuasion* by Allied Artists, the film's distributor, based on a 1952 agreement between the Screen Writers Guild and various production companies. That agreement gave studios the right to omit from the screen the name of any individual who had failed to clear himself before a duly constituted legislative committee of Congress if accused of Communist affiliations, as was the case with Wilson at the time. The Academy, in the awkward position of possibly conferring its highest honor on someone whose name had been omitted from screen credit, revised its bylaws at a special February 6, 1957, meeting. That revision, in essence, allowed that in such cases, the achievement itself could be eligible for nomination, but the specific writer would be ineligible. (The bylaw was repealed by the Academy as "unworkable" on January 12, 1959.)

Also, when nominations were announced, Edward Bernds and Elwood Ullman, the authors of a Bowery Boys quickie titled *High Society,* were among the contenders but respectfully withdrew their own names, aware that voters had probably mistaken their *High Society* with another 1956 release of the same title which was written by John Patrick and starred Bing Crosby, Grace Kelly and Frank Sinatra. There was further confusion when the final winners were announced (at the Pantages Theatre in Hollywood, plus New York's Century Theater, telecast by NBC) and the best motion picture story winner was *The Brave One,* credited to Robert Rich. The Rich name was later acknowledged as a pseudonym, with exact writer credit not officially established for several years until Dalton Trumbo was confirmed as the author; in 1956, he had been unable to work under his own name because of the earlier House Un-American Activities investigations into the motion picture industry. Shortly before Trumbo's death in 1976, the Academy's then-President Walter Mirisch presented the screenwriter his overdue Oscar.

Most-honored films of the year were *Around the World in 80 Days* (five awards, including best picture) and *The King and I* (five awards, including best actor Yul Brynner). Anthony Quinn,

140

Best Picture: **Around the World in 80 Days** *(United Artists; produced by Michael Todd). Broadway showman Michael Todd had never made a motion picture before, and he didn't tip-toe in with his first one, based on Jules Verne's lampoon of Victorian manners in which a proper Britisher of 1872 sets out to win a wager that he can circle the globe in precisely 80 days. Todd turned it into a 178-minute movie carnival—and an exceptionally super film—featuring (right) Robert Newton, Cantinflas, Shirley MacLaine and David Niven. He also coined a new show business phrase, "cameo role," to cover major stars he'd enticed into playing bit roles, including Frank Sinatra, Marlene Dietrich, Jose Greco, Ronald Colman, Noel Coward, Beatrice Lillie, Red Skelton, Victor McLaglen, Buster Keaton and others who did unexpected walk-ons. Michael Anderson directed.*

Dorothy Malone and director George Stevens were also honored and, for the first year, foreign language films were classified in a separate category, nominated and voted on along with other awards instead of being presented as an honorary award with no nominations. M.C. of the Oscar night show itself was Jerry Lewis in Hollywood, with Celeste Holm handling hostess duties on the New York sister-show.

Best Actress: **Ingrid Bergman** *as the Woman (above) in* Anastasia *(20th Century-Fox; directed by Anatole Litvak). With filming done entirely in Europe, Ingrid Bergman played a Paris derelict, saved from suicide by a trio of White Russians who train her to pose as the missing daughter of Czar Nicholas II of Russia, who had supposedly escaped death in the 1918 assassination of the Royal Family; plagued by fears of insanity and with only vague recollections of her own past, the woman* wins recognition from the Dowager Empress (Helen Hayes) and even gives evidence she might be the real Anastasia. Originally a Broadway success with Viveca Lindfors in the title role, Anastasia *brought Ingrid Bergman back into the front-line of the motion picture world after a six-year absence and earned her a second Oscar. A third one came 18 years later, for* Murder on the Orient Express.

Best Actor: **Yul Brynner** *as the King of Siam in* The King and I *(20th Century-Fox; directed by Walter Lang). Yul Brynner had appeared on screen only once before (in 1949's minor* Port of New York*) but in 1956 he made an imposing screen impression in three of the year's most conspicuous films:* The King and I, The Ten Commandments *and* Anastasia. *He won the Academy Award for the first, as the virile Siamese tyrant of the 1800s whose desire to be a cultivated and educated man clashes with his traditional, royal arrogance and with an imported governess, played by Deborah Kerr. Brynner had played the King before, on Broadway opposite Gertrude Lawrence, when the story was first set to Rodgers and Hammerstein music in 1951. The King had also been in the movies before, portrayed by Rex Harrison in a 1946 nonmusical version,* Anna and the King of Siam.

Best Supporting Actress: Dorothy Malone *as Marylee Hadley (above, with Rock Hudson) in* Written on the Wind *(Universal-International; directed by Douglas Sirk). After a long career (14 years, 39 films) of work-horse roles, the majority of them B-budget projects, Dorothy Malone had an actress's field day playing a sexually maladjusted, poor-little-rich-girl sister of Robert Stack, out to conquer family friend Rock Hudson. She won the Oscar, although the character played by Hudson forever eluded her.*

MOTION PICTURE

* **AROUND THE WORLD IN 80 DAYS**, Todd, UA, James W. Sullivan and Ken Adam; Ross J. Dowd.
FRIENDLY PERSUASION, Allied Artists. Produced by William Wyler.
GIANT, Warner Bros. Produced by George Stevens and Henry Ginsberg.
THE KING AND I, 20th Century-Fox. Produced by Charles Brackett.
THE TEN COMMANDMENTS, DeMille, Paramount. Produced by Cecil B. DeMille.

ACTOR

***YUL BRYNNER** in *The King and I*, 20th Century-Fox.
JAMES DEAN in *Giant*, Warner Bros.
KIRK DOUGLAS in *Lust for Life*, M-G-M.
ROCK HUDSON in *Giant*, Warner Bros.
SIR LAURENCE OLIVIER in *Richard III*, Olivier, Lopert Films (British).

ACTRESS

CARROLL BAKER in *Baby Doll*, Newtown, Warner Bros.
***INGRID BERGMAN** in *Anastasia*, 20th Century-Fox.
KATHARINE HEPBURN in *The Rainmaker*, Wallis, Paramount.
NANCY KELLY in *The Bad Seed*, Warner Bros.
DEBORAH KERR in *The King and I*, 20th Century-Fox.

SUPPORTING ACTOR

DON MURRAY in *Bus Stop*, 20th Century-Fox.
ANTHONY PERKINS in *Friendly Persuasion*, Allied Artists.
***ANTHONY QUINN** in *Lust for Life*, M-G-M.
MICKEY ROONEY in *The Bold and the Brave*, Filmakers Releasing, RKO Radio.
ROBERT STACK in *Written on the Wind*, U-I.

SUPPORTING ACTRESS

MILDRED DUNNOCK in *Baby Doll*, Newtown, Warner Bros.
EILEEN HECKART in *The Bad Seed*, Warner Bros.
MERCEDES McCAMBRIDGE in *Giant*, Warner Bros.
PATTY McCORMACK in *The Bad Seed*, Warner Bros.
***DOROTHY MALONE** in *Written on the Wind*, U-I.

DIRECTING

AROUND THE WORLD IN 80 DAYS, Todd, UA. Michael Anderson.
FRIENDLY PERSUASION, Allied Artists. William Wyler.
***GIANT**, Warner Bros. George Stevens.
THE KING AND I, 20th Century-Fox. Walter Lang.
WAR AND PEACE, Ponti-De Laurentiis, Paramount (Italo-American). King Vidor.

WRITING

(Motion Picture Story)

***THE BRAVE ONE**, King Bros., RKO Radio. Dalton Trumbo (aka Robert Rich).
THE EDDY DUCHIN STORY, Columbia. Leo Katcher.
HIGH SOCIETY, Allied Artists. Edward Bernds and Elwood Ullman. (Withdrawn from final ballot.)
THE PROUD AND THE BEAUTIFUL, Kingsley International (French). Jean Paul Sartre.
UMBERTO D., Harrison & Davidson Releasing (Italian). Cesare Zavattini.

(Best Screenplay — adapted)

***AROUND THE WORLD IN 80 DAYS**, Todd, UA. James Poe, John Farrow and S.J. Perelman.
BABY DOLL, Newtown, Warner Bros. Tennessee Williams.
GIANT, Warner Bros. Fred Guiol and Ivan Moffat.

LUST FOR LIFE, M-G-M. Norman Corwin.
FRIENDLY PERSUASION, Allied Artists. (Writer Michael Wilson ineligible for nomination under 1956 Academy bylaws.)

(Best Screenplay—original)

THE BOLD AND THE BRAVE, Filmakers, RKO Radio. Robert Lewin.
JULIE, Arwin, M-G-M. Andrew L. Stone.
LA STRADA, Ponti-De Laurentiis, Trans-Lux Dist. Corp. (Italian). Federico Fellini and Tullio Pinelli.
THE LADY KILLERS, Ealing, Continental Dist. (British). William Rose.
***THE RED BALLOON**, Lopert Films (French). Albert Lamorisse.

CINEMATOGRAPHY

(Black-and-White)

BABY DOLL, Newtown, Warner Bros. Boris Kaufman.
THE BAD SEED, Warner Bros. Hal Rosson.
THE HARDER THEY FALL, Columbia. Burnett Guffey.
***SOMEBODY UP THERE LIKES ME**, M-G-M. Joseph Ruttenberg.
STAGECOACH TO FURY, Regal Films, 20th Century-Fox. Walter Strenge.

(Color)

***AROUND THE WORLD IN 80 DAYS**, Todd, UA. Lionel Lindon.
THE EDDY DUCHIN STORY, Columbia. Harry Stradling.
THE KING AND I, 20th Century-Fox. Leon Shamroy.
THE TEN COMMANDMENTS, DeMille, Paramount. Loyal Griggs.
WAR AND PEACE, Ponti-De Laurentiis, Paramount (Italo-American). Jack Cardiff.

ART DIRECTION-
SET DECORATION

(Black-and-White)

THE PROUD AND THE PROFANE, Perlberg-Seaton, Paramount. Hal Pereira and A. Earl Hedrick; Samuel M. Comer and Frank R. McKelvy.
SEVEN SAMURAI, Toho, Kingsley International (Japanese). Takashi Matsuyama.
THE SOLID GOLD CADILLAC, Columbia. Ross Bellah; William R. Kiernan and Louis Diage.
***SOMEBODY UP THERE LIKES ME**, M-G-M. Cedric Gibbons and Malcolm F. Brown; Edwin B. Willis and F. Keogh Gleason.
TEENAGE REBEL, 20th Century-Fox. Lyle R. Wheeler and Jack Martin Smith; Walter M. Scott and Stuart A. Reiss.

(Color)

AROUND THE WORLD IN 80 DAYS, Todd, UA. James W. Sullivan and Ken Adam; Ross J. Dowd.
GIANT, Warner Bros. Boris Leven; Ralph S. Hurst.
***THE KING AND I**, 20th Century-Fox. Lyle R. Wheeler and John DeCuir; Walter M. Scott and Paul S. Fox.
LUST FOR LIFE, M-G-M. Cedric Gibbons, Hans Peters and Preston Ames; Edwin B. Willis and F. Keogh Gleason.
THE TEN COMMANDMENTS, DeMille, Paramount. Hal Pereira, Walter H. Tyler and Albert Nozaki; Sam M. Comer and Ray Moyer.

COSTUME DESIGN

(Black-and-White)

THE POWER AND THE PRIZE, M-G-M. Helen Rose.
THE PROUD AND THE PROFANE, Perlberg-Seaton, Paramount. Edith Head.
SEVEN SAMURAI, Toho, Kingsley International (Japanese). Kohei Ezaki.

The Brave One *(RKO Radio; produced by Maurice King and Frank King) featured Michel Ray (at right) as a young Mexican boy who attempts to save his pet bull from being sent into the bullring. The film received an Oscar for motion picture story and unintentionally spawned confusion: the name of the writer credited with authorship, Robert Rich, turned out to be an alias. Two decades later, the mystery was officially solved and the Academy statuette went to its rightful owner, screenwriter Dalton Trumbo, blacklisted in 1956 by the industry for political affiliations.*

Best Director: **George Stevens** *(above, with James Dean) for* Giant *(Warner Bros.; also produced by Stevens, with Henry Ginsberg). Based on the Edna Ferber novel,* Giant *was a mammoth (198 minutes) and sprawling epic focusing on the Benedict clan (headed by Rock Hudson with Elizabeth Taylor) of Texas. Stevens had previously won the Academy Award for 1951's* A Place in the Sun, *also with Elizabeth Taylor, and was additionally nominated in 1943 (for* The More the Merrier*), 1953 (for* Shane*) and 1959 (for* The Diary of Anne Frank*). He also received the 1953 Irving G. Thalberg Memorial Award.*

Best Supporting Actor: **Anthony Quinn** *as Paul Gauguin (above, with Kirk Douglas) in* Lust for Life *(M-G-M; directed by Vincente Minnelli). Quinn won his second Supporting Actor Oscar as the real-life Gauguin, ego-ridden painter and housemate of the tormented Vincent van Gogh. He played the role with vitality and dark humor, and it was one of the shortest performances ever to win an Academy Award, constituting only a matter of eight minutes of total screen time, a supporting performance in the best sense of the word.*

*THE SOLID GOLD CADILLAC, Columbia. Jean Louis.
TEENAGE REBEL, 20th Century-Fox. Charles LeMaire and Mary Wills.

(Color)

AROUND THE WORLD IN 80 DAYS, Todd, UA. Miles White.
GIANT, Warner Bros. Moss Mabry and Marjorie Best.
*THE KING AND I, 20th Century-Fox. Irene Sharaff.
THE TEN COMMANDMENTS, DeMille, Paramount. Edith Head, Ralph Jester, John Jensen, Dorothy Jeakins and Arnold Friberg.
WAR AND PEACE, Ponti-De Laurentiis, Paramount (Italo-American). Marie De Matteis.

SOUND RECORDING

THE BRAVE ONE, King Bros., RKO Radio. John Myers, sound director.
THE EDDY DUCHIN STORY, Columbia. Columbia Studio Sound Department; John Livadary, sound director.
FRIENDLY PERSUASION, Allied Artists. Westrex Sound Services, Inc.; Gordon R. Glennan, sound director, and Samuel Goldwyn Studio Sound Department; Gordon Sawyer, sound director.
*THE KING AND I, 20th Century-Fox. 20th Century-Fox Studio Sound Department; Carl Faulkner, sound director.
THE TEN COMMANDMENTS, DeMille, Paramount. Paramount Studio Sound Department; Loren L. Ryder, sound director.

FILM EDITING

*AROUND THE WORLD IN 80 DAYS, Todd, UA. Gene Ruggiero and Paul Weatherwax.
THE BRAVE ONE, King Bros., RKO Radio. Merrill G. White.
GIANT, Warner Bros. William Hornbeck, Philip W. Anderson and Fred Bohanan.
SOMEBODY UP THERE LIKES ME, M-G-M. Albert Akst.
THE TEN COMMANDMENTS, DeMille, Paramount. Anne Bauchens.

SPECIAL EFFECTS

FORBIDDEN PLANET, M-G-M. A. Arnold Gillespie, Irving Ries and Wesley C. Miller.
*THE TEN COMMANDMENTS, DeMille, Paramount. John Fulton.

MUSIC

(Song)

FRIENDLY PERSUASION (THEE I LOVE) (*Friendly Persuasion,* Allied Artists); Music by Dimitri Tiomkin. Lyrics by Paul Francis Webster.
JULIE (*Julie,* Arwin, M-G-M); Music by Leith Stevens. Lyrics by Tom Adair.
TRUE LOVE (*High Society,* Siegel, M-G-M); Music and Lyrics by Cole Porter.

*WHATEVER WILL BE, WILL BE (QUE SERA, SERA) (*The Man Who Knew Too Much,* Hitchcock, Paramount); Music and Lyrics by Jay Livingston and Ray Evans.
WRITTEN ON THE WIND (*Written on the Wind,* U-I); Music by Victor Young. Lyrics by Sammy Cahn.

(Scoring of a Dramatic or Comedy Picture)

ANASTASIA, 20th Century-Fox. Alfred Newman.
*AROUND THE WORLD IN 80 DAYS, Todd, UA. Victor Young.
BETWEEN HEAVEN AND HELL, 20th Century-Fox. Hugo Friedhofer.
GIANT, Warner Bros. Dimitri Tiomkin.
THE RAINMAKER, Wallis, Paramount. Alex North.

(Scoring of a Musical Picture)

THE BEST THINGS IN LIFE ARE FREE, 20th Century-Fox. Lionel Newman.
THE EDDY DUCHIN STORY, Columbia. Morris Stoloff and George Duning.
HIGH SOCIETY, Siegel, M-G-M. Johnny Green and Saul Chaplin.
*THE KING AND I, 20th Century-Fox. Alfred Newman and Ken Darby.
MEET ME IN LAS VEGAS, M-G-M. George Stoll and Johnny Green.

SHORT SUBJECTS

(Cartoon)

GERALD McBOING-BOING ON PLANET MOO, UPA, Columbia. Stephen Bosustow, producer.
THE JAYWALKER, UPA, Columbia. Stephen Bosustow, producer.
*MISTER MAGOO'S PUDDLE JUMPER, UPA, Columbia. Stephen Bosustow, producer.

(One-reel)

*CRASHING THE WATER BARRIER, Warner Bros. Konstantin Kalser, producer.
I NEVER FORGET A FACE, Warner Bros. Robert Youngson, producer.
TIME STOOD STILL, Warner Bros. Cedric Francis, producer.

(Two-reel)

*THE BESPOKE OVERCOAT, George K. Arthur, Go Pictures, Inc. Romulus Films, producer.
COW DOG, Disney, Buena Vista. Larry Lansburgh, producer.
THE DARK WAVE, 20th Century-Fox. John Healy, producer.
SAMOA, Disney, Buena Vista. Walt Disney, producer.

DOCUMENTARY

(Short Subjects)

A CITY DECIDES, Charles Guggenheim & Assocs.
THE DARK WAVE, 20th Century-Fox. John Healy, producer.
THE HOUSE WITHOUT A NAME, U-I. Valentine Davies, producer.

MAN IN SPACE, Disney, Buena Vista. Ward Kimball, producer.
*THE TRUE STORY OF THE CIVIL WAR, Camera Eye Pictures. Louis Clyde Stoumen, producer.

(Features)

THE NAKED EYE, Camera Eye Pictures. Louis Clyde Stoumen, producer.
*THE SILENT WORLD, Filmad-F.S.J.Y.C., Columbia (French). Jacques-Yves Cousteau, producer.
WHERE MOUNTAINS FLOAT, Brandon Films (Danish). The Government Film Committee of Denmark, producer.

FOREIGN LANGUAGE FILM

(First year of nominations; previously honored in the Special Award division)

THE CAPTAIN OF KOPENICK, (West Germany). Gyula Trebitsch and Walter Koppel, producers.
GERVAISE, (France). Annie Dorfmann, producer.
HARP OF BURMA, (Japan). Masayuki Takagi, producer.
*LA STRADA, (Italy). Dino De Laurentiis and Carlo Ponti, producers.
QIVITOQ, (Denmark). O. Dalsgaard-Olsen, producer.

HONORARY AND OTHER AWARDS

TO EDDIE CANTOR for distinguished service to the film industry. (statuette)

1956 IRVING G. THALBERG MEMORIAL AWARD

TO BUDDY ADLER

1956 JEAN HERSHOLT HUMANITARIAN AWARD

(New category)

TO Y. FRANK FREEMAN

SCIENTIFIC OR TECHNICAL

CLASS I (statuette)

None.

CLASS II (plaque)

None.

CLASS III (citation)

RICHARD H. RANGER of Rangertone Inc.;
TED HIRSCH, CARL HAUGE and EDWARD REICHARD of Consolidated Film Industries;
THE TECHNICAL DEPARTMENTS of PARAMOUNT PICTURES CORP;
ROY C. STEWART AND SONS of Stewart-Trans Lux Corp., DR. C.R. DAILY and the TRANSPARENCY DEPARTMENT of PARAMOUNT PICTURES CORP;
THE CONSTRUCTION DEPARTMENT of METRO-GOLDWYN-MAYER STUDIO;
DANIEL J. BLOOMBERG, JOHN POND, WILLIAM WADE and the ENGINEERING and CAMERA DEPARTMENTS of REPUBLIC STUDIO.

*INDICATES WINNER

1957
The Thirtieth Year

In newspaper parlance, 30 means "the end," but when the Academy turned thirty with the 1957 awards ceremony, March 26, 1958, it was the start of something new: for the first time in the six years Oscar shows had been televised, the show itself was TV-sponsored solely by the motion picture industry, financed by the major studios, independent producers and theater owners, who used the telecast to promote new film products instead of unallied commercial products, as had been the case. It was an auspicious idea and continued for three television years, but ultimately proved too much of an organizational and financial burden.

Voting rules were also drastically altered. Since 1946, the final voting decision on Oscars had been made by the Academy's approximately 2,000 members, but yearly nominations for awards had been chosen by more than 12,000 individuals, members of the Academy, industry guilds and unions; beginning with the 1957 awards, both the nominations *and* final selections were left strictly in the hands of the Academy members. The number of categories, which had swelled to thirty-one in the previous year, was also streamlined down to twenty-three.

Because the NBC telecast was wholly an industry affair, it was especially crowded with major box office names, several of whom—like Clark Gable and Jennifer Jones—had never appeared on television before. It was produced for

the Academy by Jerry Wald. Five people shared master of ceremonies duties (James Stewart, David Niven, Jack Lemmon, Rosalind Russell, Bob Hope) with some animated help from Donald Duck, who hosted a seven-minute combined live-action and cartoon history of the movies. The entire show came from the Pantages Theatre in Hollywood, with no New York cut-in, another first for Oscar's television career. Among the entertainment highlights of the evening was the opening number: a medley of previous Oscar-winning songs, done by Betty Grable and Harry James, Mae West and Rock Hudson, Marge and Gower Champion, Bob Hope and Rhonda Fleming, Shirley MacLaine and others.

The Bridge on the River Kwai dominated the evening's awards, winning seven, including best picture, best actor (Alec Guinness) and best director (David Lean). *Sayonara* was runner-up with four Oscars, including those for best supporting actor (Red Buttons) and best supporting actress (Miyoshi Umeki). Best actress was 28-year-old Joanne Woodward in *The Three Faces of Eve,* and Italy's *The Nights of Cabiria* was selected as best foreign language film. All the acting winners were on hand at the Pantages, except winner Guinness, who was in England filming *The Horse's Mouth.* His award was accepted by Jean Simmons.

Best Director: David Lean *and* **Best Actor:** Alec Guinness *as Colonel Nicholson for* The Bridge on the River Kwai *(Columbia; produced by Sam Spiegel). England's David Lean had been a part of the Academy Awards story since 1946 when he was twice nominated for* Brief Encounter *(as director and for co-writing the screenplay); the following year, he was again nominated in the same two divisions for* Great Expectations, *and in 1955 for directing* Summertime. *Guiness had been nominated for acting in 1952 for* The Lavender Hill Mob, *and both gentlemen won their first Oscars for 1957's* Bridge. *Both were also to collect additional Academy Awards in the years ahead.*

Best Actress: Joanne Woodward *as Eve White (above) in* The Three Faces of Eve *(20th Century-Fox; directed by Nunnally Johnson). First offered to Jean Simmons, then to Judy Garland and Carroll Baker, among others, Eve was* *based on an actual split-personality case, recorded by two Georgia psychiatrists, in which a drab housewife suffered severe headaches and during subsequent blackouts underwent a striking personality change (to Eve 'Black'), then under* *psychiatric treatment gave way to a third personality ('Jane'). It was a plump and showy role, finally entrusted to newcomer Joanne Woodward, and she gave it her own indelible mark. Eve won her the Academy Award, and made her a major star.*

Best Picture: The Bridge on the River Kwai, *which took a hot and uncomfortable three-and-a-half months to film in the Ceylon jungle. Based on Pierre Boulle's grim novel about the folly of men unwittingly invovled in the useless game of war, it paid off on film as the most realistic antiwar movie since* All Quiet on the Western Front *27 years before. It won* *seven Academy Awards including one for Alec Guinness' performance as a British colonel held captive with his men in a World War II Japanese prisoner-of-war camp. A strict disciplinarian, the colonel has a rigid conflict of wills with his Japanese captors over military protocol, and later supervises the building of a railway bridge for the Japanese without* *regard for the aid it gives the enemy, obsessed instead with proving his battalion is superior to his enemy. Guinness' fellow players included William Holden, Jack Hawkins, Sessue Hayakawa and Geoffrey Horne.*

(right) **Best Supporting Actor:** Red Buttons *as Sgt. Joe Kelly and* **Best Supporting Actress:** Miyoshi Umeki *as Katsumi (at right of James Garner and Marlon Brando) in* Sayonara *(Warner Bros.; directed by Joshua Logan). As an ill-fated interracial married couple hounded by prejudice— and military red tape—in postwar Japan, Miyoshi Umeki and Red Buttons gave poignant, touching performances in this sumptuous and romantic version of James A. Michener's novel, and both received Academy Awards. Brando played an Air Force major who champions their cause before it tragically ends in a double suicide pact.*

Special Award *to* "Broncho Billy" Anderson *(at right, with his daughter and receiving his Oscar from Hugh O'Brian). Although western movies enjoyed a long popularity with movie audiences, and more than once had to pay the studio mortgage when loftier endeavors fell short, very few films of the genre—and virtually no performers primarily associated with the western movie—received Oscar attention. But, long after he'd hung up his six-gun and deserted cardboard sagebrush, "Broncho Billy" Anderson—best known as a western hero, par excellence, of the silent screen era, received an honorary Oscar, specifically "for his contributions to the development of motion pictures as entertainment."*

MOTION PICTURE

*THE BRIDGE ON THE RIVER KWAI, Horizon, Columbia. Produced by Sam Spiegel.

PEYTON PLACE, Wald, 20th Century-Fox. Produced by Jerry Wald.

SAYONARA, Goetz, Warner Bros. Produced by William Goetz.

12 ANGRY MEN, Orion-Nova, UA. Produced by Henry Fonda and Reginald Rose.

WITNESS FOR THE PROSECUTION, Small-Hornblow, UA. Produced by Arthur Hornblow, Jr.

ACTOR

MARLON BRANDO in *Sayonara*, Goetz, Warner Bros.

ANTHONY FRANCIOSA in *A Hatful of Rain*, 20th Century-Fox.

*ALEC GUINNESS in *The Bridge on the River Kwai*, Horizon, Columbia.

CHARLES LAUGHTON in *Witness for the Prosecution*, Small-Hornblow, UA.

ANTHONY QUINN in *Wild Is the Wind*, Wallis, Paramount.

ACTRESS

DEBORAH KERR in *Heaven Knows, Mr. Allison*, 20th Century-Fox.

ANNA MAGNANI in *Wild Is the Wind*, Wallis, Paramount.

ELIZABETH TAYLOR in *Raintree County*, M-G-M.

LANA TURNER in *Peyton Place*, Wald, 20th Century-Fox.

*JOANNE WOODWARD in *The Three Faces of Eve*, 20th Century-Fox.

SUPPORTING ACTOR

*RED BUTTONS in *Sayonara*, Goetz, Warner Bros.

VITTORIO DE SICA in *A Farewell to Arms*, Selznick, 20th Century-Fox.

SESSUE HAYAKAWA in *The Bridge on the River Kwai*, Horizon, Columbia.

ARTHUR KENNEDY in *Peyton Place*, Wald, 20th Century-Fox.

RUSS TAMBLYN in *Peyton Place*, Wald, 20th Century-Fox.

SUPPORTING ACTRESS

CAROLYN JONES in *The Bachelor Party*, Norma, UA.

ELSA LANCHESTER in *Witness for the Prosecution*, Small-Hornblow, UA.

HOPE LANGE in *Peyton Place*, Wald, 20th Century-Fox.

*MIYOSHI UMEKI in *Sayonara*, Goetz, Warner Bros.

DIANE VARSI in *Peyton Place*, Wald, 20th Century-Fox.

DIRECTING

*THE BRIDGE ON THE RIVER KWAI, Horizon, Columbia. David Lean.

PEYTON PLACE, Wald, 20th Century-Fox. Mark Robson.

SAYONARA, Goetz, Warner Bros. Joshua Logan.

12 ANGRY MEN, Orion-Nova Prod., UA. Sidney Lumet.

WITNESS FOR THE PROSECUTION, Small-Hornblow, UA. Billy Wilder.

WRITING

(New classification; two awards for writing instead of three as previously given since 1940)

(Screenplay—based on material from another medium)

*THE BRIDGE ON THE RIVER KWAI, Horizon, Columbia. Pierre Boulle, Carl Foreman and Michael Wilson.
(NOTE: Because of the political climate of the time, only Pierre Boulle was given official on-screen credit, but actual screenwriters Foreman and Wilson have since been acknowledged by the Academy for their contributions.)

HEAVEN KNOWS, MR. ALLISON, 20th Century-Fox. John Lee Mahin and John Huston.

PEYTON PLACE, Wald, 20th Century-Fox. John Michael Hayes.

SAYONARA, Goetz, Warner Bros. Paul Osborn.

12 ANGRY MEN, Orion-Nova Prod., UA. Reginald Rose.

(Story and Screenplay—written directly for the screen)

*DESIGNING WOMAN, M-G-M. George Wells.

FUNNY FACE, Paramount. Leonard Gershe.

MAN OF A THOUSAND FACES, U-I. Ralph Wheelright, R. Wright Campbell, Ivan Goff and Ben Roberts.

THE TIN STAR, Perlberg-Seaton, Paramount. Barney Slater, Joel Kane and Dudley Nichols.

I VITELLONI, API-Janus (Italian). Federico Fellini, Ennio Flaiano, and Tullio Pinelli.

CINEMATOGRAPHY

(New classification; one award instead of separate awards for black-and-white and color films, for the first year since 1938)

AN AFFAIR TO REMEMBER, Wald, 20th Century-Fox. Milton Krasner.

*THE BRIDGE ON THE RIVER KWAI, Horizon, Columbia. Jack Hildyard.

FUNNY FACE, Paramount, Ray June.

PEYTON PLACE, Wald, 20th Century-Fox. William Mellor.

SAYONARA, Goetz, Warner Bros. Ellsworth Fredericks.

ART DIRECTION-SET DECORATION

(New classification; one award instead of separate awards for black-and-white and color films, for the first year since 1939)

FUNNY FACE, Paramount. Hal Pereira and George W. Davis; Sam Comer and Ray Moyer.

LES GIRLS, Siegel, M-G-M. William A. Horning and Gene Allen; Edwin B. Willis and Richard Pefferle.

PAL JOEY, Essex-Sidney, Columbia. Walter Holscher; William Kiernan and Louis Diage.

RAINTREE COUNTY, M-G-M. William A. Horning and Urie McCleary; Edwin B. Willis and Hugh Hunt.

*SAYONARA, Goetz, Warner Bros. Ted Haworth; Robert Priestly.

COSTUME DESIGN

(New classification; one award instead of separate awards for black-and-white and color films, for first time in this category)

AN AFFAIR TO REMEMBER, Wald, 20th Century-Fox. Charles LeMaire.

FUNNY FACE, Paramount. Edith Head and Hubert de Givenchy.

*LES GIRLS, Siegel, M-G-M. Orry-Kelly.

PAL JOEY, Essex-Sidney, Columbia. Jean Louis.

RAINTREE COUNTY, M-G-M. Walter Plunkett.

SOUND RECORDING

GUNFIGHT AT THE O.K. CORRAL, Wallis, Paramount. Paramount Studio Sound Dept., George Dutton, Sound Director.

LES GIRLS, Siegel, M-G-M. M-G-M Studio Sound Dept., Dr. Wesley C. Miller, Sound Director.

PAL JOEY, Essex-Sidney, Columbia. Columbia Studio Sound Dept., John P. Livadary, Sound Director.

*SAYONARA, Goetz, Warner Bros. Warner Bros. Studio Sound Dept., George Groves, Sound Director.

WITNESS FOR THE PROSECUTION, Small-Hornblow, UA. Samuel Goldwyn Studio Sound Dept., Gordon Sawyer, Sound Director.

FILM EDITING

*THE BRIDGE ON THE RIVER KWAI, Horizon, Columbia. Peter Taylor.

GUNFIGHT AT THE O.K. CORRAL, Wallis, Paramount. Warren Low.

PAL JOEY, Essex-Sidney, Columbia. Viola Lawrence and Jerome Thoms.

SAYONARA, Goetz, Warner Bros. Arthur Schmidt and Philip W. Anderson.

WITNESS FOR THE PROSECUTION, Small-Hornblow, UA. Daniel Mandell.

SPECIAL EFFECTS

*THE ENEMY BELOW, 20th Century-Fox. Walter Rossi.

THE SPIRIT OF ST. LOUIS, Hayward-Wilder, Warner Bros. Louis Lichtenfield.

MUSIC

(Song)

AN AFFAIR TO REMEMBER (*An Affair to Remember*, Wald, 20th Century-Fox); Music by Harry Warren. Lyrics by Harold Adamson and Leo McCarey.

*ALL THE WAY (*The Joker Is Wild*, Paramount); Music by James Van Heusen. Lyrics by Sammy Cahn.

APRIL LOVE (*April Love*, 20th Century-Fox); Music by Sammy Fain. Lyrics by Paul Francis Webster.

TAMMY (*Tammy and the Bachelor*, U-I); Music and Lyrics by Ray Evans and Jay Livingston.

WILD IS THE WIND (*Wild Is the Wind*, Wallis, Paramount); Music by Dimitri Tiomkin. Lyrics by Ned Washington.

(Music Scoring)

(New Classification; one award for Music Scoring instead of two, for first year since 1937)

AN AFFAIR TO REMEMBER, Wald, 20th Century-Fox. Hugo Friedhofer.

BOY ON A DOLPHIN, 20th Century-Fox. Hugo Friedhofer.

*THE BRIDGE ON THE RIVER KWAI, Horizon, Columbia. Malcolm Arnold.

PERRI, Disney, Buena Vista. Paul Smith.

RAINTREE COUNTY, M-G-M. Johnny Green.

SHORT SUBJECTS

(New rules: two categories for short subjects, instead of three as previously given.)

(Cartoons)

*BIRDS ANONYMOUS, Warner Bros. Edward Selzer, producer.

ONE DROOPY KNIGHT, M-G-M. William Hanna and Joseph Barbera, producers.

TABASCO ROAD, Warner Bros. Edward Selzer, producer.

TREES AND JAMAICA DADDY, UPA, Columbia. Stephen Bosustow, producer.

THE TRUTH ABOUT MOTHER GOOSE, Disney, Buena Vista. Walt Disney, producer.

(Live Action Subjects)

A CHAIRY TALE, National Film Board of Canada, Kingsley International. Norman McLaren, producer.

CITY OF GOLD, National Film Board of Canada, Kingsley International. Tom Daly, producer.

FOOTHOLD ON ANTARCTICA, World Wide Pictures, Schoenfeld Films. James Carr, producer.

PORTUGAL, Disney, Buena Vista. Ben Sharpsteen, producer.

*THE WETBACK HOUND, Disney, Buena Vista. Larry Lansburgh, producer.

DOCUMENTARY

(Short Subjects)

No nominations or award this year.

(Features)

*ALBERT SCHWEITZER, Hill and Anderson Prod., Louis de Rochemont Assocs. Jerome Hill, producer.

ON THE BOWERY, Rogosin, Film Representations, Inc. Lionel Rogosin, producer.

TORERO!, Producciones Barbachano Ponce, Columbia (Mexican). Manuel Barbachano Ponce, producer.

FOREIGN LANGUAGE FILM

THE DEVIL CAME AT NIGHT (Germany).

GATES OF PARIS (France).

MOTHER INDIA (India).

*THE NIGHTS OF CABIRIA (Italy).

NINE LIVES (Norway).

HONORARY AND OTHER AWARDS

TO CHARLES BRACKETT for outstanding service to the Academy. (statuette)

TO B.B. KAHANE for distinguished service to the motion picture industry. (statuette)

TO GILBERT M. ("Broncho Billy") ANDERSON, motion picture pioneer, for his contributions to the development of motion pictures as entertainment. (statuette)

TO THE SOCIETY OF MOTION PICTURE AND TELEVISION ENGINEERS for their contributions to the advancement of the motion picture industry. (statuette)

1957 IRVING G. THALBERG MEMORIAL AWARD

None given this year.

1957 JEAN HERSHOLT HUMANITARIAN AWARD

TO SAMUEL GOLDWYN

SCIENTIFIC OR TECHNICAL

CLASS I (statuette)

TODD-AO CORP. and WESTREX CORP. for developing a method of producing and exhibiting wide-film motion pictures known as the Todd-AO System.

MOTION PICTURE RESEARCH COUNCIL for the design and development of a high efficiency projection screen for drive-in theatres.

CLASS II (plaque)

SOCIETE D'OPTIQUE ET DE MECANIQUE DE HAUTE PRECISION for the development of a high speed variafocal photographic lens.

HARLAN L. BAUMBACH, LORAND WARGO, HOWARD M. LITTLE and the UNICORN ENGINEERING CORP. for the development of an automatic printer light selector.

CLASS III (citation)

CHARLES E. SUTTER, WILLIAM B. SMITH, PARAMOUNT PICTURES CORP. and GENERAL CABLE CORP.

*INDICATES WINNER

1958-1967
The Academy's Fourth Decade

U nlike the preceding years, which had seen the Academy of Motion Picture Arts and Sciences actively (and often inadvertently) involved in studio-labor disputes, political controversies and other weighty industry problems, the organization's fourth decade was one of relative serenity. Conversely, the film industry itself spent most of those ten years in a state of turmoil and confusion, caused by the ever-changing tastes of moviegoers and the tumultuous times through which everyone was living. There seemed to be one blow after another: the Vietnam war, the Cuban missile crisis, equal rights demonstrations, the assassinations of President John F. Kennedy and Martin Luther King, Jr., and social changes such as the beginning of the drug culture. On the more positive side were major advances in space exploration, medicine and technology.

The Academy, still housed in its Melrose Avenue headquarters, continued to expand, rapidly making a future move to larger quarters and a new Academy building of its own—not only a distinct possibility but a necessity. The library acquired more and more material for its research files, including clippings, still photographs, periodicals, press books and memorabilia; there was now barely room to house the numerous scrapbooks and private collections of valuable materials donated to the Academy by individuals and organizations related to the motion picture industry.

Other Academy activities also continued: private screenings for members of new and older films in the downstairs Academy Award Theater, as well as publication three times each year of both the *Academy Players Directory* and the *Screen Achievement Records Bulletin*. In 1965, the Academy also began sponsoring a scholarship program for film students (which, beginning in 1973, would also include official Student Film Awards presented by the Academy). In cooperation with the American Film Institute and the Society of Motion Picture and Television Engineers, an internship program for young filmmakers was also inaugurated.

Also, with spectacular results, the Academy Awards presentations continued to thrive and capture the interest and the imagination of the world's public and press. Since March 23, 1950, the annual ceremony had been held at the RKO Pantages Theater in the heart of Hollywood, a few doors east of the intersection of Hollywood and Vine. Beginning April 17, 1961, on the night the thirty-third Awards were distributed, the Oscar Awards were moved to a new location, the Santa Monica Civic Auditorium, in Santa Monica, California, miles away from the nearest film studio. The presentations continued there annually for eight years. Also during the decade, the Academy ceremony was telecast in color for the first time (April 18, 1966) and two new records were set: 1959's *Ben Hur* became the most honored of all Academy Award-winning films, winning eleven awards,

148

ELIZABETH TAYLOR

"The Oscar is the highest award in motion picture history given to you by your peers; therefore, I feel to every actor it's the most important one. I've known the disappointment of losing. I've known the amazing feeling of excitement of winning two Oscars. I will never forget the night I won my first one for Butterfield 8. *I had been nominated before and lost, so I had become almost superstitious about having any acceptance speech even remotely in mind.*

A great friend of mine, Yul Brynner, who had won the year before, was presenting the woman's award, and he teased me over dinner the previous evening that if my name was in the envelope he was going to milk it.

On that evening there were five of us sitting on the aisle. I watched Yul open the envelope, take the longest pause in the history of my memory, case every actress in the house and finally settle his eyes on me; then beat, beat, beat, his mischievous smile lit up and he said, 'the winner is'—and vaguely from somewhere I heard my name, somebody poking me in the ribs, somebody else telling me to stand up and walk down the aisle—

that I had won.

I have no recollection at all of what I said except thank you—I still say thank you."

Elizabeth Taylor, Best Actress, 1960; 1966
Jean Hersholt Humanitarian Award, 1992

**RICHARD M. SHERMAN &
ROBERT B. SHERMAN**

"Ever since that incredible night thirteen years ago, when we each won two Oscars, we have worn with pride the designation, 'Academy Award winners.' Now, each time we begin a new film-musical, those Golden Gentlemen are there to remind us that all it will take for us to achieve something excellent is hard work, a shipload of good luck and an army of talented people all doing their thing on the same project with us."

Richard M. Sherman
Robert B. Sherman
Music Score (Substantially Original), 1964
Music (Song), 1964

Stage full of stars: 31st awards show, April 6, 1959

and 1961's *West Side Story* became a close runner-up, winning ten awards plus a special Award voted by the Board of Governors to Jerome Robbins for his choreography on the film. Eligibility rules, especially those for judging the best foreign language film Award continued to change from year to year as the Academy Board attempted to make rules for Awards judging as fair as possible. If anything, the most rigid thing about the Academy was its determination to remain flexible.

From time to time, as before, speculation occasionally surfaced suggesting that pressures from certain studios might be responsible for the outcome of Academy members' voting, or that some members of the film community were attempting to "buy" Academy attention by purchasing full-page ads in the trade papers and Los Angeles newspapers to

David Niven, Susan Hayward (31st Awards)

GEORGE CUKOR

"The great, the unique thing about the Academy Awards is that it's on the level — absolutely on the level.

I've been around a long time, and never in my experience has anyone offered me a bribe, or tried in any way to influence me in how I voted. Even friendship doesn't count for much. You may think in advance that you will vote for a good pal, but when the chips are down, and you are alone with your God and your ballot, you find yourself voting for what you really think. It is sometimes said, disparagingly, that an Oscar is just a reward for popularity. Ina Claire told me that when she was a young star on the stage she was introduced to Sarah Bernhardt as a 'great American actress.' She modestly said, 'Oh no, I happen to be a popular actress.' Bernhardt, then at the end of her long and distinguished career, replied, 'Very well, very well, first come popular, then come great. The public is never wrong.' Old Sarah was absolutely right. True popularity means something; it cannot be faked. If you look back over the history of the Awards, in a curious way the truth does come out; the choices of the Academy withstand the test of time.

I am not one of those who think prizes are ignoble. But some are obviously more valuable than others. The Academy Award is most valuable because it is dearly won. It is an expert, professional judgment, at once the most merciless and, sometimes, the most amazingly generous.

It is good for the soul, if not very pleasant, to sit there with your nomination and be turned down in front of a hundred million people. But when you do get it, it is a glory. Mine seemed to be an inordinately long time coming, but when at last I got it, it meant more to me than any other award I have ever received."

George Cukor
Best Director, 1964

WALTER MIRISCH

"I recall sitting in the end seat of a row at the Academy Awards presentation in 1968. Sitting in front of me and behind me were the producers of Bonnie and Clyde, The Graduate, Guess Who's Coming to Dinner *and* Doctor Doolittle.

I had by then pretty well insulated myself against the disappointment of losing by the traditional method: namely, convincing myself that another film was practically a foregone certainty to win. Of course, under that method one still leaves just a tiny glimmer of hope to remain until that very last second.

As Julie Andrews began to name the Best Picture nominees, that tiny glimmer of hope suddenly rose to mountainous proportions. When she read In The Heat of the Night *and my name, the surging hope reached an unbelievable climax, and I rose almost mechanically to walk to the podium. I accepted the award from Julie and I began to speak bits and pieces of things I had sorted out just in case. In essence, 'Thank you to all.' I then walked to the wings. Sidney Poitier and Rod Steiger both came out to greet me. I threw my arms around Sidney and kissed him."*

Walter Mirisch, Best Picture, 1967
Irving G. Thalberg Memorial Award, 1977
Jean Hersholt Humanitarian Award, 1982

bring attention to a specific accomplishment. No one was more disapproving of industry pressures—if they really did exist—or more against the extravagant use of blatant advertising for votes—which was considerable—than the Academy itself. Further, the Academy issued a statement in the 1960s denouncing the latter practice, and it is something they have done almost annually since, but with only limited success at correcting the problem. The soliciting of votes proves to still be a habitual embarrassment.

Preparations for the yearly Awards show, as might be expected, require Herculean efforts on the part of the Academy's own staff. In a special section devoted to the awards in 1962, the *Hollywood Citizen News* paper reported:

"Unsung heroes of the Awards presentations are the staff members of the Academy of Motion Picture Arts and Sciences. The 30-odd employees have literally led a dog's life during the past six weeks while 'doggedly' toiling to make the affair a success.

"This 'dogged' existence hit its stride the day the nominations (for the 34th Awards presentations) were announced on February 26 at the Academy Award Theater. Many of them were 'imprisoned' there from 2 am until the announcements were made at 10 am. This is a precautionary measure taken each year to ensure secrecy of the nominations.

"Some of the staff had to come to work at 2 am to begin assembling photographs and biographies of the nominees as soon as the list was delivered in an armored car from the auditing firm which tabulated the secret ballots. They weren't allowed to leave the library area of the Theater or use telephones until the announcement, together with the photos and biographies, were released to almost 100 members of the press.

"However, that was only the forerunner of the countless hours of leg work which had to be done from then until the grand finale last night. 'Our work is just beginning now,' said Mrs. Joseph Segar, secretary to Sam Brown, assistant executive director of the Academy, following the announcements. As a ten-year employee of the Academy, she knew whereof she spoke. She

explained that between then and the grand finale last night, the staff would have to contact all the nominees and work out all the details for them or their representatives to be present, plus handling the myriad other details connected with the arrangements for the show."

"One of the female staffers' observations last night as she stood backstage watching the proceedings on a television set reflected the employees' point-of-view on the affair: 'Do you know that I wore out three typewriter ribbons, and wore an inch-long callus on my dialing finger trying to get a simple answer from that actress as to whether she was going to be here tonight, or send someone else?' "

"She was referring to a blonde smiling broadly at one of emcee Bob Hope's barbs, and explained that the actress had been moving around on movie locations in Europe for the past several months. The staffer then sighed resignedly while massaging her callused finger and said, 'And just think of all the thank-you notes we're going to have to write after all this is over for everybody else!' "

During the decade, Bob Hope continued to be Oscar's most conspicuous host, acting as master of ceremonies (at least partially) at eight of the ten Awards shows, missing only 1962 Awards and the 1963 Awards due to a conflict of interests between the sponsors of the Academy show and Hope's own television shows. There were also a few provocative and newsworthy incidents that occurred during those Academy Awards nights. The 1958 show, with Jerry Lewis as co-host, finished twenty minutes earlier than had been anticipated. In order to make the best of an ill-timed situation, Lewis took a baton, briefly conducted the orchestra, and clowned, while a stage full of stars began dancing (including Cary Grant, Ingrid Bergman, Laurence Olivier, Sophia Loren, Bette Davis, James Cagney, Gary Cooper, Irene Dunne, John Wayne, Joan Fontaine, Rock Hudson, Elizabeth Taylor, David Niven, Susan Hayward and June Allyson) until the program finally came to an embarrassing end.

Simone Signoret, Yves Montand

LILA KEDROVA

"To win the Oscar for Best Supporting Actress was not only a great honor, but was, without question, the most exciting and moving moment in my career. It opened up a new life to me, and has given me the great joy and opportunity to play in many, many countries around the world. I will always be deeply grateful to the members of the Academy who opened their hearts to 'Bouboulina!' "

Lila Kedrova
Best Supporting Actress, 1964

FREDDIE YOUNG

"Three of the highlights in my life were winning my three Oscars. Whatever anybody might say to the contrary, to win an Oscar is a very special thing.

To be nominated is very exciting, but to actually win an Oscar! Well, you just have to be lucky."

Freddie Young
Cinematography (Color), 1962; 1965
Cinematography, 1970

MAURICE JARRE

"You are a kid in Lyon, France, living under the Nazi occupation. Not much to eat, not much to smile about. But one dream to hold on to: 'I am going to be a COMPOSER some day.'

Fade out.

Paris radio announces that you have been nominated for an Academy Award for the music of a film called Lawrence of Arabia.

The excitement you feel is somewhat dampened when you hear the lugubrious voice of the producer telling you, 'Baby you haven't got a chance. The competition is ferocious.'

Okay.

So you go to bed like Harry Truman and the next thing you hear is the Paris radio announcing: 'You have WON!'

Wrestling my Oscar from the reluctant grip of the producer was perhaps the most difficult task of all. So I was determined to be present when I was in the running again for Dr. Zhivago. *This time I literally hurled myself onto the stage, took a firm hold on my gold statue*

and haltingly said the words that had been filling my heart: 'To be chosen by my fellow composers for a nomination is already the achievement. With my deep respect I say for these thrilling moments of my life, thank you, thank you all.' "

Maurice Jarre
Musical Score (Substantially Original),
1962; 1965; 1984

MARTIN BALSAM

"Aside from remembering the precise moment of my name being called, I remember feeling as if someone put a sky hook in my collar and yanked me from my chair and put me on stage to receive my Oscar.

My memories of that night include someone saying 'Don't scratch it. There may be chocolate underneath.' There wasn't. It was sturdy and solid, but sweet.

Looking at it, or it looking at me, still gives me the pleasure of a treasured moment."

Martin Balsam
Best Supporting Actor, 1965

William Wyler, Charlton Heston (32nd Awards)

Elizabeth Taylor, Burt Lancaster (33rd Awards)

Edmund O'Brien, Shelley Winters (32nd Awards)

CLAUDE LELOUCH

"Nothing is more suspect than an award...and nothing is more delightful to receive."

Claude Lelouch
Writing (Best Story and Screenplay written directly for the screen), 1966

WALTER MATTHAU

"The night I won my Academy Award I was still in a state of shock from an accident the day before. I had fallen off a bicycle on the Pacific Coast Highway. I was speeding and hit a bump in the road and flew through the air and landed heavily on my left elbow, breaking it in sixteen places and getting about three pounds of gravel into my eyes, nose and throat. And so when my name was announced as the winner of the Academy Award, I thought it was still part of the accident. I thought it was some sort of aftershock. But it seemed strange to me that an accident could be so thrilling."

Walter Matthau
Best Supporting Actor, 1966

CHARLTON HESTON

"There are many awards given to filmmakers, perhaps too many. It seems to me the reason the Academy Award remains the most highly prized is clear: it represents the opinion of your peers. When you receive an Academy nomination, it means that the people who do the work you thought you did it well. Each of us would rather have that approval than any other."

Charlton Heston
Best Actor, 1959
Jean Hersholt Humanitarian Award, 1977

HENRY MANCINI

"I would like to take my space here to thank the Academy for two marvelous nights shared with my huckleberry friend Johnny Mercer."

Henry Mancini
Music (Scoring of Dramatic or Comedy Picture), 1961
Music (Song), 1961; 1962
Music (Song Score and Adaptation Score), 1982

VINCENTE MINNELLI

"I was nominated for An American in Paris *but something happened. That 'something' was George Stevens for directing* A Place in the Sun.

So when I was nominated again for Gigi *and was leaving very early the next morning on location to direct the drama* Home from the Hill *with Robert Mitchum, I almost didn't attend the ceremony, thinking 'they'll never give an Oscar to a musical.'*

Then I heard my name called; it was a miraculous, glorious, earth-shattering feeling and one I shall treasure always."

Vincente Minelli
Best Director, 1958

MIKE NICHOLS

"I was so out of it when I received the 'Oscar' that I've often wished I could go back and do it again. This time I would really enjoy it."

Mike Nichols
Best Director, 1967

The Santa Monica Civic Auditorium, April 5, 1965

Patty Duke, Joan Crawford (35th Awards)

At the 1961 Awards ceremony, on April 9, 1962, a professional gate-crasher somehow got past an army of uniformed police guards, sprinted on stage of the Santa Monica Civic Auditorium during the program and presented a small, hand-made Oscar to a briefly startled Hope. "Who needs Price Waterhouse? What we need is a doorman," smiled the comedian. He was equally surprised four years later when he was presented the Academy's first Gold Medal, for "unique and distinguished service to the motion picture industry and the Academy," voted by the Board of Governors. Hope had pre-

viously been presented a special silver Academy plaque at the 1940 ceremony "in recognition of his unselfish services to the motion picture industry," a life membership in the Academy at the 1944 ceremony "for his many services to the Academy" a Special Award Oscar statuette in 1952 for "his contribution to the laughter of the world, his service to the motion picture industry, and his devotion to the American premise," and an Oscar statuette as winner of the 1959 Jean Hersholt Humanitarian Award.

The 1966 Oscar TV show was almost cancelled, due to a lingering strike by the theatrical union governing live

telecasts, the American Federation of Television and Radio Artists (AFTRA), but three hours before the ceremony was to begin the strike was settled, allowing telecast coverage after all.

The following year, the ceremony was postponed two days due to the assassination of Martin Luther King, Jr. The annual Board of Governors' Ball that year was cancelled altogether.

Music also played an unusually striking part in the Academy's fourth decade of existence. At the 34th Awards show on April 9, 1962, one of the nominees as Best Song of 1961, "Bachelor in Paradise," was sung by a little-known per-

GREGORY PECK

"When I was about eight years old, a typical California small-town kid (in La Jolla), freckle-faced and bare-footed, a Hollywood movie company came to town. Roped off at a safe distance with the other locals, I watched in amazement as Lew Cody, in orange make-up, eye shadow and black lips, frolicked on the beach and brandished a long cigarette holder (no fooling) at a collection of bathing beauties. Creatures from another planet, I thought.

Later on, I became one of those creatures, and eventually was voted an Academy Award for To Kill A Mockingbird. *It remains the high point of my professional life, precisely because of my respect and affection for my acting colleagues who nominated me for the honor. I had long since discovered that, orange make-up and all, performers in the theater and in films are the most interesting, the most generous, the most vulnerable, and at the same time, the most courageous people I know. I was thrilled to be honored by the Academy then, in 1962, and I still am. Incidentally, since we all have to turn in our dinner pail one day,*

it is no small comfort to know in advance that the lead line in one's obituary will read, 'Academy Award winner, etc., etc., etc.' "

Gregory Peck
Best Actor, 1962
Jean Hersholt Humanitarian Award, 1967

SHIRLEY JONES

"The funny thing about Oscar is that you actually plan your whole life to get one, from childhood on. And the little kid dream never ends, even after the little kid does. It only grows more vivid as reality brings you into some proximity. You plan further—with every picture, every script, every idea—'maybe this one,' 'maybe this one.' Then, a good roll of the dice—one of them gets near the winner's circle, and the dream is close. You plan the night, you plan the dress, and you plan the speech. And there you are—the envelope open—my God, it's me. The music, the cheers, the mike, and all the world awaiting the simple words you've been planning for twenty years. AND YOU'RE A ZOMBIE; A BAB-BLING, GIGGLING, SLOBBERING ZOMBIE—

without a two-cent string of intelligible sounds to save your soul—and nothing left but twenty years to look back and 'plan' the way it SHOULD have gone!!!

Ah, Oscar, you can WIN one, but you CAN'T WIN!!!"

Shirley Jones
Best Supporting Actress, 1960

PATRICIA NEAL

"When I was nominated for an Oscar for my part in Hud, *I was unable to attend the ceremony because I was heavily pregnant. I therefore asked my great friend Annabella to deputize for me in case I was lucky enough to win. California was then nine hours behind England in time so that when the announcement was made in Los Angeles, I was asleep in bed here at 6 a.m. the next day. At 6:15 a.m. the long-distance telephone call awoke me and the voice of Betsy Drake shouted down the phone, 'You've won!' Wasn't that lovely?"*

Patricia Neal
Best Actress, 1963

Julie Christie, Rex Harrison (38th Awards)

Jack L. Warner, Audrey Hepburn, Rex Harrison, George Cukor (37th Awards)

had a spectacular moment on the 1966 Awards show performing a mod musical interpretation of "Georgy Girl" with four male partners, as did Angela Lansbury as she Charlestoned with her partners to "Thoroughly Modern Millie" on the 1967 Awards program.

But if music and the recognition of film excellence and the myriad of other activities was an on-going fact of life to the Academy itself as the decade drew to a conclusion, so was the unavoidable problem of space—or the lack of it. The Academy had once again outgrown its home base and, in the decade ahead, would make a final, long-awaited move.

ACADEMY PRESIDENTS, THE FOURTH DECADE

June 1957–May 1958	**George Seaton**
June 1958–May 1959	**George Stevens**
June 1959–May 1960	**B.B. Kahane**
June 1960–September 1960	**B.B. Kahane***
September 1960–May 1961	**Valentine Davies**
May 1961–July 1961	**Valentine Davies****
August 1961–May 1962	**Wendell Corey**
May 1962–May 1963	**Wendell Corey**
June 1963–May 1964	**Arthur Freed**
June 1964–May 1965	**Arthur Freed**
June 1965–May 1966	**Arthur Freed**
June 1966–May 1967	**Arthur Freed**

*Died during second term
**Died during second term

former named Ann-Margret, delivered in an unabashed style that literally launched her motion picture career; Ann-Margret was never "unknown" again, and later became a two-time nominee for acting honors. Angela Lansbury, Joan Collins and Dana Wynter in 1959 did a special-material

number, "It's Bully Not To Be Nominated," a parody of a number done the previous year, "It's Great Not to Be Nominated," performed by Burt Lancaster and Kirk Douglas as a humorous "sour grapes" ballad giving tongue-in-cheek reasons they weren't in the competition for acting awards. Mitzi Gaynor

153

WENDY HILLER

"The first Oscar I ever saw was on Mr. Shaw's mantelshelf in his home at Ayot St. Lawrence. My first thought on hearing that I had got one was that if the great G.B.S. thought it was respectable then who was I to worry?"

Wendy Hiller
Best Supporting Actress, 1958

DAVID NIVEN

"Many think I am the first self-confessed drunk to win the Oscar. When my name was read out, and the odds are always four to one against this happening, I thought I had better get up on that stage before everybody changed their minds. I rushed down to the front of the theater, my coattail flapping, and fell headlong up the steps onto the stage. Not having prepared an acceptance speech for fear of attracting bad luck, I grabbed the proffered Oscar and the microphone and tried to explain my rather peculiar arrival. 'The reason I just fell over,' I said, and I intended to continue, 'was because I was so loaded with good luck charms that I was top heavy.'

Unfortunately, I made an idiot pause after the word 'loaded.' This brought down the house, and knowing I could never top that I tottered off the stage with my prize."

David Niven
Best Actor, 1958

EDITH HEAD

"When I received my first award—The Heiress, in 1950—I was so terrrified I merely mumbled 'Thank you' and scurried off.

When I received my eighth award—The Sting, in 1974—I don't actually remember what I said, but at least people laughed and applauded.

People who work in the motion picture industry have stimulating lives, but nothing will ever compare with the actual receiving of the Oscar."

Edith Head
Costume Design (Black-and-white)
1949; 1950; 1951; 1953; 1954; 1960
Costume Design (Color), 1950
Costume Design, 1973

ROBERT WISE

"In early 1962, I was assured that meeting and appearing before the Queen of England at the Command Performance of West Side Story *in London would be a memorable evening—and it was.*

However, the evening was definitely overshadowed a few weeks later by the Academy Awards and by being called to the stage twice for Oscars for my part in West Side Story. *Few experiences can match the excitement and reward of approval by one's peers."*

Robert Wise, Best Director, 1961; 1965
Best Picture, 1961; 1965
Irving G. Thalberg Memorial Award, 1966

BILL THOMAS

"Winning an 'Oscar' was the culmination of an exciting career in this exciting business of ours. It makes each new assignment even more of a challenge, hoping that the Academy might again see a possibility for a mate for Oscar Number One."

Bill Thomas
Costume Design (Color), 1960

Anew decade and a new record! On April 6, 1959, the start of Oscar's fourth decade, M-G-M's gilded *Gigi* set a new, all-time Academy record to date, with nine Oscar awards for 1958 achievement; the previous record holders had been *Gone with the Wind* (1939), *From Here to Eternity* (1953) and *On the Waterfront* (1954), with eight awards each. The *Gigi* total included awards for best picture, best director (Vincente Minnelli), best costume design (Cecil Beaton) and best song ("Gigi" by Alan Jay Lerner and Frederick Loewe), and it was additionally responsible for an honorary award to Maurice Chevalier, specifically cited for his contributions to the entertainment world for over a half century. *Gigi* didn't hold its record long (it would be broken the next year), but it was an interesting Oscar paradox on two levels: it was one of the few films to win all awards for which it had been nominated, and it was one of only eight best picture winners in the Academy's first sixty years not to receive a single acting nomination for any of its cast members. The others: *Wings* (1927-28), *All Quiet on the Western Front* (1929-30), *Grand Hotel* (1931-32), *An American in Paris* (1951), *The Greatest Show on Earth* (1952), *Around the World in 80 Days* (1956) and *The Last Emperor* (1987).

For the second year, NBC's telecast of the ceremony was fully sponsored by the motion picture industry itself, produced by Jerry Wald for the Academy; it was produced and directed for NBC by Alan Handley from the Pantages Theatre in Hollywood. Once again, six personalities shared hosting duties in turn: Bob Hope, David Niven, Tony Randall, Mort Sahl, Sir Laurence Olivier and Jerry Lewis. As the final M.C. of the night, Jerry Lewis found himself in the awkward position of having to stretch out the show when all business at hand was completed. With twenty minutes of a scheduled two hours of air time still to be filled, NBC finally switched its cameras to a sports review filler.

Susan Hayward, on her fifth nomination as best actress, won for *I Want to Live!;* David Niven, on his first, won as best actor for *Separate Tables*. Supporting awards went to Wendy Hiller (for *Separate Tables*) and Burl Ives (for *The Big Country*), and France's comedy *My Uncle* was chosen best foreign language film. It was also a big night for the durable Bugs Bunny. After a long life on the Hollywood drawing boards, he won his very first Oscar when Warner Bros.' *Knighty Knight Bugs* won the statuette as best cartoon.

THE FIRST LERNER-LOEWE MUSICAL SINCE MY FAIR LADY

LESLIE CARON
MAURICE CHEVALIER · LOUIS JOURDAN

154

Best Picture: Gigi *(M-G-M; produced by Arthur Freed)* **and Best Director: Vincente Minnelli** *for* Gigi. Gigi *was Hollywood's answer to Broadway's* My Fair Lady, *which had opened in New York in 1956 and also featured a captivating musical score by Alan Jay Lerner and Frederick Loewe, and awesome costumes by Cecil Beaton. Basis for the new project was a 60-page novelette by French writer Colette, which became a French play, later a French movie, finally a Broadway play with Audrey Hepburn. This latest reincarnation had a blithe spirit and a French sense of humor; in Paris of 1900, a teenage girl is trained by a wealthy aunt to be a courtesan in the tradition of her family, only to eventually upset the plan by putting marriage first. The cast included (right) Hermione Gingold, Louis Jourdan and Leslie Caron, plus Maurice Chevalier, Isabel Jeans, Eva Gabor and Jacques Bergerac. It set a new Academy record with nine awards plus an honorary Oscar for Chevalier.*

Best Actress: Susan Hayward *as Barbara Graham in* I Want to Live! *(United Artists; directed by Robert Wise). The story was based on fact: a California woman named Barbara Graham was executed in the San Quentin gas chamber on June 3, 1955, for allegedly joining two men in the murder of a Burbank widow during an attempted robbery. As a movie produced by Walter Wanger, the first half of the film swiftly tells how Miss Graham was caught; part two chronicles her final, agonizing days on death row, enduring stays of execution, last-minute postponements and the final walk to the gas chamber. As Barbara, Susan Hayward (being led through the gas chamber door by John Marley, at right) gave a tour de force performance, and won the Academy Award which had elusively passed her by four times previously, when she was nominated in 1947 for* Smash Up—The Story of a Woman, *in 1949 for* My Foolish Heart, *in 1952 for* With a Song in My Heart *and in 1955 for* I'll Cry Tomorrow. *"I'll admit I wanted to win. Very much," Hayward later conceded.*

155

Best Actor: David Niven *as Major Pollock and* **Best Supporting Actress: Wendy Hiller** *as Miss Cooper (right) in* Separate Tables *(United Artists; directed by Delbert Mann). When originally presented on stage, Terence Rattigan's story, set in a small English hotel on the south coast of Britain, was written as two single-act plays, with Eric Portman and Margaret Leighton each playing dual roles. The screenplay united the plays and had four starring roles instead of two. Niven played a phony major who covers up his basic fears and frustrations with boring lies about desert campaigns during World War II but is later exposed as a fake when arrested for molesting a woman in a theatre; Miss Hiller, in a small but important role, played an efficient, lonely hotel manager who loses the one interesting man in her life (Burt Lancaster) because of the unexpected arrival at the hotel of his ex-wife (Rita Hayworth). It marked first Oscars for both Hiller, a stage legend who rarely made films, and Niven, who'd made 52 films during the preceding 23 years.*

The Defiant Ones *(United Artists; directed by Stanley Kramer) was a powerful preachment about racial intolerance and brotherhood, with Sidney Poitier and Tony Curtis as convicts shackled together—a black and a white man attempting to escape prison, and each other. It won Oscars for story and screenplay (Nedrick Young and Harold Jacob Smith) and for black-and-white cinematography (Sam Leavitt).*

MOTION PICTURE

AUNTIE MAME, Warner Bros. Jack L. Warner, studio head.
CAT ON A HOT TIN ROOF, Avon, M-G-M. Produced by Lawrence Weingarten.
THE DEFIANT ONES, Kramer, UA. Produced by Stanley Kramer.
*GIGI, Freed, M-G-M. Produced by Arthur Freed.
SEPARATE TABLES, Hecht-Hill-Lancaster, UA. Produced by Harold Hecht.

ACTOR

TONY CURTIS in *The Defiant Ones*, Kramer, UA.
PAUL NEWMAN in *Cat on a Hot Tin Roof*, Avon, M-G-M.
*DAVID NIVEN, in *Separate Tables*, Hecht-Hill-Lancaster, UA.
SIDNEY POITIER in *The Defiant Ones*, Kramer, UA.
SPENCER TRACY in *The Old Man and the Sea*, Hayward, Warner Bros.

ACTRESS

*SUSAN HAYWARD in *I Want to Live!*, Figaro, UA.
DEBORAH KERR in *Separate Tables*, Hecht-Hill-Lancaster, UA.
SHIRLEY MacLAINE in *Some Came Running*, Siegel, M-G-M.
ROSALIND RUSSELL in *Auntie Mame*, Warner Bros.
ELIZABETH TAYLOR in *Cat on a Hot Tin Roof*, M-G-M.

SUPPORTING ACTOR

THEODORE BIKEL in *The Defiant Ones*, Kramer, UA.
LEE J. COBB in *The Brothers Karamazov*, Avon, M-G-M.
*BURL IVES in *The Big Country*, Anthony-Worldwide, UA.
ARTHUR KENNEDY in *Some Came Running*, Siegel, M-G-M.
GIG YOUNG in *Teacher's Pet*, Perlberg-Seaton, Paramount.

SUPPORTING ACTRESS

PEGGY CASS in *Auntie Mame*, Warner Bros.
*WENDY HILLER in *Separate Tables*, Hecht-Hill-Lancaster, UA.
MARTHA HYER in *Some Came Running*, Siegel, M-G-M.
MAUREEN STAPLETON in *Lonelyhearts*, Schary, UA.
CARA WILLIAMS in *The Defiant Ones*, Kramer, UA.

DIRECTING

CAT ON A HOT TIN ROOF, Avon, M-G-M. Richard Brooks.
THE DEFIANT ONES, Kramer, UA. Stanley Kramer.
*GIGI, Freed, M-G-M. Vincente Minnelli.
THE INN OF THE SIXTH HAPPINESS, 20th Century-Fox. Mark Robson.
I WANT TO LIVE!, Wanger-Figaro, UA. Robert Wise.

WRITING

(Screenplay—based on material from another medium)

CAT ON A HOT TIN ROOF, Avon, M-G-M. Richard Brooks and James Poe.
*GIGI, Freed, M-G-M. Alan Jay Lerner.
THE HORSE'S MOUTH, Lopert-UA (British). Alec Guiness.
I WANT TO LIVE! Wanger-Figaro, UA. Nelson Gidding and Don Mankiewicz.
SEPARATE TABLES, Hecht-Hill-Lancaster, UA. Terence Rattigan and John Gay.

(Story and Screenplay—written directly for the screen)

*THE DEFIANT ONES, Kramer, UA. Nedrick Young and Harold Jacob Smith.
THE GODDESS, Perlman, Columbia. Paddy Chayefsky.
HOUSEBOAT, Paramount. Melville Shavelson and Jack Rose.
THE SHEEPMAN, M-G-M. Story by William Bowers and James Edward Grant.
TEACHER'S PET, Perlberg-Seaton, Paramount. Fay and Michael Kanin.

CINEMATOGRAPHY

(After a one-year change in 1957, two awards again given for cinematography achievement)

(Black-and-White)

*THE DEFIANT ONES, Kramer, UA. Sam Leavitt.
DESIRE UNDER THE ELMS, Hartman, Paramount. Daniel L. Fapp.
I WANT TO LIVE!, Wanger-Figaro, Inc., UA. Lionel Lindon.
SEPARATE TABLES, Hecht-Hill-Lancaster, UA. Charles Lang, Jr.
THE YOUNG LIONS, 20th Century-Fox. Joe MacDonald.

(Color)

AUNTIE MAME, Warner Bros. Harry Stradling, Sr.
CAT ON A HOT TIN ROOF, Avon, M-G-M. William Daniels.
*GIGI, Freed, M-G-M. Joseph Ruttenberg.
THE OLD MAN AND THE SEA, Hayward, Warner Bros. James Wong Howe.
SOUTH PACIFIC, Magna Corp., 20th Century-Fox. Leon Shamroy.

ART DIRECTION-SET DECORATION

(Black-and-White or Color)

AUNTIE MAME, Warner Bros. Malcolm Bert; George James Hopkins.
BELL, BOOK AND CANDLE, Phoenix, Columbia. Cary Odell; Louis Diage.
A CERTAIN SMILE, 20th Century-Fox. Lyle R. Wheeler and John DeCuir; Walter M. Scott and Paul S. Fox.
*GIGI, Freed, M-G-M. William A. Horning and Preston Ames; Henry Grace and Keogh Gleason.
VERTIGO, Hitchcock, Paramount. Hal Pereira and Henry Bumstead; Sam Comer and Frank McKelvy.

COSTUME DESIGN

(Black-and-White or Color)

BELL, BOOK AND CANDLE, Phoenix, Columbia. Jean Louis.
THE BUCCANEER, DeMille, Paramount. Ralph Jester, Edith Head and John Jensen.
A CERTAIN SMILE, 20th Century-Fox. Charles LeMaire and Mary Wills.
*GIGI, Freed, M-G-M. Cecil Beaton.
SOME CAME RUNNING, Siegel, M-G-M. Walter Plunkett.

SOUND

(No longer categorized as 'Sound Recording')

I WANT TO LIVE!, Wanger-Figaro, UA. Samuel Goldwyn Studio Sound Dept., Gordon E. Sawyer, Sound Director.
*SOUTH PACIFIC, Magna Corp., 20th Century-Fox. Todd-AO Sound Department. Fred Hynes, sound director.
A TIME TO LOVE AND A TIME TO DIE, U-I. Universal-International Studio Sound Dept., Leslie I. Carey, Sound Director.
VERTIGO, Hitchcock, Paramount. Paramount Studio Sound Dept., George Dutton, Sound Director.
THE YOUNG LIONS, 20th Century-Fox. 20th Century-Fox Studio Sound Dept., Carl Faulkner, Sound Director.

FILM EDITING

AUNTIE MAME, Warner Bros. William Ziegler.
COWBOY, Phoenix, Columbia. William A. Lyon and Al Clark.

Best Supporting Actor: Burl Ives *as Rufus Hannassey (above with Charles Bickford) in* The Big Country *(United Artists; directed by William Wyler). Best known as a folksinger* and balladeer, Burl Ives co-starred in three important 1958 dramas without singing a note: Desire under the Elms, Cat on a Hot Tin Roof *and* The Big Country. *He won his* Academy Award for the latter, an impressive 2-hour, 46-minute western epic in which he played a tough cattle baron at war over water rights with another strong-willed rancher.

THE DEFIANT ONES, Kramer, UA. Frederic Knudtson.
*GIGI, Freed, M-G-M. Adrienne Fazan.
I WANT TO LIVE!, Wanger-Figaro, UA. William Hornbeck.

SPECIAL EFFECTS

*TOM THUMB, Pal, M-G-M. Tom Howard.
TORPEDO RUN, M-G-M. A. Arnold Gillespie and Harold Humbrock.

MUSIC

(Song)
ALMOST IN YOUR ARMS (Love Song from *Houseboat*) (*Houseboat*, Paramount); Music and Lyrics by Jay Livingston and Ray Evans.
A CERTAIN SMILE (*A Certain Smile*, 20th Century-Fox); Music by Sammy Fain. Lyrics by Paul Francis Webster.
*GIGI (*Gigi*, Freed, M-G-M); Music by Frederick Loewe. Lyrics by Alan Jay Lerner.
TO LOVE AND BE LOVED (*Some Came Running*, Siegel, M-G-M); Music by James Van Heusen. Lyrics by Sammy Cahn.
A VERY PRECIOUS LOVE (*Marjorie Morningstar*, Sperling, Warner Bros.); Music by Sammy Fain. Lyrics by Paul Francis Webster.

(NOTE: After a one-year change in 1957, two awards again given for achievement in Music Scoring)

(Scoring of a Dramatic or Comedy Picture)
THE BIG COUNTRY, Anthony-Worldwide, UA. Jerome Moross.
*THE OLD MAN AND THE SEA, Hayward, Warner Bros. Dimitri Tiomkin.
SEPARATE TABLES, Hecht-Hill-Lancaster, UA. David Raksin.
WHITE WILDERNESS, Disney, Buena Vista, Oliver Wallace.
THE YOUNG LIONS, 20th Century-Fox. Hugo Friedhofer.

(Scoring of a Musical Picture)
THE BOLSHOI BALLET, Czinner-Maxwell, Rank Releasing (British). Yuri Faier and G. Rozhdestvensky.
DAMN YANKEES, Warner Bros. Ray Heindorf.
*GIGI, Freed, M-G-M. Andre Previn.
MARDI GRAS, Wald, 20th Century-Fox. Lionel Newman.
SOUTH PACIFIC, Magna Corp., 20th Century-Fox, Alfred Newman and Ken Darby.

SHORT SUBJECTS

(Cartoons)
*KNIGHTY KNIGHT BUGS, Warner Bros. John W. Burton, Producer.
PAUL BUNYAN, Walt Disney Prods., Buena Vista Film Distribution. Walt Disney, producer.
SIDNEY'S FAMILY TREE, Terrytoons, 20th Century-Fox. William M. Weiss, producer.

(Live Action Subjects)
*GRAND CANYON, Walt Disney Prods., Buena Vista. Walt Disney, producer.
JOURNEY INTO SPRING, British Transport Films, Lester A. Schoenfeld Films. Ian Ferguson, producer.
THE KISS, Cohay Prods., Continental Distributing, Inc. John Patrick Hayes, producer.
SNOWS OF AORANGI, New Zealand Screen Board. George Brest Assocs.
T IS FOR TUMBLEWEED, Continental Distributing, Inc. James A. Lebenthal, producer.

DOCUMENTARY

(Short Subjects)
*AMA GIRLS, Disney Prods., Buena Vista. Ben Sharpsteen, producer.
EMPLOYEES ONLY, Hughes Aircraft Co. Kenneth G. Brown, producer.
JOURNEY INTO SPRING, British Transport Films, Lester A. Schoenfeld Films. Ian Ferguson, producer.
THE LIVING STONE, National Film Board of Canada. Tom Daly, producer.
OVERTURE, United Nations Film Service. Thorold Dickinson, producer.

(Features)
ANTARCTIC CROSSING, World Wide Pictures, Lester A. Schoenfeld Films. James Carr, producer.
THE HIDDEN WORLD, Small World Co. Robert Snyder, producer.
PSYCHIATRIC NURSING, Dynamic Films, Inc. Nathan Zucker, producer.
*WHITE WILDERNESS, Disney Prods., Buena Vista. Ben Sharpsteen, producer.

FOREIGN LANGUAGE FILM

ARMS AND THE MAN (Germany).
LA VENGANZA (Spain).
*MY UNCLE (France).
THE ROAD A YEAR LONG (Yugoslavia).
THE USUAL UNIDENTIFIED THIEVES (Italy).

HONORARY AND OTHER AWARDS

TO MAURICE CHEVALIER for his contributions to the world of entertainment for more than half a century. (statuette)

1958 IRVING G. THALBERG MEMORIAL AWARD

TO JACK L. WARNER

1958 JEAN HERSHOLT HUMANITRIAN AWARD

None given this year.

SCIENTIFIC OR TECHNICAL

CLASS I (statuette)
None.

CLASS II (plaque)
DON W. PRIDEAUX, LEROY G. LEIGHTON and the LAMP DIVISION of GENERAL ELECTRIC CO. for the development and production of an improved 10 kilowatt lamp for motion picture set lighting.
PANAVISION, INC., for the design and development of the Auto Panatar anamorphic photographic lens for 35mm CinemaScope photography.

CLASS III (citation)
WILLY BORBERG of the GENERAL PRECISION LABORATORY, INC.;
FRED PONEDEL, GEORGE BROWN and CONRAD BOYE of the WARNER BROS. SPECIAL EFFECTS DEPT.

*INDICATES WINNER

157

For the second year in a row, M-G-M was the noise and the news at the Academy Awards ceremony. Held April 4, 1960, at the Pantages Theatre in Hollywood, and telecast by NBC, the studio's *Ben Hur,* nominated for twelve Academy Awards, won eleven of them, a new Oscar record, topping the previous high of nine awards won by M-G-M's *Gigi* in the preceding year. The *Ben-Hur* awards included best picture, best actor (Charlton Heston), best supporting actor (Hugh Griffith) and best director (William Wyler, his third Oscar in that category). The only area where *Ben-Hur* was nominated and bested was in the best screenplay division, where Neil Paterson received the award for *Room at the Top,* a British-made drama. *Ben-Hur* was also the second remake in two years to win a best picture statuette (following 1958's *Gigi*).

Next to *Ben-Hur,* the evening had a distinctly French flavor. France's Simone Signoret, who had never appeared in a Hollywood-made motion picture, won the best actress award (for *Room at the Top*) and became the first actress to win the Academy Award for a performance in a foreign-made film (the first actor was Charles Laughton in 1932-33). France's *Black Orpheus* was chosen best foreign language film; Miss Signoret's husband Yves Montand entertained at the awards show, and two-time Oscar winner Olivia de Havilland, a resident of Paris, returned to her native Hollywood to present one of the evening's awards.

Other award winners included Shelley Winters as best supporting actress for *The Diary of Anne Frank,* which, next to *Ben-Hur,* won the most awards of the evening with a total of three, including black-and-white cinematography and black-and-white art direction. Buster Keaton received an honorary Oscar for his comedic talents. This award was not presented on the awards show but at the post-award Board of Governors Ball at the Beverly Hilton in Beverly Hills.

The telecast itself was again hosted by Bob Hope, who was also the recipient of the evening's Jean Hersholt Humanitarian Award. It was the last time, at least during Oscar's first sixty years, the motion picture industry sponsored the Academy ceremony. The financial burden had become too steep, and—due to one-studio sweeps such as *Gigi* and *Ben-Hur*—it had become increasingly difficult to get studios to pay for an expensive telecast which might spotlight a rival's product. But it had been worth the try.

Best Picture: **Ben-Hur** *(M-G-M; produced by Sam Zimbalist),* ***Best Director:*** **William Wyler** *(immediate right) and* ***Best Actor:*** **Charlton Heston** *as Judah Ben-Hur (far right) in* Ben-Hur. *M-G-M's decision to make a second version of Gen. Lew Wallace's* Ben-Hur *was risky: at the time, the studio was teetering on financial bankruptcy, and yet the decision was made to pour $15 million—an enormous investment at the time—into the single do-or-die project. But Ben turned out to be a great critical success, and a box office bonanza, saving—at least temporarily—Culver City's Lion for more roars in the future. The most awesome sequence in* Ben-Hur *was a mind-blowing chariot race which ran 11 minutes of the film's 3-hour, 32-minute running time, and Charlton Heston was equally impressive as a wealthy Jew sentenced to life as a galley slave by his once-best friend, played by Stephen Boyd. Director Wyler also deservedly received great praise for* Ben-Hur; *he proved conclusively it was possible to make a rousing spectacle in which audiences could also care about the people involved.*

Best Supporting Actress: **Shelley Winters** *as Mrs. Van Daan in* The Diary of Anne Frank *(20th Century-Fox; directed by George Stevens). She spent the first phase of her career playing svelte glamour girls, but Shelley Winters found her niche in films as a character actress—and a superb one. As Mrs. Van Daan, she was one of eight Jews attempting to survive in Nazi-occupied Amsterdam by hiding in a cramped attic for two years. She won the Academy Award, and a second one in 1965 for* A Patch of Blue.

MOTION PICTURE

ANATOMY OF A MURDER, Preminger, Columbia. Produced by Otto Preminger.
*BEN-HUR, M-G-M. Produced by Sam Zimbalist.
THE DIARY OF ANNE FRANK, 20th Century-Fox. Produced by George Stevens.
THE NUN'S STORY, Warner Bros. Produced by Henry Blanke.
ROOM AT THE TOP, Romulus, Continental (British). Produced by John and James Woolf.

ACTOR

LAURENCE HARVEY in *Room at the Top,* Romulus, Continental (British).
*CHARLTON HESTON in *Ben-Hur,* M-G-M.
JACK LEMMON in *Some Like It Hot,* Ashton, Mirisch, UA.
PAUL MUNI in *The Last Angry Man,* Kohlmar, Columbia.
JAMES STEWART in *Anatomy of a Murder,* Preminger, Columbia.

ACTRESS

DORIS DAY in *Pillow Talk,* Arwin, U-I.
AUDREY HEPBURN in *The Nun's Story,* Warner Bros.
KATHARINE HEPBURN in *Suddenly, Last Summer,* Horizon, Columbia.
*SIMONE SIGNORET in *Room at the Top,* Romulus, Continental (British).
ELIZABETH TAYLOR in *Suddenly, Last Summer,* Horizon, Columbia.

SUPPORTING ACTOR

*HUGH GRIFFITH in *Ben-Hur,* M-G-M.
ARTHUR O'CONNELL in *Anatomy of a Murder,* Preminger, Columbia.
GEORGE C. SCOTT in *Anatomy of a Murder,* Preminger, Columbia.
ROBERT VAUGHN in *The Young Philadelphians,* Warner Bros.
ED WYNN in *The Diary of Anne Frank,* 20th Century-Fox.

SUPPORTING ACTRESS

HERMIONE BADDELEY in *Room at the Top,* Romulus, Continental (British).
SUSAN KOHNER in *Imitation of Life,* U-I.
JUANITA MOORE in *Imitation of Life,* U-I.
THELMA RITTER in *Pillow Talk,* Arwin, U-I.
*SHELLEY WINTERS in *The Diary of Anne Frank,* 20th Century-Fox.

DIRECTING

*BEN-HUR, M-G-M. William Wyler.
THE DIARY OF ANNE FRANK, 20th Century-Fox. George Stevens.
THE NUN'S STORY, Warner Bros. Fred Zinnemann.
ROOM AT THE TOP, Romulus, Continental (British). Jack Clayton.
SOME LIKE IT HOT, Mirisch-Ashton, UA. Billy Wilder.

WRITING

(Screenplay—based on material from another medium)
ANATOMY OF A MURDER, Preminger, Columbia. Wendell Mayes.
BEN-HUR, M-G-M. Karl Tunberg.
THE NUN'S STORY, Warner Bros. Robert Anderson.
*ROOM AT THE TOP, Romulus. Continental (British). Neil Paterson.
SOME LIKE IT HOT, Mirisch-Ashton, UA. Billy Wilder and I.A.L. Diamond.

(Story and Screenplay—written directly for the screen)
THE 400 BLOWS, Zenith International (French). Francois Truffaut and Marcel Moussy.
NORTH BY NORTHWEST, Hitchcock, M-G-M. Ernest Lehman.
OPERATION PETTICOAT, Granart, U-I. Paul King, Joseph Stone, Stanley Shapiro and Maurice Richlin.
*PILLOW TALK, Arwin, U-I. Russell Rouse, Clarence Greene, Stanley Shapiro and Maurice Richlin.
WILD STRAWBERRIES, Janus Films (Swedish) Ingmar Bergman.

CINEMATOGRAPHY

(Black-and-White)
ANATOMY OF A MURDER, Preminger, Columbia. Sam Leavitt.
CAREER, Wallis, Paramount. Joseph LaShelle.
*THE DIARY OF ANNE FRANK, 20th Century-Fox. William C. Mellor.
SOME LIKE IT HOT, Mirisch-Ashton, UA. Charles Lang, Jr.
THE YOUNG PHILADELPHIANS, Warner Bros. Harry Stradling, Sr.

(Color)
*BEN-HUR, M-G-M. Robert L. Surtees.
THE BIG FISHERMAN, Rowland V. Lee, Buena Vista. Lee Garmes.
THE FIVE PENNIES, Dena, Paramount. Daniel L. Fapp.
THE NUN'S STORY, Warner Bros. Franz Planer.
PORGY AND BESS, Goldwyn, Columbia. Leon Shamroy.

ART DIRECTION-
SET DECORATION

(After a change in 1957-1958, two awards again given for achievements in this category)

(Black-and-White)
CAREER, Wallis, Paramount. Hal Pereira and Walter Tyler; Sam Comer and Arthur Krams.
*THE DIARY OF ANNE FRANK, 20th Century-Fox. Lyle R. Wheeler and George W. Davis; Walter M. Scott and Stuart A. Reiss.
THE LAST ANGRY MAN, Kohlmar, Columbia. Carl Anderson; William Kiernan.
SOME LIKE IT HOT, Mirisch-Ashton, UA. Ted Haworth; Edward G. Boyle.
SUDDENLY, LAST SUMMER, Horizon, Columbia. Oliver Messel and William Kellner; Scot Slimon.

(Color)
*BEN-HUR, M-G-M. William A. Horning and Edward Carfagno; Hugh Hunt.
THE BIG FISHERMAN, Rowland V. Lee, Buena Vista. John DeCuir; Julia Heron.
JOURNEY TO THE CENTER OF THE EARTH, 20th Century-Fox. Lyle R. Wheeler, Franz Bachelin and Herman A. Blumenthal; Walter M. Scott and Joseph Kish.
NORTH BY NORTHWEST, Hitchcock, M-G-M. William A. Horning, Robert Boyle and Merrill Pye; Henry Grace and Frank McKelvy.
PILLOW TALK, Arwin, U-I. Richard H. Riedel; Russell A. Gausman and Ruby R. Levitt.

COSTUME DESIGN

(After a change in 1957-1958, two awards again given for costume design achievements)

(Black-and-White)
CAREER, Wallis, Paramount. Edith Head.
THE DIARY OF ANNE FRANK, 20th Century-Fox. Charles LeMaire and Mary Willis.
THE GAZEBO, Avon, M-G-M. Helen Rose.
*SOME LIKE IT HOT, Mirisch-Ashton, UA. Orry-Kelly.
THE YOUNG PHILADELPHIANS, Warner Bros. Howard Shoup.

(Color)
*BEN-HUR, M-G-M. Elizabeth Haffenden.
THE BEST OF EVERYTHING, Wald, 20th Century-Fox. Adele Palmer.
THE BIG FISHERMAN, Rowland V. Lee, Buena Vista, Renie.
THE FIVE PENNIES, Dena, Paramount. Edith Head.
PORGY AND BESS, Goldwyn, Columbia. Irene Sharaff.

SOUND

*BEN-HUR, M-G-M. Metro-Goldwyn-Mayer Studio Sound Department; Franklin E. Milton, sound director.
JOURNEY TO THE CENTER OF THE EARTH, 20th Century-Fox. 20th Century-Fox Studio Sound Department; Carl Faulkner, sound director.
LIBEL!, M-G-M (British). Metro-Goldwyn-Mayer London Sound Department; A.W. Watkins, sound director.
THE NUN'S STORY, Warner Bros. Warner Bros. Studio Sound Department; George R. Groves, sound director.
PORGY AND BESS, Goldwyn, Columbia. Samuel Goldwyn Studio Sound Department; Gordon E. Sawyer, sound director; and Todd-AO Sound Dept., Fred Hunes, sound director.

FILM EDITING

ANATOMY OF A MURDER, Preminger, Columbia. Louis R. Loeffler.
*BEN-HUR, M-G-M. Ralph E. Winters and John D. Dunning.
NORTH BY NORTHWEST, Hitchcock, M-G-M. George Tomasini.
THE NUN'S STORY, Warner Bros. Walter Thompson.
ON THE BEACH, Kramer, UA. Frederic Knudtson.

SPECIAL EFFECTS

*BEN-HUR, M-G-M. A. Arnold Gillespie, Robert MacDonald and Milo Lory.
JOURNEY TO THE CENTER OF THE EARTH, 20th Century-Fox. L.B. Abbott, James B. Gordon and Carl Faulkner.

Best Actress: Simone Signoret *as Alice Aisgill (above, with Laurence Harvey) in* Room at the Top *(Continental Distributing; directed by Jack Clayton). "When we made the film, we thought it would be a picture we would like and some of our friends would like," said Simone Signoret. "Its success came as a great surprise." Made in England, the film was about an ambitious young schemer (Harvey) in a Yorkshire mill town who has an affair with an unhappily married woman, 10 years his senior, played by Miss Signoret; when he discards her to marry a mill owner's young daughter who can help his career, the older woman tragically dies in an automobile accident. Sultry, plumpish and frankly 40, the German-born Signoret was a new kind of leading lady to American audiences in the late 1950s, and an immediate success. In 1965 she received a second Oscar nomination, for* Ship of Fools.

Best Supporting Actor: Hugh Griffith *as Sheik Ilderim in* Ben-Hur. *In his Oscar-winning performance, England's prolific scene-stealer played the man who befriends Judah Ben-Hur (Charlton Heston) and sponsors him in a mammoth Roman chariot race. Griffith was also a nominee in 1963 as the daffy squire in* Tom Jones *and is one of only a handful of performers who have appeared in three Oscar-winning best pictures. In Griffith's case:* Ben-Hur *(1959),* Tom Jones *(1963) and* Oliver! *(1968).*

MUSIC

(Song)

THE BEST OF EVERYTHING (*The Best of Everything,* Wald, 20th Century-Fox); Music by Alfred Newman. Lyrics by Sammy Cahn.

THE FIVE PENNIES (*The Five Pennies,* Dena, Paramount); Music and Lyrics by Sylvia Fine.

THE HANGING TREE (*The Hanging Tree,* Warner Bros.); Music by Jerry Livingston. Lyrics by Mack David.

*HIGH HOPES (*A Hole in the Head,* Sincap, UA); Music by James Van Heusen. Lyrics by Sammy Cahn.

STRANGE ARE THE WAYS OF LOVE (*The Young Land,* C.V. Whitney, Columbia); Music by Dimitri Tiomkin. Lyrics by Ned Washington.

(Scoring of a Dramatic or Comedy Picture)

*BEN-HUR, M-G-M. Miklos Rozsa.

THE DIARY OF ANNE FRANK, 20th Century-Fox. Alfred Newman.

THE NUN'S STORY, Warner Bros. Franz Waxman.

ON THE BEACH, Kramer, UA. Ernest Gold.

PILLOW TALK, Arvin, U-I. Frank DeVol.

(Scoring of a Musical Picture)

THE FIVE PENNIES, Dena, Paramount. Leith Stevens.

LI'L ABNER, Panama and Frank, Paramount. Nelson Riddle and Joseph J. Lilley.

*PORGY AND BESS, Goldwyn, Columbia. Andre Previn and Ken Darby.

SAY ONE FOR ME, Crosby, 20th Century-Fox. Lionel Newman.

SLEEPING BEAUTY, Disney, Buena Vista. George Bruns.

SHORT SUBJECTS

(Cartoons)

MEXICALI SHMOES, Warner Bros. John W. Burton, producer.

*MOONBIRD, Storyboard-Harrison. John Hubley, producer.

NOAH'S ARK, Disney, Buena Vista. Walt Disney, producer.

THE VIOLINIST, Pintoff Prods., Kingsley International. Ernest Pintoff, producer.

(Live Action Subjects)

BETWEEN THE TIDES, British Transport Films, Schoenfeld Films (British). Ian Ferguson, producer.

*THE GOLDEN FISH, Les Requins Associes, Columbia (French). Jacques-Yves Cousteau, producer.

MYSTERIES OF THE DEEP, Disney, Buena Vista. Walt Disney, producer.

THE RUNNING, JUMPING AND STANDING-STILL FILM, Lion International, Kingsley-Union Films (British). Peter Sellers, producer.

SKYSCRAPER, Burstyn Film Enterprises. Shirley Clarke, Willard Van Dyke and Irving Jacoby, producers.

DOCUMENTARY

(Short Subjects)

DONALD IN MATHMAGIC LAND, Disney, Buena Vista. Walt Disney, producer.

FROM GENERATION TO GENERATION, Cullen Assocs., Maternity Center Assoc. Edward F. Cullen, producer.

*GLASS, Netherlands Government, George K. Arthur-Go Pictures (The Netherlands). Bert Haanstra, producer.

(Features)

THE RACE FOR SPACE, Wolper, Inc. David L. Wolper, producer.

*SERENGETI SHALL NOT DIE, Okapia-Film Prods., Transocean Film (German). Bernhard Grzimek, producer.

FOREIGN LANGUAGE FILM

*BLACK ORPHEUS (France).

THE BRIDGE (Germany).

THE GREAT WAR (Italy).

PAW (Denmark).

THE VILLAGE ON THE RIVER (The Netherlands).

HONORARY AND OTHER AWARDS

TO LEE DE FOREST for his pioneering inventions which brought sound to the motion picture. (statuette)

TO BUSTER KEATON for his unique talents which brought immortal comedies to the screen. (statuette)

1959 IRVING G. THALBERG MEMORIAL AWARD

None given this year.

1959 JEAN HERSHOLT HUMANITARIAN AWARD

TO BOB HOPE

SCIENTIFIC OR TECHNICAL

CLASS I (statuette)

None.

CLASS II (plaque)

DOUGLAS G. SHEARER of M-G-M, Inc., and ROBERT E. GOTTSCHALK and JOHN R. MOORE of Panavision, Inc., for the development of a system of producing and exhibiting wide film motion pictures known as Camera 65.

WADSWORTH E. POHL, WILLIAM EVANS, WERNER HOPF, S.E. HOWSE, THOMAS P. DIXON, STANFORD RESEARCH INSTITUTE and TECHNICOLOR CORP. for the design and development of the Technicolor electronic printing timer.

WADSWORTH E. POHL, JACK ALFORD, HENRY IMUS, JOSEPH SCHMIT, PAUL FASSNACHT, AL LOFQUIST and TECHNICOLOR CORP. for the development and practical application of equipment for wet printing.

DR. HOWARD S. COLEMAN, DR. A. FRANCIS TURNER, HAROLD H. SCHROEDER, JAMES R. BENFORD and HAROLD E. ROSENBERGER of the Bausch & Lomb Optical Co. for the design and development of the Balcold projection mirror.

ROBERT P. GUTTERMAN of General Kinetics, Inc., and the LIPSNER-SMITH CORP. for the design and development of the CF-2 Ultra-sonic Film Cleaner.

CLASS III (citation)

UB IWERKS of Walt Disney Prods.

E.L. STONES, GLEN ROBINSON, WINFIELD HUBBARD and LUTHER NEWMAN of the M-G-M Studio Construction Dept.

*INDICATES WINNER

For the 1960 Academy Awards presentations, Oscar moved to a new setting: the Santa Monica Civic Auditorium, sixteen and one-half miles away from the Hollywood-Los Angeles area which had played host for the previous thirty-two years. There were several reasons for the move. Interest in Oscar and the awards continued to grow, requiring more seating space for nominees, guests and supporters. Simultaneously, the audience capacity at the Pantages Theatre in Hollywood had been reduced in order to install a larger screen for a roadshow presentation of *Spartacus;* and, after investigation, no other auditorium in the area was found by the Academy to be either big enough or available on the dates required. So, on April 17, 1961, Hollywood's finest drove away from the cinema hub into nearby Santa Monica to attend the festivities. That location remained Oscar's home for the next seven awards presentations.

Also for the first time, the ceremony itself was telecast over the ABC-TV network, under a newly signed five-year contract with the Academy for exclusive television and radio rights. Richard Dunlap produced and directed for the network, while Arthur Freed produced and Vincente Minnelli directed for the Academy. Andre Previn was the evening's musical director and Bob Hope was again master of ceremonies while an estimated seventy million viewers watched. Of added interest was Elizabeth Taylor, one of the nominees (and

eventual winner) as best actress for *Butterfield 8;* she was making her first public appearance, accompanied by husband Eddie Fisher, since surviving a much-headlined bout with pneumonia. Other acting winners included Burt Lancaster (best actor for *Elmer Gantry*) and Peter Ustinov (best supporting actor in *Spartacus*).

The Apartment was the biggest winner of the evening, with five awards including Oscars for best picture, best director (Billy Wilder) and best story and screenplay (Wilder and I.A.L. Diamond). Sweden's *The Virgin Spring* was honored as best foreign language film, and — another first-time occurrence — a song from a foreign-made film was named winner in the music category (Manos Hadjidakis' "Never on Sunday").

Honorary awards went to Hayley Mills, Stan Laurel and Gary Cooper and — next to the drama surrounding Elizabeth Taylor's appearance — the Cooper award caused the major talk of the night. The actor did not attend, and his statuette was accepted by friend James Stewart, the man who had presented Cooper with his 1941 Oscar for *Sergeant York*. Stewart's speech was so emotional it caused speculation that Cooper might be ill. He was, and died one month later, on May 13, 1961.

Best Picture: **The Apartment** *(United Artists; produced by Billy Wilder) and* **Best Director:** **Billy Wilder** *for* The Apartment. *Swinging like a pendulum between farce and near-tragic drama,* The Apartment *was about a struggling insurance clerk (played by Jack Lemmon, right, with Shirley MacLaine) who lends his Manhattan apartment to company executives for their extra-curricular activities, in return for promotions. The film was the pick of 1960's films with Academy voters, and it won five awards, including three to the man behind the whole sly idea: Billy Wilder, as producer of the year's best picture, as director and as co-author, with I.A.L. Diamond.*

Best Actress: **Elizabeth Taylor** *as Gloria Wandrous (above) in* Butterfield 8 *(M-G-M; directed by Daniel Mann). Elizabeth Taylor never cared for the* Butterfield 8 *script, based on John O'Hara's novel about a New York model and part-time call girl who tragically falls in love with a wealthy, disillusioned married man. But she made the film, primarily to complete contractual ties to M-G-M, so she could be free to accept an unprecedented offer of $1 million from 20th Century-Fox to do a film about Cleopatra.* Butterfield *turned out to be her Oscar charm; after three previous nominations in a row, she won the Academy Award, her first. A second arrived six years later, for 1966's* Who's Afraid of Virginia Woolf?.

Best Supporting Actress: **Shirley Jones** *as Lulu Bains and* **Best Actor:** **Burt Lancaster** *as Elmer in* Elmer Gantry *(United Artists; directed by Richard Brooks). It was a sharp change of pace for Shirley Jones, playing a tough-talking, hardened prostitute who blows the whistle on a hypocritical do-gooder; in her previous five films, she had played soft ingenues, usually singing Rodgers and Hammerstein songs to Gordon MacRae. For Burt Lancaster,* Elmer Gantry *offered a definitive role, marvelously suited to his unique vitality and mannerisms. Both won Academy Awards for the film, based on the first half of a 33-year-old novel by Sinclair Lewis about a traveling salesman and con man who becomes a successful revivalist-preacher, sells salvation and ultimately crashes to a fall. Jean Simmons, Dean Jagger, Arthur Kennedy and Patti Page were also in the cast; director Brooks also received an Oscar for writing* Elmer's *screenplay.*

Honorary Award: **Hayley Mills** *(above, in* Pollyanna*) for "the outstanding juvenile performance during 1960." The daughter of England's acting family headed by John Mills, she was the twelfth juvenile performer (and, to date, the last) to receive the Academy's miniature Oscar, voted by the Academy's Board of Governors. Her statuette was presented at the Awards ceremony by the first talented tot to win one, Shirley Temple.*

MOTION PICTURE

THE ALAMO, Batjac, UA. Produced by John Wayne.
*THE APARTMENT, Mirisch, UA. Produced by Billy Wilder.
ELMER GANTRY, Lancaster-Brooks, UA. Produced by Bernard Smith.
SONS AND LOVERS, Wald, 20th Century-Fox. Produced by Jerry Wald.
THE SUNDOWNERS, Warner Bros. Produced by Fred Zinnemann.

ACTOR

TREVOR HOWARD in *Sons and Lovers,* Wald, 20th Century-Fox.
*BURT LANCASTER in *Elmer Gantry,* Lancaster-Brooks, UA.
JACK LEMMON in *The Apartment,* Mirisch, UA.
LAURENCE OLIVIER in *The Entertainer,* Woodfall, Continental (British).
SPENCER TRACY in *Inherit the Wind,* Kramer, UA.

ACTRESS

GREER GARSON in *Sunrise at Campobello,* Schary, Warner Bros.
DEBORAH KERR in *The Sundowners,* Warner Bros.
SHIRLEY MacLAINE in *The Apartment,* Mirisch, UA.
MELINA MERCOURI in *Never on Sunday,* Melinafilm, Lopert Pictures (Greek).
*ELIZABETH TAYLOR in *Butterfield 8,* Afton-Linebrook, M-G-M.

SUPPORTING ACTOR

PETER FALK in *Murder, Inc.,* 20th Century-Fox.
JACK KRUSCHEN in *The Apartment,* Mirisch, UA.
SAL MINEO in *Exodus,* Preminger, UA.
*PETER USTINOV in *Spartacus,* Bryna, U-I.
CHILL WILLS in *The Alamo,* Batjac, UA.

SUPPORTING ACTRESS

GLYNIS JOHNS in *The Sundowners,* Warner Bros.
*SHIRLEY JONES in *Elmer Gantry,* Lancaster-Brooks, UA.
SHIRLEY KNIGHT in *The Dark at the Top of the Stairs,* Warner Bros.
JANET LEIGH in *Psycho,* Hitchcock, Paramount.
MARY URE in *Sons and Lovers,* Wald, 20th Century-Fox.

DIRECTING

*THE APARTMENT, Mirisch, UA. Billy Wilder.
NEVER ON SUNDAY, Melinafilm, Lopert Pictures (Greek). Jules Dassin.
PSYCHO, Hitchcock, Paramount. Alfred Hitchcock.
SONS AND LOVERS, Wald, 20th Century-Fox. Jack Cardiff.
THE SUNDOWNERS, Warner Bros. Fred Zinnemann.

WRITING

*ELMER GANTRY, Lancaster-Brooks, UA. Richard Brooks.
INHERIT THE WIND, Kramer, UA. Nedrick Young and Harold Jacob Smith.
SONS AND LOVERS, Wald, 20th Century-Fox. Gavin Lambert and T.E.B. Clarke.
THE SUNDOWNERS, Warner Bros. Isobel Lennart.
TUNES OF GLORY, Lopert Pictures (British). James Kennaway.

(Story and Screenplay—written directly for the screen)
THE ANGRY SILENCE, Beaver Films, Lion International (British). Richard Gregson, Michael Craig and Bryan Forbes.
*THE APARTMENT, Mirisch, UA. Billy Wilder and I.A.L. Diamond.
THE FACTS OF LIFE, Panama and Frank, UA. Norman Panama and Melvin Frank.
HIROSHIMA, MON AMOUR, Zenith International (French-Japanese). Marguerite Duras.
NEVER ON SUNDAY, Melinafilm, Lopert Pictures (Greek). Jules Dassin.

CINEMATOGRAPHY

(Black-and-White)
THE APARTMENT, Mirisch, UA. Joseph LaShelle.
THE FACTS OF LIFE, Panama and Frank Prod., UA. Charles B. Lang, Jr.
INHERIT THE WIND, Kramer, UA. Ernest Laszlo.
PSYCHO, Hitchcock, Paramount. John L. Russell.
*SONS AND LOVERS, Wald, 20th Century-Fox. Freddie Francis.

(Color)
THE ALAMO, Batjac, UA. William H. Clothier.
BUTTERFIELD 8, Afton-Linebrook, M-G-M. Joseph Ruttenberg and Charles Harten.
EXODUS, Preminger, UA. Sam Leavitt.
PEPE, Sidney, Columbia. Joe MacDonald.
*SPARTACUS, Bryna, U-I. Russell Metty.

ART DIRECTION-SET DECORATION

(Black-and-White)
*THE APARTMENT, Mirisch, UA. Alexander Trauner; Edward G. Boyle.
THE FACTS OF LIFE, Panama and Frank, UA. Joseph McMillan Johnson and Kenneth A. Reid; Ross Dowd.
PSYCHO, Hitchcock, Paramount. Joseph Hurley and Robert Clatworthy; George Milo.
SONS AND LOVERS, Wald, 20th Century-Fox. Tom Morahan; Lionel Couch.
VISIT TO A SMALL PLANET, Wallis, Paramount. Hal Pereira and Walter Tyler; Sam Comer and Arthur Krams.

(Color)
CIMARRON, M-G-M. George W. Davis and Addison Hehr; Henry Grace, Hugh Hunt and Otto Siegel.
IT STARTED IN NAPLES, Paramount. Hal Pereira and Roland Anderson; Sam Comer and Arrigo Breschi.
PEPE, Sidney, Columbia. Ted Haworth; William Kiernan.
*SPARTACUS, Bryna, U-I. Alexander Golitzen and Eric Orbom; Russell A. Gausman and Julia Heron.
SUNRISE AT CAMPOBELLO, Schary, Warner Bros. Edward Carrere; George James Hopkins.

COSTUME DESIGN

(Black-and-White)
*THE FACTS OF LIFE, Panama and Frank Prod., UA. Edith Head and Edward Stevenson.
NEVER ON SUNDAY, Melinafilm, Lopert Pictures (Greek). Denny Vachlioti.
THE RISE AND FALL OF LEGS DIAMOND, United States Prod., Warner Bros. Howard Shoup.
SEVEN THIEVES, 20th Century-Fox. Bill Thomas.
THE VIRGIN SPRING, Janus Films (Swedish). Marik Vos.

(Color)
CAN-CAN, Suffolk-Cummings, 20th Century-Fox. Irene Sharaff.
MIDNIGHT LACE, Hunter-Arwin, U-I. Irene.
PEPE, Sidney, Columbia. Edith Head.
*SPARTACUS, Bryna, U-I. Valles and Bill Thomas.
SUNRISE AT CAMPOBELLO, Schary, Warner Bros. Marjorie Best.

Best Foreign Language Film: **The Virgin Spring** *from Sweden (Janus Films; directed by Ingmar Bergman). Birgitta Pettersson (in center, at left) was featured as an innocent Swedish maiden who is raped and murdered by three goatherds in the Middle Ages, a story based on a 13th-century Swedish legend about revenge and repentance. Academy voters chose it as the year's outstanding foreign film, the first Ingmar Bergman film so honored. In its country of origin, it was called* Jung Fru Kallan; *Max von Sydow, Birgitta Valberg and Gunnel Lindblom were also in the cast.*

SOUND

*THE ALAMO, Batjac, UA. Samuel Goldwyn Studio Sound Department, Gordon E. Sawyer, sound director; and Todd-AO Sound Department, Fred Hynes, sound director.
THE APARTMENT, Mirisch, UA. Samuel Goldwyn Studio Sound Department; Gordon E. Sawyer, sound director.
CIMARRON, M-G-M. Metro-Goldwyn-Mayer Studio Sound Department; Franklin E. Milton, sound director.
PEPE, Sidney, Columbia. Columbia Studio Sound Department; Charles Rice, sound director.
SUNRISE AT CAMPOBELLO, Schary, Warner Bros. Warner Bros. Studio Sound Department; George R. Groves, sound director.

FILM EDITING

THE ALAMO, Batjac, UA. Stuart Gilmore.
*THE APARTMENT, Mirisch, UA. Daniel Mandell.
INHERIT THE WIND, Kramer, UA. Frederic Knudtson.
PEPE, Sidney, Columbia. Viola Lawrence and Al Clark.
SPARTACUS, Bryna, U-I. Robert Lawrence.

SPECIAL EFFECTS

THE LAST VOYAGE, Stone, M-G-M. A.J. Lohman.
*THE TIME MACHINE, Pal, M-G-M. Gene Warren and Tim Baar.

MUSIC

(Song)

THE FACTS OF LIFE (*The Facts of Life,* Panama and Frank, UA); Music and Lyrics by Johnny Mercer.
FARAWAY PART OF TOWN (*Pepe,* Sidney, Columbia); Music by Andre Previn. Lyrics by Dory Langdon.
THE GREEN LEAVES OF SUMMER (*The Alamo,* Batjac, UA); Music by Dimitri Tiomkin. Lyrics by Paul Francis Webster.
*NEVER ON SUNDAY (*Never on Sunday,* Melinafilm, Lopert Pictures; Greek); Music and Lyrics by Manos Hadjidakis.
THE SECOND TIME AROUND (*High Time,* Crosby, 20th Century-Fox); Music by James Van Heusen. Lyrics by Sammy Cahn.

(Scoring of a Dramatic or Comedy Picture)

THE ALAMO, Batjac, UA. Dimitri Tiomkin.
ELMER GANTRY, Lancaster-Brooks, UA. Andre Previn.
*EXODUS, Preminger, UA. Ernest Gold.
THE MAGNIFICENT SEVEN, Mirisch-Alpha, UA. Elmer Bernstein.
SPARTACUS, Bryna, U-I. Alex North.

(Scoring of a Musical Picture)

BELLS ARE RINGING, Freed, M-G-M. Andre Previn.
CAN-CAN, Suffolk-Cummings, 20th Century-Fox. Nelson Riddle.
LET'S MAKE LOVE, Wald 20th Century-Fox. Lionel Newman and Earle H. Hagen.
PEPE, Sidney, Columbia. Johnny Green.
*SONG WITHOUT END, Goetz, Columbia. Morris Stoloff and Harry Sukman.

SHORT SUBJECTS

(Cartoons)

GOLIATH II, Disney, Buena Vista, Walt Disney, producer.
HIGH NOTE, Warner Bros.
MOUSE AND GARDEN, Warner Bros.
*MUNRO, Rembrandt Films, Film Representations. William L. Snyder, producer.
A PLACE IN THE SUN, George K. Arthur-Go Pictures (Czechoslovakian). Frantisek Vystrecil, producer.

(Live Action Subjects)

THE CREATION OF WOMAN, Trident Films, Sterling World Distributors (Indian). Charles F. Schwep and Ismail Merchant, producers.
*DAY OF THE PAINTER, Little Movies, Kingsley-Union Films. Ezra R. Baker, producer.
ISLANDS OF THE SEA, Disney, Buena Vista. Walt Disney, producer.
A SPORT IS BORN, Paramount. Leslie Winik, producer.

DOCUMENTARY

(Short Subjects)

BEYOND SILENCE, U.S. Information Agency.
A CITY CALLED COPENHAGEN, Statens Filmcentral, Danish Film Office (Danish).
GEORGE GROSZ' INTERREGNUM, Educational Communications Corp. Charles and Altina Carey, producers.
*GIUSEPPINA, Schoenfeld Films (British). James Hill, producer.
UNIVERSE, National Film Board of Canada, Schoenfeld Films (Canadian). Colin Low, producer.

Best Supporting Actor: Peter Ustinov *as Batiatus (here with* Charles Laughton*) in* Spartacus *(Universal-International; directed by Stanley Kubrick). The big-scale* Spartacus *was a saga of Roman gladiators, emperors and intrigues, and received four Academy Awards, one for Ustinov as a clownish slave in B.C. Rome, plus additional ones for color cinematography, for color art direction and for color costume design. Spartacus was based on a novel by Howard Fast and featured a distinguished cast including Kirk Douglas, Laurence Olivier, Charles Laughton, John Gavin, Tony Curtis, Nina Foch and John Dall. Ustinov was also prominent during 1960 in Fred Zinnemann's superb* The Sundowners, *and he won a second Oscar four years later, for* Topkapi.

(Features)

*THE HORSE WITH THE FLYING TAIL, Disney, Buena Vista. Larry Lansburgh, producer.
REBEL IN PARADISE, Tiare Co. Robert D. Fraser, producer.

FOREIGN LANGUAGE FILM

KAPO (Italy).
LA VERITE (France).
MACARIO (Mexico).
THE NINTH CIRCLE (Yugoslavia).
*THE VIRGIN SPRING (Sweden).

HONORARY AND OTHER AWARDS

TO GARY COOPER for his many memorable screen performances and the international recognition he, as an individual, has gained for the motion picture industry. (statuette)
TO STAN LAUREL for his creative pioneering in the field of cinema comedy. (statuette)
TO HAYLEY MILLS for *Pollyanna,* the most outstanding juvenile performance during 1960. (miniature statuette)

1960 IRVING G. THALBERG MEMORIAL AWARD

None give this year.

1960 JEAN HERSHOLT HUMANITARIAN AWARD
TO SOL LESSER

SCIENTIFIC OR TECHNICAL

CLASS I (statuette)
None.

CLASS II (plaque)
AMPEX PROFESSIONAL PRODUCTS CO. for the production of a well-engineered multi-purpose sound system combining high standards of quality with convenience of control, dependable operation and simplified emergency provisions.

CLASS III (citation)
ARTHUR HOLCOMB, PETRO VLAHOS and COLUMBIA STUDIO CAMERA DEPT.;
ANTHONY PAGLIA and the 20TH CENTURY-FOX STUDIO MECHANICAL EFFECTS DEPT.;
CARL HAUGE, ROBERT GRUBEL and EDWARD REICHARD of Consolidated Film Industries.

*INDICATES WINNER

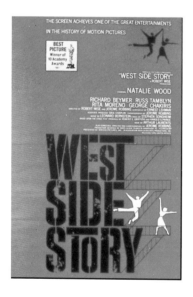

Advertising for Academy votes in Hollywood trade publications had become a major embarrassment to the Academy by the early 1960s, reaching a crescendo with a blatant campaign launched on behalf of supporting actor nominee Chill Wills. It caused the Board of Governors to issue a statement of policy on the subject. "We feel it has now become necessary to state our position in regard to all potential nominees," it read, "and we are mindful that throughout the years the great majority of those nominated, or seeking nominations, have exercised restraint in reminding the voting members of the Academy of their achievements. Regrettably, however, last year a few resorted to outright, excessive and vulgar solicitation of votes. This became a serious embarrassment to the Academy and our industry. We are hesitant to set down specific rules governing advertising (and) leave the decision for this year to the good conscience of the nominees."

The statement further requested a cooperative effort to eliminate those advertising practices "which are irrelevant to the honest evaluation of artistic and technical accomplishments and violate the principles under which the Academy was established. Any honorary organization such as the Academy can command respect only as long as its members and the nominees take unto themselves the responsibility of dignified conduct." The statement concluded: "We are hopeful this reminder will be sufficient." Unfortunately, similar admonishments have had to be made in succeeding years.

The awards for 1961 were presented April 9, 1962, again at the Santa Monica Civic Auditorium. Sophia Loren, winner as best actress for *Two Women,* wasn't on hand to accept her statuette (Greer Garson did stand-in duty for Sophia); she was at home in Rome awaiting the outcome. She was the first performer in a foreign language film to be nominated for an Academy Award, and so became Oscar's initial subtitled acting winner. It was an evening for Oscar "firsts." Maximilian Schell, chosen best actor for *Judgment at Nuremberg,* became the first performer to win an Academy Award for re-creating on screen a role he had originally done on television. Also for the initial time, two directors won in the best director category: Jerome Robbins and Robert Wise of *West Side Story.* *West Side Story* was the big winner of the year with ten awards, including ones for best picture, supporting actor (George Chakiris), supporting actress (Rita Moreno), plus a special Oscar to Robbins for his *West Side Story* choreography.

Earlier, there had been another first. Shortly after the nominations were announced, George C. Scott informed Academy officials he wished to decline his nomination in the supporting actor category; his name, however, remained on the ballot.

ABC-TV again carried the telecast, with Richard Dunlap producing-direct-

Best Picture: **West Side Story** *(United Artists; produced by Robert Wise),* **Best Directors:** **Robert Wise** *and* **Jerome Robbins** *and (right)* **Best Supporting Actor:** **George Chakiris** *as Bernardo and* **Best Supporting Actress:** **Rita Moreno** *as Anita in* West Side Story. *On the Broadway stage,* West Side Story *opened Sept. 26, 1957, and was a spellbinder; four years later, it became a 153-minute motion picture, with its qualities enhanced even further by the ability of the film medium to give limitless elbow room to its vitality. It was also* Romeo and Juliet *set to music (by Leonard Bernstein, lyrics by Stephen Sondheim), with the Capulet-Montague friction in Verona translated into a Puerto Rican-American gang rivalry on the streets of Manhattan's upper West Side. Natalie Wood, beginning her adult screen career, and Richard Beymer were the star-crossed lovers and, among the cast, George Chakiris and Rita Moreno made particularly striking impressions—and won Oscars—as the leader of the Puerto Rican "Shark" gang and his fiery girl friend.*

Considerable attention was given to the fact Marni Nixon was the off-camera singing voice for Wood; Beymer was musically dubbed by Jim Bryant. Ultimately, West Side Story *won a near-record 10 Academy Awards, including those for color cinematography, color art direction, color costume design, sound, scoring of a musical, film editing, plus a special award to Robbins for his choreography.*

ing for the network, and Arthur Freed producing for the Academy. Johnny Green was musical director, Bob Hope was master of ceremonies, and Ann-Margret, a relative newcomer to movie circles, attracted major attention when she delivered a version of "Bachelor in Paradise," one of the year's nominees as best song. There was also an unabashed (and uninvited) visitor on stage: Stan Berman, a "professional" gate crasher, bypassed 125 uniformed police guards during the evening and went on stage to hand a home-made Oscar to a surprised Bob Hope.

Nominations 1961

Best Actor: Maximillan Schell *as Hans Rolfe in* Judgment at Nuremberg *(United Artists; directed by Stanley Kramer)*. *Maximillan Schell first played Hans Rolfe in an April 1959 CBS-TV version of* Judgment at Nuremberg, *directed by George Roy Hill; when Stanley Kramer expanded the story into a 3-hour, 15-minute movie, Schell was the only actor chosen to repeat his role, and he was the least-known face among the film's powerhouse cast which included Spencer Tracy, Burt Lancaster, Richard Widmark, Montgomery Clift, Marlene Dietrich and Judy Garland. Schell played a German lawyer in the 1948 war crimes trial held in Nuremberg, Germany, defending four Nazis on trial for their part in supporting Hitler's precepts during World War II. His argument: in wartime, it was their duty—not a choice—to accept the orders of their leader and follow them. Ultimately, Hans Rolfe lost the case, but actor Schell won the Academy Award. He was again nominated as best actor in 1975 for* The Man in the Glass Booth *and as Best Supporting Actor in 1977 for* Julia. *He also co-produced and directed* First Love, *a 1970 Academy nominee as best foreign language film.*

MOTION PICTURE

FANNY, Mansfield, Warner Bros. Produced by Joshua Logan.
THE GUNS OF NAVARONE, Foreman, Columbia. Produced by Carl Foreman.
THE HUSTLER, Rossen, 20th Century-Fox. Produced by Robert Rossen.
JUDGMENT AT NUREMBERG, Kramer, UA. Produced by Stanley Kramer.
*****WEST SIDE STORY,** Mirisch-B&P Enterprises, UA. Produced by Robert Wise.

ACTOR

CHARLES BOYER in *Fanny,* Mansfield, Warner Bros.
PAUL NEWMAN in *The Hustler,* Rossen, 20th Century-Fox.
***MAXIMILIAN SCHELL** in *Judgment at Nuremberg,* Kramer, UA.
SPENCER TRACY in *Judgment at Nuremberg,* Kramer, UA.
STUART WHITMAN in *The Mark,* Buchman-Stross, Continental (British).

ACTRESS

AUDREY HEPBURN in *Breakfast at Tiffany's,* Jurow-Shepherd, Paramount.
PIPER LAURIE in *The Hustler,* Rossen, 20th Century-Fox.
***SOPHIA LOREN** in *Two Women,* Ponti, Embassy (Italian).
GERALDINE PAGE in *Summer and Smoke,* Wallis, Paramount.
NATALIE WOOD in *Splendor in the Grass,* Kazan, Warner Bros.

SUPPORTING ACTOR

***GEORGE CHAKIRIS** in *West Side Story,* Mirisch-B&P Enterprises, UA.
MONTGOMERY CLIFT in *Judgment at Nuremberg,* Kramer, UA.
PETER FALK in *Pocketful Of Miracles,* Franton, UA.
JACKIE GLEASON in *The Hustler,* Rossen, 20th Century-Fox.
GEORGE C. SCOTT in *The Hustler,* Rossen, 20th Century-Fox.

SUPPORTING ACTRESS

FAY BAINTER in *The Children's Hour,* Mirisch-Worldwide, UA.
JUDY GARLAND in *Judgment at Nuremberg,* Kramer, UA.
LOTTE LENYA in *The Roman Spring of Mrs. Stone,* Seven Arts, Warner Bros.
UNA MERKEL in *Summer and Smoke,* Wallis, Paramount.
***RITA MORENO** in *West Side Story,* Mirisch-B&P Enterprises, UA.

DIRECTING

THE GUNS OF NAVARONE, Foreman, Columbia. J. Lee Thompson.
THE HUSTLER, Rossen, 20th Century-Fox. Robert Rossen.
JUDGMENT AT NUREMBERG, Kramer, UA. Stanley Kramer.
LA DOLCE VITA, Astor Pictures (Italian). Federico Fellini.
*****WEST SIDE STORY**, Mirisch-Seven Arts, UA. Robert Wise and Jerome Robbins.

WRITING

(Screenplay—based on material from another medium)

BREAKFAST AT TIFFANY'S, Jurow-Shepherd, Paramount. George Axelrod.
THE GUNS OF NAVARONE, Foreman, Columbia. Carl Foreman.
THE HUSTLER, Rossen, 20th Century-Fox. Sidney Carroll and Robert Rossen.
***JUDGMENT AT NUREMBERG,** Kramer, UA. Abby Mann.
WEST SIDE STORY, Mirisch-Seven Arts, UA. Ernest Lehman.

(Story and Screenplay—written directly for the screen)

BALLAD OF A SOLDIER, Kingsley International-M.J.P. (Russian). Valentin Yoshov and Grigori Chukhrai.
GENERAL DELLA ROVERE, Continental Distributing (Italian). Sergio Amidei, Diego Fabbri and Indro Montanelli.
LA DOLCE VITA, Astor Pictures (Italian). Federico Fellini, Tulio Pinelli, Ennio Flaiano and Brunello Rondi.
LOVER COME BACK, Shapiro-Arwin, U-I. Stanley Shapiro and Paul Henning.
***SPLENDOR IN THE GRASS,** Kazan, Warner Bros. William Inge.

CINEMATOGRAPHY

(Black-and-White)

THE ABSENT MINDED PROFESSOR, Disney, Buena Vista. Edward Colman.
THE CHILDREN'S HOUR, Mirisch-Worldwide, UA. Franz F. Planer.
***THE HUSTLER,** Rossen, 20th Century-Fox. Eugen Shuftan.
JUDGMENT AT NUREMBERG, Kramer, UA. Ernest Laszlo.
ONE, TWO, THREE, Mirisch-Pyramid, UA. Daniel L. Fapp.

(Color)

FANNY, Logan, Warner Bros. Jack Cardiff.
FLOWER DRUM SONG, Hunter, U-I, Russell Metty.
A MAJORITY OF ONE, Warner Bros. Harry Stradling, Sr.
ONE-EYED JACKS, Pennebaker, Paramount. Charles Lang, Jr.
***WEST SIDE STORY,** Mirisch-Seven Arts, UA. Daniel L. Fapp.

ART DIRECTION-SET DECORATION

(Black-and-White)

THE ABSENT MINDED PROFESSOR, Disney, Buena Vista. Carroll Clark; Emile Kuri and Hal Gausman.
THE CHILDREN'S HOUR, Mirisch-Worldwide, UA. Fernando Carrere; Edward G. Boyle.
***THE HUSTLER,** Rossen, 20th Century-Fox. Harry Horner; Gene Callahan.
JUDGMENT AT NUREMBERG, Kramer, UA. Rudolph Sternad; George Milo.
LA DOLCE VITA, Astor Pictures (Italian); Piero Gherardi.

(Color)

BREAKFAST AT TIFFANY'S, Jurow-Shepherd, Paramount. Hal Pereira and Roland Anderson; Sam Comer and Ray Moyer.

EL CID, Bronston, Allied Artists. Veniero Colasanti and John Moore.

FLOWER DRUM SONG, Hunter, U-I. Alexander Golitzen and Joseph Wright; Howard Bristol.

SUMMER AND SMOKE, Wallis, Paramount. Hal Pereira and Walter Tyler; Sam Comer and Arthur Krams.

*WEST SIDE STORY, Mirisch-Seven Arts, UA. Boris Leven; Victor A. Gangelin.

COSTUME DESIGN

(Black-and-White)

THE CHILDREN'S HOUR, Mirisch-Worldwide, UA. Dorothy Jeakins.

CLAUDELLE INGLISH, Warner Bros. Howard Shoup.

JUDGMENT AT NUREMBERG, Kramer, UA. Jean Louis.

*LA DOLCE VITA, Astor Pictures (Italian). Piero Gherardi.

YOJIMBO, Toho Company (Japanese). Yoshiro Muraki.

(Color)

BABES IN TOYLAND, Disney, Buena Vista. Bill Thomas.

BACK STREET, Hunter, U-I. Jean Louis.

FLOWER DRUM SONG, Hunter, U-I. Irene Sharaff.

POCKETFUL OF MIRACLES, Franton, UA. Edith Head and Walter Plunkett.

*WEST SIDE STORY, Mirisch-Seven Arts, UA. Irene Sharaff.

SOUND

THE CHILDREN'S HOUR, Mirisch-Worldwide, UA. Samuel Goldwyn Studio Sound Dept.; Gordon E. Sawyer, sound director.

FLOWER DRUM SONG, Hunter, U-I. Revue Studio Sound Dept.; Waldon O. Watson, sound director.

THE GUNS OF NAVARONE, Foreman, Columbia. Shepperton Studio Sound Dept.; John Cox, sound director.

THE PARENT TRAP, Disney, Buena Vista. Walt Disney Studio Sound Dept.; Robert O. Cook, sound director.

*WEST SIDE STORY, Mirisch-Seven Arts, UA. Todd-AO Sound Dept., Fred Hynes, sound director, and Samuel Goldwyn Studio Sound Dept.; Gordon E. Sawyer, sound director.

FILM EDITING

FANNY, Logan, Warner Bros. William H. Reynolds.

THE GUNS OF NAVARONE, Foreman, Columbia. Alan Osbiston.

JUDGMENT AT NUREMBERG, Kramer, UA. Frederic Knudtson.

THE PARENT TRAP, Disney, Buena Vista. Philip W. Anderson.

*WEST SIDE STORY, Mirisch-Seven Arts, UA. Thomas Stanford.

SPECIAL EFFECTS

THE ABSENT MINDED PROFESSOR, Disney, Buena Vista. Robert A. Mattey and Eustace Lycett.

*THE GUNS OF NAVARONE, Foreman, Columbia. Bill Warrington and Vivian C. Greenham.

MUSIC

(Song)

BACHELOR IN PARADISE (Bachelor in Paradise, Richmond, M-G-M); Music by Henry Mancini. Lyrics by Mack David.

LOVE THEME FROM EL CID (El Cid, Bronston, Allied Artists); Music by Miklos Rozsa. Lyrics by Paul Francis Webster.

*MOON RIVER (Breakfast at Tiffany's, Jurow-Shepherd, Paramount); Music by Henry Mancini. Lyrics by Johnny Mercer.

POCKETFUL OF MIRACLES (Pocketful of Miracles, Franton, UA); Music by James Van Heusen. Lyrics by Sammy Cahn.

TOWN WITHOUT PITY (Town Without Pity, Mirisch-Gloria, UA); Music by Dimitri Tiomkin. Lyrics by Ned Washington.

(Scoring of a Dramatic or Comedy Picture)

*BREAKFAST AT TIFFANY'S, Jurow-Shepherd, Paramount. Henry Mancini.

EL CID, Bronston, Allied Artists. Miklos Rozsa.

FANNY, Logan, Warner Bros. Morris Stoloff and Harry Sukman.

THE GUNS OF NAVARONE, Foreman, Columbia. Dimitri Tiomkin.

SUMMER AND SMOKE, Wallis, Paramount. Elmer Bernstein.

Best Actress: *Sophia Loren* as Cesira *in* Two Women *(Embassy; directed by Vittorio DeSica). The role—volcanic, lusty and warm—was originally designed for Anna Magnani; in the hands of Sophia Loren, it became the first performance delivered in a foreign language film to win an Academy Award. Sophia played a passionate Italian widow, unable to face 1943 wartime dangers in Rome, who leaves the city with her 13-year-old daughter (Eleanora Brown) in order to sit out the war in the safety of her mountainside birthplace, miles away; on their journey, both are raped in a gutted church by Moroccan soldiers, and the resultant trauma threatens to wreck the daughter's life and the mother-daughter relationship. Filmed in Italy, in Italian,* Two Women *co-starred Jean-Paul Belmondo and Raf Vallone and was one of the first subtitled foreign language films to find a wide popular acceptance by the public in the United States; it also proved Sophia, then most famous as a movie sex symbol, could hold her own with anyone as an actress.*

(Scoring of a Musical Picture)

BABES IN TOYLAND, Disney, Buena Vista. George Bruns.

FLOWER DRUM, Hunter, U-I. Alfred Newman and Ken Darby.

KHOVANSHCHINA, Artkino (Russian). Dimitri Shostakovich.

PARIS BLUES, Pennebaker, UA. Duke Ellington.

*WEST SIDE STORY, Mirisch-Seven Arts, UA. Saul Chaplin, Johnny Green, Sid Ramin and Irwin Kostal.

SHORT SUBJECTS

(Cartoons)

AQUAMANIA, Disney, Buena Vista. Walt Disney, producer.

BEEP PREPARED, Warner Bros. Chuck Jones, producer.

*ERSATZ (The Substitute), Zagreb Film, Herts-Lion International Corp.

NELLY'S FOLLY, Warner Bros. Chuck Jones, producer.

PIED PIPER OF GUADALUPE, Warner Bros. Friz Freleng, producer.

(Live Action Subjects)

BALLON VOLE (Play Ball), Cine Documents, Kingsley International.

THE FACE OF JESUS, Jennings-Stern, Inc. Dr. John D. Jennings, producer.

ROOFTOPS OF NEW YORK, McCarty-Rush-Gaffney. Columbia.

*SEAWARDS THE GREAT SHIPS, Templar Film Studios, Schoenfeld Films.

VERY NICE, VERY NICE, National Film Board of Canada, Kingsley International.

DOCUMENTARY

(Short Subjects)

BREAKING THE LANGUAGE BARRIER, U.S. Air Force.

CRADLE OF GENIUS, Plough Prods., Lesser Films (Irish). Jim O'Connor and Tom Hayes, producers.

KAHL, Dido-Film-GmbH., AEG-Filmdienst (German).

L'UOMO IN GRIGIO (The Man In Gray), (Italian). Benedetto Benedetti, producer.

*PROJECT HOPE, Klaeger Films. Frank P. Bibas, producer.

(Features)

LA GRANDE OLIMPIADE (Olympic Games 1960), Cineriz (Italian).

*LE CIEL ET LA BOUE (Sky Above And Mud Beneath), Rank Films (French). Arthur Cohn and Rene Lafuite, producers.

FOREIGN LANGUAGE FILM

HARRY AND THE BUTLER, (Denmark).

IMMORTAL LOVE, (Japan).

THE IMPORTANT MAN, (Mexico).

PLACIDO, (Spain).

*THROUGH A GLASS DARKLY, (Sweden).

HONORARY AND OTHER AWARDS

TO WILLIAM L. HENDRICKS for his outstanding patriotic service in the conception, writing and production of the Marine Corps film, A Force in Readiness, which has brought honor to the Academy and the motion picture industry. (statuette)

TO FRED L. METZLER for his dedication and outstanding service to the Academy of Motion Picture Arts and Sciences. (statuette)

TO JEROME ROBBINS for his brilliant achievements in the art of choreography on film. (statuette)

1961 IRVING G. THALBERG MEMORIAL AWARD

TO STANLEY KRAMER

1961 JEAN HERSHOLT HUMANITARIAN AWARD

TO GEORGE SEATON

SCIENTIFIC OR TECHNICAL

CLASS I (statuette)

None.

CLASS II (plaque)

SYLVANIA ELECTRIC PRODUCTS, INC., for the development of a hand held high-power photographic lighting unit known as the Sun Gun Professional.

JAMES DALE, S. WILSON, H.E. RICE, JOHN RUDE, LAURIE ATKIN, WADSWORTH E. POHL, H. PEASGOOD and TECHNICOLOR CORP. for a process of automatic selective printing.

20TH CENTURY-FOX RESEARCH DEPT., under the direction of E.I. SPONABLE and HERBERT E. BRAGG, and DELUXE LABORATORIES, INC., with the assistance of F.D. LESLIE, R.D. WHITMORE, A.A. ALDEN, ENDEL POOL and JAMES B. GORDON for a system of decompressing and recomposing CinemaScope pictures for conventional aspect ratios.

CLASS III (citation)

HURLETRON, INC., ELECTRIC EYE DIVISION; WADSWORTH E. POHL and TECHNICOLOR CORP.

*INDICATES WINNER

Frank Sinatra made his first appearance as an Academy Awards host on April 8, 1963—the night 1962 film achievements were honored—but he almost missed the show. Running late, he forgot to apply the proper sticker to his car and was refused admittance to the Santa Monica Civic Auditorium arrival area. He had to park his car himself, then rush on foot to the stage area. Bob Hope, usually in the host spot, had to sit this one out because of a product conflict between the sponsors of the Academy telecast and his own television specials.

The thirty-fifth Academy ceremony was telecast on ABC-TV, produced for the Academy for the fifth time by Arthur Freed, with Alfred Newman as musical director. Richard Dunlap produced and directed for the network.

Lawrence of Arabia, a prize example of the kind of international movemaking becoming more prevalent in the industry, received a total of seven awards (including ones for best picture and for David Lean as best director); Gregory Peck, on his fifth nomination as best actor, won for *To Kill a Mockingbird,* and told reporters, "I hate to give it (the statuette) back to the Academy, even if it's only to have my name engraved on it!" Anne Bancroft, appearing on stage in New York in *Mother Courage,* was named best actress in *The Miracle Worker;* her award was accepted in her absence by Joan Crawford.

Sixteen-year-old Patty Duke, best supporting actress in *The Miracle Worker,* was the first under-18 performer to win a competitive Academy Award; for the preceding twenty-eight years, child actors had been honored by the Academy only in the special award division. One of her fellow nominees, Mary Badham of *To Kill a Mockingbird,* was even younger; she was nine at the time. Veteran character actor Ed Begley won as the year's best supporting actor (for *Sweet Bird of Youth*) and France's *Sundays and Cybele* was chosen best foreign language film, the sixth French film similarly honored.

A slight pre-show controversy surrounded the planned entertainment portions of the 1962 telecast. Since Ethel Merman had been asked to sing a medley of Irving Berlin songs, and Eddie Fisher had also agreed to do a medley of eleven past Oscar-winning tunes, program planners announced the five best song nominees would not be performed during the program, breaking an Oscar tradition. That decision struck a negative response from members in the Academy's Music Branch, so the songs were quickly reinstated, but with a slight alteration. This year, for the first time, they were not sung individually, but as a medley. Robert Goulet did the honors.

Best Actress: **Anne Bancroft** *as Anne Sullivan and* ***Best Supporting Actress:*** **Patty Duke** *as Helen Keller in* The Miracle Worker *(United Artists; directed by Arthur Penn). The Miracle Worker first appeared as a 1957 television play with Teresa Wright and Patty McCormack, then became a 1959 Broadway play with Anne Bancroft and Patty Duke and, finally, a 1962 motion picture, again with Bancroft and Duke (right). The story followed real-life Anne Sullivan, half-blind from a childhood illness, as she attempts to teach deaf-and-blind young Helen how to speak through the sense of touch, concurrently having to battle the girl's animal-like stubbornness. It became one of 1962's most-admired, and best-acted, dramas.*

Best Picture: Lawrence of Arabia *(Columbia; produced by Sam Spiegel). For their first reteaming after their highly successful* The Bridge on the River Kwai *in 1957, Sam Spiegel and director David Lean first toyed with the idea of filming the life of Mahatma Gandhi, then discarded it when Spiegel was able to purchase the rights to Thomas Edward Lawrence's* Seven Pillars of Wisdom. *Marlon Brando was the first choice* to play Lawrence but he was filming Mutiny on the Bounty *and unable to accept, so the role went to 28-year-old Peter O'Toole, an actor relatively unknown in film circles. Location filming went on for many months in raw temperatures, but the hardships ultimately added to the authenticity and grandeur of the finished film, a visually stunning epic which concentrated on the guerilla desert campaigns of Lawrence* at the time of World War I, leading Arab raids against the Turks; at times, it also pondered the man's mysterious nature and his occasional streaks of sadism. Lawrence *co-starred Alec Guinness, Anthony Quinn, Jack Hawkins, Jose Ferrer, Omar Sharif, Claude Rains, Arthur Kennedy, Anthony Quayle and won a total of seven Academy Awards for its excellence.*

171

Best Actor: Gregory Peck *as Atticus Finch (at left, in court) in* To Kill a Mockingbird *(Universal-International; directed by Robert Mulligan). Atticus was the mainspring of Harper Lee's best-selling novel, a wise and gentle small town Alabama lawyer of 1932, rearing his motherless offspring and defending a black man falsely accused of rape. Under the soft-spoken guidance of Atticus, his youngsters emerge from the world of childhood fantasy towards maturity, but in the court-room, Southern prejudice defeats his case. Gregory Peck's performance won him his first Academy Award after four previous nominations in 1945, 1946, 1947 and 1949; in 1967, he was voted the Jean Hersholt Humanitarian Award by the Academy's Board of Governors. He also served as Academy president for three terms, 1967-1970.*

What Ever Happened to Baby Jane? (Warner Bros.; produced by Robert Aldrich) gave rousing screen roles to Joan Crawford and Bette Davis (above) and was voted the Academy Award for Norma Koch's black-and-white costume designs. The actresses played former celebrities living like recluses in a decaying Hollywood mansion; one is an apparent cripple, the other a grotesque misfit who can't forget she was once a child star in vaudeville. Robert Aldrich directed it.

PICTURE

*LAWRENCE OF ARABIA, Horizon-Spiegel-Lean, Columbia. Produced by Sam Spiegel.
THE LONGEST DAY, Zanuck, 20th Century-Fox. Produced by Darryl F. Zanuck.
THE MUSIC MAN, Warner Bros. Produced by Morton Da Costa.
MUTINY ON THE BOUNTY, Arcola, M-G-M. Produced by Aaron Rosenberg.
TO KILL A MOCKINGBIRD, Pakula-Mulligan-Brentwood, U-I. Produced by Alan J. Pakula.

ACTOR

BURT LANCASTER in *Bird Man of Alcatraz*, Hecht, UA.
JACK LEMMON in *Days of Wine and Roses*, Manulis-Jalem, Warner Bros.
MARCELLO MASTROIANNI in *Divorce—Italian Style*, Embassy (Italian).
PETER O'TOOLE in *Lawrence of Arabia*, Horizon-Spiegel-Lean, Columbia.
*GREGORY PECK in *To Kill a Mockingbird*, Pakula-Mulligan-Brentwood, U-I.

ACTRESS

*ANNE BANCROFT in *The Miracle Worker*, Playfilms, UA.
BETTE DAVIS in *What Ever Happened to Baby Jane?*, Seven Arts-Associates & Aldrich, Warner Bros.
KATHARINE HEPBURN in *Long Day's Journey Into Night*, Landau, Embassy.
GERALDINE PAGE in *Sweet Bird of Youth*, Roxbury, M-G-M.
LEE REMICK in *Days of Wine and Roses*, Manulis-Jalem, Warner Bros.

SUPPORTING ACTOR

*ED BEGLEY in *Sweet Bird of Youth*, Roxbury, M-G-M.
VICTOR BUONO in *What Ever Happened to Baby Jane?*, Seven Arts-Associates & Aldrich, Warner Bros.
TELLY SAVALAS in *Bird Man of Alcatraz*, Hecht, UA.
OMAR SHARIF in *Lawrence of Arabia*, Horizon-Spiegel-Lean, Columbia.
TERENCE STAMP in *Billy Budd*, Harvest, Allied Artists.

SUPPORTING ACTRESS

MARY BADHAM in *To Kill a Mockingbird*, Pakula-Mulligan-Brentwood, U-I.
*PATTY DUKE in *The Miracle Worker*, Playfilms, UA.
SHIRLEY KNIGHT in *Sweet Bird of Youth*, Roxbury, M-G-M.
ANGELA LANSBURY in *The Manchurian Candidate*, M.C. Prod., UA.
THELMA RITTER in *Bird Man of Alcatraz*, Hecht, UA.

DIRECTING

DAVID AND LISA, Heller-Perry, Continental. Frank Perry.
DIVORCE—ITALIAN STYLE, Embassy Pictures (Italian). Pietro Germi.
*LAWRENCE OF ARABIA, Horizon, Columbia. David Lean.
THE MIRACLE WORKER, Playfilms, UA. Arthur Penn.
TO KILL A MOCKINGBIRD, Pakula-Mulligan, U-I. Robert Mulligan.

WRITING

(Screenplay—based on material from another medium)
DAVID AND LISA, Heller-Perry, Continental. Eleanor Perry.
LAWRENCE OF ARABIA by Robert Bolt and Michael Wilson.
LOLITA, Seven Arts, M-G-M. Vladimir Nabokov.
THE MIRACLE WORKER, Playfilms, UA. William Gibson.
*TO KILL A MOCKINGBIRD, Pakula-Mulligan, U-I. Horton Foote.

(Story and Screenplay—written directly for the screen)
*DIVORCE—ITALIAN STYLE, Embassy Pictures (Italian). Ennio de Concini, Alfredo Giannetti and Pietro Germi.
FREUD, Huston, U-I. Charles Kaufman and Wolfgang Reinhardt.
LAST YEAR AT MARIENBAD, Astor Pictures (French). Alain Robbe-Grillet.
THAT TOUCH OF MINK, Granley-Arwin-Shapiro, U-I. Stanley Shapiro and Nate Monaster.
THROUGH A GLASS DARKLY, Janus Films (Swedish). Ingmar Bergman.

CINEMATOGRAPHY

(Black-and-White)
BIRD MAN OF ALCATRAZ, Hecht, UA. Burnett Guffey.
*THE LONGEST DAY, Zanuck, 20th Century-Fox. Jean Bourgoin and Walter Wottitz.
TO KILL A MOCKINGBIRD, Pakula-Mulligan, U-I. Russell Harlan.
TWO FOR THE SEESAW, Mirisch-Argyle-Talbot-Seven Arts, UA. Ted McCord.
WHAT EVER HAPPENED TO BABY JANE?, Seven Arts-Aldrich, Warner Bros. Ernest Haller.

(Color)
GYPSY, Warner Bros. Harry Stradling, Sr.
HATARI!, Hawks, Paramount. Russell Harlan.
*LAWRENCE OF ARABIA, Horizon, Columbia. Fred A. Young.
MUTINY ON THE BOUNTY, Arcola, M-G-M. Robert L. Surtees.
THE WONDERFUL WORLD OF THE BROTHERS GRIMM, M-G-M and Cinerama. Paul C. Vogel.

MUSIC

(Song)
*DAYS OF WINE AND ROSES (*Days of Wine and Roses*, Manulis-Jalem, Warner Bros.); Music by Henry Mancini. Lyrics by Johnny Mercer.
LOVE SONG FROM MUTINY ON THE BOUNTY (Follow Me) (*Mutiny on the Bounty*, Arcola, M-G-M); Music by Bronislau Kaper. Lyrics by Paul Francis Webster.
SONG FROM TWO FOR THE SEESAW (Second Chance) (*Two for the Seesaw*, Mirisch-Argyle-Talbot-Seven Arts, UA); Music by Andre Previn. Lyrics by Dory Langdon.
TENDER IS THE NIGHT (*Tender is the Night*, 20th Century-Fox); Music by Sammy Fain. Lyrics by Paul Francis Webster.
WALK ON THE WILD SIDE (*Walk on the Wild Side*, Feldman-Famous Artists, Columbia); Music by Elmer Bernstein. Lyrics by Mack David.

(Music Score—substantially original)
(New classification)
FREUD, Huston, U-I. Jerry Goldsmith.
*LAWRENCE OF ARABIA, Horizon, Columbia. Maurice Jarre.
MUTINY ON THE BOUNTY, Arcola, M-G-M. Bronislau Kaper.
TARAS BULBA, Hecht, UA. Franz Waxman.
TO KILL A MOCKINGBIRD, Pakula-Mulligan, U-I. Elmer Bernstein.

Best Director: David Lean (left, on camera boom) for Lawrence of Arabia. Few directors racked up a portfolio to match the accomplishments of Lean who, within only a nine-year span, made 1957's The Bridge on the River Kwai *(seven Oscars), 1962's* Lawrence of Arabia *(seven Oscars) and 1965's* Doctor Zhivago *(five Oscars). Lean personally won Academy Awards for* Bridge *and* Lawrence *and was nominated for* Zhivago; *he was also a nominee again in 1984 for* A Passage to India. *In all, he received seven nominations as a director during his lifetime, the same total achieved by Fred Zinnemann, and topped only by William Wyler (with 12 nominations) and Billy Wilder (eight nominations as a director).*

(New classification)
BILLY ROSE'S JUMBO, Euterpe-Arwin, M-G-M. George Stoll.
GIGOT, Seven Arts, 20th Century-Fox. Michel Magne.
GYPSY, Warner Bros. Frank Perkins.
*THE MUSIC MAN, Warner Bros. Ray Heindorf.
THE WONDERFUL WORLD OF THE BROTHERS GRIMM, M-G-M and Cinerama. Leigh Harline.

ART DIRECTION-SET DECORATION

(Black-and-White)
DAYS OF WINE AND ROSES, Manulis-Jalem, Warner Bros. Joseph Wright; George James Hopkins.
THE LONGEST DAY, Zanuck, 20th Century-Fox. Ted Haworth, Leon Barsacq and Vincent Korda; Gabriel Bechir.
PERIOD OF ADJUSTMENT, Marten, M-G-M. George W. Davis and Edward Carfagno; Henry Grace and Dick Pefferle.
THE PIGEON THAT TOOK ROME, Llenroc, Paramount, Hal Pereira and Roland Anderson; Sam Comer and Frank R. McKelvy.
*TO KILL A MOCKINGBIRD, Pakula-Mulligan, U-I. Alexander Golitzen and Henry Bumstead; Oliver Emert.

(Color)
*LAWRENCE OF ARABIA, Horizon, Columbia. John Box and John Stoll; Dario Simoni.
THE MUSIC MAN, Warner Bros. Paul Groesse; George James Hopkins.
MUTINY ON THE BOUNTY, Arcola, M-G-M. George W. Davis and J. McMillan Johnson; Henry Grace and Hugh Hunt.
THAT TOUCH OF MINK, Granley-Arwin-Shapiro, U-I. Alexander Golitzen and Robert Clatworthy; George Milo.
THE WONDERFUL WORLD OF THE BROTHERS GRIMM, M-G-M and Cinerama. George W. Davis and Edward Carfagno; Henry Grace and Dick Pefferle.

COSTUME DESIGN

(Black-and-White)
DAYS OF WINE AND ROSES, Manulis-Jalem, Warner Bros. Don Feld.
THE MAN WHO SHOT LIBERTY VALANCE, Ford, Paramount. Edith Head.
THE MIRACLE WORKER, Playfilms, UA. Ruth Morley.
PHAEDRA, Dassin-Melinafilm, Lopert Pictures, Denny Vachiloti.
*WHAT EVER HAPPENED TO BABY JANE?, Seven Arts-Aldrich, Warner Bros. Norma Koch.

(Color)
BON VOYAGE, Disney, Buena Vista. Bill Thomas.
GYPSY, Warner Bros., Orry-Kelly.
THE MUSIC MAN, Warner Bros. Dorothy Jeakins.
MY GEISHA, Sachiko, Paramount. Edith Head.
*THE WONDERFUL WORLD OF THE BROTHERS GRIMM, M-G-M and Cinerama. Mary Wills.

SOUND
BON VOYAGE, Disney, Buena Vista. Walt Disney Studio Sound Dept.; Robert O. Cook, sound director.
*LAWRENCE OF ARABIA, Horizon, Columbia. Shepperton Studio Sound Dept.; John Cox, sound director.
THE MUSIC MAN, Warner Bros. Warner Bros. Studio Sound Dept.; George R. Groves, sound director.
THAT TOUCH OF MINK, Granley-Arwin-Shapiro, U-I. Universal City Studio Sound Dept.; Waldon O. Watson, sound director.
WHAT EVER HAPPENED TO BABY JANE?, Seven Arts-Warner Bros. Glen Glenn Sound Dept.; Joseph Kelly, sound director.

FILM EDITING
*LAWRENCE OF ARABIA, Horizon, Columbia. Anne Coates.
THE LONGEST DAY, Zanuck, 20th Century-Fox. Samuel E. Beetley.
THE MANCHURIAN CANDIDATE, Axelrod-Frankenheimer, UA. Ferris Webster.
THE MUSIC MAN, Warner Bros. William Ziegler.
MUTINY ON THE BOUNTY, Arcola, M-G-M. John McSweeney, Jr.

SPECIAL EFFECTS
*THE LONGEST DAY, Zanuck, 20th Century-Fox. Robert MacDonald and Jacques Maumont.
MUTINY ON THE BOUNTY, Arcola, M-G-M. A. Arnold Gillespie and Milo Lory.

Best Supporting Actor: Ed Begley as Boss Finley in Sweet Bird of Youth (M-G-M; directed by Richard Brooks). Tennessee Williams wrote it, Sidney Blackmer originated the character on Broadway, and (above, balking at a photographer and flanked by Rip Torn) Ed Begley played Boss Finley on film, a corrupt and powerful Florida political boss determined to keep his daughter (Shirley Knight) away from an aging beachboy-hustler (Paul Newman) who loves her. Geraldine Page co-starred as a has-been movie star on a lost weekend in the town Boss Finley controls.

SHORT SUBJECTS

(Cartoons)
*THE HOLE, Storyboard Inc., Brandon Films. John and Faith Hubley, producers.
ICARUS MONTGOLFIER WRIGHT, Format Films, UA. Jules Engel, producer.
NOW HEAR THIS, Warner Bros.
SELF DEFENSE—FOR COWARDS, Rembrandt Films, Film Representations. William L. Snyder, producer.
SYMPOSIUM ON POPULAR SONGS, Disney, Buena Vista. Walt Disney, producer.

(Live Action Subjects)
BIG CITY BLUES, Mayfair Pictures. Martina and Charles Huguenot van der Linden, producers.
THE CADILLAC, United Producers Releasing. Robert Clouse, producer.
THE CLIFF DWELLERS, (a.k.a. One Plus One), Group II Film Prods., Schoenfeld Films. Hayward Anderson, producer.
*HEUREUX ANNIVERSAIRE (Happy Anniversary), Atlantic Pictures (French). Pierre Etaix and J.C. Carriere, producers.
PAN, Mayfair Pictures. Herman van der Horst, producer.

DOCUMENTARY

(Short Subjects)
*DYLAN THOMAS, TWW Ltd., Janus Films (Welsh). Jack Howells, producer.
THE JOHN GLENN STORY, Department of the Navy, Warner Bros. William L. Hendricks, producer.
THE ROAD TO THE WALL, CBS Films, Department of Defense. Robert Saudek, producer.

(Features)
ALVORADA (Brazil's Changing Face), MW Filmproduktion (German). Hugo Niebeling, producer.
*BLACK FOX, Image Prods., Heritage Films. Louis Clyde Stoumen, producer.

FOREIGN LANGUAGE FILM
ELECTRA, (Greece).
THE FOUR DAYS OF NAPLES, (Italy).
KEEPER OF PROMISES (The Given Word), (Brazil).
*SUNDAYS AND CYBELE, (France).
TLAYUCAN, (Mexico).

HONORARY AND OTHER AWARDS
None given this year.

1962 IRVING G. THALBERG MEMORIAL AWARD
None given this year.

1962 JEAN HERSHOLT HUMANITARIAN AWARD
TO STEVE BROIDY

SCIENTIFIC OR TECHNICAL

CLASS I (statuette)
None.

CLASS II (plaque)
RALPH CHAPMAN for the design and development of an advanced motion picture camera crane.
ALBERT S. PRATT, JAMES L. WASSELL and HANS C. WOHLRAB of the Professional Division, Bell & Howell Co., for the design and development of a new and improved automatic motion picture additive color printer.
NORTH AMERICAN PHILIPS CO., INC., for the design and engineering of the Norelco Universal 70/35mm motion picture projector.
CHARLES E. SUTTER, WILLIAM BRYSON SMITH and LOUIS C. KENNELL of Paramount Pictures Corp. for the engineering and application to motion picture production of a new system of electric power distribution.

CLASS III (citation)
ELECTRO-VOICE, INC.;
LOUIS G. MacKENZIE.

*INDICATES WINNER

1963
The Thirty-Sixth Year

This was a serious year, with political questions relating to Vietnam becoming more difficult, strong actions in the civil rights corner and the assassination of President John F. Kennedy. If laughter was ever needed this was the time and, almost on cue, came a ribald, scampish British laugh-inducer named *Tom Jones*. It won great favor with audiences and Academy voters, and was honored with four Oscars, including best picture and best director (Tony Richardson). It was only the second time in Academy annals a British-made film had won the best picture statuette, the first occasion being *Hamlet's* 1948 Oscar.

Cleopatra, probably the most publicized motion picture of the decade, also won four Academy Awards: best color cinematography, best color art direction, best costume design and best special effects. Other multiple winners included *Hud* (three awards, including best actress Patricia Neal and best supporting actor Melvyn Douglas), *How the West Was Won* (three awards) and *Federico Fellini's 8½* from Italy with two awards, including best foreign language film. Sidney Poitier was named best actor for *Lilies of the Field* and became the first Black to win one of the Academy's two "upstairs" acting awards. England's Margaret Rutherford was named best supporting actress for *The V.I.P.s.*

Oscar night—April 13, 1964—showed the strong influence of English talents on the 1963 movie world: ten of the twenty acting nominees were either British-born or cited for their work in British films.

The awards were presented at the Santa Monica Civic Auditorium. Jack Lemmon was the evening's M.C. and George Sidney produced the program for the Academy. Richard Dunlap again produced and directed for the ABC network.

Among the acting winners, only Poitier was present to receive his award. Annabella accepted for Patricia Neal, who was in England, Peter Ustinov accepted for Margaret Rutherford, also in England, and Brandon de Wilde did stand-in duty for Melvyn Douglas, who was working in Spain.

Sammy Davis, Jr. provided the biggest off-the-cuff laugh of the evening. When he was handed the incorrect envelope to announce the music awards, he quipped, "Wait until the NAACP hears about this...."

Best Actor: **Sidney Poitier** *as Homer Smith (left, with Lilia Skala) in* Lilies of the Field *(United Artists; directed by Ralph Nelson). It was a little film and a labor of love, modestly budgeted at $450,000 and based on a 92-page novelette by W.E. Barrett. Sidney Poitier charmingly played a footloose handyman and ex-G.I., traveling the Arizona countryside in a station wagon, who stops to repair a farmhouse roof for five refugee German nuns; the nuns are convinced he is the answer to prayers for a helper, so they cajole him into helping them build a chapel on some desolate desert land bequeathed to them.* Lilies *helped establish a precedent for black actors in American films, spotlighting the Poitier character as an individual rather than as a black, and was free of racial preachments or violence. When Academy Awards were voted, Poitier was a popular choice for his performance as handyman Homer.*

Best Picture: Tom Jones *(United Artists; produced in England by Tony Richardson) and* **Best Director: Tony Richardson** *for* Tom Jones. *Boisterous and bawdy, it was derived from the Henry Fielding classic about a bastard baby boy, born in mysterious circumstances and raised as the son of an English squire, who is later banished from his home, pegged as a thief and almost hanged on the gallows before he is left with his rightful inheritance. Albert Finney (left, with Susannah York) starred as the lusty Tom, and director Richardson and editor Antony Gibbs (the latter curiously not nominated for his contribution) infected the picture with a frenetic pace, wild fist fights, an eye-boggling fox hunt (with cross-cuts between a hand-held camera and helicopter views), even occasional asides by the actors to the camera. Audiences loved it; Academy voters did, too. Besides being a fine film, it was probably the least stuffy costume picture ever put on celluloid.*

Best Actress: Patricia Neal *as Alma (left, with Paul Newman) in* Hud *(Paramount; directed by Martin Ritt). "I thought the days when I would be offered a part like Alma were over," said Patricia Neal. Alma was a brief role but a strong one: she's the wise but slatternly housekeeper for the Bannon household in modern Texas, which consists of an honest, cattleman father (Melvyn Douglas), his ruthless, virile son (Paul Newman) and a 17-year-old nephew (Brandon de Wilde) who's still in his formative and impressionable years. Alma cooks and cleans for the clan, mockingly aware of the son's corruption; after he attempts to rape her, she boards a bus and leaves town, well aware she's too fascinated by him to stay. Unlike most Oscar-winning roles, Alma had no high, dramatic soliloquies or moments and was played mostly in the background to the other characters, all the more credit to Patricia Neal's superb abilities as an actress to make it so memorable.*

Best Supporting Actress: Margaret Rutherford *as the Duchess of Brighton in* The V.I.P.s *(M-G-M; directed by Anthony Asquith). In the style of* Grand Hotel, *with an all-star cast of unrelated characters in a common environment,* The V.I.P.s *was written by Terence Rattigan and took place in London's bustling airport, involving the plights of travelers such as Elizabeth Taylor, Richard Burton, Louis Jourdan, Orson Welles and Maggie Smith. The tweedy Miss Rutherford was at her quivering best as a confused and eccentric dowager traveling tourist class to Florida, grounded at the terminal by fog. On hearing she'd won an Oscar, the 72-year-old actress told newsmen in England, "I'm absolutely thrilled. This may sound presumptuous at my age, but I like to feel that this will be the starting point of a new little phase for me in films."*

176

PICTURE

AMERICA AMERICA, Athena, Warner Bros. Produced by Elia Kazan.
CLEOPATRA, 20th Century-Fox. Produced by Walter Wanger.
HOW THE WEST WAS WON, M-G-M. Cinerama. Produced by Bernard Smith.
LILIES OF THE FIELD, Rainbow, UA. Produced by Ralph Nelson.
*__TOM JONES,__ Woodfall, UA-Lopert (British). Produced by Tony Richardson.

ACTOR

ALBERT FINNEY in *Tom Jones,* Woodfall, UA-Lopert (British).
RICHARD HARRIS in *This Sporting Life,* Wintle-Parkyn, Reade-Sterling-Continental (British).
REX HARRISON in *Cleopatra,* 20th Century-Fox.
PAUL NEWMAN in *Hud,* Salem-Dover, Paramount.
*__SIDNEY POITIER__ in *Lilies of the Field,* Rainbow, UA.

ACTRESS

LESLIE CARON in *The L-Shaped Room,* Romulus, Columbia (British).
SHIRLEY MacLAINE in *Irma La Douce,* Mirisch-Phalanx, UA.
*__PATRICIA NEAL__ in *Hud,* Salem-Dover, Paramount.
RACHEL ROBERTS in *This Sporting Life,* Wintle-Parkwyn, Reade-Sterling-Continental (British).
NATALIE WOOD in *Love with the Proper Stranger,* Boardwalk-Rona, Paramount.

SUPPORTING ACTOR

NICK ADAMS in *Twilight of Honor,* Perlberg-Seaton, M-G-M.
BOBBY DARIN in *Captain Newman, M.D.,* Brentwood-Reynard, Universal.
*__MELVYN DOUGLAS__ in *Hud,* Salem-Dover, Paramount.
HUGH GRIFFITH in *Tom Jones,* Woodfall, UA-Lopert (British).
JOHN HUSTON in *The Cardinal,* Preminger, Columbia.

SUPPORTING ACTRESS

DIANE CILENTO in *Tom Jones,* Woodfall, UA-Lopert (British).
DAME EDITH EVANS in *Tom Jones,* Woodfall, UA-Lopert (British).
JOYCE REDMAN in *Tom Jones,* Woodfall, UA-Lopert (British).
*__MARGARET RUTHERFORD__ in *The V.I.P.s,* M-G-M.
LILIA SKALA in *Lilies of the Field,* Rainbow, UA.

DIRECTING

AMERICA, AMERICA, Kazan, Warner Bros. Elia Kazan.
THE CARDINAL, Preminger, Columbia. Otto Preminger.
FEDERICO FELLINI'S 8 ½, Embassy Pictures (Italian). Federico Fellini.
HUD, Salem-Dover, Paramount. Martin Ritt.
*__TOM JONES,__ Woodfall, UA-Lopert (British). Tony Richardson.

WRITING

(Screenplay—based on material from another medium)
CAPTAIN NEWMAN, M.D., Brentwood-Reynard, Universal. Richard L. Breen, Phoebe and Henry Ephron.
HUD, Salem-Dover, Paramount. Irving Ravetch and Harriet Frank, Jr.
LILIES OF THE FIELD, Rainbow, UA. James Poe.
SUNDAYS AND CYBELE, Columbia (French). Serge Bourguignon and Antoine Tudal.
*__TOM JONES,__ Woodfall, UA-Lopert (British). John Osborne.

(Story and Screenplay—written directly for the screen)
AMERICA AMERICA, Kazan, Warner Bros. Elia Kazan.
FEDERICO FELLINI'S 8½, Embassy Pictures (Italian). Federico Fellini, Ennio Flaiano, Tullio Pinelli and Brunello Rondi.
THE FOUR DAYS OF NAPLES, Titanus, M-G-M (Italian). Pasquale Festa Campanile, Massino Franciosa, Nanni Loy, Vasco Pratolini and Carlo Bernari.
*__HOW THE WEST WAS WON,__ M-G-M and Cinerama. James R. Webb.
LOVE WITH THE PROPER STRANGER, Pakula-Mulligan, Paramount. Arnold Schulman.

CINEMATOGRAPHY

(Black-and-White)
THE BALCONY, Allen-Hodgdon, Reade-Sterling-Continental Dist. George Folsey.
THE CARETAKERS, Bartlett, UA. Lucien Ballard.
*__HUD,__ Salem-Dover, Paramount. James Wong Howe.
LILIES OF THE FIELD, Rainbow, UA. Ernest Haller.
LOVE WITH THE PROPER STRANGER, Pakula-Mulligan, Paramount. Milton Krasner.

(Color)
THE CARDINAL, Preminger, Columbia. Leon Shamroy.
*__CLEOPATRA,__ Wanger, 20th Century-Fox. Leon Shamroy.
HOW THE WEST WAS WON, M-G-M and Cinerama. William H. Daniels, Milton Krasner, Charles Lang, Jr. and Joseph LaShelle.
IRMA LA DOUCE, Mirisch-Alperson, UA. Joseph LaShelle.
IT'S A MAD, MAD, MAD, MAD WORLD, Kramer, UA. Ernest Laszlo.

ART DIRECTION-SET DECORATION

(Black-and-White)
*__AMERICA AMERICA,__ Kazan, Warner Bros. Gene Callahan.
FEDERICO FELLINI'S 8½, Embassy Pictures (Italian). Piero Gherardi.
HUD, Salem-Dover, Paramount. Hal Pereira and Tambi Larsen; Sam Comer and Robert Benton.
LOVE WITH THE PROPER STRANGER, Pakula-Mulligan, Paramount. Hal Pereira and Roland Anderson; Sam Comer and Grace Gregory.
TWILIGHT OF HONOR, Perlberg-Seaton, M-G-M. George W. Davis and Paul Groesse; Henry Grace and Hugh Hunt.

(Color)
THE CARDINAL, Preminger, Columbia. Lyle Wheeler; Gene Callahan.
*__CLEOPATRA,__ Wanger, 20th Century-Fox. John DeCuir, Jack Martin Smith, Hilyard Brown, Herman Blumenthal, Elven Webb, Maurice Pelling and Boris Juraga; Walter M. Scott, Paul S. Fox and Ray Moyer.
COME BLOW YOUR HORN, Essex-Tandem, Paramount. Hal Pereira and Roland Anderson; Sam Comer and James Payne.
HOW THE WEST WAS WON, M-G-M and Cinerama. George W. Davis, William Ferrari and Addison Hehr; Henry Grace, Don Greenwood, Jr. and Jack Mills.
TOM JONES, Woodfall, UA-Lopert (British). Ralph Brinton, Ted Marshall and Jocelyn Herbert; Josie MacAvin.

COSTUME DESIGN

(Black-and-White)
*__FEDERICO FELLINI'S 8½,__ Embassy Pictures (Italian). Piero Gherardi.
LOVE WITH THE PROPER STRANGER, Pakula-Mulligan, Paramount. Edith Head.
THE STRIPPER, Wald, 20th Century-Fox. Travilla.
TOYS IN THE ATTIC, Mirisch-Claude, UA. Bill Thomas.
WIVES AND LOVERS, Wallis, Paramount. Edith Head.

(Color)
THE CARDINAL, Preminger, Columbia. Donald Brooks.
*__CLEOPATRA,__ Wanger, 20th Century-Fox. Irene Sharaff, Vittorio Nino Novarese and Renie.
HOW THE WEST WAS WON, M-G-M and Cinerama. Walter Plunkett.
THE LEOPARD, Titanus, 20th Century-Fox. Piero Tosi.
A NEW KIND OF LOVE, Llenroc, Paramount. Edith Head.

SOUND

BYE BYE BIRDIE, Kohlmar-Sidney, Columbia. Columbia Studio Sound Dept. Charles Rice, sound director.
CAPTAIN NEWMAN, M.D., Brentwood-Reynard, Universal, Universal City Studio Sound Dept.; Waldon O. Watson, sound director.
CLEOPATRA, Wanger, 20th Century-Fox. 20th Century-Fox Studio Sound Dept.; James P. Corcoran, sound director, and Todd A-O Sound Dept., Fred Hynes, sound director.
*__HOW THE WEST WAS WON,__ M-G-M and Cinerama. M-G-M Studio Sound Dept.; Franklin E. Milton, sound director.
IT'S A MAD, MAD, MAD, MAD WORLD, Kramer, UA. Samuel Goldwyn Studio Sound Dept.; Gordon E. Sawyer, sound director.

FILM EDITING

THE CARDINAL, Preminger, Columbia. Louis R. Loeffler.
CLEOPATRA, Wanger, 20th Century-Fox. Dorothy Spencer.
THE GREAT ESCAPE, Mirisch-Alpha, UA. Ferris Webster.
*__HOW THE WEST WAS WON,__ M-G-M and Cinerama. Harold F. Kress.
IT'S A MAD, MAD, MAD, MAD WORLD, Kramer, UA. Frederic Knudtson, Robert C. Jones and Gene Fowler, Jr.

SPECIAL VISUAL EFFECTS

(New classification)
THE BIRDS, Hitchcock, Universal, Ub Iwerks.
*__CLEOPATRA,__ Wanger, 20th Century-Fox. Emil Kosa, Jr.

SOUND EFFECTS

(New classification)

A GATHERING OF EAGLES, Universal. Robert L. Bratton.

*IT'S A MAD, MAD, MAD, MAD WORLD, Kramer, UA. Walter G. Elliott.

MUSIC

(Song)

*CALL ME IRRESPONSIBLE (*Papa's Delicate Condition*, Amro, Paramount); Music by James Van Heusen. Lyrics by Sammy Cahn.

CHARADE (*Charade*, Donen, Universal); Music by Henry Mancini. Lyrics by Johnny Mercer.

IT'S A MAD, MAD, MAD, MAD WORLD, (*It's a Mad, Mad, Mad, Mad World*, Kramer, UA); Music by Ernest Gold. Lyrics by Mack David.

MORE (*Mondo Cane*, Cineriz Prods., Times Film); Music by Riz Ortolani and Nino Oliviero. Lyrics by Norman Newell.

SO LITTLE TIME (*55 Days at Peking*, Bronston, Allied Artists); Music by Dimitri Tiomkin. Lyrics by Paul Francis Webster.

(Music Score—substantially original)

CLEOPATRA, Wanger, 20th Century-Fox. Alex North.

55 DAYS AT PEKING, Bronston, Allied Artists. Dimitri Tiomkin.

HOW THE WEST WAS WON, M-G-M and Cinerama. Alfred Newman and Ken Darby.

IT'S A MAD, MAD, MAD, MAD WORLD, Kramer, UA. Ernest Gold.

*TOM JONES, Woodfall, UA-Lopert (British). John Addison.

(Scoring of Music—adaptation or treatment)

BYE BYE BIRDIE, Kohlmar-Sidney, Columbia. John Green.

*IRMA LA DOUCE, Mirisch-Alperson, UA. Andre Previn.

A NEW KIND OF LOVE, Llenroc, Paramount. Leith Stevens.

SUNDAYS AND CYBELE, Columbia (French). Maurice Jarre.

THE SWORD IN THE STONE, Disney, Buena Vista. George Bruns.

SHORT SUBJECTS

(Cartoons)

AUTOMANIA 2000, Pathe Contemporary Films. John Halas, producer.

*THE CRITIC, Pintoff-Crossbow Prods., Columbia. Ernest Pintoff, producer.

THE GAME (Ingra), Rembrandt Films-Film Representations. Dusan Vukotic, producer.

MY FINANCIAL CAREER, National Film Board of Canada, Walter Reade-Sterling-Continental Distributing. Colin Low and Tom Daly, producers.

PIANISSIMO, Cinema 16. Carmen D'Avino, producer.

(Live Action Subjects)

THE CONCERT, King Corp., George K. Arthur-Go Pictures. Ezra Baker, producer.

HOME-MADE CAR, Schoenfeld Films. James Hill, producer.

*AN OCCURRENCE AT OWL CREEK BRIDGE, Janus Films. Paul de Roubaix and Marcel Ichac, producers.

SIX-SIDED TRIANGLE, Lion International, Christopher Miles, producer.

THAT'S ME, Pathe Contemporary Films. Walker Stuart, producer.

DOCUMENTARY

(Short Subjects)

*CHAGALL, Auerbach-Flag Films. Simon Schiffrin, producer.

THE FIVE CITIES OF JUNE, US Information Agency. George Stevens, Jr., producer.

THE SPIRIT OF AMERICA, Spotlite News, Algernon G. Walker, producer.

THIRTY MILLION LETTERS, British Transport Films. Edgar Anstey, producer.

TO LIVE AGAIN, Wilding Inc. Mel London, producer.

(Features)

LE MAILLON ET LA CHAINE (The Link And The Chain), Films Du Centaure-Filmartic (French). Paul de Roubaix, producer.

*ROBERT FROST: A LOVER'S QUARREL WITH THE WORLD, WGBH Educational Foundation. Robert Hughes, producer.

THE YANKS ARE COMING, David L. Wolper Prods. Marshall Flaum, producer.

FOREIGN LANGUAGE FILM

*FEDERICO FELLINI'S 8½, (Italy).

KNIFE IN THE WATER, (Poland).

LOS TARANTOS, (Spain).

THE RED LANTERNS, (Greece).

TWIN SISTERS OF KYOTO, (Japan).

177

Best Supporting Actor: Melvyn Douglas *as Homer Bannon (above, being aided by Brandon de Wilde and Paul Newman) in* Hud *(Paramount; directed by Martin Ritt). Melvyn Douglas first established himself in movies as a suave, aristocratic leading man to actresses like Greta Garbo, Marlene Dietrich, Katharine Hepburn and Merle Oberon, then he concentrated his talents on the legitimate theater in the 1950s. After an 11-year absence, he returned to movie making in 1962's* Billy Budd, *then the following year he made* Hud, *playing an aging cattle rancher with old-fashioned, idealistic principles, a man in sharp contrast to a greedy, insensitive son (played by Paul Newman).* Hud *also won an Academy Award for James Wong Howe's magnificent black-and-white cinematography. Douglas won a second supporting Oscar in 1979 for* Being There.

HONORARY AND OTHER AWARDS

None given this year.

1963 IRVING G. THALBERG MEMORIAL AWARD

TO SAM SPIEGEL

1963 JEAN HERSHOLT HUMANITARIAN AWARD

None given this year.

SCIENTIFIC OR TECHNICAL

CLASS I (statuette)

None.

CLASS II (plaque)

None.

CLASS III (citation)

DOUGLAS G. SHEARER and A. ARNOLD GILLESPIE of M-G-M Studios.

*INDICATES WINNER

Two musical ladies—*Mary Poppins* and *My Fair Lady*—shared the Academy Awards spotlight on April 5, 1965, when awards for 1964 achievements were announced at the Santa Monica Civic Auditorium. *Poppins* was nominated for thirteen awards, *My Fair Lady* was nominated for twelve and they had something more in common: Julie Andrews, star of the *Poppins* movie, had earlier created the *My Fair Lady* Eliza Doolittle role on the stage. When the final tally was in, *My Fair Lady* received eight awards, including best picture, best actor (Rex Harrison) and best director (George Cukor), and *Mary Poppins* received five, including Julie Andrews as best actress. For director Cukor, it was his first Oscar in a distinguished thirty-five year career, during which he had directed five actors into Academy wins (James Stewart, Ingrid Bergman, Ronald Colman, Judy Holliday and Harrison) and some fourteen others to nominations.

Peter Ustinov received his second Academy Award as best supporting actor, this one for *Topkapi,* and Lila Kedrova was chosen best supporting actress for *Zorba the Greek.* Italy's *Yesterday, Today and Tomorrow* was named best foreign language film, and makeup expert William Tuttle was given an honorary award for his achievement on *7 Faces of Dr. Lao,* the first time the area of makeup had been singled out by the Academy's Board of Governors.

Joe Pasternak produced the presentation show for the Academy, telecast over ABC-TV, and Bob Hope was master of ceremonies. Among the presenters, Martha Raye and Jimmy Durante created an Oscar highlight when they got tongue-tied reading the names of a few foreign-born nominees. Two popular television doctors, Dr. Kildare (Richard Chamberlain) and Dr. Ben Casey (Vince Edwards), appeared together for the first time, Judy Garland sang a special medley of Cole Porter songs, and Peter Gennaro danced to Gershwin's "I Got Rhythm." It was also the last year home viewers would see an Academy Awards ceremony telecast only in black-and-white.

Best Picture: My Fair Lady *(Warner Bros.; produced by Jack L. Warner) and* **Best Actor: Rex Harrison** *as Professor Henry Higgins (right, with Audrey Hepburn) in* My Fair Lady. *The story of a Cockney flower girl named Eliza Doolittle who blooms from a weed into an orchid under the tutelage of a crusty English professor,* My Fair Lady *was a musical version of George Bernard Shaw's* Pygmalion *and had become the longest-running musical in American theater history when Warner Bros. outbid all competitors for the screen rights in 1962. On screen, it became as much of a classic as it had been on stage, with Audrey Hepburn as the movie Eliza (with her singing dubbed by Marni Nixon) and Rex Harrison—full of rascally charm and likeable brashness—playing Higgins for the 1007th time since he'd created the singing 'enry 'iggins on stage.* My Fair Lady, *in all, won eight Academy Awards.*

Best Actress: Julie Andrews *as Mary Poppins (left) in* Mary Poppins *(Buena Vista; directed by Robert Stevenson). Julie Andrews had made a major success on stage in the original* My Fair Lady *opposite Rex Harrison but was bypassed for the film version. Instead, she made her movie debut the same year for Walt Disney in his musical version of P.L. Travers' Mary Poppins books, as a 1910 English nanny who travels through the air via an open umbrella, and takes charge of two unruly children and an unsettled household, helped by liberal doses of magic. The movie won Miss Andrews the Academy Award, and received others for song ("Chim Chim Cher-ee"), original music score, film editing and visual effects, the latter a new awards category classification. It also started Julie Andrews on a popular screen career which brought additional Oscar nominations for 1965's* The Sound of Music *and 1982's* Victor/Victoria.

Best Director: George Cukor *(left, directing Audrey Hepburn) for* My Fair Lady. *Not all of the great talents of the motion picture business become Academy Award winners, and many conspicuous contributors have been inexplicably overlooked for years. George Cukor was nominated four times (for 1932-33's* Little Women, *1940's* The Philadelphia Story, *1947's* A Double Life *and 1950's* Born Yesterday*) and had directed numerous performers toward Oscars and/or nominations without receiving an Award himself. Then along came* My Fair Lady *and, at long last, Mr. Cukor got his due.*

PICTURE

BECKET, Wallis, Paramount. Produced by Hal Wallis.
DR. STRANGELOVE OR: HOW I LEARNED TO
STOP WORRYING AND LOVE THE BOMB, Hawk
Films, Columbia. Produced by Stanley Kubrick.
MARY POPPINS, Disney, Buena Vista. Produced by
Walt Disney and Bill Walsh.
*MY FAIR LADY, Warner Bros. Produced by Jack L.
Warner.
ZORBA THE GREEK, Rochley, 20th Century-Fox/
International Classics. Produced by Michael Cacoyannis.

ACTOR

RICHARD BURTON in *Becket,* Wallis, Paramount.
*REX HARRISON in *My Fair Lady,* Warner Bros.
PETER O'TOOLE in *Becket,* Wallis, Paramount.
ANTHONY QUINN in *Zorba the Greek,* Rochley, 20th
Century-Fox/International Classics.
PETER SELLERS in *Dr. Strangelove or: How I
Learned to Stop Worrying and Love the Bomb,* Hawk
Films, Columbia.

ACTRESS

*JULIE ANDREWS in *Mary Poppins,* Disney, Buena
Vista.
ANNE BANCROFT in *The Pumpkin Eater,* Romulus,
Royal Films International/Columbia (British).
SOPHIA LOREN in *Marriage Italian Style,* Champion-
Concordia, Embassy (Italian).
DEBBIE REYNOLDS in *The Unsinkable Molly Brown,*
Marten, M-G-M.
KIM STANLEY in *Seance on a Wet Afternoon,*
Attenborough-Forbes Artixo (British).

SUPPORTING ACTOR

JOHN GIELGUD in *Becket,* Wallis, Paramount.
STANLEY HOLLOWAY in *My Fair Lady,* Warner Bros.
EDMOND O'BRIEN in *Seven Days in May,* Joel,
Paramount.
LEE TRACY in *The Best Man,* Millar-Turman, UA.
*PETER USTINOV in *Topkapi,* Filmways, UA.

SUPPORTING ACTRESS

GLADYS COOPER in *My Fair Lady,* Warner Bros.
DAME EDITH EVANS in *The Chalk Garden,* Hunter,
Universal.
GRAYSON HALL in *The Night of the Iguana,* Seven
Arts, M-G-M.
*LILA KEDROVA in *Zorba the Greek,* Rochley, 20th
Century-Fox/International Classics.
AGNES MOOREHEAD in *Hush...Hush, Sweet Charlotte,*
Associates & Aldrich, 20th Century-Fox.

DIRECTING

BECKET, Wallis, Paramount. Peter Glenville.
DR. STRANGELOVE, OR: HOW I LEARNED TO
STOP WORRYING AND LOVE THE BOMB,
Kubrick, Columbia. Stanley Kubrick.
MARY POPPINS, Disney, Buena Vista. Robert
Stevenson.
*MY FAIR LADY, Warner Bros. George Cukor.
ZORBA THE GREEK, Rochley, International
Classics/20th Century-Fox. Michael Cacoyannis.

WRITING

(Screenplay—based on material from another medium)

*BECKET, Wallis, Paramount. Edward Anhalt.
DR. STRANGELOVE OR: HOW I LEARNED TO
STOP WORRYING AND LOVE THE BOMB,
Kubrick, Columbia. Stanley Kubrick, Peter George
and Terry Southern.
MARY POPPINS, Disney, Buena Vista. Bill Walsh and
Don DaGradi.
MY FAIR LADY, Warner Bros. Alan Jay Lerner.
ZORBA THE GREEK, Rochley, International Classics/
20th Century-Fox. Michael Cacoyannis.

(Story and Screenplay—written directly for the screen)

*FATHER GOOSE, Granox, Universal. S.H. Barnett,
Peter Stone and Frank Tarloff.
A HARD DAY'S NIGHT, Shenson-UA (British). Alun
Owen.
ONE POTATO, TWO POTATO, Cinema V. Orville H.
Hampton and Raphael Hayes.
THE ORGANIZER, Reade-Sterling-Continental
(Italian). Age, Scarpelli and Mario Monicelli.
THAT MAN FROM RIO, Lopert (French). Jean-Paul
Rappeneau, Ariane Mnouchkine, Daniel Boulanger
and Philippe De Broca.

CINEMATOGRAPHY

(Black-and-White)

THE AMERICANIZATION OF EMILY, Ransohoff,
M-G-M. Philip H. Lathrop.
FATE IS THE HUNTER, Arcola, 20th Century-Fox.
Milton Krasner.
HUSH...HUSH, SWEET CHARLOTTE, Aldrich, 20th
Century-Fox. Joseph Biroc.
THE NIGHT OF THE IGUANA, Seven Arts, M-G-M.
Gabriel Figueroa.
*ZORBA THE GREEK, Rochley, International Classics/
20th Century-Fox. Walter Lassally.

(Color)

BECKET, Wallis, Paramount. Geoffrey Unsworth.
CHEYENNE AUTUMN, Ford-Smith, Warner Bros.
William H. Clothier.
MARY POPPINS, Disney, Buena Vista. Edward Colman.
*MY FAIR LADY, Warner Bros. Harry Stradling.
THE UNSINKABLE MOLLY BROWN, Marten, M-G-M.
Daniel L. Fapp.

ART DIRECTION-SET DECORATION

(Black-and-White)

THE AMERICANIZATION OF EMILY, Ransohoff,
M-G-M. George W. Davis, Hans Peters and Elliot
Scott; Henry Grace and Robert R. Benton.
HUSH...HUSH, SWEET CHARLOTTE, Aldrich, 20th
Century-Fox. William Glasgow; Raphael Bretton.
THE NIGHT OF THE IGUANA, Seven Arts, M-G-M.
Stephen Grimes.
SEVEN DAYS IN MAY, Joel, Paramount. Cary Odell;
Edward G. Boyle.
*ZORBA THE GREEK, Rochley, International Classics/
20th Century-Fox. Vassilis Fotopoulos.

***Best Supporting Actor:* Peter Ustinov** *as Arthur
Simpson (above) in* Topkapi *(United Artists; directed by Jules
Dassin). Ustinov won his second Oscar (the first one came
in 1960) as a small-time con man and tourist-guide in a Greek
seaport town, mixed up in an attempt to steal an emerald-
studded dagger from a museum in Istanbul. Ustinov was
again an Academy Award nominee in 1968, as co-author of
the story and screenplay of* Hot Millions.

***Best Supporting Actress:* Lila Kedrova** *as Madame
Hortense (above, with Anthony Quinn) in* Zorba the Greek
*(20th Century-Fox; directed by Michael Cacoyannis). Born
in Leningrad and well known as a European stage actress,
she played an eccentric, aging courtesan briefly involved with
a lusty and vibrant Greek, played by Quinn. Simone Signoret*

*had begun filming the role, then withdrew, and Miss Kedrova
replaced her, and won the Academy Award. Miss Kedrova
later won a Tony award for the same role when she and Quinn
costarred on stage in a musical version of the story called,
simply,* Zorba.

(Color)

BECKET, Wallis, Paramount. John Bryan and Maurice Carter; Patrick McLoughlin and Robert Cartwright.
MARY POPPINS, Disney, Buena Vista. Carroll Clark and William H. Tuntke; Emile Kuri and Hal Gausman.
*__*MY FAIR LADY,__* Warner Bros. Gene Allen and Cecil Beaton; George James Hopkins.
THE UNSINKABLE MOLLY BROWN, Marten, M-G-M. George W. Davis and Preston Ames; Henry Grace and Hugh Hunt.
WHAT A WAY TO GO, Apjac-Orchard, 20th Century-Fox. Jack Martin Smith and Ted Haworth; Walter M. Scott and Stuart A. Reiss.

COSTUME DESIGN

(Black-and-White)

A HOUSE IS NOT A HOME, Greene-Rouse, Embassy Pictures. Edith Head.
HUSH...HUSH, SWEET CHARLOTTE, Aldrich, 20th Century-Fox. Norma Koch.
KISSES FOR MY PRESIDENT, Pearlayne, Warner Bros. Howard Shoup.
*__*THE NIGHT OF THE IGUANA,__* Seven Arts, M-G-M. Dorothy Jeakins.
THE VISIT, DeRode, 20th Century-Fox. Rene Hubert.

(Color)

BECKET, Wallis, Paramount. Margaret Furse.
MARY POPPINS, Disney, Buena Vista. Tony Walton.
*__*MY FAIR LADY,__* Warner Bros. Cecil Beaton.
THE UNSINKABLE MOLLY BROWN, Marten, M-G-M. Morton Haack.
WHAT A WAY TO GO, Apjac-Orchard, 20th Century-Fox. Edith Head and Moss Mabry.

SOUND

BECKET, Wallis, Paramount. Shepperton Studio Sound Dept.; John Cox, sound director.
FATHER GOOSE, Granox, Universal. Universal City Studio Sound Dept.; Waldon O. Watson, sound director.
MARY POPPINS, Disney, Buena Vista. Walt Disney Studio Sound Dept.; Robert O. Cook, sound director.
*__*MY FAIR LADY,__* Warner Bros. Warner Bros. Studio Sound Dept.; George R. Groves, sound director.
THE UNSINKABLE MOLLY BROWN, Marten, M-G-M. M-G-M Studio Sound Dept.; Franklin E. Milton, sound director.

FILM EDITING

BECKET, Wallis, Paramount. Anne Coates.
FATHER GOOSE, Granox, Universal. Ted J. Kent.
HUSH...HUSH, SWEET CHARLOTTE, Aldrich, 20th Century-Fox. Michael Luciano.
*__*MARY POPPINS,__* Disney, Buena Vista. Cotton Warburton.
MY FAIR LADY, Warner Bros. William Ziegler.

SPECIAL VISUAL EFFECTS

*__*MARY POPPINS,__* Disney, Buena Vista. Peter Ellenshaw, Hamilton Luske and Eustace Lycett.
7 FACES OF DR. LAO, Pal, M-G-M. Jim Danforth.

SOUND EFFECTS

*__*GOLDFINGER,__* Broccoli-Saltzman-Eon, UA (British). Norman Wanstall.
THE LIVELY SET, Universal. Robert L. Bratton.

MUSIC

(Song)

*__*CHIM CHIM CHER-EE__* (*Mary Poppins,* Disney, Buena Vista); Music and Lyrics by Richard M. Sherman and Robert B. Sherman.
DEAR HEART (*Dear Heart,* Warner Bros.); Music by Henry Mancini. Lyrics by Jay Livingston and Ray Evans.
HUSH...HUSH, SWEET CHARLOTTE, (*Hush...Hush, Sweet Charlotte,* Aldrich, 20th Century-Fox); Music by Frank DeVol. Lyrics by Mack David.
MY KIND OF TOWN, (*Robin and the 7 Hoods,* Warner Bros.); Music by James Van Heusen. Lyrics by Sammy Cahn.
WHERE LOVE HAS GONE (*Where Love Has Gone,* Embassy, Paramount); Music by James Van Heusen. Lyrics by Sammy Cahn.

(Music Score—substantially original)

BECKET, Wallis, Paramount. Laurence Rosenthal.
THE FALL OF THE ROMAN EMPIRE, Bronston, Paramount. Dimitri Tiomkin.
HUSH...HUSH, SWEET CHARLOTTE, Aldrich, 20th Century-Fox. Frank DeVol.
*__*MARY POPPINS,__* Disney, Buena Vista. Richard M. Sherman and Robert B. Sherman.
THE PINK PANTHER, Mirisch, UA. Henry Mancini.

(Scoring of Music—adaptation or treatment)

A HARD DAY'S NIGHT, Shenson, UA (British). George Martin.
MARY POPPINS, Disney, Buena Vista. Irwin Kostal.
*__*MY FAIR LADY,__* Warner Bros. Andre Previn.
ROBIN AND THE 7 HOODS, Warner Bros. Nelson Riddle.
THE UNSINKABLE MOLLY BROWN, Marten, M-G-M. Robert Armbruster, Leo Arnaud, Jack Elliott, Jack Hayes, Calvin Jackson and Leo Shuken.

SHORT SUBJECTS

(Cartoons)

CHRISTMAS CRACKER, National Film Board of Canada, Favorite Films of California.
HOW TO AVOID FRIENDSHIP, Rembrandt Films, Film Representations. William L. Snyder, producer.
NUDNIK #2, Rembrandt Films, Film Representations. William L. Snyder, producer.
*__*THE PINK PHINK,__* Mirisch-Geoffrey, UA. David H. Depatie and Friz Freleng, producers.

(Live Action Subjects)

*__*CASALS CONDUCTS: 1964,__* Thalia Films, Beckman Film Corp. Edward Schreiber, producer.
HELP! MY SNOWMAN'S BURNING DOWN, Pathe Contemporary Films. Carson Davidson, producer.
THE LEGEND OF JIMMY BLUE EYES, Topaz Film Corp. Robert Clouse, producer.

DOCUMENTARY

(Short Subjects)

BREAKING THE HABIT, American Cancer Society, Modern Talking Picture Service. Henry Jacobs and John Korty, producers.
CHILDREN WITHOUT, National Education Association, Guggenheim Productions.
KENOJUAK, National Film Board of Canada.
*__*NINE FROM LITTLE ROCK,__* US Information Agency, Guggenheim Productions.
140 DAYS UNDER THE WORLD, New Zealand National Film Unit, Rank Films. Geoffrey Scott and Oxley Hughan, producers.

(Features)

THE FINEST HOURS, Le Vien Films, Columbia. Jack Le Vien, producer.
FOUR DAYS IN NOVEMBER, David L. Wolper Prods., UA. Mel Stuart, producer.
THE HUMAN DUTCH, Haanstra Film-productie. Bert Haanstra, producer.
*__*JACQUES-YVES COUSTEAU'S WORLD WITHOUT SUN,__* Columbia. Jacques-Yves Cousteau, producer.
OVER THERE, 1914-18, Zodiac Prods., Pathe Contemporary Films. Jean Aurel, producer.

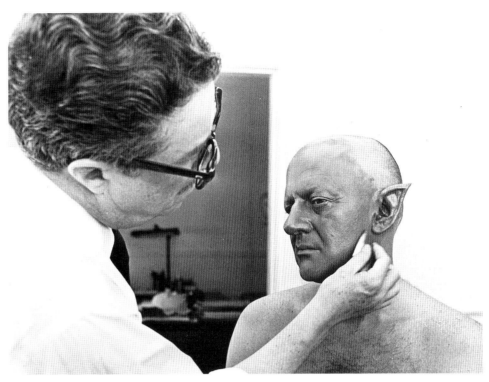

Achievements by the film industry's master makeup artists were not recognized on any regular basis until 1981. William Tuttle's tour-de-force *transformation of Tony Randall into a whole playbill's worth of characters however, for the offbeat* 7 Faces of Dr. Lao, *(M-G-M; directed by George Pal) won Tuttle an honorary Oscar for 1964.*

FOREIGN LANGUAGE FILM

RAVEN'S END (Sweden).
SALLAH (Israel).
THE UMBRELLAS OF CHERBOURG (France).
WOMAN IN THE DUNES (Japan).
*__*YESTERDAY, TODAY AND TOMORROW__* (Italy).

HONORARY AND OTHER AWARDS

TO WILLIAM TUTTLE for his outstanding make-up achievement for *7 Faces of Dr. Lao* (statuette)

1964 IRVING G. THALBERG MEMORIAL AWARD

None given this year.

1964 JEAN HERSHOLT HUMANITARIAN AWARD

None given this year.

SCIENTIFIC OR TECHNICAL

CLASS I (statuette)

PETRO VLAHOS, WADSWORTH E. POHL and **UB IWERKS** for the conception and perfection of techniques for Color Traveling Matte Composite Cinematography.

CLASS II (plaque)

SIDNEY P. SOLOW, EDWARD H. REICHARD, CARL W. HAUGE and **JOB SANDERSON** of Consolidated Film Industries for the design and development of a versatile Automatic 35mm Composite Color Printer.
PIERRE ANGENIEUX for the development of a ten-to-one Zoom Lens for cinematography.

CLASS III (citation)

MILTON FORMAN, RICHARD B. GLICKMAN and **DANIEL J. PEARLMAN** of ColorTran Industries;
STEWART FILMSCREEN CORPORATION;
ANTHONY PAGLIA and the **20TH CENTURY-FOX STUDIO MECHANICAL EFFECTS DEPT.;**
EDWARD H. REICHARD (2 citations) and **CARL W. HAUGE** (2 citations) and **LEONARD L. SOKOLOW** of Consolidated Film Industries;
NELSON TYLER.

*INDICATES WINNER

181

The first telecast of an Academy Awards ceremony in *color* took place April 18, 1966, when awards for 1965 were announced on ABC-TV, produced and directed for the network by Richard Dunlap, and produced for the Academy by Joe Pasternak. To heighten the impact given Oscar by color hues, art directors Alexander Golitzen and William Morris designed an unusually spectacular setting as a backdrop which employed forty-two fountains spraying water. Bob Hope was again M.C., and as in the preceding year, a musical—*The Sound of Music*—was named best picture.

Both *The Sound of Music* and *Doctor Zhivago* were nominated for ten awards, and both won five of them, to become the most honored films of the year. Lee Marvin in *Cat Ballou* was named best actor, Julie Christie in *Darling* was chosen best actress, and Martin Balsam in *A Thousand Clowns* was awarded the best supporting actor Oscar. Shelley Winters was named best supporting actress in *A Patch of Blue* and became the first actress to win two Oscars in that category. Robert Wise (for *The Sound of Music*) received the best director statuette, Czechoslovakia's *The Shop on Main Street* was chosen best foreign language film and Bob Hope was presented an honorary award in the form of a gold medal for his services to the Academy and the motion picture industry.

Nominated songs were sung by, among others, Liza Minnelli, Robert Goulet and Michel Legrand, and Cyd Charisse joined James Mitchell in a dance specialty to music by George Gershwin and Leonard Bernstein. An added highlight was the showing of film clips in which past Oscar winners discussed how it felt to win. It was a big and colorful evening for Oscar, but the biggest single star attraction of the night was someone not affiliated with the motion picture industry: Lynda Bird Johnson, daughter of the president of the United States was in Hollywood to attend her first Academy Awards presentation, escorted by actor George Hamilton.

Best Picture: The Sound of Music *(20th Century-Fox; produced by Robert Wise)* and **Best Director: Robert Wise** *for* The Sound of Music. *It was a rare thing: a movie everyone agreed was an improvement over its stage original. By doing extensive location filming in Salzburg, Austria, Robert Wise and his troupe (including Julie Andrews, right, with kids) were able to open up the vistas that* The Sound of Music's *real-life story required; audiences liked it as much as Oscar did, and it immediately became one of the movies' all-time best-loved entertainments. The story followed the adventures of real-life Maria Trapp, first as a music-loving postulant in Austria's Nonnberg Abbey, then as a governess to seven children, later as the wife of widower Capt. von Trapp (Christopher Plummer), a strong-willed opposer to the Nazi annexation of Austria in 1938. Eleanor Parker, Richard Haydn, Peggy Wood and Anna Lee were also in the cast; the music—a major asset—was by Richard Rodgers and Oscar Hammerstein II. Sound eventually became the first movie in 26 years to unseat* Gone with the Wind *as the all-time top grosser in motion picture history, and Wise became the president who led the Academy through its 58th, 59th and 60th years.*

Best Actor: Lee Marvin *as Kid Shelleen and as Tim Strawn in* Cat Ballou *(Columbia; directed by Elliot Silverstein). A western spoof starring Jane Fonda (left, with Marvin) and set in Wyoming, circa 1894,* Cat Ballou *was filmed in a fast 32 days, partially on location in Colorado, and became the year's most talked-about "sleeper." It also gave Lee Marvin a chance to have an actor's field day, playing two outrageous roles: one as a seedy, booze-soaked gunman who's been hired to battle a desperado even though he can barely stand; the other as the gunman's cool, evil brother who wears an artificial silver nose because "the real one was bit off in a fight." It was a daffy, beautifully conceived performance, in sharp contrast to Marvin's dramatic role the same year in* Ship of Fools, *and Academy voters chose him as best actor of the year. Receiving his award, he said "I think half of this belongs to a horse somewhere out in the Valley," referring to an animal with whom he shared some of the film's most hilarious and picturesque moments.*

Best Actress: Julie Christie *as Diana Scott in* Darling *(Embassy; directed by John Schlesinger). Told in flashback,* Darling *opens as an English beauty named Diana—now the Princess della Romita—narrates her life story, in a somewhat misleading manner, to a woman's magazine; in reality, she bounces from one affair to another, progresses from a fun-loving model to an international swinger and ends up as the* bored wife of an aging Italian prince, a victim of the very world she set out to conquer. Julie Christie, previously unknown to most film audiences, won the Academy Award as the restless Diana; during the year, she also sealed her reputation as a bright new actress in Young Cassidy and Doctor Zhivago. Dirk Bogarde and Laurence Harvey were her Darling co-stars.*

PICTURE

DARLING, Anglo-Amalgamated, Embassy (British). Produced by Joseph Janni.
DOCTOR ZHIVAGO, Sostar, S.A., M-G-M. Produced by Carlo Ponti.
SHIP OF FOOLS, Kramer, Columbia. Produced by Stanley Kramer.
*****THE SOUND OF MUSIC**, Argyle, 20th Century-Fox. Produced by Robert Wise.
A THOUSAND CLOWNS, Harrell, UA. Produced by Fred Coe.

ACTOR

RICHARD BURTON in *The Spy Who Came In from the Cold,* Salem, Paramount.
*****LEE MARVIN** in *Cat Ballou,* Hecht, Columbia.
LAURENCE OLIVIER in *Othello,* B.H.E., Warner Bros. (British).
ROD STEIGER in *The Pawnbroker,* Ely Landau, American International.
OSKAR WERNER in *Ship of Fools,* Kramer, Columbia.

ACTRESS

JULIE ANDREWS in *The Sound of Music,* Argyle, 20th Century-Fox.
*****JULIE CHRISTIE** in *Darling,* Anglo-Amalgamated, Embassy (British).
SAMANTHA EGGAR in *The Collector,* Columbia.
ELIZABETH HARTMAN in *A Patch of Blue,* Berman-Green, M-G-M.
SIMONE SIGNORET in *Ship of Fools,* Kramer, Columbia.

SUPPORTING ACTOR

*****MARTIN BALSAM** in *A Thousand Clowns,* Harrell, UA.
IAN BANNEN in *The Flight of the Phoenix,* Associates & Aldrich, 20th Century-Fox.
TOM COURTENAY in *Doctor Zhivago,* Sostar, S.A., M-G-M.
MICHAEL DUNN in *Ship of Fools,* Kramer, Columbia.
FRANK FINLAY in *Othello,* B.H.E., Warner Bros. (British).

SUPPORTING ACTRESS

RUTH GORDON in *Inside Daisy Clover,* Park Place, Warner Bros.
JOYCE REDMAN in *Othello,* B.H.E., Warner Bros. (British).
MAGGIE SMITH in *Othello,* B.H.E., Warner Bros. (British).
*****SHELLEY WINTERS** in *A Patch of Blue,* Berman-Green, M-G-M.
PEGGY WOOD in *The Sound of Music,* Argyle, 20th Century-Fox.

DIRECTING

THE COLLECTOR, Columbia. William Wyler.
DARLING, Embassy (British). John Schlesinger.
DOCTOR ZHIVAGO, Ponti, M-G-M. David Lean.
*****THE SOUND OF MUSIC**, 20th Century-Fox. Robert Wise.
WOMAN IN THE DUNES, Pathe Contemporary Films (Japanese). Hiroshi Teshigahara.

WRITING

(Screenplay—based on material from another medium)

CAT BALLOU, Hecht, Columbia. Walter Newman and Frank R. Pierson.
THE COLLECTOR, Columbia. Stanley Mann and John Kohn.
*****DOCTOR ZHIVAGO**, Ponti, M-G-M. Robert Bolt.
SHIP OF FOOLS, Kramer, Columbia. Abby Mann.
A THOUSAND CLOWNS, Harrell, UA. Herb Gardner.

(Story and Screenplay—written directly for the screen)

CASANOVA '70, Embassy (Italian). Age, Scarpelli, Mario Monicelli, Tonino Guerra, Giorgio Salvioni and Suso Cecchi D'Amico.
*****DARLING**, Embassy (British). Frederic Raphael.
THOSE MAGNIFICENT MEN IN THEIR FLYING MACHINES, 20th Century-Fox. Jack Davies and Ken Annakin.
THE TRAIN, Les Prods., UA. Franklin Coen and Frank Davis.
THE UMBRELLAS OF CHERBOURG, Landau Releasing (French). Jacques Demy.

CINEMATOGRAPHY

(Black-and-White)

IN HARM'S WAY, Preminger, Paramount. Loyal Griggs.
KING RAT, Coleytown, Columbia. Burnett Guffey.
MORITURI, Arcola-Colony, 20th Century-Fox. Conrad Hall.
A PATCH OF BLUE, Berman-Green, M-G-M. Robert Burks.
*****SHIP OF FOOLS**, Kramer, Columbia. Ernest Laszlo.

(Color)

THE AGONY AND THE ECSTASY, 20th Century-Fox. Leon Shamroy.
*****DOCTOR ZHIVAGO**, Ponti, M-G-M. Freddie Young.
THE GREAT RACE, Patricia-Jalem-Reynard, Warner Bros. Russell Harlan.
THE GREATEST STORY EVER TOLD, Stevens, UA. William C. Mellor and Loyal Griggs.
THE SOUND OF MUSIC, 20th Century-Fox. Ted McCord.

ART DIRECTION-SET DECORATION

(Black-and-White)

KING RAT, Coleytown, Columbia. Robert Emmet Smith; Frank Tuttle.
A PATCH OF BLUE, Berman-Green, M-G-M. George W. Davis and Urie McCleary; Henry Grace and Charles S. Thompson.
*****SHIP OF FOOLS**, Kramer, Columbia. Robert Clatworthy; Joseph Kish.
THE SLENDER THREAD, Paramount. Hal Pereira and Jack Poplin; Robert Benton and Joseph Kish.
THE SPY WHO CAME IN FROM THE COLD, Salem, Paramount. Hal Pereira, Tambi Larsen and Edward Marshall; Josie MacAvin.

(Color)

THE AGONY AND THE ECSTASY, 20th Century-Fox. John DeCuir and Jack Martin Smith; Dario Simoni.
*****DOCTOR ZHIVAGO**, Ponti, M-G-M. John Box and Terry Marsh; Dario Simoni.
THE GREATEST STORY EVER TOLD, Stevens, UA. Richard Day, William Creber and David Hall; Ray Moyer, Fred MacLean and Norman Rockett.
INSIDE DAISY CLOVER, Pakula-Mulligan, Warner Bros. Robert Clatworthy; George James Hopkins.
THE SOUND OF MUSIC, 20th Century-Fox. Boris Leven; Walter M. Scott and Ruby Levitt.

COSTUME DESIGN

(Black-and-White)

*****DARLING**, Embassy (British). Julie Harris.
MORITURI, Arcola-Colony, 20th Century-Fox. Moss Mabry.
A RAGE TO LIVE, Mirisch-Araho, UA. Howard Shoup.
SHIP OF FOOLS, Kramer, Columbia. Bill Thomas and Jean Louis.
THE SLENDER THREAD, Paramount. Edith Head.

(Color)

THE AGONY AND THE ECSTASY, 20th Century-Fox. Vittorio Nino Novarese.
*****DOCTOR ZHIVAGO**, Ponti, M-G-M. Phyllis Dalton.
THE GREATEST STORY EVER TOLD, Stevens, UA. Vittorio Nino Novarese and Marjorie Best.
INSIDE DAISY CLOVER, Pakula-Mulligan, Warner Bros. Edith Head and Bill Thomas.
THE SOUND OF MUSIC, 20th Century-Fox. Dorothy Jeakins.

SOUND

THE AGONY AND THE ECSTASY, 20th Century-Fox. 20th Century-Fox Studio Sound Dept.; James P. Corcoran, sound director.
DOCTOR ZHIVAGO, M-G-M. M-G-M British Studio Sound Dept., A.W. Watkins, sound director; and M-G-M Studio Sound Dept., Franklin E. Milton, sound director.
THE GREAT RACE, Patricia-Jalem-Reynard, Warner Bros. Warner Bros. Studio Sound Dept.; George R. Groves, sound director.
SHENANDOAH, Universal. Universal City Sound Dept.; Waldon O. Watson, sound director.
*****THE SOUND OF MUSIC**, 20th Century-Fox. 20th Century-Fox Studio Sound Dept., James P. Corcoran, sound director; and Todd A-O Sound Dept., Fred Hynes, sound director.

FILM EDITING

CAT BALLOU, Hecht, Columbia. Charles Nelson.
DOCTOR ZHIVAGO, Ponti, M-G-M. Norman Savage.
THE FLIGHT OF THE PHOENIX, Aldrich, 20th Century-Fox. Michael Luciano.
THE GREAT RACE, Patricia-Jalem-Reynard, Warner Bros. Ralph E. Winters.
*****THE SOUND OF MUSIC**, 20th Century-Fox. William Reynolds.

SPECIAL VISUAL EFFECTS

THE GREATEST STORY EVER TOLD, Stevens, UA. J. McMillan Johnson.
*****THUNDERBALL**, Broccoli-Saltzman-McClory, UA (British). John Stears.

SOUND EFFECTS

*****THE GREAT RACE**, Patricia-Jalem-Reynard, Warner Bros. Tregoweth Brown.
VON RYAN'S EXPRESS, 20th Century-Fox. Walter A. Rossi.

MUSIC

(Song)

THE BALLAD OF CAT BALLOU (*Cat Ballou*, Hecht,
Columbia); Music by Jerry Livingston. Lyrics by
Mack David.

I WILL WAIT FOR YOU (*The Umbrellas of Cherbourg*,
Landau Releasing; French); Music by Michel
Legrand. Lyrics by Jacques Demy.

*THE SHADOW OF YOUR SMILE (*The Sandpiper*,
Filmways-Venice, M-G-M); Music by Johnny Mandel.
Lyrics by Paul Francis Webster.

THE SWEETHEART TREE (*The Great Race*, Patricia-
Jalem-Reynard, Warner Bros.); Music by Henry
Mancini. Lyrics by Johnny Mercer.

WHAT'S NEW PUSSYCAT? (*What's New Pussycat?*,
Famous Artists-Famartists, UA); Music by Burt
Bacharach. Lyrics by Hal David.

(Music Score—substantially original)

THE AGONY AND THE ECSTASY, 20th Century-Fox.
Alex North.

*DOCTOR ZHIVAGO, Ponti, M-G-M. Maurice Jarre.

THE GREATEST STORY EVER TOLD, Stevens, UA.
Alfred Newman.

A PATCH OF BLUE, Berman-Green Prod., M-G-M.
Jerry Goldsmith.

THE UMBRELLAS OF CHERBOURG, Landau Releasing
(French). Michel Legrand and Jacques Demy.

(Scoring of Music—adaptation or treatment)

CAT BALLOU, Hecht, Columbia. DeVol.

THE PLEASURE SEEKERS, 20th Century-Fox. Lionel
Newman and Alexander Courage.

*THE SOUND OF MUSIC, 20th Century-Fox. Irwin
Kostal.

A THOUSAND CLOWNS, Harrel, UA. Don Walker.

THE UMBRELLAS OF CHERBOURG, Landau
Releasing (French). Michel Legrand.

SHORT SUBJECTS

(Cartoons)

CLAY OR THE ORIGIN OF SPECIES, Harvard
University, Pathe Contemporary Films, Eliot Noyes,
Jr., producer.

*THE DOT AND THE LINE, M-G-M. Chuck Jones and
Les Goldman, producers.

THE THIEVING MAGPIE (La Gazza Ladra), Allied
Artists. Emanuele Luzzati, producer.

(Live Action Subjects)

*THE CHICKEN (Le Poulet). Pathe Contemporary
Films (French). Claude Berri, producer.

FORTRESS OF PEACE, Farner-Looser Films,
Cinerama. Lothar Wolff, producer.

SKATERDATER, Byway Prods., UA. Marshal Backlar
and Noel Black, producers.

SNOW, Manson Distributing. Edgar Anstey, producer.

TIME PIECE, Muppets, Inc., Pathe Contemporary
Films. Jim Henson, producer.

DOCUMENTARY

(Short Subjects)

MURAL ON OUR STREET, Henry Street Settlement,
Pathe Contemporary Films, Kirk Smallman,
producer.

OUVERTURE, Mafilm Prods., Hungarofilm-Pathe
Contemporary Films.

POINT OF VIEW, Vision Associates Prod., National
Tuberculosis Assoc.

*TO BE ALIVE!, Johnson Wax. Francis Thompson, Inc.,
producer.

YEATS COUNTRY, Aengus Films for the Dept. of
External Affairs of Ireland. Patrick Carey and Joe
Mendoza, producers.

(Features)

THE BATTLE OF THE BULGE...THE BRAVE
RIFLES, Mascott Prods. Laurence E. Mascott,
producer.

*THE ELEANOR ROOSEVELT STORY, American
International. Sidney Glazier, producer.

THE FOURTH ROAD BRIDGE, Random Film Prods.,
Shell-Mex and B.P. Film Library. Peter Mills, producer.

LET MY PEOPLE GO, David L. Wolper Prods.
Marshall Flaum, producer.

TO DIE IN MADRID, Altura Films International,
Frederic Rossif, producer.

FOREIGN LANGUAGE FILM

BLOOD ON THE LAND (Greece).

DEAR JOHN (Sweden).

KWAIDAN (Japan).

MARRIAGE ITALIAN STYLE (Italy).

*THE SHOP ON MAIN STREET (Czechoslovakia).

HONORARY AND OTHER AWARDS

TO BOB HOPE for unique and distinguished service to
our industry and the Academy. (gold medal)

Best Supporting Actor: **Martin Balsam** *as Arnold
Burns in* A Thousand Clowns *(United Artists; directed by
Fred Coe). A veteran of television's early days of live drama,
Balsam was honored by the Academy for his performance as
the conventional brother of a decidedly off-beat New Yorker*

*(Jason Robards, at left above, with Balsam), the latter a cheery
rebel determined to remain a nonconformist. The screenplay
was by Herb Gardner, based on his original Broadway
comedy.*

Best Supporting Actress: **Shelley Winters** *as Rose-Ann
D'Arcy (above, screeching at Sidney Poitier) in* A Patch of Blue
*(M-G-M; directed by Guy Green). Winters, a previous support-
ing actress winner in 1959 for* The Diary of Anne Frank, *won
her second statuette as the amoral, savage mother of a blind*

*girl (Elizabeth Hartman) who was befriended by a gentle black,
played by Poitier. Winters also received two other Academy
nominations during Oscar's first 70 years; in 1951 as best
actress for* A Place in the Sun *and in 1972 for her supporting
role in* The Poseidon Adventure.

1965 IRVING G. THALBERG MEMORIAL AWARD

TO WILLIAM WYLER

1965 JEAN HERSHOLT HUMANITARIAN AWARD

TO EDMOND L. DePATIE

SCIENTIFIC OR TECHNICAL

CLASS I (statuette)

None.

CLASS II (plaque)

ARTHUR J. HATCH of the Strong Electric Corporation,
subsidiary of General Precision Equipment Corporation,
for the design and development of an Air Blown
Carbon Arc Projection Lamp.

STEFAN KUDELSKI for the design and development
of the Nagra portable ¼" tape recording system for
motion picture sound recording.

CLASS III (citation)

None.

*INDICATES WINNER

185

The telecast of the 1966 Academy Awards presentations came hairline close to being canceled on April 10, 1967, because of a strike involving the American Federation of Television and Radio Artists (AFTRA), the theatrical union governing live telecasts. The blackout of TV coverage would have meant a loss to the Academy of approximately $700,000 in revenue paid by the ABC network for rights, but the Academy was prepared to proceed with the awards at the Santa Monica Civic Auditorium without the usual TV coverage. Happily, all was settled in movie serial fashion, just three hours before the ceremony was scheduled to begin.

Most nominated picture of the year was *Who's Afraid of Virginia Woolf?* with a near-record thirteen nominations (topped only by the fourteen accorded *All About Eve* in 1950); it won in five categories, including awards to Elizabeth Taylor as best actress and to Sandy Dennis as best supporting actress. *A Man for All Seasons* won six awards, including best picture, best actor (Paul Scofield) and best director (Fred Zinnemann). Best supporting actor was Walter Matthau in *The Fortune Cookie;* Matthau received his award with a broken arm and bruised face, the result of a cycling accident. It was the first time in twenty-five years two sisters (Vanessa Redgrave and Lynn Redgrave) were both nominees in the best actress category. It had happened before in 1941 when Olivia de Havilland and Joan Fontaine were dually nominated.

The program, again telecast in color and produced for the Academy by Joe Pasternak with Bob Hope as M.C., was notable for Mitzi Gaynor's high-energy rendition of "Georgy Girl," one of the year's nominees as best song, plus an impromptu dance by Fred Astaire and Ginger Rogers when they momentarily reteamed to present one of the evening's awards. Patricia Neal, making her first Hollywood appearance since a near-fatal stroke of two years before, received a standing ovation from the audience. Among the guests in the audience was California's Governor Ronald Reagan, a long-time Academy member and supporter.

186

Best Supporting Actor: **Walter Matthau** *as Willie Gingrich (right, with Ron Rich and, in bed with neck brace, Jack Lemmon) in* The Fortune Cookie *(United Artists; directed by Billy Wilder). Matthau was a comical but shady lawyer, of the ambulance-chasing variety, who maneuvers his brother-in-law into an elaborate accident-insurance swindle. Since his role and billing were of equal size in* Fortune *to that of co-star Lemmon, there was some controversy whether or not Matthau more properly belonged in Oscar's lead, not supporting, actor category.*

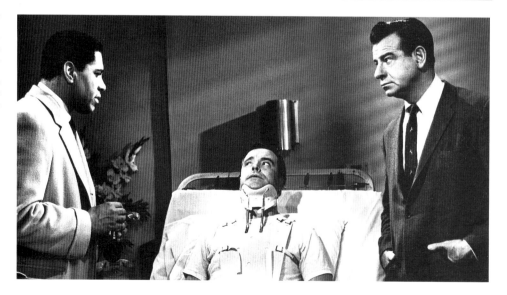

Best Picture: A Man for All Seasons *(Columbia; produced by Fred Zinnemann)*, **Best Director: Fred Zinnemann** *and* **Best Actor: Paul Scofield** *as Sir Thomas More (above) in* A Man for All Seasons. *It began as* a 1960 play by Robert Bolt, first on the London stage, then later in New York, and it told of the last seven years in the life of Sir Thomas More, the respected 16th-century English chancellor beheaded by King Henry VIII. Scofield, a superb artist generally unknown to 1966 moviegoers, re-created his original stage role and permanently preserved on celluloid one of the great performances of the decade. The film itself won a total of six awards.

Best Actress: Elizabeth Taylor *as Martha (at right, being held by George Segal as Richard Burton watches) and* **Best Supporting Actress: Sandy Dennis** *as Honey (at right, on couch) in* Who's Afraid of Virginia Woolf? *(Warner Bros.; directed by Mike Nichols). The picture itself, outspoken and sprinkled with graphic profanities, won five Oscars and was a bold step forward for those who wanted to tackle stronger themes than had previously been allowed. For Taylor, it seemed like unlikely casting: Hollywood's 33-year-old personification of beauty as Edward Albee's middle-aged, venomous Martha, a woman engaged in a drunken, all-night battle with her husband. But Taylor astounded the doubters, gave a bravura performance and enjoyed her finest hour to date as an actress. Dennis, in her second film role (the first: in Elia Kazan's 1961* Splendor in the Grass*), played the nervous and naive wife of a college professor (Segal), beyond her depth when they became the guests—and targets—at the home of the destructive and battling older couple.*

Fantastic Voyage (20th Century-Fox; produced by Saul David) was a superb example of Hollywood's ability to conjure up wild visual magic; the Academy honored it in the categories of art direction and special visual effects. Directed by Richard Fleischer and starring Stephen Boyd, Raquel Welch, Edmond O'Brien and Donald Pleasence, it had a unique premise, even for imaginative science-fiction films: a group of scientists, shrunken to minute proportions, are injected into the bloodstream of an injured man, and take an eye-boggling trip through his body.

PICTURE

ALFIE, Sheldrake, Paramount (British). Produced by Lewis Gilbert.
*A MAN FOR ALL SEASONS, Highland Films, Columbia. Produced by Fred Zinnemann.
THE RUSSIANS ARE COMING, THE RUSSIANS ARE COMING, Mirisch, UA. Produced by Norman Jewison.
THE SAND PEBBLES, Argyle-Solar, 20th Century-Fox. Produced by Robert Wise.
WHO'S AFRAID OF VIRGINIA WOOLF?, Chenault, Warner Bros. Produced by Ernest Lehman.

ACTOR

ALAN ARKIN in The Russians Are Coming, The Russians Are Coming, Mirisch, UA.
RICHARD BURTON in Who's Afraid of Virginia Woolf?, Chenault, Warner Bros.
MICHAEL CAINE in Alfie, Sheldrake, Paramount (British).
STEVE McQUEEN in The Sand Pebbles, Argyle-Solar, 20th Century-Fox.
*PAUL SCOFIELD in A Man for All Seasons, Highland Films, Columbia.

ACTRESS

ANOUK AIMEE in A Man and a Woman, Allied Artists (French).
IDA KAMINSKA in The Shop on Main Street, Prominent Films (Czechoslovakia).
LYNN REDGRAVE in Georgy Girl, Everglades, Columbia (British).
VANESSA REDGRAVE in Morgan!, Quintra Films, Cinema V (British).
*ELIZABETH TAYLOR in Who's Afraid of Virginia Woolf?, Chenault, Warner Bros.

SUPPORTING ACTOR

MAKO in The Sand Pebbles, Argyle-Solar, 20th Century-Fox.
JAMES MASON in Georgy Girl, Everglades, Columbia (British).
*WALTER MATTHAU in The Fortune Cookie, Phalanx-Jalem-Mirisch, UA..
GEORGE SEGAL in Who's Afraid of Virginia Woolf?, Chenault, Warner Bros.
ROBERT SHAW in A Man for All Seasons, Highland Films, Columbia.

SUPPORTING ACTRESS

*SANDY DENNIS in Who's Afraid of Virginia Woolf?, Chenault, Warner Bros.
WENDY HILLER in A Man for All Seasons, Highland Films, Columbia.
JOCELYNE LAGARDE in Hawaii, Mirisch, UA.
VIVIEN MERCHANT in Alfie, Sheldrake, Paramount (British).
GERALDINE PAGE in You're a Big Boy Now, Seven Arts.

DIRECTING

BLOW-UP, Ponti, Premier Productions (British). Michelangelo Antonioni.
A MAN AND A WOMAN, Les Films 13, Allied Artists (French). Claude Lelouch.
*A MAN FOR ALL SEASONS, Highland Films, Columbia. Fred Zinnemann.
THE PROFESSIONALS, Brooks, Columbia. Richard Brooks.
WHO'S AFRAID OF VIRGINIA WOOLF?, Chenault, Warner Bros. Mike Nichols.

WRITING

(Screenplay—based on material from another medium)

ALFIE, Paramount (British). Bill Naughton.
*A MAN FOR ALL SEASONS, Highland Films, Columbia. Robert Bolt.
THE PROFESSIONALS, Brooks, Columbia. Richard Brooks.
THE RUSSIANS ARE COMING, THE RUSSIANS ARE COMING, Mirisch, UA. William Rose.
WHO'S AFRAID OF VIRGINIA WOOLF?, Chenault, Warner Bros. Ernest Lehman.

(Story and Screenplay—written directly for the screen)

BLOW-UP, Ponti Premier Productions (British), Michelangelo Antonioni, Tonino Guerra and Edward Bond.
THE FORTUNE COOKIE, Phalanx-Jalem-Mirisch, UA. Billy Wilder and I.A.L. Diamond.
KHARTOUM, Blaustein, UA. Robert Ardrey.
*A MAN AND A WOMAN, Les Films 13, Allied Artists (French). Claude Lelouch and Pierre Uytterhoeven.
THE NAKED PREY, Theodora, Paramount. Clint Johnston and Don Peters.

CINEMATOGRAPHY

(Black-and-White)

THE FORTUNE COOKIE, Phalanx-Jalem-Mirisch, UA. Joseph LaShelle.
GEORGY GIRL, Columbia (British). Ken Higgins.
IS PARIS BURNING?, Transcontinenta Films-Marianne, Paramount. Marcel Grignon.
SECONDS, Paramount. James Wong Howe.
*WHO'S AFRAID OF VIRGINIA WOOLF?, Chenault, Warner Bros. Haskell Wexler.

(Color)

FANTASTIC VOYAGE, 20th Century-Fox. Ernest Laszlo.
HAWAII, Mirisch, UA. Russell Harlan.
*A MAN FOR ALL SEASONS, Highland Films, Columbia. Ted Moore.
THE PROFESSIONALS, Brooks, Columbia. Conrad Hall.
THE SAND PEBBLES, Argyle-Solar, 20th Century-Fox. Joseph MacDonald.

ART DIRECTION- SET DECORATION

(Black-and-White)

THE FORTUNE COOKIE, Phalanx-Jalem-Mirisch, UA. Robert Luthardt. Edward G. Boyle.
THE GOSPEL ACCORDING TO ST. MATTHEW, Walter Reade-Continental (Italian). Luigi Scacciancoe.
IS PARIS BURNING?, Transcontinental Films-Marianne, Paramount. Willy Holt; Marc Frederix and Pierre Guffroy.
MISTER BUDDWING, M-G-M. George W. Davis and Paul Groesse; Henry Grace and Hugh Hunt.
*WHO'S AFRAID OF VIRGINIA WOOLF?, Chenault, Warner Bros. Richard Sylbert; George James Hopkins.

(Color)

*FANTASTIC VOYAGE, 20th Century-Fox. Jack Martin Smith and Dale Hennesy; Walter M. Scott and Stuart A. Reiss.

GAMBIT, Universal. Alexander Golitzen and George C. Webb; John McCarthy and John Austin.

JULIET OF THE SPIRITS, Rizzoli Films (Italian). Piero Gherardi.

THE OSCAR, Greene-Rouse, Embassy. Hal Pereira and Arthur Lonergan; Robert Benton and James Payne.

THE SAND PEBBLES, Argyle-Solar, 20th Century-Fox. Boris Leven; Walter M. Scott, John Sturtevant and William Kiernan.

COSTUME DESIGN

(Black-and-White)

THE GOSPEL ACCORDING TO ST. MATTHEW, Walter Reade-Continental (Italian). Danilo Donati.

MANDRAGOLA, (Italian). Danilo Donati.

MISTER BUDDWING, DDD-Cherokee, M-G-M. Helen Rose.

MORGAN!, (British), Cinema V. Jocelyn Rickards.

*WHO'S AFRAID OF VIRGINIA WOOLF?, Chenault, Warner Bros. Irene Sharaff.

(Color)

GAMBIT, Universal. Jean Louis.

HAWAII, Mirisch, UA. Dorothy Jeakins.

JULIET OF THE SPIRITS, Rizzoli Films (Italian). Piero Gherardi.

*A MAN FOR ALL SEASONS, Highland Films, Columbia. Elizabeth Haffenden and Joan Bridge.

THE OSCAR, Greene-Rouse, Embassy. Edith Head.

SOUND

GAMBIT, Universal. Universal City Studio Sound Dept.; Waldon O. Watson, sound director.

*GRAND PRIX, Lewis-Frankenheimer-Cherokee, M-G-M. M-G-M Studio Sound Dept.; Franklin E. Milton, sound director.

HAWAII, Mirisch, UA. Samuel Goldwyn Studio Sound Dept.; Gordon E. Sawyer, sound director.

THE SAND PEBBLES, Argyle-Solar, 20th Century-Fox. 20th Century-Fox Studio Sound Dept.; James P. Corcoran, sound director.

WHO'S AFRAID OF VIRGINIA WOOLF?, Chenault, Warner Bros. Warner Bros. Studio Sound Dept.; George R. Groves, sound director.

FILM EDITING

FANTASTIC VOYAGE, 20th Century-Fox. William B. Murphy.

*GRAND PRIX, Lewis-Frankenheimer-Cherokee, M-G-M. Fredric Steinkamp, Henry Berman, Stewart Linder and Frank Santillo.

THE RUSSIANS ARE COMING, THE RUSSIANS ARE COMING, Mirisch, UA. Hal Ashby and J. Terry Williams.

THE SAND PEBBLES, Argyle-Solar, 20th Century-Fox. William Reynolds.

WHO'S AFRAID OF VIRGINIA WOOLF?, Chenault, Warner Bros. Sam O'Steen.

SPECIAL VISUAL EFFECTS

*FANTASTIC VOYAGE, 20th Century-Fox. Art Cruickshank.

HAWAII, Mirisch, UA. Linwood G. Dunn.

SOUND EFFECTS

FANTASTIC VOYAGE, 20th Century-Fox. Walter Rossi.

*GRAND PRIX, Lewis-Frankenheimer-Cherokee, M-G-M. Gordon Daniel.

MUSIC

(Song)

ALFIE, (Alfie, Paramount); Music by Burt Bacharach. Lyrics by Hal David.

*BORN FREE (Born Free, Open Road-Atlas Films, Columbia; British); Music by John Barry. Lyrics by Don Black.

GEORGY GIRL, (Georgy Girl, Columbia; British); Music by Tom Springfield. Lyrics by Jim Dale.

MY WISHING DOLL (Hawaii, Mirisch, UA); Music by Elmer Bernstein. Lyrics by Mack David.

A TIME FOR LOVE (An American Dream, Warner Bros.); Music by Johnny Mandel. Lyrics by Paul Francis Webster.

(Original Music Score)

THE BIBLE, DeLaurentiis-Seven Arts, 20th Century-Fox. Toshiro Mayuzumi.

*BORN FREE, Open Road-Atlas Films, Columbia (British). John Barry.

HAWAII, Mirisch, UA. Elmer Bernstein.

THE SAND PEBBLES, Argyle-Solar, 20th Century-Fox. Jerry Goldsmith.

WHO'S AFRAID OF VIRGINIA WOOLF?, Chenault, Warner Bros. Alex North.

Born Free (Columbia), based on the popular novel by Joy Adamson, starred Bill Travers and Virginia McKenna (above, at far right) and became one of the year's best-liked movies. It also won two Academy Awards for music, for its title song by John Barry and Don Black, and for its original music score by Barry. Like most films of the year, it was also photographed in color; so few black-and-white films were now being made, in fact, that the 1966 award year was the last time the Academy had separate designations for black-and-white and color films in the categories of cinematography, art direction and costume design.

(Scoring of Music—adaptation or treatment)

*A FUNNY THING HAPPENED ON THE WAY TO THE FORUM, Frank, UA. Ken Thorne.

THE GOSPEL ACCORDING TO ST. MATTHEW, Walter-Reade-Continental (Italian). Luis Enrique Bacalov.

RETURN OF THE SEVEN, Mirisch, UA. Elmer Bernstein.

THE SINGING NUN, M-G-M. Harry Sukman.

STOP THE WORLD—I WANT TO GET OFF, Warner Bros. Al Ham.

SHORT SUBJECTS

(Cartoons)

THE DRAG, National Film Board of Canada, Favorite Films. Wolf Koenig and Robert Verrall, producers.

*HERB ALPERT AND THE TIJUANA BRASS DOUBLE FEATURE, Paramount. John and Faith Hubley, producers.

THE PINK BLUEPRINT, Mirisch-Geoffrey-DePatie-Freleng, UA. David H. DePatie and Friz Freleng, producers.

(Live Action Subjects)

TURKEY THE BRIDGE, Samaritan Prods., Schoenfeld Films. Derek Williams, producer.

*WILD WINGS, British Transport Films, Manson Distributing. Edgar Anstey, producer.

THE WINNING STRAIN, Winik Films, Paramount. Leslie Winik, producer.

DOCUMENTARY

(Short Subjects)

ADOLESCENCE, M.K. Prods. Marin Karmitz and Vladimir Forgency, producers.

COWBOY, U.S. Information Agency. Michael Ahnemann and Gary Schlosser, producers.

THE ODDS AGAINST, Vision Associates Prod. for The American Foundation Institute of Corrections. Lee R. Bobker and Helen Kristt Radin, producers.

SAINT MATTHEW PASSION, Mafilm Studio, Hungarofilm.

*A YEAR TOWARD TOMORROW, Sun Dial Films for Office of Economic Opportunity. Edmond A. Levy, producer.

(Features)

THE FACE OF A GENIUS, WBZ-TV, Group W. Boston. Alfred R. Kelman, producer.

HELICOPTER CANADA, Centennial Commission, National Film Board of Canada. Peter Jones and Tom Daly, producers.

LE VOLCAN INTERDIT (The Forbidden Volcano), Cine Documents Tazieff, Athos Films. Haroun Tazieff, producer.

THE REALLY BIG FAMILY, David L. Wolper Prod. Alex Grasshoff, producer.

*THE WAR GAME, BBC Prod. for the British Film Institute, Pathe Contemporary Films. Peter Watkins, producer.

FOREIGN LANGUAGE FILM

THE BATTLE OF ALGIERS (Italy).

LOVES OF A BLONDE (Czechoslovakia).

*A MAN AND A WOMAN (France).

PHARAOH (Poland).

THREE (Yugoslavia).

HONORARY AND OTHER AWARDS

TO Y. FRANK FREEMAN for unusual and outstanding service to the Academy during his thirty years in Hollywood. (statuette)

TO YAKIMA CANUTT for achievements as a stunt man and for developing safety devices to protect stunt men everywhere. (statuette)

1966 IRVING G. THALBERG MEMORIAL AWARD
TO ROBERT WISE

1966 JEAN HERSHOLT HUMANITARIAN AWARD
TO GEORGE BAGNALL

SCIENTIFIC OR TECHNICAL

CLASS I (statuette)

None.

CLASS II (plaque)

MITCHELL CAMERA CORPORATION for the design and development of the Mitchell Mark II 35mm Portable Motion Picture Reflex Camera.

ARNOLD & RICHTER KG for the design and development of the Arriflex 35mm Portable Motion Picture Reflex Camera.

CLASS III (citation)

PANAVISION INCORPORATED;
CARROLL KNUDSON;
RUBY RAKSIN.

*INDICATES WINNER

189

"I am enormously touched," Katharine Hepburn told a reporter in Nice when informed she had won the 1967 Academy Award as best actress for *Guess Who's Coming to Dinner.* "They don't usually give these things to the old girls, you know." Miss Hepburn later cabled an official reply to the Academy, saying, "It was delightful, a total surprise. I feel I have received a big, affectionate hug from my fellow workers." The awards were presented April 10, 1968, at the Santa Monica Civic Auditorium, postponed because of the assassination of Civil Rights leader Dr. Martin Luther King, Jr. on April 4.

In the Heat of the Night received the most awards of the evening, a total of five including best picture and best actor (Rod Steiger); it was the first film in the detective genre to be honored by Academy voters through the years. Mike Nichols was named best director for *The Graduate,* George Kennedy was chosen best supporting actor in *Cool Hand Luke* and Estelle Parsons was best supporting actress for *Bonnie and Clyde.* Next to *In the Heat of the Night,* the most honored film of the year was *Camelot* with three awards.

For the fourteenth year, Bob Hope handled M.C. duties and it was Oscar's eighth visit to the Santa Monica Civic Auditorium. Arthur Freed produced for the Academy, and Richard Dunlap produced and directed for the ABC network. Due to an all-out push by the Academy's president, Gregory Peck, eighteen of the twenty acting nominees were present at the ceremony; only Miss Hepburn, filming *The Madwoman of Chaillot* in France, and the late Spencer Tracy, nominated posthumously, were missing. Alfred Hitchcock received the Irving G. Thalberg Memorial Award, Peck was presented the Jean Hersholt Humanitarian Award and the Board of Governors voted an honorary Oscar to Arthur Freed.

Color, now an integral part of Academy Awards telecasts, had also begun to dominate the motion picture screen so completely, with black-and-white films so rare, it was decided to restructure the art direction, cinematography and costume design categories to one award per division rather than continue separate awards for black-and-white and color achievements.

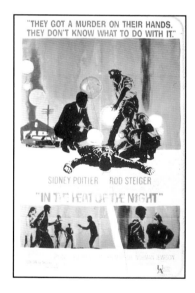

Best Picture: **In the Heat of the Night** *(United Artists; produced by Walter Mirisch) and* **Best Actor:** **Rod Steiger** *as Bill Gillespie in* In the Heat of the Night. *It was the first detective story to win Oscar's best picture honors, and centered on a fictional black detective named Virgil Tibbs from Philadelphia (played by Sidney Poitier) who is called on in a sleepy little Mississippi town to solve a murder, much to the irritation of the local police chief, who's slow-moving, bigoted and white. Directed by Norman Jewison, Rod Steiger (right, with Poitier) won the Academy Award as the drawling sheriff, and the success of the film inspired two later sequels,* They Call Me Mister Tibbs! *(1970) and* The Organization *(1971). John Ball authored the original novel, and* In the Heat of the Night *won additional awards for screenplay, sound and film editing.*

Best Actress: **Katharine Hepburn** *as Christina Drayton (left) in* Guess Who's Coming to Dinner *(Columbia; directed by Stanley Kramer). Katharine Hepburn had been totally absent from the screen for five years when she made* Guess Who's Coming to Dinner, *playing a socially prominent, liberal-thinking parent whose daughter suddenly informs the family she plans to marry a distinguished black scientist. It was one of the less demanding roles of her career, but she was enormously fond of it; it also marked the first time in her enduring career Katharine Hepburn had ever played a happily married wife and mother. It was her ninth and last film opposite Spencer Tracy, and—35 years after her first Oscar victory—she was again voted the year's best actress. Two more awards were also to follow, in 1968 and 1981.*

Best Director: **Mike Nichols** *for* The Graduate *(Embassy; produced by Lawrence Turman). One of the year's most intensely liked, and best-made, successes,* The Graduate *made a star of movie newcomer Dustin Hoffman (above, floating in pool as Nichols, in white pants, oversees). Hoffman* *played a bewildered and comical grad who is seduced by the wife of his father's law partner, then falls in love with the lady's beautiful daughter. Anne Bancroft and Katharine Ross co-starred, and* The Graduate *won the Academy Award for the man who made it all happen: Mike Nichols.*

Best Supporting Actor: George Kennedy as Dragline (right, helping Paul Newman) in Cool Hand Luke *(Warner Bros.; directed by Stuart Rosenberg). The movie was a strong essay on individuality, a pertinent and a well-liked theme in the late 1960s, and Kennedy won his Academy Award as a chain-gang convict in a Southern state who battles Luke (played by Newman) for leadership of the gang, then ends up Luke's friend and would-be protector.*

192

Best Supporting Actress: Estelle Parsons as Blanche Barrow in Bonnie and Clyde *(Warner Bros.; directed by Arthur Penn). Produced by Warren Beatty,* Bonnie and Clyde *made waves and caused talk; there was considerable controversy about whether or not it glamorized violence, but no argument whatsoever about its brilliance as a well-made motion picture or about Estelle Parsons' performance as the noisy wife of Buck Barrow (Gene Hackman) and sister-in-law of Clyde Barrow (Warren Beatty), a team of real-life bank robbers and killers in Texas and Oklahoma, just after the depression.*

PICTURE

BONNIE AND CLYDE, Tatira-Hiller, Warner Bros.-Seven Arts. Produced by Warren Beatty.
DOCTOR DOOLITTLE, Apjac, 20th Century-Fox. Produced by Arthur P. Jacobs.
THE GRADUATE, Nichols-Turman, Embassy. Produced by Lawrence Turman.
GUESS WHO'S COMING TO DINNER, Kramer, Columbia. Produced by Stanley Kramer.
*IN THE HEAT OF THE NIGHT, Mirisch, UA. Produced by Walter Mirisch.

ACTOR

WARREN BEATTY in Bonnie and Clyde, Tatira-Hiller, Warner Bros.-Seven Arts.
DUSTIN HOFFMAN in The Graduate, Nichols-Turman, Embassy.
PAUL NEWMAN in Cool Hand Luke, Jalem, Warner Bros.-Seven Arts.
*ROD STEIGER in In the Heat of the Night, Mirisch, UA.
SPENCER TRACY in Guess Who's Coming to Dinner, Kramer, Columbia.

ACTRESS

ANNE BANCROFT in The Graduate, Nichols-Turman, Embassy.
FAYE DUNAWAY in Bonnie and Clyde, Tatira-Hiller, Warner Bros.-Seven Arts.
DAME EDITH EVANS in The Whisperers, Seven Pines, UA/Lopert (British).
AUDREY HEPBURN in Wait until Dark, Warner Bros.-Seven Arts.
*KATHARINE HEPBURN in Guess Who's Coming to Dinner, Kramer, Columbia.

SUPPORTING ACTOR

JOHN CASSAVETES in The Dirty Dozen, Aldrich, M-G-M.
GENE HACKMAN in Bonnie and Clyde, Tatira-Hiller, Warner Bros.-Seven Arts.
CECIL KELLAWAY in Guess Who's Coming to Dinner, Kramer, Columbia.
*GEORGE KENNEDY in Cool Hand Luke, Jalem, Warner Bros.-Seven Arts.
MICHAEL J. POLLARD in Bonnie and Clyde, Tatira-Hiller, Warner Bros.-Seven Arts.

SUPPORTING ACTRESS

CAROL CHANNING in Thoroughly Modern Millie, Hunter, Universal.
MILDRED NATWICK in Barefoot in the Park, Wallis, Paramount.
*ESTELLE PARSONS in Bonnie and Clyde, Tatira-Hiller, Warner Bros.-Seven Arts.
BEAH RICHARDS in Guess Who's Coming to Dinner, Kramer, Columbia.
KATHARINE ROSS in The Graduate, Nichols-Turman, Embassy.

DIRECTING

BONNIE AND CLYDE, Tatira-Hiller, Warner Bros.-Seven Arts. Arthur Penn.
*THE GRADUATE, Nichols-Turman, Embassy. Mike Nichols.
GUESS WHO'S COMING TO DINNER, Kramer, Columbia. Stanley Kramer.
IN COLD BLOOD, Brooks, Columbia. Richard Brooks.
IN THE HEAT OF THE NIGHT, Mirisch, UA. Norman Jewison.

WRITING

(Screenplay—based on material from another medium)

COOL HAND LUKE, Jalem, Warner Bros.-Seven Arts. Donn Pearce and Frank R. Pierson.
THE GRADUATE, Nichols-Turman, Embassy. Calder Willingham and Buck Henry.
IN COLD BLOOD, Brooks, Columbia. Richard Brooks.
*IN THE HEAT OF THE NIGHT, Mirisch, UA. Stirling Silliphant.
ULYSSES, Walter Reade-Continental Distributing. Joseph Strick and Fred Haines.

(Story and Screenplay—written directly for the screen)

BONNIE AND CLYDE, Tatira-Hiller, Warner Bros.-Seven Arts. David Newman and Robert Benton.
DIVORCE AMERICAN STYLE, Tandem-National General, Columbia. Robert Kaufman and Norman Lear.
*GUESS WHO'S COMING TO DINNER, Kramer, Columbia. William Rose.
LA GUERRE EST FINIE, Sofracima-Europa, Brandon Films (French). Jorge Semprun.
TWO FOR THE ROAD, Donen, 20th Century-Fox. Frederic Raphael.

CINEMATOGRAPHY

(New classification; one award instead of separate awards for Black-and-White and Color achievements)

*BONNIE AND CLYDE, Tatira-Hiller, Warner Bros.-Seven Arts. Burnett Guffey.
CAMELOT, Warner Bros.-Seven Arts. Richard H. Kline.
DOCTOR DOOLITTLE, Apjac, 20th Century-Fox. Robert Surtees.
THE GRADUATE, Nichols-Turman, Embassy. Robert Surtees.
IN COLD BLOOD, Brooks, Columbia. Conrad Hall.

ART DIRECTION-SET DECORATION

(New classification: one award instead of separate awards for Black-and-White and Color achievements)

*CAMELOT, Warner Bros.-Seven Arts. John Truscott and Edward Carrere; John W. Brown.
DOCTOR DOOLITTLE, Apjac, 20th Century-Fox. Mario Chiari, Jack Martin Smith and Ed Graves; Walter M. Scott and Stuart A. Reiss.
GUESS WHO'S COMING TO DINNER, Kramer, Columbia. Robert Clatworthy; Frank Tuttle.
THE TAMING OF THE SHREW, Royal Films International, Columbia. Renzo Mongiardino, John DeCuir, Elven Webb and Giuseppe Mariani; Dario Simoni and Luigi Gervasi.
THOROUGHLY MODERN MILLIE, Hunter, Universal. Alexander Golitzen and George C. Webb; Howard Bristol.

COSTUME DESIGN

(New classification: one award instead of separate awards for Black-and-White and Color achievements)

BONNIE AND CLYDE, Tatira-Hiller, Warner Bros.-Seven Arts. Theadora Van Runkle.
*CAMELOT, Warner Bros.-Seven Arts. John Truscott.
THE HAPPIEST MILLIONAIRE, Disney, Buena Vista. Bill Thomas.
THE TAMING OF THE SHREW, Royal Films International, Columbia. Irene Sharaff and Danilo Donati.
THOROUGHLY MODERN MILLIE, Hunter, Universal. Jean Louis.

Thalberg Award winner: Alfred Hitchcock (above, receiving the award from Robert Wise). It's one of the Oscar ironies that the great and prolific Alfred Hitchcock never won an actual Academy Award statuette during his legendary career. Although his first American-made film Rebecca *received the Oscar as 1940's best picture, and despite five personal nominations (for* Rebecca, *1944's* Lifeboat, *1945's*

Spellbound, *1954's* Rear Window *and 1960's* Psycho*), and awards won by others for work in or on Hitchcock films, the master himself never received an Oscar statuette. But he became an award-winner in 1967 when he received, if not a statuette, a bust of Irving Thalberg as the prestigious Irving G. Thalberg Memorial Award for consistent high quality of production throughout his long and remarkable career.*

FAR FROM THE MADDING CROWD, Appia, M-G-M. Richard Rodney Bennett.
IN COLD BLOOD, Brooks, Columbia. Quincy Jones.
*THOROUGHLY MODERN MILLIE, Hunter, Universal. Elmer Bernstein.

(Scoring of Music—adaptation or treatment)
*CAMELOT, Warner Bros.-Seven Arts. Alfred Newman and Ken Darby.
DOCTOR DOOLITTLE, Apjac, 20th Century-Fox. Lionel Newman and Alexander Courage.
GUESS WHO'S COMING TO DINNER, Kramer, Columbia. DeVol.
THOROUGHLY MODERN MILLIE, Hunter, Universal. Andre Previn and Joseph Gershenson.
VALLEY OF THE DOLLS, Red Lion, 20th Century-Fox. John Williams.

SHORT SUBJECTS

(Cartoons)
*THE BOX, Brandon Films. Fred Wolf, producer.
HYPOTHESE BETA, Films Orzeaux, Pathe Contemporary Films. Jean-Charles Meunier, producer.
WHAT ON EARTH!, National Film Board of Canada, Columbia. Robert Verrall and Wolf Koenig, producers.

(Live Action Subjects)
PADDLE TO THE SEA, National Film Board of Canada, Favorite Films. Julian Biggs, producer.
*A PLACE TO STAND, T.D.F. Prod. for Ontario Dept. of Economics and Development, Columbia. Christopher Chapman, producer.
SKY OVER HOLLAND, Ferno Prod. for The Netherlands, Seneca International. John Ferno, producer.
STOP, LOOK AND LISTEN, M-G-M. Len Janson and Chuck Menville, producers.

DOCUMENTARY

(Short Subjects)
MONUMENT TO THE DREAM, Guggenheim Prods. Charles E. Guggenheim, producer.
A PLACE TO STAND, T.D.F. Prod. for The Ontario Department of Economics and Development. Christopher Chapman, producer.
*THE REDWOODS, King Screen Prods. Mark Harris and Trevor Greenwood, producers.
SEE YOU AT THE PILLAR, Associated British-Pathe Prod. Robert Fitchett, producer.
WHILE I RUN THIS RACE, Sun Dial Films for VISTA. Carl V. Ragsdale, producer.

(Features)
*THE ANDERSON PLATOON, French Broadcasting System. Pierre Schoendoerffer, producer.
FESTIVAL, Patchke Prods. Murray Lerner, producer.
HARVEST, U.S. Information Agency. Carroll Ballard, producer.
A KING'S STORY, Jack Le Vien Prod. Jack Le Vien, producer.
A TIME FOR BURNING, Quest Prods. for Lutheran Film Associates. William C. Jersey, producer.

FOREIGN LANGUAGE FILMS
*CLOSELY WATCHED TRAINS (Czechoslovakia).
EL AMOR BRUJO (Spain).
I EVEN MET HAPPY GYPSIES (Yugoslavia).
LIVE FOR LIFE (France).
PORTRAIT OF CHIEKO (Japan).

HONORARY AND OTHER AWARDS
TO ARTHUR FREED for distinguished service to the Academy and the production of six top-rated Awards telecasts. (statuette)

193

1967 IRVING G. THALBERG MEMORIAL AWARD
TO ALFRED HITCHCOCK

1967 JEAN HERSHOLT HUMANITARIAN AWARD
TO GREGORY PECK

SCIENTIFIC OR TECHNICAL

CLASS I (statuette)
None.

CLASS II (plaque)
None.

CLASS III (citation)
ELECTRO-OPTICAL DIVISION of the KOLLMORGEN CORPORATION;
PANAVISION INCORPORATED;
FRED R. WILSON of the SAMUEL GOLDWYN STUDIO SOUND DEPT.;
WALDON O. WATSON and the UNIVERSAL CITY STUDIO SOUND DEPT.

*INDICATES WINNER

SOUND
CAMELOT, Warner Bros.-Seven Arts. Warner Bros.-Seven Arts Studio Sound Dept.
THE DIRTY DOZEN, Aldrich, M-G-M. M-G-M Studio Sound Dept.
DOCTOR DOOLITTLE, Apjac, 20th Century-Fox. 20th Century-Fox Studio Sound Dept.
*IN THE HEAT OF THE NIGHT, Mirisch, UA. Samuel Goldwyn Studio Sound Dept.
THOROUGHLY MODERN MILLIE, Hunter, Universal. Universal City Studio Sound Dept.

FILM EDITING
BEACH RED, Theodora, UA. Frank P. Keller
THE DIRTY DOZEN. Aldrich, M-G-M. Michael Luciano.
DOCTOR DOOLITTLE, Apjac, 20th Century-Fox. Samuel E. Beetley and Marjorie Fowler.
GUESS WHO'S COMING TO DINNER, Kramer, Columbia. Robert C. Jones.
*IN THE HEAT OF THE NIGHT, Mirisch, UA. Hal Ashby.

SPECIAL EFFECTS
*DOCTOR DOOLITTLE, Apjac, 20th Century-Fox. L.B. Abbott.
TOBRUK, Gibraltar-Corman, Universal. Howard A. Anderson, Jr. and Albert Whitlock.

SOUND EFFECTS
(Not given after this year)
*THE DIRTY DOZEN, Aldrich, M-G-M. John Poyner.
IN THE HEAT OF THE NIGHT, Mirisch, UA. James A. Richard.

MUSIC
(Song)
THE BARE NECESSITIES, (The Jungle Book, Disney, Buena Vista); Music and Lyrics by Terry Gilkyson.
THE EYES OF LOVE (Banning, Universal); Music by Quincy Jones. Lyrics by Bob Russell.
THE LOOK OF LOVE (Casino Royale, Famous Artists, Columbia); Music by Burt Bacharach. Lyrics by Hal David.
*TALK TO THE ANIMALS, (Doctor Doolittle, Apjac, 20th Century-Fox); Music and Lyrics by Leslie Bricusse.
THOROUGHLY MODERN MILLIE, (Thoroughly Modern Millie, Hunter, Universal); Music and Lyrics by James Van Heusen and Sammy Cahn.

(Original Music Score)
COOL HAND LUKE, Jalem, Warner Bros.-Seven Arts. Lalo Schifrin.
DOCTOR DOOLITTLE, Apjac, 20th Century-Fox. Leslie Bricusse.

1968-1977
The Academy's Fifth Decade

The Academy's fifth decade saw the fulfillment of that dream which had been in the making for almost fifty years: a new, specially designed headquarters for the organization, and for the first time all of the Academy's many facilities would be located under one roof. At last Oscar would have a home of its own.

The new building, located at 8949 Wilshire Boulevard in Beverly Hills, was designed by Maxwell Starkman and built by the Buckeye Construction Company of Los Angeles. The Academy's activities were initially organized into the seven floors as follows:

Ground floor: grand lobby, patio, building foyer, theater manager's office, caterers' workroom;

Second floor: Samuel Goldwyn Theater (1111 seats), lobby display of one-sheet posters of past Academy Award-winning films;

Third Floor: special screening room (80 seats), projection booth, editing room, film storage area;

Fourth floor: Margaret Herrick Research Library;

Fifth floor: library storage area;

Sixth floor: Academy membership office, Academy Players Directory office, Scientific and Technical Awards office, Theater operations office, Administrative office;

Seventh floor: executive offices for the Academy president, executive director, Board of Governors' conference room.

Groundbreaking for the site took place on September 18, 1973, and the official dedication ceremony was held nearly two years later, on December 8, 1975. At that time the Academy hosted a series of grand opening parties in the lobby of the new complex for Academy members, press, civic leaders and industry friends. Among those attending the first evening were sixteen performers who had won Academy Awards during preceding years: Red Buttons, Patty Duke, Ben Johnson, Jack Lemmon, Karl Malden, Walter Matthau, Laurence Olivier, Sidney Poitier, Ginger Rogers, Harold Russell, Eva Marie Saint, Maximilian Schell, Rod Steiger, Claire Trevor, Peter Ustinov, and Shelley Winters. In addition to organized tours of the building, guests were invited into the Samuel Goldwyn Theater for a special screening of sequences from all the past Academy Award-winning Best Pictures, beginning with *Wings,* the 1927-28 winner.

The whole decade was an active one for the Academy. In 1969, it received one of its most extensive donations to date, from Paramount Pictures. The collection encompasses stills, scripts and press material from more than 2,200 Paramount releases, dating to the earliest silent film days. The opening of the new Academy building provided the space for the proper filing and storage of such collections donated to the Academy, which now included the valuable RKO Radio Studios still photos collection, the papers of writer-director Lamont Johnson, the Cecil B. DeMille still photograph books, the Howard Estabrook papers, the William Wright collection, the Technicolor Film Continuity Sheets, the Ivan Kahn collection, the Mack Sennett collection, the Lever

CARY GRANT

"I'm very grateful to the Academy's Board for this happy tribute, and to Frank for coming here especially to give it to me, and to all the fellows who worked so hard in finding and assembling those film clips....

You know, I may never look at this without remembering the quiet patience of the directors who were so kind to me, who were kind enough to put up with me more than once—some of them even three or four times. There were Howard Hawks, Alfred Hitchcock, the late Leo McCarey, George Stevens, George Cukor and Stanley Donen. And all the writers...There were Philip Barry, Dore Schary, Bob Sherwood, Ben Hecht, dear Clifford Odets, Sidney Sheldon and more recently Stanley Shapiro and Peter Stone. Well, I trust they and all the other directors, writers and producers, and leading women, have all forgiven me what I didn't know.

I realize it's conventional and usual to praise one's fellow workers on these occasions...but why not? Ours is a collaborative medium; we all need each other! And what better opportunity is there to publicly express one's appreciation and admiration and affection for all those who contribute so much to each of our welfare?

You know, I've never been a joiner or a member of any—oh, particular—social set, but I've been privileged to be a part of Hollywood's most glorious era. And yet, tonight, thinking of all the empty screens that are waiting to be filled with marvelous images, ideologies, points of view—whatever—and considering all the students who are studying film techniques in the universities throughout the world, and the astonishing young talents that are coming up in our midsts, I think there's an even more glorious era right around the corner.

So, before I leave you, I want to thank you very much for signifying your approval of this. I shall cherish it until I die...because probably no greater honor can come to any man than the respect of his colleagues.

Thank you."

Cary Grant
April 7, 1970, when receiving
his 1969 Honorary Award

John Wayne, Barbra Streisand (42nd Awards)

Cary Grant (42nd Awards)

JOHN WAYNE

"For us in the industry the Oscar is the highest and most cherished award. It is a goal for which all of us instinctively strive. It is our most coveted honor, because it means recognition from our peers.

It is also the only way we who work in front of the camera have to publicly thank those wonderful craftsmen, technicians and artists whose invention, skill and imagination make us who paint our faces popular, interesting, or at least palatable to the public taste. To these people I will be forever grateful.

I spent nearly fifty years chasing this elusive fellow with good performances and bad, so I was extremely delighted when he was handed to me by Barbra Streisand."

John Wayne
Best Actor, 1969

MARTHA RAYE

"One of the proudest moments of my life was receiving the Oscar for the Jean Hersholt Humanitarian Award. Ever grateful."

Martha Raye
Jean Hersholt Humanitarian Award, 1968

JOEL GREY

"The night I won my Oscar for Cabaret, *I went to the ceremonies all but convinced I wouldn't win so, when Diana Ross opened the envelope and the name she announced was mine, it was like this incredible shot of electricity or adrenalin swept through me and the moment seemed to stand still in time. All I remember was kissing my wife, and then I guess 'my feet did their stuff' because the next thing I knew, I was no longer in my seat but up on stage warming in the affection and approval of my peers and finally saying, 'Don't let anybody tell you this isn't terrific.'"*

Joel Grey
Best Supporting Actor, 1972

ONNA WHITE

"Dear Oscar,
It is with great pleasure that I have been made a part of your association by being named the first female choreographer for a Special Oscar. Thank you."

Onna White
Honorary Award, 1968

ALAN AND MARILYN BERGMAN

"About winning the Oscar? It's all been said—and all of it is true.

But if you want to recall that feeling up there, our advice is: win two.

Our first (for 'Windmills of Your Mind') was dazzling—a thrill—but, alas, a blur. The second was sweeter simply because we remember 'The Way We Were'!"

Alan and Marilyn Bergman
Music (Song), 1968; 1973
Original Song Score, 1983

The Dorothy Chandler Pavilion of the Los Angeles Music Center

Brothers-Lux Radio Theater collection, among others. The Margaret Herrick Library, named for the Academy's first librarian and later its executive director who retired in 1970 after forty years of service, also established a new collection of its own: the Black American Film History collection, to recognize and preserve important contributions made by blacks in the film industry.

In 1970, the Academy joined with the Writers Guild to jointly publish an extensive directory of screenwriting credits called *Who Wrote the Movie (and*

What Else Did He Write?), covering the years 1936 through 1969, filling a research need that had existed for years. Two years later, in 1972, another attempt was made in the area of publishing an on-going magazine, called *Academy Leader*, offering news, reviews and photographs about the motion picture industry. This was planned as a quarterly publication, but it only existed for three issues. A comprehensive book, *Introduction to the Photoplay*, was published in 1978 as a limited edition by the National Film Society, with the

Academy's involvement and cooperation. The book is based on previously unpublished works compiled from fifteen lectures delivered back in 1929 at the University of Southern California by leading film professionals, including Irving Thalberg, William Cameron Menzies, William C. deMille, Conrad Nagel and Benjamin Glazer.

Both the *Academy Players Directory* and the *Screen Achievement Records Bulletin* continued to flourish throughout the decade. The *Directory*, still an invaluable aid for casting purposes, had

196

INGRID BERGMAN

"I belong to the group of people who like the tradition of the Academy Award under the friendly name of Oscar. I am aware that many people find that too many artists have been overlooked. Too many people have been given awards, as they used to say, for sentimental reasons. In other words, after several nominations and losing the award, you would get it for a picture less worthy. Well, I am not against the sentimentality of these awards. I am sad that people like Greta Garbo and Ernst Lubitsch were overlooked. That people like Charles Chaplin and Jean Renoir were given Special Awards so late in their creative careers. Despite its shortcomings, it is still the most valuable award in the film industry of the entire world, and no one can deny the excitement felt by the people present at the award-giving ceremony or those watching it at home on television. I look with pride on my three and feel immensely happy and proud to have received them."

Ingrid Bergman
Best Actress, 1944; 1956
Best Supporting Actress, 1974

JOEL HIRSCHHORN

"As a youngster I used to race to the Kingsbridge Theatre in the Bronx and sit through all the popular musicals, fantasizing about the day I could be a part of Hollywood. My favorite was An American in Paris, *which I saw at least twenty times. You can imagine, then, my sense of joy and fulfillment when I won an Oscar, and the further excitement I felt being presented the award by Gene Kelly."*

Joel Hirschhorn
Music (Song), 1972; 1974

LEE GRANT

"The 'Oscar' has endured because of our yearning for excellence. Getting one is like being appointed valedictorian from the bottom of the class. The 'outs' like me, get their moment to be 'in,' for as long as it lasts."

Lee Grant
Best Supporting Actress, 1975

GENE HACKMAN

"The Academy Award did one thing for me. It made me far more patient of those sometimes protracted thank you speeches of acceptance. Standing there, feeling the weight of the statue for the first time, you suddenly are overwhelmed with the thought of thirty years of people to be thanked and how to squeeze it into thirty seconds. The Oscar meant two other things to me, two of the films I take a certain pride in having worked on. I've been told by the people who made them that the glow of that Oscar had something to do with the opportunity to get Scarecrow *and Francis Coppola's* The Conversation *made. It's hard for me to believe that the power of the scripts and the talent-value of the creators involved wouldn't have made the films inevitable. But Hollywood is filled with that kind of contradiction. If my Oscar was put into the realization of two worthwhile films, chalk another two up for Oscar."*

Gene Hackman
Best Actor, 1971
Best Supporting Actor, 1992

Roger Moore, Liv Ullmann, "Sacheen Littlefeather" (45th Awards)

Lillian Gish, Melvyn Douglas (43rd Awards)

Charlie Chaplin comes home, April 10, 1972

CLORIS LEACHMAN

"The American ethic is to be the best. From the Nobel Prize to Queen for a Day, from the Olympics to the best apple pie. At worst it is merchandising our business. It creates jobs and opportunities for everyone, and in the tradition of great American competition the Oscar reflects that.

We take turns being the catalyst for other professionals. We actors, producers, directors, writers, etc., all motivate each other. My mother always said there is plenty of room at the top. That to me means excellence. With all the ramifications of the Academy Awards, excellence encourages excellence. It nourishes each of us.

I was astonished and literally swept off my feet by the response that night I was honored. Suddenly it was no longer a committee or a faceless group, it was everybody cheering YEAH!! for you, and I can pass that on. I felt that night that it wasn't necessary at that point in my career but I certainly felt loved, and it was terrific!"

Cloris Leachman
Best Supporting Actress, 1971

CLIFF ROBERTSON

"Charly was not an easy delivery...seven years. I am indebted to all attendants. I am in debt to all who believed."

Cliff Robertson
Best Actor, 1968

GOLDIE HAWN

"I was in London when I first heard the news that I won the Award. I was so sure that I was not going to get it, that when I received the call at six in the morning, I had no idea who could be calling me at that hour. After the hysterics and tears were over, I then wished so hard that I could have been there to accept my Oscar. Receiving an Academy Award for my first motion picture was, I realized, a great achievement, but it didn't carry the impact for me as it would have, had I done other pictures prior to winning and thereby been more aware of how difficult it is to earn an Oscar.

But I am forever grateful."

Goldie Hawn
Best Supporting Actress, 1969

TATUM O'NEAL

"That night was like a shining light which never goes out. I sat with most of my beloved family and suddenly my name was called — I was lifted up into another world, leaving many childish things behind, but happily.

I love my profession. It is important and noble."

Tatum O'Neal
Best Supporting Actress, 1973

VERNA FIELDS

"Winning the Oscar is for anyone in our industry the ultimate accolade from one's peers. It is an honor to receive and a feeling of great personal pride to feel one has accomplished something to deserve it. As I glance up and see my Oscar, it reminds me of the many years it took to learn what I needed to know to achieve that honor."

Verna Fields
Film Editing, 1975

grown to include in excess of ten thousand individual players. More than fifteen hundred copies per issue were now being distributed. The *Bulletin* had become equally indispensable, as the only regularly published reference book compiling current individual screen credits.

The Student Film Awards program was inaugurated in 1973 as a program of the Academy, the Academy Foundation and later co-sponsored by the American Telephone and Telegraph Company to recognize and encourage excellence in college filmmaking. Since the annual program began, over four hundred students per year from across the United States were now taking part in the competition, vying for awards and cash grants, with their student films judged in four specific categories: dramatic, animated, documentary and experimental films. Honorary Awards were now also given to films of exceptional merit not otherwise recognized in the competition.

The Marvin Borowsky Lectureship on Screenwriting was established in 1974 by Mr. Borowsky's widow Maxine, and overseen by the Academy as a series in which noted screenwriters lecture on their craft, then answer questions posed by Academy members, students of screenwriting and professionals in attendance.

Throughout the decade, the Academy also continued to extend Hollywood beyond its own borders, with an extensive Visiting Artists Program, providing

Eileen Heckart, Joel Gray, Liza Minnelli (45th Awards)

distinguished members of the film industry for speaking engagements on college and university campuses throughout the United States. This program has been an attempt to bridge the gap between the classroom and the world of professional filmmakers, and traveling participants during the decade included such Academy members as Frank Capra, King Vidor, Robert Towne, Rouben Mamoulian, Lee Garmes, Thomas Stanford, Verna Fields, Paul Schrader and Linwood Dunn. Members waived any fees offered for their speaking services and the Academy accepted no compensation for administering the program.

One of the projects of the Academy Foundation (established in 1944) has been the annual disbursement of grants, fellowships and internships to individuals and/or organizations, to support and encourage a wide spectrum of film-related projects. The Academy Internship Program, administered by the American Film Institute, allows film students and professionals to study the making of motion pictures from inception through completion, working side by side with distinguished directors. There have also been scholarship grants to students majoring in the film sciences, selected

SIR JOHN MILLS

"Expressing my thoughts on receiving the Oscar proves rather difficult, as on that particular evening my mind was almost a complete blank, but I do know that it was one of the most exciting things that has ever happened to me. In fact, I have barely recovered from the shock yet.

I send my very best wishes to the Academy."

Sir John Mills, C.B.E.
Best Supporting Actor, 1970

GEORGE ROY HILL

"Awards for any of the arts have always struck me as unavoidably capricious and, more often than not, given for reasons other than for genuine artistic achievement. Time is going to be the final judge of merit regardless of what the contemporary awards say. But knowing this somehow did not diminish one whit my delight in receiving it. It was a hell of a thrill."

George Roy Hill
Best Director, 1973

LIONEL NEWMAN

"One of the odd sensations with respect to winning an Oscar is that the 'magic moment' and the 'Cinderella evening' inevitably have to end. Actually, upon hearing one's name called, one doesn't care about himself, but is concerned that his wife, children and friends are proud of him — to say nothing of his peers.

So many people make it all possible. I have been nominated twelve times and finally received the Oscar for Hello, Dolly! *I'm damned proud to display it where it can be seen. No bullshit about a 'doorstop' or using it as a 'paperweight.'*

I love our industry and am very grateful to be a small part of it."

Lionel Newman
Scoring of a Musical Picture
(Original or Adaptation), 1969

BEN JOHNSON

"I will always be grateful to the Academy for the fair and impartial way in which it conducts the Oscar Awards.

For an Oklahoma cowboy-turned-actor to win a major award, without a campaign or war-chest, proved to me beyond a shadow of doubt that the Academy always deals from the top of the deck. And as I said when I received the Award, 'It couldn't have happened to a nicer feller!' "

Ben Johnson
Best Supporting Actor, 1971

LIZA MINNELLI

"It was wonderful to be even nominated, and then receiving the Oscar knowing that my peers had voted for me was totally thrilling and an honor I will cherish always."

Liza Minnelli
Best Actress, 1972

Charlton Heston, Susan Hayward (46th Awards)

JOHN SCHLESINGER

"I was in England shooting Sunday Bloody Sunday *when the Academy Awards were to be announced for the previous year, and* Midnight Cowboy *was one of the nominations. Obviously, we had all prepared ourselves not to win, and although United Artists said they would stop shooting and pay for me to fly over for the occasion, I thought there would be nothing worse than the possibility of my returning empty handed to my unit, who might have been hanging around for three days waiting for a jet-lagged director.*

At 5:15 English time on the morning of the Awards, the telephone rang, and my secretary from Midnight Cowboy *(who was by now working for the Academy Awards show) was backstage, and they were just coming up to the writer awards. She certainly had a sense of timing. Everyone in my house grabbed extension phones, and we listened to the distant sounds of the Academy Awards night over the trans-Atlantic phone connected backstage, where my ex-secretary screamed with delight every time* Cowboy *won another award. In many ways it was the best way to hear the news.*

There was not much work done on the set that day — too many interruptions and celebratory drinks, but I was happy to share the occasion with my unit and cast. After all, the pleasure of winning an Academy Award is that it is an accolade from one's colleagues and peers."

John Schlesinger
Best Director, 1969

BEATRICE STRAIGHT

"Next to my marriage and the birth of my children, winning the Oscar was one of the most exciting and happy moments of my life — full of deep gratitude to my fellow actors and partners in work, and the joy of being an artist. I was also fully aware that I was only one of many, but had been lucky enough to be in the right part at the right time."

Beatrice Straight
Best Supporting Actress, 1976

EILEEN HECKART

"All the people who have touched your life win with you. You suddenly even hear from that freckle-faced boy who sat behind you in psychology class in 1942."

Eileen Heckart
Best Supporting Actress, 1972

CARMINE COPPOLA

"As I get older, I realize how much more I need to learn; how different it is than when I was a young composer, out to dazzle everyone. I knew everything.

When I received the Oscar for Best Music Score I finally realized, not only a great prize and honor, but also that possibly I had started to learn something about music and in a little while longer could learn even more. My years with Juilliard, Toscanini and Joseph Schellinger in composition served me well."

Carmine Coppola
Music (Original Dramatic Score), 1974

David Niven and friend (46th Awards)

Lawrence Weingarten, Katharine Hepburn (46th Awards)

with the cooperation of the Society of Motion Picture and Television Engineers, and financial assistance to several scholarly projects involving such fields as animation and set design.

But the decade wasn't all confined to scholarly endeavors. On May 11, 1977, fifty years to the day after the initial Academy of Motion Picture Arts and Sciences' organization meeting in the Crystal Ballroom of the Los Angeles Biltmore Hotel, a year-long celebration of Oscar's Fiftieth Anniversary officially began in the same room, filled with a towering birthday cake, attended by Academy leaders, film industry executives, civic officials and friends, and emceed by Bob Hope.

Proclamations honoring the Academy and its contributions were presented by the City of Los Angeles, the State of California, the United States Senate, the House of Representatives and President Jimmy Carter. Life memberships were presented to sixteen film professionals who were admitted to the Academy during its first year, and a twenty-two-minute film called *Oscar's First Fifty Years*, hosted by Jack Lemmon, was shown. It marked the first time the Academy had described its own broad range of activities on film, and the featurette was later made available to schools, museums, service clubs and other organizations for showing. A special seven-minute version was also made available to theaters across the country, prior to the Fiftieth Academy Awards presentation, to further enhance public interest in Oscar's golden anniversary.

While the Academy itself began a retrospective series showing all of the past Oscar-winning best picture selections in the Samuel Goldwyn Theater, the organization also participated in a series of television specials aired on the ABC-TV network. They included "Oscar's

ELLEN BURSTYN

"When I was awarded my Oscar, I couldn't be there to receive it in person because I was working in a play in New York. Two nights later, Jack Lemmon and Walter Matthau delivered my 'gold statue' to the theater in New York, then took me out to dinner with a few friends afterwards. During dinner Oscar sat on the floor in a little felt bag between Walter and me. Over coffee, I turned to Walter and said, 'What is that down there in the bag, Walter? What is an Oscar? What does it mean?' And Walter said, 'Let's put it this way, Ellen. When you die, the newspapers will say, "The Academy Award-winning actress Ellen Burstyn died today."'

'Oh,' said the Academy Award-winning actress, and finished her coffee, silent and informed."

Ellen Burstyn
Best Actress, 1974

BILL GOLDMAN

"I understand the voting is secret, the specific results never announced; and that is as it should be. But why couldn't we have a listing of the order of the five candidates? Or, if you feel that would be embarrassing, why not make some kind of note when the voting was particularly close? (Say, for example, when the second place winner was within a certain percentage of winning.)

I think this is valid for one reason and one reason only. We all know — those of us who work in the movie business — that it is an industry award. And only occasionally do we sense the mood of the industry clearly. Example: I don't think there's any doubt in most people's minds that Taylor won Best Actress in 1960, not for Butterfield 8, but because she had pneumonia and came back, and the industry properly loves survivors. Also, Taylor had not won for either Cat on a Hot Tin Roof or, most particularly, the year before in Suddenly, Last Summer.

Personally, I don't believe that movies are 'good' or 'bad' when they are released. They either 'work' or 'don't work.' I think the former terms are something only to be used when time has had a chance to operate. But the awards, as they should be, are about movies that work or don't work for the public. Has a flop ever won anything? Doubtful.

Okay, to try and sum up: if we knew who was close to winning, or the order of the five, or at least the runner-up, we would have a wonderful way of trying to gauge the sentiment and thoughts of the industry at a particular point in time."

Bill Goldman
Writing (Story and Screenplay
written directly for the screen), 1969
Writing (Screenplay based on material
from another medium), 1976

Art Carney (47th Awards)

RICHARD DREYFUSS

"The night was a complete fuzz out. At the time, it seemed highly rational that I was being considered for an Academy Award. It was only later I realized that my God, I won the Best Actor Award of 1977.

I wanted to be in control so that when I turned to the audience I could appreciate the experience moment by moment, but my mind turned to Jello and all I could do was guffaw into the microphone.

We've all participated in two rituals: one is the watching of the Academy Awards and the other is the putting down of the Academy Awards. Both are very sacred and traditional American events. I always vowed that I would never go to an Academy Award presentation that I was involved in. (This was in my days of chutzpah and cockiness.) But as the reality became closer and closer and I saw myself in a vision: driving Pacific Coast Highway alone in my car listening to the Academy Awards presentation on the radio, and hearing my name and saying to myself 'Schmuck . . . what are you doing here?' So, I decided I would go to the Oscars.

It is extraordinary, but the most relevant part of the experience to me is not from that night, but from what I have been carrying with me ever since. And that is this: I would have to work very hard to deny my success now. I would have to expend an enormous amount of effort to say that I'm not doing well in this business. The accolade, the acceptance, the acknowledgement that this award has given me, to my surprise, more whiffs of personal happiness in my soul than I ever expected it to do. Usually once every two or three days, for periods of two or three minutes at a time, an enormous giggle of happiness comes over me . . . not only that I won, that I am the winner, but that I'm here and I'm me and I can enjoy it and it's all wonderful."

Richard Dreyfuss
Best Actor, 1977

FAYE DUNAWAY

"All my years of work as an actress seemed to come together the night I won the Oscar for Network, and for a brief moment I felt that I had reached the pinnacle. That kind of elation lasts only for a few hours, but it's something I'll always remember.

In this business you go on to the next film, or play, or whatever, and it's almost like starting from scratch every time. Winning an Oscar doesn't mean you can rest on your laurels, and it certainly shouldn't become a bench mark for measuring subsequent performances because you have to approach each new role as a totally separate entity if you're going to maintain your integrity as an artist. If you dwell too long in past achievements, you're in trouble.

Success is a relative quotient, and fame can be ephemeral. An Oscar is something that becomes a part of your record, a tangible acknowledgement that your efforts have made a difference."

Faye Dunaway
Best Actress, 1976

Best Music" (telecast November 25, 1975), "Oscar's Best Movies" (February 13, 1977), "Oscar Presents the War Movies and John Wayne" (November 22, 1977) and "Oscar's Best Actors" (aired May 23, 1978). These activities culminated, with an appropriate serving of spectacle, at the actual Fiftieth Academy Awards presentation, April 3, 1978, which also set a new record to date for television viewership.

It was a far, far cry from those beginning days when only a handful of interested pioneers started it all. At the conclusion of its fifth decade, the Academy was already a survivor of wars, depressions, prosperity, political unrest, criticisms, revolutionary inventions, changing styles, even a gate-crasher and a streaker. And more noteworthy times were still to come.

ACADEMY PRESIDENTS, THE FIFTH DECADE

June 1967–May 1968 . . . . *Gregory Peck*
June 1968–May 1969 . . . . *Gregory Peck*
June 1969–May 1970 . . . . *Gregory Peck*
June 1970–May 1971 . . . . *Daniel Taradash*
June 1971–May 1972 . . . . *Daniel Taradash*
June 1972–May 1973 . . . . *Daniel Taradash*
June 1973–May 1974 . . . . *Walter Mirisch*
June 1974–May 1975 . . . . *Walter Mirisch*
June 1975–May 1976 . . . . *Walter Mirisch*
June 1976–May 1977 . . . . *Walter Mirisch*
June 1977–May 1978 . . . . *Howard W. Koch*

Ingrid Bergman (47th Awards)

BURT BACHARACH

"When I was nominated three years in a row, it was a tremendously exciting thing, but the night that I won two Oscars has to just about qualify as one of the greatest nights in my life."

Burt Bacharach
Music (Original Score), 1969
Music (Song), 1969, 1981

AL KASHA

"My father was a barber and I lived over a store in Brooklyn. The possibility of winning an award like this seemed an impossible dream. It was an overwhelming feeling that night when my name was announced. I remembered the days over that store and said to myself, 'This can't be happening to Al Kasha!'"

Al Kasha
Music (Song), 1972; 1974

MILOS FORMAN

"I was sitting in the auditorium at the Academy Awards with my two twelve-year-old sons. They had arrived the night before from Czechoslovakia. It was their first time in America and I hadn't seen them in five years. We were strangers to each other that evening. They didn't speak English, but they had learned the name of my film: Cuksunext.

The film was mentioned as a nominee for Best Supporting Actor. The boys got very excited, and when George Burns won in this category for Sunshine Boys, *my boys gave me a standing ovation.*

'Cut it,' I said. 'You are making fools of yourselves. We lost.'

They looked at me like I was making a very bad joke. After we lost four nominations in a row, Petr fell asleep and Matej started concentrating on his bubble gum. I realized that if I didn't win, the boys would never understand what they had come for.

Finally, I won. I was filled with pride and self confidence as a father. 'Tell me anything in the world you

want,' I said generously. 'I'll get it for you.'

'Anything?' They looked at each other.

'Anything.'

Without hesitation, they replied, 'We want to meet that Columbo guy Peter Falk, and then we want to see Jaws!'"

Milos Forman
Best Director, 1975, 1984

Janet Gaynor, Diane Keaton, Walter Matthau (50th Awards)

Louise Fletcher (48th Awards)

DONALD W. MacDOUGALL

" 'And the winner is,'…the sound of silence that follows those words is deafening. In that brief instant, you relive all the torturous hours spent in personal anguish breathing life into an image on the screen.

When Star Wars won Best Sound for 1977, I was immediately filled with an overwhelming sense of accomplishment and pride for my colleagues, for our work, for having made a journey filled with great adventure."

Donald W. MacDougall
Sound, 1977

JOHN BARRY

"It was without doubt the high point of my career as a designer. The number of foreign technicians who have been honored in this way illustrates the generosity of the Academy and the truly international nature of the industry."

John Barry
Art Direction, 1977

ROBERT BLALACK

"The release of Star Wars became a phenomenon in America and the world rivalled perhaps only by the Hula Hoop. My surprise at its instant success was only surpassed by my astonishment that we might win an Oscar for the visual effects. I was completely uncertain whether Close Encounters would win, and I felt that as their effects might be seen as more 'traditional,' we might well not be the Oscar recipients.

I was focused on the part of the event which was the Visual Effects Oscar, and when they started to list the contenders, I felt like I was walking a tightrope across a significant divide. 'The envelope please' statement made me want to freeze time and suspend it there: I didn't want to know the results. As Joan Fontaine started to read our names, I felt transformed, completely acknowledged, and elated. We all ran up to the stage, hugging each other and laughing uncontrollably.

I had prepared a speech in case we won, and I had been careful in it to say that the award was possible only because of the past effects workers, and the optical effects crew. I wanted to be clear that this is our Oscar.

Having received it, I am now much more credible to filmmakers and producers, and I do not have to explain or justify what I did on Star Wars.

The little fellow carries a great deal of weight."

Robert Blalack
Best Achievement in Visual Effects, 1977

GEORGE BURNS

"I was thrilled when I was nominated, but it was very, very exciting to win an Oscar. Imagine, winning an Oscar when you're eighty years old. I've been in show business all my life, and I've always played myself, George Burns. Here I make one movie, The Sunshine Boys, where for the first time I didn't play myself. I played a character 'Al Lewis' and won an Oscar. I guess that could mean I've been doing the wrong thing for the last eighty years. It's a good thing I found out before it's too late."

George Burns
Best Supporting Actor, 1975

1968
The Forty-First Year

Now
everyone
can have
m**O**re!
m**O**re!
m**O**re!
of
OLIVER!

It almost required a certified public accountant to keep tabs on the records set during the 1968 Oscar awards, held April 14, 1969. Katharine Hepburn became the first person to win three Academy Awards in either the best actor or best actress categories (Walter Brennan had earlier won three in the "supporting" classification), winning this time for *The Lion in Winter*. Having also won the preceding year, she became the third individual (following Luise Rainer and Spencer Tracy) to win the honor in consecutive years. Her eleven acting nominations were also a new industry record. Further, Miss Hepburn won this latest award in a tie with Barbra Streisand (for *Funny Girl*), the second time in history two performers had tied for a single Oscar honor.

This tie, however, was precedent setting. In 1931-32, when Fredric March and Wallace Beery were announced as co-winners as best actor, a tie was officially declared, but at that time the policy was to award a tie when any runner-up came within three votes of a winner. Beery, it was announced, had come within one vote of March's total. To share the honor under 1968 rules, both Miss Hepburn and Miss Streisand had to receive the exact same number of votes from the Academy's 3,030 voting members. Streisand was present to receive her Oscar; Hepburn was not.

For the first time in years, the Oscar show also changed residences, moving to the 3,400-seat Dorothy Chandler Pavilion of the Los Angeles Music Center for the awards presentation. Gower Champion produced, directed and choreographed the program for the Academy, while Richard Dunlap produced and directed for ABC. There was no single M.C.; instead, awards were handed out by a rotating group of ten "Friends of Oscar," including Ingrid Bergman, Rosalind Russell, Frank Sinatra, Burt Lancaster, Sidney Poitier, Walter Matthau, Jane Fonda, Natalie Wood, Diahann Carroll and Tony Curtis.

Oliver! received five awards including best picture and best director (Carol Reed), the biggest total of the evening. Cliff Robertson in *Charly* was named best actor, Jack Albertson in *The Subject Was Roses* was best supporting actor and Ruth Gordon in *Rosemary's Baby* was best supporting actress. Russia's mammoth *War and Peace* was chosen best foreign language film.

Bob Hope, in a brief appearance, received an ovation from the industry audience as did one of his former co-stars, Martha Raye. She was presented the Jean Hersholt Humanitarian Award, the first woman so honored. For the first time in forty years, the actual ceremony was not carried on any radio station, but it was telecast worldwide in thirty-seven countries, in a fifty-six minute capsule version, bringing Oscar and the awards to an estimated international audience of somewhere between two hundred fifty million and six hundred million people.

Best Picture: **Oliver!** *(Columbia; produced by John Woolf)* and **Best Director:** **Carol Reed** *for* Oliver! *Charles Dickens' 130-year-old story* Oliver Twist, *following the adventures of a nine-year-old runaway orphan in 19th-century London, had been filmed eight times as a straight Dickens drama, then was streamlined as a London stage musical in 1960 with music, lyrics and book by Lionel Bart, then became an Academy Award-winning picture. It marked a distinct change of pace for director Carol Reed, best known for mystery-dramas such as those which had won him earlier Oscar nominations, 1949's* The Fallen Idol *and 1950's* The Third Man. *The lively* Oliver! *cast included Ron Moody, Oliver Reed, Shani Wallis, Hugh Griffith, Jack Wild, and (at right, carrying empty bowl) Mark Lester. The picture won five awards, plus a special award to Onna White for her choreography.*

Best Actor: **Cliff Robertson** *as Charly Gordon in* Charly *(Cinerama Releasing; directed by Ralph Nelson). Robertson had played Charly on television, as a 1961 U.S. Steel Hour drama, then bought the property and helped bring it to the screen. He portrayed a mentally-retarded adult of thirty who undergoes an experimental brain operation and briefly becomes a man of superior intellect before tragically regressing to his former condition. Filming was done in Boston, and Claire Bloom co-starred as a therapist with whom Charly (at left, in center) has a romantic attachment.*

For the second time in Academy Awards history, two performers tied in a single acting category. **Best Actress: Katharine Hepburn** *as Eleanor of Aquitaine (above, left) in* The Lion in Winter *(Avco Embassy; directed by Anthony Harvey) and* **Best Actress: Barbra Streisand** *as Fannie Brice (above, right) in* Funny Girl *(Columbia; directed by William Wyler). For Miss Hepburn, it was her 36th film and her third Oscar for acting, a new record in that category, as the estranged wife of aging King Henry II; for Miss Streisand, it was her first film, a recreation and extension of her 1964 Broadway success as Ziegfeld's great musical comedienne.*

Best Foreign Language Film: War and Peace *from Russia. It was a truly monumental undertaking, an adaptation of Leo Tolstoy's epic novel, directed by Sergei Bondarchuk, which took five years to film at a reported cost of $100 million, and ran 7 hours and 14 minutes in its original form (but cut to 6 hours, 13 minutes for United States distribution). Filled with awesome scenes of a magnitude rarely (if ever) captured on film before,* War and Peace *set a new standard for the grandiose film, and became the first Russian-made film honored by the Academy in its foreign language film award category. Sergei Bondarchuk directed and co-starred (as Pierre), with Ludmilla Savelyeva (as Natasha) and Vyacheslav Tihonov (as Andrei).*

PICTURE

FUNNY GIRL, Rastar, Columbia. Produced by Ray Stark.
THE LION IN WINTER, Haworth, Avco Embassy. Produced by Martin Poll.
***OLIVER!,** Romulus, Columbia. Produced by John Woolf.
RACHEL, RACHEL, Kayos, Warner Bros.-Seven Arts. Produced by Paul Newman.
ROMEO AND JULIET, B.H.E.-Verona-De Laurentiis, Paramount. Produced by Anthony Havelock-Allan and John Brabourne.

ACTOR

ALAN ARKIN in *The Heart Is a Lonely Hunter,* Warner Bros.-Seven Arts.
ALAN BATES in *The Fixer,* Frankenheimer-Lewis, M-G-M.
RON MOODY in *Oliver!,* Romulus, Columbia.
PETER O'TOOLE in *The Lion in Winter,* Haworth, Avco Embassy.
***CLIFF ROBERTSON** in *Charly,* ABC-Selmur, Cinerama.

ACTRESS

***KATHARINE HEPBURN** in *The Lion in Winter,* Haworth, Avco Embassy.
PATRICIA NEAL in *The Subject Was Roses,* M-G-M.
VANESSA REDGRAVE in *Isadora,* Hakim, Universal.
***BARBRA STREISAND** in *Funny Girl,* Rastar, Columbia.
JOANNE WOODWARD in *Rachel, Rachel,* Kayos, Warner Bros.-Seven Arts.

SUPPORTING ACTOR

***JACK ALBERTSON** in *The Subject Was Roses,* M-G-M.
SEYMOUR CASSEL in *Faces,* Cassavetes, Reade-Continental.
DANIEL MASSEY in *Star!,* Wise, 20th Century-Fox.
JACK WILD in *Oliver!* Romulus, Columbia.
GENE WILDER in *The Producers,* Glazier, Avco Embassy.

SUPPORTING ACTRESS

LYNN CARLIN in *Faces,* Cassavetes, Reade-Continental.
***RUTH GORDON** in *Rosemary's Baby,* Castle, Paramount.
SONDRA LOCKE in *The Heart Is a Lonely Hunter,* Warner Bros.-Seven Arts.
KAY MEDFORD in *Funny Girl,* Rastar, Columbia.
ESTELLE PARSONS in *Rachel, Rachel,* Kayos, Warner Bros.-Seven Arts.

DIRECTING

THE BATTLE OF ALGIERS, Igor-Casbash, Allied Artists (Italian). Gillo Pontecorvo.
THE LION IN WINTER, Haworth, Avco Embassy. Anthony Harvey.
***OLIVER!,** Romulus, Columbia. Carol Reed.
ROMEO AND JULIET, B.H.E.-Verona-De Laurentiis, Paramount. Franco Zeffirelli.
2001: A SPACE ODYSSEY, Polaris, M-G-M. Stanley Kubrick.

WRITING

(Screenplay—based on material from another medium)
***THE LION IN WINTER,** Haworth, Avco Embassy. James Goldman.
THE ODD COUPLE, Koch, Paramount. Neil Simon.
OLIVER!, Romulus, Columbia. Vernon Harris.
RACHEL, RACHEL, Kayos, Warner Bros.-Seven Arts. Stewart Stern.
ROSEMARY'S BABY, Castle, Paramount. Roman Polanski.

(Story and Screenplay—written directly for the screen)
THE BATTLE OF ALGIERS, Igor-Casbah, Allied Artists (Italian). Franco Solinas and Gillo Pontecorvo.
FACES, Cassavetes, Walter Reade-Continental. John Cassavetes.
HOT MILLIONS, Alberg, M-G-M. Ira Wallach and Peter Ustinov.
***THE PRODUCERS,** Glazier, Avco Embassy. Mel Brooks.
2001: A SPACE ODYSSEY, Polaris, M-G-M. Stanley Kubrick and Arthur C. Clarke.

CINEMATOGRAPHY

FUNNY GIRL, Rastar, Columbia. Harry Stradling.
ICE STATION ZEBRA, Filmways, M-G-M. Daniel L. Fapp.
OLIVER! Romulus, Columbia. Oswald Morris.
***ROMEO AND JULIET,** B.H.E.-Verona-DeLaurentiis, Paramount. Pasqualino De Santis.
STAR!, Wise, 20th Century-Fox. Ernest Laszlo.

ART DIRECTION-SET DECORATION

***OLIVER!** Romulus, Columbia. John Box and Terence Marsh; Vernon Dixon and Ken Muggleston.
THE SHOES OF THE FISHERMAN, Englund, M-G-M. George W. Davis and Edward Carfagno.
STAR!, Wise, 20th Century-Fox. Boris Leven; Walter M. Scott and Howard Bristol.
2001: A SPACE ODYSSEY, Polaris, M-G-M. Tony Masters, Harry Lange and Ernie Archer.
WAR AND PEACE, Mosfilm, Walter Reade-Continental (Russian). Mikhail Bogdanov and Gennady Myasnikov; G. Koshelev and V. Uvarov.

COSTUME DESIGN

THE LION IN WINTER, Haworth, Avco Embassy. Margaret Furse.
OLIVER!, Romulus, Columbia. Phyllis Dalton.
PLANET OF THE APES, Apjac, 20th Century-Fox. Morton Haack.
***ROMEO AND JULIET,** B.H.E.-Verona-DeLaurentiis, Paramount. Danilo Donati.
STAR!, Wise, 20th Century-Fox. Donald Brooks.

SOUND

BULLITT, Solar, Warner Bros.-Seven Arts. Warner Bros.-Seven Arts Studio Sound Dept.
FINIAN'S RAINBOW, Warner Bros.-Seven Arts. Warner Bros.-Seven Arts Studio Sound Dept.
FUNNY GIRL, Rastar, Columbia. Columbia Studio Sound Dept.
***OLIVER,** Romulus, Columbia. Shepperton Studio Sound Dept.
STAR!, Wise, 20th Century-Fox. 20th Century-Fox Studio Sound Dept.

FILM EDITING

***BULLITT,** Solar, Warner Bros.-Seven Arts. Frank P. Keller.
FUNNY GIRL, Rastar, Columbia. Robert Swink, Maury Winetrobe and William Sands.
THE ODD COUPLE, Koch, Paramount. Frank Bracht.
OLIVER!, Romulus, Columbia. Ralph Kemplen.
WILD IN THE STREETS, American International. Fred Feitshans and Eve Newman.

SPECIAL EFFECTS

ICE STATION ZEBRA, Filmways, M-G-M. Hal Millar and J. McMillan Johnson.
***2001: A SPACE ODYSSEY,** Polaris, M-G-M. Stanley Kubrick.

MUSIC

(Song)

CHITTY CHITTY BANG BANG (*Chitty Chitty Bang Bang*, Warfield, UA); Music and Lyrics by Richard M. Sherman and Robert B. Sherman.
FOR LOVE OF IVY (*For Love of Ivy*, ABC-Palomar, Cinerama); Music by Quincy Jones. Lyrics by Bob Russell.
FUNNY GIRL (*Funny Girl*, Rastar, Columbia); Music by Jule Styne. Lyrics by Bob Merrill.
STAR! (*Star!*, Wise, 20th Century-Fox); Music by Jimmy Van Heusen. Lyrics by Sammy Cahn.
*THE WINDMILLS OF YOUR MIND (*The Thomas Crown Affair*, Mirisch-Simkoe-Solar, UA); Music by Michel Legrand. Lyrics by Alan and Marilyn Bergman.

(Original Score—for a motion picture [not a musical])

THE FOX, Stross, Claridge Pictures. Lalo Schifrin.
*THE LION IN WINTER, Haworth, Avco Embassy. John Barry.
PLANET OF THE APES, Apjac, 20th Century-Fox. Jerry Goldsmith.
THE SHOES OF THE FISHERMAN, Englund, M-G-M. Alex North.
THE THOMAS CROWN AFFAIR, Mirisch-Simkoe-Solar, UA. Michel Legrand.

(Score of a Musical Picture—[original or adaptation])

FINIAN'S RAINBOW, Warner Bros.-Seven Arts. Ray Heindorf.
FUNNY GIRL, Rastar, Columbia. Walter Scharf.
*OLIVER!, Romulus, Columbia. John Green.
STAR!, Wise, 20th Century-Fox. Lennie Hayton.
THE YOUNG GIRLS OF ROCHEFORT, Warner Bros.-Seven Arts (French). Michel Legrand and Jacques Demy.

SHORT SUBJECTS

(Cartoons)

THE HOUSE THAT JACK BUILT, National Film Board of Canada, Columbia. Wolf Koenig and Jim MacKay, producers.
THE MAGIC PEAR TREE, Bing Crosby Prods. Jimmy Murakami, producer.
WINDY DAY, Hubley Studios, Paramount. John and Faith Hubley, producers.
*WINNIE THE POOH AND THE BLUSTERY DAY, Disney, Buena Vista. Walt Disney, producer.

(Live Action Subjects)

THE DOVE, Coe-Davis, Schoenfeld Films. George Coe, Sidney Davis and Anthony Lover, producers.
DUO, National Film Board of Canada, Columbia.
PRELUDE, Prelude Company, Excelsior Dist. John Astin, producer.
*ROBERT KENNEDY REMEMBERED, Guggenheim Prods., National General. Charles Guggenheim, producer.

DOCUMENTARY

(Short Subjects)

THE HOUSE THAT ANANDA BUILT, Films Division, Government of India. Fali Bilimoria, producer.
THE REVOLVING DOOR, Vision Associates for American Foundation Institute of Corrections. Lee R. Broker, producer.
A SPACE TO GROW, Office of Economic Opportunity for Project Upward Bound. Thomas P. Kelly, Jr. producer.
A WAY OUT OF THE WILDERNESS, John Sutherland, Prods. Dan E. Weisburd, producer.
*WHY MAN CREATES, Saul Bass & Associates. Saul Bass, producer.

(Features)

A FEW NOTES ON OUR FOOD PROBLEM, U.S. Information Agency. James Blue, producer.
*JOURNEY INTO SELF, Western Behavioral Sciences Institute. Bill McGaw producer.
THE LEGENDARY CHAMPIONS, Turn Of The Century Fights. William Cayton, producer.
OTHER VOICES, DHS Films. David H. Sawyer, producer.
YOUNG AMERICANS, The Young Americans Prod. Robert Cohn and Alex Grasshoff, producers.

(NOTE: YOUNG AMERICANS was originally voted the award but later (on May 7, 1969) was declared ineligible after it was learned picture was first shown in a theater in October 1967 and therefore not eligible for a 1968 Award. JOURNEY INTO SELF, first runner-up, was announced as the official winner on May 8, 1969.)

FOREIGN LANGUAGE

THE BOYS OF PAUL STREET (Hungary).
THE FIREMEN'S BALL (Czechoslovakia).
THE GIRL WITH THE PISTOL (Italy).
STOLEN KISSES (France).
*WAR AND PEACE (Russia).

Best Supporting Actress: Ruth Gordon *as Minnie Castevet (above, with Mia Farrow) in* Rosemary's Baby *(Paramount; directed by Roman Polanski). Gordon was no stranger to the Academy's honor rolls when she won her Oscar as a mysterious neighbor (and witch) in Ira Levin's chiller story about dark powers in modern day Manhattan.*

Earlier nominated as a performer for 1965's Inside Daisy Clover, *she also had been nominated three times for her screenwriting: for 1947's* A Double Life, *1950's* Adam's Rib *and 1952's* Pat and Mike. *Receiving her first Oscar at age 72, she smiled and said, "I can't tell ya' how encouragin' a thing like this is . . . ."*

Best Supporting Actor: Jack Albertson *as Jack Cleary in* The Subject Was Roses *(M-G-M; directed by Ulu Grosbard). Author Frank Gilroy refused to sell the rights to his Pulitzer Prize-winning play unless it was agreed Jack Albertson would replay his original role in the screen version.*

Gilroy got his way, and Albertson got an Oscar for his exacting performance as the hostile husband of Patricia Neal, and the vitriolic father of Martin Sheen (above, at right, sparring with Albertson) living out their damaged lives in a Bronx apartment.

HONORARY AND OTHER AWARDS

TO JOHN CHAMBERS for his outstanding make-up achievement for *Planet Of The Apes*. (statuette)
TO ONNA WHITE for her outstanding choreography achievement for *Oliver!* (statuette)

1968 IRVING G. THALBERG MEMORIAL AWARD

None given this year.

1968 JEAN HERSHOLT HUMANITARIAN AWARD

TO MARTHA RAYE

SCIENTIFIC OR TECHNICAL

CLASS I (statuette)

PHILIP V. PALMQUIST of MINNESOTA MINING AND MANUFACTURING CO., to DR. HERBERT MEYER of the MOTION PICTURE AND TELEVISION RESEARCH CENTER, and to CHARLES D. STAFFELL of the RANK ORGANISATION for the development of a successful embodiment of the reflex background projection system for composite cinematography.
EASTMAN KODAK COMPANY for the development and introduction of a color reversal intermediate film for motion pictures.

CLASS II (plaque)

DONALD W. NORWOOD for the design and development of the Norwood Photographic Exposure Meters.
EASTMAN KODAK COMPANY and PRODUCERS SERVICE COMPANY for the development of a new high-speed step-optical reduction printer.
EDMUND M. DIGIULIO, NIELS G. PETERSEN and NORMAN S. HUGHES of the CINEMA PRODUCT DEVELOPMENT COMPANY for the design and application of a conversion which makes available the reflex viewing system for motion picture cameras.
OPTICAL COATING LABORATORIES, INC., for the development of an improved anti-reflection coating for photographic and projection lens systems.
EASTMAN KODAK COMPANY for the introduction of a new high speed motion picture color negative film.
PANAVISION INCORPORATED for the conception, design and introduction of a 65mm hand-held motion picture camera.
TODD-AO COMPANY and the MITCHELL CAMERA COMPANY for the design and engineering of the Todd-AO hand-held motion picture camera.

CLASS III (citation)

CARL W. HAUGE and EDWARD H. REICHARD of CONSOLIDATED FILM INDUSTRIES and E. MICHAEL MEAHL and ROY J. RIDENOUR of RAMTRONICS;
EASTMAN KODAK COMPANY and CONSOLIDATED FILM INDUSTRIES.

*INDICATES WINNER

The 1969 Academy Awards had a distinctly western flavor. *Butch Cassidy and the Sundance Kid,* a blockbuster about two real-life turn-of-the century gunmen, received the most Oscars for the year—four, including two statuettes to composer Burt Bacharach for his music. *Midnight Cowboy,* a stark contemporary drama about a different sort of western 'hero,' won three awards, including best picture and best director (John Schlesinger). And the most durable cowboy of all, John Wayne, was named best actor for *True Grit,* playing a paunchy and fictional U.S. marshal.

The awards were presented April 7, 1970, again at the Dorothy Chandler Pavilion of the Los Angeles Music Center, produced by M.J. Frankovich and directed by Jack Haley, Jr., with Richard Dunlap producing and directing for the ABC-TV network. For the second year, there was no official master of ceremonies. Awards were presented by seventeen "Friends of Oscar": Bob Hope, John Wayne, Barbra Streisand, Fred Astaire, Jon Voight, Myrna Loy, Clint Eastwood, Raquel Welch, Candice Bergen, James Earl Jones, Katharine Ross, Cliff Robertson, Ali McGraw, Barbara McNair, Elliott Gould, Claudia Cardinale and—wearing a much-publicized $1.5 million diamond—Elizabeth Taylor.

The year's best actress award went to England's Maggie Smith for *The Prime of Miss Jean Brodie,* Goldie Hawn was named best supporting actress for *Cactus Flower* and Gig Young was chosen best supporting actor for *They Shoot Horses, Don't They? Z,* also nominated in the best picture category, was honored as the best foreign language film, possible under 1969 qualification rules.

Possibly the most popular award of the evening was the honorary statuette presented to Cary Grant, a durable screen contributor who had never been honored previously by Academy voters. He received a standing ovation after a montage of film clips from his thirty-four-year screen career was shown. Frank Sinatra made the presentation to Grant, an actor and gentleman whose image was a 180⁰ turn from the cowboy image that dominated the rest of the evening.

Best Actress: **Maggie Smith** *as Jean Brodie in* The Prime of Miss Jean Brodie *(20th Century-Fox; directed by Ronald Neame). Miss Brodie, an odd and spinsterish Edinburgh schoolteacher with a flair for unconsciously imparting dangerous misinformation to her students, was created on the London stage by Vanessa Redgrave and on Broadway by Zoe Caldwell; in her screen incarnation, she was played by Maggie Smith—and played brilliantly. Maggie was a winner again in 1978, for her supporting performance in* California Suite.

Best Picture: **Midnight Cowboy** *(United Artists; produced by Jerome Hellman) and* **Best Director:** **John Schlesinger** *for* Midnight Cowboy. *At the time, Midnight Cowboy had been given an X-rating by the Motion Picture Association of America, making it the first film with that rating to win the Academy's highest award; in later years, however, it was re-classified to an R (for Restricted). Tough and hard-hitting, it took a compassionate look at some humanity encased at the bottom of the world, and starred (right) Dustin Hoffman as a sickly con man and Jon Voight as a would-be male hustler, attempting to survive together. It also won an Oscar for Waldo Salt's screenplay.*

Best Actor: **John Wayne** *as Rooster Cogburn in* True Grit *(Paramount; directed by Henry Hathaway). Hollywood's durable Duke, at age 62, celebrated his 40th year in the film business with a towering role and performance, as a hard-drinking, one-eyed old U.S. marshal who helps a young girl (Kim Darby) and a Texas ranger (Glen Campbell) avenge a murder in 1880 Arkansas. Wayne had also been an Academy Award nominee in 1949 for* Sands of Iwo Jima *and again played crusty Rooster in a 1975 sequel,* Rooster Cogburn, *with Katharine Hepburn. He made his final public appearance at an Academy Award telecast, in April 1979, just two months before his death.*

Butch Cassidy and the Sundance Kid *(20th Century-Fox; produced by John Foreman) told the tongue-in-cheek exploits of two real-life, turn-of-the-century outlaws, played by Paul Newman and Robert Redford (above), and was a genuine audience pleaser. It was also the year's most honored film by Academy voters, with four awards: for story and screenplay (by William Goldman), cinematography (Conrad Hall), song ("Raindrops Keep Fallin' on My Head" by Burt Bacharach and Hal David) and original score of a non-musical (Burt Bacharach).*

Best Suppporting Actor: Gig Young *as Rocky in* They Shoot Horses, Don't They? *(Cinerama Releasing; directed by Sydney Pollack). Nominated for Oscars in 1951 for* Come Fill the Cup *and in 1958 for* Teacher's Pet, *and best known as a light comedian, Gig Young won his Academy statuette as a jaded, puffy-eyed and dissipated dance marathon emcee of the Depression years in the drama based on a 1935 novel by Horace McCoy. The cast also included Jane Fonda, Michael Sarrazin, Susannah York, Red Buttons and Bruce Dern.*

PICTURE

ANNE OF THE THOUSAND DAYS, Wallis, Universal. Produced by Hal Wallis.
BUTCH CASSIDY AND THE SUNDANCE KID, Hill-Monash, 20th Century-Fox. Produced by John Foreman.
HELLO, DOLLY!, Chenault, 20th Century-Fox. Produced by Ernest Lehman.
*****MIDNIGHT COWBOY,** Hellman-Schlesinger, UA. Produced by Jerome Hellman.
Z, Reggane Films-O.N.C.I.C., Cinema V (Algerian). Produced by Jacques Perrin and Hamed Rachedi.

ACTOR

RICHARD BURTON in *Anne of the Thousand Days,* Wallis, Universal.
DUSTIN HOFFMAN in *Midnight Cowboy,* Hellman-Schlesinger, UA.
PETER O'TOOLE in *Goodbye, Mr. Chips,* Apjac, M-G-M.
JON VOIGHT in *Midnight Cowboy,* Hellman-Schlesinger, UA.
*****JOHN WAYNE** in *True Grit,* Wallis, Paramount.

ACTRESS

GENEVIEVE BUJOLD in *Anne of the Thousand Days,* Wallis, Universal.
JANE FONDA in *They Shoot Horses, Don't They?,* Chartoff-Winkler-Pollack, ABC Pictures, Cinerama.
LIZA MINNELLI in *The Sterile Cuckoo,* Boardwalk, Paramount.
JEAN SIMMONS in *The Happy Ending,* Pax Films.
*****MAGGIE SMITH** in *The Prime of Miss Jean Brodie,* 20th Century-Fox.

SUPPORTING ACTOR

RUPERT CROSSE in *The Reivers,* Ravetch-Kramer-Solar, Cinema Center/National General.
ELLIOTT GOULD in *Bob & Carol & Ted & Alice,* Frankovich, Columbia.
JACK NICHOLSON in *Easy Rider,* Pando-Raybert, Columbia.
ANTHONY QUAYLE in *Anne of the Thousand Days,* Wallis, Universal.
*****GIG YOUNG** in *They Shoot Horses, Don't They?,* Chartoff-Winkler-Pollack, ABC Pictures, Cinerama.

SUPPORTING ACTRESS

CATHERINE BURNS in *Last Summer,* Perry-Alsid, Allied Artists.
DYAN CANNON in *Bob & Carol & Ted & Alice,* Frankovich, Columbia.
*****GOLDIE HAWN** in *Cactus Flower,* Frankovich, Columbia.
SYLVIA MILES in *Midnight Cowboy,* Hellman-Schlesinger, UA.
SUSANNAH YORK in *They Shoot Horses, Don't They?,* Chartoff-Winkler-Pollack, ABC Pictures, Cinerama.

DIRECTING

ALICE'S RESTAURANT, Florin Prod., UA. Arthur Penn.
BUTCH CASSIDY AND THE SUNDANCE KID, Hill-Monash, 20th Century-Fox. George Roy Hill.
*****MIDNIGHT COWBOY,** Hellman-Schlesinger, UA. John Schlesinger.
THEY SHOOT HORSES, DON'T THEY?, Chartoff-Winkler-Pollack, ABC Pictures, Cinerama. Sydney Pollack.
Z, Reggane Films-O.N.C.I.C., Cinema V (Algerian). Costa-Gavras.

WRITING

(Screenplay—based on material from another medium)

ANNE OF THE THOUSAND DAYS, Wallis, Universal. John Hale, Bridget Boland and Richard Sokolove.
GOODBYE COLUMBUS, Willow Tree, Paramount. Arnold Schulman.
*****MIDNIGHT COWBOY,** Hellman-Schlesinger, UA. Waldo Salt.
THEY SHOOT HORSES, DON'T THEY?, Chartoff-Winkler-Pollack, ABC Pictures, Cinerama. James Poe and Robert E. Thompson.
Z, Reggane Films-O.N.C.I.C., Cinema V (Algerian). Jorge Semprun and Costa-Gavras.

(Story and Screenplay—based on material not previously published or produced)

BOB & CAROL & TED & ALICE, Frankovich, Columbia. Paul Mazursky and Larry Tucker.
*****BUTCH CASSIDY AND THE SUNDANCE KID,** Hill-Monash, 20th Century-Fox. William Goldman.
THE DAMNED, Pegaso-Praesidens, Warner Bros. Nicola Badalucco, Enrico Medioli and Luchino Visconti.
EASY RIDER, Pando-Raybert, Columbia. Peter Fonda, Dennis Hopper and Terry Southern.
THE WILD BUNCH, Feldman, Warner Bros. Walon Green, Roy N. Sickner and Sam Peckinpah.

CINEMATOGRAPHY

ANNE OF THE THOUSAND DAYS, Wallis, Universal. Arthur Ibbetson.
BOB & CAROL & TED & ALICE, Frankovich, Columbia. Charles B. Lang.
*****BUTCH CASSIDY AND THE SUNDANCE KID,** Hill-Monash, 20th Century-Fox. Conrad Hall.
HELLO, DOLLY!, Chenault, 20th Century-Fox. Harry Stradling.
MAROONED, Frankovich-Sturges, Columbia. Daniel Fapp.

ART DIRECTION-SET DECORATION

ANNE OF THE THOUSAND DAYS, Wallis, Universal. Maurice Carter and Lionel Couch; Patrick McLoughlin.
GAILY, GAILY, Mirisch-Cartier, UA. Robert Boyle and George B. Chan; Edward Boyle and Carl Biddiscombe.

Best Supporting Actress: Goldie Hawn *as Toni Simmons in* Cactus Flower *(Columbia; directed by Gene Saks). Goldie came to the movies from TV's successful* Laugh-In *series and won the Academy Award for her first post-*Laugh-In *performance, as a kookie Greenwich Village girl pursued by a middle-aged dentist (Walter Matthau) who pretends to be married to an "unfaithful" wife (Ingrid Bergman), who is in reality only his dental assistant, all adding to many comical situations.*

*HELLO, DOLLY!, Chenault, 20th Century-Fox. John DeCuir, Jack Martin Smith and Herman Blumenthal; Walter M. Scott, George Hopkins and Raphael Bretton.
SWEET CHARITY, Universal. Alexander Golitzen and George C. Webb; Jack D. Moore.
THEY SHOOT HORSES, DON'T THEY?, Chartoff-Winkler-Pollack, ABC Pictures, Cinerama. Harry Horner; Frank McKelvey.

COSTUME DESIGN

*ANNE OF THE THOUSAND DAYS, Wallis, Universal. Margaret Furse.
GAILY, GAILY, Mirisch-Cartier, UA. Ray Aghayan.
HELLO, DOLLY!, Chenault, 20th Century-Fox. Irene Sharaff.
SWEET CHARITY, Universal. Edith Head.
THEY SHOOT HORSES, DON'T THEY?, Chartoff-Winkler-Pollack, ABC Pictures, Cinerama. Donfeld.

SOUND

ANNE OF THE THOUSAND DAYS, Wallis, Universal. John Aldred.
BUTCH CASSIDY AND THE SUNDANCE KID, Hill-Monash, 20th Century-Fox. William Edmundson and David Dockendorf.
GAILY, GAILY, Mirisch-Cartier, UA. Robert Martin and Clem Portman.
*HELLO, DOLLY!, Chenault, 20th Century-Fox. Jack Solomon and Murray Spivack.
MAROONED, Frankovich-Sturges, Columbia. Les Fresholtz and Arthur Piantadosi.

FILM EDITING

HELLO, DOLLY!, Chenault, 20th Century-Fox. William Reynolds.
MIDNIGHT COWBOY, Hellman-Schlesinger, UA. Hugh A. Robertson.
THE SECRET OF SANTA VITTORIA, Kramer, UA. William Lyon and Earle Herdan.
THEY SHOOT HORSES, DON'T THEY?, Chartoff-Winkler-Pollack, ABC Pictures, Cinerama. Fredric Steinkamp.
*Z, Reggane Films-O.N.C.I.C., Cinema V (Algerian). Francoise Bonnot.

SPECIAL VISUAL EFFECTS

KRAKATOA, EAST OF JAVA, ABC Pictures, Cinerama. Eugene Lourie and Alex Weldon.
*MAROONED, Frankovich-Sturges, Columbia. Robbie Robertson.

MUSIC

(Song)
COME SATURDAY MORNING (The Sterile Cuckoo, Boardwalk, Paramount); Music by Fred Karlin. Lyrics by Dory Previn.
JEAN (The Prime of Miss Jean Brodie, 20th Century-Fox); Music and Lyrics by Rod McKuen.

*RAINDROPS KEEP FALLIN' ON MY HEAD (Butch Cassidy and the Sundance Kid, Hill-Monash, 20th Century-Fox); Music by Burt Bacharach. Lyrics by Hal David.
TRUE GRIT (True Grit, Wallis, Paramount); Music by Elmer Bernstein. Lyrics by Don Black.
WHAT ARE YOU DOING FOR THE REST OF YOUR LIFE? (The Happy Ending, Brooks, UA); Music by Michel Legrand. Lyrics by Alan and Marilyn Bergman.

(Original Score—for a motion picture [not a musical])
ANNE OF THE THOUSAND DAYS, Wallis, Universal. Georges Delerue.
*BUTCH CASSIDY AND THE SUNDANCE KID, Hill-Monash, 20th Century-Fox. Burt Bacharach.
THE REIVERS, Ravetch-Kramer-Solar, Cinema Center Films, National General. John Williams.
THE SECRET OF SANTA VITTORIA, Kramer, UA. Ernest Gold.
THE WILD BUNCH, Feldman, Warner Bros. Jerry Fielding.

(Score of a Musical Picture—[original or adaptation])
GOODBYE, MR. CHIPS, Apjac, M-G-M. Leslie Bricusse and John Williams.
*HELLO, DOLLY!, Chenault, 20th Century-Fox. Lennie Hayton and Lionel Newman.
PAINT YOUR WAGON, Lerner, Paramount. Nelson Riddle.
SWEET CHARITY, Universal. Cy Coleman.
THEY SHOOT HORSES, DON'T THEY?, Chartoff-Winkler-Pollack, ABC Pictures, Cinerama. John Green and Albert Woodbury.

SHORT SUBJECTS

(Cartoons)
*IT'S TOUGH TO BE A BIRD, Disney, Buena Vista. Ward Kimball, producer.
OF MEN AND DEMONS, Hubley Studios, Paramount. John and Faith Hubley, producers.
WALKING, National Film Board of Canada, Columbia. Ryan Larkin, producer.

(Live Action Subjects)
BLAKE, National Film Board of Canada, Vaudeo Inc. Doug Jackson, producer.
*THE MAGIC MACHINES, Fly-By-Night Prods., Manson Distributing. Joan Keller Stern, producer.
PEOPLE SOUP, Pangloss Prods., Columbia. Marc Merson, producer.

DOCUMENTARY

(Short Subjects)
*CZECHOSLOVAKIA 1968, Sanders-Fresco Film Makers for U.S. Information Agency. Denis Sanders and Robert M. Fresco, producers.
AN IMPRESSION OF JOHN STEINBECK: WRITER, Donald Wrye Prods. for U.S. Information Agency. Donald Wrye, producer.
JENNY IS A GOOD THING, A.C.I. Prod. for Project Head Start. Joan Horvath, producer.

LEO BEUERMAN, Centron Prod. Arthur H. Wolf and Russell A. Mosser, producers.
THE MAGIC MACHINES, Fly-By-Night Prods., Manson Distributing. Joan Keller Stern, producer.

(Features)
*ARTHUR RUBINSTEIN—THE LOVE OF LIFE, Midem, Prod. Bernard Chevry, producer.
BEFORE THE MOUNTAIN WAS MOVED, Robert K. Sharpe Prods. for The Office of Economic Opportunity. Robert K. Sharpe, producer.
IN THE YEAR OF THE PIG, Emile de Antonio Prod. Emile de Antonio, producer.
THE OLYMPICS IN MEXICO, Film Section of the Organizing Committee for the XIX Olympic Games.
THE WOLF MEN, M-G-M. Irwin Rosten, producer.

FOREIGN LANGUAGE FILM

ADALEN '31, (Sweden).
THE BATTLE OF NERETVA, (Yugoslavia).
THE BROTHERS KARAMAZOV, (U.S.S.R.).
MY NIGHT WITH MAUD, (France).
*Z, (Algeria).

HONORARY AND OTHER AWARDS

TO CARY GRANT for his unique mastery of the art of screen acting with the respect and affection of his colleagues. (statuette)

1969 IRVING G. THALBERG MEMORIAL AWARD

None given this year.

1969 JEAN HERSHOLT HUMANITARIAN AWARD

TO GEORGE JESSEL

SCIENTIFIC OR TECHNICAL

CLASS I (statuette)
None.

CLASS II (plaque)
HAZELTINE CORPORATION for the design and development of the Hazeltine Color Film Analyzer.
FOUAD SAID for the design and introduction of the Cinemobile series of equipment trucks for location motion picture production.
JUAN DE LA CIERVA and DYNA-SCIENCES CORPORATION for the design and development of the Dynalens optical image motion compensator.

CLASS III (citation)
OTTO POPELKA of Magna-Tech Electronics Do., Inc.;
FENTON HAMILTON of M-G-M Studios;
PANAVISION INCORPORATED;
ROBERT M. FLYNN and RUSSELL HESSEY of Universal City Studios, Inc.

*INDICATES WINNER

In a movie year dominated by escalating admission prices at the box office, a widespread invasion of pornographic movies and extensive unemployment among film craftsmen, 20th Century-Fox's *Patton* dominated the 1970 Academy Awards, presented April 15, 1971, at the Dorothy Chandler Pavilion of the Los Angeles Music Center. *Patton* won seven awards, including best picture, best actor (George C. Scott), best director (Franklin J. Schaffner) and best story and screenplay (Francis Ford Coppola and Edmund H. North).

Scott chose to decline the nomination and the award, but it remained an Academy Award fact. As explained by then-President of the Academy Daniel Taradash, "Nominations and awards are voted for achievements as they appear on the screen; therefore a person responsible for the achievement cannot decline the nomination after it is voted. Actually, Mr. Scott is not involved. It is his performance in *Patton* which is involved."

Except for *Patton,* the only other 1970 release to win more than one award was *Ryan's Daughter,* with two, best supporting actor (John Mills) and best cinematography (Freddie Young). The rest of the year's honors were evenly distributed over ten other films, including *Love Story, M*A*S*H, Woodstock, Tora! Tora! Tora!, Cromwell* and Italy's *Investigation of a Citizen above Suspicion.* Glenda Jackson was named best actress for *Women in Love,* and Helen Hayes was named best supporting actress for *Airport.* Miss Hayes, a best actress Oscar winner in 1931-32, became the first actor or actress to receive Academy Awards in the two categories honoring performers. The Beatles also became Academy Award winners, for their original song score for *Let It Be.*

The telecast was produced for the Academy by Robert E. Wise, and aired over NBC-TV for the first time in eleven years, produced and directed for the network by Richard Dunlap. Award presentation and hosting duties were handled by thirty-two different "Friends of Oscar," including Merle Oberon, Steve McQueen, Jeanne Moreau, Bob Hope, Maggie Smith, Walter Matthau, Joan Blondell and the first Oscar winner, Janet Gaynor. Ingmar Bergman was voted the 1970 Irving G. Thalberg Memorial Award, Frank Sinatra received the Jean Hersholt Humanitarian Award and honorary Oscars went to two motion picture legends "for their superlative and distinguished service in the making of motion pictures:" Lillian Gish and Orson Welles.

***Best Actress:* Glenda Jackson** *as Gudrun Brangwen in* Women in Love *(United Artists; directed by Ken Russell). Glenda Jackson was a powerful, fascinating newcomer to film audiences when she first appeared as D.H. Lawrence's ill-fated Gudrun, at once vulnerable, domineering, confident, brutal and always memorable, caught in a tragic affair with a gruff, earthy coal-mining executive (Oliver Reed, left, with Jackson). She created her own unique niche as a screen actress, won the Academy Award and, three years later, won a second one for 1973's* A Touch of Class. *She also received nominations in 1971 for* Sunday Bloody Sunday *and in 1975 for* Hedda.

Best Picture: Patton *(20th Century-Fox; produced by Frank McCarthy);* **Best Director: Franklin J. Schaffner** *and* **Best Actor: George C. Scott** *as Gen. George S. Patton, Jr. (above) in* Patton. *Producer McCarthy began in 1951 trying to ignite interest in a screen biography of World War II's flamboyant General Patton, but the project generated no interest for eighteen years, until it received the green light from 20th Century-Fox. In its final form, it turned out to be* a brilliant film and a riveting examination of a controversial soldier in wartime, following Patton from 1943 in North Africa when he assumed command of the Second Army, to 1945, just before he died in an auto accident. George C. Scott dominated the film as the complex man—dedicated but disobedient, merciless but compassionate, persevering and swaggering—and Patton *ultimately received seven Academy* Awards, including ones for story and screenplay, art direction, sound and film editing. Expected to be an extremely tough sell in a world preoccupied with the pros and cons of America's involvement in the then-current Vietnam war, this drama about a World War II tyrant turned out not only to be well respected by critics but a popular attraction with the ticket-buying public as well.

PICTURE

AIRPORT, Hunter, Universal. Produced by Ross Hunter.
FIVE EASY PIECES, BBS Productions, Columbia. Produced by Bob Rafelson and Richard Wechsler.
LOVE STORY, Paramount. Produced by Howard G. Minsky.
M*A*S*H, Aspen, 20th Century-Fox. Produced by Ingo Preminger.
*****PATTON,** 20th Century-Fox. Produced by Frank McCarthy.

ACTOR

MELVYN DOUGLAS in *I Never Sang for My Father,* Jamel, Columbia.
JAMES EARL JONES in *The Great White Hope,* Turman, 20th Century-Fox.
JACK NICHOLSON in *Five Easy Pieces,* BBS Productions, Columbia.
RYAN O'NEAL in *Love Story,* Paramount.
*****GEORGE C. SCOTT** in *Patton,* 20th Century-Fox.

ACTRESS

JANE ALEXANDER in *The Great White Hope,* Turman, 20th Century-Fox.
*****GLENDA JACKSON** in *Women in Love,* Kramer-Rosen, UA.
ALI MacGRAW in *Love Story,* Paramount.
SARAH MILES in *Ryan's Daughter,* Faraway, M-G-M.
CARRIE SNODGRESS in *Diary of a Mad Housewife,* Perry, Universal.

SUPPORTING ACTOR

RICHARD CASTELLANO in *Lovers and Other Strangers,* ABC Pictures, Cinerama.
CHIEF DAN GEORGE in *Little Big Man,* Hiller-Stock-bridge, Cinema Center Films/National General.
GENE HACKMAN in *I Never Sang for My Father,* Jamel, Columbia.
JOHN MARLEY in *Love Story,* Paramount.
*****JOHN MILLS** in *Ryan's Daughter,* Faraway, M-G-M.

SUPPORTING ACTRESS

KAREN BLACK in *Five Easy Pieces,* BBS Productions, Columbia.
LEE GRANT in *The Landlord,* Mirisch-Carter, UA.
*****HELEN HAYES** in *Airport,* Hunter, Universal.
SALLY KELLERMAN in *M*A*S*H,* Aspen, 20th Century-Fox.
MAUREEN STAPLETON in *Airport,* Hunter, Universal.

DIRECTING

FELLINI SATYRICON, Frimaldi, UA (Italian). Federico Fellini.
LOVE STORY, Paramount. Arthur Hiller.
M*A*S*H, Aspen, 20th Century-Fox. Robert Altman.
*****PATTON,** 20th Century-Fox. Franklin J. Schaffner.
WOMEN IN LOVE, Kramer-Rosen, UA. Ken Russell.

WRITING

(Screenplay—based on material from another medium)

AIRPORT, Hunter, Universal. George Seaton.
I NEVER SANG FOR MY FATHER, Jamel, Columbia. Robert Anderson.
LOVERS AND OTHER STRANGERS, ABC Pictures, Cinerama. Renee Taylor, Joseph Bologna and David Zelag Goodman.
*****M*A*S*H,** Aspen, 20th Century-Fox. Ring Lardner, Jr.
WOMEN IN LOVE, Kramer-Rosen, UA. Larry Kramer.

(Story and Screenplay—based on factual material or material not previously published or produced)

FIVE EASY PIECES, BBS Prods., Columbia. Bob Rafelson and Adrien Joyce.
JOE, Cannon Group, Cannon Releasing. Norman Wexler.
LOVE STORY, Paramount. Erich Segal.
MY NIGHT AT MAUD'S, Pathe Contemporary (French). Eric Rohmer.
*****PATTON,** 20th Century-Fox. Francis Ford Coppola and Edmund H. North.

CINEMATOGRAPHY

AIRPORT, Hunter, Universal. Ernest Laszlo.
PATTON, 20th Century-Fox. Fred Koenekamp.
*****RYAN'S DAUGHTER,** Faraway Prods., M-G-M. Freddie Young.
TORA! TORA! TORA!, 20th Century-Fox. Charles F. Wheeler, Osami Furuya, Sinsaku Himeda and Masamichi Satoh.
WOMEN IN LOVE, Kramer-Rosen, UA. Billy Williams.

ART DIRECTION-SET DECORATION

AIRPORT, Hunter, Universal. Alexander Golitzen and E. Preston Ames; Jack D. Moore and Mickey S. Michaels.
THE MOLLY MAGUIRES, Tamm Prods., Paramount. Tambi Larsen; Darrell Silvera.
*****PATTON,** 20th Century-Fox. Urie McCleary and Gil Parrondo; Antonio Mateos and Pierre-Louis Thevenet.
SCROOGE, Waterbury Films, Cinema Center Films, National General. Terry Marsh and Bob Cartwright; Pamela Cornell.
TORA! TORA! TORA!, 20th Century-Fox. Jack Martin Smith, Yoshiro Muraki, Richard Day and Taizoh Kawashima; Walter M. Scott, Norman Rockett and Carl Biddiscombe.

COSTUME DESIGN

AIRPORT, Hunter, Universal. Edith Head.
*****CROMWELL,** Irving Allen, Columbia. Nino Novarese.
DARLING LILI, Geoffrey Prods., Paramount. Donald Brooks and Jack Bear.
THE HAWAIIANS, Mirisch, UA. Bill Thomas.
SCROOGE, Waterbury Films, Cinema Center Films, National General. Margaret Furse.

SOUND

AIRPORT, Hunter, Universal. Ronald Pierce and David Moriarty.
*****PATTON,** 20th Century-Fox. Douglas Williams and Don Bassman.
RYAN'S DAUGHTER, Faraway Prods., M-G-M. Gordon K. McCallum and John Bramall.
TORA! TORA! TORA!, 20th Century-Fox. Murray Spivack and Herman Lewis.
WOODSTOCK, Wadleigh-Maurice. Warner Bros. Dan Wallin and Larry Johnson.

FILM EDITING

AIRPORT, Hunter, Universal. Stuart Gilmore.
M*A*S*H, Aspen, 20th Century-Fox. Danford B. Greene.
*****PATTON,** 20th Century-Fox. Hugh S. Fowler.
TORA! TORA! TORA!, 20th Century-Fox. James E. Newcom, Pembroke J. Herring and Inoue Chikaya.
WOODSTOCK, Wadleigh-Maurice, Warner Bros. Thelma Schoonmaker.

Best Supporting Actress: **Helen Hayes** *as Ada Quonsett in* Airport *(Universal; directed by George Seaton). Helen Hayes hadn't made a film in the 14 years since 1956's* Anastasia *when she signed on as the elderly stowaway in* Airport, *inadvertently on a jet flight with a psychopathic bomber among its passengers. A previous Academy winner as best actress of 1931-32, she became the first performer to win Oscars in both the leading and supporting acting categories.* Airport *spawned a series of subsequent movies which used the original film's title and formula, and kept MCA-Universal stockholders smiling for several seasons.*

Best Supporting Actor: **John Mills** *as Michael in* Ryan's Daughter *(M-G-M; directed by David Lean). Mills (at right, center, with Trevor Howard and Leo McKern) played a gentle but misshapen village mute in David Lean's epic drama, set during the 1916 Irish Revolution and filmed in Ireland and Africa. It was Mill's fifth performance under Lean's direction, and he became the second member of his acting family honored by the Academy; daughter Hayley had won an honorary award as a juvenile performer in 1960.*

M*A*S*H *(20th Century-Fox; produced by Ingo Preminger) was made by director Robert Altman in a snappy 42 days and was a series of adventures and pranks unraveling around a* *Military Army Surgical Hospital behind the battle lines in Korea. The cast included Donald Sutherland, Elliott Gould, Sally Kellerman, Robert Duvall, Michael Murphy, Gary* *Burghoff and Bud Cort and it won the Academy Award for Ring Lardner Jr.'s screenplay. Later, it also became the basis for a hugely successful television series.*

SPECIAL VISUAL EFFECTS

PATTON, 20th Century-Fox. Alex Weldon.
*TORA! TORA! TORA!, 20th Century-Fox. A.D. Flowers and L.B. Abbott.

MUSIC

(Song)

*FOR ALL WE KNOW (*Lovers and Other Strangers*, ABC Pictures, Cinerama); Music by Fred Karlin. Lyrics by Robb Royer and James Griffin aka Robb Wilson and Arthur James.
PIECES OF DREAMS (*Pieces of Dreams*, RFB Enterprises, UA); Music by Michel Legrand. Lyrics by Alan and Marilyn Bergman.
THANK YOU VERY MUCH (*Scrooge*, Waterbury Films, Cinema Center Films, National General); Music and Lyrics by Leslie Bricusse.
TILL LOVE TOUCHES YOUR LIFE (*Madron*, Four Star-Excelsior Releasing); Music by Riz Ortolani. Lyrics by Arthur Hamilton.
WHISTLING AWAY THE DARK (*Darling Lili*, Geoffrey Prods., Paramount); Music by Henry Mancini. Lyrics by Johnny Mercer.

(Original Score)

AIRPORT, Hunter, Universal. Alfred Newman.
CROMWELL, Irving Allen, Columbia. Frank Cordell.
*LOVE STORY, Paramount. Francis Lai.
PATTON, 20th Century-Fox. Jerry Goldsmith.
SUNFLOWER, Sostar Prod., Avco Embassy. Henry Mancini.

(Original Song Score)

THE BABY MAKER, Robert Wise Prod., National General. Fred Karlin and Tylwyth Kymry.
A BOY NAMED CHARLIE BROWN, Mendelson-Melendez, Cinema Center Films, National General. Rod McKuen, John Scott Trotter, Bill Melendez, Al Shean and Vince Guaraldi.
DARLING LILI, Geoffrey Prods., Paramount. Henry Mancini and Johnny Mercer.
*LET IT BE, Beatles-Apple Prods., UA. The Beatles.
SCROOGE, Waterbury Films, Cinema Center Films, National General. Leslie Bricusse, Ian Fraser and Herbert W. Spencer.

SHORT SUBJECTS

(Cartoons)

THE FURTHER ADVENTURES OF UNCLE SAM: PART TWO, Haboush Company, Goldstone Films. Robert Mitchell and Dale Case, producers.
*IS IT ALWAYS RIGHT TO BE RIGHT?, Stephen Bosustow Prods., Schoenfeld Films. Nick Bosustow, producer.

THE SHEPHERD, Cameron Guess and Associates, Brandon Films. Cameron Guess, producer.

(Live Action Subjects)

*THE RESURRECTION OF BRONCHO BILLY, University of Southern California, Dept. of Cinema, Universal. John Longenecker, producer.
SHUT UP...I'M CRYING, Robert Siegler Prods., Schoenfeld Films. Robert Siegler, producer.
STICKY MY FINGERS...FLEET MY FEET, American Film Institute, Schoenfeld Films. John Hancock, producer.

DOCUMENTARY

(Short Subjects)

THE GIFTS, Richter-McBride Prods. for The Water Quality Office of the Environmental Protection Agency. Robert McBride, producer.
*INTERVIEWS WITH MY LAI VETERANS, Laser Film Corp. Joseph Strick, producer.
A LONG WAY FROM NOWHERE, Robert Aller Prods. Bob Aller, producer.
OISIN, An Aengue Film. Vivien and Patrick Carey, producers.
TIME IS RUNNING OUT, Gesellschaft fur bidende Filme, Horst Dallmayr and Robert Menegoz, producers.

(Features)

CHARIOTS OF THE GODS, Terra-Filmkunst GmbH. Dr. Harald Reinl, producer.
JACK JOHNSON, The Big Fights. Jim Jacobs, producer.
KING: A FILMED RECORD...MONTGOMERY TO MEMPHIS, Commonwealth United Prod. Ely Landau, producer.
SAY GOODBYE, A Wolper Prod. David H. Vowell, producer.
*WOODSTOCK, Wadleigh-Maurice, Warner Bros. Bob Maurice, producer.

FOREIGN LANGUAGE FILM

FIRST LOVE (Switzerland).
HOA-BINH (France).
*INVESTIGATION OF A CITIZEN ABOVE SUSPICION (Italy).
PAIX SUR LES CHAMPS (Belgium).
TRISTANA (Spain).

HONORARY AND OTHER AWARDS

TO LILLIAN GISH for superlative artistry and for distinguished contribution to the progress of motion pictures. (statuette)
TO ORSON WELLES for superlative artistry and versatility in the creation of motion pictures. (statuette)

1970 IRVING G. THALBERG MEMORIAL AWARD

TO INGMAR BERGMAN

1970 JEAN HERSHOLT HUMANITARIAN AWARD

TO FRANK SINATRA

SCIENTIFIC OR TECHNICAL

CLASS I (statuette)

None.

CLASS II (plaque)

LEONARD SOKOLOW and EDWARD H. REICHARD of Consolidated Film Industries for the concept and engineering of the Color Proofing Printer for motion pictures.

CLASS III (citation)

SYLVANIA ELECTRIC PRODUCTS, INC.;
B.J. LOSMANDY;
EASTMAN KODAK COMPANY and PHOTO ELECTRONICS CORPORATION;
ELECTRO SOUND INCORPORATED.

*INDICATES WINNER

1971
The Forty-Fourth Year

harles Chaplin, just a week away from his eighty-third birthday, returned to Hollywood for the first time in twenty years to receive the Academy's honorary Oscar, officially for "the incalculable effect he has had in making motion pictures the art form of the century." Out of respect, no other special awards were voted for 1971, and the presentation to Chaplin by Jack Lemmon was the evening's last order of business on April 10, 1972, at the Dorothy Chandler Pavilion of the Los Angeles Music Center. Chaplin had received a special Academy Award at the very first Oscar ceremony (for achievement during 1927-28) but had not been honored subsequently for his work. It was undeniably a high point of the evening, and brought unusually heavy international attention to the Academy and the Oscars.

The French Connection received the most Academy Awards of any 1971 film, winning five, including best picture, best actor (Gene Hackman) and best director (William Friedkin); *Fiddler on the Roof* won three awards, *The Last Picture Show* garnered two (for best supporting actor Ben Johnson and best supporting actress Cloris Leachman), *Nicholas and Alexandra* received two, and seven others won one each. Jane Fonda was chosen the year's best actress for her performance in *Klute,* and Italy's *The Garden of the Finzi-Continis* was named best foreign language film. Isaac Hayes' "Theme From Shaft" was the Oscar winner for best

song, and was the subject of spectacular staging by Ron Field during the night's telecast on NBC-TV.

Howard W. Koch produced the telecast for the Academy, Robert Finkel was the executive producer for the network and Marty Pasetta directed the telecast. Helen Hayes, Alan King, Sammy Davis, Jr. and Jack Lemmon shared master of ceremony turns, and presenters included Frank Capra, Tennessee Williams, Raquel Welch, Betty Grable and Dick Haymes.

Among the highlights of the night, in addition to Hollywood's welcome back to the legendary Chaplin, was a knockout opening number called "Lights, Camera, Action." It was choreographed by Ron Field, written by Billy Barnes, interpreted by Joel Grey and took a swooping musical look at Hollywood's past.

216

Best Picture: **The French Connection** *(20th Century-Fox; produced by Philip D'Antoni),* **Best Director:** **William Friedkin** *and (right)* **Best Actor:** **Gene Hackman** *as Detective Jimmy Doyle in* The French Connection. *From the best-selling book by Robin Moore, based on experiences of two real-life detectives (Eddie "Popeye" Egan and Sonny Grosso) who stumbled onto a case in 1962 which involved the seizure of $32 million in heroin smuggled into New York from Marseilles, this was action moviemaking at its best. Also among the best: Hackman's performance as the colorful Egan (here named Doyle). The film's giant success inspired a 1975 sequel,* French Connection II, *again starring Hackman.*

Fiddler on the Roof *(United Artists; produced by Norman Jewison) won three Oscars: for cinematography, music scoring and sound. At the time it was put on film, Fiddler had become Broadway's all-time longest-running stage play; on film, Topol* (above) played the likeable milkman named Tevye who had his hands full with five marriageable daughters, a sharp-tongued wife, and a lame horse.*

Best Actress: Jane Fonda *as Bree in* Klute *(Warner Bros.; directed by Alan Pakula). Previously nominated in 1969 as best actress for* They Shoot Horses, Don't They?, *actress Fonda won for her skillful portrait of a worn-but-wise Manhattan call girl threatened by an unknown, would-be killer. Donald Sutherland played the title role of Klute, the detective who helped Bree set a trap for her shadowy assailant. Fonda (above) won a second Oscar as best actress for 1978's* Coming Home.

Nicholas and Alexandra *(Columbia; produced by Sam Spiegel) was based on the mammoth historical novel by Robert K. Massie and starred (dancing, above) Michael Jayston and Janet Suzman as the ill-fated Russian royalty whose family* was executed on July 16, 1918. Sumptuously produced and tastefully made, it won two Academy Awards, for art direction/set decoration and for costume design.*

Best Supporting Actor: Ben Johnson *as Sam the Lion in* The Last Picture Show *(Columbia; directed by Peter Bogdanovich). Johnson, a 30-year veteran of cinematic sagebrush wars, had his finest film role to date as a graying old cowboy in a decaying Texas town, circa 1951, who owned the local pool hall, cafe and movie theater, and befriended teenagers Sonny (Timothy Bottoms) and Duane (Jeff Bridges). Said Bogdanovich: "Having Ben Johnson in the picture was having the real thing."*

PICTURE

A CLOCKWORK ORANGE, Hawk Films, Warner Bros. Produced by Stanley Kubrick.
FIDDLER ON THE ROOF, Mirisch-Cartier, UA. Produced by Norman Jewison.
*THE FRENCH CONNECTION, D'Antoni-Schine-Moore, 20th Century-Fox. Produced by Philip D'Antoni.
THE LAST PICTURE SHOW, BBS Productions, Columbia. Produced by Stephen J. Friedman.
NICHOLAS AND ALEXANDRA, Horizon, Columbia. Produced by Sam Spiegel.

ACTOR

PETER FINCH in *Sunday Bloody Sunday,* Janni, UA.
*GENE HACKMAN in *The French Connection,* D'Antoni-Schine-Moore, 20th Century-Fox.
WALTER MATTHAU in *Kotch,* ABC Pictures, Cinerama.
GEORGE C. SCOTT in *The Hospital,* Gottfried-Chayefsky-Hiller, UA.
TOPOL in *Fiddler on the Roof,* Mirisch-Cartier, UA.

ACTRESS

JULIE CHRISTIE in *McCabe & Mrs. Miller,* Altman-Foster, Warner Bros.
*JANE FONDA in *Klute,* Gus, Warner Bros.
GLENDA JACKSON in *Sunday Bloody Sunday,* Janni, UA.
VANESSA REDGRAVE in *Mary, Queen of Scots,* Wallis, Universal.
JANET SUZMAN in *Nicholas and Alexandra,* Horizon, Columbia.

SUPPORTING ACTOR

JEFF BRIDGES in *The Last Picture Show,* BBS Productions, Columbia.
LEONARD FREY in *Fiddler on the Roof,* Mirisch-Cartier, UA.
RICHARD JAECKEL in *Sometimes a Great Notion,* Newman-Foreman, Universal.
*BEN JOHNSON in *The Last Picture Show,* BBS Productions, Columbia.
ROY SCHEIDER in *The French Connection,* D'Antoni-Schine-Moore, 20th Century-Fox.

SUPPORTING ACTRESS

ELLEN BURSTYN in *The Last Picture Show,* BBS Productions, Columbia.
BARBARA HARRIS in *Who Is Harry Kellerman and Why Is He Saying Those Terrible Things about Me?,* Cinema Center Films/National General.
*CLORIS LEACHMAN in *The Last Picture Show,* BBS Productions, Columbia.
MARGARET LEIGHTON in *The Go-Between,* World Film Series, Columbia.
ANN-MARGRET in *Carnal Knowledge,* Icarus, Avco Embassy.

DIRECTING

A CLOCKWORK ORANGE, Hawk Films, Warner Bros. Stanley Kubrick.
FIDDLER ON THE ROOF, Mirisch-Cartier, UA. Norman Jewison.
*THE FRENCH CONNECTION, 20th Century-Fox. William Friedkin.
THE LAST PICTURE SHOW, BBS Prods., Columbia. Peter Bogdanovich.
SUNDAY BLOODY SUNDAY, Janni, UA. John Schlesinger.

WRITING

(Screenplay—based on material from another medium)
A CLOCKWORK ORANGE, Hawk Films, Warner Bros. Stanley Kubrick.
THE CONFORMIST, Paramount (Italian). Bernardo Bertolucci.
*THE FRENCH CONNECTION, 20th Century-Fox. Ernest Tidyman.
THE GARDEN OF THE FINZI-CONTINIS, Cinema V (Italian). Ugo Pirro and Vittorio Bonicelli.
THE LAST PICTURE SHOW, BBS Prods., Columbia. Larry McMurtry and Peter Bogdanovich.

(Story and Screenplay—based on factual material or material not previously published or produced)
*THE HOSPITAL, Gottfried-Chayefsky-Hiller, UA. Paddy Chayefsky.
INVESTIGATION OF A CITIZEN ABOVE SUSPICION, Columbia (Italian). Elio Petri and Ugo Pirro.
KLUTE, Gus Prod. Warner Bros. Andy and Dave Lewis.
SUMMER OF '42, Mulligan-Roth, Warner Bros. Herman Raucher.
SUNDAY BLOODY SUNDAY, Janni, UA. Penelope Gilliatt.

ART DIRECTION-SET DECORATION

THE ANDROMEDA STRAIN, Robert Wise Prods., Universal. Boris Leven and William Tuntke; Ruby Levitt.
BEDKNOBS AND BROOMSTICKS, Disney, Buena Vista. John B. Mansbridge and Peter Ellenshaw; Emile Kuri and Hal Gausman.
FIDDLER ON THE ROOF, Mirisch-Cartier, UA. Robert Boyle and Michael Stringer; Peter Lamont.
MARY, QUEEN OF SCOTS, Wallis, Universal. Terence Marsh and Robert Cartwright; Peter Howitt.
*NICHOLAS AND ALEXANDRA, Horizon, Columbia. John Box, Ernest Archer, Jack Maxsted and Gil Parrondo; Vernon Dixon.

COSTUME DESIGN

BEDKNOBS AND BROOMSTICKS, Disney, Buena Vista. Bill Thomas.
DEATH IN VENICE, Alfa Cinematografica-P.E.C.F., Warner Bros. Piero Tosi.
MARY QUEEN OF SCOTS, Wallis, Universal. Margaret Furse.
*NICHOLAS AND ALEXANDRA, Horizon, Columbia. Yvonne Blake and Antonio Castillo.
WHAT'S THE MATTER WITH HELEN? Filmways-Raymax, UA. Morton Haack.

SOUND

DIAMONDS ARE FOREVER, Broccoli-Saltzman, UA. Gordon K. McCallum, John Mitchell and Alfred J. Overton.
*FIDDLER ON THE ROOF, Mirisch-Cartier, UA. Gordon K. McCallum and David Hildyard.
THE FRENCH CONNECTION, 20th Century-Fox. Theodore Soderberg and Christopher Newman.
KOTCH, ABC Pictures, Cinerama. Richard Portman and Jack Solomon.
MARY, QUEEN OF SCOTS, Wallis, Universal. Bob Jones and John Aldred.

FILM EDITING

THE ANDROMEDA STRAIN, Robert Wise Prod., Universal. Stuart Gilmore and John W. Holmes.
A CLOCKWORK ORANGE, Hawk Films, Warner Bros. Bill Butler.
*THE FRENCH CONNECTION, 20th Century-Fox. Jerry Greenberg.
KOTCH, ABC Pictures, Cinerama. Ralph E. Winters.
SUMMER OF '42, Mulligan-Roth, Warner Bros. Folmar Blangsted.

CINEMATOGRAPHY

*FIDDLER ON THE ROOF, Mirisch-Cartier, UA. Oswald Morris.
THE FRENCH CONNECTION, 20th Century-Fox. Owen Roizman.
THE LAST PICTURE SHOW, BBS Prods., Columbia. Robert Surtees.
NICHOLAS AND ALEXANDRA, Horizon, Columbia. Freddie Young.
SUMMER OF '42, Mulligan-Roth, Warner Bros. Robert Surtees.

SHORT SUBJECTS

(New classification: designation of first category changed from 'cartoons' to 'animated films')

(Animated Films)
*THE CRUNCH BIRD, Maxwell-Petok-Petrovich Prods., Regency Films. Ted Petok, producer.
EVOLUTION, National Film Board of Canada, Columbia. Michael Mills, producer.
THE SELFISH GIANT, Potterton Prods., Pyramid Films. Peter Sander and Murray Shostak, producers.

(Live Action Film)
GOOD MORNING, E/G Films, Seymour Borde & Associates. Denny Evans and Ken Greenwald, producers.
THE REHEARSAL, Cinema Verona Prod., Schoenfeld Films. Stephen F. Verona, producer.
*SENTINELS OF SILENCE, Producciones Concord, Paramount. Manuel Arango and Robert Amram, producers.

MUSIC

(Song)
THE AGE OF NOT BELIEVING (*Bedknobs and Broomsticks,* Disney, Buena Vista); Music and Lyrics by Richard M. Sherman and Robert B. Sherman.
ALL HIS CHILDREN (*Sometimes a Great Notion,* Newman-Foreman, Universal); Music by Henry Mancini. Lyrics by Alan and Marilyn Bergman.
BLESS THE BEASTS & CHILDREN (*Bless the Beasts & Children,* Columbia); Music and Lyrics by Barry DeVorzon and Perry Botkin, Jr.
LIFE IS WHAT YOU MAKE IT (*Kotch,* ABC Pictures, Cinerama); Music by Marvin Hamlisch. Lyrics by Johnny Mercer.

Special Honorary Award to **Charles Chaplin** *(above). On the eve of his 83rd birthday, (he was born April 16, 1889), the movies' legendary Charlie-the-Tramp returned to the town he helped create in order to receive an Honorary Oscar from the Academy's Board of Governors. Presented the Oscar by Jack Lemmon (above, on left) Chaplin received a standing ovation from the in-theater audience of 3,200 and, repressing tears, said simply, "Words seem, oh, so futile, so feeble. This is a very emotional moment for me. You are wonderful…sweet people." Then, once more, he donned the Tramp's bowler hat. It was the last visit for Chaplin to the town in which he'd earlier done the work that made him famous, rich, and a symbol of filmmaking genius.*

Best Supporting Actress: **Cloris Leachman** *as Ruth Popper in* The Last Picture Show *(Columbia; directed by Peter Bogdanovich). In her Oscar-winning role, she played the lonely, sexually deprived wife of a small-town coach who stumbles into an affair with one of her husband's high school students (Timothy Bottoms, above with Leachman) and is eventually deserted by him. Says the actress: "I based my characterization on some Ruth Poppers I knew when I was growing up in Des Moines."*

*THEME FROM SHAFT (*Shaft*, M-G-M); Music and Lyrics by Isaac Hayes.

(Original Dramatic Score)

MARY, QUEEN OF SCOTS, Wallis, Universal. John Barry.
NICHOLAS AND ALEXANDRA, Horizon, Columbia. Richard Rodney Bennett.
SHAFT, M-G-M. Isaac Hayes.
STRAW DOGS, ABC Pictures, Cinerama. Jerry Fielding.
*SUMMER OF '42, Mulligan-Roth, Warner Bros. Michel Legrand.

(Scoring: Adaptation and Original Song Score)

BEDKNOBS AND BROOMSTICKS, Disney, Buena Vista. Richard M. Sherman, Robert B. Sherman and Irwin Kostal.
THE BOY FRIEND, Russflix, M-G-M. Peter Maxwell Davies and Peter Greenwell.
*FIDDLER ON THE ROOF, Mirisch-Cartier, UA. John Williams.
TCHAIKOVSKY, Dimitri Tiomkin-Mosfilm Studios (U.S.S.R.). Dimitri Tiomkin.
WILLY WONKA AND THE CHOCOLATE FACTORY, Wolper, Paramount. Leslie Bricusse, Anthony Newley and Walter Scharf.

SPECIAL VISUAL EFFECTS

(Not given as an annual Award after this year)

*BEDKNOBS AND BROOMSTICKS, Disney, Buena Vista. Alan Maley, Eustace Lycett and Danny Lee.
WHEN DINOSAURS RULED THE EARTH, Hammer, Warner Bros. Jim Danforth and Roger Dicken.

DOCUMENTARY

(Short Subjects)

ADVENTURES IN PERCEPTION, Han van Gelder Filmproduktie for Netherlands Information Service. Han van Gelder, producer.
ART IS…, Henry Strauss Associates for Sears Roebuck Foundation. Julian Krainin and DeWitt L. Sage, Jr., producers.
THE NUMBERS START WITH THE RIVER, A WH Picture for U.S. Information Agency. Donald Wrye, producer.
*SENTINELS OF SILENCE, Producciones Concord, Paramount. Manuel Arango and Robert Amram, producers.
SOMEBODY WAITING, Snider Prods., for University of California Medical Film Library. Hal Riney, Dick Snider and Sherwood Omens, producers.

(Features)

ALASKA WILDERNESS LAKE, Alan Landsburg Prods. Alan Landsburg, producer.
*THE HELLSTROM CHRONICLE, David L. Wolper, Cinema V. Walon Green, producer.
ON ANY SUNDAY, Brown-Solar, Cinema V. Bruce Brown, producer.
THE RA EXPEDITIONS, Swedish Broadcasting Company, Interwest Film Corp. Lennart Ehrenborg and Thor Heyerdahl, producers.
THE SORROW AND THE PITY, Cinema V (French). Marcel Ophuls, producer.

FOREIGN LANGUAGE FILM

DODES'KA-DEN (Japan)
THE EMIGRANTS (Sweden)
*THE GARDEN OF THE FINZI-CONTINIS (Italy)
THE POLICEMAN (Israel)
TCHAIKOVSKY (U.S.S.R.)

HONORARY AND OTHER AWARDS

TO CHARLES CHAPLIN for the incalculable effect he has had in making motion pictures the art form of this century. (statuette)

1971 IRVING G. THALBERG MEMORIAL AWARD

None given this year.

1971 JEAN HERSHOLT HUMANITARIAN AWARD

None given this year.

SCIENTIFIC OR TECHNICAL

CLASS I (statuette)
None.

CLASS II (plaque)

JOHN N. WILKINSON of Optical Radiation Corporation for the development and engineering of a system of xenon arc lamphouses for motion picture projection.

CLASS III (citation)

THOMAS JEFFERSON HUTCHINSON, JAMES R. ROCHESTER and **FENTON HAMILTON;**
PHOTO RESEARCH, A Division of Kollmorgen Corporation;
ROBERT D. AUGUSTE and **CINEMA PRODUCTS CO.;**
PRODUCERS SERVICE CORPORATION and **CONSOLIDATED FILM INDUSTRIES;** and to **CINEMA RESEARCH CORPORATION** and **RESEARCH PRODUCTS, INC.;**
CINEMA PRODUCTS CO.

*INDICATES WINNER

1972
The Forty-Fifth Year

The Godfather and Cabaret dominated the 1972 Academy Awards presentations, March 27, 1973, held for the fifth year at the Dorothy Chandler Pavilion of the Los Angeles Music Center and telecast on NBC-TV. Cabaret won eight awards, including best actress (Liza Minelli), best director (Bob Fosse) and best supporting actor (Joel Grey), more than any other picture in Academy history which didn't go on to also win the best picture statuette. That award went to The Godfather, along with awards for best actor (Marlon Brando) and best screenplay (Mario Puzo and Francis Ford Coppola). Brando rejected the award—his second as best actor—and had his reasons read by a young Indian girl, Sacheen Littlefeather, later identified as an actress named Maria Cruz. His primary objections were to the industry's treatment of Indians in films, on TV and in movie reruns.

The awards were produced by Howard W. Koch and directed by Marty Pasetta. M.C.s were Carol Burnett, Michael Caine, Charlton Heston and Rock Hudson; Heston fell victim to a flat tire on his way to the ceremony and arrived fifteen minutes after his first show entrance was scheduled, so Clint Eastwood was grabbed out of the audience to briefly do stand-in duty.

Among the musical segments was an opulent opening, "Make a Little Magic," written by Billy Barnes, choreographed by Carl Jablonski and featuring Angela Lansbury, in the tradition of bygone Hollywood musical production numbers. A musical salute to Walt Disney Studios' fiftieth anniversary, featured, among others, the durable Mickey Mouse.

The Jean Hersholt Humanitarian Award went to Rosalind Russell, and other honorary awards went to the late Edward G. Robinson who had died just two months earlier, industry veteran Charles Boren and to The Poseidon Adventure for its special visual effects. Eileen Heckart was named best supporting actress for Butterflies Are Free, France's The Discreet Charm of the Bourgeoisie was selected as best foreign language film. And, as in the preceding year, Charles Chaplin was once again an Academy Award winner. Along with the late Raymond Rasch and Larry Russell, he won the 1972 best original dramatic score award for Limelight, a movie made in 1952. Its belated eligibility was due to the fact the film had never been shown in Los Angeles until 1972, and only then qualified for award consideration.

There was also a new rule in 1972 related to short subjects and documentary eligibility. For the first time, short subjects which also qualified as documentary short subjects could compete in either category, but not in both, as in previous years. The choice of area consideration was to be designated by the producers involved at the time the entry was submitted to the Academy for preliminary voting.

220

Best Supporting Actress: **Eileen Heckart** *as Mrs. Baker in* Butterflies Are Free *(Columbia; directed by Milton Katselas). Re-creating her original 1969 Broadway role, she played a Hillsborough mother who has difficulty cutting the umbilical cord from a blind son (Edward Albert, right, with Heckart) who wants to live in his own San Francisco apartment and attempt to make it without Mama but with a saucy neighbor played by Goldie Hawn. It was Heckart's second Academy nomination (the first one: 1956's* The Bad Seed*), and her first win.*

Best Director: Bob Fosse, *and (above)* Best Actress: Liza Minnelli *as Sally Bowles and* Best Supporting Actor: Joel Grey *as the master of ceremonies in* Cabaret *(ABC Pictures/Allied Artists; produced by Cy Feuer). Cabaret was the newest reincarnation of Christopher Isherwood's original* Berlin Stories *(earlier made into a 1951 play and a 1955 movie both called* I Am a Camera*) and focused on five lives tangled together in pre-Hitler Germany of the 1930s. Liza Minnelli was the "divinely decadent" and available cabaret singer with green fingernails, saucer eyes and flexible morals; Joel Grey recreated his Broadway role of the white-faced, rouge-lipped M.C. of the Kit Kat Klub who symbolized the decay which helped the Nazi menace gain momentum.*

221

Best Picture: The Godfather *(Paramount; produced by Albert Ruddy) and* Best Actor: Marlon Brando *as Don Vito Corleone in* The Godfather. *Mario Puzo's powerful and popular novel about organized crime made a bang-up movie, rich in detail and performances, as it inspected the fall of a powerful Cosa Nostra chieftain (Brando, above) and the concurrent rise to power of his son, a fresh-faced Ivy Leaguer who becomes a cool, lethal hood (played by Al Pacino). Brando, at age 46, was almost unrecognizable as the elderly Italian Don, and he dominated the film, which included in its cast Robert Duvall, Talia Shire, Morgana King, James Caan, Diane Keaton, Richard Conte, Sterling Hayden and others, directed by Francis Ford Coppola. Two years later, there was a sequel:* The Godfather Part II, *which also became an Academy Award-winning best picture of the year.*

Nominations 1972

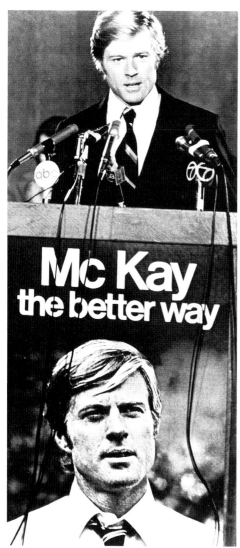

The Candidate *(Warner Bros.; produced by Walter Coblenz) starred Robert Redford (above) as a political candidate caught between idealism and the realities of the political system of the 1970s. It won writer Jeremy Larner an Oscar for its story and screenplay.*

Limelight *(Columbia; produced by Charles Chaplin) was a true Oscar oddity. Starring Charles Chaplin (right, applying makeup as Buster Keaton watches), it was made by Chaplin in 1952 and shown in only a few cities at that time via United Artists. Its limited distribution was primarily due to the political climate at the time as it affected Chaplin. The film never played Los Angeles until 20 years later, when it thereby became eligible for Academy Award consideration. And not only did it garner a nomination in the music category, for original dramatic score, it went on to win two decades after its production.*

PICTURE

CABARET, ABC Pictures, Allied Artists. Produced by Cy Feuer.
DELIVERANCE, Warner Bros. Produced by John Boorman.
THE EMIGRANTS, Svensk Filmindustri, Warner Bros. (Swedish). Produced by Bengt Forslund.
*****THE GODFATHER,** Ruddy, Paramount. Produced by Albert S. Ruddy.
SOUNDER, Radnitz/Mattel, 20th Century-Fox. Produced by Robert B. Radnitz.

ACTOR

*****MARLON BRANDO** in *The Godfather,* Ruddy, Paramount.
MICHAEL CAINE in *Sleuth,* Palomar, 20th Century-Fox.
LAURENCE OLIVIER in *Sleuth,* Palomar, 20th Century-Fox.
PETER O'TOOLE in *The Ruling Class,* Keep Films, Avco Embassy.
PAUL WINFIELD in *Sounder,* Radnitz/Mattel, 20th Century-Fox.

ACTRESS

*****LIZA MINNELLI** in *Cabaret,* ABC Pictures, Allied Artists.
DIANA ROSS in *Lady Sings the Blues,* Motown-Weston-Furie, Paramount.
MAGGIE SMITH in *Travels with My Aunt,* Fryer, M-G-M.
CICELY TYSON in *Sounder,* Radnitz/Mattel, 20th Century-Fox.
LIV ULLMANN in *The Emigrants,* Svensk Filmindustri, Warner Bros. (Swedish).

SUPPORTING ACTOR

EDDIE ALBERT in *The Heartbreak Kid,* Palomar, 20th Century-Fox.
JAMES CAAN in *The Godfather,* Ruddy, Paramount.
ROBERT DUVALL in *The Godfather,* Ruddy, Paramount.
*****JOEL GREY** in *Cabaret,* ABC Pictures, Allied Artists.
AL PACINO in *The Godfather,* Ruddy, Paramount.

SUPPORTING ACTRESS

JEANNIE BERLIN in *The Heartbreak Kid,* Palomar, 20th Century-Fox.
*****EILEEN HECKART** in *Butterflies Are Free,* Frankovich, Columbia.
GERALDINE PAGE in *Pete 'N' Tillie,* Ritt-Epstein, Universal.
SUSAN TYRRELL in *Fat City,* Rastar, Columbia.
SHELLEY WINTERS in *The Poseidon Adventure,* Irwin Allen, 20th Century-Fox.

DIRECTING

*****CABARET,** ABC Pictures, Allied Artists. Bob Fosse.
DELIVERANCE, Warner Bros. John Boorman.
THE EMIGRANTS, Svensk Filmindustri, Warner Bros. (Swedish). Jan Troell.
THE GODFATHER, Ruddy, Paramount. Francis Ford Coppola.
SLEUTH, Palomar, 20th Century-Fox. Joseph L. Mankiewicz.

WRITING

(Screenplay—based on material from another medium)

CABARET, ABC Pictures, Allied Artists. Jay Allen.
THE EMIGRANTS, Svensk Filmindustri, Warner Bros. (Swedish). Jan Troell and Bengt Forslund.
*****THE GODFATHER,** Ruddy, Paramount. Mario Puzo and Francis Ford Coppola.
PETE 'N' TILLIE, Ritt-Epstein, Universal. Julius J. Epstein.
SOUNDER, Radnitz/Mattel, 20th Century-Fox. Lonne Elder, III.

(Story and Screenplay—based on factual material or material not previously published or produced)

*****THE CANDIDATE,** Redford-Ritchie, Warner Bros. Jeremy Larner.
THE DISCREET CHARM OF THE BOURGEOISIE, Silberman, 20th Century-Fox (French). Luis Bunuel and Jean-Claude Carriere.
LADY SINGS THE BLUES, Motown-Weston-Furie, Paramount. Terence McCloy, Chris Clark and Suzanne de Passe.
MURMUR OF THE HEART, Continental Distributing (French). Louis Malle.
YOUNG WINSTON, Open Road Films, Columbia. Carl Foreman.

CINEMATOGRAPHY

BUTTERFLIES ARE FREE, Frankovich, Columbia. Charles B. Lang.
*****CABARET,** ABC Pictures, Allied Artists. Geoffrey Unsworth.
THE POSEIDON ADVENTURE, Irwin Allen, 20th Century-Fox. Harold E. Stine.
"1776," Jack L. Warner, Columbia. Harry Stradling, Jr.
TRAVELS WITH MY AUNT, Fryer, M-G-M. Douglas Slocombe.

ART DIRECTION-SET DECORATION

*****CABARET,** ABC Pictures, Allied Artists. Rolf Zehetbauer and Jurgen Kiebach. Herbert Strabel.
LADY SINGS THE BLUES, Motown-Weston-Furie, Paramount. Carl Anderson; Reg Allen.
THE POSEIDON ADVENTURE, Irwin Allen, 20th Century-Fox. William Creber; Raphael Bretton.
TRAVELS WITH MY AUNT, Fryer, M-G-M. John Box, Gil Parrondo and Robert W. Laing.
YOUNG WINSTON, Open Road Films, Columbia. Don Ashton, Geoffrey Drake, John Graysmark and William Hutchinson; Peter James.

COSTUME DESIGN

THE GODFATHER, Ruddy, Paramount. Anna Hill Johnstone.
LADY SINGS THE BLUES, Motown-Weston-Furie, Paramount. Bob Mackie, Ray Aghayan and Norma Koch.
THE POSEIDON ADVENTURE, Irwin Allen, 20th Century-Fox. Paul Zastupnevich.
*****TRAVELS WITH MY AUNT,** Fryer, M-G-M. Anthony Powell.
YOUNG WINSTON, Open Road Films, Columbia. Anthony Mendleson.

Best Foreign Language Film: **The Discreet Charm of the Bourgeoisie** *from France (above). Produced by Serge Silberman,* Discreet *was a black comedy through which 72-year-old cinemagician Luis Bunuel as director took jabs* at everything from the upper classes and the Church, to South American politics and military inanities, all interspersed with surrealistic explorations of four diverse people who arrive at a rich couple's home for dinner, only to discover it is the wrong day. The cast included Fernando Rey, Delphine Seyrig, Stephane Audran and Jean-Pierre Cassel.

SOUND

BUTTERFLIES ARE FREE, Frankovich, Columbia. Arthur Piantadosi and Charles Knight.
*CABARET, ABC Pictures, Allied Artists. Robert Knudson and David Hildyard.
THE CANDIDATE, Redford-Ritchie, Warner Bros. Richard Portman and Gene Cantamessa.
THE GODFATHER, Ruddy, Paramount. Bud Grenzbach, Richard Portman and Christopher Newman.
THE POSEIDON ADVENTURE, Irwin Allen, 20th Century-Fox. Theodore Soderberg and Herman Lewis.

FILM EDITING

*CABARET, ABC Pictures, Allied Artists. David Bretherton.
DELIVERANCE, Warner Bros. Tom Priestley.
THE GODFATHER, Ruddy, Paramount. William Reynolds and Peter Zinner.
THE HOT ROCK, Landers-Roberts, 20th Century-Fox. Frank P. Keller and Fred W. Berger.
THE POSEIDON ADVENTURE, Irwin Allen, 20th Century-Fox. Harold F. Kress.

SHORT SUBJECTS

(Animated Films)

*A CHRISTMAS CAROL, American Broadcasting Company Film Services. Richard Williams, producer.
KAMA SUTRA RIDES AGAIN, Lion International Films. Bob Godfrey, producer.
TUP TUP, Zagreb Film-Corona Cinematografica, Manson Distributing. Nedejiko Dragic, producer.

(Live Action Films)

FROG STORY, Gidron Productions, Schoenfeld Films. Ron Satlof and Ray Gideon, producers.
*NORMAN ROCKWELL'S WORLD...AN AMERICAN DREAM, Concepts Unlimited, Columbia. Richard Barclay, producer.
SOLO, Pyramid Films, UA. David Adams, producer.

DOCUMENTARY

(Short Subjects)

HUNDERTWASSER'S RAINY DAY, Argos Films-Schamoni Film Prod. Peter Schamoni, producer.
K-Z, Nexus Films. Giorgio Treves, producer.
SELLING OUT, Unit Productions Films. Tadeusz Jaworski, producer.
*THIS TINY WORLD, A Charles Huguenot van der Linden Production. Charles and Martina Huguenot van der Linden, producers.
THE TIDE OF TRAFFIC, BP-Greenpark. Humphrey Swingler, producer.

(Features)

APE AND SUPER-APE, Netherlands Ministry of Culture, Recreation and Social Welfare. Bert Haanstra, producer.
MALCOLM X, Warner Bros. Marvin Worth and Arnold Perl, producers.

MANSON, Merrick International. Robert Hendrickson and Laurence Merrick, producers.
*MARJOE, Cinema X, Cinema 5, Ltd. Howard Smith and Sarah Kernochan, producers.
THE SILENT REVOLUTION, Leonaris Films. Eckehard Munck, producer.

FOREIGN LANGUAGE FILM

THE DAWNS ARE QUIET (U.S.S.R.).
*THE DISCREET CHARM OF THE BOURGEOISIE (France).
I LOVE YOU ROSA (Israel).
MY DEAREST SENORITA (Spain).
THE NEW LAND (Sweden).

MUSIC

(Song)

BEN (*Ben*, Bing Crosby Prods., Cinerama); Music by Walter Scharf. Lyrics by Don Black.
COME FOLLOW, FOLLOW ME (*The Little Ark*, Radnitz, Cinema Center Films, National General); Music by Fred Karlin. Lyrics by Marsha Karlin.
MARMALADE, MOLASSES & HONEY (*The Life and Times of Judge Roy Bean*, First Artists, National General); Music by Maurice Jarre. Lyrics by Marilyn and Alan Bergman.
*THE MORNING AFTER, (*The Poseidon Adventure*, Irwin Allen, 20th Century-Fox); Music and Lyrics by Al Kasha and Joel Hirschhorn.
STRANGE ARE THE WAYS OF LOVE (*The Stepmother*, Crown International); Music by Sammy Fain. Lyrics by Paul Francis Webster.

(Original Dramatic Score)

IMAGES, Hemdale-Lion's Gate Films, Columbia. John Williams.
*LIMELIGHT, Charles Chaplin, Columbia. Charles Chaplin, Raymond Rasch and Larry Russell.
NAPOLEON AND SAMANTHA, Disney, Buena Vista. Buddy Baker.
THE POSEIDON ADVENTURE, Irwin Allen, 20th Century-Fox. John Williams.
SLEUTH, Palomar Pictures, 20th Century-Fox. John Addison.
(Note: *The Godfather* score, composed by Nino Rota, was originally announced as one of the five official nominees, but was later declared ineligible and withdrawn when it was disclosed portions of the composition had previously been used in Rota's score for the 1958 Italian film *Fortunella*. Additionally, *Limelight*, made in 1952, was belatedly eligible for 1972 consideration because it had not previously been shown in a Los Angeles theater as Academy rules require.)

(Scoring: Adaptation and Original Song Score)

*CABARET, ABC Pictures, Allied Artists. Ralph Burns.
LADY SINGS THE BLUES, Motown-Weston-Furie, Paramount. Gil Askey.
MAN OF LA MANCHA, PEA Produzioni Europee Associate Prod., UA. Laurence Rosenthal.

SPECIAL ACHIEVEMENT AWARD

(New classification)
For Visual Effects: L.B. ABBOTT and A.D. FLOWERS for *The Poseidon Adventure,* Irwin Allen, 20th Century-Fox.

HONORARY AND OTHER AWARDS

TO CHARLES BOREN, Leader for 38 years of the industry's enlightened labor relations and architect of its policy of non-discrimination. With the respect and affection of all who work in films. (statuette)
TO EDWARD G. ROBINSON who achieved greatness as a player, a patron of the arts and a dedicated citizen...in sum, a Renaissance man. From his friends in the industry he loves. (statuette)

1972 IRVING G. THALBERG MEMORIAL AWARD

None given this year.

1972 JEAN HERSHOLT HUMANITARIAN AWARD

TO ROSALIND RUSSELL

SCIENTIFIC OR TECHNICAL

CLASS I (statuette)

None.

CLASS II (plaque)

JOSEPH E. BLUTH for research and development in the field of electronic photography and transfer of video tape to motion picture film.
EDWARD H. REICHARD and HOWARD T. LaZARE of Consolidated Film Industries, and EDWARD EFRON of IBM for the engineering of a computerized light valve monitoring system for motion picture printing.
PANAVISION INCORPORATED for the development and engineering of the Panaflex motion picture camera.

CLASS III (citation)

PHOTO RESEARCH, a Division of Kollmorgen Corporation, and PCS TECHNOLOGY INC., Acme Products Division;
CARTER EQUIPMENT COMPANY, INC. and RAMTRONICS;
DAVID DEGENKOLB, HARRY LARSON, MANFRED MICHELSON and FRED SCOBEY of Deluxe General Inc.;
JIRO MUKAI and RYUSHO HIROSE of Canon, Inc. and WILTON R. HOLM of the AMPTP Motion Picture and Television Research Center.;
PHILIP V. PALMQUIST and LEONARD L. OLSON of the 3M Company, and FRANK P. CLARK of the AMPTP Motion Picture and Television Research Center.
E.H. GEISSLER and G.M. BERGGREN of Wil-Kin Inc.

*INDICATES WINNER

223

1973
The Forty-Sixth Year

"'m the living proof someone can wait forty-one years to be unselfish," Katharine Hepburn told the Academy Awards audience April 2, 1974, gathered to honor 1973 motion picture achievements. Miss Hepburn had won three Academy Awards as best actress in the past—an Oscar record—but had never attended an Academy presentation before. She put aside her own dislike of public appearances to appear at the Dorothy Chandler Pavilion of the Los Angeles Music Center and present the Academy's Irving G. Thalberg Memorial Award to her friend producer Lawrence Weingarten. Wearing a black Mao-type pantsuit, she told the surprised, delighted audience, "I'm so glad no one called out, "It's about time!" Susan Hayward also made a rare public appearance which, unknown at the time, would be her final one.

The Sting won a total of seven 1973 Academy Awards, including best picture, best director (George Roy Hill), and best costume design (Edith Head, her eighth Oscar, an industry record among women). Jack Lemmon was named best actor for *Save the Tiger;* it was his second Oscar, but his first in that category, having won previously as the best supporting actor of 1955 in *Mister Roberts.* Glenda Jackson also became a two-time Academy Award winner, named best actress for *A Touch of Class,* after winning three years before in that same category. John Houseman, age seventy-one and best known as a distinguished producer, was chosen best supporting actor in *The Paper Chase,* and Tatum O'Neal, age ten, became the youngest winner ever in a competitive Academy Awards category when she was named best supporting actress in *Paper Moon.*

Marvin Hamlisch set a new Oscar record when he won all three of the year's music awards: best song (with Alan and Marilyn Bergman), best original dramatic score, and best scoring. Special awards went to comedian Groucho Marx and French film curator Henri Langlois, and Lew Wasserman of Universal/MCA received the Jean Hersholt Humanitarian Award.

Jack Haley, Jr. produced the show, Marty Pasetta directed for NBC and hosting duties were handled by John Huston, Diana Ross, Burt Reynolds and David Niven. Liza Minnelli performed a vivacious opening number, "Oscar," written especially for the night by Fred Ebb and John Kanter, staged by Broadway's Ron Field.

Moments before David Niven announced Elizabeth Taylor as one of the evening's presenters, there was another Oscar first: a streaker, fully stripped, unexpectedly charged across the large Music Center stage. "Isn't it fascinating," quipped Niven, "to think that probably the only laugh that man will ever get in his life is by stripping off his clothes and showing his shortcomings." Later identified as thirty-three-year-old Robert Opal, he made news again five years later, when he was found murdered in San Francisco.

224

Best Picture: **The Sting** *(Universal; produced by Tony Bill, Michael and Julia Phillips) and* **Best Director: George Roy Hill** *for* The Sting. *The movie starred (at right, facing each other) Paul Newman and Robert Redford and was lightweight, impish and diverting; It was also a movie-movie that brilliantly accomplished exactly what it set out to do: entertain. The Sting not only possessed a soundtrack bouncing with ragtime tunes by the late Scott Joplin (adapted by Marvin Hamlisch) but contained enough plot twists, deceptions, counteractions and complications by screenwriter David S. Ward to fill a dozen films, as con men Redford and Newman get revenge on a racketeer (Shaw) by fleecing him in a phony off-track horse-betting ploy. Set in the Depression days, the film opened with Universal Studio's old trademark logo of that era, which hadn't been used in decades.*

Best Actress: Glenda Jackson *as Vicki Allessio in* A Touch of Class *(Avco Embassy; directed by Melvin Frank). Three years after winning her first Academy Award (for 1970's dramatic* Women in Love*), Glenda Jackson was again a winner, this time in a comedy role, as a partially liberated, London-based business woman of the 1970s, laboriously trying to have a light love affair with an American fellow who's married (George Segal, left, toasting with Jackson). It was a win that surprised everyone, including actress Jackson who later said, "I gave both my Oscars to my mother in Cheshire. It's not that I don't treasure them, but if I display them in my own home, I'm afraid people will think I'm big-headed."*

225

Best Actor: Jack Lemmon *as Harry Stoner (left) in* Save the Tiger *(Paramount; directed by John G. Avildsen). Lemmon had been a Supporting Oscar winner in 1955 for* Mister Roberts *and a nominee in 1959 (for* Some Like It Hot*), 1960 (for* The Apartment*), and 1962 (for* Days of Wine and Roses*). He would subsequently be nominated in 1979 (for* The China Syndrome*), 1980 (for* Tribute*) and 1982 (for* Missing*). As* Tiger's *Harry Stoner, he won his second Award, but his first as best actor, playing a middle-aged, disillusioned businessman living through a day of crisis in which he comes to grips with the realization his great American dream has gone far astray. The film was a pet project of producer-writer Steve Shagan and, said Lemmon, "I'm very proud of the film we finally got. I also believe very deeply in what it has to say."*

Best Supporting Actor: John Houseman *as Professor Kingsfield (above, standing) in* The Paper Chase *(20th Century-Fox; directed by James Bridges). Houseman, age 71, had acted in only one previous film (1964's* Seven Days in May*) but between 1945-1962 he had produced 18 important features (including* The Bad and the Beautiful, Julius Ceasar *and* Lust for Life*) and was also a stalwart contributor to the legitimate theater. He stepped into his* Paper Chase *role when previously signed James Mason had to bow out, and then won the Oscar for his playing of an academic dictator in Harvard's law school, a man who looms over his students (including Timothy Bottoms, Edward Herrmann and James Naughton) like a quietly arrogant Goliath. Houseman later replayed his role of Kingsfield in a much-respected* Paper Chase *television series.*

226

PICTURE

AMERICAN GRAFFITI, Universal-Lucasfilm, Ltd.-Coppola Co. Prod., Universal. Francis Ford Coppola, producer, Gary Kurtz, co-producer.
CRIES AND WHISPERS, Svenska Filminstitutet-Cinematograph AB Prod., New World Pictures. Ingmar Bergman, producer.
THE EXORCIST, Hoya Prods., Warner Bros. William Peter Blatty, producer.
***THE STING,** Universal-Bill/Phillips-George Roy Hill Film Prod., Zanuck/Brown Presentation, Universal. Tony Bill, Michael and Julia Phillips, producers.
A TOUCH OF CLASS, Brut Prods., Avco Embassy, Melvin Frank, producer.

ACTOR

MARLON BRANDO in *Last Tango in Paris,* UA.
***JACK LEMMON** in *Save the Tiger,* Filmways-Jalem-Cirandinha, Paramount.
JACK NICHOLSON in *The Last Detail,* Acrobat, Columbia.
AL PACINO in *Serpico,* De Laurentiis, Paramount.
ROBERT REDFORD in *The Sting,* Bill/Phillips-Hill, Zanuck/Brown, Universal.

ACTRESS

ELLEN BURSTYN in *The Exorcist,* Hoya, Warner Bros.
***GLENDA JACKSON** in *A Touch of Class,* Brut, Avco Embassy.
MARSHA MASON in *Cinderella Liberty,* Sanford, 20th Century-Fox.
BARBRA STREISAND in *The Way We Were,* Rastar, Columbia.
JOANNE WOODWARD in *Summer Wishes, Winter Dreams,* Rastar, Columbia.

SUPPORTING ACTOR

VINCENT GARDENIA in *Bang the Drum Slowly,* Rosenfield, Paramount.
JACK GILFORD in *Save the Tiger,* Filmways-Jalem-Cirandinha, Paramount.
***JOHN HOUSEMAN** in *The Paper Chase,* Thompson-Paul, 20th Century Fox.
JASON MILLER in *The Exorcist,* Hoya, Warner Bros.
RANDY QUAID in *The Last Detail,* Acrobat, Columbia.

SUPPORTING ACTRESS

LINDA BLAIR in *The Exorcist,* Hoya, Warner Bros.
CANDY CLARK in *American Graffiti,* Lucasfilm-Coppola, Universal.
MADELINE KAHN in *Paper Moon,* Directors Company, Paramount.
***TATUM O'NEAL** in *Paper Moon,* Directors Company, Paramount.
SYLVIA SIDNEY in *Summer Wishes, Winter Dreams,* Rastar, Columbia.

DIRECTING

AMERICAN GRAFFITI, Lucasfilm/Coppola Company, Universal. George Lucas.
CRIES AND WHISPERS, New World Pictures (Swedish). Ingmar Bergman.
THE EXORCIST, Hoya Prods., Warner Bros. William Friedkin.
LAST TANGO IN PARIS, UA. Bernardo Bertolucci.
***THE STING,** Bill/Phillips-Hill-Zanuck/Brown, Universal. George Roy Hill.

WRITING

(Best Screenplay—based on material from another medium)
***THE EXORCIST,** Hoya Prods., Warner Bros. William Peter Blatty.
THE LAST DETAIL, Acrobat Films, Columbia. Robert Towne.
THE PAPER CHASE, Thompson-Paul Prods., 20th Century-Fox. James Bridges.
PAPER MOON, Directors Company, Paramount. Alvin Sargent.
SERPICO, De Laurentiis, Paramount. Waldo Salt and Norman Wexler.

(Best Story and Screenplay—based on factual material or material not previously published or produced)
AMERICAN GRAFFITI, Lucasfilm/Coppola Company, Universal. George Lucas, Gloria Katz and Willard Huyck.
CRIES AND WHISPERS, New World Pictures (Swedish). Ingmar Bergman.
SAVE THE TIGER, Filmways-Jalem-Cirandinha, Paramount. Steve Shagan.
***THE STING,** Bill/Phillips-Hill-Zanuck/Brown, Universal. David S. Ward.
A TOUCH OF CLASS, Brut, Avco Embassy. Melvin Frank and Jack Rose.

CINEMATOGRAPHY

***CRIES AND WHISPERS,** New World Pictures (Swedish). Sven Nykvist.
THE EXORCIST, Hoya Prods., Warner Bros. Owen Roizman.
JONATHAN LIVINGSTON SEAGULL, Bartlett, Paramount. Jack Couffer.
THE STING, Bill/Phillips-Hill-Zanuck/Brown, Universal. Robert Surtees.
THE WAY WE WERE, Rastar, Columbia. Harry Stradling, Jr.

ART DIRECTION-SET DECORATION

BROTHER SUN SISTER MOON, Euro International-Vic Film Ltd., Paramount. Lorenzo Mongiardino and Gianni Quaranta; Carmelo Patrono.
THE EXORCIST, Hoya Prods., Warner Bros. Bill Malley; Jerry Wunderlich.
***THE STING,** Bill/Phillips-Hill-Zanuck/Brown, Universal. Henry Bumstead; James Payne.
TOM SAWYER, Jacobs, Reader's Digest, UA. Philip Jefferies; Robert de Vestel.
THE WAY WE WERE, Rastar, Columbia. Stephen Grimes; William Kiernan.

COSTUME DESIGN

CRIES AND WHISPERS, New World Pictures (Swedish). Marik Vos.
LUDWIG, Mega Film S.p.A. Prod., M-G-M. Piero Tosi.
***THE STING,** Bill/Phillips-Hill-Zanuck/Brown, Universal. Edith Head.
TOM SAWYER, Jacobs, Reader's Digest, UA. Donfeld.
THE WAY WE WERE, Rastar, Columbia. Dorothy Jeakins and Moss Mabry.

SOUND

THE DAY OF THE DOLPHIN, Icarus, Avco Embassy. Richard Portman and Lawrence O. Jost.
***THE EXORCIST,** Hoya Prods., Warner Bros. Robert Knudson and Chris Newman.
THE PAPER CHASE, Thompson-Paul Prods., 20th Century-Fox. Donald O. Mitchell and Lawrence O. Jost.
PAPER MOON, Directors Company, Paramount. Richard Portman and Les Fresholtz.
THE STING, Bill/Phillips-Hill-Zanuck/Brown, Universal. Ronald K. Pierce and Robert Bertrand.

FILM EDITING

AMERICAN GRAFFITI, Lucasfilm/Coppola Company, Universal. Verna Fields and Marcia Lucas.
THE DAY OF THE JACKAL, Warwick Films, Universal. Ralph Kemplen.
THE EXORCIST, Hoya Prods., Warner Bros. Jordan Leondopoulos, Bud Smith, Evan Lottman and Norman Gay.
JONATHAN LIVINGSTON SEAGULL, Bartlett, Paramount. Frank P. Keller and James Galloway.
***THE STING,** Bill/Phillips-Hill-Zanuck/Brown, Universal. William Reynolds.

MUSIC

(Song)
ALL THAT LOVE WENT TO WASTE (*A Touch of Class,* Brut, Avco Embassy); Music by George Barrie. Lyrics by Sammy Cahn.
LIVE AND LET DIE (*Live and Let Die,* Eon, UA); Music and Lyrics by Paul and Linda McCartney.
LOVE (*Robin Hood,* Disney, Buena Vista); Music by George Bruns. Lyrics by Floyd Huddleston.
***THE WAY WE WERE** (*The Way We Were,* Rastar, Columbia); Music by Marvin Hamlisch. Lyrics by Alan and Marilyn Bergman.
NICE TO BE AROUND (*Cinderella Liberty,* Sanford Prod., 20th Century-Fox); Music by John Williams. Lyrics by Paul Williams.

(Best Original Dramatic Score)
CINDERELLA LIBERTY, Sanford Prod., 20th Century-Fox. John Williams.
THE DAY OF THE DOLPHIN, Icarus Prods., Avco Embassy, Georges Delerue.
PAPILLON, Corona-General Productions, Allied Artists. Jerry Goldsmith.
A TOUCH OF CLASS, Brut, Avco Embassy. John Cameron.
***THE WAY WE WERE,** Rastar, Columbia. Marvin Hamlisch.

(Best Scoring: Original Song Score and/or Adaptation)
JESUS CHRIST SUPERSTAR, Jewison-Stigwood, Universal. Andre Previn, Herbert Spencer and Andrew Lloyd Webber.
***THE STING,** Bill/Phillips-Hill-Zanuck/Brown, Universal. Marvin Hamlisch.
TOM SAWYER, Jacobs, Reader's Digest, UA. Richard M. Sherman, Robert B. Sherman and John Williams.

Best Foreign Language Film: Day for Night *from France, directed by François Truffaut (at right with Jacqueline Bisset). Truffaut, a great movie fan as well as moviemaker, turned his cameras on the filmmaking process itself in* Day for Night, *observing all the funny, serious, self-indulgent, maddening details that can happen during the shooting of a movie, from the traumas of an aging actress no longer able to remember her lines, to the horizontal activities off-camera of various crew and cast members. His expert cast included Bisset, Valentina Cortesa, Jean-Pierre Aumont, Jean-Pierre Leaud, Nathalie Baye and Truffaut himself.*

SHORT SUBJECTS

(Animated Films)

*FRANK FILM, Frank Mouris Production, Frank Mouris, producer.
THE LEGEND OF JOHN HENRY, Bosustow-Pyramid Films. Nick Bosustow and David Adams, producers.
PULCINELLA, Luzzati-Gianini Prod. Emanuele Luzzati and Giulio Gianini, producers.

(Live Action Films)

*THE BOLERO, Allan Miller Production. Allan Miller and William Fertik, producers.
CLOCKMAKER, James Street Prods. Richard Gayer, producer.
LIFE TIMES NINE, Insight Prods. Pen Densham and John Watson producers.

DOCUMENTARY

(Short Subjects)

BACKGROUND, D'Avino and Fucci-Stone Prods. Carmen D'Avino, producer.
CHILDREN AT WORK, (Paisti Ag Obair), Gael-Linn Films. Louis Marcus, producer.
CHRISTO'S VALLEY CURTAIN, Maysles Films. Albert and David Maysles, producers.
FOUR STONES FOR KANEMITSU, A Tamarind Prod. Terry Sanders and June Wayne, producers.
*PRINCETON: A SEARCH FOR ANSWERS, Krainin-Sage Prods. Julian Krainin and DeWitt L. Sage, Jr., producers.

(Features)

ALWAYS A NEW BEGINNING, Goodell Motion Pictures, John D. Goodell, producer.
BATTLE OF BERLIN, Chronos Film. Bengt von zur Muehlen, producer.
*THE GREAT AMERICAN COWBOY, Merrill-Rodeo Film Prods. Kieth Merrill, producer.
JOURNEY TO THE OUTER LIMITS, National Geographic Society and Wolper Prods. Alex Grasshoff, producer.
WALLS OF FIRE, Mentor Prods. Gertrude Ross Marks and Edmund F. Penney, producers.

FOREIGN LANGUAGE FILM

*DAY FOR NIGHT (France).
THE HOUSE ON CHELOUCHE STREET (Israel).
L'INVITATION (Switzerland).
THE PEDESTRIAN (Federal Republic of West Germany).
TURKISH DELIGHT (The Netherlands).

HONORARY AND OTHER AWARDS

TO HENRI LANGLOIS for his devotion to the art of film, his massive contributions in preserving its past and his unswerving faith in its future. (statuette)
TO GROUCHO MARX in recognition of his brilliant creativity and for the unequalled achievements of the Marx Brothers in the art of motion picture comedy. (statuette)

SPECIAL ACHIEVEMENT AWARD

None given this year.

Best Supporting Actress: Tatum O'Neal *as Addie Pray (above) in* Paper Moon *(Paramount; directed by Peter Bogdanovich). Tatum, age 10 and a first-time performer, co-starred with her real-life father, Ryan O'Neal, as a street-wise, cigarette-puffing moppet in the Depression days of the 1930s who teams up with a dandy; together they con their way into billfolds all across Kansas and Missouri, bilking without a blink. With her win, Tatum became the youngest recipient to date to be voted an Oscar in a regular Academy Awards category.*

1973 IRVING G. THALBERG MEMORIAL AWARD
TO LAWRENCE WEINGARTEN

1973 JEAN HERSHOLT HUMANITARIAN AWARD
TO LEW WASSERMAN

SCIENTIFIC OR TECHNICAL

CLASS I (statuette)
None.

CLASS II (plaque)
JOACHIM GERB and ERICH KASTNER of The Arnold and Richter Company for the development and engineering of the Arriflex 35BL motion-picture camera.

MAGNA-TECH ELECTRONIC CO., INC. for the engineering and development of a high-speed re-recording system for motion-picture production.
WILLIAM W. VALLIANT of PSC Technology Inc., HOWARD F. OTT of Eastman Kodak, Company, and GERRY DIEBOLD of The Richmark Camera Service Inc. for the development of a liquid-gate system for motion picture printers.
HAROLD A. SCHEIB, CLIFFORD H. ELLIS and ROGER W. BANKS of Research Products Incorporated for the concept and engineering of the Model 2101 optical printer for motion picture optical effects.

CLASS III (citation)
ROSCO LABORATORIES, INC.;
RICHARD H. VETTER of the Todd-AO Corporation.

*INDICATES WINNER

otion picture showmanship was fully evident during 1974 via a number of so-called "disaster" epics (or, according to some, "survival" pictures), most of them laden with famous faces, spectacular special effects and a nerve-wracking premise which audiences could vicariously enjoy without leaving the safety of their theater seats. When 1974 Academy Awards for achievement were handed out, April 8, 1975, at the Dorothy Chandler Pavilion of the Los Angeles Music Center, two of the "disaster" genre were well represented: *The Towering Inferno* with three technical awards, and *Earthquake* with two, including a special achievement award for special effects.

The most conspicuous films of the night, however, had less to do with awesome effects than they did with powerhouse melodrama: *Chinatown* and *The Godfather Part II,* both from Paramount Studios, were each nominated for eleven Oscars. When the award totals were tallied, *Chinatown* won one (for Robert Towne's best original screenplay), and *The Godfather Part II* received six, including best picture, best director (Francis Ford Coppola), best supporting actor (Robert De Niro) and best adapted screenplay (Coppola and Mario Puzo). It thus became the first motion picture sequel to win the Academy's best picture statuette, just as the original, *The Godfather,* had done two years before.

In other categories, Art Carney was named best actor (for *Harry and Tonto*), Ellen Burstyn was chosen best actress (for *Alice Doesn't Live Here Anymore*) and Ingrid Bergman won her third Academy Award, as best supporting actress in *Murder on the Orient Express,* the first time she had been honored in that division. (She had previously won as best actress in 1945 and in 1956.) She also became the first Academy winner to devote an acceptance speech to praising the virtues of a competitor. After complimenting the performance of fellow nominee Valentina Cortese in *Day for Night,* she charmingly complained, "Now I'm her rival, and I don't like it at all. Please forgive me, Valentina. I didn't mean to (win)..." Special awards went to directors Howard Hawks and Jean Renoir, and Italy's *Amarcord* was named best foreign language film.

The ceremony was again telecast on NBC, with a quartet of masters of ceremonies in charge: Sammy Davis, Jr., Bob Hope, Shirley MacLaine and Frank Sinatra. Howard W. Koch produced the show, and Marty Pasetta directed.

During the program, there was some controversy over the political implications in a telegram read by producer Bert Schneider when he accepted an Oscar for his best documentary feature *Hearts and Minds,* a film about the Vietnamese war; before the show ended, an impromptu disclaimer in the name of the Academy was read from the stage by Frank Sinatra. Since Article II of the Academy's bylaws specifically states that "The Academy is expressly pro-

Best Picture: The Godfather Part II *(Paramount; produced by Francis Ford Coppola) and* **Best Supporting Actor:** **Robert De Niro** *as Vito Corleone (right) in* The Godfather Part II. *A mammoth and magnificent follow-up to 1972's Academy Award-winning* The Godfather, *it showed the rise to power of the young Vito Corleone, played by De Niro, and the decline of his son, Michael (played by Al Pacino) decades later, shifting back and forth in time between the two generations and forming a prologue and epilogue around that first* Godfather *feature.* Godfather II *became the first sequel to an Oscar-winning film to duplicate the award success of its predecessor and, by virtue of De Niro's own Academy Award, it also marked the first time two different actors (De Niro, and Marlon Brando as Vito Corleone in the original* Godfather) *received Oscars for playing different age spans of the same character.*

hibited from concerning itself with economic, political or labor issues," it was thought best to make the announcement, as Sinatra did, that "The Academy is not responsible for any political references on this program, and we are sorry that they had to take place this evening."

Best Actor: Art Carney *as Harry in* Harry and Tonto *(20th Century-Fox; directed by Paul Mazursky). Harry and Tonto was a series of gentle vignettes with 55-year-old Art Carney as a 72-year-old widower who gets evicted from his New York apartment and decides to open up his shrinking world by traveling cross-country with his cat, Tonto; at the end of their journey, he loses Tonto to old age but has regained his own vitality and self-esteem. It was one of the year's most pleasant movie surprises with an unusual theme for the blood-and-thunder 1970s: life is available to anyone, at any age, who wants it. Among Carney's coplayers in the film was Ellen Burstyn, who had her own triumph, and her own Oscar, in 1974 with* Alice Doesn't Live Here Anymore.

229

Best Actress: Ellen Burstyn *as Alice Hyatt in* Alice Doesn't Live Here Anymore *(Warner Bros.; directed by Martin Scorsese). The script had been rejected by several producers and stars before Ellen Burstyn found it, and played the spunky new widow who works her way across the Southwest, with a 12-year-old son in tow, singing in dives and working in hash houses as she attempts to reconstruct her life. Burstyn, left, with Kris Kristofferson, had earlier been nominated for Academy Awards in 1971 as supporting actress in* The Last Picture Show *and in 1973 as best actress in* The Exorcist, *and later received additional nominations in 1978 and 1980. Alice later became the basis for a successful weekly television series starring Linda Lavin.*

Best Director: Francis Ford Coppola *for* The Godfather Part II. *Coppola (at right, in striped shirt) won his first Academy Award at age 31, for co-writing the story and screenplay of 1970's* Patton; *two years later, he won another for co-writing the screenplay of* The Godfather *(1972), and he received an additional nomination as 1972's best director. In 1974, there was more Coppola everywhere; he won three Academy Awards (as producer of the year's best picture, as director, and as co-author of the screenplay of* The Godfather Part II*) and was also nominated twice for* The Conversation *(as producer, and as sole author of its original screenplay). A busy year, a talented creator.*

Best Supporting Actress: Ingrid Bergman *as Gretta Ohlsson (right, listening to Lauren Bacall) in* Murder on the Orient Express *(Paramount; directed by Sidney Lumet). Ingrid Bergman's contribution to the film was short, but a prime example of why the Academy instigated supporting awards categories in the first place: to properly honor well-played smaller roles and gem-like junior performances which add so immeasurably to motion pictures. As a mousey, nervous Swedish missionary riding on the Orient Express, she basically had but one lengthy scene, interrogated by detective Hercule Poirot (Albert Finney) about an unsolved murder in their midst. It was a true cameo performance, and it brought her a third Academy Award, her first in the supporting division. Earlier, she won for* Gaslight *(1944) and* Anastasia *(1956).*

230

PICTURE

CHINATOWN, Evans, Paramount. Produced by Robert Evans.

THE CONVERSATION, Directors Company, Paramount. Produced by Francis Ford Coppola.

* THE GODFATHER PART II, Coppola Company, Paramount. Produced by Francis Ford Coppola; Co-Produced by Gray Frederickson and Fred Roos.

LENNY, Worth, UA. Produced by Marvin Worth.

THE TOWERING INFERNO, Irwin Allen, 20th Century-Fox/Warner Bros. Produced by Irwin Allen.

ACTOR

*ART CARNEY in *Harry and Tonto,* 20th Century-Fox.

ALBERT FINNEY in *Murder on the Orient Express,* G.W. Films, Paramount.

DUSTIN HOFFMAN in *Lenny,* Worth, UA.

JACK NICHOLSON in *Chinatown,* Evans, Paramount.

AL PACINO in *The Godfather Part II,* Coppola Company, Paramount.

ACTRESS

*ELLEN BURSTYN in *Alice Doesn't Live Here Anymore,* Warner Bros.

DIAHANN CARROLL in *Claudine,* Third World Cinema-Selznick-Pine, 20th Century-Fox.

FAYE DUNAWAY in *Chinatown,* Evans, Paramount.

VALERIE PERRINE in *Lenny,* Worth, UA.

GENA ROWLANDS in *A Woman under the Influence,* Faces International.

SUPPORTING ACTOR

FRED ASTAIRE in *The Towering Inferno,* Irwin Allen, 20th Century-Fox/Warner Bros.

JEFF BRIDGES in *Thunderbolt and Lightfoot,* Malpaso, UA.

*ROBERT DE NIRO in *The Godfather Part II,* Coppola Company, Paramount.

MICHAEL V. GAZZO in *The Godfather Part II,* Coppola Company, Paramount.

LEE STRASBERG in *The Godfather Part II,* Coppola Company, Paramount.

SUPPORTING ACTRESS

*INGRID BERGMAN in *Murder on the Orient Express,* G.W. Films, Paramount.

VALENTINA CORTESE in *Day for Night* (French), Warner Bros.

MADELINE KAHN in *Blazing Saddles,* Warner Bros.

DIANE LADD in *Alice Doesn't Live Here Anymore,* Warner Bros.

TALIA SHIRE in *The Godfather Part II,* Coppola Company, Paramount.

DIRECTING

CHINATOWN, Robert Evans, Paramount. Roman Polanski.

DAY FOR NIGHT, Warner Bros. (French). François Truffaut.

*THE GODFATHER PART II, Coppola Company.

Paramount. Francis Ford Coppola.
LENNY, Marvin Worth, UA. Bob Fosse.
A WOMAN UNDER THE INFLUENCE, Faces International. John Cassavetes.

WRITING
(New classifications)

(Original Screenplay)
ALICE DOESN'T LIVE HERE ANYMORE, Warner Bros. Robert Getchell.
*CHINATOWN, Robert Evans, Paramount. Robert Towne.
THE CONVERSATION, Directors Company, Paramount. Francis Ford Coppola.
DAY FOR NIGHT, Warner Bros. (French). Francois Truffaut, Jean-Louis Richard and Suzanne Schiffman.
HARRY AND TONTO, 20th Century-Fox. Paul Mazursky and Josh Greenfeld.

(Screenplay Adapted From Other Material)
THE APPRENTICESHIP OF DUDDY KRAVITZ, International Cinemedia Centre, Paramount. Mordecai Richler and Lionel Chetwynd.
*THE GODFATHER PART II, Coppola Company, Paramount. Francis Ford Coppola and Mario Puzo.
LENNY, Marvin Worth, UA. Julian Barry.
MURDER ON THE ORIENT EXPRESS, G.W. Films, Ltd., Paramount. Paul Dehn.
YOUNG FRANKENSTEIN, Gruskoff/Venture Films-Crossbow-Jouer, 20th Century-Fox. Gene Wilder and Mel Brooks.

CINEMATOGRAPHY
CHINATOWN, Robert Evans, Paramount. John A. Alonzo.
EARTHQUAKE, Robson-Filmakers Group, Universal. Philip Lathrop.
LENNY, Marvin Worth, UA. Bruce Surtees.
MURDER ON THE ORIENT EXPRESS, G.W. Films, Ltd., Paramount. Geoffrey Unsworth.
*THE TOWERING INFERNO, Irwin Allen, 20th Century-Fox/Warner Bros. Fred Koenekamp and Joseph Biroc.

ART DIRECTION-
SET DECORATION
CHINATOWN, Robert Evans, Paramount. Richard Sylbert and W. Stewart Campbell; Ruby Levitt.
EARTHQUAKE, Robson-Filmakers Group, Universal. Alexander Golitzen and E. Preston Ames; Frank McKelvy.
*THE GODFATHER PART II, Coppola Company, Paramount. Dean Tavoularis and Angelo Graham; George R. Nelson.
THE ISLAND AT THE TOP OF THE WORLD, Disney, Buena Vista. Peter Ellenshaw, John B. Mansbridge, Walter Tyler and Al Roelofs; Hal Gausman.
THE TOWERING INFERNO, Irwin Allen, 20th Century-Fox/Warner Bros. William Creber and Ward Preston; Raphael Bretton.

COSTUME DESIGN
CHINATOWN, Robert Evans, Paramount. Anthea Sylbert.
DAISY MILLER, Directors Company, Paramount. John Furness.
THE GODFATHER PART II, Coppola Company, Paramount. Theadora Van Runkle.
*THE GREAT GATSBY, David Merrick, Paramount. Theoni V. Aldredge.
MURDER ON THE ORIENT EXPRESS, G.W. Films, Ltd., Paramount. Tony Walton.

SOUND
CHINATOWN, Robert Evans, Paramount. Bud Grenzbach and Larry Jost.
THE CONVERSATION, Directors Company, Paramount. Walter Murch and Arthur Rochester.
*EARTHQUAKE, Robson-Filmakers Group, Universal. Ronald Pierce and Melvin Metcalfe, Sr.
THE TOWERING INFERNO, Irwin Allen, 20th Century-Fox/Warner Bros. Theodore Soderberg and Herman Lewis.
YOUNG FRANKENSTEIN, Gruskoff/Venture Films-Crossbow-Jouer, 20th Century-Fox. Richard Portman and Gene Cantamessa.

FILM EDITING
BLAZING SADDLES, Warner Bros. John C. Howard and Danford Greene.
CHINATOWN, Robert Evans, Paramount. Sam O'Steen.
EARTHQUAKE, Robson-Filmakers Group, Universal. Dorothy Spencer.
THE LONGEST YARD, Ruddy, Paramount. Michael Luciano.
*THE TOWERING INFERNO, Irwin Allen, 20th Century-Fox/Warner Bros. Harold F. Kress and Carl Kress.

MUSIC
(Song)
BENJI'S THEME (I FEEL LOVE) (*Benji*, Mulberry Square); Music by Euel Box. Lyrics by Betty Box.
BLAZING SADDLES (*Blazing Saddles*, Warner Bros.); Music by John Morris. Lyrics by Mel Brooks.
LITTLE PRINCE (*The Little Prince*, Stanley Donen, Paramount); Music by Frederick Loewe. Lyrics by Alan Jay Lerner.
*WE MAY NEVER LOVE LIKE THIS AGAIN (*The Towering Inferno*, Irwin Allen, 20th Century-Fox/Warner Bros.); Music and Lyrics by Al Kasha and Joel Hirschhorn.
WHEREVER LOVE TAKES ME (*Gold*, Avton, Allied Artists); Music by Elmer Bernstein. Lyrics by Don Black.

(Original Dramatic Score)
CHINATOWN, Robert Evans, Paramount. Jerry Goldsmith.
*THE GODFATHER PART II, Coppola Company, Paramount. Nino Rota and Carmine Coppola.
MURDER ON THE ORIENT EXPRESS, G.W. Films, Ltd., Paramount. Richard Rodney Bennett.
SHANKS, William Castle, Paramount. Alex North.
THE TOWERING INFERNO, Irwin Allen, 20th Century-Fox/Warner Bros. John Williams.

(Scoring: Original Song Score and/or Adaptation)
*THE GREAT GATSBY, David Merrick, Paramount. Nelson Riddle.
THE LITTLE PRINCE, Stanley Donen, Paramount. Alan Jay Lerner, Frederick Loewe; Angela Morley and Douglas Gamley.
PHANTOM OF THE PARADISE, Harbor Prods., 20th Century-Fox. Paul Williams and George Aliceson Tipton.

SHORT FILMS
(Previously listed as Short Subjects)

(Animated Films)
*CLOSED MONDAYS, Lighthouse Productions. Will Vinton and Bob Gardiner, producers.
THE FAMILY THAT DWELT APART, National Film Board of Canada. Yvon Mallette and Robert Verrall, producers.
HUNGER, National Film Board of Canada. Peter Foldes and Rene Jodoin, producers.
VOYAGE TO NEXT, Hubley Studio. Faith and John Hubley, producers.
WINNIE THE POOH AND TIGGER TOO, Disney, Buena Vista. Wolfgang Reitherman, producer.

(Live Action Films)
CLIMB, Dewitt Jones Productions. Dewitt Jones, producer.
THE CONCERT, The Black And White Colour Film Company, Ltd. Julian and Claude Chagrin, producers.
*ONE-EYED MEN ARE KINGS, C.A.P.A.C. Productions (Paris). Paul Claudon and Edmond Sechan, producers.
PLANET OCEAN, Graphic Films. George V. Casey, producer.
THE VIOLIN, Sincinkin, Ltd. Andrew Welsh and George Pastic, producers.

DOCUMENTARY
(Short Subjects)
CITY OUT OF WILDERNESS, Francis Thompson Inc. Francis Thompson, producer.
*DON'T, R.A. Films. Robin Lehman, producer.
EXPLORATORIUM, Jon Boorstin Prod. Jon Boorstin, producer.
JOHN MUIR'S HIGH SIERRA, Dewitt Jones Prods. Dewitt Jones and Lesley Foster, producers.
NAKED YOGA, Filmshop Prod. Ronald S. Kass and Mervyn Lloyd, producers.

(Features)
ANTONIA: A PORTRAIT OF THE WOMAN, Rocky Mountain Prods. Judy Collins and Jill Godmilow, producers.
THE CHALLENGE...A TRIBUTE TO MODERN ART, World View. Herbert Kline, producer.
THE 81ST BLOW, Ghetto Fighters House. Jacquot Ehrlich, David Bergman and Haim Gouri, producers.
*HEARTS AND MINDS, Touchstone-Audjeff-BBS Prod., Zuker/Jaglom-Rainbow Pictures. Peter Davis and Bert Schneider, producers.
THE WILD AND THE BRAVE, E.S.J.-Tomorrow Entertainment-Jones/Howard Ltd. Natalie R. Jones and Eugene S. Jones, producers.

FOREIGN LANGUAGE FILM
*AMARCORD (Italy).
CATSPLAY (Hungary).
THE DELUGE (Poland).
LACOMBE, LUCIEN (France).
THE TRUCE (Argentina).

HONORARY AND OTHER AWARDS
TO HOWARD HAWKS—A master American filmmaker whose creative efforts hold a distinguished place in world cinema. (statuette)
TO JEAN RENOIR—A genius who, with grace, responsibility and enviable devotion through silent film, sound film, feature, documentary and television, has won the world's admiration. (statuette)

SPECIAL ACHIEVEMENT AWARDS
For Visual Effects: FRANK BRENDEL, GLEN ROBINSON and ALBERT WHITLOCK for *Earthquake*, a Universal-Mark Robson-Filmakers Group Production, Universal.

1974 IRVING G. THALBERG MEMORIAL AWARD
None given this year.

1974 JEAN HERSHOLT HUMANITARIAN AWARD
TO ARTHUR B. KRIM

SCIENTIFIC OR TECHNICAL
CLASS I (statuette)
None.

CLASS II (plaque)
JOSEPH D. KELLY of Glen Glenn Sound for the design of new audio control consoles which have advanced the state of the art of sound recording and rerecording for motion picture production.
THE BURBANK STUDIOS Sound Department for the design of new audio control consoles engineered and constructed by the Quad-Eight Sound Corporation.
SAMUEL GOLDWYN STUDIOS Sound Department for the design of a new audio control console engineered and constructed by the Quad-Eight Sound Corporation.
QUAD-EIGHT SOUND CORPORATION for the engineering and construction of new audio control consoles designed by The Burbank Studios Sound Department and by the Samuel Goldwyn Studios Sound Department.
WALDON O. WATSON, RICHARD J. STUMPF, ROBERT J. LEONARD and the UNIVERSAL CITY STUDIOS Sound Department for the development and engineering of the Sensurround System for motion picture presenation.

CLASS III (citation)
ELEMACK COMPANY of Rome, Italy;
LOUIS AMI of the Universal City Studios.

*INDICATES WINNER

One *Flew Over the Cuckoo's Nest,* a project which took years to get off the Hollywood drawing boards, justified the tenacity of its backers by winning five major awards at the 1975 Academy Awards presentations, held March 29, 1976. *Cuckoo's Nest* won the awards for best picture, best actor (Jack Nicholson), best actress (Louise Fletcher), best director (Milos Forman) and best screenplay adaptation (Lawrence Hauben and Bo Goldman). It was the first film to win all four of the Academy's most famous awards—picture, actor, actress, director—since *It Happened One Night* forty-two years earlier.

The awards ceremony was held again at the Dorothy Chandler Pavilion of the Los Angeles Music Center and telecast over ABC for the first time in six years. Howard W. Koch produced for the Academy, Marty Pasetta directed for ABC, and co-hosts of the evening were Walter Matthau, Robert Shaw, George Segal, Goldie Hawn and Gene Kelly. Ray Bolger and 24 dancers opened the show with a special number, "Hollywood Honors Its Own," and Elizabeth Taylor closed it by leading a salute to the country's Bicentennial.

George Burns, age eighty, was named best supporting actor of the year (for *The Sunshine Boys*), and thus became the oldest performer to win an Academy Award. Lee Grant was named best supporting actress (for *Shampoo*). The Soviet Union's *Dersu Uzala* was picked as best foreign language film, Mervyn

LeRoy received the Irving G. Thalberg Memorial Award and Dr. Jules Stein was honored with the Jean Hersholt Humanitarian Award.

Two ladies—one a Hollywood veteran, the other a newcomer—dominated the show. Mary Pickford, one of the industry's bona fide legends and a past Academy Award winner, received an honorary Oscar from the Academy's Board of Governors, specifically "in recognition of her unique contributions to the film industry and the development of film as an artistic medium." She accepted the statuette from Academy President Walter Mirisch in a ceremony pre-taped at her Pickfair estate. Later, best actress winner Louise Fletcher gave her acceptance speech partially in sign language to her deaf parents watching at home in Birmingham, Alabama, which rated as one of the most moving Oscar moments on record. "I want to say thank you...for teaching me to have a dream," she told them. "You are seeing...my dream come true."

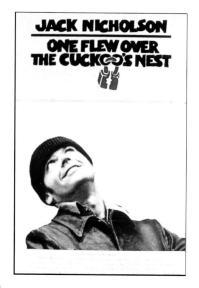

Best Supporting Actor: **George Burns** *as Al Lewis (right, with Walter Matthau) in* The Sunshine Boys *(M-G-M/United Artists; directed by Herbert Ross). The role was created on Broadway by Sam Levene and was for Burns his first role in a motion picture in thirty-six years (since 1939's* Honolulu*). He played a long-retired vaudevillian in the midst of making a one-shot comeback on television with a former partner with whom he's been on the outs for years. Said Burns, age 80: "This is all so exciting, I've decided to keep making one movie every thirty-six years." His winning role had earlier been earmarked for Jack Benny, who died, and then for Red Skelton, who turned it down.*

Best Picture: One Flew Over the Cuckoo's Nest (United Artists; produced by Saul Zaentz and Michael Douglas), **Best Director: Milos Forman,** and (above) **Best Actress: Louise Fletcher** as Nurse Ratched and **Best Actor: Jack Nicholson** as Randle P. McMurphy in One Flew Over the Cuckoo's Nest. It took over 13 years to get Ken Kesey's powerful anti-establishment novel on the screen, but the result hit the jackpot, with five of 1975's top Academy Awards honors. Filmed at the Oregon State Hospital in Salem, Oregon, it was the story of a non-conforming con man (played by Nicholson) who feigns insanity to avoid prison work, and is sent to a mental hospital where he is ultimately destroyed when he tries to go against "the system"—and a poisonous nurse, played by Miss Fletcher. The cast also included Danny DeVito, Brad Dourif, Scatman Crothers, William Redfield, Christopher Lloyd and Will Sampson and was an instant classic.

233

Best Supporting Actress: Lee Grant as Felicia Karpf (left) in Shampoo (Columbia; directed by Hal Ashby). Previously nominated in 1951 for Detective Story and in 1970 for The Landlord, Lee Grant won her Academy Award as the frisky wife of a wealthy Los Angeles businessman (Jack Warden), a lady with an interest in her hairdresser (Warren Beatty) beyond his ability to comb curls. She was nominated again in 1976 for The Voyage of the Damned and in the 1980s began concentrating more on directing films than acting in them.

Best Original Song: "I'm Easy" *from* Nashville *(Paramount), with music and lyrics by Keith Carradine (above). Carradine became the first person to win an Oscar for composing a song he also introduced in a movie. In* Nashville, *directed by Robert Altman, he played a soft-spoken rock star briefly involved with a married woman (Lily Tomlin).*

PICTURE

BARRY LYNDON, Hawk Films, Warner Bros. Produced by Stanley Kubrick.
DOG DAY AFTERNOON, Warner Bros. Produced by Martin Bregman and Martin Elfand.
JAWS, Zanuck/Brown, Universal. Produced by Richard D. Zanuck and David Brown.
NASHVILLE, ABC Entertainment-Weintraub-Altman, Paramount. Produced by Robert Altman.
***ONE FLEW OVER THE CUCKOO'S NEST,** Fantasy Films, UA. Produced by Saul Zaentz and Michael Douglas.

ACTOR

WALTER MATTHAU in *The Sunshine Boys,* Stark, M-G-M.
***JACK NICHOLSON** in *One Flew over the Cuckoo's Nest,* Fantasy Films, UA.
AL PACINO in *Dog Day Afternoon,* Warner Bros.
MAXIMILIAN SCHELL in *The Man in the Glass Booth,* Landau, AFT Distributing.
JAMES WHITMORE in *Give 'em Hell, Harry!,* Theatrovision, Avco Embassy.

ACTRESS

ISABELLE ADJANI in *The Story of Adele H.,* New World Pictures (French).
ANN-MARGRET in *Tommy,* Stigwood, Columbia.
***LOUISE FLETCHER** in *One Flew over the Cuckoo's Nest,* Fantasy Films, UA.
GLENDA JACKSON in *Hedda,* Royal Shakespeare-Barrie/Enders, Brut Productions.
CAROL KANE in *Hester Street,* Midwest Films.

SUPPORTING ACTOR

***GEORGE BURNS** in *The Sunshine Boys,* M-G-M.
BRAD DOURIF in *One Flew over the Cuckoo's Nest,* Fantasy Films, UA.
BURGESS MEREDITH in *The Day of the Locust,* Hellman, Paramount.
CHRIS SARANDON in *Dog Day Afternoon,* Warner Bros.
JACK WARDEN in *Shampoo,* Rubeeker, Columbia.

SUPPORTING ACTRESS

RONEE BLAKLEY in *Nashville,* ABC Entertainment-Weintraub-Altman, Paramount.
***LEE GRANT** in *Shampoo,* Rubeeker, Columbia.
SYLVIA MILES in *Farewell, My Lovely.* Kastner-ITC, Avco Embassy.
LILY TOMLIN in *Nashville,* ABC Entertainment-Weintraub-Altman, Paramount.
BRENDA VACCARO in *Jacqueline Susann's Once Is Not Enough,* Koch, Paramount.

DIRECTING

AMARCORD, New World Pictures (Italian). Federico Fellini.
BARRY LYNDON, Hawk Films, Warner Bros. Stanley Kubrick.
DOG DAY AFTERNOON, Warner Bros. Sidney Lumet.
NASHVILLE, ABC Entertainment-Weintraub-Altman, Paramount. Robert Altman.
***ONE FLEW OVER THE CUCKOO'S NEST,** Fantasy Films, UA. Milos Forman.

WRITING

(Original Screenplay)

AMARCORD, New World Pictures (Italian). Federico Fellini and Tonino Guerra.
AND NOW MY LOVE, Avco Embassy (French). Claude Lelouch and Pierre Uytterhoeven.
***DOG DAY AFTERNOON,** Warner Bros. Frank Pierson.
LIES MY FATHER TOLD ME, Pentimento-Pentacle VIII, Columbia. Ted Allan.
SHAMPOO, Rubeeker, Columbia. Robert Towne and Warren Beaty.

(Screenplay Adapted From Other Material)

BARRY LYNDON, Hawk Films, Warner Bros. Stanley Kubrick.
THE MAN WHO WOULD BE KING, Columbia/Allied Artists. John Huston and Gladys Hill.
***ONE FLEW OVER THE CUCKOO'S NEST,** Fantasy Films, UA. Lawrence Hauben and Bo Goldman.
SCENT OF A WOMAN, Dean Films, 20th Century-Fox (Italian). Ruggero Maccari and Dino Risi.
THE SUNSHINE BOYS, Ray Stark, M-G-M. Neil Simon.

CINEMATOGRAPHY

***BARRY LYNDON,** Hawk Films, Warner Bros. John Alcott.
THE DAY OF THE LOCUST, Jerome Hellman, Paramount. Conrad Hall.
FUNNY LADY, Rastar, Columbia. James Wong Howe.
THE HINDENBURG, Robert Wise-Filmakers Group, Universal. Robert Surtees.
ONE FLEW OVER THE CUCKOO'S NEST, Fantasy Films, UA. Haskell Wexler and Bill Butler.

ART DIRECTION-SET DECORATION

***BARRY LYNDON,** Hawk Films, Warner Bros. Ken Adam and Roy Walker, Vernon Dixon.
THE HINDENBURG, Robert Wise-Filmakers Group, Universal. Edward Carfagno; Frank McKelvy.
THE MAN WHO WOULD BE KING, Columbia/Allied Artists. Alexander Trauner and Tony Inglis; Peter James.
SHAMPOO, Rubeeker, Columbia. Richard Sylbert and W. Stewart Campbell; George Gaines.
THE SUNSHINE BOYS, Ray Stark, M-G-M. Albert Brenner, Marvin March.

COSTUME DESIGN

***BARRY LYNDON,** Hawk Films, Warner Bros. Ultra-Britt Soderlund and Milena Canonero.
THE FOUR MUSKETEERS, Salkind, 20th Century-Fox. Yvonne Blake, Ron Talsky.
FUNNY LADY, Rastar, Columbia. Ray Aghayan and Bob Mackie.
THE MAGIC FLUTE, Furrogate Releasing (Swedish). Henny Noremark and Karin Erskine.
THE MAN WHO WOULD BE KING, Columbia/Allied Artists. Edith Head.

Honorary Award: **Mary Pickford** *(right, with Academy President Walter Mirisch). No star ever held quite such a grasp on the world of movies, or its audiences, as Mary Pickford, and the Academy Board of Governors saluted her in appreciation of her numerous accomplishments and contributions to the industry. One of the original founders of the Academy, she was also a winner in 1928-29 for her performance in* Coquette. *Her pre-taped appearance on the Academy Award telecast was her first public appearance in many years, and was a major conversation piece.*

SOUND

BITE THE BULLET, Brooks, Columbia. Arthur Piantodosi, Les Fresholtz, Richard Tyler and Al Overton, Jr.

FUNNY LADY, Rastar, Columbia. Richard Portman, Don MacDougall, Curly Thirlwell and Jack Solomon.

THE HINDENBURG, Robert Wise-Filmakers Group, Universal. Leonard Peterson, John A. Bolger, Jr., John Mack and Don K. Sharpless.

*JAWS, Zanuck/Brown, Universal. Robert L. Hoyt, Roger Heman, Earl Madery and John Carter.

THE WIND AND THE LION, Herb Jaffee. M-G-M. Harry W. Tetrick, Aaron Rochin, William McCaughey and Roy Charman.

FILM EDITING

DOG DAY AFTERNOON, Warner Bros. Dede Allen.

*JAWS, Zanuck/Brown, Universal. Verna Fields.

THE MAN WHO WOULD BE KING, Columbia/Allied Artists. Russell Lloyd.

ONE FLEW OVER THE CUCKOO'S NEST, Fantasy Films, UA. Richard Chew, Lynzee Klingman and Sheldon Kahn.

THREE DAYS OF THE CONDOR, De Laurentiis, Paramount, Fredric Steinkamp and Don Guidice.

MUSIC

(Song)

HOW LUCKY CAN YOU GET (Funny Lady, Rastar, Columbia); Music and Lyrics by Fred Ebb and John Kander.

*I'M EASY, (Nashville, ABC-Weintraub-Altman, Paramount); Music and Lyrics by Keith Carradine.

NOW THAT WE'RE IN LOVE (Whiffs, Brut, 20th Century-Fox); Music by George Barrie. Lyrics by Sammy Cahn.

RICHARD'S WINDOW, (The Other Side of the Mountain, Filmways-Larry Peerce, Universal); Music by Charles Fox. Lyrics by Norman Gimbel.

THEME FROM MAHOGANY (DO YOU KNOW WHERE YOU'RE GOING TO) (Mahogany, Jobete, Paramount); Music by Michael Masser. Lyrics by Gerry Goffin.

(Original Score)

BIRDS DO IT, BEES DO IT, Wolper, Columbia. Gerald Fried.

BITE THE BULLET, Brooks, Columbia. Alex North.

*JAWS, Zanuck/Brown, Universal. John Williams.

ONE FLEW OVER THE CUCKOO'S NEST. Fantasy Films, UA. Jack Nitzsche.

THE WIND AND THE LION, Herb Jaffee. M-G-M. Jerry Goldsmith.

(Scoring: Original Song Score and/or Adaptation)

*BARRY LYNDON, Hawk Films, Warner Bros. Leonard Rosenman.

FUNNY LADY, Rastar, Columbia. Peter Matz.

TOMMY, Stigwood Organization, Columbia. Peter Townshend.

SHORT FILMS

(Animated Films)

*GREAT, Grantstern, British Lion Films Ltd. Bob Godfrey, producer.

KICK ME, Swarthe Productions. Robert Swarthe, producer.

MONSIEUR POINTU, National Film Board of Canada. Rene Jodoin, Bernard Longpre and Andre Leduc, producers.

SISYPHUS, Hungarofilms. Marcell Jankovics, producer.

(Live Action)

*ANGEL AND BIG JOE, Salzman Productions. Bert Salzman, producer.

CONQUEST OF LIGHT, Louis Marcus Films Ltd. Louis Marcus, producer.

DAWN FLIGHT, Lansburgh and Brian Lansburgh, producers.

A DAY IN THE LIFE OF BONNIE CONSOLO, Barr Films. Barry Spinello, producer.

DOUBLETALK, Beattie Productions. Alan Beattie, producer.

DOCUMENTARY

(Short Subjects)

ARTHUR AND LILLIE, Department of Communication, Stanford University. Jon Else, Steven Kovacs and Kristine Samuelson, producers.

*THE END OF THE GAME, Opus Films Ltd. Claire Wilbur and Robin Lehman, producers.

MILLIONS OF YEARS AHEAD OF MAN, BASF. Manfred Baier, producer.

PROBES IN SPACE, Graphic Films. George V. Casey, producer.

WHISTLING SMITH, National Film Board of Canada. Barrie Howells and Michael Scott, producers.

Jaws (Universal; produced by Zanuck/Brown) won three Academy Awards: for its film editing by Verna Fields, its sound by Robert L. Hoyt, Roger Heman, Earl Madery and John Carter, and its original music score by John Williams. The year's most financially successful movie, it also helped re-define the then-popular "disaster" movie genre and also inspired several sequels. Taut, suspenseful and commercial, it was excellently made from the first frame to its last bite, all about a killer shark and the havoc it causes during the tourist season at a normally peaceful beach town.

(Features)

THE CALIFORNIA REICH, Yasny Talking Pictures. Walter F. Parkes and Keigh F. Critchiow, producers.

FIGHTING FOR OUR LIVES, A Farm Worker Film. Glen Pearcy, producer.

THE INCREDIBLE MACHINE, The National Geographic Society, Wolper Prods. Irwin Rosten, producer.

*THE MAN WHO SKIED DOWN EVEREST, Crawley Films. F.R. Crawley, James Hager and Dale Hartleben, producers.

THE OTHER HALF OF THE SKY: A CHINA MEMOIR, MacLaine Productions. Shirley MacLaine, producer.

FOREIGN LANGUAGE FILM

*DERSU UZALA (U.S.S.R.).

LAND OF PROMISE (Poland).

LETTERS FROM MARUSIA (Mexico).

SANDAKAN NO. 8 (Japan).

SCENT OF A WOMAN (Italy).

HONORARY AND OTHER AWARDS

TO MARY PICKFORD in recognition of her unique contributions to the film industry and the development of film as an artistic medium. (statuette)

SPECIAL ACHIEVEMENT AWARDS

For Sound Effects: PETER BERKOS for The Hindenburg. Robert Wise-Filmakers Group, Universal.

For Visual Effects: ALBERT WHITLOCK and GLEN ROBINSON for The Hindenburg. Robert Wise-Filmakers Group, Universal.

1975 IRVING G. THALBERG MEMORIAL AWARD

TO MERVYN LeROY

1975 JEAN HERSHOLT HUMANITARIAN AWARD

TO JULES C. STEIN

SCIENTIFIC OR TECHNICAL

CLASS I (statuette)

None.

CLASS II (plaque)

CHADWELL O'CONNOR of the O'Connor Engineering Laboratories for the concept and engineering of a fluid-damped camera-head for motion-picture photography.

WILLIAM F. MINER of Universal City Studios, Inc. and the WESTINGHOUSE ELECTRIC CORPORATION for the development and engineering of a solid-state, 500 kilowatt, direct-current static rectifier for motion-picture lighting.

CLASS III (citation)

LAWRENCE W. BUTLER and ROGER BANKS:

DAVID J. DEGENKOLB and FRED SCOBEY of Deluxe General Inc. and JOHN C. DOLAN and RICHARD DUBOIS of the Akwaklame Company;

JOSEPH WESTHEIMER;

CARTER EQUIPMENT CO., INC. and RAMTRONICS;

THE HOLLYWOOD FILM COMPANY;

BELL & HOWELL;

FREDRIK SCHLYTER.

*INDICATES WINNER

235

Three films dominated the 1976 Academy Awards: *Network* (with four awards), *All the President's Men* (also with four Oscars) and *Rocky* (with three awards, including best picture of the year statuette). It was also a triumphant night for Sylvester Stallone, although he didn't win an award; he was only the third person in the Oscar record books to be nominated in a single year both as an actor and as a screenwriter (preceded by Charles Chaplin in 1940 and Orson Welles in 1941).

It was a year for several records to be set. *Network* became the only motion picture other than 1951's *A Streetcar Named Desire* to win three awards for acting to date: best actress (Faye Dunaway), best supporting actress (Beatrice Straight) and best actor (Peter Finch). Finch, who died two months before the Academy Awards winners were announced on March 29, 1977, was the first performer to win a posthumous Oscar. It was accepted by his widow.

Barbra Streisand, a best actress winner in 1968, became the first Oscar-winner performer to also be an Academy Award-winning composer; her song, "Evergreen" from *A Star Is Born,* written with Paul Williams, was named the year's best song. John Avildsen was named best director for *Rocky,* and among his competition was Lina Wertmuller, the first woman ever nominated in that category. Jason Robards in *All the President's Men* was chosen best supporting actor, Pandro S. Berman was voted the Irving G. Thalberg Memorial Award and special visual effects awards went to both *King Kong* and *Logan's Run. Black and White in Color,* a film from the Ivory Coast, was chosen best foreign language film.

The show, originating from the Dorothy Chandler Pavilion of the Los Angeles Music Center, was telecast over ABC, produced by William Friedkin and directed by Marty Pasetta. Co-hosts for the evening were Richard Pryor, Jane Fonda, Ellen Burstyn and Warren Beatty. Among the show's entertainment highlights were Barbra Streisand, appearing on an Oscar show for the first time as a performer, and Muhammad Ali—unannounced and unexpected—good naturedly sparring for an abbreviated round with a flabbergasted "Rocky" Stallone.

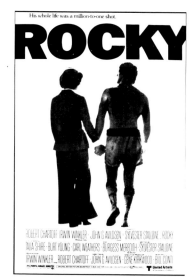

His whole life was a million-to-one shot.

ROBERT CHARTOFF · IRWIN WINKLER · JOHN G. AVILDSEN · SYLVESTER STALLONE · ROCKY
TALIA SHIRE · BURT YOUNG · CARL WEATHERS · BURGESS MEREDITH · SYLVESTER STALLONE
IRWIN WINKLER · ROBERT CHARTOFF · JOHN G. AVILDSEN · GENE KIRKWOOD · BILL CONTI
United Artists

236

Best Picture: **Rocky** *(United Artists; produced by Irwin Winkler and Robert Chartoff) and* **Best Director:** **John G. Avildsen** *for* Rocky. *It was the 'sleeper of the season, economically made for $960,000 in twenty-eight days, and it grew into the year's best-loved movie, the story of a likeable but deadweight fighter named Rocky Balboa (Sylvester Stallone, right, with Burgess Meredith) who miraculously gets picked for a heavyweight title bout and, in the final analysis, wins his own self-respect and dignity. Stallone also wrote the screenplay, and* Rocky *won a third Oscar for film editing. The cast also included Talia Shire, Burt Young and Carl Weathers. The film inspired a series of subsequent* Rocky *films which featured a consistently more sculptured and muscled Stallone than his original incarnation.*

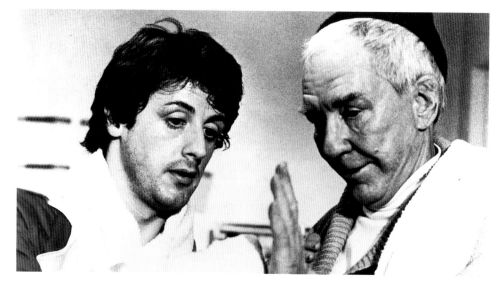

Best Actor: Peter Finch *as Howard Beale (above) in* Network *(M-G-M/United Artists; directed by Sidney Lumet).* Network, *by Paddy Chayefsky, took a biting, semi-satirical look at television in the 1970s and its eagerness for high* program ratings. Beale (played by Finch) is a fictional newsman who attracts high ratings by promising to commit suicide on camera; at the same time, he begs viewers to take a stand against current TV programming by exclaiming "I'm mad as hell and I'm not going to take it anymore!" Finch died on January 14, 1977, just a month before the 1976 Oscar nominations were announced.

237

Best Actress: Faye Dunaway *as Diana Christensen (above) in* Network. *Playing a ruthless head of network programming in the Chayefsky screenplay, Dunaway/Diana was not above plotting an assassination, or other skulduggery, to hype her company's Nielsen numbers. It also made for a smashing role for Dunaway, previously nominated for 1967's* Bonnie and Clyde *and 1974's* Chinatown. *Among the other Academy Awards won by* Network *was an Oscar to Paddy Chayefsky for original screenplay; he was, without question, a man highly gifted with words and ideas.*

Best Supporting Actress: Beatrice Straight *as Louise Schumacher in* Network. *It took only three days of rehearsal and three more days of filming (at the classic old Apthorp apartment building in New York City) for her role, but Beatrice Straight gave a superb supporting Oscar performance in every sense of the word; she played the wife of William Holden, attempting to retain her dignity—and her sanity—when her husband admits he is in love with a younger woman.*

Special Award: **King Kong** *(Paramount; produced by Dino De Laurentiis) with Jessica Lange, above, was voted a Special Achievement Award for its visual effects by the Board of Governors, and presented to Carlo Rambaldi, Glen Robinson and Frank Van der Veer. From 1939 through 1971 (excluding a three-year period, 1951-1953), visual effects were honored via a regular awards category; between 1972 and 1976, such achievements were saluted by a special award, not mandatory each year, voted "at such times as in the judgment of the Board of Governors there is an achievement which makes an exceptional contribution to the motion picture for which it was created, but for which there is no annual awards category."*

PICTURE

ALL THE PRESIDENT'S MEN, Wildwood, Warner Bros. Produced by Walter Coblenz.
BOUND FOR GLORY, UA. Produced by Robert F. Blumofe and Harold Leventhal.
NETWORK, Gottfried/Chayefsky, M-G-M/UA. Produced by Howard Gottfried.
*__ROCKY,__ Chartoff-Winkler, UA. Produced by Irwin Winkler and Robert Chartoff.
TAXI DRIVER, Bill/Phillips-Scorsese, Columbia. Produced by Michael Phillips and Julia Phillips.

ACTOR

ROBERT DE NIRO in *Taxi Driver,* Bill/Phillips-Scorsese, Columbia.
*__PETER FINCH__ in *Network,* Gottfried/Chayefsky, M-G-M/UA.
GIANCARLO GIANNINI in *Seven Beauties,* Cinema 5 (Italian).
WILLIAM HOLDEN in *Network,* Gottfried/Chayefsky, M-G-M/UA.
SYLVESTER STALLONE in *Rocky,* Chartoff-Winkler, UA.

ACTRESS

MARIE-CHRISTINE BARRAULT in *Cousin, Cousine,* Northal Films (French).
*__FAYE DUNAWAY__ in *Network,* Gottfried/Chayefsky, M-G-M/UA.
TALIA SHIRE in *Rocky,* Chartoff-Winkler, UA.
SISSY SPACEK in *Carrie,* Redbank Films, UA.
LIV ULLMANN in *Face to Face,* Paramount (Swedish).

SUPPORTING ACTOR

NED BEATTY in *Network,* Gottfried/Chayefsky, M-G-M/UA.
BURGESS MEREDITH in *Rocky,* Chartoff-Winkler, UA.
LAURENCE OLIVIER in *Marathon Man,* Evans-Beckerman, Paramount.
*__JASON ROBARDS__ in *All the President's Men,* Wildwood, Warner Bros.
BURT YOUNG in *Rocky,* Chartoff-Winkler, UA.

SUPPORTING ACTRESS

JANE ALEXANDER in *All the President's Men,* Wildwood, Warner Bros.
JODIE FOSTER in *Taxi Driver,* Bill/Phillips-Scorsese, Columbia.
LEE GRANT in *Voyage of the Damned,* ITC, Avco Embassy.
PIPER LAURIE in *Carrie,* Redbank Films, UA.
*__BEATRICE STRAIGHT__ in *Network,* Gottfried/Chayefsky, M-G-M/UA.

DIRECTING

ALL THE PRESIDENT'S MEN, Wildwood, Warner Bros. Alan J. Pakula.
FACE TO FACE, Cinematograph, A.B., Paramount (Swedish). Ingmar Bergman.
NETWORK, Gottfried/Chayefsky, M-G-M/UA. Sidney Lumet.
*__ROCKY,__ Chartoff-Winkler, UA. John G. Avildsen.
SEVEN BEAUTIES, Medusa Distribuzione, Cinema 5 (Italian). Lina Wertmuller.

WRITING

(Screenplay Written Directly For The Screen)

COUSIN, COUSINE, Northal Film Distributors Ltd. (French). Jean-Charles Tacchella and Daniele Thompson.
THE FRONT, Columbia. Walter Bernstein.
*__NETWORK,__ Gottfried/Chayefsky, M-G-M/UA. Paddy Chayefsky.
ROCKY, Chartoff-Winkler, UA. Sylvester Stallone.
SEVEN BEAUTIES, Medusa Distribuzione, Cinema 5 (Italian). Lina Wertmuller.

(Screenplay Based On Material From Another Medium)

*__ALL THE PRESIDENT'S MEN,__ Wildwood, Warner Bros. William Goldman.
BOUND FOR GLORY, UA. Robert Getchell.
FELLINI'S CASANOVA, Universal (Italian). Federico Fellini and Bernadino Zapponi.
THE SEVEN-PER-CENT SOLUTION, Herbert Ross/Winitsky-Sellers, Universal. Nicholas Meyer.
VOYAGE OF THE DAMNED, ITC Entertainment, Avco Embassy. Steve Shagan and David Butler.

CINEMATOGRAPHY

*__BOUND FOR GLORY,__ UA. Haskell Wexler.
KING KONG, De Laurentiis, Paramount, Richard H. Kline.
LOGAN'S RUN, Saul David, M-G-M. Ernest Laszlo.
NETWORK, Gottfried/Chayefsky, M-G-M/UA. Owen Roizman.
A STAR IS BORN, Barwood/Peters-First Artists, Warner Bros. Robert Surtees.

ART DIRECTION-
SET DECORATION

*__ALL THE PRESIDENT'S MEN,__ Wildwood, Warner Bros. George Jenkins; George Gaines.
THE INCREDIBLE SARAH, Helen M. Strauss-Reader's Digest, Seymour Borde & Associates. Elliot Scott and Norman Reynolds.
THE LAST TYCOON, Spiegel-Kazan, Paramount, Gene Callahan and Jack Collis; Jerry Wunderlich.
LOGAN'S RUN, Saul David, M-G-M. Dale Hennesy; Robert de Vestel.
THE SHOOTIST, Frankovich/Self-De Laurentiis, Paramount. Robert F. Boyle; Arthur Jeph Parker.

COSTUME DESIGN

BOUND FOR GLORY, UA. William Theiss.
*__FELLINI'S CASANOVA,__ Universal (Italian). Danilo Donati.
THE INCREDIBLE SARAH, Helen M. Strauss-Reader's Digest, Seymour Borde & Associates. Anthony Mendleson.
THE PASSOVER PLOT, Coast Industries-Golan-Globus, Atlas Films. Mary Wills.
THE SEVEN-PER-CENT SOLUTION, Herbert Ross/Winitsky-Sellers, Universal. Alan Barrett.

SOUND

*__ALL THE PRESIDENT'S MEN,__ Wildwood, Warner Bros. Arthur Piantadosi, Les Fresholtz, Dick Alexander and Jim Webb.
KING KONG, De Laurentiis, Paramount. Harry Warren Tetrick, William McCaughey, Aaron Rochin and Jack Solomon.
ROCKY, Chartoff-Winkler, UA. Harry Warren Tetrick, William McCaughey, Lyle Burbridge and Bud Alper.
SILVER STREAK, Frank Yablans, 20th Century-Fox. Donald Mitchell, Douglas Williams, Richard Tyler and Hal Etherington.
A STAR IS BORN, Barwood/Peters-First Artists, Warner Bros. Robert Knudson, Dan Wallin, Robert Glass and Tom Overton.

FILM EDITING

ALL THE PRESIDENT'S MEN, Wildwood, Warner Bros. Robert L. Wolfe.
BOUND FOR GLORY, UA. Robert Jones and Pembroke J. Herring.
NETWORK, Gottfried/Chayefsky, M-G-M/UA. Alan Heim.
*__ROCKY,__ Chartoff-Winkler, UA. Richard Halsey and Scott Conrad.
TWO-MINUTE WARNING, Filmways/Peerce-Feldman, Universal. Eve Newman and Walter Hannemann.

MUSIC

(Song)

AVE SATANI (*The Omen,* 20th Century-Fox); Music and Lyrics by Jerry Goldsmith.
COME TO ME (*The Pink Panther Strikes Again,* Amjo, UA); Music by Henry Mancini. Lyrics by Don Black.
*__EVERGREEN (Love Theme from A Star Is Born)__ (*A Star Is Born,* Barwood/Peters-First Artists, Warner Bros.); Music by Barbra Streisand. Lyrics by Paul Williams.
GONNA FLY NOW (*Rocky,* Chartoff-Winkler, UA); Music by Bill Conti. Lyrics by Carol Connors and Ayn Robbins.
A WORLD THAT NEVER WAS (*Half a House,* Lenro Productions, First American Films); Music by Sammy Fain. Lyrics by Paul Francis Webster.

(Original Score)

OBSESSION, Litto, Columbia. Bernard Herrmann.
*__THE OMEN,__ 20th Century-Fox. Jerry Goldsmith.
THE OUTLAW JOSEY WALES, Malpaso, Warner Bros. Jerry Fielding.
TAXI DRIVER, Bill/Phillips-Scorsese, Columbia. Bernard Herrmann.
VOYAGE OF THE DAMNED, ITC Entertainment, Avco Embassy. Lalo Schifrin.

(Original Song Score and Its Adaptation or Best Adaptation Score)

*__BOUND FOR GLORY,__ UA. Leonard Rosenman.
BUGSY MALONE, Goodtimes Enterprises, Paramount, Paul Williams.
A STAR IS BORN, Barwood/Peters-First Artists, Warner Bros. Roger Kellaway.

SHORT FILMS

(Animated Films)

DEDALO, Cineteam Realizzazioni. Manfredo Manfredi, producer.
*__LEISURE,__ Film Australia. Suzanne Baker, producer.
THE STREET, National Film Board of Canada. Caroline Leaf and Guy Glover, producers.

(Live Action)

*IN THE REGION OF ICE, American Film Institute. Andre Guttfreund and Peter Werner, producers.

KUDZU, A Short Production. Marjorie Anne Short, producer.

THE MORNING SPIDER, The Black and White Colour Film Company. Julian Chagrin and Claude Chagrin, producers.

NIGHTLIFE, Opus Films, Ltd. Claire Wilbur and Robin Lehman, producers.

NUMBER ONE, Number One Productions. Dyan Cannon and Vince Cannon, producers.

DOCUMENTARY

(Short Subjects)

AMERICAN SHOESHINE, Titan Films, Sparky Greene, producer.

BLACKWOOD, National Film Board of Canada. Tony Ianzelo and Andy Thompson, producers.

THE END OF THE ROAD, Pelican Films. John Armstrong, producer.

*NUMBER OUR DAYS, Community Television of Southern California. Lynne Littman, producer.

UNIVERSE, Graphic Films Corp. for NASA. Lester Novros, producer.

(Features)

*HARLAN COUNTY, U.S.A., Cabin Creek Films, Barbara Kopple, producer.

HOLLYWOOD ON TRIAL, October Films/Cinema Associates. James Gutman and David Helpern, Jr., producers.

OFF THE EDGE, Pentacle Films. Michael Firth, producer.

PEOPLE OF THE WIND, Elizabeth E. Rogers Productions. Anthony Howarth and David Koff, producers.

VOLCANO: AN INQUIRY INTO THE LIFE AND DEATH OF MALCOLM LOWRY, National Film Board of Canada. Donald Brittain and Robert Duncan, producers.

FOREIGN LANGUAGE FILM

*BLACK AND WHITE IN COLOR, (Ivory Coast).

COUSIN, COUSINE, (France).

JACOB, THE LIAR, (German Democratic Republic).

NIGHTS AND DAYS, (Poland).

SEVEN BEAUTIES, (Italy).

HONORARY AND OTHER AWARDS

None given this year.

SPECIAL ACHIEVEMENT AWARDS

For Visual Effects: **CARLO RAMBALDI, GLEN ROBINSON** and **FRANK VAN DER VEER** for *King Kong*, De Laurentiis, Paramount.

For Visual Effects: **L.B. ABBOTT, GLEN ROBINSON** and **MATTHEW YURICICH** for *Logan's Run*, Saul David, M-G-M.

1976 IRVING G. THALBERG MEMORIAL AWARD

TO PANDRO S. BERMAN

1976 JEAN HERSHOLT HUMANITARIAN AWARD

None given this year.

SCIENTIFIC OR TECHNICAL

CLASS I (statuette)

None.

CLASS II (plaque)

CONSOLIDATED FILM INDUSTRIES and the BARNEBEY-CHENEY COMPANY for the development of a system for the recovery of film-cleaning solvent vapors in a motion-picture laboratory.

WILLIAM L. GRAHAM, MANFRED G. MICHELSON, GEOFFREY F. NORMAN and SIEGFRIED SEIBERT of Technicolor for the development and engineering of a continuous, high-speed, Color Motion Picture Printing System.

CLASS III (citation)

FRED BARTSCHER of the Kollmorgen Corporation and to GLENN BERGGREN of the Schneider Corporation.

PANAVISION INCORPORATED;

HIROSHI SUZUKAWA of Canon and WILTON R. HOLM of AMPTP Motion Picture and Television Research Center;

CARL ZEISS COMPANY;

PHOTO RESEARCH DIVISION of the KOLLMORGEN CORPORATION.

*INDICATES WINNER

Best Supporting Actor: **Jason Robards** *as Ben Bradlee in* All the President's Men *(Warner Bros.; directed by Alan J. Pakula). Robards played the real-life Bradlee, editor of the* Washington Post *and the man who gave the final go-ahead (and continued support) to reporters Carl Bernstein and Bob Woodward in their investigation of the Watergate coverup in Washington, D.C. The film also won Academy Awards for screenplay (based on material from another medium), art direction, and sound. Robards, above in foreground talking to Robert Redford, Jack Warden and Dustin Hoffman, was also to win a second Oscar the following year for once again playing a real-life person, Dashiell Hammett in* Julia.

239

Bound for Glory *(United Artists; produced by Robert F. Blumofe) featured David Carradine (above) in a biography of the late Woody Guthrie, a spirited and sensitive troubadour deeply affected by America's Depression era of the 1930s. The film received Academy awards for Haskell Wexler's cinematography and for Leonard Rosenman's scoring: adaptation.*

Here it was at last: fifty years after that initial gathering at the Hollywood Roosevelt Hotel, the Academy celebrated its first half-century birthday, stronger than ever, with Oscar the acknowledged final word on motion picture achievement. The celebration took place April 3, 1978, again at the Dorothy Chandler Pavilion of the Los Angeles Music Center, with a stage full of stars, including the first Oscar winner Janet Gaynor, two-time champions such as Bette Davis and Olivia de Havilland, plus current box office names like John Travolta and Sylvester Stallone taking part. The show was telecast on ABC-TV, produced by Howard W. Koch and directed by Marty Pasetta.

Star Wars won six statuettes for the biggest award total of the night, all of them in the technical division; it also received a seventh award, voted by the Academy Board of Governors, for its special achievement (by Benjamin Burtt, Jr.) in the creation of alien creature and robot voices. *Annie Hall* received four awards, including best picture, best actress (Diane Keaton), best director (Woody Allen) and best original screenplay (Woody Allen and Marshall Brickman). Richard Dreyfuss was chosen best actor (for *The Goodbye Girl*), France's *Madame Rosa* was selected best foreign language film, Vanessa Redgrave was named best supporting actress in *Julia* and Jason Robards was chosen best supporting actor (for *Julia*). Robards, winner in the same category the previous year, became the fourth performer in Academy history to win in subsequent years (following Luise Rainer in 1936-1937, Spencer Tracy in 1937-1938, and Katharine Hepburn in 1967-1968). Miss Redgrave caused controversy when she used her acceptance speech to criticize "militant Zionist hoodlums" for protesting her political beliefs and actions.

Overall, it was a friendly, glamorous and star-studded night for Oscar, a fitting finale to the first fifty years of activity. And there was good news the morning after, when the ratings came tumbling in: the telecast had attracted the largest television audience for any Oscar show to date.

WOODY ALLEN
DIANE KEATON
TONY ROBERTS
CAROL KANE
PAUL SIMON
JANET MARGOLIN
SHELLEY DUVALL
CHRISTOPHER WALKEN
COLLEEN DEWHURST

"ANNIE HALL"

A nervous romance.

Best Picture: **Annie Hall** *(United Artists; produced by Charles H. Joffe),* **Best Director:** Woody Allen *and* **Best Actress:** Diane Keaton *as Annie (right, with Allen as Alvy Singer) in* Annie Hall. *Annie's a budding singer, and Alvy is a TV-nightclub comic; they meet in Manhattan, have a brief entanglement, then split. Told with penetrating insights into modern relationships (and generously sprinkled with Woody Allen's unique deadpan humor)* Annie Hall *won four Oscars, including two for Mr. Allen, as director and as co-author (with Marshall Brickman) of the original screenplay, and one for the infectious title performance by Miss Keaton.*

Star Wars *(20th Century-Fox; produced by Gary Kurtz) was the blockbuster of the year, a sweeping, energetic, and absolutely splendid space-adventure-fantasy which reawakened the world's interest in sci-fi films and showed what movies could do better than any other entertainment* medium. *The film won six awards, the most of any film of 1977: for costume design, film editing, art direction, sound, original music score, visual effects plus a special achievement award, voted by the Academy's Board of Governors. It was the first of a trilogy of* Star Wars *films which included 1980's* The Empire Strikes Back *and 1983's* Return of the Jedi, *blockbusters all. The stars of all three films were Harrison Ford, Carrie Fisher and Mark Hamill.*

Best Actor: Richard Dreyfuss *as Elliot Garfield in* The Goodbye Girl *(M-G-M/Warner Bros.; directed by Herbert Ross). Dreyfuss, with words written by Neil Simon, played an aspiring actor in New York, grudgingly sharing a small Manhattan apartment with a grumbling young mother (Marsha Mason) and her precocious daughter (Quinn Cummings), while concurrently struggling to star in an off-Broadway and off-beat version of* Richard III. *It was his first Academy nomination. For Dreyfuss (at right with Mason), 1977 was an important career year: besides his potent* Goodbye *role, he also starred in Steven Spielberg's imposing and popular* Close Encounters of the Third Kind.

Best Supporting Actress: **Vanessa Redgrave** *as* Julia *(right, with Jane Fonda) in* Julia *(20th Century-Fox; directed by Fred Zinnemann).* Julia *was based on Lillian Hellman's* Pentimento, *with Jane Fonda playing author Hellman, reminiscing about her early life and especially a childhood friend (played by Miss Redgrave), who grew into an impassioned activist in World War II Europe and was eventually murdered by Nazi factions. Previously, Vanessa Redgrave had been an Academy nominee for* Morgan! *(1966),* Isadora *(1968) and* Mary, Queen of Scots *(1971). She was also the first from her distinguished acting family to win an Oscar; later she was also nominated for* The Bostonians *(1984) and* Howards End *(1992). By virtue of her* Julia *win, she became the only person in Oscar's first 70 years to win a supporting Academy Award for playing the title role in a movie.*

PICTURE

*ANNIE HALL, Rollins-Joffe, UA. Produced by Charles H. Joffe.
THE GOODBYE GIRL, Stark, M-G-M/Warner Bros. Produced by Ray Stark.
JULIA, 20th Century-Fox. Produced by Richard Roth.
STAR WARS, 20th Century-Fox. Produced by Gary Kurtz.
THE TURNING POINT, Hera Productions, 20th Century-Fox. Produced by Herbert Ross and Arthur Laurents.

ACTOR

WOODY ALLEN in *Annie Hall,* Rollins-Joffe UA.
RICHARD BURTON in *Equus,* Winkaast, UA.
*RICHARD DREYFUSS in *The Goodbye Girl,* Stark, M-G-M/Warner Bros.
MARCELLO MASTROIANNI in *A Special Day,* Canafox Films, Cinema 5 (Italian).
JOHN TRAVOLTA in *Saturday Night Fever,* Stigwood, Paramount.

ACTRESS

ANNE BANCROFT in *The Turning Point,* Hera Prods., 20th Century-Fox.
JANE FONDA in *Julia,* 20th Century-Fox.
*DIANE KEATON in *Annie Hall,* Rollins-Joffe, UA.
SHIRLEY MacLAINE in *The Turning Point,* Hera Prods., 20th Century-Fox.
MARSHA MASON in *The Goodbye Girl,* Stark, M-G-M/Warner Bros.

SUPPORTING ACTOR

MIKHAIL BARYSHNIKOV in *The Turning Point,* Hera Productions, 20th Century-Fox.
PETER FIRTH in *Equus,* Winkast, UA.
ALEC GUINNESS in *Star Wars,* 20th Century-Fox.
*JASON ROBARDS in *Julia,* 20th Century-Fox.
MAXIMILIAN SCHELL in *Julia,* 20th Century-Fox.

SUPPORTING ACTRESS

LESLIE BROWNE in *The Turning Point,* Hera Productions, 20th Century-Fox.
QUINN CUMMINGS in *The Goodbye Girl,* Stark, M-G-M/Warner Bros.
MELINDA DILLON in *Close Encounters Of The Third Kind,* Columbia.
*VANESSA REDGRAVE in *Julia,* 20th Century-Fox.
TUESDAY WELD in *Looking for Mr. Goodbar,* Fields, Paramount.

DIRECTING

*ANNIE HALL, Rollins-Joffe, UA. Woody Allen.
CLOSE ENCOUNTERS OF THE THIRD KIND, Columbia. Steven Spielberg.
JULIA, 20th Century-Fox. Fred Zinnemann.
STAR WARS, 20th Century-Fox. George Lucas.
THE TURNING POINT, Hera Productions, 20th Century-Fox. Herbert Ross.

WRITING

(Screenplay Written Directly For The Screen)

*ANNIE HALL, Rollins-Joffe, Woody Allen and Marshall Brickman.
THE GOODBYE GIRL, Ray Stark, M-G-M/Warner Bros. Neil Simon.
THE LATE SHOW, Lion's Gate, Warner Bros. Robert Benton.
STAR WARS, 20th Century-Fox, George Lucas.
THE TURNING POINT, Hera Productions, 20th Century-Fox. Arthur Laurents.

(Screenplay Based On Material From Another Medium)

EQUUS, Winkast Company, UA. Peter Shaffer.
I NEVER PROMISED YOU A ROSE GARDEN, Scherick/Blatt, New World Pictures. Gavin Lambert and Lewis John Carlino.
*JULIA, 20th Century-Fox. Alvin Sargent.
OH, GOD!, Warner Bros. Larry Gelbart.
THAT OBSCURE OBJECT OF DESIRE, First Artists (Spain). Luis Bunuel and Jean-Claude Carriere.

CINEMATOGRAPHY

*CLOSE ENCOUNTERS OF THE THIRD KIND, Columbia. Vilmos Zsigmond.
ISLANDS IN THE STREAM, Bart/Palevsky, Paramount. Fred J. Koenekamp.
JULIA, 20th Century-Fox. Douglas Slocombe.
LOOKING FOR MR. GOODBAR, Freddie Fields, Paramount. William A. Fraker.
THE TURNING POINT, Hera Productions, 20th Century-Fox. Robert Surtees.

ART DIRECTION-
SET DECORATION

AIRPORT '77, Jennings Lang, Universal. George C. Webb; Mickey S. Michaels.
CLOSE ENCOUNTERS OF THE THIRD KIND, Columbia. Joe Alves and Dan Lomino; Phil Abramson.
THE SPY WHO LOVED ME, Eon, UA. Ken Adam and Peter Lamont; Hugh Scaife.
*STAR WARS, 20th Century-Fox. John Barry, Norman Reynolds and Leslie Dilley; Roger Christian.
THE TURNING POINT, Hera Productions, 20th Century-Fox. Albert Brenner; Marvin March.

COSTUME DESIGN

AIRPORT '77, Jennings Lang, Universal. Edith Head and Burton Miller.
JULIA, 20th Century-Fox. Anthea Sylbert.
A LITTLE NIGHT MUSIC, Sascha-Wien/Elliott Kastner, New World Pictures. Florence Klotz.
THE OTHER SIDE OF MIDNIGHT, Frank Yablans, 20th Century-Fox. Irene Sharaff.
*STAR WARS, 20th Century-Fox. John Mollo.

Best Supporting Actor: Jason Robards *as Dashiell Hammett in* Julia. *For the second year in a row, Jason Robards won the Academy's supporting actor award; for the second year in a row, he was also portraying a real-life person, this time,*

Dashiell Hammett, the author of The Thin Man *and* The Maltese Falcon, *and—as portrayed in* Julia—*the man who loved author Lillian Hellman (played by Jane Fonda) and helped her evolve into a noted author and playwright.*

SOUND

CLOSE ENCOUNTERS OF THE THIRD KIND, Columbia. Robert Knudson, Robert J. Glass, Don MacDougall and Gene S. Cantamessa.

THE DEEP, Casablanca Filmworks, Columbia. Walter Goss, Dick Alexander, Tom Beckert and Robin Gregory.

SORCERER, Friedkin, Paramount/Universal. Robert Knudson, Robert J. Glass, Richard Tyler and Jean-Louis Ducarme.

*****STAR WARS,** 20th Century-Fox. Don MacDougall, Ray West, Bob Minkler and Derek Ball.

THE TURNING POINT, Hera Productions, 20th Century-Fox. Theodore Soderberg, Paul Wells, Douglas O. Williams and Jerry Jost.

FILM EDITING

CLOSE ENCOUNTERS OF THE THIRD KIND, Columbia. Michael Kahn.

JULIA, 20th Century-Fox. Walter Murch and Marcel Durham.

SMOKEY AND THE BANDIT, Rastar, Universal. Walter Hannemann and Angelo Ross.

*****STAR WARS,** 20th Century-Fox. Paul Hirsch, Marcia Lucas and Richard Chew.

THE TURNING POINT, Hera Productions, 20th Century-Fox. William Reynolds.

VISUAL EFFECTS

CLOSE ENCOUNTERS OF THE THIRD KIND, Columbia. Roy Arbogast, Douglas Trumbull, Matthew Yuricich, Gregory Jein and Richard Yuricich.

*****STAR WARS,** 20th Century-Fox. John Stears, John Dykstra, Richard Edlund, Grant McCune and Robert Blalack.

MUSIC

(Song)

CANDLE ON THE WATER (*Pete's Dragon,* Disney, Buena Vista); Music and Lyrics by Al Kasha and Joel Hirschhorn.

NOBODY DOES IT BETTER (*The Spy Who Loved Me,* Eon, UA); Music by Marvin Hamlisch. Lyrics by Carole Bayer Sager.

THE SLIPPER AND THE ROSE WALTZ (He Danced With Me/She Danced With Me) (*The Slipper and the Rose—The Story of Cinderella,* Paradine Co-Productions, Universal); Music and Lyrics by Richard M. Sherman and Robert B. Sherman.

SOMEONE'S WAITING FOR YOU (*The Rescuers,* Disney, Buena Vista); Music by Sammy Fain. Lyrics by Carol Conners and Ayn Robbins.

*****YOU LIGHT UP MY LIFE** (*You Light Up My Life,* Session Company, Columbia); Music and Lyrics by Joseph Brooks.

(Original Score)

CLOSE ENCOUNTERS OF THE THIRD KIND, Columbia. John Williams.

JULIA, 20th Century-Fox. Georges Delerue.

MOHAMMAD-MESSENGER OF GOD, Filmco International, Irwin Yablans Company. Maurice Jarre.

THE SPY WHO LOVED ME, Eon, UA. Marvin Hamlisch.

*****STAR WARS,** 20th Century-Fox. John Williams.

(Original Song Score and Its Adaptation or Best Adaptation Score)

*****A LITTLE NIGHT MUSIC,** Sascha-Wien/Elliott Kastner, New World Pictures. Jonathon Tunick.

PETE'S DRAGON, Disney, Buena Vista. Al Kasha, Joel Hirschhorn and Irwin Kostal.

THE SLIPPER AND THE ROSE—THE STORY OF CINDERELLA, Paradine Co-Productions, Universal. Richard M. Sherman, Robert B. Sherman and Angela Morley.

SHORT FILMS

(Animated Films)

THE BEAD GAME, National Film Board of Canada. Ishu Patel, producer.

THE DOONESBURY SPECIAL, Hubley Studio. John and Faith Hubley and Gary Trudeau, producers.

JIMMY THE C, Motionpicker Production. James Picker, Robert Grossman and Craig Whitaker, producers.

*****SAND CASTLE,** National Film Board of Canada. Co Hoedeman, producer.

(Live Action)

THE ABSENT-MINDED WAITER, Aspen Film Society. William E. McEuen, producer.

FLOATING FREE, Trans World International. Jerry Butts, producer.

*****I'LL FIND A WAY,** National Film Board of Canada. Beverly Shaffer and Yuki Yoshida, producers.

NOTES ON THE POPULAR ARTS, Saul Bass Films. Saul Bass, producer.

SPACEBORNE, Lawrence Hall of Science Production for the Regents of the University of California with the cooperation of NASA. Philip Dauber, producer.

DOCUMENTARY

(Short Subjects)

AGUEDA MARTINEZ: OUR PEOPLE, OUR COUNTRY, Esparza Production. Moctesuma Esparza, producer.

FIRST EDITION, Sage Productions. Helen Whitney and DeWitt L. Sage, Jr., producers.

*****GRAVITY IS MY ENEMY,** Joseph Production. John Joseph and Jan Stussy, producers.

OF TIME, TOMBS AND TREASURES, Charlie/Papa Production. James R. Messenger and Paul N. Raimondi, producers.

THE SHETLAND EXPERIENCE, Balfour Films. Douglas Gordon, producer.

(Features)

THE CHILDREN OF THEATRE STREET, Mack-Vaganova Company. Robert Dornhelm and Earle Mack, producers.

HIGH GRASS CIRCUS, National Film Board of Canada. Bill Brind, Torben Schjoler and Tony Lanzelo, producers.

HOMAGE TO CHAGALL—THE COLOURS OF LOVE, CBC Production. Harry Rasky, producer.

UNION MAIDS, Klein, Reichert, Mogulescu Production. James Klein, Julia Reichert and Miles Mogulescu, producers.

*****WHO ARE THE DeBOLTS? AND WHERE DID THEY GET NINETEEN KIDS?,** Korty Films/Charles M. Schulz, Sanrio Films. John Korty, Dan McCann and Warren L. Lockhart, producers.

FOREIGN LANGUAGE FILM

IPHIGENIA, (Greece).

*****MADAME ROSA,** (France).

OPERATION THUNDERBOLT, (Israel).

A SPECIAL DAY, (Italy).

THAT OBSCURE OBJECT OF DESIRE, (Spain).

HONORARY AND OTHER AWARDS

TO MARGARET BOOTH for her exceptional contribution to the art of film editing in the motion picture industry.

GORDON E. SAWYER and **SIDNEY P. SOLOW** in appreciation for outstanding service and dedication in upholding the high standards of the Academy of Motion Picture Arts and Sciences. (medal of commendation)

SPECIAL ACHIEVEMENT AWARDS

For Sound Effects Editing: **FRANK WARNER** for *Close Encounters Of The Third Kind,* Columbia.

For Sound Effects Creations: **BENJAMIN BURTT, JR.** for *Star Wars,* 20th Century-Fox.

1977 IRVING G. THALBERG MEMORIAL AWARD

TO WALTER MIRISCH

1977 JEAN HERSHOLT HUMANITARIAN AWARD

TO CHARLTON HESTON

SCIENTIFIC OR TECHNICAL

CLASS I (statuette)

GARRETT BROWN and the **CINEMA PRODUCTS CORP. ENGINEERING STAFF UNDER THE SUPERVISION OF JOHN JURGENS** for the invention and development of Steadicam.

CLASS II (plaque)

JOSEPH D. KELLY, EMORY M. COHEN, BARRY K. HENLEY, HAMMOND H. HOLT and **JOHN AGALSOFF** of **GLEN GLENN SOUND** for the concept and development of a post-production audio processing system for motion picture films.

PANAVISION INCORPORATED for the concept and engineering of the improvements incorporated in the Panaflex Motion Picture Camera.

N. PAUL KENWORTHY, JR. and **WILLIAM R. LATADY** for the invention and development of the Kenworthy Snorkel Camera System for motion picture photography.

JOHN C. DYKSTRA for the development of the Dykstraflex Camera and **ALVAH J. MILLER** and **JERRY JEFFRESS** for the engineering of the Electronic Motion Control System used in concert for multiple exposure visual effects motion picture photography.

THE EASTMAN KODAK COMPANY for the development and introduction of a new duplicating film for motion pictures.

STEFAN KUDELSKI of Nagra Magnetic Recorders, Incorporated, for the engineering of the improvements incorporated in the Nagra 4.2L sound recorder for motion picture production.

CLASS III (citation)

ERNST NETTMANN of the Astrovision Division of Continental Camera Systems, Inc.;

EECO (ELECTRONIC ENGINEERING COMPANY OF CALIFORNIA);

DR. BERNARD KUHL and **WERNER BLOCK** of **OSRAM,** GmbH;

PANAVISION, INCORPORATED (2 citations);

PICLEAR, INC.

*****INDICATES WINNER**

243

1978-1987
The Academy's Sixth Decade

By the start of the Academy's sixth decade, membership in its twelve branches had reached 4190; the number rose to 4489 by 1983 and by 1987 the total tallied in at almost exactly 5000. And membership totals weren't the only thing blooming within the Academy structure.

Old programs were constantly being refined, new ones were instigated and, during the decade, there were so many additional archival acquisitions that the storage facilities of the Academy and its Margaret Herrick Library were fairly bulging at the seams. Prompted by the need for more space, the library underwent some major remodeling and further plans were afoot for the future: the Academy acquired a long-term lease on a structure on La Cienega Boulevard at Olympic in Los Angeles, former home of the Beverly Hills water pumping and purification plant, where the entire library and film archive could eventually move, and expand.

Among the priceless new acquisitions were all George Cukor's personal papers, scripts, photographs and memorabilia, donated by Mr. Cukor himself before his death in 1983. An extensive Alfred Hitchcock collection was donated by his daughter Patricia Hitchcock O'Connell, and Metro-Goldwyn-Mayer gave the Academy a collection of two million historical photographs, covering nearly all the MGM films produced between 1923 and 1972. The Academy also acquired, directly from Mary Pickford and her husband Buddy Rogers,

rare stills, scrapbooks and various papers relating to the actress's remarkable career.

Other collections included the papers of John Huston, scripts of James Wong Howe, costume sketches of Edith Head, the Hal Wallis files covering the 1945-1975 period of his career as an independent producer. Also: the Fred Zinnemann collection, scrapbooks of columnist Louella O. Parsons, and extensive papers and collections of Shirley Temple Black, Fred Zinnemann, Henry King, George Stevens, Sam Peckinpah, Lewis Milestone and Jean Hersholt among the many. Besides full collections, there were also single gems of note such as a shooting script of the 1929-30 Academy Award winner *All Quiet on the Western Front,* donated by William Bakewell, one of the stars of the film.

Throughout the decade, the Academy archivists also continued their Sherlocking to find a one-sheet pre-Oscar poster representing each film that had received a best picture Academy Award, something akin to hunting needles in the proverbial haystack. One of the rewards of the search came with the gift to the Academy of the one-sheet poster for the very first best picture champ, *Wings.* It was donated by Morris Everett, a collector from Cleveland, and is the only such poster on the film known to exist. The poster is on permanent display in the second floor lobby of the Academy's headquarters in Beverly Hills, along with

---

VIVIENNE VERDON-ROE

The second time I was nominated for an Academy Award, I won. It was even more fun!

My film was called Women—for America, for the World. *When the presenter opened the envelope and announced, "The winner is Wo . . . ", I leapt out of my seat and began sprinting down the aisle. Only one film title in my category began with "W"! When he heard we'd won, my husband, Michael, turned to me in excitement—but I was already gone! All that remained on my seat was my evening bag. Instead of graciously kissing my husband and gliding up to the stage, as the actresses usually do, I looked as though I was doing the 100 yard dash. I guess I was afraid they might say, "Oops—got it wrong!"*

Halfway up the aisle, I crashed into an usher. At the last second, I saw we were going to collide, and I managed to swing her around to stop the momentum of my "dash." At least we didn't land on the floor in a heap.

I had rehearsed my acceptance speech a thousand times. I was nervous. All the nominees had been

warned, "At 45 seconds the red light above the TV cameras will come on; at 50 seconds, it will start blinking; at 60 seconds, the music will come up and we will cut to a commercial. DON'T TALK FOR MORE THAN ONE MINUTE! And please, NO POLITICAL SPEECHES!" My films are political (if saving the planet from nuclear war is considered political). I didn't want to offend anyone, but I knew I would never forgive myself if I won an Oscar, but lost the chance to say something that might move the hearts and the minds of one billion people.

I was just about to launch forth, when I felt a tap on my shoulder, and Matthew Broderick, one of the presenters, whispered, "Don't you want this?" In his hand, he held an Oscar.

At last I got to give my speech.

"What a wonderful recognition of all the people who work so hard to end the arms race! Our country is only as good as we make it. Last year, in the United States, 10,000 children died as a direct result of poverty. Not one human being on earth need suffer starvation if, each year, we used the resources of just four days of

John Wayne, Johnny Carson (51st Awards)

Lord Olivier (51st Awards)

Robert DeNiro (53rd Awards)

Robert Redford (53rd Awards)

other rare posters of Oscar-winning films. Utilizing miniature reproductions of those posters, the Academy also commissioned a "Best Picture Poster," which became an immediate collector's item in 1986.

Other acquisitions throughout the decade extended beyond papers, posters and memorabilia. Stanley Kramer donated 35mm copies of several of his films to the Academy archives; an extremely rare nitrate print of the 1915 *Birth of a Nation* was also acquired. Michael Eisner, while president of Paramount Pictures, presented the Academy with a new and complete print of *Wings*, aiding the Academy's goal to eventually obtain one print of every film nominated through the years for the best picture Academy Award. At the end of the 1978-87 decade, the Academy's film archives housed more than 2000 individual films, dating from 1903 to the present.

Most of the films weren't allowed to linger on shelves or rest in vault cans, either. During the decade, the Academy continued — and accelerated — its policy of frequent special showings of the films. Among the most-discussed was a reconstructed print of the early John Wayne epic *The Big Trail*, circa 1930, shown in its original Fox Grandeur wide-screen format. Giorgio Moroder's reconstructed version of Fritz Lang's *Metropolis* also had a first show-

ing at the Academy, as did newly preserved prints of films such as Raoul Walsh's *The Bowery* and George Cukor's *A Bill of Divorcement,* which introduced Katharine Hepburn. A new "Film Classics Revisited" series was also inaugurated in which artists from all branches of the Academy who contributed to a particular film were assembled for a screening of that film, followed by a post-screening discussion. The first in the series was Richard Brooks' *The Blackboard Jungle;* one of the most popular was an evening devoted to *The Wizard of Oz*, bringing together such *Oz* alumni as producer Mervyn LeRoy, makeup artist William Tuttle and performers Ray Bolger and Margaret Hamilton.

Extensive film was also unspooled during the Academy's many retrospective film tributes, given to a wide array of film folk including Groucho Marx, Rudolph Valentino, W.C. Fields, Mary Pickford, James Dean, Judy Garland, Cecil B. DeMille, Allan Dwan, Nunnally Johnson, Mae West, Mickey Mouse, Douglas Fairbanks, Tennessee Williams and Eleanor Powell. Miss Powell herself hosted an evening of film se-

world military spending. Let's improve our efforts to care for each other."

At this point, the audience applauded. I realized this was not just one more rehearsal—this was it! I literally couldn't feel my feet on the ground. I floated off the stage.

I thought I had taken a big risk by doing something other than thanking my mum and dad in my acceptance speech. But at the end of the show, when all the Oscar winners were invited back onto the stage, the President of the Academy turned to me and said, "Thank you for giving one of the most significant speeches of the evening."

The moral of that fits my philosophy of life — "Go for it!"

Vivienne Verdon-Roe
Documentary Short Subject, 1986

SIR JOHN GIELGUD

Of course I was greatly flattered, as well as surprised, when I received my Oscar. The honour was

so entirely unexpected, and I know how much I was indebted to the extremely generous help of Dudley Moore and Liza Minnelli, as well as the author and director, Steve Gordon, whose sudden death, just after the film had been greeted with such success, saddened me very much. It was immensely gratifying to be singled out with such a very prestigious award and to be praised for work so entirely different from that of my long career in the live theatre over more than sixty years.

My occasional forays in early films (I even made a couple of silent ones in my salad days) proved to be remarkably uninteresting, giving me no confidence in my adaptability, although I had always been a devotee of the cinema as a member of the audience.

It was not until 1951, when I first came to Hollywood to act with James Mason and Marlon Brando in the Mankiewicz film Julius Caesar that I really began to appreciate the fascinating subtleties of screen acting, with its endlessly complicated schedules and demands.

Since then I have enjoyed memorable associations with a great number of fine players and gifted directors both in Europe and America, and I feel very lucky to

be able to appear on the screen so long as health and memory allow. I shall always be grateful to have won a good opinion from the leaders of the film world, and to find encouragement from the figure on my mantelpiece.

John Gielgud
Best Supporting Actor, 1981

SIR RICHARD ATTENBOROUGH

"If you work in movies, being awarded an Oscar marks the absolute pinnacle of your career. There is nothing in the world to beat it. As a film maker who happens to be British, I profoundly appreciate the Academy's extraordinary and continuing generosity towards technicians, actors and actresses from other countries. In paying tribute to their endeavours, the membership has, over the years, effectively elevated this essentially twentieth century medium into an art form truly worthy of international recognition.

Sir Richard Attenborough, Best Director, 1982
Best Picture, 1982

Warren Beatty (54th Awards)

Mickey Rooney congratulated by Carol Burnett, Walter Matthau, Liza Minnelli and assorted gentlemen (55th Awards)

quences saluting the work of dance directors; other salutes and tributes were devoted to Luise Rainer, swash-buckling films, Max von Sydow, ASCAP members, even Donald Duck. One such evening in 1985, devoted to Shirley Temple Black, ended with a surprise. After the showing of highlights from many of the Temple films (interspersed with a question-and-answer session), the former child star was handed a new, shiny, full-size Oscar to replace the miniature one awarded her back in the 1934 awards year.

Academy screenings also took place outside of the Hollywood area. A special tribute to Myrna Loy was given by the Academy at New York's Carnegie Hall in 1985, followed by a dinner in Miss Loy's honor at the Grand Ballroom of the Waldorf-Astoria. In 1983, the Academy also sponsored a six-city tour of a newly reconstructed version of the 1954 *A Star is Born.* The first "return" screening was given July 7 before a sold-out audience at the 6200-seat Radio City Music Hall in New York City; that was followed by gala showings in Washington D.C., Oakland, Los Angeles, Chicago and Dallas. The *Star* tour was designed not only to drama-

William Hurt, Sally Field (58th Awards)

246

JOHN PATRICK SHANLEY

Here I am. I'm sitting there. In this immense room full of celebrities. I've been sitting there for three hours. My category is best original screenplay. For some reason that's near the end.

Now I should explain that all my life I haven't gotten nominated for anything and, what's more, I've gotten bad reviews. I had been working in theater for over ten years. Theater is mad dogs in the gutter fighting over a bare bone. In short, I'd learned to survive on no recognition and very little money. I was a man who was used to living in the desert. And here I am, this artistic camel, a creature designed to survive an extremely harsh environment, sitting in a tuxedo waiting for my category. And I'm dying. I'm like a man with a parachute but I'm not jumping out of a plane. I've got nothing to do. There is nothing to do. My life has stopped. This clock is ticking.

One shoe fell. I was nominated for an Academy Award. More than I ever hoped for. And this was only my second movie. I told everyone. I'm happy with this.

A man at my stage of things. A nomination is an incredible honor. But then sick little voices began to whisper, Well, maybe you'll win. Or worse, You know, I think you're going to win. Or, the ultimate set-up for disaster, I KNOW YOU'RE GOING TO WIN! I tried to fight it. But how far gone I was, in crediting or discrediting these voices, I could not know. Only when the announcement And the Winner Is was made would I truly know what, in my heart of hearts, I had prepared myself for.

And now, I'm there, it's been three hours, and my category is coming up. Audrey Hepburn and Gregory Peck come out to deliver the news. I'm sunk in my chair. My wife is patting my arm. I feel like I'm looking into my own open grave. And then Audrey Hepburn opens the envelope and Gregory Peck reads, And the Winner Is: John Patrick Shanley, for Moonstruck!

I'm totally shocked. I had completely prepared myself to lose. And I won. I kiss my wife. I say to her, I won? She nods. I get up and head for the stage. I know what I'm going to do. I'm going to shake hands with Gregory

Peck and kiss Audrey Hepburn. I get up there. I do it. I think, You just kissed Audrey Hepburn. I got this gold statue in my hand. This statue I've seen all my life. I look out at this enormous audience, and I think, John, let this happen to you. Let this in. And I did. Like the sunshine. I let this good moment in my life happen to me. I was happy. And I'm still happy when I think of it now.

John Patrick Shanley
Screenplay Directly for the Screen, 1987

BO GOLDMAN

"There are years between for all writers when there are no awards. I would like to thank some (people) who have helped me and whom I love." A piece of my speech and it still holds; I always feel I am in the years between.

Bo Goldman
Adapted Screenplay, 1975; 1980

tize the cause of film preservation, but also to generate funds for further preservation needs.

But not all of the Academy tributes were done via sprocket-holes. Throughout the decade, numerous exhibits were presented in the main lobby of the Academy headquarters, and open free to the public. One display, saluting costume designers, featured 18 Oscar-nominated or winning costumes displayed on mannequins, accompanied by their designers' original sketches. Other displays were devoted to a spectrum of subjects including the work of art directors, the making of *Gone With the Wind*, the 75th anniversary of Hollywood, portrait photographers and, one of the most unusual, film personalities as subjects of *Time Magazine* covers from 1923-1985.

There was also much attention given during the decade to the various activities which had started and taken root in earlier years, such as the Student Film competitions and awards; also various scholarships and grants. The Academy's Visiting Artists Program continued to send filmmakers representing the various Academy branches to U.S. colleges for lectures, seminars, workshops and discussions. Participants included Vincente Minnelli traveling to Northern Arizona University, Edward Dmytryk to Purdue University, Frank Capra to the New York State University at Buffalo, Arthur Penn to Syracuse University, Gordon Parks to D.C.'s Black Film Institute, Tony Bill to Alaska Pacific University, and many others.

During her presidency, Fay Kanin also traveled extensively on behalf of the Academy, including a trip in 1981 to the People's Republic of China, arranged by the cultural arm of the State Department, to show the first American films to be widely seen there since 1945. The films she took: *The*

Barbara Stanwyck and admirer at post-Awards ball

Shirley MacLaine (56th Awards)

RICK BAKER

At the age of ten I decided to become a makeup artist. I was determined to try and become one of the best; I worked hard at my hobby, hoping that someday it would become my profession. I dreamed if I worked hard enough, one day I might be honored with an Oscar.

I'll never forget hearing Vincent Price saying "And the winner is Rick Baker." At that moment my childhood dream came true.

Rick Baker
Makeup, 1981; 1987; 1994; 1996; 1997

CHARLES L. CAMPBELL

I grew up during the Depression when movies were the great escape. The bill changed twice a week with a special matinee for kids on Saturday. It was a good time for me, and those hours in the darkened theater helped shape my life and give me a dream.

I remember seeing lights in the sky one night in those long ago days and I remember my Uncle Mac taking

me on the four-block walk to Fort Street and the Lincoln Square Theatre where the giant klieg lights were clustered around a stake-back truck. There were steps that led to a wooden viewing platform around the truck that contained a live rhinoceros. To see with my own eyes and smell a creature that had only existed before in the pages of my grandfather's National Geographics, overwhelmed me. The occasion was the Detroit premiere of an Osa and Martin Johnson film documenting their exploits in Africa.

My fate was sealed: I would see Africa and work in the business of my idols, Jack Holt, Richard Dix, Cagney, Powell, Cooper, and Osa and Martin Johnson.

Happy endings; I've been to Africa, won two Oscars and live in a house where on a clear day, I can see the ocean. If that is not enough in the realm of my good fortune, I was selected by my peers as a Governor of the Academy of Motion Picture Arts and Sciences, the greatest honor of all.

However, to bring this all into perspective, I reflect

back to my first Academy Award, after having the last dance on the floor and the last drink at the bar with an arm grown weak with the weight of my prize; my proud wife, Maxine, and I were limo'ed home where I sat traumatized until 4 a.m., staring at the culmination of my dreams.

My morning came at noon, and at an over-the-shoulder glance as I left the house, I still couldn't believe the "Golden Man" had come to stay.

Late as I was, yet hungry, I stopped at the Deli at the bottom of my hill for a sandwich to get me through the day on the dubbing stage.

When Joe, the Deli Manager, saw me amid the crowd at his counter, he smiled and wiggled a long finger close to my face. "I saw you, I saw you on television last night." I was tired, humble, but proud. I felt a lot of eyes searching my face; I felt very special. My celebrity ended suddenly, when Joe asked, "Who catered?"

Charles L. Campbell
Sound Effects Editing, 1982; 1985; 1988

Anjelica Huston (58th Awards)

Marlee Matlin (59th Awards)

Steven Spielberg (59th Awards)

Black Stallion, Guess Who's Coming to Dinner, Singin' in the Rain, Shane and *Snow White and the Seven Dwarfs.* The Academy's Executive Director James M. Roberts also traveled to Taipei as a guest of the government of the Republic of China; Gene Allen, during his presidency, also represented the Academy in China and in other far-from-Hollywood areas including five East European nations. Robert Wise, the decade's final president, carried the Academy's message to the Soviet Union and South America.

The *Academy Players Directory* also celebrated its 50th anniversary during the decade, with 17,000 actors listed in the birthday edition, compared to the 1200 that graced Issue number one. In 1982, the Academy decided to reprint that first (1937) edition of the Directory and hosted a party to honor the 26 players listed in both the first and the latest editions. Among those attending the nostalgic gathering as honorees were Ginger Rogers, John Payne, Jane Withers, Marsha Hunt, Edith Fellows, Harry Ritz, Gene Raymond, Keye Luke and Rudy Vallee. The *Annual Index to*

Motion Picture Credits also continued to thrive during the decade.

The "Marvin Borowsky Memorial Lecture in Writing for the Screen," given annually by the Academy, also continued successfully, presented through the decade by a succession of screenwriters including Richard Brooks, Carl Foreman, Waldo Salt, Jay Pressen Allen, Lawrence Kasdan and Philip Dunne. And joining the Borowsky lectures, three other "recurring lectures" on the art of motion pictures were added to the Academy's programming agenda. In 1981, the Academy began an annual "George Pal Lecture on Fantasy in Film," established in memory of the famous science-fiction director. It was delivered in its first year by Ray Bradbury, and in later years by Carl Sagan, Richard Matheson, Jim Hensen and others.

The "Jack Oakie Lecture on Comedy in Film" began in 1982, designed to mix an analysis of comic strategies with illustrations of their proper use. Larry Gelbart was the first speaker in this series, and was succeeded by Gene Wilder, Jerry Lewis and others. The

first "George Stevens Lecture on Directing" was also held in 1982 with Robert Benton as lecturer.

One of the most immediately popular new Academy functions also made its debut during the sixth decade, and became an instant success. On March 9, 1982, the Academy for the first time hosted a luncheon honoring all of the year's Academy Award nominees. It was designed as a casual gathering where nominees could comfortably visit with their peers, away from the hysteria of the actual Oscar evening, and it was a megahit with all, a highpoint in the whole Oscar award structure. At the end of the luncheon, the nominees also received their official nomination certificates and posed for a group photograph. After that first get-together, Steven Spielberg told a reporter, "It was wonderful! They made you feel like all the nominees were winners, which is the way it should be." Voila!, a new Oscar tradition was born.

And new traditions didn't stop there, either. There were other activities, other duties, other functions, each

CARLO RAMBALDI

I have had the distinct honor to be awarded three Oscars, (for King Kong, for Alien, and for E.T.), yet I never believed I would ever win even one since in Europe the word was that the Americans were very nationalistic and hence almost never gave the Academy Award to foreigners except for the category of best foreign film.

But now I know that such talk in Europe consisted simply of false rumors.

Now I know that the members of the Academy are not prejudiced when they judge the work of those who make motion pictures.

For me winning an Oscar is the physical proof of the huge and warm applause of the Academy members, testifying to the winner's deep professional seriousness and the high quality of his work.

Even in Europe the Oscar is recognized as the highest award a film maker can receive. It is just as highly-coveted in Italy as it is here; perhaps even more so, since so few Europeans are fortunate enough to be awarded an Oscar.

Perhaps the most important of my three Oscars is the one awarded me for having created E.T. for the movie of the same name.

It proved that a mechanical actor can excite the emotions of motion picture audiences just as much as can a human actor, and became a worldwide phenomenon in doing so. One thing I will always remember is how a family of American tourists visiting Los Angeles postponed their departure for home by two days just so they could track me down and meet me.

The Oscar also conferred upon me a worldwide fame which otherwise I feel sure I would not have enjoyed.

Carlo Rambaldi
Visual Effects, 1976; 1979; 1982

OLIVER STONE

It reinforces the sense in me that I am not totally worthless as a human being...but then again, I still have doubts.

Oliver Stone
Screenplay Based on Another Medium, 1978
Best Director, 1986; 1989

VITTORIO STORARO

I never thought I could be so moved if my name were to be called at the opening of the envelope for my first nomination, for Apocalypse Now. I still don't remember how I was able to put one step after another in order to reach the stage; I still don't remember how I was able to put one word after another in order to say my speech.

When my envelope was opened the second time for Reds my entire body got paralyzed. I will never forget my suffering with each step I took and with any single word I said.

When I was called the third time for The Last Emperor my heart was jumping up and down so that I thought I might have a heart attack before arriving at the podium. When I reached the statuette and I looked at the audience, I understood once more, that that moment is one of the greatest possible emotions in life. You can never get used to it. If I am ever nominated again in my life, I think I will take a doctor with me, just in case.

Vittorio Storaro
Cinematography 1979; 1981; 1987

part of the Academy's continued involvement in devoting time and muscle to representing, encouraging and preserving the best aspects of the motion picture arena. Good times and bad, the Academy also tried to keep in step, and to stay fair.

A good example occured in 1985 when the Academy caught up on some 28-year-old unfinished business. Back in 1957, in accordance with the official screen credits on *The Bridge on the River Kwai,* the Academy had given the Oscar for the screenplay of *Kwai* to Pierre Boulle, the author of the book on which the script was based. The actual screenwriters had been Carl Foreman and Michael Wilson who, at the time, were denied the credit due to tempers of the time, and sentiment in some industry quarters, stemming from the House Un-American Activities probes of the time. So, in response to a motion from the Writers Branch Governors, the Academy Board unanimously voted to correct the historical record by, at last, officially recognizing Foreman and Wilson as the true collaborators on that winning *Kwai* script of nearly three decades before. In a special ceremony on March 16, 1985, the families of the two writers, both deceased, were presented with Academy Award statuettes. It was a symbolic gesture but one that suggested the Academy was still doing its best to correctly honor achievement in filmmaking.

ACADEMY PRESIDENTS, THE SIXTH DECADE

May 1978–July 1979	*Howard W. Koch*
July 1979–July 1980	*Fay Kanin*
July 1980–July 1981	*Fay Kanin*
July 1981–July 1982	*Fay Kanin*
July 1982–July 1983	*Fay Kanin*
July 1983–July 1984	*Gene Allen*
July 1984–July 1985	*Gene Allen*
July 1985–July 1986	*Robert Wise*
July 1986–July 1987	*Robert Wise*
July 1987–July 1988	*Robert Wise*

Paul Newman (60th Awards)

Cher (60th Awards)

BEN KINGSLEY

We are gladiators; benign gladiators; after the sweat, dust, thrill of the event, we turn to the emperor for a sign. The craft. The applause. A symbiotic relationship—the one cannot live without the other. I cannot turn my back on pomp, ceremony, occasion, glamour. I know the motive behind my craft is modest and pure—to please.

When I was nominated for the Oscar, my fellow gladiators were Hoffman, Lemmon, O'Toole, Newman. Honestly, it was enough to be placed in the arena with them, my competitors, my heroes, my colleagues.

I live in a small farming village; Doris cycles round with the post each morning. "Would you sign for this, Dear?" she said, hauling a hefty package out of the basket of her bicycle.

My Oscar had arrived.
I had pleased.
The emperor had spoken.
Thank You.

Ben Kingsley
Best Actor, 1982

DAME PEGGY ASHCROFT

To be nominated for an Oscar award was certainly something I would not have believed could happen to me—after a life-time in the theatre and very occasional ventures into the film world. That it should actually have been conferred was still more astonishing! Amazement—and, of course, gratitude—were my predominant feelings. Perhaps I have still a slight sense of disbelief that it has happened, all the more because illness sadly prevented me from receiving it in person. But the honour and the gratitude remain—all the more as I feel I have been welcomed into a world in which I feel I am a visitor.

Peggy Ashcroft
Best Supporting actress, 1984

F. MURRAY ABRAHAM

As for the general speculation about an "Oscar-jinx," what hogwash. The Oscar is the single most important event of my career. I have dined with kings, shared equal billing with my idols, lectured at Harvard and Columbia, and am professor of theater at the City University in Brooklyn. I am privileged to have taken part in the greatest international gathering of artists in the world. If this is a jinx, I'll take two.

F. Murray Abraham
Best Actor, 1984

MAUREEN STAPLETON

To paraphrase Leigh Hunt
Say I'm weary
Say I'm sad
Say that health
And wealth have
Missed me,
Say I'm growing old
But add
"Oscar" kissed me.

Maureen Stapleton
Best Supporting Actress, 1981

The Lord and the Duke—both legends, both former Oscar winners, both survivors despite debilitating bouts of ill health—put a powerhouse finale on the first Oscar show of the Academy's second half-century. England's Laurence Olivier, age seventy-one, and America's John Wayne, also seventy-one, each made a special appearance near the conclusion of the 51st Academy Award festivities on April 9, 1979, and each brought the audience to its feet, in respect and in awe. Olivier was receiving his third Oscar (following a special one for 1946's *Henry V* and his best actor trophy for 1948's *Hamlet*), this latest one on behalf of his entire body of film work. Wayne, recently out of the hospital, was on hand to present the best picture award. There was some irony, under the circumstances. The winner, announced by the Duke, was the Vietnam war drama *The Deer Hunter,* a far cry from the kind of war films Wayne had often made in his own movie past.

Vietnam was highly in evidence throughout the night, in fact. *Coming Home,* which focused on the rehabilitation of a disabled Viet vet, won Oscars for Jane Fonda and Jon Voight as the best actress and best actor of the year; *Home* also won for its original screenplay. *The Deer Hunter* also received awards for the direction by Michael Cimino, for best supporting actor (Christopher Walken) plus nods for film editing and sound. Prior to the presentations at the Los Angeles Music Center,

police had some scuffles with demonstrators who objected to *The Deer Hunter* as a "racist" film and as a "fantasy picturization" of the Vietnam cause. As tempers flared, several arrests were made. Cimino later told the press, "I was trying to just make a movie, not rewrite history."

Maggie Smith was named best supporting actress for *California Suite,* considered a major surprise of the night. Honorary awards went to Walter Lantz, director King Vidor and New York's Museum of Modern Art. France's *Get Out Your Handkerchiefs* was named the top foreign language film of the year and Columbia Pictures' chairman of the board Leo Jaffe received the Jean Hersholt Humanitarian Award.

For Oscar's 51st show there was also a new master-of-ceremonies: Johnny Carson, making his first appearance on an Oscarcast. In evidence, but not participating in the show, was Warren Beatty, seated in the audience with girlfriend Diane Keaton. Beatty was the year's most conspicuous nominee, the first man since Orson Welles (in 1941) to be nominated in four separate Oscar categories in a single year, all of them for *Heaven Can Wait,* a feat he was to repeat three years later with 1981's *Reds.* For the first time in Academy history, the five nominated songs were sung by the singers who introduced them in the films; Sammy Davis, Jr. and Steve Lawrence delivered a production number built around songs through the years that were never nominated for an Oscar.

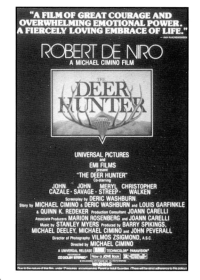

250

Best Picture: The Deer Hunter *(Universal; produced by Barry Spikings, Michael Deeley, Michael Cimino and John Peverall) and* **Best Director: Michael Cimino** *(right, with Robert DeNiro) for* The Deer Hunter. *Although it was undeniably the most stinging anti-war film since* All Quiet on the Western Front, *director Michael Cimino denied that* The Deer Hunter *was really about war at all. "It is a film about people in a crisis," he said. "The war is incidental." Nevertheless, the Vietnam war was a brutal aspect of the excellent film, in which Robert DeNiro, Christopher Walken and John Savage played three close buddies from a rural Pennsylvania steel mill town, all drafted into the Vietnam situation with tragic consequences for each.*

But it was Olivier and Wayne who really gave punch to the long-winded, three-hour-and-25-minute show. Said the Duke, looking thin and wan, "Oscar and I have something in common. Oscar first came to Hollywood in 1928; so did I. We're both a little weatherbeaten but we're still here, and plan to be around for a whole lot longer." Unfortunately the words on his own durability turned out to be inaccurate. Two months and two days later, John Wayne died of cancer.

Best Actor: **Jon Voight** *as Luke Martin and* **Best Actress:** **Jane Fonda** *as Sally Hyde in* Coming Home *(United Artists; directed by Hal Ashby). For Fonda, it was the second time in the winner's circle, following 1971's* Klute, *but she said "This one means much more, because the film means so much to me. I've been living with it for eight years." She had been one of the instigators of the project, a compelling drama about the wife (Fonda) of a gung-ho marine officer (Bruce Dern) who re-meets and falls in love with an old high-school classmate (Voight) who's been crippled in the Vietnam war. By virtue of the Oscar wins by costars Voight and Fonda,* Coming Home *became the fourth film in 51 years to spawn both a best actor and best actress winner (following 1934's* It Happened One Night, *1975's* One Flew over the Cuckoo's Nest *and 1976's* Network*).*

Best Supporting Actor: **Christopher Walken** *as Nick (at right with Robert DeNiro, Chuck Aspegren, John Savage and John Cazale) in* The Deer Hunter. *Walken was unknown to most filmgoers when he made* The Deer Hunter *and it was a smashing introduction: his character is a blue-collar American ultimately sent to Vietnam and captured by the Viet Cong. Tortured both mentally and physically, heavily drugged and half-insane, he is killed while playing Russian roulette in a Saigon gambling den, a needless casualty of a complicated war.*

Best Supporting Actress: **Maggie Smith** *as Diana Barry in* California Suite *(Columbia; produced by Ray Stark). Based on a Neil Simon play comprised of four separate playlets set in the common environment of the Beverly Hills Hotel, the movie version of* Suite, *directed by Herbert Ross, kept the setting but integrated the stories into one revolving plotline. Most fun of the situations involved Maggie Smith (right, with Michael Caine as her husband), deliciously playing an actress holed up at the hotel while awaiting the outcome of Oscar night. Besides being a nervous nominee, she also has to cope with a hubby whose sexual tastes are different, yet similar, to her own. It was a second Academy Award for Smith (her first was for 1969's* The Prime of Miss Jean Brodie); *via* California Suite *she also became the first person to become an Oscar winner for playing an Oscar loser.*

PICTURE

COMING HOME, Hellman, UA. Produced by Jerome Hellman.
*__**THE DEER HUNTER,** EMI/Cimino, Universal. Produced by Barry Spikings, Michael Deeley, Michael Cimino and John Peverall.
HEAVEN CAN WAIT, Dogwood, Paramount. Produced by Warren Beatty.
MIDNIGHT EXPRESS, Casablanca, Columbia. Produced by Alan Marshall and David Puttnam.
AN UNMARRIED WOMAN, 20th Century-Fox. Produced by Paul Mazursky and Tony Ray.

ACTOR

WARREN BEATTY in *Heaven Can Wait,* Dogwood, Paramount.
GARY BUSEY in *The Buddy Holly Story,* Innovisions-ECA, Columbia.
ROBERT DE NIRO in *The Deer Hunter,* EMI/Cimino, Universal.
LAURENCE OLIVIER in *The Boys From Brazil,* ITC, 20th Century-Fox.
*__**JON VOIGHT** in *Coming Home,* Hellman, UA.

ACTRESS

INGRID BERGMAN in *Autumn Sonata,* Personafilm GmbH, Grade-Starger-ITC, New World Pictures.
ELLEN BURSTYN in *Same Time, Next Year,* Mirisch-Mulligan, Universal.
JILL CLAYBURGH in *An Unmarried Woman,* 20th Century-Fox.
*__**JANE FONDA** in *Coming Home,* Hellman, UA.
GERALDINE PAGE in *Interiors,* Rollins-Joffe, UA.

SUPPORTING ACTOR

BRUCE DERN in *Coming Home,* Hellman, UA.
RICHARD FARNSWORTH in *Comes a Horseman,* Chartoff-Winkler, UA.
JOHN HURT in *Midnight Express,* Casablanca, Columbia.
*__**CHRISTOPHER WALKEN** in *The Deer Hunter,* EMI/Cimino, Universal.
JACK WARDEN in *Heaven Can Wait,* Dogwood, Paramount.

SUPPORTING ACTRESS

DYAN CANNON in *Heaven Can Wait,* Dogwood, Paramount.
PENELOPE MILFORD in *Coming Home,* Hellman, UA.
*__**MAGGIE SMITH** in *California Suite,* Stark, Columbia.
MAUREEN STAPLETON in *Interiors,* Rollins-Joffe, UA.
MERYL STREEP in *The Deer Hunter,* EMI/Cimino, Universal.

DIRECTING

COMING HOME, Hellman, UA. Hal Ashby.
*__**THE DEER HUNTER,** EMI/Cimino, Universal. Michael Cimino.
HEAVEN CAN WAIT, Dogwood, Paramount. Warren Beatty and Buck Henry.
INTERIORS, Rollins-Joffe, UA. Woody Allen.
MIDNIGHT EXPRESS, Casablanca, Columbia. Alan Parker.

WRITING

(Screenplay Written Directly For The Screen)

AUTUMN SONATA, Personafilm GmbH, Grade-Starger-ITC, New World Pictures. Ingmar Bergman.
*__**COMING HOME,** Hellman, UA. Nancy Dowd, Waldo Salt and Robert C. Jones.
THE DEER HUNTER, EMI/Cimino, Universal. Michael Cimino, Deric Washburn, Louis Garfinkle, Quinn K. Redeker and Deric Washburn.
INTERIORS, Rollins-Joffe, UA. Woody Allen.
AN UNMARRIED WOMAN, 20th Century-Fox. Paul Mazursky.

(Screenplay Based On Material From Another Medium)

BLOODBROTHERS, Warner Bros. Walter Newman.
CALIFORNIA SUITE, Stark, Columbia. Neil Simon.
HEAVEN CAN WAIT, Dogwood, Paramount. Elaine May and Warren Beatty.
*__**MIDNIGHT EXPRESS,** Casablanca, Columbia. Oliver Stone.
SAME TIME, NEXT YEAR, Mirisch-Mulligan, Universal. Bernard Slade.

CINEMATOGRAPHY

*__**DAYS OF HEAVEN,** OP, Paramount. Nestor Almendros.
THE DEER HUNTER, EMI/Cimino, Universal. Vilmos Zsigmond.
HEAVEN CAN WAIT, Dogwood, Paramount. William A. Fraker.
SAME TIME, NEXT YEAR, Mirisch-Mulligan, Universal. Robert Surtees.
THE WIZ, Motown, Universal. Oswald Morris.

ART DIRECTION-
SET DECORATION

THE BRINK'S JOB, De Laurentiis, Universal. Dean Tavoularis, and Angelo Graham; George R. Nelson and Bruce Kay.
CALIFORNIA SUITE, Stark, Columbia. Albert Brenner; Marvin March.

*HEAVEN CAN WAIT, Dogwood, Paramount. Paul
  Sylbert and Edwin O'Donovan; George Gaines.
INTERIORS, Rollins-Joffe, UA. Mel Bourne; Daniel
  Robert.
THE WIZ, Motown, Universal. Tony Walton and Philip
  Rosenberg; Edward Stewart and Robert Drumheller.

COSTUME DESIGN

CARAVANS, Ibex-F.I.D.C.I., Universal. Renie Conley.
DAYS OF HEAVEN, OP, Paramount. Patricia Norris.
*DEATH ON THE NILE, Brabourne-Goodwin,
  Paramount. Anthony Powell.
THE SWARM, Warner Bros. Paul Zastupnevich.
THE WIZ, Motown, Universal. Tony Walton.

SOUND

THE BUDDY HOLLY STORY, Innovisions-ECA,
  Columbia. Tex Rudloff, Joel Fein, Curly Thirlwell
  and Willie Byrton.
DAYS OF HEAVEN, OP, Paramount. John K.
  Wilkinson, Robert W. Glass, Jr., John T. Reitz and
  Barry Thomas.
*THE DEER HUNTER, EMI/Cimino, Universal. Richard
  Portman, William McCaughey, Aaron Rochin and
  Darin Knight.
HOOPER, Warner Bros. Robert Knudson, Robert J.
  Glass, Don MacDougall and Jack Solomon.
SUPERMAN, Dovemead, Salkind, Warner Bros.
  Gordon K. McCallum, Graham Hartstone, Nicolas Le
  Messurier and Roy Charman.

FILM EDITING

THE BOYS FROM BRAZIL, ITC, 20th Century-Fox.
  Robert E. Swink.
COMING HOME, Hellman, UA. Don Zimmerman.
*THE DEER HUNTER, EMI/Cimino, Universal. Peter
  Zinner.
MIDNIGHT EXPRESS, Casablanca, Columbia. Gerry
  Hambling.
SUPERMAN, Dovemead, Salkind, Warner Bros. Stuart
  Baird.

MUSIC

(Song)

HOPELESSLY DEVOTED TO YOU (Grease,
  Stigwood/Carr, Paramount); Music and Lyrics by
  John Farrar.
*LAST DANCE (Thank God It's Friday, Casablanca-
  Motown, Columbia); Music and Lyrics by Paul
  Jabara.
THE LAST TIME I FELT LIKE THIS (Same Time,
  Next Year, Mirisch-Mulligan, Universal); Music by
  Marvin Hamlisch. Lyrics by Alan and Marilyn
  Bergman.
READY TO TAKE A CHANCE AGAIN (Foul Play,
  Miller-Milkis/Higgins, Paramount); Music by Charles
  Fox. Lyrics by Norman Gimbel.
WHEN YOU'RE LOVED (The Magic of Lassie, Lassie
  Productions, The International Picture Show
  Company); Music and Lyrics by Richard M. Sherman
  and Robert B. Sherman.

(Original Score)

THE BOYS FROM BRAZIL, ITC, 20th Century-Fox.
  Jerry Goldsmith.
DAYS OF HEAVEN, OP, Paramount. Ennio Morricone.
HEAVEN CAN WAIT, Dogwood, Paramount. Dave
  Grusin.
*MIDNIGHT EXPRESS, Casablanca, Columbia. Giorgio
  Moroder.
SUPERMAN, Dovemead, Salkind, Warner Bros. John
  Williams.

(Original Song Score and its Adaptation or Best Adaptation Score)

*THE BUDDY HOLLY STORY, Innovisions-ECA,
  Columbia. Joe Renzetti.
PRETTY BABY, Malle, Paramount. Jerry Wexler.
THE WIZ, Motown, Universal. Quincy Jones.

SHORT FILMS

(Animated Films)

OH MY DARLING, Nico Crama Production. Nico
  Crama, producer.
RIP VAN WINKLE, A Will Vinton/Billy Budd Film.
  Will Vinton, producer.
*SPECIAL DELIVERY, National Film Board of Canada.
  Eunice Macaulay and John Weldon, producers.

(Live Action)

A DIFFERENT APPROACH, A Jim
  Belcher/Brookfield Production. Jim Belcher and
  Fern Field, producers.
MANDY'S GRANDMOTHER, Illumination Films.
  Andrew Sugerman, producer.
STRANGE FRUIT, The American Film Institute. Seth
  Pinsker, producer.
*TEENAGE FATHER, New Visions Inc. for the
  Children's Home Society of California. Taylor
  Hackford, producer.

DOCUMENTARY

(Short Subjects)

THE DIVIDED TRAIL: A NATIVE AMERICAN
  ODYSSEY, A Jerry Aronson Production. Jerry
  Aronson, producer.
AN ENCOUNTER WITH FACES, Films Division,
  Government of India. K.K. Kapil, producer.
*THE FLIGHT OF THE GOSSAMER CONDOR, A
  Shedd Production. Jacqueline Phillips Shedd and
  Ben Shedd, producer.
GOODNIGHT MISS ANN, An August Cinquegrana
  Films Production. August Cinquegrana, producer.
SQUIRES OF SAN QUENTIN, The J. Gary Mitchell
  Film Company. J. Gary Mitchell, producer.

(Features)

THE LOVERS' WIND, Ministry of Culture & Arts of
  Iran. Albert Lamorisse, producer.
MYSTERIOUS CASTLES OF CLAY, A Survival Anglia
  Ltd. Production. Alan Root, producer.
RAONI, A Franco-Brazilian Production. Jean-Pierre
  Dutilleux, Barry Williams and Michel Gast,
  producers.
*SCARED STRAIGHT!, A Golden West Television
  Production. Arnold Shapiro, producer.
WITH BABIES AND BANNERS: STORY OF THE
  WOMEN'S EMERGENCY BRIGADE, A Women's
  Labor History Film Project Production. Anne
  Bohlen, Lyn Goldfarb and Lorraine Gray, producers.

FOREIGN LANGUAGE FILM

*GET OUT YOUR HANDKERCHIEFS (France).
THE GLASS CELL (German Federal Republic).
HUNGARIANS (Hungary).
VIVA ITALIA! (Italy).
WHITE BIM BLACK EAR (U.S.S.R.).

HONORARY AND OTHER AWARDS

TO WALTER LANTZ for bringing joy and laughter to
  every part of the world through his unique animated
  motion pictures.
TO THE MUSEUM OF MODERN ART,
  DEPARTMENT OF FILM for the contribution it has
  made to the public's perception of movies as an art
  form.
TO LAURENCE OLIVIER for the full body of his
  work, for the unique achievements of his entire
  career and his lifetime of contribution to the art of
  film.
TO KING VIDOR for his incomparable achievements
  as a cinematic creator and innovator.
TO LINWOOD G. DUNN, LOREN L. RYDER and
  WALDON O. WATSON in appreciation for
  outstanding service and dedication in upholding the
  high standards of the Academy of Motion Picture
  Arts and Sciences. (Medals of Commendation)

SPECIAL ACHIEVEMENT AWARDS

For Visual Effects: LES BOWIE, COLIN CHILVERS,
  DENYS COOP, ROY FIELD, DEREK MEDDINGS
  and ZORAN PERISIC for "Superman," a Dovemead
  Ltd. Production, Alexander Salkind Presentation,
  Warner Bros.

1978 IRVING G. THALBERG MEMORIAL AWARD

None given this year.

1978 JEAN HERSHOLT HUMANITARIAN AWARD

TO LEO JAFFE

SCIENTIFIC OR TECHNICAL AWARDS

Effective this year, Class I became Academy Award of Merit,
  Class II became Scientific and Engineering Award and
  Class III became Technical Achievement Award.

(Academy Award of Merit)

EASTMAN KODAK COMPANY for the research and
  development of a Duplicating Color Film for Motion
  Pictures.
STEFAN KUDELSKI of Nagra Magnetic Recorders,
  Incorporated, for the continuing research, design
  and development of the Nagra Production Sound
  Recorder for Motion Pictures.
PANAVISION, INCORPORATED. and its engineering
  staff under the direction of Robert E. Gottschalk, for
  the concept, design and continuous development of
  the Panaflex Motion Picture Camera System.

(Scientific and Engineering Award)

RAY M. DOLBY, IOAN R. ALLEN, DAVID P.
  ROBINSON, STEPHEN M. KATZ and PHILLIP S.
  J. BOOLE of Dolby Laboratories, Incorporated, for
  the development and implementation of an
  improved Sound Recording and Reproducing System
  for Motion Picture Production and Exhibition.

(Technical Achievement Award)

KARL MACHER and GLENN M. BERGGREN of Isco
  Optische Werke for the development and
  introduction of the Cinelux-ULTRA Lens for 35mm
  Motion Picture Projection.
DAVID J. DEGENKOLB, ARTHUR L. FORD and
  FRED J. SCOBEY of DeLuxe General, Incorporated,
  for the development of a Method to Recycle Motion
  Picture Laboratory Photographic Wash Waters by Ion
  Exchange.
KIICHI SEKIGUCHI of CINE-FI International for the
  development of the CINE-FI Auto Radio Sound
  System for Drive-In Theaters.
LEONARD CHAPMAN of Leonard Equipment
  Company, for the design and manufacture of a small,
  mobile, motion picture camera platform known as
  the Chapman Hustler Dolly.
JAMES L. FISHER of J.L. Fisher, Incorporated, for
  the design and manufacture of a small, mobile,
  motion picture camera platform known as the Fisher
  Model Ten Dolly.
ROBERT STINDT of Production Grip Equipment
  Company, for the design and manufacture of a small,
  mobile, motion picture camera platform known as
  the Stindt Dolly.

*INDICATES WINNER

Dustin Hoffman, winning his first Academy Award (for 1979's *Kramer vs. Kramer*), included thanks in his acceptance speech to his parents "for not practicing birth control"; that remark was perhaps the most unexpected delivery in an evening notable for its lack of surprises. Four months before the 52nd Oscars were handed out on April 14, 1980, the Los Angeles Film Critics Association had voted its annual bests to *Kramer vs. Kramer* as best picture, to Hoffman as best actor, Sally Field as best actress, Melvyn Douglas and Meryl Streep for supporting performances and to Robert Benton for direction and screenplay. Other groups basically seconded the motion, and it was only left to Oscar to make it all official. If there was any expectation of an upset, it came in the pint-sized form of Mickey Rooney, in the midst of a gigantic career on Broadway. Many bets were on Rooney winning the supporting actor prize over Douglas, but it didn't happen.

Once again there had been considerable controversy when the nominations were disclosed, especially over the missing names of two cinematographers: Caleb Deschanel of *The Black Stallion* and Gordon Willis of *Manhattan*. Some felt there had been deliberate snubs. Cinematographer Haskell Wexler, who was nominated, said, "I think it's a disgrace and I'm indignant"; Willis, a New Yorker, figured, "Maybe if I bought a house in Hollywood, I'd have a better chance," but fellow lensman Conrad

Hall had the last word. "Unfortunately, somebody's always left out," he reminded everyone. "Injustice in the Academy is something people have to accept." Another definite newsmaker at nomination time was Justin Henry. Eight years old, he became the youngest nominee for a competitive award in the Academy's history.

For the second year in a row, Johnny Carson was the host for the Oscar show, again held at the Dorothy Chandler Pavilion of the Los Angeles Music Center. Presenters ran the gamut from Douglas Fairbanks Jr. and Gene Kelly to Dolly Parton and Bo Derek, and a major musical highlight was Donald O'Connor and 32 dancers saluting famous movie choreographers and the musical film genre in a number called "Dancin' on the Silver Screen." *The Tin Drum* was voted the best foreign language film award, Ray Stark received the Irving Thalberg award, Robert Benjamin received the Jean Hersholt Humanitarian Award and Alec Guinness, previously a best actor winner back in 1957, received an honorary Oscar "for advancing the art of screen acting through a host of memorable and distinguished performances." Commented Sir Alec, after receiving a standing ovation, "I feel very fraudulent taking this. But," he added with a smile, and making a quick exit, "I'm grabbing this while the going's good." Among those who stayed on stage longer: The Muppets' Kermit the Frog, singing one of the year's nominated songs, "The Rainbow Connection."

Kramer
vs.
Kramer

Dustin Hoffman
Kramer vs. Kramer

Meryl Streep · Jane Alexander

Nestor Almendros · Avery Corman
Stanley R. Jaffe · Robert Benton

254

Best Supporting Actress: **Meryl Streep** *as Joanna Kramer in* Kramer vs. Kramer *(Columbia; produced by Stanley R. Jaffe). The film was a touching, emotionally punching story about divorce, with Meryl Streep as a young wife and mother who exits her family to seek an independent life style, only to return later to claim her young son as "a mother's prerogative," a move that sets off a court battle with her ex-husband (Dustin Hoffman, right, with Streep). Also nominated for an Academy Award the preceding year, Streep was on her way to a striking Oscar tally: in her first 18 years in film, she was nominated ten times (in 1978, 1979, 1981, 1982, 1983, 1986, 1987, 1988, 1990, and 1995), winning twice en route for 1979's* Kramer *and again in 1982 for* Sophie's Choice.

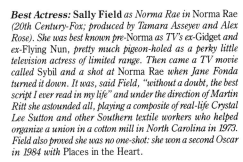

Best Actress: Sally Field as Norma Rae in Norma Rae *(20th Century-Fox; produced by Tamara Asseyev and Alex Rose). She was best known pre-*Norma *as TV's ex-*Gidget *and ex-*Flying Nun, *pretty much pigeon-holed as a perky little television actress of limited range. Then came a TV movie called* Sybil *and a shot at* Norma Rae *when Jane Fonda turned it down. It was, said Field, "without a doubt, the best script I ever read in my life" and under the direction of Martin Ritt she astounded all, playing a composite of real-life Crystal Lee Sutton and other Southern textile workers who helped organize a union in a cotton mill in North Carolina in 1973. Field also proved she was no one-shot: she won a second Oscar in 1984 with* Places in the Heart.

255

Best Picture: Kramer vs. Kramer *(Columbia),* **Best Director: Robert Benton** *for* Kramer vs. Kramer, *and* **Best Actor: Dustin Hoffman** *as Ted Kramer. What happens when divorce suddenly collapses a young family? Based on Avery Corman's insightful novel,* Kramer *explored the issues and adventures of an advertising executive (Hoffman, left, with Justin Henry) who finds himself parenting a six-year-old son he barely knows. Benton also wrote the screenplay (for which he was also Oscared) and directed with sensitivity, warmth and enough of a light touch to make the film tremendously appealing. Besides Meryl Streep as the leave-taking mother, the cast also included Jane Alexander, Howard Duff, Jobeth Williams and, effortlessly stealing most of the scenes he was in, pint-sized Justin Henry as the Kramer's son and arguing point.*

All That Jazz *(Columbia/20th Century-Fox; produced by Robert Alan Aurthur). Directed by Bob Fosse,* Jazz *was speculated to be based on Fosse's own life as it took an undiluted look at the hard days and driven nights of a workaholic director-choreographer bent on self-destruction. It won four Academy Awards, for art direction, film editing, costume design and original music score, making it the most honored film of the year next to* Kramer vs. Kramer *(with five awards). Roy Scheider (above) starred as the focal* Jazz *character, the womanizer preoccupied with dance and death, and the cast included Jessica Lange, Ben Vereen and, way down in the credits, a newcomer named John Lithgow.*

PICTURE

ALL THAT JAZZ, 20th Century-Fox. Produced by Robert Alan Aurthur.
APOCALYPSE NOW, Omni Zoetrope, UA. Produced by Francis Coppola. Co-produced by Fred Roos, Gray Frederickson and Tom Sternberg.
BREAKING AWAY, 20th Century-Fox. Produced by Peter Yates.
*****KRAMER VS. KRAMER,** Jaffe, Columbia. Produced by Stanley R. Jaffe.
NORMA RAE, 20th Century-Fox. Produced by Tamara Asseyev and Alex Rose.

ACTOR

*****DUSTIN HOFFMAN** in *Kramer vs. Kramer,* Jaffe, Columbia.
JACK LEMMON in *The China Syndrome,* Douglas/IPC, Columbia.
AL PACINO in *...And Justice for All,* Malton, Columbia.
ROY SCHEIDER in *All That Jazz,* 20th Century-Fox.
PETER SELLERS in *Being There,* Lorimar-Fernsehproduktion GmbH, UA.

ACTRESS

JILL CLAYBURGH in *Starting Over,* Pakula/Brooks, Paramount.
*****SALLY FIELD** in *Norma Rae,* 20th Century-Fox.
JANE FONDA in *The China Syndrome,* Douglas/IPC, Columbia.
MARSHA MASON in *Chapter Two,* Stark, Columbia.
BETTE MIDLER in *The Rose,* 20th Century-Fox.

SUPPORTING ACTOR

*****MELVYN DOUGLAS** in *Being There,* Lorimar-Fernsehproduktion GmbH, UA.
ROBERT DUVALL in *Apocalypse Now,* Omni Zoetrope, UA.
FREDERIC FORREST in *The Rose,* 20th Century-Fox.
JUSTIN HENRY in *Kramer vs. Kramer,* Jaffe, Columbia.
MICKEY ROONEY in *The Black Stallion,* Omni Zoetrope, UA.

SUPPORTING ACTRESS

JANE ALEXANDER in *Kramer vs. Kramer,* Jaffe, Columbia.
BARBARA BARRIE in *Breaking Away,* 20th Century-Fox.
CANDICE BERGEN in *Starting Over,* Pakula/Brooks, Paramount.
MARIEL HEMINGWAY in *Manhattan,* Rollins-Joffee, UA.
***** MERYL STREEP** in *Kramer vs. Kramer,* Jaffe, Columbia.

DIRECTING

ALL THAT JAZZ, 20th Century-Fox. Bob Fosse.
APOCALYPSE NOW, Omni Zoetrope, UA. Francis Coppola.
BREAKING AWAY, 20th Century-Fox. Peter Yates.
*****KRAMER VS. KRAMER,** Jaffe, Columbia. Robert Benton.
LA CAGE AUX FOLLES, SPA, UA. Edouard Molinaro.

WRITING

(Screenplay Written Directly for the Screen)

ALL THAT JAZZ, 20th Century-Fox. Robert Alan Aurthur and Bob Fosse
...AND JUSTICE FOR ALL, Malton, Columbia. Valerie Curtin and Barry Levinson.
*****BREAKING AWAY,** 20th Century-Fox. Steve Tesich.
THE CHINA SYNDROME, Douglas/IPC, Columbia. Mike Gray, T.S. Cook and James Bridges.
MANHATTAN, Rollins-Joffe, UA. Woody Allen and Marshall Brickman.

(Screenplay Based on Material from Another Medium)

APOCALYPSE NOW, Omni Zoetrope, UA. John Milius and Francis Coppola.
*****KRAMER VS. KRAMER,** Jaffe, Columbia. Robert Benton.
LA CAGE AUX FOLLES, SPA, UA. Francis Veber, Edouard Molinaro, Marcello Danon and Jean Poiret.
A LITTLE ROMANCE, Pan Arts, Orion. Allan Burns.
NORMA RAE, 20th Century-Fox. Irving Ravetch and Harriet Frank, Jr.

CINEMATOGRAPHY

ALL THAT JAZZ, 20th Century-Fox. Giuseppe Rotunno.
***APOCALYPSE NOW,** Omni Zoetrope, UA. Vittorio Storaro.
THE BLACK HOLE, Disney. Frank Phillips.
KRAMER VS. KRAMER, Jaffe, Columbia. Nestor Almendros.
1941, Spielberg, Universal. William A. Fraker.

ART DIRECTION-
SET DECORATION

ALIEN, 20th Century-Fox. Michael Seymour, Les Dilley and Roger Christian; Ian Whittaker.

*****ALL THAT JAZZ,** 20th Century-Fox. Philip Rosenberg and Tony Walton; Edward Stewart and Gary Brink.
APOCALYPSE NOW, Omni Zoetrope, UA. Dean Tavoularis and Angelo Graham; George R. Nelson.
THE CHINA SYNDROME, Douglas/IPC, Columbia. George Jenkins; Arthur Jeph Parker.
STAR TREK—THE MOTION PICTURE, Century Associates, Paramount. Harold Michelson, Joe Jennings, Leon Harris and John Vallone; Linda DeScenna.

COSTUME DESIGN

AGATHA, Sweetwall-Casablanca-First Artists, Warner Bros. Shirley Russell.
***** ALL THAT JAZZ,** 20th Century-Fox. Albert Wolsky.
BUTCH AND SUNDANCE: THE EARLY DAYS, 20th Century-Fox. William Ware Theiss.
THE EUROPEANS, Merchant Ivory, Levitt-Pickman. Judy Moorcroft.
LA CAGE AUX FOLLES, Les Productions Artistes Associes/Da Ma, UA. Piero Tosi, Ambra Danon.

SOUND

*****APOCALYPSE NOW,** Omni Zoetrope, UA. Walter Murch, Mark Berger, Richard Beggs and Nat Boxer.
THE ELECTRIC HORSEMAN, Rastar/Wildwood/Pollack, Columbia. Arthur Piantadosi, Les Fresholtz, Michael Minkler and Al Overton.
METEOR, American International. William McCaughey, Aaron Rochin, Michael J. Kohut and Jack Solomon.
1941, Spielberg, Universal. Robert Knudson, Robert J. Glass, Don MacDougall and Gene S. Cantamessa.
THE ROSE, 20th Century-Fox. Theodore Soderberg, Douglas Williams, Paul Wells and Jim Webb.

FILM EDITING

*****ALL THAT JAZZ,** 20th Century-Fox. Alan Heim.
APOCALYPSE NOW, Omni Zoetrope, UA. Richard Marks, Walter Murch, Gerald B. Greenberg and Lisa Fruchtman.
THE BLACK STALLION, Omni Zoetrope, UA. Robert Dalva.
KRAMER VS. KRAMER, Jaffe, Columbia. Jerry Greenberg.
THE ROSE, 20th Century-Fox. Robert L. Wolfe and C. Timothy O'Meara.

VISUAL EFFECTS

*****ALIEN,** 20th Century-Fox. H.R. Giger, Carlo Rambaldi, Brian Johnson, Nick Allder and Denys Ayling.
THE BLACK HOLE, Disney. Peter Ellenshaw, Art Cruickshank, Eustace Lycett, Danny Lee, Harrison Ellenshaw and Joe Hale.
MOONRAKER, Eon, UA. Derek Meddings, Paul Wilson and John Evans.
1941, Spielberg, Universal. William A. Fraker, A.D. Flowers and Gregory Jein.
STAR TREK—THE MOTION PICTURE, Century Associates, Paramount. Douglas Trumbull, John Dykstra, Richard Yuricich, Robert Swarthe, Dave Stewart and Grant McCune.

MUSIC

(Song)

*****IT GOES LIKE IT GOES** (*Norma Rae,* 20th Century-Fox); Music by David Shire. Lyrics by Norman Gimbel.
THE RAINBOW CONNECTION (*The Muppet Movie,* Henson/Grade/Starger, Associated Film Distribution); Music and Lyrics by Paul Williams and Kenny Ascher.
IT'S EASY TO SAY (*10,* Geoffrey, Orion); Music by Henry Mancini. Lyrics by Robert Wells.
THROUGH THE EYES OF LOVE (*Ice Castles,* Cinemedia, Columbia); Music by Marvin Hamlisch. Lyrics by Carole Bayer Sager.
I'LL NEVER SAY "GOODBYE" (*The Promise,* Weintraub-Heller, Universal); Music by David Shire. Lyrics by Alan and Marilyn Bergman.

(Original Score)

THE AMITYVILLE HORROR, American International Pictures. Lalo Schifrin.
THE CHAMP, M-G-M. Dave Grusin.
***A LITTLE ROMANCE,** Pan Arts, Orion. Georges Delerue.
STAR TREK—THE MOTION PICTURE, Century Associates, Paramount. Jerry Goldsmith.
10, Geoffrey, Orion. Henry Mancini.

(Original Song and Score and its Adaptation or Best Adaptation Score)

*****ALL THAT JAZZ,** 20th Century-Fox. Ralph Burns.
BREAKING AWAY, 20th Century-Fox. Patrick Williams.
THE MUPPET MOVIE, Henson/Grade/Starger, Associated Film Distribution. Paul Williams and Kenny Ascher; Paul Williams.

SHORT FILMS

(Animated Films)

Melvyn Douglas *as Benjamin Rand in* Being There *(United Artists; directed by Hal Ashby). Douglas had been an Oscar winner before, in 1963 for* Hud; *his second win came for a gem-like contribution to this comedy-fable by Jerzy* *Kosinski about the improbable rise of a childlike gardener (Peter Sellers) to a position of esteemed national importance, all because his simplicity is interpreted by others as having some deep significance. Douglas (above, with Shirley* *MacLaine) played a Capitol Hill kingmaker who, in his dying days, comes under the influence of the gardener, and vice versa.*

DREAM DOLL, Bob Godfrey Films/Zagreb Films/Halas and Batchelor, FilmWright. Bob Godfrey and Zlatko Grgic, producers.
*EVERY CHILD, National Film Board of Canada. Derek Lamb, producer.
IT'S SO NICE TO HAVE A WOLF AROUND THE HOUSE, AR&T Productions for Learning Corporation of America. Paul Fierlinger, producer.

(Live Action)
*BOARD AND CARE, Ron Ellis Films. Sarah Pillsbury and Ron Ellis, producers.
BRAVERY IN THE FIELD, National Film Board of Canada. Roman Kroitor and Stefan Wodoslawsky, producers.
OH BROTHER, MY BROTHER, Ross Lowell Productions, Pyramid Films, Inc. Carol and Ross Lowell, producers.
THE SOLAR FILM, Wildwood Enterprises Inc. Saul Bass and Michael Britton, producers.
SOLLY'S DINER, Mathias/Zukerman/Hankin Productions. Harry Mathias, Jay Zuckerman and Larry Hankin, producers.

DOCUMENTARY

(Short Subjects)
DAE, Vardar Film/Skopje. Risto Teofilovski, producer.
KORYO CELADON, Charlie/Papa Productions, Inc. Donald A. Connolly and James R. Messenger, producers.
NAILS, National Film Board of Canada. Phillip Borsos, producer.
*PAUL ROBESON; TRIBUTE TO AN ARTIST, Janus Films Inc., Saul J. Turell, producer.
REMEMBER ME, Dick Young Productions, Ltd. Dick Young, producer.

(Features)
*BEST BOY, Only Child Motion Pictures, Inc. Ira Wohl, producer.
GENERATION ON THE WIND, More Than One Medium. David A. Vassar, producer.
GOING THE DISTANCE, National Film Board of Canada. Paul Cowan and Jacques Bobet, producers.
THE KILLING GROUND, ABC News Closeup Unit. Steve Singer and Tom Priestley, producers.

THE WAR AT HOME, Catalyst Films/Madison Film Production Co. Glenn Silber and Barry Alexander Brown, producers.

FOREIGN LANGUAGE FILM
THE MAIDS OF WILKO (Poland).
MAMA TURNS A HUNDRED (Spain).
A SIMPLE STORY (France).
*THE TIN DRUM (Federal Republic of Germany).
TO FORGET VENICE (Italy).

HONORARY AND OTHER AWARDS
TO ALEC GUINNESS for advancing the art of screen acting through a host of memorable and distinguished performances.
TO HAL ELIAS for his dedication and distinguished service to the Academy of Motion Picture Arts and Sciences.
TO JOHN O. AALBERG, CHARLES G. CLARKE and JOHN G. FRAYNE in appreciation for outstanding service and dedication in upholding the high standards of the Academy of Motion Picture Arts and Sciences. (Medals of Commendation)

SPECIAL ACHIEVEMENT AWARDS
For Sound Editing: ALAN SPLET for "The Black Stallion," Omni Zoetrope, UA.

1979 IRVING G. THALBERG MEMORIAL AWARD
TO RAY STARK

1979 JEAN HERSHOLT HUMANITARIAN AWARD
TO ROBERT BENJAMIN

SCIENTIFIC OR TECHNICAL AWARDS

(Academy Award of Merit)
MARK SERRURIER for the progressive development of the Moviola from the 1924 invention of his father, Iwan Serrurier, to the present Series 20 sophisticated film editing equipment.

(Scientific and Engineering Award)
NEIMAN-TILLAR ASSOCIATES for the creative development and to MINI-MICRO SYSTEMS, INCORPORATED, for the design and engineering of an Automated Computer-Controlled Editing Sound System (ACCESS) for motion picture post-production.

(Technical Achievement Award)
MICHAEL V. CHEWEY, WALTER G. EGGERS and ALLEN HECHT of M-G-M Laboratories for the development of a Computer-Controlled Paper Tape Programmer System and its applications in the motion picture laboratory.
IRWIN YOUNG, PAUL KAUFMAN, and FREDRIK SCHLYTER of Du Art Film Laboratories, Incorporated, for the development of a Computer-Controlled Paper Tape Programmer System and its applications in the motion picture laboratory.
JAMES S. STANFIELD and PAUL W. TRESTER for the development and manufacture of a device for the repair or protection of sprocket holes in motion picture film.
ZORIN PERISIC of Courier Films., Limited, for the Zoptic Special Optical Effects Device for motion picture photography.
A.D. FLOWERS and LOGAN R. FRAZEE for the development of a device to control flight patterns of miniature airplanes during motion picture photography.
PHOTO RESEARCH DIVISION OF KOLLMORGEN CORPORATION for the development of the Spectra Series II Cine Special Exposure Meter for motion picture photography.
BRUCE LYON and JOHN LAMB for the development of a Video Animation System for testing motion picture animation sequences.
ROSS LOWELL of Lowel-Light Manufacturing, Incorporated, for the development of compact lighting equipment for motion picture photography.

*INDICATES WINNER

1980
The Fifty-Third Year

Henry Fonda, after a 46-year, 83-film career that had established him as one of the genuine giants of the acting profession, finally received his first Academy Award when the 53rd Oscars were dispensed March 31, 1981. That same night Robert Redford also won his first Academy recognition but, ironically, neither Fonda nor Redford got those initial trophies for one of the year's acting performances. Fonda's award came as an honorary Oscar "in recognition of his brilliant accomplishments and enduring contribution to the art of motion pictures." Redford received his prize not for acting but as the year's best director via *Ordinary People*, a film that not only marked Redford's debut as a film director but also won top prizes as the year's best picture, for Timothy Hutton as the best supporting actor and for Alvin Sargent's screenplay. Fonda told the audience at the Dorothy Chandler Pavilion of the Los Angeles Music Center "this has got to be the climax," unaware it was but an omen of things to come: the following year he would again receive an Oscar, a competitive one, as best actor of the year for *On Golden Pond*.

There was a tinge of real-life drama surrounding the award night itself: the Academy presentations had been postponed twenty-four hours from their originally scheduled date because of an assassination attempt on the life of President Ronald Reagan. A pre-taped message from the President, who was hospitalized, was played on the show.

Real-life drama was also prevalent in the winner's circle: for the first time in Academy history, three of the four awards for acting in a single year went to actors portraying real people: Robert DeNiro as boxer Jake LaMotta in *Raging Bull,* Sissy Spacek as country-western singer Loretta Lynn in *Coal Miner's Daughter* and Mary Steenburgen as the first wife of would-be Howard Hughes heir Melvin Dummar in *Melvin and Howard.*

The evening's m.c., for the third year in a row, was Johnny Carson; Lucie Arnaz was featured in an elaborate "Hooray for Hollywood" production number and Irene Cara did rousing renditions of the two nominated songs from "Fame," including the title song which eventually went on to become the winner. *Tess,* embroiled in some controversy because of the complicated legal/illegal status of its director Roman Polanski (he'd earlier fled from Los Angeles to France on the eve of being sentenced in a case involving his relationship with a minor), won three of the evening's Oscars: for cinematography, art direction and costume design. Among the stars participating in the show were *Tess* star Nastassia Kinski, as well as Lillian Gish, Lily Tomlin, Steve Martin, George Cukor, King Vidor and Diana Ross. The latter's date for the evening was Michael Jackson.

After the evening had come to a halt, there was some bad news for the Academy. Despite the star power, the telecast had pulled the lowest rating in the

Best Picture: **Ordinary People** *(Paramount; produced by Ronald L. Schwary),* **Best Director:** **Robert Redford** *for* Ordinary People *and* **Best Supporting Actor:** **Timothy Hutton** *as Conrad Jarrett (right, with Redford) in* Ordinary People. *Robert Redford, marking his first time at bat as a motion picture director, had a real winner: a compelling study of how the drowning death of a "favored" son affects a family, especially a younger brother (Hutton) who's convinced his parents (Mary Tyler Moore and Donald Sutherland) hold him partially responsible. It was based on Judith Guest's best-seller and the cast included Judd Hirsch, Elizabeth McGovern and Adam Baldwin.*

29-year history of Academy Award telecasts. But there was good news for Paramount. It was reported that business at theaters playing *Ordinary People* had jumped an amazing 92 percent due to that best picture trophy and Oscar praise.

***Best Actress:* Sissy Spacek** *as Loretta Lynn in* Coal Miner's Daughter *(Universal; produced by Bernard Schwartz). Sissy Spacek used her own singing voice to expertly render the life of real-life country-western music queen Loretta Lynn, a rags-to-riches saga which begins with a poverty-laden childhood in the backwoods of rural Kentucky and ends with Lynn's great success as a beloved entertainer. Spacek, right, was directed by Michael Apted; Tommy Lee Jones played Lynn's husband, Beverly D'Angelo was the ill-fated Patsy Cline.*

***Best Actor:* Robert DeNiro** *as Jake LaMotta in* Raging Bull *(United Artists; produced by Irwin Winkler and Robert Chartoff). Also based on a real-life personality, Raging Bull was directed by Martin Scorsese and spotlighted the life of middleweight boxing champ Jake LaMotta from his days as a well-chiseled force in the ring during the 1940s (above, left) to* later depths as a bloated has-been reduced to working as an emcee in second-rate strip joints *(above, right). Filmed almost entirely in black-and-white, the film had raw, brute-force power, especially in its graphic prize-fight sequences. There was also added punch from the fact DeNiro gained 50 pounds in order to more authentically portray the later LaMotta.*

*Honorary Oscar to **Henry Fonda**. Despite 45 years of consistently strong screen performances, Fonda had yet to receive an Academy award by the 1980 award year; in fact, he'd only been nominated once, for 1940's The Grapes of Wrath. The neglect cued the Board of Governors to vote him a special Oscar in recognition of his many accomplishments. No one knew at the time but, the following year, he'd also be an Oscar winner, as best actor.*

*Best Supporting Actress: **Mary Steenburgen** as Lynda Dummar in Melvin and Howard (Universal; directed by Jonathan Demme). Yet another 1980 portrayal of a real-life character went on to receive Oscar gold, this time for Mary Steenburgen as the wife, then ex-wife, of Melvin Dummar (played by Paul Le Mat), an impoverished fellow who, by fluke or hoax, briefly was said to be the possible beneficiary of $165,000,000 from the estate of the late Howard Hughes.*

PICTURE

COAL MINER'S DAUGHTER, Schwartz, Universal. Produced by Bernard Schwartz.
THE ELEPHANT MAN, Brooksfilms, Paramount. Produced by Jonathan Sanger.
*ORDINARY PEOPLE,** Wildwood, Paramount. Produced by Ronald L. Schwary.
RAGING BULL, Chartoff-Winkler, UA. Produced by Irwin Winkler and Robert Chartoff.
TESS, Renn-Burrill, Columbia. Produced by Claude Berri. Co-produced by Timothy Burrill.

ACTOR

*ROBERT DE NIRO in *Raging Bull*, Chartoff-Winkler, UA.
ROBERT DUVALL in *The Great Santini*, Orion-Crosby, Orion.
JOHN HURT in *The Elephant Man*, Brooksfilms, Paramount.
JACK LEMMON in *Tribute*, Turman-Foster, 20th Century-Fox.
PETER O'TOOLE in *The Stunt Man*, Simon, 20th Century-Fox.

ACTRESS

ELLEN BURSTYN in *Resurrection*, Universal.
GOLDIE HAWN in *Private Benjamin*, Warner Bros.
MARY TYLER MOORE in *Ordinary People*, Wildwood, Paramount.
GENA ROWLANDS in *Gloria*, Columbia.
*SISSY SPACEK in *Coal Miner's Daughter*, Schwartz, Universal.

SUPPORTING ACTOR

JUDD HIRSCH in *Ordinary People*,Wildwood, Paramount.
*TIMOTHY HUTTON in *Ordinary People*, Wildwood, Paramount.
MICHAEL O'KEEFE in *The Great Santini*, Orion-Crosby, Orion.
JOE PESCI in *Raging Bull*, Chartoff-Winkler, UA.
JASON ROBARDS in *Melvin and Howard*, Linson/Phillips/Demme, Universal.

SUPPORTING ACTRESS

EILEEN BRENNAN in *Private Benjamin*, Warner Bros.
EVA LE GALLIENNE in *Resurrection*, Universal.
CATHY MORIARTY in *Raging Bull*, Chartoff-Winkler, UA.
DIANA SCARWID in *Inside Moves*, Goodmark, AFD (Associated Film Distribution).
*MARY STEENBURGEN in *Melvin and Howard*, Linson/Phillips/Demme, Universal.

DIRECTING

THE ELEPHANT MAN, Brooksfilms, Paramount. David Lynch.
*ORDINARY PEOPLE,** Wildwood, Paramount. Robert Redford.
RAGING BULL, Chartoff-Winkler, UA. Martin Scorsese.
THE STUNT MAN, Simon, 20th Century-Fox. Richard Rush.
TESS, Renn-Burrill, Columbia. Roman Polanski.

WRITING

(Screenplay Written Directly for the Screen)

BRUBAKER, 20th Century-Fox. W.D. Richter and Arthur Ross.
FAME, M-G-M. Christopher Gore.
*MELVIN AND HOWARD,** Linson/Phillips/Demme, Universal. Bo Goldman
MON ONCLE D'AMERIQUE, Dussart-Andrea, New World. Jean Gruault.
PRIVATE BENJAMIN, Warner Bros. Nancy Meyers, Charles Shyer and Harvey Miller.

(Screenplay Based on Material from Another Medium)

BREAKER MORANT,Pact Productions, New World. Jonathan Hardy, David Stevens and Bruce Beresford.
COAL MINER'S DAUGHTER, Schwartz, Universal. Tom Rickman.
THE ELEPHANT MAN, Brooksfilms, Paramount. Christopher DeVore, Eric Bergren and David Lynch.
*ORDINARY PEOPLE,** Wildwood, Paramount. Alvin Sargent.
THE STUNT MAN, Simon, 20th Century-Fox. Lawrence B. Marcus and Richard Rush.

CINEMATOGRAPHY

THE BLUE LAGOON, Columbia. Nestor Almendros.
COAL MINER'S DAUGHTER, Schwartz, Universal. Ralf D. Bode.
THE FORMULA, M-G-M. James Crabe.
RAGING BULL, Chartoff-Winkler, UA. Michael Chapman.
*TESS, Renn-Burrill, Columbia. Geoffrey Unsworth and Ghislain Cloquet.

ART DIRECTION-
SET DECORATION

COAL MINER'S DAUGHTER, Schwartz, Universal. John W. Corso; John M. Dwyer.
THE ELEPHANT MAN, Brooksfilms, Paramount. Stuart Craig and Bob Cartwright; Hugh Scaife.
THE EMPIRE STRIKES BACK, Lucasfilm, 20th Century-Fox. Norman Reynolds, Leslie Dilley, Harry Lange, and Alan Tomkins; Michael Ford.
KAGEMUSHA (The Shadow Warrior), Toho-Kurosawa, 20th Century-Fox. Yoshiro Muraki.
*TESS, Renn-Burrill, Columbia. Pierre Guffroy and Jack Stephens.

COSTUME DESIGN

THE ELEPHANT MAN, Brooksfilms, Paramount. Patricia Norris.
MY BRILLIANT CAREER, Analysis Film Releasing. Anna Senior.
SOMEWHERE IN TIME, Rastar-Deutsch, Universal. Jean-Pierre Dorleac.
*TESS, Renn-Burrill, Columbia. Anthony Powell.
WHEN TIME RAN OUT, Warner Bros. Paul Zastupnevich.

SOUND

ALTERED STATES, Warner Bros. Arthur Piantadosi, Les Fresholtz, Michael Minkler and Willie D. Burton.
COAL MINER'S DAUGHTER, Schwartz, Universal. Richard Portman, Roger Heman and Jim Alexander.
*THE EMPIRE STRIKES BACK,** Lucasfilm, 20th Century-Fox. Bill Varney, Steve Maslow, Gregg Landaker and Peter Sutton.
FAME, M-G-M. Michael J. Kohut, Aaron Rochin, Jay M. Harding and Chris Newman.
RAGING BULL, Chartoff-Winkler, UA. Donald O. Mitchell, Bill Nicholson, David J. Kimball and Les Lazarowitz.

FILM EDITING

COAL MINER'S DAUGHTER, Schwartz, Universal. Arthur Schmidt.
THE COMPETITION, Rastar, Columbia. David Blewitt.
THE ELEPHANT MAN, Brooksfilms, Paramount. Anne V. Coates.
FAME, M-G-M. Gerry Hambling.
*RAGING BULL,** Chartoff-Winkler, UA. Thelma Schoonmaker.

MUSIC

(Song)

*FAME (*Fame*, M-G-M); Music by Michael Gore. Lyrics by Dean Pitchford.
NINE TO FIVE (*Nine To Five*, 20th Century-Fox); Music and Lyrics by Dolly Parton.
ON THE ROAD AGAIN (*Honeysuckle Rose*, Warner Bros.); Music and Lyrics by Willie Nelson.
OUT HERE ON MY OWN (*Fame*, M-G-M); Music by Michael Gore. Lyrics by Lesley Gore.
PEOPLE ALONE (*The Competition*, Rastar, Columbia); Music by Lalo Schifrin. Lyrics by Wilbur Jennings.

(Original Score)

ALTERED STATES, Warner Bros. John Corigliano.
THE ELEPHANT MAN, Brooksfilms, Paramount. John Morris.
THE EMPIRE STRIKES BACK,Lucasfilm, 20th Century-Fox. John Williams.
*FAME,** M-G-M. Michael Gore.
TESS, Renn-Burrill, Columbia. Philippe Sarde.

SHORT FILMS

(Animated Films)

ALL NOTHING, Radio Canada. Frederic Back, producer.
*THE FLY,** Pannonia Film, Budapest. Ferenc Rofusz, producer.
HISTORY OF THE WORLD IN THREE MINUTES FLAT, Michael Mills Productions Ltd. Michael Mills, producer.

(Live Action)

*THE DOLLAR BOTTOM,** Rocking Horse Films Limited, Paramount. Lloyd Phillips, producer.
FALL LINE, Sports Imagery, Inc. Bob Carmichael and Greg Lowe, producers.
A JURY OF HER PEERS, Sally Heckel Productions. Sally Heckel, producer.

DOCUMENTARY

(Short Subjects)

DON'T MESS WITH BILL, John Watson and Pen Densham's Insight Productions Inc. John Watson and Pen Densham, producers.
THE ERUPTION OF MOUNT ST. HELENS, Graphic Films Corporation. George Casey, producer.
IT'S THE SAME WORLD, Dick Young Productions, Ltd. Dick Young, producer.

Fame (M-G-M; produced by David De Silva and Alan Marshall) was set in New York's famous High School of Performing Arts and featured an energetic cast of actors and dancers gyrating through a series of ups, downs and successes, many set to music. Alan Parker directed the cast which included Irene Cara, Gene Anthony Ray, Lee Curreri, Laura Dean, Barry Miller, Anne Meara and Albert Hauge. Fame won wide popularity with audiences as well as two Oscars for its music. It also inspired a long-running TV series.

*KARL HESS: TOWARD LIBERTY, Halle/Ladue, Inc. Roland Halle and Peter W. Ladue, producers.
LUTHER METKE AT 94, U.C.L.A. Ethnographic Film Program. Richard Hawkins and Jorge Preloran, producers.

(Features)
AGEE, James Agee Film Project. Ross Spears, producer.
THE DAY AFTER TRINITY, Jon Else Productions. Jon Else, producer.
*FROM MAO TO MOZART: ISAAC STERN IN CHINA, The Hopewell Foundation. Murray Lerner, producer.
FRONT LINE, David Bradbury Productions. David Bradbury, producer.
THE YELLOW STAR—THE PERSECUTION OF THE JEWS IN EUROPE 1933-45, Chronos Films. Bengt von zur Muehlen and Arthur Cohn, producers.

FOREIGN LANGUAGE FILM

CONFIDENCE (Hungary).
KAGEMUSHA (The Shadow Warrier) (Japan).
THE LAST METRO (France).
*MOSCOW DOES NOT BELIEVE IN TEARS (U.S.S.R.).
THE NEST (Spain).

HONORARY AND OTHER AWARDS

TO HENRY FONDA, the consummate actor, in recognition of his brilliant accomplishments and enduring contribution to the art of motion pictures.
TO FRED HYNES, in appreciation for outstanding service and dedication in upholding the high standards of the Academy of Motion Picture Arts and Sciences. (Medal of Commendation)

SPECIAL ACHIEVEMENT AWARDS

For Visual Effects: BRIAN JOHNSON, RICHARD EDLUND, DENNIS MUREN and BRUCE NICHOLSON for The Empire Strikes Back, a Lucasfilm, Ltd. Production, 20th Century-Fox.

1980 IRVING G. THALBERG MEMORIAL AWARD

None given this year.

1980 JEAN HERSHOLT HUMANITARIAN AWARD

None given this year.

SCIENTIFIC OR TECHNICAL AWARDS

(Academy Award of Merit)
LINWOOD G. DUNN, CECIL D. LOVE and ACME TOOL AND MANUFACTURING COMPANY for the concept, engineering and development of the Acme-Dunn Optical Printer for motion picture special effects.

(Scientific and Engineering Award)
JEAN-MARIE LAVALOU, ALAIN MASSERON and DAVID SAMUELSON of Samuelson Alga Cinema S.A. and Samuelson Film Service, Limited, for the engineering and development of the Louma Camera Crane and remote control system for motion picture production.
EDWARD B. KRAUSE of Filmline Corporation for the engineering and manufacture of the micro-demand drive for continuous motion picture film processors.
ROSS TAYLOR for the concept and development of a system of air guns for propelling objects used in special effects motion picture production.
DR. BERNHARD KUHL and DR. WERNER BLOCK of OSRAM GmbH, for the progressive engineering and manufacture of the OSRAM HMI light source for motion picture color photography.
DAVID A. GRAFTON for the optical design and engineering of a telecentric anamorphic lens for motion picture optical effects printers.

(Technical Achievement Awards)
CARTER EQUIPMENT COMPANY for the development of a continuous contact, total immersion, additive color motion picture printer.
HOLLYWOOD FILM COMPANY for the development of a continuous contact, total immersion, additive color motion picture printer.
ANDRE DeBRIE S.A. for the development of a continuous contact, total immersion, additive color, motion picture printer.
CHARLES VAUGHN and EUGENE NOTTINGHAM of Cinetron Computer Systems, Incorporated, for the development of a versatile general purpose computer system for animation and optical effects motion picture photography.
JOHN W. LANG, WALTER HRASTNIK and CHARLES J. WATSON of Bell and Howell Company for the development and manufacture of a modular continuous contact motion picture film printer.
WORTH BAIRD of LaVezzi Machine Works, Incorporated, for the advanced design and manufacture of a film sprocket for motion picture projectors.
PETER A. REGLA and DAN SLATER of Elicon for the development of a follow-focus system for motion picture optical effects printers and animation stands.

*INDICATES WINNER

Even at age fifty-four, Oscar could still deliver a good punch and an even bigger surprise. It was, in fact, one of the biggest upsets in the Academy Award history books so far: all the pre-show betting had been on 1981's best picture prize going to the popular *On Golden Pond* or *Raiders of the Lost Ark,* the massive *Reds* or the highly praised *Atlantic City,* but along came the British-made *Chariots of Fire* to run off with the gold. It was also the first time in the 18 years since 1963's *Tom Jones* that a film from England had won Hollywood's top award.

The whole evening, in fact, turned out to be full of upsets and surprises. First, there was a downpour that continued on through showtime. Then, Katharine Hepburn became the first actor or actress to win a fourth Academy Award for performing, this time for *On Golden Pond;* heaviest betting had been on Diane Keaton or Meryl Streep to win. (The Academy's most honored lady, however, was still Edith Head, with eight Oscars for costume design.) Henry Fonda, Hepburn's costar in *Pond,* was named the year's best actor; it was the first competitive Oscar he'd won. The best supporting actor was John Gielgud in *Arthur,* best supporting actress was Maureen Stapleton in *Reds* and Warren Beatty was named best director, also for *Reds.*

Most of the major winners, however, were no-shows at the party, held March 29, 1982, again at the Dorothy Chandler Pavilion of the Los Angeles Music Cen-

ter. Hepburn was in Washington, D.C., starring in *West Side Waltz,* a new play by Ernest Thompson, the author of *Pond* and himself a new Academy Award winner for *Pond's* screenplay. Fonda was ill and unable to attend the ceremony but watched the awards on television at his home in Beverly Hills; he died less than five months later. Gielgud was in Munich working in *Wagner* with Richard Burton.

But Beatty and Stapleton were both in person to accept their statuettes. Stapleton thanked, among others, "My inspiration, Joel McCrea." Backstage she also told the press, "I hope this is only the beginning. Next I want to win as best actress, then best supporting actor, best actor, all of it." Hepburn later told reporters in Washington, "I was very surprised I won. But I knew Hank would get it. He was amazing on that film. He wasn't feeling very well, you know, but you never would have known it."

Makeup artists were honored for the first time in a regular category of their own; the initial winner was Rick Baker for *An American Werewolf in London. Mephisto* from Hungary was named the year's best foreign language film and the most Oscars of the night went to *Raiders of the Lost Ark* with five awards: for art direction, sound, film editing, visual effects and a special achievement award for sound effects editing.

The most memorable moments on the show were due to two very different ladies, Bette Midler and Barbara Stanwyck. Midler, presenting the best song award, was outrageous with some off-

Best Picture: **Chariots of Fire** *(Ladd Company/Warner Bros.; produced by David Puttnam). The seeds for a film about two track aces competing at the 1924 Paris Olympics were planted when "The Official History of the Olympics" turned out to be the only book producer David Puttnam could find to browse through in a newly rented home. The British-made* Chariots, *directed by Hugh Hudson, marked the screen debuts of Ben Cross and Ian Charlson as Olympic runners each spurred on by different motives. The film included a haunting music score by Vangelis which was also rewarded with an Academy Award. Producer Puttnam later said he was "a little embarrassed by the film's win because, in all honesty, I don't think it's as good a film as I think should be given Oscars." Few in 1981 agreed.*

the-cuff remarks; Stanwyck delivered one from the heart. Accepting an honorary Oscar for a lifetime of screen work, Stanwyck received the evening's sole standing ovation. It was her first Academy Award, despite four previous nominations and, after thanking "the remarkable crews we had the privilege to work with," she gave a brief testimony to the late William Holden. "A few years ago, I stood on this stage with William Holden as a presenter," she said. "I loved him very much and I miss him. He always wished that I would get an Oscar." Raising the statue she said, on the verge of tears, "And so tonight, my golden boy, you've got your wish!"

Best Director: Warren Beatty *for* Reds *(Paramount; produced by Beatty) and* **Best Supporting Actress: Maureen Stapleton** *as Emma Goldman (above, with Beatty) in* Reds. *A long (200 minutes) and ambitious inspection of journalist-activist John Reed and his involvement in American and Russian political affairs prior to World War I,* Reds *was far more than a one-man show although Beatty's hand was everywhere: he starred as Reed, produced the film and directed it, winning much respect in the process. The rich supporting cast included Diane Keaton and Jack Nicholson (as Eugene O'Neill), and actress Stapleton had one of her strongest screen hours as the real-life Goldman, an anarchist and feminist who helped stir the political climate that influenced Reed.*

Best Actor: Henry Fonda *as Norman Thayer and* **Best Actress: Katharine Hepburn** *as Ethel Thayer in* On Golden Pond *(Universal; produced by Bruce Gilbert). She'd already won three Academy Awards; he'd received only one, a special award in the preceding year. And despite long careers and legendary status, Katharine Hepburn and Henry Fonda had never worked together on stage or screen until they joined director Mark Rydell in filming Ernest Thompson's 1978 play about a retired professor (Fonda) facing his 80th birthday as he and his wife (Hepburn) spend their 48th— and possibly last—summer together at their New England cottage. Filled with poignancy, humor and—above all—superb performances by two much-revered performers,* Pond *became one of the year's best-liked movies by young and old alike, and won Oscars for both its stars. Jane Fonda played their daughter, a woman intimidated by her father and, much to his displeasure, about to marry a gent (Dabney Coleman) who comes to the family with a salty-tongued 13-year-old son (Doug McKeon), all of which threatens the serenity of the summer on Golden Pond.*

Best Foreign Language Film: Mephisto *from Hungary. It was directed by Istvan Szabo, based on a book by Klaus Mann and it starred Klaus Maria Brandauer (above) as a German actor who climbs to the top of his profession in the 1920s and 1930s by using women and by insinuating himself into the upper echelons of Nazi power, all so he can have choice roles to play in Berlin theatres. A parable about the corruption of power, it was the first film from Hungary to be voted the Academy's foreign language film prize.*

264

PICTURE

ATLANTIC CITY, ICC, Paramount. Produced by Denis Heroux and John Kemeny.
*****CHARIOTS OF FIRE,** Enigma, The Ladd Company/Warner Bros. Produced by David Puttnam.
ON GOLDEN POND, ITC/IPC, Universal. Produced by Bruce Gilbert.
RAIDERS OF THE LOST ARK, Lucasfilm, Paramount. Produced by Frank Marshall.
REDS, J.R.S., Paramount. Produced by Warren Beatty.

ACTOR

WARREN BEATTY in *Reds,* J.R.S., Paramount.
*****HENRY FONDA** in *On Golden Pond,* ITC/IPC, Universal.
BURT LANCASTER in *Atlantic City,* ICC, Paramount.
DUDLEY MOORE in *Arthur,* Rollins, Joffe, Morra and Brezner, Orion.
PAUL NEWMAN in *Absence of Malice,* Mirage, Columbia.

ACTRESS

*****KATHARINE HEPBURN** in *On Golden Pond,* ITC/IPC, Universal.
DIANE KEATON in *Reds,* J.R.S., Paramount.
MARSHA MASON in *Only When I Laugh,* Columbia.
SUSAN SARANDON in *Atlantic City,* ICC, Paramount.
MERYL STREEP in *The French Lieutenant's Woman,* Parlon, UA.

SUPPORTING ACTOR

JAMES COCO in *Only When I Laugh,* Columbia.
*****JOHN GIELGUD** in *Arthur,* Rollins, Joffe, Morra and Brezner, Orion.
IAN HOLM in *Chariots of Fire,* Enigma, The Ladd Company/Warner Bros.
JACK NICHOLSON in *Reds,* J.R.S., Paramount.
HOWARD E. ROLLINS, JR. in *Ragtime,* Paramount.

SUPPORTING ACTRESS

MELINDA DILLON in *Absence of Malice,* Mirage, Columbia.
JANE FONDA in *On Golden Pond,* ITC/IPC, Universal.
JOAN HACKETT in *Only When I Laugh,* Columbia.
ELIZABETH McGOVERN in *Ragtime,* Paramount.
*****MAUREEN STAPLETON** in *Reds,* J.R.S., Paramount.

DIRECTING

ATLANTIC CITY, ICC, Paramount. Louis Malle.
CHARIOTS OF FIRE, Enigma, The Ladd Company/Warner Bros. Hugh Hudson.
ON GOLDEN POND, ITC/IPC, Universal. Mark Rydell.
RAIDERS OF THE LOST ARK, Lucasfilm, Paramount. Steven Spielberg.
*****REDS,** J.R.S., Paramount. Warren Beatty.

WRITING

(Screenplay Written Directly for the Screen)
ABSENCE OF MALICE, Mirage, Columbia. Kurt Luedtke.
ARTHUR, Rollins, Joffe, Morra and Brezner, Orion. Steve Gordon.
ATLANTIC CITY, ICC, Paramount. John Guare.
*****CHARIOTS OF FIRE,** Enigma, The Ladd Company/Warner Bros. Colin Welland.
REDS, J.R.S., Paramount. Warren Beatty and Trevor Griffiths.

(Screenplay Based on Material from Another Medium)
THE FRENCH LIEUTENANT'S WOMAN, Parlon, UA. Harold Pinter.
*****ON GOLDEN POND,** ITC/IPC, Universal. Ernest Thompson.
PENNIES FROM HEAVEN, Ross/Hera, M-G-M. Dennis Potter.
PRINCE OF THE CITY, Orion/Warner Bros. Jay Presson Allen and Sidney Lumet.
RAGTIME, Paramount. Michael Weller.

CINEMATOGRAPHY

EXCALIBUR, Orion. Alex Thomson.
ON GOLDEN POND, ITC/IPC, Universal. Billy Williams.
RAGTIME, Paramount. Miroslav Ondricek.
RAIDERS OF THE LOST ARK, Lucasfilm, Paramount. Douglas Slocombe.
*****REDS,** J.R.S., Paramount. Vittorio Storaro.

ART DIRECTION-SET DECORATION

THE FRENCH LIEUTENANT'S WOMAN, Parlon, UA. Assheton Gorton; Ann Mollo.
HEAVEN'S GATE, Partisan, UA. Tambi Larsen; Jim Berkey.
RAGTIME, Paramount. John Graysmark, Patrizia Von Brandenstein and Anthony Reading; George de Titta, Sr., George de Titta, Jr. and Peter Howitt.
*****RAIDERS OF THE LOST ARK,** Lucasfilm, Paramount. Norman Reynolds and Leslie Dilley; Michael Ford.
REDS, J.R.S., Paramount. Richard Sylbert; Michael Seirton.

COSTUME DESIGN

*****CHARIOTS OF FIRE,** Enigma, The Ladd Company/Warner Bros. Milena Canonero.
THE FRENCH LIEUTENANT'S WOMAN, Parlon, UA. Tom Rand.
PENNIES FROM HEAVEN, Ross/Hera, M-G-M. Bob Mackie.
RAGTIME, Paramount. Anna Hill Johnstone.
REDS, J.R.S., Paramount. Shirley Russell.

SOUND

ON GOLDEN POND, ITC/IPC, Universal. Richard Portman and David Ronne.
OUTLAND, The Ladd Company. John K. Wilkinson, Robert W. Glass, Jr., Robert M. Thirwell and Robin Gregory.
PENNIES FROM HEAVEN, Ross/Hera, M-G-M. Michael.J. Kohut, Jay M. Harding, Richard Tyler and Al Overton.
*****RAIDERS OF THE LOST ARK,** Lucasfilm, Paramount. Bill Varney, Steve Maslow, Gregg Landaker and Roy Charman.
REDS, J.R.S., Paramount. Dick Vorisek, Tom Fleischman and Simon Kaye.

FILM EDITING

CHARIOTS OF FIRE, Enigma, The Ladd Company/Warner Bros. Terry Rawlings.
THE FRENCH LIEUTENANT'S WOMAN, Parlon, UA. John Bloom.
ON GOLDEN POND, ITC/IPC, Universal. Robert L. Wolfe.
*****RAIDERS OF THE LOST ARK,** Lucasfilm, Paramount. Michael Kahn.
REDS, J.R.S., Paramount. Dede Allen and Craig McKay.

VISUAL EFFECTS

DRAGONSLAYER, Barwood/Robbins, Paramount. Dennis Muren, Phil Tippett, Ken Ralston and Brian Johnson.
*****RAIDERS OF THE LOST ARK,** Lucasfilm, Paramount. Richard Edlund, Kit West, Bruce Nicholson and Joe Johnston.

MUSIC

(Song)
*****ARTHUR'S THEME (Best That You Can Do)** (*Arthur,* Rollins, Joffe, Morra and Brezner, Orion); Music and Lyrics by Burt Bacharach, Carole Bayer Sager, Christopher Cross and Peter Allen.
ENDLESS LOVE (*Endless Love,* Barish/Lovell, Universal); Music and Lyrics by Lionel Richie.
THE FIRST TIME IT HAPPENS (*The Great Muppet Caper,* Henson/ITC, Universal); Music and Lyrics by Joe Raposo.
FOR YOUR EYES ONLY (*For Your Eyes Only,* EON, UA); Music by Bill Conti. Lyrics by Mick Leeson.
ONE MORE HOUR (*Ragtime,* Paramount); Music and Lyrics by Randy Newman.

(Original Score)
*****CHARIOTS OF FIRE,** Enigma, The Ladd Company/Warner Bros. Vangelis.
DRAGONSLAYER, Barwood/Robbins, Paramount. Alex North.
ON GOLDEN POND, ITC/IPC, Universal. Dave Grusin.
RAGTIME, Paramount. Randy Newman.
RAIDERS OF THE LOST ARK, Lucasfilm, Paramount. John Williams.

MAKEUP

*****AN AMERICAN WEREWOLF IN LONDON,** Lycanthrope/Polygram, Universal. Rick Baker.
HEARTBEEPS, Phillips, Universal. Stan Winston.

SHORT FILMS

(Animated Films)
*****CRAC,** Societe Radio-Canada. Frederic Back, producer.
THE CREATION, Will Vinton Productions. Will Vinton, producer.
THE TENDER TALE OF CINDERELLA PENGUIN, National Film Board of Canada. Janet Perlman, producer.

(Live Action)
COUPLES AND ROBBERS, Flamingo Pictures Ltd. Christine Oestreicher, producer.
FIRST WINTER, National Film Board of Canada. John N. Smith, producer.
*****VIOLET,** The American Film Institute. Paul Kemp and Shelley Levinson, producers.

DOCUMENTARY

(Short Subjects)

AMERICAS IN TRANSITION, Americas in Transition, Inc. Obie Benz, producer.
*__CLOSE HARMONY,__ A Nobel Enterprise. Nigel Nobel Enterprise.
JOURNEY FOR SURVIVAL, Dick Young Productions, Inc. Dick Young, producer.
SEE WHAT I SAY, Michigan Women Filmmakers Productions. Linda Chapman, Pam LeBlanc and Freddi Stevens, producers..
URGE TO BUILD, Roland Halle Productions, Inc. Roland Halle and John Hoover, producers.

(Features)

AGAINST WIND AND TIDE: A CUBAN ODYSSEY, Seven League Productions, Inc. Suzanne Bauman, Paul Neshamkin and Jim Burroughs, producers.
BROOKLYN BRIDGE, Florentine Films. Ken Burns, producer.
EIGHT MINUTES TO MIDNIGHT: A PORTRAIT OF DR. HELEN CALDICOTT, The Caldicott Project. Mary Benjamin, Susanne Simpson and Boyd Estus, producers.
EL SALVADOR: ANOTHER VIETNAM, Catalyst Media Productions. Glenn Silber and Tete Vasconcellos, producers.
*__GENOCIDE,__ Arnold Schwartzman Productions, Inc. Arnold Schwartzman and Rabbi Marvin Hier, producers.

FOREIGN LANGUAGE FILM

THE BOAT IS FULL (Switzerland).
MAN OF IRON (Poland).
*__MEPHISTO__ (Hungary).
MUDDY RIVER (Japan).
THREE BROTHERS (Italy).

HONORARY

TO BARBARA STANWYCK, for superlative creativity and unique contribution to the art of screen acting.

SPECIAL ACHIEVEMENT AWARDS

For Sound Effects Editing: **BEN BURTT** and **RICHARD L. ANDERSON** for "Raiders of the Lost Ark," Lucasfilm, Paramount.

1981 IRVING G. THALBERG MEMORIAL AWARD

TO ALBERT A. BROCCOLI

1981 JEAN HERSHOLT HUMANITARIAN AWARD

TO DANNY KAYE

1981 GORDON E. SAWYER AWARD

(First year given)

TO JOSEPH B. WALKER

SCIENTIFIC OR TECHNICAL AWARDS

(Academy Award of Merit)

The **FUJI PHOTO FILM COMPANY, LTD.** for the research, development and introduction of a new Ultra-high-speed color negative film for motion pictures.

(Scientific and Engineering Award)

NELSON TYLER for the progressive development and improvement of the Tyler Helicopter motion picture camera platform.
LEONARD SCKOLOW for the concept and design and to **HOWARD T. LaZARE** for the development of the Consolidated Film Industries' Stroboscan motion picture film viewer.
RICHARD EDLUND and **INDUSTRIAL LIGHT AND MAGIC, INCORPORATED** for the concept and engineering of a beam-splitter optical composite motion picture printer.
RICHARD EDLUND and **INDUSTRIAL LIGHT AND MAGIC, INCORPORATED** for the engineering of the Empire Motion Picture Camera System.
EDWARD J. BLASKO and **DR. RODERICK T. RYAN** of the Eastman Kodak Company for the application of the Prostar Microfilm Processor for motion picture title and special optical effects production.

(Technical Achievement Award)

HAL LANDAKER for the concept and to **ALAN D. LANDAKER** for the engineering of the Burbank Studios' Production Sound Department 24-frame color video system.
BILL HOGAN of Ruxton, Ltd. and **RICHARD J. STUMPF** and **DANIEL R. BREWER** of Universal City Studios' Production Sound Department for the engineering of a 24-frame color video system.
JOHN DeMUTH for the engineering of a 24-frame video system.
ERNST F. NETMANN of Continental Camera Systems, Inc., for the development of a pitching lens for motion picture photography.
BILL TAYLOR of Universal City Studios for the concept and specifications for a Two Format, Rotating Head, Aerial Image Optical Printer.
PETER D. PARKS of Oxford Scientific Films for the development of the OSF microcosmic zoom device for microscopic photography.
DR. LOUIS STANKIEWICZ and **H. L. BLACHFORD** for the development of Baryfol sound barrier materials.
DENNIS MUREN and **STUART ZIFF** of Industrial Light and Magic, Incorporated for the development of a Motion Picture Figure Mover for animation photography.

*__INDICATES WINNER__

Best Supporting Actor: **John Gielgud** *as Hobson in* Arthur *(Orion/Warner Bros.; directed by Steve Gordon) was a tolerant but acidly sarcastic valet to Dudley Moore, a wildly rich playboy with a love for booze and good times. Gielgud's performance made a hilarious addition to a merry comedy caper which also included Liza Minnelli and Geraldine Fitzgerald in the cast. Gielgud, one of the most respected Sirs in the British theater, also appeared in 1981's best picture champ* Chariots of Fire *and, despite the fact his character expires at the end of* Arthur, *he nevertheless popped up in the 1988 sequel* Arthur 2 on the Rocks.

Raiders of the Lost Ark *(Paramount; directed by Steven Spielberg) introduced a new name to movie audiences: Indiana Jones. Played by Harrison Ford, Mr. Jones was involved in a wild series of adventures beginning with a close escape from a crushing boulder (above) as he attempted to plunder a South American jungle tomb, all of which left audiences breathless. And happy. Raiders was nominated for eight awards including best picture and it won five of them, making it the single most Oscared film of the year.*

For the majority of moviegoers, 1982 was quintessentially the year of *E.T. The Extra-Terrestrial,* a film that was by Hollywood terms a true "sleeper," a quietly made project of little expectations that had gone on to become the biggest money-making movie of all time, and one of the best liked. The Steven Spielberg project was also much respected by Oscar, pulling nine nominations when the 1982 awards rolled around. It eventually won four of those prizes, but on Oscar night, April 11, 1983, even *E.T.* took a back seat to *Gandhi.* Sir Richard Attenborough's epic was nominated for eleven awards and achieved a virtual sweep by collecting eight of them. Among the *Gandhi* gatherings: trophies for best picture of the year, for Ben Kingsley as best actor and for Sir Richard as best director.

Tootsie, also extremely well liked among 1982 movies, was nominated for 10 Academy Awards but took home only one, for Jessica Lange's supporting performance. For Lange, it was a double-whammy year: she was nominated both as best supporting actress and as best actress, in the latter category for her work in *Frances.* It was only the fourth time in the Academy's 55 years a performer had competed in two acting categories the same year. Her predecessors: Fay Bainter in 1938, Teresa Wright in 1942 and Barry Fitzgerald in 1944.

It was also a big night for pregnant Meryl Streep, named best actress for *Sophie's Choice.* It was the second Oscar she'd received in her short film career.

The year's best supporting actor award went to Louis Gossett, Jr. for *An Officer and a Gentleman;* Gossett was the third black to win a competitive Oscar, and the first to do so in that category. He was in close competition with first-time nominee but long-time film veteran Robert Preston, nominated for *Victor/Victoria.* That picture, curiously, was one of several films of the year (including *Tootsie* and *The World According to Garp*) pulling numerous Oscar nominations for performers playing in drag, portraying transsexuals or cross-dressers.

The award ceremony itself was hosted by Walter Matthau, Liza Minnelli, Dudley Moore and Richard Pryor, and presenters included two-time Oscar winner Luise Rainer, 1940s pin-up queen Jane Russell and Bob Hope, presenting an honorary Oscar to Mickey Rooney for his "years of versatility in a variety of memorable film performances." One of the musical highlights of the evening was a salute to Irving Berlin, scheduled to be sung by Ethel Merman but done instead by Bernadette Peters and Peter Allen. It was later revealed that Merman, while readying to leave New York for the California show, had suffered a stroke, one from which she never fully recovered before her death in 1984.

On a lighter side, presenters Kristy McNichol and Matt Dillon gave decidedly new pronunciations to names they had to read, such as Zbigniew Rybczynski, Michael Toshiyuki Uno and Christine Oestreicher. Rybczynski, winner for his animated short *Tango,* also

266

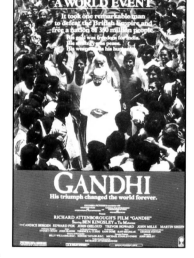

Best Picture: **Gandhi** *(Columbia; produced by Richard Attenborough),* ***Best Director:*** **Richard Attenborough** *for* Gandhi *and* ***Best Actor:*** **Ben Kingsley** *as Mahatma Gandhi. It took Richard Attenborough a full 20 years to realize an ambition to make a movie on the life of saintly Mahatma Gandhi, the wise but complex man who helped his native India achieve independence from imperial Britain. Covering more than a half century of India's turmoil, the biographical film cost $22 million to make, ran over three hours (188 minutes) and became the picture of the year, thanks in no small measure to the pivotal performance of 38-year-old Ben Kingsley (right), a veteran of England's Royal Shakespeare Company. The cast also included John Gielgud, John Mills, Trevor Howard, Martin Sheen and Candice Bergen, the latter as photographer Margaret Bourke-White.*

became the first Oscar winner known to spend some of his night of triumph behind bars. Briefly leaving the Dorothy Chandler Pavilion for a cigarette break during the show, he was barred by a guard from re-entering, resulting in a scuffle and a brief stretch in the slammer before he was identified and charges were dropped.

Meanwhile, among those in the audience watching the festivities and applauding the winners: Oscar rebel George C. Scott, obviously thinking more kindly toward Oscar in the 1980s than he had in 1970 when he refused to show up and accept a trophy of his own.

Best Actress: **Meryl Streep** as Sophie Zawistowska in Sophie's Choice *(Universal/AFD; produced by Alan Pakula and Keith Barish). One of the choices Sophie has to make is forced on her during World War II: Nazi guards at the Auschwitz concentration camp say they will spare the life of just one of her two children, but Sophie herself must decide which one. It's an agonizing moment which thereafter dooms Sophie, long after she's survived the war and moved to Brooklyn, temporarily finding a new life with a lover (Kevin Kline) and a compassionate neighbor (Peter MacNichol, at right with Streep) who's the film's narrator. Streep, directed by Alan Pakula and required to speak Polish, German, then English with a Polish accent for the role, was superb and won her second Oscar, her first in the best actress category.*

Best Supporting Actress: **Jessica Lange** as Julie in Tootsie *(Columbia; produced by Sydney Pollack and Dick Richards). It was a great year for Jessica Lange with two diverse roles, both released at virtually the same time for a one-two punch: the first as real-life actress Frances Farmer in the intense bio-drama* Frances, *which brought her a best actress nomination; the second as a fictional TV actress in the sparkling comedy* Tootsie, *for which she won the year's supporting actress Oscar. In the latter, directed by Sydney Pollack, she played a performer in a television soap opera befriended by her TV costar "Dorothy Michaels" who, unbeknownst to Lange, is really an actor in drag (Dustin Hoffman, right with Lange).*

267

Best Supporting Actor: Louis Gossett, Jr. *as Sergeant Foley in* An Officer and a Gentleman *(Paramount/Lorimar; produced by Martin Elfand). Playing a super-tough drill sergeant at a Naval Aviation Officer Candidate school, Gossett (right, shaping up recruits including Richard Gere, at far left) virtually stole the show in the muscular romantic drama. Directed by Taylor Hackford, the film focused on the relationship of Gere with Debra Winger and David Keith with Lisa Blount, while the would-be gents endured 13 weeks of agony to become Navy officers. Gossett supplied the agony but it was, of course, all for the cause.*

PICTURE

E.T. THE EXTRA-TERRESTRIAL, Universal. Produced by Steven Spielberg and Kathleen Kennedy.
*****GANDHI,** Columbia. Produced by Richard Attenborough.
MISSING, Lewis, Universal. Produced by Edward Lewis and Mildred Lewis.
TOOTSIE, Mirage/Punch, Columbia. Produced by Sydney Pollack and Dick Richards.
THE VERDICT, Zanuck/Brown, 20th Century-Fox. Produced by Richard D. Zanuck and David Brown.

ACTOR

DUSTIN HOFFMAN in *Tootsie*, Mirage/Punch, Columbia.
*****BEN KINGSLEY** in *Gandhi*, Columbia.
JACK LEMMON in *Missing*, Lewis, Universal.
PAUL NEWMAN in *The Verdict*, Zanuck/Brown, 20th Century-Fox.
PETER O'TOOLE in *My Favorite Year*, Brooksfilm/Gruskoff, M-G-M/UA.

ACTRESS

JULIE ANDREWS in *Victor/Victoria*, M-G-M/UA.
JESSICA LANGE in *Frances*, Brooksfilm/EMI, Universal/A.F.D.
SISSY SPACEK in *Missing*, Lewis, Universal.
*****MERYL STREEP** in *Sophie's Choice*, ITC/Pakula-Barish, Universal/A.F.D.
DEBRA WINGER in *An Officer and a Gentleman*, Lorimar/Elfand, Paramount.

SUPPORTING ACTOR

CHARLES DURNING in *The Best Little Whorehouse in Texas*, Miller-Milkis-Boyett, Universal.
*****LOUIS GOSSETT, JR.** in *An Officer and a Gentleman*, Lorimar/Elfand, Paramount.
JOHN LITHGOW in *The World According to Garp*, Warner Bros.
JAMES MASON in *The Verdict*, Zanuck/Brown, 20th Century-Fox.
ROBERT PRESTON in *Victor/Victoria*, M-G-M/UA.

SUPPORTING ACTRESS

GLENN CLOSE in *The World According to Garp*, Warner Bros.
TERI GARR in *Tootsie*, Mirage/Punch, Columbia.
*****JESSICA LANGE** in *Tootsie*, Mirage/Punch, Columbia.

KIM STANLEY in *Frances*, Brooksfilm/EMI, Universal/A.F.D.
LESLEY ANN WARREN in *Victor/Victoria*, M-G-M/UA.

DIRECTING

DAS BOOT, Bavaria Atelier GmbH, Columbia/PSO. Wolfgang Peterson.
E.T. THE EXTRA-TERRESTRIAL, Universal. Steven Spielberg.
*****GANDHI,** Columbia. Richard Attenborough.
TOOTSIE, Mirage/Punch, Columbia. Sydney Pollack.
THE VERDICT, Zanuck/Brown, 20th Century-Fox. Sidney Lumet.

WRITING

(Screenplay Written Directly for the Screen)

DINER, Weintraub, M-G-M/UA. Barry Levinson.
E.T. THE EXTRA-TERRESTRIAL, Universal. Melissa Mathison.
*****GANDHI,** Columbia. John Briley.
AN OFFICER AND A GENTLEMAN, Lorimar/Elfand, Paramount. Douglas Day Stewart.
TOOTSIE, Mirage/Punch, Columbia. Larry Gelbart, Murray Schisgal and Don McGuire.

(Screenplay Based on Material from Another Medium)

DAS BOOT, Bavaria Atelier GmbH, Columbia/PSO. Wolfgang Petersen.
*****MISSING,** Lewis, Universal. Costas-Gavras and Donald Stewart.
SOPHIE'S CHOICE, ITC/Pakula-Barish, Universal/A.F.D. Alan J. Pakula.
THE VERDICT, Zanuck/Brown, 20th Century-Fox. David Mamet.
VICTOR/VICTORIA, M-G-M/UA. Blake Edwards.

CINEMATOGRAPHY

DAS BOOT, Bavaria Atelier GmbH, Columbia/PSO. Jost Vacano.
E.T. THE EXTRA-TERRESTRIAL, Universal. Allen Daviau.
*****GANDHI,** Columbia. Billy Williams and Ronnie Taylor.
SOPHIE'S CHOICE, ITC/Pakula-Barish, Universal/A.F.D. Nestor Almendros.
TOOTSIE, Mirage/Punch, Columbia. Owen Roizman.

ART DIRECTION-SET DECORATION

ANNIE, Rastar, Columbia. Dale Hennesy; Marvin March.
BLADE RUNNER, Deeley-Scott, The Ladd Company/Sir Run Run Shaw. Lawrence G. Paull and David L. Snyder; Linda DeScenna.
*GANDHI, Columbia. Stuart Craig and Bob Laing; Michael Seirton.
LA TRAVIATA, Accent, Universal Classics. Franco Zeffirelli; Gianni Quaranta.
VICTOR/VICTORIA, M-G-M/UA. Rodger Maus, Tim Hutchinson and William Craig Smith; Harry Cordwell.

COSTUME DESIGN

*GANDHI, Columbia. John Mollo and Bhanu Athaiya.
LA TRAVIATA, Accent, Universal Classics. Piero Tosi.
SOPHIE'S CHOICE, ITC/Pakula-Barish, Universal/A.F.D. Albert Wolsky
TRON, Disney. Elois Jenssen and Rosanna Norton.
VICTOR/VICTORIA, M-G-M/UA. Patricia Norris.

SOUND

DAS BOOT, Bavaria Atelier GmbH, Columbia/PSO. Milan Bor, Trevor Pyke and Mike Le-Mare.
*E.T. THE EXTRA-TERRESTRIAL, Universal. Robert Knudson, Robert Glass, Don Digirolamo and Gene Cantamessa.
GANDHI, Columbia. Gerry Humphreys, Robin O'Donoghue, Jonathan Bates and Simon Kaye.
TOOTSIE, Mirage/Punch, Columbia. Arthur Piantadosi, Les Fresholtz, Dick Alexander and Les Lazarowitz.
TRON, Disney. Michael Minkler, Bob Minkler, Lee Minkler and Jim La Rue.

FILM EDITING

DAS BOOT, Bavaria Atelier GmbH, Columbia/PSO. Hannes Nikel.
E.T. THE EXTRA-TERRESTRIAL, Universal. Carol Littleton.
*GANDHI, Columbia. John Bloom.
AN OFFICER AND A GENTLEMAN, Lorimar/Elfand, Paramount. Peter Zinner.
TOOTSIE, Mirage/Punch, Columbia. Fredric Steinkamp and William Steinkamp.

VISUAL EFFECTS

BLADE RUNNER, Deeley-Scott, The Ladd Company/Sir Run Run Shaw. Douglas Trumbull, Richard Yuricich and David Dryer.
*E.T. THE EXTRA-TERRESTRIAL, Universal. Carlo Rambaldi, Dennis Muren and Kenneth F. Smith.
POLTERGEIST, Spielberg, M-G-M/UA. Richard Edlund, Michael Wood and Bruce Nicholson.

SOUND EFFECTS EDITING
(New designation)

DAS BOOT, Bavaria Atelier GmbH, Columbia/PSO. Mike Le-Mare.
*E.T. THE EXTRA-TERRESTRIAL, Universal. Charles L. Campbell and Ben Burtt.
POLTERGEIST, Spielberg, M-G-M/UA. Stephen Hunter Flick and Richard L. Anderson.

MUSIC
(Song)

EYE OF THE TIGER (Rocky III, Chartoff-Winkler, M-G-M/UA); Music and Lyrics by Jim Peterik and Frankie Sullivan III.
HOW DO YOU KEEP THE MUSIC PLAYING? (Best Friends, Timberlane, Warner Bros.); Music by Michel Legrand. Lyrics by Alan and Marilyn Bergman.
IF WE WERE IN LOVE (Yes, Giorgio, M-G-M/UA); Music by John Williams. Lyrics by Alan and Marilyn Bergman.
IT MIGHT BE YOU (Tootsie, Mirage/Punch, Columbia); Music by Dave Grusin. Lyrics by Alan and Marilyn Bergman.
*UP WHERE WE BELONG (An Officer and a Gentleman, Lorimar/Elfand, Paramount); Music by Jack Nitzsche and Buffy Sainte-Marie. Lyrics by Will Jennings.

(Original Score)

*E.T. THE EXTRA-TERRESTRIAL, Universal. John Williams.
GANDHI, Columbia. Ravi Shankar and George Fenton.
AN OFFICER AND A GENTLEMAN, Lorimar/Elfand, Paramount. Jack Nitzsche.
POLTERGEIST, Spielberg, M-G-M/UA. Jerry Goldsmith.
SOPHIE'S CHOICE, ITC/Pakula-Barish, Universal/A.F.D. Marvin Hamlisch.

(Original Song Score and its Adaptation or Best Adaptation Score)

ANNIE, Rastar, Columbia. Ralph Burns.
ONE FROM THE HEART, Zoetrope, Columbia. Tom Waits.

*VICTOR/VICTORIA, M-G-M/UA. Henry Mancini and Leslie Bricusse.

MAKEUP

GANDHI, Columbia. Tom Smith.
*QUEST FOR FIRE, ICC, 20th Century-Fox. Sarah Monzani and Michele Burke.

SHORT FILMS
(Animated Films)

THE GREAT COGNITO, Will Vinton Productions. Will Vinton, producer.
THE SNOWMAN, Snowman Enterprises Ltd. John Coates, producer.
*TANGO, Film Polski. Zbigniew Rybczynski, producer.

(Live Action)

BALLET ROBOTIQUE, Bob Rogers and Company. Bob Rogers, producer.
*A SHOCKING ACCIDENT, Flamingo Pictures Ltd. Christine Oestreicher, producer.
THE SILENCE, The American Film Institute. Michael Toshiyuki Uno and Joseph Benson, producers.
SPLIT CHERRY TREE, Learning Corporation of America. Jan Saunders, producer.
SREDNI VASHTAR, Laurentic Film Productions Ltd. Andrew Birkin, producer.

DOCUMENTARY
(Short Subject)

GODS OF METAL, A Richter Productions Film. Robert Richter, producer.
*IF YOU LOVE THIS PLANET, National Film Board of Canada. Edward Le Lorrain and Terri Nash, producers.
THE KLAN: A LEGACY OF HATE IN AMERICA, Guggenheim Productions, Inc. Charles Guggenheim and Werner Schumann, producers.
TO LIVE OR LET DIE, American Film Foundation. Freida Lee Mock, producer.
TRAVELING HOPEFULLY, Arnuthfonyus Films, Inc. John G. Avildsen, producer.

(Features)

AFTER THE AXE, National Film Board of Canada. Sturla Gunnarsson and Steve Lucas, producers.
BEN'S MILL, Public Broadcasting Associates—ODYSSEY. John Karol and Michel Chalufour, producers.
IN OUR WATER, A Foresight Films Production. Meg Switzgable, producer.
*JUST ANOTHER MISSING KID, Canadian Broadcasting Corporation. John Zaritsky, producer.
A PORTRAIT OF GISELLE, ABC Video Enterprises, Inc. in association with Wishupon Productions, Inc. Joseph Wishy, producer.

FOREIGN LANGUAGE FILM

ALSINO AND THE CONDOR (Nicaragua).
COUP DE TORCHON ("Clean Slate") (France).
THE FLIGHT OF THE EAGLE (Sweden).
PRIVATE LIFE (U.S.S.R.).
*VOLVER A EMPEZAR (Spain).

HONORARY

TO MICKEY ROONEY, in recognition of his 60 years of versatility in a variety of memorable film performances.

1982 IRVING G. THALBERG MEMORIAL AWARD

None given this year.

1982 JEAN HERSHOLT HUMANITARIAN AWARD
TO WALTER MIRISCH

1982 GORDON E. SAWYER AWARD
TO JOHN O. AALBERG

SCIENTIFIC OR TECHNICAL AWARDS

(Academy Award of Merit)

AUGUST ARNOLD and ERICH KAESTNER of Arnold & Richter, GmbH, for the concept and engineering of the first operational 35mm, hand-held, spinning-mirror reflex, motion picture camera.

(Scientific and Engineering Award)

COLIN F. MOSSMAN and THE RESEARCH AND DEVELOPMENT GROUP OF RANK FILM LABORATORIES, LONDON, for the engineering and implementation of a 4,000 meter printing system for motion picture laboratories.
SANTE ZELLI and SALVATORE ZELLI of Elemack Italia S.4.1., Rome, Italy, for the continuing engineering, design and development that has resulted in the Elemack Camera Dolly Systems for motion picture production.
LEONARD CHAPMAN for the engineering design, development and manufacture of the PeeWee Camera Dolly for motion picture production.
DR. MOHAMMAD S. NOZARI of Minnesota Mining and Manufacturing Company for the research and development of the 3M Photogard protective coating for motion picture film.
BRIANNE MURPHY and DONALD SCHISLER of Mitchell Insert Systems, Incorporated, for the concept, design and manufacture of the MISI Camera Insert Car and Process Trailer.
JACOBUS L. DIMMERS for the engineering and manufacture of the Teccon Enterprises' magnetic transducer for motion picture sound recording the playback.

(Technical Achievement Award)

RICHARD W. DEATS for the design and manufacture of the "Little Big Crane" for motion picture production.
CONSTANT TRESFON and ADRIAAN DE ROOY of Egripment, and to ED PHILLIPS AND CARLOS DE MATTOS of Matthews Studio Equipment, Incorporated, for the design and manufacture of the "Tulip Crane" for motion picture production.
BRAN FERREN of Associates and Ferren for the design and development of a computerized lighting effect system for motion picture photography.
CHRISTIE ELECTRIC CORPORATION and LaVEZZI MACHINE WORKS, INCORPORATED, for the design and manufacture of the Ultramittent film transport for Christie motion picture projectors.

*INDICATES WINNER

There was almost as much noise and newsprint expended over who wasn't nominated for the 1983 Academy Awards as who was. One furor arose over *Yentl,* the $16 million production Barbra Streisand had produced, directed, co-authored and starred in. Before the nominations were announced, the Washington *Post* had commented, "It would constitute a Hollywood scandal if Barbra Streisand was denied an Oscar nomination for her direction of *Yentl,*" but when the final five choices were announced, Streisand's name was not among them. *Yentl* itself received five nominations but none of them for any of La Barbra's contributions. Bob Fosse's *Star 80* also caused an uproar; it failed to receive a single nomination. Writer-director Philip Kaufman also was bypassed for recognition although his film *The Right Stuff* received eight nominations elsewhere, and there was much discussion of the fact that only one (Glenn Close) of the ensemble cast of the well-liked *The Big Chill* had been singled out for an Oscar nomination.

But when the awards were finally handed out on April 9, 1984, there was little argument, or surprise, over the final champs. Shirley MacLaine, as expected, was named best actress for *Terms of Endearment,* Jack Nicholson was named best supporting actor from the same film and *Terms* also won Oscars for James L. Brooks' direction and screenplay plus the biggie: best picture of the year. MacLaine, in accepting her award, praised the "turbulent brilliance" of costar Debra Winger, with whom she'd competed for the best actress trophy; she also said, "God bless that potential we all have for making anything possible if we think we deserve it." She smilingly added, "I deserve this!"

Best actor of the year was Robert Duvall for *Tender Mercies,* Linda Hunt was named best supporting actress for her performance as a man in *The Year of Living Dangerously* and Ingmar Bergman's *Fanny & Alexander* was named best foreign language film. Since the Swedish film won a total of four awards (including those for cinematography, art direction and costume design), it became the most honored foreign film to date in Oscar annals.

Veteran filmmaker Hal Roach, 92, was voted an honorary statuette; M.J. "Mike" Frankovich received the Jean Hersholt Humanitarian Award and *Return of the Jedi* was given a special visual effects Oscar. George Lucas, the mastermind behind *Jedi,* was thanked no less than seven times by the four who won that visual effects prize during their combined acceptance speech. But Irene Cara, co-winner in the music division, went them one step further. She specifically thanked two dozen individuals while at the podium.

Johnny Carson was once again the evening's host, and among the participants were Shirley Temple, Mel Gibson, Frank Capra, Matthew Broderick, Rock Hudson, Joan Collins and the duet of

Best Actor: Robert Duvall *as Mac Sledge in* Tender Mercies *(Universal/AFD; produced by Philip S. Hobel). The screenplay was by Horton Foote, author of the film version of* To Kill a Mockingbird*; the director was Australia's Bruce Beresford making his first American film.* Tender *was a small tale, gently told, although danger always seemed imminent as it followed Robert Duvall as an ex-country/western singer on the skids but getting a second chance when he marries a young widow (Tess Harper) and acquires a stepson (Allan Hubbard, right, with Duvall). Duvall had previously been nominated as best supporting actor for* The Godfather *(1972) and* Apocalypse Now *(1979) and as best actor for 1980's* The Great Santini.

Sylvester Stallone and Dolly Parton. At one point, winner MacLaine had commented to the Dorothy Chandler audience, "This show has been as long as my career." She wasn't far from the truth. When the 1983 extravaganza finally wound to a close, it clocked at 3 hours, 42 minutes, two minutes longer than *Gone with the Wind* and the lengthiest Oscar show on record, to date.

Best Supporting Actress: **Linda Hunt** *as Billy Kwan in* The Year of Living Dangerously *(M-G-M; produced by Jim McElroy). It had never happened before, at least not within Oscar range: an actress playing a male role, and winning a best supporting actress award for it. Director Peter Weir says he cast Linda Hunt in the part of a Chinese-Australian dwarf-cameraman because he was unable to find a short male actor who could properly play it. The casting turned out to be inspired, adding a bizarre quality to the Kwan character, an enigmatic gent who comes to the aid of an Australian journalist (Mel Gibson) in Indonesia during the final days of the Sukarno regime.*

271

Best Picture: **Terms of Endearment** *(Paramount; produced by James L. Brooks),* **Best Director: James L. Brooks** *for* Terms of Endearment, *Best Actress:* **Shirley MacLaine** *as Aurora Greenway,* **Best Supporting Actor: Jack Nicholson** *as Garrett Breedlove. Jennifer Jones was the first to see possibilities of a 24-karat, four-handkerchief* movie in Larry McMurtry's story of the rocky relationship of a mother and daughter, often at screeching odds but tightly bonded when the daughter suddenly falls seriously ill. Miss Jones optioned the property, later sold it to Paramount and it was finally made with Shirley MacLaine (above, with Debra Winger and Jack Nicholson). It also took MacLaine to the *Academy Award podium for the first time after four previous nominations for acting (and one as a documentary producer); it brought Nicholson his second Oscar, his first in the supporting division, as he played MacLaine's boozing, potbellied neighbor and sometimes bed-partner, a role first offered to Burt Reynolds.*

The Right Stuff *(The Ladd Company/Warner Bros.; produced by Irwin Winkler and Robert Chartoff)* was a soaring film version of Tom Wolfe's best-seller about 16 years leading up to the successful space flight of the Project Mercury astronauts. Sam Shepard (above) played Chuck Yeager among a cast including Dennis Quaid, Scott Glenn, Ed Harris, Fred Ward, Charles Frank and—on the ground—Kim Stanley, Barbara Hershey and Veronica Cartwright. Directed and scripted by Philip Kaufman, it won Oscars for sound, film editing, original score and sound effects editing.

272

Best Foreign Language Film: Fanny & Alexander *from Sweden. It was one of Ingmar Bergman's most accessible films and, winning four Oscars, tallied the highest total number of Academy Awards of any foreign language film to date. Fanny ran 188 minutes and was grand to watch, a rich tapestry of Swedish family life among the affluent in the early 1900s, with several concurrent stories to pique interest and, as with all Bergman films, plenty to analyze afterwards. Bertil Guve and Pernilla Allwin (left) played the ten-year-old Alexander and his eight-year-old sister, the youngest members of the clan in question.*

PICTURE

THE BIG CHILL, Carson, Columbia. Produced by Michael Shamberg.
THE DRESSER, Goldcrest, Columbia. Produced by Peter Yates.
THE RIGHT STUFF, Chartoff-Winkler, The Ladd Company through Warner Bros. Produced by Irwin Winkler and Robert Chartoff.
TENDER MERCIES, EMI, Universal/AFD. Produced by Philip S. Hobel.
*TERMS OF ENDEARMENT, Brooks, Paramount. Produced by James L. Brooks.

ACTOR

MICHAEL CAINE in *Educating Rita,* Acorn, Columbia.
TOM CONTI in *Reuben, Reuben,* Saltair/Shenson, 20th Century Fox International Classics.
TOM COURTENAY in *The Dresser,* Goldcrest, Columbia.
*ROBERT DUVALL in *Tender Mercies,* EMI, Universal/AFD.
ALBERT FINNEY in *The Dresser,* Goldcrest, Columbia.

ACTRESS

JANE ALEXANDER in *Testament,* Entertainment Events, Paramount.
*SHIRLEY MacLAINE in *Terms of Endearment,* Brooks, Paramount.
MERYL STREEP in *Silkwood,* ABC, 20th Century-Fox.
JULIE WALTERS in *Educating Rita,* Acorn, Columbia.
DEBRA WINGER in *Terms of Endearment,* Brooks, Paramount.

SUPPORTING ACTOR

CHARLES DURNING, in *To Be or Not To Be,* Brooksfilms, 20th Century-Fox.
JOHN LITHGOW in *Terms of Endearment,* Brooks, Paramount.
*JACK NICHOLSON in *Terms of Endearment,* Brooks, Paramount.
SAM SHEPARD in *The Right Stuff,* Chartoff-Winkler, The Ladd Company through Warner Bros.
RIP TORN in *Cross Creek,* Radnitz/Ritt/Thorn EMI, Universal.

SUPPORTING ACTRESS

CHER in *Silkwood,* ABC, 20th Century Fox.
GLENN CLOSE in *The Big Chill,* Carson, Columbia.
*LINDA HUNT in *The Year of Living Dangerously,* Fields, M-G-M/UA.
AMY IRVING in *Yentl,* Ladbroke/Barwood, M-G-M/UA.
ALFRE WOODARD in *Cross Creek,* Radnitz/Ritt/Thorn EMI, Universal.

DIRECTING

THE DRESSER, Goldcrest, Columbia. Peter Yates.
FANNY & ALEXANDER, Embassy. Ingmar Bergman.
SILKWOOD, ABC, 20th Century Fox. Mike Nichols.
TENDER MERCIES, EMI, Universal/AFD. Bruce Beresford.
*TERMS OF ENDEARMENT, Brooks, Paramount. James L. Brooks.

*JAMES L. BROOKS for *Terms of Endearment*, Brooks, Paramount.

WRITING

(Screenplay Written Directly for the Screen)

THE BIG CHILL, Carson, Columbia. Lawrence Kasdan and Barbara Benedek.
FANNY & ALEXANDER, Embassy. Ingmar Bergman.
SILKWOOD, ABC, 20th Century Fox. Nora Ephron and Alice Arlen.
*TENDER MERCIES, EMI, Universal/AFD. Horton Foote.
WARGAMES, Goldberg, M-G-M/UA. Lawrence Lasker and Walter F. Parkes.

(Screenplay Based on Material from Another Medium)

BETRAYAL, Horizon, 20th Century Fox International Classics. Harold Pinter.
THE DRESSER, Goldcrest, Columbia. Ronald Harwood.
EDUCATING RITA, Acorn, Columbia. Willy Russell.
REUBEN, REUBEN, Saltair/Shenson, 20th Century Fox International Classics. Julius J. Epstein.
*TERMS OF ENDEARMENT, Brooks, Paramount. James L. Brooks.

CINEMATOGRAPHY

*FANNY & ALEXANDER, Embassy. Sven Nykvist.
FLASHDANCE, Polygram, Paramount. Don Peterman.
THE RIGHT STUFF, Chartoff-Winkler, The Ladd Company through Warner Bros. Caleb Deschanel.
WARGAMES, Goldberg, M-G-M/UA. William A. Fraker.
ZELIG, Rollins and Joffe, Orion/Warner Bros. Gordon Willis.

ART DIRECTION-SET DECORATION

*FANNY & ALEXANDER, Embassy. Anna Asp.
RETURN OF THE JEDI, Lucasfilm, 20th Century Fox. Norman Reynolds, Fred Hole and James Schoppe; Michael Ford.
THE RIGHT STUFF, Chartoff-Winkler, The Ladd Company through Warner Bros. Geoffrey Kirkland, Richard J. Lawrence, W. Stewart Campbell and Peter Romero; Pat Pending and George R. Nelson.
TERMS OF ENDEARMENT, Brooks, Paramount. Polly Platt and Harold Michelson; Tom Pedigo and Anthony Mondello.
YENTL, Ladbroke/Barwood, M-G-M/UA. Roy Walker and Leslie Tomkins; Tessa Davies.

COSTUME DESIGN

CROSS CREEK, Radnitz/Ritt/Thorn EMI, Universal. Joe I. Tompkins.
*FANNY & ALEXANDER, Embassy. Marik Vos.
HEART LIKE A WHEEL, Aurora, 20th Century Fox. William Ware Theiss.
THE RETURN OF MARTIN GUERRE, Marcel Dassault—FR3, European International Distribution. Anne-Marie Marchand.
ZELIG, Rollins and Joffe, Orion/Warner Bros. Santo Loquasto.

SOUND

NEVER CRY WOLF, Disney. Alan R. Splet, Todd Boekelheide, Randy Thom and David Parker.
RETURN OF THE JEDI, Lucasfilm, 20th Century Fox. Ben Burtt, Gary Summers, Randy Thom and Tony Dawe.
*THE RIGHT STUFF, Chartoff-Winkler, The Ladd Company through Warner Bros. Mark Berger, Tom Scott, Randy Thom and David MacMillan.
TERMS OF ENDEARMENT, Brooks, Paramount. Donald O. Mitchell, Rick Kline, Kevin O'Connell and Jim Alexander.
WARGAMES, Goldberg, M-G-M/UA. Michael J. Kohut, Carlos de Larios, Aaron Rochin and Willie D. Burton.

FILM EDITING

BLUE THUNDER, Rastar, Columbia. Frank Morriss and Edward Abroms.
FLASHDANCE, Polygram, Paramount. Bud Smith and Walt Mulconery.
*THE RIGHT STUFF, Chartoff-Winkler, The Ladd Company through Warner Bros. Glenn Farr, Lisa Fruchtman, Stephen A. Rotter, Douglas Stewart and Tom Rolf.
SILKWOOD, ABC, 20th Century Fox. Sam O'Steen.
TERMS OF ENDEARMENT, Brooks, Paramount. Richard Marks.

SOUND EFFECTS EDITING

RETURN OF THE JEDI, Lucasfilm, 20th Century Fox. Ben Burtt.
*THE RIGHT STUFF, Chartoff-Winkler, The Ladd Company through Warner Bros. Jay Boekelheide.

MUSIC

(Song)

*FLASHDANCE...WHAT A FEELING (*Flashdance,* Polygram, Paramount); Music by Giorgio Moroder. Lyrics by Keith Forsey and Irene Cara.
MANIAC (*Flashdance,* Polygram, Paramount); Music and Lyrics by Michael Sembello and Dennis Matkosky.
OVER YOU (*Tender Mercies,* EMI, Universal/AFD); Music and Lyrics by Austin Roberts and Bobby Hart.
PAPA, CAN YOU HEAR ME? (*Yentl,* Ladbroke/Barwood, M-G-M/UA); Music by Michel Legrand. Lyrics by Alan and Marilyn Bergman.
THE WAY HE MAKES ME FEEL (*Yentl,* Ladbroke/Barwood, M-G-M/UA); Music by Michel Legrand. Lyrics by Alan and Marilyn Bergman.

(Original Score)

CROSS CREEK, Radnitz/Ritt/Thorn EMI, Universal. Leonard Rosenman.
RETURN OF THE JEDI, Lucasfilm, 20th Century Fox. John Williams.
*THE RIGHT STUFF, Chartoff-Winkler, The Ladd Company through Warner Bros. Bill Conti.
TERMS OF ENDEARMENT, Brooks, Paramount. Michael Gore.
UNDER FIRE, Lions Gate, Orion. Jerry Goldsmith.

(Original Song Score and its Adaptation or Best Adaptation Score)

THE STING II, Lang, Universal. Lalo Schifrin.
TRADING PLACES, Russo, Paramount. Elmer Bernstein.
*YENTL, Ladbroke/Barwood, M-G-M/UA. Michel Legrand, Alan and Marilyn Bergman.

SHORT FILMS

(Animated Films)

MICKEY'S CHRISTMAS CAROL, Disney. Burny Mattinson, producer.
SOUND OF SUNSHINE—SOUND OF RAIN, A Hallinan Plus Production. Eda Godel Hallinan, producer.
*SUNDAE IN NEW YORK, A Motionpicker Production, Jimmy Picker, producer.

(Live Action)

*BOYS AND GIRLS, An Atlantis Films Ltd. Production. Janice L. Platt, producer.
GOODIE-TWO-SHOES, A Timeless Films Production, Paramount. Ian Emes, producer.
OVERNIGHT SENSATION, A Bloom Film Production. Jon H. Bloom, producer.

DOCUMENTARY

(Short Subjects)

*FLAMENCO AT 5:15, A National Film Board of Canada Production. Cynthia Scott and Adam Symansky, producers.
IN THE NUCLEAR SHADOW: WHAT CAN THE CHILDREN TELL US?, An Impact Production. Vivienne Verdon-Roe and Eric Thiermann, producers.
SEWING WOMAN, A DeepFocus Production. Arthur Dong, producer.
SPACES: THE ARCHITECTURE OF PAUL RUDOLPH, An Eisenhardt Production. Robert Eisenhardt, producer.
YOU ARE FREE (IHR ZENT FREI), A Brokman/Landis Production. Dea Brokman and Ilene Landis, producers.

(Features)

CHILDREN OF DARKNESS, A Children of Darkness Production. Richard Kotuk and Ara Chekmayan, producers.
FIRST CONTACT, An Arundel Production. Bob Connolly and Robin Anderson, producers.
*HE MAKES ME FEEL LIKE DANCIN', An Edgar J. Scherick Associates Production. Emile Ardolino, producer.
THE PROFESSION OF ARMS (WAR SERIES FILM #3), A National Film Board of Canada Production. Michael Bryans and Tina Viljoen, producers.
SEEING RED, A Heartland Production. James Klein and Julia Reichert, producers.

FOREIGN LANGUAGE FILM

CARMEN (Spain).
ENTRE NOUS (France).
*FANNY & ALEXANDER (Sweden)
JOB'S REVOLT (Hungary).
LE BAL (Algeria).

HONORARY

TO HAL ROACH, in recognition of his unparalled record of distinguished contributions to the motion picture art form.

SPECIAL ACHIEVEMENT AWARD

For Visual Effects: RICHARD EDLUND, DENNIS MUREN, KEN RALSTON and PHIL TIPPETT for ''Return of the Jedi,'' Lucasfilm, 20th Century Fox.

1983 IRVING G. THALBERG MEMORIAL AWARD

None given this year.

1983 JEAN HERSHOLT HUMANITARIAN AWARD

TO M.J. FRANKOVICH

1983 GORDON E. SAWYER AWARD

TO DR. JOHN G. FRAYNE

SCIENTIFIC OR TECHNICAL AWARDS

(Academy Award of Merit)

DR. KURT LARCHE of OSRAM GmbH for the research and development of xenon short-arc discharge lamps for motion picture projection.

(Scientific and Engineering Award)

JONATHAN ERLAND and ROGER DORNEY of Apogee, Incorporated, for the engineering and development of a reverse bluescreen traveling matte process for special effects photography.
GERALD L. TURPIN of Lightflex International Limited for the design, engineering and development of an on-camera device providing contrast control, sourceless fill light and special effects for motion picture photography.
GUNNAR P. MICHELSON for the engineering and development of an improved, electronic, high-speed, precision light valve for use in motion picture printing machines.

(Technical Achievement Awards):

WILLIAM G. KROKAUGGER of Mole-Richardson Company for the design and engineering of a portable, 12,000 watt, lighting-control dimmer for use in motion picture production.
CHARLES J. WATSON , LARRY L. LANGREHR and JOHN H. STEINER for the development of the BHP (electro-mechanical) fader for use on continuous motion picture contact printers.
ELIZABETH D. DE LA MARE of De La Mare Engineering, Incorporated, for the progressive development and continuous research of special effects pyrotechnics originally designed by Glenn W. De La Mare for motion picture production.
DOUGLAS FRIES, JOHN LACEY and MICHAEL SIGRIST for the design and engineering of a 35mm reflex conversion camera system for special effects photography.
JACK CASHIN of Ultra-Stereo Labs, Incorporated, for the engineering and development of a 4-channel, stereophonic, decoding system for optical motion picture sound track reproduction.
DAVID J. DEGENKOLB for the design and development of an automated device used in the silver recovery process in motion picture laboratories.

*INDICATES WINNER

1984
The Fifty-Seventh Year

ajor efforts were expended to turn the 1984 Academy Award ceremony into a faster, snappier show than the long-run marathons they had increasingly become over the years. But, when all was said and tallied at the end of the evening, March 25, 1985, the show at the Dorothy Chandler Pavilion of the Los Angeles Music Center still rolled in at 3 hours and 10 minutes, shorter by 32 minutes than the previous year but still a bit long by most yardsticks.

There was a new host for the evening, Jack Lemmon, and something for everyone; everything, that is, except brevity. Prince, a nominee (and eventual winner) in the music category, made a splashy entrance wearing a purple sequined-and-hooded cape. Cary Grant was simpler: he wore a tuxedo and dazzling smile. Laurence Olivier was also there; so were Tom Selleck, Steven Spielberg, Steve Martin, Diana Ross, Gene Kelly, Kirk Douglas, Burt Lancaster, even Placido Domingo, all of them involved in presenting the evening's awards.

And most of those awards went strictly in one direction: to Orion's *Amadeus.* Nominated for eleven Oscars, it won eight of them, including awards for best picture, best actor—F. Murray Abraham—and best director—Milos Forman. It was a second win for Forman, who'd been in that same winner's circle nine years earlier via *One Flew Over the Cuckoo's Nest.* For Abraham, it was a first nomination, a first win and a first

real introduction to international fame. "It would be a lie if I told you I didn't know what to say," he told the Dorothy Chandler audience. "I've been working on this speech for about 25 years!"

It was also a triumphant night for Sally Field, winning her second best actress trophy, this time for *Places in the Heart.* She also delivered an acceptance speech that came back to haunt her. "This means so much more to me this time, I don't know why," she told the audience. "I think the first time I hardly felt it because it was all too new. I haven't had an orthodox career and I wanted more than anything to have your respect." She added, "The first time I didn't feel it but this time I feel it and I can't deny the fact you like me. Right now, you *like* me!" Her words were praised by many as a warm, spontaneous reaction, but years later she was still being kidded about what came to be known as her "you *like* me!" speech.

British stage legend Dame Peggy Ashcroft was named best supporting actress of the year for *A Passage to India;* the seventy-seven-year-old actress wasn't present in Hollywood to receive her award so it was placed in her hands one week later in London by Sir Richard Attenborough. The best supporting actor award went to Dr. Haing S. Ngor in *The Killing Fields,* and David Wolper, one of the men responsible for bringing the 1984 Summer Olympics to Los Angeles, received the Jean Hersholt Humanitarian Award.

274

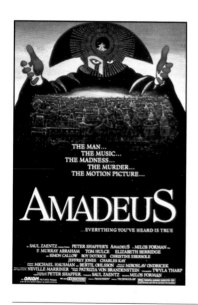

Best Picture: Amadeus *(Orion; produced by Saul Zaentz),* **Best Director: Milos Forman** *for* Amadeus *and* **Best Actor: F. Murray Abraham** *as Antonio Salieri in* Amadeus. *Written by Peter Shaffer,* Amadeus *was a fictionalized account of the rise to prominence of Wolfgang Amadeus Mozart and the overwhelming jealousy of Vienna's court composer Salieri, owing to his recognition of Mozart's genius and, by comparison, his own mediocrity. The play was first presented successfully on stage in London with Paul Scofield, then on Broadway with Ian McKellen. Little-known actor F. Murray Abraham (right, having his hand kissed) was cast in the screen version and won the Oscar for his performance as the green-eyed rival of brattish Mozart (played by Tom Hulce). Under the direction of Milos Forman, it became the year's most honored film.*

Among the nominees, at least one name inspired smiles: P.H. Vazak, listed as co-writer with Michael Austin of *Greystoke, the Legend of Tarzan, Lord of the Apes.* The name actually belonged to a sheepdog, owned by writer Robert Towne. Towne had borrowed the name as a pseudonym on the script when he wanted to distance himself from *Greystoke,* a film he'd once been set to direct. Neither Towne nor the sheepdog won.

Fewer smiles were inspired by the morning-after news: for the second consecutive year, the Oscar viewing audience had declined. True, the show had been seen in an estimated 23.5 million American homes, a staggering number, but nearly 1.9 million fewer than the year before.

Best Actress: **Sally Field** *as Edna Spalding in* Places in the Heart *(Tri-Star; produced by Arlene Donovan). Set in Waxahachie, Texas, in 1935,* Places *gave Sally Field (above) an excellent role as a young widow with true grit, coping with the problems of raising two small children, keeping her homestead from foreclosure and battling the treacheries of nature and neighbors. Directed by Robert Benton, himself a native of Waxahachie, the film brought Field her second Oscar (the first: five years earlier for 1979's* Norma Rae) *and initially had competition from two other 1984 dramas emphasizing struggles in rural life,* Country *with Jessica Lange and* The River *with Sissy Spacek.*

275

Best Supporting Actor: **Haing S. Ngor** *as Dith Pran in* The Killing Fields *(Warner Bros.; produced by David Puttnam). An actual Cambodian refugee, 36-year-old Haing S. Ngor was the first non-professional to win an Academy Award for acting since Harold Russell in 1946 for* The Best Years of Our Lives. *In* The Killing Fields, *directed by Roland Joffe, he played the real-life Cambodian assistant to New York Times reporter Sydney Schanberg (played by Sam Waterston, above left with Ngor) during the fall of Cambodia in 1975, after which Pran was tortured at the hands of Khmer Rouge soldiers before he eventually escaped. Ngor got the role by chance: a doctor by profession in his homeland, he'd moved to Los Angeles and accidentally met a casting director at a wedding, unaware of the size of the* Killing *role until he was in Thailand to begin shooting. Ironically, having escaped Pol Pot's killing fields, he would be murdered by a Los Angeles street gang in 1996.*

Best Supporting Actress: **Peggy Ashcroft** *as Mrs. Moore in* A Passage to India *(Columbia; produced by John Brabourne and Richard Goodwin). Peggy Ashcroft had made her professional debut in 1926 at the age of 18 on stage in London and through the years became one of the British theater's greatest stars, playing such classic roles as Ophelia, Electra, Cleopatra and Desdemona. Although she occasionally worked in films, her screen portfolio was sparse—by choice—but she became a familiar face to international audiences via a pair of 1984 projects, both set in India: a British-made TV mini-series* The Jewel in the Crown, *then David Lean's film version of E.M. Forster's* A Passage to India *in which she played a free-thinking British matron on a spiritual journey. Having become Dame Peggy Ashcroft in 1956, she was England's first Dame of the Theater to also win an Academy Award.*

Purple Rain *(Warner Bros.; directed by Albert Magnoli) gave rock star Prince (right) his first motion picture role in a snappy-fitting vehicle emphasizing, to great effect, the star's own unique persona. Heavy on music (naturally), even when the storyline flowed,* Purple *was wall-to-wall with original songs written by Prince, who won the Oscar in the Academy's music category for best original song score and its adaptation. For the record, his real name in full is Prince Rogers Nelson.*

PICTURE

*AMADEUS, Zaentz, Orion. Produced by Saul Zaentz.
THE KILLING FIELDS, Enigma, Warner Bros. Produced by David Puttnam.
A PASSAGE TO INDIA, G.W. Films, Columbia. Produced by John Brabourne and Richard Goodwin.
PLACES IN THE HEART, Tri-Star. Produced by Arlene Donovan.
A SOLDIER'S STORY, Caldix, Columbia. Produced by Norman Jewison, Ronald L. Schwary and Patrick Palmer.

ACTOR

*F. MURRAY ABRAHAM in *Amadeus,* Zaentz, Orion.
JEFF BRIDGES in *Starman,* Columbia.
ALBERT FINNEY in *Under the Volcano,* Ithaca, Universal.
TOM HULCE in *Amadeus,* Zaentz, Orion.
SAM WATERSTON in *The Killing Fields,* Enigma, Warner Bros.

ACTRESS

JUDY DAVIS in *A Passage to India,* G.W. Films, Columbia.
*SALLY FIELD in *Places in the Heart,* Tri-Star.
JESSICA LANGE in *Country,* Touchstone, Buena Vista.
VANESSA REDGRAVE in *The Bostonians,* Merchant Ivory, Almi.
SISSY SPACEK in *The River,* Universal.

SUPPORTING ACTOR

ADOLPH CAESAR in *A Soldier's Story,* Caldix, Columbia.
JOHN MALKOVICH in *Places in the Heart,* Tri-Star.
NORIYUKI "PAT" MORITA in *The Karate Kid,* Columbia.
*HAING S. NGOR in *The Killing Fields,* Enigma, Warner Bros.
RALPH RICHARDSON in *Greystoke: The Legend of Tarzan, Lord of the Apes,* Warner Bros.

SUPPORTING ACTRESS

*PEGGY ASHCROFT in *A Passage to India,* G.W. Films, Columbia.
GLENN CLOSE in *The Natural,* Tri-Star.
LINDSAY CROUSE in *Places in the Heart,* Tri-Star.
CHRISTINE LAHTI in *Swing Shift,* Warner Bros.
GERALDINE PAGE in *The Pope of Greenwich Village,* Koch/Kirkwood, M-G-M/UA.

DIRECTING

*AMADEUS, Zaentz, Orion. Milos Forman.
BROADWAY DANNY ROSE, Rollins and Joffe, Orion. Woody Allen.
THE KILLING FIELDS, Enigma, Warner Bros. Roland Joffe.
A PASSAGE TO INDIA, G.W. Films, Columbia. David Lean.
PLACES IN THE HEART, Tri-Star. Robert Benton.

WRITING

(Screenplay Written Directly for the Screen)
BEVERLY HILLS COP, Simpson/Bruckheimer, Paramount. Daniel Petrie, Jr. and Danilo Bach.
BROADWAY DANNY ROSE, Rollins/Joffe, Orion. Woody Allen.
EL NORTE, Cinecom International/Island Alive. Gregory Nava and Anna Thomas.
*PLACES IN THE HEART, Tri-Star. Robert Benton.
SPLASH, Touchstone, Buena Vista. Lowell Ganz, Babaloo Mandel, Bruce Jay Friedman and Brian Grazer.

(Screenplay Based on Material from Another Medium)
*AMADEUS, Zaentz, Orion. Peter Shaffer.
GREYSTOKE: THE LEGEND OF TARZAN, LORD OF THE APES, Warner Bros. P.H. Vazak and Michael Austin.
THE KILLING FIELDS, Enigma, Warner Bros. Bruce Robinson.
A PASSAGE TO INDIA, G.W. Films, Columbia. David Lean.
A SOLDIER'S STORY, Caldix, Columbia. Charles Fuller.

CINEMATOGRAPHY

AMADEUS, Zaentz, Orion. Miroslav Ondricek.
*THE KILLING FIELDS, Enigma, Warner Bros. Chris Menges.
THE NATURAL, Tri-Star. Caleb Deschanel.
A PASSAGE TO INDIA, G.W. Films, Columbia. Ernest Day.
THE RIVER, Universal. Vilmos Zsigmond.

ART DIRECTION-
SET DECORATION

*AMADEUS, Zaentz, Orion. Patrizia Von Brandenstein; Karel Cerny.
THE COTTON CLUB, Orion. Richard Sylbert; George Gaines and Les Bloom.
THE NATURAL, Tri-Star. Angelo Graham, Mel Bourne, James J. Murakami and Speed Hopkins; Bruce Weintraub.
A PASSAGE TO INDIA, G.W. Films, Columbia. John Box and Leslie Tomkins; Hugh Scaife.
2010, Hyams, M-G-M/UA. Albert Brenner; Rick Simpson.

COSTUME DESIGN

*AMADEUS, Zaentz, Orion. Theodor Pistek.
THE BOSTONIANS, Merchant Ivory, Almi. Jenny Beavan and John Bright.
A PASSAGE TO INDIA, G.W. Films, Columbia. Judy Moorcroft.
PLACES IN THE HEART, Tri-Star. Ann Roth.
2010, Hyams, M-G-M/UA. Patricia Norris.

SOUND

*AMADEUS, Zaentz, Orion. Mark Berger, Tom Scott, Todd Boekelheide and Chris Newman.
DUNE, De Laurentiis, Universal. Bill Varney, Steve Maslow, Kevin O'Connell and Nelson Stoll.
A PASSAGE TO INDIA, G.W. Films, Columbia. Graham V. Hartstone, Nicolas Le Messuier, Michael A. Carter and John Mitchell.
THE RIVER, Universal. Nick Alphin, Robert Thirlwell, Richard Portman and David Ronne.
2010, Hyams, M-G-M/UA. Michael J. Kohut, Aaron Rochin, Carlos De Larios and Gene S. Cantamessa. ·

FILM EDITING

AMADEUS, Zaentz, Orion. Nena Danevic and Michael Chandler.
THE COTTON CLUB, Orion. Barry Malkin and Robert Q. Lovett.
*THE KILLING FIELDS, Enigma, Warner Bros. Jim Clark.
A PASSAGE TO INDIA, G.W. Films, Columbia. David Lean.
ROMANCING THE STONE, El Corazon, 20th Century Fox. Donn Cambern and Frank Morriss.

VISUAL EFFECTS

GHOSTBUSTERS, Columbia. Richard Edlund, John Bruno, Mark Vargo and Chuck Gaspar.
*INDIANA JONES AND THE TEMPLE OF DOOM, Lucasfilm, Paramount. Dennis Muren, Michael McAlister, Lorne Peterson and George Gibbs.
2010, Hyams, M-G-M/UA. Richard Edlund, Neil Krepela, George Jenson and Mark Stetson.

MUSIC

(Song)

AGAINST ALL ODDS (TAKE A LOOK AT ME NOW) (Against All Odds, New Visions, Columbia); Music and Lyrics by Phil Collins.
FOOTLOOSE (Footloose, Melnick, Paramount); Music and Lyrics by Kenny Loggins and Dean Pitchford.
GHOSTBUSTERS (Ghostbusters, Columbia); Music and Lyrics by Ray Parker, Jr.
*I JUST CALLED TO SAY I LOVE YOU (The Woman in Red, Orion); Music and Lyrics by Stevie Wonder.
LET'S HEAR IT FOR THE BOY (Footloose, Melnick, Paramount); Music and Lyrics by Tom Snow and Dean Pitchford.

(Original Score)

INDIANA JONES AND THE TEMPLE OF DOOM, Lucasfilm, Paramount. John Williams.
THE NATURAL, Tri-Star. Randy Newman.
*A PASSAGE TO INDIA, G.W. Films, Columbia. Maurice Jarre.
THE RIVER, Universal. John Williams
UNDER THE VOLCANO, Ithaca, Universal. Alex North.

(Original Song Score and Its Adaptation or Best Adaptation Score)

THE MUPPETS TAKE MANHATTAN, Tri-Star. Jeff Moss.
*PURPLE RAIN, Warner Bros. Prince.
SONGWRITER, Tri-Star. Kris Kristofferson.

MAKEUP

*AMADEUS, Zaentz, Orion. Paul LeBlanc and Dick Smith.
GREYSTOKE: THE LEGEND OF TARZAN, LORD OF THE APES, Warner Bros. Rick Baker and Paul Engelen.
2010, Hyams, M-G-M/UA. Michael Westmore.

SHORT FILMS

(Animated Films)

*CHARADE, A Sheridan College Production. Jon Minnis, Producer.
DOCTOR DE SOTO, Michael Sporn Animation, Inc. Morton Schindel and Michael Sporn, Producers.
PARADISE, National Film Board of Canada. Ishu Patel, Producer.

(Live Action)

THE PAINTED DOOR, Atlantis Films Limited in association with the National Film Board of Canada. Michael MacMillan and Janice L. Platt, producer.
TALES OF MEETING AND PARTING, The American Film Institute—Directing Workshop for Women. Sharon Oreck and Lesli Linka Glatter, Producers.
*UP, Pyramid Films. Mike Hoover, Producer.

DOCUMENTARY

(Short Subjects)

THE CHILDREN OF SOONG CHING LING, UNICEF and The Soong Ching Ling Foundation. Gary Bush and Paul T.K. Lin, Producers.
CODE GRAY: ETHICAL DILEMMAS IN NURSING, The Nursing Ethics Project/Fanlight Productions. Ben Achtenberg and Joan Sawyer, Producers.
THE GARDEN OF EDEN, Florentine Films. Lawrence R. Hott and Roger M. Sherman, Producers.
RECOLLECTIONS OF PAVLOVSK, Leningrad Documentary Film Studio. Irina Kalinina, Producer.
*THE STONE CARVERS, Paul Wagner Productions. Marjorie Hunt and Paul Wagner, Producers.

(Features)

HIGH SCHOOLS, Guggenheim Productions, Inc. Charles Guggenheim and Nancy Sloss, Producers.
IN THE NAME OF THE PEOPLE, Pan American Films. Alex W. Drehsler and Frank Christopher, Producers.
MARLENE, Zev Braun Pictures, Inc./OKO Film Produktion. Karel Dirka and Zev Braun, Producers.
STREETWISE, Bear Creek Productions, Inc. Cheryl McCall, Producer.
*THE TIMES OF HARVEY MILK, Black Sand Educational Productions, Inc. Robert Epstein and Richard Schmiechen, Producers.

FOREIGN LANGUAGE FILM

BEYOND THE WALLS (Israel).
CAMILA (Argentina).
*DANGEROUS MOVES (Switzerland).
DOUBLE FEATURE (Spain).
WARTIME ROMANCE (U.S.S.R.).

HONORARY AND OTHER AWARDS

TO JAMES STEWART for his fifty years of memorable performances. For his high ideals both on and off the screen. With the respect and affection of his colleagues.
TO THE NATIONAL ENDOWMENT FOR THE ARTS in recognition of its 20th anniversary and its dedicated commitment to fostering artistic and creative activity and excellence in every area of the arts.

SPECIAL ACHIEVEMENT AWARDS

For Sound Effects Editing: KAY ROSE for The River, a Universal Pictures Production.

1984 IRVING G. THALBERG MEMORIAL AWARD

None given this year.

1984 JEAN HERSHOLT HUMANITARIAN AWARD

TO DAVID L. WOLPER

1984 GORDON E. SAWYER AWARD

TO LINWOOD G. DUNN

SCIENTIFIC OR TECHNICAL AWARDS

(Academy Award of Merit)

None.

(Scientific And Engineering Award)

DONALD A. ANDERSON and DIANA REINERS of 3M Company for the development of "Cinetrak" Magnetic Film #350/351 for motion picture sound recording.

BARRY M. STULTZ, RUBEN AVILA and WES KENNEDY of Film Processing Corporation for the development of FPC 200 PB Fullcoat Magnetic Film for motion picture sound recording.
BARRY M. STULTZ, RUBEN AVILA and WES KENNEDY of Film Processing Corporation for the formulation and application of an improved sound track stripe to 70mm motion picture film, and to JOHN MOSELY for the engineering research involved therein.
KENNETH RICHTER of Richter Cine Equipment for the design and engineering of the R-2 Auto-Collimator for examining image quality at the focal plane of motion picture camera lenses.
GUNTHER SCHAIDT and ROSCO LABORATORIES, INCORPORATED, for the development of an improved, non-toxic fluid for creating fog and smoke for motion picture production.
JOHN WHITNEY, JR. and GARY DEMOS of Digital Productions, Incorporated, for the practical simulation of motion picture photography by means of computer-generated images.

(Technical Achievement Award)

NAT TIFFEN of Tiffen Manufacturing Corporation for the production of high-quality, durable, laminated color filters for motion picture photography.
DONALD TRUMBULL, JONATHAN ERLAND, STEPHEN FOG and PAUL BURK of Apogee, Incorporated, for the design and development of the "Blue Max" high-power, blue-flux projector for traveling matte composite photography.
JONATHAN ERLAND and ROBERT BEALMEAR of Apogee, Incorporated, for an innovative design for front projection screens and an improved method for their construction.
HOWARD J. PRESTON of Preston Cinema Systems for the design and development of a variable speed control device with automatic exposure compensation for motion picture cameras.

*INDICATES WINNER

1985
The Fifty-Eighth Year

Out of Africa virtually swept the 58th Academy Awards, winning seven Oscars and easily outdistancing its closest runners-up *Cocoon* and *Witness,* each of which won two statuettes. And among the *Africa* windfall was the prize that counted most: best picture of the year. It also brought an Oscar for its direction by Sydney Pollack, and its screenplay by Kurt Luedtke, based on Isak Dinesen's account of her experiences in Kenya in 1914. *Africa* had been nominated for eleven awards, as had Steven Spielberg's *The Color Purple.*

The biggest conversation puller, once the verdicts were in, wasn't that *Africa* had done so well but that *The Color Purple* had fared so poorly, ending up totally Oscarless. Earlier, there had also been a *Color* controversy stirred when Spielberg, the film's director, had failed to be nominated in Oscar's director division, despite those eleven nominations elsewhere. And even more confusion reigned when Spielberg was named best director of the year by the Director's Guild of America, a group comprised of at least some of those also involved in deciding the Oscar nominees in that category. By virtue of its eleven-nomination but zero-win status, *The Color Purple* joined 1977's *The Turning Point* as the two most nominated non-winning films in the Academy's history. *Turning* had also been an 11-0 puzzler.

Among the more positive emotional peaks of Oscar night on March 24, 1986, was the win by Geraldine Page as best actress for *The Trip to Bountiful;* Page had previously been a nominee seven times without a win. Obviously delighted, she received a standing ovation from the crowd at the Dorothy Chandler Pavilion. Another standing ovation went to seventy-seven-year-old Don Ameche, named best supporting actor for *Cocoon,* and winning on his very first nomination after a screen career that began a full 40 years earlier.

Hosts for the Oscar show were Jane Fonda, Alan Alda and Robin Williams; Stanley Donen produced for the first time, and musical numbers were staged by Ron Field who had done similar duties for the opening ceremonies at the 1984 Summer Olympics. Among the high points: Howard Keel singing to a bevy of movie musical leading ladies, including Jane Powell, Esther Williams, Kathryn Grayson, June Allyson, Leslie Caron, Debbie Reynolds, Cyd Charisse and Ann Miller. Less successful was an opening number featuring Teri Garr, a chorus line, some elaborate staging, intercut film clips and pyrotechnics. After that, things improved considerably.

William Hurt was named best actor for *Kiss of the Spider Woman,* Anjelica Huston was chosen best supporting actress for her work in her father John Huston's film *Prizzi's Honor* and Argentina's *The Official Story* was picked as best foreign language film. Charles "Buddy" Rogers received the year's Jean Hersholt Humanitarian Award and composer Alex North was honored for a lifetime of achievement on film. Paul

278

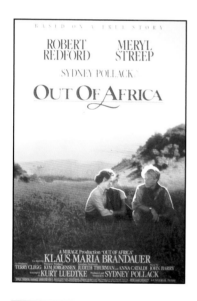

Best Actor: **William Hurt** *as Molina in* Kiss of the Spider Woman *(Island Alive; produced by David Weisman). It was a daring role for William Hurt, and one originally tagged for Raul Julia until the two actors decided to switch parts. Hurt played a homosexual, locked up in a South American prison, sharing his cell and private thoughts with a journalist (Julia) who's in for a stretch because of political writings. Hector Babenco directed and kept the action and ideas moving even though much of the screenplay by Leonard Schrader, from Manuel Puig's novel, was confined behind bars. Hurt, wearing dyed hair and an effeminate manner, created a character both off-putting and endearing. He was nominated again the following year for 1986's* Children of a Lesser God *and yet again in 1987 for* Broadcast News.

Newman also received an honorary Oscar for his film career and accepted his award via videotape from Chicago where he was filming *The Color of Money.* "I am especially grateful that this did not come wrapped in a gift certificate to Forest Lawn," he smiled, adding "(I) hope that my best work is down the pike, ahead of me and not behind." Those words proved to be prophetic. The very next year Newman would again receive an Academy Award.

Best Actress: **Geraldine Page** *as Mrs. Watts in* The Trip to Bountiful *(Island; produced by Sterling VanWagenen and Horton Foote). For a time it looked as if Geraldine Page would go into the records as Oscar's most nominated non-winner among actors. She'd been nominated seven times without carrying home a prize, a dubious distinction she shared with Peter O'Toole and the late Richard Burton. But for Page* number eight was the charm, and the charmer, when she played a Texas woman of advancing years, determined to travel back to a town called Bountiful where she'd once lived in happier times. Peter Masterson was the director. The Horton Foote story had earlier been done as a 1953 teleplay, then as a Broadway play, both starring Lillian Gish.

Best Picture: **Out of Africa** *(Universal; produced by Sydney Pollack) and* **Best Director: Sydney Pollack** *for* Out of Africa. Africa *was a striking change of pace for director Pollack after 1982's comedy* Tootsie. *Beginning in Kenya in 1914, it told the story of real-life writer Karen Blixen, who was* published under the pen name Isak Dinesen, seeing her through a loveless marriage to one man (played by Klaus Maria Brandauer) and a romantic but frustrating relationship with another (Robert Redford). Meryl Streep (above) played Blixen and the film was a constant eye-dazzler, encompassing some of the most beautiful visuals yet seen on film. Besides being named the year's best picture, it brought Oscars to director Pollack and cinematographer David Watkin and was honored as well for its screenplay, art direction, music score and sound.

Best Supporting Actress: Anjelica Huston as Maerose Prizzi in Prizzi's Honor (ABC/20th Century-Fox; produced by John Foreman). "I feel like a dynasty," Anjelica Huston said after she'd won the Oscar as the year's best supporting actress. Justifiably. Her granddad Walter Huston had been an Academy Award winner in a performance directed by Anjelica's father John Huston; John, too, had won an Oscar and now Anjelica had one as well, hers for a role in which she'd been directed by her dad. In Prizzi's she played the black-sheep daughter in a Mafia dynasty, in love with a hit man (Jack Nicholson) who's much more interested in Kathleen Turner who, to his surprise, turns out to be a hit (wo)man, too.

280

PICTURE

THE COLOR PURPLE, Warner Bros. Produced by Steven Spielberg, Kathleen Kennedy, Frank Marshall and Quincy Jones.
KISS OF THE SPIDER WOMAN, Island Alive. Produced by David Weisman.
*****OUT OF AFRICA,** Universal. Produced by Sydney Pollack.
PRIZZI'S HONOR, ABC, 20th Century Fox. Produced by John Foreman.
WITNESS, Feldman, Paramount. Produced by Edward S. Feldman.

ACTOR

HARRISON FORD in Witness, Feldman, Paramount.
JAMES GARNER in Murphy's Romance, Fogwood, Columbia.
*****WILLIAM HURT** in Kiss of the Spider Woman, Island Alive.
JACK NICHOLSON in Prizzi's Honor, ABC, 20th Century Fox.
JON VOIGHT in Runaway Train, Cannon.

ACTRESS

ANNE BANCROFT in Agnes of God, Columbia.
WHOOPI GOLDBERG in The Color Purple, Warner Bros.
JESSICA LANGE in Sweet Dreams, HBO, Tri-Star.
*****GERALDINE PAGE** in The Trip to Bountiful, Island.
MERYL STREEP in Out of Africa, Universal.

SUPPORTING ACTOR

*****DON AMECHE** in Cocoon, Zanuck-Brown, 20th Century Fox.
KLAUS MARIA BRANDAUER in Out of Africa, Universal.
WILLIAM HICKEY in Prizzi's Honor, ABC, 20th Century Fox.
ROBERT LOGGIA in Jagged Edge, Columbia.
ERIC ROBERTS in Runaway Train, Cannon.

SUPPORTING ACTRESS

MARGARET AVERY in The Color Purple, Warner Bros.
*****ANJELICA HUSTON** in Prizzi's Honor, ABC, 20th Century Fox.
AMY MADIGAN in Twice in a Lifetime, Bud Yorkin Productions.
MEG TILLY in Agnes of God, Columbia.
OPRAH WINFREY in The Color Purple, Warner Bros.

DIRECTING

KISS OF THE SPIDER WOMAN, Island Alive. Hector Babenco.
*****OUT OF AFRICA,** Universal. Sydney Pollack.
PRIZZI'S HONOR, ABC, 20th Century Fox. John Huston.
RAN, Orion Classics. Akira Kurosawa.
WITNESS, Feldman, Paramount. Peter Weir.

WRITING

(Screenplay Written Directly for the Screen)
BACK TO THE FUTURE, Amblin, Universal. Robert Zemeckis and Bob Gale.
BRAZIL, Embassy International, Universal. Terry Gilliam, Tom Stoppard and Charles McKeown.
THE OFFICIAL STORY, Almi. Luis Puenzo and Aida Bortnik.
THE PURPLE ROSE OF CAIRO, Rollins and Joffe, Orion. Woody Allen.
*****WITNESS,** Feldman, Paramount. William Kelley, Pamela Wallace and Earl W. Wallace.

(Screenplay Based on Material from Another Medium)
THE COLOR PURPLE, Warner Bros. Menno Mayjes.
KISS OF THE SPIDER WOMAN, Island Alive. Leonard Schrader.
*****OUT OF AFRICA,** Universal. Kurt Luedtke.
PRIZZI'S HONOR, ABC, 20th Century Fox. Richard Condon and Janet Roach.
THE TRIP TO BOUNTIFUL, Island. Horton Foote.

CINEMATOGRAPHY

THE COLOR PURPLE, Warner Bros. Allen Daviau.
MURPHY'S ROMANCE, Fogwood, Columbia. William A. Fraker.
*****OUT OF AFRICA,** Universal. David Watkin.
RAN, Orion Classics. Takao Saito, Masaharu Ueda and Asakazu Nakai.
WITNESS, Feldman, Paramount. John Seale.

ART DIRECTION-SET DECORATION

BRAZIL, Embassy International, Universal. Norman Garwood; Maggie Gray.
THE COLOR PURPLE, Warner Bros. J. Michael Riva and Robert W. Welch; Linda DeScenna.
*****OUT OF AFRICA,** Universal. Stephen Grimes; Josie MacAvin.

RAN, Orion Classics. Yoshiro Muraki and Shinobu Muraki.
WITNESS, Feldman, Paramount. Stan Jolley; John Anderson.

COSTUME DESIGN

THE COLOR PURPLE, Warner Bros. Aggie Guerard Rodgers.
THE JOURNEY OF NATTY GANN, Disney and Silver Screen Partners II, Buena Vista. Albert Wolsky.
OUT OF AFRICA, Universal. Milena Canonero.
PRIZZI'S HONOR, ABC, 20th Century Fox. Donfeld.
*****RAN,** Orion Classics. Emi Wada.

SOUND

BACK TO THE FUTURE, Amblin, Universal. Bill Varney, B. Tennyson Sebastian II, Robert Thirlwell and William B. Kaplan.
A CHORUS LINE, Embassy/Polygram, Columbia. Donald O. Mitchell, Michael Minkler, Gerry Humphreys and Chris Newman.
LADYHAWKE, Warner Bros. Les Fresholtz, Dick Alexander, Vern Poore and Bud Alper.
*****OUT OF AFRICA,** Universal. Chris Jenkins, Gary Alexander, Larry Stensvold and Peter Handford.
SILVERADO, Columbia. Donald O. Mitchell, Rick Kline, Kevin O'Connell and David Ronne.

FILM EDITING

A CHORUS LINE, Embassy/Polygram, Columbia. John Bloom.
OUT OF AFRICA, Universal. Fredric Steinkamp, William Steinkamp, Pembroke Herring and Sheldon Kahn.
PRIZZI'S HONOR, ABC, 20th Century Fox. Rudi Fehr and Kaja Fehr.
RUNAWAY TRAIN, Cannon. Henry Richardson.
*****WITNESS,** Feldman, Paramount. Thom Noble.

VISUAL EFFECTS

*****COCOON,** Zanuck-Brown, 20th Century Fox. Ken Ralston, Ralph McQuarrie, Scott Farrar and David Berry.
RETURN TO OZ, Disney and Silver Screen Partners II, Buena Vista. Will Vinton, Ian Wingrove, Zoran Perisic and Michael Lloyd.
YOUNG SHERLOCK HOLMES, Amblin/Winkler/Birnbaum, Paramount. Dennis Muren, Kit West, John Ellis and David Allen.

SOUND EFFECTS EDITING

*****BACK TO THE FUTURE,** Amblin, Universal. Charles L. Campbell and Robert Rutledge.
LADYHAWKE, Warner Bros. Bob Henderson and Alan Murray.
RAMBO: FIRST BLOOD PART II, Tri-Star. Frederick J. Brown.

MUSIC

(Song)
MISS CELIE'S BLUES (SISTER) (The Color Purple, Warner Bros.); Music by Quincy Jones and Rod Temperton. Lyrics by Quincy Jones, Rod Temperton and Lionel Richie.
THE POWER OF LOVE (Back to the Future, Amblin, Universal); Music by Chris Hayes and Johnny Colla. Lyrics by Huey Lewis.
*****SAY YOU, SAY ME** (White Nights, Columbia); Music and Lyrics by Lionel Richie.
SEPARATE LIVES (White Nights, Columbia); Music and Lyrics by Stephen Bishop.
SURPRISE, SURPRISE (A Chorus Line, Embassy/Polygram, Columbia); Music by Marvin Hamlisch. Lyrics by Edward Kleban.

(Original Score)
AGNES OF GOD, Columbia, Georges Delerue.
THE COLOR PURPLE, Warner Bros. Quincy Jones, Jeremy Lubbock, Rod Temperton, Caiphus Semenya, Andrae Crouch, Chris Boardman, Jorge Calandrelli, Joel Rosenbaum, Fred Steiner, Jack Hayes, Jerry Hey and Randy Kerber.
*****OUT OF AFRICA,** Universal. John Barry.
SILVERADO, Columbia. Bruce Broughton.
WITNESS, Feldman, Paramount. Maurice Jarre.

MAKEUP

THE COLOR PURPLE, Warner Bros. Ken Chase.
*****MASK,** Universal. Michael Westmore and Zoltan Elek.
REMO WILLIAMS: THE ADVENTURE BEGINS, Clark/Spiegel/Bergman, Orion. Carl Fullerton.

SHORT FILMS

(Animated Films)
*****ANNA & BELLA,** The Netherlands. Cilia Van Dijk, Producer.
THE BIG SNIT, National Film Board of Canada. Richard Condie and Michael Scott, Producers.

Best Supporting Actor: **Don Ameche** *as Art Selwyn in* Cocoon *(20th Century-Fox; produced by Richard Zanuck, David Brown and Lili Fini Zanuck). At 77, Don Ameche had been in movies, and a star, for 49 years, most famous for his 1939 portrayal of Alexander Graham Bell and a popular* leading man to almost every leading lady in town, including Claudette Colbert, Myrna Loy and Carmen Miranda. But he'd never been within call of an Oscar nomination and his screen career seemed perhaps a thing of the past when he was cast in Cocoon, directed by Ron Howard. He played an old *duffer in a Florida retirement home who, with Hume Cronyn, Jack Gilford, Maureen Stapleton, Gwen Verdon (above), Jessica Tandy and others, is rejuvenated with some help from outer space. Ameche's career was rejuvenated, too, and at long last he was an Academy champ.*

SECOND CLASS MAIL, National Film & Television
School. Alison Snowden, Producer.

(Live Action Films)

GRAFFITI, The American Film Institute. Dianna
Costello, Producer.
*MOLLY'S PILGRIM, Phoenix Films. Jeff Brown and
Chris Pelzer, Producers.
RAINBOW WAR, Bob Rogers and Company. Bob
Rogers, Producers.

DOCUMENTARY

(Short Subjects)

THE COURAGE TO CARE, a United Way Production.
Robert Gardner, Producer.
KEATS AND HIS NIGHTINGALE: A Blind Date, a
Production of the Rhode Island Committee for the
Humanities. Michael Crowley and James Wolpaw,
Producers.
MAKING OVERTURES—The Story of a Community
Orchestra, a Rhombus Media, Inc. Production.
Barbara Willis Sweete, Producer.
*WITNESS TO WAR: Dr. Charlie Clements, a Skylight
Picture Production. David Goodman, Producer.
THE WIZARD OF THE STRINGS, a Seventh Hour
Production. Alan Edelstein, Producer.

(Features)

*BROKEN RAINBOW, an Earthworks Films
Production. Maria Florio and Victoria Mudd,
Producers.
LAS MADRES—The Mothers of Plaza de Mayo,
Sponsored by Film Arts Foundation. Susana Munoz
and Lourdes Portillo, Producers.
SOLDIERS IN HIDING, a Filmworks, Inc. Production.
Japhet Asher, Producer.

THE STATUE OF LIBERTY, a Florentine Films
Production. Ken Burns and Buddy Squires,
Producers.
UNFINISHED BUSINESS, a Mouchette Films
Production. Steven Okazaki, Producer.

FOREIGN LANGUAGE FILM

ANGRY HARVEST (Federal Republic of Germany).
COLONEL REDL (Hungary).
*THE OFFICIAL STORY (Argentina).
THREE MEN AND A CRADLE (France).
WHEN FATHER WAS AWAY ON BUSINESS
(Yugoslavia).

HONORARY AND OTHER AWARDS

TO PAUL NEWMAN in recognition of his many and
memorable compelling screen performances and for
his personal integrity and dedication to his craft.
TO ALEX NORTH in recognition of his brilliant
artistry in the creation of memorable music for a
host of distinguished motion pictures.
TO JOHN H. WHITNEY, SR. for Cinematic Pioneering
(Medal of Commendation)

1985 IRVING G. THALBERG MEMORIAL AWARD

None given this year.

1985 JEAN HERSHOLT HUMANITARIAN AWARD

TO CHAS. (BUDDY) ROGERS

1985 GORDON E. SAWYER AWARD

None given this year.

SCIENTIFIC OR TECHNICAL AWARDS

Academy Award of Merit (Oscar)
None.

Scientific and Engineering Award (Academy Plaque)

IMAX SYSTEMS CORPORATION for a method of
filming and exhibiting high-fidelity, large-format,
wide-angle motion pictures.
ERNST NETTMAN of E. F. Nettman & Associates for
the invention, and to EDWARD PHILLIPS and
CARLOS DeMATTOS of Matthews Studio Equipment,
Inc., for the development, of the Cam-Remote for
motion picture photography.
MYRON GORDIN, JOE P. CROOKHAM, JIM DROST
and DAVID CROOKHAM of Musco Mobile Lighting,
Ltd., for the invention of a method of transporting
adjustable, high-intensity Luminaires and their
application to the motion picture industry.

Technical Achievement Award (Academy Certificate)

DAVID W. SPENCER for the development of an
Animation Photo Transfer (APT) process.
HARRISON & HARRISON, OPTICAL ENGINEERS,
for the invention and development of Harrison
Diffusion Filters for motion picture photography.
LARRY BARTON of Cinematography Electronics, Inc.,
for a Precision Speed, Crystal-controlled Device for
motion picture photography.
ALAN LANDAKER of the Burbank Studios for the
Mark III Camera Drive for motion picture
photography.

*INDICATES WINNER

281

Patience paid off for Paul Newman: at age sixty-two, with seven Oscar nominations to his credit during a 28-year, 45-film span, the actor finally won his first competitive Academy Award at the Academy's 59th gathering, March 30, 1987. True, he'd been voted an honorary statue the preceding year but this, at last, was The Big One. Newman, however, wasn't there to accept it in person. He was, in fact, 3000 miles away from the Los Angeles Music Center, watching the ABC-TV telecast at his home in New York. His reason? "I've been there six times and lost," he said. "Maybe if I stay away I'll win." He did, and he did.

So did at least two others, one by necessity, the other by choice. Michael Caine, named best supporting actor for his work in Woody Allen's *Hannah and Her Sisters* was unable to attend the ceremony in Los Angeles; he was in the Bahamas, delayed there because of filming complications on *Jaws: The Revenge.* Woody Allen, a winner for his *Hannah* screenplay and a consistent no-show at award functions, stayed true to form and remained in New York, playing clarinet at Michael's Pub while his name was announced at the Dorothy Chandler Pavilion.

But Dianne Wiest was on hand to accept her supporting actress award for *Hannah;* so was Marlee Matlin, the first deaf actress to be nominated for an Academy Award. She was named the year's best actress for *Children of a Lesser God.*

Over all, it still turned out to be Oliver Stone's night. Personally nominated for three Oscars (as director and screenwriter of *Platoon,* and competing against himself as co-screenwriter of *Salvador*), Stone won the best director prize and his *Platoon* marched on to become the year's most honored film, with four awards including the best picture of the year trophy. Accepting the latter, Stone said "I think through this award you're really acknowledging that for the first time you really understand what happened over there (in Vietnam). And I think what you're saying is that it should never in our lifetime happen again."

The Assault was named best foreign language film and became the first from the Netherlands honored in that Oscar category. Veteran actor Ralph Bellamy, eighty-three, received an honorary Oscar and Steven Spielberg was voted the Irving G. Thalberg Memorial Award. At thirty-nine, Spielberg was the youngest recipient of the Academy's highest award since Jerry Wald had won it in 1949, at the age of thirty-seven.

One thing was becoming a common denominator: Oscar was still one of the longer shows in town, this one coming in at three hours and 20 minutes. The hosts were Chevy Chase, Goldie Hawn and Paul Hogan, the latter also a nominee in the original screenplay division for his Australian-made *"Crocodile" Dundee.* Bernadette Peters was featured in a 16-minute production number and the entire show was produced, for the

Best Picture: **Platoon** *(Orion; produced by Arnold Kopelson) and* **Best Director:** **Oliver Stone** *for* Platoon. *Oliver Stone, himself a Vietnam veteran, delivered a wrenching, rarely screened vision of war in* Platoon, *using his own first-hand visions of men in war to create a striking drama. He also introduced wide audiences to a platoon of new actors, including Tom Berenger and Willem Dafoe, both of whom were nominated as supporting actors, and Charlie Sheen as a fresh-faced new soldier thrown headlong into a nightmare of bullets, brutality, death, dope and a fraternity he never chose. Filmed with the Philippines subbing for Vietnam,* Platoon *won four awards, including Stone's director prize and that best-of-the-crop picture award.*

first time, by Samuel Goldwyn, Jr. Presenters included a combination of new stars (William Hurt, Matthew Broderick, Molly Ringwald, Oprah Winfrey, Tom Hanks), movie legends (Elizabeth Taylor, Jennifer Jones, Anthony Quinn, Bugs Bunny) and at least two Bettes— Midler and Davis, the latter caught in a confusion of mis-cues and crossed signals when attempting to present the year's best actor prize. The incident was heavily discussed for days after and proved that Oscar, at age fifty-nine, and Bette Davis, five days before her 79th birthday, could still make waves and cause talk, intentionally or not.

Best Actor: **Paul Newman** *as Fast Eddie Felson in* The Color of Money *(Touchstone/Buena Vista; produced by Irving Axelrad and Barbara De Fina). Newman had first played Fast Eddie Felson, a pool hustler, 25 years earlier in 1961's* The Hustler *and received an Academy Award nomination for it. In this belated sequel-of-sorts, directed by Martin* Scorsese, Newman's Eddie was still fast, still able to sink a nine ball but now older, wiser and the teacher of a younger sport (Tom Cruise) who gets tips from the old pro on his way to big-time pool games. Newman won the Oscar after six earlier nominations; he'd also received an honorary Oscar the preceding year for his body of work.

Best Actress: **Marlee Matlin** *as Sarah Norman in* Children of a Lesser God *(Paramount; produced by Burt Sugarman and Patrick Palmer). Randa Haines became the first woman in Academy history to direct a performer to a "leading role" Oscar, in this story of a young deaf woman who resists making the adjustments she feels the hearing world demands as its price for acceptance. Matlin received her award from her co-star William Hurt (above), the presenter by virtue of his best actor win the previous year.*

The Mission *(Warner Bros.; produced by Fernando Ghia and David Puttnam) starred Robert DeNiro (above) and Jeremy Irons and won an Oscar for its striking cinematography by Chris Menges. It was also nominated for six other awards, including best picture and best director (Rolland Joffe).*

PICTURE

CHILDREN OF A LESSER GOD, Sugarman, Paramount. Produced by Burt Sugarman and Patrick Palmer.
HANNAH AND HER SISTERS, Rollins and Joffee, Orion. Produced by Robert Greenhut.
THE MISSION, Warner Bros. Produced by Fernando Ghia and David Puttnam.
*****PLATOON,** Hemdale, Orion. Produced by Arnold Kopelson.
A ROOM WITH A VIEW, Merchant Ivory, Cinecom. Produced by Ismail Merchant.

ACTOR

DEXTER GORDON in *'Round Midnight,* Winkler, Warner Bros.
BOB HOSKINS in *Mona Lisa,* Island.
WILLIAM HURT in *Children of a Lesser God,* Sugarman, Paramount.
*****PAUL NEWMAN** in *The Color of Money,* Touchstone with Silver Screen Partners II, Buena Vista.
JAMES WOODS in *Salvador,* Hemdale.

ACTRESS

JANE FONDA in *The Morning After,* Lorimar, 20th Century Fox.
*****MARLEE MATLIN** in *Children of a Lesser God,* Sugarman, Paramount.
SISSY SPACEK in *Crimes of the Heart,* De Laurentiis Entertainment Group.
KATHLEEN TURNER in *Peggy Sue Got Married,* Rastar, Tri-Star.
SIGOURNEY WEAVER in *Aliens,* 20th Century Fox.

SUPPORTING ACTOR

TOM BERENGER in *Platoon,* Hemdale, Orion.
*****MICHAEL CAINE** in *Hannah and Her Sisters,* Rollins and Joffe, Orion.
WILLEM DAFOE in *Platoon,* Hemdale, Orion.
DENHOLM ELLIOTT in *A Room with a View,* Merchant Ivory, Cinecom.
DENNIS HOPPER in *Hoosiers,* de Haven, Orion.

SUPPORTING ACTRESS

TESS HARPER in *Crimes of the Heart,* De Laurentiis Entertainment Group.
PIPER LAURIE in *Children of a Lesser God,* Sugarman, Paramount.
MARY ELIZABETH MASTRANTONIO in *The Color of Money,* Touchstone with Silver Screen Partners II, Buena Vista.
MAGGIE SMITH in *A Room with a View,* Merchant Ivory, Cinecom.
*****DIANNE WIEST** in *Hannah and Her Sisters,* Rollins and Joffe, Orion.

DIRECTING

BLUE VELVET, De Laurentiis Entertainment Group. David Lynch.
HANNAH AND HER SISTERS, Rollins and Joffe, Orion. Woody Allen.
THE MISSION, Warner Bros. Roland Joffe.
*****PLATOON,** Hemdale, Orion. Oliver Stone.
A ROOM WITH A VIEW, Merchant Ivory, Cinecom. James Ivory.

WRITING

(Screenplay Written Directly for the Screen)
"CROCODILE" DUNDEE, Rimfire, Paramount. Paul Hogan, Ken Shadie and John Cornell.
*****HANNAH AND HER SISTERS,** Rollins and Joffe, Orion. Woody Allen.
MY BEAUTIFUL LAUNDRETTE, Orion Classics. Hanif Kureishi
PLATOON, Hemdale, Orion. Oliver Stone.
SALVADOR, Hemdale. Oliver Stone and Richard Boyle.

(Screenplay Based on Material from Another Medium)
CHILDREN OF A LESSER GOD, Sugarman, Paramount. Hesper Anderson and Mark Medoff.
THE COLOR OF MONEY, Touchstone with Silver Screen Partners II, Buena Vista. Richard Price.
CRIMES OF THE HEART, De Laurentiis Entertainment Group. Beth Henley.
*****A ROOM WITH A VIEW,** Merchant Ivory, Cinecom. Ruth Prawer Jhabvala.
STAND BY ME, Act III, Columbia. Raynold Gideon and Bruce A. Evans.

CINEMATOGRAPHY

*****THE MISSION,** Warner Bros. Chris Menges.
PEGGY SUE GOT MARRIED, Rastar, Tri-Star. Jordan Cronenweth.
PLATOON, Hemdale, Orion. Robert Richardson.
A ROOM WITH A VIEW, Merchant Ivory, Cinecom. Tony Pierce-Roberts.
STAR TREK IV: THE VOYAGE HOME, Bennett, Paramount. Don Peterman.

ART DIRECTION-
SET DECORATION

ALIENS, 20th Century Fox. Peter Lamont; Crispian Sallis.
THE COLOR OF MONEY, Touchstone with Silver Screen Partners II, Buena Vista. Boris Leven; Karen A. O'Hara.
HANNAH AND HER SISTERS, Rollins and Joffe, Orion. Stuart Wurtzel; Carol Joffe.
THE MISSION, Warner Bros. Stuart Craig; Jack Stephens.
*****A ROOM WITH A VIEW,** Merchant Ivory, Cinecom. Gianni Quaranta and Brian Ackland-Snow; Brian Savegar and Elio Altramura.

COSTUME DESIGN

THE MISSION, Warner Bros. Enrico Sabbatini.
OTELLO, Cannon. Anna Anni and Maurizio Millenotti.
PEGGY SUE GOT MARRIED, Rastar, Tri-Star. Theadora Van Runkle.
PIRATES, Cannon. Anthony Powell.
*****A ROOM WITH A VIEW,** Merchant Ivory, Cinecom. Jenny Beavan and John Bright.

SOUND

ALIENS, 20th Century Fox. Graham V. Hartstone, Nicolas Le Messurier, Michael A. Carter and Roy Charman.
HEARTBREAK RIDGE, Warner Bros. Les Fresholtz, Dick Alexander, Vern Poore and William Nelson.
*****PLATOON,** Hemdale, Orion. John K. Wilkinson, Richard Rogers, Charles "Bud" Grenzbach and Simon Kaye.
STAR TREK IV: THE VOYAGE HOME, Bennett, Paramount. Terry Porter, Dave Hudson, Mel Metcalfe and Gene S. Cantamessa.
TOP GUN, Simpson/Bruckheimer, Paramount. Donald O. Mitchell, Kevin O'Connell, Rick Kline and William B. Kaplan.

FILM EDITING

ALIENS, 20th Century Fox. Ray Lovejoy.
HANNAH AND HER SISTERS, Rollins and Joffe, Orion. Susan E. Morse.
THE MISSION, Warner Bros. Jim Clark.
*****PLATOON,** Hemdale, Orion. Claire Simpson.
TOP GUN, Simpson/Bruckheimer, Paramount. Billy Weber and Chris Lebenzon.

SOUND EFFECTS EDITING

*****ALIENS,** 20th Century Fox. Don Sharpe.
STAR TREK IV: THE VOYAGE HOME, Benett, Paramount. Mark Mangini.
TOP GUN, Simpson/Bruckheimer, Paramount. Cecelia Hall and George Watters II.

VISUAL EFFECTS

*****ALIENS,** 20th Century Fox. Robert Skotak, Stan Winston, John Richardson and Suzanne Benson.
LITTLE SHOP OF HORRORS, Geffen, through Warner Bros. Lyle Conway, Bran Ferren and Martin Gutteridge.
POLTERGEIST II: THE OTHER SIDE, Victor-Grais, M-G-M. Richard Edlund, John Bruno, Garry Waller and William Neil.

Best Supporting Actress: **Dianne Wiest** *as Holly (above) and* **Best Supporting Actor:** **Michael Caine** *as Elliot (below, with Mia Farrow) in* Hannah and Her Sisters *(Orion; produced by Robert Greenhut). In a world according to Woody Allen, Hannah (Farrow) has two sisters: Lee (Barbara Hershey) and Holly (Wiest). Hannah's also got a family loaded with problems, not the least of which is Holly's being a flaky neurotic, jumping between careers, men and shrinks until she re-meets Hannah's ex-husband (Woody Allen), with whom she unexpectedly finds the relationship she's always wanted. Caine played Hannah's current husband, himself involved in an affair with sister-in-law Lee. It was one of Allen's best movies, given special sparks by the performances of Wiest and Caine, both of whom were awarded for their work. It was a first Oscar for each.*

A Room with a View *(Merchant Ivory; produced by Ismail Merchant), a small, brilliantly worked jewel of a picture, was directed by James Ivory and nominated in eight categories. The British production took home prizes for art direction,* *costume design and for Ruth Prawer Jhabvala's script from the E.M. Forster novel. Helena Bonham Carter and Daniel Day-Lewis (above) highlighted an ensemble cast that also included Denholm Elliot, Julian Sands and Maggie Smith.*

MUSIC

(Song)

GLORY OF LOVE (*The Karate Kid Part II*, Columbia); Music by Peter Cetera and David Foster. Lyrics by Peter Cetera and Diane Nini.
LIFE IN A LOOKING GLASS (*That's Life*, Columbia); Music by Henry Mancini. Lyrics by Leslie Bricusse.
MEAN GREEN MOTHER FROM OUTER SPACE (*Little Shop of Horrors*, The Geffen Company through Warner Bros.); Music by Alan Menken. Lyrics by Howard Ashman.
SOMEWHERE OUT THERE (*An American Tail*, Amblin, Universal); Music by James Horner and Barry Mann. Lyrics by Cynthia Weil.
*****TAKE MY BREATH AWAY** (*Top Gun*, Simpson/Bruckheimer, Paramount); Music by Giorgio Moroder. Lyrics by Tom Whitlock.

(Original Score)

ALIENS, 20th Century Fox. James Horner.
HOOSIERS, De Haven, Orion. Jerry Goldsmith.
THE MISSION, Warner Bros. Ennio Morricone.
*****'ROUND MIDNIGHT**, Winkler, Warner Bros. Herbie Hancock.
STAR TREK IV: THE VOYAGE HOME, Bennett, Paramount. Leonard Rosenman.

MAKEUP

THE CLAN OF THE CAVE BEAR, Warner Bros. Michael G. Westmore and Michele Burke.
*****THE FLY**, Brooksfilms, 20th Century Fox. Chris Walas and Stephan Dupuis.
LEGEND, Universal. Rob Bottin and Peter Robb-King.

SHORT FILMS

(Animated Films)

THE FROG, THE DOG AND THE DEVIL, New Zealand National Film Unit. Bob Stenhouse, producer.
*****A GREEK TRAGEDY**, CineTe pvba. Linda Van Tulden and Willem Thijssen, producers.
LUXO JR., Pixar Productions. John Lasseter and William Reeves, producers.

(Live Action)

EXIT, Rai Radiotelevisione Italiana/RAI-UNO. Stefano Reali and Pino Quartullo, producers.

LOVE STRUCK, Rainy Day Productions. Fredda Weiss, producer.
*****PRECIOUS IMAGES**, Calliope Films, Inc. Chuck Workman, producer.

DOCUMENTARY

(Short Subjects)

DEBONAIR DANCERS, an Alison Nigh-Strelich Production. Alison Nigh-Strelich, producer.
THE MASTERS OF DISASTER, Indiana University Audio Visual Center. Sonya Friedman, producer.
RED GROOMS; SUNFLOWER IN A HOTHOUSE, a Polaris Entertainment Production. Thomas L. Neff and Madeline Bell, producers.
SAM, a Film by Aaron D. Weisblatt. Aaron D. Weisblatt, producer.
*****WOMEN—FOR AMERICA, FOR THE WORLD**, Educational Film & Video Project. Vivienne Verdon-Roe, producer.

(Features)

*****ARTIE SHAW: TIME IS ALL YOU'VE GOT**, a Bridge Film Production. Brigitte Berman, producer.
CHILE: HASTA CUANDO?, a David Bradbury Production. David Bradbury, producer.
*****DOWN AND OUT IN AMERICA**, a Joseph Feury Production. Joseph Feury and Milton Justice, producers.
ISAAC IN AMERICA: A Journey with Isaac Bashevis Singer, Amram Nowak Associates. Kirk Simon and Amram Nowak, producers.
WITNESS TO APARTHEID, a Production of Developing News Inc. Sharon I. Sopher, producer.

FOREIGN LANGUAGE FILM

*****THE ASSAULT** (The Netherlands).
BETTY BLUE (France).
THE DECLINE OF THE AMERICAN EMPIRE (Canada).
MY SWEET LITTLE VILLAGE (Czechoslovakia).
"38" (Austria).

HONORARY AND OTHER AWARDS

TO RALPH BELLAMY, for his unique artistry and his distinguished service to the profession of acting.

TO E.M. (AL) LEWIS, in appreciation for outstanding service and dedication in upholding the high standards of the Academy of Motion Picture Arts and Sciences.

1986 IRVING G. THALBERG MEMORIAL AWARD
TO STEVEN SPIELBERG

1986 JEAN HERSHOLT HUMANITARIAN AWARD
None given this year.

1986 GORDON E. SAWYER AWARD
None given this year.

SCIENTIFIC OR TECHNICAL AWARDS

Academy Award of Merit (Oscar)
None.

Scientific and Engineering Award (Academy Plaque)

BRAN FERREN, CHARLES HARRISON and **KENNETH WISNER** of Associates and Ferren for the concept and design of an advanced optical printer.
RICHARD BENJAMIN GRANT and **RON GRANT** of Auricle Control Systems for their invention of the Film Composer's Time Processor.
ANTHONY D. BRUNO and **JOHN L. BAPTISTA** of Metro-Goldwyn-Mayer Laboratories, Incorporated, and to **MANFRED G. MICHELSON** and **BRUCE W. KELLER** of Technical Film Systems, Incorporated, for the design and engineering of a Continuous-Feed Printer.
ROBERT GREENBERG, JOEL HYNEK and **EUGENE MAMUT** of R/Greenberg Associates, Incorporated, and to **DR. ALFRED THUMIM, ELAN LIPSHITZ** and **DARRYL A. ARMOUR** of the Oxberry Division of Richmark Camera Service, Incorporated, for the design and development of the RGA/Oxberry Compu-Quad Special Effects Optical Printer.
PROFESSOR FRITZ SENNHEISER of Sennheiser Electronic Corporation for the invention of an interference tube directional microphone.
RICHARD EDLUND, GENE WHITEMAN, DAVID GRAFTON, MARK WEST, JERRY JEFFRESS and **BOB WILCOX** of Boss Film Corporation for the design and development of a Zoom Aerial (ZAP) 65mm Optical Printer.
WILLIAM L. FREDRICK and **HAL NEEDHAM** for the design and development of the Shotmaker Elite camera car and crane.

Technical Achievement Award (Academy Certificate)

LEE ELECTRIC (LIGHTING) LIMITED for the design and development of an electronic, flicker-free, discharge lamp control system.
PETER D. PARKS of Oxford Scientific Films' Image Quest Division for the development of a live aero-compositor for special effects photography.
MATT SWEENEY and **LUCINDA STRUB** for the development of an automatic capsule gun for simulating bullet hits for motion picture special effects.
CARL HOLMES of Carl E. Holmes Company and to **ALEXANDER BRYCE** of The Burbank Studios for the development of a mobile DC power supply unit for motion picture production photography.
BRAN FERREN of Associates and Ferren for the development of a laser synchro-cue system for applications in the motion picture industry.
JOHN L. BAPTISTA of Metro-Goldwyn-Mayer Laboratories, Inc. for the development and installation of a computerized silver recovery operation.
DAVID W. SAMUELSON for the development of programs incorporated into a pocket computer for motion picture cinematographers, and to **WILLIAM B. POLLARD** for contributing new algorithms on which the programs are based.
HAL LANDAKER and **ALAN LANDAKER** of The Burbank Studios for the development of the Beat System low-frequency cue track for motion picture production sound recording.

*****INDICATES WINNER**

285

Some things, obviously, never change. The Academy Award had been born in the midst of industry strife and unrest, and on the night of Oscar's 60th birthday party April 11, 1988, there was again dissension within the motion picture arena, this time due to a heated writers' strike. Still there was a wide chasm between most aspects of the awards given for that first year 1927-28 and the 60th, for 1987. Categories now numbered 23 instead of 13, Oscar was now a world-wide symbol of film excellence and considerably more than 270 people watched the golden boys being handed out to winners.

Actually, the 60th award ceremony unintentionally turned out to be as much of a celebration for Bernardo Bertolucci's epic *The Last Emperor* as it did for Oscar. Nominated for nine awards, *Emperor* waltzed to the stage to collect all of them, nine for nine, one of the rare times any film had ended up with every prize for which it was nominated. Among the nods, *Emperor* was named best picture of the year, and Bertolucci best director. And by virtue of those nine Oscars, the film became the fourth most honored film in the Academy's 60-year history, after *Ben-Hur* (1959) with eleven awards, *West Side Story* (1961) with ten and *Gigi* (1958) also with nine.

Michael Douglas, already with an Oscar to his credit as co-producer of the 1975 Oscar winner *One Flew Over the Cuckoo's Nest,* was named best actor for *Wall Street;* in his acceptance remarks

he added thanks to "my father...for helping a son step out of a shadow." Cher was honored as best actress for *Moonstruck;* Olympia Dukakis was best supporting actress for the same film and shouted "Okay, Michael, let's go!," referring to her cousin Michael Dukakis, then in the throes of campaigning to be the Democratic choice for President in the 1988 election. Most popular winner of the night, hands down, was Sean Connery, named best supporting actor for *The Untouchables.* Biggest surprise was the announcement of Denmark's *Babette's Feast* as best foreign language film; pre-show predictions had indicated a shoo-in for Louis Malle's much-liked *Au Revoir les Infants* from France.

Most of the immediate talk, pre-show and post-show, however, had less to do with the evening's champs and oversights than with a horrendous traffic jam that snarled the streets, freeways and by-ways at show time near the Los Angeles Shrine Auditorium, where the Oscar ceremony was being held for the first time in 40 years. Many of the nominees, presenters and guests had to abandon their limos, grab their dates and semi-jog in their tuxedoes and gowns down neighborhood streets in an attempt to make the show's opening. No one was immune, including presenter Olivia de Havilland, who'd flown in from Paris to present an award early in the evening's program, and Glenn Close, a nominee and quite pregnant. The jam was so intense, the show's producer Samuel Goldwyn, Jr. and director Marty

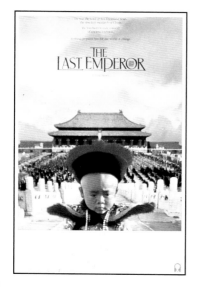

Best Picture: **The Last Emperor** *(Hemdale/Columbia; produced by Jeremy Thomas) and* **Best Director:** **Bernardo Bertolucci** *for* The Last Emperor. *Filmed on location in China, it was the first western production to be made about modern China with the full cooperation of that nation's government; it was also an epic in the truest sense of the word, a visual feast with a giant cast and 19,000 extras. Taking only a few dramatic liberties, it followed the saga of Pu Yi, who was made Emperor of China at the age of three but who ended up a gardener at the time of his death in 1967. It was Bertolucci's first film in six years and the cast (none of whom was nominated for an Oscar) included Peter O'Toole. It won nine Oscars, including the big one.*

Pasetta had to make a last-minute scratch of an elaborate segment involving players from each of the 59 preceding best picture winners since 1927-28. The traffic problems made the execution of the segment impossible.

If the traffic was a headache, though, the news from the TV ratings more than helped erase them. After a downward trend that had become a worry, ratings were up for the second consecutive year. It seemed a positive way to close the book on the Academy's first 60 years, too, although anyone who'd been through Oscar wars and Oscar history knew there'd undoubtedly be see-saw times ahead. And new "firsts" to put in future record books. Even the latest awards were no exception to that challenge. For proof: the 60th Oscars marked the first time an Academy Award nominee was actively being sought by police. On the night of the awards, many of L.A.'s finest were on the hunt for Gustav Hasford, a nominee in the screenplay division, wanted in connection with grand theft charges involving a large collection of library books. Hasford did not win and, as far as anyone knew, did not attend the ceremony. But he had inadvertently added yet another salty footnote to a checkered but firm history, and a tradition that seems to grow more golden each decade.

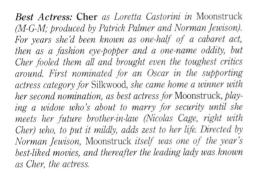

Best Actress: **Cher** *as Loretta Castorini in* Moonstruck *(M-G-M; produced by Patrick Palmer and Norman Jewison). For years she'd been known as one-half of a cabaret act, then as a fashion eye-popper and a one-name oddity, but Cher fooled them all and brought even the toughest critics around. First nominated for an Oscar in the supporting actress category for* Silkwood, *she came home a winner with her second nomination, as best actress for* Moonstruck, *playing a widow who's about to marry for security until she meets her future brother-in-law (Nicolas Cage, right with Cher) who, to put it mildly, adds zest to her life. Directed by Norman Jewison,* Moonstruck *itself was one of the year's best-liked movies, and thereafter the leading lady was known as Cher, the actress.*

Best Actor: **Michael Douglas** *as Gordon Gekko in* Wall Street *(20th Century-Fox; produced by Edward R. Pressman). Michael Douglas, in the Academy Award race for the first time as an actor, won his Oscar playing a chilly Wall Street wheeler-dealer, a man both calculating and dangerous, whether manipulating a merger or cynically educating a young broker (Charlie Sheen). Oliver Stone directed from his own screenplay, penned with Stanley Weiser, and made New York's financial district seem as treacherous as the battlefronts he presented in* Platoon. *Douglas was dynamic in his role, the second juicy one he had in 1987 which began for him with* Fatal Attraction.

Best Supporting Actress: Olympia Dukakis *as Rose Castorini in* Moonstruck *(M-G-M; directed by Norman Jewison). As the mother of Cher and the wife of Vincent Gardenia, Olympia Dukakis created one of the year's favorite performances as a warm, supportive mama of a noisy Italian clan who is, no contest, the centerpiece of the family. Pre-*Moonstruck, *Dukakis was primarily a stage actress but the popular movie made her close to a household word, just as her cousin Michael was becoming the same via the political route.*

PICTURE

BROADCAST NEWS, 20th Century Fox. Produced by James L. Brooks.

FATAL ATTRACTION, Jaffe/Lansing, Paramount. Produced by Stanley R. Jaffe and Sherry Lansing.

HOPE AND GLORY, Davros, Columbia. Produced by John Boorman.

*THE LAST EMPEROR, Hemdale, Columbia. Produced by Jeremy Thomas.

MOONSTRUCK, M-G-M. Produced by Patrick Palmer and Norman Jewison.

ACTOR

WILLIAM HURT in *Broadcast News,* 20th Century Fox.

*MICHAEL DOUGLAS in *Wall Street,* Oaxatal, 20th Century Fox.

ROBIN WILLIAMS in *Good Morning, Vietnam,* Touchstone with Silver Screen Partners III, Buena Vista.

MARCELLO MASTROIANNI in *Dark Eyes,* Excelsior, Island Pictures.

JACK NICHOLSON in *Ironweed,* Taft/Barish, Tri-Star.

ACTRESS

*CHER in *Moonstruck,* Palmer/Jewison, M-G-M.

MERYL STREEP in *Ironweed,* Taft/Barish, Tri-Star.

SALLY KIRKLAND in *Anna,* Magnus, Vestron.

GLENN CLOSE in *Fatal Attraction,* Jaffe/Lansing, Paramount.

HOLLY HUNTER in *Broadcast News,* 20th Century Fox.

SUPPORTING ACTOR

ALBERT BROOKS in *Broadcast News,* 20th Century Fox.

MORGAN FREEMAN in *Street Smart,* Cannon.

*SEAN CONNERY in *The Untouchables,* Linson, Paramount.

DENZEL WASHINGTON in *Cry Freedom,* Marble Arch, Universal.

VINCENT GARDENIA in *Moonstruck,* Palmer/Jewison, M-G-M.

SUPPORTING ACTRESS

NORMA ALEANDRO in *Gaby—A True Story,* Brimmer, Tri-Star.

ANN SOTHERN in *The Whales of August,* Alive Films.

*OLYMPIA DUKAKIS in *Moonstruck,* Palmer/Jewison, M-G-M.

ANNE ARCHER in *Fatal Attraction,* Jaffe/Lansing, Paramount.

ANNE RAMSEY in *Throw Momma from the Train,* Rollins, Morra, & Brezner, Orion.

DIRECTING

FATAL ATTRACTION, Jaffe/Lansing, Paramount. Adrian Lyne.

HOPE AND GLORY, Davros, Columbia. John Boorman.

*THE LAST EMPEROR, Hemdale, Columbia. Bernardo Bertolucci.

MOONSTRUCK, Palmer/Jewison, M-G-M. Norman Jewison.

MY LIFE AS A DOG, Svensk Filmindustri/Filmteknik, Skouras Pictures. Lasse Hallstrom.

WRITING

(Screenplay Written Directly for the Screen)

AU REVOIR LES ENFANTS (GOODBYE, CHILDREN), NEF, Orion Classics. Louis Malle.

BROADCAST NEWS, 20th Century Fox. James L. Brooks.

HOPE AND GLORY, Davros, Columbia. John Boorman.

*MOONSTRUCK, Palmer/Jewison, M-G-M. John Patrick Shanley.

RADIO DAYS, Rollins and Joffe, Orion. Woody Allen.

(Screenplay Based on Material from Another Medium)

THE DEAD, Liffey, Vestron. Tony Huston.

FATAL ATTRACTION, Jaffe/Lansing, Paramount. James Dearden.

FULL METAL JACKET, Nataunt, Warner Bros. Stanley Kubrick, Michael Herr and Gustav Hasford.

*THE LAST EMPEROR, Hemdale, Columbia. Mark Peploe and Bernardo Bertolucci.

MY LIFE AS A DOG, Svensk Filmindustri/Filmteknik, Skouras Pictures. Lasse Hallstrom, Reidar Jonsson, Brasse Brannstrom and Per Berglund.

CINEMATOGRAPHY

BROADCAST NEWS, 20th Century Fox. Michael Ballhaus.

*THE LAST EMPEROR, Hemdale, Columbia. Vittorio Storaro.

HOPE AND GLORY, Davros, Columbia. Philippe Rousselot.

MATEWAN, Red Dog, Cinecom. Haskell Wexler.

EMPIRE OF THE SUN, Warner Bros. Allen Daviau.

ART DIRECTION- SET DECORATION

*THE LAST EMPEROR, Hemdale, Columbia. Ferdinando Scarfiotti; Bruno Cesari and Osvaldo Desideri.

RADIO DAYS, Rollins and Joffe, Orion. Santo Loquasto; Carol Joffe, Les Bloom and George DeTitta, Jr.

HOPE AND GLORY, Davros, Columbia. Anthony Pratt; Joan Woolard.

THE UNTOUCHABLES, Linson, Paramount. Patrizia Von Brandenstein and William A. Elliott; Hal Gausman.

EMPIRE OF THE SUN, Warner Bros. Norman Reynolds; Harry Cordwell.

COSTUME DESIGN

MAURICE, Merchant Ivory, Cinecom. Jenny Beavan and John Bright.

EMPIRE OF THE SUN, Warner Bros. Bob Ringwood.

THE UNTOUCHABLES, Linson, Paramount. Marilyn Vance-Straker.

THE DEAD, Liffey, Vestron. Dorothy Jeakins.

*THE LAST EMPEROR, Hemdale, Columbia. James Acheson.

SOUND

EMPIRE OF THE SUN, Warner Bros. Robert Knudson, Don Digirolamo, John Boyd and Tony Dawe.

*THE LAST EMPEROR, Hemdale, Columbia. Bill Rowe and Ivan Sharrock.

LETHAL WEAPON, Warner Bros. Les Fresholtz, Dick Alexander, Vern Poore and Bill Nelson.

ROBOCOP, Tobor, Orion. Michael J. Kohut, Carlos de Larios, Aaron Rochin and Robert Wald.

THE WITCHES OF EASTWICK, Warner Bros. Wayne Artman, Tom Beckert, Tom Dahl and Art Rochester.

Best Supporting Actor: Sean Connery *as Jim Malone in* The Untouchables *(Paramount; produced by Art Linson),* The Untouchables *had started as a black-and-white TV series starring Robert Stack as law enforcer Elliot Ness; Brian DePalma's colorful and big-scale reworking centered on Ness (Kevin Costner) attempting to bring down mobster kingpin Al Capone (Robert De Niro) during Chicago's Prohibition era. One of Ness's helpers is a likable, tough street cop played by Sean Connery who takes the younger lawman under his wing. Connery (left, holding Costner) walked off with the show and also, at long last, he walked off with an Oscar. He had never been a winner or even a nominee before.*

Best Foreign Language Film: Babette's Feast from Denmark. Adapted from an Isak Dinesen short story, Babette's Feast was the delightful tale of two Danish sisters, carrying on the stern Lutheran traditions of their late father, and their loyal housekeeper Babette who prepares "a real

French meal" of staggering sumptuousness for the sisters and a group of their ascetic fellow-parishioners. Winning the foreign language film award, Feast became the first film from Denmark to do so.

FILM EDITING

*THE LAST EMPEROR, Hemdale, Columbia. Gabriella Cristiani.
FATAL ATTRACTION, Jaffe/Lansing, Paramount. Michael Kahn and Peter E. Berger.
ROBOCOP, Tobor, Orion. Frank J. Urioste.
EMPIRE OF THE SUN, Warner Bros. Michael Kahn.
BROADCAST NEWS, 20th Century Fox. Richard Marks.

VISUAL EFFECTS

PREDATOR, 20th Century Fox. Joel Hynek, Robert M. Greenberg, Richard Greenberg and Stan Winston.
*INNERSPACE, Warner Bros. Dennis Muren, William George, Harley Jessup and Kenneth Smith.

MUSIC

(Song)

CRY FREEDOM, (Cry Freedom, Marble Arch, Universal); Music and Lyrics by George Fenton and Jonas Gwangwa.
*(I'VE HAD) THE TIME OF MY LIFE (Dirty Dancing, Vestron); Music by Franke Previte, John DeNicola and Donald Markowitz. Lyrics by Franke Previte.
NOTHING'S GONNA STOP US NOW (Mannequin, Gladden, 20th Century Fox); Music and Lyrics by Albert Hammond and Diane Warren.
SHAKEDOWN (Beverly Hills Cop II, Simpson/Bruckheimer, Paramount); Music by Harold Faltermeyer and Keith Forsey. Lyrics by Harold Faltermeyer, Keith Forsey and Bob Seger.
STORYBOOK LOVE (The Princess Bride, Act III, 20th Century Fox); Music and Lyrics by Willy DeVille.

(Original Score)

CRY FREEDOM, Marble Arch, Universal. George Fenton and Jonas Gwangwa.
EMPIRE OF THE SUN, Warner Bros. John Williams.
*THE LAST EMPEROR, Hemdale, Columbia. Ryuichi Sakamoto, David Byrne and Cong Su.
THE WITCHES OF EASTWICK, Warner Bros. John Williams.
THE UNTOUCHABLES, Linson, Paramount. Ennio Morricone.

MAKEUP

*HARRY AND THE HENDERSONS, Amblin, Universal. Rick Baker.
HAPPY NEW YEAR, Columbia. Bob Laden.

SHORT FILMS

(Animated Films)

GEORGE AND ROSEMARY, National Film Board of Canada. Eunice Macaulay, producer.
*THE MAN WHO PLANTED TREES, Societe Radio-Canada/Canadian Broadcasting Corporation. Frederic Back, producer.
YOUR FACE, Bill Plympton Productions. Bill Plympton, producer.

(Live Action)

MAKING WAVES, The Production Pool Ltd. Ann Wingate, producer.
*RAY'S MALE HETEROSEXUAL DANCE HALL, Chanticleer Films. Jonathan Sanger and Jana Sue Memel, producers.
SHOESHINE, Tom Abrams Productions. Robert A. Katz, producer.

DOCUMENTARY

(Short Subjects)

FRANCES STELOFF: MEMOIRS OF A BOOKSELLER, a Winterlude Films, Inc. Production. Deborah Dickson, producer.
IN THE WEE WEE HOURS. . . , School of Cinema/TV, University of Southern California. Dr. Frank Daniel and Izak Ben-Meir, producers.
LANGUAGE SAYS IT ALL, a Tripod Production. Megan Williams, producer.
SILVER INTO GOLD, Department of Communications, Stanford University. Lynn Mueller, producer.
*YOUNG AT HEART, a Sue Marx Films, Inc. Production. Sue Marx and Pamela Conn, producers.

(Features)

EYES ON THE PRIZE: AMERICA'S CIVIL RIGHTS YEARS/Bridge to Freedom 1965, a Blackside, Inc. Production. Callie Crossley and James A. DeVinney, producers.

HELLFIRE: A JOURNEY FROM HIROSHIMA, John Junkerman and John W. Dower, producers.
RADIO BIKINI, a Production of Crossroads Film Project, Ltd. Robert Stone, producer.)
A STITCH FOR TIME, a Production of Peace Quilters Production Company, Inc. Barbara Herbich and Cyril Christo, producers.
*THE TEN-YEAR LUNCH: THE WIT AND LEGEND OF THE ALGONQUIN ROUND TABLE, an Aviva Films Production. Aviva Slesin, producer.

FOREIGN LANGUAGE FILMS

AU REVOIR LES ENFANTS (GOODBYE, CHILDREN) (France).
*BABETTE'S FEAST (Denmark).
COURSE COMPLETED (Spain).
THE FAMILY (Italy).
PATHFINDER (Norway).

SPECIAL ACHIEVEMENT AWARDS

For Sound Effects Editing: **STEPHEN FLICK** and **JOHN POSPISIL** for "Robocop."

1987 IRVING G. THALBERG MEMORIAL AWARD

TO BILLY WILDER

1987 JEAN HERSHOLT HUMANITARIAN AWARD

None given this year.

1987 GORDON E. SAWYER AWARD

TO FRED HYNES

SCIENTIFIC OR TECHNICAL AWARDS

Academy Award of Merit (Statuette)

BERNARD KUHL and **WERNER BLOCK** and to the **OSRAM GmbH RESEARCH AND DEVELOPMENT DEPARTMENT** for the invention and the continuing improvement of the OSRAM HM1 light source for motion picture photography.

Scientific and Engineering Award (Academy Plaque)

WILLI BURTH and **KINOTONE CORPORATION** for the invention and development of the Non-rewind Platter System for motion picture exhibition.
MONTAGE GROUP, LTD. for the development, and to **RONALD C. BARKER** and **CHESTER L. SCHULER** for the invention, of the Montage Picture Processor electronic film editing system.
COLIN F. MOSSMAN and **RANK FILM LABORATORIES' DEVELOPMENT GROUP** for creating a fully-automated film handling system for improving productivity of high speed film processing.
EASTMAN KODAK COMPANY for the development of Eastman Color High Speed Daylight Negative Film 5297/7297.
EASTMAN KODAK COMPANY for the development of Eastman Color High Speed SA Negative Film 5295 for blue-screen traveling matte photography.
FRITZ GABRIEL BAUER for the invention and development of the improved features of the Moviecam Camera System.
ZORAN PERISIC of Courier Films Ltd. for the Zoptic dual-zoom front projection system for visual effects photography.
CARL ZEISS COMPANY for the design and development of a series of super-speed lenses for motion picture photography.

Technical Achievement Award (Academy Certificate)

IOAN ALLEN of Dolby Laboratories, Inc., for the Cat. 43 playback-only noise reduction unit and its practical application to motion picture sound recordings.
JOHN EPPOLITO, WALLY GENTLEMAN, WILLIAM MESA, LES PAUL ROBLEY and **GEOFFREY H. WILLIAMSON** for refinements to a dual screen, front projection, image-compositing system.
JAN JACOBSEN for the application of a dual screen, front projection system to motion picture special effects photography.
THAINE MORRIS and **DAVID PIER** for the development of DSC Spark Devices for motion picture special effects.
TADEUZ KRZANOWSKI of Industrial Light and Magic, Inc., for the development of a Wire Rig Model Support Mechanism used to control the movements of miniatures in special effects.
DAN C. NORRIS and **TIM COOK** of Norris Film Products for the development of a single-frame exposure system for motion picture photography.

*INDICATES WINNER

289

1988-1997
The Academy's Seventh Decade

One of the primary accomplishments of the Academy's seventh decade was to continue tidying up oversights, amending the Academy records that had shortchanged several artists during the McCarthy-House Un-American Activities era of the 1950s. That period had sent a reign of terror through the Hollywood studios, blacklisting writers accused of having "unfriendly" political sympathies, even erasing names from film credits and, therefore, from their due acknowledgment on the Academy honor rolls. Back in 1975, writer Dalton Trumbo had been given a long overdue Oscar for his 1956 story for *The Brave One*, awarded at the time to "Robert Rich," a pen name Trumbo had used during his blacklisted days. Although Trumbo had died in 1976, in 1992 he was additionally given Academy credit for writing the 1953 Oscar-winning story for *Roman Holiday*, which had always been credited to Ian McClellan Hunter, co-author of the screenplay with John Dighton. Trumbo, it was revealed, had actually written the original story for *Roman* but had to enlist Hunter, a friend and fellow screenwriter, to act as a front for him in those tumultuous Fifties. On May 10, 1993, Trumbo's widow, Cleo, and their three children were officially presented a belated Oscar in the writer's name for his work on *Roman Holiday*. Other blacklisted writers such as Michael Wilson also had their names, at long last, rightfully written into the Academy records where they belonged.

Another major event of the Academy's Decade VII occurred in 1990: the move of the Academy's extensive Margaret Herrick Library from the AMPAS headquarters in Beverly Hills to its own 40,000 square-foot building a few blocks east at the corner of La Cienega and Olympic boulevards. Named the Center for Motion Picture Study, the new acquisition was a sixty-three-year-old structure that had formerly housed the Beverly Hills Waterworks; the move and renovations cost $6 million and for the first time brought under one roof the holdings of the Margaret Herrick Library and the Academy Film Archive. It officially opened its doors in January, 1991, following four nights of grand-opening events.

The construction and conversion of the new center were paid for with monies the Academy had on hand; at the same time, a campaign to build a $15 million endowment to support the facility, the Academy's first-ever fund raising effort, was launched. Led by successive Academy presidents Karl Malden and Robert Rehme, it brought donations from a wide spectrum of contributors, including $1 million each from Bob Hope and the Cecil B. DeMille Foundation.

During the same period, major renovations were also done on the theaters at the Academy's headquarters, keeping them state-of-the-art facilities. The 1,022-seat Samuel Goldwyn Theater was upgraded to include all three of the recently introduced digital sound formats, a JBL three-way speaker system, computerized theatrical lighting controls, a 24-channel professional sound mixing console for live events and a unique computerized projection moni-

LILI FINI ZANUCK

"All my life I've imagined winning an Academy Award, and all my life, whenever I fantasized about it, I would see myself with some kind of Winner's Dress on. It was a red dress with a train, or maybe a big bright yellow dress—a big fantasy dress. But once you're nominated, you get to thinking: What if you lose? You don't want to be galumphing around the Governors Ball in a big Winners' Dress when you've just lost in front of a billion people. So now you're preparing for the biggest event of your life by buying the plainest dress you can find. As for your fantasy of entering the Dorothy Chandler Pavilion brandishing a long cigarette holder and flanked by twin Afghan hounds—forget about it.

As the weeks go by, you get scared and superstitious.

The day arrives. My husband is so nervous he won't let me talk to him, not even during the ceremony. We're sitting there in silence and at last, Driving Miss Daisy *wins Best Makeup. This means I can put my hand on his arm. An hour and half later, Alfred Uhry wins Best Screenplay; polite conversation is permitted. When* Jessica Tandy *wins Best Actress, we can continue the polite conversation, but we also get to hold hands—and cross our fingers. Then the nominations for Best Picture are announced, and you see clips from them all, and suddenly I just can't believe how terrific the other nominated movies are. And then . . .*

. . . the envelope is opened and your name is read, and somehow, mysteriously, you float to the podium.

And the thing I discovered that night was this: even though I didn't have a speech written, I had total clarity about whom to thank. I didn't forget anybody, and I remembered them in exactly the order that they helped get the picture made. I remembered them all because in that moment, the biggest moment of my life, nothing was clearer to me than my gratitude."

Lili Fini Zanuck
Best Picture, 1989

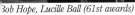
Bob Hope, Lucille Ball (61st awards)

Tom Hanks, Rita Wilson (61st awards)

"Under the Sea" production number with Geoffrey Holder (62nd awards)

RICHARD D. ZANUCK

"As a young man I grew up mesmerized by the three Academy Awards and the three Irving G. Thalberg Awards lined up atop the living room fireplace at our home at the beach. My father had won the Academy Awards for How Green Was My Valley, Gentleman's Agreement, *and* All About Eve. *The Thalbergs had been spread throughout his career and after he had won for the third time, the Academy passed a ruling by which no member could win this award more than once. I would often stare at these golden testaments of Academy triumphs and lifetime achievements and contemplate whether or not something like this or a fraction thereof would be in my future. It was something I dreamed of and fantasized about as I grew up.*

I don't have to elaborate for you how it felt stepping up to the podium the night they presented the Award for Best Picture of 1989. Driving Miss Daisy, *the film that no one wanted to make and the film that apparently directed itself, since Bruce Beresford was not one of its nine nominees, became after all these years the unlikely conduit between Oscar and me.*

Happily, my Oscar is not lonely on my mantel as it is joined by the one brought home that night in 1989 by my fellow producer, partner, and wife, Lili Fini Zanuck.

The following year the Academy bestowed upon me its greatest honor, the Irving G. Thalberg Award, and now my mantel runneth over.

Boyhood dreams can come true, you know."

Richard D. Zanuck
Best Picture, 1989
Irving G. Thalberg Award, 1990

ALFRED UHRY

"I went through the Academy Awards show on automatic pilot. They didn't get to my category until almost the end. When my name was announced by Jane Fonda, it seemed like it was happening to somebody else. A few days later—back home in New York—I watched the show on tape. I went through all the appropriate emotions. Alone in my apartment, I was apprehensive, frightened, hopeful. I was elated when I won. I choked up. And I realized that the Academy Awards presenta-

tion only seemed real to me on television because that's how I'd seen it my whole life. It was a remarkable and bizarre experience."

Alfred Uhry
Screenplay Based on Material from Another
Medium, 1989

CLINT EASTWOOD

"I was sitting in the theater next to my 85-year-old mother thinking, "What if I had her come all this way and we go home empty?" I was mulling over this thought while they read the names for Best Director and when they announced that I had won, I got up and thanked everyone EXCEPT my mother. I got off the stage thinking that I had to win for Best Picture if only to get back up on stage and rectify my error. The theme that year was The Year of the Woman, and luckily I got to thank the greatest woman on earth: my mother."

Clint Eastwood
Best Picture and Best Director, 1992
Irving G. Thalberg Award 1994

Jodie Foster (61st awards)

Kevin Costner (63rd awards)

Madonna (63rd awards)

toring system designed exclusively for the Academy. In addition, the Grand Lobby of the theater was given a complete new look, and the building's 67-seat Little Theater was entirely rebuilt. That wasn't the end of renovations, however. An earthquake on January 17, 1994, severely shook up things, including a high-pressure roof-top water pipe on the Academy's main building, with enough flooding and damage resulting that several weeks of reconstruction were required.

During the decade, there were many gala events in the Academy's Goldwyn Theater, beginning with a salute to the late composer Irving Berlin, hosted by Jack Lemmon, with a live orchestra under the direction of Peter Matz and the participation of many celebrities. Later tributes during this decade included evenings devoted to the careers of Mary Pickford, Joseph L. Mankiewicz, Johnny Green, Hermes Pan, Betty Comden and Adolph Green, Georges Méliès, Marlene Dietrich, Federico Fellini, Buster Keaton, Stanley Donen, Bernardo Bertolucci, Jay Livingston and Ray Evans and the Kanin clan, composed of brothers Garson and Michael Kanin and their wives Ruth Gordon and Fay Kanin. Several of the tributes were first done at New York's Museum of Modern Art as a joint effort of MoMA and the Academy; others were initially done at the Academy's L.A. headquarters, then

Billy Crystal (63rd awards)

ANTHONY HOPKINS

"When I was nominated for the Academy Award, it all seemed very unreal.

When Kathy Bates announced my name, 'And the Oscar goes to. . .', everything went into dream time. I got up onto the stage and thought 'I've just been given an Oscar! I've been given an Oscar! Now what the hell do I say?' So instead of thanking Orion Pictures and the Academy, I just said 'Hello' to my mother at home in Wales. So if it is not too late, 'Thank you Academy. And thank you everyone at Orion Pictures.'

It was the sweetest moment in my life."

Anthony Hopkins
Best Actor, 1991

EMMA THOMPSON

"I was sitting next to my mother, who turned to me and said 'You haven't got a snowball's chance in hell.'

When Tony said my name I sat stock-still for about half an hour worrying about my high heels. It took ages
to get to him. The only person I could see was Mother, leaning forward in her seat with a very concentrated and serious expression, like the ones she wore at school assembly when I was a child. Then I went backstage and met Jane Fonda. I felt like the Queen on a very good day."

Emma Thompson
Best Actress, 1992
Screenplay Based on Material Previously Produced
or Published, 1995

TED TALLY

"During the ceremony itself, I was remarkably composed. I don't know why. Even when Robert Duvall opened the envelope and announced my name, I remained in an eerie calm, as if I were floating twenty feet above the auditorium floor, watching someone else embrace his wife, hug his director, walk towards the stage. . .

The next morning I walked from my hotel to a nearby shopping center to get the papers. I sat on a bench and read them. And that's when it finally hit me. Five Oscars. Only the third film in history to sweep those par-
ticular awards. One of the papers had printed a list of all the Best Picture winners, going back through time, and as I read them I started to tremble. Gone with the Wind. Casablanca. Lawrence of Arabia. West Side Story. On and on, that astonishing roll call. . . movies that had amazed and thrilled and inspired me my whole life. And there we were, too, The Silence of the Lambs, now listed forever alongside those masterpieces. All my mysterious calm vanished at last, and I sat on that bench with tears in my eyes, shaking like a leaf."

Ted Tally
Screenplay Based on Material Previously Produced
or Published, 1991

NEIL TRAVIS

"The Oscar gave me such a feeling of acceptance that I was, automatically, able to break a fifty-year-old habit of biting my fingernails. I know it sounds strange, but Sally Field had the right of it."

Neil Travis
Film Editing, 1990

epeated at MoMA. Still others, such as those saluting the careers of Celeste Holm and Esther Williams, were coordinated by the Academy but presented only at MoMA's New York headquarters. One of the most ambitious events was a salute to Hollywood's role in World War II, called "Films for the Fight," specifically created to commemorate the 50th anniversary of the D-Day Invasion celebrated at the Deauville Film Festival in France in 1995. The program was later repeated in both New York and Los Angeles.

During the decade, numerous screenings open to the public were also held in the Academy's theater. The selection included both off-beat films as well as treasures from the archives, the latter giving attendees a rare chance to see, again or for the first time, classic Oscar-winning films on a big screen, in mint 35mm condition. Seminars relating to all aspects of filmmaking—acting, directing, writing, marketing, et al—also continued at full-steam and, for the first time, the Academy allowed the historic archival footage from past Oscar telecasts to be publicly released on video, in an arrangement with Columbia TriStar Home Video. Profits from "Oscar's Greatest Moments," a compilation of highlights from the then-most-recent 21 years of Oscar telecasts, were earmarked to benefit the Endowment Fund of the Academy's Center for Motion Picture Study.

Also for the first time, on November 1, 1988, the Academy was honored in a genuinely royal manner by its British cousins. A gala dinner hosted by the British Academy of Film and Television Arts was given in England in the great dining room of Hampton Court Palace, Henry VIII's favorite restaurant, specifically to salute the many British subjects who had won Academy Awards in Hollywood. The guest list included many Sirs (among them, David Lean, John Mills, Richard Attenborough) and such spectacular talent as Peter Ustinov (who later in the decade

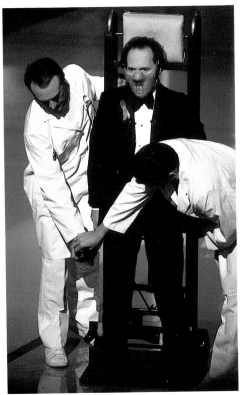

Billy Crystal (64th awards)

Hal Roach (64th awards)

Whoopi Goldberg, Denzel Washington (63rd awards)

ALAN MENKEN

"In 1990 I was nominated for the best score for The Little Mermaid *and two songs, "Under the Sea" and "Kiss the Girl." From the moment we arrived, everything pointed to a night spent traversing that immense distance to that stage. One fellow nominee said, "I don't know who's winning tonight but I'm told that a couple of statues have fins on them." I mentally prepared myself, but nothing quite prepares you for the tension that builds as your moment arrives.*

Score came first and I'll never forget Steve Martin saying my name, Janis kissing me and, most of all, Howard Ashman reaching over and congratulating me. He had made it all possible.

I spent the next hour and a half praying for a best song award for the two of us.

I often watch the video of us rising to accept our Oscar for "Under the Sea" and look at the happiness in Howard's face. It was a wonderful night. Two days later Howard told me he was sick with AIDS. He was gone within a year."

Alan Menken
Music (Original Score), 1989; 1991; 1992; 1995
Music (Song), 1989; 1991; 1992; 1995

RONALD BASS

"As our award was being announced, I sat in the third row, convinced that none of this affected me. The smart money was on another writer as heavy favorite in our category. The podium was on the far side of the stage, and so I watched a huge screen directly in front of me filled with the beautiful face of our presenter, Amy Irving, a sweet and loyal friend. As Amy opened the envelope, something in her expression told me I had won, and reflexively, I simply stood up. By the time my name was actually read, my wife was looking up at me in amazement at how I could already be standing. I often reflect on what a long way down it would have been to my seat, if that reflex had been mistaken."

Ronald Bass
Screenplay Written Directly for the Screen, 1988

STEVEN SPIELBERG

"Believe me when I say, "It's a lot easier imagining an Oscar than winning one." When that moment finally arrived, even though I had been nagged at by friends and associates that I could actually take one home, I honestly never believed any of them until Clint Eastwood opened the envelope and read my name out loud.

What made it so hard for me to believe was that in the entire history of the Academy Awards, representing the thousands of movies and films, spanning nearly a century of American picture making, I had been selected as one of only 66 directors to receive this highest honor.

It's been four years since I won the Academy Award for Schindler's List, *but to me, it still seems like yesterday."*

Steven Spielberg
Irving G. Thalberg Award, 1986
Best Picture and Best Director, 1993

would also become a Sir), Olivia de Havilland, Ben Kingsley, Jack Cardiff among the many, with HRH Princess Anne also in attendance. Hampton Court was chosen for the gathering because of its own Oscar connection: the very first British film to win a major Academy Award was *The Private Life of Henry VIII*, much of it set in Hampton Court and a film which earned the 1932-33 "best actor" award for Charles Laughton.

On January 28, 1993, the Academy enlisted photographer Theo Westenberger to record another historic gathering: 67 Oscar-winning women (out of the 158 living at the time) brought together in one place at one time. The photograph was taken in the Goldwyn Theater at the Academy headquarters, during a reception which quickly grew into a genuine party. The reason for the massive get together was to call added attention to the upcoming 65th Oscar ceremonies which were subtitled "Oscar Celebrates Women and the Movies," as well as to increase general awareness of the numerous and important contributions by women to all areas of filmmaking.

In February of 1995, the Board of Governors voted to inaugurate the first new Academy branch in 42 years, giving the roughly 130 visual effects members a branch of their own. It was the first increase in the number of Academy branches since 1953.

Various individuals and groups continued to donate valuable film-related collections to the Margaret Herrick Library. Sid Avery and the Los Angeles County Museum of Art contributed more than 35,000 photographs and negatives that originally had been part of the Hollywood Photographers Archive. The Turner/MGM script collection, encompassing some 50,000 individual items, arrived in January 1994 via 1,500 boxes transported by three moving vans, the largest single donation of archival materials yet. (It included a completely handwritten first-draft script for *Meet Me in St. Louis*.) Other important collections

Marcello Mastroianni, Federico Fellini, Sophia Loren (65th awards)

belonging to Paul Mazursky, William Friedkin, Jerry Goldsmith, Sam Peckinpah, Bryan Forbes, Hal Ashby, Leo "K" Kuter, Gregory Peck, Alex North, Sammy Cahn, Richard Brooks, David Niven, Mervyn LeRoy, John Engstead and others were received, as well as documents relating to the careers of Cary Grant, Warner Baxter and others. The Edward Mapp Collection of 900 movie posters documenting African-American filmmakers also became a part of the Academy's archives.

In September 1991, the Academy also acquired two historic Academy Award statuettes which had been reported stolen from the home of director Lewis Milestone in 1978 and were being offered for sale to Los Angeles-area memorabilia dealers. The Oscars, won by Milestone for his direction of *Two Arabian Knights* (1927-28) and *All Quiet on the Western Front* (1929–30), were reclaimed by the Academy via a court order and eventually surrendered without

objection by a North Hollywood resident. In 1995, Margaret O'Brien was also overjoyed to get back the long-missing miniature Oscar she had been presented in 1944 as "the outstanding child actress" of that year. Two baseball memorabilia collectors had bought it at a swap meet and returned it to Ms. O'Brien upon learning it had been stolen some 40 years earlier.

Also, thanks to a surprising and generous gesture in 1997, the Academy acquired the Oscar won by the late Clark Gable for 1934's *It Happened One Night*. The statuette had been put into auction by Gable's son, John Clark Gable, and, despite the Academy's efforts to acquire it, the auction proceeded with an anonymous buyer paying $550,000 for the award. (With fees and commissions added, the final total was an awesome $607,500.) A few days later, the statue arrived at the Academy as a gift from the bidder, who turned out to be Steven Spielberg. He had bought it, he said,

TOM SCHULMAN

"When I won my Academy Award, my presenter was Jane Fonda, and having her accompany me quickly put the whole thing into perspective.

Right after I made my acceptance speech, I stepped into the wings and went into full-blown panic. I had neglected to thank three very important people. Jane asked me what was wrong and when I told her, she said, 'Oh, don't be silly. You'll thank them next time.' Hmm. I was somehow not consoled.

It was a great night. One I will never forget. I am waiting to win again so I can thank those three wonderful people."

Tom Schulman
Screenplay Written Directly for the Screen, 1989

MARK JOHNSON

"For weeks, even months, before the actual ceremony everyone, and I mean everyone, predicted a win for our movie. Every phone call would close with some well-meaning voice assuring me that the Oscar was mine. Even my dry cleaner said it was a lock.

It got to the point that had Rain Man *not won, I would have been made to feel as though I had disappointed everyone, as though I had deliberately done something to undermine a sure winner. Rather than be gloriously content with a nomination, I would have been, so I was beginning to think, a loser. The pressure to perform, to win, was relentless. Finally, when all was over and done with, my overriding joy was not one of triumph, but one of relief! The element of surprise was never allowed me. What crazy and wonderful times!"*

Mark Johnson
Best Picture, 1988

GEORGE WATTERS II

"The fastest couple of minutes in your life is from the moment your name is announced as a winner of an Academy Award until you are walking off stage carrying it. You don't remember anything you said until you are reminded at home while you watch yourself on a tape on your VCR. Maybe someday it will sink in that I won, but after three years I still can't believe it."

George Watters II
Sound Effects Editing, 1990

xpressly so it would be returned to the \academy. "A sanctuary for Gable's only)scar," said Spielberg.

Earlier, in 1988, the Academy found it necessary to bring a lawsuit against a Chicago trophy company called Creative House Promotions which had been manufacturing and selling a close replica of the copyrighted Oscar statuette. Three years later a 1991 ruling by the U.S. 9th Circuit Court of Appeals on the case concluded that "the Academy's sleek, muscular gold statuette known as 'Oscar,' which is recognized worldwide as a distinctive symbol of outstanding achievement in film, . . . should be given the strongest possible protection against infringement." Creative House was required to pay the Academy $300,000 for its violation and to discontinue the manufacture and sale of the design in question. Disputes with other trophy manufacturers were similarly settled. One paid a substantial sum to the Academy and agreed to discontinue the production of its Oscar clone; a second voluntarily modified its trophy to eliminate similarities to the Academy's famous symbol.

During the Academy's seventh decade, James M. Roberts decided to retire. Roberts, a 35-year veteran of the AMPAS, had begun his career with the Academy in 1954 as the organization's controller; since 1971, he had served as the Academy's Executive Director. He retired July 31, 1989, succeeded by Bruce Davis, who had been the Academy's Executive Administrator before accepting his new post.

ACADEMY PRESIDENTS, 1988–1997

July 88–July 89	Richard Kahn
July 89–July 90	Karl Malden
July 90–July 91	Karl Malden
July 91–July 92	Karl Malden
July 92–July 93	Robert Rehme
July 93–July 94	Arthur Hiller
July 94–July 95	Arthur Hiller
July 95–July 96	Arthur Hiller
July 96–July 97	Arthur Hiller
July 97–July 98	Robert Rehme

Callie Khouri, Geena Davis, Becky Johnston at Nominees Luncheon (64th awards)

Anthony Hopkins hugging Jodie Foster (64th awards)

DOUG SMYTHE

"The audience was hushed. The timpani rolled. The names were read—our names. The moment I had dreamt of had arrived. I followed my co-winners up to the stage to accept our awards and attempt the impossible: to deliver four acceptance speeches before the orchestra struck the chords that would lead the viewers at home into a commercial break, cutting off a stunned Oscar recipient mid-sentence.

It's all simple mathematics, really—winners are allotted forty-five seconds to present their words of gratitude, and since there were four of us, that meant we each had eleven seconds to speak. There were so many people I wanted to mention, but time was so limited—what to do? What Billy Crystal later figured to be a 'new record' for speed-accepting: thirteen names in ten seconds.

It was truly a magical night. Thank you to all."

Doug Smythe
Visual Effects, 1992

MERCEDES RUEHL

"On the night of the Academy Awards, all of my anxiety coalesced into one obsessive fear: that if I won, and was summoned to the podium, I would trip and fall en route. And shortly after my name was called, I nearly did. The rail-less steps that led up to the stage were strewn at the base with a tangle of cables transmitting the show to Mr. and Mrs. America, every country in the world, and all the ships at sea. As I picked my way through them in a dream—and, more to the point, in four-inch heels provided by Valentino—I listed dangerously to starboard. A hand came out of nowhere to steady me. Following the hand up its arm to a face, I discovered it to be Warren Beatty's, smiling 'Oh, my,' a breathy voice very far away inside me said. I proceeded on to the podium. I was armed with one line that would save me—I had come up with it in the bathtub of the Bel Air Hotel the night before—should any further mishap upend me before a billion viewers and land me in a humiliated heap of designer gown and borrowed jewels before the microphone. The line was, 'I have arrived! Not with standing!'"

Mercedes Ruehl
Supporting Actress, 1991

JESSICA YU

"A lot of people ask, "What was going through your mind when you heard your name?" The answer is nothing, a white buzz, what my cat thinks when it hears a loud noise. It wasn't until I was walking up to the stage that I had my first coherent thought. I was looking down at the steps so I wouldn't stumble in my unfamiliar spike heels when I thought, "Gee, these stairs are kind of scuffed. They're just ordinary stairs." Then I got up there and saw the crowd all lit up; it seemed like everyone was smiling at me. My one billion new close friends.

After running the gauntlet of press rooms (all those elbows jostling to take my picture?) I went to the lobby to call Mark O'Brien. He was holding an Oscar party in his Berkeley apartment, and when he answered the phone I heard this roar. When I got back to my seat I told my husband, 'For a guy in an iron lung, Mark sure can yell.'

My goal had been simply to enjoy the moment if I won. I had a blast."

Jessica Yu
Best Documentary (Short Subject), 1996

"Rain" fell on the sixty-first Academy Awards ceremonies, held March 29, 1989, at the Shrine Civic Auditorium in downtown Los Angeles. That was the simple part, compared to the storm that brewed immediately after. For Oscar statisticians, it was definitely the year of *Rain Man*; for others, it became known as the year of *l'affair de Blanche Neige*.

It came as no surprise to the pre-show quarterbackers when *Rain Man* walked off with several of the year's top awards. The drama was named best picture of the year; Dustin Hoffman also followed pre-show predictions by winning as the year's best actor, his second award in that category. Barry Levinson of the same film, as prophesied, won the director's prize, his first.

Many of the evening's other winners caught handicappers decidedly off guard. Kevin Kline, instead of odds-on-favorite Martin Landau, nabbed the best supporting actor award. Geena Davis was announced as the year's best supporting actress; most had Sigourney Weaver to win in that division. Weaver had been nominated twice in 1988, once as best actress (for *Gorillas in the Mist*) and again in the supporting actress category. This was the first time anyone with two such nominations had ended up empty-handed at the end of an Oscar ceremony. Jodie Foster was chosen as best actress for *The Accused*; it was a popular win but had been far from a sure thing.

For the second year in a row, a film from Denmark was named Oscar's favorite foreign language film. In 1988 the winner was *Pelle the Conqueror*, directed by Bille August and starring Max von Sydow; the previous year the winner had been the Danish-made *Babette's Feast*. On the domestic front, *Rain Man* and *Who Framed Roger Rabbit* ended up in a tie as the year's most honored films, with four awards each, hardly a sweep for either.

Ultimately it was not the results but the telecast itself that caused the most lingering rain clouds. The three-hour-nineteen-minute show, carried over ABC-TV, had been produced by showman Allan Carr with good intentions but some unforeseen fall-out, most stemming from the show's opening sequence. Carr had borrowed it from a satirical San Francisco musical called "Beach Blanket Babylon" and used Eileen Bowman as a clone of Disney's Snow White performing alongside a singing-dancing Rob Lowe. When the Disney Company saw Miss White playing such a prominent and—in the studio's view—undignified role in the proceedings, it objected and even briefly threatened a lawsuit. After an apology from the Academy, though, AMPAS-Disney relations quickly returned to a cordial state.

Reviews were mixed on the rest of the show as well. A sequence set in a mockup of the old Cocoanut Grove nightclub presented some welcome, durable stars from Hollywood's

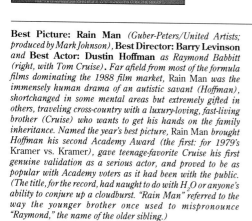

Best Picture: Rain Man *(Guber-Peters/United Artists; produced by Mark Johnson)*, **Best Director: Barry Levinson** and **Best Actor: Dustin Hoffman** *as Raymond Babbitt (right, with Tom Cruise). Far afield from most of the formula films dominating the 1988 film market,* Rain Man *was the immensely human drama of an autistic savant (Hoffman), shortchanged in some mental areas but extremely gifted in others, traveling cross-country with a luxury-loving, fast-living brother (Cruise) who wants to get his hands on the family inheritance. Named the year's best picture,* Rain Man *brought Hoffman his second Academy Award (the first: for 1979's* Kramer vs. Kramer*), gave teenage-favorite Cruise his first genuine validation as a serious actor, and proved to be as popular with Academy voters as it had been with the public. (The title, for the record, had naught to do with H_2O or anyone's ability to conjure up a cloudburst. "Rain Man" referred to the way the younger brother once used to mispronounce "Raymond," the name of the older sibling.)*

golden era (Alice Faye, Tony Martin, Cyd Charisse, Dorothy Lamour, Merv Griffin, Buddy Rogers, Roy Rogers and Dale Evans, Vincent Price, Coral Browne) but failed to generate the kind of genuine glamour that had been anticipated. There was also a musical number showcasing nineteen Hollywood newcomers that did not inspire much confidence about the industry's future.

But it was far from a throwaway show. The ratings were the highest in years, and producer Carr, in attempting to add some old-style Hollywood glitz and fun to the telecast, had managed to entice a formidable number of stars to participate. Most

of them were introduced in familiar pairs, such as James Stewart and Kim Novak, costars in *Bell, Book and Candle* and *Vertigo*; Dudley Moore and Bo Derek of *10*; dancers Sammy Davis, Jr., and Gregory Hines; newly married Bruce Willis and Demi Moore; father and son Donald and Keifer Sutherland; and Sean Connery and Michael Caine, who had earlier teamed in John Huston's *The Man Who Would Be King*. Connery and Caine were eventually joined on stage by Roger Moore, the man who had succeeded Connery as the movies' James Bond. Two classic clowns also appeared together and received a standing ovation: for Bob Hope, it

was his twenty-sixth appearance on an Oscar show. For Lucille Ball, the night was destined to be her last public appearance; she died less than a month later, on April 16, 1989.

Although the ceremony was again held at the Shrine Civic Auditorium, there were none of the traffic snarls, late arrivals, and heated tempers that had complicated the previous year's Academy Award party. Thanks to some extraordinary troubleshooting and preplanning, this time everything went off without a hitch.

Best Actress: Jodie Foster *as Sarah Tobias in* The Accused *(Jaffe-Lansing/Paramount; directed by Jonathan Kaplan). Inspired by a true 1983 incident in Massachusetts,* The Accused *chronicled the aftereffects of a gang-rape on a gutsy, hard-drinking waitress (Foster, left, with Kelly McGillis) who finds life just as brutal in court when her case is heard. Tough and cynical, the film provoked considerable controversy because of its morality issues; it also gave Foster the juiciest role of her career to date and, eventually, an Academy Award after a lifetime in front of movie cameras and a long romance with Oscar. (Her first nomination had come in 1976 at the age of 14 for* Taxi Driver.*) Three years later, she was to win again, as 1991's best actress in* The Silence of the Lambs.

Best Supporting Actor: Kevin Kline *as Otto West in* A Fish Called Wanda *(MGM; directed by Charles Crichton). Kevin Kline had been acknowledged as one of the theater's funniest fellows, thanks to over-the-wall performances delivered on Broadway in "On the Twentieth Century" (1978) and "The Pirates of Penzance" (1980), both of which won him Tony awards. By contrast his screen life had been markedly subdued until he played a thuggish, would-be Italian stallion in* A Fish Called Wanda, *a wacky British-flavored comedy about a blundering gang of jewel thieves that was written for the screen by Monty Python vet John Cleese. As a guy named Otto, Kline (left, with Jamie Lee Curtis) turned out to be at once bonkers, insensitive, and hilarious.* Wanda *costarred Cleese and fellow Python alumnus Michael Palin. It also reaffirmed that, as in the days when Alec Guinness and Peter Sellers were making small-scale but extremely witty comedies, the Brits were still masters at tickling ribs.*

Best Supporting Actress: Geena Davis *as Muriel Pritchett in* The Accidental Tourist *(Warner Bros.; directed by Lawrence Kasdan). Voted the year's best picture by the New York Film Critics,* Tourist *was based on a best-selling novel by Anne Tyler about an uptight, fastidious travel writer (William Hurt) who is despondent over the death of his twelve-year-old son and the subsequent breakup of a long marriage, until he meets a spontaneous, upbeat and kooky dog trainer (Geena Davis). Davis' plucky performance was showy and memorable; her subsequent Oscar win also propelled her immediately into a mainstream career that made her one of the few bankable actresses of the early 1990s.*

Who Framed Roger Rabbit *(Buena Vista) tied with* Rain Man *as the year's most honored film, collecting four Oscars: for visual effects, editing, sound effects editing, and a special achievement award for the film's animation director, Richard Williams.* Rabbit, *executive produced by Steven Spielberg and Kathleen Kennedy, was an eye-popping combination of live actors (led by Bob Hoskins and Christopher Lloyd) sharing the screen with a whole stable of famous cartoon stars, including classic 'toon characters from both Warner Bros. and Disney, working in tandem for the very first time.*

PICTURE

THE ACCIDENTAL TOURIST, Warner Bros. Produced by Lawrence Kasdan, Charles Okun and Michael Grillo.
DANGEROUS LIAISONS, Warner Bros. Produced by Norma Heyman and Hank Moonjean.
MISSISSIPPI BURNING, Frederick Zollo, Orion. Produced by Frederick Zollo and Robert F. Colesberry.
*** RAIN MAN,** Guber-Peters, United Artists. Produced by Mark Johnson.
WORKING GIRL, 20th Century Fox. Produced by Douglas Wick.

ACTOR

GENE HACKMAN in *Mississippi Burning*, Frederick Zollo, Orion.
TOM HANKS in *Big*, 20th Century Fox.
*** DUSTIN HOFFMAN** in *Rain Man*, Guber-Peters, United Artists.
EDWARD JAMES OLMOS in *Stand and Deliver*, Menendez/Musca & Olmos, Warner Bros.
MAX VON SYDOW in *Pelle the Conqueror*, Per Holst/Kaerne, Miramax Films.

ACTRESS

GLENN CLOSE in *Dangerous Liaisons*, Warner Bros.
*** JODIE FOSTER** in *The Accused*, Jaffe-Lansing, Paramount.
MELANIE GRIFFITH in *Working Girl*, 20th Century Fox.
MERYL STREEP in *A Cry in the Dark*, Cannon Entertainment/Golan-Globus, Warner Bros.
SIGOURNEY WEAVER in *Gorillas in the Mist*, Warner Bros./Universal.

SUPPORTING ACTOR

ALEC GUINNESS in *Little Dorrit*, Sands Films, Cannon.
*** KEVIN KLINE** in *A Fish Called Wanda*, Michael Shamberg-Prominent Features, M-G-M.
MARTIN LANDAU in *Tucker the Man and His Dream*, Lucasfilm, Paramount.
RIVER PHOENIX in *Running on Empty*, Lorimar, Warner Bros.
DEAN STOCKWELL in *Married to the Mob*, Mysterious Arts-Demme, Orion.

SUPPORTING ACTRESS

JOAN CUSACK in *Working Girl*, 20th Century Fox.
*** GEENA DAVIS** in *The Accidental Tourist*, Warner Bros.
FRANCES McDORMAND in *Mississippi Burning*, Frederick Zollo, Orion.
MICHELLE PFEIFFER in *Dangerous Liaisons*, Warner Bros.
SIGOURNEY WEAVER in *Working Girl*, 20th Century Fox.

DIRECTING

A FISH CALLED WANDA, Michael Shamberg-Prominent Features, M-G-M. Charles Crichton.
THE LAST TEMPTATION OF CHRIST, Testament, Universal/Cineplex Odeon. Martin Scorsese.
MISSISSIPPI BURNING, Frederick Zollo, Orion. Alan Parker.
***RAIN MAN,** Guber-Peters Company, United Artists. Barry Levinson.
WORKING GIRL, 20th Century Fox. Mike Nichols.

WRITING

(Screenplay Written Directly for the Screen)
BIG, 20th Century Fox. Gary Ross and Anne Spielberg.
BULL DURHAM, Mount Company, Orion. Ron Shelton.
A FISH CALLED WANDA, Michael Shamberg-Prominent Features, M-G-M. Screenplay by John Cleese. Story by John Cleese and Charles Crichton.
*** RAIN MAN,** Guber-Peters Company, United Artists. Screenplay by Ronald Bass and Barry Morrow. Story by Barry Morrow.
RUNNING ON EMPTY, Lorimar Production, Warner Bros. Naomi Foner.

(Screenplay Based on Material from Another Medium)
THE ACCIDENTAL TOURIST, Warner Bros. Frank Galati and Lawrence Kasdan.
*** DANGEROUS LIAISONS,** Warner Bros. Christopher Hampton.
GORILLAS IN THE MIST, Warner Bros./Universal. Screenplay by Anna Hamilton Phelan. Story by Anna Hamilton Phelan and Tab Murphy.
LITTLE DORRIT, Sands Films, Cannon. Christine Edzard.
THE UNBEARABLE LIGHTNESS OF BEING, Saul Zaentz Company, Orion. Jean-Claude Carriere and Philip Kaufman.

CINEMATOGRAPHY

*** MISSISSIPPI BURNING,** Frederick Zollo, Orion. Peter Biziou.
RAIN MAN, Guber-Peters Company, United Artists. John Seale.
TEQUILA SUNRISE, Mount Company Production, Warner Bros. Conrad L. Hall.
THE UNBEARABLE LIGHTNESS OF BEING, Saul Zaentz Company, Orion. Sven Nykvist.
WHO FRAMED ROGER RABBIT, Amblin Entertainment and Touchstone Pictures, Buena Vista. Dean Cundey.

ART DIRECTION-SET DECORATION

BEACHES, Touchstone Pictures in Association with Silver Screen Partners III, Buena Vista. Albert Brenner; Garrett Lewis.
*** DANGEROUS LIAISONS,** Warner Bros. Stuart Craig; Gerard James.
RAIN MAN, Guber-Peters Company, United Artists. Ida Random; Linda DeScenna.
TUCKER THE MAN AND HIS DREAM, Lucasfilm, Paramount. Dean Tavoularis; Armin Ganz.
WHO FRAMED ROGER RABBIT, Amblin Entertainment and Touchstone Pictures, Buena Vista. Elliot Scott; Peter Howitt.

Hotel Terminus: The Life and Times of Klaus Barbie *was Marcel Ophuls' four-and-one-half-hour chronicle of the infamous Nazi war criminal responsible for the extermination and/or deportation of thousands of French Jews. It was named the year's best documentary feature.*

COSTUME DESIGN
COMING TO AMERICA, Eddie Murphy, Paramount. Deborah Nadoolman.
* **DANGEROUS LIAISONS**, Warner Bros. James Acheson.
A HANDFUL OF DUST, Stage Screen, New Line. Jane Robinson.
SUNSET, Hudson Hawk, Tri-Star. Patricia Norris.
TUCKER THE MAN AND HIS DREAM, Lucasfilm, Paramount. Milena Canonero.

SOUND
* **BIRD**, Malpaso, Warner Bros. Les Fresholtz, Dick Alexander, Vern Poore and Willie D. Burton.
DIE HARD, 20th Century Fox. Don Bassman, Kevin F. Cleary, Richard Overton and Al Overton.
GORILLAS IN THE MIST, Warner Bros./Universal. Andy Nelson, Brian Saunders and Peter Handford.
MISSISSIPPI BURNING, Frederick Zollo, Orion. Robert Litt, Elliot Tyson, Rick Kline and Danny Michael.
WHO FRAMED ROGER RABBIT, Amblin Entertainment and Touchstone Pictures, Buena Vista. Robert Knudson, John Boyd, Don Digirolamo and Tony Dawe.

FILM EDITING
DIE HARD, 20th Century Fox. Frank J. Urioste and John F. Link.
GORILLAS IN THE MIST, Warner Bros./Universal. Stuart Baird.
MISSISSIPPI BURNING, Frederick Zollo, Orion. Gerry Hambling.
RAIN MAN, Guber-Peters Company, United Artists. Stu Linder.
* **WHO FRAMED ROGER RABBIT**, Amblin Entertainment and Touchstone Pictures, Buena Vista. Arthur Schmidt.

SOUND EFFECTS EDITING
DIE HARD, 20th Century Fox. Stephen H. Flick and Richard Shorr.
* **WHO FRAMED ROGER RABBIT**, Amblin Entertainment-Touchstone, Buena Vista. Charles L. Campbell and Louis L. Edemann.
WILLOW, Lucasfilm with Imagine Entertainment, M-G-M. Ben Burtt and Richard Hymns.

VISUAL EFFECTS
DIE HARD, 20th Century Fox. Richard Edlund, Al DiSarro, Brent Boates and Thaine Morris.
* **WHO FRAMED ROGER RABBIT**, Amblin Entertainment-Touchstone, Buena Vista. Ken Ralston, Richard Williams, Edward Jones and George Gibbs.
WILLOW, Lucasfilm with Imagine Entertainment, M-G-M. Dennis Muren, Michael McAlister, Phil Tippett and Chris Evans.

MUSIC
(Song)
CALLING YOU (*Bagdad Cafe*, Pelemele Film, Island); Music and lyrics by Bob Telson.
* **LET THE RIVER RUN** (*Working Girl*, 20th Century Fox); Music and lyrics by Carly Simon.
TWO HEARTS (*Buster*, N.F.H., Hemdale); Music by Lamont Dozier. Lyrics by Phil Collins.

(Original Score)
THE ACCIDENTAL TOURIST, Warner Bros. John Williams.
DANGEROUS LIAISONS, Warner Bros. George Fenton.
GORILLAS IN THE MIST, Warner Bros./Universal. Maurice Jarre.
* **THE MILAGRO BEANFIELD WAR**, Robert Redford/ Moctesuma Esparza, Universal. Dave Grusin.
RAIN MAN, Guber/Peters, United Artists. Hans Zimmer.

MAKEUP
* **BEETLEJUICE**, Geffen/Warner Bros. Ve Neill, Steve LaPorte and Robert Short.
COMING TO AMERICA, Eddie Murphy, Paramount. Rick Baker.
SCROOGED, Art Linson, Paramount. Tom Burman and Bari Dreiband-Burman.

SHORT FILMS
(Animated)
THE CAT CAME BACK, National Film Board of Canada. Cordell Barker.
TECHNOLOGICAL THREAT, Kroyer Films, Inc. Bill Kroyer and Brian Jennings.
* **TIN TOY**, Pixar. John Lasseter and William Reeves.

(Live Action)
* **THE APPOINTMENTS OF DENNIS JENNINGS**, Schooner Productions, Inc. Dean Parisot and Steven Wright.
CADILLAC DREAMS, Cadillac Dreams Production. Matia Karrell and Abbee Goldstein.
GULLAH TALES, Georgia State University. George deGolian and Gary Moss.

DOCUMENTARY
(Short Subjects)
THE CHILDREN'S STOREFRONT, a Simon and Goodman Picture Company Production. Karen Goodman, producer.
FAMILY GATHERING, a Lise Yasui Production. Lise Yasui and Ann Tegnell, producers.
GANG COPS, Produced at the Center for Visual Anthropology and the School of Cinema/Television, University of Southern California. Thomas B. Fleming and Daniel J. Marks, producers.
PORTRAIT OF IMOGEN, A Pacific Pictures Production. Nancy Hale and Meg Partridge, producers.
* **YOU DON'T HAVE TO DIE**, a Tiger Rose Production in Association with Filmworks, Inc. William Guttentag and Malcolm Clarke, producers.

(Features)
THE CRY OF REASON– BEYERS NAUDE: AN AFRIKANER SPEAKS OUT, a production of Worldwide Documentaries, Inc. Robert Bilheimer and Roland Mix, producers.
* **HOTEL TERMINUS: THE LIFE AND TIMES OF KLAUS BARBIE**, a production of The Memory Pictures Company. Marcel Ophuls, producer.
LET'S GET LOST, a production of Little Bear Films, Inc. Bruce Weber and Nan Bush, producers.
PROMISES TO KEEP, a production of Durrin Productions, Inc. Ginny Durrin, producer.
WHO KILLED VINCENT CHIN?, a production of Film News Now Foundation and Detroit Educational Television Foundation. Renee Tajima and Christine Choy, producers.

FOREIGN LANGUAGE FILMS
HANUSSEN (Hungary)
THE MUSIC TEACHER (Belgium)
* **PELLE THE CONQUEROR** (Denmark)
SALAAM BOMBAY! (India)
WOMEN ON THE VERGE OF A NERVOUS BREAKDOWN (Spain)

SPECIAL ACHIEVEMENT AWARD
For Animation Direction: **RICHARD WILLIAMS** for *Who Framed Roger Rabbit.*

HONORARY AND OTHER AWARDS
TO **NATIONAL FILM BOARD OF CANADA** in recognition of its 50th anniversary and its dedicated commitment to originate artistic, creative and technological activity and excellence in every area of film making.
TO **EASTMAN KODAK COMPANY** in recognition of the company's fundamental contributions to the art of motion pictures during the first century of film history.

IRVING G. THALBERG MEMORIAL AWARD
None given this year.

JEAN HERSHOLT HUMANITARIAN AWARD
None given this year.

1988 GORDON E. SAWYER AWARD
GORDON HENRY COOK

SCIENTIFIC OR TECHNICAL AWARDS
Academy Award of Merit (Statuette)
RAY DOLBY and **IOAN ALLEN** of Dolby Laboratories Incorporated for their continuous contributions to motion picture sound through the research and development programs of Dolby Laboratories.

Scientific and Engineering Award (Academy Plaque)
ROY W. EDWARDS and the Engineering Staff of **PHOTO-SONICS, INCORPORATED** for the design and development of the Photo-Sonics 35mm-4ER High-Speed Motion Picture Camera with Reflex Viewing and Video Assist.
THE ARNOLD & RICHTER Engineering Staff, **OTTO BLASCHEK** and **ARRIFLEX CORPORATION** for the concept and engineering of the Arriflex 35-3 Motion Picture Camera.
BILL TONDREAU of Tondreau Systems/**ALVAH MILLER** and **PAUL JOHNSON** of Lynx Robotics/**PETER A. REGLA** of ELICON/DAN SLATER/ BUD ELAM, JOE PARKER and BILL BRYAN of Interactive Motion Control/and **JERRY JEFFRESS, RAY FEENEY, BILL HOLLAND** and **KRIS BROWN** for their individual contributions and the collective advancements they have brought to the motion picture industry in the field of motion control technology.

Technical Achievement Award (Academy Certificate)
GRANT LOUCKS of Alan Gordon Enterprises Incorporated for the design concept, and **GEOFFREY H. WILLIAMSON** of Wilcam for the mechanical and electrical engineering, of the Image 300 35mm High-Speed Motion Picture Camera.
MICHAEL V. CHEWEY III for the development of the motion picture industry's first paper tape reader incorporating microprocessor technology.
BHP, Inc., successor to the Bell & Howell Professional Equipment Division, for the development of a high-speed reader incorporating microprocessor technology for motion picture laboratories.
HOLLYWOOD FILM COMPANY for the development of a high-speed reader incorporating microprocessor technology for motion picture laboratories.
BRUCE W. KELLER and **MANFRED G. MICHELSON** of Technical Film Systems for the design and development of a high-speed light valve controller and constant current power supply for motion picture laboratories.
DR. ANTAL LISZIEWICZ and **GLENN M. BERGGREN** of ISCO-OPTIC GmbH for the design and development of the Ultra-Star series of motion picture lenses.
JAMES K. BRANCH of Spectra Cine, Incorporated, and **WILLIAM L. BLOWERS** and **NASIR J. ZAIDI** for the design and development of the Spectra CineSpot one-degree spotmeter for measuring the brightness of motion picture screens.
BOB BADAMI, DICK BERNSTEIN and **BILL BERNSTEIN** of Offbeat Systems for the design and development of the Streamline Scoring System, Mark IV, for motion picture music editing.
GARY ZELLER of Zeller International Limited for the development of Zel-Jel fire protection barrier for motion picture stunt work.
EMANUEL TRILLING of Trilling Resources Limited for the development of Stunt-Gel fire protection barrier for motion picture stunt work.
PAUL A. ROOS for the invention of a method known as Video Assist, whereby a scene being photographed on motion picture film can be viewed on a monitor and/or recorded on video tape.

*INDICATES WINNER

The sixty-second Academy Award ceremonies were a triumph for the little guys. Oscar's top prize went to *Driving Miss Daisy*, a gentle film made for under $10 million in an era when the average cost of a movie hovered between $16 and $20 million. *Daisy* had pulled nine nominations and won five awards, including the best actress statuette for Jessica Tandy. *My Left Foot*, made in Britain for an even slimmer $3 million, received two of the night's top statuettes, for Daniel Day Lewis as best actor and for Brenda Fricker as the year's best supporting actress.

All the year's acting winners were also first-time champs. Denzel Washington, named best supporting actor for *Glory*, became the fourth African-American to receive a competitive Oscar for acting, following Hattie McDaniel (1939), Sidney Poitier (1963), and Louis Gossett, Jr. (1982). For Tandy it was a record of another kind. She was eighty years old (plus 293 days) at the time she was handed her award, making her the oldest performer ever to receive a competitive Oscar. When that distinction was pointed out to her backstage she said, somewhat surprised, "Am I?" then after a pause added cheerily, "Well, good for me!" She also said, "I'm walking on air."

The main competition for *Miss Daisy* had been Oliver Stone's Vietnam drama *Born on the Fourth of July*. Nominated for eight awards, it received only two, for Stone's direc-

tion and for the editing by David Brenner and Joe Hutshing. Despite some pre-show controversy over foreign language film rules, Italy's *Cinema Paradiso* was named the winner in that category. For several weeks it had been questioned whether or not the version of *Paradiso* submitted by Italy to the Academy and shown in U.S. theaters was actually the same version that had been exhibited in its home country, a necessity under Academy rules.

After two years of award-dispensing at L.A.'s Shrine Auditorium, the March 26, 1990, awards ceremonies returned to the Dorothy Chandler Pavilion, where the seating capacity was smaller but the parking lots more familiar. There were also two newcomers aboard: Gilbert Cates produced for the first time and Billy Crystal took his first shot as an Oscar show MC. With his irreverent wit, amiable jabs, and lightning-fast ad libs, Crystal was an immediate hit, making the show speed along like a locomotive despite its considerable length of three hours, thirty-seven minutes. Several portions of the show originated from distant international locales via worldwide satellite hookups. Mel Gibson and Glenn Close, filming *Hamlet* in England, opened the envelope live from London, Bryan Brown and Rachel Ward participated from Sydney, Charlton Heston and Norma Aleandro from Buenos Aires, and Jack Lemmon hosted a segment from Moscow.

Best Picture: Driving Miss Daisy *(Zanuck Company/ Warner Bros.; produced by Richard D. Zanuck and Lili Fini Zanuck) and* **Best Actress: Jessica Tandy** *as Daisy Werthan in* Driving Miss Daisy. *For the first time, a movie based on an off-Broadway play—never produced on Broadway's main stem— captured the Academy's highest honor; at the same time it brought long-deserved recognition to the eighty-year-old Tandy, who had spent most of her career playing distinguished roles in the theater that, to her chagrin, were then given to other actresses when they were transferred to film. This time she got a role every actress over age fifty had wanted. As Miss Daisy, she was a chilly, stubborn Jewish widow in Atlanta who, initially against her will, acquires a black chauffeur (Morgan Freeman; right, with Tandy). Over a period of twenty-five years, they become true, indispensable friends. Scripted by Alfred Uhry from his original play,* Miss Daisy *touched Oscar voters as it had the 1989 movie audiences who had turned it into a surprise box-office hit.* Miss Daisy *was liked enough at ballot time to capture nine nominations, the most of any film of the year, although its director, Bruce Beresford, was not nominated in his category. The last time a picture had been chosen "best" without its director being nominated was fifty-seven years earlier: in 1931-32,* Grand Hotel *won the Academy's best picture prize, but the film's director, Edmund Goulding, was not a nominee in his category.*

Other high points of the show included George Lucas and Steven Spielberg handing a special Oscar to Japan's mighty film master Akira Kurosawa for his "cinematic accomplishments that have inspired, delighted, enriched and entertained worldwide audiences and influenced filmmakers throughout the world." It was a birthday present of sorts for Kurosawa; three days earlier, on March 23, he had turned eighty. An animated Bugs Bunny—celebrating his own fiftieth anniversary as a Hollywood star—was among the Oscar presenters. Howard W. Koch received the Jean Hersholt Humanitarian Award, and Diana Ross led the audience in a singalong of "Over the Rainbow," segueing from a clip of Judy Garland doing the same in 1939's memorable *The Wizard of Oz*.

For the first time in nearly four decades, an official Oscar night party was also simultaneously held on the East Coast. Numerous New York-based Academy members gathered together at the famous Russian Tea Room to watch the results and cheer the winners, along with one billion others estimated to be watching worldwide.

Best Actor: Daniel Day Lewis *as Christy Brown in* My Left Foot *(Miramax; directed by Jim Sheridan). It was highly unlikely material for a movie, commercial or otherwise, in the late 1980s: a young Irish boy, born with cerebral palsy into an extremely poor family, overcomes the liabilities of his handicap to become a world-famous writer and painter.* My Left Foot *was based on the life of Ireland's renowned artist Christy Brown and, despite the downbeat theme, turned out to be a highly entertaining, uplifting movie. If it was a decidedly hard sell, it also had a commanding asset: the central performance of Daniel Day Lewis as Brown. Prior to filming, Day Lewis spent eight intense weeks of research with cerebral palsy victims; during the entire six-week shoot in Dublin, he remained in a wheelchair, never breaking character, even to the point of being hand-fed by the cast and crew. The result was acting of the highest order: powerful, earnest, unforgettable.*

301

Best Supporting Actress: Brenda Fricker *as Mrs. Brown in* My Left Foot. *Although Daniel Day Lewis dominated the film,* My Left Foot *was full of acting riches, including a brilliant turn by Fricker as Christy Brown's mother, the wife of a poor Irish bricklayer who helps her young son (initially played by Hugh O'Connor, then Day Lewis) not only survive but triumph beyond his debilitating handicap. Fricker, best known for her work in a British TV serial, was remarkable in the role. One of the film's great moments came when young Christy, written off by many as akin to a dumb animal, slowly picked up a piece of chalk with his left foot, the only part of his body he was able to control, then determinedly scrawled the letter A, then his first word, "mother."*

Best Supporting Actor: Denzel Washington *as Private Trip in* Glory *(Freddie Fields/ TriStar; directed by Edward Zwick). Set during the Civil War,* Glory *was an eloquent epic about the real-life Col. Robert Gould Shaw (played by Matthew Broderick), who was a white soldier still wet behind the ears put in charge of training the country's first black military regiment, the six-hundred-man 54th Massachusetts Voluntary Infantry. Extremely rich in photographic detail and characterizations, the film had a strong supporting cast, with Washington particularly memorable as a hostile runaway slave who becomes a proud but unbending soldier as well as Broderick's primary adviser. Besides winning him an Oscar,* Glory *also provided Washington's breakthrough role, immediately after which he went to starring roles and international recognition.*

Nominations 1989

Best Director: Oliver Stone *for* Born on the Fourth of July *(Universal; produced by A. Kitman Ho and Oliver Stone). Three years after* Platoon, *Oliver Stone again turned to the Vietnam War for a lengthy (144 minutes), passionate antiwar statement; again he won an Oscar for the result. Very much a Stone project (besides directing, he co-wrote the script with Ron Kovic and co-produced),* Born *was based on Kovic's own real-life journey from willing combatant in the controversial Vietnam fight to passionate, wheelchair-bound activist. Tom Cruise played Kovic; the supporting cast included Willem Dafoe; and the final film stirred talk, both pro and con, not unusual in a Stone endeavor. But even those who had complaints about the film itself did not complain about Cruise's performance or deny that Stone was a master at putting his unique stamp on a movie.*

PICTURE
BORN ON THE FOURTH OF JULY, A. Kitman Ho & Ixtlan, Universal. Produced by A. Kitman Ho and Oliver Stone.
DEAD POETS SOCIETY, Touchstone Pictures with Silver Screen Partners IV, Buena Vista. Produced by Steven Haft, Paul Junger Witt and Tony Thomas.
* **DRIVING MISS DAISY,** Zanuck Company, Warner Bros. Produced by Richard D. Zanuck and Lili Fini Zanuck.
FIELD OF DREAMS, Gordon Company, Universal. Produced by Lawrence Gordon and Charles Gordon.
MY LEFT FOOT, Ferndale/Granada, Miramax. Produced by Noel Pearson.

ACTOR
KENNETH BRANAGH in *Henry V,* Renaissance Films with BBC, Samuel Goldwyn Company.
TOM CRUISE in *Born on the Fourth of July,* A. Kitman Ho & Ixtlan, Universal.
* **DANIEL DAY LEWIS** in *My Left Foot,* Ferndale/Granada, Miramax.
MORGAN FREEMAN in *Driving Miss Daisy,* Zanuck Company, Warner Bros.
ROBIN WILLIAMS in *Dead Poets Society,* Touchstone Pictures with Silver Screen Partners IV, Buena Vista.

ACTRESS
ISABELLE ADJANI in *Camille Claudel,* Films Christian Fechner-Lilith Films-Gaumont-A2 TV France-Films A2-DD, Orion Classics.
PAULINE COLLINS in *Shirley Valentine,* Lewis Gilbert/Willy Russell, Paramount.
JESSICA LANGE in *Music Box,* Carolco, Tri-Star.
MICHELLE PFEIFFER in *The Fabulous Baker Boys,* Gladden Entertainment, Mirage, 20th Century Fox.
* **JESSICA TANDY** in *Driving Miss Daisy,* Zanuck Company, Warner Bros.

SUPPORTING ACTOR
DANNY AIELLO in *Do the Right Thing,* Forty Acres and a Mule Filmworks, Universal.
DAN AYKROYD in *Driving Miss Daisy,* Zanuck Company, Warner Bros.
MARLON BRANDO in *A Dry White Season,* Paula Weinstein, M-G-M.
MARTIN LANDAU in *Crimes and Misdemeanors,* Jack Rollins and Charles H. Joffe, Orion.
* **DENZEL WASHINGTON** in *Glory,* Tri-Star.

SUPPORTING ACTRESS
* **BRENDA FRICKER** in *My Left Foot,* Ferndale /Granada, Miramax.
ANJELICA HUSTON in *Enemies, a Love Story,* Morgan Creek, 20th Century Fox.
LENA OLIN in *Enemies, a Love Story,* a Morgan Creek, 20th Century Fox.
JULIA ROBERTS in *Steel Magnolias,* Rastar Production, Tri-Star.
DIANNE WEIST in *Parenthood,* Imagine Entertainment, Universal.

DIRECTING
* **BORN ON THE FOURTH OF JULY,** A. Kitman Ho & Ixlan, Universal. Oliver Stone.
CRIMES AND MISDEMEANORS. Jack Rollins and Charles H. Joffe, Orion. Woody Allen.
DEAD POETS SOCIETY, Touchstone Pictures with Silver Screen Partners IV, Buena Vista. Peter Weir.
HENRY V, Renaissance Films with BBC, Samuel Goldwyn Company. Kenneth Branagh.
MY LEFT FOOT, Ferndale/Granada, Miramax. Jim Sheridan.

WRITING
(Screenplay Written Directly for the Screen)
CRIMES AND MISDEMEANORS, Jack Rollins and Charles H. Joffe, Orion. Woody Allen.
* **DEAD POETS SOCIETY,** Touchstone with Silver Screen Partners IV, Buena Vista. Tom Schulman.
DO THE RIGHT THING, Forty Acres and a Mule Filmworks, Universal. Spike Lee.
SEX, LIES, AND VIDEOTAPE, Outlaw , Miramax. Steven Soderbergh.
WHEN HARRY MET SALLY..., Castle Rock, Columbia. Nora Ephron.

(Screenplay Based on Material from Another Medium)
BORN ON THE FOURTH OF JULY, A. Kitman Ho & Ixtlan, Universal. Oliver Stone and Ron Kovic.
* **DRIVING MISS DAISY,** Zanuck Company, Warner Bros. Alfred Uhry.
ENEMIES, A LOVE STORY, Morgan Creek, 20th Century Fox. Roger L. Simon and Paul Mazursky.
FIELD OF DREAMS, Gordon Company, Universal. Phil Alden Robinson.
MY LEFT FOOT, Ferndale/Granada, Miramax. Jim Sheridan and Shane Connaughton.

CINEMATOGAPHY
THE ABYSS, 20th Century Fox. Mikael Salomon.
BLAZE, Touchtone with Silver Screen Partners IV, Buena Vista. Haskell Wexler.
BORN ON THE FOURTH OF JULY, A. Kitman Ho & Ixtlan, Universal. Robert Richardson.
THE FABULOUS BAKER BOYS, Gladden Entertainment, Mirage, 20th Century Fox. Michael Ballhaus.
* **GLORY,** Tri-Star Pictures, Tri-Star, Freddie Francis.

ART DIRECTION-SET DECORATION
THE ABYSS, 20th Century Fox. Leslie Dilley; Anne Kuljian.
THE ADVENTURES OF BARON MUNCHAUSEN, Prominent Features & Laura Film, Columbia. Dante Feretti; Francesca Lo Schiavo.
* **BATMAN,** Warner Bros. Anton Furst; Peter Young.
DRIVING MISS DAISY, Zanuck Company, Warner Bros. Bruno Rubeo; Crispian Sallis.
GLORY, Tri-Star Pictures, Tri-Star. Norman Garwood; Garret Lewis.

COSTUME DESIGN
THE ADVENTURES OF BARON MUNCHAUSEN, Prominent Features & Laura Film, Columbia. Gabriella Pescucci.
DRIVING MISS DAISY, Zanuck, Warner Bros. Elizabeth McBride.
HARLEM NIGHTS, Eddie Murphy, Paramount. Joe I. Tompkins.
* **HENRY V,** Renaissance Films with BBC, Samuel Goldwyn Company. Phyllis Dalton.
VALMONT, Claude Berri and Renn, Orion. Theodor Pistek.

SOUND
THE ABYSS, 20th Century Fox. Don Bassman, Kevin F. Cleary, Richard Overton and Lee Orloff.
BLACK RAIN, Jaffe/Lansing with Michael Douglas, Paramount. Donald O. Mitchell, Kevin O'Connell, Greg P. Russell and Keith A. Wester.
BORN ON THE FOURTH OF JULY, A. Kitman Ho & Ixtlan, Universal. Michael Minkler, Gregory H. Watkins, Wylie Stateman and Tod A. Maitland.
* **GLORY,** Tri-Star. Donald O. Mitchell, Gregg C. Rudloff, Elliot Tyson and Russell Williams II.
INDIANA JONES AND THE LAST CRUSADE, Lucasfilm, Paramount. Ben Burtt, Gary Summers, Shawn Murphy and Tony Dawe.

FILM EDITING
THE BEAR, Renn, Tri-Star. Noelle Boisson.
* **BORN ON THE FOURTH OF JULY,** A. Kitman Ho & Ixtlan, Universal. David Brenner and Joe Hutshing.
DRIVING MISS DAISY, Zanuck Company Production, Warner Bros. Mark Warner.
THE FABULOUS BAKER BOYS, Gladden Entertainment, Mirage, 20th Century Fox. William Steinkamp.
GLORY, Tri-Star. Steven Rosenblum.

SOUND EFFECTS EDITING
BLACK RAIN, Jaffe/Lansing with Michael Douglas, Paramount. Milton C. Burrow and William L. Manger.
* **INDIANA JONES AND THE LAST CRUSADE,** Lucasfilm, Paramount. Ben Burtt and Richard Hymns.
LETHAL WEAPON 2, Warner Bros. Robert Henderson and Alan Robert Murray.

Best Foreign Language Film: Cinema Paradiso *from Italy. Amazingly, it was not a success in its own country; Cinema Paradiso, in fact, was a dud at the box office in Italy, even when it was brought back for a second try after winning wide acceptance (and an Oscar) elsewhere. Outside the Boot, however,* *writer-director Giuseppe Tornatore's valentine to the movie business was universally embraced; even those who normally avoided any movie carrying even the hint of a subtitle loved Cinema Paradiso. It centered on the effects of a movie theater in a small Sicilian village on the life of a lad who grows from being* *the theater mascot (played by Salvatore Cascio; above, with Philippe Noiret) to the movie house's young projectionist (Marco Leonardi), and finally to a successful film director (Jacques Perrin) in Rome.*

VISUAL EFFECTS
* **THE ABYSS**, 20th Century Fox. John Bruno, Dennis Muren, Hoyt Yeatman and Dennis Skotak.
  THE ADVENTURES OF BARON MUNCHAUSEN, Prominent Features & Laura Film, Columbia. Richard Conway and Kent Houston.
  BACK TO THE FUTURE PART II, Universal Pictures/Amblin Entertainment, Universal. Ken Ralston, Michael Lantieri, John Bell and Steve Gawley.

MUSIC
(Song)
  AFTER ALL (*Chances Are*, Tri-Star); Music by Tom Snow. Lyrics by Dean Pitchford.
  THE GIRL WHO USED TO BE ME (*Shirley Valentine*, Lewis Gilbert/ Willy Russell , Paramount); Music by Marvin Hamlisch. Lyrics by Alan and Marilyn Bergman.
  I LOVE TO SEE YOU SMILE (*Parenthood*, Imagine Entertainment, Universal); Music and lyrics by Randy Newman.
  KISS THE GIRL (*The Little Mermaid*, Walt Disney Pictures with Silver Screen Partners IV, Buena Vista); Music by Alan Menken. Lyrics by Howard Ashman.
* **UNDER THE SEA** (*The Little Mermaid*, Walt Disney Pictures with Silver Screen Partners IV, Buena Vista); Music by Alan Menken. Lyrics by Howard Ashman.

(Original Score)
  BORN ON THE FOURTH OF JULY, A. Kitman Ho & Ixtlan, Universal. John Williams.
  THE FABULOUS BAKER BOYS, Gladden Entertainment, Mirage, 20th Century Fox. David Grusin.
  FIELD OF DREAMS, Gordon Company, Universal. James Horner.
  INDIANA JONES AND THE LAST CRUSADE, Lucasfilm, Paramount. John Williams.
* **THE LITTLE MERMAID**, Walt Disney Pictures with Silver Screen Partners IV, Buena Vista. Alan Menken.

MAKEUP
  THE ADVENTURES OF BARON MUNCHAUSEN, Prominent Features & Laura Film, Columbia. Maggie Weston and Fabrizio Sforza.
  DAD, Universal Pictures/Amblin Entertainment, Universal. Dick Smith, Ken Diaz and Greg Nelson.
* **DRIVING MISS DAISY**, Zanuck Company, Warner Bros. Manlio Rocchetti, Lynn Barber and Kevin Haney.

SHORT FILMS
(Animated Films)
* **BALANCE**, a Lauenstein Production. Christoph Lauenstein and Wolfgang Lauenstein.
  THE COW, The "Pilot" Co-op Animated Film Studio with VPTO Videofilm. Alexander Petrov.
  THE HILL FARM, National Film & Television School. Mark Baker.

(Live Action)
  AMAZON DIARY, Determined Production, Inc. Robert Nixon.
  THE CHILDEATER, Stephen-Tammuz Productions, Ltd. Jonathan Tammuz.
* **WORK EXPERIENCE**, North Inch Production, Ltd. James Hendrie.

DOCUMENTARY
(Short Subjects)
  FINE FOOD, FINE PASTRIES, OPEN 6 TO 9, a production of David Petersen Productions. David Petersen, producer.
* **THE JOHNSTOWN FLOOD**, a production of Guggenheim Production, Inc. Charles Guggenheim, producer.
  YAD VASHEM: PRESERVING THE PAST TO ENSURE THE FUTURE, a Ray Errol Fox Production. Ray Errol Fox, producer.

(Features)
  ADAM CLAYTON POWELL, a production of RKB Productions. Richard Killberg and Yvonne Smith, producers.
* **COMMON THREADS: STORIES FROM THE QUILT**, a Telling Pictures and The Couturie Company Production. Robert Epstein and Bill Couturie, producers.
  CRACK USA: COUNTY UNDER SIEGE, a production of Half-Court Productions, Ltd. Vince DiPersio and William Guttentag, producers.
  FOR ALL MANKIND, a production of Apollo Associates/FAM Productions Inc. Al Reinert and Betsy Broyles Breier, producers.
  SUPER CHIEF: THE LIFE AND LEGACY OF EARL WARREN, a Quest Production. Judith Leonard and Bill Jersey, producers.

FOREIGN LANGUAGE FILMS
  CAMILLE CLAUDEL (France)
* **CINEMA PARADISO** (Italy)
  JESUS OF MONTREAL (Canada)
  WALTZING REGITZE (Denmark)
  WHAT HAPPENED TO SANTIAGO (Puerto Rico)

HONORARY AND OTHER AWARDS
  TO **AKIRA KUROSAWA**, for accomplishments that have inspired, delighted, enriched and entertained audiences and influenced filmmakers throughout the world.

  The Academy of Motion Picture Arts and Sciences' Board of Governors commends the contributions of the members of the **ENGINEERING COMMITTEES OF THE SOCIETY OF MOTION PICTURE AND TELEVISION ENGINEERS** (SMPTE). By establishing industry standards, they have greatly contributed to making film a primary form of international communication (Special Commendation)

Honorary Oscar *to* **Akira Kurosawa**. *George Lucas and Steven Spielberg presented the award "To Akira Kurosawa for accomplishments that have inspired, delighted, enriched and entertained audiences and influenced filmmakers throughout the world."*

SPECIAL ACHIEVEMENT AWARD
None given this year.

1989 IRVING G. THALBERG MEMORIAL AWARD
None given this year.

1989 JEAN HERSHOLT HUMANITARIAN AWARD
TO HOWARD W. KOCH

1989 GORDON E. SAWYER AWARD
TO PIERRE ANGENIEUX

SCIENTIFIC OR TECHNICAL AWARDS
Academy Award of Merit (Statuette)
  None.
Scientific and Engineering Award (Academy Plaque)
  JAMES KETCHUM of JSK Engineering, for the excellence in engineering and the broad adaptability of the SDA521B Advance/Retard system for magnetic film sound dubbing.
  J. NOXON LEAVITT, for the invention of, and **ISTEC, INCORPORATED**, for the Continuing development of the Wescam Stabilized Camera System.
  GEOFFREY H. WILLIAMSON of Wilcam Photo Research, Incorporated, for the design and development, and to **ROBERT D. AUGUSTE** for the electronic design and development of the Wilcam W-7 200 frames-per-second VistaVision Rotating Mirror Reflex Camera.
  J.L. FISHER of J.L. Fisher, Incorporated, for the design and manufacture of a small, mobile motion picture camera platform known as the Fisher Model Ten Dolly.
  KLAUS RESCH for the design, **ERICH FITZ** and **FGV SCHMIDLE & FITZ** for the development of the Super Panther MS-180 Camera Dolly.

Technical Achievement Award (Academy Certificate)
  DR. LEO CATOZZO for the design and development of the CIR-Catozzo Self-Perforating Adhesive Tape Film Splicer.
  MAGNA-TECH ELECTRONIC COMPANY for the introduction of the first remotely controlled Advance/Retard function for magnetic film sound dubbing.

*INDICATES WINNER

303

I t was the year of Kevin Costner. A first-time director, Costner had managed against all odds to turn some unlikely subject matter into an epic film that was praised by critics and loved by all kinds of movie audiences, both cornbelt and sophisticate. On March 25, 1991, Oscar concurred. With twelve Oscar nominations to its credit, *Dances With Wolves* captured seven final prizes, including the Big One as best picture of the year. It was clearly a sweep, more than double the number of awards given the two closest runners-up, *Dick Tracy* (three awards) and *Ghost* (two awards).

Two of the seven Oscars won by *Dances* went to Costner himself, as co-producer of the year's best film and as best director; his grand adventure also won trophies for adapted screenplay, cinematography, editing, original score, and sound. Costner was also nominated for best actor for the film but, in one of his few reversals of fortune of the night, saw the Oscar in that category go to Jeremy Irons for a film called *Reversal of Fortune*.

Kathy Bates in *Misery* was named best actress. Joe Pesci of *Good Fellas*, who won as best supporting actor, delivered one of the shortest Oscar acceptance speeches on record, six words in all: "It was my privilege. Thank you," he said, then exited. In an extremely popular win, Whoopi Goldberg was named best supporting actress for *Ghost*. Visibly moved, she enthusiastically exclaimed, "Ever since I was a little kid, I wanted this!"

The biggest upset of the evening was the best foreign language film win by the Swiss-made *Journey of Hope*; most soothsayers had figured the prize would go, in an easy race, to France's *Cyrano de Bergerac*, which had also earned a best actor nomination for Gerard Depardieu. *Cyrano* had to be content with a single win, for best costume design.

By far the most sentimental moments of the night came when two special honorary awards were handed to two legendary leading ladies. Long-time favorite Myrna Loy received her Oscar during a live satellite hookup from her New York apartment; Sophia Loren was in person at the Shrine Auditorium, and she tearfully accepted hers. When she briefly mentioned her husband, Carlo Ponti, during her thank-you remarks, he stood for a bow. It was the first time within memory that the recipient of an Oscar recipient's thanks had gone so far as to take the spotlight for himself, however briefly. It delighted the audience.

Richard Zanuck and David Brown, former producing partners, were presented the Irving G. Thalberg Award for excellence in production, and among those performing the year's nominated songs were Jon Bon Jovi, Harry Connick, Jr., Reba McEntire,

304

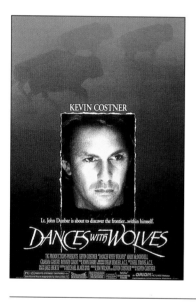

Best Picture: Dances With Wolves *(Orion; produced by Jim Wilson and Kevin Costner) and* Best Director: Kevin Costner *for* Dances With Wolves. *Early on they were calling it "Kevin's Gate," a negative reference to Michael Cimino's over-long, over-budget, and ultimately unsuccessful western epic,* Heaven's Gate. *But Kevin Costner had the last laugh. True, he'd never directed a film before, but he felt keenly enough about the potential of* Dances With Wolves *that he even helped finance the $18 million project with his own money when* Wolves *began slipping over budget during its seventeen-week shoot in South Dakota. More ominous, his final cut ran 183 minutes even after considerable footage had been slashed away. Considered a further liability was the fact that much of the dialogue was spoken in the Lakota language, accompanied by English subtitles. But both Costner and* Dances *ultimately triumphed: the final film was proclaimed a magnificent piece of work, with both critics and ticket buyers embracing it. Immeasurably aided by the spectacular cinematography of Dean Semler and by Costner's own fresh directorial style,* Dances *was a sweeping, warm-blooded tale of a white man's heroic adventure among the Sioux Indians on the Dakota plains, circa the late 1860s. Besides being the driving force behind the film as both director and co-producer, Costner also played the lead, a Union officer in the Civil War who ultimately chooses to live in the far reaches of the American frontier "because I want to see it before it disappears." Although his name is John Dunbar, the Sioux eventually rename him "Dances With Wolves."*

nd Madonna, the latter offering a Marilyn Monroe imitation as she performed Stephen Sondheim's "Sooner or Later" from the movie *Dick Tracy*. The song went on to win Sondheim his first Oscar; Madonna caused a pre-and-post-show buzz by attending on the arm of Michael Jackson.

The theme of the telecast, produced by Gilbert Cates, was "100 Years at the Movies." For the second year in a row, Billy Crystal was the evening's inspired MC; in a puckishly shameless plug for his own upcoming release, *City Slickers*, Crystal made his initial entrance on stage via horseback.

Outside the Shrine, it was far from fun and games. Earlier in the day, rain had fallen over California in heavy doses, soaking Los Angeles, drenching the forecourt of the giant auditorium, and sending TV newsmen scurrying to wrap their cameras in nylon jackets while Academy workmen quickly tented the forecourt area with plastic covers. By show time, the rain had ceased but the dampness remained.

And, in a sign of the times, so did a need for unprecedented security measures. Because of a complicated international political climate and security hangovers from the Persian Gulf War, everyone who entered the Shrine had to be checked through metal detectors, with all handbags and packages searched. It slowed entrances considerably and added a definite jolt of reality to a night honoring make-believe.

Best Actress: Kathy Bates *as Annie Wilkes in* Misery *(Columbia; directed by Rob Reiner). Based on a tale by Stephen King,* Misery *used the often awkward relationship between a celebrity and an obsessive fan as the basis for a shiveringly good spooker. In King's story, screenwritten by William Goldman, a popular novelist (James Caan) is injured in a car wreck on an isolated Colorado mountain road, then finds himself the virtual prisoner of a plump, mousy woman played by Bates. Claiming to be the writer's "No. 1 fan," she turns out to be a Jekyll-Hyde psychopath, not above breaking the writer's legs to keep him in her power. It was a no-holds-barred role in a year not rampant with important parts for women; under Rob Reiner's superb direction, Bates became a first-time Oscar nominee and soon after was named the year's best actress.*

Best Actor: Jeremy Irons *as Claus von Bulow in* Reversal of Fortune *(Warner Bros.; directed by Barbet Schroeder). The very real Claus von Bulow story had all the elements of great movie fiction: In March 1982, von Bulow, a European aristocrat, was found guilty of attempting to murder his wife Sunny, a wealthy socialite, by means of insulin injections. Later, New York lawyer Alan Dershowitz was hired to appeal the conviction. In its chilling screen translation, Glenn Close (above, with a pet*

tiger cub and Irons) played the ill-fated Sunny, Ron Silver was Dershowitz, and, most flawlessly, Irons played the cool, calculating von Bulow, a cad whose public image was determined as much by his imperious, cold personality as by his ultimate guilt or innocence. At one point Dershowitz/Silver says to von Bulow/Irons: "You're a strange guy, Claus." Replies the man, with a sardonic smile, "You have no idea."

Best Supporting Actor: Joe Pesci *as Tommy DeVito in* Good Fellas *(Warner Bros.; directed by Martin Scorsese). One of the most chilling indictments yet of mob manners and Mafia matters, Martin Scorsese used Nicholas Pileggi's best-seller,* Wiseguy, *as the basis for* Good Fellas; *he was forced to drop the book's title for the film version in order to avoid confusion with a concurrent TV series that bore no other relation to the Scorsese project. Scorsese's thunderbolt was in a class quite its own, filled with alarming characters, played with bravado by an ace cast including Robert DeNiro, Ray Liotta, Lorraine Bracco, and Paul Sorvino. None, however, shined brighter than Joe Pesci as a pint-sized, cold-blooded psycho-mobster with a short fuse. If* Good Fellas *was chilling, it was Pesci who gave the film its ice and icing: at Oscar time he was resoundingly remembered, and rewarded.*

305

Myrna Loy *was a curious Academy statistic: Although she had starred in two films selected as best pictures (1936's* The Great Ziegfeld, *1946's* The Best Years of Our Lives*) and had delivered unique, outstanding performances during six decades, she'd never been nominated for an Oscar, an oversight that confused everyone. At the age of 85, she was finally voted a special statuette "in recognition of her extraordinary qualities both on screen and off, and with appreciation for a lifetime's worth of indelible performances." In frail health and unable to attend the ceremonies in Hollywood, Loy accepted her Oscar via a satellite hookup from her apartment in New York City. "You've made me very happy. Thank you very much," she said as she held the elusive award that finally, and deservedly, had come her way.*

Best Supporting Actress: Whoopi Goldberg *as Oda Mae Brown (above, with Demi Moore) in* Ghost *(Paramount; directed by Jerry Zucker). It was a role Goldberg begged to play, even after she'd been told it was targeted to go in another direction altogether. It was a case where tenacity paid off: as Oda Mae, a bogus medium who gets unwittingly intertwined with real ghosts, Goldberg incorporated her own unique* Whoopiness into an amusing role for a perfect fit, one that u her an Academy Award and a new level of popularity u audiences. Ghost *itself turned out to be a genuine sleeper, a of the biggest Hollywood had had in years, and did much advance many careers, including those of her co-stars Moc Patrick Swayze, and newcomer Tony Goldwyn.*

PICTURE

AWAKENINGS, Columbia. Produced by Walter F. Parkes and Lawrence Lasker.
* **DANCES WITH WOLVES,** Tig, Orion. Produced by Jim Wilson and Kevin Costner.
GHOST, Howard W. Koch, Paramount. Produced by Lisa Weinstein.
THE GODFATHER, PART III, Zoetrope Studios, Paramount. Produced by Francis Ford Coppola.
GOOD FELLAS, Warner Bros. Produced by Irwin Winkler.

ACTOR

KEVIN COSTNER in *Dances With Wolves*, Tig, Orion.
ROBERT DE NIRO in *Awakenings*, Columbia.
GERARD DEPARDIEU in *Cyrano de Bergerac*, Hachette Premiere/Camera One, Orion Classics.
RICHARD HARRIS in *The Field*, Granada, Avenue Pictures.
* **JEREMY IRONS** in *Reversal of Fortune*, Reversal Films, Warner Bros.

ACTRESS

* **KATHY BATES** in *Misery*, Castle Rock Entertainment, Columbia.
ANJELICA HUSTON in *The Grifters*, Martin Scorsese, Miramax.
JULIA ROBERTS in *Pretty Woman*, Touchstone Pictures, Buena Vista.
MERYL STREEP in *Postcards from the Edge*, Columbia.
JOANNE WOODWARD in *Mr. & Mrs. Bridge*, Merchant Ivory, Miramax.

SUPPORTING ACTOR

BRUCE DAVISON in *Longtime Companion*, American Playhouse, Samuel Goldwyn Company.
ANDY GARCIA in *The Godfather, Part III*, Zoetrope Studios, Paramount.
GRAHAM GREENE in *Dances With Wolves*, Tig, Orion.
AL PACINO in *Dick Tracy*, Touchstone Pictures, Buena Vista.
* **JOE PESCI** in *Good Fellas*, Warner Bros.

SUPPORTING ACTRESS

ANNETTE BENING in *The Grifters*, Martin Scorsese, Miramax.
LORRAINE BRACCO in *Good Fellas*, Warner Bros.
* **WHOOPI GOLDBERG** in *Ghost*, Howard W. Koch, Paramount.
DIANE LADD in *Wild at Heart*, Polygram/Propaganda Films, Samuel Goldwyn Company.
MARY McDONNELL in *Dances With Wolves*, Tig, Orion.

DIRECTING

*DANCES WITH WOLVES, Tig, Orion. Kevin Costner.
THE GODFATHER, PART III, Zoetrope Studios, Paramount. Francis Ford Coppola.
GOOD FELLAS, Warner Bros. Martin Scorsese.
THE GRIFTERS, Martin Scorsese, Miramax. Stephen Frears.
REVERSAL OF FORTUNE, Reversal Films, Warner Bros. Barbet Schroeder.

WRITING

(Screenplay Written Directly for the Screen)
ALICE, Jack Rollins and Charles H. Joffe, Orion. Woody Allen.
AVALON, Tri-Star. Barry Levinson.
* **GHOST,** Howard W. Koch, Paramount. Bruce Joel Rubin.
GREEN CARD, Green Card Company, Buena Vista. Peter Weir.
METROPOLITAN, Westerly Film-Video, New Line. Whit Stillman.

(Screenplay Based on Material from Another Medium)
AWAKENINGS, Columbia. Steven Zaillian.
* **DANCES WITH WOLVES,** Tig, Orion. Michael Blake.
GOOD FELLAS, Warner Bros. Nicholas Pileggi and Martin Scorsese.
THE GRIFTERS, Martin Scorsese, Miramax. Donald E. Westlake.
REVERSAL OF FORTUNE, Reversal Films, Warner Bros. Nicholas Kazan.

CINEMATOGRAPHY

AVALON, Tri-Star, Tri-Star. Allen Daviau.
* **DANCES WITH WOLVES,** Tig, Orion. Dean Semler.
DICK TRACY, Touchstone Pictures, Buena Vista. Vittorio Storaro.
THE GODFATHER, PART III, Zoetrope Studios, Paramount. Gordon Willis.
HENRY & JUNE, Walrus & Associates, Universal. Philippe Rousselot.

ART DIRECTION-SET DECORATION

CYRANO DE BERGERAC, Hachette Premiere/Camera One, Orion Classics. Ezio Frigerio; Jacques Rouxel.
DANCES WITH WOLVES, Tig, Orion. Jeffrey Beecroft; Lisa Dean.
* **DICK TRACY,** Touchstone Pictures, Buena Vista. Richard Sylbert; Rick Simpson.
THE GODFATHER, PART III, Zoetrope Studios, Paramount. Dean Tavoularis; Gary Fettis.
HAMLET, Icon, Warner Bros. Dante Ferretti; Francesca Lo Schiavo.

COSTUME DESIGN

AVALON, Tri-Star. Gloria Gresham.
* **CYRANO DE BERGERAC,** Hachette Premiere/Camera One, Orion Classics. Franca Squarciapino.
DANCES WITH WOLVES, Tig, Orion. Elsa Zamparelli.
DICK TRACY, Touchstone Pictures, Buena Vista. Milena Canonero.
HAMLET, Icon, Warner Bros. Maurizio Millenotti.

SOUND
* **DANCES WITH WOLVES,** Tig, Orion. Jeffrey Perkins, Bill W. Benton, Greg Watkins and Russell Williams II.
DAYS OF THUNDER, Don Simpson and Jerry Bruckheimer, Paramount. Donald O. Mitchell, Rick Kline, Kevin O'Connell and Charles Wilborn.
DICK TRACY, Touchstone Pictures, Buena Vista. Chris Jenkins, David E. Campbell, D.M. Hemphill and Thomas Causey.
THE HUNT FOR RED OCTOBER, Mace Neufeld/Jerry Sherlock, Paramount. Don Bassman, Richard Overton, Kevin F. Cleary and Richard Bryce Goodman.
TOTAL RECALL, Carolco Pictures, Tri-Star. Michael J. Kohut, Carlos de Larios, Aaron Rochin and Nelson Stoll.

FILM EDITING
* **DANCES WITH WOLVES,** Tig, Orion. Neil Travis.
GHOST, Howard W. Koch, Paramount. Walter Murch.
THE GODFATHER, PART III, Zoetrope Studios, Paramount. Barry Malkin, Lisa Fruchtman and Walter Murch.
GOOD FELLAS, Warner Bros. Thelma Schoonmaker.
THE HUNT FOR RED OCTOBER, Mace Neufeld/Jerry Sherlock, Paramount. Dennis Virkler and John Wright.

SOUND EFFECTS EDITING
FLATLINERS, Stonebridge Entertainment Production, Columbia. Charles L. Campbell and Richard Franklin.
* **THE HUNT FOR RED OCTOBER,** Mace Neufeld/Jerry Sherlock, Paramount. Cecelia Hall and George Watters II.
TOTAL RECALL, Carolco Pictures, Tri-Star. Stephen H. Flick.

MUSIC
(Song)
BLAZE OF GLORY (*Young Guns II*, Morgan Creek, 20th Century Fox); Music and Lyrics by Jon Bon Jovi.
I'M CHECKIN' OUT, in (*Postcards from the Edge*, Columbia); Music and Lyrics by Shel Silverstein.
PROMISE ME YOU'LL REMEMBER (*The Godfather, Part III,* Zoetrope Studios, Paramount); Music by Carmine Coppola. Lyrics by John Bettis.
SOMEWHERE IN MY MEMORY (*Home Alone,* 20th Century Fox); Music by John Williams. Lyrics by Leslie Bricusse.
* **SOONER OR LATER (I ALWAYS GET MY MAN)** (*Dick Tracy,* Touchstone Pictures, Buena Vista); Music and Lyrics by Stephen Sondheim.

(Original Score)
AVALON, Tri-Star. Randy Newman.
* **DANCES WITH WOLVES,** Tig, Orion. John Barry.
GHOST, Howard W. Koch, Paramount. Maurice Jarre.
HAVANA, Universal Pictures Limited, Universal. David Grusin.
HOME ALONE, 20th Century Fox. John Williams.

MAKEUP
CYRANO DE BERGERAC, Hachette Premiere/Camera One, Orion Classics. Michele Burke and Jean-Pierre Eychenne.
* **DICK TRACY,** Touchstone Pictures, Buena Vista. John Caglione, Jr. and Doug Drexler.
EDWARD SCISSORHANDS, 20th Century Fox. Ve Neill and Stan Winston.

SHORT FILMS
(Animated)
* **CREATURE COMFORTS,** an Aardman Animations Limited Production. Nick Park, producer.
A GRAND DAY OUT, a National Film and Television School Production. Nick Park, producer.
GRASSHOPPERS (CAVALLETTE), a Bruno Bozzetto Production. Bruno Bozzetto, producer.

(Live Action)
BRONX CHEERS, an American Film Institute Production. Raymond De Felitta and Matthew Gross, producers.
DEAR ROSIE, a World's End Production. Peter Cattaneo and Barnaby Thompson, producers.
* **THE LUNCH DATE,** an Adam Davidson Production. Adam Davidson, producer.
SENZENI NA? (WHAT HAVE WE DONE?), an American Film Institute Production. Bernard Joffa and Anthony E. Nicholas, producers.
12:01 PM, a Chanticleer Films Production. Hilary Ripps and Jonathan Heap, producers.

DOCUMENTARY
(Short Subjects)
BURNING DOWN TOMORROW, an Interscope Communications, Inc. Production. Kit Thomas, producer.
CHIMPS: SO LIKE US, a Simon & Goodman Picture Company Production. Karen Goodman and Kirk Simon, producers.
* **DAYS OF WAITING,** a Mouchette Films Production. Steven Okazaki, producer.
JOURNEY INTO LIFE: THE WORLD OF THE UNBORN, an ABC/Kane Productions International, Inc. Production. Derek Bromhall, producer.
ROSE KENNEDY: A LIFE TO REMEMBER, a production of Sanders & Mock Productions and American Film Foundation. Freida Lee Mock and Terry Sanders, producers.

Dick Tracy won three Academy Awards, making it the year's most Oscared film after Dances With Wolves. The Tracy prizes came for its art direction/set decoration by Richard Sylbert and Rick Simpson, its makeup by John Caglione, Jr., and John Drexler, and the original song "Sooner or Later (I Always Get My Man)" with music and lyrics by Broadway's master music man Stephen Sondheim, who had never before been an Oscar nominee or winner.

(Features)
* **AMERICAN DREAM,** a Cabin Creek Films Production. Barbara Kopple and Arthur Cohn, producers.
BERKELEY IN THE SIXTIES, a production of Berkeley in the Sixties Production Partnership. Mark Kitchell, producer.
BUILDING BOMBS, a Mori/Robinson Production. Mark Mori and Susan Robinson, producers.
FOREVER ACTIVISTS: STORIES FROM THE VETERANS OF THE ABRAHAM LINCOLN BRIGADE, a Judith Montell Production. Judith Montell, producer.
WALDO SALT: A SCREENWRITER'S JOURNEY, a Waldo Productions, Inc. Production. Robert Hillmann and Eugene Corr, producers.

FOREIGN LANGUAGE FILM
CYRANO DE BERGERAC (France).
* **JOURNEY OF HOPE** (Switzerland).
JU DOU (People's Republic of China).
THE NASTY GIRL (Germany).
OPEN DOORS (Italy).

HONORARY AND OTHER AWARDS
TO SOPHIA LOREN, one of the genuine treasures of world cinema who, in a career rich with memorable performances, has added permanent luster to our art form.
TO MYRNA LOY, in recognition of her extraordinary qualities both on screen and off, with appreciation for a lifetime's worth of indelible performances.
TO RODERICK T. RYAN, DON TRUMBULL and **GEOFFREY H. WILLIAMSON,** in appreciation for outstanding service and dedication in upholding the high standards of the Academy of Motion Picture Arts and Sciences. (Medals of Commendation)

SPECIAL ACHIEVEMENT AWARDS
For Visual Effects: **ERIC BREVIG, ROB BOTTIN, TIM McGOVERN** and **ALEX FUNKE** for *Total Recall,* a Carolco Pictures Production, Tri-Star.

1990 IRVING G. THALBERG MEMORIAL AWARD
TO **RICHARD D. ZANUCK** and **DAVID BROWN**

1990 JEAN HERSHOLT HUMANITARIAN AWARD
None given this year.

1990 GORDON E. SAWYER AWARD
TO **STEFAN KUDELSKI**

SCIENTIFIC OR TECHNICAL AWARDS
Academy Award of Merit (Statuette)
EASTMAN KODAK COMPANY for the development of T-Grain technology and the introduction of EXR color negative films which utilize this technology.

Sceintific and Engineering Award (Academy Plaque)
BRUCE WILTON and **CARLOS ICINKOFF** of Mechanical Concepts, Incorporated, for the development of the Mechanical Concepts Optical Printer Platform.
ENGINEERING DEPARTMENT of ARNOLD & RICHTER for the continued design improvements of the Arriflex BL Camera System, culminating in the 35BL-4S model.
FUJI PHOTO FILM COMPANY, LIMITED, for the development and introduction of the F-Series of color negative films covering the range of film speeds from EI 64 to EI 500.
MANFRED G. MICHELSON of Technical Film Systems, Incorporated, for the design and development of the first sprocket-driven film transport system for color print film processors which permits transport speeds in excess of 600 feet per minute.
JOHN W. LANG, WALTER HRASTNIK and **CHARLES J. WATSON** of Bell and Howell Company for the development and manufacture of a modular continuous contact motion picture film printer.

Technical Achievement Award (Academy Certificate)
WILLIAM L. BLOWERS of Belco Associates, Incorporated, and **THOMAS F. DENOVE** for the development and manufacture of the Belco/Denove Cinemeter. This digital/analog exposure meter was specifically and uniquely designed for the cinematographer.
IAIN NEIL for optical design; **TAKUO MIYAGISHIMA** for the mechanical design; and **PANAVISION, INCORPORATED,** for the concept and development of the Primo Series of spherical prime lenses for 35mm cinematography.
CHRISTOPHER S. GILMAN and **HARVEY HUBERT, JR.,** of the Diligent Dwarves Effects Lab for the development of the Actor Climate System, consisting of heat-transferring undergarments.
JIM GRAVES of J&G Enterprises for the development of the Cool Suit System, consisting of heat-transferring undergarments.
BENJT O. ORHALL, KENNETH LUND, BJORN SELIN and **KJELL HOGBERG** of AB Film-Teknik for the development and manufacture of the Mark IV film subtitling processor, which has increased the speed, simplified the operation and improved the quality of subtitling.
RICHARD MULA and **PETE ROMANO** of HydroImage, Incorporated, for the development of the SeaPar 1200 watt HMI Underwater Lamp.
DEDO WEIGERT of Dedo Weigert Film GmbH for the development of the Dedolight, a miniature low-voltage tungsten-halogen lighting fixture.
DR. FRED KOLB, JR., and **PAUL PREO** for the concept and development of a 35mm projection test film.
PETER BALDWIN for the design; **DR. PAUL KIANKHOOY** and the Lightmaker Company for the development of the Lightmaker AC/DC HMI Ballast.
ALL-UNION CINEMA AND PHOTO RESEARCH INSTITUTE (NIKFI) for continuously improving and providing 3-D presentations to Soviet motion picture audiences for the last 25 years.

*INDICATES WINNER

The *Silence of the Lambs* devoured the competition at the sixty-fourth Academy Award festivities on March 30, 1992. The first psychological thriller to win the Academy's best picture prize, *Silence* also romped off with four other awards: best actor (Anthony Hopkins), best actress (Jodie Foster), best director (Jonathan Demme), and best adapted screenplay (Ted Tally), the first time a single film had won the Academy's top five awards since 1975's *One Flew over the Cuckoo's Nest.*

Silence bucked the conventional wisdom that says a film must open late in the calendar year to be a success at Oscar time. With a February 1991 release, the film had not only been in theaters for over a year by Oscar night, it also became the first best picture champ already released on video cassette at the time of its victory. The film's Oscar success additionally marked something of a bittersweet victory for Orion Pictures. It was the second year in a row Orion had made a film named by the Academy as the best of the year, following the company's 1990 bellringer *Dances With Wolves.* Yet despite the double Oscar whammy, the company was in bankruptcy, a victim of the foibles of the movie business of the 1990s.

It was the second Oscar in three years for Foster; she dedicated it "to all the women who came before me who never had the chances I've had." For Hopkins it was a personal first and the third time in three years that a British actor had copped Oscar's top male acting prize.

Oscar show host Billy Crystal also got caught up in the *Silence* mode: for his first entrance at the Dorothy Chandler Pavilion he was wheeled on stage strapped to a dolly, wearing a replica of the "Hannibal Lecter" mask Hopkins had worn in the film. (Quipped Crystal, "I look like the goalie from the SAG hockey team.")

Jack Palance also gave Crystal some juicy material to satirize. When the crusty Palance was named the best supporting actor for *City Slickers,* he took time between his thank yous to do some one-handed push-ups, his way of defending so-called dispensable older actors being bypassed for film work because of age. For the remainder of the telecast, Crystal kept ad-libbing good-natured but saucy references to Palance and his penchant for push-ups.

Mercedes Ruehl won the year's supporting actress prize for *The Fisher King.* Indian director Satyajit Ray, honored with a special Oscar for his thirty-six-year, thirty-film career, accepted his award from a hospital bed in Calcutta where he was being treated for a heart ailment. In a segment that had been pretaped at the hospital two weeks before Oscar night, Ray thanked all Hollywood filmmakers for the inspiration they had given him in pursuing his own career in India. A month later, on April 23, 1992, the great filmmaker was dead.

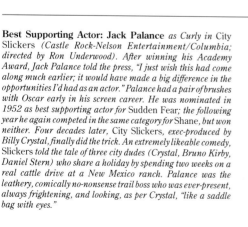

Best Supporting Actor: Jack Palance *as Curly in* City Slickers *(Castle Rock-Nelson Entertainment/Columbia; directed by Ron Underwood). After winning his Academy Award, Jack Palance told the press, "I just wish this had come along much earlier; it would have made a big difference in the opportunities I'd had as an actor." Palance had a pair of brushes with Oscar early in his screen career. He was nominated in 1952 as best supporting actor for* Sudden Fear; *the following year he again competed in the same category for* Shane, *but won neither. Four decades later,* City Slickers, *exec-produced by Billy Crystal, finally did the trick. An extremely likeable comedy,* Slickers *told the tale of three city dudes (Crystal, Bruno Kirby, Daniel Stern) who share a holiday by spending two weeks on a real cattle drive at a New Mexico ranch. Palance was the leathery, comically no-nonsense trail boss who was ever-present, always frightening, and looking, as per Crystal, "like a saddle bag with eyes."*

Alan Menken went home with two Academy Awards, as composer of the year's best original score and the best original song, both written for Disney's *Beauty and the Beast*. He had written the latter with lyricist Howard Ashman, who had died a year earlier; Ashman thus became the first victim of AIDS to receive an Academy Award posthumously. Robert Richardson, winning for his cinematography on *JFK*, became the first American cinematographer to win in that category in sixteen years, since Haskell Wexler's 1976 award for *Bound for Glory*.

Film pioneer Hal Roach, one hundred years of age, was given a standing ovation when introduced to the Dorothy Chandler audience and caught the show's director by surprise when he decided to deliver some impromptu remarks despite the absence of a microphone. Jumping in to save an awkward situation, Crystal commented to the crowd, which had heard nothing, "I think that's fitting, because Mr. Roach started in silent pictures."

Once again, Oscar was not without controversy. When the nominations had been announced on February 19, there were several roars of protest because Barbra Streisand's name was not among the nominees for best director; her direction of *The Prince of Tides* had earlier been put forward as one of the year's five best for the Director's Guild award, nomination for which was viewed by some as a forecast of the eventual five Academy nominees. Adding further fuel to this fire was the fact that *Tides* had been nominated as one of the Oscars' five best picture contenders. On Oscar night, those protests were subordinated to another, more vocal complaint. An estimated one thousand protesters chanted and carried signs outside the Dorothy Chandler Pavilion, some indignant about Streisand but many more suggesting that two of the year's most conspicuous films, *The Silence of the Lambs* and *JFK*, had portrayed gays in an unflattering light.

Best Picture: The Silence of the Lambs *(Orion).* **Best Director: Jonathan Demme, Best Actor: Anthony Hopkins** *(right) as Dr. Hannibal Lecter, and* **Best Actress: Jodie Foster** *(above) as Clarice Starling. It had happened only twice before in Academy history: in 1934* It Happened One Night *had won five top Academy Awards (for picture, actor, actress, direction, screenplay); it took 41 years and* One Flew Over the Cuckoo's Nest *in 1975 to equal that record. Sixteen years later, the harrowing film adaptation of Thomas Harris' novel did the same. Silence also became the first genuine psychological thriller to win Oscar's top prize. As in Harris' book, the story followed a young FBI recruit (Foster) as she enters the terrifying world of a serial killer named Dr. Hannibal Lecter (Hopkins), also known as "Hannibal the Cannibal" because of the way he disposed of his victims. In an era not known for a wealth of strong roles for women, Silence offered a multidimensional diving board for Foster's talents, and she came through with a radiant, riveting performance. Hopkins didn't have as much footage, but he nevertheless dominated the film as the chillingly hypnotic sociopath, the personification of unrepentant evil, brilliant enough to manage an escape from even the most heavily secured prison. It was, Hopkins said later, "so beautifully written it was easy to play." Silence marked the second screen appearance of Dr. Lecter: he was also a principal character, played by Brian Cox, in the 1986 film* Manhunter.

Best Supporting Actress: Mercedes Ruehl *as Anne Napolitano (right, with Robin Williams, Jeff Bridges, and Amanda Plummer) in* The Fisher King *(TriStar; directed by Terry Gilliam). Most of* The Fisher King *focused on a radio shock-jock (Bridges), saved from suicide and befriended by a maniacal derelict (Williams) whose life had been disastrously affected by the on-air ramblings of that same radio jock. Both actors received high praise for their work, and Williams went on to become one of the year's nominees as best actor. But Mercedes Ruehl went one step further: In a smaller role as Bridges' brassy, man-hungry girlfriend, she copped the Oscar. Ruehl ruled at more than one award party that year. When Broadway's Tony awards were handed out, she was also named the year's best actress for her performance in Neil Simon's play "Lost in Yonkers," a role she would later re-create on film.*

Terminator 2: Judgment Day *(TriStar) won four Academy Awards, making it the year's most Oscared film after* The Silence of the Lambs. *A futuristic smorgasbord full of eye-boggling special effects, the James Cameron-directed spectacle was about a primitive Terminator (Arnold Schwarzenegger) battling it out with a villainous man-machine (Robert Patrick) in order to save the world from destruction. The film took a truckload of prizes from the technical end of the Academy honors list: for its stunning visual effects, sound effects editing, sound, and makeup.*

George Lucas *received the Irving G. Thalberg Award from his longtime pal and sometime collaborator Steven Spielberg. Lucas, the creator of four of the top ten box-office hits of all time as of 1992 (Star Wars, Return of the Jedi, Raiders of the Lost Ark, The Empire Strikes Back), thanked "the thousands of men, women, robots and aliens" with whom he'd shared the creative process, with a special mention to Francis Ford Coppola "for being my mentor" and to his daughters for being "current teachers."*

PICTURE

BEAUTY AND THE BEAST, Walt Disney Pictures, Buena Vista. Produced by Don Hahn.
BUGSY, TriStar. Produced by Mark Johnson, Barry Levinson and Warren Beatty.
JFK, Camelot, Warner Bros. Produced by A. Kitman Ho and Oliver Stone.
THE PRINCE OF TIDES, Barwood/Longfellow , Columbia. Produced by Barbra Streisand and Andrew Karsch.
* **THE SILENCE OF THE LAMBS**, Strong Heart/Demme, Orion. Produced by Edward Saxon, Kenneth Utt and Ron Bozman.

ACTOR

WARREN BEATTY in *Bugsy*, TriStar.
ROBERT DE NIRO in *Cape Fear*, Amblin Entertainment with Cappa Films and Tribeca Productions, Universal.
* **ANTHONY HOPKINS** in *The Silence of the Lambs*, Strong Heart/Demme, Orion.
NICK NOLTE in *The Prince of Tides*, Barwood/Longfellow, Columbia.
ROBIN WILLIAMS in *The Fisher King*, TriStar.

ACTRESS

GEENA DAVIS in *Thelma & Louise*, Pathe Entertainment, M-G-M.
LAURA DERN in *Rambling Rose*, Carolco, Seven Arts.
* **JODIE FOSTER** in *The Silence of the Lambs*, Strong Heart/ Demme, Orion.
BETTE MIDLER in *For the Boys*, 20th Century Fox.
SUSAN SARANDON in *Thelma & Louise*, Pathe Entertainment, M-G-M.

SUPPORTING ACTOR

TOMMY LEE JONES in *JFK*, Camelot, Warner Bros.
HARVEY KEITEL in *Bugsy*, TriStar.
BEN KINGSLEY in *Bugsy*, TriStar.
MICHAEL LERNER in *Barton Fink*, Barton Circle, 20th Century Fox.
* **JACK PALANCE** in *City Slickers*, Castle Rock Entertainment, Columbia.

SUPPORTING ACTRESS

DIANE LADD in *Rambling Rose*, Carolco Pictures, Seven Arts.
JULIETTE LEWIS in *Cape Fear*, Amblin Entertainment with Cappa Films and Tribeca, Universal.
KATE NELLIGAN in *The Prince of Tides*, Barwood/Longfellow , Columbia.
* **MERCEDES RUEHL** in *The Fisher King*, TriStar.
JESSICA TANDY in *Fried Green Tomatoes*, Act III Communications with Electric Shadow, Universal.

DIRECTING

BOYZ N THE HOOD, Columbia. John Singleton.
BUGSY, TriStar. Barry Levinson.
JFK, Camelot, Warner Bros. Oliver Stone.
***THE SILENCE OF THE LAMBS**, Strong Heart/Demme, Orion. Jonathan Demme.
THELMA & LOUISE, Pathe Entertainment, M-G-M. Ridley Scott.

WRITING

(Screenplay Written Directly for the Screen)
BOYZ N THE HOOD, Columbia. John Singleton.
BUGSY, TriStar. James Toback.
THE FISHER KING, TriStar. Richard LaGravenese.
GRAND CANYON, 20th Century Fox. Lawrence Kasdan and Meg Kasdan.
* **THELMA & LOUISE**, Pathe Entertainment M-G-M. Callie Khouri.

(Screenplay Based on Material Previously Produced or Published)
EUROPA EUROPA, CCC-Filmkunst and Les Films du Losange, Orion Classics. Agnieszka Holland.
FRIED GREEN TOMATOES, ACT III Communications with Electric Shadow, Universal. Fannie Flagg and Carol Sobieski.
JFK, Camelot, Warner Bros. Oliver Stone and Zachary Sklar.
THE PRINCE OF TIDES, Barwood/Longfellow, Columbia. Pat Conroy and Becky Johnston.
* **THE SILENCE OF THE LAMBS**, Strong Heart/Demme, Orion. Ted Tally.

CINEMATOGRAPHY

BUGSY, TriStar. Allen Daviau.
* **JFK**, Camelot, Warner Bros. Robert Richardson.
THE PRINCE OF TIDES, Barwood/Longfellow, Columbia. Stephen Goldblatt.
TERMINATOR 2: JUDGMENT DAY, a Carolco, TriStar. Adam Greenberg.
THELMA & LOUISE, Pathe Entertainment, M-G-M. Adrian Biddle.

ART DIRECTION-SET DECORATION

BARTON FINK, Barton Circle, 20th Century Fox. Dennis Gassner; Nancy Haigh.
* **BUGSY**, TriStar. Dennis Gassner; Nancy Haigh.
THE FISHER KING, TriStar. Mel Bourne; Cindy Carr.
HOOK, TriStar. Norman Garwood; Garrett Lewis.
THE PRINCE OF TIDES, Barwood/Longfellow, Columbia. Paul Sylbert; Caryl Heller.

COSTUME DESIGN

THE ADDAMS FAMILY, Scott Rudin, Paramount. Ruth Myers.
BARTON FINK, Barton Circle, 20th Century Fox. Richard Hornung.
* **BUGSY**, TriStar. Albert Wolsky.
HOOK, TriStar. Anthony Powell.
MADAME BOVARY, MK2/C.E.D./FR3 Films, Samuel Goldwyn Company. Corinne Jorry.

SOUND

BACKDRAFT, Trilogy Entertainment Group/Brian Grazer, Universal. Gary Summers, Randy Thom, Gary Rydstrom and Glenn Williams.
BEAUTY AND THE BEAST, Walt Disney Pictures, Buena Vista. Terry Porter, Mel Metcalfe, David J. Hudson and Doc Kane.
JFK, Camelot, Warner Bros. Michael Minkler, Gregg Landaker and Tod A. Maitland.
THE SILENCE OF THE LAMBS, Strong Heart/Demme, Orion. Tom Fleischman and Christopher Newman.
* **TERMINATOR 2: JUDGMENT DAY**, Carolco, TriStar. Tom Johnson, Gary Rydstrom, Gary Summers and Lee Orloff.

FILM EDITING

THE COMMITMENTS, Beacon Communications, 20th Century Fox. Gerry Hambling.
* **JFK**, Camelot, Warner Bros. Joe Hutshing and Pietro Scalia.
THE SILENCE OF THE LAMBS, Strong Heart/Demme, Orion. Craig McKay.
TERMINATOR 2: JUDGMENT DAY, Carolco, TriStar. Conrad Buff, Mark Goldblatt and Richard A. Harris.
THELMA & LOUISE, Pathe Entertainment, M-G-M. Thom Noble.

SOUND EFFECTS EDITING

BACKDRAFT, Trilogy Entertainment Group/Brian Grazer, Universal. Gary Rydstrom and Richard Hymns.
STAR TREK VI: THE UNDISCOVERED COUNTRY, Paramount Pictures, Paramount. George Watters II and F. Hudson Miller.
* **TERMINATOR 2: JUDGMENT DAY**, Carolco, TriStar. Gary Rydstrom and Gloria S. Borders.

ISUAL EFFECTS
BACKDRAFT, Trilogy Entertainment Group/Brian Grazer, Universal. Mikael Salomon, Allen Hall, Clay Pinney and Scott Farrar.
HOOK, TriStar. Eric Brevig, Harley Jessup, Mark Sullivan and Michael Lantieri.
TERMINATOR 2: JUDGMENT DAY, Carolco, TriStar. Dennis Muren, Stan Winston, Gene Warren, Jr., and Robert Skotak.

MUSIC
(Song)
BE OUR GUEST (*Beauty and the Beast,* Walt Disney Pictures, Buena Vista); Music by Alan Menken. Lyrics by Howard Ashman.
BEAUTY AND THE BEAST (*Beauty and the Beast,* Walt Disney Pictures, Buena Vista); Music by Alan Menken. Lyrics by Howard Ashman.
BELLE (*Beauty and the Beast,* Walt Disney Pictures, Buena Vista); Music by Alan Menken. Lyric by Howard Ashman.
(EVERYTHING I DO) I DO IT FOR YOU (*Robin Hood: Prince of Thieves,* Morgan Creek, Warner Bros); Music by Michael Kamen. Lyrics by Bryan Adams and Robert John Lange.
WHEN YOU'RE ALONE (*Hook,* TriStar Pictures, TriStar); Music by John Williams. Lyrics by Leslie Bricusse.

(Original Score)
BEAUTY AND THE BEAST, Walt Disney Pictures, Buena Vista. Alan Menken.
BUGSY, TriStar. Ennio Morricone.
THE FISHER KING, TriStar. George Fenton.
JFK, Camelot, Warner Bros. John Williams.
THE PRINCE OF TIDES, Barwood/Longfellow, Columbia. James Newton Howard.

MAKEUP
HOOK, TriStar. Christina Smith, Monty Westmore and Greg Cannom.
STAR TREK VI: THE UNDISCOVERED COUNTRY, Paramount. Michael Mills, Edward French and Richard Snell.
* **TERMINATOR 2: JUDGMENT DAY,** Carolco, TriStar. Stan Winston and Jeff Dawn.

SHORT FILMS
(Animated)
BLACKFLY, a National Film Board of Canada Production. Christopher Hinton.
* **MANIPULATION,** a Tandem Films Production. Daniel Greaves.
STRINGS, a National Film Board of Canada Production. Wendy Tilby.

(Live Action)
BIRCH STREET GYM, a Chanticleer Films Production. Stephen Kessler and Thomas R. Conroy.
LAST BREEZE OF SUMMER, an American Film Institute Production. David M. Massey.
* **SESSION MAN,** a Chanticleer Films Production. Seth Winston and Rob Fried.

DOCUMENTARY
(Short Subjects)
BIRDNESTERS OF THAILAND (aka "Shadow Hunters"), an Antenne 2/National Geographic Society/M.D.I./Wind Horse Production. Eric Valli and Alain Majani, producers.
* **DEADLY DECEPTION: GENERAL ELECTRIC, NUCLEAR WEAPONS AND OUR ENVIRONMENT,** a Women's Educational Media, Inc. Production. Debra Chasnoff, producer.
A LITTLE VICIOUS, a Film and Video Workshop, Inc. Production. Immy Humes, producer.
THE MARK OF THE MAKER, a McGowan Film and Video, Inc. Production. David McGowan, producer.
MEMORIAL: LETTERS FROM AMERICAN SOLDIERS, a Couturie Company Production. Bill Couturie and Bernard Edelman, producers.

(Features)
DEATH ON THE JOB, a Half-Court Pictures, Ltd. Production. Vince DiPersio and William Guttentag, producers.
DOING TIME: LIFE INSIDE THE BIG HOUSE, a Video Verite Production. Alan Raymond and Susan Raymond, producers.
* **IN THE SHADOW OF THE STARS,** a Light-Saraf Films Production. Allie Light and Irving Saraf, producers.
THE RESTLESS CONSCIENCE, a Hava Kohav Beller Production. Hava Kohav Beller, producer.
WILD BY LAW, a Florentine Films Production. Lawrence Hott and Diane Garey, producers.

FOREIGN LANGUAGE FILM
CHILDREN OF NATURE (Iceland).
THE ELEMENTARY SCHOOL (Czechoslovakia).
* **MEDITERRANEO** (Italy).
THE OX (Sweden).
RAISE THE RED LANTERN (Hong Kong).

HONORARY AND OTHER AWARDS
TO SATYAJIT RAY, in recognition of his rare mastery of the art of motion pictures, and of his profound humanitarian outlook, which has had an indelible influence on filmmakers and audiences throughout the world.

Beauty and the Beast (*Buena Vista*) *managed a coup no other animated feature in film history had achieved, not even the much-revered* Snow White and the Seven Dwarfs, Pinocchio *or* Fantasia: Beauty *pulled a nomination as best picture of the year. It was an honor that struck cold fear into the heart of many an unemployed actor, fearing the accolade could encourage more producers to bypass live performers in favor of pencil marks.* Beauty *lost to* The Silence of the Lambs *on the final tally but it did win two trophies, both in the music category. One was for Alan Menken's original score and one for Menken's and Howard Ashman's "Beauty and the Beast" as the year's best song. In the latter category, they competed against themselves: two of their other songs from* Beauty *were also nominees, "Be Our Guest" and "Belle."*

TO PETE COMANDINI, RICHARD T. DAYTON, DONALD HAGANS and RICHARD T. RYAN of YCM Laboratories for the creation and development of a motion picture film restoration process using liquid gate and registration correction on a contact printer. (Award of Commendation – Special Plaque)
TO RICHARD J. STUMPF and JOSEPH WESTHEIMER for outstanding service and dedication in upholding the high standards of the Academy of Motion Picture Arts and Sciences. (Medals of Commendation)

1991 IRVING G. THALBERG MEMORIAL AWARD
TO GEORGE LUCAS

1991 JEAN HERSHOLT HUMANITARIAN AWARD
None given this year.

1991 GORDON E. SAWYER AWARD
TO RAY HARRYHAUSEN

SCIENTIFIC OR TECHNICAL AWARDS
Academy Award of Merit (Statuette)
None.

Scientific and Engineering Award (Academy Plaque)
IAIN NEIL for the optical design; ALBERT SAIKI for the mechanical design; and PANAVISION, INCORPORATED, for the concept and development of the Primo Zoom Lens for 35mm cinematography.
GEORG THOMA for the design; HEINZ FEIERLEIN and the engineering department of Sachtler AG for the development of a range of fluid tripod heads.
HARRY J. BAKER for the design and development of the first full fluidaction tripod head with adjustable degrees of viscous drag.
GUIDO CARTONI for his pioneering work in developing the technology to achieve selectable and repeatable viscous drag modules in fluid tripod heads.
RAY FEENEY, RICHARD KEENEY and RICHARD J. LUNDELL for the software development and adaptation of the Solitaire Film Recorder that provides a flexible, cost-effective film recording system.
FAZ FAZAKAS, BRIAN HENSON, DAVE HOUSMAN, PETER MILLER and JOHN STEPHENSON for the development of the Henson Performance Control System.
MARIO CELSO for his pioneering work in the design, development and manufacture of equipment for carbon arc and xenon power supplies and igniters used in motion picture projection.
RANDY CARTWRIGHT, DAVID B. COONS, LEM DAVIS, THOMAS HAHN, JAMES HOUSTON, MARK KIMBALL, PETER NYE, MICHAEL SHANTZIS, DAVID F. WOLF and the Walt Disney Feature Animation Department for the design and development of the 'CAPS' production system for feature film animation.

GEORGE WORRALL for the design, development and manufacture of the Worrall geared camera head for motion picture production.

Technical Achievement Award (Academy Certificate)
ROBERT W. STOKER, JR., for the design and development of a cobweb gun, for applying non-toxic cobweb effects on motion picture sets with both safety and ease of operation.
JAMES DOYLE for the design and development of the Dry Fogger, which uses liquid nitrogen to produce a safe, dense, low-hanging fog effect.
DICK CAVDEK, STEVE HAMERSKI and OTTO NEMENZ INTERNATIONAL, INCORPORATED for the opto-mechanical design and development of the Canon/Nemenz Zoom Lens.
KEN ROBINGS and CLAIRMONT CAMERA for the opto-mechanical design and development of the Canon/Clairmont Camera Zoom Lens.
CENTURY PRECISION OPTICS for the opto-mechanical design and development of the Canon/Century Precision Optics Zoom Lens.

*INDICATES WINNER

311

1992
The Sixty-Fifth Year

For Clint Eastwood, March 29, 1993, was a triumphant night to remember. After thirty years of being dismissed by too many as a moviemaker of little consequence, the estimable Eastwood went home with not one but two Academy Awards, as the year's best director and for producing the year's best film, *Unforgiven*. He took it all in leisurely stride. Backstage he told reporters, "I think winning means more to me now. If you win early in your career, you wonder where to go from that point. And maybe, at that time in your life, you might start wearing leggings and a monocle and taking yourself too seriously." Eastwood was the fourth actor in Oscar history to win an Academy Award for directing a movie he also starred in, following Woody Allen (1977), Warren Beatty (1981), and Kevin Costner (1990).

The two most nominated films of the year had been Eastwood's American-made *Unforgiven* and the British-born *Howards End* from Merchant Ivory, each with nine nominations. After the sixty-fifth Oscars were disbursed, *Unforgiven* had received four (including nods for Gene Hackman's supporting actor performance and Joel Cox's editing) while *Howards End* tallied three (best actress Emma Thompson, best adapted screenplay by Ruth Prawer Jhabvala, best art direction by Luciana Arrighi, with set decoration by Ian Whittaker).

Just as Eastwood had finally made it into the winner's circle after a long haul, so had Al Pacino. Nominated six times during the preceding two decades without a win, Pacino was up for two 1992 acting awards, for best supporting actor (in *Glengarry Glen Ross*) and best actor (in *Scent of a Woman*). He won for the latter. "You broke my streak," he told the Academy audience. Pacino, Thompson, Hackman, and Eastwood had all been favored to win in their divisions. Marisa Tomei, named best supporting actress for *My Cousin Vinny*, had definitely been a dark horse. Her victory was rated as the night's biggest surprise.

For the first time, there were only four official nominees in the category of best foreign language film. A fifth contender, *A Place in the World*, had been nominated as an entry from Uruguay but was later disqualified when it came to the Academy's attention that the film was essentially an Argentine, not a Uruguayan, production. The French-made *Indochine*, which had brought Catherine Deneuve a nomination as best actress, was named the year's best foreign language film, the first time since 1978 a French film had been so honored.

For the second year in a row, music man Alan Menken won two Oscars, one for best original score, another for best original song ("Whole New World" from Disney's animated *Aladdin*). Menken accepted

Best Picture: Unforgiven *(Malpaso/Warner Bros.; produced by Clint Eastwood),* **Best Director: Clint Eastwood,** *and* **Best Supporting Actor: Gene Hackman** *as Little Bill Daggett (right, with Eastwood). It was no relation to John Huston's 1960 western* The Unforgiven; *indeed, Clint Eastwood's* Unforgiven *stood squarely in its own unique boots as the first genuine western to win Oscar's premier prize. Admittedly, several earlier best picture winners (such as 1930-31's* Cimarron *and 1990's* Dances With Wolves*) had shared a kindred spirit of the Old West; just as true, Eastwood's sagebrush saga was a million light-years from the basic western movie form popularized by John Wayne and Roy Rogers in which the lines between heroes and villains were clearly defined. In* Unforgiven, *Eastwood showed a dark, unglamorized glimpse into the Old West, the "hero" (played by Eastwood) a retired hell-raiser who, in need of money, takes on the job of hunting down two bad guys who carved up a prostitute in a Wyoming town called Big Whiskey. His assignment eventually brings him in touch with Morgan Freeman, Richard Harris, and Gene Hackman, the latter the unrelenting sheriff who rules Big Whiskey with an iron fist. Hackman's character ends up in a showdown with Eastwood; Hackman himself ended up with an Academy Award for supporting actor, his first after winning in 1971 as the best actor of the year for* The French Connection.

the latter award, his sixth in a four-year span, with the song's lyricist, Tim Rice.

The Crying Game had been the year's giant sleeper. Opening without fanfare, the British-made drama went on to become extremely popular with moviegoers and a favorite topic of discussion because of several surprise twists in its storyline. At Oscar time, it also generated enough steam to win six nominations, including one as the year's best picture. However, when the votes were counted, *Crying* ended up with only a single trophy, for Neil Jordan's original screenplay.

Jean Hersholt Humanitarian Awards went to both Elizabeth Taylor and Audrey Hepburn, and Italy's great director Federico Fellini received a special honorary Oscar for "his cinematic accomplishments that have thrilled and entertained worldwide audiences." His Oscar was presented by two other Italian landmarks, Sophia Loren and Marcello Mastroianni, while Mrs. Fellini, actress Giulietta Masina, wept in the audience. During his thank-you speech, Fellini included a request to her: "Please stop crying, Giulietta."

For the fourth consecutive year, Billy Crystal was the night's MC, this time making his entrance onto the stage of the Dorothy Chandler Pavilion whip in hand, riding atop a giant Oscar pulled by Jack Palance. After Palance did a reprise of the one-arm push-ups he'd done at the preceding year's Academy Awards ceremonies, Crystal jumped off the Oscar and declared, "I am Spartacus . . ."

The theme of the show, "Oscar Salutes Women and the Movies," had stirred some controversy prior to the telecast, particularly among those whose conception of "women in film" was restricted to actresses. It had been an especially lean year in terms of strong roles for women, they argued, and so it was ironic or worse for the Academy to select a theme relating to women. Producer Gil Cates patiently pointed out that he was celebrating the many vital contributions that women had made through the entire history of movies, behind the screen as well as on it, and asked whether it wasn't better to light candles than to curse darkness. His position seemed vindicated when women won Oscars in nine of the evening's twenty-three categories, a record showing and strong evidence that women were progressing toward equality of contributions to the art form.

Best Actress: Emma Thompson *as Margaret Schlegel in* Howards End *(Merchant Ivory/Sony Pictures Classics; directed by James Ivory). Before* Howards End, *Emma Thompson was barely known to movie audiences; to those who were aware of her, she was most familiar as the wife of actor-director Kenneth Branagh and the leading lady of her husband's films* Henry V *and* Dead Again. *Then came the British-made* Howards End, *based on E. M. Forster's 1910 novel; Thompson was positively illuminating as a bright, well-bred Englishwoman near the end of the Edwardian era, devoted to her headstrong sister (Helena Bonham Carter) and eventually intertwined with a dynamic family of means headed by Anthony Hopkins and Vanessa Redgrave. For her performance as the compassionate Miss Schlegel, Thompson won the Academy Award, acquired an identity quite her own, and began her own front-line screen career thanks to* Howards End, *a literate, leisurely comedy-drama of manners and morals, done with taste and intelligence by the team of (Ismail) Merchant/(James) Ivory, earlier responsible for a superb screen version of Forster's* A Room with a View.

Best Actor: Al Pacino *as Frank Slade in* Scent of a Woman *(Universal; directed by Martin Brest). It looked as though Al Pacino was destined always to be a bridesmaid, never a bride, at least as far as a wedding with Oscar was concerned. Since his first nomination in 1972 (for* The Godfather*) he had accumulated a total of six nominations without ever carrying home a statuette. (Among actors, only Peter O'Toole and the late Richard Burton topped him, both gents with seven nominations but zero wins on their tally sheets.) In 1992, Pacino received two more nominations, one as best supporting actor for* Glengarry Glen Ross, *another as best actor for* Scent of a Woman. *The latter finally did the trick.* Scent *was a remake of the 1975 Italian movie of the same name, which had starred Vittorio Gassman. (Ironically, that 1975 screenplay by Ruggiero Maccari and Dino Risi lost the Oscar to* One Flew Over the Cuckoo's Nest *by Laurence Hauben and Bo Goldman; Goldman wrote the screenplay for the new version of* Scent.*)*

Best Supporting Actress: Marisa Tomei as *Mona Lisa Vito* in *My Cousin Vinny (20th Century Fox; directed by Jonathan Lynn)*. *If anything came near an Academy upset in 1992, it was Marisa Tomei's win for* My Cousin Vinny. *The title referred to a swaggering, inept lawyer named Vincent Gambini (Joe Pesci) who gets in over his head while trying to plead a court case in Alabama involving a cousin named Bill (Ralph Macchio). Despite the fun at hand, it was Tomei who stole the show as Cousin Vinny's crazy-making girlfriend Mona Lisa Vito, who accompanies him south and is in a constant tizzy because her biological clock is ticking loudly. American-born Tomei won her Oscar over a field that included four of the best from overseas: Joan Plowright, Miranda Richardson, Vanessa Redgrave, and Judy Davis.*

Never before had two Jean Hersholt Humanitarian Awards been presented in a single year; on January 13, 1993, it was announced that Elizabeth Taylor (above) and Audrey Hepburn had both been chosen by the Board of Governors for the honor, the third and fourth women so named. Taylor was acknowledged for her extensive work on behalf of AIDS sufferers, Hepburn for her work as a UNICEF ambassador helping millions of third world children. Unfortunately, only Taylor was able to receive her Humanitarian Award in person; the much-loved Hepburn had succumbed to cancer on January 20, only a week after the announcement of her award had been made to the world.

PICTURE

THE CRYING GAME, Palace Pictures, Miramax. Produced by Stephen Woolley.
A FEW GOOD MEN, Castle Rock Entertainment, Columbia. Produced by David Brown, Rob Reiner, and Andrew Scheinman.
HOWARDS END, Merchant Ivory, Sony Pictures Classics. Produced by Ismail Merchant.
SCENT OF A WOMAN, Universal Release/City Lights Films, Universal. Produced by Martin Brest.
* **UNFORGIVEN,** Warner Bros. Produced by Clint Eastwood.

ACTOR

ROBERT DOWNEY, JR. in *Chaplin*, Carolco Pictures, TriStar.
CLINT EASTWOOD in *Unforgiven*, Warner Bros.
* **AL PACINO** in *Scent of a Woman*, Universal Release/City Lights Films, Universal.
STEPHEN REA in *The Crying Game*, Palace Pictures, Miramax.
DENZEL WASHINGTON in *Malcolm X*, By Any Means Necessary Cinema, Universal.

ACTRESS

CATHERINE DENEUVE in *Indochine*, Paradis Films/La Generale d'Images/BAC Films/Orly Films/Cine Cinq, Sony Pictures Classics.
MARY McDONNELL in *Passion Fish*, Atchafalaya Films, Miramax.
MICHELLE PFEIFFER in *Love Field*, Sanford/Pillsbury, Orion.
SUSAN SARANDON in *Lorenzo's Oil*, Kennedy Miller Films, Universal.
* **EMMA THOMPSON** in *Howards End*, Merchant Ivory, Sony Pictures Classics.

SUPPORTING ACTOR

JAYE DAVIDSON in *The Crying Game*, Palace Pictures, Miramax.
* **GENE HACKMAN** in *Unforgiven*, Warner Bros.
JACK NICHOLSON in *A Few Good Men*, Castle Rock Entertainment, Columbia.
AL PACINO in *Glengarry Glen Ross*, Stephanie Lynn, New Line.
DAVID PAYMER in *Mr. Saturday Night*, Castle Rock Entertainment, Columbia.

SUPPORTING ACTRESS

JUDY DAVIS in *Husbands and Wives*, TriStar.
JOAN PLOWRIGHT in *Enchanted April*, BBC Films with Greenpoint Films, Miramax.
VANESSA REDGRAVE in *Howards End*, Merchant Ivory, Sony Pictures Classics.
MIRANDA RICHARDSON in *Damage*, SKREBA/Damage/NEF/Le Studio Canal+, New Line.
* **MARISA TOMEI** in *My Cousin Vinny*, 20th Century Fox.

DIRECTING

THE CRYING GAME, Palace Pictures, Miramax. Neil Jordan.
HOWARDS END, Merchant Ivory, Sony Pictures Classics. James Ivory.
THE PLAYER, Avenue Pictures, Fine Line. Robert Altman.
SCENT OF A WOMAN, Universal Release/City Lights Films, Universal. Martin Brest.
*****UNFORGIVEN,** Warner Bros. Clint Eastwood.

WRITING

(Screenplay Written Directly for the Screen)
* **THE CRYING GAME,** Palace Pictures, Miramax. Neil Jordan.
HUSBANDS AND WIVES, TriStar. Woody Allen.
LORENZO'S OIL, Kennedy Miller Films, Universal. George Miller and Nick Enright.
PASSION FISH, Atchafalaya Films, Miramax. John Sayles.
UNFORGIVEN, Warner Bros. David Webb Peoples.

(Screenplay Based on Material Previously Produced or Published)
ENCHANTED APRIL, BBC Films with Greenpoint Films, Miramax. Peter Barnes.
* **HOWARDS END,** Merchant Ivory, Sony Pictures Classics. Ruth Prawer Jhabvala.
THE PLAYER, Avenue Pictures, Fine Line. Michael Tolkin.
A RIVER RUNS THROUGH IT, Columbia. Richard Friedenberg.
SCENT OF A WOMAN, Universal Release/City Lights Films, Universal. Bo Goldman.

CINEMATOGRAPHY

HOFFA, 20th Century Fox. Stephen H. Burum.
HOWARDS END, Merchant Ivory, Sony Pictures Classics. Tony Pierce-Roberts.
THE LOVER, Renn/Burrill Productions/Films A2, M-G-M/UA. Robert Fraisse.
* **A RIVER RUNS THROUGH IT,** Columbia. Philippe Rousselot.
UNFORGIVEN, Warner Bros. Jack N. Green.

ART DIRECTION - SET DECORATION

BRAM STOKER'S DRACULA, Columbia. Thomas Sanders; Garrett Lewis.
CHAPLIN, Carolco Pictures, TriStar. Stuart Craig; Chris A. Butler.
* **HOWARDS END,** Merchant Ivory, Sony Pictures Classics. Luciana Arrighi; Ian Whittaker.
TOYS, 20th Century Fox. Ferdinando Scarfiotti; Linda DeScenna.
UNFORGIVEN, Warner Bros. Henry Bumstead; Janice Blackie-Goodine.

COSTUME DESIGN

BRAM STOKER'S DRACULA, Columbia. Eiko Ishioka.
ENCHANTED APRIL, BBC Films with Greenpoint Films,
  Miramax. Sheena Napier.
HOWARDS END, Merchant Ivory , Sony Pictures Classics.
  Jenny Beavan and John Bright.
MALCOLM X, By Any Means Necessary Cinema, Warner Bros.
  Ruth Carter.
TOYS, 20th Century Fox. Albert Wolsky.

SOUND

ALADDIN, Walt Disney Pictures, Buena Vista. Terry Porter, Mel
  Metcalfe, David J. Hudson, and Doc Kane.
A FEW GOOD MEN, Castle Rock Entertainment, Columbia.
  Kevin O'Connell, Rick Kline, and Bob Eber.
* **THE LAST OF THE MOHICANS**, 20th Century Fox. Chris
  Jenkins, Doug Hemphill, Mark Smith, and Simon Kaye.
UNDER SIEGE, Northeast, Warner Bros. Donald O. Mitchell,
  Frank A. Montano, Rick Hart, and Scott Smith.
UNFORGIVEN, Warner Bros. Les Fresholtz, Vern Poore, Dick
  Alexander, and Rob Young.

FILM EDITING

BASIC INSTINCT, Carolco, TriStar. Frank J. Urioste.
THE CRYING GAME, Palace Pictures, Miramax. Kant Pan.
A FEW GOOD MEN, Castle Rock Entertainment, Columbia.
  Robert Leighton.
THE PLAYER, Avenue Pictures, Fine Line. Geraldine Peroni.
* **UNFORGIVEN**, Warner Bros. Joel Cox.

SOUND EFFECTS EDITING

ALADDIN, Walt Disney Pictures, Buena Vista. Mark Mangini.
* **BRAM STOKER'S DRACULA**, Columbia. Tom C. McCarthy
  and David E. Stone.
UNDER SIEGE, Northeast, Warner Bros. John Leveque and
  Bruce Stambler.

VISUAL EFFECTS

ALIEN³, 20th Century Fox. Richard Edlund, Alec Gillis, Tom
  Woodruff, Jr., and George Gibbs.
BATMAN RETURNS, Warner Bros. Michael Fink, Craig Barron,
  John Bruno, and Dennis Skotak.
* **DEATH BECOMES HER**, Universal. Ken Ralston, Doug
  Chiang, Doug Smythe, and Tom Woodruff, Jr.

MUSIC

(Song)
BEAUTIFUL MARIA OF MY SOUL (*The Mambo Kings*,
  Northwest, Warner Bros.); Music by Robert Kraft. Lyrics by
  Arne Glimcher.
FRIEND LIKE ME (*Aladdin*, Walt Disney Pictures, Buena
  Vista); Music by Alan Menken. Lyrics by Howard Ashman.
I HAVE NOTHING (*The Bodyguard*, Warner Bros.); Music by
  David Foster. Lyrics by Linda Thompson.
RUN TO YOU (*The Bodyguard*, Warner Bros.); Music by Jud
  Friedman. Lyrics by Allan Rich.
* **A WHOLE NEW WORLD** (*Aladdin*, Walt Disney Pictures,
  Buena Vista); Music by Alan Menken. Lyrics by Tim Rice.

(Original Score)
* **ALADDIN**, Walt Disney Pictures, Buena Vista. Alan Menken.
BASIC INSTINCT, Carolco, TriStar. Jerry Goldsmith.
CHAPLIN, Carolco, TriStar. John Barry.
HOWARDS END, Merchant Ivory, Sony Pictures Classics.
  Richard Robbins.
A RIVER RUNS THROUGH IT, Columbia. Mark Isham.

MAKEUP

BATMAN RETURNS, Warner Bros. Ve Neill, Ronnie Specter,
  and Stan Winston.
* **BRAM STOKER'S DRACULA**, Columbia. Greg Cannom,
  Michele Burke, and Matthew W. Mungle.
HOFFA, 20th Century Fox. Ve Neill, Greg Cannom, and
  John Blake.

SHORT FILMS

(Animated)
ADAM, an Aardman Animations Ltd. Production. Peter Lord,
  producer.
* **MONA LISA DESCENDING A STAIRCASE**, a Joan C. Gratz
  Production. Joan C. Gratz, producer.
RECI, RECI, RECI... (WORD, WORDS, WORDS), a Kratky
  Film Production. Michaela Pavlatova, producer.
THE SANDMAN, a Batty Berry Mackinnon Production.
  Paul Berry, producer.
SCREEN PLAY, a Bare Boards Film Production. Barry J.C.
  Purves, producer.

(Live Action)
CONTACT, a Chanticleer Films, Inc. Production. Jonathan Darby
  and Jana Sue Memel, producers.
CRUISE CONTROL, a Palmieri Pictures Production. Matt
  Palmieri, producer.
THE LADY IN WAITING, a Taylor Made Films Production.
  Christian M. Taylor, producer.
* **OMNIBUS**, a Lazennec tout court/Le C.R.R.A.V. Production.
  Sam Karmann, producer.
SWAN SONG, a Renaissance Films PLC Production. Kenneth
  Branagh and David Parfitt, producers.

Best Foreign Language Film: Indochine *from France.
Directed by Régis Wargnier and starring Catherine Deneuve,
Indochine was a lengthy (155 minutes), sweeping romantic
saga that eavesdropped on two women and a man during the
final twenty-five years of French rule in Indochina, before it*
*became Vietnam. The film not only unleashed tearducts and
also won the Academy's highest praise from overseas. It brought
Deneuve her first Academy Award nomination, making her one
of the few performers honored for work in foreign language films.*

DOCUMENTARY

(Short Subjects)
**AT THE EDGE OF CONQUEST: THE JOURNEY OF
  CHIEF WAI-WAI**, a Realis Pictures Inc. Production. Geoffrey
  O'Connor, producer.
**BEYOND IMAGINING: MARGARET ANDERSON AND
  THE "LITTLE REVIEW,"** a Wendy L. Weinberg Production.
  Wendy L. Weinberg, producer.
**THE COLOURS OF MY FATHER: A PORTRAIT OF SAM
  BORENSTEIN**, an Imageries P.B. Ltd. Production in
  coproduction with the National Film Board of Canada. Richard
  Elson and Sally Bochner, producers.
* **EDUCATING PETER**, a State of the Art, Inc. Production.
  Thomas C. Goodwin and Gerardine Wurzburg, producers.
WHEN ABORTION WAS ILLEGAL: UNTOLD STORIES, a
  Concentric Media Production. Dorothy Fadiman, producer.

(Features)
**CHANGING OUR MINDS: THE STORY OF DR. EVELYN
  HOOKER**, an Intrepid Production. David Haugland, producer.
FIRES OF KUWAIT, a Black Sun Films, Ltd./IMAX Corporation
  Production. Sally Dundas, producer.
**LIBERATORS: FIGHTING ON TWO FRONTS IN WORLD
  WAR II**, a Miles Educational Film Productions, Inc. Production.
  William Miles and Nina Rosenblum, producers.
MUSIC FOR THE MOVIES: BERNARD HERRMANN, an
  Alternate Current Inc./Les Films d'Ici Production. Margaret
  Smilow and Roma Baran, producers.
* **THE PANAMA DECEPTION**, an Empowerment Project
  Production. Barbara Trent and David Kasper, producers.

FOREIGN LANGUAGE FILM

CLOSE TO EDEN (Russia).
DAENS (Belgium).
* **INDOCHINE** (France).
SCHTONK (Germany).

HONORARY AND OTHER AWARDS

TO FEDERICO FELLINI, in recognition of his place as one of
  the screen's master storytellers.
TO PETRO VLAHOS in appreciation for outstanding service and
  dedication in upholding the high standards of the Academy of
  Motion Picture Arts and Sciences. (Medal of Commendation)

1992 IRVING G. THALBERG MEMORIAL AWARD

None given this year.

1992 JEAN HERSHOLT HUMANITARIAN AWARD

TO AUDREY HEPBURN
TO ELIZABETH TAYLOR

1992 GORDON E. SAWYER AWARD

TO ERICH KAESTNER

SCIENTIFIC AND TECHNICAL AWARDS

Academy Award of Merit (Statuette)
CHADWELL O'CONNOR of the O'Connor Engineering
  Laboratories for the concept and engineering of the fluid-
  damped camera-head for motion picture photography.

Scientific and Engineering Award (Academy Plaque)
**LOREN CARPENTER, ROB COOK, ED CATMULL, TOM
  PORTER, PAT HANRAHAN, TONY APODACA**, and
  DARWYN PEACHEY for the development of "RenderMan"
  software which produces images used in motion pictures from
  3D computer descriptions of shape and appearance.
CLAUS WIEDEMANN and **ROBERT ORBAN** for the
  design and Dolby Laboratories for the development of the Dolby
  Labs "Container."
KEN BATES for the design and development of the Bates
  Decelerator System for accurately and safely arresting the
  descent of stunt persons in high freefalls.
AL MAYER for the camera design; **IAIN NEIL** and **GEORGE
  KRAEMER** for the optical design; **HANS SPIRAWSKI** and
  BILL ESLICK for the opto-mechanical design; and **DON EARL**
  for technical support in developing the Panavision System 65
  Studio Sync Sound Reflex Camera for 65mm motion picture
  photography.
DOUGLAS TRUMBULL for the concept; **GEOFFREY H.
  WILLIAMSON** for the movement design; **ROBERT D.
  AUGUSTE** for the electronic design and **EDMUND M.
  DIGIULIO** for the camera system design of the CP-65
  Showscan Camera System for 65mm motion picture
  photography.
ARRIFLEX CORPORATION, OTTO BLASCHEK, and the
  ENGINEERING DEPARTMENT OF ARRI, AUSTRIA for
  the design and development of the Arriflex 765 Camera System
  for 65mm motion picture photography.

Technical Achievement Award (Academy Certificate)
IRA TIFFEN of Tiffen Manufacturing Corporation for the
  production of the Ultra Contrast Filter Series for motion picture
  photography.
ROBERT R. BURTON of Audio Rents, Incorporated, for the
  development of the Model S-27, 4-Band Splitter/Combiner.
IAIN NEIL for the optical design and **KAZ FUDANO** for the
  mechanical design of the Panavision Slant Focus Lens for
  motion picture photography.
TOM BRIGHAM for the original concept and pioneering
  work; and **DOUGLAS SMYTHE** and the Computer Graphics
  Department of Industrial Light & Magic for the development
  and the first implementation in feature motion pictures of the
  "MORF" system for digital metamorphosis of high resolution
  images.

*INDICATES WINNER

1993
The Sixty-Sixth Year

"This is the best drink of water after the longest drought in my life," said Steven Spielberg at the 66th Academy Awards after winning his first competitive Academy Award, two actually, one for directing *Schindler's List,* the other as a coproducer of that film, which was named the best of the year. It was Spielberg's night all the way: two films indelibly stamped with Spielberg's name won a total of 10 awards, seven for *Schindler's* and three for the phenomenonally successful *Jurassic Park.* Backstage, proudly clutching his two statues, Spielberg told the press, "I swear I have never held one before. This is the first time I have ever held one in my hand." (A previous award from the Academy, the 1986 Irving G. Thalberg Award, had come in the form of a bust of Thalberg, not an Oscar statuette.) All four of the year's acting champs were also first time A.A. winners. Tom Hanks, named best actor of the year as a gay AIDS patient in *Philadelphia,* gave a passionate and tearful acceptance speech in which he paid homage to a gay teacher, Rawley Farnsworth, from his high school. (The situation was later used as the basis of the 1997 comedy *In & Out,* in which a joyful Oscar winner, during his acceptance speech in front of millions, inadvertently outs a teacher.)

Holly Hunter, without saying a word in the independent film *The Piano,* garnered the year's best actress honors; her teammate in that film, 11-year-old Anna Paquin,

was named best supporting actress in what was her first screen role. Veteran Tommy Lee Jones was chosen best supporting actor for *The Fugitive,* and Spain's *Belle Epoque,* a comedy about an Army deserter who becomes romantically involved with four sisters, was selected in the foreign language film category. It wasn't all first-timers, however: Paul Newman, previously the winner of an Honorary Oscar (in 1985) and the best actor award (in 1986), received a third statuette, this time the Jean Hersholt Humanitarian Award.

Deborah Kerr, long retired from acting, flew from her home in Switzerland to receive both an honorary Oscar and a standing ovation at the ceremony, held March 21, 1994, at the Dorothy Chandler Pavilion of the Los Angeles Music Center. The 72-year-old actress came close to dropping the statuette when it was handed her by Glenn Close. "I've never been so frightened in all my life," said Kerr, adding "but I feel better now because I know I'm among friends." Whoopi Goldberg, by virtue of her role as the evening's emcee, became the first woman and/or African-American to serve as the solo host of an Oscar show, this one telecast on the ABC television network and clocked at 3 hours 18 minutes. Among the highlights was Bruce Springsteen singing "Streets of Philadelphia," a song he composed for *Philadelphia,* and which went on to win as the year's best original song. It was the first time The Boss had written music for any motion picture.

Best Picture: **Schindler's List** *(Universal/Amblin Entertainment; produced by Steven Spielberg, Gerald R. Molen and Branko Lustig),* **Best Director:** **Steven Spielberg** *(left) for* Schindler's List. *There had long been speculation that, perhaps, Academy voters were anti-Spielberg. Not true: prior to 1993 he'd been Oscar-nominated five times, both as a director (in 1977, 1981, 1982) and as a producer (1982, 1985). But it took his daunting, 185-minute* Schindler's *to finally take him the distance. The film, shot in black and white, was by far his most personal and accomplished work to that time, based on the real-life exploits of Oskar Schindler, a German businessman credited with saving the lives of thousands of Jews in World War II. Filming was done in Poland, primarily in Krakow in locales where many of the events had actually happened. Liam Neeson (right) played the complicated, fascinating Schindler; Ralph Fiennes drew his first international attention as a sadistic S.S. commander. By virtue of its win in the best film category,* Schindler's *became the first essentially non-color feature in 33 years (since 1960's* The Apartment*) to be selected for the Academy's highest praise.*

Best Actor: Tom Hanks *as Andrew Beckett in* Philadelphia *(TriStar; directed by Jonathan Demme). It was a tour de force year for Tom Hanks: earlier in 1993, he'd had a popular success in the romantic comedy* Sleepless in Seattle; *then came this drama from an original script by Ron Nyswaner, with Hanks portraying a man dying of AIDS who is fired from a powerful law firm, causing him to take his former employers to court. He does so with the support of his lover (Antonio Banderas) and the help of an attorney (Denzel Washington) who initially has his own prejudices against his client. Compassionately delivered,* Philadelphia *was criticized in some quarters for a sugar-coated treatment of the harsh realities it exposed; others applauded the fact that, better late than never, it was the first mainstream Hollywood film to deal with a health crisis which had been a part of the landscape since 1981. No one quarreled, however, about Hanks' stirring, nuanced performance as the victim.*

Best Actress: Holly Hunter *as Ada (above, right) and* **Best Supporting Actress:** Anna Paquin *as Flora (above, left) in* The Piano *(Miramax; directed by Jane Campion). Set in the 19th century, this striking drama cast Hunter as a mute woman who travels from Scotland to an undeveloped area of New Zealand to marry a man she's never met (Sam Neill). Physically unable to articulate her frustrations, she is ultimately comforted only by her young daughter (Paquin), her piano and an illiterate, charismatic settler (Harvey Keitel) who lives nearby. Paquin, at age 11, became one of the youngest performers to win a competitive Oscar; Hunter, by virtue of the fact that she never speaks a word throughout the film's duration, became the seventh Academy winner to win for a performance virtually without spoken dialogue (her predecessors: Janet Gaynor, Emil Jannings, Jane Wyman, John Mills, Patty Duke, and Marlee Matlin).*

Best Supporting Actor: Tommy Lee Jones *as Deputy Samuel Gerard in* The Fugitive *(Warner Bros.; directed by Andrew Davis). Speeding like a runaway train throughout most of its 127 minutes,* Fugitive *was based on characters created by Roy Huggins for a popular 1960s television series which had starred David Janssen as a Chicago physician on the run for his life after being accused of a murder he didn't commit. In this Tiffany-style film version, Harrison Ford played the man forever on the lam, and Jones was the obsessive U.S. Marshal tenaciously on his tail, a man ruthless and razor-sharp who also comes to respect the bravado and brilliance of the fellow he's bloodhounding.*

Honorary Award to Deborah Kerr. Despite six past Academy nominations (in 1949, 1953, 1956, 1957, 1958, 1960), Deborah Kerr had never ended up with a gold statuette. In order to make up that oversight (spurred perhaps by the fact that several sequences featuring Kerr and Cary Grant from the 1957 An Affair to Remember *had considerably livened up the 1993 hit* Sleepless in Seattle, *while reminding everyone of Kerr's enduring magical presence as an actress) the Academy at long last presented that elusive Oscar to her, specifically "In appreciation for a full career's worth of elegant and beautifully crafted performances."*

PICTURE

THE FUGITIVE, Warner Bros. Arnold Kopelson, Producer.
IN THE NAME OF THE FATHER, Hell's Kitchen/Gabriel Byrne, Universal. Jim Sheridan, Producer.
THE PIANO, Jan Chapman & CIBY 2000, Miramax. Jan Chapman, Producer.
THE REMAINS OF THE DAY, Mike Nichols/John Calley/Merchant Ivory, Columbia. Mike Nichols, John Calley and Ismail Merchant, Producers.
* SCHINDLER'S LIST, Universal/Amblin, Universal. Steven Spielberg, Gerald R. Molen and Branko Lustig, Producers.

ACTOR

DANIEL DAY-LEWIS in *In the Name of the Father,* Hell's Kitchen/Gabriel Byrne, Universal.
LAURENCE FISHBURNE in *What's Love Got to Do with It,* Touchstone, Buena Vista.
* TOM HANKS in *Philadelphia,* TriStar.
ANTHONY HOPKINS in *The Remains of the Day,* Mike Nichols/John Calley/Merchant Ivory, Columbia.
LIAM NEESON in *Schindler's List,* Universal/Amblin, Universal.

ACTRESS

ANGELA BASSETT in *What's Love Got to Do with It,* Touchstone, Buena Vista.
STOCKARD CHANNING in *Six Degrees of Separation,* MGM/UA.
* HOLLY HUNTER in *The Piano,* Jan Chapman & CIBY 2000, Miramax.
EMMA THOMPSON in *The Remains of the Day,* Mike Nichols/John Calley/Merchant Ivory, Columbia.
DEBRA WINGER in *Shadowlands,* Shadowlands Production, Savoy.

SUPPORTING ACTOR

LEONARDO DICAPRIO in *What's Eating Gilbert Grape,* Matalon Teper Ohlsson, Paramount.
RALPH FIENNES in *Schindler's List,* Universal/Amblin, Universal.
* TOMMY LEE JONES in *The Fugitive,* Warner Bros.
JOHN MALKOVICH in *In the Line of Fire,* Castle Rock, Columbia.
PETE POSTLETHWAITE in *In the Name of the Father,* Hell's Kitchen/Gabriel Byrne, Universal.

SUPPORTING ACTRESS

HOLLY HUNTER in *The Firm,* John Davis/Scott Rudin/Mirage, Paramount.
* ANNA PAQUIN in *The Piano,* Jan Chapman & CIBY 2000, Miramax.
ROSIE PEREZ in *Fearless,* Warner Bros.
WINONA RYDER in *The Age of Innocence,* Cappa/De Fina, Columbia.
EMMA THOMPSON in *In the Name of the Father,* Hell's Kitchen/Gabriel Byrne, Universal.

DIRECTING

IN THE NAME OF THE FATHER, Hell's Kitchen/Gabriel Byrne, Universal. Jim Sheridan.
THE PIANO, Jan Chapman & CIBY 2000, Miramax. Jane Campion.
THE REMAINS OF THE DAY, Mike Nichols/John Calley/Merchant Ivory, Columbia. James Ivory.
*SCHINDLER'S LIST, Universal/Amblin, Universal. Steven Spielberg.
SHORT CUTS, Avenue Pictures, Fine Line Features. Robert Altman.

WRITING

(Screenplay Based on Material Previously Produced or Published)

THE AGE OF INNOCENCE, Cappa/De Fina, Columbia. Jay Cocks, Martin Scorsese.
IN THE NAME OF THE FATHER, Hell's Kitchen/Gabriel Byrne, Universal. Terry George, Jim Sheridan.
THE REMAINS OF THE DAY, Mike Nichols/John Calley/Merchant Ivory, Columbia. Ruth Prawer Jhabvala.
* SCHINDLER'S LIST, Universal/Amblin, Universal. Steven Zaillian.
SHADOWLANDS, Shadowlands Production, Savoy. William Nicholson.

(Screenplay Written Directly for the Screen)

DAVE, Warner Bros. Gary Ross.
IN THE LINE OF FIRE, Castle Rock, Columbia. Jeff Maguire.
PHILADELPHIA, TriStar. Ron Nyswaner.
* THE PIANO, Jan Chapman & CIBY 2000, Miramax. Jane Campion.
SLEEPLESS IN SEATTLE, TriStar. Screenplay by Nora Ephron, David S. Ward, Jeff Arch; Story by Jeff Arch.

ART DIRECTION-SET DECORATION

ADDAMS FAMILY VALUES, Scott Rudin, Paramount. Ken Adam; Marvin March.
THE AGE OF INNOCENCE, Cappa/De Fina, Columbia. Dante Ferretti; Robert J. Franco.
ORLANDO, Adventures Pictures, Sony Pictures Classics. Ben Van Os, Jan Roelfs.
THE REMAINS OF THE DAY, Mike Nichols/John Calley/Merchant Ivory, Columbia. Luciana Arrighi; Ian Whittaker.
* SCHINDLER'S LIST, Universal/Amblin, Universal. Allan Starski; Ewa Braun.

CINEMATOGRAPHY

FAREWELL MY CONCUBINE, Tomson (HK) Films, Miramax. Gu Changwei.
THE FUGITIVE, Warner Bros. Michael Chapman.
THE PIANO, Jan Chapman & CIBY 2000, Miramax. Stuart Dryburgh.
* SCHINDLER'S LIST, Universal/Amblin, Universal. Janusz Kaminski.
SEARCHING FOR BOBBY FISCHER, Scott Rudin/Mirage, Paramount. Conrad L. Hall.

COSTUME DESIGN

* THE AGE OF INNOCENCE, Cappa/De Fina, Columbia. Gabriella Pescucci.
ORLANDO, Adventures Pictures, Sony Pictures Classics. Sandy Powell.
THE PIANO, Jan Chapman & CIBY 2000, Miramax. Janet Patterson.
THE REMAINS OF THE DAY, Mike Nichols/John Calley/Merchant Ivory, Columbia. Jenny Beavan, John Bright.
SCHINDLER'S LIST, Universal/Amblin, Universal. Anna Biedrzycka-Sheppard.

FILM EDITING

THE FUGITIVE, Warner Bros. Dennis Virkler, David Finfer, Dean Goodhill, Don Brochu, Richard Nord, Dov Hoenig.
IN THE LINE OF FIRE, Castle Rock, Columbia. Anne V. Coates.

The Age of Innocence (Columbia; directed by Martin Scorsese) was an impeccably made adaptation of Edith Wharton's romantic novel about the restraints imposed on passion in New York's upper social circles of the 1870s. It starred Daniel Day-Lewis and Winona Ryder (left, with Miriam Margolyes sitting) along with Michelle Pfeiffer and was notable for its rich recreation of a bygone era. The film was nominated for five Academy Awards and won one: for its exquisite costumes designed by Gabriella Pescucci.

Jurassic Park *(Universal; directed by Steven Spielberg) couldn't have been more unlike Spielberg's other 1993 bellringer,* Schindler's List. *Whereas* Schindler's *was dark, dramatic and devastating,* Jurassic *abounded in vivid colors, lively special effects and spunky fantasy. It swiftly became one of the industry's all-time highest money grossers (at the time, second only to* Spielberg's own E.T. The Extra-Terrestrial*) and won three Academy Awards, one for its visual effects, the others for sound and sound effects editing.* Jurassic *also offered good visual proof that it can be damaging to one's health to hang around angry dinosaurs.*

IN THE NAME OF THE FATHER, Hell's Kitchen/Gabriel Byrne, Universal. Gerry Hambling.
THE PIANO, Jan Chapman & CIBY 2000, Miramax. Veronika Jenet.
* SCHINDLER'S LIST, Universal/Amblin, Universal. Michael Kahn.

MAKEUP
* MRS. DOUBTFIRE, 20th Century Fox. Greg Cannom, Ve Neill, Yolanda Toussieng.
PHILADELPHIA, TriStar. Carl Fullerton, Alan D'Angerio.
SCHINDLER'S LIST, Universal/Amblin, Universal. Christina Smith, Matthew Mungle, Judy Alexander Cory.

MUSIC
(Song)
AGAIN *(Poetic Justice,* Columbia). Music and Lyric by Janet Jackson, James Harris III, Terry Lewis.
THE DAY I FALL IN LOVE *(Beethoven's 2nd,* Universal). Music and Lyric by Carole Bayer Sager, James Ingram, Clif Magness.
PHILADELPHIA *(Philadelphia,* TriStar). Music and Lyric by Neil Young.
* STREETS OF PHILADELPHIA *(Philadelphia,* TriStar). Music and Lyric by Bruce Springsteen.
A WINK AND A SMILE *(Sleepless in Seattle,* TriStar). Music by Marc Shaiman; Lyric by Ramsey McLean.

(Original Score)
THE AGE OF INNOCENCE, Cappa/De Fina, Columbia. Elmer Bernstein.
THE FIRM, John Davis/Scott Rudin/Mirage, Paramount. Dave Grusin.
THE FUGITIVE, Warner Bros. James Newton Howard.
THE REMAINS OF THE DAY, Mike Nichols/John Calley/Merchant Ivory, Columbia. Richard Robbins.
* SCHINDLER'S LIST, Universal/Amblin, Universal. John Williams.

SOUND
CLIFFHANGER, Cliffhanger B.V., TriStar. Michael Minkler, Bob Beemer, Tim Cooney.
THE FUGITIVE, Warner Bros. Donald O. Mitchell, Michael Herbick, Frank A. Montaño, Scott D. Smith.
GERONIMO: AN AMERICAN LEGEND, Columbia. Chris Carpenter, D. M. Hemphill, Bill W. Benton, Lee Orloff.
* JURASSIC PARK, Amblin, Universal. Gary Summers, Gary Rydstrom, Shawn Murphy, Ron Judkins.
SCHINDLER'S LIST, Universal/Amblin, Universal. Andy Nelson, Steve Pederson, Scott Millan, Ron Judkins.

SOUND EFFECTS EDITING
CLIFFHANGER, Cliffhanger B.V., TriStar. Wylie Stateman, Gregg Baxter.
THE FUGITIVE, Warner Bros. John Leveque, Bruce Stambler.
* JURASSIC PARK, Amblin, Universal. Gary Rydstrom, Richard Hymns.

VISUAL EFFECTS
CLIFFHANGER, Cliffhanger B.V. Production; TriStar. Neil Krepela, John Richardson, John Bruno, Pamela Easley.
* JURASSIC PARK, Amblin Entertainment Production; Universal. Dennis Muren, Stan Winston, Phil Tippett, Michael Lantieri.
THE NIGHTMARE BEFORE CHRISTMAS, Touchstone Pictures Production; Buena Vista. Pete Kozachik, Eric Leighton, Ariel Velasco Shaw, Gordon Baker.

DOCUMENTARY
(Feature)
THE BROADCAST TAPES OF DR. PETER, Canadian Broadcasting Corporation/HBO Films Production. (Canada) David Paperny and Arthur Ginsberg.
CHILDREN OF FATE, Young/Friedson Production. Susan Todd and Andrew Young.
FOR BETTER OR FOR WORSE, David Collier Production. David Collier and Betsy Thompson.
* I AM A PROMISE: THE CHILDREN OF STANTON ELEMENTARY SCHOOL, Verité Films Production. Susan Raymond and Alan Raymond.
THE WAR ROOM, R.J. Cutler/Wendy Ettinger/Frazer Pennebaker Production. D. A. Pennebaker and Chris Hegedus.

(Short Subject)
BLOOD TIES: THE LIFE AND WORK OF SALLY MANN, Moving Target Production. Steven Cantor and Peter Spirer.
CHICKS IN WHITE SATIN, University of Southern California School of Cinema/Television. Elaine Holliman and Jason Schneider.
* DEFENDING OUR LIVES, Cambridge Documentary Films Production. Margaret Lazarus and Renner Wunderlich.

FOREIGN LANGUAGE FILM
* BELLE EPOQUE, (Spain).
FAREWELL MY CONCUBINE, (Hong Kong).
HEDD WYN, (United Kingdom/Wales)
THE SCENT OF GREEN PAPAYA, (Vietnam).
THE WEDDING BANQUET, (Taiwan).

SHORT FILMS
(Animated)
BLINDSCAPE, National Film & Television School. Stephen Palmer.
THE MIGHTY RIVER, Canadian Broadcasting Corporation/Société Radio-Canada Production. Frédéric Back, Hubert Tison.
SMALL TALK, Bob Godfrey Films, Ltd. Bob Godfrey, Kevin Baldwin.
THE VILLAGE, Pizazz Pictures Production. Mark Baker.
* THE WRONG TROUSERS, Aardman Animations Limited Production. Nick Park.

(Live Action)
* BLACK RIDER (SCHWARZFAHRER), Trans-Film GmbH Production. Pepe Danquart.

DOWN ON THE WATERFRONT, Stacy Title/Jonathan Penner Production. Stacy Title, Jonathan Penner.
THE DUTCH MASTER, Regina Ziegler Film Production. Susan Seidelman, Jonathan Brett.
PARTNERS, Chanticleer Films. Peter Weller, Jana Sue Memel.
THE SCREW (LA VIS), Perla Films Production. Didier Flamand.

HONORARY AND OTHER AWARDS
TO DEBORAH KERR in appreciation for a full career's worth of elegant and beautifully crafted performances.

1993 IRVING G. THALBERG MEMORIAL AWARD
None given this year.

1993 JEAN HERSHOLT HUMANITARIAN AWARD
TO PAUL NEWMAN

1993 GORDON E. SAWYER AWARD
TO PETRO VLAHOS

SCIENTIFIC AND TECHNICAL AWARDS
Academy Award of Merit (Statuette)
PANAVISION for the Auto Panatar anamorphic photographic lens.
MANFRED G. MICHELSON of Technical Film Systems, Incorporated, for the design and development of the first sprocket-driven film transport system for color print film processors which permits transport speeds in excess of 600 feet per minute.

Scientific and Engineering Award (Plaque)
MARK LEATHER, LES DITTERT, DOUGLAS SMYTHE and GEORGE JOBLOVE for the concept and development of the Digital Motion Picture Retouching System for removing visible rigging and dirt/damage artifacts from original motion picture imagery.
FRITZ GABRIEL BAUER for the design, development and manufacture of the Moviecam Compact Modular 35mm motion picture camera system.

Technical Achievement Award (Certificate)
WALLY MILLS for the concept; and GARY STADLER and GUSTAVE PARADA for the design of the Cinemills Lamp Protection System.
GARY NUZZI, DAVID JOHNSRUD and WILLIAM BLETHEN for the design and development of the Unilux H3000 Strobe Lighting System.
HARRY J. BAKER for the design and development of the Ronford-Baker Metal Tripods for motion picture photography.
MICHAEL DORROUGH for the design and development of the compound meter known as the Dorrough Audio Level Meter.
DAVID DEGENKOLB for the development of a Silver Recovery Ion Exchange System to eliminate hazardous waste (silver ion) in wash water and allow recycling of this water.

t hadn't happened in 56 years: one individual winning two Oscars in the "best actor" category back-to-back. Not since Spencer Tracy won consecutive best actor awards in 1937 and 1938 had an actor accomplished such a feat, but at the Academy's 67th party Tom Hanks matched the Tracy record when, following his 1993 award for *Philadelphia,* he was again named actor of the year for 1994's *Forrest Gump.* (In Oscar's first 70 years, only five performers won consecutive Oscars: the first was Luise Rainer in 1936 and 1937, then Tracy, later Katharine Hepburn, supporting actor Jason Robards and, finally, Hanks.) Something even rarer happened at the 67th Oscar party, held March 27, 1995, at the Los Angeles Shrine Auditorium: Jessica Lange was named the year's best actress for her work in a 1994 release called *Blue Sky,* a film which had been completed three years earlier, in 1991.

In many aspects, this particular show had a distinctly familiar look: three of the four acting winners (Hanks, Lange and supporting actress winner Dianne Wiest for *Bullets over Broadway*) had previously been in the winner's circle; only supporting actor champ Martin Landau (for *Ed Wood*) was a newcomer in the ranks. Among the films, the big winner of the night was *Gump,* which walked off with six awards, including best picture of the year, best director (Robert Zemeckis) and adapted screenplay (Eric Roth).

For the fifth time in Academy history there was a tie: in the live action short film category *Franz Kafka's It's a Wonderful Life* and *Trevor* received exactly the same number of votes, and each received an Oscar. An honorary award went to 82-year-old Italian director Michelangelo Antonioni; it was presented by Jack Nicholson, who'd starred in Antonioni's 1975 film *The Passenger.* Clint Eastwood received the Irving G. Thalberg award, Quincy Jones was presented the Jean Hersholt Humanitarian award and *Burnt by the Sun* from Russia was chosen best foreign language film.

Major pre-show attention, televised once again by ABC and seen by an audience approaching one billion in more than 100 countries worldwide, focused on late-night television host David Letterman making his debut as an Oscar show emcee. There was also considerable press attention given to the failure of *Hoop Dreams* to be nominated in the best feature documentary category. The latter incident did ultimately contribute to changes being made in the nomination procedures for that category. Much of the post-show talk centered around a dress. It was worn by Australian designer Lizzy Gardiner, a co-winner in the costume design category (for *The Adventures of Priscilla, Queen of the Desert*) and was created entirely out of American Express Gold Cards. Quipped Letterman later, "While we were gone, her dress expired."

Best Actress: **Jessica Lange** as *Carly Marshall in* Blue Sky *(Orion; produced by Robert H. Solo). Lange, center, won her second Academy Award (the first: as 1982's best supporting actress for* Tootsie*) as a manic-depressive housewife whose severe mood swings put a strain on her relationship with both her daughter and her husband, an Army scientist (Tommy Lee Jones, left); the wife's overt sexuality is also resoundingly misunderstood by others, including a military man (Powers Boothe, right), a commanding officer at the Alabama military base where her husband is assigned. The film itself initially possessed all the elements of a hard luck saga: shot in 1991, its director Tony Richardson had died soon after it was completed; the studio distributing it then went bankrupt and the film languished in a vault for three years, some suspecting it would never reach theaters. Little did anyone suspect that, once in release, it would end up with such notable Oscar attention.*

Best Picture: **Forrest Gump** *(Paramount; produced by Wendy Finerman, Steve Tisch and Steve Starkey),* **Best Actor:** **Tom Hanks** *as Forrest Gump (below, right) in* Forrest Gump *and* **Best Director:** **Robert Zemeckis** *(below, left) for* Forrest Gump. *It came from a solid source: a novel by Winston Groom about a kind-hearted, painfully honest simpleton who whimsically careens through four decades of life, often succeeding in the most spectacular ways in spite of himself. The Gump philosophy: "Life is like a box of choco-lates—you never know what you're going to get." It was extremely tricky material to interpret on screen, and it took nine years before a major studio was willing to gamble on a screen version. The final film, however, displayed such charm, style and good-naturedness it immediately became one of the giant grossers of all time, and became the picture of the year, nominated for a near-record 13 Academy awards and winning six of them, including one for visual effects, which allowed Hanks as the amiable Gump to interact in newsreel footage with the likes of John F. Kennedy, Lyndon Johnson, and Richard Nixon.*

Best Supporting Actor: **Martin Landau** *as Bela Lugosi (right) in* Ed Wood *(Buena Vista; directed by Tim Burton). Looking eerily like the real Lugosi, in his prime the famed horror star of* Dracula, *Landau had an actor's field day in this homage to the man who directed Lugosi's final films, a 1940's movie maverick and grade-Z filmmaker named Ed Wood, often described as "the worst film director of all time." Lugosi, his star days long past and his mind addled with drugs, became a pathetic caricature of himself; Landau's performance as the aging Lugosi perfectly captured his egomania, madness and poignancy during those days working with Wood. The role required Landau to spend three hours each day in a makeup chair; not surprisingly, at Oscar time the award for makeup went to Rick Baker, Ve Neill, and Yolanda Toussieng for* Ed Wood.

Best Supporting Actress: Dianne Wiest as Helen Sinclair (above left) in Bullets over Broadway (Miramax; directed by Woody Allen). Once again, Dianne Wiest had reason to be grateful there was a man in her life named Woody. Eight years before, in 1986, she'd won a Supporting Oscar for a film directed by Allen, Hannah and Her Sisters. Here she was again, an Academy Award in hand, thanks to a dazzling performance in a Woody Allen film. This time Wiest was playing a 1920s stage diva, signed to star in a debut work by a fledgling playwright (John Cusack, above right). A woman every bit as theatrical off stage as on, she was the year's funniest movie creation, never more so than when silencing Cusack's ongoing attempts at a disussion by melodramatically throwing up her hands and commanding, as if lives depended upon it, "Don't . . . speak!"

Best Cinematography: Legends of the Fall (Tristar), set amid the rugged beauty of Montana, won the year's Cinematography prize for John Toll's awesome scenic images. The Legends story centered on the three Ludlow brothers (Aidan Quinn, Brad Pitt, Henry Thomas, below left to right), raised on a remote ranch by a stern father (Anthony Hopkins), and later torn apart by sibling rivalries, World War I fervor and the fact that all the Ludlows are stirred by a refined and initially-repressed beauty from the East named Susannah (Julia Ormond, right).

PICTURE

* **FORREST GUMP**, Steve Tisch/Wendy Finerman, Paramount. Wendy Finerman, Steve Tisch and Steve Starkey, Producers.
FOUR WEDDINGS AND A FUNERAL, Working Title, Gramercy. Duncan Kenworthy, Producer.
PULP FICTION, A Band Apart/Jersey Films, Miramax. Lawrence Bender, Producer.
QUIZ SHOW, Hollywood Pictures/Wildwood/Baltimore Pictures, Buena Vista. Robert Redford, Michael Jacobs, Julian Krainin and Michael Nozik, Producers.
THE SHAWSHANK REDEMPTION, Castle Rock, Columbia. Niki Marvin, Producer.

ACTOR

MORGAN FREEMAN in *The Shawshank Redemption*, Castle Rock, Columbia.
* **TOM HANKS** in *Forrest Gump*, Steve Tisch/Wendy Finerman, Paramount.
NIGEL HAWTHORNE in *The Madness of King George*, Close Call Films, Goldwyn/Channel Four.
PAUL NEWMAN in *Nobody's Fool*, Scott Rudin/Cinehaus, Paramount/Capella International.
JOHN TRAVOLTA in *Pulp Fiction*, A Band Apart/Jersey Films, Miramax.

ACTRESS

JODIE FOSTER in *Nell*, 20th Century Fox.
* **JESSICA LANGE** in *Blue Sky*, Robert H. Solo, Orion.
MIRANDA RICHARDSON in *Tom & Viv*, New Era, Miramax.
WINONA RYDER in *Little Women*, Di Novi, Columbia.
SUSAN SARANDON in *The Client*, Client Production, Warner Bros.

SUPPORTING ACTOR

SAMUEL L. JACKSON in *Pulp Fiction*, A Band Apart/Jersey Films, Miramax.
* **MARTIN LANDAU** in *Ed Wood*, Touchstone, Buena Vista.
CHAZZ PALMINTERI in *Bullets over Broadway*, Jean Doumanian, Miramax.
PAUL SCOFIELD in *Quiz Show*, Hollywood Pictures/Wildwood/Baltimore Pictures, Buena Vista.
GARY SINISE in *Forrest Gump*, Steve Tisch/Wendy Finerman, Paramount.

SUPPORTING ACTRESS

ROSEMARY HARRIS in *Tom & Viv*, New Era, Miramax.
HELEN MIRREN in *The Madness of King George*, Close Call Films, Goldwyn/Channel Four.
UMA THURMAN in *Pulp Fiction*, A Band Apart/Jersey Films, Miramax.
JENNIFER TILLY in *Bullets over Broadway*, Jean Doumanian, Miramax.
* **DIANNE WIEST** in *Bullets over Broadway*, Jean Doumanian, Miramax.

DIRECTING

BULLETS OVER BROADWAY, Jean Doumanian, Miramax. Woody Allen.
* **FORREST GUMP**, Steve Tisch/Wendy Finerman, Paramount. Robert Zemeckis.
PULP FICTION, A Band Apart/Jersey Films, Miramax. Quentin Tarantino.
QUIZ SHOW, Hollywood Pictures/Wildwood/ Baltimore Pictures, Buena Vista. Robert Redford.
RED, CAB/MK2/TOR, Miramax. Krzysztof Kieslowski.

WRITING

(Screenplay Based on Material Previously Produced or Published)
* **FORREST GUMP**, Steve Tisch/Wendy Finerman, Paramount. Eric Roth.
THE MADNESS OF KING GEORGE, Close Call Films, Goldwyn/Channel Four. Alan Bennett.
NOBODY'S FOOL, Scott Rudin/Cinehaus, Paramount/Capella International. Robert Benton.
QUIZ SHOW, Hollywood Pictures/Wildwood/Baltimore Pictures, Buena Vista. Paul Attanasio.

THE SHAWSHANK REDEMPTION, Castle Rock, Columbia. Frank Darabont.
(Screenplay Written Directly for the Screen)
BULLETS OVER BROADWAY, Jean Doumanian, Miramax. Woody Allen, Douglas McGrath.
FOUR WEDDINGS AND A FUNERAL, Working Title, Gramercy. Richard Curtis.
HEAVENLY CREATURES, Wingnut, Miramax. Frances Walsh, Peter Jackson.
* **PULP FICTION**, A Band Apart/Jersey Films, Miramax. Screenplay by Quentin Tarantino. Stories by Quentin Tarantino & Roger Avary.
RED, CAB/MK2/TOR, Miramax. Krzysztof Piesiewicz, Krzysztof Kieslowski.

ART DIRECTION-SET DECORATION

BULLETS OVER BROADWAY, Jean Doumanian, Miramax. Santo Loquasto; Susan Bode.
FORREST GUMP, Steve Tisch/Wendy Finerman, Paramount. Rick Carter; Nancy Haigh.
INTERVIEW WITH THE VAMPIRE, Geffen, Warner Bros. Dante Ferretti; Francesca Lo Schiavo.
LEGENDS OF THE FALL, TriStar. Lilly Kilvert; Dorree Cooper.
* **THE MADNESS OF KING GEORGE**, Close Call Films, Goldwyn/Channel Four. Ken Adam; Carolyn Scott.

CINEMATOGRAPHY

FORREST GUMP, Steve Tisch/Wendy Finerman, Paramount. Don Burgess.
* **LEGENDS OF THE FALL**, TriStar. John Toll.
RED, CAB/MK2/TOR, Miramax. Piotr Sobocinski.
THE SHAWSHANK REDEMPTION, Castle Rock, Columbia. Roger Deakins.
WYATT EARP, Tig, Warner Bros. Owen Roizman.

COSTUME DESIGN

* **THE ADVENTURES OF PRISCILLA, QUEEN OF THE DESERT**, Latent Images, Gramercy. Lizzy Gardiner, Tim Chappel.
BULLETS OVER BROADWAY, Jean Doumanian, Miramax. Jeffrey Kurland.
LITTLE WOMEN, Di Novi, Columbia. Colleen Atwood.
MAVERICK, Icon, Warner Bros. April Ferry.
QUEEN MARGOT, Renn, Miramax. Moidele Bickel.

FILM EDITING

* **FORREST GUMP**, Steve Tisch/Wendy Finerman, Paramount. Arthur Schmidt.
HOOP DREAMS, Kartemquin, Fine Line Features. Frederick Marx, Steve James, Bill Haugse.
PULP FICTION, A Band Apart/Jersey Films, Miramax. Sally Menke.
THE SHAWSHANK REDEMPTION, Castle Rock, Columbia. Richard Francis-Bruce.
SPEED, 20th Century Fox. John Wright.

MAKEUP

* **ED WOOD**, Touchstone, Buena Vista. Rick Baker, Ve Neill, Yolanda Toussieng.
FORREST GUMP, Steve Tisch/Wendy Finerman, Paramount. Daniel C. Striepeke, Hallie D'Amore, Judith A. Cory.
MARY SHELLEY'S FRANKENSTEIN, TriStar. Daniel Parker, Paul Engelen, Carol Hemming.

MUSIC

(Song)
* **CAN YOU FEEL THE LOVE TONIGHT** (*The Lion King*, Disney, Buena Vista). Music by Elton John; Lyric by Tim Rice.
CIRCLE OF LIFE (*The Lion King*, Buena Vista). Music by Elton John; Lyric by Tim Rice.
HAKUNA MATATA (*The Lion King*, Disney, Buena Vista). Music by Elton John; Lyric by Tim Rice.
LOOK WHAT LOVE HAS DONE (*Junior*, Northern Lights, Universal). Music and Lyric by Carole Bayer Sager, James Newton Howard, James Ingram, Patty Smyth.
MAKE UP YOUR MIND (*The Paper*, Imagine, Universal). Music and Lyric by Randy Newman.

(Original Score)
FORREST GUMP, Steve Tisch/Wendy Finerman, Paramount. Alan Silvestri.
INTERVIEW WITH THE VAMPIRE, Geffen, Warner Bros. Elliot Goldenthal.
* **THE LION KING**, Disney, Buena Vista. Hans Zimmer.
LITTLE WOMEN, Di Novi, Columbia. Thomas Newman.
THE SHAWSHANK REDEMPTION, Castle Rock, Columbia. Thomas Newman.

SOUND

CLEAR AND PRESENT DANGER, Mace Neufeld/Robert Rehme, Paramount. Donald O. Mitchell, Michael Herbick, Frank A. Montaño, Arthur Rochester.
FORREST GUMP, Steve Tisch/Wendy Finerman, Paramount. Randy Thom, Tom Johnson, Dennis Sands, William B. Kaplan.
LEGENDS OF THE FALL, TriStar. Paul Massey, David Campbell, Christopher David, Douglas Ganton.
THE SHAWSHANK REDEMPTION, Castle Rock, Columbia. Robert J. Litt, Elliot Tyson, Michael Herbick, Willie Burton.
* **SPEED**, 20th Century Fox. Gregg Landaker, Steve Maslow, Bob Beemer, David R. B. MacMillan.

SOUND EFFECTS EDITING

CLEAR AND PRESENT DANGER, Mace Neufeld/Robert Rehme, Paramount. Bruce Stambler, John Leveque.

FORREST GUMP, Steve Tisch/Wendy Finerman, Paramount. Gloria S. Borders, Randy Thom.
* **SPEED,** 20th Century Fox. Stephen Hunter Flick.

VISUAL EFFECTS
* **FORREST GUMP,** Steve Tisch/Wendy Finerman Productions; Paramount. Ken Ralston, George Murphy, Stephen Rosenbaum, Allen Hall.
  MASK, Katja Motion Picture Production; New Line. Scott Squires, Steve Williams, Tom Bertino, Jon Farhat.
  TRUE LIES, Lightstorm Entertainment Production; 20th Century Fox. John Bruno, Thomas L. Fisher, Jacques Stroweis, Patrick McClung.

DOCUMENTARY
(Feature)
  COMPLAINTS OF A DUTIFUL DAUGHTER, D/D Production. Deborah Hoffmann.
  D-DAY REMEMBERED, Guggenheim Productions, Inc. Production for the National D-Day Museum. Charles Guggenheim.
  FREEDOM ON MY MIND, Clarity Film Production. Connie Field, Marilyn Mulford.
  A GREAT DAY IN HARLEM, Jean Bach Production; Castle Hill. Jean Bach.
* **MAYA LIN: A STRONG CLEAR VISION,** American Film Foundation/Sanders and Mock Productions. Freida Lee Mock, Terry Sanders.

(Short Subject)
  BLUES HIGHWAY, Half-Court Pictures, Ltd./National Geographic Society Production. Vince DiPersio, Bill Guttentag.
  89MM OD EUROPY (89MM FROM EUROPE), Studio Filmowe "Kalejdoskop"/Telewizja Polska Production. (Poland) Marcel Lozinski.
  SCHOOL OF ~~THE AMERICAS~~ ASSASSINS, A Richter Productions Film. Robert Richter.
  STRAIGHT FROM THE HEART, Woman Vision Production. Dee Mosbacher, Frances Reid.
* **A TIME FOR JUSTICE,** Guggenheim Productions, Inc. Production for the Southern Poverty Law Center. Charles Guggenheim.

FOREIGN LANGUAGE FILM
  BEFORE THE RAIN, (Macedonia).
* **BURNT BY THE SUN,** (Russia).
  EAT DRINK MAN WOMAN, (Taiwan).
  FARINELLI: IL CASTRATO, (Belgium).
  STRAWBERRY AND CHOCOLATE, (Cuba).

SHORT FILMS
(Animated)
  THE BIG STORY, Spitting Image Production. Tim Watts, David Stoten.
* **BOB'S BIRTHDAY,** Snowden Fine Animation for Channel Four/National Film Board of Canada Production. Alison Snowden, David Fine.
  THE JANITOR, Vanessa Schwartz Production. Vanessa Schwartz.
  THE MONK AND THE FISH, Folimage Valence Production. Michael Dudok de Wit.
  TRIANGLE, Gingco Ltd. Production for Channel Four. Erica Russell.

The Lion King (Buena Vista), the 32nd animated feature from The Walt Disney Company, won two Academy Awards: one for Hans Zimmer's original music score and another for the year's best original song, "Can You Feel the Love Tonight," music by Elton John and lyric by Tim Rice. This was The Walt Disney Company's fourth double win in six years in the Academy's music division (following similar victories for The Little Mermaid *in 1989,* Beauty and the Beast *in 1991 and* Aladdin *in 1992), a remarkable record repeated yet again in 1995, with* Pocahontas. The Lion King, *like* Beauty and the Beast, *also became the basis for a successful live Broadway version.*

Pulp Fiction (Miramax; directed by Quentin Tarantino) with Uma Thurman and John Travolta (above) was a Palme d'Or winner at the Cannes Film Festival and brought Travolta back into Oscar contention for the first time since he was nominated in 1977 for his breakthrough performance in Saturday Night Fever. Pulp *was a mad, imaginative mix of stories about life among big-time gangsters and small-time hoods in Los Angeles. Both daring and imaginative, it brought writer-director Tarantino two personal nominations among the total of seven received by the film. It won one award, for Tarantino's original screenplay, which was based on stories by Tarantino and Roger Avary.*

(Live Action)
* **FRANZ KAFKA'S IT'S A WONDERFUL LIFE,** Conundrum Films Production. Peter Capaldi, Ruth Kenley-Letts.
  KANGAROO COURT, Lava Entertainment Production. Sean Astin, Christine Astin.
  ON HOPE, Chanticleer Films. JoBeth Williams, Michele McGuire.
  SYRUP, First Choice Production. Paul Unwin, Nick Vivian.
* **TREVOR,** Rajski/Stone Production. Peggy Rajski, Randy Stone.

HONORARY AND OTHER AWARDS
  TO MICHELANGELO ANTONIONI in recognition of his place as one of the cinema's master visual stylists.
  TO JOHN A. BONNER in appreciation for outstanding service and dedication in upholding the high standards of the Academy of Motion Picture Arts and Sciences. (Medal of Commendation)

1994 IRVING G. THALBERG MEMORIAL AWARD
  TO CLINT EASTWOOD

1994 JEAN HERSHOLT HUMANITARIAN AWARD
  TO QUINCY JONES

1994 GORDON E. SAWYER AWARD
  None given this year.

SCIENTIFIC AND TECHNICAL AWARDS
Academy Award of Merit (Statuette)
  PETRO VLAHOS and **PAUL VLAHOS** for the conception and development of the Ultimatte Electronic Blue Screen Compositing Process for motion pictures.
  EASTMAN KODAK COMPANY for the development of the Eastman EXR Color Intermediate Film 5244.

Scientific and Engineering Awards (Plaque)
  GARY DEMOS and **DAN CAMERON** of Information International, **DAVID DiFRANCESCO** and **GARY STARKWEATHER** of Pixar, and **SCOTT SQUIRES** of Industrial Light & Magic for their pioneering work in the field of film input scanning.
  RAY FEENEY, WILL McCOWN and **BILL BISHOP** of RFX, Inc., and **LES DITTERT** of Pacific Data Images for their development work with area array CCD (Charge Coupled Device) film input scanning systems.
  LINCOLN HU and **MICHAEL MACKENZIE** of Industrial Light & Magic and **GLENN KENNEL** and **MIKE DAVIS** of Eastman Kodak for their joint development work on a linear array CCD (Charge Coupled Device) film input scanning system.
  IAIN NEIL for the optical design, **AL SAIKI** for the mechanical design and **PANAVISION INTERNATIONAL L.P.** for the development of the Panavision 11:1 Primo Zoom Lens for motion picture photography.
  JAMES KETCHAM of JSK Engineering for the concept and design of the MC211 microprocessor-based motion controller for synchronizing sprocketed film with timecode-based machines.
  WILLIAM J. WARNER and **ERIC C. PETERS** for the concept, **MICHAEL E. PHILLIPS** and **TOM A. OHANIAN**

for the system design and **PATRICK D. O'CONNOR** and **JOE H. RICE** for the engineering of the Avid Film Composer for motion picture editing.
  PAUL BAMBOROUGH for the concept, **NICK POLLACK** and **ARTHUR WRIGHT** for the hardware development and **NEIL HARRIS** and **DUNCAN MacLEAN** for the software development of The Lightworks Editor for motion picture editing.
  GEORGE SAUVE, BILL BISHOP, ARPAG DADOURIAN, RAY FEENEY and **RICHARD PATTERSON** for the Cinefusion software, implementation of the Ultimatte Blue Screen Compositing Technology.

Technical Achievement Awards (Certificate)
  B. RUSSELL HESSEY of Special Effects Spectacular, Inc., and **VINCENT T. KELTON** for the hardware design and **GEORGE JACKMAN** of De La Mare Engineering, Inc. for the pyrotechnic development which together comprise the non-gun safety blank firing system.
  FRIEDER HOCHHEIM, GARY SWINK, DR. JOE ZHOU and **DON NORTHROP** for the development of the Kino Flo Portable, Flicker-Free, High-Output Fluorescent Lighting System for motion picture set illumination.
  EMANUEL PREVINAIRE of Flying-Cam for his pioneering concept and for the development of mounting a motion picture camera on a remotely controlled miniature helicopter.
  JACQUES SAX of Sonosax for the design and development of the Sonosax SX-S portable audio mixer.
  CLAY DAVIS and **JOHN CARTER** of Todd-AO for the pioneering effort of computer controlled list management style ADR (Automated Dialogue Replacement).
  STEPHEN W. POTTER, JOHN B. ASMAN, CHARLES PELL and **RICHARD LARSON** of LarTec Systems for the advancement and refinement of the computer controlled list management style ADR (Automated Dialogue Replacement) system via the LarTec ADR System that has established itself as a standard of the industry.
  AUDIO TRACKS, INC. for the design and development of the ADE (Advanced Data Encoding) System which creates an encoded timecode track and database during the initial transfer of the production sound "dailies."
  COLIN BROAD of CB Electronics for the design and development of the EDL (Edit Decision List) lister which creates an encoded timecode track and database during the initial transfer of the production sound "dailies."
  DIETER STURM of Sturm's Special Effects Int'l, for the creation and development of the Bio-Snow 2 Flake.
  DAVID A. ADDLEMAN and **LLOYD A. ADDLEMAN** for the development of the Cyberware 3030 3D Digitizer.
  MARK R. SCHNEIDER, HERBERT R. JONES, CHRISTOPHER D. CONOVER and **JOHN R.B. BROWN** for the development of the Polhemus 3 Space Digitizing System.
  JACK C. SMITH, MICHAEL CRICHTON and **EMIL SAFIER** for pioneering computerized motion picture budgeting and scheduling.
  STEPHEN GREENFIELD and **CHRIS HUNTLEY** of Screenplay Systems for development of the "Scriptor" software.
  ART FRITZEN of the California Fritzen Propeller Company as the designer and sole manufacturer of the Eight-Bladed Ritter Fan Propellers.
  DR. MIKE BOUDRY of the Computer Film Company for his pioneering work in the field of film input scanning.

Soothsayers were caught napping this time: *Braveheart,* the film named by the Academy voters as 1995's best picture, hadn't collected a single best picture prize from any other award group prior to Academy Award night on March 25, 1996. Compounding the surprise, the historical epic ended up with a bigger total of prizes than any other film of the year, five in all. No other 1995 feature won more than two Oscars. The *Braveheart* awards included ones for best direction (Mel Gibson), best makeup, best sound effects editing and best cinematography, the latter going to John Toll who'd won in that same division the preceding year for his cinematography of *Legends of the Fall.* Gibson, who'd never been nominated as an actor during his 19-year film career, went home with two statuettes, one for his direction, the other because he'd been one of the producers of *Braveheart,* along with Alan Ladd, Jr. and Bruce Davey. Said Gibson, "Like most directors, I suppose what I really want to do is act."

It was a year when all the acting champs were first-timers in the winner's circle. Nicolas Cage was named as best actor for *Leaving Las Vegas,* Susan Sarandon was best actress for *Dead Man Walking* and the supporting winners were Kevin Spacey for *The Usual Suspects* and Mira Sorvino in *Mighty Aphrodite.* For Sarandon and Sorvino the night was decidedly a family affair. Sarandon's companion of eight years Tim Robbins had written, directed and produced her film ("This is yours as much as mine," Sarandon said to Robbins in her acceptance speech. "Thank God we live together.") Sorvino's proud papa dissolved in tears as his daughter told the audience, "When you give me this award you honor my father, Paul Sorvino, who has taught me everything I know about acting." Kirk Douglas, age 79, received an Honorary Oscar and, speaking with difficulty from the effects of a recent stroke, acknowledged his four sons sitting in the auditorium, saying "They're proud of the old man. And I'm proud, too—proud to be a part of Hollywood for 50 years." Another special award went to legendary animator Chuck Jones, who quipped, "I stand guilty before the world of directing over 300 cartoons. I hope this means you've forgiven me."

Whoopi Goldberg, after a one-year lay-off, was again the emcee of the Oscar Show, beamed from the Dorothy Chandler Pavilion of the Los Angeles Music Center and produced for the first time by Quincy Jones and David Salzman. Among the highpoints was Emma Thompson, after winning the screenplay adaptation award for her script of Jane Austen's *Sense and Sensibility,* saying, "I went to visit Jane Austen's grave in Winchester Cathedral to pay my respects. . . and tell her about the grosses. I don't know how she would react to an evening like this but I do hope she knows how big she is in Uruguay." Two films about the Holocaust won documentary awards. *One Survivor Remembers* received the prize for best documentary short subject, and *Anne Frank Remem-*

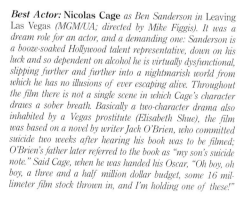

Best Actor: **Nicolas Cage** *as Ben Sanderson in* Leaving Las Vegas *(MGM/UA; directed by Mike Figgis). It was a dream role for an actor, and a demanding one: Sanderson is a booze-soaked Hollywood talent representative, down on his luck and so dependent on alcohol he is virtually dysfunctional, slipping further and further into a nightmarish world from which he has no illusions of ever escaping alive. Throughout the film there is not a single scene in which Cage's character draws a sober breath. Basically a two-character drama also inhabited by a Vegas prostitute (Elisabeth Shue), the film was based on a novel by writer Jack O'Brien, who committed suicide two weeks after hearing his book was to be filmed; O'Brien's father later referred to the book as "my son's suicide note." Said Cage, when he was handed his Oscar, "Oh boy, oh boy, a three and a half million dollar budget, some 16 millimeter film stock thrown in, and I'm holding one of these!"*

bered was chosen best feature documentary. One of several emotional moments in the evening occured with the appearance on stage of Christopher Reeve, in a wheelchair and partially paralyzed from a horse-riding accident almost a year earlier. His participation in the telecast had been kept a secret; he appeared to introduce a selection of highlights from films of the past which dealt with social issues. After a long and enthusiastic ovation from the audience, Reeve spoke, quietly and with measured speech, challenging current filmmakers "to do more, to take risks, to tackle the issues."

Best Picture: **Braveheart** *(Paramount; produced by Mel Gibson, Alan Ladd, Jr. and Bruce Davey) and* ***Best Director:*** **Mel Gibson** *for* Braveheart. *Running nearly three hours in length,* Braveheart *spun the tale of the legendary 13th century Scottish freedom fighter William Wallace (played by Gibson, leading a charge, below), famous for the rebellion he led against England's tyrannical King Edward I, following his father's credo that "It's our wits that make us men." Done on an ambitious scale, and reading at times like a medieval-style western, the film was full of battles, burrs, blood, bravado and beheadings. It also had stunning cinematography by John Toll which was also honored, as were the film's achievements in sound effects editing and makeup. For Mel Gibson, it was a particular triumph:* Braveheart *was only his second attempt at directing a film (the first: the small-scale* Man without a Face *in 1993) and brought him two statuettes for his mantel.*

Best Actress: **Susan Sarandon** *as Sister Helen Prejean in* Dead Man Walking *(Gramercy; directed by Tim Robbins). After four previous best actress nominations, Sarandon finally went home an Academy winner for her performance as a real-life Louisiana nun who tries to awaken the conscience of a convicted murderer (Sean Penn) as he awaits execution at the* Angola Prison in New Orleans. Inspired by Prejean's 1993 bestseller, it was a drama which covered extremely tricky cinematic terrain, as the sister begins a fight for the convict's soul, even though she is appalled by the details of his criminal acts. Meanwhile, with great power but without preachment, Dead Man *also deftly examined the pros and cons of capital punishment.*

325

Nominations 1995

Babe *(Universal; directed by Chris Noonan) was made in Australia and became the year's most-talked-about and endearing film, so well liked it landed a spot as one of the year's five Best Picture nominees. ("A picture about a pig up for the top Oscar prize? It doesn't seem quite kosher," commented one writer.) The title character is a sweet-natured but free-spirited barnyard piglet who, more than anything else, wants to be a sheepdog, ultimately accomplishing that lofty aim by winning a sheep-herding contest. The ham who played* Babe *was actually 48 different piglets, and real animals were blended with computer animation and puppets, but all done so seamlessly that* Babe *went on to win the year's award for Visual Effects.*

PICTURE
APOLLO 13, Imagine, Universal. Brian Grazer, Producer.
BABE, Kennedy Miller, Universal. George Miller, Doug Mitchell and Bill Miller, Producers.
* BRAVEHEART, Icon/Ladd Company, Paramount. Mel Gibson, Alan Ladd, Jr. and Bruce Davey, Producers.
THE POSTMAN (IL POSTINO), Cecchi Gori Group Tiger Cinematografica Production/Pentafilm/Esterno Mediterraneo/Blue Dahlia, Miramax. Mario Cecchi Gori, Vittorio Cecchi Gori and Gaetano Daniele, Producers.
SENSE AND SENSIBILITY, Mirage, Columbia. Lindsay Doran, Producer.

ACTOR
* NICOLAS CAGE in *Leaving Las Vegas,* Initial Productions, MGM/UA.
RICHARD DREYFUSS in *Mr. Holland's Opus,* Hollywood Pictures/Interscope Communications, Buena Vista.
ANTHONY HOPKINS in *Nixon,* Hollywood Pictures/Cinergi, Buena Vista.
SEAN PENN in *Dead Man Walking,* Working Title/Havoc, Gramercy.
MASSIMO TROISI in *The Postman (Il Postino),* Cecchi Gori Group Tiger Cinematografica Production/Pentafilm/Esterno Mediterraneo/Blue Dahlia, Miramax.

ACTRESS
* SUSAN SARANDON in *Dead Man Walking,* Working Title/Havoc, Gramercy.
ELISABETH SHUE in *Leaving Las Vegas,* Initial Productions, MGM/UA.
SHARON STONE in *Casino,* Universal.
MERYL STREEP in *The Bridges of Madison County,* Amblin/Malpaso, Warner Bros.
EMMA THOMPSON in *Sense and Sensibility,* Mirage, Columbia.

SUPPORTING ACTOR
JAMES CROMWELL in *Babe,* Kennedy Miller, Universal.
ED HARRIS in *Apollo 13,* Imagine, Universal.
BRAD PITT in *12 Monkeys,* Atlas/Classico, Universal.
TIM ROTH in *Rob Roy,* United Artists, MGM/UA.
* KEVIN SPACEY in *The Usual Suspects,* Blue Parrot, Gramercy.

SUPPORTING ACTRESS
JOAN ALLEN in *Nixon,* Hollywood Pictures/Cinergi, Buena Vista.
KATHLEEN QUINLAN in *Apollo 13,* Imagine, Universal.
* MIRA SORVINO in *Mighty Aphrodite,* Sweetheart, Miramax.
MARE WINNINGHAM in *Georgia,* CIBY 2000, Miramax.
KATE WINSLET in *Sense and Sensibility,* Mirage, Columbia.

DIRECTING
BABE, Kennedy Miller, Universal. Chris Noonan.
*BRAVEHEART, Icon/Ladd Company, Paramount. Mel Gibson.
DEAD MAN WALKING, Working Title/Havoc, Gramercy. Tim Robbins.
LEAVING LAS VEGAS, Initial Productions; MGM/UA. Mike Figgis.
THE POSTMAN (IL POSTINO), Cecchi Gori Group Tiger Cinematografica Production/Pentafilm/Esterno Mediterraneo/Blue Dahlia, Miramax. Michael Radford.

WRITING
(Screenplay Based on Material Previously Produced or Published)
APOLLO 13, Imagine, Universal. William Broyles, Jr., Al Reinert.
BABE, Kennedy Miller, Universal. George Miller, Chris Noonan.
LEAVING LAS VEGAS, Initial Productions; MGM/UA. Mike Figgis.
THE POSTMAN (IL POSTINO), Cecchi Gori Group Tiger Cinematografica Production/Pentafilm/Esterno Mediterraneo/Blue Dahlia, Miramax. Anna Pavignano, Michael Radford, Furio Scarpelli, Giacomo Scarpelli, Massimo Troisi.
* SENSE AND SENSIBILITY, Mirage, Columbia. Emma Thompson.

(Screenplay Written Directly for the Screen)
BRAVEHEART, Icon/Ladd Company, Paramount. Randall Wallace.
MIGHTY APHRODITE, Sweetheart, Miramax. Woody Allen.
NIXON, Hollywood Pictures/Cinergi, Buena Vista. Stephen J. Rivele, Christopher Wilkinson, Oliver Stone.
TOY STORY, Disney/Pixar, Buena Vista. Screenplay by Joss Whedon, Andrew Stanton, Joel Cohen, Alec Sokolow; Story by John Lasseter, Peter Docter, Andrew Stanton, Joe Ranft.
* THE USUAL SUSPECTS, Blue Parrot, Gramercy. Christopher McQuarrie.

ART DIRECTION-SET DECORATION
APOLLO 13, Imagine, Universal. Michael Corenblith; Merideth Boswell.
BABE, Kennedy Miller, Universal. Roger Ford; Kerrie Brown.
A LITTLE PRINCESS, Warner Bros. Bo Welch; Cheryl Carasik.
* RESTORATION, Segue/Avenue Pictures/Oxford Film Company, Miramax. Eugenio Zanetti
RICHARD III, Richard III Limited Production, MGM/UA. Tony Burrough.

CINEMATOGRAPHY
BATMAN FOREVER, Warner Bros. Stephen Goldblatt.
* BRAVEHEART, Icon/Ladd Company, Paramount. John Toll.
A LITTLE PRINCESS, Warner Bros. Emmanuel Lubezki.
SENSE AND SENSIBILITY, Mirage, Columbia. Michael Coulter.
SHANGHAI TRIAD, Shanghai Film Studios, Sony Pictures Classics. Lu Yue.

COSTUME DESIGN
BRAVEHEART, Icon/Ladd Company, Paramount. Charles Knode.
* RESTORATION, Segue/Avenue Pictures/Oxford Film Company, Miramax. James Acheson.
RICHARD III, Richard III Limited Production, MGM/UA. Shuna Harwood.
SENSE AND SENSIBILITY, Mirage, Columbia. Jenny Beavan, John Bright.
12 MONKEYS, Atlas/Classico, Universal. Julie Weiss.

FILM EDITING
* APOLLO 13, Imagine, Universal. Mike Hill, Dan Hanley.
BABE, Kennedy Miller, Universal. Marcus D'Arcy, Jay Friedkin.
BRAVEHEART, Icon/Ladd Company, Paramount. Steven Rosenblum.
CRIMSON TIDE, Hollywood Pictures, Buena Vista. Chris Lebenzon.
SEVEN, Juno Pix, New Line. Richard Francis-Bruce.

MAKEUP
* BRAVEHEART, Icon/Ladd Company, Paramount. Peter Frampton, Paul Pattison, Lois Burwell.
MY FAMILY, MI FAMILIA, New Line. Ken Diaz, Mark Sanchez.
ROOMMATES, Hollywood Pictures/Interscope, Buena Vista. Greg Cannom, Bob Laden, Colleen Callaghan.

MUSIC
(Song)
* COLORS OF THE WIND (*Pocahontas,* Disney, Buena Vista). Music by Alan Menken; Lyric by Stephen Schwartz.
DEAD MAN WALKIN' (*Dead Man Walking,* Working Title/Havoc, Gramercy). Music and Lyric by Bruce Springsteen.
HAVE YOU EVER REALLY LOVED A WOMAN (*Don Juan DeMarco,* Juno Pix, New Line). Music and Lyric by Michael Kamen, Bryan Adams, Robert John Lange.
MOONLIGHT (*Sabrina,* Mirage/Scott Rudin/Sandollar, Paramount/Constellation Films). Music by John Williams; Lyric by Alan Bergman, Marilyn Bergman.
YOU'VE GOT A FRIEND IN ME (*Toy Story,* Disney/Pixar, Buena Vista). Music and Lyric by Randy Newman.

(Original Dramatic Score)
APOLLO 13, Imagine, Universal. James Horner.
BRAVEHEART, Icon/Ladd Company, Paramount. James Horner.
NIXON, Hollywood Pictures/Cinergi, Buena Vista. John Williams.
* THE POSTMAN (IL POSTINO), Cecchi Gori Group Tiger Cinematografica Production/Pentafilm/Esterno Mediterraneo/Blue Dahlia, Miramax. Luis Enrique Bacalov.
SENSE AND SENSIBILITY, Mirage, Columbia. Patrick Doyle.

(Original Musical or Comedy Score)
THE AMERICAN PRESIDENT, Castle Rock, Columbia. Marc Shaiman.
* POCAHONTAS, Disney, Buena Vista. Music by Alan Menken; Lyrics by Stephen Schwartz; Orchestral Score by Alan Menken.
SABRINA, Mirage/Scott Rudin/Sandollar, Paramount/Constellation Films. John Williams.
TOY STORY, Disney/Pixar, Buena Vista. Randy Newman.
UNSTRUNG HEROES, Hollywood Pictures, Buena Vista. Thomas Newman.

Sense and Sensibility *(Columbia; directed by Ang Lee) was a lush and witty adaptation of Jane Austen's first novel, starring Emma Thompson (above) as one of three lively daughters left in reduced circumstances after the death of their father. All are either wooed by or delightfully manipulating would-be suitors in turn-of-the-19th-century England. For*

Thompson, Sense *was a particular triumph: the film brought her an Academy nomination as the year's best actress, and she won the award for writing the year's best adapted screenplay. Since she'd previously won a best actress award in 1992 for* Howards End, *she thus became the first woman to win Oscars in both the writing and acting divisions.*

Best Supporting Actor: Kevin Spacey as *Verbal Kint* in The Usual Suspects *(Gramercy; directed by Bryan Singer). In a film filled with flashbacks and a maze of twisty subplots, Spacey essayed a con man with a bum leg and an inclination for chatter, grilled by a U.S. customs agent (Chazz Palminteri) about a bungled crime caper involving five hoods (Spacey, Gabriel Byrne, Stephen Baldwin, Kevin Pollak, Benicio Del Toro) who'd initially been brought together in a police lineup, then joined forces for a successful emerald heist, followed by a disastrous involvement in a multimillion dollar cocaine deal.*

Best Supporting Actress: Mira Sorvino as *Linda Ash (above, with Michael Rapaport) in* Mighty Aphrodite *(Miramax; directed by Woody Allen). It was the second year in a row that filmmaker Allen had directed an actress to Oscar success in a supporting role; the preceding year, he'd done the same for Dianne Wiest in* Bullets over Broadway*. In* Aphrodite*, Allen portrayed a Manhattan sportswriter determined to seek out the biological mother of the near-genius son he and his wife (Helena Bonham Carter) had adopted as an infant; the real mom turns out to be Sorvino, a sweet-natured, flirty bubble-head who, to Allen's chagrin, is also a call girl and dedicated porno star.*

SOUND
* **APOLLO 13**, Imagine, Universal. Rick Dior, Steve Pederson, Scott Millan, David MacMillan.
  BATMAN FOREVER, Warner Bros. Donald O. Mitchell, Frank A. Montaño, Michael Herbick, Petur Hliddal.
  BRAVEHEART, Icon/Ladd Company, Paramount. Andy Nelson, Scott Millan, Anna Behlmer, Brian Simmons.
  CRIMSON TIDE, Hollywood Pictures, Buena Vista. Kevin O'Connell, Rick Kline, Gregory H. Watkins, William B. Kaplan.
  WATERWORLD, Universal. Steve Maslow, Gregg Landaker, Keith A. Wester.

SOUND EFFECTS EDITING
BATMAN FOREVER, Warner Bros. John Leveque, Bruce Stambler.
* **BRAVEHEART**, Icon/Ladd Company, Paramount. Lon Bender, Per Hallberg.
  CRIMSON TIDE, Hollywood Pictures, Buena Vista. George Watters II.

VISUAL EFFECTS
APOLLO 13, Imagine; Universal. Robert Legato, Michael Kanfer, Leslie Ekker, Matt Sweeney.
* **BABE**, Kennedy Miller Pictures; Universal. Scott E. Anderson, Charles Gibson, Neal Scanlon, John Cox.

DOCUMENTARY
(Feature)
* **ANNE FRANK REMEMBERED**, Jon Blair Film Company Limited Production; Sony Pictures Classics. Jon Blair.
  THE BATTLE OVER CITIZEN KANE, Lennon Documentary Group Production for The American Experience. Thomas Lennon, Michael Epstein.
  FIDDLEFEST—ROBERTA TZAVARAS AND HER EAST HARLEM VIOLIN PROGRAM, Four Oaks Foundation Production. Allan Miller, Walter Scheuer.
  HANK AARON: CHASING THE DREAM, Turner Original Production. Mike Tollin, Fredric Golding.
  TROUBLESOME CREEK: A MIDWESTERN, West City Films, Inc., Production. Jeanne Jordan, Steven Ascher.

(Short Subject)
JIM DINE: A SELF-PORTRAIT ON THE WALLS, Outside in July, Inc., Production. Nancy Dine, Richard Stilwell.
THE LIVING SEA, MacGillivray Freeman Films Production. Greg MacGillivray, Alec Lorimore.
NEVER GIVE UP: THE 20TH CENTURY ODYSSEY OF HERBERT ZIPPER, American Film Foundation. Terry Sanders, Freida Lee Mock.
* **ONE SURVIVOR REMEMBERS**, Home Box Office and The United States Holocaust Memorial Museum Production. Kary Antholis.
  THE SHADOW OF HATE, Guggenheim Productions, Inc. Production for the Southern Poverty Law Center. Charles Guggenheim.

FOREIGN LANGUAGE FILM
ALL THINGS FAIR, (Sweden).
* **ANTONIA'S LINE**, (The Netherlands).
  DUST OF LIFE, (Algeria).

O QUATRILHO, (Brazil).
THE STAR MAKER, (Italy).

SHORT FILMS
(Animated)
THE CHICKEN FROM OUTER SPACE, Stretch Films, Inc./Hanna-Barbera Cartoons, Inc./Cartoon Network Production. John R. Dilworth.
* **A CLOSE SHAVE**, Aardman Animations Limited Production. Nick Park.
  the end, Alias/Wavefront Production. Chris Landreth, Robin Bargar.
  GAGARIN, Second Frog Animation Group Production. Alexij Kharitidi.
  RUNAWAY BRAIN, Walt Disney Pictures Production. Chris Bailey.

(Live Action)
BROOMS, Yes/No Production. Luke Cresswell, Steve McNicholas,
DUKE OF GROOVE, Chanticleer Films. Griffin Dunne, Thom Colwell.
* **LIEBERMAN IN LOVE**, Chanticleer Films. Christine Lahti, Jana Sue Memel.
  LITTLE SURPRISES, Chanticleer Films. Jeff Goldblum, Tikki Goldberg.
  TUESDAY MORNING RIDE, Chanticleer Films. Dianne Houston, Joy Ryan.

HONORARY AND OTHER AWARDS
TO KIRK DOUGLAS for fifty years as a creative and moral force in the motion picture community.
TO CHUCK JONES for the creation of classic cartoons which have brought worldwide joy for more than half a century.

1995 SPECIAL ACHIEVEMENT AWARD
TO JOHN LASSETER for his inspired leadership of the Pixar *Toy Story* team, resulting in the first feature-length computer-animated film.

1995 IRVING G. THALBERG MEMORIAL AWARD
None given this year.

1995 JEAN HERSHOLT HUMANITARIAN AWARD
None given this year.

1995 GORDON E. SAWYER AWARD
TO DONALD C. ROGERS

SCIENTIFIC AND TECHNICAL AWARDS
Scientific and Engineering Award (Plaque)
HOWARD FLEMMING and **RONALD UHLIG** for their pioneering work leading to motion picture digital sound.
DIGITAL THEATER SYSTEMS for the design and development of the DTS Digital Sound System for motion picture exhibition.
DOLBY LABORATORIES for the design and development of the SR-D Digital Sound System for motion picture exhibition.
SONY CORPORATION for the design and development of the SDDS Digital Sound System for motion picture exhibition.

COLIN MOSSMAN, JOE WARY, HANS LEISINGER, GERALD PAINTER and **DELUXE LABORATORIES** for the design and development of the Deluxe Quad Format Digital Sound Printing Head.
DAVID GILMARTIN, JOHANNES BORGGREBE, JEAN-PIERRE GAGNON, FRANK RICOTTA and **TECHNICOLOR, INC.** for the design and development of the Technicolor Contact Printer Sound Head.
RONALD C. GOODMAN, ATTILA SZALAY, STEVEN SASS and **SPACECAM SYSTEMS, INC.** for the design of the SpaceCam gyroscopically stabilized camera system.
MARTIN S. MUELLER for the design and development of the MSM 9801 IMAX 65mm/15 perf production motion picture camera.
IAIN NEIL for the optical design; **RICK GELBARD** for the mechanical design; **ERIC DUBBERKE** for the engineering and **PANAVISION INTERNATIONAL, L.P.**, for the development of the Primo 3:1 Zoom Lens.
ARNOLD AND RICHTER CINE TECHNIK for the development of the Arriflex 535 Series of Cameras for motion picture cinematography.
ALVY RAY SMITH, ED CATMULL, THOMAS PORTER and **TOM DUFF** for their pioneering inventions in digital image compositing.

Technical Achievement Award (Certificate)
DAVID PRINGLE and **YAN ZHONG FANG** for the design and development of "Lightning Strikes," a flexible, high-performance electronic lightning effect system.
AL JENSEN, CHUCK HEADLEY, JEAN MESSNER and **HAZEM NABULSI** of CEI Technology for producing a self-contained, flicker-free Color Video-Assist Camera.
PETER DENZ of Prazisions-Entwicklung Denz for developing a flicker-free Color Video-Assist Camera.
GARY DEMOS, DAVID RUHOFF, DAN CAMERON and **MICHELLE FERAUD** for their pioneering efforts in the creation of the Digital Productions Digital Film Compositing System.
DOUGLAS SMYTHE, LINCOLN HU, DOUGLAS S. KAY and **INDUSTRIAL LIGHT AND MAGIC** for their pioneering efforts in the creation of the ILM Digital Film Compositing System.
COMPUTER FILM COMPANY for their pioneering efforts in the creation of the CFC Digital Film Compositing System.
JOE FINNEGAN (a.k.a. Joe Yrigoyen) for his pioneering work in developing the Air Ram for motion picture stunt effects.
INSTITUT NATIONAL POLYTECHNIQUE DE TOULOUSE for the concept; **KODAK PATHE CTP CINE** for the prototype; and **ECLAIR LABORATORIES** and **MARTINEAU INDUSTRIES** for the development and further implementation of the Toulouse Electrolytic Silver Recovery Cell.
BHP, INCORPORATED for their pioneering efforts in developing digital sound printing heads for motion pictures.
JAMES DEAS of the Warner Bros. Studio Facility for the design and subsequent development of an Automated Patchbay and Metering System for motion picture sound transfer and dubbing operations.
CLAY DAVIS and **JOHN CARTER** of Todd AO for their pioneering efforts in creating an Automated Patchbay System for motion picture sound transfer and dubbing operations.
PASCAL CHEDEVILLE for the design of the L.C. Concept Digital Sound System for motion picture exhibition.

t had never happened before: when the final tally was in on the 69th Academy Awards, not one major Hollywood studio had been responsible for making, or releasing, the films that swept the highest-profile prizes. On March 24, 1997 at the Los Angeles Shrine Auditorium, the best picture award went to *The English Patient* from Miramax, still considered an indie operation despite recent ownership by the Walt Disney company; the supporting actress winner (Juliette Binoche) and best director (Anthony Minghella) also were from that same Miramax film. Further, Geoffrey Rush won as best actor for *Shine,* a drama from Fine Line; best actress winner Frances McDormand was tagged for *Fargo,* from Gramercy, and Cuba Gooding Jr. was named the year's top supporting actor for *Jerry Maguire,* from Sony/TriStar. Unlike years past when the Academy scorecards were dotted with towering studio names like MGM, Paramount, Warner Bros., 20th Century Fox, Universal and Columbia, the victors for 1996 were from predominantly indie organizations, and adamantly proud of it. A new Oscar era had begun.

Competition was keen in several categories, but none more so than in the best actor division where all the nominees—Tom Cruise, Ralph Fiennes, Woody Harrelson, Billy Bob Thornton and Rush—had strong pools of support. The supporting actress category was thought by some to be a shoo-in for Lauren Bacall in *The Mirror Has Two Faces* but, as TV cameras were zeroing in on Bacall at the moment of

truth, near the top of the show, French actress Binoche was named instead. Even the winner seemed genuinely surprised. "I didn't prepare anything," said Binoche. "I thought Lauren Bacall was going to get it . . . I think she deserves it. This is a dream. It must be a French dream." No winner, however, seemed more genuinely pleased to be holding an Oscar than Gooding. Bouncing with enthusiasm, he jubilantly danced around the podium, thanking a myriad of names in the process.

Director-choreographer Michael Kidd, introduced by Julie Andrews as "my favorite curmudgeon," received an Honorary Oscar in recognition of his contributions to film musicals; Saul Zaentz, the producer of *English Patient,* also received the Irving G. Thalberg Memorial Award and, by virtue of having produced three Oscar-winning films to date (the others: 1975's *One Flew over the Cuckoo's Nest,* 1984's *Amadeus*), became only the third person in history to have accomplished such a feat, his predecessors being Darryl F. Zanuck and Sam Spiegel. One of the major emotional moments of the evening came when former heavyweight boxing champ Muhammad Ali, suffering from Parkinson's Disease, came to the stage with fellow champion George Foreman after the Academy Award for best feature documentary went to *When We Were Kings,* a film which depicts the 1974 Ali-Foreman championship bout in Zaire. *Kolya,* the first film from the Czech Republic nominated by the Academy, won as the year's best foreign language film.

Best Actor: **Geoffrey Rush** *as David Helfgott in* Shine *(Fine Line Features; directed by Scott Hicks). Made in Australia and based on the life of then-45-year-old Helfgott,* Shine *told of the downward spiral then triumphant comeback of Helfgott, plagued in his youth by a bullying father and an obsessive drive for musical perfection, initially showing great promise as a concert pianist but his potential and career cut short because of nervous breakdowns and years spent in mental institutions. Three actors played the central character: Alex Rafalowicz played Helfgott as a child, Noah Taylor was the young David, and Rush (right, at piano) portrayed the adult who ultimately managed to triumph over his physical limitations and that painful past.*

The host for the evening was Billy Crystal, returning to that post for the first time in four years; he opened in crackerjack fashion and with the help of special effects by injecting himself into key scenes from some of the year's nominated films. Among those making music on the show was Céline Dion, slated to sing one of the year's nominated songs but, at the last minute, she stepped in to sing a second one as well when Natalie Cole fell ill. Also performing was David Helfgott, the pianist portrayed by "best actor" Rush in his Oscar-winning performance. Helfgott performed "Flight of the Bumble Bee."

Best Actress: **Frances McDormand** *as Police Chief Marge Gunderson in* Fargo *(Gramercy; directed by Joel Coen). Coen, as cowriter and director, specifically fashioned the quirky* Fargo *for McDormand, his wife, and she responded with a funny, off-beat interpretation of a very pregnant chief of police who waddles into action and leaves no stone unturned when a kidnapping scheme goes wildly out of control and produces a trio of homicides in the town in which she's in charge. Based on a true incident which occured in 1987, the film's odd-ball, wry humor carried through to its title: though called* Fargo, *the majority of the film was set not in North Dakota but in the small Minnesota burg of Brainerd.*

Best Picture: **The English Patient** *(Miramax; produced by Saul Zaentz),* **Best Director:** **Anthony Minghella** *for* The English Patient. *A sweeping, romantic and poetic adaptation of the prize-winning novel by Michael Ondaatje,* English *starred Ralph Fiennes and Kristen Scott Thomas (above) as two star-crossed lovers embroiled in an affair complicated by separations, war, desert heat, betrayal and a husband. The film, like Ondaatje's book, continually switched from past to present, telling of a handsome Hungarian Count (Fiennes) as he meets a married woman (Scott Thomas) while both are in the Sahara in the 1930s on a mapping expedition;* *years later, the Count is the victim of a plane crash, hideously burned and covered in bandages, recalling fragmented incidents of his haunted past as he waits to die. Full of stunning images and possessing a mystic charm,* English *won nine Academy Awards in all, making it one of the most honored films of the Academy's first seven decades, alongside* Ben-Hur *(11 awards),* West Side Story *(10),* Gigi *(9),* The Last Emperor *(9), and the White Star liner looming just over the horizon.*

Best Supporting Actor: **Cuba Gooding Jr.** *as Rod Tidwell in* Jerry Maguire *(Sony/TriStar; directed by Cameron Crowe). As a tale of the greed and ruthlessness in professional sports,* Jerry Maguire *hit a bullseye, with Tom Cruise as a slick sports agent with a top company who eventually gets bounced and loses all his clients except for a brash, loud-mouthed wide receiver who displays as much confidence and moxie as he does athletic prowess. In the latter role, Gooding virtually stole the show with a sassy, hilarious performance accented by a line of dialogue which swiftly became a national catch phrase: says Gooding as Tidwell, not once but several times, "Show . . . me . . . the money!"*

PICTURE

* **THE ENGLISH PATIENT,** Tiger Moth, Miramax. Saul Zaentz, Producer.
FARGO, Working Title, Gramercy. Ethan Coen, Producer.
JERRY MAGUIRE, TriStar. James L. Brooks, Laurence Mark, Richard Sakai and Cameron Crowe, Producers.
SECRETS & LIES, CIBY 2000/Thin Man Films, October Films. Simon Channing-Williams, Producer.
SHINE, Momentum Films, Fine Line Features. Jane Scott, Producer.

ACTOR

TOM CRUISE in *Jerry Maguire,* TriStar.
RALPH FIENNES in *The English Patient,* Tiger Moth, Miramax.
WOODY HARRELSON in *The People vs. Larry Flynt,* Ixtlan, Columbia.
* **GEOFFREY RUSH** in *Shine,* Momentum Films, Fine Line Features.
BILLY BOB THORNTON in *Sling Blade,* Shooting Gallery, Miramax.

ACTRESS

BRENDA BLETHYN in *Secrets & Lies,* CIBY 2000/Thin Man Films, October Films.
DIANE KEATON in *Marvin's Room,* Marvin's Room Production, Miramax.
* **FRANCES McDORMAND** in *Fargo,* Working Title, Gramercy.
KRISTIN SCOTT THOMAS in *The English Patient,* Tiger Moth, Miramax.
EMILY WATSON in *Breaking the Waves,* Zentropa Entertainment/ Trust Film Svenska/ Liberator/Argus Film/Northern Lights, October Films.

SUPPORTING ACTOR

* **CUBA GOODING, JR.** in *Jerry Maguire,* TriStar.
WILLIAM H. MACY in *Fargo,* Working Title, Gramercy.
ARMIN MUELLER-STAHL in *Shine,* Momentum Films, Fine Line Features.
EDWARD NORTON in *Primal Fear,* Gary Lucchesi, Paramount in assoc. w/Rysher Entertainment.
JAMES WOODS in *Ghosts of Mississippi,* Castle Rock, Columbia.

SUPPORTING ACTRESS

JOAN ALLEN in *The Crucible,* 20th Century Fox.
LAUREN BACALL in *The Mirror Has Two Faces,* TriStar.
* **JULIETTE BINOCHE** in *The English Patient,* Tiger Moth, Miramax.
BARBARA HERSHEY in *The Portrait of a Lady,* Polygram, Gramercy.
MARIANNE JEAN-BAPTISTE in *Secrets & Lies,* CIBY 2000/Thin Man Films, October Films.

DIRECTING

* **THE ENGLISH PATIENT,** Tiger Moth, Miramax. Anthony Minghella.
FARGO, Working Title, Gramercy. Joel Coen.
THE PEOPLE VS. LARRY FLYNT, Ixtlan, Columbia. Milos Forman.
SECRETS & LIES, CIBY 2000/Thin Man Films, October Films. Mike Leigh.
SHINE, Momentum Films, Fine Line Features. Scott Hicks.

WRITING

(Screenplay Based on Material Previously Produced or Published)
THE CRUCIBLE, 20th Century Fox. Arthur Miller.
THE ENGLISH PATIENT, Tiger Moth, Miramax. Anthony Minghella.
HAMLET, Castle Rock, Columbia. Kenneth Branagh.

* **SLING BLADE,** Shooting Gallery, Miramax. Billy Bob Thornton.
TRAINSPOTTING, Channel Four Films, Miramax. John Hodge.

(Screenplay Written Directly for the Screen)
* **FARGO,** Working Title, Gramercy. Ethan Coen, Joel Coen.
JERRY MAGUIRE, TriStar. Cameron Crowe.
LONE STAR, Castle Rock, Sony Pictures Classics. John Sayles.
SECRETS & LIES, CIBY 2000/Thin Man Films, October Films. Mike Leigh.
SHINE, Momentum Films, Fine Line Features. Screenplay by Jan Sardi; Story by Scott Hicks.

ART DIRECTION- SET DECORATION

THE BIRDCAGE, United Artists, MGM/UA. Bo Welch; Cheryl Carasik.
* **THE ENGLISH PATIENT,** Tiger Moth, Miramax. Stuart Craig; Stephenie McMillan.
EVITA, Hollywood Pictures/Cinergi Pictures, Buena Vista. Brian Morris; Philippe Turlure.
HAMLET, Castle Rock, Columbia. Tim Harvey.
WILLIAM SHAKESPEARE'S ROMEO & JULIET, 20th Century Fox. Catherine Martin; Brigitte Broch.

CINEMATOGRAPHY

* **THE ENGLISH PATIENT,** Tiger Moth, Miramax. John Seale.
EVITA, Hollywood Pictures/Cinergi Pictures, Buena Vista. Darius Khondji.
FARGO, Working Title, Gramercy. Roger Deakins.
FLY AWAY HOME, Sandollar, Columbia. Caleb Deschanel.
MICHAEL COLLINS, Geffen Pictures, Warner Bros. Chris Menges.

COSTUME DESIGN

ANGELS AND INSECTS, Playhouse International, Goldwyn. Paul Brown.
EMMA, Matchmaker Films/Haft Entertainment, Miramax. Ruth Myers.
* **THE ENGLISH PATIENT,** Tiger Moth, Miramax. Ann Roth.
HAMLET, Castle Rock, Columbia. Alex Byrne.
THE PORTRAIT OF A LADY, Polygram, Gramercy. Janet Patterson.

FILM EDITING

* **THE ENGLISH PATIENT,** Tiger Moth, Miramax. Walter Murch.
EVITA, Hollywood Pictures/Cinergi Pictures, Buena Vista. Gerry Hambling.
FARGO, Working Title, Gramercy. Roderick Jaynes.
JERRY MAGUIRE, TriStar. Joe Hutshing.
SHINE, Momentum Films, Fine Line Features. Pip Karmel.

MAKEUP

GHOSTS OF MISSISSIPPI, Castle Rock, Columbia. Matthew W. Mungle, Deborah La Mia Denaver.
* **THE NUTTY PROFESSOR,** Imagine, Universal. Rick Baker, David LeRoy Anderson.
STAR TREK: FIRST CONTACT, Rick Berman, Paramount. Michael Westmore, Scott Wheeler, Jake Garber.

MUSIC
(Song)

BECAUSE YOU LOVED ME, (*Up Close and Personal,* Touchstone, Buena Vista). Music and Lyric by Diane Warren.
FOR THE FIRST TIME, (*One Fine Day,* 20th Century Fox). Music and Lyric by James Newton Howard, Jud J. Friedman, Allan Dennis Rich.
I FINALLY FOUND SOMEONE (*The Mirror Has Two Faces,* TriStar). Music and Lyric by Barbra Streisand, Marvin Hamlisch, Bryan Adams, Robert "Mutt" Lange.
THAT THING YOU DO! (*That Thing You Do!,* 20th Century Fox). Music and Lyric by Adam Schlesinger.
* **YOU MUST LOVE ME** (*Evita,* Hollywood Pictures/Cinergi Pictures, Buena Vista). Music by Andrew Lloyd Webber; Lyric by Tim Rice.

(Original Dramatic Score)
* **THE ENGLISH PATIENT,** Tiger Moth, Miramax. Gabriel Yared.
HAMLET, Castle Rock, Columbia. Patrick Doyle.
MICHAEL COLLINS, Geffen Pictures, Warner Bros. Elliot Goldenthal.
SHINE, Momentum Films, Fine Line Features. David Hirschfelder.
SLEEPERS, Propaganda Films, Warner Bros. John Williams.

Best Foreign Language Film: **Kolya** *from the Czech Republic. In the film's title role, young Andrej Chalimon, left, was a captivating Russian five-year-old who, by happenstance, gets left in the care of a womanizing Czech musician (Zdenek Sverak) who grudgingly becomes a temporary guardian to the boy whose language he doesn't understand, and whose youthful needs and behavior at first mystify him. Set during the early days of the 1989 revolution which ended Communist rule in Czechoslovakia,* Kolya *was the fourth feature of 31-year-old director Jan Sverak, whose father both scripted the film and costarred in it as Kolya's reluctant benefactor.*

(Original Musical or Comedy Score)
* EMMA, Matchmaker Films/Haft Entertainment, Miramax. Rachel Portman.
THE FIRST WIVES CLUB, Scott Rudin, Paramount. Marc Shaiman.
THE HUNCHBACK OF NOTRE DAME, Walt Disney, Buena Vista. Music by Alan Menken; Lyrics by Stephen Schwartz; Orchestral Score by Alan Menken.
JAMES AND THE GIANT PEACH, Walt Disney, Buena Vista. Randy Newman.
THE PREACHER'S WIFE, Touchstone/Goldwyn, Buena Vista. Hans Zimmer.

SOUND
* THE ENGLISH PATIENT, Tiger Moth, Miramax. Walter Murch, Mark Berger, David Parker, Chris Newman.
EVITA, Hollywood Pictures/Cinergi Pictures, Buena Vista. Andy Nelson, Anna Behlmer, Ken Weston.
INDEPENDENCE DAY, 20th Century Fox. Chris Carpenter, Bill W. Benton, Bob Beemer, Jeff Wexler.
THE ROCK, Hollywood Pictures, Buena Vista. Kevin O'Connell, Greg P. Russell, Keith A. Wester.
TWISTER, Warner Bros./Universal. Steve Maslow, Gregg Landaker, Kevin O'Connell, Geoffrey Patterson.

SOUND EFFECTS EDITING
DAYLIGHT, Davis Entertainment/Joseph M. Singer, Universal. Richard L. Anderson, David A. Whittaker.
ERASER, Warner Bros. Alan Robert Murray, Bub Asman.
* THE GHOST AND THE DARKNESS, Douglas/Reuther, Paramount. Bruce Stambler.

VISUAL EFFECTS
DRAGONHEART, Raffaella De Laurentiis, Universal. Scott Squires, Phil Tippett, James Straus, Kit West.
* INDEPENDENCE DAY, 20th Century Fox. Volker Engel, Douglas Smith, Clay Pinney, Joseph Viskocil.
TWISTER, Warner Bros./Universal. Stefen Fangmeier, John Frazier, Habib Zargarpour, Henry La Bounta.

DOCUMENTARY
(Feature)
THE LINE KING: THE AL HIRSCHFELD STORY, New York Times History Production; Castle Hill. Susan W. Dryfoos.
MANDELA, Clinica Estetico, Ltd. Production; Island Pictures. Jo Menell, Angus Gibson.
SUZANNE FARRELL: ELUSIVE MUSE, Seahorse Films, Inc. Production. Anne Belle, Deborah Dickson.
TELL THE TRUTH AND RUN: GEORGE SELDES AND THE AMERICAN PRESS, Never Tire Production. Rick Goldsmith.
* WHEN WE WERE KINGS, DASFilms Ltd. Production; Gramercy. Leon Gast, David Sonenberg.

(Short Subject)
* BREATHING LESSONS: THE LIFE AND WORK OF MARK O'BRIEN, Inscrutable Films/Pacific News Service Production. Jessica Yu.
COSMIC VOYAGE, Cosmic Voyage Inc. Production. Jeffrey Marvin, Bayley Silleck.
AN ESSAY ON MATISSE, Great Projects Film Company, Inc. Production. Perry Wolff.
SPECIAL EFFECTS, NOVA/WGBH Boston Production. Susanne Simpson, Ben Burtt.
THE WILD BUNCH: AN ALBUM IN MONTAGE, Tyrus Entertainment Production. Paul Seydor, Nick Redman.

FOREIGN LANGUAGE FILM
A CHEF IN LOVE, (Georgia).
* KOLYA, (Czech Republic).
THE OTHER SIDE OF SUNDAY, (Norway).
PRISONER OF THE MOUNTAINS, (Russia).
RIDICULE, (France).

SHORT FILMS
(Animated)
CANHEAD, Timothy Hittle Production. Timothy Hittle, Chris Peterson.
LA SALLA, National Film Board of Canada. Richard Condie.
* QUEST, Thomas Stellmach Animation Production. Tyron Montgomery, Thomas Stellmach.
WAT'S PIG, Aardman Animations Limited Production. Peter Lord.

(Live Action)
DE TRIPAS, CORAZÓN, IMCINE/DPC/Universidad de Guadalajara Production. Antonio Urrutia.
* DEAR DIARY, DreamWorks SKG Production. David Frankel, Barry Jossen.
ERNST & LYSET, M & M Production. Kim Magnusson, Anders Thomas Jensen.
ESPOSADOS, Zodiac Films/Juan Carlos Fresnadillo P.C. Production. Juan Carlos Fresnadillo.
WORDLESS, Film Trust Italia Production. Bernadette Carranza, Antonello De Leo.

HONORARY AND OTHER AWARDS
TO MICHAEL KIDD in recognition of his services to the art of the dance in the art of the screen.
TO VOLKER W. BAHNEMANN and BURTON "BUD" STONE in appreciation for outstanding service and dedication in upholding

Best Supporting Actress: Juliette Binoche *as Hana in* The English Patient. *Despite that "supporting" designation, Binoche's Hana was a main focus and force of* The English Patient, *a beautiful Canadian nurse who, internally scarred by the carnage she's seen on the front lines during World War II, sequesters herself in an adandoned Tuscan monastery to look after a dying patient, becoming his private nurse, protector and, eventually, trusted confidant. Binoche became the second French-born actress to win an Oscar, after 1934's Claudette Colbert. (1959 winner Simone Signoret, though she worked primarily in French films, was actually born in Germany.)*

the high standards of the Academy of Motion Picture Arts and Sciences. (John A. Bonner Medals of Commendation)
TO JOE LOMBARDI in celebration of fifty years in the motion picture industry. His knowledge and leadership in the field of pyrotechnics and special effects along with his uncompromising promotion of safety on the set have established the standard for today's special effects technicians. (Award of Commendation plaque)

1996 IRVING G. THALBERG MEMORIAL AWARD
TO SAUL ZAENTZ

1996 JEAN HERSHOLT HUMANITARIAN AWARD
None given this year.

1996 GORDON E. SAWYER AWARD
None given this year.

SCIENTIFIC AND TECHNICAL AWARDS
Academy Award of Merit (Statuette)
IMAX CORPORATION for the method of filming and exhibiting high-fidelity, large-format, wide-angle motion pictures.

Scientific and Engineering Awards (Plaque)
JOHN SCHLAG, BRIAN KNEP, ZORAN KAČIČ-ALESIĆ and THOMAS WILLIAMS for the development of the Viewpaint 3D Paint System for film production work.
WILLIAM REEVES for the original concept and the development of particle systems used to create computer generated visual effects in motion pictures.

JIM HOURIHAN for the primary design and development of the interactive language-based control of particle systems as embodied in the Dynamation software package.
JONATHAN ERLAND and KAY BEVING ERLAND for the development of the Digital Series Traveling Matte Backing System used for composite photography in motion pictures.

Technical Achievement Awards (Certificate)
PERRY KIVOLOWITZ, for the primary design, and DR. GARTH A. DICKIE for the development of the algorithms for the shape-driven warping and morphing subsystem of the Elastic Reality Special Effects System.
KEN PERLIN for the development of Perlin Noise, a technique used to produce natural appearing textures on computer-generated surfaces for motion picture visual effects.
NESTOR BURTNYK and MARCELI WEIN of the National Research Council of Canada for their pioneering work in the development of software techniques for Computer Assisted Key Framing for Character Animation.
GRANT LOUCKS for the concept and specifications of the Mark V Director's Viewfinder.
BRIAN KNEP, CRAIG HAYES, RICK SAYRE and THOMAS WILLIAMS for the creation and development of the Direct Input Device.
JAMES KAJIYA and TIMOTHY KAY for their pioneering work in producing computer-generated fur and hair in motion pictures.
JEFFREY YOST, CHRISTIAN ROUET, DAVID BENSON and FLORIAN KAINZ for the development of a system to create and control computer-generated fur and hair in motion pictures.
RICHARD A. PREY and WILLIAM N. MASTEN for the design and development of the Nite Sun II lighting crane and camera platform.

One word not applicable to Oscar's 70th birthday party was Lilliputian. It was *Titanic* all the way. James Cameron's watery epic about the ill-fated ocean liner was, hands down, the film of the year, amassing 14 Academy Award nominations, which tied *T* with 1950's *All about Eve* for the most nominations ever pulled by a single film. When the final Oscar prizes were announced at the Los Angeles Shrine Auditorium on March 23, 1998, *Titanic* tallied a total equal to 1959's *Ben-Hur* as the most Academy Awarded film of all time, winning 11 statuettes—for best picture, directing, cinematography, art direction, film editing, costume design, sound, sound effects editing, visual effects, original dramatic music score and original song. (Such a windfall caused the film's producer-director Cameron to exclaim, quoting a line from his film, "I'm the king of the world!") Also in a titanic mode, the award show itself, hosted by Billy Crystal, was the second longest ever. At 3 hours, 45 minutes it also pulled the largest audience of any Oscar telecast to date with an estimated 87 million people watching in the U.S., eclipsing the previous high of 82 million domestic viewers in 1995.

The awards for best actor and best actress went to Jack Nicholson and Helen Hunt in *As Good As It Gets,* marking the seventh time in seventy years of the Oscar that a leading actor and actress from the same film received top Oscar prizes (following Clark Gable and Claudette Colbert in 1934, Jack Nicholson and Louise Fletcher in 1975, Peter Finch and Faye Dunaway in 1976, Jon Voight and Jane Fonda in 1978, Henry Fonda and Katharine Hepburn in 1981, and Anthony Hopkins and Jodie Foster in 1991). Kim Basinger was named best supporting actress for *L.A. Confidential,* and Robin Williams was tapped as the year's best supporting actor in *Good Will Hunting,* a film in which—despite his "supporting" classification—Williams had received first-position billing. *Hunting* also bagged Oscars for its two writers, boyhood friends Matt Damon and Ben Affleck. Their win also marked the fourth consecutive year actor-writers won Academy Awards in the screenplay category, following 1996's Billy Bob Thornton, 1995's Emma Thompson and (to stretch a point), 1994's Quentin Tarantino. *Character* from the Netherlands was named the year's best foreign language film.

Billy Crystal was the emcee for the sixth time and in his opening moments, as in the previous year, he mercilessly kidded the year's five best picture nominees by editing himself into some of those films' key scenes. Another highpoint was the acceptance speech of honorary Oscar winner Stanley Donen, who sang his "thank you" via Irving Berlin's "Cheek to Cheek," finishing with a brief tap dance. As a special salute to the Academy's seventieth anniversary year, near the finish of the telecast, producer Gil Cates brought together on stage "Oscar's Family Album," a live gathering of seventy previous winners of Academy Awards for acting, competitive and honorary, seated on four tiers, in alphabetical order from Anne Bancroft to Teresa Wright. Included were two winners from

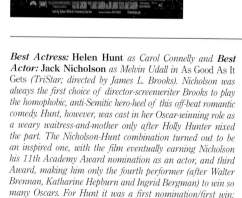

Best Actress: **Helen Hunt** *as Carol Connelly and* **Best Actor:** **Jack Nicholson** *as Melvin Udall in* As Good As It Gets *(TriStar; directed by James L. Brooks). Nicholson was always the first choice of director-screenwriter Brooks to play the homophobic, anti-Semitic hero-heel of this off-beat romantic comedy. Hunt, however, was cast in her Oscar-winning role as a weary waitress-and-mother only after Holly Hunter nixed the part. The Nicholson-Hunt combination turned out to be an inspired one, with the film eventually earning Nicholson his 11th Academy Award nomination as an actor, and third Award, making him only the fourth performer (after Walter Brennan, Katharine Hepburn and Ingrid Bergman) to win so many Oscars. For Hunt it was a first nomination/first win; she became the first performer to win a "leading role" acting Oscar while concurrently starring in a TV series.*

the 1930s (Shirley Temple Black, 1934; Luise Rainer, the first performer to win Academy Awards back-to-back, in 1936 and 1937), seven winners from the 1940s (Celeste Holm, Claude Jarman Jr., Jennifer Jones, Mercedes McCambridge, Harold Russell, Claire Trevor and Ms. Wright), eight from the 1950s (Ernest Borgnine, Red Buttons, Charlton Heston, Jack Lemmon, Karl Malden, Eva Marie Saint, Vincent Winter, Shelley Winters), and the rest from the succeeding four decades. It was the first time so many Academy Award-winning actors had ever been gathered together in one spot—another Titanic touch to the Oscar party MCMXCVII.

Best Supporting Actress: **Kim Basinger** *as Lynn Bracken in* L.A. Confidential *(Warner Bros.; directed by Curtis Hanson). It was a role Basinger nearly declined, as a call girl who's been physically altered to resemble '40s screen siren Veronica Lake. A determined agent, however, eventually convinced Basinger to play the part, the result bringing her the best reviews of her career, her first Academy nomination and, on Oscar Night, the big enchilada. The film itself was also named one of the year's best and pulled a total of nine nominations. Based on a James Ellroy novel, it was a stunner about three cops working the back alleys and other, more exotic locales of 1950s Los Angeles.*

333

Best Picture: **Titanic** *(A Lightstorm Entertainment Production, 20th Century Fox and Paramount; produced by James Cameron and Jon Landau) and* **Best Director:** **James Cameron** *for* Titanic. *Early speculation was that the film might sink faster than the real luxury liner had done on April 15, 1912, but to the contrary, the $200 million epic was an immediate box office phenomenon, reaching an unprecedented worldwide box office gross of $1.8 billion. Covering the* final days and hours of the supposedly "unsinkable" ship on its maiden voyage from Southampton to New York, fact was intertwined with a fictional story about a lost jewel and a steerage-class Romeo (Leonardo DiCaprio) who woos a debutante from the upper deck (Kate Winslet), until an iceberg interferes. The film's story and scope clearly had enormous affect both within and outside the Academy and, in the final Oscar tally, Titanic remained immense: winning 11 awards, tying with 1959's *Ben-Hur as the most Oscared of all motion pictures. In spite of reported bickering between the two studios responsible for Titanic's budget—Fox and Paramount—it was the second time in three years that a film distributed by those same two studios won the best picture award (1995's* Braveheart *was the other). It was also one of the longest of the Academy's best picture winners, running 3 hours 14 minutes, or as its producers preferred to clock it, "2 hours and 74 minutes."*

The Full Monty (Fox Searchlight; produced by Uberto Pasolini) was made in England for peanuts and became one of the year's surprise hits. It was a first feature by director Peter Cattaneo, following six steelworkers from a Yorkshire burg who lose their jobs because of industrial cutbacks and, to support themselves and their families, and despite less-than-Adonis-like bodies, raise funds by creating a Chippendale's-type dance act in which, for a finale, they drop their drawers. Besides winning the Oscar for Anne Dudley's "best original musical or comedy score," Monty also became the year's biggest profit-maker: costing a miniscule $3 million to make, it went on to collect over $200 million in worldwide grosses.

PICTURE

AS GOOD AS IT GETS, Gracie Films, TriStar. James L. Brooks, Bridget Johnson and Kristi Zea, Producers.
THE FULL MONTY, Redwave Films, Fox Searchlight. Uberto Pasolini, Producer.
GOOD WILL HUNTING, Be Gentlemen, Miramax. Lawrence Bender, Producer.
L.A. CONFIDENTIAL, Arnon Milchan/David L. Wolper, Warner Bros. Arnon Milchan, Curtis Hanson and Michael Nathanson, Producers.
* TITANIC, Lightstorm Entertainment, 20th Century Fox and Paramount. James Cameron and Jon Landau, Producers.

ACTOR

MATT DAMON in *Good Will Hunting*, Be Gentlemen, Miramax.
ROBERT DUVALL in *The Apostle*, Butcher's Run, October Films.
PETER FONDA in *Ulee's Gold*, Nunez-Gowan/Clinica Estetico, Orion.
DUSTIN HOFFMAN in *Wag the Dog*, New Line.
* JACK NICHOLSON in *As Good As It Gets*, Gracie Films, TriStar.

ACTRESS

HELENA BONHAM CARTER in *The Wings of the Dove*, Renaissance Films, Miramax.
JULIE CHRISTIE in *Afterglow*, Moonstone Entertainment, Sony Pictures Classics.
JUDI DENCH in *Mrs. Brown*, Ecosse Films, Miramax.
* HELEN HUNT in *As Good As It Gets*, Gracie Films, TriStar.
KATE WINSLET in *Titanic*, Lightstorm Entertainment, 20th Century Fox and Paramount.

SUPPORTING ACTOR

ROBERT FORSTER in *Jackie Brown*, Mighty, Mighty Afrodite, Miramax.
ANTHONY HOPKINS in *Amistad*, DreamWorks.
GREG KINNEAR in *As Good As It Gets*, Gracie Films, TriStar.
BURT REYNOLDS in *Boogie Nights*, New Line.
* ROBIN WILLIAMS in *Good Will Hunting*, Be Gentlemen, Miramax.

SUPPORTING ACTRESS

* KIM BASINGER in *L.A. Confidential*, Arnon Milchan/David L. Wolper, Warner Bros.
JOAN CUSACK in *In & Out*, Scott Rudin, Paramount in association with Spelling Films.
MINNIE DRIVER in *Good Will Hunting*, Be Gentlemen, Miramax.
JULIANNE MOORE in *Boogie Nights*, New Line.
GLORIA STUART in *Titanic*, Lightstorm Entertainment, 20th Century Fox and Paramount

DIRECTING

THE FULL MONTY, Redwave Films, Fox Searchlight. Peter Cattaneo.
GOOD WILL HUNTING, Be Gentlemen, Miramax. Gus Van Sant.
L.A. CONFIDENTIAL, Arnon Milchan/David L. Wolper, Warner Bros. Curtis Hanson.
THE SWEET HEREAFTER, Ego Film Arts, Fine Line Features. Atom Egoyan.
*TITANIC, Lightstorm Entertainment, 20th Century Fox and Paramount. James Cameron.

WRITING

(Screenplay Based on Material from Another Medium)

DONNIE BRASCO, Mandalay Entertainment, TriStar. Paul Attanasio.
* L.A. CONFIDENTIAL, Arnon Milchan/David L. Wolper, Warner Bros. Brian Helgeland and Curtis Hanson.
THE SWEET HEREAFTER, Ego Film Arts, Fine Line Features. Atom Egoyan.
WAG THE DOG, New Line. Hilary Henkin and David Mamet.
THE WINGS OF THE DOVE, Renaissance Films, Miramax. Hossein Amini.

(Screenplay Written Directly for the Screen)

AS GOOD AS IT GETS, Gracie Films, TriStar. Mark Andrus and James L. Brooks.
BOOGIE NIGHTS, New Line. Paul Thomas Anderson.
DECONSTRUCTING HARRY, Jean Doumanian, Fine Line Features. Woody Allen.
THE FULL MONTY, Redwave Films, Fox Searchlight. Simon Beaufoy.
* GOOD WILL HUNTING, Be Gentlemen, Miramax. Ben Affleck and Matt Damon.

CINEMATOGRAPHY

AMISTAD, DreamWorks. Janusz Kaminski.
KUNDUN, Touchstone Pictures, Buena Vista. Roger Deakins.
L.A. CONFIDENTIAL, Arnon Milchan/David L. Wolper, Warner Bros. Dante Spinotti.
* TITANIC, Lightstorm Entertainment, 20th Century Fox and Paramount. Russell Carpenter.
THE WINGS OF THE DOVE, Renaissance Films, Miramax. Eduardo Serra.

ART DIRECTION-SET DECORATION

GATTACA, Jersey Films, Columbia. Jan Roelfs; Nancy Nye.
KUNDUN, Touchstone Pictures, Buena Vista. Dante Ferretti; Francesca Lo Schiavo.
L.A. CONFIDENTIAL, Arnon Milchan/David L. Wolper, Warner Bros. Jeannine Oppewall; Jay R. Hart.
MEN IN BLACK, Amblin Entertainment, Columbia. Bo Welch; Cheryl Carasik.
* TITANIC, Lightstorm Entertainment, 20th Century Fox and Paramount. Peter Lamont; Michael Ford.

COSTUME DESIGN

AMISTAD, DreamWorks. Ruth E. Carter.
KUNDUN, Touchstone Pictures, Buena Vista. Dante Ferretti.
OSCAR AND LUCINDA, Dalton Films, Fox Searchlight. Janet Patterson.
* TITANIC, Lightstorm Entertainment, 20th Century Fox and Paramount. Deborah L. Scott.
THE WINGS OF THE DOVE, Renaissance Films, Miramax. Sandy Powell.

SOUND

AIR FORCE ONE, Beacon Pictures/Columbia Pictures, Columbia. Paul Massey, Rick Kline, D. M. Hemphill and Keith A. Wester.
CON AIR, Touchstone Pictures, Buena Vista. Kevin O'Connell, Greg P. Russell and Arthur Rochester.
CONTACT, Warner Bros. Randy Thom, Tom Johnson, Dennis Sands and William B. Kaplan.
L.A. CONFIDENTIAL, Arnon Milchan/David L. Wolper, Warner Bros. Andy Nelson, Anna Behlmer and Kirk Francis.
* **TITANIC,** Lightstorm Entertainment, 20th Century Fox and Paramount. Gary Rydstrom, Tom Johnson, Gary Summers and Mark Ulano.

FILM EDITING

AIR FORCE ONE, Beacon Pictures/Columbia Pictures, Columbia. Richard Francis-Bruce.
AS GOOD AS IT GETS, Gracie Films, TriStar. Richard Marks.
GOOD WILL HUNTING, Be Gentlemen, Miramax. Pietro Scalia.
L.A. CONFIDENTIAL, Arnon Milchan/David L. Wolper, Warner Bros. Peter Honess
* **TITANIC,** Lightstorm Entertainment, 20th Century Fox and Paramount. Conrad Buff, James Cameron and Richard A. Harris.

SOUND EFFECTS EDITING

FACE/OFF, Douglas/Reuther/WCG/David Permut, Paramount and Touchstone. Mark P. Stoecklinger and Per Hallberg.
THE FIFTH ELEMENT, Gaumont, Columbia. Mark Mangini.
* **TITANIC,** Lightstorm Entertainment, 20th Century Fox and Paramount. Tom Bellfort and Christopher Boyes.

MUSIC

(Song)

GO THE DISTANCE, (*Hercules,* Walt Disney Pictures, Buena Vista); Music by Alan Menken; Lyric by David Zippel.
HOW DO I LIVE, (*Con Air,* Touchstone Pictures, Buena Vista); Music and Lyric by Diane Warren.
JOURNEY TO THE PAST (*Anastasia,* 20th Century Fox); Music by Stephen Flaherty; Lyric by Lynn Ahrens.
MISS MISERY, (*Good Will Hunting,* Be Gentlemen, Miramax); Music and Lyric by Elliott Smith.
* **MY HEART WILL GO ON,** (*Titanic,* Lightstorm Entertainment, 20th Century Fox and Paramount); Music by James Horner; Lyric by Will Jennings.

(Original Dramatic Score)

AMISTAD, DreamWorks. John Williams.
GOOD WILL HUNTING, Be Gentlemen, Miramax. Danny Elfman.
KUNDUN, Touchstone Pictures, Buena Vista. Philip Glass.
L.A. CONFIDENTIAL, Arnon Milchan/David L. Wolper, Warner Bros. Jerry Goldsmith.
* **TITANIC,** Lightstorm Entertainment, 20th Century Fox and Paramount. James Horner.

(Original Musical or Comedy Score)

ANASTASIA, 20th Century Fox. Music by Stephen Flaherty; Lyrics by Lynn Ahrens; Orchestral Score by David Newman.
AS GOOD AS IT GETS, Gracie Films, TriStar. Hans Zimmer.
* **THE FULL MONTY,** Redwave Films, Fox Searchlight. Anne Dudley.
MEN IN BLACK, Amblin Entertainment, Columbia. Danny Elfman.
MY BEST FRIEND'S WEDDING, Jerry Zucker/Predawn, TriStar. James Newton Howard.

MAKEUP

* **MEN IN BLACK,** Amblin Entertainment, Columbia. Rick Baker and David LeRoy Anderson.
MRS. BROWN, Ecosse Films, Miramax. Lisa Westcott, Veronica Brebner and Beverley Binda.
TITANIC, Lightstorm Entertainment, 20th Century Fox and Paramount. Tina Earnshaw, Greg Cannom and Simon Thompson.

SHORT FILMS

(Animated)

FAMOUS FRED, TVC London Production for Channel 4 and S4C. Joanna Quinn.
* **GERI'S GAME,** Pixar Animation Studios Production. Jan Pinkava.
LA VIEILLE DAME ET LES PIGEONS (THE OLD LADY AND THE PIGEONS), Productions Pascal Blais/Les Armateurs/Odec Kid Cartoons Production. Sylvain Chomet.
THE MERMAID, Film Company "DAGO"/"SHAR" School-Studio/ Studio "PANORAMA", Yaroslavl Production. Alexander Petrov.
REDUX RIDING HOOD, Walt Disney Television Animation Production. Steve Moore and Dan O'Shannon.

(Live Action)

DANCE LEXIE DANCE, Raw Nerve Production for Northern Lights. Pearse Moore and Tim Loane.
IT'S GOOD TO TALK, Feasible Films Production. Roger Goldby and Barney Reisz.
SWEETHEARTS?, Metronome Productions/Victoria Film Production. Birger Larsen and Thomas Lydholm.
* **VISAS AND VIRTUE,** Cedar Grove Production. Chris Tashima and Chris Donahue.
WOLFGANG, M & M Production for Dansk Novellefilm. Kim Magnusson and Anders Thomas Jensen.

DOCUMENTARY

(Short Subjects)

ALASKA: SPIRIT OF THE WILD, Graphic Films Corporation. George Casey and Paul Novros.
AMAZON, Ogden Entertainment Production. Kieth Merrill and Jonathan Stern.

DAUGHTER OF THE BRIDE, Terri Randall Film and Video Production. Terri Randall.
STILL KICKING: THE FABULOUS PALM SPRINGS FOLLIES, Little Apple Film Production. Mel Damski and Andrea Blaugrund.
* **A STORY OF HEALING,** Dewey-Obenchain Films Production. Donna Dewey and Carol Pasternak.

(Features)

AYN RAND: A SENSE OF LIFE, A G Media Corporation Limited Production, Strand Releasing. Michael Paxton.
COLORS STRAIGHT UP, Echo Pictures Production. Michele Ohayon and Julia Schachter.
4 LITTLE GIRLS, HBO Documentary Film/40 Acres and a Mule Filmworks Production. Spike Lee and Sam Pollard.
* **THE LONG WAY HOME,** Moriah Films Production at the Simon Wiesenthal Center, Seventh Art. Rabbi Marvin Hier and Richard Trank.
WACO: THE RULES OF ENGAGEMENT, SomFord Entertainment/ Fifth Estate Production. Dan Gifford and William Gazecki.

FOREIGN LANGUAGE FILM

BEYOND SILENCE (Germany)
* **CHARACTER** (The Netherlands)
FOUR DAYS IN SEPTEMBER (Brazil)
SECRETS OF THE HEART (Spain)
THE THIEF (Russia)

VISUAL EFFECTS

THE LOST WORLD: JURASSIC PARK, Universal/Amblin Entertainment, Universal. Dennis Muren, Stan Winston, Randal M. Dutra and Michael Lantieri.
STARSHIP TROOPERS, TriStar Pictures/Touchstone Pictures, TriStar. Phil Tippett, Scott E. Anderson. Alec Gillis and John Richardson.
* **TITANIC,** Lightstorm Entertainment, 20th Century Fox and Paramount. Robert Legato, Mark Lasoff, Thomas L. Fisher and Michael Kanfer.

HONORARY AWARDS

TO STANLEY DONEN in appreciation of a body of work marked by grace, elegance, wit and visual innovation.
TO PETE CLARK, in appreciation for outstanding service and dedication in upholding the high standards of the Academy of Motion Picture Arts and Sciences. (John A. Bonner Medal of Commendation)

1997 GORDON E. SAWYER AWARD
TO DON IWERKS

1997 IRVING G. THALBERG AWARD
None given this year

1997 JEAN HERSHOLT HUMANITARIAN AWARD
None given this year

SCIENTIFIC AND TECHNICAL AWARDS
Academy Award of Merit (Statuette)

GUNNAR P. MICHELSON for the engineering and development of an improved, electronic, high-speed, precision light valve for use in motion picture printing machines.

Scientific and Engineering Awards (Plaque)

WILLIAM KOVACS for his creative leadership and **ROY HALL** for his principal engineering efforts that led to the Wavefront Advanced Visualizer computer graphics system.
JOHN GIBSON, ROB KRIEGER, MILAN NOVACEK, GLEN OZYMOK and **DAVE SPRINGER** for the development of the geometric modeling component of the Alias PowerAnimator System.
DOMINIQUE BOISVERT, RÉJEAN GAGNÉ, DANIEL LANGLOIS and **RICHARD LAPERRIÈRE** for the development of the "Actor" animation component of the Softimage computer animation system.
EBEN OSTBY, WILLIAM REEVES, SAMUEL J. LEFFLER and **TOM DUFF** for the development of the Marionette Three-Dimensional Computer Animation Systemn.
CRAIG W. REYNOLDS for his pioneering contributions to the development of three-dimensional computer animation for motion picture production.
RICHARD SHOUP, ALVY RAY SMITH and **THOMAS PORTER** for their pioneering efforts in the development of digital paint systems used in motion picture production.
KIRK HANDLEY, RAY MELUCH, SCOTT ROBINSON, WILSON H. ALLEN and **JOHN NEARY** for the design, development and implementation of the Dolby CP500 Digital Cinema Processor.
JOEL W. JOHNSON of the OConnor Laboratories for the unique design improvement in fluid head counter-balancing techniques as used in their Model 2575.
AL JENSEN, CHUCK HEADLEY, JEAN MESSNER and **HAZEM NABULSI** of CEI Technology for the production of a self-contained, flicker-free, Color Video-Assist Camera.

Technical Achievement Awards (Certificate)

CLARK F. CRITES for the design and development of the Christie ELF 1-C Endless Loop Film Transport and Storage System.
DAN LEIMETER and **ROBERT WEITZ** for the development and implementation of a Portable Adjustment Tool for T-Style Slit Lens Assemblies.
PHILIP C. CORY for the design and development of the Special Effects Spark Generator.
JAMES M. REILLY, DOUGLAS W. NISHIMURA and **MONIQUE C. FISCHER** of the Rochester Institute of Technology for the creation of A-D Strips, a diagnostic tool for the detection of the presence of vinegar syndrome in processed acetate-based motion picture film.
JIM FRAZIER, for the design concept, and **IAIN NEIL** and **RICK GELBARD** for the further design and development of the Panavision/Frazier Lens System for motion picture photography.
JAMES F. FOLEY, CHARLES E. CONVERSE and **F. EDWARD GARDNER** of UCISCO; and to **ROBERT W. STOKER, JR.** and **MATT SWEENEY** for the development and realization of Liquid Synthetic Air.
JACK CASHIN, ROGER HIBBARD and **LARRY JACOBSON** for the design, development and implementation of a projection system analyzer.
RICHARD CHUANG, GLENN ENTIS and **CARL ROSENDAHL** for the concept and architecture of the Pacific Data Images (PDI) Animation System.
GREG HERMANOVIC, KIM DAVIDSON, MARK ELENDT and **PAUL H. BRESLIN** for the development of the procedural modeling and animation components of the Prisms software package.
JAMES J. KEATING, MICHAEL WAHRMAN and **RICHARD HOLLANDER** for their contributions that led to the Wavefront Advanced Visualizer computer graphics system.

Best Supporting Actor: **Robin Williams** *(above right, with Matt Damon as Will Hunting), as Sean McGuire in* Good Will Hunting *(Miramax; directed by Gus Van Sant). It was Williams' participation that gave the film its initial stature and attention. The screenplay had been through a five-year period of ups, downs and turnarounds, written and rewritten by struggling actors Damon and Boston buddy Ben Affleck who, wisely, included juicy roles for themselves. At* Oscar time, their penetrating story of a young South Boston school janitor (Damon) who turns out to be a math whiz not only brought them Oscars for writing the year's best original screenplay, it also earned a statuette for Williams as a psychology professor who, initially downbeat and semi-hostile, eventually lightens up his own life while insuring the prodigy's future by encouraging the boy to embrace life.

After Academy Award statuettes had been dispensed in myriad different locales during its first seven decades—in various dining rooms, banquet halls, theaters and auditoriums from Hollywood to West Hollywood to downtown Los Angeles to Santa Monica and back to Los Angeles again—it seemed high time Oscar should have a home of his own.

At the beginning of the Academy's eighth decade, its executives started laying down roots to that very effect, entering into an agreement with the TrizecHahn Corporation to fashion a theater at a choice location, designed to meet the specific needs of an Academy Awards broadcast. Fittingly, the chosen site is where Hollywood Boulevard meets Highland Boulevard, in the heart of Hollywood itself and, ironically, only a few steps east and across the street from the Hollywood Roosevelt Hotel, where the very first Academy Award huddle had occurred on May 16, 1929. Oscar was about to come full circle.

Initial plans had been for the $94 million Kodak Theatre to make its debut in the spring of 2001 to help usher Oscar into the new millennium, but the first awards weren't actually presented from the Kodak stage until one year later. The space, designed by Chicago-born, New York-based architect David Rockwell, was specifically created with state-of-the-art technology to optimize the venue as an ideal setting for presenting, recording and broadcasting not only a world-class live entertainment such as the annual Academy Awards telecast, but also concerts, Broadway shows and other performing-arts events.

Once the dream for a permanent home was set in motion, the Academy negotiated an exclusive eight-year contract extension with ABC Television, which provided not only a new night (Sunday) for the annual Academy telecasts but also an earlier time slot and a network-aired pre-show.

Meanwhile, Oscar himself took time for a bit of a facelift. It seems that some 30 years of extensive use of its one-of-a-kind mold had caused the statuette to begin looking a little soft around the ears and chin. After a general agreement that a tuck was needed, the Academy ordered a new mold struck that would strengthen Oscar's chin and give his neck the same chiseled look he possessed when George Stanley sculpted the first statuettes on the Academy's behalf 70-plus years earlier.

During the eighth decade, composer Jerry Goldsmith gave the Academy two special gifts. One was, at long last, an official musical theme for the Academy Awards Show titled "Fanfare for Oscar." His other gift was his presentation to the Margaret Herrick Library of his own original handwritten musical sketches from more than a hundred film scores from 1957 to 1996. The decade also saw several other important donations to the library. From William Wyler's estate the library received scripts, story files, production files, correspondence and photographs. Paramount augmented its

JULIAN FELLOWES

"All of my life I had been convinced that if you were the winner of an Oscar, someone would tip you off. It didn't seem feasible that they would risk your being struck dumb or simply passing out with shock. When the day came and no hint had been received, I therefore assumed that I couldn't have won and I carefully arranged my face to look generous and undisappointed. When Miss Paltrow read out my name it was therefore like a kick from a mule. After that, I was in a dream. I hadn't prepared a speech except for the names to be thanked (and that was only because the producer at the Nominees' Luncheon had been so fierce about keeping them to a minimum) but I was filled with gratitude towards America and in the year of September 11th I am very glad to have had the opportunity of saying so. Perhaps the most surreal moment came after I had been taken upstairs for interviews and general carry-on. I was waiting in a side room to return to my seat, watching the monitor with a couple of others and we were chatting. It was only as I was leaving that I real-ized my companions had been Robert Redford and Barbra Streisand. Given the fact that I was also clutching an Oscar in my hands, that was truly a moment when I felt I had stepped through the looking glass."

Julian Fellowes
Original Screenplay 2001

PHIL COLLINS

"Ever since I can remember, I've watched the Oscar shows. Watching all those great actors, writers and directors receiving the Holy Grail. I never thought in a million years that I'd get a nomination. As years rolled by I was lucky enough to be included a couple of times. When my third time came with Tarzan, I truly didn't believe it would be me. When Cher opened the envelope and said "Ph..." you could have knocked me down with a feather. It really was, and is, an incredible feeling. Of all the awards I've been fortunate to collect over the years, the Oscar is the most treasured."

Phil Collins
Original Song 1999

Roberto Benigni climbs over Steven Spielberg (71st Awards)

Kevin Spacey (72nd Awards)

Hilary Swank (72nd Awards)

1977 gift of screenplays with a hundred more boxes of scripts covering the years 1963–1980. Additions were made as well to the Samuel Goldwyn Collection, including rare music scores from Goldwyn's 1939 *Wuthering Heights* and his 1946 *The Best Years of Our Lives*. Papers of the late visual-effects wizard Linwood Dunn, who died in May 1998, were also given to the library, as were the drawings, animation cels, scripts, photographs, production records and posters of designer and Oscar winner Saul Bass.

Also during this period, the Academy *Players Directory* marked its 60th anniversary with a gala hosted by director John Badham and attended by almost 800 actors and casting directors (including the only two actors whose photos appeared in the first and the latest issues of the *Players Directory*, Mickey Rooney and Frank Coghlan).

The Academy saluted, on opposite

Itzhak Perlman, Yo Yo Ma (73rd Awards)

337

JOHN CORIGLIANO

"When I attended the Oscars that year, I felt I was attending less as a motion-picture artist—which I'm not, really, I'm a concert composer who's scored three films—than as an awed tourist in the magic kingdom of Hollywood. There they all are, these creatures I'd only seen onscreen! Jude Law sipping wine! Catherine Deneuve checking her wrap! The possibility of actually winning the award felt as improbable as Alice tumbling through the looking-glass or Jeff Daniels stepping off the screen into the world of The Purple Rose of Cairo.

Which is as good a definition as any of how I felt when my name was called. Suddenly I was not only at the show, but in a show – the show, the show of shows, what David Mamet once called one of the two high holy days (the other being the Super Bowl) of American culture. I had never even seen an actual Oscar statue, only images of one: and now the first one I'd ever seen was to be my own! Does it get any better than that?"

John Corigliano
Music Score 1999

MARCIA GAY HARDEN

"Oscar Night was fun! Big, bold fun! I hadn't expected to win, but wanted to be remembered anyway, so I chose a very glamourous Randolph Duke dress, scarlet red with plenty of cleavage. And lots of Harry Winston diamonds! My Dad had been very ill, so I was ecstatic that he and Mom were there. When Nicolas Cage read the names, I was sure he took a nap between 'And the Oscar goes to'...nap nap nap... 'Marcia Gay Harden.' I gasped. I heard a cheer go up in the balcony. I could see out of the corner of my eye, my big Navy Captain father on his feet, arms waving above his head, bellowing, 'Bravo! Bravo!' And he and my mom were crying. My husband was crying, cheering and grinning from ear to ear, and Ed Harris, my director, producer and co-star, was beaming, literally glowing, he was so proud.

The next morning, I thought I would open the door, and there would be rainbows in the sky, birds singing, and probably Steven Spielberg waiting patiently on the lawn with the brand new script that Bo Goldman had written just for me. Waaangh-Waanngh. There were no rainbows, no birds, no Spielberg, and no Bo. There was instead a pending actors strike, and then the Septem-

ber 11 attack. There was a shortage of work, a recession, my father died in February and there was a huge sadness everywhere I looked. What? No one seemed to care that I had won? It was in this starkness that I understand the meaning of the Oscar, and it was intensely personal. And for me, it was an accomplishment of the heart, and a validation of 18 years of struggle, and a result of Ed's intense passion and generosity as a director. It didn't translate to larger roles or fat paychecks. It was a reward, an acknowledgment, and a night of pure joy, celebrating good work. It was a gift from my peers."*

Marcia Gay Harden
Supporting Actress 2000

HOWARD SHORE

"A suspended magic moment in time. One that I will remember all my life. An honor to be included amongst the composers who have walked up onto that stage during the 75 years of Oscar."

Howard Shore
Music Score 2001

Laura Linney, Ed Harris (73rd Awards)

Renée Zellweger hosting the Scientific and Technical Awards (73rd Awards)

Ang Lee, Joan Allen (73rd Awards)

coasts, former costars Sidney Poitier and Richard Widmark—Widmark at New York's Museum of Modern Art for his 50-year career in films, Poitier with a two-day event at the Academy's Samuel Goldwyn Theater in Beverly Hills. Other tributes were given to late greats Fred Astaire and Gary Cooper on both the West and East Coasts; Karl Malden, Teresa Wright and Sidney Lumet were given tributes by the Academy in New York, while in Los Angeles special honorees included Jeanne Moreau and the late Mary Pickford and Preston Sturges. A special evening at the Goldwyn Theater was devoted to 98-year-old caricaturist Al Hirschfeld, who participated in a lively question-and-answer session while extensive samples of his artwork and film posters, some dating back to the silent-screen era, were on display in the Goldwyn Theater lobby and in the building's fourth-floor gallery.

There were also several cast-and-crew reunions thrown by the Academy during these years, including one for the first public screening in several decades of the 1950 musical *Annie Get Your Gun,* along with 25th-anniversary celebrations of *American Graffiti* and *Nashville,* special screenings of *Close Encounters of the Third Kind* and newly restored editions of David O. Selznick's *Duel in the Sun,* the Oscar-winning *Oliver!, Easy Rider* and *In Cold Blood,* with stars from each of those films participating in post-screening panel discussions. The Academy's London chapter hosted a restored-print screening of *The Lion in Winter,* attended by the film's star Peter O'Toole, cast members Jane Merrow and Timothy Dalton, producer Martin Poll and editor John Bloom, with Richard Harris and Omar Sharif also present.

Something else the Academy began during 2002: screenings of pristine new prints of each of the past 74 Best Picture winners, starting with the second year's winning film, *The Broadway Melody,* and going in order through the decades to culminate with the 75th Best Picture. (The first Best Picture, *Wings,* was undergoing restoration when the series commenced, and was screened in its pristine state well along in the series, on the actual date of the organization's 75th Anniversary.)

Film preservation remained a heavy Academy focus and commitment, with some 37 preservation projects on its archive docket at the decade's midpoint. Among those films newly preserved were

---

JOHN IRVING

"As a novelist who spent thirteen years adapting my 1985 novel The Cider House Rules *to a film script, I was neither an experienced screenwriter nor a fast writer in any form–and I knew almost nothing about the Academy Awards. (From a distance, I thought Oscar was a naked gold man holding what was commonly mistaken for his sword.) The nominating process was a revelation; that I was nominated by my fellow writers, and only by them, was deeply moving. When Kevin Spacey handed me the Oscar, my speaking voice became as accelerated as my heart. On a stationary bike in the gym, earlier that afternoon, I had carefully timed what I would say if I won–on the bike peddling hard, it took forty-five seconds. That evening at the Shrine, I spoke for only thirty-five seconds and I didn't leave out a word. I know now that I lost those ten seconds to the thrill of the moment. The moment meant a lot to me. I keep my Oscar on my desk, where I work every day."*

John Irving
Adapted Screenplay 1999

DOUGLAS WICK

"The sweetest moment of victory came a full day after receiving the award. The night itself had been a blur of adrenaline and anxiety. The next morning, I took my daughter to school. When I entered her fourth grade classroom all of the kids stood up and cheered. I have never felt prouder."

Douglas Wick
Best Picture 2000

TAN DUN

"When I heard 'the best original score goes to Tan Dun,' I jumped out of my seat, hugged my wife Jane and the 'Tiger team' around me, then started running to the podium. I felt the distance from there to here was as long as hundreds of years passed and thousands of miles crossed; as from the village where I was a rice planter, as the Peking Opera House where I was a fiddle player, as from New York where I am a classical music composer.

My music is to dream without boundaries. That night, I saw boundaries were crossed once again – a

human story with a Chinese cast and told in its Chinese language won four Oscars, which has created a historical record for the world film industry.

In the following months, during my numerous music tours to Europe and Asia, I was further convinced by the fact that this Oscar Night was truly celebrated by millions of people throughout the world, from various cultures and speaking different languages.

This world is no longer separated by oceans and languages. And the Academy had embraced a new world of audience."

Tan Dun
Music Score 2000

six Best Pictures *(All the King's Men, All about Eve, In the Heat of the Night, Oliver!, One Flew over the Cuckoo's Nest,* and *Amadeus),* as well as William Wellman's *The Story of G.I. Joe, Hearts and Minds,* and *Olympia en México,* along with the archive's first serious restoration of a large-format film *(Lord Jim)* and an ongoing effort to preserve all the films of director Satyajit Ray. It's worth noting that to keep track of the tens of thousands of items now in the Academy's collection, the archive switched during the decade to MAVIS, a new database system from Australia, the first to be built and designed from scratch by film archivists specifically for use in cataloging film archives.

To the nearly 24,000 movie posters currently stored at the Margaret Herrick Library in its Charles M. Powell Repository of Motion Picture Marketing Materials, the decade added two of its rarest acquisitions: two vintage *King Kong* three-sheets, each of a different design and among the rarest movie ad art. The first was donated to the library in 1999 by the Cecil B. DeMille Foundation, which bought it at auction for $244,500 (the second-highest price ever paid for a movie poster) so it might be mounted in the library's DeMille Reading Room. The other *Kong* poster arrived two years later, a gift from director John Landis and his wife, costume designer Deborah Nadoolman.

Other noteworthy Academy business during the decade included the Board of Governors' unanimous decision to name

Wolfgang Puck at the Governors Ball (73rd Awards)

the Margaret Herrick Library's collection of still photographs the Roddy McDowall Photograph Archive, after the actor and Academy governor, himself a dedicated photographer, who died in 1998. The building housing the library and its McDowall Archive, which had been known since its 1990 opening as the Center for Motion Picture Study, had its name expanded in 2002 to the Fairbanks Center for Motion Picture Study, as a way of honoring the man who, in 1927, both led the civic campaign to have the building constructed and served the Academy as its first president. Late in 2002 the Fairbanks Center acquired a mate, as the Academy's third major Los Angeles facility was christened the Pickford Center for Motion Picture Study. The Academy had purchased the sprawling historic television studio complex at the corner of Fountain and Vine Streets, and had begun converting its sound stages—one at a time, in a process not to be completed for decades—into chilled and dehumidified vaults that would

eventually house all the holdings of the Academy Film Archive except those on nitrate film.

In addition to the archive staff, the Players Directory personnel and offices also relocated to the new facility, rendering the Academy, like ancient Gaul, divided into three parts.

The first new Academy Award category in a long time was created when the Board decided that a sufficient number of feature-length animated pictures were being released most years to justify a set of nominations. It was decided that if as many as eight feature-length animation films were released during a calendar year, an award would be given. (The first winner was 2001's *Shrek.*) Some 150 documentary-filmmaking Academy members shifted from at-large to Branch status, and elected Oscar-recipient Freida Lee Mock their first governor. Two additional governors were added the next year, giving the new branch the standard contingent of three.

There were two grand glitches during

AKIVA GOLDSMAN

"I was sitting with my better half, Rebecca Spikings, clutching her hand so hard I think she still has little fingerprints indented in her palm. Rebecca's father had won an Academy Award for producing The Deer Hunter *when he was 39, the same age I was on Oscar night. All I could think, as the envelope was opened, was that if somehow I won, I would be institutionalizing a rather daunting family tradition. When my name was actually read, my mind was instantly replaced by a dial tone. I have only little flashes: walking to the podium...hugging Ethan Hawke and Gwyneth Paltrow...looking out at so many faces (everyone smiles at you when you're up there)...realizing, as I read my speech, that I'd printed it on three-hole punch paper. I moved through the parties on autopilot. It was only at about five a.m., sitting in our bed eating pizza, that it really hit me. I had won an Oscar. And I promptly burst into tears. Having the award is still endlessly remarkable, like a Christmas gift you keep getting every day. I just hope any potential offspring don't go into the business. Now, there's just going to be way too much pressure."*

Akiva Goldsman
Adapted Screenplay 2001

BRUCE COHEN

"In April, 1970, I was 8 years old, my parents were out of town, and my two grandmothers let me stay up to watch the Academy Awards. I had never seen anything like the extraordinary excitement and glamour of the event and was very taken by the clips from the Best Picture nominees, especially the classic 'We've got to jump off the cliff together' scene from Butch Cassidy and the Sundance Kid. *And all this little kid could think of, watching the parade of winners giving their acceptance speeches while clutching their shiny gold men, was 'Someday, I want one of those.'"*

Two years later, when my parents refused to let me stay up and watch that year's edition of the Oscars, I felt I had no choice but to run away from home. I left behind a note expressing my anger and concluding with 'I may still love you, but I no longer need you'.

On the night before the Academy Awards, at which I was nominated along with my producing partner Dan Jinks for Best Picture, a group of my 15 closest family members and friends, including my mom and dad, gathered for dinner. I shared my memories of my first Oscars in 1970 and then my mom reached into her

purse and produced the note I had written 1972, which she read out loud to the table, much to all of our amazement.

And so on the following evening, as Clint Eastwood opened the envelope and announced 'And the Oscar goes to...American Beauty,' I jumped out of my seat to join the illustrious parade of winners giving their acceptance speeches while clutching their shiny gold men with the complete awareness that this was literally my lifelong dream coming true."

Bruce Cohen
Best Picture 1999

the decade, the kinds that cause royal headaches but eventually add color and spunk to the Oscar legend. Three weeks before the 72nd Academy Awards telecast was to take place, it was discovered that the entire batch of final ballots sent to members in Southern California had been lost in the mail. After replacement ballots had been made up and mailed out, those previously missing ballots suddenly turned up in the U.S. Postal Service's bulk mail sorting center in Bell, California. The nightmare wasn't over. The following Monday, several crates containing 55 Oscar statuettes—essentially, the full supply for that year's ceremonies—disappeared from a shipping dock, also in Bell, California. With the clock ticking away, an S.O.S. was sent to the manufacturer in Chicago, which heroically cast, plated, polished and delivered another supply in time for the show. By the time they arrived, the AWOL awards had mysteriously turned up in a convenience-store parking lot, and three employees of the shipping company eventually found their way into police custody.

The past five years had been a time of tremendous changes within the film industry at large, with new techniques and inventions dotting the horizons, new movie magicians coming to the forefront, other careers having their last hurrahs but no one as yet in possession of a crystal ball reliable enough to forecast what the future would hold for the film community in general. The industry's credo, as well as the Academy's, remained "ex-

Woody Allen (74th Awards)

pect the unexpected," something that had extra meaning when five days before Oscar officially celebrated his 75th anniversary in March of 2003, America found itself at war again, requiring major changes in that year's Academy Award celebration. But Oscar, stout fellow, quickly adjusted as needed, and began prepping for his next seventy-five years.

ACADEMY PRESIDENTS, 1998–2002

July 98–July 99	Robert Rehme
July 99–July 00	Robert Rehme
July 00–July 01	Robert Rehme
July 01–July 02	Frank Pierson
July 02–July 03	Frank Pierson

Sidney Poitier (74th Awards)

Nicole Kidman (74th Awards)

ARON WARNER

"Being a naturally, well, obsessive person, I barely ate or slept for the three weeks prior to the awards. I kept thinking 'You're not just representing yourself but also the 500 or so people who helped make this film, you damn well better do a job worthy of all of them.' Thinking about that over and over probably wasn't such a great idea....

I was fine until the first award was given out. Andrew Adamson, one of our directors, was sitting with me. At one point he turned and said, 'Are you going to throw up?' I assured him I wasn't but he looked skeptical. While I was on stage, what I remember most was a sound: a huge jet engine-like roar. I know I wasn't really hearing it, but I'm convinced that somehow it was the sound of my friends around the country who were watching and with me up there on the stage.

I feel immensely lucky to be able to work in a creative field, even luckier to be able to work with smart, funny and good-hearted people. Winning an Oscar is a permanent reminder of all the good things in my life."

Aron Warner
Animated Feature 2001

CHRIS WEDGE

"The greatest thrill in the whole affair was our very first taste of Oscar: being nominated in the first place. That event played in the sphere of our everyday lives, and the glamour of everything that followed, rarified as it was, was disadvantaged without that contrast of routine to surround it.

I had held my breath for the three months after our film qualified, until that morning in February when the nominees were announced. Usually the news reaches New York when I am in the car, and I find out who the nominees are when I get to work. I stayed home that morning, pacing compulsively through the house. It was surreal: dust on things, half-dried flakes of cereal in bowls on the breakfast table, a little pile of yesterday's clothes on the floor, impossibly normal in the presence of my anxiety.

The telecast came and went. Why did I assume that 'Animated Short Subject' would be announced on national television?

We ran downstairs to the computer and logged on to the Academy website. It looked the same as it had for the previous few weeks. The announcements weren't there

yet. We hit it again and again for a while, no change. I searched for other sites that might be posting the complete list of nominees and then checked the Academy site again. Nada. Maybe I should go to work. A half-hour of this and suddenly the site had had a complete facelift. There was a section for nominees! I zipped down through the list and didn't see anything. Nothing about animation. I must have missed it. From the top again, in measured click, click, click, clicks....There it was! Bunny! Our movie! My wife screeched and jumped crying into my lap.

I had tried for months to stay cool about this, to pretend that it wasn't on my mind, but there it was: the little title that only a few of us knew about joined in a list by the biggest names in the business. Oscar's glory shone into our household that moment and every corner dust-ball swooned. It felt like the rest of the world could see us there.

*It started sinking in. What to do next, the changes, the plans. 'Holy ****!' we said to each other. "We're going to the Academy Awards!"*

Chris Wedge
Animated Short Film, 1997

Halle Berry (74th Awards)

Steve Martin (75th Awards)

Sixty-four Oscar-winning actors on stage at the Kodak Theatre (75th Awards)

BILL CONDON

"In my year, the writing awards were given out three-and-a-half hours into the show. By the time my name was announced, I'd heard the words 'we're broadcasting live to a billion people worldwide' so often that they started to seem like a threat, a warning against possible global humiliation...Later, I ran the backstage gauntlet of bookers for the morning television shows, with the distributor's publicity woman screaming, 'I've got Bill Condon, he just won, who wants Bill?' The response was immediate and unanimous, a dozen variations on 'Are you kidding?' It was funny and strangely liberating; life wasn't going to change in any meaningful way, which was a great relief. I realized and had a wonderful time for the rest of the night."

Bill Condon
Adapted Screenplay 1998

JAMES MOLL

"Hearing my name called was incredible, but it was not the best moment. Giving my speech was not the best moment either. That perfect moment didn't come until I walked off the stage, Oscar in hand, knowing that my paranoia about tripping and falling in front of the world was gone. Knowing that there was no way I was going to appear in one of those 'Worst Moments in Oscar History' reels. I stood in the wings with presenters Matt Damon and Ben Affleck who both knew exactly how I felt (they won Oscars the year before). They knew I was having the 'backstage moment' and their grins were as big as mine. It was awesome."

James Moll
Documentary Feature, 1998

DAN JINKS

"While winning the Academy Award was certainly the most exciting night of my life, it was also the must surreal. Winning an Oscar is the kind of thing that happens to OTHER people. So many people told us that we were going to win, but I didn't want to believe it. I was too
afraid of expecting it, and than not winning. I remember walking up on stage as they announced that our film, American Beauty, had won best picture. I looked down at my feet for a moment and I decided to remember that moment for the rest of my life. I was walking up on stage to accept the Academy Award in front of a billion people. Wow. My speech was pretty much a blur until I looked out and saw Annette Bening's beautiful face in the audience, looking at me with her supportive eyes. She was eight and a half months pregnant at the time. When my producing partner and I walked offstage, there was Sam Mendes, our director, and Steven Spielberg, who had greenlit the movie for Dreamworks. The four of us had a warm, wonderful moment where we celebrated our win.

The next day I watched a tape of the broadcast. The seemingly long moment where I looked down at my feet was just a quick glance down on television. But unexpectedly, the moment with Steven and Sam was broadcast. I had no idea there were cameras backstage. It was so nice to see the excitement in all of our eyes without knowing that the world was watching."

Dan Jinks
Best Picture 1999

In his 71st year, Oscar found himself up to his bootstraps in love and war, with all of the year's best picture nominees featuring either sagas of the 44-year reign of Elizabeth I or the four-year ordeal of World War II. The war seized three of the five spots: Terrence Malick soldiered on to Guadalcanal (via his remaking of James Jones's novel *The Thin Red Line),* Steven Spielberg did his Longest D-Day *(Saving Private Ryan)* and Roberto Benigni strove throughout the Holocaust to prove *Life Is Beautiful.* The other two nominees offered contrasting views of the Virgin Queen: a centerpiece close-up of her power struggles *(Elizabeth)* and an extended cameo of her as a member of the Bard's intimate circle *(Shakespeare in Love).* It was oddly fitting that Henry VIII—the only character ever to put three different actors in the Oscar running (Charles Laughton, Robert Shaw and Richard Burton)—produced a daughter who could beget two different Oscar-nominated portrayals in the same year, in this case Cate Blanchett's title performance in *Elizabeth* and Judi Dench's eight-minute bit in *Shakespeare in Love.* Blanchett's queen lost the best actress award to Gwyneth Paltrow in *Shakespeare in Love,* but Dench won the supporting actress nod. Only once before in Oscar history had two actresses been nominated in the same Academy Award year for playing the same character, the two being Kate Winslet and Gloria Stuart in 1997's *Titanic.*

Just as in the movies, when Oscar's love-versus-war standoff climaxed on March 21, 1999, at the Dorothy Chandler Pavilion of the Los Angeles Music Center, love won all over the place. *Shakespeare in Love* emerged as the year's most-Oscared entry, with seven awards. In addition to raking in both awards in the female-acting divisions, it won the prizes for picture, original screenplay, art direction, original musical score and costume design. Meanwhile, back on the World War II front, *Saving Private Ryan* scored five direct hits in all, including a directing Oscar for Spielberg to go with one he received five years earlier for another World War II–era drama, *Schindler's List.* Italy's Benigni, nominated both as best director and best actor, triumphed in the latter category, making him only the second performer to be honored for work in a foreign language film—the other being Sophia Loren in 1961's *Two Women*—and the second one (after Olivier) to direct himself to a best actor statuette; *Life Is Beautiful* also became the second film in Academy history to be nominated both as best picture and best foreign language film. Like 1969's *Z,* which had also been nominated in both categories, *Life* won in the foreign language division. James Coburn, with his first Academy nomination, was named the year's best supporting actor, for *Affliction.* Norman Jewison was presented the Thalberg Award.

The evening was not without controversy. There was some protesting and ado over the Board of Governors' voting an Honorary Award to twice-Oscared Elia Kazan for his brilliant screen contributions; the uproar was due to the un-

LOVE IS THE ONLY INSPIRATION

GWYNETH
PALTROW

JOSEPH
FIENNES

GEOFFREY
RUSH

COLIN
FIRTH

BEN
AFFLECK

JUDI
DENCH

SHAKESPEARE IN LOVE

Best Picture: **Shakespeare in Love** *(Miramax Films; produced by David Parfitt, Donna Gigliotti, Harvey Weinstein, Edward Zwick and Marc Norman) and* **Best Actress:** **Gwyneth Paltrow** *as Viola De Lesseps in* Shakespeare in Love, *a buoyant, merry film that conjures up Shakespeare at the starting gate as an aspiring, but uninspired, scribe working his way through writer's block. Paltrow plays a luminous muse who motivates the smitten young Will (Joseph Fiennes) to write* Romeo and Juliet, *no small order; and if that's not the way it actually happened, the film's telling was so delightful, even the historians didn't complain. Screenwriter Marc Norman credited his son with coming up with the basic idea, which he eventually turned over to Tom Stoppard, an old manhandler of the Bard in the past (*Rosencrantz and Guildenstern Are Dead*) for additional dashes of Elizabethan wit. The result weighed in with a near-record 13 nominations and made good on seven of those.*

popular appearances Kazan had made before the House Un-American Activities Committee 47 years earlier. Despite the brouhaha, 89-year-old Kazan showed up to collect the prize, which was presented to him by Robert De Niro and Martin Scorsese; some in the audience did not stand or applaud as a form of protest, while many others did.

Whoopi Goldberg hosted this ABC-broadcast event for nigh-onto four hours in a variety of giddy get-ups, starting out in Elizabethan drag and identifying herself as the African Queen. Something brand new for Oscar: for the first time in the golden boy's 71-year history, awards were handed out on a Sunday.

Best Actor: **Roberto Benigni** *as Guido in* Life Is Beautiful *(Miramax Films; directed by Roberto Benigni). In* Life Is Beautiful, *Benigni gambles with his own life to convince his son (Giorgio Cantarini, right) that the life they've been forced to endure in a World War II concentration camp is actually an elaborate child's game. The film was a stunning mix of Chaplinesque comedy, heartwarming emotion and fine-tuned drama, and became the most profitable foreign language film in history. Also, with seven nominations, it was the most-nominated foreign language film in the Academy's record books. When it copped the foreign language prize, Benigni was handed the award by the only other person to win an acting Oscar for a foreign language film,* Two Women's *one woman, Sophia Loren, a fellow Italian. Benigni was the only foreign filmmaker to score an Oscar-nomination trifecta for acting, directing and screenwriting in the same year.*

343

Best Supporting Actress: **Judi Dench** *as Queen Elizabeth I in* Shakespeare in Love *(Miramax Films; directed by John Madden). For her second consecutive royal-role nomination (she received a best actress nomination the year before as Queen Victoria in* Mrs. Brown), *Dame Judi emerged victorious—at a fraction. "I feel for eight minutes on the screen I should only get a little bit of him," she said, almost apologetically, as she hugged her new trophy. It was one of the shortest performances on record to win an Oscar. Never one to rest on her laurels, Dame Judi proceeded directly to Broadway to do David Hare's play* Amy's View *and wound up among an elite half-dozen who managed to win a Tony in the same year that they won an Oscar, her peers including Fredric March, Shirley Booth, Audrey Hepburn, Ellen Burstyn and Mercedes Ruehl.*

Best Directing: Steven Spielberg *for* Saving Private Ryan *(DreamWorks Pictures and Paramount Pictures; produced by Spielberg, Ian Bryce, Mark Gordon and Gary Levinsohn). Ryan related the efforts of an eight-man Army squad in World War II, led by Tom Hanks (left) and Edward Burns (right), to recover—and return to his mother—a private (Matt Damon) whose three brothers had been killed in battle. This noble operation proved an emotional maelstrom for audiences, who were ambushed at the outset by a graphic, no-holds-barred 24-minute preamble depicting D-Day in the most gruesome terms. Many of the director's creative collaborators on this savage sequence—in sound, sound effects editing, film editing, and cinematography—preceded him to the Oscar podium. In nominations (11) as well as in wins (5), Ryan was 1998's second most honored film, and its harrowing curtain-raiser made it virtually impossible ever to look at a war movie in the same way again.*

PICTURE

ELIZABETH, Working Title Production, Gramercy Pictures. Alison Owen, Eric Fellner and Tim Bevan, Producers.
LIFE IS BEAUTIFUL, Melampo Cinematografica Production, Miramax Films. Elda Ferri and Gianluigi Braschi, Producers.
SAVING PRIVATE RYAN, Amblin Entertainment Production in association with Mutual Film Company, DreamWorks Pictures and Paramount Pictures. Steven Spielberg, Ian Bryce, Mark Gordon and Gary Levinsohn, Producers.
* **SHAKESPEARE IN LOVE,** Miramax Films, Universal Pictures, Bedford Falls Company Production, Miramax Films. David Parfitt, Donna Gigliotti, Harvey Weinstein, Edward Zwick and Marc Norman, Producers.
THE THIN RED LINE, Fox 2000 Pictures Presentation from Phoenix Pictures in association with George Stevens, Jr., 20th Century Fox. Robert Michael Geisler, John Roberdeau and Grant Hill, Producers.

ACTOR

* **ROBERTO BENIGNI** in *Life Is Beautiful,* Melampo Cinematografica Production, Miramax Films.
TOM HANKS in *Saving Private Ryan,* Amblin Entertainment Production in association with Mutual Film Company, DreamWorks Pictures and Paramount Pictures.
IAN McKELLEN in *Gods and Monsters,* Regent Pictures, Lions Gate Films.
NICK NOLTE in *Affliction,* Tormenta Production, Lions Gate Films.
EDWARD NORTON in *American History X,* Turman-Morrissey Company Production, New Line.

ACTRESS

CATE BLANCHETT in *Elizabeth,* Working Title Production, Gramercy Pictures.
FERNANDA MONTENEGRO in *Central Station,* Arthur Cohn Production, Sony Pictures Classics.
* **GWYNETH PALTROW** in *Shakespeare in Love,* Miramax Films, Universal Pictures, Bedford Falls Company Production, Miramax Films.
MERYL STREEP in *One True Thing,* Universal Pictures Production, Universal.
EMILY WATSON in *Hilary and Jackie,* Oxford Film Company Production, October Films.

SUPPORTING ACTOR

* **JAMES COBURN** in *Affliction,* Tormenta Production, Lions Gate Films.
ROBERT DUVALL in *A Civil Action,* Touchstone Pictures and Paramount Pictures Production, Buena Vista.
ED HARRIS in *The Truman Show,* Scott Rudin Production, Paramount.
GEOFFREY RUSH in *Shakespeare in Love,* Miramax Films, Universal Pictures, Bedford Falls Company Production, Miramax Films.
BILLY BOB THORNTON in *A Simple Plan,* Mutual Film Company Production, Paramount and Mutual Film Company in association with Savoy Pictures.

SUPPORTING ACTRESS

KATHY BATES in *Primary Colors,* Universal Pictures Production, Universal and Mutual Film Company.
BRENDA BLETHYN in *Little Voice,* Scala Production, Miramax Films.
* **JUDI DENCH** in *Shakespeare in Love,* Miramax Films, Universal Pictures, Bedford Falls Company Production, Miramax Films.
RACHEL GRIFFITHS in *Hilary and Jackie,* Oxford Film Company Production, October Films.
LYNN REDGRAVE in *Gods and Monsters,* Regent Pictures, Lions Gate Films.

DIRECTING

LIFE IS BEAUTIFUL, Melampo Cinematografica Production, Miramax Films. Roberto Benigni.
* **SAVING PRIVATE RYAN,** Amblin Entertainment Production in association with Mutual Film Company, DreamWorks Pictures and Paramount Pictures. Steven Spielberg.
SHAKESPEARE IN LOVE, Miramax Films, Universal Pictures, Bedford Falls Company Production, Miramax Films. John Madden.
THE THIN RED LINE, Fox 2000 Pictures Presentation from Phoenix Pictures in association with George Stevens, Jr., 20th Century Fox. Terrence Malick.
THE TRUMAN SHOW, Scott Rudin Production, Paramount. Peter Weir.

WRITING

(Screenplay Based on Material Previously Produced or Published)
* **GODS AND MONSTERS,** Regent Pictures, Lions Gate Films. Bill Condon.
OUT OF SIGHT, Jersey Films Production, Universal. Scott Frank.
PRIMARY COLORS, Universal Pictures Production, Universal and Mutual Film Company. Elaine May.
A SIMPLE PLAN, Mutual Film Company Production, Paramount and Mutual Film Company in association with Savoy Pictures. Scott B. Smith.
THE THIN RED LINE, Fox 2000 Pictures Presentation from Phoenix Pictures in association with George Stevens, Jr., 20th Century Fox. Terrence Malick.

(Screenplay Written Directly for the Screen)
BULWORTH, 20th Century Fox. Warren Beatty, Jeremy Pikser.
LIFE IS BEAUTIFUL, Melampo Cinematografica Production, Miramax Films. Vincenzo Cerami, Roberto Benigni.
SAVING PRIVATE RYAN, Amblin Entertainment Production in association with Mutual Film Company, DreamWorks Pictures and Paramount Pictures. Robert Rodat.
* **SHAKESPEARE IN LOVE,** Miramax Films, Universal Pictures, Bedford Falls Company Production, Miramax Films. Marc Norman, Tom Stoppard.
THE TRUMAN SHOW, Scott Rudin Production, Paramount. Andrew Niccol.

ART DIRECTION—SET DECORATION

ELIZABETH, Working Title Production, Gramercy Pictures. John Myhre; Peter Howitt.
PLEASANTVILLE, Larger Than Life Production, New Line. Jeannine Oppewall; Jay Hart.
SAVING PRIVATE RYAN, Amblin Entertainment Production in association with Mutual Film Company, DreamWorks Pictures and Paramount Pictures. Tom Sanders; Lisa Dean Kavanaugh.
* **SHAKESPEARE IN LOVE,** Miramax Films, Universal Pictures, Bedford Falls Company Production, Miramax Films. Martin Childs; Jill Quertier.
WHAT DREAMS MAY COME, Interscope Communications Production in association with Metafilmics, PolyGram. Eugenio Zanetti; Cindy Carr.

CINEMATOGRAPHY

A CIVIL ACTION, Touchstone Pictures and Paramount Pictures Production, Buena Vista. Conrad L. Hall.
ELIZABETH, Working Title Production, Gramercy Pictures. Remi Adefarasin.
* **SAVING PRIVATE RYAN,** Amblin Entertainment Production in association with Mutual Film Company, DreamWorks Pictures and Paramount Pictures. Janusz Kaminski.
SHAKESPEARE IN LOVE, Miramax Films, Universal Pictures, Bedford Falls Company Production, Miramax Films. Richard Greatrex.
THE THIN RED LINE, Fox 2000 Pictures Presentation from Phoenix Pictures in association with George Stevens, Jr., 20th Century Fox. John Toll.

Best Supporting Actor: James Coburn *as Glen Whitehouse in* Affliction *(Lions Gate Films; directed by Paul Schrader). The sins of the father (Coburn, second from left) were visited on his sons (Oscar nominee Nick Nolte, left, and Willem Dafoe, right) and daughter-in-law (Sissy Spacek) in* Affliction, *a harrowing drama coproduced by Nolte. None of Coburn's 60 or so earlier films had prepared him to play this abusive patriarch, who ran so counter to the charm-laden characters he'd played in such past films as* The Great Escape, The Magnificent Seven *and* Our Man Flint. *It almost cost him the gig. "Not charming," director Paul Schrader stressed to him. "I don't want to see charm in this guy, because he definitely is not charming." Coburn did as he was told and got the gold.*

COSTUME DESIGN
BELOVED, Touchstone Pictures Production, Buena Vista. Colleen Atwood.
ELIZABETH, Working Title Production, Gramercy Pictures. Alexandra Byrne.
PLEASANTVILLE, Larger Than Life Production, New Line. Judianna Makovsky.
* SHAKESPEARE IN LOVE, Miramax Films, Universal Pictures, Bedford Falls Company Production, Miramax Films. Sandy Powell.
VELVET GOLDMINE, Zenith/Killer Films Production, Miramax Films. Sandy Powell.

FILM EDITING
LIFE IS BEAUTIFUL, Melampo Cinematografica Production, Miramax Films. Simona Paggi.
OUT OF SIGHT, Jersey Films Production, Universal. Anne V. Coates.
* SAVING PRIVATE RYAN, Amblin Entertainment Production in association with Mutual Film Company, DreamWorks Pictures and Paramount Pictures. Michael Kahn.
SHAKESPEARE IN LOVE, Miramax Films, Universal Pictures, Bedford Falls Company Production, Miramax Films. David Gamble.
THE THIN RED LINE, Fox 2000 Pictures Presentation from Phoenix Pictures in association with George Stevens, Jr., 20th Century Fox. Billy Weber, Leslie Jones and Saar Klein.

MAKEUP
* ELIZABETH, Working Title Production, Gramercy Pictures. Jenny Shircore.
SAVING PRIVATE RYAN, Amblin Entertainment Production in association with Mutual Film Company, DreamWorks Pictures and Paramount Pictures. Lois Burwell, Conor O'Sullivan and Daniel C. Striepeke.
SHAKESPEARE IN LOVE, Miramax Films, Universal Pictures, Bedford Falls Company Production, Miramax Films. Lisa Westcott, Veronica Brebner.

MUSIC
(Original Dramatic Score)
ELIZABETH, Working Title Production, Gramercy Pictures. David Hirschfelder.
* LIFE IS BEAUTIFUL, Melampo Cinematografica Production, Miramax Films. Nicola Piovani.
PLEASANTVILLE, Larger Than Life Production, New Line. Randy Newman.
SAVING PRIVATE RYAN, Amblin Entertainment Production in association with Mutual Film Company, DreamWorks Pictures and Paramount Pictures. John Williams.
THE THIN RED LINE, Fox 2000 Pictures Presentation from Phoenix Pictures in association with George Stevens, Jr., 20th Century Fox. Hans Zimmer.

(Original Musical or Comedy Score)
A BUG'S LIFE, Walt Disney Pictures/Pixar Animation Studios Production, Buena Vista. Randy Newman.
MULAN, Walt Disney Pictures Production, Buena Vista. Music by Matthew Wilder; Lyric by David Zippel; Orchestral Score by Jerry Goldsmith.
PATCH ADAMS, Universal Pictures Production, Universal. Marc Shaiman.
THE PRINCE OF EGYPT, DreamWorks SKG Production, DreamWorks. Music and Lyric by Stephen Schwartz; Orchestral Score by Hans Zimmer.
* SHAKESPEARE IN LOVE, Miramax Films, Universal Pictures, Bedford Falls Company Production, Miramax Films. Stephen Warbeck.

(Original Song)
I DON'T WANT TO MISS A THING (Armageddon, Touchstone Pictures Production, Buena Vista); Music and Lyric by Diane Warren.
THE PRAYER (Quest for Camelot, Warner Bros.); Music by Carole Bayer Sager and David Foster; Lyric by Carole Bayer Sager, David Foster, Tony Renis and Alberto Testa.
A SOFT PLACE TO FALL (The Horse Whisperer, Touchstone Pictures Production, Buena Vista); Music and Lyric by Allison Moorer and Gwil Owen.
THAT'LL DO (Babe: Pig in the City, Kennedy Miller Media Pty. Ltd. Production, Universal); Music and Lyric by Randy Newman.
* WHEN YOU BELIEVE (The Prince of Egypt, DreamWorks SKG Production, DreamWorks); Music and Lyric by Stephen Schwartz.

SOUND
ARMAGEDDON, Touchstone Pictures Production, Buena Vista. Kevin O'Connell, Greg P. Russell and Keith A. Wester.
THE MASK OF ZORRO, Amblin Entertainment Production, TriStar. Kevin O'Connell, Greg P. Russell and Pud Cusack.
* SAVING PRIVATE RYAN, Amblin Entertainment Production in association with Mutual Film Company, DreamWorks Pictures and Paramount Pictures. Gary Rydstrom, Gary Summers, Andy Nelson and Ronald Judkins.
SHAKESPEARE IN LOVE, Miramax Films, Universal Pictures, Bedford Falls Company Production, Miramax Films. Robin O'Donoghue, Dominic Lester and Peter Glossop.
THE THIN RED LINE, Fox 2000 Pictures Presentation from Phoenix Pictures in association with George Stevens, Jr., 20th Century Fox. Andy Nelson, Anna Behlmer and Paul Brincat.

SOUND EFFECTS EDITING
ARMAGEDDON, Touchstone Pictures Production, Buena Vista. George Watters II.
THE MASK OF ZORRO, Amblin Entertainment Production, TriStar. David McMoyler.
* SAVING PRIVATE RYAN, Amblin Entertainment Production in association with Mutual Film Company, DreamWorks Pictures and Paramount Pictures. Gary Rydstrom and Richard Hymns.

VISUAL EFFECTS
ARMAGEDDON, Touchstone Pictures Production, Buena Vista. Richard R. Hoover, Pat McClung and John Frazier.
MIGHTY JOE YOUNG, Walt Disney Pictures Production, Buena Vista. Rick Baker, Hoyt Yeatman, Allen Hall and Jim Mitchell.
* WHAT DREAMS MAY COME, Interscope Communications Production in association with Metafilmics, PolyGram. Joel Hynek, Nicholas Brooks, Stuart Robertson and Kevin Mack.

SHORT FILMS
(Animated)
* BUNNY, Blue Sky Studios, Inc., Production. Chris Wedge.
THE CANTERBURY TALES, S4C/BBC Wales/HBO Production. Christopher Grace and Jonathan Myerson.
JOLLY ROGER, Astley Baker/Silver Bird Production for Channel Four. Mark Baker.
MORE, Bad Clams Productions/Swell Productions/Flemington Pictures Production. Mark Osborne and Steve Kalafer.
WHEN LIFE DEPARTS, A. Film Production. Karsten Kiilerich and Stefan Fjeldmark.

(Live Action)
CULTURE, False Alarm Pictures Production. Will Speck and Josh Gordon.
* ELECTION NIGHT (VALGAFTEN), M & M Production. Kim Magnusson and Anders Thomas Jensen.
HOLIDAY ROMANCE, Jovy Junior Enterprises Ltd. Production. Alexander Jovy and JJ Keith.
LA CARTE POSTALE (THE POSTCARD), K2 S.A. Production. Vivian Goffette.
VICTOR, Bergvall Bilder/Hemikrania Production. Simon Sandquist and Joel Bergvall.

DOCUMENTARY
(Feature)
DANCEMAKER, Four Oaks Foundation Production. Matthew Diamond, Jerry Kupfer.
THE FARM: ANGOLA, U.S.A., Gabriel Films Production. Jonathan Stack, Liz Garbus.
* THE LAST DAYS: SURVIVORS OF THE SHOAH VISUAL HISTORY FOUNDATION PRODUCTION, October Films. James Moll, Ken Lipper.
LENNY BRUCE: SWEAR TO TELL THE TRUTH, Whyaduck Productions. Robert B. Weide.
REGRET TO INFORM, Sun Fountain Production. Barbara Sonneborn, Janet Cole.

(Short Subject)
* THE PERSONALS: IMPROVISATIONS ON ROMANCE IN THE GOLDEN YEARS, Keiko Ibi Film Production. Keiko Ibi.
A PLACE IN THE LAND, Guggenheim Productions. Charles Guggenheim.
SUNRISE OVER TIANANMEN SQUARE, National Film Board of Canada Production. Shui-Bo Wang, Donald McWilliams.

FOREIGN LANGUAGE FILM
CENTRAL STATION (Brazil)
CHILDREN OF HEAVEN (Iran)
THE GRANDFATHER (Spain)
* LIFE IS BEAUTIFUL (Italy)
TANGO (Argentina)

HONORARY AWARDS
TO ELIA KAZAN in recognition of his indelible contributions to the art of motion picture direction. [s(Statuette)]
TO DAVID W. GRAY in appreciation for outstanding service and dedication in upholding the high standards of the Academy of Motion Picture Arts and Sciences. [(John A. Bonner Medal of Commendation)]

1998 IRVING G. THALBERG MEMORIAL AWARD
TO NORMAN JEWISON

1998 JEAN HERSHOLT HUMANITARIAN AWARD
None given this year.

1998 GORDON E. SAWYER AWARD
None given this year.

SCIENTIFIC AND TECHNICAL AWARDS
Academy Award of Merit (Statuette)
AVID TECHNOLOGY, INC., for the concept, system design and engineering of the Avid Film Composer for motion picture editing.

Scientific and Engineering Awards (Academy Plaque)
DR. THOMAS G. STOCKHAM, JR., and ROBERT B. INGEBRETSEN for their pioneering work in the areas of waveform editing, crossfades and cut-and-paste techniques for digital audio editing.

JAMES A. MOORER for his pioneering work in the design of digital signal processing and its application to audio editing for film.
STEPHEN J. KAY of K-Tec Corporation for the design and development of the Shock Block.
GARY TREGASKIS for the primary design, and DOMINIQUE BOISVERT, PHILIPPE PANZINI and ANDRÉ LEBLANC for the development and implementation, of the Flame and Inferno software.
ROBERT PREDOVICH, JOHN SCOTT, MOHAMED KEN T. HUSAIN and CAMERON SHEARER for the design and implementation of the Soundmaster Integrated Operations Nucleus operating environment.
ROY B. FERENCE, STEVEN R. SCHMIDT, RICHARD J. FEDERICO, ROCKWELL YARID and MICHAEL E. MCCRACKAN for the design and development of the Kodak Lightning Laser Recorder.
COLIN MOSSMAN, HANS LEISINGER and GEORGE JOHN ROWLAND of Deluxe Laboratories for the concept and design of the Deluxe High Speed Spray Film Cleaner.
ARNOLD & RICHTER CINE TECHNIK, and ARRI USA, INC., for the concept and engineering of the Arriflex 435 Camera System.
ARNOLD & RICHTER CINE TECHNIK and THE CARL ZEISS COMPANY for the concept and optical design of the Carl Zeiss/Arriflex Variable Prime Lenses.
DEREK C. LIGHTBODY of OpTex for the design and development of Aurasoft Luminaires.
MARK ROBERTS, RONAN CARROLL, ASSAFF RAWNER, PAUL BARTLETT and SIMON WAKLEY for the creation of the Milo Motion-Control Crane.
MICHAEL SORENSEN and RICHARD ALEXANDER of Sorensen Designs International, and Donald Trumbull for advancing the state-of-the-art of real-time motion-control, as exemplified in the Gazelle and Zebra camera dolly systems.
RONALD E. UHLIG, THOMAS F. POWERS and FRED M. FUSS of the Eastman Kodak Company for the design and development of KeyKode latent-image barcode key numbers.
IAIN NEIL for the optical design, TAKUO MIYAGISHIMA for the mechanical design, and PANAVISION, INCORPORATED, for the concept and development of the Primo Series of spherical prime lenses for 35mm cinematography.

Technical Achievement Awards (Academy Certificate)
GARRETT BROWN and JERRY HOLWAY for the creation of the Skyman flying platform for Steadicam operators.
JAMES RODNUNSKY, JAMES WEBBER and BOB WEBBER of Cablecam Systems, and Trou Bayliss for the design and engineering of Cablecam.
DAVID DIFRANCESCO, BALA S. MANIAN and THOMAS L. NOGGLE for their pioneering efforts in the development of laser film recording technology.
MICHAEL MACKENZIE, MIKE BOLLES, UDO PAMPEL and JOSEPH FULMER of Industrial Light & Magic for their pioneering work in motion-controlled silent camera dollies.
BARRY WALTON, BILL SCHULTZ, CHRIS BARKER and DAVID CORNELIUS of Sony Pictures Imageworks for the creation of an advanced motion-controlled silent camera dolly.
BRUCE WILTON and CARLOS ICINKOFF of Mechanical Concepts for their modular system of motion-control rotators and movers for use in motion-control.
REMY SMITH for the software and electronic design and development,; and JAMES K. BRANCH and NASIR J. ZAIDI for the design and development of the Spectra Professional IV-A digital exposure meter.
IVAN KRUGLAK for his commitment to the development of a wireless transmission system for video-assisted images for the motion picture industry, and his pioneering concept and the development of the Coherent Time Code Slate.
DR. DOUGLAS R. ROBLE for his contribution to tracking technology and for the design and implementation of the TRACK system for camera position calculation and scene reconstruction.
THADDEUS BEIER for the design and implementation of ras_track, a system for 2D tracking, stabilization and 3D camera and object tracking.
MANFRED N. KLEMME and DONALD E. WETZEL for the design and development of the K-Tek Microphone Boom Pole and accessories for on-set motion picture sound recording.
NICK FOSTER for his software development in the field of water simulation systems.
CARY PHILLIPS for the design and development of the "Caricature" Animation System at Industrial Light & Magic.
DR. MITCHELL J. BOGDANOWICZ of the Eastman Kodak Company, and JIM MEYER and STAN MILLER of Rosco Laboratories, Inc., for the design of the CalColor Calibrated Color Effects Filters.
DR. A. TULSI RAM, RICHARD C. SEHLIN, DR. CARL F. HOLTZ and DAVID F. KOPPERL of the Eastman Kodak Company for the research and development of the concept of molecular sieves applied to improve the archival properties of processed photographic film.
TAKUO MIYAGISHIMA and ALBERT K. SAIKI of Panavision, Inc., for the design and development of the Eyepiece Leveler.
EDMUND M. DI GIULIO and JAMES BARTELL of Cinema Products for the design of the KeyKode Sync Reader.
IVAN KRUGLAK for his pioneering concept and the development of the Coherent Time Code Slate.
MIKE DENECKE for refining and further developing electronic time code slates.
ED ZWANEVELD and FREDERICK GASOI of the National Film Board of Canada, and MIKE LAZARIDIS and DALE BRUBACHER-CRESSMAN of Research in Motion for the design and development of the DigiSync Film KeyKode Reader.

Back at the 1942 Oscars, an honorary prize had been passed out "To Metro-Goldwyn-Mayer Studio for its achievement in representing the American way of life in the production of the Andy Hardy series of films." By millennium's end, just how far movies had moved out of the Hardy hometown of Carvel was abundantly apparent in the arm wrestling that went on for 1999's best picture prize: on the one hand there was *American Beauty,* a kinky, darkly comical portrayal of a dysfunctional family coming apart at the seams in the suburbs; there was also a coming-of-age story backdropped by a theme of abortion in Maine (*The Cider House Rules*), an unusual and potent prison story (*The Green Mile*), a supernatural thriller (*The Sixth Sense*) and a political mystery based on a true story (*The Insider*). It was all a long way from *Love Finds Andy Hardy.*

On March 26, 2000, at the Los Angeles Shrine Auditorium, DreamWorks's *American Beauty* eventually plucked off more "bests" than any of its competition—five big ones: picture, actor, director, original screenplay and cinematography. Kevin Spacey, named the year's best actor in *Beauty,* became the 10th performer to win Oscars in both the starring and supporting categories, following Helen Hayes, Jack Lemmon, Ingrid Bergman, Maggie Smith, Robert De Niro, Meryl Streep, Jack Nicholson, Gene Hackman and Jessica Lange. In his acceptance speech, Spacey dedicated his Oscar to one of that number, Lemmon, with whom

he'd worked in 1992's *Glengarry Glen Ross.* Lemmon, said Spacey, was "the man who inspired my performance, a man who has been my friend and my mentor and, since my father died, a little bit like my father. Wherever you are," added Spacey, "thank you, thank you, thank you." Lemmon was watching the Oscars at the home of the Gregory Pecks and was "overwhelmed."

Hilary Swank was named best actress for playing a girl brutalized for wanting to be a male in *Boys Don't Cry.* Michael Caine as the kindly country abortionist in *The Cider House Rules* won his second supporting actor prize. For supporting actress winner Angelina Jolie in *Girl, Interrupted* it was a first nomination and first award. It was not the first Oscar in Jolie's family tree, however: her father, Jon Voight, was Oscar's best actor winner in 1978 for *Coming Home.* The only previous father-daughter pair of acting Oscar winners had been the Fondas, daughter Jane in 1971 and 1978, father Henry in 1981. On this Oscar night, Jane Fonda, off the screen for several years, reentered Hollywood society to present an honorary award to Polish director Andrzej Wajda. Warren Beatty received the prestigious Irving Thalberg Award.

Billy Crystal made his seventh appearance as an Oscar show host. Producers of the show were Richard Zanuck and his wife, Lili Fini Zanuck, making her the first woman to produce the event. It also turned out to be the longest Academy Award show to date, clocking in at four hours and eight minutes.

Best Picture: **American Beauty** *(DreamWorks; produced by Bruce Cohen and Dan Jinks).* **Best Directing:** **Sam Mendes** *for* American Beauty *and* **Best Actor:** **Kevin Spacey** *as Lester Burnham in* American Beauty. *DreamWorks's Steven Spielberg set this project in motion on a Saturday, when he read Alan Ball's cutting-edge psychocomedy about a chaotic household under fire and put in a successful bid for the film rights the following Monday. Instead of directing it himself, he took a gamble and gave it to a cinematically untested British theater director, Sam Mendes, who made it through beautifully with the help of veteran cinematographer Conrad L. Hall. Spacey, heading a strong cast, particularly shone as a cuckolded husband who consoled himself with erotic rose-covered fantasies about a glamorous gal-pal of his teenage daughter.*

Best Supporting Actor: **Michael Caine** *as Dr. Wilbur Larch in* The Cider House Rules *(Miramax Films; directed by Lasse Hallström). If they gave Oscars for acceptance speeches, Caine might have won that, too. Not since Ingrid Bergman apologized to fellow nominee Valentina Cortese at the 1974 Oscars had a winner displayed quite such class and generosity of spirit. "I was thinking of how the Academy changed [announcing] 'The winner is . . .' to 'The Oscar goes to . . .'," Caine remarked. "If ever there was a category where the Oscar goes to someone without there being a 'winner,' it's this one." He cheered the work of his four competitors, ending with, "So really I'm basically up here, guys, to represent you as what I hope you will all be: a survivor." As he left the stage, statuette in hand, his rivals for the award—Tom Cruise, Jude Law, Michael Clarke Duncan and young Haley Joel Osment—were leading a standing ovation.*

Best Supporting Actress: **Angelina Jolie** *as Lisa in* Girl, Interrupted *(Columbia; directed by James Mangold). Considering that it was designed as a vehicle for Winona Ryder (far left) and produced by Ms. Ryder, Girl was true to its title, the girl in this case upstaged by Jolie's stunning supporting performance as a seductive, flamboyantly off-the-padded-wall sociopath. The role was too juicy not to have stolen the glory in this filming of Susanna Kaysen's autobiographical account of her stay in a mental hospital in the '60s, where the author saw herself as sane compared to those around her. Jolie's bravura interpretation as the girl's constant yardstick, the ward firebrand who was ferociously "out there," struck exactly the right note, and Oscar voters took notice.*

Best Actress: **Hilary Swank** *as Brandon Teena (a.k.a. Teena Brandon) in* Boys Don't Cry *(Fox Searchlight; directed by Kimberly Peirce). Cross-dressing had worked wonders for Linda Hunt, voted best supporting actress in 1983 for playing a male in* The Year of Living Dangerously. *Oscar's other gender-benders have been gay deceivers—nominees Jaye Davidson (a male playing a transvestite in 1992's* The Crying Game*) and Julie Andrews (attempting the triple somersault—a female playing a male playing a female—in 1982's* Victor/Victoria*), and now Swank's tragically true case in point of a young woman who reinvents herself as a man. Her layered portrayal of this compelling and complex human being was stunning, as life-affirming as the story was dark, sinister and compelling. Produced independently and on a minimum budget, it paid great dividends to Swank by bringing her international stardom. Chloë Sevigny (left) was also Oscar-nominated as the object of Swank's affections.*

347

Best Director: Sam Mendes *for* American Beauty *(DreamWorks). Thirty-four years old and English-born, Mendes came to films while also extremely active as a stage director. He had been running the experimental Donmar Warehouse Theatre in London since 1992 and often directed for the Royal Shakespeare Company, the National Theatre and in the West End; he first caught Broadway's attention with an edgy and eroticized 1998 revival of* Cabaret. Beauty *marked his debut as a film director and, containing as it did the kind of refreshing, off-beat and often jolting approach to storytelling that had marked many of the Mendes theatrical endeavors, he was named the year's best director, one of the few times in Oscar's history that a newcomer to the film ranks took home the big prize for his very first film effort.*

PICTURE
* **AMERICAN BEAUTY,** Jinks/Cohen Company Production, DreamWorks. Bruce Cohen and Dan Jinks, Producers.
THE CIDER HOUSE RULES, FilmColony Production, Miramax Films. Richard N. Gladstein, Producer.
THE GREEN MILE, Castle Rock Production, Warner Bros. David Valdes and Frank Darabont, Producers.
THE INSIDER, Touchstone Pictures Production, Buena Vista. Michael Mann and Pieter Jan Brugge, Producers.
THE SIXTH SENSE, Kennedy/Marshall/Barry Mendel Production, Buena Vista. Frank Marshall, Kathleen Kennedy and Barry Mendel, Producers.

ACTOR
RUSSELL CROWE in *The Insider,* Touchstone Pictures Production, Buena Vista.
RICHARD FARNSWORTH in *The Straight Story,* Walt Disney Pictures Production, Buena Vista.
SEAN PENN in *Sweet and Lowdown,* Jean Doumanian Production, Sony Pictures Classics.
* **KEVIN SPACEY** in *American Beauty,* Jinks/Cohen Company Production, DreamWorks.
DENZEL WASHINGTON in *The Hurricane,* Beacon Pictures Production, Universal and Beacon.

ACTRESS
ANNETTE BENING in *American Beauty,* Jinks/Cohen Company Production, DreamWorks.
JANET McTEER in *Tumbleweeds,* Spanky Pictures/Filmtribe in association with River One Films Production, Fine Line Features.
JULIANNE MOORE in *The End of the Affair,* Stephen Woolley Production, Columbia.
MERYL STREEP in *Music of the Heart,* Craven/Maddalena Films Production, Miramax Films.
* **HILARY SWANK** in *Boys Don't Cry,* Killer Films/Hart-Sharp Entertainment Production, Fox Searchlight.

SUPPORTING ACTOR
* **MICHAEL CAINE** in *The Cider House Rules,* FilmColony Production, Miramax Films.
TOM CRUISE in *Magnolia,* JoAnne Sellar/Ghoulardi Film Company Production, New Line.
MICHAEL CLARKE DUNCAN in *The Green Mile,* Castle Rock Production, Warner Bros.
JUDE LAW in *The Talented Mr. Ripley,* Mirage Enterprises/ Timnick Films Production, Paramount & Miramax.
HALEY JOEL OSMENT in *The Sixth Sense,* Kennedy/Marshall/Barry Mendel Production, Buena Vista.

SUPPORTING ACTRESS
TONI COLLETTE in *The Sixth Sense,* Kennedy/Marshall/Barry Mendel Production, Buena Vista.
* **ANGELINA JOLIE** in *Girl, Interrupted,* Red Wagon/Columbia Pictures Production, Columbia.
CATHERINE KEENER in *Being John Malkovich,* Propaganda Films/Single Cell Pictures Production, USA Films.
SAMANTHA MORTON in *Sweet and Lowdown,* Jean Doumanian Production, Sony Pictures Classics.
CHLOË SEVIGNY in *Boys Don't Cry,* Killer Films/Hart-Sharp Entertainment Production, Fox Searchlight.

DIRECTING
* **AMERICAN BEAUTY,** Jinks/Cohen Company Production, DreamWorks. Sam Mendes.
BEING JOHN MALKOVICH, Propaganda Films/Single Cell Pictures Production, USA Films. Spike Jonze.
THE CIDER HOUSE RULES, FilmColony Production, Miramax Films. Lasse Hallström.
THE INSIDER, Touchstone Pictures Production, Buena Vista. Michael Mann.
THE SIXTH SENSE, Kennedy/Marshall/Barry Mendel Production, Buena Vista. M. Night Shyamalan.

WRITING
(Screenplay Based on Material Previously Produced or Published)
* **THE CIDER HOUSE RULES,** FilmColony Production, Miramax Films. John Irving.
ELECTION, MTV Films in association with Bona Fide Production, Paramount. Alexander Payne and Jim Taylor.
THE GREEN MILE, Castle Rock Production, Warner Bros. Frank Darabont.
THE INSIDER, Touchstone Pictures Production, Buena Vista. Eric Roth and Michael Mann.
THE TALENTED MR. RIPLEY, Mirage Enterprises/Timnick Films Production, Paramount & Miramax. Anthony Minghella.

(Screenplay Written Directly for the Screen)
* **AMERICAN BEAUTY,** Jinks/Cohen Company Production, DreamWorks. Alan Ball.
BEING JOHN MALKOVICH, Propaganda Films/Single Cell Pictures Production, USA Films. Charlie Kaufman.
MAGNOLIA, JoAnne Sellar/Ghoulardi Film Company Production, New Line. Paul Thomas Anderson.
THE SIXTH SENSE, Kennedy/Marshall/Barry Mendel Production, Buena Vista. M. Night Shyamalan.
TOPSY-TURVY, Simon Channing-Williams Production, USA Films. Mike Leigh.

ART DIRECTION—SET DECORATION
ANNA AND THE KING, Fox 2000 Pictures Production, 20th Century Fox. Luciana Arrighi; Ian Whittaker.
THE CIDER HOUSE RULES, FilmColony Production, Miramax Films. David Gropman; Beth Rubino.
* **SLEEPY HOLLOW,** Scott Rudin/American Zoetrope Production, Paramount and Mandalay. Rick Heinrichs; Peter Young.
THE TALENTED MR. RIPLEY, Mirage Enterprises/Timnick Films Production, Paramount & Miramax. Roy Walker; Bruno Cesari.
TOPSY-TURVY, Simon Channing-Williams Production, USA Films. Eve Stewart; Eve Stewart and John Bush.

CINEMATOGRAPHY
* **AMERICAN BEAUTY,** Jinks/Cohen Company Production, DreamWorks. Conrad L. Hall.
THE END OF THE AFFAIR, Stephen Woolley Production, Columbia. Roger Pratt.
THE INSIDER, Touchstone Pictures Production, Buena Vista. Dante Spinotti.
SLEEPY HOLLOW, Scott Rudin/American Zoetrope Production, Paramount and Mandalay. Emmanuel Lubezki.
SNOW FALLING ON CEDARS, Kennedy/Marshall/Harry J. Ufland/Ron Bass Production, Universal. Robert Richardson.

COSTUME DESIGN
ANNA AND THE KING, Fox 2000 Pictures Production, 20th Century Fox. Jenny Beavan.
SLEEPY HOLLOW, Scott Rudin/American Zoetrope Production, Paramount and Mandalay. Colleen Atwood.
THE TALENTED MR. RIPLEY, Mirage Enterprises/Timnick Films Production, Paramount & Miramax. Ann Roth and Gary Jones.
TITUS, Clear Blue Sky Production, Fox Searchlight. Milena Canonero.
* **TOPSY-TURVY,** Simon Channing-Williams Production, USA Films. Lindy Hemming.

FILM EDITING
AMERICAN BEAUTY, Jinks/Cohen Company Production, DreamWorks. Tariq Anwar and Christopher Greenbury.
THE CIDER HOUSE RULES, FilmColony Production, Miramax Films. Lisa Zeno Churgin.
THE INSIDER, Touchstone Pictures Production, Buena Vista. William Goldenberg, Paul Rubell and David Rosenbloom.
* **THE MATRIX,** Matrix Films Pty Ltd. Production, Warner Bros. Zach Staenberg.
THE SIXTH SENSE, Kennedy/Marshall/Barry Mendel Production, Buena Vista. Andrew Mondshein.

The Matrix (Warner Bros.) made off with four Academy Awards, which in turn made it the second-most-honored film of the year after American Beauty. *Throughout this action-driven sci-fi thriller directed by the Brothers Wachowski, men flew through the air with the greatest of ease, thanks to state-of-the-art movie wizardry, much of it rewarded with awards (in sound, sound effects editing, film editing and visual effects). Right, from left, Keanu Reeves and Hugo Weaving demonstrate.*

MAKEUP

AUSTIN POWERS: THE SPY WHO SHAGGED ME, Eric's Boy, Moving Pictures & Team Todd Production, New Line. Michèle Burke and Mike Smithson.

BICENTENNIAL MAN, Touchstone Pictures/Columbia Pictures Production, Buena Vista. Greg Cannom.

LIFE, Universal Pictures and Imagine Entertainment Production, Universal. Rick Baker.

* **TOPSY-TURVY,** Simon Channing-Williams Production, USA Films. Christine Blundell and Trefor Proud.

MUSIC

(Original Score)

AMERICAN BEAUTY, Jinks/Cohen Company Production, DreamWorks. Thomas Newman.

ANGELA'S ASHES, David Brown/Scott Rudin/Dirty Hands Production, Paramount-Universal Pictures International. John Williams.

THE CIDER HOUSE RULES, FilmColony Production, Miramax Films. Rachel Portman.

* **THE RED VIOLIN,** Rhombus Media Production, Lions Gate Films. John Corigliano.

THE TALENTED MR. RIPLEY, Mirage Enterprises/Timnick Films Production, Paramount & Miramax. Gabriel Yared.

(Original Song)

BLAME CANADA *(South Park: Bigger, Longer & Uncut,* Scott Rudin and Trey Parker/Matt Stone in association with Comedy Central Production, Paramount and Warner Bros.); Music and Lyric by Trey Parker and Marc Shaiman.

MUSIC OF MY HEART *(Music of the Heart,* Craven/Maddalena Films Production, Miramax Films); Music and Lyric by Diane Warren.

SAVE ME *(Magnolia,* JoAnne Sellar/Ghoulardi Film Company Production, New Line); Music and Lyric by Aimee Mann.

WHEN SHE LOVED ME *(Toy Story 2,* Walt Disney Pictures/Pixar Animation Studios Production, Buena Vista); Music and Lyric by Randy Newman.

* **YOU'LL BE IN MY HEART** *(Tarzan,* Walt Disney Pictures Production, Buena Vista); Music and Lyric by Phil Collins.

SOUND

THE GREEN MILE, Castle Rock Production, Warner Bros. Robert J. Litt, Elliot Tyson, Michael Herbick and Willie D. Burton.

THE INSIDER, Touchstone Pictures Production, Buena Vista. Andy Nelson, Doug Hemphill and Lee Orloff.

* **THE MATRIX,** Matrix Films Pty Ltd. Production, Warner Bros. John Reitz, Gregg Rudloff, David Campbell and David Lee.

THE MUMMY, Alphaville Production, Universal. Leslie Shatz, Chris Carpenter, Rick Kline and Chris Munro.

STAR WARS EPISODE I: THE PHANTOM MENACE, Lucasfilm, Ltd. Production, 20th Century Fox. Gary Rydstrom, Tom Johnson, Shawn Murphy and John Midgley.

SOUND EFFECTS EDITING

FIGHT CLUB, Fox 2000 Pictures and New Regency Production, 20th Century Fox. Ren Klyce and Richard Hymns.

* **THE MATRIX,** Matrix Films Pty Ltd. Production, Warner Bros. Dane A. Davis.

STAR WARS EPISODE I: THE PHANTOM MENACE, Lucasfilm, Ltd. Production, 20th Century Fox. Ben Burtt and Tom Bellfort.

VISUAL EFFECTS

* **THE MATRIX,** Matrix Films Pty Ltd. Production, Warner Bros. John Gaeta, Janek Sirrs, Steve Courtley and Jon Thum.

STAR WARS EPISODE I: THE PHANTOM MENACE, Lucasfilm, Ltd. Production, 20th Century Fox. John Knoll, Dennis Muren, Scott Squires and Rob Coleman.

STUART LITTLE, Douglas Wick and Franklin/Waterman and Columbia Pictures Production, Columbia. John Dykstra, Jerome Chen, Henry F. Anderson III and Eric Allard.

SHORT FILMS

(Animated)

HUMDRUM, Aardman Animations Limited Production. Peter Peake.

MY GRANDMOTHER IRONED THE KING'S SHIRTS, National Film Board of Canada & Studio Magica a.s. Production. Torill Kove.

* **THE OLD MAN AND THE SEA,** Productions Pascal Blais/ Imagica Corp./Dentsu Tech./NHK Enterprise 21/Panorama Studio of Yaroslavl Production. Alexander Petrov.

3 MISSES, CinéTé Film Production. Paul Driessen.

WHEN THE DAY BREAKS, National Film Board of Canada Production. Wendy Tilby and Amanda Forbis.

(Live Action)

BROR, MIN BROR (TEIS AND NICO), Nimbus Film & Dansk Novellefilm Production. Henrik Ruben Genz and Michael W. Horsten.

KILLING JOE, Joy Films and Chelsea Pictures Production. Mehdi Norowzian and Steve Wax.

KLEINGELD (SMALL CHANGE), A Production of Die Hochschule für Film und Fernsehen "Konrad Wolf" Potsdam-Babelsberg. Marc-Andreas Bochert and Gabriele Lins.

MAJOR AND MINOR MIRACLES, Dramatiska Institutet Production. Marcus Olsson.

* **MY MOTHER DREAMS THE SATAN'S DISCIPLES IN NEW YORK,** Kickstart Production, American Film Institute. Barbara Schock and Tammy Tiehel.

Best Foreign Language Film: All about My Mother *(Sony Pictures Classics) from Spain. Director Pedro Almodóvar was born in a small town (Calzada de Calatrava) in the impoverished Spanish region of La Mancha six months after* All about Eve *made its then-unequaled march to Oscar's history books, but Eve had obviously caught up with him—such is the international language of film. He lovingly echoed the Joseph Mankiewicz film throughout this paean to womenfolk everywhere, on stage and off.*

DOCUMENTARY

(Feature)

BUENA VISTA SOCIAL CLUB, Road Movies Production, Artisan. Wim Wenders and Ulrich Felsberg.

GENGHIS BLUES, Wadi Rum Production, Roxie Releasing. Roko Belic and Adrian Belic.

ON THE ROPES, Highway Films Production, WinStar Cinema. Nanette Burstein and Brett Morgen.

* **ONE DAY IN SEPTEMBER,** Arthur Cohn Production. Arthur Cohn and Kevin Macdonald.

SPEAKING IN STRINGS, CounterPoint Films Production, Seventh Art. Paola di Florio and Lilibet Foster.

(Short Subject)

EYEWITNESS, Marbert Art Foundation Production, Seventh Art. Bert Van Bork.

* **KING GIMP,** Whiteford-Hadary/University of Maryland/Tapestry International Production. Susan Hannah Hadary and William A. Whiteford.

THE WILDEST SHOW IN THE SOUTH: THE ANGOLA PRISON RODEO, Gabriel Films Production, Seventh Art. Simeon Soffer and Jonathan Stack.

FOREIGN LANGUAGE FILM

* **ALL ABOUT MY MOTHER** (Spain)

CARAVAN (Nepal)

EAST-WEST (France)

SOLOMON AND GAENOR (United Kingdom)

UNDER THE SUN (Sweden)

HONORARY AWARDS

To **ANDRZEJ WAJDA** in recognition of five decades of extraordinary film direction. (Statuette)

To **EDMUND M. DI GIULIO** in appreciation for outstanding service and dedication in upholding the high standards of the Academy of Motion Picture Arts and Sciences. (John A. Bonner Medal of Commendation)

To **TAKUO MIYAGISHIMA** in appreciation for outstanding service and dedication in upholding the high standards of the Academy of Motion Picture Arts and Sciences. (John A. Bonner Medal of Commendation)

To **FPC, INCORPORATED,** under the leadership of Barry M. Stultz and Milton Jan Friedman, for the development and implementation of an environmentally responsible program to recycle or destroy discarded motion picture prints. (Award of Commendation - Special Award Plaque)

1999 IRVING G. THALBERG MEMORIAL AWARD
TO WARREN BEATTY

1999 JEAN HERSHOLT HUMANITARIAN AWARD
None given this year.

1999 GORDON E. SAWYER AWARD
TO RODERICK T. RYAN

SCIENTIFIC AND TECHNICAL AWARDS

Scientific and Engineering Awards (Academy Plaque)

NICK PHILLIPS for the design and development of the three-axis Libra III remote control camera head.

FRITZ GABRIEL BAUER for the concept, design and engineering of the Moviecam Superlight 35mm Motion Picture Camera.

IAIN NEIL for the optical design, **RICK GELBARD** for the mechanical design, and **PANAVISION, INC.,** for the development of the Millennium Camera System viewfinder.

HUW GWILYM, KARL LYNCH and **MARK V. CRABTREE** for the design and development of the AMS Neve Logic Digital Film Console for motion picture sound mixing.

JAMES MOULTRIE for the mechanical design, and **MIKE SALTER** and **MARK CRAIG GERCHMAN** for the optical design of the Cooke S4 Range of Fixed Focal Length Lenses for 35mm motion picture photography.

MARLOWE A. PICHEL for development of the process for manufacturing Electro-formed Metal Reflectors, which, when combined with the DC Short Arc Xenon Lamp, became the worldwide standard for motion picture projection systems.

L. RON SCHMIDT for the concept, design and engineering of the Linear Loop Film Projectors.

NAT TIFFEN of Tiffen Manufacturing Corporation for the production of high-quality, durable, laminated color filters for motion picture photography.

Technical Achievement Awards (Academy Certificate)

VIVIENNE DYER and **CHRIS WOOLF** for the design and development of the Rycote Microphone Windshield Modular System.

LESLIE DREVER for the design and development of the Light Wave microphone windscreens and isolation mounts from Light Wave Systems.

RICHARD C. SEHLIN for the concept, and **DR. MITCHELL J. BOGDANOWICZ** and **MARY L. SCHMOEGER** of the Eastman Kodak Company for the design and development of the Eastman Lamphouse Modification Filters.

HOYT H. YEATMAN, JR., of Dream Quest Images; and **JOHN C. BREWER** of the Eastman Kodak Company, for the identification and diagnosis leading the elimination of the "red fringe" artifact in traveling matte composite photography.

I t was not enough that Steven Soderbergh helmed two of 2000's five Oscar-contending best picture nominees, *Erin Brockovich* and *Traffic,* each with its own Oscar-winning performance (best actress Julia Roberts and best supporting actor Benicio Del Toro, respectively), the first time that had happened since the 1948 Oscars, when John Huston directed winners Claire Trevor and his own dad, Walter Huston, to the Oscar podium. Soderbergh went a step further and got himself nominated twice for best director as well, the first time *that* had happened since the 1938 awards, when Michael Curtiz went *mano a mano* with himself for directing the films *Angels with Dirty Faces* and *Four Daughters.* When the moment of truth came up on March 25, 2001, at the Los Angeles Shrine Auditorium, the 38-year-old director proceeded to rewrite Oscar history by going on to win, something Curtiz had not managed to do. The two most nominated films of the year were Ridley Scott's sword-and-scandal Roman spectacle *Gladiator,* with 12 nominations, and Ang Lee's high-flying martial arts exercise *Crouching Tiger, Hidden Dragon* with 10, the latter the third film in the Academy's history to be nominated in the same year for both best picture and best foreign language film (as had 1969's *Z* and 1998's *Life Is Beautiful*). Both *Gladiator* and *Crouching Tiger* were strong on action, an aspect of filmmaking that had never been given much attention in Oscar's past.

Gladiator ended up the big champ with five awards, including best picture, the first film since 1949's *All the King's Men* to win that prize without either its writer or director also Oscared. *Crouching Tiger* took home four awards, including the foreign language trophy. *Traffic* also took home four, one to Del Toro as supporting actor, the other three to a Steven and two Stephens (director Soderbergh, screenwriter Gaghan and film editor Mirrione). Another honor for *Crouching Tiger:* it trumped 1998's *Life Is Beautiful* as the top-grossing and most Oscar-laden foreign language film to date.

Best actor Russell Crowe and best actress Julia Roberts did their Oscar work in title roles, he as the gladiator, she as Erin Brockovich, and Marcia Gay Harden did hers supporting a title character, painter Jackson Pollock. Joaquin Phoenix's nomination as *Gladiator*'s evil emperor in the same supporting actor category in which his late brother, River Phoenix, had competed 12 years earlier for *Running on Empty* made them the first pair of Oscar-nominated acting brothers.

The 73rd Annual Academy Awards allowed another Academy first: a cinematographer was finally presented an Honorary Oscar—Jack Cardiff, with such films to his credit as 1947's *Black Narcissus,* 1948's *The Red Shoes* and 1951's *The African Queen.* By a coincidence, Cardiff's portfolio also includes three films (1956's *War and Peace,* 1984's *Conan the Destroyer* and 1985's

Best Picture: **Gladiator** *(DreamWorks and Universal; produced by Douglas Wick, David Franzoni and Branko Lustig) and* **Best Actor:** **Russell Crowe** *as Maximus in* Gladiator, *directed by Ridley Scott. Behaving much as* Ben-Hur *had 41 years earlier, winning Oscars for best picture and its title player,* Gladiator *revived the old toga saga in all its epic SPQR glory, revamping it with the full brutality of the era and filling its sports arena with a computer-generated populace. (CGI, computer-generated-imagery, even completed the performance of Oliver Reed, who died two days before finishing the film.) Crowe, playing Maximus to the maximum, dominated the film—at $100 million, the most expensive of the five nominees—as a Roman general demoted to thumbs-up-or-down fun and games, a sharp contrast to his modern role in* The Insider, *which had brought him an Academy nomination as best actor the previous year.*

Cat's Eye) he had photographed for producer Dino De Laurentiis, who received the night's Irving Thalberg Award. Writer Ernest Lehman also received an Honorary Oscar.

Steve Martin, making his first appearance as an Oscar host, accomplished what some were beginning to think was impossible: he helped bring the ABC telecast in 37 minutes under the four-hour (and often longer) durations of the recent past.

Best Supporting Actor: **Benicio Del Toro** *as Javier Rodriguez in* Traffic *(USA Films; directed by Steven Soderbergh). As an incorruptible, sometimes volatile, often quietly desperate Mexican border cop in the middle of a drug war, Del Toro smoldered more than he spoke and rarely spoke in* English. *His was, in fact, the first Oscar-winning performance delivered almost exclusively in Spanish. Prior to this, Oscar acting had been done entirely in English or Italian (Sophia Loren in* Two Women, *Robert De Niro in* The Godfather Part II *and Roberto Benigni in* Life Is Beautiful).

Best Directing: **Steven Soderbergh** *for* Traffic. *Of Soderbergh's two 2000 nominations in the best directing category, for* Erin Brockovich *and* Traffic, *it was the latter film, a tricky contemporary thriller, that put him over the top. It was formidable storytelling, requiring him to twirl three full plates of plots, all grimly demonstrating how the U.S. was losing the drug war on the international front, at the border and, most personally of all, in the home. Some figured the director's double nomination would cancel his chances for a win, especially since he resolutely refused to say which film he himself favored. "I'm just proud of both movies," he told the press, and let the Academy voters decide, which they did, in his favor.*

351

Best Actress: **Julia Roberts** *as Erin Brockovich in* Erin Brockovich *(Universal and Columbia; directed by Steven Soderbergh). "Think* A Civil Action *with cleavage," said one critic in characterizing both the film and the role that won Roberts her Oscar. She played a real-life twice-divorced single mom who, in her menial job as a legal-aid researcher, goes after a corporate Goliath (California's monolithic Pacific Gas & Electric) in wobbly stiletto heels and trailer-trash attire and ultimately brings the erring company to its knees in a landmark $333 million water-contamination suit. Roberts's acceptance speech was the night's longest (three minutes and two seconds beyond the allotted 45 seconds), and to her later chagrin, she still forgot to thank her "inspiration," the real Ms. Brockovich.*

PICTURE

CHOCOLAT, David Brown Production, Miramax Films. David Brown, Kit Golden and Leslie Holleran, Producers.

CROUCHING TIGER, HIDDEN DRAGON, Zoom Hunt International Production, Sony Pictures Classics. Bill Kong, Hsu Li Kong and Ang Lee, Producers.

ERIN BROCKOVICH, Jersey Films Production, Universal and Columbia. Danny DeVito, Michael Shamberg and Stacey Sher, Producers.

* **GLADIATOR,** Douglas Wick in association with Scott Free Production, DreamWorks and Universal. Douglas Wick, David Franzoni and Branko Lustig, Producers.

TRAFFIC, Bedford Falls/Laura Bickford Production, USA Films. Edward Zwick, Marshall Herskovitz and Laura Bickford, Producers.

ACTOR

JAVIER BARDEM in *Before Night Falls,* Grandview Pictures Production, Fine Line Features.

* **RUSSELL CROWE** in *Gladiator,* Douglas Wick in association with Scott Free Production, DreamWorks and Universal.

TOM HANKS in *Cast Away,* ImageMovers/Playtone Production, 20th Century Fox and DreamWorks.

ED HARRIS in *Pollock,* Brant/Allen Films/Zeke Films/Fred Berner Films Production, Sony Pictures Classics.

GEOFFREY RUSH in *Quills,* Industry Entertainment/Walrus & Associates, Ltd. Production, Fox Searchlight.

ACTRESS

JOAN ALLEN in *The Contender,* Battleground in association with the SE8 Group Production, DreamWorks and Cinerenta/Cinecontender.

JULIETTE BINOCHE in *Chocolat,* David Brown Production, Miramax Films.

ELLEN BURSTYN in *Requiem for a Dream,* Thousand Words Production, Artisan.

LAURA LINNEY in *You Can Count on Me,* Shooting Gallery/Hart Sharp Entertainment Production, Paramount Classics/ Shooting Gallery/Hart Sharp Entertainment in association with Cappa Productions.

* **JULIA ROBERTS** in *Erin Brockovich,* Jersey Films Production, Universal and Columbia.

SUPPORTING ACTOR

JEFF BRIDGES in *The Contender,* Battleground in association with the SE8 Group Production, DreamWorks and Cinerenta/Cinecontender.

WILLEM DAFOE in *Shadow of the Vampire,* Saturn Films Production, Lions Gate Films.

* **BENICIO DEL TORO** in *Traffic,* Bedford Falls/Laura Bickford Production, USA Films.

ALBERT FINNEY in *Erin Brockovich,* Jersey Films Production, Universal and Columbia.

JOAQUIN PHOENIX in *Gladiator,* Douglas Wick in association with Scott Free Production, DreamWorks and Universal.

SUPPORTING ACTRESS

JUDI DENCH in *Chocolat,* David Brown Production, Miramax Films.

* **MARCIA GAY HARDEN** in *Pollock,* Brant/Allen Films/Zeke Films/Fred Berner Films Production, Sony Pictures Classics.

KATE HUDSON in *Almost Famous,* Vinyl Films Production, DreamWorks and Columbia.

FRANCES McDORMAND in *Almost Famous,* Vinyl Films Production, DreamWorks and Columbia.

JULIE WALTERS in *Billy Elliot,* Working Title Films Production, Universal Focus.

DIRECTING

BILLY ELLIOT, Working Title Films Production, Universal Focus. Stephen Daldry.

CROUCHING TIGER, HIDDEN DRAGON, Zoom Hunt International Production, Sony Pictures Classics. Ang Lee.

ERIN BROCKOVICH, Jersey Films Production, Universal and Columbia. Steven Soderbergh.

GLADIATOR, Douglas Wick in association with Scott Free Production, DreamWorks and Universal. Ridley Scott.

* **TRAFFIC,** Bedford Falls/Laura Bickford Production, USA Films. Steven Soderbergh.

WRITING

(Screenplay Based on Material Previously Produced or Published)

CHOCOLAT, David Brown Production, Miramax Films. Robert Nelson Jacobs.

CROUCHING TIGER, HIDDEN DRAGON, Zoom Hunt International Production, Sony Pictures Classics. Wang Hui Ling, James Schamus and Tsai Kuo Jung.

O BROTHER, WHERE ART THOU?, Working Title Production, Buena Vista. Ethan Coen and Joel Coen.

* **TRAFFIC,** Bedford Falls/Laura Bickford Production, USA Films. Stephen Gaghan.

WONDER BOYS, Scott Rudin/Curtis Hanson Production, Paramount and Mutual Film Company. Steve Kloves.

(Screenplay Written Directly for the Screen)

* **ALMOST FAMOUS,** Vinyl Films Production, DreamWorks and Columbia. Cameron Crowe.

BILLY ELLIOT, Working Title Films Production, Universal Focus. Lee Hall.

ERIN BROCKOVICH, Jersey Films Production, Universal and Columbia. Susannah Grant.

GLADIATOR, Douglas Wick in association with Scott Free Production, DreamWorks and Universal. David Franzoni, John Logan and William Nicholson.

YOU CAN COUNT ON ME, Shooting Gallery/Hart Sharp Entertainment Production, Paramount Classics/Shooting Gallery/Hart Sharp Entertainment in association with Cappa Productions. Kenneth Lonergan.

ART DIRECTION—SET DECORATION

* **CROUCHING TIGER, HIDDEN DRAGON,** Zoom Hunt International Production, Sony Pictures Classics. Tim Yip.

DR. SEUSS' HOW THE GRINCH STOLE CHRISTMAS, Universal Pictures and Imagine Entertainment Production, Universal. Michael Corenblith; Merideth Boswell.

GLADIATOR, Douglas Wick in association with Scott Free Production, DreamWorks and Universal. Arthur Max; Crispian Sallis.

QUILLS, Industry Entertainment/Walrus & Associates, Ltd. Production, Fox Searchlight. Martin Childs; Jill Quertier.

VATEL, Légende Enterprises-Gaumont in association with Nomad, Timothy Burrill, T.F.1 Films Production, Miramax Films. Jean Rabasse; Françoise Benoit-Fresco.

CINEMATOGRAPHY

* **CROUCHING TIGER, HIDDEN DRAGON,** Zoom Hunt International Production, Sony Pictures Classics. Peter Pau.

GLADIATOR, Douglas Wick in association with Scott Free Production, DreamWorks and Universal. John Mathieson.

MALÈNA, Medusa Film in collaboration with TELE+ Production, Miramax Films. Lajos Koltai.

O BROTHER, WHERE ART THOU?, Working Title Production, Buena Vista. Roger Deakins.

THE PATRIOT, Mutual Film Company/Centropolis Entertainment Production, Sony Pictures Releasing. Caleb Deschanel.

COSTUME DESIGN

CROUCHING TIGER, HIDDEN DRAGON, Zoom Hunt International Production, Sony Pictures Classics. Tim Yip.

DR. SEUSS' HOW THE GRINCH STOLE CHRISTMAS, Universal Pictures and Imagine Entertainment Production, Universal. Rita Ryack.

* **GLADIATOR,** Douglas Wick in association with Scott Free Production, DreamWorks and Universal. Janty Yates.

102 DALMATIANS, Walt Disney Pictures Production, Buena Vista. Anthony Powell.

QUILLS, Industry Entertainment/Walrus & Associates, Ltd., Production, Fox Searchlight. Jacqueline West.

FILM EDITING

ALMOST FAMOUS, Vinyl Films Production, DreamWorks and Columbia. Joe Hutshing and Saar Klein.

CROUCHING TIGER, HIDDEN DRAGON, Zoom Hunt International Production, Sony Pictures Classics. Tim Squyres.

GLADIATOR, Douglas Wick in association with Scott Free Production, DreamWorks and Universal. Pietro Scalia.

* **TRAFFIC,** Bedford Falls/Laura Bickford Production, USA Films. Stephen Mirrione.

WONDER BOYS, Scott Rudin/Curtis Hanson Production, Paramount and Mutual Film Company. Dede Allen.

MAKEUP

THE CELL, Caro-McLeod/Radical Media Production, New Line. Michèle Burke and Édouard Henriques.

* **DR. SEUSS' HOW THE GRINCH STOLE CHRISTMAS,** Universal Pictures and Imagine Entertainment Production, Universal. Rick Baker and Gail Ryan.

SHADOW OF THE VAMPIRE, Saturn Films Production, Lions Gate Films. Ann Buchanan and Amber Sibley.

Best Foreign Language Film: Crouching Tiger, Hidden Dragon *(Sony Pictures Classics) from Taiwan. Never one to be typecast, Taiwan-born director Ang Lee has pole-vaulted from epoch to epoch, from Jane Austen's England (1995's* Sense and Sensibility) *to suburban Connecticut in the 1970s (1997's* The Ice Storm) *to the American Civil War (1999's* Ride with the Devil). *With Tiger/Dragon, he returned to his roots, to the land of his parents, mainland China of the 19th century, and he arrived there flying. Or at least his cast was airborne (including Michelle Yeoh, below, bolting off walls). Lee achieved gravity-defying athletics with unseen cables—a longtime staple of action-driven supernatural sagas from Hong Kong—but added a magical touch by imbuing the film with its own unique drama, charm and resonance, a case of a serious, cerebral filmmaker putting mind over martial arts and creating a true wonder show.*

MUSIC

(Original Score)
  CHOCOLAT, David Brown Production, Miramax Films. Rachel Portman.
* CROUCHING TIGER, HIDDEN DRAGON, Zoom Hunt International Production, Sony Pictures Classics. Tan Dun.
  GLADIATOR, Douglas Wick in association with Scott Free Production, DreamWorks and Universal. Hans Zimmer.
  MALÈNA, Medusa Film in collaboration with TELE+ Production, Miramax Films. Ennio Morricone.
  THE PATRIOT, Mutual Film Company/Centropolis Entertainment Production, Sony Pictures Releasing. John Williams.

(Original Song)
  A FOOL IN LOVE *(Meet the Parents,* Universal Pictures Production, Universal and DreamWorks); Music and Lyric by Randy Newman.
  I'VE SEEN IT ALL *(Dancer in the Dark,* Fine Line Features/Zentropa Entertainments 4/Trust Film Svenska/Film I Vast/Liberator Production, Fine Line Features); Music by Björk; Lyric by Lars von Trier and Sjon Sigurdsson.
  A LOVE BEFORE TIME *(Crouching Tiger, Hidden Dragon,* Zoom Hunt International Production, Sony Pictures Classics); Music by Jorge Calandrelli and Tan Dun; Lyric by James Schamus.
  MY FUNNY FRIEND AND ME *(The Emperor's New Groove,* Walt Disney Pictures Production, Buena Vista); Music by Sting and David Hartley; Lyric by Sting.
* THINGS HAVE CHANGED *(Wonder Boys,* Scott Rudin/Curtis Hanson Production, Paramount and Mutual Film Company); Music and Lyric by Bob Dylan.

SOUND

  CAST AWAY, ImageMovers/Playtone Production, 20th Century Fox and DreamWorks. Randy Thom, Tom Johnson, Dennis Sands and William B. Kaplan.
* GLADIATOR, Douglas Wick in association with Scott Free Production, DreamWorks and Universal. Scott Millan, Bob Beemer and Ken Weston.
  THE PATRIOT, Mutual Film Company/Centropolis Entertainment Production, Sony Pictures Releasing. Kevin O'Connell, Greg P. Russell and Lee Orloff.
  THE PERFECT STORM, Warner Bros. Pictures Production, Warner Bros. John Reitz, Gregg Rudloff, David Campbell and Keith A. Wester.
  U-571, Dino De Laurentiis Production, Universal and StudioCanal. Steve Maslow, Gregg Landaker, Rick Kline and Ivan Sharrock.

SOUND EDITING

  SPACE COWBOYS, Warner Bros. Pictures Production, Warner Bros. Alan Robert Murray and Bub Asman.
* U-571, Dino De Laurentiis Production, Universal and StudioCanal. Jon Johnson.

VISUAL EFFECTS

* GLADIATOR, Douglas Wick in association with Scott Free Production, DreamWorks and Universal. John Nelson, Neil Corbould, Tim Burke and Rob Harvey.
  HOLLOW MAN, Columbia Pictures Production, Sony Pictures Releasing. Scott E. Anderson, Craig Hayes, Scott Stokdyk and Stan Parks.
  THE PERFECT STORM, Warner Bros. Pictures Production, Warner Bros. Stefen Fangmeier, Habib Zargarpour, John Frazier and Walt Conti.

SHORT FILMS

(Animated)
* FATHER AND DAUGHTER, CinéTé Filmproductie bv/Cloudrunner Ltd. Production. Michael Dudok de Wit.
  THE PERIWIG-MAKER, Ideal Standard Film Production. Steffen Schäffler and Annette Schäffler.
  REJECTED, Bitter Films Production. Don Hertzfeldt.

(Live Action)
  BY COURIER, Two Tequila Production. Peter Riegert and Ericka Frederick.
  ONE DAY CROSSING, Open Eyes Production. Joan Stein and Christina Lazaridi.
* QUIERO SER (I WANT TO BE . . .), Mondragon Films Production. Florian Gallenberger.
  SERAGLIO, Seraglio Production. Gail Lerner, Colin Campbell.
  A SOCCER STORY (UMA HISTORIA DE FUTEBOL), UM Filmes Production. Paulo Machline.

DOCUMENTARY

(Feature)
* INTO THE ARMS OF STRANGERS: STORIES OF THE KINDERTRANSPORT, Sabine Films Production, Warner Bros. Mark Jonathan Harris and Deborah Oppenheimer.
  LEGACY, Nomadic Pictures Production. Tod Lending.
  LONG NIGHT'S JOURNEY INTO DAY, Iris Films Production, Seventh Art. Frances Reid and Deborah Hoffmann.
  SCOTTSBORO: AN AMERICAN TRAGEDY, Social Media Production. Barak Goodman and Daniel Anker.
  SOUND AND FURY, Production of Aronson Film Associates and Public Policy Productions, Artistic License Films. Josh Aronson and Roger Weisberg.

Best Supporting Actress: **Marcia Gay Harden** *as Lee Krasner in* Pollock *(Sony Pictures Classics; directed by Ed Harris). Artist, critic, wife, lover, caretaker, tormentor, Ms. Krasner embraced all those roles while turbulently married to artist Jackson Pollock during his comet ride into the 1950s New York art scene; in this long-time-coming film bio, Harden personified those aspects of Krasner as well, bringing her a first Academy nomination and, amid competition that included Dame Judi Dench, Frances McDormand, Julie Walters and Kate Hudson, making her an Oscar winner.*

(Short Subject)
* BIG MAMA, Birthmark Production. Tracy Seretean.
  CURTAIN CALL, NJN/White Whale Production. Chuck Braverman and Steve Kalafer.
  DOLPHINS, MacGillivray Freeman Films Production. Greg MacGillivray and Alec Lorimore.
  THE MAN ON LINCOLN'S NOSE, Adama Films Production. Daniel Raim.
  ON TIPTOE: GENTLE STEPS TO FREEDOM, On Tip Toe Production. Eric Simonson and Leelai Demoz.

FOREIGN LANGUAGE FILM

  AMORES PERROS (Mexico)
* CROUCHING TIGER, HIDDEN DRAGON (Taiwan)
  DIVIDED WE FALL (Czech Republic)
  EVERYBODY FAMOUS! (Belgium)
  THE TASTE OF OTHERS (France)

HONORARY AWARDS

  TO JACK CARDIFF, master of light and color. (Statuette)
  TO ERNEST LEHMAN, in appreciation of a body of varied and enduring work. (Statuette)
  TO IOAN ALLEN for the concept, ROBIN BRANSBURY for the design and MARK HARRAH for the implementation of the Trailer Audio Standards Association (TASA) Loudness Standard. The adoption of the TASA loudness standard has led directly to better sound in the cinema for trailers and features alike. (Award of Commendation—Special Award Plaque)
  TO N. PAUL KENWORTHY, JR., in appreciation for outstanding services and dedication in upholding the high standards of the Academy of Motion Picture Arts and Sciences. (John A. Bonner Medal of Commendation)

2000 IRVING G. THALBERG AWARD
TO DINO DE LAURENTIIS

2000 JEAN HERSHOLT HUMANITARIAN AWARD
  None given this year.

2000 GORDON E. SAWYER AWARD
TO IRWIN W. YOUNG

SCIENTIFIC AND TECHNICAL AWARDS
Academy Award of Merit (Statuette)
  ROB COOK, LOREN CARPENTER and ED CATMULL for their significant advancements the field of motion picture rendering, as exemplified by Pixar's "Renderman."

Scientific and Engineering Awards (Academy Plaque)
  AL MAYER, SR., and AL MAYER, JR., for the mechanical design, IAIN NEIL for the optical design and BRIAN DANG for the electronic design of the Panavision Millennium XL Camera System.
  JOE WARY, GERALD PAINTER and COLIN F. MOSSMAN for the design and development of the Deluxe Laboratories Multi Roller Film Transport System.
  ALVAH J. MILLER and PAUL JOHNSON of Lynx Robotics for the electronic and software design of the Lynx C-50 Camera Motor System.
  AKAI DIGITAL for the design and development of the DD8plus digital audio dubber specifically designed for the motion picture industry.
  FAIRLIGHT for the design and development of the DAD digital audio dubber specifically designed for the motion picture industry.
  ADVANCED DIGITAL SYSTEMS GROUP (ADSG) for the design and development of the Sony DADR 5000 digital audio dubber specifically designed for the motion picture industry.
  TIMELINE, INCORPORATED, for the design and development of the MMR 8 digital audio dubber specifically designed for the motion picture industry.

Technical Achievement Awards (Academy Certificate)
  LEONARD PINCUS, ASHOT NALBANDYAN, GEORGE JOHNSON, THOMAS KONG and DAVID PRINGLE for the design and development of the SoftSun low-pressure xenon long-arc light sources, their power supplies and fixtures.
  VIC ARMSTRONG for the refinement and application the film industry of the Fan Descender for accurately and safely arresting the descent of stunt persons in high freefalls.
  PHILIP GREENSTREET of Rosco Laboratories for the concept and development of the Roscolight Day/Night Backdrop.
  UDO SCHAUSS, HILDEGARD EBBESMEIER and KARL LENHARDT for the optical design, and RALF LINN and NORBERT BRINKER for the mechanical design of the Schneider Super Cinelux lenses for motion picture projection.
  GLENN M. BERGGREN for the concept, HORST LINGE for research and development, and WOLFGANG REINECKE for the optical design of the ISCO Ultra-Star Plus lenses for motion picture projection.
  BILL TONDREAU of Kuper Systems, ALVAH J. MILLER and PAUL JOHNSON of Lynx Robotics, and DAVID STUMP of Visual Effects Rental Services for the conception, design and development of data capture systems that enable superior accuracy, efficiency and economy in the creation of composite imagery.
  VENKAT KRISHNAMURTHY for the creation of the Paraform Software for 3D Digital Form Development.
  GEORGE BORSHUKOV, KIM LIBRERI and DAN PIPONI for the development of a system for image-based rendering allowing choreographed camera movements through computer graphic reconstructed sets.
  JOHN P. PYTLAK for the development of the Laboratory Aim Density (LAD) system.

353

Oscar's 74th birthday party marked a historic night for the Academy and for African Americans in the motion picture industry. On March 24, 2002, Sidney Poitier, the only African American ever to win an Academy Award for best actor (for 1963's *Lilies of the Field),* returned to the Oscar-winner's circle in his own 75th year, this time to pick up a special Honorary Oscar. The 85-second standing ovation accorded Poitier's return to the podium was the longest and warmest in a night that proved to be one of the most emotionally rich in Oscar annals. It didn't stop there. Shortly after Poitier was honored, Denzel Washington became the second black actor to win the Academy's top male acting prize, for his raw portrayal of a rogue narc cop in *Training Day.* Even more history was made when the envelope was opened to disclose the year's best actress. Halle Berry, in what was considered a neck-and-neck race with her four competitors (Nicole Kidman in *Moulin Rouge,* Dame Judi Dench in *Iris,* Sissy Spacek in *In the Bedroom* and Renée Zellweger in *Bridget Jones's Diary),* was declared the winner, making her the first black actress in the Academy's history to win in that category. Such a sweep for African Americans added all sorts of new asterisks to the Academy records, including Washington, becoming the first black performer to win in both the leading and supporting acting categories. Poitier became the second black actor to receive an honorary Oscar, the first having been James Baskett in 1947 for "his able and heart-warming characterization of Uncle Remus, friend and story teller to the children of the world in Walt Disney's *Song of the South."* (Less than four months after receiving the award, the 44-year-old Baskett died of a heart ailment.) Other firsts occurred during Oscar's 74th time at the plate: a whole new category was inaugurated to honor the best animated feature, with the award going to *Shrek.* And the year's best foreign language film, *No Man's Land,* was a first win for a film from Bosnia and Herzegovina. The evening also provided a first for song-writer/composer Randy Newman, who, with 15 previous nominations and no wins to his credit, finally cashed his 16th nomination in for gold as the writer of the year's best song, "If I Didn't Have You," from *Monsters, Inc.* With tongue in cheek, he thanked the music branch of the Academy for "giving me so many chances to be humiliated."

Hosting the evening was Whoopi Goldberg, herself a black Oscar winner (for 1990's *Ghost).* The show was telecast on ABC and, for the fourth year in a row, was held on a Sunday. Clocking in at 257 minutes, it also turned out to be the longest Oscarcast ever. *A Beautiful Mind* was named the year's best picture, with its director Ron Howard and supporting actress Jennifer Connelly also in the winner's circle. *Mind* also won a fourth award, for Akiva Goldsman's screenplay adaptation. Also winning four awards was *The Lord of the Rings: The Fellowship of the Ring,* named best in the categories of cin-

Best Picture: **A Beautiful Mind** *(Universal and Dream-Works; produced by Brian Grazer and Ron Howard; directed by Ron Howard) and* ***Best Supporting Actress:*** *Jennifer* **Connelly** *as Alicia Larde Nash in* A Beautiful Mind. *Like Marcia Gay Harden, who had won in the supporting actress category the year before for* Pollock, *Connelly had the difficult task of playing the helpless helpmate of a crazed and driven genius. The danger of paling by comparison to her partner's heavy-duty histrionics was ever-present, but Connelly skillfully played a woman who was anchored, angry and deeply damaged by the domestic fallout. The film itself, with Russell Crowe as the real-life John Forbes Nash, a man hampered but undeterred by severe bouts of schizophrenia, was unusual screen material, but was executed with an honesty, flair and passion that pleased Academy voters more than any other film of the year.*

ematography, music score, makeup and visual effects. Jim Broadbent was named best supporting actor for his work in *Iris*, Arthur Hiller was voted the Jean Hersholt Humanitarian Award, and, like Poitier, Robert Redford received an Honorary Oscar. It was also a night when Oscar moved to a brand new home, the 3,300-seat Kodak Theatre at Hollywood Boulevard and Highland Avenue, the first time since 1960 that the Oscars were actually presented in Hollywood, rather than in Santa Monica or downtown Los Angeles. Ironically, and fittingly, the new theater brought Oscar full circle in his septuagenarian years: the new location was only one city block away from the Hollywood Roosevelt Hotel, where the very first Academy Awards had been handed out on May 16, 1929.

Best Actress: **Halle Berry** *as Leticia Musgrove in* Monster's Ball *(Lions Gate Films; directed by Marc Forster). Berry, who had earlier won an Emmy award for playing the late Dorothy Dandridge, the first black woman nominated for the best actress Academy Award, became the first black woman to win in that same Oscar category. It was a juicy role, that of a contemporary Southern woman who loses her* husband *to death row and her son to a hit-and-run accident but finds solace in an interracial affair. At the podium on Oscar night, winner Berry gave the year's most tearful speech ("More an aria than an acceptance speech," wrote one critic), which acknowledged her debt to such pioneering spirits as Dandridge, Lena Horne and Oprah Winfrey.*

Best Supporting Actor: **Jim Broadbent** *as John Bayley in* Iris *(Miramax; directed by Richard Eyre). Even if he had not been voted best supporting actor of the year, Broadbent would still have been the year's most conspicuous supporting actor. As the master of ceremonies in* Moulin Rouge, *the daddy in* Bridget Jones's Diary *and the hubby of* Iris, *he spurred and sparred on screen with three-fifths of the year's best actress contenders: Nicole Kidman, Renée Zellweger and Judi Dench. His portrayal of the latter's frustrated, loving caretaker—the real-life John Bayley, who, like his wife Iris Murdoch, was a writer of note—suffered the horror and heartbreak of a man watching his mate fade into the dark fog of Alzheimer's.*

Best Actor: **Denzel Washington** *as Det. Sgt. Alonzo Harris in* Training Day *(Warner Bros.; directed by Antoine Fuqua). "No more Mister Nice Guy" might have been Washington's mantra during the making of* Training Day, *an intense and violence-edged drama about a renegade cop apparently born with ice water running through his veins. His courageous performance and casting against type paid off in Oscar gold: it brought Washington his second Academy Award but his first win in the best actor category, following his supporting performance victory in 1989 for* Glory. *Riding shotgun with him in the film was Ethan Hawke, whose own performance as a rookie under Washington's corrupt wing was so good he was himself nominated as one of the year's five best supporting actors.*

355

Best Directing: Ron Howard *for* A Beautiful Mind *(Universal and DreamWorks; produced by Brian Grazer and Howard). A film director since 1977 with such popular successes to his credit as* Splash, Cocoon *and* Apollo 13, *the fellow formerly known as TV's Opie was working a long way from his days as a child actor on* The Andy Griffith Show *when he attempted to render onscreen the brilliant, if profoundly troubled, mind of John Forbes Nash, Jr., the Princeton prof who, despite galloping schizophrenia, earned a Nobel prize in 1994. Howard began by introducing Nash as a conspicuously idiosyncratic, tad-too-deeply-dedicated academician, played by Russell Crowe, and then struck a profoundly dramatic chord as the bookworm's illness turned him nasty and neurotic.*

Moulin Rouge *(20th Century Fox; produced by Martin Brown, Baz Luhrmann and Fred Baron). Like John Huston's 1952* Moulin Rouge, *which contended for the best picture Oscar 49 years earlier, the Baz Luhrmann* Moulin *of 2001 was a visual stunner that won Academy Awards for its dazzling sets and ravishing costumes. Mrs. Luhrmann, Catherine Martin, had a hand in both, collaborating on the art direction with set decorator Brigitte Broch and the costumes with Angus Strathie. Below, the stars of the film, Nicole Kidman and Ewan McGregor, cavort among the fine feathers and backdrops of Martin's creations. The new* Moulin Rouge *received eight nominations, one more than the '52 version.*

PICTURE

* **A BEAUTIFUL MIND,** Universal Pictures and Imagine Entertainment Production, Universal and DreamWorks. Brian Grazer and Ron Howard, Producers.

   GOSFORD PARK, Sandcastle 5 in association with Chicagofilms and Medusa Film Production, USA Films. Robert Altman, Bob Balaban and David Levy, Producers.

   IN THE BEDROOM, Good Machine/GreeneStreet Production, Miramax Films. Graham Leader, Ross Katz and Todd Field, Producers.

   THE LORD OF THE RINGS: THE FELLOWSHIP OF THE RING, New Line Cinema and Wingnut Films Production, New Line. Peter Jackson, Fran Walsh and Barrie M. Osborne, Producers.

   MOULIN ROUGE, 20th Century Fox Production, 20th Century Fox. Martin Brown, Baz Luhrmann and Fred Baron, Producers.

ACTOR

   RUSSELL CROWE in *A Beautiful Mind,* Universal Pictures and Imagine Entertainment Production, Universal and DreamWorks.

   SEAN PENN in *I Am Sam,* New Line Cinema/Bedford Falls Company/Red Fish, Blue Fish Films Production, New Line.

   WILL SMITH in *Ali,* Columbia Pictures Production, Sony Pictures Releasing.

* **DENZEL WASHINGTON** in *Training Day,* Training Day Production, Warner Bros.

   TOM WILKINSON in *In the Bedroom,* Good Machine/GreeneStreet Production, Miramax Films.

ACTRESS

* **HALLE BERRY** in *Monster's Ball,* Monster Production, Lions Gate Films.

   JUDI DENCH in *Iris,* Mirage Enterprises, Robert Fox/Scott Rudin Production, Miramax Films.

   NICOLE KIDMAN in *Moulin Rouge,* 20th Century Fox Production, 20th Century Fox.

   SISSY SPACEK in *In the Bedroom,* Good Machine/GreeneStreet Production, Miramax Films.

   RENÉE ZELLWEGER in *Bridget Jones's Diary,* Working Title Production, Miramax/ Universal/StudioCanal.

SUPPORTING ACTOR

* **JIM BROADBENT** in *Iris,* Mirage Enterprises, Robert Fox/Scott Rudin Production, Miramax Films.

   ETHAN HAWKE in *Training Day,* Training Day Production, Warner Bros.

   BEN KINGSLEY in *Sexy Beast,* Sexy RPC Limited and Kanzaman S.A. Production, Fox Searchlight.

   IAN McKELLEN in *The Lord of the Rings: The Fellowship of the Ring,* New Line Cinema and Wingnut Films Production, New Line.

   JON VOIGHT in *Ali,* Columbia Pictures Production, Sony Pictures Releasing.

SUPPORTING ACTRESS

* **JENNIFER CONNELLY** in *A Beautiful Mind,* Universal Pictures and Imagine Entertainment Production, Universal and DreamWorks.

   HELEN MIRREN in *Gosford Park,* Sandcastle 5 in association with Chicagofilms and Medusa Film Production, USA Films.

   MAGGIE SMITH in *Gosford Park,* Sandcastle 5 in association with Chicagofilms and Medusa Film Production, USA Films.

   MARISA TOMEI in *In the Bedroom,* Good Machine/GreeneStreet Production, Miramax Films.

   KATE WINSLET in *Iris,* Mirage Enterprises, Robert Fox/Scott Rudin Production, Miramax Films.

DIRECTING

* **A BEAUTIFUL MIND,** Universal Pictures and Imagine Entertainment Production, Universal and DreamWorks. Ron Howard.

   BLACK HAWK DOWN, Revolution Studios Production, Sony Pictures Releasing. Ridley Scott.

   GOSFORD PARK, Sandcastle 5 in association with Chicagofilms and Medusa Film Production, USA Films. Robert Altman.

   THE LORD OF THE RINGS: THE FELLOWSHIP OF THE RING, New Line Cinema and Wingnut Films Production, New Line. Peter Jackson.

   MULHOLLAND DRIVE, Les Films Alain Sarde/Asymmetrical Production, Universal and StudioCanal. David Lynch.

WRITING

(Screenplay Based on Material Previously Produced or Published)

* **A BEAUTIFUL MIND,** Universal Pictures and Imagine Entertainment Production, Universal and DreamWorks. Akiva Goldsman.

   GHOST WORLD, Mr. Mudd Production, United Artists through MGM. Daniel Clowes and Terry Zwigoff.

   IN THE BEDROOM, Good Machine/GreeneStreet Production, Miramax Films. Rob Festinger and Todd Field.

   THE LORD OF THE RINGS: THE FELLOWSHIP OF THE RING, New Line Cinema and Wingnut Films Production, New Line. Fran Walsh, Philippa Boyens and Peter Jackson.

   SHREK, PDI/DreamWorks Production, DreamWorks. Ted Elliott, Terry Rossio, Joe Stillman and Roger S. H. Schulman.

(Screenplay Written Directly for the Screen)

   AMÉLIE, UGC Images Production, Miramax Zoë. Guillaume Laurant and Jean-Pierre Jeunet.

* **GOSFORD PARK,** Sandcastle 5 in association with Chicagofilms and Medusa Film Production, USA Films. Julian Fellowes.

   MEMENTO, Team Todd Production, Newmarket Films. Christopher Nolan and Jonathan Nolan.

   MONSTER'S BALL, Monster Production, Lions Gate Films. Milo Addica and Will Rokos.

   THE ROYAL TENENBAUMS, Touchstone Pictures Production, Buena Vista. Wes Anderson and Owen Wilson.

ART DIRECTION—SET DECORATION

   AMÉLIE, UGC Images Production, Miramax Zoë. Aline Bonetto; Marie-Laure Valla.

   GOSFORD PARK, Sandcastle 5 in association with Chicagofilms and Medusa Film Production, USA Films. Stephen Altman; Anna Pinnock.

   HARRY POTTER AND THE SORCERER'S STONE, Warner Bros. Ltd. Production, Warner Bros. Stuart Craig; Stephenie McMillan.

   THE LORD OF THE RINGS: THE FELLOWSHIP OF THE RING, New Line Cinema and Wingnut Films Production, New Line. Grant Major; Dan Hennah.

* **MOULIN ROUGE,** 20th Century Fox Production, 20th Century Fox. Catherine Martin; Brigitte Broch.

CINEMATOGRAPHY

   AMÉLIE, UGC Images Production, Miramax Zoë. Bruno Delbonnel.

   BLACK HAWK DOWN, Revolution Studios Production, Sony Pictures Releasing. Slawomir Idziak.

* **THE LORD OF THE RINGS: THE FELLOWSHIP OF THE RING,** New Line Cinema and Wingnut Films Production, New Line. Andrew Lesnie.

   THE MAN WHO WASN'T THERE, Working Title Production, USA Films. Roger Deakins.

   MOULIN ROUGE, 20th Century Fox Production, 20th Century Fox. Donald M. McAlpine.

COSTUME DESIGN

   THE AFFAIR OF THE NECKLACE, Alcon Entertainment Production, Warner Bros. Milena Canonero.

   GOSFORD PARK, Sandcastle 5 in association with Chicagofilms and Medusa Film Production, USA Films. Jenny Beavan.

   HARRY POTTER AND THE SORCERER'S STONE, Warner Bros. Ltd. Production, Warner Bros. Judianna Makovsky.

   THE LORD OF THE RINGS: THE FELLOWSHIP OF THE RING, New Line Cinema and Wingnut Films Production, New Line. Ngila Dickson and Richard Taylor.

* **MOULIN ROUGE,** 20th Century Fox Production, 20th Century Fox. Catherine Martin and Angus Strathie.

FILM EDITING

   A BEAUTIFUL MIND, Universal Pictures and Imagine Entertainment Production, Universal and DreamWorks. Mike Hill and Dan Hanley.

* **BLACK HAWK DOWN,** Revolution Studios Production, Sony Pictures Releasing. Pietro Scalia.

   THE LORD OF THE RINGS: THE FELLOWSHIP OF THE RING, New Line Cinema and Wingnut Films Production, New Line. John Gilbert.

   MEMENTO, Team Todd Production, Newmarket Films. Dody Dorn.

   MOULIN ROUGE, 20th Century Fox Production, 20th Century Fox. Jill Bilcock.

MAKEUP

   A BEAUTIFUL MIND, Universal Pictures and Imagine Entertainment Production, Universal and DreamWorks. Greg Cannom and Colleen Callaghan.

* **THE LORD OF THE RINGS: THE FELLOWSHIP OF THE RING,** New Line Cinema and Wingnut Films Production, New Line. Peter Owen and Richard Taylor.

   MOULIN ROUGE, 20th Century Fox Production, 20th Century Fox. Maurizio Silvi and Aldo Signoretti.

MUSIC

(Original Score)

A.I. ARTIFICIAL INTELLIGENCE, Warner Bros. Pictures and DreamWorks Pictures Production, Warner Bros. John Williams.

A BEAUTIFUL MIND, Universal Pictures and Imagine Entertainment Production, Universal and DreamWorks. James Horner.

HARRY POTTER AND THE SORCERER'S STONE, Warner Bros. Ltd. Production, Warner Bros. John Williams.

* THE LORD OF THE RINGS: THE FELLOWSHIP OF THE RING, New Line Cinema and Wingnut Films Production, New Line. Howard Shore.

MONSTERS, INC., Walt Disney Pictures/Pixar Animation Studios Production, Buena Vista. Randy Newman.

(Original Song)

* IF I DIDN'T HAVE YOU (Monsters, Inc., Walt Disney Pictures/Pixar Animation Studios Production, Buena Vista); Music and Lyric by Randy Newman.

MAY IT BE (The Lord of the Rings: The Fellowship of the Ring, New Line Cinema and Wingnut Films Production, New Line); Music and Lyric by Enya, Nicky Ryan and Roma Ryan.

THERE YOU'LL BE (Pearl Harbor, Touchstone Pictures/Jerry Bruckheimer Films Production, Buena Vista); Music and Lyric by Diane Warren.

UNTIL (Kate & Leopold, Konrad Pictures Production, Miramax Films); Music and Lyric by Sting.

VANILLA SKY (Vanilla Sky, Cruise/Wagner-Vinyl Films Production, Paramount); Music and Lyric by Paul McCartney.

SOUND

AMÉLIE, UGC Images Production, Miramax Zoë. Vincent Arnardi, Guillaume Leriche and Jean Umansky.

* BLACK HAWK DOWN, Revolution Studios Production, Sony Pictures Releasing. Michael Minkler, Myron Nettinga and Chris Munro.

THE LORD OF THE RINGS: THE FELLOWSHIP OF THE RING, New Line Cinema and Wingnut Films Production, New Line. Christopher Boyes, Michael Semanick, Gethin Creagh and Hammond Peek.

MOULIN ROUGE, 20th Century Fox Production, 20th Century Fox. Andy Nelson, Anna Behlmer, Roger Savage and Guntis Sics.

PEARL HARBOR, Touchstone Pictures/Jerry Bruckheimer Films Production, Buena Vista. Kevin O'Connell, Greg P. Russell and Peter J. Devlin.

SOUND EDITING

MONSTERS, INC., Walt Disney Pictures/Pixar Animation Studios Production, Buena Vista. Gary Rydstrom and Michael Silvers.

* PEARL HARBOR, Touchstone Pictures/Jerry Bruckheimer Films Production, Buena Vista. George Watters II and Christopher Boyes.

VISUAL EFFECTS

A.I. ARTIFICIAL INTELLIGENCE, Warner Bros. Pictures and DreamWorks Pictures Production, Warner Bros. Dennis Muren, Scott Farrar, Stan Winston and Michael Lantieri.

* THE LORD OF THE RINGS: THE FELLOWSHIP OF THE RING, New Line Cinema and Wingnut Films Production, New Line. Jim Rygiel, Randall William Cook, Richard Taylor and Mark Stetson.

PEARL HARBOR, Touchstone Pictures/Jerry Bruckheimer Films Production, Buena Vista. Eric Brevig, John Frazier, Ed Hirsh and Ben Snow.

SHORT FILMS

(Animated)

FIFTY PERCENT GREY, Zanita Films Production. Ruairi Robinson and Seamus Bryne.

* FOR THE BIRDS, Pixar Animation Studios Production. Ralph Eggleston.

GIVE UP YER AUL SINS, Irish Film Board/Radio Telefis Eireann/Arts Council/Brown Bag Films Production. Cathal Gaffney and Darragh O'Connell.

STRANGE INVADERS, National Film Board of Canada Production. Cordell Barker.

STUBBLE TROUBLE, Calabash Animation Production. Joseph E. Merideth.

(Live Action)

* THE ACCOUNTANT, Ginny Mule Pictures Production. Ray McKinnon and Lisa Blount.

COPY SHOP, Virgil Widrich/Multimediaproduktions G.m.b.H Production. Virgil Widrich.

GREGOR'S GREATEST INVENTION, Südwest Film Filmproduktion. Johannes Kiefer.

A MAN THING (MESKA SPRAWA), Polish National Film School Production. Slawomir Fabicki and Bogumil Gofrejow.

SPEED FOR THESPIANS, Lester Films Ltd. Production. Kalman Apple and Shameela Bakhsh.

DOCUMENTARY

(Feature)

CHILDREN UNDERGROUND, Belzberg Films Production. Edet Belzberg.

LALEE'S KIN: THE LEGACY OF COTTON, Maysles Films Production. Susan Froemke and Deborah Dickson.

* MURDER ON A SUNDAY MORNING, Maha Productions/Pathé Doc/France 2/HBO Production. Jean-Xavier de Lestrade and Denis Poncet.

PROMISES, Promises Film Project Production. Justine Shapiro and B. Z. Goldberg.

WAR PHOTOGRAPHER, Christian Frei Filmproductions, Films Transit. Christian Frei.

Best Animated Feature: Shrek (DreamWorks; produced by Aron Warner). The Academy's historic admiration for animated features had been evidenced by its special Oscars for the advances represented by 1938's Snow White, 1988's Who Framed Roger Rabbit and 1995's Toy Story, as well as by the 1991 best picture nomination for Beauty and the Beast. But the Academy Board had been dissuaded from establishing a regular category for animated features by the sparse 'toon output: for most of the Academy's history fewer than five animated features were released in a year, and a category in which every eligible contender became a nominee was unappealing. By the turn of the new century, though, enough cel, clay animation and computer-animated pictures were being released each year to justify a new category. Shrek, a fairy-tale spoof about a troll and his donkey sidekick trudging to the rescue of a beautiful princess, became the category's first award recipient.

(Short Subject)

ARTISTS AND ORPHANS: A TRUE DRAMA, Not by Chance Production. Lianne Klapper McNally.

SING!, KCET/Hollywood and American Film Foundation Production. Freida Lee Mock and Jessica Sanders.

* THOTH, Amateur Rabbit Production. Sarah Kernochan and Lynn Appelle.

ANIMATED FEATURE FILM

JIMMY NEUTRON: BOY GENIUS, O Entertainment Production, Paramount and Nickelodeon Movies. Steve Oedekerk and John A. Davis.

MONSTERS, INC., Walt Disney Pictures/Pixar Animation Studios Production, Buena Vista. Pete Docter and John Lasseter.

* SHREK, PDI/DreamWorks Production, DreamWorks. Aron Warner.

FOREIGN LANGUAGE FILM

AMÉLIE (France)

ELLING (Norway)

LAGAAN (India)

* NO MAN'S LAND (Bosnia and Herzegovina)

SON OF THE BRIDE (Argentina)

HONORARY AWARDS

TO SIDNEY POITIER, in recognition of his remarkable accomplishments as an artist and as a human being. (Statuette)

TO ROBERT REDFORD, actor, director, producer, creator of Sundance, inspiration to independent and innovative filmmakers everywhere. (Statuette)

TO RUNE ERICKSON for his pioneering development and thirty years of dedication to the Super-16mm format for motion pictures. The Super-16mm format has achieved a significant impact on the worldwide film industry by playing a major role in empowering low-budget films to be produced for theatrical release. (Award of Commendation—Special Award Plaque)

TO the AMERICAN SOCIETY OF CINEMATOGAPHERS (ASC) for the continued publication of The American Cinematographers Manual. Born from The Cinematographic Annual first published by the ASC in 1930, The American Cinematographers Manual has become an essential bible for cinematographers. Currently in its eighth edition, this premier reference manual has had a significant impact on decades of motion picture photography around the world. (Award of Commendation—Special Award Plaque)

TO RAY FEENEY in appreciation for outstanding service and dedication in upholding the high standards of the Academy of Motion Picture Arts and Sciences. (John A. Bonner Medal of Commendation)

2001 IRVING G. THALBERG MEMORIAL AWARD

None given this year.

2001 JEAN HERSHOLT HUMANITARIAN AWARD

TO ARTHUR HILLER

2001 GORDON E. SAWYER AWARD

TO EDMUND M. DI GIULIO

SCIENTIFIC AND TECHNICAL AWARDS

Scientific and Engineering Awards (Academy Plaque)

JOHN M. EARGLE, D. B. "DON" KEELE and MARK E. ENGEBRETSON for the concept, design and engineering of the modern constant-directivity, direct-radiator style motion picture loudspeaker systems.

IAIN NEIL for the concept and optical design and AL SAIKI for the mechanical design of the Panavision Primo Macro Zoom Lens (PMZ).

FRANZ KRAUS, JOHANNES STEURER and WOLFGANG RIEDEL for the design and development of the Arrilaser Film Recorder.

PETER KURAN for the invention, and SEAN COUGHLIN, JOSEPH A. OLIVIER and WILLIAM CONNER for the engineering and development, of the RCI-Color Film Restoration Process.

MAKOTO TSUKADA, SHOJI KANEKO and the technical staff of Imagica Corporation, and DAIJIRO FUJIE of Nikon Corporation for the engineering excellence and the impact on the motion picture industry of the Imagica 65/35 Multi-Format Optical Printer.

STEVEN GERLACH, GREGORY FARRELL and CHRISTIAN LURIN for the design, engineering and implementation of the Kodak Panchromatic Sound Recording Film.

PAUL J. CONSTANTINE and PETER M. CONSTANTINE for the design and development of the CELCO Digital Film Recorder products.

Technical Achievement Awards (Academy Certificate)

PETE ROMANO for the design and development of the Remote Aqua-Cam, an underwater camera housing system for use in motion pictures.

JORDAN KLEIN for his pioneering efforts in the development and application of underwater camera housings for motion pictures.

BERNARD M. WERNER and WILLIAM GELOW for the engineering and design of filtered line arrays and screen-spreading compensation as applied to motion picture loudspeaker systems.

TOMLINSON HOLMAN for the research and systems integration resulting in the improvement of motion picture loudspeaker systems.

GEOFF JACKSON and ROGER WOODBURN for their DMS 120S Camera Motor.

THOMAS MAJOR BARRON for the overall concept and design; CHAS SMITH for the structural engineering; and GORDON SEITZ for the mechanical engineering of the Bulldog Motion Control Camera Crane.

JOHN R. ANDERSON, JIM HOURIHAN, CARY PHILLIPS and SEBASTIAN MARINO for the development of the ILM Creature Dynamics System.

STEVE SULLIVAN and ERIC R. L. SCHAFER for the development of the ILM Motion and Structure Recovery System (MARS).

CARL LUDWIG and JOHN M. CONSTANTINE, JR., for their contributions to CELCO Digital Film Recorder products.

BILL SPITZAK, PAUL VAN CAMP, JONATHAN EGSTAD and PRICE PETHEL for their pioneering effort on the NUKE-2D Compositing Software.

DR. LANCE J. WILLIAMS for his pioneering influence in the field of computer-generated animation and effects for motion pictures.

DR. UWE SASSENBERG and ROLF SCHNEIDER for the development of "3D Equalizer," an advanced and robust camera and object match-moving system.

DR. GARLAND STERN for the concept and implementation of the Cel Paint Software System.

MIC RODGERS and MATT SWEENEY for the concept, design and realization of the "Mic Rig."

The first seventy-five years of the Academy couldn't have ended on a more dramatic note: five days before the awards were scheduled to be handed out at the Kodak Theatre in Hollywood, on March 23, 2003, the United States officially declared war on Iraq, with American and British troops marching toward Baghdad. It was a move that stirred enormous controversy worldwide, and, initially, Academy officials considered postponing the award ceremony altogether. As the clock ticked on, however, it was decided to proceed as originally planned, holding open the possibility of postponement if necessary. If the show were to go on, it would be under highly modified conditions—with no pre-show red carpet festivities, scant press coverage, a minimum of photographers and hoopla—in keeping with the seriousness of the national situation. For the next few days planning progressed, but everything stayed flexible. The possibility existed that the ceremonies would be held in the Kodak, but that a portion of them would be lost to the viewing public owing to cutaways for war news coverage. It made for the most sobering Oscar event since Hollywood had handed out Oscars sixty-one years before, twelve weeks after the United States had entered World War II. It turned out nonetheless to be a remarkably good show, shorn of much of the usual razzle-dazzle but crisp, relevant, respectful, and swift.

Chicago, which had been nominated for a hefty thirteen awards, won six of them, including best picture and best supporting actress (Catherine Zeta-Jones). Its closest runner-up was *The Pianist,* with three awards, including best actor Adrien Brody and best director Roman Polanski. *The Lord of the Rings: The Two Towers* and *Frida* received two awards each; eight other pictures received one award. Nicole Kidman was named the year's best actress in *The Hours;* Chris Cooper in *Adaptation* was chosen as best supporting actor. The most neglected film of the night was Martin Scorsese's *The Gangs of New York:* nominated for ten awards, it failed to pick up any of them.

It was a year that set several imposing records. Meryl Streep, receiving her thirteenth Oscar nomination (this time in the best supporting actress category, for *Adaptation),* remained the most nominated performer in Oscar history, topping Katharine Hepburn's twelve nominations (although all of Hepburn's had been for lead performances); Jack Nicholson, nominated as best actor for *About Schmidt,* tied Hepburn's twelve, and became the most nominated male performer to date. Julianne Moore, nominated both as best actress (for *Far from Heaven)* and best supporting actress (for *The Hours),* became one of nine in the exclusive club of actors nominated for awards in two acting categories in the same Oscar year, the first being Fay Bainter in 1938, the most recent before Moore being Emma Thompson and Holly Hunter in 1993.

Steve Martin was the evening's host, Bill Conti the musical director, and the

Best Picture: Chicago *(Miramax; Producer Circle Co., Zadan/Meron; directed by Rob Marshall)* and **Best Supporting Actress: Catherine Zeta-Jones** *as Velma Kelly in* Chicago. *Broadway producer Martin Richards had been trying to spearhead a film version of Bob Fosse's 1975 Broadway musical* Chicago *for twenty-seven years; his initial plan had been for Fosse himself to direct, with Liza Minnelli and Goldie Hawn as the story's two sassy leading ladies. But mountains of roadblocks, including the director-choreographer's death in 1987, squelched that plan; later efforts by Richards to produce it with other star combinations got no further, and, at several turns, the project looked to be dead. But Richards persevered unrelentingly, and what finally did emerge was bright, noisy, tantalizing, and spirited, and found great favor with Academy voters, taking home statuettes for best picture, art direction, costume design, film editing, and sound, and one for Zeta-Jones as a singing-dancing cabaret star with a passion for publicity, murder, "and all that jazz." There had been two earlier, non-musical movie versions based on the same source material, the 1926 play* Chicago, *written by Maurine Dallas Watkins. One was a 1927 silent with Phyllis Haver, the other a 1942 sound version called* Roxie Hart, *with Ginger Rogers in the title role, which had been a big success.*

telecast was produced by Gil Cates and directed by Louis J. Horvitz. Musical numbers were limited to nominated songs, one of them a spirited version of John Kander and Fred Ebb's "I Move On" from *Chicago*, delivered by Queen Latifah and an eight-months-pregnant Catherine Zeta-Jones. A high point of the night for many came near the end of the evening, when two-time Oscar winner Olivia de Havilland introduced a stage full of fifty-nine former acting winners, from "A" as in Julie Andrews (1964) to "W" as in Teresa Wright (1942), including nonagenarian Luise Rainer, the first performer to win Oscars back to back (in 1936 and 1937). The night was not without its lightning. Although even the most politically outspoken of stars participating in the show steered clear of specifically criticizing the war, a number did express a hope for peace. Outside, some 3,000 demonstrators gathered near the Kodak Theatre to protest —and, in smaller numbers, support— the military action. When *Bowling for Columbine* was named best documentary feature, its producer-director Michael Moore was initially greeted with applause, then boos when he began a blistering speech directed at U.S. president George W. Bush. Soon after, Adrien Brody, clutching his *Pianist* prize, gave an impromptu four-minute thank-you speech which included an impassioned and touching prayer for peace. It gave the evening an unusually strong emotional finish and brought Brody two separate standing ovations.

Best Actress: **Nicole Kidman,** *as Virginia Woolf in* The Hours *(Paramount and Miramax; directed by Stephen Daldry). One of the year's most admired and arresting dramas, this screen version of Michael Cunningham's Pulitzer Prize-winning novel also had an unusual structure: three stories set in different time periods, showing Woolfian themes in each of them. With Meryl Streep and Julianne Moore as the other two women, it offered acting tours de force from all three performers, especially Kidman, virtually unrecognizable behind a long, false nose created by prosthetic makeup artists Conor O'Sullivan and Jo Allen to make Kidman look like the brilliant, real-life Woolf. Kidman, for the record, is the first actress to win an Oscar for a performance with a false beak, although several actors, including José Ferrer, Lee Marvin, and Robert De Niro, have done so.*

Best Documentary Feature: **Bowling for Columbine** *(United Artists and Alliance Atlantis). Written and directed by Michael Moore, this 120-minute documentary also features Moore on camera, mixed with archival and new footage of George W. Bush, Dick Cheney, Bill Clinton, Charlton Heston, and others, as Moore takes a blistering look at what he sees as America's passion for violence, the government's continued promotion of world unrest, and an acceleration of homicides.*

Best Actor: **Adrien Brody,** *as Wladyslaw Szpilman in* The Pianist *(Focus Features; directed by Roman Polanski). Brody was unknown to most moviegoers when* The Pianist *was initially released; soon after, at age twenty-nine, he became the youngest performer to win a leading actor Oscar, a year younger than thirty-year-old Richard Dreyfuss when he won in 1977 for* The Goodbye Girl. *Already slim, Brody shed some thirty pounds to play the real-life Szpilman, a Polish-Jewish musician determined to survive the destruction of the Warsaw Ghetto of World War II; he also learned to play Chopin proficiently and gave a film performance that was at once delicate, powerful, rich, and unforgettable.*

Peter O'Toole: *It had been exactly forty years since the seventy-year-old O'Toole first came to prominence in 1962's* Lawrence of Arabia, *a film that brought him the first of seven Academy Award nominations but, to date, no statuette of his own. The Academy's Board of Governors decided it was high time to make up for the oversight, voting O'Toole an Honorary Oscar. It's an honor O'Toole initially rejected ("Since I'm still in the game, I would rather try to win one on my own," he said), but then, after second thoughts, he agreed to accept. When Meryl Streep handed him the statuette, he said, "I have my very own Oscar now, to be with me until death do us part," adding, "I wish the Academy to know I am as delighted as I am honored, and I am honored."*

Best Directing: Roman Polanski, *for* The Pianist *(Focus Features). Through the years, several Oscar winning directors have not been present to pick up their Oscar statues in person; William Wyler, for one, was in an airplane on a World War II military mission when he won the Oscar for directing 1942's* Mrs. Miniver; *Woody Allen was playing clarinet in a favorite New York haunt when his name was announced in Hollywood for his directing work on 1977's* Annie Hall. *When Polanski was announced as the winner for 2002, he was at his home in France, watching the show live on TV with his wife, actress Emmanuelle Seigner. He has been in exile in Europe since 1978, when he left the United States to avoid being sentenced in a Los Angeles legal case. But his award for* The Pianist *brought him, in absentia, one of the evening's nine standing ovations.*

BEST PICTURE

* **CHICAGO,** Producer Circle Co., Zadan/Meron Production, Miramax. Martin Richards, Producer.
  GANGS OF NEW YORK, Alberto Grimaldi Production, Miramax. Alberto Grimaldi and Harvey Weinstein, Producers.
  THE HOURS, Scott Rudin/Robert Fox Production, Paramount & Miramax. Scott Rudin and Robert Fox, Producers.
  THE LORD OF THE RINGS: THE TWO TOWERS, New Line Cinema and Wingnut Films Production, New Line. Barrie M. Osborne, Fran Walsh and Peter Jackson, Producers.
  THE PIANIST, R.P. Productions, Heritage Films, Studio Babelsberg, Runtime LTD. Production, Focus Features. Roman Polanski, Robert Benmussa and Alain Sarde, Producers.

ACTOR

* **ADRIEN BRODY** in *The Pianist,* R.P. Productions, Heritage Films, Studio Babelsberg, Runtime LTD. Production, Focus Features.
  NICOLAS CAGE in *Adaptation,* Columbia Pictures/Intermedia Films Production, Sony Pictures Releasing.
  MICHAEL CAINE in *The Quiet American,* Mirage Enterprises/ Saga Pictures/IMF Production, Miramax and Intermedia.
  DANIEL DAY-LEWIS in *Gangs of New York,* Alberto Grimaldi Production, Miramax.
  JACK NICHOLSON in *About Schmidt,* Michael Besman/Harry Gittes Production, New Line.

ACTRESS

  SALMA HAYEK in *Frida,* Ventanarosa in association with Lions Gate Films Production, Miramax.
* **NICOLE KIDMAN** in *The Hours,* Scott Rudin/Robert Fox Production, Paramount & Miramax.
  DIANE LANE in *Unfaithful,* Fox 2000 Pictures and Regency Enterprises Production, 20th Century Fox.
  JULIANNE MOORE in *Far from Heaven,* Vulcan, Section Eight, Killer Films Production, Focus Features.
  RENÉE ZELLWEGER in *Chicago,* Producer Circle Co., Zadan/Meron Production, Miramax.

SUPPORTING ACTOR

* **CHRIS COOPER** in *Adaptation,* Columbia Pictures/Intermedia Films Production, Sony Pictures Releasing.
  ED HARRIS in *The Hours,* Scott Rudin/Robert Fox Production, Paramount & Miramax.
  PAUL NEWMAN in *Road to Perdition,* Zanuck Company Production, DreamWorks and 20th Century Fox.
  JOHN C. REILLY in *Chicago,* Producer Circle Co., Zadan/Meron Production, Miramax.
  CHRISTOPHER WALKEN in *Catch Me If You Can,* Kemp Company and Splendid Pictures Production, a Parkes/MacDonald Production, DreamWorks.

SUPPORTING ACTRESS

  KATHY BATES in *About Schmidt,* Michael Besman/Harry Gittes Production, New Line.
  JULIANNE MOORE in *The Hours,* Scott Rudin/Robert Fox Production, Paramount & Miramax.
  QUEEN LATIFAH in *Chicago,* Producer Circle Co., Zadan/Meron Production, Miramax.
  MERYL STREEP in *Adaptation,* Columbia Pictures/Intermedia Films Production, Sony Pictures Releasing.
* **CATHERINE ZETA-JONES** in *Chicago,* Producer Circle Co., Zadan/Meron Production, Miramax.

DIRECTING

  CHICAGO, Producer Circle Co., Zadan/Meron Production, Miramax. Rob Marshall.
  GANGS OF NEW YORK, Alberto Grimaldi Production, Miramax. Martin Scorsese.
  THE HOURS, Scott Rudin/Robert Fox Production, Paramount & Miramax. Stephen Daldry.
* **THE PIANIST,** R.P. Productions, Heritage Films, Studio Babelsberg, Runtime LTD. Production, Focus Features. Roman Polanski.
  TALK TO HER, El Deseo S.A. Production, Sony Pictures Classics. Pedro Almodóvar.

WRITING

(Adapted Screenplay)

  ABOUT A BOY, Tribeca/Working Title Production, Universal. Peter Hedges, Chris Weitz and Paul Weitz.
  ADAPTATION, Columbia Pictures/Intermedia Films Production, Sony Pictures Releasing. Charlie Kaufman and Donald Kaufman.
  CHICAGO, Producer Circle Co., Zadan/Meron Production, Miramax. Bill Condon.
  THE HOURS, Scott Rudin/Robert Fox Production, Paramount & Miramax. David Hare.
* **THE PIANIST,** R.P. Productions, Heritage Films, Studio Babelsberg, Runtime LTD. Production, Focus Features. Ronald Harwood.

(Original Screenplay)

  FAR FROM HEAVEN, Vulcan, Section Eight, Killer Films Production, Focus Features. Todd Haynes.
  GANGS OF NEW YORK, Alberto Grimaldi Production, Miramax. Jay Cocks, Steve Zaillian and Kenneth Lonergan.
  MY BIG FAT GREEK WEDDING, Playtone Production, IFC/Gold Circle Films. Nia Vardalos.
* **TALK TO HER,** El Deseo S.A. Production, Sony Pictures Classics. Pedro Almodóvar.
  Y TU MAMÁ TAMBIÉN, Producciones Anhelo Production, IFC Films. Carlos Cuarón and Alfonso Cuarón.

ART DIRECTION - SET DECORATION

* **CHICAGO,** Producer Circle Co., Zadan/Meron Production, Miramax. John Myhre; Gordon Sim.
  FRIDA, Ventanarosa in association with Lions Gate Films Production, Miramax. Felipe Fernandez del Paso; Hania Robledo.
  GANGS OF NEW YORK, Alberto Grimaldi Production, Miramax. Dante Ferretti; Francesca Lo Schiavo.
  THE LORD OF THE RINGS: THE TWO TOWERS, New Line Cinema and Wingnut Films Production, New Line. Grant Major; Dan Hennah and Alan Lee.
  ROAD TO PERDITION, Zanuck Company Production, DreamWorks and 20th Century Fox. Dennis Gassner; Nancy Haigh.

CINEMATOGRAPHY

  CHICAGO, Producer Circle Co., Zadan/Meron Production, Miramax. Dion Beebe.
  FAR FROM HEAVEN, Vulcan, Section Eight, Killer Films Production, Focus Features. Edward Lachman.
  GANGS OF NEW YORK, Alberto Grimaldi Production, Miramax. Michael Ballhaus.
  THE PIANIST, R.P. Productions, Heritage Films, Studio Babelsberg, Runtime LTD. Production, Focus Features. Pawel Edelman.
* **ROAD TO PERDITION,** Zanuck Company Production, DreamWorks and 20th Century Fox. Conrad L. Hall.

COSTUME DESIGN

* **CHICAGO,** Producer Circle Co., Zadan/Meron Production, Miramax. Colleen Atwood.
  FRIDA, Ventanarosa in association with Lions Gate Films Production, Miramax. Julie Weiss.
  GANGS OF NEW YORK, Alberto Grimaldi Production, Miramax. Sandy Powell.
  THE HOURS, Scott Rudin/Robert Fox Production, Paramount & Miramax. Ann Roth.
  THE PIANIST, R.P. Productions, Heritage Films, Studio Babelsberg, Runtime LTD. Production, Focus Features. Anna Sheppard.

FILM EDITING

* **CHICAGO,** Producer Circle Co., Zadan/Meron Production, Miramax. Martin Walsh.
  GANGS OF NEW YORK, Alberto Grimaldi Production, Miramax. Thelma Schoonmaker.
  THE HOURS, Scott Rudin/Robert Fox Production, Paramount & Miramax. Peter Boyle.
  THE LORD OF THE RINGS: THE TWO TOWERS, New Line Cinema and Wingnut Films Production, New Line. Michael Horton.
  THE PIANIST, R.P. Productions, Heritage Films, Studio Babelsberg, Runtime LTD. Production, Focus Features. Hervé de Luze.

MUSIC

(Original Score)

  CATCH ME IF YOU CAN, Kemp Company and Splendid Pictures Production, a Parkes/MacDonald Production, DreamWorks. John Williams.
  FAR FROM HEAVEN, Vulcan, Section Eight, Killer Films Production, Focus Features. Elmer Bernstein.
* **FRIDA,** Ventanarosa in association with Lions Gate Films Production, Miramax. Elliot Goldenthal.
  THE HOURS, Scott Rudin/Robert Fox Production, Paramount & Miramax. Philip Glass.
  ROAD TO PERDITION, Zanuck Company Production, DreamWorks and 20th Century Fox. Thomas Newman.

(Original Song)

BURN IT BLUE (*Frida*, Ventanarosa in association with Lions Gate Films Production, Miramax); Music by Elliot Goldenthal; Lyric by Julie Taymor.

FATHER AND DAUGHTER (*The Wild Thornberrys Movie*, Klasky Csupo Production, Paramount and Nickelodeon Movies); Music and Lyric by Paul Simon.

THE HANDS THAT BUILT AMERICA (*Gangs of New York*, Alberto Grimaldi Production, Miramax); Music and Lyric by Bono, The Edge, Adam Clayton and Larry Mullen.

I MOVE ON (*Chicago*, Producer Circle Co., Zadan/Meron Production, Miramax); Music by John Kander; Lyric by Fred Ebb.

* LOSE YOURSELF (*8 Mile*, Universal Pictures and Imagine Entertainment Production, Universal); Music by Eminem, Jeff Bass and Luis Resto; Lyric by Eminem.

SOUND

* CHICAGO, Producer Circle Co., Zadan/Meron Production, Miramax. Michael Minkler, Dominick Tavella and David Lee.

GANGS OF NEW YORK, Alberto Grimaldi Production, Miramax. Tom Fleischman, Eugene Gearty and Ivan Sharrock.

THE LORD OF THE RINGS: THE TWO TOWERS, New Line Cinema and Wingnut Films Production, New Line. Christopher Boyes, Michael Semanick, Michael Hedges and Hammond Peek.

ROAD TO PERDITION, Zanuck Company Production, DreamWorks and 20th Century Fox. Scott Millan, Bob Beemer and John Patrick Pritchett.

SPIDER-MAN, Columbia Pictures Production, Sony Pictures Releasing. Kevin O'Connell, Greg P. Russell and Ed Novick.

SOUND EDITING

* THE LORD OF THE RINGS: THE TWO TOWERS, New Line Cinema and Wingnut Films Production, New Line. Ethan Van der Ryn and Michael Hopkins.

MINORITY REPORT, 20th Century Fox and DreamWorks Pictures Production, 20th Century Fox and DreamWorks. Richard Hymns and Gary Rydstrom.

ROAD TO PERDITION, Zanuck Company Production, DreamWorks and 20th Century Fox. Scott A. Hecker.

VISUAL EFFECTS

* THE LORD OF THE RINGS: THE TWO TOWERS, New Line Cinema and Wingnut Films Production, New Line. Jim Rygiel, Joe Letteri, Randall William Cook and Alex Funke.

SPIDER-MAN, Columbia Pictures Production, Sony Pictures Releasing. John Dykstra, Scott Stokdyk, Anthony LaMolinara and John Frazier.

STAR WARS EPISODE II ATTACK OF THE CLONES, Lucasfilm, Ltd., Production, 20th Century Fox. Rob Coleman, Pablo Helman, John Knoll and Ben Snow.

MAKEUP

* FRIDA, Ventanarosa in association with Lions Gate Films Production, Miramax. John Jackson and Beatrice De Alba.

THE TIME MACHINE, Parkes/MacDonald Production, DreamWorks and Warner Bros. John M. Elliott, Jr., and Barbara Lorenz.

SHORT FILMS

(Animated)

THE CATHEDRAL, Platige Image Production. Tomek Baginski.

* THE CHUBBCHUBBS!, Sony Pictures Imageworks Production, Columbia. Eric Armstrong.

DAS RAD, Filmakademie Baden-Württemberg GmbH Production. Chris Stenner and Heidi Wittlinger.

MIKE'S NEW CAR, Pixar Animation Studios Production, Buena Vista. Pete Docter and Roger Gould.

MT. HEAD, Yamamura Animation Production. Koji Yamamura.

(Live Action)

FAIT D'HIVER, Another Dimension of an Idea Production. Dirk Beliën and Anja Daelemans.

I'LL WAIT FOR THE NEXT ONE . . . (J'ATTENDRAI LE SUIVANT . . .), La Boîte Production. Philippe Orreindy and Thomas Gaudin.

INJA (DOG), Australian Film TV & Radio School (AFTRS) Production. Steven Pasvolsky and Joe Weatherstone.

JOHNNY FLYNTON, Red Corner Production. Lexi Alexander and Alexander Buono.

* THIS CHARMING MAN (DER ER EN YNDIG MAND), M&M Productions for Novellefilm Production. Martin Strange-Hansen and Mie Andreasen.

DOCUMENTARY

(Feature)

* BOWLING FOR COLUMBINE, Salter Street Films/VIF 2/Dog Eat Dog Films Production, United Artists and Alliance Atlantis. Michael Moore and Michael Donovan.

DAUGHTER FROM DANANG, Interfaze Educational Production, Balcony Releasing in association with Cowboy Pictures. Gail Dolgin and Vicente Franco.

PRISONER OF PARADISE, Média Vérité/Café Production, Alliance Atlantis. Malcolm Clarke and Stuart Sender.

SPELLBOUND, Blitz/Welch Production, THINKFilm. Jeffrey Blitz and Sean Welch.

WINGED MIGRATION, Galatée Films/France 2 Cinéma/France 3 Cinéma/Les Productions de la Guéville/Bac Films/Pandora Film/Les Productions JMH/Wanda Vision/Eyescreen Production, Sony Pictures Classics. Jacques Perrin.

Best Animated Feature: **Spirited Away** (*Buena Vista; directed by Hayao Miyazaki). For the second year, the Academy honored animated features via their own separate category; this year's champion was a dubbed-into-English version of Hayao Miyazaki's Japanese-made* Sen *and the Mysterious Disappearance of Chihiro, a strikingly creative tale of a dispirited ten-year-old girl who, like Alice in Wonderland, inadvertently wanders into a magical world ruled by monsters, witches, and trickery. It is, in the words of one critic, "a fairy tale that can be thoroughly enjoyed by nippers but will be most appreciated by grown-ups who appreciate true wit and imagination."*

(Short Subject)

THE COLLECTOR OF BEDFORD STREET, An Alice Elliott Production. Alice Elliott.

MIGHTY TIMES: THE LEGACY OF ROSA PARKS, Tell the Truth Pictures Production. Robert Hudson and Bobby Houston.

* TWIN TOWERS, Wolf Films/Shape Pictures/Universal/Mopo Entertainment Production. Bill Guttentag and Robert David Port.

WHY CAN'T WE BE A FAMILY AGAIN?, Public Policy Production. Roger Weisberg and Murray Nossel.

ANIMATED FEATURE FILM

ICE AGE, 20th Century Fox Production, 20th Century Fox. Chris Wedge.

LILO & STITCH, Walt Disney Pictures Production, Buena Vista. Chris Sanders.

SPIRIT: STALLION OF THE CIMARRON, DreamWorks Animation LLC, DreamWorks Pictures Production, DreamWorks. Jeffrey Katzenberg.

* SPIRITED AWAY, Studio Ghibli Production, Buena Vista. Hayao Miyazaki.

TREASURE PLANET, Walt Disney Pictures Production, Buena Vista. Ron Clements.

FOREIGN LANGUAGE FILM

EL CRIMEN DEL PADRE AMARO (Mexico)

HERO (People's Republic of China)

THE MAN WITHOUT A PAST (Finland)

* NOWHERE IN AFRICA (Germany)

ZUS & ZO (The Netherlands)

HONORARY AWARDS

TO PETER O'TOOLE, whose remarkable talents have provided cinema history with some of its most memorable characters. (Statuette)

TO CURT R: BEHLMER and RICHARD B. GLICKMAN for outstanding service and dedication in upholding the high standards of the Academy. (John A. Bonner Medal of Commendation)

2002 IRVING G. THALBERG MEMORIAL AWARD

None given this year.

2002 JEAN HERSHOLT HUMANITARIAN AWARD

None given this year.

2002 GORDON E. SAWYER AWARD

None given this year.

SCIENTIFIC AND TECHNICAL AWARDS

Academy Award of Merit (Oscar Statuette)

ALIAS/WAVEFRONT for the development of a 3D-animation, -dynamics, -modeling and -rendering production tool known as Maya.

ARNOLD & RICHTER CINE TECHNIK and PANAVISION INC. for their continuing development and innovation in the design and manufacturing of advanced camera systems specifically designed for the motion picture entertainment industry.

Scientific and Engineering Awards (Academy Plaque)

GLENN SANDERS and HOWARD STARK of Zaxcom for the concept, design and engineering of the portable Deva Digital Audio Disk Recorder.

MARK ELENDT, PAUL H. BRESLIN, GREG HERMANOVIC and KIM DAVIDSON for their continued development of the procedural modeling and animation components of their Prisms program, as exemplified in the Houdini software.

DR. LESLIE GUTIERREZ, DIANE E. KESTNER, JAMES MERRILL and DAVID NIKLEWICZ for the design and development of the Kodak Vision Premier Color Print Film 2393.

DEDO WEIGERT for the concept, DR. DEPU JIN for the optical calculations, and FRANZ PETTERS for the mechanical construction of the Dedolight 400D.

Technical Achievement Awards (Academy Certificate)

DICK WALSH for the development of the PDI/DreamWorks Facial Animation System.

THOMAS DRIEMEYER and the team of mathematicians, physicists and software engineers of Mental Images for their contributions to the Mental Ray rendering software for motion pictures.

ERIC DANIELS, GEORGE KATANICS, TASSO LAPPAS and CHRIS SPRINGFIELD for the development of the Deep Canvas rendering software.

JIM SONGER for his contributions to the technical development of video-assist in the motion picture industry.

PIERRE CHABERT of Airstar for the introduction of balloons with internal light sources to provide set lighting for the motion picture industry.

RAWDON HAYNE and ROBERT W. JEFFS of Leelium Tubelites for their contributions to the development of internally lit balloons for motion picture lighting.

Best Supporting Actor: **Chris Cooper**, *as John Laroche in* Adaptation *(Sony Pictures Releasing; directed by Spike Jonze). Mixing fact and fiction, truth and outrageously drawn characters and situations, screenwriter Charlie Kaufman converted Susan Orlean's book* The Orchid Thief *into one of the year's most unusual films; it had Cooper as the real-life Laroche who, as depicted in this often-hilarious, always outrageous film, is part outlaw, part avid collector, a borderline madman and toothless wonder, at once tortured, troubled, and touching. Cooper played the part fearlessly, becoming an Oscar winner with his first nomination.*

Awards Ceremonies
The First Seventy-Five Years

Frank Borzage

1st Awards: May 16, 1929
Thursday, 8:00 PM
Blossom Room of the Hollywood Roosevelt Hotel (banquet)
   Hosts—Douglas Fairbanks, Academy
   President, William C. deMille

2nd Awards: April 3, 1930
Thursday, 8:00 PM
The Coconut Grove of the Ambassador Hotel, Los Angeles (banquet)
   Host—William C. deMille, Academy
   President

3rd Awards: November 5, 1930
Wednesday, 8:00 PM
Fiesta Room of the Ambassador Hotel, Los Angeles (banquet)
   Host—Conrad Nagel

4th Awards: November 10, 1931
Tuesday, 8:00 PM
Sala D'Oro of the Biltmore Hotel, Los Angeles (banquet)
   MC—Lawrence Grant

5th Awards: November 18, 1932
Friday, 8:00 PM
Fiesta Room of the Ambassador Hotel, Los Angeles (banquet)
   Host—Conrad Nagel, Academy
   President

6th Awards: March 16, 1934
Friday, 8:00 PM
Fiesta Room of the Ambassador Hotel, Los Angeles (banquet)
   MC—Will Rogers

7th Awards: February 27, 1935
Wednesday, 8:00 PM
The Biltmore Bowl of the Biltmore Hotel, Los Angeles (banquet)
   MC—Irvin S. Cobb

8th Awards: March 5, 1936
Thursday, 8:00 PM
The Biltmore Bowl of the Biltmore Hotel, Los Angeles (banquet)
   Host—Frank Capra, Academy
   President

9th Awards: March 4, 1937
Thursday, 8:00 PM
The Biltmore Bowl of the Biltmore Hotel, Los Angeles (banquet)
   MC—George Jessel

10th Awards: March 10, 1938
Thursday, 8:15 PM (postponed from March 3rd)
The Biltmore Bowl of the Biltmore Hotel, Los Angeles (banquet)
   MC—Bob Burns

11th Awards: February 23, 1939
Thursday, 8:30 PM
The Biltmore Bowl of the Biltmore Hotel, Los Angeles (banquet)
   Host—Frank Capra, Academy
   President

12th Awards: February 29, 1940
Thursday, 8:30 PM
The Coconut Grove of the Ambassador Hotel, Los Angeles (banquet)
   MC—Bob Hope (for last half only)

13th Awards: February 27, 1941
Thursday, 8:45 PM
The Biltmore Bowl of the Biltmore Hotel, Los Angeles (banquet)
   Banquet addressed by President
   Franklin D. Roosevelt via direct-line
   radio from Washington, D.C.
   Host—Walter Wanger, Academy
   President

14th Awards: February 26, 1942
Thursday, 7:45 PM
The Biltmore Bowl of the Biltmore Hotel, Los Angeles (dinner)
   Wendell Willkie, principal speaker
   MC—Bob Hope

15th Awards: March 4, 1943
Thursday, 8:30 PM
The Coconut Grove of the Ambassador Hotel, Los Angeles (banquet)
   MC—Bob Hope

16th Awards: March 2, 1944
Thursday, 8:00 PM
Grauman's Chinese Theatre, Hollywood
   MC—Jack Benny (for overseas
   broadcast)

17th Awards: March 15, 1945
Thursday, 8:00 PM
Grauman's Chinese Theatre, Hollywood
   MCs—John Cromwell (for first half),
   Bob Hope (for last half)
   Program Director—Charles Brackett
   General Stage Director—Mervyn LeRoy
   Musical Director—Franz Waxman

First Awards Banquet, May 16, 1929

18th Awards: March 7, 1946
Thursday, 8:00 PM
Grauman's Chinese Theatre, Hollywood
   MCs—Bob Hope, James Stewart
   Produced and Staged by—Dore Schary
   Musical Director—Johnny Green

19th Awards: March 13, 1947
Thursday, 8:45 PM
Shrine Civic Auditorium, Los Angeles
   MC—Jack Benny
   Produced and Staged by—Mervyn
LeRoy
   Musical Direction—Leo Forbstein

20th Awards: March 20, 1948
Saturday, 8:15 PM
Shrine Civic Auditorium, Los Angeles
   Produced and Directed by—Delmer
Daves
   Musical Direction—Ray Heindorf

21st Awards: March 24, 1949
Thursday, 8:00 PM
Academy Award Theater, Hollywood
   MC—Robert Montgomery
   General Director—William Dozier
   Musical Director—Johnny Green

22nd Awards: March 23, 1950
Thursday, 8:00 PM
RKO Pantages Theatre, Hollywood
   MC—Paul Douglas
   General Director—Johnny Green
   Musical Director—Robert Emmett
Dolan

23rd Awards: March 29, 1951
Thursday, 8:00 PM
RKO Pantages Theatre, Hollywood
   MC—Fred Astaire
   General Director—Richard Breen
   Musical Director—Alfred Newman

Lionel Barrymore, Clark Gable, Irvin S. Cobb at the 1934 (7th) Awards

24th Awards: March 20, 1952
Thursday, 8:00 PM
RKO Pantages Theatre, Hollywood
   MC—Danny Kaye
   General Director—Arthur Freed
   Musical Director—Johnny Green
   Script—Sylvia Fine, Richard Breen

25th Awards: March 19, 1953
Thursday, 7:30 PM (first telecast)
RKO Pantages Theatre, Hollywood
   MC—Bob Hope
   Produced and Directed by—Johnny
Green
   Musical Director—Adolph Deutsch
   Script—Richard L. Breen
   NBC-TV Director—William A.
Bennington
*NBC International Theatre, New York
City*
   MC—Conrad Nagel
   Presentations—Fredric March

26th Awards: March 25, 1954
Thursday, 8:00 PM
RKO Pantages Theatre, Hollywood
   MC—Donald O'Connor
   General Director—Mitchell Leisen
   Musical Director—Andre Previn
   Script—Hal Kanter
   NBC-TV Director—William A.
Bennington
NBC Century Theatre, New York City
   MC—Fredric March
   Presentations—Jean Hersholt
   NBC-TV Director—Gray Lockwood

27th Awards: March 30, 1955
Wednesday, 7:30 PM
RKO Pantages Theatre, Hollywood
  MC—Bob Hope
  Producer and General Director—Jean
  Negulesco
  Musical Director—David Rose
  Script—Richard L. Breen, Melville
  Shavelson, Jack Rose
  NBC-TV Director—William A.
  Bennington
NBC Century Theatre, New York City
  MC—Thelma Ritter
  Presentations—Conrad Nagel
  NBC-TV Director—Gray Lockwood

28th Awards: March 21, 1956
Wednesday, 7:30 PM
RKO Pantages Theatre, Hollywood
  MC—Jerry Lewis
  Producer—Robert Emmett Dolan
  Director—George Seaton
  Musical Director—Andre Previn
  Script—Melville Shavelson, Jack Rose,
  Richard L. Breen
  NBC-TV Director—William A.
  Bennington
NBC Century Theatre, New York City
  Representing the Academy—Claudette
  Colbert, Joseph L. Mankiewicz
  NBC-TV Director—Richard Schneider

29th Awards: March 27, 1957
Wednesday, 7:30 PM
RKO Pantages Theatre, Hollywood
  MC—Jerry Lewis
  General Director—Valentine Davies
  Musical Director—Johnny Green
  Script—Arthur Phillips, Harry Crane,
  Hal Kanter
  NBC-TV Director—William A.
  Bennington
NBC Century Theatre, New York City
  MC—Celeste Holm
  Producer—Robert Emmett Dolan
  NBC-TV Director—Max Miller

30th Awards: March 26, 1958
Wednesday, 7:30 PM
RKO Pantages Theatre, Hollywood
  MCs—Bob Hope, Jack Lemmon, David
  Niven, Rosalind Russell, James Stewart
  and Donald Duck (on film)
  Producer—Jerry Wald
  Musical Director—Alfred Newman
  Script—Richard Breen, Melvin Frank,
  John Michael Hayes, Hal Kanter,
  Norman Panama, Jack Rose, Mel
  Shavelson
  NBC-TV Producer-Director—Alan
  Handley

364

31st Awards: April 6, 1959
Monday, 7:30 PM
RKO Pantages Theatre, Hollywood
  MCs—Bob Hope, Jerry Lewis, David
  Niven, Sir Laurence Olivier, Tony
  Randall, Mort Sahl
  General Chairman—Valentine Davies
  Producer—Jerry Wald
  Musical Director—Lionel Newman
  Script—Richard Breen, Harry Crane,
  I.A.L. Diamond, Hal Kanter, Mort
  Lachman, Arthur Phillips, Jack Rose,
  Mel Shavelson
  NBC-TV Producer-Director—Alan
  Handley

Spencer Tracy, Bette Davis at the 1938 (11th) Awards

Walter Pidgeon, Greer Garson, Ronald Colman at the 1942 Awards Banquet

32nd Awards: April 4, 1960
Monday, 7:30 PM
RKO Pantages Theatre, Hollywood
  MC—Bob Hope
  General Chairman—Valentine Davies
  Producer—Arthur Freed
  Musical Director—Andre Previn
  Directors—Vincente Minnelli, John
  Houseman, Joe Parker
  Script—Richard Breen, Hal Kanter,
  Jack Rose, Mel Shavelson
  NBC-TV Producer-Director—Alan
  Handley
(Honorary Awards and Scientific or
Technical Awards were presented during
the Governors' Ball at the Hilton Hotel
later in the evening)

33rd Awards: April 17, 1961
Monday, 7:30 PM
*Santa Monica Civic Auditorium, Santa
Monica*
  MC—Bob Hope
  General Chairman—Steve Broidy
  Producer—Arthur Freed
  Musical Director—Andre Previn
  Director—Vincente Minnelli
  Script—Richard Breen, Hal Kanter,
  Jack Rose, Mel Shavelson
  ABC-TV Producer-Director—Richard
  Dunlap

1956 Awards telecast

34th Awards: April 9, 1962
Monday, 7:30 PM
Santa Monica Civic Auditorium, Santa Monica

    MC—Bob Hope
    General Chairman—Steve Broidy
    Producer—Arthur Freed
    Music Director—John Green
    Script—Richard Breen, Hal Kanter
    ABC-TV Producer-Director—Richard
    Dunlap

35th Awards: April 8, 1963
Monday, 7:00 PM
Santa Monica Civic Auditorium, Santa Monica

    MC—Frank Sinatra
    Producer—Arthur Freed
    Music Director—Alfred Newman
    Script—George Axelrod, Richard
    Breen, Hal Kanter, Stanley Roberts
    ABC-TV Producer-Director—Richard
    Dunlap

36th Awards: April 13, 1964
Monday, 7:00 PM
Santa Monica Civic Auditorium, Santa Monica

    MC—Jack Lemmon
    Producer—George Sidney
    Music Director—John Green
    Script—George Axelrod, Richard
    Breen, Mort Lachman, Stanley
    Roberts, Melville Shavelson
    ABC-TV Producer-Director—Richard
    Dunlap

Frank Sinatra, Sophia Loren at the 1962 (35th) Awards

37th Awards: April 5, 1965
Monday, 7:00 PM
Santa Monica Civic Auditorium, Santa Monica

    MC—Bob Hope
    Producer—Joe Pasternak
    Music Director—John Green
    Script—Richard Breen, Hal Kanter,
    Milt Rosen
    ABC-TV Producer-Director—Richard
    Dunlap

38th Awards: April 18, 1966
Monday, 7:00 PM (first telecast in color)
Santa Monica Civic Auditorium, Santa Monica

    MC—Bob Hope
    Producer—Joe Pasternak
    Music Director & Conductor—John
    Green
    Script—Hal Kanter
    ABC-TV Producer-Director—Richard
    Dunlap

39th Awards: April 10, 1967
Monday, 7:00 PM
Santa Monica Civic Auditorium, Santa Monica
   MC—Bob Hope
   Producer—Joe Pasternak
   Music Director & Conductor—John Green
   Script—Hal Kanter, I.A.L. Diamond, Mort Lachman
   ABC-TV Producer-Director—Richard Dunlap

40th Awards: April 10, 1968
Wednesday, 7:00 PM (postponed from April 8th)
Santa Monica Civic Auditorium, Santa Monica
   MC—Bob Hope
   Producer—Arthur Freed
   Music Director & Conductor—Elmer Bernstein
   Script—Hal Kanter, I.A.L. Diamond, Mort Lachman
   Script for Historical Sequences—Daniel Taradash
   ABC-TV Producer-Director—Richard Dunlap

41st Awards: April 14, 1969
Monday, 7:00 PM
Dorothy Chandler Pavilion, Los Angeles County Music Center
   The Friends of Oscar—Ingrid Bergman, Diahann Carroll, Tony Curtis, Jane Fonda, Burt Lancaster, Walter Matthau, Sidney Poitier, Rosalind Russell, Frank Sinatra, Natalie Wood
   Producer-Director-Choreographer—Gower Champion
   Music Director—Henry Mancini
   Writers—Tom Waldman, Frank Waldman
   ABC-TV Producer-Director—Richard Dunlap

42nd Awards: April 7, 1970
Tuesday, 7:00 PM
Dorothy Chandler Pavilion, Los Angeles County Music Center
   Producer—M.J. Frankovich
   Director—Jack Haley, Jr.
   Music Director—Elmer Bernstein
   Writers—Hal Kanter, Frank Pierson, Mary Loos
   ABC-TV Producer-Director—Richard Dunlap

366

43rd Awards: April 15, 1971
Thursday, 7:00 PM
Dorothy Chandler Pavilion, Los Angeles County Music Center
   Producer—Robert E. Wise
   Associate to Mr. Wise—Saul Chaplin
   Music Director—Quincy Jones
   Writers—I.A.L. Diamond, Leonard Spigelgass, William Bowers
   NBC-TV Producer-Director—Richard Dunlap

44th Awards: April 10, 1972
Monday, 7:00 PM
Dorothy Chandler Pavilion, Los Angeles County Music Center
   MCs—Helen Hayes, Alan King, Sammy Davis, Jr., Jack Lemmon
   Producer—Howard W. Koch
   Director—Marty Pasetta
   Writers—Leonard Spigelgass, William Ludwig, Hal Kanter
   Music Director—Henry Mancini
   Telecast on NBC-TV

45th Awards: March 27, 1973
Tuesday, 7:00 PM
Dorothy Chandler Pavilion, Los Angeles County Music Center
   MCs—Carol Burnett, Michael Caine, Charlton Heston, Rock Hudson
   Producer—Howard W. Koch
   Director—Marty Pasetta
   Writers—Leonard Spigelgass, William Ludwig
   Music Director—John Williams
   Telecast on NBC-TV

46th Awards: April 2, 1974
Tuesday, 7:00 PM
Dorothy Chandler Pavilion, Los Angeles County Music Center
   MCs—John Huston, Diana Ross, Burt Reynolds, David Niven
   Producer—Jack Haley, Jr.
   Director—Marty Pasetta
   Writer—Marty Farrell
   Music Director—Henry Mancini
   Telecast on NBC-TV

47th Awards: April 8, 1975
Tuesday, 7:00 PM
Dorothy Chandler Pavilion, Los Angeles County Music Center
   MCs—Sammy Davis, Jr., Bob Hope, Shirley MacLaine, Frank Sinatra
   Producer—Howard W. Koch
   Director—Marty Pasetta
   Writers—Hal Kanter, William Ludwig, Leonard Spigelgass
   Music Director—John Green
   Telecast on NBC-TV
(Scientific or Technical Awards were presented April 3, 1975, at a 4:00 PM press call in the Champagne Room of the Beverly Wilshire Hotel)

48th Awards: March 29, 1976
Monday, 7:00 PM
Dorothy Chandler Pavilion, Los Angeles County Music Center
   MCs—Walter Matthau, Robert Shaw, George Segal, Goldie Hawn, Gene Kelly
   Producer—Howard W. Koch
   Director—Marty Pasetta
   Writers—Hal Kanter, William Ludwig, Leonard Spigelgass
   Music Director—John Williams
   Telecast on ABC-TV
(Scientific or Technical Awards were presented March 24, 1976, at a 4:00 PM press call in the Academy Lobby)

Sidney Poitier, Anne Bancroft at the 1963 (36th) Awards

Laurence Olivier at the 1978 (51st) Awards

49th Awards: March 28, 1977
Monday, 7:00 PM
Dorothy Chandler Pavilion, Los Angeles County Music Center
   MCs—Richard Pryor, Jane Fonda, Ellen Burstyn, Warren Beatty
   Producer—William Friedkin
   Director—Marty Pasetta
   Writers—Ray Bradbury, Hal Kanter
   Music Director—Bill Conti
   Telecast on ABC-TV
(Scientific or Technical Awards were presented March 24, 1977, at a 7:00 PM cocktail party in the Academy Lobby)

Groucho Marx at the 1973 (46th) Awards

50th Awards: April 3, 1978
Monday, 7:00 PM
*Dorothy Chandler Pavilion, Los Angeles
County Music Center*
    MC—Bob Hope
    Producer—Howard W. Koch
    Director—Marty Pasetta
    Writers—William Ludwig, Leonard
    Spigelgass
    Special Material—Hal Kanter
    Musical Director—Nelson Riddle
    Telecast on ABC-TV
(Scientific or Technical Awards were
presented March 29, 1978, in the
Versailles Room of The Beverly Hilton)

51st Awards: April 9, 1979
Monday, 7:00 PM
*Dorothy Chandler Pavilion, Los Angeles
County Music Center*
    MC—Johnny Carson
    Producer—Jack Haley, Jr.
    Director—Marty Pasetta
    Writers—Buz Kohan, Tony Thomas,
    Rod Warren
    Music Directors—Jack Elliott, Allyn
    Ferguson
    Telecast on ABC-TV
(Scientific or Technical Awards were
presented April 6, 1979, in the Versailles
Room of The Beverly Hilton)

52nd Awards: April 14, 1980
Monday, 6:00 PM
*Dorothy Chandler Pavilion, Los Angeles
County Music Center*
    MC—Johnny Carson
    Producer—Howard W. Koch
    Director—Marty Pasetta
    Writers—Buz Kohan, Leonard
    Spigelgass, Rod Warren
    Music Arranged and Conducted by—
    Henry Mancini
    Telecast on ABC-TV
(Scientific or Technical Awards were
presented April 11, 1980, in the Grand
Ballroom of The Beverly Hilton)

53rd Awards: March 31, 1981
Tuesday, 7:00 PM (postponed from
March 30th)
*Dorothy Chandler Pavilion, Los Angeles
County Music Center*
    MC—Johnny Carson
    Producer—Norman Jewison
    Director—Marty Pasetta
    Writers—Buz Kohan, Hal Kanter, Rod
    Warren
    Music Arranged and Conducted by—
    Henry Mancini
    Telecast on ABC-TV
(Scientific or Technical Awards were
presented March 15, 1981, in the Grand
Ballroom of The Beverly Hilton)

54th Awards: March 29, 1982
Monday, 6:00 PM
*Dorothy Chandler Pavilion, Los Angeles
County Music Center*
    MC—Johnny Carson
    Produced by—Howard W. Koch, Melvin
    Frank
    Director—Marty Pasetta
    Creative Consultant/Chief Writer—Hal
    Kanter
    Writers—Melville Shavelson, Jack
    Rose, Melvin Frank
    Special Material—Leonard Spigelgass
    Music Arranged and Conducted by—
    Bill Conti
    Telecast on ABC-TV
(Scientific or Technical Awards were
presented March 21, 1982, in the Grand
Ballroom of The Beverly Hilton)

55th Awards: April 11, 1983
Monday, 6:00 PM
*Dorothy Chandler Pavilion, Los Angeles
County Music Center*
    Hosts—Liza Minnelli, Dudley Moore,
    Richard Pryor, Walter Matthau
    Produced by—Howard W. Koch
    Director—Marty Pasetta
    Creative Consultant/Chief Writer—Hal
    Kanter
    Writers—Jack Rose, Rod Warren,
    Leonard Spigelgass
    Music Arranged and Conducted by—
    Bill Conti
    Telecast on ABC-TV
(Scientific or Technical Awards were
presented March 27, 1983, in the Grand
Ballroom of The Beverly Hilton)

56th Awards: April 9, 1984
Monday, 6:00 PM
*Dorothy Chandler Pavilion, Los Angeles
County Music Center*
    MC—Johnny Carson
    Produced by—Jack Haley, Jr.
    Director—Marty Pasetta
    Written by—Rod Warren, Tony Thomas
    Musical Director—Ian Fraser
    Telecast on ABC-TV
(Scientific or Technical Awards were
presented March 31, 1984, in the Grand
Ballroom of The Beverly Hilton)

57th Awards: March 25, 1985
Monday, 6:00 PM
*Dorothy Chandler Pavilion, Los Angeles
County Music Center*
    Host—Jack Lemmon
    Co-Hosts—Candice Bergen, Jeff
    Bridges, Glenn Close, Michael Douglas,
    Gregory Hines, William Hurt, Amy
    Irving, Diana Ross, Tom Selleck,
    Kathleen Turner
    Produced by—Gregory Peck, Robert E.
    Wise, Larry Gelbart, Gene Allen
    Director—Marty Pasetta
    Written by—Larry Gelbart
    Music Director—Bill Conti
    Telecast on ABC-TV
(Scientific or Technical Awards were
presented March 17, 1985, in the Grand
Ballroom of The Beverly Hilton)

58th Awards: March 24, 1986
Monday, 6:00 PM
*Dorothy Chandler Pavilion, Los Angeles
County Music Center*
    Hosts—Alan Alda, Jane Fonda, Robin
    Williams
    Produced by—Stanley Donen
    Directed by—Marty Pasetta
    Written by—Glenn Gordon Caron,
    Douglas Wyman, Larry Gelbart
    Music Supervised and Conducted by—
    Lionel Newman
    Associate Musical Director—Dominic
    Frontiere
    Telecast on ABC-TV
(Scientific or Technical Awards were
presented March 16, 1986, in the Grand
Ballroom of The Beverly Hilton)

59th Awards: March 31, 1987
Monday, 6:00 PM
*Dorothy Chandler Pavilion, Los Angeles
County Music Center*
    Hosts—Chevy Chase, Goldie Hawn,
    Paul Hogan
    Produced by—Samuel Goldwyn, Jr.
    Directed by—Marty Pasetta
    Written by—Jeffrey Barron, Ernest
    Lehman, Jack Rose, Melville Shavelson
    Music Supervised and Conducted by—
    Lionel Newman
    Telecast on ABC-TV
(Scientific or Technical Awards were
presented March 22, 1987, in the Grand
Ballroom of The Beverly Hilton)

60th Awards: April 11, 1988
Monday, 6:00 PM
Shrine Civic Auditorium, Los Angeles
    Host—Chevy Chase
    Produced by—Samuel Goldwyn, Jr.
    Directed by—Marty Pasetta
    Written by—Ernest Lehman, Jack
    Rose, Melville Shavelson
    Music Supervised and Conducted by—
    Bill Conti
    Telecast on ABC-TV
(Scientific or Technical Awards were
presented March 27, 1988, in the Grand
Ballroom of The Beverly Hilton)

Shirley MacLaine, at the 1986 (59th) Awards

Robin Williams, at the 1988 (61st) Awards

61st Awards: March 29, 1989
Wednesday, 6:00 PM
Shrine Civic Auditorium, Los Angeles
    Produced by—Allan Carr
    Directed by—Jeff Margolis
    Written by—Bruce Vilanch,
    Hildy Parks
    Music Supervised and Composed
    by—Marvin Hamlisch
    Telecast on ABC-TV
(Scientific or Technical Awards were
presented March 19, 1989, in the Crystal
Room of The Beverly Hills Hotel)

62nd Awards: March 26, 1990
Monday, 6:00 PM
Dorothy Chandler Pavilion, Los Angeles
County Music Center
    Host—Billy Crystal
    Produced by—Gilbert Cates
    Directed by—Jeff Margolis
    Written by—Ernest Lehman,
    Mel Shavelson, Marty Farrell
    Special Material by—Robert Wuhl
    Music Director—Bill Conti
    Telecast on ABC-TV
(Scientific or Technical Awards were
presented March 3, 1990, in the Grand
Ballroom of the Beverly Hilton Hotel)

368

63rd Awards: March 25, 1991
Monday, 6:00 PM
Shrine Civic Auditorium, Los Angeles
    Host—Billy Crystal
    Produced by—Gilbert Cates
    Directed by—Jeff Margolis
    Written by—Hal Kanter, Buz Kohan
    Special Material by—Bruce Vilanch,
    Robert Wuht
    Music Director—Bill Conti
    Telecast on ABC-TV
(Scientific or Technical Awards were
presented March 2, 1991, in the Grand
Ballroom of the Beverly Hilton Hotel)

64th Awards: March 30, 1992
Monday, 6:00 PM
Dorothy Chandler Pavilion, Los Angeles
County Music Center
    Host—Billy Crystal
    Produced by—Gilbert Cates
    Directed by—Jeff Margolis
    Written by—Hal Kanter and
    Buz Kohan
    Special Material by—Billy Crystal,
    David Steinberg, Bruce Vilanch
    and Robert Wuhl
    Music Director—Bill Conti
    Telecast on ABC-TV
(Scientific or Technical Awards were
presented March 7, 1992, in the
Los Angeles Ballroom of the Century
Plaza Hotel)

65th Awards: March 29, 1993
Monday, 6:00 PM
Dorothy Chandler Pavilion, Los Angeles
County Music Center
    Host—Billy Crystal
    Produced by—Gilbert Cates
    Directed by—Jeff Margolis
    Written by—Hal Kanter, Buz Kohan
    and Sheila Benson
    Special Material by—Billy Crystal,
    David Steinberg, Bruce Vilanch and
    Robert Wuhl
    Music Director—Bill Conti
    Telecast on ABC-TV
(Scientific and Technical Awards were
presented March 6, 1993, in the
Los Angeles Ballroom of the Century
Plaza Hotel)

Marisa Tomei, at the 1992 (65th) Awards

Spike Lee, Denzel Washington, Danny Aiello at the 1989 (62nd) Awards Board of Governor's Ball

Callie Khouri, at the 1991 (64th) Awards

369

Production Number, "Whole New World", at the 1992 (65th) Awards

66th Awards: March 21, 1994
Monday, 6:00 PM
Dorothy Chandler Pavilion, Los Angeles County Music Center
    Host—Whoopi Goldberg
    Produced by—Gilbert Cates
    Directed by—Jeff Margolis
    Written by—Hal Kanter and Buz Kohan
    Special Material by—Bruce Vilanch, Billy Grundfest, Drake Sather
    Music Director—Bill Conti
    Telecast on ABC-TV
(Scientific and Technical Awards were presented February 26, 1994, in the Grand Ballroom of the Beverly Hilton Hotel)

67th Awards: March 27, 1995
Monday, 6:00 PM
Shrine Auditorium, Los Angeles
    Host—David Letterman
    Produced by—Gilbert Cates
    Directed by—Jeff Margolis
    Written by—Hal Kanter, Buz Kohan, Bruce Vilanch
    Special Material by—Rob Burnett, Mike Barrie, Jon Beckerman, Donick Cary, Al Franken, Larry Jacobson, Jim Mulholland, Gerry Mulligan, Bill Scheft
    Music Director—Bill Conti
    Telecast on ABC-TV
(Scientific and Technical Awards were presented March 4, 1995, in the Ballroom of the Regent Beverly Wilshire Hotel)

68th Awards: March 25, 1996
Monday, 6:00 PM
Dorothy Chandler Pavilion, Los Angeles County Music Center
    Host—Whoopi Goldberg
    Executive Producer—Quincy Jones
    Produced by—Quincy Jones, David Salzman
    Directed by—Jeff Margolis
    Written by—Stephen Pouliot, Bruce Vilanch
    Special Material by—Jay Cocks, Daniel M. Salzman, Alec Berg, Jeff Schaffer
    Music Director—Tom Scott
    Telecast on ABC-TV
(Scientific and Technical Awards were presented March 2, 1996, in the Ballroom of the Regent Beverly Wilshire Hotel)

Clint Eastwood and Arnold Schwarzenegger at the 1994 (67th) Awards

69th Awards: March 24, 1997
Monday, 6:00 PM
Shrine Auditorium, Los Angeles
    Host—Billy Crystal
    Produced by—Gil Cates
    Directed by—Louis J. Horvitz
    Written by—Hal Kanter, Carrie Fisher, Buz Kohan
    Special Material by—Billy Crystal, Joe Bolster, Ed Driscoll, Jon Macks, Billy Martin, Marc Shaiman, David Steinberg, Bruce Vilanch
    Music Director—Bill Conti
    Telecast on ABC-TV
(Scientific and Technical Awards were presented March 1, 1997, in the Ballroom of the Regent Beverly Wilshire Hotel)

70th Awards: March 23, 1998
Monday, 6:00 PM
Shrine Auditorium, Los Angeles
    Host–Billy Crystal
    Produced by-Gil Cates
    Directed by-Louis J. Horvitz
    Written by–Rita Cash, Billy Grundfest, Hal Kanter and Buz Kohan
    Special Material by–Billy Crystal, Dave Boone, Ed Driscoll, Jon Macks, Billy Martin, Marc Shaiman, David Steinberg, Bruce Vilanch
    Music Director–Bill Conti
    Telecast on ABC-TV
(Scientific and Technical Awards were presented February 28, 1998, in the Ballroom of the Regent Beverly Wilshire Hotel)

Quincy Jones at the 1994 (67th) Awards

Christopher Reeve at the 1995 (68th) Awards

Whoopi Goldberg at the 1995 (68th) Awards

Kim Basinger at the 1997 (70th) Awards

Cuba Gooding, Jr. at the 1996 (69th) Awards

Robin Williams at the 1997 (70th) Awards

Bruce Springsteen at the 1993 (66th) Awards

71st Awards: March 21, 1999
Sunday, 5:30 PM (with a half-hour Pre-Show preceding)
Dorothy Chandler Pavilion, Los Angeles County Music Center
    Host—Whoopi Goldberg
    Producer—Gil Cates
    Directed by—Louis J. Horvitz
    Written by—Rita Cash, Hal Kanter, Buz Kohan
    Special Material by—Whoopi Goldberg, Jon Macks, Billy Martin, Bruce Vilanch
    Music Director—Bill Conti
    Telecast on ABC-TV
(Scientific and Technical Awards were presented February 27, 1999, in the Ballroom of the Regent Beverly Wilshire Hotel)

72nd Awards: March 26, 2000
Sunday, 5:30 PM (with a half-hour Pre-Show preceding)
Shrine Auditorium & Expo Center
    Host—Billy Crystal
    Producers—Richard D. Zanuck, Lili Fini Zanuck
    Directed by—Louis J. Horvitz
    Written by—Bruce Vilanch, Rita Cash, Carol Leifer, Jonathan Tolins
    Special Material by—Billy Crystal, Dave Boone, Ed Driscoll, Jon Macks, Billy Martin, Jeffrey Ross, Marc Shaiman, David Steinberg
    Music Directors—Burt Bacharach, Don Was
    Telecast on ABC-TV
(Scientific and Technical Awards were presented March 4, 2000, in the Ballroom of the Regent Beverly Wilshire Hotel)

73rd Awards: March 25, 2001
Sunday, 5:30 PM (with a half-hour Pre-Show preceding)
Shrine Auditorium & Expo Center
    Host—Steve Martin
    Producer—Gil Cates
    Directed by—Louis J. Horvitz
    Written by—Rita Cash, Hal Kanter, Buz Kohan
    Special Material by—Andy Breckman, Jon Macks, Steve Martin, Rita Rudner, Bruce Vilanch
    Music Director—Bill Conti
    Telecast on ABC-TV
(Scientific and Technical Awards were presented March 3, 2001, in the Ballroom of the Regent Beverly Wilshire Hotel)

Presenters Tommy Lee Jones and Ashley Judd receive the Best Film Editing envelope from PricewaterhouseCoopers at the 1999 (72nd) Awards

74th Awards: March 24, 2002
Sunday, 5:30 PM (with a half-hour Pre-Show preceding)
Kodak Theatre, Hollywood & Highland
    Host—Whoopi Goldberg
    Producer—Laura Ziskin
    Directed by—Louis J. Horvitz
    Written by—Bruce Vilanch, Dave Boone, Carrie Fisher, Chris Henchy, Carol Leifer, Jon Macks, Chuck Martin, Rita Rudner, Wanda Sykes, Jonathan Tolins
    Special Material by—Alan and Marilyn Bergman, James Cameron, Ethan and Joel Coen, Cameron Crowe, Buck Henry, David Mamet
    Music Director—John Williams
    Telecast on ABC-TV
(Scientific and Technical Awards were presented March 2, 2002, in the Ballroom of the Regent Beverly Wilshire Hotel)

75th Awards: March 22, 2003
Sunday, 5:30 PM (with a half-hour Pre-Show preceding)
Kodak Theatre, Hollywood & Highland
    Host—Steve Martin
    Producer—Gil Cates
    Directed by—Louis J. Horvitz
    Written by—Rita Cash, Hal Canter, Buz Kohan
    Special Material by—Steve Martin, Beth Armogida, Dave Barry, Dave Boone, Andy Breckman, Jon Macks, Rita Rudner, Bruce Vilanch
    Music Supervised and Composed by—Bill Conti
    Telecast on ABC-TV
(Scientific and Technical Awards were presented March 1, 2003, in the Ballroom of the Regent Beverly Wilshire Hotel)

Arrivals at the 1999 (72nd) Awards

Bruce Paltrow, Gwyneth Paltrow, Blythe Danner at the 1998 (71st) Awards

Presenters John Travolta and Sharon Stone backstage at the 2001 (74th) Awards

Paul McCartney at the 2001 (74th) Awards

Salma Hayek and Elliot Goldenthal at the 2002 (75th) Awards

ACADEMY FACTS AND RECORDS

(Through the First Seventy-Five Years)

ELEVEN ACADEMY AWARDS:
BEN-HUR (1959)
TITANIC (1997)

TEN ACADEMY AWARDS:
WEST SIDE STORY (1961)

NINE ACADEMY AWARDS:
GIGI (1958)
THE LAST EMPEROR (1987)
THE ENGLISH PATIENT (1996)

EIGHT ACADEMY AWARDS:
GONE WITH THE WIND (1939)
FROM HERE TO ETERNITY (1953)
ON THE WATERFRONT (1954)
MY FAIR LADY (1964)
CABARET (1972)
GANDHI (1982)
AMADEUS (1984)

MOST NOMINATED MOTION PICTURES:
ALL ABOUT EVE (1950), 14 nominations
TITANIC (1997), 14 nominations
GONE WITH THE WIND (1939), 13 nominations
FROM HERE TO ETERNITY (1953), 13 nominations
MARY POPPINS (1964), 13 nominations
WHO'S AFRAID OF VIRGINIA WOOLF? (1966), 13 nominations
FORREST GUMP (1994), 13 nominations
SHAKESPEARE IN LOVE (1998), 13 nominations
THE LORD OF THE RINGS: THE FELLOWSHIP OF THE RING (2001), 13 nominations
CHICAGO (2002), 13 nominations

MOST HONORED PERFORMER:
KATHARINE HEPBURN, winner of 4 Academy Awards for acting, all of them in the Best Actress category, 1932/33, 1967, 1968, 1981.

MOST NOMINATED ACTRESSES:
MERYL STREEP, 13 nominations
KATHARINE HEPBURN, 12 nominations
BETTE DAVIS, 10 nominations

MOST NOMINATED ACTORS:
JACK NICHOLSON, 12 nominations
LAURENCE OLIVIER, 10 nominations for acting (Lord Olivier was also nominated as a Director and received two Honorary Oscars, in 1946 and 1978.)
SPENCER TRACY, 9 nominations

MOST HONORED INDIVIDUALS:
(male) WALT DISNEY, personally credited with 26 Awards, including 12 Cartoon Awards, plus multiple Awards in the categories of Short Subjects, Documentaries and Honorary.
(female) EDITH HEAD, 8 Academy Awards for Costume Design, 1949, 1950 (2), 1951, 1953, 1954, 1960, 1973.

MOST HONORED DIRECTORS:
JOHN FORD, 4 Awards, 1935, 1940, 1941, 1952
FRANK CAPRA, 3 Awards
WILLIAM WYLER, 3 Awards

MOST NOMINATED DIRECTORS:
WILLIAM WYLER, 12 nominations
BILLY WILDER, 8 nominations

MOST NOMINATED NON-WINNING MOVIES:
THE TURNING POINT (1977), 11 nominations
THE COLOR PURPLE (1985), 11 nominations

THE ONLY SILENT FILM TO WIN AN OSCAR AS BEST PICTURE:
WINGS (1927/28)

THE FIRST SOUND FILM TO WIN AN OSCAR FOR BEST PICTURE:
THE BROADWAY MELODY (1928/29)

THE ONLY TELEPLAY TO BE MADE INTO A FEATURE WHICH WON A BEST PICTURE OSCAR:
MARTY (1955)

THE FIRST MOVIE IN COLOR TO WIN A BEST PICTURE OSCAR:
GONE WITH THE WIND (1939)

THE LAST ENTIRELY BLACK-AND-WHITE MOVIE TO WIN A BEST PICTURE AWARD:
THE APARTMENT (1960) [Schindler's List (1993) had some color elements.]

THE ONLY SEQUEL TO WIN AN OSCAR AS BEST PICTURE:
THE GODFATHER PART II (1974)

THE FIRST NON-HOLLYWOOD FILM TO WIN AN ACADEMY AWARD:
THE PRIVATE LIFE OF HENRY VIII (1932/33), which won a Best Actor Award for Charles Laughton.

THE FIRST NON-HOLLYWOOD FILM TO WIN THE BEST PICTURE AWARD:
HAMLET (1948), financed and filmed in England.

THE FIRST FOREIGN-LANGUAGE PERFORMANCE TO WIN AN ACADEMY AWARD:
SOPHIA LOREN, named 1961's Best Actress for her work in the Italian film *Two Women*.

BEST PICTURE OSCAR WINNERS THAT RECEIVED NO NOMINATIONS FOR ACTING:
WINGS (1927/28)
THE BROADWAY MELODY (1928/29)
ALL QUIET ON THE WESTERN FRONT (1929/30)
GRAND HOTEL (1931/32)
AN AMERICAN IN PARIS (1951)
THE GREATEST SHOW ON EARTH (1952)
AROUND THE WORLD IN 80 DAYS (1956)
GIGI (1958)
THE LAST EMPEROR (1987)
BRAVEHEART (1995)

FILMS IN WHICH THE ENTIRE CAST WAS NOMINATED FOR OSCARS:
SLEUTH (1972)
GIVE 'EM HELL, HARRY (1975)

THE ONLY MOTION PICTURES TO WIN AWARDS FOR BEST PICTURE, DIRECTION, ACTRESS, ACTOR AND SCREENPLAY:
IT HAPPENED ONE NIGHT (1934)
ONE FLEW OVER THE CUCKOO'S NEST (1975)
THE SILENCE OF THE LAMBS (1991)

THE ONLY PERFORMERS TO WIN CONSECUTIVE ACADEMY AWARDS:
LUISE RAINER, 1936 and 1937
SPENCER TRACY, 1937 and 1938
KATHARINE HEPBURN, 1967 and 1968
JASON ROBARDS, 1976 and 1977
TOM HANKS, 1993 and 1994

THE ONLY FILMS TO WIN THREE ACADEMY AWARDS FOR ACTING:
A STREETCAR NAMED DESIRE (1951)
NETWORK (1976)
(To date, no film has won all four of the Oscar Awards for acting.)

THE ONLY FILMS TO WIN BOTH BEST ACTOR AND BEST ACTRESS AWARDS:
IT HAPPENED ONE NIGHT (1934)
ONE FLEW OVER THE CUCKOO'S NEST (1975)
NETWORK (1976)
COMING HOME (1978)
ON GOLDEN POND (1981)
THE SILENCE OF THE LAMBS (1991)
AS GOOD AS IT GETS (1997)

THE ONLY PERFORMERS NOMINATED FOR PLAYING THE SAME CHARACTER IN THE SAME FILM:
KATE WINSLET as "Rose DeWitt Bukater" and GLORIA STUART as "Old Rose" in *Titanic* (1997)
KATE WINSLET as "Young Iris Murdoch" and JUDI DENCH as "Iris Murdoch" in *Iris* (2001)

THE ONLY PERFORMERS NOMINATED TWICE FOR THE SAME ROLE BUT IN TWO DIFFERENT FILMS:
BING CROSBY as Father O'Malley in 1944's *Going My Way** and in 1945's *The Bells of St. Mary's*
PAUL NEWMAN as Fast Eddie Felson in 1961's *The Hustler* and in 1986's *The Color of Money**
PETER O'TOOLE as King Henry II in 1964's *Becket* and in 1968's *Lion in Winter*
AL PACINO as Michael Corleone in 1972's *The Godfather* and in 1974's *The Godfather Part II*
(*Indicates the performance won an Academy Award)

THE FIRST POSTHUMOUS OSCAR WINNER:
SIDNEY HOWARD, 1939 winner for writing the Screenplay of *Gone with the Wind*.

THE FIRST POSTHUMOUS OSCAR WINNER AMONG PERFORMERS:
PETER FINCH, 1976, for *Network*.

ONLY YEAR OF A TIE IN THE BEST ACTOR CATEGORY:
1931/32, **WALLACE BEERY** in The Champ tied with **FREDRIC MARCH** in *Dr. Jekyll and Mr. Hyde.*

ONLY YEAR OF A TIE IN THE BEST ACTRESS CATEGORY:
1968, **KATHARINE HEPBURN** in *The Lion in Winter* tied with **BARBRA STREISAND** in *Funny Girl.*

THE ONLY YEAR TWO OSCARS WERE GIVEN FOR BEST DIRECTOR:
1961, **ROBERT WISE** and **JEROME ROBBINS**, co-directors of *West Side Story.*

THE ONLY PERSON TO WIN AN OSCAR FOR PLAYING AN OSCAR LOSER:
MAGGIE SMITH, 1978, in *California Suite.*

THE ONLY PERFORMER TO WIN AN OSCAR FOR PLAYING A MEMBER OF THE OPPOSITE SEX:
LINDA HUNT, 1983, for *The Year of Living Dangerously.*

THE ONLY PERFORMER NOMINATED TWICE FOR THE SAME PERFORMANCE:
BARRY FITZGERALD 1944, nominated both as Best Actor and Best Supporting Actor for *Going My Way.* (Such a feat is not possible under present Academy rules.)

THE ONLY PERFORMER TO WIN TWO OSCARS FOR THE SAME PERFORMANCE:
HAROLD RUSSELL, 1946, voted Best Supporting Actor for *The Best Years of Our Lives,* and voted an Honorary Oscar that year for his performance.

THE MOST NOMINATED NON-WINNING PERFORMERS:
RICHARD BURTON, 7 nominations, no wins
PETER O'TOOLE, 7 nominations, no wins (one honorary Oscar)

THE ONLY PERFORMERS TO WIN THREE OR MORE OSCARS FOR ACTING:
KATHARINE HEPBURN, 4 wins
WALTER BRENNAN, 3 wins
INGRID BERGMAN, 3 wins
JACK NICHOLSON, 3 wins

PERFORMERS WHO'VE WON TWO OSCARS FOR ACTING:
MARLON BRANDO, MICHAEL CAINE, GARY COOPER, BETTE DAVIS, OLIVIA DE HAVILLAND, ROBERT DE NIRO, MELYVN DOUGLAS, SALLY FIELD, JANE FONDA, JODIE FOSTER, GENE HACKMAN, TOM HANKS, HELEN HAYES, DUSTIN HOFFMAN, GLENDA JACKSON, JESSICA LANGE, VIVIEN LEIGH, JACK LEMMON, FREDRIC MARCH, ANTHONY QUINN, LUISE RAINER, JASON ROBARDS, MAGGIE SMITH, KEVIN SPACEY, MERYL STREEP, ELIZABETH TAYLOR, SPENCER TRACY, PETER USTINOV, DENZEL WASHINGTON, DIANNE WIEST, SHELLEY WINTERS.

THE ONLY WOMEN NOMINATED AS BEST DIRECTOR:
LINA WERTMULLER, 1976
JANE CAMPION, 1993

DIRECTORS RESPONSIBLE FOR THE MOST OSCAR-WINNING PERFORMANCES:
WILLIAM WYLER, 14
ELIA KAZAN, 9
FRED ZINNEMANN, 7

DIRECTORS RESPONSIBLE FOR THE MOST OSCAR-NOMINATED PERFORMANCES:
WILLIAM WYLER, 35
ELIA KAZAN, 24
FRED ZINNEMAN, 20

THE ONLY PERSONS TO DIRECT THEMSELVES TO A COMPETITIVE ACTING OSCAR:
LAURENCE OLIVIER, 1948. (Director of and Best Actor for *Hamlet)*
ROBERTO BENIGNI, 1998. (Director of and Best Actor in a Leading Role for *Life is Beautiful)*

THE FIRST PERSON NOMINATED AS A PRODUCER, DIRECTOR, ACTOR AND SCREENWRITER IN A SINGLE YEAR:
ORSON WELLES, 1941, for *Citizen Kane.*

THE FIRST PERSON TO WIN OSCARS AS DIRECTOR AND SCREENWRITER:
LEO MCCAREY, 1944, for *Going My Way.*

THE ONLY THREE-GENERATION OSCAR FAMILY:
THE HUSTONS. (Walter Huston won as Best Supporting Actor in 1948, son John Huston won as Best Director in 1948, granddaughter Anjelica Huston won as Best Supporting Actress in 1985.)

THE ONLY BROTHER AND SISTER TO WIN ACTING OSCARS:
LIONEL BARRYMORE, 1931/32
ETHEL BARRYMORE, 1944

THE ONLY SISTERS TO WIN ACTING OSCARS:
JOAN FONTAINE, 1941
OLIVIA DE HAVILLAND, 1946 and 1949

THE ONLY TWINS TO WIN OSCARS:
JULIUS J. EPSTEIN and **PHILIP G. EPSTEIN**, 1943. (With Howard Koch, they scripted that year's winning screenplay *Casablanca.)*
CHRISTOPH LAUENSTEIN and **WOLFGANG LAUENSTEIN**, 1989. (They produced the winning animated short film, *Balance.)*

THE ONLY BROTHERS TO WIN CONSECUTIVE OSCARS:
Screenwriter **JAMES GOLDMAN**, 1968, for *The Lion in Winter;*
Screenwriter **WILLIAM GOLDMAN**, 1969, for *Butch Cassidy and the Sundance Kid.*

THE ONLY MARRIED COUPLES TO WIN OSCARS FOR ACTING:
LAURENCE OLIVIER (1948) and **VIVIEN LEIGH** (1951). (They were not yet married when Vivien Leigh won her first Academy Award as Best Actress of 1939.)
PAUL NEWMAN (1986) and **JOANNE WOODWARD** (1957). (The couple were married in January of 1958, prior to her receiving 1957's Best Actress award.)

THE ONLY OSCAR WINNER WITH PARENTS WHO BOTH RECEIVED OSCARS:
LIZA MINNELLI. (Her mother Judy Garland received an Honorary miniature Oscar in 1939; father Vincente Minnelli won as Best Director of 1958; Ms. Minnelli herself won as Best Actress of 1972.)

THE FIRST PERSON TO REFUSE AN OSCAR:
DUDLEY NICHOLS, 1935, winner for his Screenplay of *The Informer.*

THE ONLY CONSECUTIVE DOUBLE OSCAR WINNERS:
JOSEPH L. MANKIEWICZ. (In 1949, he won Oscars as Director and Screenwriter of *A Letter to Three Wives;* in 1950, he repeated wins in those same two categories for *All about Eve.)*
ALAN MENKEN. (For 1991's *Beauty and the Beast,* he won Oscars for original score and original song; the next year, for 1992's *Aladdin,* he again won Academy Awards in those same two categories.)

THE ONLY OSCAR GIVEN FOR WORK DONE 20 YEARS EARLIER:
The 1972 award for **BEST MUSIC SCORE** for Charles Chaplin's *Limelight,* made in 1952. The film was shown in a few key U.S. cities but was never commercially shown in Los Angeles until 1972 and thus was not eligible for Academy Award consideration until that calendar year.

THE ONLY WRITE-IN OSCAR WINNER:
HAL MOHR, 1935, for his Cinematography of *A Midsummer Night's Dream.* (He won without having been a nominee, a feat not possible under today's Academy rules.)

THE YOUNGEST PERFORMER TO BE NOMINATED FOR AN ACADEMY AWARD:
JUSTIN HENRY, 1979, for *Kramer vs. Kramer.* He was 8 years old at the time.

THE YOUNGEST PERFORMER TO RECEIVE AN ACADEMY AWARD:
SHIRLEY TEMPLE, Special Award winner in 1934. (6 years, 10 months)

THE YOUNGEST PERFORMER TO WIN A COMPETITIVE ACADEMY AWARD:
TATUM O'NEAL, 1973, for *Paper Moon.* (10 years old)

THE YOUNGEST WINNER AS BEST ACTOR:
ADRIEN BRODY, 2002, for *The Pianist.* (29 years old)

THE YOUNGEST WINNER AS BEST ACTRESS:
MARLEE MATLIN, 1986, for *Children of a Lesser God.* (21 years old)

THE YOUNGEST SUPPORTING ACTOR WINNER:
TIMOTHY HUTTON, 1980, for *Ordinary People.* (20 years old)

THE OLDEST SUPPORTING ACTOR WINNER:
GEORGE BURNS, 1975, for *The Sunshine Boys.* (80 years, 69 days)

THE OLDEST WINNER AS BEST ACTOR:
HENRY FONDA, 1981, for *On Golden Pond.* (76 years, 317 days)

THE OLDEST PERFORMER TO RECEIVE AN ACADEMY AWARD:
GROUCHO MARX, Honorary Award winner in 1973. (83 years old)

THE OLDEST PERFORMER TO WIN A COMPETITIVE ACADEMY AWARD:
JESSICA TANDY, 1989, for *Driving Miss Daisy.* (80 years old)

THE MOST OSCARS AWARDED TO ONE PERSON AT A SINGLE CEREMONY:
FOUR, to Walt Disney, in 1953, for the categories of Documentary Feature, Documentary Short Subject, Cartoon Short Subject and Two-reel Short Subject.

Index
The First
Seventy-Five
Years of
Academy
Awards
Nominees

Alphabetizing is word by word, except for compound names of people (like De Niro), which are treated as solid words. Films with identical titles are further identified by year (the year of the Oscars nomination, not the production year, is used). Illustrations are indicated by *italic* page references.

382

384

389

396

400

407

410

411